THE LIBRARY OF LIVING PHILOSOPHERS

THE PHILOSOPHY OF RUDOLF CARNAP

THE LIBRARY OF LIVING PHILOSOPHERS

PAUL ARTHUR SCHILPP, *Editor*

Already Published:

THE PHILOSOPHY OF JOHN DEWEY (1939)
THE PHILOSOPHY OF GEORGE SANTAYANA (1940)
THE PHILOSOPHY OF ALFRED NORTH WHITEHEAD (1941)
THE PHILOSOPHY OF G. E. MOORE (1942)
THE PHILOSOPHY OF BERTRAND RUSSELL (1944)
THE PHILOSOPHY OF ERNST CASSIRER (1949)
ALBERT EINSTEIN: PHILOSOPHER-SCIENTIST (1949)
THE PHILOSOPHY OF SARVEPALLI RADHAKRISHNAN (1952)
THE PHILOSOPHY OF KARL JASPERS (1957)
THE PHILOSOPHY OF C. D. BROAD (1959)
THE PHILOSOPHY OF RUDOLF CARNAP (1963)

In Preparation:

THE PHILOSOPHY OF MARTIN BUBER
THE PHILOSOPHY OF C. I. LEWIS
THE PHILOSOPHY OF KARL R. POPPER

Other volumes to be announced later

Rudolf Carnap

THE LIBRARY OF LIVING PHILOSOPHERS
VOLUME XI

THE PHILOSOPHY OF RUDOLF CARNAP

EDITED BY
PAUL ARTHUR SCHILPP
NORTHWESTERN UNIVERSITY

LA SALLE, ILLINOIS • OPEN COURT • ESTABLISHED 1887
LONDON • CAMBRIDGE UNIVERSITY PRESS

THE PHILOSOPHY OF RUDOLF CARNAP

FIRST EDITION

Library of Congress Catalog Card Number: 62-9577

Printed in the United States of America

GENERAL INTRODUCTION*
TO
"THE LIBRARY OF LIVING PHILOSOPHERS"

According to the late F. C. S. Schiller, the greatest obstacle to fruitful discussion in philosophy is "the curious etiquette which apparently taboos the asking of questions about a philosopher's meaning while he is alive." The "interminable controversies which fill the histories of philosophy," he goes on to say, "could have been ended at once by asking the living philosophers a few searching questions."

The confident optimism of this last remark undoubtedly goes too far. Living thinkers have often been asked "a few searching questions," but their answers have not stopped "interminable controversies" about their real meaning. It is none the less true that there would be far greater clarity of understanding than is now often the case, if more such searching questions had been directed to great thinkers while they were still alive.

This, at any rate, is the basic thought behind the present undertaking. The volumes of *The Library of Living Philosophers* can in no sense take the place of the major writings of great and original thinkers. Students who would know the philosophies of such men as John Dewey, George Santayana, Alfred North Whitehead, G. E. Moore, Bertrand Russell, Ernst Cassirer, Karl Jaspers, Rudolf Carnap, Martin Buber, *et al.*, will still need to read the writings of these men. There is no substitute for first-hand contact with the original thought of the philosopher himself. Least of all does this *Library* pretend to be such a substitute. The *Library* in fact will spare neither effort nor expense in offering to the student the best possible guide to the published writings of a given thinker. We shall attempt to meet this aim by providing at the end of each volume in our series a complete bibliography of the published work of the philosopher in question. Nor should one overlook the fact that the essays in each volume cannot but finally lead to this same goal. The interpretative and critical discussions of the various phases of a great thinker's work and, most of all, the reply of the thinker himself, are bound to lead the reader to the works of the philosopher himself.

At the same time, there is no denying the fact that different experts find different ideas in the writings of the same philosopher. This is as true of the appreciative interpreter and grateful disciple as it is of the critical opponent. Nor can it be denied that such differences of reading and of interpretation on the part of other experts often leave the neo-

*This *General Introduction,* setting forth the underlying conception of this *Library,* is purposely reprinted in each volume (with only very minor changes).

phyte aghast before the whole maze of widely varying and even opposing interpretations. Who is right and whose interpretation shall he accept? When the doctors disagree among themselves, what is the poor student to do? If, in desperation, he decides that all of the interpreters are probably wrong and that the only thing for him to do is to go back to the original writings of the philosopher himself and then make his own decision—uninfluenced (as if this were possible) by the interpretation of any one else—the result is not that he has actually come to the meaning of the original philosopher himself, but rather that he has set up one more interpretation, which may differ to a greater or lesser degree from the interpretations already existing. It is clear that in this direction lies chaos, just the kind of chaos which Schiller has so graphically and inimitably described.[1]

It is curious that until now no way of escaping this difficulty has been seriously considered. It has not occurred to students of philosophy that one effective way of meeting the problem at least partially is to put these varying interpretations and critiques before the philosopher while he is still alive and to ask him to act at one and the same time as both defendant and judge. If the world's great living philosophers can be induced to co-operate in an enterprise whereby their own work can, at least to some extent, be saved from becoming merely "dessicated lecture-fodder," which on the one hand "provides innocuous sustenance for ruminant professors," and, on the other hand, gives an opportunity to such ruminants and their understudies to "speculate safely, endlessly, and fruitlessly, about what a philosopher must have meant" (Schiller), they will have taken a long step toward making their intentions clearly comprehensible.

With this in mind, *The Library of Living Philosophers* expects to publish at more or less regular intervals a volume on each of the greater among the world's living philosophers. In each case it will be the purpose of the editor of the *Library* to bring together in the volume the interpretations and criticisms of a wide range of that particular thinker's scholarly contemporaries, each of whom will be given a free hand to discuss the specific phase of the thinker's work which has been assigned to him. All contributed essays will finally be submitted to the philosopher with whose work and thought they are concerned, for his careful perusal and reply. And, although it would be expecting too much to imagine that the philosopher's reply will be able to stop all differences of interpretation and of critique, this should at least serve the purpose of stopping certain of the grosser and more general kinds of misinterpretations. If no further gain than this were to come from the present

[1]In his essay on "Must Philosophers Disagree?" in the volume by the same title Macmillan, London, 1934), from which the above quotations were taken.

and projected volumes of this *Library*, it would seem to be fully justified.

In carrying out this principal purpose of the *Library*, the editor announces that (in so far as humanly possible) each volume will conform to the following pattern:

First, a series of expository and critical articles written by the leading exponents and opponents of the philosopher's thought;

Second, the reply to the critics and commentators by the philosopher himself;

Third, an intellectual autobiography of the thinker whenever this can be secured; in any case an authoritative and authorized biography; and

Fourth, a bibliography of writings of the philosopher to provide a ready instrument to give access to his writings and thought.

The editor has deemed it desirable to secure the services of an Advisory Board of philosophers to aid him in the selection of the subjects of future volumes. The names of the six prominent American philosophers who originally consented to serve appear below.* To each of them the editor expresses his sincere gratitude.

Future volumes in this series will appear in as rapid succession as is feasible in view of the scholarly nature of this *Library*. The next two volumes in this series will be those of Martin Buber and C. I. Lewis.

Through the generosity of the Edward C. Hegeler Foundation, the publication of each new volume of the *Library* is assured on completion of the manuscript. However, funds are still required for editorial purposes in order to place the entire project of *The Library of Living Philosophers* on a sound financial foundation. The *Library* would be deeply grateful, therefore, for gifts and donations. Moreover, since November 6th, 1947, any gifts or donations made to The Library of Living Philosophers, Inc., are deductible by the donors in arriving at their taxable net income in conformity with the Internal Revenue Code of the Treasury Department of the United States of America.

DEPARTMENT OF PHILOSOPHY
NORTHWESTERN UNIVERSITY
EVANSTON, ILLINOIS

P. A. S.
Editor

ACKNOWLEDGEMENTS
by the editor

The editor hereby gratefully acknowledges his obligation and sincere gratitude to all the publishers of Professor Carnap's books and publications for their kind and uniform courtesy in permitting us to quote —sometimes at some length—from Professor Carnap's writings.

PAUL A. SCHILPP

ACKNOWLEDGEMENTS
by Professor Carnap

I wish to express my gratitude to all those who read parts of my manuscript for the present volume and who made numerous helpful suggestions for improvements.

My friends, Herbert Feigl, Carl G. Hempel, and Maria Reichenbach, read the original, much longer version of the autobiography and helped me greatly in the selection of the material to be retained; they suggested improvements in the content and the form of the autobiography and of some of the replies.

I wish to thank especially Maria Reichenbach, who generously devoted much time and effort in going over most parts of the manuscripts with great care; she gave me most valuable help by proposing clarifications and improving the style.

I am also indebted for help on various aspects, regarding both content and form, to Herbert G. Bohnert, Adolf Grünbaum, Brownlee Haydon, Olaf Helmer, David B. Kaplan, Ruth Anna Mathers, Gordon Matthews, and Larry Travis.

Most of all I wish to thank my dear wife for her devotion and co-operation in my work, without which my contributions to this volume might never have been completed.

RUDOLF CARNAP

TABLE OF CONTENTS

II. DESCRIPTIVE AND CRITICAL ESSAYS ON THE PHILOSOPHY OF RUDOLF CARNAP

PREFACE

A volume on *The Philosophy of Rudolf Carnap* has been inevitable ever since the inception of our LIBRARY OF LIVING PHILOSOPHERS. And this both because of the world-wide importance and influence of the philosophies of logical empiricism in general and because of the leading role the thought and work of Rudolf Carnap has played in this philosophical movement of the twentieth century.

The contents of this book will promptly convince any knowledgeable reader with its importance and lasting value. The seriousness with which Professor Carnap has taken both the unfolding and development of his own philosophical thought (in his detailed Autobiography) and the critical comments on and discussions of his philosophical contemporaries (in his careful and closely reasoned "Reply") make it possible to say, without fear of contradiction, that the present volume constitutes the definitive work on Carnap's philosophy. If it was a long time coming, it was more than worth waiting for.

The editor's most heart-felt gratitude is due, therefore, first and foremost to Professor Carnap himself for his painstaking efforts and kind and never failing helpful co-operation. But it is due to each of the contributors as well without whose kind co-operation this work could not have come into existence. It is only fair to add that Professor Herbert Feigl should be singled out for special mention. For it was he who in the first place helped this work to take shape and upon whose unselfish advice the editor has always been able to rely. The laborious task of assembling as nearly perfect and complete a bibliography as possible of Professor Carnap's writings was admirably and graciously carried to successful conclusion by Mr. Arthur Benson. And the Index—always a labor of love with little love for the labor—was kindly compiled by Robert P. Sylvester. To all these our sincere thanks.

It is with profound regret and deep sorrow that we have to record the passing of three contributors to this volume, namely, Professors Robert Feys of Louvain, Belgium, Paul Henle of the University of Michigan, and Arthur Pap of Yale University, and of three members of the Advisory Board of the *Library of Living Philosophers,* Professors George P. Adams of the University of California, Fritz Kaufmann of the University of Buffalo, and Arthur E. Murphy of the University of Texas. Their loss is far more deeply felt than we can express here.

The order of the essays in Part II was determined by the order in which Professor Carnap replied to his critics in Part III.

The publication of this book was unduly delayed because of a variety of circumstances over which the editor had no control.

* * * * *

It is a pleasure to call our readers' attention to the fact that, with the publication of this the XIth volume of our LIBRARY, the series will be appearing under the imprint of a new publisher. On May 30, 1961 we had the privilege of entering into a new contract with the Open Court Publishing Company of LaSalle, Illinois, by the terms of which Open Court will not merely publish all future volumes of this LIBRARY, but also has agreed to keep all volumes of this series in print.

In this connection it is particularly gratifying to be able to report that the painstaking, laborious, tedious, time-consuming, but exceedingly necessary and important task of proof-reading has been all but completely lifted from the shoulders of the editor by virtue of the fact that the very able and conscientious editor of Open Court, Dr. Eugene Freeman, in his capacity of Editorial Consultant to *The Library's* Editor, has undertaken to assume this onerous burden; a task in which he has been greatly strengthened and assisted by the grand lady who is truly proving to be his helpmate, Mrs. Ann Freeman. No words of the editor could suffice to express his sincerely felt gratitude to this gracious and hard working couple. If any typographical errors should still be left in this book, it will be through no fault of theirs; for they have spared neither time nor effort nor energy nor greatest care and scrutiny to make this volume as nearly letter-perfect as human fallibility can achieve.

* * * * *

The editor is happy, once again, to express his sincere gratitude and appreciation to the Graduate Research Council of Northwestern University and specifically to Vice-President Payson S. Wild and Dean Moody E. Prior of the Graduate School for the continuance of a small annual grant-in-aid to help defray some of the editorial expenses of this as well as of other volumes in our LIBRARY.

Volume XII, on *The Philosophy of Martin Buber* is scheduled to be published in 1964, Volume XIII, on *The Philosophy of C. I. Lewis,* in 1965, and Volume XIV, on *The Philosophy of Karl R. Popper,* in 1967.

BRENTANO HALL OF PHILOSOPHY
NORTHWESTERN UNIVERSITY
EVANSTON, ILLINOIS
SPRING, 1963

PAUL ARTHUR SCHILPP

Editor

RUDOLF CARNAP

INTELLECTUAL AUTOBIOGRAPHY

I was born in 1891 in Ronsdorf near Barmen, in Northwest Germany. My father, Johannes S. Carnap, came from a family of poor weavers, but had, in a long, industrious life, acquired a prosperous & respected position. The forebears of my mother, Anna Carnap nee Dörpfeld, were teachers, pastors, + peasants. When I was a child, my mother worked for years on a large book describing the life, work, & ideas of her late father, the teacher & pedagogical author Friedrich Wilhelm Dörpfeld. I was fascinated by the magical activity of putting thought on paper, & I have loved it ever since.

FACSIMILE REPRODUCTION OF CARNAP'S HANDWRITING

I

THE DEVELOPMENT OF MY THINKING

1. My Student Years

I WAS born in 1891 in Ronsdorf near Barmen, in Northwest Germany. My father, Johannes S. Carnap, came from a family of poor weavers, but had in a long, industrious life acquired a prosperous and respected position. The forebears of my mother, Anna Carnap nee Dörpfeld, were teachers, pastors, and peasants. When I was a child, my mother worked for years on a large book describing the life, work, and ideas of her late father, the teacher and pedagogical author, Friedrich Wilhelm Dörpfeld. I was fascinated by the magical activity of putting thought on paper, and I have loved it ever since.

My parents were deeply religious; their faith permeated their whole lives. My mother used to impress upon us that the essential in religion was not so much the acceptance of a creed, but the living of the good life; the convictions of another were for her morally neutral, as long as he sought seriously for the truth. This attitude made her very tolerant toward people with other beliefs.

When my sister and I reached school age, my mother, having been a teacher, obtained permission to teach us herself at home. She did so for three years, but for only an hour each day. She did not believe much in the quantity of material learned; she aimed rather at helping us to acquire a clear and interconnected knowledge of each item and, above all, to develop the ability to think for ourselves.

After the death of my father in 1898 we moved to Barmen. I attended the *Gymnasium,* whose curriculum was based on the classical languages. The subjects I liked most were mathematics, which attracted me by the exactness of its concepts and the possibility of proving results by mere thinking, and Latin with its rational structure.

In 1909 we moved to Jena. From 1910 to 1914 I studied at the Universities of Jena and Freiburg/i.B. First I concentrated on philosophy and mathematics; later, physics and philosophy were my major fields. In the selection of lecture courses I followed only my own interests without thinking about examinations or a professional career. When I did not like a lecture course, I dropped it and studied the subject by reading books in the field instead.

Within the field of philosophy, I was mainly interested in the theory of knowledge and in the philosophy of science. On the other hand, in the field of logic, lecture courses and books by philosophers appeared to me dull and entirely obsolete after I had become acquainted with a genuine logic through Frege's lectures. I studied Kant's philosophy with Bruno Bauch in Jena. In his seminar, the *Critique of Pure Reason* was discussed in detail for an entire year. I was strongly impressed by Kant's conception that the geometrical structure of space is determined by the form of our intuition. The after-effects of this influence were still noticeable in the chapter on the space of intuition in my dissertation, *Der Raum* (written in 1920, see the next section).

I remember with special pleasure and gratitude the seminars of Hermann Nohl (at that time a young instructor in Jena), in philosophy, education, and psychology, even when the topic, for example, Hegel's *Rechtsphilosophie,* was often somewhat remote from my main interests. My friends and I were particularly attracted by Nohl because he took a personal interest in the lives and thoughts of his students, in contrast to most of the professors in Germany at that time, and because in his seminars and in private talks he tried to give us a deeper understanding of philosophers on the basis of their attitude toward life *("Lebensgefühl")* and their cultural background.

On the whole, I think I learned much more in the field of philosophy by reading and by private conversations than by attending lectures and seminars.

I greatly enjoyed the study of mathematics. In contrast to the endless controversies among the various schools of philosophy, the results in mathematics could be proven exactly and there was no further controversy. But the most fruitful inspiration I received from university lectures did not come from those in the fields of philosophy proper or mathematics proper, but rather from the lectures of Frege on the borderlands between those fields, namely, symbolic logic and the foundations of mathematics.

Gottlob Frege (1848-1925) was at that time, although past 60, only Professor Extraordinarius (Associate Professor) of mathematics in Jena. His work was practically unknown in Germany; neither mathematicians nor philosophers paid any attention to it. It was obvious that Frege was deeply disappointed and sometimes bitter about this dead silence. No publishing house was willing to bring out his main work, the two volumes of *Grundgesetze der Arithmetik;* he had it printed at his own expense. In addition, there was the disappointment over Russell's discovery of the famous antinomy which occurs both in Frege's system and in Cantor's set theory. I do not remember that he ever discussed in his lectures the problem of this antinomy and the question of possible modifications of his system in order to eliminate it. But from the Appendix of the second volume it is clear that he was confident that a satisfactory way for overcoming the difficulty could be found. He did not share the pessimism with respect to the "foundation crisis" of mathematics sometimes expressed by other authors.

In the fall of 1910, I attended Frege's course "Begriffsschrift" (conceptual notation, ideography), out of curiosity, not knowing anything either of the man or the subject except for a friend's remark that somebody had found it interesting. We found a very small number of other students, there. Frege looked old beyond his years. He was of small stature, rather shy, extremely introverted. He seldom looked at the audience. Ordinarily we saw only his back, while he drew the strange diagrams of his symbolism on the blackboard and explained them. Never did a student ask a question or make a remark, whether during the lecture or afterwards. The possibility of a discussion seemed to be out of the question.

Toward the end of the semester Frege indicated that the new logic to which he had introduced us, could serve for the construction of the whole of mathematics. This remark aroused our curiosity. In the summer semester of 1913, my friend and I decided to attend Frege's course "Begriffsschrift II". This time the entire class consisted of the two of us and a retired major of the army who studied some of the new ideas in mathematics as a hobby. It was from the major that I first heard about Cantor's set theory, which no professor had ever mentioned. In this small group Frege felt more at ease and thawed out a bit more. There were still no questions or discussions. But Frege occasionally made critical remarks about other conceptions, sometimes with irony and even sarcasm. In particular he attacked the formalists, those who declared that numbers were mere symbols. Although his main works do not show much of his witty irony, there exists a delightful little satire *Ueber die Zahlen des Herrn H. Schubert.*[1] In this pamphlet he ridicules the definition which H. Schubert had given in an article on the foundations of mathematics, which was published as the first article in the first volume of the first edition of the large *Enzyklopädie der mathematischen Wissenschaften.* (Schubert's article fortunately was replaced in the second edition by an excellent contribution by Hermes and Scholz.) Frege points out that Schubert discovered a new principle, which Frege proposed to call the principle of the non-distinction of the distinct, and he showed further that his principle could be used in a most fruitful way in order

[1] I own a copy of this pamphlet which was privately published by Frege (Jena, 1899, 32 pp.). I have not seen any reference to it (except for that in Church's Bibliography of Symbolic Logic, based on my information). I do not know whether any library possesses it. I have also a micro-film copy and shall be glad to have copies made for anyone interested in it.

to reach the most amazing conclusions.

In the advanced course on *Begriffsschrift,* Frege explained various applications, among them some which are not contained in his publications, e.g., a definition of the continuity of a function, and of the limit of a function, the distinction between ordinary convergence and uniform convergence. All these concepts were expressible with the help of the quantifiers, which appear in his system of logic for the first time. He gave also a demonstration of the logical mistake in the ontological proof for the existence of God.

Although Frege gave quite a number of examples of interesting applications of his symbolism in mathematics, he usually did not discuss general philosophical problems. It is evident from his works that he saw the great philosophical importance of the new instrument which he had created, but he did not convey a clear impression of this to his students. Thus, although I was intensely interested in his system of logic, I was not aware at that time of its great philosophical significance. Only much later, after the first world war, when I read Frege's and Russell's books with greater attention, did I recognize the value of Frege's work not only for the foundations of mathematics, but for philosophy in general.

In the summer semester of 1914 I attended Frege's course, *Logik in der Mathematik*. Here he examined critically some of the customary conceptions and formulations in mathematics. He deplored the fact that mathematicians did not even seem to aim at the construction of a unified, well-founded *system* of mathematics, and therefore showed a lack of interest in foundations. He pointed out a certain looseness in the customary formulation of axioms, definitions, and proofs, even in works of the more prominent mathematicians. As an example he quoted Weyerstrass' definition: "A number is a series of things of the same kind" (". . .*eine Reihe gleichartiger Dinge*"). He criticized in particular the lack of attention to certain fundamental distinctions, e.g., the distinction between the symbol and the symbolized, that between a logical concept and a mental image or act, and that between a function and the value of the function. Unfortunately, his admonitions go mostly unheeded even today.

Among the empirical sciences physics was for me the most attractive. I was strongly impressed by the fact that it is possible to state laws with exact numerical relations by which events can be generally described and thus explained, and future events predicted.

In 1913 I began experimental research in physics, aimed at a doctoral dissertation. The problem concerned the emission of electrons from a heated electrode in a vacuum. This task was technically difficult, and I was certainly not a good experimenter. Thus the progress of the investigation was slow. It came to an abrupt end in August 1914 with the outbreak of the war. The professor with whom I had studied was killed in the very first days of the war.

I was also interested in other fields of knowledge. I read books in many fields and pondered whether to study some of them more thoroughly. But psychology was the only field in which I attended courses and seminars and did a little experimental work. What was disturbing to me in all fields of empirical science except physics, was the lack of clarity in the explanation of the concepts and in the formulation of the laws, and the great number of insufficiently connected facts.

During my pre-university years I had gradually begun to doubt the religious doctrines about the world, man, and God. As a student I turned away from these beliefs more deliberately and definitely. Under the influence of books and conversations with friends, I recognized that these doctrines, if interpreted literally, were incompatible with the results of modern science, especially with the theory of evolution in biology and determinism in physics. The freethinker movement in Germany was at that time mainly represented by the *Monistenbund* (Society of Monists). I studied eagerly the works of the leaders of this movement, e.g., the zoologist Ernst Haeckel and the prominent chemist Wilhelm Ostwald. Although most of these books could not be regarded as serious philosophical writings but belonged rather to popular literature, and from the point of view of the theory of knowledge their formulations seemed to me often quite primitive, I was nevertheless in sympathy with their insistence that the scientific method was the only method of obtaining well-founded, systematically coherent knowledge and with their humanist aim of improving the life of mankind by rational means.

The transformation of my basic beliefs occurred however not suddenly, but in a gradual development. First the supernatural features in the doctrines of religion disappeared. Christ was regarded not as divine, but as a man among men, distinguished as an important leader in the development of humane morality. Later the idea of God as a personal, though immaterial being, interfering in the course of nature and history in order to reward and punish, was abandoned and replaced by a kind of pantheism. This conception had certain Spinozist features, which came to me less from the works of Spinoza himself than from those of men like Goethe, whose work, personality, and *Lebensweisheit* (wisdom of life) I esteemed very highly. Since my pantheism was thus more influenced by poetical than by philosophical works, it had more an ethical than a theoretical nature; that is to say, it was more a matter of the attitude toward the world and fellow human beings than of explicitly formulated doctrines. Later I became more and more convinced that pantheism, if taken not as an emotional-ethical attitude but as a doctrine, could not be scientifically grounded, inasmuch as the events in nature, including those in man and society as a part of nature, can be explained by the scientific method without the need of any idea of God.

Together with the belief in a personal God, I abandoned also the belief in immortality as the survival of a personal, conscious soul. The main factor in this development was a strong impression of the continuity in the scientific view of the world. Man has gradually developed from lower forms of organisms without sudden changes. All mental processes are intimately connected with the brain; how can they continue when the body disintegrates? Thus I arrived gradually at a clear naturalistic conception: everything that happens is part of nature, man is a higher form of organism and dies like all other organisms. There remained the question of an explanation of the historical fact that the belief in one or several gods and in immortality was very widespread in all known cultures. This, however, was not a philosophical problem but a historical and psychological one. I gradually found an answer based on anthropological results concerning the historical evolution of religious conceptions. Much later I gained important insights into the development of the individual's picture of the world through the results of Freud's investigations and in particular his discovery of the origin of the conception of God as a substitute for the father.

Since I experienced the positive effect of a living religion in the lives of my parents and in my own life during childhood, my respect for any man whose character I esteem highly is not diminished by the fact that he embraces some form of religion, traditional or otherwise. At the present stage of development of our culture, many people still need religious mythological symbols and images. It seems to me wrong to try to deprive them of the support they obtain from these ideas, let alone to ridicule them.

An entirely different matter is the question of theology, here understood as a system of doctrines in distinction to a system of valuations and prescriptions for life. Systematic theology claims to represent knowledge concerning alleged beings of a supernatural order. A claim of this kind must be examined according to the same rigorous standards as any other claim of knowledge. Now in my considered opinion this examination has clearly shown that traditional theology is a remnant of earlier times, entirely out of line with the scientific way of thinking in the present century. Any system of traditional theological dogmas can usually be interpreted in many different ways. If they are taken in a direct and literal sense, for example, based on a literal interpretation of statements in the Bible or other "holy scriptures," then most of the dogmas are refuted by the results of science. If, on the other hand, this crude literal interpretation is rejected and instead a refined reformulation is accepted which puts theological questions outside the scope of the scientific method, then the dogmas have the same character as statements of traditional metaphysics. As I shall explain later, I came in my philosophical development first to the insight that the main statements of traditional metaphysics are outside the realm of science and irrelevant for scientific knowledge, and later to the more radical conviction that they are devoid of any cognitive content. Since that time I have been convinced that the same holds for most of the statements of contemporary Christian theology.

The transformation and final abandonment of my religious convictions led at no time to a nihilistic attitude towards moral questions. My moral valuations were afterwards essentially the same as before. It is not easy to characterize these valuations in a few words, since they are not based on explicitly formulated principles, but constitute rather an implicit lasting attitude. The following should therefore be understood as merely a rough and brief indication of certain basic features. The main task of an individual seems to me the development of his personality and the creation of fruitful and healthy relations among human beings. This aim implies the task of co-operation in the development of society and ultimately of the whole of mankind towards a community in which every individual has the possibility of leading a satisfying life and of participating in cultural goods. The fact that everybody knows that he will eventually die, need not make his life meaningless or aimless. He himself gives meaning to his life if he sets tasks for himself, struggles to fulfill them to the best of his ability, and regards all the specific tasks of all individuals as parts of the great task of humanity, whose aim goes far beyond the limited span of each individual life.

The outbreak of the war in 1914 was for me an incomprehensible catastrophe. Military service was contrary to my whole attitude, but I accepted it now as a duty, believed to be necessary in order to save the fatherland. Before the war, I, like most of my friends, had been uninterested and ignorant in political matters. We had some general ideals, including a just, harmonious and rational organization within the nation and among the nations. We realized that the existing political and economic order was not in accord with these ideals, and still less the customary method of settling conflicts of interests among nations by war. Thus the general trend of our political thinking was pacifist, anti-militarist, anti-monarchist, perhaps also socialist. But we did not think much about the problem of how to implement these ideals by practical action. The war suddenly destroyed our illusion that everything was already on the right path of continuous progress.

During the first years of the war I was at the front most of the time. In the summer of 1917 I was transferred to Berlin. I remained an officer in the army, but I served as a physicist in a military institution which worked on the development of the new wireless telegraph and, toward the end of the war, of the wireless telephone. In Berlin I had opportunities to study political problems by reading and talking with friends; my aim was to understand the causes of the war and possible ways of ending it and of avoiding future wars. I observed that in various countries the labor parties were the only large groups which had preserved at least a remnant of the aims of internationalism and of the anti-war attitude. I gradually gained a clearer understanding of the connection between the international order and the economic order, and I began to study the ideas of the socialist workers' movement in greater detail. I also sent out circular letters in which all these problems were discussed by a larger circle of friends and acquaintances.

My friends in Berlin and I welcomed the German revolution at least for its negative effect, the liberation from the old powers. Similarly, we had welcomed the revolution in Russia one year earlier. In both cases we had some hope for the future, mixed with doubts. In both cases, after a few years, we saw that the promised high ideals were not realized.

Even during the war, my scientific and philosophical interests were not entirely neglected. During a quiet period at the Western Front in 1917 I read many books in various fields, e.g., about the world situation and the great questions of politics, problems of *Weltanschauung,* poetry, but also science and philosophy. At that time I became acquainted with Einstein's theory of relativity, and was strongly impressed and enthusiastic about the magnificent simplicity and great explanatory power of the basic principles. Later, in Berlin, I studied the theory of relativity more thoroughly and was especially interested in the methodological problems connected with it. I also wrote circular letters about the theory to a few friends; I included an article or small book by Einstein or others and added detailed explanations with diagrams. Thus I tried to share my great intellectual enjoyment of the theory with friends.

2. *The Beginning of My Work in Philosophy (1919-1926)*

After the war, I lived for a while in Jena, and then in Buchenbach near Freiburg/i.B. In this period, I first passed my examinations, and then I began my own research in philosophy, first in relative isolation, but later in contact with Reichenbach and others who worked in a similar direction. This period ended in 1926, when I went to Vienna and joined the Vienna Circle.

Before the war I had studied according to my own interests without any clear practical plans. I had the idea that some day I would be a university teacher, but I had not decided whether in philosophy or in physics. When I came back from more than four years of service in the war, I was still equally interested in both fields. However, I now saw clearly that I did not wish to do experimental work in physics, because my inclination and abilities were purely theoretical. Therefore I tried to combine my interests in theoretical physics and in philosophy.

Around 1919 I studied the great work *Principia Mathematica* by Whitehead and Russell, to which Frege had sometimes referred in his lectures. I was strongly impressed by the development of the theory of relations in this work. The beginnings of a symbolic logic of relations were also in Frege's system, but in *P.M.* the theory was developed in a very comprehensive way and represented by a much more convenient notation. I began to apply symbolic notation, now more frequently in the *Principia* form than in Frege's, in my own thinking about philosophical problems or in the formulation of axiom systems. When I considered a concept or a proposition occurring in a scientific or philosophical discussion, I thought that I understood it clearly only if I felt that I could express it, if I wanted to, in symbolic language. I performed the actual symbolization, of course, only in special cases where it seemed necessary or useful.

In particular, I began the construction of an *axiom system* for a physical theory of *space and time,* using as primitives two relations, the coincidence *C* of world points of two physical elements, and the time relation *T* between the world points of the same physical element. I thought that I might develop this axiom system into a doctor's dissertation in theoretical physics. I wrote a brief outline of it, called "Axiomatic Foundations of Kinematics", and showed it to Professor Max Wien, the head of the Institute of Physics at the University of Jena. After I gave some explanations, he said that it might be an interesting project, but certainly not in physics. He suggested that I might show the outline to Professor Bruno Bauch with whom I had studied philosophy. Bauch took more interest, but his final judgment was that this project belonged to physics rather than philosophy. He suggested my submitting it to Professor Wien. But in the end we came to an agreement that I would choose another project in philosophy, namely the philosophical foundations of geometry.

This experience with my thesis project, which seemed to fit neither into physics nor into philosophy, made clear to me for the first time what difficulties I would continually have to face in the future. If one is interested in the relations between fields which, according to customary academic divisions, belong to different departments, then he will not be welcomed as a builder of bridges, as he might have expected, but will rather be regarded by both sides as an outsider and troublesome intruder.

In my doctoral dissertation, *Der Raum* [1921][2], I tried to show that

[2]Notations like "[1921]" or "[1932-4]" refer to items in the Bibliography at the end of the present volume.

the contradictory theories concerning the nature of space, maintained by mathematicians, philosophers, and physicists, were due to the fact that these writers talked about entirely different subjects while using the same term "space". I distinguished three meanings of this term, namely, formal space, intuitive space, and physical space. Formal space is an abstract system, constructed in mathematics, and more precisely in the logic of relations; therefore our knowledge of formal space is of a logical nature. Knowledge of intuitive space I regarded at that time, under the influence of Kant and the neo-Kantians, especially Natorp and Cassirer, as based on "pure intuition" and independent of contingent experience. But, in contrast to Kant, I limited the features of intuitive space grasped by pure intuition to certain topological properties; the metrical structure (in Kant's view, the Euclidean structure) and the three-dimensionality I regarded not as purely intuitive, but rather as empirical. Knowledge of physical space I already considered as entirely empirical, in agreement with empiricists like Helmholtz and Schlick. In particular, I discussed the role of non-Euclidean geometry in Einstein's theory.

My own philosophical work began with the doctoral dissertation just mentioned. The men who had the strongest effect on my philosophical thinking were Frege and Russell. I was influenced by Frege first through his lectures and later, perhaps even to a greater extent, through his works, most of which I read only after the war. His main work, *Die Grundgesetze der Arithmetik* (2 vols., 1893 and 1903), I studied in 1920. From Frege I learned carefulness and clarity in the analysis of concepts and linguistic expressions, the distinction between expressions and what they stand for, and concerning the latter between what he called *"Bedeutung"* (denotation or *nominatum*) and what he called *"Sinn"* (sense or *significatum*). From his analysis I gained the conviction that knowledge in mathematics is analytic in the general sense that it has essentially the same nature as knowledge in logic. I shall later explain how this view became more radical and precise, chiefly through the influence of Wittgenstein. Furthermore the following conception, which derives essentially from Frege, seemed to me of paramount importance: It is the task of logic and of mathematics within the total system of knowledge to supply the forms of concepts, statements, and inferences, forms which are then applicable everywhere, hence also to non-logical knowledge. It follows from these considerations that the nature of logic and mathematics can be clearly understood only if close attention is given to their application in non-logical fields, especially in empirical science. Although the greater part of my work belongs to the fields of pure logic and the logical foundations of mathematics, nevertheless great weight is given in my thinking to the application of logic to non-logical knowledge. This point of view is an important factor in the motivation for some of my philosophical positions, for example, for the choice of forms of languages, for my emphasis on the fundamental distinction between logical and non-logical knowledge. The latter position, which I share with many contemporary philosophers, differs from that of some logicians like Tarski and Quine, with whom I agree on many other basic questions. From Frege I learned the requirement to formulate the rules of inference of logic without any reference to meaning, but also the great significance of meaning analysis. I believe that here are the roots of my philosophical interest—on the one hand in logical syntax, and on the other hand in that part of semantics which may be regarded as a theory of meaning.

Whereas Frege had the strongest influence on me in the fields of logic and semantics, in my philosophical thinking in general I learned most from Bertrand Russell. In the winter of 1921 I read his book, *Our Knowledge of the External World, as a Field For Scientific Method in Philosophy*. Some passages made an especially vivid impression on me because they formulated clearly and explicitly a view of the aim and method of philosophy which I had implicitly held for some time. In the Preface he speaks about "the logical-analytic method of philosophy" and refers to Frege's work as the first complete example of this method. And on the very last pages of the book he gives a summarizing characterization of this philosophical method in the following words:

> The study of logic becomes the central study in philosophy: it gives the method of research in philosophy, just as mathematics gives the method in physics. . . .
>
> All this supposed knowledge in the traditional systems must be swept away, and a new beginning must be made. . . . To the large and still growing body of men engaged in the pursuit of science, . . . the new method, successful already in such time-honored problems as number, infinity, continuity, space and time, should make an appeal which the older methods have wholly failed to make. . . . The one and only condition, I believe, which is necessary in order to secure for philosophy in the near future an achievement surpassing all that has hitherto been accomplished by philosophers, is the creation of a school of men with scientific training and philosophical interests, unhampered by the traditions of the past, and not misled by the literary methods of those who copy the ancients in all except their merits.

I felt as if this appeal had been directed to me personally. To work in this spirit would be my task from now on! And indeed henceforth the application of the new logical instrument for the purposes of analyzing scientific concepts and of clarifying philosophical problems has been the essential aim of my philosophical activity.

I now began an intensive study of Russell's books on the theory of knowledge and the methodology of science. I owe very much to his work, not only with respect to philosophical method, but also in the solution of special problems.

I also continued to occupy myself with symbolic logic. Since the *Principia Mathematica* was not easily accessible, I began work on a textbook in symbolic logic. There was no copy of the *Principia* in the University Library at Freiburg. The price of a new copy was out of reach because of the inflation in Germany. Since my efforts to find a secondhand copy in England were unsuccessful, I asked Russell whether he could help me in finding one. Instead, he sent me a long list containing all the most important definitions of *Principia*, handwritten by himself, on 35 pages, which I still cherish as a priceless possession. In 1924 I wrote the first version of the later book, *Abriss der Logistik* [1929]. It was based on *Principia*. Its main purpose was to give not only a system of symbolic logic, but also to show its application for the analysis of concepts and the construction of deductive systems.

Among all those who worked in Germany in a similar direction in philosophy and in the foundations of science, Hans Reichenbach was the one whose philosophical outlook was nearest to mine. He was at that time Instructor of Physics at the Technological Institute in Stuttgart. Both of us came from physics and had the same interest in its philosophical foundations, and especially in the methodological problems created by Einstein's theory of relativity. Furthermore, we had a common interest in the theory of knowledge and in logic. At first we communicated only by correspondence. It was not until March 1923, that we met at a small conference in Erlangen, which we organized with a few others who were likewise working in the field of symbolic logic and its use for the development of a scientific philosophy. Among the participants were Heinrich Behmann, Paul Hertz, and Kurt Lewin. There were addresses on pure logic, e.g., a new symbolism, the decision problem, relational structures, and on applied logic, e.g., the relation between physical objects and sense-data, a theory of knowledge without metaphysics, a comparative theory of sciences, the topology of time, and the use of the axiomatic method in physics. Our points of view were often quite divergent, and the debates were very vivid and sometimes heated. Nevertheless, there was a common basic attitude and the common aim of developing a sound and exact method in philosophy. We were gratified to realize that there was a considerable number of men in Germany who worked toward this same aim. The Erlangen Conference may be regarded as the small but significant initial step in the movement of a scientific philosophy in Germany.

After the Erlangen Conference I met Reichenbach frequently. Each of us, when hitting upon new ideas, regarded the other as the best critic. Since Reichenbach remained in close contact with physics through his teaching and research, whereas I concentrated more on other fields, I often asked him for explanations in recent developments, for example, in quantum-mechanics. His explanations were always excellent in bringing out the main points with great clarity. I sometimes explained to him developments in special problems of logic or the logical foundations of mathematics.

I continued my work on the foundations of physics. In an article on the task of physics [1923] I imagined the ideal system of physics as consisting of three volumes: The first was to contain the basic physical laws, represented as a formal axiom system; the second to contain the phenomenal-physical dictionary, that is to say, the rules of correspondence between observable qualities and physical magnitudes; the third to contain descriptions of the physical state of the universe for two arbitrary time points. From these descriptions, together with the laws contained in the first volume, the state of the world for any other time-point would be deducible (Laplace's form of determinism), and from this result, with the help of the rules of correspondence, the qualities could be derived which are observable at any position in space and time. The distinction between the laws represented as formal axioms and the correlations to observables was resumed and further developed many years later in connection with the theoretical language.

In an article [1924], I made an analysis of the structure of causal determination in physics and of its connection with the structure of space. My strongly conventionalist attitude in this article and in [1923] was influenced by Poincaré's books and by Hugo Dingler. However, I did not share Dingler's radical conventionalism and still less his rejection of Einstein's general theory of relativity.

About this time I worked again on the axiom system of space-time-topology (*C-T* system). I explained the philosophical basis of this system in the paper [1925]. The main ideas were first that the spatial order of events is based on the structure of the causal connection or signal relation, in the sense that the spatial distance between two bodies is the greater, the more time is needed for a signal from the one to the other; and secondly, that the signal relation in turn is definable on the basis of the temporal relation "earlier than".[3]

In this period I also wrote a monograph, *Physikalische Begriffsbildung* [1926]. Among other things I specified here the form of the rules which must be set up for the specification of a quantitative physical magnitude. Furthermore, I described the world of physics as an abstract system of ordered quadruples of real numbers to which values of certain functions are co-ordinated; the quadruples represent the space-time-points, and the

[3]The treatise "Topology of the Space-Time-System", which I announced in the paper as forthcoming, was never published. I gave a summary of the axiom system in the logistics book [1929], and a more detailed exposition in the later books [1954-3] and [1958-2] (§§48-50).

philosophers who are in contact with scientific work. Only gradually, in the course of years, did I recognize clearly that my way of thinking was neutral with respect to the traditional controversies, e.g., realism vs. idealism, nominalism vs. Platonism (realism of universals), materialism vs. spiritualism, and so on. When I developed the system of the *Aufbau,* it actually did not matter to me which of the various forms of philosophical language I used, because to me they were merely modes of speech, and not formulations of positions. Indeed, in the book itself, in the description of the system of construction or constitution, I used in addition to the neutral language of symbolic logic three other languages, in order to facilitate the understanding for the reader; namely, first, a simple translation of the symbolic formula of definition into the word language; second, a corresponding formulation in the realistic language as it is customary in natural science; and third, a reformulation of the definition as a rule of operation for a constructive procedure, applicable by anybody, be it Kant's transcendental subject or a computing machine.

The system of concepts was constructed on a phenomenalistic basis; the basic elements were experiences, as mentioned before. However, I indicated also the possibility of constructing a total system of concepts on a physicalistic basis. The main motivation for my choice of a phenomenalistic basis was the intention to represent not only the logical relations among the concepts but also the equally important epistemological relations. The system was intended to give, though not a description, still a rational reconstruction of the actual process of the formation of concepts. The choice of a phenomenalistic basis was influenced by some radical empiricist or positivist German philosphers of the end of the last century whom I had studied with interest, in the first place Ernst Mach, and further Richard Avenarius, Richard von Schubert-Soldern, and Wilhelm Schuppe. For the construction of scientific concepts on the phenomenal basis I found fruitful suggestions in the works of Mach and Avenarius, and, above all, in the logical constructions made by Russell. With respect to the problem of the basis, my attitude was again ontologically neutral. For me it was simply a methodological question of choosing the most suitable basis for the system to be constructed, either a phenomenalistic or a physicalistic basis. The ontological theses of the traditional doctrines of either phenomenalism or materialism remained for me entirely out of consideration.

This neutral attitude toward the various philosophical forms of language, based on the principle that everyone is free to use the language most suited to his purpose, has remained the same throughout my life. It was formulated as "principle of tolerance" in *Logical Syntax* and I still hold it today, e.g., with respect to the contemporary controversy about a nominalist or Platonic language. On the other hand, regarding the criticism of traditional metaphysics, in the *Aufbau* I merely refrained from taking sides; I added that, if one proceeds from the discussion of language forms to that of the corresponding metaphysical theses about the reality or unreality of some kind of entities, he steps beyond the bounds of science. I shall later speak of the development towards a more radical anti-metaphysical position.

For the construction of the world of physics on the basis of the temporal sequence of sensory experiences, I used the following method. A system of ordered quadruples of real numbers serves as the system of co-ordinates of space-time-points. To these quadruples, sensory qualities, e.g., colors, are assigned first, and then numbers as values of physical state magnitudes. These assignments are made according to general rules of maximization: for example, the assignments should be in accordance with the experiences as far as possible, there should be a minimum of change in the course of time, and a maximum of regularity. As Quine[4] has pointed out correctly, this procedure is different from the methods of concept formation used elsewhere in my book. In general, I introduced concepts by explicit definitions, but here the physical concepts were introduced instead on the basis of general principles of correspondence, simplicity, and analogy. It seems to me that the procedure which I used in the construction of the physical world, anticipates the method which I recognized explicitly much later, namely the method of introducing theoretical terms by postulates and rules of correspondence.

The first version of the book was finished in 1925, before I went to Vienna. Later it was revised, and then published in 1928. I emphasized in the book that all details in the construction of the system were only tentative. I believed that my proposal of the system would soon induce others to make new attempts or improvements either in the system as a whole or in certain particular points. I should have been very happy if in this way my book had soon been superseded by better systems. But for a long time nobody worked in this direction. The first proposal for an improved system with the same general aim was presented in Nelson Goodman's book, *The Structure of Appearance* (1951). In the meantime I myself did not work on these problems. Part of the reason was the fact that some years later a physicalistic basis appeared to me more suitable for a system of all scientific concepts than a phenomenalistic one; therefore the specific problems of the system of the *Aufbau* lost their interest for me. While writing the present section, I looked at the old book for the first time in many years. I had the impression that the problems raised and the general features of the methods used are still fruitful, and perhaps also some of the answers I gave to particular

[4]Quine, "Two Dogmas of Empiricism", reprinted in *From a Logical Point of View*, 40.

problems. But it might chiefly be of interest to those who still prefer a phenomenalistic basis for the construction of the total system of concepts.

3. The Vienna Circle (1926-1935)

In the summer of 1924, through Reichenbach, I had become acquainted with Moritz Schlick. Schlick told me that he would be happy to have me as an instructor in Vienna. In 1925 I went for a short time to Vienna and gave some lectures in Schlick's Philosophical Circle. From the fall of 1926 to the summer of 1931 I was an instructor of philosophy at the University of Vienna.

For my philosophical work the period in Vienna was one of the most stimulating, enjoyable, and fruitful periods of my life. My interests and my basic philosophical views were more in accord with those of the Circle than with any group I ever found. From the very beginning, when in 1925 I explained in the Circle the general plan and method of *Der logische Aufbau,* I found a lively interest. When I returned to Vienna in 1926, the typescript of the first version of the book was read by the members of the Circle, and many of its problems were thoroughly discussed. Especially the mathematician Hans Hahn, who was strongly interested in symbolic logic, said that he had always hoped that somebody would carry out Russell's program of an exact philosophical method using the means of symbolic logic, and welcomed my book as the fulfillment of these hopes. Hahn was strongly influenced by Ernst Mach's phenomenalism, and therefore recognized the importance of the reduction of scientific concepts to a phenomenalistic basis, which I had attempted in the book.

Schlick, like Reichenbach and myself, had come to philosophy from physics. In 1922 he had been called to the University of Vienna and occupied the chair for the philosophy of the inductive sciences, which had been held previously by philosophically interested physicists like Ernst Mach and Ludwig Boltzmann. Since then he had begun to gather a group of men who were interested in the philosophical foundations of science; this group was later called the Vienna Circle. Among those who were particularly active in the discussions of the Circle were Hahn, the economist and sociologist Otto Neurath, the philosopher Victor Kraft, and, among the younger members, Friedrich Waismann and Herbert Feigl. Later the mathematicians Karl Menger, Kurt Gödel, and Gustav Bergmann joined the Circle. The physicist Philipp Frank came often from Prague to Vienna and visited the Circle. The philosopher of law, Felix Kaufmann, attended the meetings often, but did not count himself as a member, because his philosophical position was rather remote from ours. He was chiefly influenced by Husserl's phenomenology;

but later, in America, he came closer to the point of view of empiricism.

The task of fruitful collaboration, often so difficult among philosophers, was facilitated in our Circle by the fact that all members had a first-hand acquaintance with some field of science, either mathematics, physics or social science. This led to a higher standard in clarity and responsibility than is usually found in philosophical groups, particularly in Germany. Also, the members of the Circle were familiar with modern logic. This made it possible to represent the analysis of a concept or proposition under discussion symbolically and thereby make the arguments more precise. Furthermore, there was agreement among most of the members to reject traditional metaphysics. However, very little time was wasted in a polemic against metaphysics. The anti-metaphysical attitude showed itself chiefly in the choice of the language used in the discussion. We tried to avoid the terms of traditional philosophy and to use instead those of logic, mathematics, and empirical science, or of that part of the ordinary language which, though more vague, still is in principle translatable into a scientific language.

Characteristic for the Circle was the open and undogmatic attitude taken in the discussions. Everyone was willing constantly to subject his views to a re-examination by others or by himself. The common spirit was one of co-operation rather than competition. The common purpose was to work together in the struggle for clarification and insight.

The congenial atmosphere in the Circle meetings was due above all to Schlick's personality, his unfailing kindness, tolerance, and modesty. Both by his personal inclination toward clarity and by his training in physics, he was thoroughly imbued with the scientific way of thinking. He was one of the first philosophers to analyze the methodological foundations of Einstein's theory of relativity and to point out its great significance for philosophy. Schlick's important philosophical work has unfortunately not found the attention it deserves. His very first book (*Erkenntnislehre,* 1918) contains many ideas that anticipate the core of later, often more elaborate and formalized developments by other authors. Examples are his conception of the task of philosophy as an analysis of the foundations of knowledge and, in particular, of science, in other words, a clarification of meaning; the conception of meaning as given by the rules of the language for the use of a sign; the view that knowledge is characterized by symbolization and is thus fundamentally different from mere experience; the emphasis on the procedure, suggested by Hilbert's formalistic method, of introducing concepts by so-called implicit definitions, i.e., by postulates; the conception of truth as consisting in the unique co-ordination of a statement to a fact; the view that the distinction between the physical and the mental is not a distinction between two kinds of entities, but merely a difference of two languages; the rejection of the alleged incompatibility of freedom of the will and determinism as based on a confusion of regularity with compulsion. By his clear, sober, and realistic way of thinking, Schlick often exerted a sound moderating influence on the discussions of the Circle. Sometimes he warned against an exaggerated thesis or against an explication that appeared too artificial, and he appealed to what might be called a scientifically refined common sense.

I shall not relate in detail the content of the discussions in the Circle. Some of the problems will be dealt with in Part Two. More detailed reports of the activities and the views of the Vienna Circle have been published by other authors.[5]

I should, however, like to describe some aspects of Neurath's activity in the Circle and his influence on my own thinking, because very little has been written about this in the earlier publications. One of the important contributions made by Neurath consisted in his frequent remarks on the social and historical conditions for the development of philosophical conceptions. He criticized strongly the customary view, held among others by Schlick and by Russell, that a wide-spread acceptance of a philosophical doctrine depends chiefly on its truth. He emphasized that the sociological situation in a given culture and in a given historical period is favorable to certain kinds of ideology or philosophical attitude and unfavorable to others. For example, with the development of urban life and of industry, the dependence on uncontrollable factors like the weather is decreased and thereby also the tendency toward supernaturalistic religion. He shared our hopeful belief that the scientific way of thinking in philosophy would grow stronger in our era. But he emphasized that this belief is to be based, not simply on the correctness of the scientific way of thinking, but rather on the historical fact that the Western world at the present time, and soon also the other parts of the world, will be compelled for economic reasons to industrialize more and more. Therefore, in his view, on the one hand the psychological need for theological or metaphysical ways of thinking will decrease, and on the other hand the cultivation of the natural sciences will be strongly increased because they are needed by the technology of industrialization. Consequently the general cultural atmosphere will become more favorable toward the scientific way of thinking.

Up to this point Neurath did not find much opposition. But he went

[5]See, for example, Hahn, Neurath, Carnap, *Wissenschaftliche Weltauffassung: Der Wiener Kreis* (Wien, 1929); Otto Neurath, *Le développement du cercle de Vienne*, Paris (1925); Jörgen Jörgensen, *The Development of Logical Empiricism*, Int. Encycl. of Unified Science II, 9 (Chicago, 1951); Victor Kraft, *The Vienna Circle* (New York, 1953). A concise picture of Schlick's basic philosophical ideas and his personality is given by Herbert Feigl, "Moritz Schlick", *Erkenntnis* VII (1939), 393-419.

further and often presented arguments of a more pragmatic-political rather than of a theoretical nature for the desirability or undesirability of certain logical or empirical investigations. All of us in the Circle were strongly interested in social and political progress. Most of us, myself included, were socialists. But we liked to keep our philosophical work separated from our political aims. In our view, logic, including applied logic, and the theory of knowledge, the analysis of language, and the methodology of science, are, like science itself, neutral with respect to practical aims, whether they are moral aims for the individual, or political aims for a society. Neurath criticized strongly this neutralist attitude, which in his opinion gave aid and comfort to the enemies of social progress. We in turn insisted that the intrusion of practical and especially of political points of view would violate the purity of philosophical methods. Neurath, for example, reproached Hahn because he was not only theoretically interested, as I was, in parapsychological investigations, but took active part in séances in an attempt to introduce stricter scientific methods of experimentation (without success, unfortunately). Neurath pointed out that such séances served chiefly to strengthen super-naturalism and thereby to weaken political progress. We in turn defended the right to examine objectively and scientifically all processes or alleged processes without regard for the question of whether other people use or misuse the results.

Another problem was more closely connected with the interests of the Circle. For Neurath the aim of a unified science was of vital importance. The sharp distinction between natural sciences and *Geisteswissenschaften* (humanities), which was strongly emphasized in contemporary German philosophy, was in his view an obstacle on the road towards our social goal, because it impeded the extension of the empirico-logical method to the social sciences. Among the possible forms of a unified language of science he gave strong preference to a physicalistic language as against a phenomenalistic one. We conceded that the acceptance of a physicalistic language might possibly have a positive correlation with social progress. But we thought it advisable to disregard this fact in our investigations, so as to avoid any prejudice in examining the possibility of a unified physicalistic language. Neurath rejected these doubts and warnings. He would deride those purist philosophers who sit on their icy glaciers and are afraid they might dirty their hands if they were to come down and tackle the practical problems of the world.

In spite of the difference of opinion between Neurath and the other members of the Circle at certain points, we certainly owed very much to his collaboration. Of particular importance for me personally was his emphasis on the connection between our philosophical activity and the great historical processes going on in the world: Philosophy leads to an improvement in scientific ways of thinking and thereby to a better understanding of all that is going on in the world, both in nature and in society; this understanding in turn serves to improve human life. In numerous private conversations I came into even closer contact with Neurath's ideas. He liked to spice the talks with a lot of wit and sarcasm, criticizing the views and attitudes of others, including myself and of philosophers whom I appreciated highly, such as Schlick and Russell. These talks were always most lively and stimulating; and in spite of my frequent opposition, I learned a great deal from them.

Neurath's views about social problems were strongly influenced by Marx. But he was not a dogmatic Marxist; for him every theory must be further developed by constant criticism and re-examination. In a series of private discussion meetings with me and some younger members of the Circle, he explained the basic ideas of Marxism and showed their relevance to a better understanding of the sociological function of philosophy. He believed that our form of physicalism was an improved, non-metaphysical and logically unobjectionable version which today should supersede both the mechanistic and the dialectical forms of nineteenth century materialism. His expositions and the subsequent discussions were very illuminating for all of us. But most of us could not accept certain points, in particular the dialectic in its Marxist form, which we rejected no less than the Hegelian dialectic when it claimed to fulfill the function of logic. Dialectical logic seemed to us, including Neurath, incompatible with modern symbolic logic, which we regarded as the best developed form of logic so far.

In the Vienna Circle, a large part of Ludwig Wittgenstein's book *Tractatus Logico-Philosophicus* was read aloud and discussed sentence by sentence. Often long reflections were necessary in order to find out what was meant. And sometimes we did not find any clear interpretation. But still we understood a good deal of it and then had lively discussions about it. I had previously read parts of Wittgenstein's work when it was published as an article in Ostwald's *Annalen der Natur-und Kulturphilosophie*. I found in it many interesting and stimulating points. But at that time I did not make the great effort required to come to a clear understanding of the often obscure formulations; for this reason I had not read the whole treatise. Now I was happy to see that the Circle was interested in this work and that we undertook to study it together.

Wittgenstein's book exerted a strong influence upon our Circle. But it is not correct to say that the philosophy of the Vienna Circle was just Wittgenstein's philosophy. We learned much by our discussions of the book, and accepted many views as far as we could assimilate them to our basic conceptions. The degree of influence varied, of course, for the different members.

For me personally, Wittgenstein was perhaps the philosopher who, besides Russell and Frege, had the greatest influence on my thinking. The most important insight I gained from his work was the conception that the truth of logical statements is based only on their logical structure and on the meaning of the terms. Logical statements are true under all conceivable circumstances; thus their truth is independent of the contingent facts of the world. On the other hand, it follows that these statements do not say anything about the world and thus have no factual content.

Another influential idea of Wittgenstein's was the insight that many philosophical sentences, especially in traditional metaphysics, are pseudo-sentences, devoid of cognitive content. I found Wittgenstein's view on this point close to the one I had previously developed under the influence of anti-metaphysical scientists and philosophers. I had recognized that many of these sentences and questions originate in a misuse of language and a violation of logic. Under the influence of Wittgenstein, this conception was strengthened and became more definite and more radical.

In 1927 Schlick became personally acquainted with Wittgenstein. Schlick conveyed to him the interest of our Circle in his book and his philosophy and also our urgent wish that he meet with us and explain certain points in his book which had puzzled us. But Wittgenstein was not willing to do this. Schlick had several talks with him; and Wittgenstein finally agreed to meet with Waismann and me. Thus the three of us met several times with Wittgenstein during the summer of 1927. Before the first meeting, Schlick admonished us urgently not to start a discussion of the kind to which we were accustomed in the Circle, because Wittgenstein did not want such a thing under any circumstances. We should even be cautious in asking questions, because Wittgenstein was very sensitive and easily disturbed by a direct question. The best approach, Schlick said, would be to let Wittgenstein talk and then ask only very cautiously for the necessary elucidations.

When I met Wittgenstein, I saw that Schlick's warnings were fully justified. But his behavior was not caused by any arrogance. In general, he was of a sympathetic temperament and very kind; but he was hypersensitive and easily irritated. Whatever he said was always interesting and stimulating, and the way in which he expressed it was often fascinating. His point of view and his attitude toward people and problems, even theoretical problems, were much more similar to those of a creative artist than to those of a scientist; one might almost say, similar to those of a religious prophet or a seer. When he started to formulate his view on some specific philosophical problem, we often felt the internal struggle that occurred in him at that very moment, a struggle by which he tried to penetrate from darkness to light under an intense and painful strain, which was even visible on his most expressive face. When finally, sometimes after a prolonged arduous effort, his answer came forth, his statement stood before us like a newly created piece of art or a divine revelation. Not that he asserted his views dogmatically. Although some of the formulations of the *Tractatus* sound as if there could not be any possibility of a doubt, he often expressed the feeling that his statements were inadequate. But the impression he made on us was as if insight came to him as through a divine inspiration, so that we could not help feeling that any sober rational comment or analysis of it would be a profanation.

Thus there was a striking difference between Wittgenstein's attitude toward philosophical problems and that of Schlick and myself. Our attitude toward philosophical problems was not very different from that which scientists have toward their problems. For us the discussion of doubts and objections of others seemed the best way of testing a new idea in the field of philosophy just as much as in the fields of science; Wittgenstein, on the other hand, tolerated no critical examination by others, once the insight had been gained by an act of inspiration. I sometimes had the impression that the deliberately rational and unemotional attitude of the scientist and likewise any ideas which had the flavor of "enlightenment" were repugnant to Wittgenstein. At our very first meeting with Wittgenstein, Schlick unfortunately mentioned that I was interested in the problem of an international language like Esperanto. As I had expected, Wittgenstein was definitely opposed to this idea. But I was surprised by the vehemence of his emotions. A language which had not "grown organically" seemed to him not only useless but despicable. Another time we touched the topic of parapsychology, and he expressed himself strongly against it. The alleged messages produced in spiritualistic séances, he said, were extremely trivial and silly. I agreed with this, but I remarked that nevertheless the question of the existence and explanation of the alleged parapsychological phenomena was an important scientific problem. He was shocked that any reasonable man could have any interest in such rubbish.

Once when Wittgenstein talked about religion, the contrast between his and Schlick's position became strikingly apparent. Both agreed of course in the view that the doctrines of religion in their various forms had no theoretical content. But Wittgenstein rejected Schlick's view that religion belonged to the childhood phase of humanity and would slowly disappear in the course of cultural development. When Schlick, on another occasion, made a critical remark about a metaphysical statement by a classical philosopher (I think it was Schopenhauer), Wittgenstein surprisingly turned against Schlick and defended the philosopher and his work.

These and similar occurrences in our conversations showed that there was a strong inner conflict in Wittgenstein between his emotional life and his intellectual thinking. His intellect, working with great intensity and penetrating power, had recognized that many statements in the field of religion and metaphysics did not, strictly speaking, say anything. In his characteristic absolute honesty with himself, he did not try to shut his eyes to this insight. But this result was extremely painful for him emotionally, as if he were compelled to admit a weakness in a beloved person. Schlick, and I, by contrast, had no love for metaphysics or metaphysical theology, and therefore could abandon them without inner conflict or regret. Earlier, when we were reading Wittgenstein's book in the Circle, I had erroneously believed that his attitude toward metaphysics was similar to ours. I had not paid sufficient attention to the statements in his book about the mystical, because his feelings and thoughts in this area were too divergent from mine. Only personal contact with him helped me to see more clearly his attitude at this point. I had the impression that his ambivalence with respect to metaphysics was only a special aspect of a more basic internal conflict in his personality from which he suffered deeply and painfully.

When Wittgenstein talked about philosophical problems, about knowledge, language and the world, I usually was in agreement with his views and certainly his remarks were always illuminating and stimulating. Even at the times when the contrast in *Weltanschauung* and basic personal attitude became apparent, I found the association with him most interesting, exciting and rewarding. Therefore I regretted it when he broke off the contact. From the beginning of 1929 on, Wittgenstein wished to meet only with Schlick and Waismann, no longer with me or Feigl, who had also become acquainted with him in the meantime, let alone with the Circle. Although the difference in our attitudes and personalities expressed itself only on certain occasions, I understood very well that Wittgenstein felt it all the time and, unlike me, was disturbed by it. He said to Schlick that he could talk only with somebody who "holds his hand". Schlick himself was very strongly influenced by Wittgenstein both philosophically and personally. During the subsequent years, I had the impression that he sometimes abandoned his usually cool and critical attitude and accepted certain views and positions of Wittgenstein's without being able to defend them by rational arguments in the discussions of our Circle.

Waismann worked on a book in which he not only explained Wittgenstein's ideas but also developed a detailed systematic representation on this basis. We regarded it as very important that Wittgenstein's ideas should be explained to many who would not be able to read his treatise. Because Waismann had frequently talked with Wittgenstein and had a great ability for lucid representation, he seemed most suitable for this task. He actually wrote the book, which was for several years announced under the title, *Logik, Sprache, Philosophie; Kritik der Philosophie durch die Logik; mit Vorrede von M. Schlick,* and was to appear as Volume I of the collection, "Schriften zur Wissenschaftlichen Weltauffassung". Unfortunately, the book never appeared. Several times when Wittgenstein came to Vienna, he requested thoroughgoing changes and Waismann undertook the task of comprehensive and time-consuming revision. Finally, after Waismann had written and rewritten the book over a period of years, Wittgenstein suddenly declared that he did not want to see his thoughts represented in a "popularized" form. Waismann consequently could never make up his mind to have the book published. Since Schlick was convinced that the publication of the book could soon be expected, he had his Preface printed and gave proof-copies of it to his friends.

The thinking of our Circle was strongly influenced by Wittgenstein's ideas, first because of our common reading of the *Tractatus* and later by virtue of Waismann's systematic exposition of certain conceptions of Wittgenstein's on the basis of his talks with him. At the same time, in the course of our discussions through the years, some divergencies became more and more apparent. Neurath was from the beginning very critical of Wittgenstein's mystical attitude, of his philosophy of the "ineffable", and of the "higher things" *(das "Höhere")*. I shall now briefly indicate the most important points of difference, especially with reference to my own conceptions.

All of us in the Circle had a lively interest in science and mathematics. In contrast to this, Wittgenstein seemed to look upon these fields with an attitude of indifference and sometimes even with contempt. His indirect influence on some students in Vienna was so strong that they abandoned the study of mathematics. It seems that later in his teaching activities in England he had a similar influence on even wider circles there. This is probably at least a contributing factor to the divergence between the attitude represented by many recent publications in analytic philosophy in England and that of logical empiricism in the United States.

Closely related is Wittgenstein's view of the philosophical relevance of constructed language systems. Chiefly because of Frege's influence, I was always deeply convinced of the superiority of a carefully constructed language and of its usefulness and even indispensability for the analysis of statements and concepts, both in philosophy and in science. All members of the Vienna Circle had studied at least the elementary parts of *Principia Mathematica.* For students of mathematics Hahn gave a lecture course and a seminar on the foundations of mathematics, based on the *Principia.* When I came to Vienna I continued these courses for students both of mathematics and of philosophy. In the Circle discussions we often made use of symbolic logic for the representation of analyses or examples. When we found in Wittgenstein's book statements about "the language", we interpreted them as referring to an ideal language; and this meant for us a formalized symbolic language. Later Wittgenstein explicitly rejected this view. He had a skeptical and sometimes even a negative view of the importance of a symbolic language for the clarification and correction of the confusions in ordinary language and also in the customary language of philosophers which, as he had shown himself, were often the cause of philosophical puzzles and pseudo-problems. On this point, the majority of British analytic philosophers share Wittgenstein's view, in contrast to the Vienna Circle and to the majority of analytical philosophers in the United States.

Furthermore, there is a divergence on a more specific point which, however, was of great importance for our way of thinking in the Circle. We read in Wittgenstein's book that certain things show themselves but cannot be said; for example the logical structure of sentences and the relation between the language and the world. In opposition to this view, first tentatively, then more and more clearly, our conception developed that it is possible to talk meaningfully about language and about the relation between a sentence and the fact described. Neurath emphasized from the beginning that language phenomena are events *within* the world, not something that refers to the world from outside. Spoken language consists of sound waves; written language consists of marks of ink on paper. Neurath emphasized these facts in order to reject the view that there is something "higher", something mysterious, "spirtual", in language, a view which was prominent in German philosophy. I agreed with him, but pointed out that only the structural pattern, not the physical properties of the ink marks, were relevant for the function of language. Thus it is possible to construct a theory about language, namely the geometry of the written pattern. This idea led later to the theory which I called "logical syntax" of language.

Among philosophical groups at other places which were close to our philosophical conceptions in the Vienna Circle, I wish to mention especially Reichenbach's circle in Berlin and the Warsaw philosophical group. Reichenbach had been teaching at the University of Berlin since 1928 and had gathered a group of people with similar philosophical interests, which later developed into the Society for Empirical Philosophy. Among the active participants in the discussions were Walter Dubislav, Kurt Grelling, and Carl G. Hempel, and also some scientists with philosophical interest, among them the psychologists Kurt Lewin and Wolfgang Köhler. I sometimes went to Berlin, gave talks in the Society and in Reichenbach's seminar, and had intensive private discussions with Reichenbach and his friends.

The first contact between the Vienna Circle and the Warsaw group was made when, at the invitation of the Mathematics Department, Alfred Tarski came to Vienna in February 1930, and gave several lectures, chiefly on metamathematics. We also discussed privately many problems in which we were both interested. Of special interest to me was his emphasis that certain concepts used in logical investigations, e.g., the consistency of axioms, the provability of a theorem in a deductive system, and the like, are to be expressed not in the language of the axioms (later called the object language), but in the metamathematical language (later called the metalanguage).

Tarski gave a lecture in our Circle on the metamathematics of the propositional calculus. In the subsequent discussion the question was raised whether metamathematics was of value also for philosophy. I had gained the impression in my talks with Tarski that the formal theory of language was of great importance for the clarification of our philosophical problems. But Schlick and others were rather skeptical at this point. At the next meeting of our Circle, when Tarski was no longer in Vienna. I tried to explain that it would be a great advantage for our philosophical discussions if a method were developed by which not only the analyzed object language, e.g., that of mathematics or of physics, would be made exact, but also the philosophical metalanguage used in the discussion. I pointed out that most of the puzzles, disagreements, and mutual misunderstandings in our discussions arose from the inexactness of the metalanguage.

My talks with Tarski were fruitful for my further studies of the problem of speaking about language, a problem which I had often discussed, especially with Gödel. Out of these reflections and talks grew my theory of logical syntax. There was one problem, however, on which I disagreed with Tarski. In contrast to our view that there is a fundamental difference between logical and factual statements, since logical statements do not say anything about the world, Tarski maintained that the distinction was only a matter of degree. This divergence exists even today.

In November 1930 I went to Warsaw for a week. I gave three lectures at the invitation of the Warsaw Philosophical Society, and had many private conversations and discussions. My lectures dealt with psychology formulated in the physical language, the elimination of metaphysics, and the tautological character of logical inference. I was impressed and gratified by the fact that a great number of professors and students had interest in problems of this kind, and that many were well versed in modern logic. In private discussions I talked especially with Tarski, Lesniewski, and Kotarbinski. Stanislaw Lesniewski was strongly influenced by Frege. This explained his emphasis that the formalistic conception, which in the meantime under Hilbert's influence had become strong and widely accepted, should be supplemented by an account of the meaning of expressions. On the other side, Lesniewski demanded, likewise in agreement with Frege, that the rules of inference of a deductive system should be formulated in a strictly formal way. This program made the development of a formal metamathematics and metalogic imperative. Tadeusz Kotarbinski's ideas were related to our physicalism. He maintained conceptions which he called "reism" and "pansomatism", i.e., the conception that all names are names of things and that all objects are material things. Both Lesniewski and Kotarbinski had worked for many years on semantical problems. I expressed my regret that this comprehensive research work of Lesniewski and Kotarbinski was inaccessible to us and to most philosophers in the world, because it was published only in the Polish language, and I pointed out the need for an international language, especially for science.

I found that the Polish philosophers had done a great deal of thoroughgoing and fruitful work in the field of logic and its applications to foundation problems, in particular the foundations of mathematics, and in the theory of knowledge and the general theory of language, the results of which were almost unknown to philosophers in other countries. I left Warsaw grateful for the many stimulating suggestions and the fruitful exchange of ideas which I had enjoyed.

Among philosophers in Vienna who did not belong to the Circle I found the contact with Karl Popper most stimulating, first by my reading of the manuscript of his book *Logik der Forschung*, and later in discussions with him. I remember with pleasure the talks I had with him and Feigl in the summer of 1932, in the Tyrolean Alps. His basic philosophical attitude was quite similar to that of the Circle. However, he had a tendency to overemphasize our differences. In his book he was critical of the "positivists", by which he seemed to mean chiefly the Vienna Circle, and in contrast emphasized his agreement with Kant and other traditional philosophers. He thereby antagonized some of the leading figures in our movement, e.g., Schlick, Neurath, and Reichenbach. Feigl and I tried in vain to effect a better mutual understanding and a philosophical reconciliation.

Even as a young author, Popper produced many interesting ideas which were discussed in our Circle. With some of his conceptions we could not agree, but some positively influenced my thinking and that of others in the Circle, especially Feigl. This is the case, for example, with Popper's views on protocol sentences, i.e., those sentences which are confirmed by observations more directly than others and serve as confirmation basis for others. Popper emphasized that no sentence could be regarded as an "absolute" protocol sentence, but that every sentence might be revised under certain circumstances. Furthermore, he pointed out that sentences about observable physical events were more suitable as protocol sentences, because, in contrast to sentences about subjective experiences, they can be tested intersubjectively. These views of his helped in clarifying and strengthening the physicalistic conception which I had developed together with Neurath. On the other hand, there were certain definite divergencies between my views and Popper's. The most important one arose later when I began to develop a system of inductive logic. He rejected, and still rejects, the possibility of any inductive logic and maintains in contrast to it a radical "deductivism".

Philipp Frank, a theoretical physicist and the successor to Einstein at the German University in Prague, came frequently to Vienna. He made important contributions to the discussions in the Circle or in private talks and also by his publications. He was familiar with the history of science and much interested in the sociology of scientific activity, for which he collected comprehensive materials from history. Both because of his historical interest and his sound common sense, he was often wary of any proposed thesis that seemed to him overly radical, or of any point of view that seemed too formalistic. Thus, in a way similar to Neurath, he often brought the abstract discussion among the logicians back to the consideration of concrete situations. Later he brought about my joining the University in Prague, and during my stay there (1931-35) we were in continuous close contact. I received many fruitful ideas from my talks with him, especially on the foundations of physics. In 1938, he, too, came to America.

As early as 1923, when Reichenbach and I announced our plans for the Erlangen Conference, we found that many people were interested in our type of philosophical thinking. Reichenbach suggested the idea of a new periodical as a forum for our kind of philosophy. However, it was only years later that his efforts were successful. Our periodical, *Erkenntnis,* began to appear in 1930. It published not only articles but also reports on conferences and congresses of our movement, beginning with the report of the First Conference on the Epistemology of the Exact Sciences, which took place in Prague in September 1929.

During my time in Vienna two earlier works of mine were completed and published: *Der logische Aufbau der Welt* [1928-1] and the *Abriss der Logistik* [1929-2], Schlick urged me to prepare the *Logistik* for publication because he felt the need for an introduction to symbolic logic which emphasized its application in non-logical fields and which thus could also be used in our philosophical work. With the appearance of this book the collection, "Schriften zur wissenschaftlichen Weltauffassung", edited by Schlick and Frank, began. I used in my book a hierarchy of logical types, like Russell and Whitehead's *Principia Mathematica,* but in a simplified form. A system with type distinctions seemed to me a more natural form for the total language of science. However, I was also interested in a form of logic without type distinctions. In 1927 I had planned a logic system of this form, to be based on the Zermelo-Fraenkel axiom system of set theory, but restricted in the sense of a constructivist method. However, I did not find the time to carry out this plan. In my later book, *Logical Syntax,* I again used a language with types.

From 1931 to 1935, I lived in Prague, Czechoslovakia. There, in the Division of the Natural Sciences of the German University, I had a chair for Natural Philosophy, which had been newly created at the suggestion of Philipp Frank. My life in Prague, without the Circle, was more solitary than it had been in Vienna. I used most of my time for concentrated work, especially on the book on logical syntax. By frequent visits I also stayed in close contact with my philosophical friends in Vienna.

In the fall of 1934 I spent several weeks in England. Susan Stebbing, whom I hold in grateful memory and appreciation, had invited me to give three lectures at the University of London (later published as [1935-1]), in which I tried to explain in non-technical language the nature of logical syntax and its significance for philosophy. I welcomed the opportunity to become personally acquainted with British philosophers. Above all I enjoyed meeting Bertrand Russell for the first time. I visited him in his residence some distance south of London. We talked on various problems of philosophy and also on the world situation. Among other topics he asked me whether anybody had made use of his logic and arithmetic of relations. I told him that his concept of relation number (relational structure) played an important rôle in our philosophy. I mentioned also my axiom system of space-time-topology using only relational logic but not real numbers. He expressed the conviction that it should be possible to go much further in representing the essential content of Einstein's general theory of relativity in the same framework without using differential equations or co-ordinate systems. I was deeply impressed by his personality, the wide horizon of his ideas from technicalities of logic to the destiny of mankind, his undogmatic attitude in both theoretical and practical questions, and the high perspective from which he looked at the world and at the actions of men.

I also had interesting discussions with other scholars. I talked often with C. K. Ogden, mainly about language and logic, his Basic English and international languages. With J. H. Woodger I discussed especially his project of applying symbolic logic to biology. I also had discussions with some of the younger philosophers, among them Alfred Ayer, who had been in Vienna for some time when I was already in Prague, R. B. Braithwaite, and Max Black; they were interested in recent ideas of the Vienna Circle, such as physicalism and logical syntax.

With the beginning of the Hitler regime in Germany in 1933, the political atmosphere, even in Austria and Czechoslovakia, became more and more intolerable. The great majority of the people in Czechoslovakia, like Benes's government, had a clearly democratic point of view. But the Nazi ideology spread more and more among the German-speaking population of the Sudeten region and therewith among the students of our university and even among some of the professors. Furthermore, there was the danger of an intervention by Hitler. Therefore, I initiated efforts to come to America, at least for a time. In December of 1935 I left Prague and came to the United States.

4. America (Since 1936)

A. My Life in the United States

In 1934 I became acquainted with two American philosophers who visited my friends in Vienna and afterwards visited me in Prague; Charles W. Morris of the University of Chicago, and W. V. Quine, of Harvard University. Both were strongly attracted by our way of philosophizing and later helped to make it known in America. Furthermore, both exerted themselves in order to make it possible for me to come to the United States. Harvard University invited me to participate in its Tercentenary Celebration, September 1936. The University of Chicago asked me to teach there in the Winter Quarter of 1936, and later offered me a permanent position, which I held from the fall of 1936 until 1952. I was very happy to remain permanently in America and, in 1941, I became a citizen of the United States. I was not only relieved to escape the stifling political and cultural atmosphere and the danger of war in Europe, but was also very gratified to see that in the United States there was a considerable interest, especially among the younger philosophers, in the scientific method of philosophy, based on modern logic, and that this interest was growing from year to year.

In Chicago Charles Morris was closest to my philosophical position. He tried to combine ideas of pragmatism and logical empiricism. Through him I gained a better understanding of the Pragmatic philosophy, especially of Mead and Dewey.

For several years in Chicago we had a colloquium, founded by Morris, in which we discussed questions of methodology with scientists from various fields of science and tried to achieve a better understanding among representatives of different disciplines and greater clarity on the essential characteristics of the scientific method. We had many stimulating lectures; but, on the whole, the productivity of the discussions was somewhat limited by the fact that most of the participants, although interested in foundation problems, were not sufficiently acquainted with logical and methodological techniques. It seems to me an important task for the future to see to it that young scientists, during their graduate education, learn to think about these problems both from a systematic and from an historical point of view.

In the year 1937-38 I gave a research seminar in which several colleagues took part. With the (financial) help of the Rockefeller Foundation, it was possible to ask Carl G. Hempel and Olaf Helmer to join me as research associates. They too remained in America. The three of us talked often about logical problems, mainly those of semantics, which I was trying to develop systematically, and in particular about the semantical concept of L-truth and related concepts, with which I was concerned at the time.

In the winter of 1939 Russell was at the University of Chicago and gave a seminar on questions of meaning and truth, which became the basis of his book, *Inquiry into Meaning and Truth.* Morris and I attended this seminar. Russell had the felicitous ability to create an atmosphere in which every participant did his best to contribute to the common task.

In August 1939, just a few days after the beginning of the second world war, we had our Fifth International Congress for the Unity of Science at Harvard. I was glad, in this critical hour, to see some of my friends from Europe who came to the Congress, especially Neurath, who lived then in Holland (whence he later escaped in a small boat and was picked up by a British Navy vessel) ; as well as Jörgen Jörgensen from Copenhagen and J. H. Woodger from England. Tarski had recently come to America with the intention of remaining here. In spite of the exciting world events, we found it possible to devote ourselves to the theoretical discussions of the Congress, which clearly demonstrated how strong the interest in an exact philosophy was in this country.

During the year 1940-41 I was a visiting professor at Harvard. During the first semester Russell was there too, giving the William James lectures, and I was glad to have an even better opportunity for talks with him on questions of philosophy as well as on social and political issues. Tarski spent the same year at Harvard. We formed a group for the discussion of logical problems; Russell, Tarski, Quine and I were its most active members. I gave several talks on the nature of logic and on the possibility of defining logical truth as a semantical concept. I discovered that in these questions, even though my thinking on semantics had originally started from Tarski's ideas, a clear discrepancy existed between my position and that of Tarski and Quine, who rejected the sharp distinction I wished to make between logical and factual truth.

In other problems we came to a closer agreement. I had many private conversations with Tarski and Quine, most of them on the construction of a language of science on a finitistic basis. I shall later report on these talks in more detail. Nelson Goodman joined some of our discussions. He had just taken his Ph.D. degree with an excellent dissertation, *A Study of Qualities*. In it he gave a detailed and critical analysis of the system developed in my book, *Der logische Aufbau der Welt*, and made suggestions for important improvements; he also developed, by a similar method but in a new direction, his own system which led to his book, *The Structure of Appearance* (1951).

Philipp Frank had come from Prague to the United States and was professor of physics at Harvard. Together with him and the psychologist S. S. Stevens, I arranged a colloquium on the foundations of science. Of special interest to me were lectures on probability by Richard von Mises and by Feigl and the discussions which followed. As a result, I also began to think about the problems of probability and induction more systematically than I had done up to that time.

From 1942 to 1944 I had a research grant from the Rockefeller Foundation. During this time, which I spent near Santa Fe, New Mexico, I was first occupied with the logic of modalities and the new semantical method of extension and intension. Later I turned to the problems of probability and induction.

From 1944 until 1952 I was back in Chicago, with the exception of the spring semester 1950 when I taught at the University of Illinois in Urbana.

From 1952 to 1954 I was at the Institute of Advanced Study in Princeton. There I could devote all my time to my research work. I became acquainted with the mathematician and philosopher, John G. Kemeny, and for a year we worked together on problems of inductive logic. In particular, we dealt with the important problems of probabilities for a language with several families of predicates. Kemeny's fertile mathematical imagination, his ability to anticipate intuitively what types of solutions might be mathematically possible, and furthermore his co-operative spirit made this one of my best experiences in active collaboration.

I had some talks separately with John von Neumann, Wolfgang Pauli, and some specialists in statistical mechanics on some questions of theoretical physics with which I was concerned. I certainly learned very much from these conversations; but for my problems in the logical and methodological analysis of physics, I gained less help than I had hoped for. At that time I was trying to construct an abstract mathematical concept of entropy, analogous to the customary physical concept of entropy. My main object was not the physical concept, but the use of the abstract concept for the purposes of inductive logic. Nevertheless, I also examined the nature of the physical concept of entropy in its classical statistical form, as developed by Boltzmann and Gibbs, and I arrived at certain objections against the customary definitions, not from a factual-experimental, but from a logical point of view. It seemed to me that the customary way in which the statistical concept of entropy is defined or interpreted makes it, perhaps against the intention of the physicists, a purely logical instead of physical concept; if so, it can no longer be, as it was intended to be, a counterpart to the classical macro-concept of entropy introduced by Clausius, which is obviously a physical and not a logical concept. The same objection holds in my opinion against the recent view that entropy may be regarded as identical with the negative amount of information. I had expected that in the conversations with the physicists on these problems, we would reach, if not an agreement, then at least a clear mutual understanding. In this, however, we did not succeed, in spite of our serious efforts, chiefly, it seems, because of great differences in point of view and in language. I recognized the fundamental difference between our methodological positions when one of the physicists said: "Physics is not like geometry; in physics there are no definitions and no axioms."

In Princeton I had some interesting talks with Einstein, whom I had known personally years before. Although a short time before he had suffered a serious illness and looked pale and aged, he was lively and cheerful in conversation. He liked to make jokes and would then burst into hearty laughter. For me personally these talks were impressive and valuable, particularly because they reflected not only his great mind but also his fascinating human personality. Most of the time I listened to him and observed his gestures and his expressive face; only occasionally I indicated my opinion.

Once Einstein said that the problem of the Now worried him seriously. He explained that the experience of the Now means something special for man, something essentially different from the past and the future, but that this important difference does not and cannot occur within physics. That this experience cannot be grasped by science seemed to him a matter of painful but inevitable resignation. I remarked that all that occurs objectively can be described in science; on the one hand the temporal sequence of events is described in physics; and, on the other hand, the peculiarities of man's experiences with respect to time, including his different attitude towards past, present, and future, can be described and (in principle) explained in psychology. But Einstein thought that these scientific descriptions cannot possibly satisfy our human needs; that there is something essential about the Now which is just outside of the realm of science. We both agreed that this was not a question of a defect for which science could be blamed, as Bergson thought. I did not wish to press the point, because I wanted primarily to understand his personal attitude to the problem rather than to clarify the theoretical situation. But I definitely had the impression that Einstein's thinking on this point involved a lack of distinction between experience and knowledge. Since science in principle can say all that can be said, there is no unanswerable question left. But though there is no theoretical question left, there is still the common human emotional experience, which is sometimes disturbing for special psychological reasons.

On one occasion Einstein said that he wished to raise an objection against positivism concerning the question of the reality of the physical world. I said that there was no real difference between our views on this question. But he insisted that he had to make an important point here. Then he criticized the view, going back to Ernst Mach, that the sense data are the only reality, or more generally, any view which presumes something as an absolutely certain basis of all knowledge. I explained that we had abandoned these earlier positivistic views, that we did no longer believe in a "rockbottom basis of knowledge"; and I mentioned Neurath's simile that our task is to reconstruct the ship while it is floating on the ocean. He emphatically agreed with this metaphor and this view. But then he added that, if positivism were now liberalized to such an extent, there would no longer be any difference between our conception and any other philosophical view. I said that there was indeed no basic difference between our conception and his and other scientists' in general, even though they often formulate it in the language of realism; but that there was still an important difference between our view and that of those traditional philosophical schools which look for an absolute knowledge.

At another time, Einstein raised a fundamental problem concerning the concept formation in contemporary physics, namely the fact that magnitudes of two entirely different kinds are used, those with continuous scales and those with discrete scales. He regarded this combination of heterogeneous concepts as intolerable in the long run. In his view, physics must finally become either pure field physics with all magnitudes having continuous scales, or else all magnitudes, including those of space and time, must be discrete. At the present time it is not yet possible to foresee which of these two forms will develop. For a pure field physics there is among others the great difficulty of explaining why electric charges do not occur in all possible values but only as multiples of the elementary charge. Then he mentioned the problem of explaining, on the basis of fundamental laws, which presumably would be symmetrical with respect to positive and negative electricity, the fact that all atomic nuclei must have a positive charge. Perhaps originally both kinds of nuclei did actually occur, but finally the positive ones devoured the others, at least in our part of the universe. (This assumption was confirmed after Einstein's death by the discovery of anti-protons.)

Once I referred in a talk with Einstein to the strong conformism in the United States, the insistence that the individual adjust his behavior to the generally accepted standards. He agreed emphatically and mentioned as an example that a complete stranger had written him that he ought to have his hair cut: "Don't forget that you now live in America."

In 1953, when Reichenbach's creative activity was suddenly ended by his premature death, our movement lost one of its most active leaders. But his published work and the fruit of his personal influence live on. In 1954 I accepted the chair which he had occupied at the University of California at Los Angeles. I was happy to see how much the spirit of scientific philosophy was alive among the philosophers at this university.

B. The Situation of Philosophy in the United States

In Vienna, there were rarely philosophical discussions with colleagues outside of our Circle. In Prague I had even fewer opportunities for discussions with philosophers, especially because there I did not belong to the Philosophical Division (i.e., the Humanities), but to the Division of the Natural Sciences. It is only when I came to live in the United States and was a member of a philosophy department, that I had frequent and close contact with other philosophers. In Chicago we had not only private conversations, but also discussions in the Department Seminar for faculty members and Ph.D. candidates, and very extensive oral examinations for the Ph.D. degree, which were attended by the entire department staff.

In this section I wish to make some remarks, mainly meant for philosophically interested readers in other countries, about the state of philosophy as I found it in the United States and especially in Chicago, and my personal reactions to it.

The contrast to the situation of philosophy in Central Europe, in particular in Germany, was remarkable and for me very heartening. Modern logic, almost unknown among philosophers in Germany, was here regarded by many as an important field of philosophy and was taught at some of the leading universities. The Association for Symbolic Logic and its *Journal* were founded in 1936. During the past twenty years, while I could observe the development, the recognition of modern logic became more and more widespread. The possibility of its application for the clarification of philosophical problems is by now widely recognized at least in principle, and the majority of philosophers understand at least the elementary parts of symbolic logic. It is true that only a minority make active use of this method, and there is still disagreement as to the range of its useful application; but at least this question is seriously discussed by all sides.

In 1936, when I came to this country, the traditional schools of philosophy did not have nearly the same influence as on the European continent. The movement of German idealism, in particular Hegelianism, which had earlier been quite influential in the United States, had by then almost completely disappeared. Neo-Kantian philosophical conceptions were represented here and there, not in an orthodox form but rather influenced by recent developments of scientific thinking, much like the conceptions of Cassirer in Germany. Phenomenology had a number of adherents mostly in a liberalized form, not in Husserl's orthodox form, and even less in Heidegger's version.

Most influential were those philosophical movements which had an empiricist tendency in a wide sense. Pragmatic ways of thinking, mostly in the version derived from John Dewey, were widely represented both among philosophers and in the movement of progressive education, which had won great influence on the methods practically applied in public schools. Many philosophers called themselves realists; their conception came from the movements of Critical Realism and of Neo-Realism, which had arisen in the beginning of this century as a reaction against the formerly strong idealism, and which therefore also had an empiricist tendency. Most of the followers of the movements mentioned rejected metaphysics and emphasized the importance of scientific ways of thinking for the solution of all theoretical problems. In the last twenty years, the ideas of analytic philosophy gained more and more acceptance, partly through the influence of logical empiricism, and also through that of the British movement stemming from G. E. Moore and Wittgenstein.

Thus I found in this country a philosophical atmosphere which, in striking contrast to that in Germany, was very congenial to me. Under the strong impression of this contrast, I expected perhaps sometimes too much, so that I became unduly impatient when I saw that philosophical thinking was still lagging far behind science even in this country with the most advanced development of philosophy.

In order to be more concrete I should like to make some remarks about the state of philosophy at the place where I spent most of my time and could observe it most closely, namely in the Department of Philosophy at the University of Chicago. These remarks are not meant as an objective report, but rather as a description of my personal impressions and feelings about what appeared to me as strengths or weaknesses in the situation. In this department great emphasis was placed on the history of philosophy. More frequently than in most other universities of the country, Ph.D. theses were based on a thorough knowledge of the philosophical sources in Greek and Latin of ancient and medieval times. The methodological attitude toward the history of philosophy which the students learned was characterized by a thorough study of the sources and by emphasis on the requirement that the doctrine of a philosopher must be understood immanently, that is, from his own point of view, inasmuch as a criticism from outside would not do justice to the peculiarity of the philosopher in question and his place in the historical development. This education in historical carefulness and a neutral attitude seemed to me useful and proper for the purpose of historical studies, but not sufficient for training in philosophy itself. The task of the history of philosophy is not essentially different from that of the history of science. The historian of science gives not only a description of the scientific theories, but also a critical judgment of them from the point of view of our present scientific knowledge. I think the same should be required in the history of philosophy. This view is based on the conviction that in philosophy, no less than in science, there is the possibility of cumulative insight and therefore of progress in knowledge. This view, of course, would be rejected by historicism in its pure form.

As an illustration of what might be called historical neutralism, I remember a Ph.D. thesis on the ontological proof for the existence of God. The thesis contained chiefly a historical study and a comparative analysis of the various forms of this proof and also a discussion of some later objections to the proof. From the thesis and the oral examination it became clear that the candidate knew that later philosophers, e.g., Kant and Russell, had rejected the proof; but for him this fact seemed merely one more example of the old rule that any assertion of a philosopher is rejected by some other philosopher. He had no idea of the fact that modern logic, independently of any particular philosophical point of view, had definitely shown the alleged proof to be logically invalid. In his view, as in that of some of my colleagues, the ontological proof was not only of historical importance which no doubt is the case, but also represented a problem which must still be taken seriously.

On some occasions, for example, in the examination mentioned and even more in discussions with colleagues in the Department Seminar, I was depressed to see that certain philosophical views which seemed to me long superseded by the development of critical thought and in some cases completely devoid of any cognitive content, were either still maintained or at least treated as deserving serious consideration.

One of the most striking examples of this cultural lag in contemporary philosophy seemed to me a lecture given by Mortimer Adler as a visitor in the Department Seminar. He declared that he could demonstrate on the basis of purely metaphysical principles the impossibility of of man's descent from "brute", i.e., subhuman forms of animals. I had of course no objection to someone's challenging a widely accepted scientific theory. What I found startling was rather the kind of arguments used. They were claimed to provide with complete certainty an answer to the question of the validity or invalidity of a biological theory, without making this answer dependent upon those observable facts in biology and paleontology, which are regarded by scientists as relevant and decisive for the theory in question.

In some philosophical discussion meetings I had the weird feeling that I was sitting among a group of medieval learned men with long beards and solemn robes. This feeling was perhaps further strengthened when I looked out of the window at the other university buildings with their medieval Gothic style. I would perhaps dream that one of my colleagues raised the famous question of how many angels could dance on the point of a needle. Or I might imagine that the colleagues who were sitting around me were not philosophers but astronomers and that one of them proposed to discuss the astrological problem whether it was more favorable for the character and fate of a person if the planet Mars stood in Taurus or in Virgo at the hour of his birth. I heard myself expressing a humble doubt whether this problem fitted well into the twentieth century. But then I heard the imaginary astronomical colleagues declaring that we must be open-minded and never exclude by personal prejudice any question from the discussion.

Of course, there were also times when I told myself not to be too impatient. It was clear anyhow that for thousands of years philosophy had been one of the most tradition-bound fields of human thinking. Philosophers, like anybody else, tend to follow the customary patterns of thinking; even movements which regard themselves as very revolutionary, such as existentialism as a philosophical doctrine (in distinction to existentialism as an attitude in life), are often basically merely a modification of an ancient metaphysical pattern, namely a certain feeling or attitude toward the world in a pseudo-theoretical disguise. I often see also the brighter aspects of the picture. It is encouraging to remember that philosophical thinking has made great progress in the course of two thousand years through the work of men like Aristotle, Leibniz, Hume, Kant, Dewey, Russell, and many others, who were basically thinking in a scientific way. Personally I regard myself as very fortunate to be living in a country with the greatest progress in philosophical thinking and to be working together with friends on the basis of a common philosophical attitude. Above all I am gratified by the fact that many young people of the generation now growing up show promise of working in philosophy in a way which will tend to diminish the cultural lag.

II

PHILOSOPHICAL PROBLEMS

In this part I shall report more systematically on my philosophical activities from the Vienna period to the present time. In each section, a certain problem or complex of problems will be dealt with. Although the order is roughly determined by the time at which the problem became prominent in my thinking, the considerations, discussions and publications on which I shall report in each of the sections often continued through many years, so that certain sections will overlap chronologically.

5. Pseudo Problems in Philosophy

During the time while I was writing the *Logischer Aufbau,* I arrived more and more at a neutral attitude with respect to the language forms used by the various philosophical schools, e.g., the phenomenalistic language about sense data and the realistic language about perceptible things and events in the so-called external world. This neutral attitude did not mean, however, that I regarded the differences between the various language forms as unimportant. On the contrary, it seemed to me one of the most important tasks of philosophers to investigate the various possible language forms and discover their characteristic properties. While working on problems of this kind, I gradually realized that such an investigation, if it is to go beyond common-sense generalities and to aim at more exact results, must be applied to artificially constructed symbolic languages. The investigation of versions of the ordinary word language, corresponding to various philosophical points of view, may certainly be useful, but only as a preparation for the more exact work on artificial language systems. Only after a thorough investigation of the various language forms has been carried through, can a well-founded choice of one of these languages be made, be it as the total language of science or as a partial language for specific purposes.

This neutral attitude with respect to different language forms led me later to adopt the principle of tolerance in *Logical Syntax.*

Even in the pre-Vienna period, most of the controversies in traditional metaphysics appeared to me sterile and useless. When I compared this kind of argumentation with investigations and discussions in empirical science or in the logical analysis of language, I was often struck by the vagueness of the concepts used and by the inconclusive nature of the arguments. I was depressed by disputations in which the opponents talked at cross purposes; there seemed hardly any chance of mutual understanding, let alone of agreement, because there was not even a common criterion for deciding the controversy. I developed this skeptical attitude toward metaphysics under the influence of anti-metaphysically inclined scientists like Kirchhoff, Hertz, and Mach, and of philosophers like Avenarius, Russell, and Wittgenstein. I also saw that the metaphysical argumentations often violated logic. Frege had pointed out an example of such a violation in the ontological proof for the existence of God. I found other examples in certain kinds of logical confusion, among them those which I labelled "mixing of spheres" *("Sphärenvermengung")* in the *Logischer Aufbau,* that is, the neglect of distinctions in the logical types of various kinds of concepts.

The most decisive development in my view of metaphysics occurred later, in the Vienna period, chiefly under the influence of Wittgenstein. I came to hold the view that many theses of traditional metaphysics are not only useless, but even devoid of cognitive content. They are pseudo-sentences, that is to say, they seem to make assertions because they have the grammatical form of declarative sentences, and the words occurring in them have many strong and emotionally loaded associations, while in fact they do not make any assertions, do not express any propositions, and are therefore neither true nor false. Even the apparent questions to which these sentences allegedly give either an affirmative or a negative answer, e.g., the question "is the external world real?" are not genuine questions but pseudo-questions. The view that these sentences and questions are non-cognitive was based on Wittgenstein's principle of verifiability. This principle says first, that the meaning of a sentence is given by the conditions of its verification and, second, that a sentence is meaningful if and only if it is in principle verifiable, that is, if there are possible, not necessarily actual, circumstances which, if they did occur, would definitely establish the truth of the sentence. This principle of verifiability was later replaced by the more liberal principle of confirmability.

Unfortunately, following Wittgenstein, we formulated our view in the Vienna Circle in the oversimplified version of saying that certain metaphysical theses are "meaningless". This formulation caused much unnecessary opposition, even among some of those philosophers who basically agreed with us. Only later did we see that it is important to distinguish the various meaning components, and therefore said in a more precise way that such theses lack cognitive or theoretical meaning. They often have other meaning components, e.g., emotive or motivative ones, which, although not cognitive, may have strong psychological effects.

The general view that many sentences of traditional metaphysics are pseudo-sentences was held by most members of the Vienna Circle and by many philosophers in other empiricist groups, such as Reichenbach's group in Berlin. In the discussions of the Vienna Circle I maintained from the beginning the view that a characterization as pseudo-sentences must also be applied to the thesis of realism concerning the reality of the external world, and to the countertheses, say, those of idealism, solipsism, and the like. I presented and discussed this view in the monograph *Scheinprobleme* [1928-2]. By contrast, Schlick had up to this time regarded himself as a realist. He and Reichenbach, like Russell, Einstein and many of the leading scientists, believed that realism was the indispensable basis of science. I maintained that what was needed for science was merely the acceptance of a realistic language, but that the thesis of the reality of the external world was an empty addition to the system of science. Under the influence of our discussions, Schlick abandoned realism. Reichenbach gave a reinterpretation of the realist thesis in the form of an empirical statement asserting that the causal structure of the world is such that inductive inferences can be successfully made. Later Feigl offered a similar reinterpretation. I agreed, of course, that such versions of the thesis are unobjectionable. But I doubted whether the label "thesis of realism" for these proposed statements was sufficiently in agreement with what had been understood by this name historically.

6. *The Foundations of Mathematics*

The conception of the nature of mathematics which we developed in the discussions of the Vienna Circle came chiefly from the following sources. I had learned from Frege that all mathematical concepts can be defined on the basis of the concepts of logic and that the theorems of mathematics can be deduced from the principles of logic. Thus the truths of mathematics are analytic in the general sense of truth based on logic alone. The mathematician Hans Hahn, one of the leading members of the Circle, had accepted the same conception under the influence of Whitehead and Russell's work, *Principia Mathematica*. Furthermore, Schlick, in his book *Allgemeine Erkenntnislehre* (1918), had clarified and emphasized the view that logical deduction cannot lead to new knowledge but only to an explication or transformation of the knowledge contained in the premises. Wittgenstein formulated this view in the more radical form that all logical truths are tautological, that is, that they hold necessarily in every possible case, therefore do not exclude any case, and do not say anything about the facts of the world.

Wittgenstein demonstrated this thesis for molecular sentences (i.e., those without variables) and for those with individual variables. It was not clear whether he thought that the logically valid sentences with variables of higher levels, e.g., variables for classes, for classes of classes, etc., have the same tautological character. At any rate, he did not count the theorems of arithmetic, algebra, etc., among the tautologies. But to the members of the Circle there did not seem to be a fundamental difference between elementary logic and higher logic, including mathematics. Thus we arrived at the conception that all valid statements of mathematics are analytic in the specific sense that they hold in all possible cases and therefore do not have any factual content.

What was important in this conception from our point of view was the fact that it became possible for the first time to combine the basic tenet of empiricism with a satisfactory explanation of the nature of logic and mathematics. Previously, philosophers had only seen two alternative positions: either a non-empiricist conception, according to which knowledge in mathematics is based on pure intuition or pure reason, or the view held, e.g., by John Stuart Mill, that the theorems of logic and of mathematics are just as much of an empirical nature as knowledge about observed events, a view which, although it preserved empiricism, was certainly unsatisfactory. Among us it was especially Hahn who emphasized, both in our discussions and in his publications, this important advance in the development of empiricism.

We discussed repeatedly and in great detail the difficulties involved in the construction of mathematics on the basis of logic. We did not see any difficulty concerning the definitions of mathematical concepts on the basis of logical concepts. But the purely logical character of some of the axioms used in the system of *Principia Mathematica* seemed problematic, namely, that of the axiom of reducibility, the axiom of infinity, and the axiom of choice. We were gratified to learn from the studies on the foundations of mathematics made by F. P. Ramsey that the so-called ramified theory of types used in the *Principia* is unnecessary, that a simple system of types is sufficient, and that therefore the axiom of reducibility can be dispensed with. With respect to the other two axioms we realized that either a way of interpreting them as analytic must be found or, if they are interpreted as non-analytic, they cannot be regarded as principles of mathematics. I was inclined towards analytic interpretations; but during my time in Vienna we did not achieve complete clarity on these questions. Later I came to the conviction that the axiom of choice is analytic, if we accept that concept of class which is used in classical mathematics in contrast to a narrower constructivist concept. Furthermore, I found several possible interpretations for the axiom of infinity, different from Russell's interpretation, of such a kind that they make this axiom analytic. The result is achieved, e.g., if not things but positions are taken as individuals.

In the field of the foundations of mathematics, three main positions have evolved in the twentieth century: the doctrine of logicism, founded by Frege and Russell, the formalism of Hilbert and his followers, and intuitionism, represented chiefly by L.E.J. Brouwer and Hermann Weyl. Most of us in the Circle accepted the logicist conception; but we made great efforts in detailed discussions to determine the validity and scope of the two other approaches. We had a good deal of sympathy with the formalist method of Hilbert, because it was in agreement with our emphasis on the hypothetico-deductive method, and we learned much from this school about the construction and analysis of formal systems. Later, in my book *Logical Syntax,* this influence became clearly visible. On the other hand, we were not satisfied with Hilbert's skepticism about the possibility of giving an interpretation to the total formal system of mathematics. Frege had already strongly emphasized that the foundation problems of mathematics can only be solved if we look not solely at pure mathematics but also at the use of mathematical concepts in factual sentences. He had found his explication of cardinal numbers by asking himself the question: What does "five" mean in contexts like "I have five fingers on my right hand"? Since Schlick and I came to philosophy from physics, we looked at mathematics always from the point of view of its application in empirical science. The idea occurred to me that from the point of view of this application there seemed to be a possibility of reconciling the conflict between logicism and formalism. Suppose that mathematics is first constructed as a purely formal system in Hilbert's way, and that rules are then added for the application of the mathematical symbols and sentences in physics, and for the use of mathematical theorems for deductions within the language of physics. Then, it seemed to me, these latter rules must implicitly give an interpretation of mathematics. I was convinced that this interpretation would essentially agree with the logicist interpretation of Frege and Russell. When we and Reichenbach's group organized a conference on the methodology of the exact sciences within the framework of the Congress of Physicists and Mathematicians, which took place in September 1930 in Königsberg, I arranged a symposium on the foundations of mathematics. J. von Neumann represented Hilbert's point of view, A. Heyting the intuitionist conception, and I the logicist position. In my conference paper [1931-4] and in another article [1930-5] I gave some indications of a way for reaching an agreement between logicism and formalism.[6]

In the Circle we also made a thorough study of intuitionism. Brou-

[6]In his contribution to this volume, E. W. Beth has made interesting remarks on the development and motivation of my ideas.

wer came to Vienna and gave a lecture on his conception, and we had private talks with him. We tried hard to understand his published or spoken explanations, which was sometimes not easy. The empiricist view of the Circle was of course incompatible with Brouwer's view, influenced by Kant, that pure intuition is the basis of all mathematics. On this view there was, strangely enough, agreement between intuitionism and the otherwise strongly opposed camp of formalism, especially as represented by Hilbert and Bernays. But the constructivist and finitist tendencies of Brouwer's thinking appealed to us greatly. Felix Kaufmann worked at that time on his book, *Das Unendliche in der Mathematik und seine Ausschaltung;* his finitism was strongly influenced by Brouwer and Wittgenstein. The mathematician Karl Menger, who took part in the Circle discussions, went for a year to Amsterdam to work with Brouwer. But later Menger's attitude toward intuitionism became more critical. He showed, and some members of our Circle were inclined to agree with him, that there was some measure of arbitrariness in the choice of the boundary line between admissible and inadmissible concepts and forms of deduction.

I had a strong inclination toward a constructivist conception. In my book, *Logical Syntax,* I constructed a language, called "Language I", which fulfilled the essential requirements of constructivism and which seemed to me to have some advantages in comparison with Brouwer's form of language. But in the same book I constructed another language comprehensive enough for the formulation of classical mathematics. According to my principle of tolerance, I emphasized that, whereas it is important to make distinctions between constructivist and non-constructivist definitions and proofs, it seems advisable not to prohibit certain forms of procedure but to investigate all practically useful forms. It is true that certain procedures, e.g., those admitted by constructivism or intuitionism, are safer than others. Therefore it is advisable to apply these procedures as far as possible. However, there are other forms and methods which, though less safe because we do not have a proof of their consistency, appear to be practically indispensable for physics. In such a case there seems to be no good reason for prohibiting these procedures so long as no contradictions have been found.

In the foregoing, the term "mathematics" is meant to include the theory of numbers of various kinds and their functions, furthermore abstract fields, e.g., abstract algebra, abstract group theory and the like, but to exclude geometry. With respect to the problems of the foundations of geometry, our discussions in the Circle led to a complete agreement among us. We emphasized the distinction between mathematical geometry and physical geometry. The former is to be regarded as a part of mathematics or of the logic of relations (as in Russell's book, *Principles of Mathematics,* 1903), and physical geometry as a part of physics. The question as to which of the mathematically possible structures of space, either the Euclidean or one of the various non-Euclidean structures, is that of the space of nature as described in physics, becomes an empirical question once the necessary definitions or rules, e.g., for the determination of congruence, are laid down. Schlick, in agreement with Einstein, had clearly expounded this view as early as 1917.[7] This conception was systematically developed and presented in great detail by Reichenbach, mainly in his book of 1928,[8] which I still regard as the basic work on the empiricist conception of space and time. As mentioned earlier, I had maintained the empirical character of physical geometry in my doctor's thesis, *Der Raum;* but at that time this view was combined with some Kantian ideas which I abandoned during the Vienna period.

7. Physicalism and the Unity of Science

I explained earlier that we had regarded the theses of phenomenalism, materialism, realism and so on in their traditional forms as pseudo-theses. On the other hand, we believed that we obtained fruitful philosophical problems if we directed our attention not to the traditional ontological problems, but rather to the questions, either theoretical or practical, concerning the corresponding language forms.

In our discussions we were especially interested in the question of whether a phenomenalistic language or a physicalistic language was preferable for the purposes of philosophy. By a phenomenalistic language we meant one which begins with sentences about sense data, such as "there is now a red triangle in my visual field." The sentences of the physicalistic language or thing-language speak of material things and ascribe observable properties to them, e.g., "this thing is black and heavy". Under the influence of some philosophers, especially Mach and Russell, I regarded in the *Logischer Aufbau* a phenomenalistic language as the best for a philosophical analysis of knowledge. I believed that the task of philosophy consists in reducing all knowledge to a basis of certainty. Since the most certain knowledge is that of the immediately given, whereas knowledge of material things is derivative and less certain, it seemed that the philosopher must employ a language which uses sense-data as a basis. In the Vienna discussions my attitude changed gradually toward a preference for the physicalistic language. Against the conception that this language may serve as a total language for all knowledge, sometimes the objection was raised that on a physicalistic basis it is impossible to reach the concepts of psychology. But I did not

7M. Schlick, *Raum und Zeit in der gegenwärtigen Physik* (Berlin, 1917) English translation: *Space and Time in Contemporary Physics* (Oxford and New York, 1920).

8H. Reichenbach, *Philosophie der Raum-Zeit-Lehre* (Berlin, 1928). English translation: *The Philosophy of Space and Time* (New York, 1958).

find this argument convincing. In the *Logischer Aufbau* I had indicated the possibility of taking a physicalistic basis instead of the phenomenalistic one actually used in the book. Furthermore, I had explained the construction of concepts concerning other minds *("das Fremdpsychische")* on the basis of the observed behavior of other human bodies; these considerations refute the objection mentioned above, and offer the possibility of choosing either the one or the other basis.

In our discussions Neurath, in particular, urged the development toward a physicalistic attitude. I say deliberately "attitude" and not "belief" because it was a practical question of preference, not a theoretical question of truth. In the beginning, Neurath defended materialism against idealism, both understood in the sense of the German philosophical movements of the 19th century. For him the strongest motive for this position was the fact that, during the last hundred years, materialism was usually connected with progressive ideas in political and social matters, while idealism was associated with reactionary attitudes. Schlick and I, however, asked for philosophical arguments instead of sociological correlations. I argued in detail that the thesis of materialism was just as much a pseudo-thesis as that of idealism. After a long struggle Neurath accepted this point. But he maintained that in the case of idealism the meaninglessness pervaded the whole doctrine, whereas in the case of materialism it was merely peripheral and could easily be eliminated without abandoning the basic idea of materialism, which he characterized as closeness to actual life and acceptance of a scientific attitude. Neurath admitted that the philosophical arguments of materialists, e.g., Ludwig Büchner and Ernst Haeckel, were often inadequate as measured by our logical standards. On the other hand, we agreed with him that their general attitude and way of thinking was closer to sound scientific method than the thinking of German idealists like Fichte, Schelling, and Hegel. When I suggested that we should not discuss the theses of idealism and materialism but rather the problem of the choice of a language, Neurath accepted this point but tried to turn my weapon against me. The choice of a language form is a practical decision, he argued, just as the choice of a route for a railroad or that of a constitution for a government. He emphasized that all practical decisions are interconnected and should therefore be made from the point of view of a general goal. The decisive criterion would be how well a certain language form, or a railroad, or a constitution, could be expected to serve the community which intended to use it. His emphasis on the interdependence of all decisions, including those in theoretical fields, and his warning against isolating the deliberation of any practical question, even that of the choice of a language form, made a strong impression upon my own thinking and that of my friends.

In my view, one of the most important advantages of the physicalistic language is its intersubjectivity, i.e., the fact that the events described in this language are in principle observable by all users of the language.

In our discussions, chiefly under the influence of Neurath, the principle of the unity of science became one of the main tenets of our general philosophical conception. This principle says that the different branches of empirical science are separated only for the practical reason of division of labor, but are fundamentally merely parts of one comprehensive unified science. This thesis must be understood primarily as a rejection of the prevailing view in German contemporary philosophy that there is a fundamental difference between the natural sciences and the *Geisteswissenschaften* (literally "spiritual sciences", understood as the sciences of mind, culture, and history, thus roughly corresponding to the social sciences and the humanities). In contrast to this customary view, Neurath maintained the monistic conception that everything that occurs is a part of nature, i.e., of the physical world. I proposed to make this thesis more precise by transforming it into a thesis concerning language, namely, the thesis that the total language encompassing all knowledge can be constructed on a physicalistic basis. I tried to show the validity of the thesis of physicalism in this sense in two articles "Die physikalische Sprache als Universalsprache der Wissenschaft" [1932-4], (translated as *Unity of Science* [1934-4]) and "Psychologie in physikalischer Sprache" [1932-5], translated as "Psychology in Physical Language" [1959-10].

The thesis of physicalism, especially in its application to psychology dealt with in my second article, and to social science, as propounded in detail in many publications by Neurath, met much opposition. This seems quite understandable in view of the fact that the thesis either was or seemed to be incompatible with many widely held views. Some of the objections deserved and obtained serious consideration from us. But some of the criticisms were based on a misunderstanding, attributing to me the assertion that sentences about other minds are meaningless; whereas in fact, my assertion was explicitly a conditional one: "*If* the physicalistic interpretation of the sentence 'Mr. A. is now excited' is rejected, then the sentence becomes meaningless." This and similar misunderstandings have been repeated up to the present time, although I thought I had cleared them up in my paper [1932-6], and although Hempel[9] gave an especially clear exposition of the meaning of the physicalistic thesis as applied to psychology.

Our initial formulations of physicalism in the publications just mentioned can only be regarded as a first rough attempt. In view of the

[9]Hempel, "Analyse logique de la psychologie", *Revue de Synthèse,* X, 1935. An English translation is contained in: Feigl-Sellars, *Readings*. The quotations from a Ms. by Hempel which I gave in my paper [1932-6] pp. 187f. were later published in this article.

liberalization of the empiricist conception which was achieved some years later, the assertion of the definability of psychological terms on the basis of the terms of the thing-language must be weakened to an assertion of reducibility. A reformulation of the principle of physicalism in this sense was given in my article [1938-2].

In recent years the thesis was further clarified in conversations with friends, especially with Feigl and Hempel, on the basis of the distinction between observation language and theoretical language. In my second paper [1932-5], I had said that the sentence "Mr. A. is now excited" refers to the physical micro-state of the body of A. I had added that in the physicalistic translation of that sentence the state of the body is not specified in micro-terms, i.e., it is not described either in physical micro-terms concerning atoms or in physiological micro-terms concerning the cells of the central nervous system; instead the state is characterized only in terms of possible effects, namely, those which may be taken as symptoms for the state. In our present conception, the reference to the micro-state is emphasized, just as before. But the distinction between a micro-state and the disposition to respond to certain external stimuli with certain observable responses is carried through more clearly.

8. *The Logical Syntax of Language*

I mentioned earlier that the members of the Circle, in contrast to Wittgenstein, came to the conclusion that it is possible to speak about language and, in particular, about the structures of linguistic expressions. On the basis of this conception, I developed the idea of the logical syntax of a language as the purely analytic theory of the structure of its expressions. My way of thinking was influenced chiefly by the investigations of Hilbert and Tarski in metamathematics, which I mentioned previously. I often talked with Gödel about these problems. In August 1930 he explained to me his new method of correlating numbers with signs and expressions. Thus a theory of the forms of expressions could be formulated with the help of concepts of arithmetic. He told me that, with the help of this method of arithmetization, he had proved that any formal system of arithmetic is incomplete and incompletable. When he published this result in 1931, it marked a turning point in the development of the foundation of mathematics.

After thinking about these problems for several years, the whole theory of language structure and its possible applications in philosophy came to me like a vision during a sleepless night in January 1931, when I was ill. On the following day, still in bed with a fever, I wrote down my ideas on forty-four pages under the title "Attempt at a metalogic". These shorthand notes were the first version of my book *Logical Syntax of Language* [1934-6]. In the spring of 1931 I changed the form of language dealt with in this essay to that of a co-ordinate language of about the same form as that later called "language I" in my book. Thus arithmetic could be formulated in this language, and by use of Gödel's method, even the metalogic of the language could be arithmetized and formulated in the language itself. In June of 1931 I gave three lectures on metalogic in our Circle.

In the metalogic I emphasized the distinction between that language which is the object of the investigation, which I called the "object language", and the language in which the theory of the object language, in other words the metalogic, is formulated, which I called the "metalanguage". One of my aims was to make the metalanguage more precise so that an exact conceptual system for metalogic could be constructed in it. Whereas Hilbert intended his metamathematics only for the special purpose of proving the consistency of a mathematical system formulated in the object language, I aimed at the construction of a general theory of linguistic forms.

At that time I defined the term "metalogic" as the theory of the forms of the expressions of a language. Later I used the term "syntax" instead of "metalogic", or, in distinction to syntax as part of linguistics, "logical syntax".

I thought of the logical syntax of language in the strictly limited sense of dealing exclusively with the forms of the expressions of the language, the form of an expression being characterized by the specification of the signs occurring in it and of the order in which the signs occur. No reference to the meaning of the signs and expressions is made in logical syntax. Since only the logical structure of the expressions is involved, the syntax language, i.e., the metalanguage serving for the formulation of logical syntax, contains only logical constants.

My interest in the development of logical syntax was chiefly determined by the following points of view. First, I intended to show that the concepts of the theory of formal deductive logic, e.g., provability, derivability from given premises, logical independence, etc., are purely syntactical concepts, and that therefore their definitions can be formulated in logical syntax, since these concepts depend merely on the forms of the sentences, not on their meanings.

Second, it seemed important to me to show that many philosophical controversies actually concern the question whether a particular language form should be used, say, for the language of mathematics or of science. For example, in the controversy about the foundations of mathematics, the conception of intuitionism may be construed as a proposal to restrict the means of expression and the means of deduction of the language of mathematics in a certain way, while the classical conception leaves the language unrestricted. I intended to make available in syntax the conceptual means for an exact formulation of controversies of this kind. Furthermore, I wished to show that everyone is free to choose the rules of his language and thereby his logic in any way he wishes. This I called the "principle of tolerance"; it might perhaps be called more exactly the "principle of the conventionality of language forms". As a consequence, the discussion of controversies of the kind mentioned need only concern first, the syntactical properties of the various forms of language, and second, practical reasons for preferring one or the other form for given purposes. In this way, assertions that a particular language is the correct language or represents the correct logic such as often occurred in earlier discussions, are eliminated, and traditional ontological problems, in contradistinction to the logical or syntactical ones, for example, problems concerning "the essence of number", are entirely abolished. The various language forms which are to be investigated and compared and from which one or several are to be chosen for a given purpose comprise, of course, not only historically given language forms, like the natural word languages or the historically developed symbolic languages of mathematics, but also any new form that anyone may wish to construct. This possibility of constructing new languages was essential from our point of view.

The chief motivation for my development of the syntactical method, however, was the following. In our discussions in the Vienna Circle it had turned out that any attempt at formulating more precisely the philosophical problems in which we were interested ended up with problems of the logical analysis of language. Since in our view the issue in philosophical problems concerned the language, not the world, these problems should be formulated, not in the object language, but in the metalanguage. Therefore it seemed to me that the development of a suitable metalanguage would essentially contribute toward greater clarity in the formulation of philosophical problems and greater fruitfulness in their discussions.

Although the investigation of philosophical problems was originally the main reason for the development of syntax, in the beginning the content of my work on the syntactical method was not much influenced by this purpose. Instead, my efforts were directed toward developing the formal features of the syntactical method. In the first chapter of my book I exhibited the method by giving syntactical rules for two model languages, called "language I" and "language II". Language I is restricted so as to admit only the definition of those concepts and the formulation of those propositions which fulfill some strict requirements of constructivism. By contrast, language II is very comprehensive; it makes available sufficient sentential forms for the formulation of everything that occurs in classical mathematics and in classical physics. Originally, in agreement with the finitist ideas with which we sympathized in the Circle, I had the intention of constructing only language I. But later, guided by my own principle of tolerance, it seemed desirable to me to develop also the language form II as a model of classical mathematics. It appeared more fruitful to develop both languages than to declare the first language to be the only correct one or to enter into a controversy about which of the two languages is preferable. I added a chapter on general syntax, that is to say, a system of syntactical concepts applicable to languages of any form. My purpose was mainly to show the desirability and possibility of general syntax. Yet this chapter was not much more than a programmatic sketch for future work. The program was carried out in a fragmentary way and sometimes in a way which I now regard as not quite satisfactory.

In writing the first version of my syntax book, my main attention was directed toward the formal construction of the theory and the definition of the concepts. To all of us in the Circle it was obvious, by virtue of the practical experience in our discussions, that an exact method of language analysis would be of great importance for the treatment of philosophical problems, as soon as someone constructed such a method. Therefore I believed, erroneously, that this would also be clear to all those readers of the book who were interested in a more exact philosophy. It was only on the urging of my friends that I added the last chapter to the book, called "Philosophy and Syntax", in which I tried to show by numerous examples how philosophical questions and statements should be interpreted as statements of the logic of science (which was the common conception of the Vienna Circle, the Berlin Circle and other related groups) and that they could therefore be formulated with the help of syntactical concepts. I am sure that without this chapter it would have taken much longer for the philosophers working in similar directions to accept the main thesis of my book, namely the importance of the metatheory for philosophy.

A few years after the publication of the book, I recognized that one of its main theses was formulated too narrowly. I had said that the problems of philosophy or of the philosophy of science are merely syntactical problems; I should have said in a more general way that these problems are metatheoretical problems. The narrower formulation is historically explained by the fact that the syntactical aspect of language had been the first to be investigated by exact means by Frege, Hilbert, the Polish logicians, and in my book. Later we saw that the metatheory must also include semantics and pragmatics; therefore the realm of philosophy must likewise be conceived as comprising these fields.

9. Liberalization of Empiricism

The simplicity and coherence of the system of knowledge, as most of us in the Vienna Circle conceived it, gave it a certain appeal and strength in the face of criticisms. On the other hand, these features caused a certain rigidity, so that we were compelled to make some radical changes in order to do justice to the open character and the inevitable uncertainty of all factual knowledge.

According to the original conception, the system of knowledge, although growing constantly more comprehensive, was regarded as a closed system in the following sense. We assumed that there was a certain rock bottom of knowledge, the knowledge of the immediately given, which was indubitable. Every other kind of knowledge was supposed to be firmly supported by this basis and therefore likewise decidable with certainty. This was the picture which I had given in the *Logischer Aufbau;* it was supported by the influence of Mach's doctrine of the sensations as the elements of all knowledge, by Russell's logical atomism, and finally by Wittgenstein's thesis that all propositions are truth-functions of the elementary propositions. This conception led to Wittgenstein's principle of verifiability, which says that it is in principle possible to obtain either a definite verification or a definite refutation for any meaningful sentence.

Looking back at this view from our present position, I must admit that it was difficult to reconcile with certain other conceptions which we had at that time, especially in the methodology of science. Therefore the development and clarification of our methodological views led inevitably to an abandonment of the rigid frame in our theory of knowledge. The important feature in our methodological position was the emphasis on the hypothetical character of the laws of nature, in particular, of physical theories. This view was influenced by men like Poincaré and Duhem, and by our study of the axiomatic method and its application in the empirical sciences with the help of co-ordinative definitions or rules. It was clear that the laws of physics could not possibly be completely verified. This conclusion led Schlick, under the influence of Wittgenstein, to the view that physical laws should no longer be regarded as general sentences but rather as rules for the derivation of singular sentences. Others, however, began to doubt the adequacy of the principle of verifiabilty.

The next step in the development of our conception concerned the nature of the knowledge of singular facts in the physical world. Neurath had always rejected the alleged rock bottom of knowledge. According to his view, the totality of what is known about the world is always uncertain and continually in need of correction and transformation; it is like a ship for which there is no dry dock and which therefore has to be repaired and rebuilt while floating on the open ocean. The influence of Karl Popper's book *Logik der Forschung* worked in the same direction. Thus some of us, especially Neurath, Hahn and I, came to the conclusion that we had to look for a more liberal criterion of significance than verifiability. This group was sometimes called the left wing of the Circle, in contrast to the more conservative right wing, chiefly represented by

Schlick and Waismann, who remained in personal contact with Wittgenstein and were inclined to maintain his views and formulations.

Although we abandoned the principle of verifiability, we did not yet see clearly what criterion of significance should take its place. But I recognized at least the general direction in which we would have to move.

In December 1932, when I returned to Vienna on one of my frequent visits from Prague, I learned that Neurath and some younger members of the Circle were occupied with the task of reformulating Freud's psychoanalytic theory in accordance with our view. They approached this task by "physicalizing" one of Freud's treatises sentence by sentence, that is, by translating each sentence into a behavioristic language. I advised against this approach and proposed that they analyze concepts rather than single sentences. For some of the concepts, I thought, it would be possible to find behavioristic and thus physicalistic definitions. But the more fundamental concepts of Freud's theory should be treated as hypothetical concepts, that is, introduced with the help of hypothetical laws in which they occur and of co-ordinative rules, which would permit the derivation of sentences about observable behavior from sentences involving the fundamental concepts of the theory. I pointed out the analogy between concepts like "ego", "id", "complex" and the field concepts in physics. My remarks were intended merely to express some ideas which, I believed, had been generally accepted by the left wing. I was surprised that they were regarded as something radically new. I believe, however, that my conception had been developed on the basis of our common view on hypotheses in science and the axiomatic method, and was influenced by talks I had had with Gödel and Popper.

The development towards a more liberal criterion of significance took a number of years, and various forms were proposed. Reichenbach had always rejected the principle of verifiability; he proposed instead a probability theory of meaning. According to his theory, a sentence is accepted as meaningful if it is possible to determine its weight on the basis of given observations; and two sentences have the same meaning if they have equal weight with respect to all possible observations. I agreed with Reichenbach in this view. But I did not follow him when he identified his concept of weight with probability in the frequency interpretation.

During the thirties, while I was in Prague, I began a systematic investigation of the logical relations between scientific concepts and basic concepts, say, observable properties of material things. The results were published in the article "Testability and Meaning" [1936-10]. I shall now explain some of these considerations.

Hypotheses about unobserved events of the physical world can never be completely verified by observational evidence. Therefore I suggested that we should abandon the concept of verification and say instead that the hypothesis is more or less confirmed or disconfirmed by the evidence. At that time I left the question open whether it would be possible to define a quantitative measure of confirmation. Later I introduced the quantitative concept of degree of confirmation or logical probability. I proposed to speak of confirmability instead of verifiability. A sentence is regarded as confirmable if observation sentences can contribute either positively or negatively to its confirmation.

Furthermore, I investigated possible sentence forms and methods for the introduction of new predicates on the basis of given primitive predicates for observable properties of things. My aim was to choose the sentence forms and methods of concept formation in such a way that the confirmability of the resulting sentences was assured. If a concept is introduced by a method which fulfills this requirement on the basis of given primitive predicates, then I called it reducible to those primitive predicates.

In addition to the requirement of complete verifiability we must abandon the earlier view that the concepts of science are explicitly definable on the basis of observation concepts; more indirect methods of reduction must be used. For this purpose I proposed a particular form of reduction sentences. In the course of further investigations it became clear that a schema of this simple form cannot suffice to introduce concepts of theoretical science. Still, the proposed simple form of reduction sentences was useful because it exhibited clearly the open character of the scientific concepts, i.e., the fact that their meanings are not completely fixed.

I made a distinction between confirmability and a somewhat stronger concept for which I proposed the term "testability". A sentence which is confirmable by possible observable events is, moreover, testable if a method can be specified for producing such events at will; this method is then a test procedure for the sentence. I considered the question of whether we should take testability or only confirmability as an empiricist criterion of significance. I proposed to take the more liberal requirement of confirmability. The stronger requirement of testability corresponds approximately to Bridgman's principle of operationism.

The thesis of physicalism, as originally accepted in the Vienna Circle, says roughly: Every concept of the language of science can be explicitly defined in terms of observables; therefore every sentence of the language of science is translatable into a sentence concerning observable properties. I suggested that only reducibility to observation predicates need be required of scientific concepts, since this requirement is sufficient for the confirmability of sentences involving those concepts.

Furthermore, I showed that our earlier thesis of phenomenalistic positivism was in need of a more liberal reformulation in an analogous way, so that translatability was replaced by confirmability.

10. Semantics

Language analysis, in our view the most important tool of philosophy, was first systematized in the form of logical syntax; but this method studies only the forms of the expressions, not their meanings. An important step in the development of language analysis consisted in the supplementation of syntax by semantics, i.e., the theory of the concepts of meaning and truth. Concepts of this kind have always been used in philosophical investigations. Exact analyses of such concepts were first given by logicians of the Warsaw school, especially Lesniewski and Kotarbinski. Subsequently Tarski, in his great treatise on the concept of truth,[10] developed a method by which adequate definitions of the concept of truth and of other semantical concepts became possible for the first time, and important results were obtained.

Even before the publication of Tarski's article I had realized, chiefly in conversations with Tarski and Gödel, that there must be a mode, different from the syntactical one, in which to speak about language. Since it is obviously admissible to speak about facts and, on the other hand, Wittgenstein notwithstanding, about expressions of a language, it cannot be inadmissable to do both in the same metalanguage. In this way it becomes possible to speak about the relations between language and facts. In our philosophical discussions we had, of course, always talked about these relations; but we had no exact systematized language for this purpose. In the new metalanguage of semantics, it is possible to make statements about the relation of designation and about truth.

When Tarski told me for the first time that he had constructed a definition of truth, I assumed that he had in mind a syntactical definition of logical truth or provability. I was surprised when he said that he meant truth in the customary sense, including contingent factual truth. Since I was thinking only in terms of a syntactical metalanguage, I wondered how it was possible to state the truth-condition for a simple sentence like "this table is black". Tarski replied: "This is simple; the sentence 'this table is black' is true if and only if this table is black".

In his treatise Tarski developed a general method for constructing exact definitions of truth for deductive language systems, that is, for stating rules which determine for every sentence of such a system a necessary and sufficient condition of its truth. In order to formulate these rules, it is necessary to use a metalanguage which contains the sentences of the object language or translations of them and which, therefore, may contain descriptive constants, e.g., the word "black" in the example men-

[10]Tarski, "Der Wahrheitsbegriff in den formalisierten Sprachen", *Studia Philosophica*, I, 1936, 261-405; separately printed in 1935. The original in Polish had been published in 1933. An English translation, "The Concept of Truth in Formalized Languages", is contained in his book *Logic, Semantics, Methamathematics* (Oxford, 1956).

tioned. In this respect, the semantical metalanguage goes beyond the limits of the syntactical metalanguage. This new metalanguage evoked my strongest interest. I recognized that it provided for the first time the means for precisely explicating many concepts used in our philosophical discussions.

When I met Tarski again in Vienna in the spring of 1935, I urged him to deliver a paper on semantics and on his definition of truth at the International Congress for Scientific Philosophy to be held in Paris in September. I told him that all those interested in scientific philosophy and the analysis of language would welcome this new instrument with enthusiasm, and would be eager to apply it in their own philosophical work. But Tarski was very skeptical. He thought that most philosophers, even those working in modern logic, would be not only indifferent, but hostile to the explication of the concept of truth. I promised to emphasize the importance of semantics in my paper and in the discussion at the Congress, and he agreed to present the suggested paper.

At the Congress it became clear from the reactions to the papers delivered by Tarski[11] and myself[12] that Tarski's skeptical predictions had been right. To my surprise, there was vehement opposition even on the side of our philosophical friends. Therefore we arranged an additional session for the discussion of this controversy outside the official program of the Congress. There we had long and heated debates between Tarski, Mrs. Lutman-Kokoszynska, and myself on one side, and our opponents Neurath, Arne Ness, and others on the other. Neurath believed that the semantical concept of truth could not be reconciled with a strictly empiricist and anti-metaphysical point of view. Similar objections were raised in later publications by Felix Kaufmann and Reichenbach. I showed that these objections were based on a misunderstanding of the semantical concept of truth, the failure to distinguish between this concept and concepts like certainty, knowledge of truth, complete verification and the like; I had already emphasized the necessity of this distinction in my Congress paper. Other misunderstandings and objections were clarified in a later article by Tarski[13] and in my [1946-2].

I began intensive work in the newly opened field. In the Encyclopedia monograph *Foundations of Logic and Mathematics* [1939-1] I explained

[11]Tarski, "Grundlegung der wissenschaftlichen Semantik", *Acts du Congrès Int. de Phil. Scient.* (Paris, 1935), Paris, 1936, Fasc. III, 1-8. Tarski gave also another interesting paper on semantics: "Über den Begriff der logischen Folgerung", *ibid.*, Fasc. VII, 1-11. English translations of both papers are contained in Tarski's book of 1956; see the previous footnote.

[12]Carnap, "Wahrheit und Bewährung" [1936-5], see also [1949-1].

[13]Tarski, "The Semantic Conception of Truth and the Foundations of Semantics", *Phil. Phen. Res.* IV, 1944, 341-76; reprinted in Linsky, *Semantics*, 1952. This paper and parts of mine are reprinted in Feigl and Sellars, *Readings in Philosophical Analysis* (1949).

in a more elementary, non-technical way the difference between syntax and semantics and the rôle of semantics in the methodology of science, especially as a theory of interpretation of formal systems, e.g., axiom systems in physics. A few years later the *Introduction to Semantics* [1942-2] followed, which explained both the theory of truth and the theory of logical deduction dealing with concepts like logical implication, logical truth and the like. My conception of semantics starts from the basis given in Tarski's work, but differs from his conception by the sharp distinction which I draw between logical and non-logical constants, and between logical and factual truth. I shall shortly return to this question. Some years later I published two more books on semantics, *Formalization of Logic* [1943] and *Meaning and Necessity* [1947-2].

As Tarski had foreseen, most of the philosophers were rather skeptical and sometimes opposed to the new theory of semantics. Today, when the importance of semantical concepts for philosophical investigations is widely recognized, it may be difficult for younger readers to imagine how strong the skepticism and active resistance was in the beginning. The reaction of many philosophers may be summed up as follows: "Semantics is an entirely new invention; we have done very well without it so far, and there is no reason why we should need it now." To me the usefulness of semantics for philosophy was so obvious that I believed no further arguments were required and it was sufficient to list a great number of customary concepts of a semantical nature; this I did in my books *Introduction* and *Formalization*. Throughout my life I have often made the psychological mistake of underestimating the inertial resistance of philosophers not only to new concepts and new views, but even to new explications and systematizations of old, familiar concepts.

At the present time in the United States, only a small number of philosophers have retained serious doubts about the usefulness of the semantical method for philosophy. The objections nowadays are usually directed not against semantics in general but against the reference in semantics to abstract entities like propositions, classes, properties, etc. This is indeed a serious problem about which I shall say more later.

The logic of *modalities* had been constructed for many years in the framework of symbolic logic, beginning mainly with the work of C. I. Lewis (1918). However, so far no clear interpretation of the modal terms had been given. After defining semantical concepts like logical truth and related ones, I proposed to interpret the modalities as those properties of propositions which correspond to certain semantical properties of the sentences expressing the propositions. For example, a proposition is logically necessary if and only if a sentence expressing it is logically true. When I was at Harvard in 1941, I talked about these ideas with Quine. He was interested, but he thought that the logical modalities were in themselves too vague and unclear to warrant the effort of constructing an exact explication. In a conversation with Lewis I indicated my interpretation of the modalities and said that this interpretation leads to a system corresponding to the strongest of his systems (S5). I assumed that he too would prefer his strongest system, although he did not say so in his book. However, he said that he regarded system S5 as too strong and preferred weaker systems just because they leave certain questions open which are settled in system S5 in a specific way. I was surprised, because the question of the validity of any of the modal formulas in Lewis' symbolic language seemed to me a purely logical question, since these formulas do not contain any non-logical constants. Therefore I would prefer a system in which these formulas are decidable.

In 1942 I worked again on the modalities. I constructed logical systems, combining modalities with variables. For systems with this combination Quine had pointed out certain difficulties which he regarded as insuperable. But in my systems these difficulties did not occur. I showed the possibilities of constructing both syntactical and semantical systems for the logic of modalities; the semantical rules in the systems represent the interpretation of the modalities briefly indicated above. These results were later published in the article [1946-1].

At the same time I developed a semantical method influenced by Frege's distinction between the *nominatum ("Bedeutung"*, i.e., the named entity) and the sense (*"Sinn"*) of an expression. I tried to explicate the distinction between *extension,* i.e., contingent reference or denotation, and *intension,* i.e., connotation or meaning, and I proposed to take these two concepts as a basis for a new method of semantical analysis. I showed the applicability of this method also for a language containing terms for logical modalities. In 1943, I wrote a book manuscript, called "Extension and Intension". With both Quine and Alonzo Church, who read copies of it, I had detailed discussions by correspondence which greatly helped to clarify my conceptions. Later, I worked out a considerably changed and extended version which appeared under the title *Meaning and Necessity* [1947-2].

I mentioned above the problem of the distinction between *logical* and *factual truth,* which constitutes a point of divergence among those working in semantics. To me it had always seemed to be one of the most important tasks to explicate this distinction, in other words, to construct a definition of logical truth or analyticity. In my search for an explication I was guided, on the one hand, by Leibniz' view that a necessary truth is one which holds in all possible worlds, and on the other hand, by Wittgenstein's view that a logical truth or tautology is characterized by holding for all possible distributions of truth-values. Therefore the various forms of my definition of logical truth are based either on the definition of logically possible states or on the definition of sentences describing those states (state-descriptions). I had given the first definition of logical truth in my book on syntax. But now I recognized that logical truth in the customary sense is a semantical concept. The concept which I had defined was the syntactical counterpart of the semantical concept. Therefore, using some of Tarski's results, I defined L-truth in semantics as an explication for the familiar concept of logical truth, and related concepts such as L-implication and L-equivalence. In this way, the distinction between logical and factual truth, which had always been regarded in our discussions in the Vienna Circle as important and fundamental, was at last vindicated. In this distinction we had seen the way out of the difficulty which had prevented the older empiricism from giving a satisfactory account of the nature of knowledge in logic and mathematics. Since empiricism had always asserted that *all* knowledge is based on experience, this assertion had to include knowledge in mathematics. On the other hand, we believed that with respect to this problem the rationalists had been right in rejecting the old empiricist view that the truth of "$2 + 2 = 4$" is contingent upon the observation of facts, a view that would lead to the unacceptable consequence that an arithmetical statement might possibly be refuted tomorrow by new experiences. Our solution, based on Wittgenstein's conception, consisted in asserting the thesis of empiricism only for factual truth. By contrast, the truths in logic and mathematics are not in need of confirmation by observations, because they do not state anything about the world of facts, they hold for any possible combination of facts.

The distinction between logical and factual truth leads also to a sharp boundary line between syntax as the theory of form alone, and semantics as the theory of meaning, and thus to the distinction between uninterpreted formal systems and their interpretations. These distinctions are meant not as assertions, but rather as proposals for the construction of a metalanguage for the analysis of the language of science. In this way we obtain also a clear distinction between questions about contingent facts and questions about meaning relations. This difference seems to me philosophically important; answering questions of the first kind is not part of the philosopher's task, though he may be interested in analyzing them; but answers to questions of the second kind lie often within the field of philosophy or applied logic.

Some of those who accept the semantical concept of truth reject a sharp distinction between logical and factual truth. Most prominent among them are Tarski and Quine. During the academic year 1940-41, when all three of us were at Harvard, we discussed this problem in great detail. They believed that, at best, a distinction of degree could be made. At that time I gave a talk on the relation of mathematics to empirical science in a large discussion group of faculty members interested in the foundations of science. My main thesis was that mathematics has no factual content and, therefore, is not in need of empirical confirmation, but that it nevertheless has a very important function in empirical science as an instrument of deduction. I thought that this was an old story and at any rate a purely academic question. But to my great surprise, the audience responded with vehement emotions. Even before I had finished my lecture, excited objections were raised. Afterwards we had a long and heated discussion in which several people often talked at the same time. Richard von Mises stated bluntly that the sentence "$2 + 2 = 4$" (if taken, not as a theorem in an uninterpreted axiom system, but in its customary interpretation) was just as much of an empirical nature as the sentence "Solid bodies expand when heated". I thought: are we now back with John Stuart Mill? The attacks by Tarski and Quine were even more spirited, but also more discerning. Many others rejected my view. I think Feigl was the only one who clearly shared my position. But, on the whole, the discussion was too vehement to permit a good mutual understanding.

A specific objection which has been raised from the beginning against my approach to semantics is directed against any reference to *abstract entities,* e.g., classes, properties, numbers, and the like. Some philosophers reject this way of speaking as a "hypostatization" of entities; in their view, it is either meaningless or at least in need of proof that such entities "do actually exist." From my point of view, which goes back to that of the Vienna Circle and of Wittgenstein, an utterance like "there are no classes" is a typical pseudo-sentence. These objections which seemed to me to involve metaphysical pseudo-questions, were, however, not made by metaphysicians but by anti-metaphysical empiricists—like Ernest Nagel, W. V. Quine, Nelson Goodman, and others. At the time each of the two parties seemed to criticize the other for using bad metaphysics.

Perhaps it will help to make clearer my way of thinking about such problems if I point out that most of the members of the Vienna Circle were trained primarily in a field of science or mathematics and that this training had a strong influence on our thinking in philosophy. It was due to this background that, when we contrasted legitimate and illegitimate concepts, questions, or ways of thinking, we usually took as typical examples, on the one hand, formulations in the exact sciences or, on the other hand, certain formulations in traditional metaphysics. Of course, this does not mean that we immediately accepted as admissible all concepts used by scientists. We certainly regarded it as our task to examine and clarify the customary concepts. Nevertheless, through our analyses, we had arrived at the conclusion that most concepts which occur, e.g., in the language of physics, are basically free of metaphysical components and hence legitimate, although they may still be in need of more exact explications. Thus the experience in our investigations and discussions led us to the following practical attitude. We regarded terms of the traditional philosophical language with suspicion or at least with caution and accepted them only when they passed a careful examination; in contrast, we regarded terms of mathematics and physics as innocent and permitted their use in our discussions unless cogent reasons had shown them to be untenable. If this point of view is applied to abstract terms like "class", "property", "natural number", "real number", etc., and similarly to variables of corresponding types, then we have to recognize first, that these are logical, not descriptive signs, and second that these terms have for centuries been in general use in mathematics and physics. Therefore, in our view, very strong reasons must be offered if such terms are to be condemned as incompatible with empiricism or as illegitimate and unscientific. To label the use of such terms as indicating Platonism or even more specifically, Platonic realism, as was sometimes done by the critics, seemed to me misleading; this view neglects the fundamental distinction between, say, physical laws containing real number variables and ontological theses like those of the reality or irreality of universals.

What I have just said is, of course, not meant to be a theoretical argument for the legitimacy of abstract terms, but merely an explanation of my reaction to those objections and of my impression that no sufficiently compelling reasons for them were given. Nevertheless, I thought that these objections deserved to be given careful and serious consideration. This I did in my article "Empiricism, Semantics, and Ontology" [1950-1]. In accord with my old principle of tolerance, I proposed to admit any forms of expression as soon as sufficient logical rules for their use are given. If a philosopher asks a question like "are there natural numbers?", he means it as a question so-to-speak outside the given language, raised for the purpose of examining the admissibility of such a language. Therefore I called philosophical questions of existence of this kind external questions. But then I pointed out that for these questions no interpretation as *theoretical* questions has been given by the philosophers. I proposed to the philosophers who discuss such questions that they interpret them as *practical* questions, i.e., as questions about the decision whether or not to accept a language containing expressions for the particular kind of entities. Various reasons may influence the decision about the acceptance or non-acceptance of the framework for such expressions. My main point is the rejection of the customary view that the introduction of a linguistic framework is legitimate only if the affirmative answer to the external question of existence (e.g., "there are natural numbers") can be shown to be true. In my view, the introduction of the framework is legitimate in any case. Whether or not this introduction is advisable for certain purposes is a practical question of language engineering, to be decided on the basis of convenience, fruitfulness, simplicity, and the like.

I have the impression that, among empiricists today, there is no longer strong opposition to abstract entities, either in semantics or in any field of mathematics or empirical science. In particular, Quine has recently taken a tolerant, pragmatistic attitude which seems close to my position.[14]

The concept of intension or meaning is closely related to that of logical truth. Recently Quine has declared that this concept is unintelligible to him. He has challenged those who regard it as scientifically meaningful to offer not only a semantical criterion for the concept of intension with respect to an artificially constructed language system, but in the first place an empirical, behavioristic criterion in pragmatics with respect to natural languages. To me it seemed clear that it should be possible to provide a criterion of this kind, since linguists in their empirical investigations have always studied the meaning of expressions. In a paper [1955-3] on meaning in natural languages, I have tried to give a pragmatical criterion of the kind required. The controversy about the admissibility and usefulness of concepts such as logical truth and intension is still going on.

11. *Language Planning*

Throughout my life I have been fascinated by the phenomenon of language. How amazing and how gratifying it is that we are capable of communicating with one another by spoken sounds or written marks, to describe facts or express thoughts and feelings, to influence the actions of others. In school I was interested in languages, especially Latin. I often thought of becoming a linguist. However, I was more inclined toward theoretical construction and systematization than toward description of facts. Therefore I had more interest in those problems of language which involved planning and construction.

There are two entirely different fields in which problems of language construction always held a vivid interest for me. The first is the construction of language systems in symbolic logic; the second is the problem of the construction of an auxiliary language for international communication. The two problems and the possible methods for their solution are utterly different. Nevertheless, there seems to be a psychological affinity between these two enterprises. A number of men from Leibniz to Peano were actively interested in both objectives. I shall now report upon my interests in language construction in each of these two fields.

First let us consider that aspect of the logician's work which has to do with the planning of new forms of *languages in symbolic logic*. When I became acquainted with Frege's symbolic system, which was for me the

[14]W. V. Quine, *From a Logical Point of View* (1953); see in particular Essays I and IV, originally published in 1948 and 1950, respectively.

first system of symbolic logic, the question of planning did not immediately occur to me, because Frege simply exhibited his kind of notation and the structure of his language, proved theorems and showed applications, but said very little about his motivation for the choice of this particular language form. Only later, when I became acquainted with the entirely different language forms of *Principia Mathematica,* the modal logic of C. I. Lewis, the intuitionistic logic of Brouwer and Heyting, and the typeless systems of Quine and others, did I recognize the infinite variety of possible language forms. On the one hand, I became aware of the problems connected with the finding of language forms suitable for given purposes; on the other hand, I gained the insight that one cannot speak of "the correct language form", because various forms have different advantages in different respects. The latter insight led me to the principle of tolerance. Thus, in time, I came to recognize that our task is one of *planning* forms of languages. Planning means to envisage the general structure of a system and to make, at different points in the system, a choice among various possibilities, theoretically an infinity of possibilities, in such a way that the various features fit together and the resulting total language system fulfills certain given desiderata.

Wittgenstein made some limited use of symbolic logic in his *Tractatus.* I think that some of the most important concepts in his philosophical conception could hardly have been found by him or accepted by other philosophers without a study of symbolic logic. This holds, e.g., for the following of his concepts based on truth-functional connectives, whose analysis he presumably learned from the work of Frege: the concepts of truth possibilities, of the range ("*Spielraum*") of a statement, his explications of logical truth ("tautology") and of logical implication in terms of ranges. But the *Tractatus* shows that he did not have a special affection for symbolism. And it seems that in his later period in England he took a more negative attitude toward constructed language systems, as can be seen from his *Lecture Notes,* the *Philosophical Investigations* and the attitude of those British philosophers who were chiefly influenced by him.

Only slowly did I recognize how large the divergence is between the views of the two wings of analytic philosophy in the question of natural versus constructed languages: the view which I shared with my friends in the Vienna Circle and later with many philosophers in the United States, and the view of those philosophers who are chiefly influenced by G. E. Moore and Wittgenstein. It seems to me that one explanation of this divergence is the fact that in the Vienna Circle mathematics and empirical science were taken as models representing knowledge in its best, most systematized form, toward which all philosophical work on problems of knowledge should be oriented. By contrast, Wittgenstein's indifferent and sometimes even negative attitude toward mathematics and science was accepted by many of his followers, impairing the fruitfulness of their philosophical work.

With the second kind of language planning, whose aim is an *international language,* I became acquainted much earlier than with language planning in symbolic logic. At the age of about fourteen I found by chance a little pamphlet called "The World Language Esperanto". I was immediately fascinated by the regularity and ingenious construction of the language, and I learned it eagerly. When a few years later I attended an international Esperanto congress, it seemed like a miracle to see how easy it was for me to follow the talks and the discussions in the large public meetings, and then to talk in private conversations with people from many other countries, while I was unable to hold conversations in those languages which I had studied for many years in school. One of the high points of the congress was the performance of Goethe's *Iphigenie* in an Esperanto translation. It was a stirring and uplifting experience for me to hear this drama, inspired by the ideal of one humanity, expressed in the new medium which made it possible for thousands of spectators from many countries to understand it, and to become united in spirit.

After the first World War, I had some opportunities of observing the practical use of Esperanto. The most extensive experience was in 1922, in connection with the Esperanto Congress in Helsingfors, Finland. There I became acquainted with a Bulgarian student; for four weeks we were almost constantly together and became close friends. After the Congress we traveled and hiked through Finland and the new Baltic republics of Estonia, Latvia, and Lithuania. We stayed with hospitable Esperantists and made contact with many people in these countries. We talked about all kinds of problems in public and in personal life, always, of course, in Esperanto. For us this language was not a system of rules but simply a living language. After experiences of this kind, I cannot take very seriously the arguments of those who assert that an international auxiliary language might be suitable for business affairs and perhaps for natural science, but could not possibly serve as an adequate means of communication in personal affairs, for discussions in the social sciences and the humanities, let alone for fiction or drama. I have found that most of those who make these assertions have no practical experience with such a language.

The motives which in my youth evoked my interest in an international language were, on the one hand the humanitarian ideal of improving the understanding between nations, and on the other, the pleasure of using a language which combined a surprising flexibility in the means of expression with a great simplicity of structure. Later I became more interested in the theoretical problems of the points of view which should guide the planning of an international language. Therefore I studied the most important language projects. I was especially interested in the theoretical discussions by the founders of these projects and the reasons which they gave for their new, improved language forms.

First I studied the language *Ido* proposed by L. Couturat, who emphasizes regularity and logic of word formation. By contrast, the "naturalistic" school stresses more the psychological factor of the continuity with the development of natural languages. To this school belong G. Peano's *Latino sine flexione,* E. de Wahl's *Occidental,* and *Interlingua.* The latter was developed on the basis of many years of research by linguists on the research staff of IALA (International Auxiliary Language Association), among them Edward Sapir, Edward L. Thorndike, and André Martinet. The final form of *Interlingua* was worked out by Alexander Gode.

Among some of the adherents of these and other language projects, heated sectarian debates are going on. Just as I pleaded for the principle of tolerance in the field of logical languages, I am in the field of international languages on the side of those who emphasize the common aim and the similarity of the proposed means. Being chiefly based on the Romance languages, the five language forms which I have mentioned, from Esperanto to Interlingua, are indeed so similar to each other that they may be regarded as variants of one language. They represent Standard Average European, as Gode put it, using a term coined by Benjamin Lee Whorf. It is true that every living language uses a particular conceptual system for the description of the world, a system that has grown out of the specific cultural background of the language. This fact, which has been explained in detail by Whorf, is sometimes used as an objection against the possibility of a constructed international language. However, the existing international language does possess a specific cultural background, as was emphasized by Gode. This background is the Western culture, more specifically, its modern science and technology, which originated in the Occident but which are now, together with their scientific terminology, the common property of many nations all over the world.

The two problems, the construction of language systems in symbolic logic and the construction of international languages, are entirely different from a practical point of view. Leibniz was the first to recognize the importance of both problems, to see their connection but also their difference. Throughout his life, he envisaged the idea of a *characteristica universalis,* a kind of logical symbolism or *Begriffsschrift* in Frege's sense. He also thought about the possibility of constructing a universal language as a means of international communication. Leibniz intended to base this language on Latin, but he planned to give it a simple and regular grammatical structure. Leibniz' second aim has been fulfilled in our time by the various forms of an international language.

Although the two problems are different and are directed toward different aims, working on them is somehow psychologically similar. As I see it, both must appeal to those whose thinking about means of expression or about language in the widest sense is not only descriptive and historical but also constructive, whose concern is the problem of finding those possible forms of expression which would be most suitable for certain linguistic functions. I think it might lead to fruitful results if some of those logicians who find satisfaction and enjoyment in designing new symbolic systems would follow the example of Leibniz, Descartes, Peano, and Couturat and direct their thought to the problem of planning an international language.

12. Probability and Inductive Logic

In our discussions on probability in the Vienna Circle, we took for granted the frequency conception, according to which probability is, roughly speaking, the same as relative frequency in the long run. This was the only interpretation of probability for which at that time there existed satisfactory explications, the explication given by Richard von Mises and by Reichenbach (as the limit of the relative frequency in an infinite sequence), and the explication accepted in statistics (based on an axiom system, e.g., that of Kolmogoroff, with rules of application referring to relative frequency). We regarded the classical conception of probability, represented chiefly by Jacob Bernoulli and Laplace, as definitely refuted by the criticism of the frequentists. The classical conception was essentially based on the principle of insufficient reason or indifference according to which two events must be regarded as having the same probability if we have no more reason to expect the one than the other. The critics of the classical conception pointed out correctly that certain consequences which the classical authors had drawn from this principle were absurd; furthermore, it was objected that this principle puts a premium on ignorance. (Today I still regard the first of these two arguments as valid, but not the second.) John Maynard Keynes' conception (1921), according to which probability is a logical concept but indefinable and only to be grasped by a kind of logical intuition, was likewise regarded by us as superseded by the development of the frequency conception; in addition, his system of axioms and definitions appeared to us to be formally unsatisfactory.

In his *Tractatus,* Wittgenstein gave a definition of probability which was based not on frequency but on the logical ranges of propositions. This conception would make a probability statement analytic, not synthetic, as the frequency conception does. Wittgenstein's remarks were, however, very brief and in the beginning did not receive much attention in our Circle. Later, Waismann developed a probability conception based on Wittgenstein's ideas. (His paper was delivered at our Conference in Prague 1929 and published in *Erkenntnis* 1931.) Waismann's approach excited much interest among us. It seems that his concept was not a purely logical one but combined the logical point of view of ranges with the empirical point of view of frequencies. This feature is indicated by his remark that the basic values of probability must be chosen in such a way that they are in accord with empirically determined frequencies.

In the spring of 1941 I began to reconsider the whole problem of probability. It seemed to me that at least in certain contexts probability should be interpreted as a purely logical concept. I think that influence in this direction came on the one hand from Wittgenstein and Waismann, on the other hand from Keynes. But I tried a new approach. I believed that the logical concept of probability should supply an exact quantitative explication of a concept which is basic in the methodology of empirical science, viz., the concept of the confirmation of a hypothesis with respect to a given body of evidence. For this reason I chose as a technical term for the explication of logical probability the term "degree of confirmation", which I had used in several papers informally in a similar sense. I continue to use the term "probability" (or "logical probability") in informal explanations. I would have preferred to use it also as a technical term, especially since I became convinced that the classical authors had used it chiefly in the logical and not in the frequency sense. I recognized, however, that this use would be inadvisable for practical reasons; because its use in the frequency sense was very wide-spread, particularly in the literature of mathematical statistics. Therefore it seemed to me that there was no other way but to use a new term.

One of the basic tenets of my conception was that the logical concept of probability is the basis for all inductive inferences, i.e., all those which do not hold with deductive necessity. Therefore I sometimes use the phrase "inductive probability" as synonymous with "logical probability". I believe that if it were possible to find a satisfactory definition and theory of logical probability, this would at last supply a clear rational basis for the controversial procedure of inductive inference. Therefore I called the theory of logical probability "inductive logic".

My reflections on logical probability in 1941 led me back to Keynes' book, *A Treatise on Probability,* with which I was only superficially acquainted. I saw that we had given too little attention to this book. I found that, in spite of its insufficiency in the formal part, it offers valuable suggestions in its general discussions of the sense and use of probability and in its historical expositions.

It was clear to me that for a purely logical concept of probability the statements of specified values would be analytic and that therefore the determination of the basic probability values could not be founded on experience but had to be based on considerations of logical relations, including logical symmetry. For these considerations a principle of indifference would be necessary. Yet I recognized that, in contrast to the very strong principle in its classical form which had been correctly criticized, we had to take a much weaker, essentially restricted version of the principle.

Somewhat later I studied Harold Jeffreys' *Theory of Probability* (1939). I was gratified to see that our conceptions of the logical nature of probability were in agreement in the essential points. But whereas Keynes and Jeffreys rejected the frequency interpretation of probability, I thought from the beginning that this concept, for which we may use the term "statistical probability", is also important but fulfills a function entirely different from that of the concept of logical probability. The statements on statistical probability, both singular and general statements, e.g., probability laws in physics or in economics, are synthetic and serve for the description of general features of facts. Therefore these statements occur *within* science, for example, in the language of physics (taken as object language). On the other hand, the statements of logical or inductive probability are analytic; they express a logical relation between given evidence and a hypothesis, a relation similar to logical implication but with numerical values. Thus these statements speak *about* statements of science; therefore they do not belong to science proper but to the logic or methodology of science, formulated in the metalanguage. The two concepts of probability, the statistical and the logical, should be acknowledged and investigated separately. The statistical concept is generally accepted today. I tried to show that in addition the logical concept is needed, which could serve as the basis of inductive logic.

I published the basic ideas of my conception on probability in several articles, beginning with [1945-2]. Later in my book, *Logical Foundations of Probability* [1950-4], I offered a more detailed and systematic presentation. I explained and discussed in detail the philosophical ideas underlying the system, and I presented a formal development of the foundations of inductive logic.

The system developed in my book also contains a general theory of estimation. In contemporary mathematical statistics there is no commonly accepted general theory of estimation. There is no agreement on the question which estimate function for a given magnitude is most adequate, or even what requirements must be fulfilled by any acceptable estimate function. I recognized very soon that the theory of estimation should be an essential part of inductive logic. But there arose the problem of whether, for this purpose, a new primitive was necessary or whether perhaps the degree of confirmation *c* would suffice. I discovered that *c* is indeed sufficient, moreover that it is not necessary to search for a new suitable estimate function with respect to every kind of magnitude. It is possible to define, on the basis of *c*, a general method of estimation, i.e., one applicable to all magnitudes. (The following explanations presuppose that a system of inductive logic for the language of science is available, i.e., a function *c* which is applicable to any sentences of the language of science. Actually we are still far from this aim.) If *c* is given, the estimate of any magnitude *u* on the basis of any given evidence *e* is defined as the weighted mean of the possible values of *u*, taking as weights the logical probabilities, repesented by *c*, of the values of *u* with respect to *e*.

On the basis indicated, a rule determining the rational choice by a person *X* of a practical decision out of a class of possible decisions can be formulated. It is presupposed for this rule that, first, a function *c* is available and, second, that the utility function for the person *X* is given which determines for every possible outcome of any possible action of *X* the resulting utility, i.e., the degree of satisfaction (positive or negative) which *X* would obtain from the outcome in question. The rule says that a rational decision by *X* consists in choosing that action for which the estimate of the utility is a maximum. This rule is analogous to customary conceptions. But it seems to me that my version of the rule is more adequate than the customary one because it uses the concept of logical probability and not that of statistical probability or other statistical concepts. It seems clear to me that a rule for a rational decision by the person *X* at a time *T* must use only that knowledge *e* which is available to *X* at the time *T*. The relevant values of statistical probability are, however, in general not known to *X;* therefore the rule should not refer to them. On the other hand, the values of logical probability are determined on the basis of the given evidence by purely logical procedures.

While I was still working on the book, I began the construction of a system of possible inductive methods which fulfill certain fundamental axioms. This was explained in the monograph, *The Continuum of Inductive Methods* [1952-1]. Each method of the kind mentioned consists of a *c*-function (degree of confirmation) and an estimate function based on it in the way indicated above. My investigations referred only to a simple language with predicates; therefore only estimate functions for frequencies are dealt with. I found that it is possible to characterize these inductive methods with the help of a single parameter λ in such a way that each method is uniquely and completely determined by the chosen value of λ. This fact makes it much easier to examine the properties of the various methods. Furthermore, I defined a measure of success for any given inductive method with respect to any possible (finite) world, based on the errors of estimates of relative frequencies of certain properties; these estimates are to be determined by the inductive method in question on the basis of the given evidence. For a given world structure it is then easy to determine that inductive method which in a world of this structure has the greatest measure of success, i.e., the smallest sum of the squares of the errors for the total system of estimates. The method thus obtained I call the optimum inductive method for the considered world structure. I found that inversely, for any given inductive method of the λ-system, we can determine a possible world structure for which this method is the optimum method.

As far as we can judge the situation at the present time, it seems that an observer is free to choose any of the admissible values of λ and thereby an inductive method. If we find that the person *X* chooses a greater value of λ than the person *Y*, then we recognize that *X* is more cautious than *Y*, i.e., *X* waits for a larger class of observational data than *Y* before he is willing to deviate in his estimate of relative frequency by a certain amount from its a priori value.

Soon after finishing the monograph *Continuum* I arrived at the conviction that the methods developed there are entirely adequate only if the probability statements involve not more than one family of predicates. If several families of predicates are considered, e.g., the family of colors or the family of heat qualities, in order to determine the degree of confirmation of a prediction, we have also to take into account the statistical dependencies among the predicates of different families as shown in the given data. The determination of the degree of confirmation in a situation of this kind belongs in my opinion to the fundamental problems of the theory of probability; but in the vast literature on probability this problem has hardly ever been touched and no solution has so far been proposed. In the years 1952-1953 I had the good fortune of meeting John G. Kemeny in Princeton, who became interested in problems in this field. We found that the problem mentioned, although essentially of an elementary nature, involved unexpected difficulties; but after working at it together for a long time we arrived at a first solution which so far has not been published. We have since made further efforts to improve our solution.

In the year 1952 I made investigations concerning the connection between degree of order and inductive probability. The results have not been published thus far. For a state-description (so to speak, a possible world) with respect to a family of predicates, the degree of order can be defined in such a way that it is in accord with the customary but vague concept of uniformity; that is to say, if in some possible world more universal laws hold than in another, the degree of order of the first is higher than that of the second. Furthermore, the initial (or a priori) probability of a possible world is proportional to its degree of order. I found that for many other problems the concepts of degree of order and degree of disorder, defined as the reciprocal of the degree of order, have considerable interest. With the help of these concepts I could clarify a certain ambiguity which is found in many books on mathematical statistics, even some of the best, an ambiguity based on a confusion of randomness and disorder. For the concept of randomness, the books give the generally accepted definition, which is clear and unobjectionable. But then the term "randomness" is sometimes used in the same book to refer to something like high degree of disorder, e.g., in connection with so-called tests of randomness. It is further used in discussions of the design of experiments, where a random distribution is proposed. What would actually be required for such a design is a high degree of disorder, not randomness.

In the years 1949 to 1951 I investigated several ways of explicating the concept of amount of information. My thinking on this problem was stimulated by a definition of amount of information in Norbert Wiener's book *Cybernetics*. However, I based my concept not on statistical probability, but on inductive probability, and I used the semantical concept of the content of a statement. Whereas the customary concept, which was suggested by Wiener and then developed by Claude Shannon and others, depends merely on the frequencies of the messages, my concept depends on the meanings of the statements. Thereby it actually corresponds to what a scientist has in mind when he says for example that a certain report on observations, although shorter than another, supplies more information. I elaborated this theory of the semantical amount of information in collaboration with Yehoshua Bar-Hillel.[15]

From the beginning it was clear to me that my conception of probability and inductive logic would meet strong opposition. Even some of my closest philosophical friends shook their heads: "Have you not told us yourself that the interpretation of probability must be based on frequencies and that probability statements are empirical? Do you really intend to return to the old and long-refuted principle of indifference? Is this not the beginning of a dangerous apriorism or rationalism"? Thus, on the one hand, I had to defend my right to change certain views which we had held in common for many years; on the other, I had to show that the new conception in no way violated our common empiricist principles. I pointed out that the logical interpretation of probability was far from being something radically new; that, on the contrary, it was older than the frequency conception because it was already clearly represented by the most important authors of the classical period of the theory of probability

[15]The results are published in our articles [1953-3] and [1953-6] and in Bar-Hillel, "An Examination of Information Theory", *Phil. of Science* XXII (1955).

in the 18th century. My position was understood more clearly when in 1950 my book appeared, which discussed in detail the purpose and the limits of inductive logic and the meaning of logical or inductive probability and which presented the construction of an exact system. Some of my empiricist friends gradually inclined to the view that logical probability and analytic inductive logic were tenable and important for the theory of knowledge, although they might still have some doubts about particular points, e.g., about the possibility of extending the theory developed in my book for simple languages with one-place predicates to richer languages. I was well aware that for scientists and statisticians the comprehensive technical apparatus in my book involving symbolic logic would have a deterrent effect. But the interest of some of them was awakened by less technical articles and lectures by myself and others. My later monograph, the *Continuum* [1952-1], used very little symbolic logic, and some of the results should be of interest not only to logicians. I showed, for example, that some methods of estimation frequently used by statisticians have serious disadvantages, which in certain cases are so strong that their application seems unacceptable to me; by contrast, the methods of estimation of frequency which I exhibited within the framework of the λ-system are free from these disadvantages. I had expected that statisticians would offer counter-arguments to defend their customary methods; but so far I have seen none. I have often noticed in discussions that it seems very difficult for those who have worked for years within the given framework of mathematical statistics to adapt their thinking to the unfamiliar concept of logical probability. In general, I have found that most scientists and philosophers are willing to discuss a new assertion, if it is formulated in the customary conceptual framework; but it seems very difficult for most of them even to consider and discuss new concepts.

13. The Theoretical Language

Theoretical physics has long used concepts which do not refer to anything directly observable; let us call them theoretical concepts. In spite of their practical usefulness, their special character was recognized and their methodological and logical analysis was developed only in recent decades. As mentioned earlier, the conceptions of the Vienna Circle on these problems were influenced by two different factors: the explicit development of the axiomatic method by Hilbert and his collaborators, and the emphasis on the importance and function of hypotheses in science, especially in physics, by men like Poincaré and Duhem. These two influences affected also the methodological ideas of some physicists, e.g., of Einstein, and led them to emphasize theoretical postulates and their relative autonomy. The early influence of these two schools of thought on my philosophical thinking is noticeable in my paper on the task of physics

[1923] and in the two small companion volumes on physics by myself and by Feigl[16] written when we were in Vienna. In my article on Testability [1936-10] I stressed the open character of scientific concepts, their incomplete interpretation, and the impossibility of translating the sentences of the scientific language into terms designating observables. This position provided a greater freedom of choice of linguistic forms and of procedures for the introduction of new concepts.

Soon I proceeded further in this direction. In *Foundations of Logic and Mathematics* ([1939-1] §§ 23-25), I showed how the system of science or of a particular scientific field, e.g., physics, can be constructed as a calculus whose axioms represent the fundamental laws of the field in question. This calculus is not directly interpreted. It is rather constructed as a "freely floating system", i.e., as a network of primitive theoretical concepts which are connected with one another by the axioms. On the basis of these primitive concepts, further theoretical concepts are defined. Eventually, some of these are closely related to observable properties and can be interpreted by semantical rules which connect them with observables. Thus e.g., '*Fe*' may be defined in terms of a certain configuration of particles and '*Y*' in terms of a certain distribution of the *EH*-field (the electromagnetic field). Then rules like the following may be stated for these terms: "'*Fe*' designates iron", "'*Y*' designates a certain shade of yellow". By these rules the floating network is "anchored to the solid ground of observable facts". Since the rules involve only certain derivative concepts, the interpretation of the theoretical terms supplied by the rules is incomplete. But this incomplete interpretation is sufficient for an understanding of the theoretical system, if "understanding" means being able to use in practical applications; this application consists in making predictions of observable events, based on observed data, with the help of the theoretical system. For this purpose it is sufficient that certain derivative terms of the theoretical system are interpreted by the semantical rules.

In subsequent years I frequently considered the problem of the possible forms of constructing such a system, and I often discussed these problems with friends. I preferred a form of construction in which the total language consists of two parts: the observation language which is presupposed as being completely understood, and the theoretical language of the network. The partial interpretation for the theoretical language is then given by rules of correspondence which permit the derivation of sentences of the one language from sentences of the other. It is important to realize that these rules involve only a particular class of terms and sentences of the theoretical language. The observation language speaks about observables. But "observability" is a rather vague term which

[16]Carnap, R., *Physikalische Begriffsbildung,* [1925]; H. Feigl, *Theorie und Erfahrung in der Physik,* Karlsruhe (1929).

may be understood in a narrower or wider sense. I gradually preferred to exclude from the observation language more and more scientific terms, even some of those which many physicists regard as observation terms because they refer to magnitudes for which there are simple procedures of measurement, e.g., "mass" and "temperature".

My thinking on these problems received fruitful stimulation from a series of conversations which I had with Tarski and Quine during the academic year 1940-41, when I was at Harvard; later Nelson Goodman participated in these talks. We considered especially the question of which form the basic language, i.e., the observation language, must have in order to fulfill the requirement of complete understandability. We agreed that the language must be nominalistic, i.e., its terms must not refer to abstract entities but only to observable objects or events. Nevertheless, we wanted this language to contain at least an elementary form of arithmetic. To reconcile arithmetic with the nominalistic requirement, we considered among others the method of representing the natural numbers by the observable objects themselves which were supposed to be ordered in a sequence; thus no abstract entities would be involved. We further agreed that for the basic language the requirements of finitism and constructivism should be fulfilled in some sense. We examined various forms of finitism. Quine preferred a very strict form; the number of objects was assumed to be finite and consequently the numbers occurring in arithmetic could not exceed a certain maximum number. Tarski and I preferred a weaker form of finitism, which left it open whether the number of all objects is finite or infinite. Tarski contributed important ideas on the possible forms of a finitistic arithmetic. In order to fulfill the requirement of constructivism I proposed to use certain features of my Language I in my *Logical Syntax*. We planned to have the basic language serve, in addition, as an elementry syntax language for the formulation of the basic syntactical rules of the total language. The latter language was intended to be comprehensive enough to contain the whole of classical mathematics and physics, represented as syntactical systems. The syntactical rules of transformation were to comprise not only the axioms of mathematics and physics, but also the rules of correspondence connecting the two parts of the language and thereby supplying a partial interpretation of the theoretical language. Quine demonstrated his well-known ingenuity in the invention of language forms. The fruitful collaboration in our discussions was very enjoyable to all of us. So far nobody has carried out the whole project as we had planned it. But various aspects have been investigated.[17]

[17] In their article "Steps Toward a Constructive Nominalism", *Journal Symb. Logic* XII (1947) Goodman and Quine have constructed a nominalistic and finitistic language for arithmetic and syntax.

More recently, I investigated the problem of the construction of the theoretical language and of the logical nature and scientific function of theoretical concepts, and discussed them with friends, in particular, in conversations with Feigl and Hempel and in conferences arranged by the Minnesota Center for Philosophy of Science. Some of the results have appeared in the volumes published by the Center, among them my article "The Methodological Character of Theoretical Concepts" [1956-4].

As mentioned above, the interpretation of theoretical terms is always incomplete, and the theoretical sentences are in general not translatable into the observation language. These disadvantages are more than balanced by the great advantages of the theoretical language, viz. the great freedom of concept formation and theory formation, and the great explanatory and predictive power of a theory. These advantages have so far been used chiefly in the field of physics; the prodigious growth of physics since the last century depended essentially upon the possibility of referring to unobservable entities like atoms and fields. In our century, other branches of science such as biology, psychology, and economics, have begun to apply the method of theoretical concepts to some extent.

What does the empiricist criterion of meaningfulness say with respect to theoretical terms? Even at the time of the earlier liberalization of the empiricist requirement, some empiricists, e.g., Quine and Hempel, expressed doubts whether it was still possible to make a clear distinction between meaningful and meaningless terms or whether this distinction should rather be taken as a matter of degree. With respect to the theoretical language, the reason for doubts of this kind seemed even stronger. Since the connection between a theoretical term t and observation terms, which is the basis of the interpretation, becomes weaker as the chain from observation terms through rules of correspondence and postulates to the term t becomes longer, it seemed plausible to think that in this context we must speak of a degree of significance. This view has been maintained chiefly by Hempel. By contrast, I have, in the article [1956-4] mentioned above, formulated tentative criteria of significance for theoretical terms and sentences, based on the following idea. A theoretical term t is significant if there is an assumption A involving t such that from A and additional assumptions involving other theoretical terms that have already been recognized as significant it is possible to derive with the help of the postulates and the rules of correspondence an observation sentence that cannot be derived without the assumption A. This criterion is meant as a minimum requirement. For sentences I proposed the following criterion. An expression of the language L containing theoretical terms is a significant sentence if it satisfies the rules of formation for L and if all theoretical terms occurring in it are significant. The proposed criteria are not yet in final form. But I am inclined to believe that it is somehow possible, even in the wider framework of the theoretical language, to make a clear distinction between those terms and sentences which are cognitively significant and those which are not.

14. Values and Practical Decisions

In our discussions in the Vienna Circle we were much concerned with clarifying the logical nature of value statements. We distinguished between absolute or unconditional value statements, e.g., one that says that a certain action is morally good in itself, and relative or conditional value statements, e.g., one saying that an action is good in the sense of being conducive toward reaching certain aims. Statements of the latter kind are obviously empirical, even though they may contain value terms like "good". On the other hand, absolute value statements that speak only about what ought to be done are devoid of cognitive meaning according to the empiricist criterion of significance. They certainly possess non-cognitive meaning components, especially emotive or motivating ones, and their effect in education, admonition, political appeal, etc., is based on these components. But, since they are not cognitive, they cannot be interpreted as assertions. The fact that they are often expressed, not in the most appropriate form as imperatives such as "love thy neighbor", but in the grammatical form of declarative sentences such as "it is thy duty to love thy neighbor", has misled many philosophers to consider them as assertive, cognitive sentences.

This result of a logical analysis of value statements and the controversies concerning them may appear as a purely academic matter without any practical interest. But I have found that the lack of distinction between factual questions and pure value questions leads to confusions and misunderstandings in discussions of moral problems in personal life or of political decisions. If the distinction is clearly made, the discussion will be more fruitful, because with respect to the two fundamentally different kinds of questions the approach most appropriate to each will be used; thus for factual questions arguments of factual evidence will be offered; whereas persuasion, educational influence, appeal, and the like will be brought to bear upon decisions concerning pure value questions.

On the other hand, I have often found philosophers who, in their criticism of our conception, ascribed to the problem of the logical nature of value statements an exaggerated practical significance. According to these critics, to deny to value statements the status of theoretical assertions and thereby the possibility of demonstrating their validity must necessarily lead to immorality and nihilism. In Prague I found a striking example of this view in Oskar Kraus, the leading representative of the philosophy of Franz Brentano. I heard from the students that in one of his seminars he characterized my thesis of the nature of value statements as so dangerous for the morality of youth that he had seriously pondered the question whether it was not his duty to call on the state authorities to put me in jail. But, he said, he finally came to the conclusion that this would not be the right thing to do because, though my doctrine was very wrong, I was not actually a wicked man. Somewhat later, when we became personally acquainted, we understood each other very well in spite of our philosophical differences. I had very high respect for his sincerity and absolute honesty in philosophical discussions, and his kindness and warmheartedness had a great personal appeal. Many of those philosophers who maintain the thesis of a special source for the alleged knowledge of absolute values think that anyone who rejects their particular source cannot possibly have any moral values at all. I am inclined to think quite generally that someone's acceptance or rejection of any particular thesis concerning the logical nature of value statements and the kind and source of their validity has usually a very limited influence upon his practical decisions. The behavior in given situations and the general attitude of people is chiefly determined by their character and very little, if at all, by the theoretical doctrines to which they adhere.

My view that the practical effect of our own thesis is similarly limited, seems to be supported by the fact that there is no agreement on it even among empiricists who share the same basic philosophical position. The thesis of the non-cognitive character of value statements is accepted by most of those who regard themselves as belonging to the movement of logical empiricism, but it is rejected by most of those empiricists who regard themselves as pragmatists or who are at least strongly influenced by Dewey's philosophy. It seems to me that the divergence in this point between the two groups of empiricists is theoretically interesting and should lead to further thorough discussions, but is relatively unimportant in its influence on practical life. In my personal experience I do not know of any case in which the difference in attitude between an empiricist of the first group and one of the second group with respect to a moral problem ever arose from the difference in their philosophical positions concerning the nature of value statements.

The view that recognition of the non-cognitive nature of value statements is either conducive to or symptomatic of a loss of interest in moral or political problems seems clearly refuted by my own experience. I have maintained the thesis for about thirty years. But throughout my life, from my childhood to the present day, I have always had an intense interest in moral problems, both those concerning the life of individuals and, since the First World War, those of politics. I have not been active in party politics, but I was always interested in political principles and I have never shied away from professing my point of view. All of us in the Vienna Circle took a strong interest in the political events in our country, in Europe, and in the world. These problems were discussed privately, not in the Circle which was devoted to theoretical questions. I think that nearly all of us shared the following three views as a matter of course which hardly needed any discussion. The first is the view that man has no supernatural protectors or enemies and that therefore whatever can be done to improve life is the task of man himself. Second, we had the conviction that mankind is able to change the conditions of life in such a way that many of the sufferings of today may be avoided and that the external and the internal situation of life for the individual, the community, and finally for humanity will be essentially improved. The third is the view that all deliberate action presupposes knowledge of the world, that the scientific method is the best method of acquiring knowledge and that therefore science must be regarded as one of the most valuable instruments for the improvement of life. In Vienna we had no names for these views; if we look for a brief designation in American terminology for the combination of these three convictions, the best would seem to be "scientific humanism".

I shall now try to indicate more concretely, beyond these general principles, the views about ends and means which I have held at least since the Vienna time, if not earlier, and which I still hold today. A number of my friends in the Vienna Circle probably shared these views in their essential features; but in detail, naturally, there were important differences. It was and still is my conviction that the great problems of the organization of economy and the organization of the world at the present time, in the era of industrialization, cannot possibly be solved by "the free interplay of forces", but require rational planning. For the organization of economy this means socialism in some form; for the organization of the world it means a gradual development toward a world government. However, neither socialism nor world government are regarded as absolute ends; they are only the organizational means which, according to our present knowledge, seem to give the best promise of leading to a realization of the ultimate aim. This aim is a form of life in which the well-being and the development of the individual is valued most highly, not the power of the state. Removing the obstacles, the main causes of suffering, such as war, poverty, disease, is merely the negative side of the task. The positive side is to improve and enrich the life of the individuals and their relations in family, friendship, professional work, and community. Enrichment of life requires that all individuals be given the possibility to develop their potential abilities and the opportunity to participate in cultural activities and experiences. If we look at the problem from the point of view of this aim, we shall recognize the dangers lying in the constant increase in the power of the state; this increase is necessary because the national states must fuse into larger units and the states must take over many functions of the economy. Therefore it will be of prime importance to take care that the civil liberties and the democratic institutions are not merely preserved but constantly developed and improved. Thus one of the main problems, perhaps the most important and the most difficult one after the terribly urgent problem of the avoidance of atomic war, is the task of finding ways of organizing society which will reconcile the personal and cultural freedom of the individual with the development of an efficient organization of state and economy.

Rudolf Carnap

Department of Philosophy
University of California at Los Angeles

DESCRIPTIVE AND CRITICAL ESSAYS ON THE PHILOSOPHY OF RUDOLF CARNAP

1

Charles Morris

PRAGMATISM AND LOGICAL EMPIRICISM

It is slightly more than twenty years ago that I first became acquainted with the work of Rudolf Carnap and other members of the Vienna Circle. My own thought was, and is, near to that of Mead and the pragmatists. At first sight there seems to be an unbridgeable gap between the bio-social orientation of a Mead and the logico-analytical orientation of a Carnap. But at that time it appeared to me that pragmatism and logical empiricism had many features in common and much to contribute to each other, and that the further growth of each would be such that the two movements would become convergent. In a number of articles written at that period I tried to analyze some of the similarities and differences between the two groups, and to outline a position (called scientific empiricism) toward which they might converge.[1] The purpose of the present paper is to see how matters now stand nearly two decades later. Since it is impossible to deal fully with this problem in an article, attention will be focused upon the development of Carnap's thought.

Pragmatics

It is well known how Carnap went beyond his early interest in the syntactical aspects of language into a consideration of its semantical aspects, thereby extending his early conception of logic as pure syntactics to include pure semantics. It is perhaps not so clearly recognized that

[1]The articles in question were as follows: "Pragmatism and Metaphysics," *Philosophical Review,* XLIII (1934), 549-564; "Philosophy of Science and Science of Philosophy," *Philosophy of Science,* II (1935), 271-286; "The Relation of the Formal and Empirical Sciences within Scientific Empiricism," *Erkenntnis,* V (1935), 6-14; "Semiotic and Scientific Empiricism," *Actes du Congrès International de Philosophie Scientifique* (1935), published in Paris in 1936; "The Concept of Meaning in Pragmatism and Logical Positivism," *Actes de Huitième Congrès International de Philosophie* (1934), published in Prague in 1936; "Scientific Empiricism," in *Encyclopedia and Unified Science,* vol. 1, no. 1 of the *International Encyclopedia of Unified Science,* 63-75, published in 1938. These articles, with the exception of the last, formed the collection of essays *Logical Positivism, Pragmatism, and Scientific Empiricism* (Paris, 1937).

Carnap has since crossed the threshold of pragmatics, not merely in the sense of admitting the legitimacy and importance of this domain,[2] but in being himself a contributor to this field. I refer here primarily to Chapter III of *Testability and Meaning.*

This essay appeared in *Philosophy of Science* in 1936 and 1937. In the reprint of the essay which was published in 1950 under the sponsorship of the Graduate Philosophy Club of Yale University, with certain corrections and additions, Carnap tells us to add after the first paragraph on page 432 the following:

> According to present terminology, we divide the theory of language (semiotic) into three parts: pragmatics, semantics, and logical syntax. The descriptive concepts mentioned belong to pragmatics; logical analysis belongs either to semantics (if referring to meaning and interpretation) or to syntax (if formalized).

The "descriptive concepts" in question are those developed in Chapter III: observable, realizable, confirmable, and testable.

In what sense do the corresponding terms belong to pragmatics? Pragmatics is characterized by Carnap as follows: "If in an investigation explicit reference is made to the speaker, or, to put it in more general terms, to the user of a language, then we assign it to the field of pragmatics."[3] The terms in question belong then to pragmatics in that they contain reference not merely to a language but to persons who use the language.

It is to be noted that Carnap calls these terms "descriptive" rather than "logical", and entitles the chapter which deals with them "Empirical Analysis of Confirmation and Testing". This fits in with his general tendency to regard pragmatics as an empirical discipline, and not to recognize the possibility of a pure pragmatics coordinate with pure semantics and pure syntactics. "Our considerations," he writes, "belong, strictly speaking, to a biological or psychological theory of language as a kind of human behavior, and especially as a kind of reaction to observations."[4] It seems to me, however, that a distinction of pure and descriptive pragmatics is justifiable, and that Carnap's own work in the chapter in question is in pure pragmatics. If it be said that such terms as 'observable' require reference to persons who use a language, then it might be replied that in Carnap's treatment this reference is not to actual persons any more than his references to languages in pure syntactics or to

[2]"A theory of pragmatical concepts would certainly be of interest, and a further development of such a theory from the present modest beginnings is highly desirable" *Logical Foundations of Probability,* 216.

[3]*Introduction to Semantics,* 9. In *Signs, Language, and Behavior* I characterized pragmatics as "that portion of semiotic which deals with the origin, uses, and effects of signs within the behavior in which they occur," 219.

[4]*Testability and Meaning,* 454.

properties in pure semantics are to actual languages or properties. If we are to develop a language to talk about the users of signs, then we need a body of terms to do so, and the introduction of these terms and the study of their relations seems as "pure" as is the development of languages to talk about the structures and significations of signs. If this be so, then it might be wise to extend the term 'logic' to cover the whole field of pure semiotic. This would be in accord with Peirce's view that logic is "the science of the general necessary laws of Signs."[5]

That pragmatics plays an important place in Carnap's later thought may be shown by reference to two discussions in which he has been engaged.

In the recent controversy concerning the relation between the analytic and the synthetic, Carnap has found it necessary to defend his view of a sharp distinction between them by the introduction of the concept of "meaning postulates".[6] Meaning postulates rest on decisions, as the word 'postulate' suggests. Thus whether a sentence such as 'All ravens are black' is or is not analytic depends upon what decisions have been made as to the meaning of certain terms, i.e, to what meanings are accepted. Thus the distinction between the analytic and synthetic is made by an appeal to pragmatical considerations, since it is relative to a decision (an acceptance). If this is so it shows that pragmatics may have an unsuspected importance for dealing with central issues in logic, for Carnap states that explicit definitions, contextual definitions, and reduction sentences for the introduction of disposition predicates can be regarded as meaning postulates.[7]

Another place where pragmatics enters Carnap's thought is in his recent stress upon linguistic frameworks—such as the frameworks of integers and rational numbers, the framework of real numbers, the framework of thing properties, the framework of a spatial-temporal coordinate system.[8] In each case he maintains that

> the introduction of the new ways of speaking does not need any theoretical justification because it does not imply any assertion of reality. To be sure, we have to face at this point an important question; but it is a practical, not a

[5]*Collected Papers,* II, 52. See also 134.

[6]"Meaning Postulates," *Philosophical Studies,* III (1952), 65-73.

[7]*Ibid.,* 71. It may be recalled that for C. I. Lewis the isolation of the analytic requires reference to "sense-meanings" or "criteria-in-mind," and hence to the users of signs. The matter is discussed at length in Book I ("Meaning and Analytic Truth") of his *Analysis of Knowledge and Valuation.* See also "Concepts Without Primitives," C. West Churchman, *Philosophy of Science* XX (1953), 262; *Meaning, Communication, and Value,* by Paul Kecskemeti, 69.

[8]"Empiricism, Semantics, and Ontology," *Revue International de Philosophie,* XI (1950), 20-40.

theoretical question; it is the question of whether or not to accept the new linguistic forms. The acceptance cannot be judged as being either true or false because it is not an assertion. It can only be judged as being more or less expedient, fruitful, conducive to the aim for which the language is intended.[9]

Carnap has of course long stressed the importance of linguistic stipulations in logic and empirical science, and the influence of considerations of efficiency, simplicity, and fruitfulness in their choice.[10] But the fact that he is here introducing such matters to clarify the status of abstract entities shows once more that the growth of Carnap's thought has given pragmatics a central and not merely a peripheral place.

It seems to me, on the basis of such considerations, that an explicit concern with pure pragmatics becomes an urgent task. Such work does not take the place of pure semantics and syntactics, and indeed was not in a technical sense possible until these disciplines were considerably advanced. But now it is desirable to bring to explicit attention that which has so far only been in the background. Pure pragmatics will be important not only for the problems of logic, but as supplying a framework for the intensive studies in descriptive pragmatics now under way in psychology, the social sciences, and the philosophy of science.

Pragmatism

Pragmatics is not, however, pragmatism. Pragmatism has indeed made important contributions to pragmatics (hence the original choice of the latter term); but a worker in the field of pragmatics need not be interested in philosophy, and if interested need not be a pragmatist. Peirce, it is true, said that his version of pragmatism (pragmaticism) was a logical theory, and so a part of semiotic, rather than a system of philosophy. The term 'pragmatism' has, however, generally come to signify philosophy as interpreted in terms of, and as constructed upon Peirce's pragmatic maxim,[11] or some similar theory of meaning. Peirce himself stressed the bearing of this maxim upon philosophy:

> What will remain of philosophy will be a series of problems capable of investigation by the observational methods of the true sciences . . . . In this regard pragmaticism is a species of prope-positivism. But what distinguishes it from other species is, first, its retention of a purified philosophy; secondly, its full

[9] *Ibid.*, 31, 32.

[10] *Der logische Aufbau der Welt,* 107; *Logische Syntax der Sprache,* 248.

[11] In one formulation: "The theory that a *conception,* that is, the rational purport of a word or other expression, lies exclusively in its conceivable bearing upon the conduct of life; so that, since obviously nothing that might not result from experiment can have any direct bearing upon conduct, if one can define accurately all the conceivable experimental phenomena which the affirmation or denial of a concept could imply, one will have therein a complete definition of the concept, and *there is absolutely nothing more in it,*" *Collected Papers,* V, 273.

acceptance of the main body of our instinctive beliefs; and thirdly, its strenuous insistence upon the truth of scholastic realism (or a close approximation to that . . .). So, instead of merely jeering at metaphysics, like other prope-positivists, whether by long drawn-out parodies or otherwise, the pragmaticist extracts from it a precious essence, which will serve to give life and light to cosmology and physics. At the same time the moral applications of the doctrine are positive and potent.[12]

Peirce predicted that "pragmatism is going to be the dominant philosophical position of the twentieth century."[13]

In the course of the movement various pragmatists have been concerned with the pragmatics of philosophical systems, but also they have constructed theories of mind, of knowing, ethical and esthetical theories, philosophies of science, and cosmologies. In my opinion the views of the major pragmatists, in spite of considerable difference on certain points, can be given a more or less organized and systematic form on the basis of a number of central doctrines held in common; for present purposes I shall assume that this is so and not attempt to argue the point.

Now what is the relation of logical empiricism to pragmatism as a philosophy? Has logical empiricism made obsolete even the "purified philosophy" which pragmatism has sought to attain by more strictly applying a theory of meaning which is in many ways similar to that which the pragmatists professed to apply in the construction of their philosophy? I think not. On the contrary, I believe that in many respects the logical empiricist has with the passage of time come closer to certain pragmatic doctrines than was originally the case. I think that this could be shown in many thinkers of the movement, but here again I will limit myself to some phases of Carnap's thought.

Carnap has not, of course, been directly concerned with pragmatism as a philosophy. His references to pragmatists are primarily to Lewis and Peirce, and to them as logicians. He notes a "great similarity" between his and Lewis's approach to probability,[14] and a "striking similarity" between his and Lewis's analysis of basic semantical concepts.[15] He writes: "I believe that Morris is right in saying that by the step described, i.e. the adoption of a generalized language which is able to express physical laws in a satisfactory way, we ("logical positivists") come to a closer agreement with pragmatism."[16] His most general statement (written in 1936) is as follows: "It seems to me there is agreement on the main points between the present views of the Vienna Circle . . . and those of

[12] *Ibid.*, 282.

[13] *Collected Papers,* VI, 346.

[14] *Logical Foundations of Probability,* ix.

[15] *Meaning and Necessity,* 64ff.

[16] *Testability and Meaning,* 26

Pragmatism, as interpreted e.g. by Lewis."[17] His only general criticism of the pragmatists (at least with respect to the phases of their work which he has considered) is that in the formulation of their views they rely too heavily upon the material rather than the formal mode of speech.[18]

There are a number of respects in which Carnap's later formulations seem to me nearer to some pragmatic doctrines than were his original formulations.

The pragmatists have placed great stress upon the category of the social, and hence upon the social factors in inquiry. "No mind," Peirce wrote, "can take one step without the aid of other minds."[19] Carnap's early stress in *Der logische Aufbau der Welt* on "methodological solipsism," with first-person experience taken as the base for epistemological construction, might have seemed a continuance of the epistemological individualism to which Peirce was opposed. But in *Testability and Meaning* Carnap discontinues the use of the phrase "methodological solipsism" with the following comment:

> I wished to indicate by it nothing more than the simple fact, that everybody in testing any sentence empirically cannot do otherwise than refer finally to his own observations; he cannot use the results of other people's observations unless he has become acquainted with them by his own observations, e.g. by hearing or reading the other man's report. No scientist, as far as I know, denies this rather trivial fact.[20]

Nor no pragmatist, as far as I know.

A related point of contention was whether, because of this "rather trivial fact," we could "know other minds." I am not sure that Carnap in *Scheinprobleme in der Philosophie* denied that we "know" psychical events other than our own, but certainly he came very close to the position that we can know only what we personally can experience. However, in *Testability and Meaning*,[21] using the distinction between confirmable and observable, Carnap can and does allow psychological predicates which are "intersubjectively confirmable but only *subjectively* observable,"—though he does not in his own construction choose these as primitive predicates. I further believe that Carnap's recent and novel justification of inference by analogy[22] could also be used to support the claim that we know of occurrences in other persons which we cannot observe in them but only in ourselves.

[17] *Ibid.*, 427.

[18] *Ibid.*, 428.

[19] *Collected Papers*, II, 129.

[20] *Testability and Meaning*, 423, 424.

[21] Pp. 11-12.

[22] *Logical Foundations of Probability*, 569-570.

Connected with the issue of "other minds" is the general question of "realism." The pragmatists have in the main been "realists" or "naturalists" in believing that human minds arise and function within an evolutionary process wider in scope than themselves. Carnap has of course never denied "empirical reality," i.e., has never denied the legitimacy of such questions as to whether a given mountain is legendary or really exists.[23] His opposition has been to "metaphysical reality," which he has said is often stated as independence from a knowing consciousness.[24] But in *Testability and Meaning,* again as the result of the introduction of terms in pragmatics, he is able to say of the sentence "If all minds (or: living beings) should disappear from the universe, the stars would go on in their courses," that it is "confirmable and even testable, though incompletely."[25] And he adds: "The same is true for any sentence about past, present or future events, which refers to events other than those we have actually observed, provided it is sufficiently connected with such events by confirmable laws."[26] It seems to me that pragmatism neither needs nor is entitled to more realism than this provides.

Finally, to conclude this section we may consider Carnap's doctrine of physicalism (or methodological materialism) as a possible area of disagreement between logical empiricism and pragmatism. If space permitted it would be interesting to consider in detail the history of the terms 'physical' and 'physics' in Carnap's writing. In *Physikalische Begriffsbildung,* physics is said to investigate the most general properties of the perceivable, and it is repeatedly stated that it does not do away with qualities or replace them by quantities but names them by numbers.[27] It is not immediately clear what is the relation of this position to the later statement that "given direct experiences are physical facts, i.e. spatio-temporal events."[28] It is true that this statement is phrased in the material mode of speech. But the corresponding formulation in the formal mode ("statements in protocol language . . . can be translated into physical language") throws us back again to the problem of the criterion for 'physical language.'

The whole issue, however, takes on a new form in *Testability and Meaning:*

In former explanations of physicalism we used to refer to the physical language as a basis of the whole language of science. It now seems to me that what

[23]*Scheinprobleme in der Philosophie,* 35.

[24]*Der logische Aufbau der Welt,* 237ff.

[25]P. 37.

[26]P. 38.

[27]Pp. 4, 47.

[28]*The Unity of Science,* 76.

we really had in mind as such a basis was rather the thing-language, or even more narrowly, the observable predicates of the thing-language,[29]

where by 'thing-language' is meant "that language which we use in every-day life in speaking about the perceptible things surrounding us."[30] The thesis of physicalism is then formulated via Carnap's pragmatical terms: "Every descriptive predicate of the language of science is confirmable on the basis of observable thing-predicates."[31] When so formulated I find nothing incompatible in the doctrine with the pragmatic theory of meaning or with pragmatic cosmology. And the reference to "the perceptible things surrounding us" makes one think of Peirce's "critical commonsensism," and of Mead's "the world that is there" in which all theories arise and to which they are returned for testing.[32]

Value Judgments and Philosophy

We now approach two areas of greater difference between the pragmatists and the logical empiricists: the nature of value judgments and the nature of philosophy.

It has been a central tenet of the pragmatists, no matter how great their other differences, that judgments of value are empirical in nature, and so have a cognitive or theoretical character amenable in principle to control by scientific methods. Stated in another way, the pragmatists have believed that judgments of value as well as the statements of science conform to the pragmatic maxim and are meaningful in the same sense. Carnap has certainly affirmed the opposite. He has maintained that we can deduce no proposition about future experience from the sentence 'Killing is evil,' and that value judgments, of which this is an example, are "not verifiable" and so have "no theoretical sense."[33] The opposition seems complete.

The issues are complex, and I will not attempt fully to resolve them. But I wish to draw attention to several points that seem to make the apparent opposition less certain.

In the *Logische Aufbau*[34] Carnap indicates how he would at that

[29] P. 467.

[30] P. 466.

[31] P. 468.

[32] A point in passing: Peirce had said: "Indeed, it is the reality of some possibilities that pragmaticism is most concerned to insist upon," *Collected Papers,* V, 306. Carnap, in distinguishing various meanings of the term 'probable,' writes that "*statistical probability* is a certain quantitative physical characteristic of physical sytems. Like any other physical magnitude, it is to be established empirically by observations," "Inductive Logic and Science," *Proc. Amer. Acad. of Arts and Sciences,* LXXX (1953), 190.

[33] *Philosophy and Logical Syntax,* 25.

[34] Pp. 203-204.

time deal with values: they would be constituted on the basis of certain terms already in the terminological system plus certain "value experiences" such as the sense of duty and esthetic satisfaction. It is interesting that Lewis adopted a similar point of view in *An Analyis of Knowledge and Valuation,* starting from value experiences as the primary data for a theory of value. But Lewis goes on to interpret value judgments as assertions about such value experiences, and hence as empirical and controllable by evidence as are scientific statements. Carnap once said in conversation that he could in general agree with what Lewis had written about value judgments in this book, and that the question of his relation to Lewis' analysis would depend upon what Lewis would do with ethical judgments (which he, Lewis, had there denied to be empirical statements). This suggests that Carnap and the pragmatists have in common a large area in which they can agree that value judgments are empirical, but that Carnap further believes that there are other types of value judgment which do not fall within an empirical criterion of meaningfulness. Thus in *The Unity of Science*[35] he rejects questions concerning "the basis of validity of moral standards (principles of value) and of the specification of valid norms" on the ground that they are "metaphysical."

It would seem that even within Carnap's framework other possibilities lie open. I suppose there is no term more basic in Carnap's work than that of 'rule,' though so far as I know he never explicates the term. There are constitution rules, syntactical rules, semantical rules; language is regarded as a system of rules; and in *Logical Foundations of Probability* Carnap is much concerned with rules for making decisions. Now rules, when formulated, are certainly not to be regarded as "meaningless," and since they are not predictions they seem to have a normative rather than a statemental character. It is quite possible then that some judgments of value may be rules for the regulation of conduct. Rules are adopted with respect to purposes to be achieved, and Carnap has expressly said that questions concerning "the efficiency, fruitfulness and simplicity" of the employment of linguistic expressions are "indeed of a theoretical nature."[36]

My point is that while Carnap officially restricts his analysis to statements, his own procedure makes use of types of linguistic symbols (such as 'rule') which if explicated might turn out to be of the same nature as certain types of value terms. And if this is so the apparent opposition between his statements about value judgments and those of certain pragmatists (such as Dewey) may be more apparent than real.

Connected with the problem of judgments of value is the question

[35]*The Unity of Science,* 23-24.

[36]"Empiricism, Semantics, and Ontology," *op. cit.,* 23-24.

as to the nature of philosophy. Carnap's conception of the nature of philosophy was given (in 1942) in his *Introduction to Semantics,* where he reformulates the position he had taken in *Logische Syntax der Sprache:*

> The *chief thesis* of Part V, if split up into two components, was like this:
> a. "(Theoretical) *philosophy* is the logic of science."
> b. "Logic of science is the syntax of the language of science." (a) remains valid. It is a terminological question whether to use the term 'philosophy' in a wider sense, including certain empirical problems. If we do so, then it seems that these empirical problems will turn out to belong mostly to pragmatics. Thesis (b), however, needs modification by adding semantics to syntax. Thus *the whole thesis is changed to the following: the task of philosophy is semiotical analysis;* the problems of philosophy concern—not the ultimate nature of being but—the semiotical structure of the language of science, including the theoretical part of everyday language. We may distinguish between those problems which deal with the activities of gaining and communicating knowledge and the problems of logical analysis. Those of the first kind belong to pragmatics, those of the second kind to semantics or syntax—to semantics, if designata ("meaning") are taken into consideration; to syntax, if the analysis is purely formal.[37]

Though Carnap has thus widened progressively his conception of philosophy (adding semantical considerations to purely syntactical ones, and pragmatical considerations to both), the abiding direction of his thought has been to define philosophy in relation to science. In fact, seen in perspective, science has been the norm or model controlling the entire development of logical empiricism. The progressive widening of the criterion of meaningfulness was due to the recognition that the earlier formulations excluded certain kinds of terms and sentences that occurred in the "best" sciences. And since science was taken as the norm, philosophy too had to be defined in relation to science: philosophy as the logic of science was the result. In this way, as Carnap made clear in the Foreword to *Der logische Aufbau der Welt,* it was hoped to build by cooperative work a philosophy that could advance as science advances.

This intention is strikingly similar to that of Peirce. Peirce had written: "I wish philosophy to be a strict science, passionless and severely fair."[38] And one of the guiding motives in his proposal of the pragmatic maxim was his belief that its acceptance would make philosophy cooperative and progressive in the manner of science.

But there is still an important difference between the pragmatists' conception of philosophy and that of the logical empiricists. The pragmatists have, without exception I believe, wished philosophy to become

[37] *Introduction to Semantics,* 250.

[38] *Collected Papers,* V, 375.

as scientific as possible, but have not limited philosophy to the philosophy of science. A scientific philosophy need not be a philosophy of science—unless one decides to define 'philosophy' in this way.

What then are the alternatives? In other writings I have considered this problem,[39] and do not now wish to cover the same ground in any detail. But some points may be noted that are especially relevant in the present context of discussion.

It may be unwise to attempt in the strict sense to define the term 'philosophy.' It may well be that the term embraces a variety of significations, and that these change in emphasis and number at different times. 'Philosophy' might then best be regarded as a residual category. Instead of definitions there might be explications, and corresponding to these explications there would be a set of terms, 'philosophy_1,' 'philosophy_2,' 'philosophy_n.' The choice between them, if it is to be made, becomes a problem in pragmatics.

Carnap's analysis of 'philosophy,' which we have quoted at length, cannot, from this point of view, be regarded as a "thesis" which is "valid" (or "invalid"), but as one explication of the term. Let us call it 'philosophy_1.' That it is an important explication is not to be denied; I know of no better if the task is to explicate philosophy as philosophy of science.

But certainly it is not the only possible explication. It obviously does not supply the criterion by which a historian singles out philosophers or a librarian classifies books as philosophical. It does not even cover some of the views that Carnap and other logical empiricists have held. Thus in the *Logische Aufbau* Carnap writes that life has many dimensions other than science, and the restriction of the term 'knowledge' to science is helpful to the friendly relation between the various spheres of life, for the admission of complete heterogeneity would lessen the strife between them.[40] This may or may not be the case, but the statement is certainly more than a logical analysis of science. It contains a recommendation or proposal, made in terms of a theory of the relation of science to other human activities.

There is another explication of 'philosophy' which would find a place for such considerations. It would run as follows: Philosophy is concerned with the comparison, the criticism, and the proposal of the most general linguistic frameworks. Let us call this 'philosophy_2.'

I think that this explication is compatible with the philosophical traditions of diverse cultures, and I do not see that it is incompatible

[39]"Philosophy of Science and Science of Philosophy," *Philosophy of Science,* II (1935), 271-286; *Signs, Language, and Behavior,* 233-238.

[40]Pp. 257-258.

with the main body of Carnap's work.[41] It is true that a follower in Carnap's steps need not be concerned with the most general frameworks. This is a matter of choice. He would then be a philosopher in sense 1 but not in sense 2. If he chose to be a philosopher in sense 2 he might still use Carnap's terminology and techniques. Thus he might find that much of what has been called metaphysics can be explicated as the analytic portion of these general or philosphical frameworks, a possibility that Carnap does not seem to have considered in his discussion of metaphysics. If the philosopher in question chose to go further, and to defend or propose a general framework, he could still choose to do it in as scientific a manner as possible. There can in this sense be a scientific philosophy which is not simply a philosophy of science.

It is such a scientific philosophy which the pragmatists have envisaged and in various ways and degrees proposed. I believe that Carnap is right in saying that the formulations of the pragmatists have often suffered by confusing the material and the formal mode of speech. Even more basic, in my opinion, is the fact that though pragmatism was given a semiotical orientation by Peirce, it never developed a semiotic sufficient to deal with all the phases and functions of a philosophical framework. With the present growth of pragmatics, coupled with the syntactical and semantical tools which Carnap and others have made available, it seems to me that the time is ripe for a re-examination of the pragmatic movement, and for those who care to do so, to continue work on its unfinished task.

CHARLES MORRIS

DEPARTMENT OF PHILOSOPHY
UNIVERSITY OF FLORIDA

[41]Cf. "The 'Political' Philosophy of Logical Empiricism," Warner A. Wick, *Philosophical Studies,* II (1951), 49-56.

2

Robert S. Cohen

DIALECTICAL MATERIALISM AND CARNAP'S LOGICAL EMPIRICISM[1]

I. *Introduction*

1. A FEW years ago, the distinguished logical empiricist, Herbert Feigl, wrote that "nothing is more urgent for education today than a social philosophy that will be appropriate and workable in an age of science," and he added that "naturalism *and* humanism should be our maxim."[2] A century earlier, Karl Marx wrote that "communism as a complete naturalism is humanism, and as a complete humanism is naturalism."[3] Although separated by time and milieu, by knowledge and mood, Marx and Feigl are united in two fundamental respects: they wish to reject Utopian fantasy as unrealistic in its appraisal of social possibilities; and they wish to preclude supernaturalism as seductively autistic in its cognitive claims. Both are scientific humanists.

Nevertheless Marxism and modern empiricism developed in different ways. Whereas Marx's dialectical naturalism was grounded upon studies of man in society, that is upon social theory, logical empiricism depended primarily upon studies of the natural order, that is upon physical theory. It is not surprising that Marx, developing Hegel's speculations about history and the Enlightenment's belief in progress, stresses human affairs, and that the central problem for his philosophy is elucidation of the nec-

[1]This essay was written during tenure of a Faculty Fellowship from the Fund for the Advancement of Education and I want to record my gratitude for this help. I am also indebted to the Faculty Research Committee of Wesleyan University for financial assistance.

[2]Herbert Feigl, "The Scientific Outlook: Naturalism and Humanism," *American Quarterly* I (1949) 135-148, reprinted in *Readings in the Philosophy of Science,* ed. Herbert Feigl and May Brodbeck (New York, 1953) , 9, 18.

[3]Karl Marx, "Oekonomisch-philosophische Manuskripte (1844)," *Marx-Engels Gesamtausgabe,* I/3 (Berlin, 1932), 114, as translated by T. B. Bottomore in *The Sociology and Social Philosophy of Karl Marx* (London, 1956) , 244. See also the complete translation by M. Milligan, *Economic and Philosophic Manuscripts of 1844* (Moscow and London, 1959), 102.

essary conditions for genuine humanism. Nor is it surprising that Mach and Carnap, developing Hume's skeptical analyses, stress cognitive caution, and that the central problem for their philosophy is the elucidation of the necessary conditions for genuine naturalism.

In the revolutionary era of 1848, social thinkers confronted situations of degradation and violence with undeveloped theories, and their conceptual weakness was matched by the ineffective organization of social movements. Natural scientists, on the other hand, could discuss matters which seemed cognitively isolated from human affairs with a success and confidence that appeared to have no limits. The application of scientific social theory was minimal; the application of physical theory was already masterful and ubiquitous. The contrast in scientific resources was reflected in the different goals of Marxist and empiricist thinkers, and it is illuminating to compare this contrast with differing social attitudes. Thus, empiricism sought criteria which would furnish cognitive agreement among equal and rational observers of the given world-order. These observers comprise a "republic of science"; their own social relations should be that of liberal democracy; their theory of knowledge is empiricist; and their conception of group intercourse is one of education, experience, and rational persuasion. But Marx was a scholar immersed in no such ideal world; 1848 had failed. And Marxism, in turning from immediate concern with the world-order, observed the conflicts and irrational arrangements within a given social-order, the deep disagreements of unequal observers who are at once unequal members of that order. Experience of conflict is matched by conflicting theories as much as by theories of conflict. From the Marxist viewpoint, a rational and coherent social order, within which all participant-observers would agree, is not yet given to experience; it must be created.

Such contrasts of emphasis yield striking formulae: agreement about the given, vs. criticism of the given; induction vs. construction; reason as static and formal, vs. reason as dynamic and concrete. The empiricist philosophy of science and Marxist social theory are each vital parts of contemporary thought, and it is interesting to consider how each may bear upon the other. For clearly, empirical natural science, and its philosophy too, are social activities, ultimately to be dealt with as such; and, just as clearly, social theory is conceived by men, who are products of nature, living in society.

> That which is perceptive to the senses (Sinnlichkeit) must be the basis of all science, but only when it emerges in the double form of material consciousness as well as material need, i.e. only if science starts from nature is it real science . . . . History itself is a real part of natural history, of the development of nature into man. Later natural science will include the science

of man in the same way as the science of man will include natural science. There will be only one science.[4]

2. For more than a century, then, a unified scientific outlook has been sought by certain dialectical philosophers and by empiricists. To be sure, forms of dialectic are found in theological discussions, and a peculiar empirical attitude appears in philosophies of existence, pure experience, and mysticism. But the attempt to preserve the role of human reasoning in a context of respect for observed facts and for scientific methods of inquiry, without recourse to supernatural explanation, has been pressed mainly by two major traditions whose contemporary exponents are logical empiricists and dialectical materialists.[5] It is doubly necessary to ask whether empiricism and dialectic are alike or supplementary or whether they are unlike or incompatible, first, because these philosophic tendencies have been associated with contending forces in practical affairs, and, second, because each has given renewed intellectual force to classic answers to human problems.

Empiricism and dialectic have usually been taken to be mutually hostile. Each has been severely criticized by adherents of the other. In controversy, creative developments tend to be ignored and dogmatic inadequacies exaggerated. As an observer who has participated in neither school but who shares their repudiation of unconfirmable fancies and undisciplined speculations, I will attempt to illuminate the issues. In such an analysis, criticism of thinkers for their pejorative associations, and dismissal of ideas because of their social origin, have no place. Such attacks have unfortunately been too frequent in this divided world. Scientific and humanist thinkers deny their own premises when they dispute in that manner.[6]

4Marx, *op. cit.,* 122, as translated by J. D. Bernal in *Marx and Science* (London and New York, 1952), 27. See Milligan translation, 111.

5These are rough labels. They cover associated groups: in the first case pragmatists, some analytic philosophers, naturalists, and realists of various kinds; in the second case those independent dialectical philosophers who work mainly in social theory, and also adherents of several different political as well as philosophical tendencies.

6In contrast to the empiricist and analytic philosophers many Marxist writers have adopted such arguments. These Marxists have confused analysis and evaluation of the social function of a given system of thought with examination of the rational and objective cogency of that system, an error which is all too easy to commit and which often generates spurious intellectual victories. Compare, e.g. Maurice Cornforth, *Science Versus Idealism* (London, 1955), Harry K. Wells, *Pragmatism* (New York, 1954), and D. P. Gorski "The Neopositivist Solutions to the Fundamental Questions of Philosophy," *Voprosy Filosofii* Nr. 3, 123-136 (1956) with Margaret Macdonald, "Things and Processes," *Analysis* VI (1938; reprinted in *Philosophy and Analysis,* ed. M. Macdonald, Oxford, 1954) and Philipp Frank, "Logisierender Empirismus in der Philosophie der U.S.S.R.," *Actes du Congrès International de Philosophie Scientifique* (Paris, 1936; reprinted in his *Modern Science and its Philosophy,* Cambridge, Mass.,

In this essay for Rudolf Carnap, it is certainly proper to note that he has never engaged in slanderous exchange, to praise his humane response to questions of human freedom and economic democracy, and especially to admire his intellectual and civic courage. Nor are these qualities of his mind and his activities divorced from Carnap's technical scholarship. Science and its philosophy were once unqualifiedly part of the foundations of human enlightenment, the creators of human independence, and the forces which might eliminate practical miseries and spiritual illusions. Carnap has always been a man of this enlightenment, writing with the hope that science will be joined with social movements which work toward a rational and cooperative society.

We cannot conceal from ourselves that metaphysical and religious movements which oppose our orientation are once again quite influential. Why are we nonetheless confident that our demand for clarity, and for the elimination of metaphysics from science, will win out? It is the awareness, or, to put it more cautiously, the belief that these hostile forces belong to the past. We feel an inner affinity between the attitude that is basic to our philosophic endeavor and the intellectual attitude which is making its mark in entirely different spheres of life; we detect this attitude in the arts, especially in architecture, and in the movements which seek a meaningful organization of human life, both personal and communal, in education and in social institutions at large. In all these areas, we sense the same fundamental orientation, the same creative

1949). But the empiricist tendency to ignore or to dismiss Marxist philosophy has hardly led to any more fruitful thought.

However in both philosophical traditions there are wise men who recognize their own need to take their intellectual opponents at the strongest, to avoid the practical error of intellectual self-delusion. Thus the well-known words of John Stuart Mill: "Nor is it enough that he should hear the arguments of adversaries from his own teachers, presented as they state them, and accompanied by what they offer as refutations. That is not the way to do justice to the arguments . . . . He must know them in their most plausible and persuasive form; he must feel the whole force of the difficulty which the true view of the subject has to encounter . . . ," *On Liberty*, ed. R. B. McCallum, (Oxford, 1948), 32. And the judgment of the foremost Italian Marxist, Antonio Gramsci: "We must not conceive of a scientific discussion as if it were a courtroom proceeding in which there are a defendant and a prosecutor who, by duty of his office, must show the defendant guilty . . . the most advanced thinker is he who understands that his adversary may express a truth which should be incorporated in his own ideas, even if in a minor way. To understand and evaluate realistically the position and reasons of one's adversary (and sometimes the adversary is the entire thought of the past) means to have freed oneself from the prison of ideologies, in the sense of blind fanaticism. One has then arrived at a critical frame of mind, the only fruitful stance in scientific research." "Problemi di Filosofia e di Storia", *Opere di Antonio Gramsci* II (Rome, 1953) 21, as translated by Carl Marzani, *The Open Marxism of Antonio Gramsci* (New York, 1957) 58; see the extended discussion in "Critical Notes on an Attempt at a Popular Presentation of Marxism by Bukharin," section 2, in Gramsci, *op. cit.*, 130, in the translation of Louis Marks, *The Modern Prince and other Writings*, (London and New York, 1957), 94ff., esp. 97. Ideas are not merely symptoms; a sick man can have a healthy idea.

style of thinking and working. It is the disposition which seeks clarity everywhere, yet recognizes that the intertwinings of life are never wholly discriminated; it is a concern for careful treatment of detail which is linked with scope for the whole, a concern for a fraternal union of human beings together with the free development of the individual. Our work is inspired by the belief that the future belongs to this outlook.[7]

3. Our times have been marked by great revolutions, gigantic wars, massive economic crises, and persistent trends toward the mechanization of human life and culture. The Communist movement, which sought vigorously to overcome deep-rooted social injustice and to bring about individual self-fulfillment, itself fell victim to the generally callous necessities of industrializing society, the more brutally so as Communists found themselves coming to power under circumstances which demanded rigorous controls and enforced capital investment, the more viciously so whenever their leaders and institutions reflected and exaggerated the repressive postponements of freedom and pleasure. Meanwhile in those few countries where liberal democracy had traditional roots, the growing manipulation of popular life and the new vigor of supernaturalist movements and anti-scientific illusions have been no less marked. Finally, the negation of such positive aspects of modern civilization as social betterment and individual liberty found its total expression under fascist regimes. How far away seem those creative trends in all spheres of life to which Carnap referred in 1928! How urgent it is to ascertain the causes of their frustration, and to formulate rational procedures for reestablishing scientific enlightenment where it has been weakened, and for stimulating it where it has been lacking!

Dialectic has been moved by the need to develop a scientific outlook which can comprehend and overcome the inherent inadequacies of the classic industrial social order. Empiricism has been moved by its traditional scepticism of closed and complete systems of ideas to clarify the methods and structure of scientific knowledge. Thus we may perhaps say that the motives of dialectic and empiricism are not opposed,[8] but rather that the manner in which they have been exercised has led to a fundamental divergence of approach. In this essay, I shall report the critique which dialectic has offered of modern empiricism, particularly

[7]Rudolf Carnap, *Der logische Aufbau der Welt* (Berlin, 1928), translated from the preface, v-vi.

[8]Thus an American Marxist commented: "Logical positivism is . . . a literary weapon against the favorite philosophies of the fascists, and though it must show itself in the end a two-edged sword, and quite incapable of coping with the heavy artillery of its enemies, the resistance it offers to reaction should be recognized," by V. J. McGill, "An Evaluation of Logical Positivism," *Science and Society* I (1936), 78.

as represented by Carnap, and indicate to what extent these criticisms are no longer valid in terms of current developments.[9]

The words to be used need definition. Philosophical labels easily degenerate into slogans, pejorative or panegyrical. Dialectical materialism is avowed as the partisan philosophy of Communist parties throughout the world with a consequent stream of invective in intellectual discussion.[10] In the area of beliefs and ideas, empiricism, under the name of logical positivism, also played an aggressive and revolutionary role, the

[9]It is well to add that the new developments are in no way a response to Marxist or other dialectical criticism!

Since Professor Carnap surely cannot be expected to defend dialectical materialism, I shall not here discuss the vital critique of dialectic which has been offered by empiricists and others. But it will be evident from this essay that dialectic too has many unfulfilled tasks which are central to its clarification of cognition. On another occasion, I hope to consider the ensemble of proposals, hypotheses, scientific achievements, *aperçus,* doctrines, and moral discourse which make up dialectical thought.

The foundations of Marxian *dialectic* are expounded by authors of diverse outlooks. Among the most lucid expositions are: Konrad Bekker, *Marx' philosophische Entwicklung, sein Verhältnis zu Hegel* (Zurich and New York, 1940); Jean-Yves Calvez, *La Pensée de Karl Marx* (Paris, 1956); Auguste Cornu, *Karl Marx. De l'Hégélianisme au matérialisme historique* (Paris, 1934); Sidney Hook, *From Hegel to Marx* (New York, 1935); Karl Korsch, *Marxismus und Philosophie* (2nd ed., Leipzig, 1930); Otis Lee, *Existence and Inquiry,* Part II (Chicago, 1949); Henri Lefèbvre, *Le Matérialisme dialectique* (3rd ed., Paris, 1949), *Pour connaître la pensée de Karl Marx* (3rd ed., Paris, 1956), and *Logique formelle, logique dialectique* (Paris, 1947); Josef Maier, *On Hegel's Critique of Kant* (New York, 1939); Herbert Marcuse, *Reason and Revolution: Hegel and the Rise of Social Theory* (2nd ed., New York and London, 1954); Émile Meyerson, *De l'explication dans les sciences,* esp. Livre III (Paris, 1921); George Politzer, *Principes fondamentaux de philosophie,* an introductory textbook (rev. ed. by Guy Besse and Maurice Caveing, Paris, 1954); M. M. Rosental, *Die marxistische dialektische Methode* (Berlin, 1953: translated by Josef Harhammer from the Russian edition, Moscow, 1952); Max Raphael, *La Théorie marxiste de la connaissance* (Paris, 1937: translated by L. Gara from a revised version of *Zur Erkenntnistheorie der konkreten Dialektik,* Paris, 1934); E. Troeltsch, "Die Marxistische Dialektik" in *Gesammelte Schriften,* III (Tübingen, 1922).

Useful expositions of the current Marxist view of scientific *materialism* as applied to problems of cognition are given by Roger Garaudy, *La Théorie matérialiste de la connaisance* (Paris, 1953), F. I. Chasschatschich, *Materie und Bewusstsein* (Berlin, 1958; trans. from the posthumous Russian ed., Moscow, 1951), M. N. Rutkewitsch, *Die Praxis als Grundlage der Erkenntnis und als Kriterium der Wahrheit* (Berlin, 1957; trans. from the Russian ed., Moscow, 1952, with supplementary critical essays by the author and others from *Voprosy Filosofii,* 1954-55).

[10]E.g. Howard Selsam (ed.), *Handbook of Philosophy* (New York, 1949), adapted from M. Rosental and P. Yudin, *Short Philosophical Dictionary* (Moscow, 1940). There have been attempts to achieve mutual understanding and fruitful discussion, e.g. the international symposium *Democracy in a World of Tensions* ed., Richard McKeon (Chicago and London, 1951); the Marxist essays of John Lewis, *Marxism and the Open Mind* (London and New York, 1957); Christian philosophical discussions in D. M. Mackinnon (ed.), *Christian Faith and Communist Faith* (London, 1953) and Jean-Yves Calvez, *op. cit.*; empiricist essays of Philipp Frank, *op cit.,* and Otto Neurath, *Empirische Soziologie* (Vienna, 1931).

terms 'metaphysical' and 'positivist' having become abusive epithets in many discussions. I shall try to avoid polemical usage. 'Dialectic' will be used to indicate the doctrine of several schools of philosophic thought which use dialectical analysis in their accounts of human knowledge and human nature, and (with less assurance in some quarters) of the order of nature. 'Materialism' or 'realism' will refer to any consistent doctrine of an objective world external to cognition, ontologically and epistemologically prior to cognition. 'Empiricism' will refer to the epistemological demand for a basis in experience, which is the link of so many Western thinkers. Thus empiricism deals with the conditions of knowing, while materialism deals mainly with the nature of reality, and at first their relationship is ambiguous. 'Positivism' refers to the phenomenalist tendency within the empiricist tradition; 'neo-positivism' refers to those recent views whose consequences may be shown to be phenomenalistic. In these terms, we may ask whether Schaff is correct in criticizing Carnap as a neopositivist[11] and whether Feigl is correct in praising Carnap as an empirical realist.[12]

4. To put the argument of this essay briefly:

Empiricism is inadequate and dangerous to the extent that it is a form of either solipsism, pure conventionalism, monadic atomism, or phenomenalism. To dialectic, such varieties of subjectivist thinking seem inadequate as an account of scientific knowledge and dangerous in the restrictions they place upon the use of reason in human affairs. But, dominant as positivist trends have been in the empiricist tradition, at least since Berkeley and Hume, empiricism is not inextricably committed to any of these subjectivist positions. Not only have many empiricists held eclectic combinations of subjectivist and materialist views, but such noted representatives as Schlick, Reichenbach, Feigl, and Carnap have offered anti-subjectivist interpretations of the empiricist attitude. In particular, the new physicalism, an empiricist materialism, now distinguishes between the empirical basis for confirmation of scientific statements and the existential, material, or referential meaning of concepts and theories. Thus, meaning and verification are no longer fused. Moreover, recent discussions of dispositions, natural laws, emergence, and other matter-of-fact relations have loosened the empiricists' commitment to material implications and the reductive interpretations of extensional logic, much as earlier critical discussions weakened their commitment to either logical or epistemological atomism. Old alterna-

11Adam Schaff, *Zu einigen Fragen der marxistischen Theorie der Wahrheit* (trans. from Polish; Berlin, 1954), esp. Ch. 8.

12Herbert Feigl, "Physicalism, Unity of Science, and the Foundations of Psychology" (this volume).

tives are re-opened, and newly fertile modes of thinking can be expected in place of the arid style of so much empiricist analysis in the biological and social sciences.

Nevertheless, despite common devotion to a naturalistic approach to nature and man, dialectic and empiricism still differ. Dialectic offers a historical analysis of the empiricist tradition and of the social function of empiricism. The recurrent *tendency* of empiricist thought to invoke phenomenalistic categories, and its delusive trends toward subjective certainty, become essential, according to the dialectical criticism, because the failure to overcome such positivism distorts social thought and incapacitates philosophy for its role as critic. Apart from any technical limitations it may have for philosophical analysis, unmodified positivism can undermine the possibility of a rational critique of any given state of man or society; for example, the strict empiricist requirements of factual confirmability and intersubjective unanimity in principle deny scientific significance to appraisal of given facts, on the one hand, and of potential facts and novel developments, on the other.

Thus, for the positivists, appearance and reality are identified once more. The positivist ethic is basically private and arbitrary, however relevant publicly objective factors may be in an instrumental relation.[13] When not liberated from positivism, the empiricist theory of knowledge lacks an account of the qualitative transition from ignorance to knowledge, for its notion of verification shows small regard for the sensuously creative practical aspect of man's cognitive encounter with his environment. Finally, the empiricist philosophy, however accurately it may understand technical control of physical processes, acquires an obscurantist character if it is extended *unchanged,* to understanding the domination of man in mass societies.[14] Unfortunately, science is no longer the wholly enlightening ally of human progress that it once seemed to be. A dialectical critic concludes that positive science is not enough; science and its philosophy must transcend the conceptual limitations implicit in any model of a scientifically 'rationalized' social order if it is to be liberated from its own ideological distortions and inhumane implications.

The crisis which this criticism precipitates is unusually thorough. If

[13]Hans Reichenbach, "Everybody is entitled to set up his own moral imperatives and to demand that everyone follow these imperatives," *The Rise of Scientific Philosophy* (Berkeley and Los Angeles, 1951), 295.

[14]The distinguishing characteristics of Marx's conceptual approach to social science, and the relation between phenomena and theory, are discussed in the valuable exploration by M. M. Rosental, *Die Dialektik in Marx' "Kapital"* Berlin, 1957, translated from the Russian by J. Harhammer, Moscow, 1955), and the studies by Heinrich Popitz, *Der entfremdete Mensch* (Basel, 1953), and Karl Korsch, *Karl Marx* (London, 1938); related epistemological discussion is to be found in Konrad Bekker, *op. cit.* An empiricist approach to the social sciences is given e.g. by Ernest Nagel, "A Formalization of Functionalism," *Logic Without Metaphysics* (Glencoe, 1956), 247-283.

the truth in science as well as in philosophy is to be so deeply immersed in the given facts of experience, then appearance and reality are alleged to be one; and even more damaging, belief in the rational structure of the world, including of experience, is undermined. The authority of bare fact unleashes unreason, for, in Whitehead's words, "Faith in reason is the faith that at the basis of things we shall not find mere arbitrary mystery." How to pass from the solipsistic embrace of fact to knowledge of past and future, or to an ordered understanding of temporally-developed regularities, seems beyond the ability of Hume for whom custom, not reason, is the guide of life.[15] If reason, and logic, being merely manipulation of symbols, have no authority over fact, then they have none over custom, either. This is the social and ethical sting within positivist thought.[16]

The road to constructive thought does not now, at any rate, lie in a return to earlier dogma. It is not to be found in the denial of science or scientific philosophy but rather in the liberation of science from a mechanistic treatment of human lives as mere objects, in the extension of science to the understanding of man as a sensuous conscious agent. Science has at last provided the means for surmounting the historical epoch of societies under the restrictive stresses of natural economic necessity. As science itself is liberated from modes of thought which are ultimately restrictive when extrapolated beyond the tasks of that epoch, it will show the way into a new historic era of abundance. And with such a change, it may be expected that cognition will change too. A new relation between man and nature will promise an understanding of that reunion of man as sensuous organism with man as impersonal object for which the mastery of objective nature was prerequisite; enlarged cognitive standards and opportunities will prevail in place of the mechanism and isolation of modern technology and its societies. These speculations require a host of empirical studies as well as philosophical clarification.[17] We will see to what extent they are presently connected with a dialectical critique of empiricism. And we will see the

[15]". . . belief is more properly an act of the sensitive, than of the cogitative part of our natures," David Hume, *Treatise of Human Nature* I, iv, Sect. 1 (ed. Selby-Bigge, Oxford, 1896), 183. This core of Hume's outlook is discussed in Norman Kemp Smith, *The Philosophy of David Hume* (London, 1941), Ch. XXV.

[16]Mr. Gradgrind is the empiricist run wild: "In this life, we want nothing but Facts, sir; nothing but Facts!" Dickens, *Hard Times*, Ch. 1.

[17]Pioneer studies of these questions have been made by Joseph Needham, *Science and Civilization in China*, especially the second volume, *History of Scientific Thought*, *passim* (Cambridge, England, 1956); Herbert Marcuse, *Eros and Civilization* (Boston and London, 1955); and Norman O. Brown, *Life Against Death* (London and Middletown, Conn., 1959). See also Pierre-Maxime Schuhl, *Machinisme et philosophie* (2nd ed., Paris, 1947).

substantial number of common problems for both of these scientific philosophies.

II. *Kant, Mach, and Positivism*

1. Modern empiricism has two quests: empirical meaning, and an assured way of ascribing truth to knowledge. Sensations seemed sufficent for both. The sceptical arguments of Berkeley and Hume had transformed Bacon's hard-headed observations of things into a concentrated study of the sensuously given. Knowledge was certified only when undoubted evidence was available, and when all doubt had been removed there seemed no way of transcending the content of sensations. The world, insofar as we can reasonably know it, comes to be only our sensations. A categorical a priori might survive such criticism, but to save merely the formal appearance of universals and laws in scientific language; but in so doing Kant saved the language of science only to propose a metaphysical world which was split into subjective categories and unknowable objects. Empirical science can hardly escape being a matter of subjective meanings for Kant as much as for Hume.

2. Subsequent to Kant, physics itself seemed to furnish another reason for rejecting a materialist interpretation of scientific knowledge. Thermodynamics had its classic growth in the early nineteenth century, turning from the study of heat phenomena to the general science of energy transformations.[18] By mid-century, thermodynamical laws had been interpreted in terms of classical dynamics, but it was realized that the mathematical equations of energy transfer and transformation did not require such interpretation. Indeed Carnot's researches on heat engines showed that understanding of the principles of heat engines needed no knowledge of the particular working substance; in fact, thermodynamics needed no picture of the nature of matter at all. To those who embraced this new science, then called 'energetics,'[19] it was a matter of some importance that natural phenomena might be described as varying appearances of energy. No need to seek the causes of apparent motion; and also, no need to restrict the entities (which undergo motions) to material particles or rigid bodies, so long as there are observed numerical correlations between the energy manifestations. Transition to an attitude hostile to hypothesis was easily made, the nature of energy coming to be as much a discredited subject as the nature of matter.[20]

[18]The subsequent remarks are adapted from R. S. Cohen "Hertz's Philosophy of Science," introductory to H. Hertz, *Principles of Mechanics* (New York, 1956).

[19]A concise account is given by René Dugas, *A History of Mechanics,* Bk. IV, Ch. x (Neuchatel and New York, 1955); and there is a detailed contemporary study by G. Helm, *Die Energetik nach ihrer geschichtlichen Entwicklung* (Leipzig, 1898).

[20]See the Marxist discussion by R. L. Worrell, *Energy and Matter* (London, 1948).

Ernst Mach provided an epistemology for this science of correlated observations, linking energetics with pure sensationism. For a scientific object to exist meant, in Mach's view, that its symbol is the name of a set of particular perceptions; for it to persist as an entity, the perceptions must persist as a correlated set through the observer's flux of sensations. This phenomenalistic basis for scientific statements served several purposes: (1) it provided a means whereby the various sciences of inanimate, animate and psychic nature might be unified into a general science of sensed experiences; (2) it eliminated metaphysical (unobservable) aspects of scientific theories; (3) it seemed faithful to the trend toward structural isomorphism in physics, as contrasted with previous picture-thinking; (4) it provided an account of cognition which might accord with the scientific demand for evolutionary interpretation of all biological phenomena, including the adaptive cognitive behavior of the brain;[21] finally, (5) it dissolved some old problems of philosophy, freeing experimental science from them by carrying a long tradition of nominalism and empiricism to a refined conclusion.

By so doing, Mach's phenomenalistic positivism returned the philosophy of science to an ancient position, one which natural philosophers had distrusted at least since Democritus and Plato, namely to a dependence upon sensuous appearances. Newton, thinking of gravitational forces acting at a distance, had expressed the modesty of physical explanation when he said that he had only *described* natural processes, albeit simply and completely. When echoed by Kirchhoff, the modesty grew extremely restrictive, such that the legitimate critique of sense-perception, patent in classical physics, was abandoned. In 1888, Boltzmann summarized Kirchhoff's view:

> The aim is not to produce bold hypotheses as to the essence of matter, or to explain the movements of a body from that of molecules, but to present equations which, free from hypothesis, are as far as possible true and quantitatively correct correspondents of the phenomenal world, careless of the essence of things and forces. In his book on Mechanics, Kirchhoff will ban all metaphysical concepts, such as force, the cause of a motion; he seeks only the equations which correspond so far as possible to observed motions.[22]

Just as Bacon, the older empiricist, rejected the Copernican astronomy because it violated the testimony of the senses, so the new empiricists, Mach and Ostwald, going beyond Kirchhoff, initially rejected the

[21]The apparent incompatibility of Mach's doctrine of "neutral elements" (which are held to be neither physical nor psychological in character) with his materialist conception of the mental life as an instrument of biological survival is discussed by Robert Bouvier, *La Pensée d'Ernst Mach* (Paris, 1923), esp. ch. 6 and 9. Mach, e.g. held that sensations release a biological reaction whose accompaniment is the adaptation of ideas to facts.

[22]Cited in Harald Hoffding, *Modern Philosophers* (English translation, London, 1920), 320. Boltzmann wrote as a critic of Kirchhoff.

atomic theory because it, too, violated sense perception. Ostwald expressed his victory over mechanical explanation (he called it his "conquest of scientific materialism") by citing that notable injunction against pictorial thinking and model making: "Thou shalt not make unto thee any graven image . . . !" Functional relations, which coordinate phenomena with other phenomena, are the essentials of scientific explanation in Mach's view.

3. Such pure empiricism has much in common with Kant's theory of science in its ontological aspects, however much they differ in methodology. Scientific entities seem both to Kant and to Mach only to be ordered collections of sensed perceptions. In Kant's view, the perceptions are put in order by a synthetic procedure due to the intrinsic and a priori conceptual techniques of the understanding. In Mach's view, itself akin to an early view of Kant's, perceptions are conveniently wrapped into bundles, a process to be described by laws of physiological psychology which are still largely unexplored. But their moods differ. Evidently Kant *praises* the creative role of the mind whereas Mach *laments* that mental weakness which requires logical ordering of individual perceptions. Mach's persisting account of the shorthand nature of all theory is expressed in his earliest philosophical essay: "If all the individual facts—all the individual phenomena, knowledge of which we desire—were immediately accessible to us, a science would never have arisen."[23]

During this period, neo-Kantian interpretations of science were developed, and the doctrine of *conventionalism* was exaggerated into a full denial of the objective character of systematic knowledge. Natural laws and relations were taken to be matters of convenience; reality consisted of the givens. The phenomenalist program was also advanced when the new and powerful extensional logic of truth-functions was taken to be the model for the structure of scientific theories. This interpretation of the new logic suggested that nature was to be conceived as a set of disconnected atomic facts, that the flux of sensations can be analyzed into individual observation-protocols, and that the correlations of these protocols would serve as reconstruction of the empirical content of scientific knowledge, by means either of logical construction or of conventional systematization.

4. The positivist content of these several empirical philosophies was evident in the early years of this century. The phenomena with which

[23]Ernst Mach, *History and Root of the Principle of the Conservation of Energy*, (Eng. tr. Open Court, Chicago, 1911), 54. The ontological disagreement was important: for Mach the "bundles" of sensations are ontological as well as methodological, and he was to be an opponent of the conception of atoms; Kant was not so opposed, because his ordered collections were only methodological in nature.

science deals were assumed to be isolated sensations or single observations. The relations among the given phenomena were subjective matters of efficient but arbitrary ordering of the data; hypothetical entities and relations were viewed as fictions or as shorthand; and the monadic character of atomic sensations was assumed a priori but made empirically plausible by a program of reductive definition of scientific concepts in terms of individual observation reports. But to press the highly subjective nature of knowledge, conceived thus, meant to reinstitute egocentric solipsism, and indeed to deny cognitive import to the knowing self as much as to the known object. Whereas the empiricists doggedly (and correctly) stressed the essential role of sensations in the attainment of factual knowledge, and investigated the ways in which sense-data reports might be arranged, their critics feared that this emphasis upon the received or subjective factor brought false notions of scientific cognition, of verification, and of the place of science among human activities.[24] Moreover, the early empiricists of this century seemed to give an incorrect account of the subjective factor itself, first because they kept their primary data apart from any objective investigations, whether physiological or sociological, and second because they rejected out-of-hand the methodological scrutiny of sense-perception. Positivistic empiricism was said to combine subjectivism, scepticism, and abstract a priori metaphysics. It was to be expected, therefore, that the positivist tenets would be criticized as though they were variants of the epistemologies of Berkeley, Hume, and Kant, and indeed they were frequently defended in these terms.

III. *Solipsism, Conventionalism, Philosophical Atomism, Phenomenalism*

Dialectic was dismayed at these three components of positivism. In their own development, Hegelians and Marxists had propounded the objectivity of knowledge (vs. subjectivism), its relative but well-founded status (vs. scepticism), and the active dialectic of knower and known (vs. the static separation of a passive unformed given and an active a priori formalism). From such a point of view, positivistic empiricism was severely criticized. When exaggerated, subjectivism becomes solipsism; when formulated as an exaggerated critique of philosophical founda-

[24]Such empiricism did *not*, however, miss the predictive, organizing, or instrumental function of science. The view that theories are only devices for calculation rather than conjectures about reality has recently been criticized in strong terms by K. R. Popper, who argues that "instruments, even theories *so far as they are instruments*, cannot be refuted" and again that "by neglecting falsification, and stressing application, instrumentalism proves to be as obscurantist a philosophy as essentialism," (the doctrine that science aims at ultimate and absolute explanations). See his "Three Views Concerning Human Knowledge" in *Contemporary British Philosophy*, 3rd series, ed. H. D. Lewis (London and New York, 1956), 380.

tions, scepticism becomes total conventionalism; when the reaction against scepticism combines with a desire for certainty, one focus lies with an arbitrarily extended logic of philosophical atomism; and the same combination has another focus in the allegedly certain world of the given, in a doctrine of pure phenomenalism. Typically, the dialectical critic took each component in these pure forms, asking where each would lead *if unmitigated*, and with what each would conflict *if completed*.

1. Solipsism is so radical as to transform all statements about past, future, and distant events into statements about a momentary sensed immediacy. It declares memory to be an illusory mental state which refers to the present. The idea of the present collapses into that of a (psychological) instant, communicable neither to others nor to oneself, for communication takes time. Indeed, communication is close to meaningless, not only because it is a temporal process but also because it presumes at least two persons, speaker and hearer, distinguished in space-time. Nor are the ideas of process and matter to be conceivable in a solipsistic world, for change and persistence are equally mysterious. Without memory, matter, or process, both direct and hypothetical propositions of science lose their reference for they would be restricted to denoting the single sensuous ensemble of immediacy which they "describe" for the moment, correctly or not. Both the subjective world and objective world would disappear, and knowledge with them.[25]

Even though solipsism is an unbelievable and barely stateable doctrine, its dual value should nevertheless be noted. First it reveals the distorting and utterly private nature of sensations which have been conceived as brutally given and hence passive. Moreover it may serve as a criterion of partial falsifiability for those philosophies which entail it.[26]

2. Conventionalism, if taken as a *complete* philosophy of science, runs counter to an objective conception of a natural order. Just as the cognitive and ontological intuitions of Kant and Husserl, conventionalist criteria seem to be clear and distinct. But in contrast to those appar-

[25]Thus Ludwig Wittgenstein wrote in the *Tractatus*: "I am my world (the microcosm)" (5.63), and a few lines previous, "In fact what solipsism *intends* is quite correct, only it cannot be *said*, but it shows itself. That the world is *my* world shows itself in the fact that the limits of language *(the* language, which I alone understand) means the limits of my world." (5.62) And then: "Here we see that solipsism strictly carried out coincides with pure realism. The I in solipsism shrinks to an extensionless point and there remains the reality coordinated with it." (5.64) J. O. Urmson comments that "this appears to be the cold comfort of being consoled for having no friends by the fact that I have no transcendental ego either," *Philosophical Analysis,* (Oxford, 1956), 136. Compare A. N. Whitehead's discussion which concludes that "there is no nature at an instant" in *Nature and Life* (London, 1934) 48, and G. H. Mead's analysis of "the fiction of the knife-edge present" in *The Philosophy of the Act,* ed. C. W. Morris (Chicago, 1938), esp. Essay XV.

[26]This utility of solipsism has been pointed out many times, e.g. by Susan Stebbing, "Logical Positivism and Analysis," *Proc. Brit. Acad.* XIX (1933), 27.

ently assured intuitions, the new criteria are arbitrary despite their compelling esthetic or utilitarian appeal. And if, despite its invariant or absolute character, Kant's a priori ordering of experience lacks an objective basis, then conventionalism turns toward a subjectivist conception with added force. The several criteria by which theories may be chosen, when alternatives present themselves, include: convenience, efficiency, comprehensiveness, simplicity, and elegance. When restricted to the working choice of *de facto* theory, no objection will be found to the use of these criteria; indeed, from every philosophical viewpoint, the logical clarification of scientific knowledge demands delineation of factual and definitional components, of objective from arbitrary.[27] But when swollen beyond its normal scope into a full theory of knowledge, conventionalism can become malignant for then it wipes out the distinction between factual and conventional, so that even the basic sentences of the observational base are thus construed. The conventionalist criteria of choice are, in themselves, logically as arbitrary as the laws they legitimate, with the result that the system of propositions which describe the cosmic order is merely the preference of the scientific temperament, itself determined, we may surmise, by personal and historical factors. A demand for partial (or universal) cosmic chaos is equally arbitrary, institutes its corresponding criteria, and can be just as thoroughgoing in its choice of the protocols.

Since the discipline of facts has generally been thought to constrain conventionalism from dependence on the vagaries of a purely subjective reason, it is in the acceptance or rejection of the primitive observation reports at the basis of an empirical language that its arbitrary character should be sought. In Carnap's empiricism of 1931, truth meant coherence with a set of basic protocols (observation-statements), and these in turn were taken to be a direct report of the given; but the given was no longer certain.[28] The legitimate problem of interpreting basic observations became, in part, a problem of identifying them. In contrast to the philosopher, who must accept the foundations of knowledge as provided by reputable science, the scientist's own choice of his basic protocols was considered to be a matter of (largely unexamined) socio-historical deter-

[27]Hans Reichenbach long ago emphasized that the correct analysis of conventional elements in scientific knowledge need not entail that scientists must deal with subjective arbitrariness; instead it has the opposite result. Accordingly "only by discovering the points of arbitrariness, by identifying them as such and by classifying them as definitions, can we obtain objective measuring results in physics," *The Philosophy of Space and Time* (New York, 1957; translated from the German ed., Berlin, 1928), 37.

[28]One could not tell *what* is certain, nor *whether* the reports were certain. A detailed critique of "self-authenticating" givens, of which primitive observation statements were direct reports, was given in Wilfrid Sellars' London Lectures, "The Myth of the Given," now published as "Empiricism and the Philosophy of Mind." in *Minnesota Studies in the Philosophy of Science,* I (Minneapolis, 1956), 253-329.

minations. If the question is raised, whose observation-reports are to be accepted, then to be sure certain physically-objective conditions were recognized by the physicalism of 1932; it was these physical conditions which were thought to make observations trustworthy within a scientific community. Most notable is the contingent agreement of different observers in their determination of the quantitative properties of space-time events, contingent because their agreement is not logically necessary. But agreement among observers, however contingent it may be, still permits wide latitude to the philosopher who reconstructs scientific knowledge. Sanction must be given to any group of natural or social scientists in their stipulation of the ("empirical") basis from which statements shall be judged acceptable or inacceptable (and ultimately true or false) so long as they are competent or, at any rate, socially reputed to be such. In his "principle of tolerance,"[29] Carnap formalized a fundamental doctrine of conventionally-chosen basic-truths. The larger doctrine of the logical syntax of cognitive language incorporated the further notion that truths in general are internally coherent with the conventionally stipulated base.

It was difficult to see how a widely accepted delusion about the foundations of any science might meaningfully be stated to be delusive, much less rationally disputed. Fairy tales are wishful thinking. However, when it comes to ghosts and witches we cannot so easily dismiss the evidence. With a sufficient quantity of convenient protocols, whether authoritative or self-authenticating, an elegant and comprehensive science of witchcraft would have to be accepted; the conventional empiricism of protocol-basic languages could have no reasonable quarrel with it. Has conventionalism a philosophically meaningful way of asserting that an entire community is in error, except by reference to an arbitrarily chosen later (or earlier) community?[30]

Thus, complete conventionalism, e.g., a relativized basis of empirical

[29]Rudolf Carnap, *The Logical Syntax of Language* (London, 1937), section 17, *et seq.*, especially in the two forms: "It is not our business to set up prohibitions, but to arrive at conventions." and "In logic, there are no morals." Perhaps the limitations of a purely syntactical approach with regard to the danger of pure conventionalism might, if heeded, have encouraged Carnap's concern with semantical and pragmatic questions. In any case, even in the *Logical Syntax,* 51, the analogy to Euclidean and non-Euclidean geometrical investigations merely raises once more, rather than clarifies, the conventionalist question with regard to 'facts' while retaining the legitimate role of conventional stipulations with regard to theories. Whatever the systematic danger, Carnap himself always recognized the evolving connection between objectively acceptable, or true, protocol-statements and historical practice; see, e.g. his reply to this serious charge of ambiguity in his "Erwiderung auf die vorstehenden Aufsätze von E. Zilsel und K. Duncker," *Erkenntnis* III (1932), 177-188, esp. 182-183.

[30]Max Horkheimer bitterly protested against the logical toleration espoused by some forms of conventionalism in his major essay "Der neueste Angriff auf die Metaphysik," *Zeitschrift für Sozialforschung* VI (1937), 4-51 esp. 28-30, 40. In his attempt to refute

knowledge, is fatal to science. It cannot responsibly distinguish facts from ghosts. Its criteria for accepting protocols are as non-empirical as Kant's synthetic a priori. And conventionalists are constrained to invoke a covertly anti-conventionalist theory of the meaning of historical statements when they offer historical interpretations of the causes of scientific agreement. Insofar as any particular empiricist theory of truth embraces or entails a thoroughgoing conventionalist doctrine of coherence, however inadvertently, it must, to that degree, suffer these same inadequacies. The ease with which a partial conventionalist analysis of science can, first, obscure the non-conventional (and essential) components of science, and, then, provide systematic support for subjectivist doctrines, requires that careful conclusions should be drawn concerning the role of conventions at all levels of scientific inquiry: facts, concepts, theories, and meta-scientific reconstructions.

That there have been serious discussions of this matter during the past half-century is of course well-known, notably the criticisms of the conventionalist doctrines of Dingler and Eddington by Planck, Schlick, Popper, and Reichenbach among others. But anti-objectivist interpretations of natural science have repeatedly adduced support from conventionalist arguments. Carnap early stressed, with Reichenbach, that physical geometry has an inescapable non-conventional element.[31] However his later repeated use of the term 'empirical' as in opposition to 'conventional'

neo-positivist restriction of philosophy to syntactical questions, Horkheimer acutely discussed the possibility of a rational critique of both human knowledge and social realities.

The similarity between the neo-positivism of Carnap and Neurath in the 1930's and the Machism with which Lenin disputed thirty years earlier is striking. Compare, say, Hempel's and Neurath's early discussions of the conventional bases of truth (where they speak of truth in physics as the acceptable statements of "the physicists of our culture-circle") with the following remark of A. Bogdanov: "The objectivity of physical bodies which we encounter in our experience depends in the last resort on the establishment of a common conviction and concordance between the assertions of different people . . . the physical world consists of nothing more than socially agreed, socially harmonized — in a word, of socially organized experience," *Empirio-monism: Essays in Philosophy* (3rd ed., Moscow, 1908), I, 23, cited by Gustav Wetter, *Dialectical Materialism: a Historical and Systematic Survey of Philosophy in the Soviet Union* (tr. Peter Heath, London and New York, 1958, from 4th German edition), 93f. That this conception is not dead may be seen, e.g. in John Hartland-Swann's *An Analysis of Knowing* (London, 1957), where the truth is the "dominant-decision of the experts."

The contemporary expert agreement on the evidence for magic and witchcraft is set forth, e.g. in D. P. Walker, *Spiritual and Demonic Magic* (London, 1958), esp. part two; Henry C. Lea, *Materials Toward a History of Witchcraft,* ed. A. C. Howland (New York, 1957), esp. part two and part four; Lynn Thorndike, *A History of Magic and Experimental Science,* esp. *7* and *8* (New York, 1958); and the two detailed studies of the evidence by a modern believer, Montague Summers, *The History of Witchcraft and Demonology* (London, 1926; New York, 1956), and *The Geography of Witchcraft* (London, 1927; Evanston, 1958).

[31]In *Der Raum* (Berlin, 1922), and *Physikalische Begriffsbildung* (Karlsruhe, 1926), 31.

still permitted the ambiguities of the conventional *basis* to reappear. But, on other grounds (as I hope to show) Carnap's empiricism has come to a realistic or materialist reference and basis for scientific knowledge, and hence we may now use 'empirical' and 'conventional' as antonyms. That Poincaré's views, as distinguished from others' conceptions of his views, were as empirical *in this realistic sense* as Carnap's has convincingly been demonstrated by Adolf Grünbaum[32] but the subjectivist pitfall of conventionalism, when its analytic function is misunderstood, is shown by the historical career of these same mis-conceptions of Poincaré's arguments.[33]

3. Atomism, the hypothesis that reality is composed of fully independent momentary (or perhaps timeless) monads, or atomic facts, was a useful failure.[34] By a Socratic dialectic of its own, the philosophy of logical atomism proposed hypotheses (about our knowledge and its sources, and about our ways of expressing that knowledge) and then transformed them by much the same sort of criticism that dialectical and metaphysical spectators had offered.

(a) The language of *Principia Mathematica* was seen to be arbitrary, one among many alternatives. Since philosophical atomism had initially assumed the ontological validity of that language, it was, therefore, in atomistic terms, at first a new a priori Kantianism, and later with the development of alternatives, it came to resemble conventionalism.

(b) The names of the atomic constituents were to be defined by direct

[32]Adolf Grünbaum, "Carnap's Views on the Foundations of Geometry" (this volume), and "Conventionalism in Geometry," *Symposium on the Axiomatic Method,* ed. P. Suppes (Amsterdam, 1959). Abraham Edel made a similar observation about Poincaré's stand against conventionalist extremists in his essay on conventional elements in philosophy and science, "Interpretation and the Selection of Categories," *Meaning and Interpretation (U. Cal. Pub. Phil.* XXV, Berkeley, 1950), 57-95. The usual Poincaré-interpretation in its wider context is persuasively argued in René Berthelot, *Un Romantisme utilitaire: Etude sur le mouvement pragmatiste* (Paris, 1911), 201-413, and Georges Sorel, "L'Experience dans la physique moderne," in *De l'utilité du pragmatisme* (Paris, 1921), 288-356.

[33]The debate within Polish philosophical circles well illustrates all these aspects; see Adam Schaff, *op. cit.,* chapter vi, esp. section 5. That Marxists run risks of being conventionalist pseudo-scientists has been urged briefly by Karl Popper in "Philosophy of Science: a Personal Report," *British Philosophy in the Mid-Century,* ed. C. A. Mace (London, 1957) and in his *The Open Society and Its Enemies* (revised, Princeton, 1952), ch. 15, and indeed, whatever the merit of his other considerations of Marxism in its several forms, the argument against conventionalism has repeatedly been expounded with incisive clarity in Popper's writings on the role of falsifiability in a scientific outlook, e.g. *The Logic of Scientific Discovery* (London and New York, 1959). Schaff's book fails to come to terms with the acute discussion in chapters 9-10 of Leon Chwistek, *The Limits of Science* (Warsaw, 1935; rev. English ed., New York, 1948).

[34]The criticisms of logical atomism which are succinctly presented by J. O. Urmson, *op. cit.,* chapter 9, are similar at some points to those of Lenin, summarized below. Jacob Loewenberg put it all cryptically by reciting the last line of Humpty-Dumpty to the analytic logicians.

denotation. If this program were to be carried out, the language of science would have come to resemble a dictionary and grammar of truth-functional shorthand in which the primitive terms were purely subjective observation-reports. Solipsism would be unavoidable and an inter-subjective language incomprehensible unless the atomic facts could achieve public status. But only an unexplained and trans-experiential factor could provide knowledge of that status.

(c) The status of atomic observation-reports was unhappy in another respect. These reports were thought to be certain, unambiguous, communicable, but in fact they were scientifically almost useless since they were at best non-descriptive ostensive signs. It was difficult to characterize their relation both to the facts which they were intended to state (whether by an explication of formal similarity, or otherwise) and to the theories whose predictions they were to test.

(d) Nor was it ever shown that the world is an ensemble of atomic facts. The proposed reductive analysis of cognitive statements (and, prior to all others, of statements about the entities of macroscopic physics) was never carried to a successful conclusion. Such analyses were attempted but common and scientific usage alike eluded the analysts.[35] They were compelled to offer re-statements of the problem in place of solution: either, as in Mill's discussion of matter, hypothetical phenomenalism; or, as in the epistemologically nearly uncommitted analyses of the present, a new quasi-empirical scrutiny of the linguistic puzzles which tangle thinking; or, conventionally chosen artificial languages whose basic sentences are parts of an axiomatic reconstruction of a given scientific theory rather than independently certified reports of direct experiences.

4. Phenomenalism has suffered from the several defects of solipsism, conventionalism, and logical atomism. Indeed, when pressed, these different doctrines each require a subjectivist metaphysic in order to certify their foundations or to legitimate their constructions. Unfortunately phenomenalist positivism has no compensating merit in elucidating scientific theories; on the contrary, we shall see that it brings inexplicable contingency into the center of the scientific enterprise.

(a) Phenomenalism regards sensations as an obstacle between subject and object, between observer and observed; it finds difficulty in maintaining any objects at all. In Ayer's modern formulation, phenome-

[35] ". . . the extra entities in the universe of discourse all went up in smoke, though from the fictional entities there lingered still a peculiar smell," John Wisdom, "Metaphysics and Verification" (1938), as reprinted in his *Philosophy and Psychoanalysis* (Oxford and New York, 1953), 59. In a somewhat similar connection, Marx discussed the autonomy of the individual and remarked that both scientific and philosophical understanding required precisely an understanding of his non-autonomous nature: "the complexity of the individual depends on the complexity of his relationships," in *The German Ideology, Marx-Engels Archiv* VII (1928), 286.

nalism is said to reject the view that "to speak about material things is to speak about something altogether different from sense-data" and further to deny even that "it is to speak about sense-data but about something else besides."[36] Even if the dangers of solipsism, convention, and pure chance were evaded, the effect upon science would be devastating. Since Galileo, science has distrusted bare facts however much it begins with those facts. Taken at first sight, the perceived world is illusory, for it is a collection of largely disconnected bits, a realm of irrational and often unexpected occurrences. With its ability to go beyond appearances, scientific explanation rejects the allegedly ultimate authority of presently contingent facts *as we experience them.*[37] The subsumptive character of scientific explanation is not thereby anti-factual nor anti-experiential, but it is anti-subjective. Subjective and phenomenal events should be construed as a very useful sub-class of objective events. But phenomenalism, however helpful it may be for the descriptive psychology of learning (and hence however valuable in the technical theory of perceptual knowledge, which itself requires independent knowledge of both object and percipient by the technical observer of both) cannot *alone* give meaning to scientific explanation.

As Paul Marhenke has commented, these and other formulae of phenomenalism can be viewed merely as attempts to connect cognition with some form of direct and observable experience. As such they are innocent and (as I argue below) correct since in such usage they would distinguish existential meaning from confirmation.[38] But many phenomenalists have meant what Ayer's sentences actually state: i.e. some form of reducibility, or synonymy, of cognitive statements to statements about sensations. The most cogent recent defense,[39] stresses that phenomenalism is not to be thought of as a theory of knowledge (nor *a fortiori* of reality) ; it is a logical hypothesis about certain relations among ideas, or

[36]A. J. Ayer, *The Foundations of Empirical Knowledge* (London and New York, 1940), 241. According to a Marxist description of phenomenalism, "between the object and consciousness, sensation stands as an impassable barrier; the result is that the influence of the object on our senses, instead of putting us in touch with it, cuts us off from it," Lyubov Axelrod, *Philosophical Studies* (cited by Wetter, *op. cit.*, 151; Russian ed., St. Petersburg, 1906).

[37]"Sense organs separate the world into elements, the mind restores it," Sandor Ferenczi, *Final Contributions to the Problems and Methods of Psychoanalysis* (London, 1955), 192.

[38]Paul Marhenke, "Phenomenalism" in *Philosophical Analysis,* ed. Max Black (Ithaca, 1950). It is necessary to retain phenomenalistic or sense-datum statements along with statements about material objects, and also to recognize their irreducibility; see C. A. Fritz, "Sense-perception and Material Objects," *Phil. and Phen. Res.* XVI (1956), 303-316.

[39]Nelson Goodman, in this volume and *The Structure of Appearance* (Cambridge, Mass., 1951). See also the general discussion in Henryk Mehlberg, "Positivisme et science, I," *Studia Philosophica* III, 1939-46 (pub. Poznan 1948), 211-294.

in Carnap's word of 1928, a "structural description" (Strukturbeschreibung), rather than a "full-color portrait of reality".[40] Such modesty, both correct and admirable on an issue which has generated much heat, admits the inadequacy of phenomenalism as a complete philosophy of science while claiming its adequacy for certain restricted tasks and for mental experiments. But the ambivalence of this "structural description" is that it claims to be *somewhat* true about the very nerve of our knowledge or else it collapses into utter common sense. Compare A. J. Ayer's recent alternative: ". . .the solution of the problem of perception may be to treat our beliefs about physical objects as constituting a theory, the function of which is to explain the course of our sensory experiences. . . (to explain) how is the physical-object language possible?"[41] a view which can permit a legitimate *scientific* (rather than philosophical) role for phenomenalist analyses.

(b) A factual example will show the need for a materialist reconstruction of the phenomenalist doctrine. 'My copy of *Leaves of Grass* is on the bookshelf in my Connecticut home,'[42] upon phenomenalist analysis, is equivalent to an indefinite set of assertions of the type 'If I were now in my home in Connecticut under certain normal conditions, I would have certain book-ish sense-data.' This excludes the further categorical assertion 'Even though I am not in my home in Connecticut, my copy of *Leaves of Grass* is on the bookshelf there,' which is certainly what I mean to assert. This categorical statement is excluded because it, in turn, is equivalent to the conjunction of 'If I were now in my home . . . I would have certain book-ish sense-data' and 'I am not now in my home in Connecticut.' Whatever might confirm the first part of this conjunction, disconfirms the second part and hence the whole. Whatever confirms the second part, neither confirms nor disconfirms the first part (unless one takes the first part as an instance of material implication; but, despite the discussion of 1936,[43] this is surely not the phenomenalist intention, for it would lead to the inadmissable conclusion that *not* observing can confirm the original categorical statement, to the effect that a factual situation obtains even though I do not observe it). Thus, the categorical statement, being indeterminate in truth-value, is empirically without meaning in the phenomenalist language, and hence it must

[40]Nelson Goodman, "The Revision of Philosophy" in *American Philosophers at Work,* ed. Sidney Hook (New York, 1956), 87.

[41]A. J. Ayer, "Phenomenalism," *Philosophical Essays,* ch. 6, (London and New York, 1954).

[42]This sentence was written in Cambridge, England. I have since found that the example is similar to an argument of Winston H. F. Barnes, *The Philosophical Predicament* (London, 1950), ch. 8.

[43]See Carnap's criticism of phenomenalism in "Testability and Meaning," *Philosophy of Science* III (1936), 420.

be excluded from a phenomenalist reconstruction of the original statement. The original statement has its intended meaning only in an objectivist language, whether of divinely supported sensibilia or of material existence. The idea that empirical confirmation need not be linked with purely experiential meanings appeared in physicalism.[44] In that case, empirical practice is an inexpugnable part of science; it has little to do with the troublesome logical constructions of a sensationist epistemology, and it is part of an empirical description of rational scientific procedure.

(c) Phenomenalism is vulnerable within its own domain. Phenomena do not show their nature. They require analysis and interpretive argument. The assurance of sensuous certainty, which phenomenalism asserts, deserved the classic rebuke which Hegel administered; insofar as positivism follows Hume in this regard, Hegel's critique is still pertinent.[45] This is so since the discussion of the basis of knowledge, at the hands of Locke and Hume, finds its counterpart in the discussion of basic sentences at the hands of Schlick, Neurath, and Carnap, wherein probability statements often serve in the empiricist escape from bondage to sense-certainty (and to its representations by observation-predicates) as did the statistical laws of psychological association in Hume's day.

Positivism in general holds to extreme nominalism. It recognizes only the particular given. Reason becomes extensional logic; logic turns to manipulation of symbols and symbolic equivalences; and general ideas, as Hume says, can serve only to represent the particulars from which they have been abstracted.

No less than Hume, Hegel's first concern was to find an *empirical* basis for general ideas and universal laws. Writing as he did, after Kant's analysis of the world order, Hegel turned his strictures against Kant as well as Hume, for the Kantian transcendental consciousness only unites the several knowing subjects with one another, the knowers of the scientific community, but it fails to unite knower with known. A priori subjective universals and sensed objective particulars cannot be united so

[44]That the dangers of a narrow basis for knowledge are not automatically avoided by this step have been pointed out, e.g., by Goodman, *op. cit.*

[45]I think that the clearest recent statement of the critique of any immediately meaningful pre-interpreted given is that of J. Loewenberg, "The Futile Flight from Interpretation," *Meaning and Interpretation, op. cit.*, 169-197. He points out that analysis cannot begin with the constituents of entities but only with a discriminable complex which is the true pre-analytic datum and which is *said* to contain, e.g. atomic sensations. Then what is *last* in analysis is taken to be *first* in awareness. Immediacy, as an epistemologically primitive state of awareness, "is an imaginative if not an imaginary notion." And in any case it leads to the (empiricist's) paradox of immediacy (178): "Of immediacy, we cannot say what we mean and we do not mean what we say." Compare Wilfrid Sellars, *op. cit.*, and C. G. Hempel's continued reappraisals of the possibilities of using denotative definitions for concept formation, e.g. *Fundamentals of Concept Formation in Empirical Science* (Chicago, 1952), sect. 6-8.

long as they remain respectively subjective and objective; and just so long will rational thought and sense-perception be split apart. What other job does philosophy have than to investigate this split and propose a reunion?

The split was genuine enough. There are knowing subjects, each with a given set of sensuous experiences, which are related to one another temporally, that is historically.

Hegel begins with a phenomenalist language, with such observation reports as Carnap's "Blue-Here-Now." How shall we proceed to analyze the stream of such reports? Can we observe temporal succession or spatial relations? Can we abstract from several reports? Can we differentiate the reports from one another, or from possible ones? We can do these and much more in our dealings with experience but we cannot say that the activities of analysis and comparison are, themselves, Here-Now reports. Whether we turn to analyze our treatment of the reports or whether we simply look at the essential similarities in the reports we will find tacit universals. What else can we make of the notion of 'similarity'? And how can we evade the *general* idea of Here-Now?[46] Understanding this aspect of empirical knowledge reveals an inner dialectic in the process of understanding itself, a spurious simplicity in the item which was taken to be brute and primary; the sense datum, which Hegel demonstrated to be "mediated simplicity," has become unclear, i.e. complex, and incomplete. It fairly groans with paradoxes to be resolved, since we are faced, even at this elementary stage, with a striking conclusion: that which commonly and essentially characterizes *all* sense experience is not the objective given, the sensed particular experience, nor even the slippery universal "particularity," but it is instead universality which this experience proves. Since Hume is correct in that we cannot sense a universal, or, to put the matter differently, that the object of empirically purified knowledge is everywhere a particular fact, it seems that the truth to which we are led by sense-experience must be non-empirical truth, a matter of reasoned knowledge.

Nor would we find release from this, and all the succeeding arguments to which this is the prelude, if we were to start with a physicalist basis of things perceived rather than experiences sensed. Hegel's critique is focused on the nominalistic certainty of whatever particularistic terms apply to things or to experiences; and the curious point is that his idealist argument on behalf of the role of the reasoning knowing subject is, at

[46]". . . take the *Here* . . . The Here is, e.g. the tree. I turn about and this truth has disappeared and has changed round into its opposite: The Here is not a tree but a house. The Here itself does not disappear; it *is* and remains in the disappearance of the house, tree, and so on, and is indifferently house, tree. The This is shown thus . . . to be *mediated simplicity,* in other words, to be *universality.*" Hegel, *The Phenomenology of Mind,* tr. J. B. Baillie (London, 1931), 152f.

heart, aimed not against the objective character of knowledge but rather at inadequate accounts of objective knowledge and of the known.[47]

5. Hegel's analysis of sense-certainty compels him to turn from sensation to perception, to the realm of things, taken as universals or at least as clusters of universals. Here again a direct confrontation of empirical description shows the essential role of the reasoning subject. Are the observed characteristics of the perceived thing a fortuitous togetherness? Is the particular thing to be considered as the *arbitrary* locus of these many universals? But every thing, momentary or persistent, challenges common sense and science to overcome such a view. We rest satisfied at this stage only if the properties cohere as a unit, if, as Hegel would put it, the unity (Gestalt) of the object filters out the myriads of *arbitrary* possible properties, precluding *their* existence therein, and permitting only the ones proper for its nature. And yet, this idea of a natural unity cannot arise in perception, for we have started by admitting that we perceive the object as merely the locus of multiple characteristics. Nor is the unity a mysterious substance *sui generis*; it rests in the very same kind of relation that the precluding showed. These outward relations are the factors which determine the unity of the cluster. They show the thing as it exists in the perspective of other entities; and among those others there can be singled out the human knower. But every property can be truly comprehended in such an outward manner, at least in principle, for each is knowable; hence, in Hegel's view, the external relations of *cognitive* being-for-another provide a guide to the objective unity of the object's internal structure, its *material* being-for-itself. The natural unity is thereby enlarged by the cognitive encounter.[48]

In its own terms, phenomenalism issues into a form of objective idealism; on the other hand, when cognition is investigated as a natural event, phenomenalism yields to a doctrine which can deal more successfully with the empirical, complex, and unavoidable questions of communicable meanings, inter-subjective agreements, and inferred entities. This was later to be the task of physicalism. But before we discuss this development, we must consider the motivations and sources of the hostility of dialectical thought toward both covert and overt subjectivism.

IV. *The Dangers of Subjectivism*

1. The empiricist movement has embraced positivist and realist think-

[47]This is still explicit in Marxist thinking. "Our practice proves that things perceived cannot be readily understood by us and that only things understood can be more profoundly perceived. Perception only solves the problem of phenomena; reason alone solves the problem of essence," from Mao Tse-tung, "On Practice," 1937, in *Selected Works* I (London and New York, 1954), 286.

[48]See Paul Tillich, "Participation and Knowledge," *Sociologica*, ed. T. W. Adorno and W. Dirks (Frankfurt, 1955), 201-209, for a brief but suggestive analysis.

ers. Individual philosophers have experimented with both outlooks. It has frequently been held to be a matter of interpretive convenience, of only minor importance, whether the language that best clarifies the content of scientific knowledge is phenomenal or material. (At one time the two were thought to be equivalent, although the equivalence later turned out to be one of correlation rather than synonymy.) This indifference was possible because the philosophy of science was predicated upon the existence of valid bodies of scientific knowledge, and only to a much lesser extent upon the philosophical function of judging the sciences. If clarification is taken to mean axiomatic re-statement in various ways, then the varying contents of the sciences (and of the questionable sciences, e.g. astrology, as well) become unquestioned raw material for philosophy. Instead of the basis of scientific knowledge being itself scrutinized, epistemology is plunged into the midst of things. The effect of this is not wholly negative, for the task of technical philosophy of science *does* consist in the clarification of the methods and results of science. One powerful argument in support of any theory of evidence, entities, or definition, is that it makes clear what scientists, in fact, say, do, and know.[49] Insofar as the philosophy of science is a relative discipline which is subsidiary to the sciences, it can be expected to unify the instrumental appendix for a world-outlook. Doubtless every *Weltanschauung* or *general* philosophy proposes certain views about the nature of the world, and in that sense should draw upon the entire range of science and upon technical philosophic elaboration and clarification of science. But when a general philosophy goes on to consider the realistic possibilities of personal and social life, it must distinguish the neo-positivistic interpretation of scientific knowledge from the knowledge itself. Thus, pure empiricist philosophers of science can treat the distinction between phenomenalism and realism as a matter of linguistic convenience only because, being ancillary to science, they are under no obligation to explicate the foundations of science in the epistemological process itself. A choice of primitive terms would be validated by their sufficiency for axiomatization of the theories into which they enter; and although this is undoubtedly a major criterion for their *use*, it cannot decide their *status*. Primitive observation-terms and primitive thing-terms may serve two functions: first, as the basic dictionary for logically-coherent expression of a theory, and, second, as a confirmation basis for that theory; but they remain unclarified, tentative, a part of an implicit metaphysic

[49]R. B. Braithwaite, *Scientific Explanation* (Cambridge, England, 1953), ch. i and xi, expounds this view; presumably the technical philosopher of science would then have to agree that there are other philosophical specialties which deal with such metaphysical questions as perception, the status of scientific knowledge, the logical nature of paradox, and of metaphysical language itself. Thus the metaphysical inquiries of Wisdom, *op. cit., passim* would be supplementary to those of Braithwaite.

(rather than science) of the cognitive process so long as these two functions are rather sharply separated.

2. Linguistic and conceptual tools change from time to time but the empirical tradition has persistently been motivated by the highest intellectual aim of rational men, namely to free us from illusion. Even as it approaches this goal, far from establishing positive truth, pure empiricism merely provides a test for establishing falsity or nonsense, helping in Locke's sense "to remove some of the rubbish that lies in the way to knowledge." But it does hint at the provision of a more practical and general criterion of truth and meaning, and it is strange that factual verifiability was not explicitly proposed in the eighteenth century.[50] For then empiricism was a liberating conception. It continues to provide an adequate theory of inquiry so long as science has to fight a two-front battle *against* dogmas and *for* facts, *against* mythological beings and *for* rational explanations. In the neo-positivist account, the nature of the facts, both as apprehended and as changeable, is shrouded, filed away among questions to be answered by a future sensationist psychology, if the positivist uses phenomenalist language; or by physiological and physical correlations, if he is a behaviorist; or, what is easier but even less adequate, the 'facts' are simply assumed to be those of the particular science whose language, in any particular philosophical analysis, is being clarified. Thus, the class of "sentences about the objects of our personal macroscopic environment (concreta) at a certain moment"[51] are taken to be both psychologically prior to, and adequate for, the reconstruction of the inferred and unobservable as well as the observable entities of the sciences. But it is these basic sentences with which a complete methodical analysis would deal. The development of such analysis challenges the view that *bare* experience, taken as the psychically or physically given, is the sole source and content of knowledge, however essential it may be as its test. For the philosopher of science the facts and ideas of science are abstracted from the relevant social process at the risk of artificiality; to grasp them with full insight requires a grasp of the whole historical situation. "The problem of descending from the world of thought to the real world changes into the problem of descending from language to life."[52]

Dialectic recognizes the coherence of an objective cognitive process with the reality that is known, and hence with the knowledge thereby attained. Therefore it has made the repudiation of subjectivism an acid test of an accurate scientific philosophy. Why is subjectivism (the dis-

[50]See Karl Popper, "Note on Berkeley as Precursor of Mach," *Brit. J. Phil. Sci.* IV (1953), 26-36.

[51]Hans Reichenbach, "Verifiability Theory of Meaning," *Proc. Amer. Acad. Arts & Sci.* LXXX (1951), 50.

[52]Marx and Engels, *The German Ideology, Marx-Engels Gesamtausgabe,* I, 5 (Berlin, 1932), 424. See also note 112.

tinctive burden of neo-positivism as well as of classic positivism) felt to be dangerous to that coherence? Why is this not a matter of terminological tolerance? Why is phenomenalism relatively harmless for axiomatic re-statement of existing special theories (though, as we have suggested, inadequate) but harmful if generalized to a total view? We shall see that the dangers of positivism are alleged to be both systematic and historical.

3. But first I must stress again that the criteria which Rudolf Carnap imposed on his thought—logical clarity and factual adequacy—have compelled this exceedingly careful thinker to develop and change, to rethink and re-construct. As the horizon of his technical philosophy enlarged, and as the quest for certainty abated, earlier criticisms seemed to become of greater relevance, and were taken with gravity. Carnap's views have been imbedded in the epistemological presuppositions of mathematics and concrete physical science rather than of social theory. The logical positivists have battled intellectual and emotional obscurantism by developing mathematically rigorous standards of logical reconstruction.

Nevertheless, rigor is not enough. It seems that few critics have found fault with Carnap's standards of inquiry (and, indeed, most of them can only hope to have standards as high). It is the source of the rigor that arouses suspicion. Whatever may have been Carnap's vision of a unified physical and social science, which serves a free and cooperative mankind, logical empiricism has thus far been less than universal in its own scope and technique. It has been conceptualized parallel with the technological demands of modern industry. Nor is this blame, for empiricism has sought to be the philosophical approach which is adequate for both theoretical and practical science.

4. The criteria of a successfully engineered factory show how adequate the empiricist canon is: *precision*; *simplicity*; *analysis* into components; *impersonal*, unidentifiable, and completely standardized workers and supplies; *economy* of tools and materials; *efficiency* of administration and labor; *unified*, consistently harmonious, and *complete* development from raw materials to finished product; and *determinate* relations between inputs and outputs. Any adequate philosophy for modern man would deal with these same criteria in terms which reflect the industrial foundations of our times.[53] Thus science, in its mutual relation with industry, also mediates between the social order and philosophy. But the

[53]For another consideration of the characteristics of the industrial order in their cultural relations to cognition, see Sigmund Freud's treatment of order, parsimony, and obstinacy, in, e.g. *Collected Papers* II (London, 1950), 45-50, and, for their direct relation to concepts and methods of empirical science (as discussed by Sombart and Weber), see Erich Fromm "Die psychoanalytische Charakterologie und ihre Bedeutung für die Sozialpsychologie" *Zeitschrift für Sozialforschung* I (1932), 253-277. An economic approach from the same general point of view suggests that the money

social order has two sides, rationalized technology and varying social relations among men. It may be legitimate to restrict the range of philosophy to consideration of man as worker and technologist, and philosophy may even be limited in its function to lucid axiomatization of those sciences that have been nurtured by, and creative of, technological civilization. But such a limited philosophy (i.e. philosophy when restricted to philosophy of the natural sciences) will have a dialectical pitfall within it. The accompaniment, in social practice, of *incomplete* technology has been a partially dehumanized society wherein working and living are divorced, individual enlightenment turns into imposed social coordination, and humanity becomes labor.[54] On the other hand, *complete* technology, the total use of precise automatic and efficient science, will be one pre-condition, *not* of a totally dehumanized society, but of its opposite: a newly humanized society founded upon an automatic, dehumanized production. A positivist sociology which draws *only* upon the rigor of technical facts can discuss neither the possibility of a culture which has transcended technology, nor the historical transition to such a culture.

The material basis for human life retains its necessary role in an automatically productive culture. This is a common-place which, however, should be supplemented by the observation that freedom from necessary and dehumanizing labor, *if taken as the mark of a civilization and not just of a leisure class*, poses certain fundamental problems of knowledge and morality anew.

Traditionally, naturalism and materialism have been the tough-minded or empirical component of expanding industrial culture. Along-

economy reflected *and promoted* a scientific manner of thought, (abstract, impersonal, objective, quantitative, rational) in as efficacious a manner as the technology itself. See, besides Freudian references, *op. cit.*, Georg Simmel, *Die Philosophie des Geldes* (Munich, 1922), 480-501; Oswald Spengler, *The Decline of the West* (London, 1932), II, 482, 489f.; Joseph Schumpeter, *Capitalism, Socialism and Democracy* (3rd ed. New York, 1950), ch. 11. But the *irrational* aspects of technology and of a money economy require equal investigation for they question the rational status of the mode of thought which this functional complex of technology-money-science utilizes; see N. O. Brown, *op. Cit.*, ch. 15. This has just as little been investigated by Marxists as by empiricists.

[54] In this way, "consciousness, increasingly less burdened by autonomy, tends to be reduced to the task of regulating the coordination of the individual with the whole . . . the individual's awareness of the prevailing repression is blunted by the manipulated restriction of his consciousness. This process alters the contents of happiness", Herbert Marcuse, *Eros and Civilization* (Boston and London, 1955), 103, see also ch. 4 "The Dialectic of Civilization." This stimulating essay in dialectical naturalism combines a metaphorical and speculative style with a rational hypothetical content. Although Marcuse took the philosophical explication of Freud in historical terms as his purpose, his achievement is, independently, of methodological and conceptual significance. See, also, Marcuse, "Zur Kritik des Hedonismus," *Zeitschrift für Sozialforschung* VII (1938), 55-87; John Dewey, *Human Nature and Conduct* (New York, 1922), Part II, Sect. 3; and P.-M. Schuhl, *op. cit.*

side their theory of the tools, procedures, weapons, and materials of construction and conquest, they developed a theory of nature as a whole. Furthermore their successes have been those of the mastery of natural processes, wrought by three kinds of men, men of science, men of capital and industry, and vast numbers of laboring men and women. But, since they are tough-minded, their corresponding *general* philosophic outlook drew mainly upon the successful sciences, indeed sponsored them to success, upon mathematics and physics and chemistry, projecting from their efficient analytic methods[55] to a world-view. The consistent accompaniment was behaviorism in theoretical psychology, manipulation of the human "objects" in applied psychology, mathematical formalization in economics, a distrust of what was felt to be unverifiable historical theory and hence the divorce of history from social science, and the abandonment of philosophy as a constructive guide to social and personal life.

Perhaps large-scale application of social science will bring about a transformation of social life with the same magnitude as did the industrial applications of classical physics. In that case, the genuinely positivistic social theorist would have as little to say about it as did the physicists, chemists, and engineers about the social transformations which their activities made possible. Physics cannot criticize physical nature; but also physics does not discuss nature at large, for its concepts do not include the physicist or his socio-historical sources and behavior. Social theory, and social philosophy, have no such excuse. Social theory must account for the social theorist.[56] In this matter, as in so many others, the decisive difference between a pure empiricist philosophy of the social sciences and a dialectical social theory is between their respective attitudes toward indubitable facts and toward the role of the theorist himself. To empiricism, there have been only two attitudes: passive acceptance of the social universe of observed facts, or rejection of the issue of acceptance and rejection as non-cognitive and philosophically irrelevant. To dialectical philosophers, there have also been two possibilities: Utopian rejection of unpalatable facts, and with them of science as well, or an *appraisal* of the present facts with respect to their genesis, development, epistemic relations, and potentialities. Such appraisal is

[55]See also the similarly conceived "methodological individualism" of the entrepreneur, e.g. Joseph Schumpeter, *The Theory of Economic Development* (New York, 1938).

[56]The empiricists, upon reflection, recognized that this penetrated their own attitude toward social science also. Much might have been made of Otto Neurath's remark that "The general revolution of our age is the ground of a scientific sociology," in *Empirische Soziologie* (Vienna, 1931), 146, if he had not already repudiated any rational assessment of prospective *fundamental* social change; "We must wait for the new phenomena in order that we might then discover lawlike regularities for them in their turn," *ibid.*, 106.

foreign to classical science as much as to positivist philosophy; this suggests a reappraisal of the limited nature of present knowledge in the light of the biological and socio-historical character *of the knowing activity.*[57]

A unified science of knowledge is prerequisite to an adequate philosophy of knowledge. The science of knowledge receives its broadest base as part of a general historical sociology. To be sure, such a general science of society must have a confirmable mode of knowing. But its circularity is benign because the theory is reflexive. In this way the dialectic of objective historical development is materially and systematically prerequisite to an empirically trustworthy epistemology. If so, then the distinction between phenomenalism and realism[58] is the old distinction between an idealism which holds "that there is a Mind with a world in it" and a materialism which holds that "there exists a world with minds in it."[59] And instead of being a trivial distinction between equivalent languages, this is the important distinction between the metaphysical postulate of phenomenalism (metaphysical because beyond empirical validation) and a broadly empirical theory of the ontogeny and phylogeny of human knowledge (a realistic theory which is empirical because its assertions are open to disciplined confirmation).

5. The subjectivist and relativist tendency in neo-positivism can lead to a complete denial of historical meaning and of historical explanation.[60] One of the results for political theory has been a denial of all but technological predictions. To those who have a practical outlook in political affairs, loss of the predictive power of a scientific social theory is a matter of some urgency. Unlike doctrines of a metaphysical absolute, scientific historical explanation could not and need not give vast descrip-

[57]Such a view is not restricted to Marxist thinkers, as is shown by Gaston Bachelard's historical and psychoanalytical investigations in the philosophy of science, e.g. *L'Eau et les rêves* (Paris, new ed., 1947), *La Formation de l'esprit scientifique* (Paris 1947), *Le Matérialisme rationnel* (Paris, 1953), *La Poétique de l'espace* (Paris, 1957). Marxists and non-Marxists have written little to illumine this dialectical theme of the historically-relative status of objective (scientific) knowledge; but the theme is itself a scientific one, and a profound study of it would further and liberate science, particularly the sciences of man.

[58]As Herbert Feigl terms it, e.g. "Existential Hypotheses: Realistic vs. Phenomenalistic Interpretations," *Philosophy of Science* XVII (1950), 35-62.

[59]These expressions are from Winston Barnes, *op. cit.*, 34. The situation would be *less* clear if the phenomenalist theory of history were *more* convincing. See G. E. M. Anscombe's criticism "The Reality of the Past," *Philosophical Analysis* ed. Max Black, (Ithaca, 1950), and A. M. MacIver "Historical Explanation" *Logic and Language,* second series, ed. Antony Flew (Oxford, 1953) which concludes that "in history we may say that pure Idealism meets its Waterloo, because in history we cannot do without 'things in themselves,' and the problem has to be faced, how they are 'represented.'" We may substitute 'phenomenalism' for MacIver's 'Idealism' without distortion.

[60]It is positivism and conventionalist relativism, rather than dialectical materialism,

which support the public philosophy of Big Brother in George Orwell's political novel *1984*. Whenever a political regime undertakes to provide a theoretical defense of its manipulative distortions we see what subjectivist weakness in theory may legitimate in practical life, e.g. rewriting history. Thus, when the editors of the *Large Soviet Encyclopedia* instructed their subscribers to remove the old page about the late L. Beria in order to substitute not an objectively corrected page about Beria but a new discourse about the Bering Sea, they abandoned, *in social practice,* the Marxist idea of objective truth, and embraced relativism. The inability of positivist thinkers to cope with relativism in social theory is linked with their subjectivism; Max Horkheimer pointed to the "naive" espousal of relativism by such distinguished positivist thinkers as the sociologist Otto Neurath and the legal theorist Hans Kelsen, (whose political commitments were genuinely democratic), and he contrasted Mussolini's realistic appraisal of the ideologically subversive role of relativism. See Horkheimer, *op. cit.*, 33, where e.g. he cites Mussolini: "Aus dem Umstand, dass all Ideologien einander wert, nämlich alle miteinander blosse Fictionen sind, schliesst der moderne Relativist, dass jedermann das Recht hat, sich die seine zu machen, und ihr mit aller Energie, zu der er nur fähig ist, Geltung zu verschaffen," translated from "Relativismo e fascismo" *Diuturna* (Milano, 1924), 374. Orwell clarifies the philosophical argument by attributing to the secret police the anti-materialist view that "we make the laws of Nature" *1984* (Penguin edition, London, 1954), 213; but when the hero, Smith, engages in epistemological discussion of the grounds for his belief and argues that certain events did occur, (despite the destruction of documents and the rewriting of historical accounts), he cites memory as meaningful ground as well as evidential basis. Then, in the *positivist* situation of *1984,* Smith has surrendered, for his police interrogator, O'Brien, simply replies "I do not remember it," *ibid.*, 198, and Smith, after torture and hypnosis and consequent self-doubt, agrees. "Doublethink," Orwell's term for the doctrine that there is no truth beyond what is *present* to human sensations and human consciousness, is exaggerated and fanatical positivism. It is exaggerated and fanatical because it is an ideology for *manipulated* consciousness. It is theoretically possible because a normal and reasonable positivism cannot transcend normal consciousness, that is it cannot account, in its own terms, for the *practical* unanimity of sense perceptions; and this is due to its subjectivism. Existence, and human knowledge of it, differ: if philosophers do not make that distinction, they cannot repudiate the nightmare of *1984*. *Theoretical relativism permits practical cynicism.* (Hans Freistadt in a private communication first called my attention to Orwell in this connection; see his "Dialectical Materialism: a Further Discussion" *Phil. Sci.* XXIV (1957), 25-40; Orwell's own positivist attitude toward social problems conditioned his bleak pessimism in *1984;* "generalizations about social forces, social trends, and historic inevitabilities made him bristle with suspicion" and "turn for political explanations to absolute 'sadistic power-hunger,'" according to Isaac Deutscher, "*1984*—the Mysticism of Cruelty", *Heretics and Renegades* (London, 1955), 47f.

But may we challenge the above assertion (that the governing clique in such a total dictatorship is "fanatically positivist") because surely Orwell's Big Brother distinguished self-deception from objective reality? Is the massive public philosophy, Orwell's "collective solipsism," *op. cit.*, 214, an effect which is imposed by dictators who *act* as though they believe, who *pretend?* If so, then they are materialists whose ideological manipulations of public consciousness conform to an exaggerated and distorted dialectic, similar to what Aristotle long ago condemned as a sophistical dialectic. But not only Orwell's hero, Smith, succumbs; to Orwell it also seemed clear that O'Brien, the police intellectual, had the consistent rationality of the insane, namely that O'Brien believed his own evidence, and his own sophistry. Altogether it appears to matter little whether an actor shows a mask or his true face so long as the logic of the drama dominates his behavior and moulds his audience. The actor may be a dialectical cynic; the play is positivist. Perhaps the most subtle statement of political relativism and mythmakers is that of Georges Sorel, *De l'utilité du pragmatisme* (Paris, 1921).

tive generalizations which lack specific causal hypotheses about social evolution; nor could any such social generalization be applied without knowledge of explicit particular data. Insofar as similar characteristics prevail in different periods, such general causal laws are conceivable and confirmable. Compare this statement by the eminent empiricist, C. G. Hempel:

> . . . the sweeping assertion that economic (or geographic, or any other kind of) conditions 'determine' the development and change of all other aspects of human society, has explanatory value only insofar as it can be substantiated by explicit laws which state just what kind of change in human culture will regularly follow upon specific changes in the economic (geographic, etc.) conditions. Only the establishment of concrete laws can fill the general thesis with scientific content, make it amenable to empirical tests, and confer upon it an explanatory function. The elaboration of such laws with as much precision as possible seems clearly to be the direction in which progress in scientific explanation and understanding has to be sought.[61]

with a remark of Marx and Engels:

> The premises from which we begin are not arbitrary ones, not dogmas, but real premises from which abstraction can only be made in the imagination . . . (to) be verified in a purely empirical way.[62]

Unlike the natural sciences which can study generally *repeatable* occurrences, and even unlike those, such as geophysics, which study kinds of processes which are less frequently repeated, history is essentially dependent upon *comparative* studies. Comparison may be of events or characteristics which are separated in time or space.[63] Causal laws are *useful* on those occasions when the independent variables are subject to human influence; they are cognitively meaningful on many other occasions.

It was generally clear to Marxists and empiricists alike that the major features of historical cultures are largely independent of individual

[61]"The Function of General Laws in History," *Readings in Philosophical Analysis,* ed. H. Feigl and W. Sellars (New York, 1949), 459-471.

[62]*The German Ideology,* tr. by Roy Pascal (London and New York, 1939), 6f., from *Marx-Engels Gesamtausgabe* I, 5 (Berlin, 1932), 10.

[63]See the illuminating case studies in: Rushton Coulborn, ed., *Feudalism in History* (Princeton, 1956); Joseph Needham's comparison of a recurrent ideological phenomenon in different societies, "The Pattern of Nature-Mysticism and Empiricism in the Philosophy of Science: Third Century B.C. China, Tenth Century A.D. Arabia, and Seventeenth Century A.D. Europe," *Science, Medicine and History* II (Oxford, 1953), 362-388; Paul M. Sweezy *et. al., The Transition from Feudalism to Capitalism* (New York, 1954); F. J. Teggart, *Rome and China* (Berkeley, 1939); S. Yushkov's parallel analysis of several pre-feudal societies, "On the Question of the Pre-Feudal State," *Voprosy Istorii* (1946), no. 7; Edgar Zilsel, "Physics and the Problem of Historico-Sociological Laws," *Philosophy of Science* VIII (1941), 567-579. Extensive analysis of this approach is given in *Theory and Practice in Historical Study,* Social Science Research Council, Bull. LIV (New York, 1946) and *The Social Sciences in Historical Study,* Social Science Research Council, Bull. LXIV (New York, 1954).

desires, wills, and efforts, and that, on the contrary, human behavior (including conscious behavior) is, to a considerable extent, the consequence of factors outside consciousness. If science is interpreted to provide only efficient correlation of similar and repeated observations, then an objective and causal account of the history of thought[64] and a nonarbitrary theory of action are impossible. It was in this fashion that Lenin faced the extension of positivism into the Marxist political thinking of pre-revolutionary Russia.

6. When the century began, empiricism was largely phenomenalist; scientific phenomena were interpreted either as thoroughly subjective or as 'neutral.' Lenin's well-known critique of positivism[65] was motivated not only by his fear that phenomenalism would undermine the theoretical foundations of the Bolshevik movement, but also (to be sure, less immediately) by his concern that an incorrect account of scientific knowledge might distort research in both the natural and the social sciences. Interpreted as a retreat back from Hegel to Humean and Berkeleyan scepticism, Mach's positivism was thought to threaten the advanced intellectual achievements of bourgeois society. It seemed to Lenin that phenomenalism, if carried thoroughly into practice, could have but two results: either complete scepticism, with the result that knowledge of experience can provide no rational assistance to practical living; or supernatural theology, the abandonment of independent science. Hume himself had drawn the former conclusion from his pure empiricism, Berkeley the latter from his immaterialism.

Materialism and Empirio-Criticism is a polemic against *Studies in the Philosophy of Marxism*,[66] a collection of essays largely concerned with positivist reconstruction of the materialist approach to nature and society. Lenin considered positivism to be a masked and inconsistent form of subjective idealism, unable to unmask because the scientific practice of its exponents is materialist, unable to be consistent because the positivists so honestly try to make their epistemology faithful to

[64]Compare Teggart, *op. cit.*, where correlations lead to interrelations of spatially distant events, with Joseph Needham, *Science and Civilization in China*, I, II, and esp. III, sect. 19(k), (Cambridge, 1954, 1956, and 1959), where the application of Mill's methods to historical explanation is illustrated with respect to history of science, as temporally separate instances of similar types.

[65]V. I. Lenin, *Materialism and Empirio-Criticism*, Eng. tr. in *Selected Works*, XI (New York, 1943), 87-409, originally published in 1908.

[66]By A. A. Malinovski (A. Bogdanov), *et al.*, (St. Petersburg, 1908). The decisive appeal of Machism for the Bogdanov group lay in Mach's struggle for a monistic interpretation of scientific knowledge: to him every sort of dualism is a more or less hidden expression of fetishism and the replacement of fetishism in social relations (by means of revolution) must be prepared and accompanied by a "positivistic annihilation of all intellectual fetishes" (by means of a genuine philosophy of "scientific monism"). See the non-Marxist account in T. G. Masaryk, *The Spirit of Russia* II, Ch. 18, iii and iv (2nd ed., London and New York, 1955).

science. Likewise, Lenin was convinced that idealism in general, and subjectivism in particular, serve reactionary social ends, whereas materialism serves progressive goals. Unfortunately neither Lenin nor other Marxist scholars have furnished a comparative study of the history of the social relations of philosophy. The recent Marxist and non-Marxist literature indicates that this problem of the social functions of philosophy has no simple solution.[67] Thus, specific idealisms, specific materialisms and specific positivisms have certainly played their ideological roles, but it is clearly necessary that we be wary of generalizations about *Weltanschauungen* which cross cultures or epochs. At the very least, so-called 'world-views' are deceptively and only verbally similar attitudes which are abstracted for purposes of analysis from materially distinct situations.

If, for example, we consider empiricism, rationalism, and mysticism, three attitudes toward nature and society which are known to occur in quite different social settings, the variety of possible social roles which these three philosophic attitudes may play becomes evident.[68] At various junctures, rationalism has undermined superstition, empiricism has

[67]E.g. Georg Lukacs, *Goethe und seine Zeit* (Berne, 1947), and *Der junge Hegel* (Zürich, 1949); Jean-T. Desanti, *Introduction a l'histoire de la philosophie,* esp. part two, "Recherches a propos de Spinoza" (Paris, 1956); I. Luppol *et al., Spinoza in Soviet Philosophy,* ed. G. L. Kline (London and New York, 1954); Lewis S. Feuer, *Spinoza and the Rise of Liberalism* (Boston, 1958); Henri Lefebvre, *Diderot* (Paris, 1949) and *Descartes* (Paris, 1947); Ch. N. Momdshian, *Helvetius* (tr. from Russian, Berlin, 1958); Irving L. Horowitz, *Claude Helvetius* (New York, 1954); Valentin Asmus, "Emmanuel Kant," *Recherches Sovietiques* I (tr. from *Voprosy Filosofii,* 1954; Paris 1956) 129-155; I. Luppol, *Diderot* (Paris, 1936); Franz Mehring, *Zur Geschichte der Philosophie* (Berlin, 1931) *passim;* Franz Borkenau, *Der Uebergang vom feudalen zum bürgerlichen Weltbild* (Paris, 1934), and the critique by Henryk Grossmann, "Die gesellschaftlichen Grundlagen der mechanistischen Philosophie," *Zeitschrift für Sozialforschung* IV (1935), 161-231; Otto Bauer, "Das Weltbild des Kapitalismus," *Der lebendige Marxismus* (Kautsky Festgabe), ed. O. Jennssen (Jena, 1924), 407-464; Benjamin Farrington, *Greek Science* (London and Baltimore, 1954); George Thomson, *Studies in Ancient Greek Society,* II, *The First Philosophers* (London, 1955), and the critiques by F. M. Cornford, "The Marxist View of Ancient Philosophy," *The Unwritten Philosophy* (London, 1950), 117-137, and by Ludwig Edelstein, "Recent Trends in the Interpretation of Ancient Science," *J. Hist. Ideas* XIII (1952), 573-604, reprinted in *Roots of Scientific Thought,* ed. P. P. Wiener and A. Noland (New York, 1957), 90-121; Joseph Needham, *op. cit., passim;* Paul Landsberg, "Zur Soziologie der Erkenntnistheorie," *Schmollers Jahrbuch* (1931), 55; Paul Honigsheim, "Zur Soziologie der mittelalterlichen Scholastik (Die soziologische Bedeutung der nominalistischen Philosophie," *Hauptprobleme der Soziologie: Erinnerungsgabe für Max Weber,* II, ed. M. Palyi (Munich, 1923); Ernst Bloch, *Avicenna und die aristotelische Linke* (Berlin, 1952); Hermann Ley, *Studie zur Geschichte des Materialismus im Mittelalter,* (Berlin, 1957).

[68]See, e.g. Joseph Needham, *op. cit.,* and David Thomson, "Scientific Thought and Revolutionary Movements," *Impact of Science on Society* VI (1955), 3-29. The logical positivists early stressed the practical and progressive social role of empiricism throughout history. E.g. Hans Hahn praised Democritus, distinguished medieval Realists as

shaken dogma, mysticism has revolted against orthodoxy. At other times, rationalism has codified oppression, empiricism has sceptically ridiculed social re-construction, mysticism has led to a retreat from reality.

Even within the comparatively brief history of modern Europe, the ideological characteristics of these philosophic activities are complex. Furthermore, it is necessary to distinguish logical relations, which may link a theoretical philosophy with a practical social theory, from the (historically determined) causal relations, both antecedent and subsequent, of the theoretical philosophies of individual thinkers. These concrete relations may appear to be systematically illogical and incoherent. Lenin thought that *consistent* positivism would corrupt the hypothetical character of advanced physical theory[69] while encouraging the supernatural theological religion of established and reactionary churches. But, in fact, Machism certainly helped to stimulate both Einstein's constructive critique of orthodox physics and the anti-theological perspectives of the Vienna Circle.[70] Mach himself was an atheist and a socialist. On the other hand, Lenin documented his book with other witnesses, scientists and theologians alike, to the effect that Machism hindered acceptance of the atomic theory and fortified conservative theology. Although these effects were causal rather than logical, it is important to note that Lenin's critique did not as such depend upon a causal analysis of social functioning. While it was couched in tendentious language, it consisted mainly of an epistemological argument with historical references. It will be useful to expound the major part of his argument for several purposes: (1) his book, including his polemical references, has been the dominant text in subsequent philosophic publications in the Soviet Union and therefore it is a principal source for understanding the Soviet Marxist attitude toward modern empiricism;[71] (2) he summarizes, perhaps without deliberate intention, a half-century of reaction

"other-worldly" escapists and Nominalists as "this-worldly" progressive thinkers, and stressed the historical link between the emergence of British democracy and empirical "this-worldly" philosophy; see his *Ueberflüssige Wesenheiten,* (Vienna, 1929).

69Compare the discussion of "homocentric operationism" in Adolf Grünbaum, "Operationism and Relativity," *The Validation of Scientific Theories,* ed. Philipp Frank (Boston, 1957), 84-94.

70Einstein describes this, "Autobiographical Notes," in P. A. Schilpp (ed.) *Albert Einstein, Philosopher-Scientist* (Evanston, 1949), 21, 53, and *Physikalische Zeit.* XVII (1916), 101.

71A representative example is M. Mitin's recent lecture to a Soviet conference on philosophy of science, "Lenins Werk 'Materialismus und Empiriokritizismus'—eine starke ideologische Waffe zur Erkenntnis und Umgestaltung der Welt," German tr. in *Sowjetwiss., Gesellschaftswiss. Beiträge* (1959), 133-149 from *Kommunist* (Moscow, 1958, no. 14). The literature on Soviet Marxism is immense. Some helpful sources, with diverse vantage points, are I. Luppol, *Lenin und die Philosophie* (German translation from Russian, Berlin, 1929); Henri Lefebvre's exposition of Lenin's

to a purely empiricist approach to science; (3) his argument extends and elaborates both that reaction and the program of a sociological approach to ideas;[72] (4) an exposition of his analysis will make it possible to show, in the subsequent section, to how considerable an extent the Leninist criticisms of logical empiricism have been overcome by developments since the first decade of this century;[73] (5) the theme of countering epistemological and ontological subjectivism runs throughout *Materialism and Empirio-Criticism;* if this subjectivism remains today as only a trap for the empiricist philosophy of science rather than an essential presupposition, it will nevertheless be illuminating to see how deep the trap has been and might yet be.

7. We shall set forth Lenin's discussion as a set of cumulative theses. He maintains:

(1) that Berkeleyan immaterialism must be subjectivist, that a Divine Subject does not change the cognitive status of immaterialist notions;[74]

(2) that Hume carried the non-theological interpretations of subjective idealism to its proper end, solipsism; and drew the proper conclusions, scepticism, and/or obedience to custom;[75]

thought, *op. cit.;* Herbert Marcuse, *Soviet Marxism* (New York, 1958); Gustav Wetter, *op. cit.;* John Somerville, *Soviet Philosophy* (New York, 1946); and the collective work, *Osnovy marksistskoi filosofii (Fundamentals of Marxist Philosophy)* ed. F. V. Konstantinov (Moscow, 1958); see also B. Kedrow, "Lenin über die Beziehungen von Philosophie und Naturwissenschaft," *Sowjetwiss., Gessellschaftswiss. Beiträge,* (1959), Heft 3, 279-299 (trans. from Russian, *Kommunist,* 1958, No. 15).

[72]The sociological approach has excited hostility, among empiricist and positivist thinkers, especially those working in the social sciences; e.g. Hans Kelsen's systematic analysis of *The Communist Theory of Law* (London, 1955), 46, 81-88, 174-175, which contrasts with the same author's incisive sociological analysis of the idea of causality, *Society and Nature* (Chicago and London, 1948). Compare the exposition in Rudolf Schlesinger, *Soviet Legal Theory* (London and New York, 1945).

[73]Contemporary Marxists generally overlook the developments and changes of logical empiricism which will be clear to readers of this essay and indeed of this volume; for a typical Marxist essay which characteristically limits itself to logical positivist writings of the earliest period, see Waltraud Seidel-Höppner, "Zur Kritik der Auffassung des Positivismus über das Verhältnis von Philosophie und Naturwissenschaften," *Deutsche Zeitschrift für Philosophie* VI (1958), 708-731.

[74]Cf. Ingemar Hedenius, *Sensationalism and Theology in Berkeley's Philosophy* (Oxford and Uppsala, 1936).

[75]Hume also drew from his reflections an intense "philosophic melancholy," to be overcome by the unphilosophical zest of daily life; like Wittgenstein, he can be thought to abandon reasonable knowledge the closer he comes to the problems of life, and thereby to cling to the mystical where it is already strongest. The foundations of modern philosophy, in Lenin's view, show a continual struggle with irrationalist scepticism; a comprehensive summary of the relevant philosophical development to Hume is given by Richard Popkin, "The Sceptical Crisis and the Rise of Modern Philosophy," *Rev. Metaphysics* VII (1953), 133-151, 307-322, 499-510; the related struggle to achieve a materialist outlook has been widely recognized, e.g. Aram Vartanian, *Diderot and Descartes* (Princeton, 1953).

(3) that Kant offered desperate expedients in his attempt to save valid knowledge, such that, with no possibility of confirmation,

(a) the *objective* entities of the world are (metaphysically) isolated from any possibility of cognition, and

(b) *subjective* a priori absolute principles are required to supply the world's order.

But, at the same time,

(4) Kant's discussion of Hume's scepticism clarifies the active, ever-creative role of the mind. He was correct in his denial that we gain knowledge by a passive reception of sensations. He was wrong in his failure to link this mental activity with a bio-physical activity. "Idealism is a one-sided, exaggerated . . development . . . of one of the characteristic aspects or limits of knowledge into an absolute."[76]

Furthermore,

(5) Hume was correct in insisting that sensations are the primary source of knowledge. But their interpretation is the crucial issue:

(a) they may be taken as ultimate and hence as the main category of subjective sensationalism (in this interpretation we perceive sensations), or

(b) they may be explained as the result of varying interactions of percipient bodies and other entities,[77] and hence as the main data of objective sensationalism, or materialism (in this interpretation we perceive *through* sensations).

Lenin holds that,

(6) this alternation is exhaustive, and, hence, post-Kantian theories of knowledge are often to be suspected of concealing subjectivist reductions by verbally deceptive accounts of the role of sensations. As such accounts, he lists: Mach's doctrine of "neutral elements" and his logical construction of scientific entities as complexes of sensations; Avenarius's (and Fichte's) "coordination" of self and not-self as components of inexplicable experience; Mill's definition of matter, which was adopted by Pearson as the doctrine of sense-impressions.

(7) Subjective idealism in science may lead in other domains to the acceptance of doctrines for which empirical tests are irrelevant, for intersubjective agreements about unconfirmable doctrines have been painfully frequent. Thus subjectivism may lead to the promulgation of

[76] V. I. Lenin, "On Dialectics," *op. cit.*, 84.

[77] This explanation was a program. Lenin wrote of it: "Materialism clearly formulates the as yet unsolved problem and thereby stimulates the attempt to solve it, to undertake further experimental investigation. Machism . . . sidetracks it." *Op. cit.*, 113.

religious cosmologies and leave the door open to superstition.[78] Less directly,

(8) subjectivist positivism prepares for such illusory beliefs, as is shown by honest religious thinkers[79] and by the positivists' epistemologically neutral attitude toward religious beliefs. Moreover,

(9) subjectivism strikes into the heart of scientific knowledge itself, for its advocates confuse *objective* knowledge with *absolute* knowledge;[80]

(10) it mistakenly identifies objective truth with the ever-corrigible criteria for judging the truth or falsity of statements, that is, it confuses

[78]It goes without saying that Lenin saw the general social role of religion as a pernicious one. But the Marxist attitude toward religion is not a simple hostility to an alleged cognitive illusion, as that of the early logical positivists tended to be. For the positivist attitude A. J. Ayer, *Language, Truth and Logic* (London, 1936), ch. 6; Rudolf Carnap, *Scheinprobleme in der Philosophie* (Berlin, 1928), and *Von Gott und Seele* (lecture to Verein Ernst Mach, June, 1929); and Hans Hahn, *et al., Wissenschaftliche Weltauffassung* (Vienna, 1929). For the Marxist position, see Karl Marx, *Kritik des Hegelschen Staatsrechts* in *Marx-Engels Gesamtausgabe* I/1/1 (Berlin, 1927; in T. B. Bottomore's translation, *op. cit.*, 26-27) and the Christian studies by Alasdair MacIntyre, *Marxism an Interpretation* (London, 1953); Henri Chambre, *Le Marxisme en Union Soviétique* (Paris, 1955); and J. Y. Calvez, *op. cit.*, Parts I and V. Thus Chambre: "Marxist atheism does not believe in God but in man; it does not battle with gods but with idols, fetishes, i.e. it disputes the supremacy of things over men" *op. cit.*, 334. J. Miller adds, in his review of Chambre's book, that "if all gods are idols, the problem of the nature of idol-producing thought becomes central to intellectual work; and leads on to the larger problem of the common relation of all thinking to that which is thought about." *Soviet Studies* VIII (1957), 255. An intermediate position between Marxist and empiricist critiques of religion was given by the positivists Hans Hahn, *Überflüssige Wesenheiten* (Vienna, 1929), and Otto Neurath, *Empirische Soziologie* (Vienna, 1931). See also Max Adler, "Über den kritischen Begriff der Religion," *Festschrift für Wilhelm Jerusalem* (Vienna, 1915), 3-46; Charles Hainchelin, *Les Origines de la religion* (new ed., Paris, 1955); Christopher Caudwell, "The Breath of Discontent: a Study in Bourgeois Religion," *Further Studies in a Dying Culture* (London and New York, 1949), 15-76; and the basic collection of Marx and Engels, *On Religion* (Moscow, 1957, and London 1958).

[79]Jacques Maritain praised the positivist movement because it was able "to disontologize science" (cited by Philipp Frank, *Modern Science and its Philosophy,* Cambridge, 1949, 175). See also James Ward, *Naturalism and Agnosticism* (4th ed., London, 1955); Pierre Duhem's views on the "autonomy" of science and religion, "Physics of a Believer" *Annales de Phil. chrétienne* IV/1 (1905), 44, 133 as translated by P. P. Wiener in appendix to *The Aim and Structure of Physical Theory* (Princeton, 1954), 273-311; Général Vouillemin, *Science et Philosophie* (Paris, 1945), ch. 13. Two other viewpoints are of interest: a recent scholastic defense of neo-Kantianism and Machian positivism by Gavin Ardley, *Aquinas and Kant* (London, 1950); and the persuasive comparison of Wittgenstein (in the *Tractatus)* with the theologian Rudolf Otto (in *The Idea of the Holy)* by Thomas McPherson, "Religion as the Inexpressible," *New Essays in Philosophical Theology,* ed. A. Flew and A. MacIntyre (London, 1955), 131-143.

[80]See, in Neurath's last essay: "When other people speak of 'facts,' the 'truth' of which is 'objective' or 'absolute,' Logical Empiricists speak of accepted protocol-statements as a basis of further discussion" in "Prediction and Induction," *Analysis* III (1946), 5.

active perception by men with meaningful reference of concepts;

(11) it reduces objectivity either to inexplicable and surd subjectivity, or

(12) to a culturally relative "collective experience" which, however, itself would be explicable only by an objectivist account of cultural history.

(13) Thus, for Lenin, even the formation of concepts and theories is affected, since a consistently subjectivist sensationalism requires of scientific ideas that they be reducible to perceptions (Mach), or mental projections (Avenarius), or conscious apprehensions (Fichte), or direct perceptions (Berkeley).

(14) In its search for certainty, subjectivism has been known to combine ultimate scepticism about ordinary reliability with an absolute faith in either metaphysical a priori categories or positive sense-data, (or both).

(15) With its program for reductive definition, subjectivism arbitrarily identifies meaning with verification, and hence precludes an objective account of the semantic relation of idea and reference; thus semantics is interpreted in a subjectivist manner, and

(16) this tends to undermine the possibility of a socio-biological explanation of the cognitive process. Yet such explanations are scientifically feasible in sociological and historical studies of different cultures and of the history of ideas, as well as in the physiological investigation of perception. Similarly,

(17) subjectivism's logical analysis converts causality into a mere, though convenient, habit of thought, offering no account of the ground for such convenience, although paradoxically encouraging a materialist physiological "causal" account of habit formation. Thus, while denying objective status to the causal connections between events, subjectivism offers no alternative explanation for the highly confirmed concrete regularities which have been observed in nature. Instead, it suggests with Kant, and apparently counter to empiricism itself, that causality is abstract, an epistemological necessity rather than a general factual relation.[81] In this manner,

[81]Lenin was concerned with the *objective* character of causal matter-of-fact relations. 'Universality,' if joined with a concept of the genidentity of persistent entities would be sufficient for *this* purpose; he might well have deleted 'necessity' from his notion of 'physical necessity' for what he described was interaction according to natural laws and objective properties. Nevertheless the general purposes of using causal descriptions seem to require 'necessity.' Marxist discussion of philosophical categories and empiricist discussion of dispositions and modal logic deserve careful comparison. Arthur Pap correctly insisted on the importance of discerning "universal propositions that are but *accidental*" in "Disposition Concepts and Extensional Logic," *Minn. Studies in the Phil. of Sci.* II (Minneapolis, 1958), 204.

The defence of Mach against Lenin, offered by Philipp Frank in *Das Kausalgesetz und seine Grenzen* (Vienna, 1932), esp. ch. x/13-14, alleges that the confusion of

(18) sceptical subjectivism discourages rational inquiry into internal (causal) relations of development, whether of nations or of men or of other objects of scientific study, *or of the process of inquiry;* that is, it isolates events, preferring to "account" for their interrelations and development by wholly inexplicable relations of conjunction and disjunction.[82] Therefore, and in particular,

(19) it fails to understand the central issue of epistemology, the *acquiring* of knowledge, itself a natural phenomenon to be investigated causally. What is known at one stage of science was not yet known at an earlier stage; and from this, Lenin concludes that a *scientific* epistemology would be able to treat the transformation relations of unknown to known. Further, this transformation, if fully accepted, can only be explained by a materialist theory of external objects that are perceptually known under circumstances which a scientific philosopher should be at pains to understand.[83] Therefore philosophy of science is a theory of perception, of instruments, and of measurements, as well as of objects known.

(20) The contrary view, that scientific entities are constructions from

mechanism and objectivity is avoided in a correct reading of Mach, but Lenin's charge of *reductive* subjectivism is not rebutted. Both here and in *Modern Science and Its Philosophy* (Cambridge, Mass., 1949), Frank correctly notes many points of agreement of dialectical materialist and logical empiricist requirements upon scientific knowledge.

[82]See Hans Reichenbach, *Nomological Statements and Admissible Operations* (Amsterdam, 1954), for a similar criticism.

[83]Lenin's own use of the metaphor of reflection unfortunately conceals rather than illuminates many of the problems involved in the materialist doctrine of perception and of semantics in general. It has been developed somewhat by Adam Schaff, *op. cit.*, P. Dosev (T. Pavlov) *The Theory of Reflection: Studies in the Theory of Knowledge of Dialectical Materialism* (in Russian, Moscow and Leningrad, 1936), and Roger Garaudy, *op. cit.* Most recent Marxist attempts to use the theory of reflection have invoked the current physiological theories, e.g. Assen Kisselintschew, *Die marxistisch-leninistische Widerspiegelungstheorie und die Lehre I. P. Pavlovs von der höheren Nerventätigkeit* (tr. from Bulgarian; Berlin, 1957; original ed., Sofia, 1954). But there is also a recent essay along logical and historical lines by Johannes H. Horn, *Widerspiegelung und Begriff* (Berlin, 1958) which deserves serious attention. G. A. Paul showed that the idea of, say, mirror reflection was similar to perception only in the case of indirect comparison of image with object, but his conclusion that this weakens the metaphorical strength seems to forget that Lenin wrote within an objectivist context; thus indirect (or projective) comparison was all that Lenin needed, as Schaff suggests, although it is true that this must not be thought to be the merely symbolic relation which Plekhanov suggested by his theory of hieroglyphics. See G. A. Paul, "Lenin's Theory of Perception," *Philosophy and Analysis*, ed. Margaret Macdonald (Oxford, 1954), 278-286. An interesting explication of Lenin's "theory of reflection" is given by Henri Lefebvre, *Pour connaître la penseé de Lénine* (Paris, 1957), 133-140; Lenin's text is supplemented in his reading notes which have been published posthumously as *Aus dem philosophischen Nachlass* (2nd German ed., Berlin, 1949) and in another selection as *Cahiers Philosophiques* (Paris, 1955), wherein the complexity of the reflective process is especially noted in his "Notes sur la métaphysique d'Aristote." Cf. Maurice Merleau-Ponty's criticism of Leninist oversimplification in *Les Aventures de la dialectique* (Paris, 1955), ch. 3.

known sense-data, gives no account of the acquisition of knowledge even if it does grasp, in an exaggerated manner, the central importance of sensuous activity in that acquisition.

(21) Now it seems that the idea of objective entities, independent of cognitive activity, is necessary to articulate cognition. If so, even a successful account of scientific objects *as perceived,* carried out by means of logical constructions out of sense-data, must be inadequate, and thus

(22) the sense-data construction must reject any but a momentary and limited notion of a single, clear, atomic sensation.

(23) Since the positivists have always maintained their interest in empirical science, Lenin thought that they have practiced objectively and philosophized subjectively, a muddling and inconsistent eclecticism being the result. In the process, many silly doctrines have been put forth, Avenarius' brainless thought, Willy's fellowship with worms, Mach's proposed linkage of particular sensations with particular processes of the brain which in turn is a complex of sensations.[84] Indeed, in Lenin's judgment, the key to the persistent stream of inconsistencies and inadequacies in a positivism which seeks a scientific basis is its subjectivism; for subjectivism eventually leads back to Berkeley and Hume and thence to Diderot's delightfully insane piano.[85] Finally,

(24) positivism endangers the social sciences directly, even while Machist thinkers assert that their view is compatible with affirmation of some of the theses of historical materialism. Lenin argued that a consistent positivism, in historical investigations, must abandon the use of causal reasoning as metaphysical, and the use of functional descriptive terms, such as 'capitalist' and 'worker,' as Platonic ontology;[86] abandon the discovery of specifically social characteristics as neglect of the individual; and consider any partisan social theory as hostile to the program of validating scientific generalizations by impersonally observed social facts.[87]

(25) On the other hand, Lenin recognized that individual positivists generally take a liberal attitude toward human betterment, favoring a harmonious society, seeking to avoid instability and violence, and wishing to increase freedom in individual and social life, sympathizing with the unfortunate, and deploring human exploitation. But from Lenin's

84Lenin, *op. cit.,* 110, 146.

85"That moment of insanity when (Diderot's) sentient piano imagined that it was the only piano in the world, and that the whole harmony of the universe resided within it," cited in Lenin, *op. cit.,* 105. This anticipates a twentieth-century notion. Thus, R. E. Money-Kyrle discusses the relation of subjectivism to insanity, infancy and the unconscious in "The World of the Unconscious and the World of Commonsense," *Brit. J. Phil. Sci.* VII (1956), 86-96.

86See J. O. Urmson, *op. cit.,* 151-153, for an analytic discussion of the term 'nation.'

87See below, note 122.

cognitivist view of the dialectic of ethics and sociology, these views run the danger of becoming *ineffective,* because they are not grounded in scientific knowledge. Nor do they cohere with the subjectivist epistemology of positivism for they presume the possibility of a science of social reality, existing objectively though known only relatively.

(26) Just as positivism in physics reduces 'physical reality' to those sensations in consciousness which may be grouped together as "inanimate" types, so positivism in sociology reduces 'social reality' to a basis of "social" types of consciousness. In addition to being a philosophical principle of analyzing social scientific statements, this is an empirical hypothesis about social reality, and moreover, it is as highly disconfirmed as its physical counterpart. Social science proceeds from the study of concrete men in objective social and natural circumstances; it does not begin with the study of social consciousness, neither the consciousness of the men whose society is being studied, nor the consciousness of the investigator himself. Both are derivative, and to be explained by a historical materialist sociology.

(27) Lenin might sum up his argument in this way: Positivism is a philosophy of untroubled, passive, isolated and fixed, atomic facts; it is false to the world of troubled, active, interrelated and developing natural entities. It is mechanically true to the stable aspects of society; it makes no sense of the unstable aspects.

8. We can formulate the critique of subjectivist sensations in social terms. Thus, we might grant that logical empiricism is faithful to modern natural science, but we assert that this itself might be questioned as incomplete. Possibly the tension of reason and unreason in industrial society is based on the wide gap between a rational approach to and mastery of the productive process as a means, and an irrational approach to the human life of mass society, wherein means are treated as ends.[88] If this is so, the tension and conflict can be thought to be revealed in a disparity between science and ideology. Insofar as science may be distinguished from its philosophic interpretations, social situations may be reflected in the latter, physical reality in the former, each with accuracy. Related conceptual correlations suggest themselves. Technical mastery in production side by side with the uncertainty of general happiness is reflected in the incompatibility of body and mind. The isolated and alienated individual in the crowd is reflected in a monadic philosophy of isolated and externally related atomic entities. Successively the search for philosophical certainty has led from a naive objective and mechanical materialism to scepticism, and then from scepticism to the subjective idealist certainty of sense-data. In turn, due to the technology

[88] This explanation would be the philosophical approach to socialist theory, and it would continue to play such a role in a socialist society too.

of mass production and the social relations of mass consumption, modern society seeks agreement and certainty in mass ideologies. As a result, the empiricist tradition, flirting with hypothetical or Humean solipsism, comes under the suspicion of deleting from its interpretive account of the success of the natural sciences certain of their virtues. For whatever their relative limitations in completeness and in scope, the natural sciences have obtained a large measure of *objective* as well as useful truth about the behavior and possible developments of inanimate and animate nature. Scientific information is the result of a special kind of confrontation with an unknown but indisputable and generally unavoidable external reality.[89] In passing from ignorance to knowledge, in whatever way this may have been stimulated from time to time,[90] man acts and reacts, remembers, analyzes, analogizes and imagines; he perceives, and extends his organs of perception, artificially and socially. But the transition from ignorance to knowledge can only be comprehended if the primary epistemological assumption is that of the objective existence of the entities with which cognition deals. And, further, this transition can be encountered only if the secondary assumption is that of an existence which is categorically different from the cognitive process itself. The source and basis of knowledge for both materialism and empiricism are socially active and biologically extended utilizations of sensations, coordinated by the neurological organs of behavior. But only materialism can say so.

V. *Empirical Materialism*

1. One effect of Lenin's discussion of positivism has been the interminable search for subjectivism in the Marxists' scrutiny of contemporary philosophy and in their self-criticism.[91] The relative lack of development of Lenin's philosophical programme, and the harsh dogmatism of so many re-statements of his opinions and arguments, understandably have led to a continued lack of productive cooperation and constructive criticism between the two groups of philosophers.

But, in this period, new surges of pessimism, even nihilism, both

[89]By 'matter,' Lenin meant, in his many different ways of saying it, a principle of objectivity, providing a reliable basis of meaningful external reference. See Abraham Edel, "Interpretation and the Selection of Categories," *op. cit.,* esp. 87.

[90]For a sketch of the possible cultural interactions, see R. S. Cohen, "Alternative Interpretations of the History of Science," *Validation of Scientific Theories,* ed. Philipp Frank (Boston, 1956).

[91]Repeatedly Marxists have stressed the hypothetical (non-observational) aspect of social science as well as of physical science. This is one theme of Mao Tse-Tung's two philosophical essays, "On Practice" and "On Contradiction," *Selected Works* I (Yenan, 1937; English tr., London, 1954), 282-297 and *ibid.,* II, 13-53, and his later exhortation against dogmatic inertia. "Reform our Study," *ibid.,* IV (Yenan, 1941; English tr., London, 1954), 12-20.

atheist and theological, have been evident, accompanied in the latter case by argued rejections both of scientific method and of the industrial culture in which it has been embedded. Subtle, and informed by scientific knowledge, the new theological orthodoxy has attacked the notion of a complete naturalistic outlook more persuasively than the older metaphysical theologies and idealistic social theories of Central and Eastern Europe, against which both Marxists and positivists have separately battled. The new anti-science has taken as its target a "scientific philosophy," which is compounded of mechanistic metaphysics and neo-positivist epistemology. Neither dialectic nor empiricism will recognize itself in this compound. This attack certainly contains a persistently valuable religious protest against the inhumanity of a mechanized and atomized society; but it is often associated with a revival of irrationalism. Previous social protests by religious and philosophical idealism were unrealistically Utopian, but nevertheless they were realistic about what they criticized, and rational in how they argued.[92] Today, however, the serious religious protest often rejects critical reason along with the rest of science, identifying the social ills of the present with rationalized techniques of mass production and mass manipulation. Hence the dominant religious protest of today reflects four intellectually retrogressive tendencies: (1) sometimes merely and hopefully a search for a simpler mode of human relations; (2) at other times a retreat from all cognitive and causal discussion of human affairs; (3) frequently an insistence on the need for an ultimate authority in matters of social policy and individual behavior; and (4) distrust of science just where empirical realism and critical reasoning are so radically needed.

It has become customary to contrast man's conquest of nature with the anxiety of man's society; but the conquest of nature which is an achievement of reason, is still incompletely fulfilled because the social order is the result of unreason. In its attempt to bring about a total eclipse of reason[93] present day theological anti-science strengthens the force of those very irrational social relations which it deplores.[94] There is little doubt that those who are guided by super-naturalistic faith characterize naturalistic positivists and naturalistic materialists *alike* as believers in a corrupted religion of scientism and humanism.

We may ask whether so technical a philosophy as empiricism can also

[92]Hence it is dangerous, even for a naturalist, to become totally and abstractly anti-metaphysical.

[93]The phrase is Max Horkheimer's. See *Eclipse of Reason* (New York, 1947), ch. 2, which is, unfortunately, less accurate in its account of contemporary empiricism than of other trends of thought.

[94]This is a problem even for such incisive and self-perceptive authors as Paul Tillich, *The Protestant Era* (Chicago, 1946); D. M. Mackinnon, ed., *op. cit;* and A. C. MacIntyre, *op. cit.*

be a philosophy of scientific humanism. Has it matured beyond scepticism and subjectivism, and the myopic search for certainty? Is empiricist social theory sufficiently free of devotion to the facts of appearance so that it can undertake a developmental analysis of social-historical reality? If not, then the clash of dialectic and empiricism will persist, for then empiricism will simultaneously affirm scientific humanism but reject the application of critical reason to social nature and human potentialities.

But the answers are no longer negative. And, despite Marxist and other critics, they never were wholly negative. At least since 1925, an objectivist realism has been an alternative to phenomenalist positivism. From the early twenties, Frank, Neurath, and Russell have stressed the social nature of scientific inquiry. Repeatedly Carnap, Hempel, Ayer, and others have criticized the sceptical sterility of successive positivist criteria for meaning. Despite Poincaré's own misleading statements on the conventional grounds for scientific theories, it is on the basis of his writings and of the pioneer studies of Reichenbach and Schlick that empiricists have worked at the vital task of disentangling the factual from the stipulational components of science. We have repeatedly pointed to subjectivist tendencies within empiricism and to the dangers these may entail. But is it true that empiricists have ever wholly succumbed to these tendencies whether temporarily or permanently?

2. Perhaps a very brief history of Carnap's development will clarify this question.

Traditional philosophies rest upon diverse conceptions of the interdependent relations among the entities of the world, as much as upon diverse conceptions of the entities themselves. To these conceptions empiricism has been hostile. At first, Carnap accepted the Humean arguments, that experience reveals no such dependent relations (and hence none can be known), and that experience provides us with a deeply individuated reality (which must therefore be treated by the method of analysis into simple elements).

Initially a positivist, Carnap wrote *Der logische Aufbau der Welt* with subjectivist notions, although both the undefined intuitive idea of objective similarity, and the author's avowal that the whole scheme was at most a hypothetical or methodical use of solipsistic analysis, showed the incomplete nature of his subjectivism.[95]

Reminiscent of earlier empiricist discussions, the solipsist language in Carnap's essay was inadequate to account for practical science and, *a fortiori*, for practical life. One could not see how it accounted for, or

[95]There is also an objective idealist component in Carnap's functionalization of reality; thus "The concept and its object are identical," *Der logische Aufbau der Welt*, 6.

even gave meaning to, the intersubjective character of scientific entities; for the status of the temporally and spatially remote; for the character of inductive inference; for the distinction between an experimental device and the entity thereby explored. Moreover, in the customary empiricist search for a secure basis, the *Logische Aufbau* obscured the process of perception; the acquisition of observations and the enunciation of observation-statements, were the least examined of the several stages of scientific inquiry. Represented by observation-statements, the given facts were passively taken, assumed to be simple, and granted the status of the most empirical of all categories, brute contingency.[96] All inroads upon the existential unassailability of these sensed phenomena were repudiated, whether those of Hegel or Kant, Condillac or Berkeley. While these philosophers were dismissed for holding empirically (i.e. observationally) unverifiable views critical of the given observed nature of things, empirical reconsideration of perception as a basis for scientific knowledge was ignored or postponed. In this way, *natural*-scientific appraisals of the observational basis of knowledge was undermined: as a factual enterprise, its independence was so limited by the imposition of epistemological assumptions that Carnap subsequently expressed the hope that modern empiricism had not unduly restricted the formation of concepts.[97] Similarly, *socio*-scientific appraisals of the status of the observational basis were, with a few hopeful acknowledgments of the need for a sociology of knowledge, neglected.

These and other criticisms gradually became apparent. In the light of continuing discussion with his colleagues, Carnap changed his views considerably. Empiricists have always regarded their achievements as partial, in the same sense that a scientific theory may be adequate to account for a portion of the materials at hand but quite inappropriate for the whole, or for observations yet to come. It is enlightening to read the critical accounts of these discussions, by Ayer, Hempel, Feigl and others, in this volume and elsewhere. To those who criticized *ab extra* however, it must have seemed strange that so long a time was needed to appreciate such fundamental matters as the limitations upon meaning-explication of pure syntax; the *cul-de-sac* of any solipsist or neo-solipsist approach; the a priori character of the choice of a set of basic sentences; the inadequate and arbitrary nature of truth by coherence with conventional basic sentences; the metaphysical aspects of the verification theory; the ineradicable presence of potentialities and dispositions in any description of nature; the frailty of an outlook which came to be a pro-

96See Carnap "Die alte und die neue Logik," *Erkenntnis* I (1930), esp. 23f.

97Rudolf Carnap, "The Methodological Character of Theoretical Concepts," *Minn. Studies Phil. Sci.*, I (Minneapolis, 1956), 70.

gram for a proposal for a theory of meaning.[98] Herbert Feigl[99] recognizes that verification ("confirmability in principle") is a way to specify a necessary (and sufficient) condition for meaning, and that meaning is not identical with degree of specification of meaning; and he goes on to admit that the various empiricist criteria for meaning are pragmatic proposals, which "cannot be validated," and which, indeed, can only exclude from discussion those "hypotheses which are proof against disproof." Thus the empiricist doctrine reaches a formulation with which all scientific thinkers can agree; and thereby it abandons any detailed analysis of metaphysical and theological hypotheses, presumably to scientific analysis by other critical doctrines which can be drawn from the sociology of religion as well as from physical cosmology. Indeed, Feigl speaks of a meaningful (although false) "natural theology." In this way logical empiricism loses its distinctive (and phenomenalistic) radicalism but gains a scientific realism that recognizes that it may talk about the universe as well as about observations without attributing "unanswerable problems or unsolvable riddles" to the universe.

Carnap, at any rate, has recognized these and other difficulties, because of those qualities which are evident throughout his writings: a vigorous common sense which seems to smile at all these tongue-in-cheek attempts to reconstruct the world by various unbelievable (i.e. merely methodological) hypotheses; an attentive desire to comprehend the facts and theories of contemporary science; an uncompromising repudiation of irrational and authoritarian dogma; both personal and impersonal modesty, recognizing that the logic of science merely clarifies and never reveals factual affairs, while the factual sciences are ever to be corrected and extended; a faith that these corrigible sciences nevertheless possess partially true and wholly respectable knowledge.

3. The materialist trend of Carnap's views is open to examination on three main questions: the nature of truth, the theory of knowledge, and the status of scientific entities. In each case, subjective idealist views can be compared with successive stages of logical empiricism.

In Carnap's early investigation of theories of space,[100] he speaks of immediately intuited essences along with empirically furnished knowledge. Within a few years, he had begun his distinguished career as a de-

[98]C. G. Hempel, "Problems and Changes in the Empiricist Criterion of Meaning," *Rev. Int. de Phil.* IV (1950), 41-63, and A. J. Ayer, *Language, Truth and Logic* (2nd ed. London, 1946), discuss the non-cognitive nature of this criterion but, on grounds of explicatory efficiency with respect to scientific usage, they would reject the charge of frailty.

[99]"Some Major Issues and Developments in the Philosophy of Science of Logical Empiricism," *Proc. 1954 Int. Cong. Phil. Sci.* (Neuchâtel, 1955), and *Minn. Studies Phil. Sci.* I, *op. cit*, 3-37.

[100]*Der Raum, op. cit.*

fender of a thoroughly empirical knowledge, which is open to qualified observers by rationally specifiable procedures. But in the phenomenological empiricism of 1928, he seeks verifications by reductions to sense data which have the same direct, certain and intuitive character as Husserl's intentions.[101] By 1931, Carnap erected the structure of scientific theories on a contingent foundation of similarly intuited (but not necessarily sensationist) protocols, contingent in the sense that the primitive protocols are records of direct experience[102] for which empirical or logical justification is neither needed nor possible. Direct experience was interpreted through observation-statements, either as Machian sense-data, or as phenomenal *Gestalten,* or as naively perceived physical objects. Each provides a different language of science. At that time, the empiricist could give no method for identifying protocols beyond the ambiguous notion of direct immediacy. The theory held that the meaning of a statement was given by the mode of certifying or confirming its truth. Subjectivism was therefore persistent, not only because truth was, at first, coherence with phenomenal properties, and then coherence with conventionally basic thing-sentences, but also because the empiricists steadily maintained with Schlick that the *central* idea of the verification theory was that the meaning of a statement is given by the mode of its verification (falsification, confirmation. . . .) *in experience.*

Carnap's liberalized formulation of 1936, *Testability and Meaning,* presented the criterion of confirmation merely as a test in terms of observation predicates of an empiricist language rather than as an equivalence, but again the primitive terms of that language were subject to conventional choice. The unsatisfactory conventional nature of the attempts to give syntactical rules for relating meaningful statements to an empirically guaranteed base came out clearly whenever genuine disagreement about protocols was envisaged. In such a situation, logical syntax could only ensure that the differing scholars would speak different and mutually incomprehensible languages.[103] It was thus only our good

101Marvin Farber discusses this in "Experience and Subjectivism," *Philosophy for the Future,* (New York, 1949), 591-632.

102Rudolf Carnap, *The Unity of Science* (London, 1934), 42.

103When world outlooks which have cognitive status are involved, such basic disagreements could only be eliminated provided the observers have a common epistemological ground. But this is what is denied by a theory of class ideology. Whether the common biological component of different observers' cognitions is a consistent source for basic agreement is perhaps to be answered affirmatively even by dialectic, since species-wide behavior is relatively invariant. But to this, dialectic adds the hypothesis that *basic* agreement, on those matters which have been socially divisive in the past, can be achieved only in a social order which is non-exploitative, free from social classes and class-ideological differences. For an elementary discussion, see R. S. Cohen, "On the Marxist Philosophy of Education," in *Modern Philosophies and Education,* ed. Nelson B. Henry (Chicago, 1955), esp. 184-192.

historical fortune that this situation has not arisen, at any rate not in the natural sciences. An objective or materialist view of history could explain this social fact, for it is due to cultural determination of scientific endeavors and to biologically determined similarity of scientists' perceptions. A subjectivist view, or a pseudo-objective conventionalist view, leaves such inter-subjective agreement to chance, or simply treats it as axiomatic.

Thus, while some form of relativist conventionalism remained after the discussions of 1936,[104] it was true, at any rate, that the classic stumbling block of natural powers and natural dispositions seemed to have eliminated any thoroughly phenomenalist interpretation of empirical science.[105] The usual subjunctive mood itself suggests this, for it is an unresolved form of compromise between subjectivity and objectivity. It seemed that no empiricist really believed in the possibility of ultimate disagreement about protocols, at least not in natural science or in behaviorist psychology, and, on the other hand, it was generally known that conventional components are present in every formal means for expressing factual knowledge. Therefore, while the attack on complete relativism or purely conventional definition awaited the development of a semantic theory, the *extended* conception of physicalism revived the possibility of including an objective reference in the empiricist account of scientific knowledge. Physicalism was not *merely* an improved mode of speaking in a materialistic manner, despite what Carnap and his Marxist critics have said.[106] It may be seen as Neurath's attempt to *express* the material foundation of knowledge, for the persistent recognition that he and Carnap paid to the natural fact of socially intersubjective agreement is one root of their anti-conventional, anti-phenomenalist attitude. The function of intersubjective agreement in actual life is to provide agreement about the *grounds* for judgments. In their use of a physicalist lan-

[104]Chiefly in this very complex field of the historical sociology of science, and of the sociology of cognition (presumably part of descriptive pragmatics,). See, e.g. Paul Landsberg, *op. cit.*, and Edgar Zilsel, *The Sociological Roots of Science*, ed. R. S. Cohen (London, to be published).

[105]R. J. Spilsbury, "Dispositions and Phenomenalism," *Mind* LXII (1953), 339-354. Cf. C. G. Hempel's discussion of the abandonment of translatability, *ibid.*, and his *Fundamentals of Concept Formation in Empirical Science* (Chicago, 1952), Sec. 6-8. And Nelson Goodman's conventionalist discussion focuses upon the central question "when are two things of the same kind?" in his *Fact, Fiction and Forecast* (London, 1954), 47.

[106]*The Unity of Science* (London, 1934), ch. 4; Maurice Cornforth, *Science vs. Idealism* (rev. ed., London, 1955), 10f. See Herbert Feigl (this volume) for the detailed development of physicalism. Compare Carnap's attitude toward materialism as a method with Pavlov's celebrated remark: "I am neither a materialist nor an idealist; I am a monist, or, if one must commit oneself, a methodological materialist" (cited by Wetter, *op. cit.*, from F. P. Mayorov, "On the World-outlook of I. P. Pavlov," *Vestnik Akad. Nauk,* (1936), 17).

guage, sceptical observers show each other their common standard for confirmation; this can be recognized without gratuitously adding that these are exhaustive standards for meaning as well.[107] For that ignores the very same social facts which provide the intersubjective agreement with which physicalism begins; it is not an agreement of behavioristically defined men, but rather of (introspectively) conscious observers, not objects of study but subjects who engage in inquiry.

At first physicalists seemed to exaggerate the possibilities of reducing all meanings to definitions or reductions in terms of the purely physical observation-meanings of individual space-time attributes. Thereby physicalism gave to the thesis of the unity of science an unduly narrow perspective. But this was unnecessary. Theoretical terms can be introduced in a less restrictive manner while preserving the physicalist confirmation basis.[108] When the physicalist thesis was propounded, Carnap might have been led to investigate alternative explanations of the intersubjective character of scientific knowledge, perhaps to formulate a reconstruction of such classical epistemologies as those of Aristotle, Spinoza, and Hegel. More likely, he might have been led to empirical considerations of a descriptive pragmatic, for which objectivity would be prior, both in theory and in fact, to intersubjectivity (as well as to the causes of subjective awareness) and hence also an axiom for cognitive communication via scientific language.

4. This did not happen. Carnap took intersubjectivity as a fortunately valid axiom rather than as a scientific and epistemological problem. Since his attendant physicalist theory of space-time properties need *not* be interpreted subjectively,[109] Carnap's abandonment of pure syntax and his fusion of physicalism with a semantic interpretation of truth came under different criticism, the charge of reductive materialism. This criticism, as well as the view which stimulated it, was unnecessary, for it was made clear that the verification theory had confused the search for a confirmation-basis of cognition with the search for scientific meaning.

[107] A classic statement of empirical realism is part of Hans Reichenbach's essay "Ziele und Wege der physikalischen Erkenntnis," *Handbuch der Physik* IV (Berlin, 1929), sec. 6, "Das Realitätsproblem," 16-24, wherein he concluded: ". . . Wahrnehmbarkeit ist zwar das *Kriterium* der Existenz, nicht aber ihre *Definition*," 13. There is extended and convincing discussion in Moritz Schlick, *Allgemeine Erkenntnislehre* (2nd ed., Berlin, 1925), esp. Part 3. To their loss, dialectical materialists apparently ignored this entire trend. Brand Blanshard put part of the argument neatly by calling the identification of meaning and evidence "an illegitimate assimilation of the cause to the effect" in "The New Philosophy of Analysis," *Proc. Am. Phil. Soc.* XCVI (1951), 230. See also the perceptive critique in E. Study, *Die realistische Weltansicht und die Lehre vom Raum* (Braunschweig, 1914), which is, however, written entirely from a Newtonian viewpoint.

[108] Rudolf Carnap, "The Methodological Character of Theoretical Concepts," *op. cit.*

[109] Adolf Grünbaum, "Carnap's Views on the Foundations of Geometry," (this volume), §5.

The verification theory stated conditions for use, that is, for the presence of meaning, but it did not state a definition of meaning. While such an identification of cognitive meaning with empirical evidence was consistent with phenomenalist theories, it was hopelessly restrictive for a (non-phenomenalist) physicalist theory of meaning. The verification theory could be seen to be itself metaphysical and ambiguous.[110] It was not merely a conventional proposal to be adopted on grounds of utility, nor an explicated tautology; instead it was either inadequate to account for the explanatory function of hypothetical entities in deductively formulated science, or misleading in its ultimate identification of acquaintance, reference, and description. Empiricism exhibits positivist and physicalist trends. The positivist tendency toward *individual* relativism and *private* subjectivism is based primarily upon recognition of one aspect of scientific confirmation: its sensuous basis in the individual body and its sensuous presentation in the individual mind. The physicalist tendency toward *group* relativism and *inter*-subjectivism modified this positivism because of the inadequacy of all solipsistic reductions of science. What is prerequisite for a consistently non-subjectivist physicalism, and constitutes its historical and biological foundations, is a theory of similar, causally-produced, sensuously-presented, interactions of human individuals, under specifiable conditions, with ascertainable entities.

After partial confirmability had replaced verifiability, and partial conditional definitions had been introduced, two factors entered logical empiricism and strengthened its defense against relativism. Empiricist conceptions of scientific meaning had evolved from a radical slogan to a continuing program for explicating meaning and usage in existing science; tests now were relevant to, but not necessarily identical with, the meaning of the propositions whose truth is tested. And this was the material nub. Testability, and whatever other formulations might follow, properly and merely provided a technical account of confirming or evidencing activity.

Physicalism, then, combines a number of propositions:

(1) an *inductive generalization* that all knowledge, whether of subjective or of objective reality, has a common sensory basis of confirmation;

(2) a *proposal* for explicating the epistemological relations (*within* each special science) between the physiological and social psychology of sensuous perception, the physics of experimental and measurement technology, and the scientific entities being known;

[110] John Wisdom, "Metaphysics and Verification," *op. cit.;* and Norman Malcolm in "The Verification Argument," *Philosophical Analysis,* ed. Max Black (Ithaca, 1950), 244-298, examine the relativist position, inherent in the verification (confirmation) theory as used after 1936, that there is no certain knowledge of matters of fact.

(3) an empirical *hypothesis* that the world is everywhere knowable in principle (though never completely in practice), because of, and by means of, the relations of causal interaction just mentioned;

(4) the additional and more tentative *hypotheses* first, that the nature of all entities is ultimately explicable in terms of physics proper, and, second, that there are no objectively emergent properties.

So far as the first three propositions are concerned, physicalism today agrees with the *relevant* parts of Marx's materialism of 1844 and Lenin's of 1908. The property of emergence might be covered by the fourth proposition of this *empirical materialism* (for that is what physicalism has become) either by trivializing the term 'physics' to include all natural properties whatsoever, or by enriching the program of the unity of science so as to include empirical investigation and systematic clarification of the relations among the clusters of natural properties that constitute the subject matter of different sciences. [111]

If seen as a joint task of descriptive pragmatics, social theory, and semantic analysis, the philosophy of knowledge might do what both Carnap and his materialist critics have wanted.[112] It would clarify the knowledge attained in a given scientific enterprise by examination of the whole

[111]Rudolf Carnap, "Remarks on Physicalism and Related Topics" (unpublished), Herbert Feigl, this volume, and P. E. Meehl and Wilfrid Sellars, "The Concept of Emergence," *Minn. Studies Phil. Sci.* I (Minneapolis, 1956), 239-252, give reconsideration to an old positivist dragon. See also Carl G. Hempel and Paul Oppenheim, "The Logic of Explanation," Pt. II, *Phil. Sci.* XV (1948); Paul Henle, "The Status of Emergence," *J. Phil.* XXXIX (1942), 486-493; C. D. Broad, *The Mind and its Place in Nature* (London, 1925), ch. II and XIV; Arthur Pap, "The Concept of Absolute Emergence," *Brit. J. Phil. Sci.* II (1952), 302-311; Ernest Nagel, *op. cit.;* James K. Feibleman, *Ontology* (Baltimore, 1951) esp. ch. 4, and the same author's "Theory of Integrative Levels," *Brit. J. Phil. Sci.* V (1954), 59-66; David Bohm's discussion of "Modes of Being" in *Causality and Chance in Modern Physics* (London and Princeton, 1957), ch. 5; Joseph Needham, "A Biologist's View of Whitehead's Philosophy" in *The Philosophy of Alfred North Whitehead* (2nd ed., New York, 1951), 241-271 and "Integrative Levels" (Oxford, 1937) both reprinted in his *Time: the Refreshing River* (London, 1943). The historical, mystical, empirical and rational strands in the notions of 'emergence' and 'integrative levels' are examined in several brief but stimulating passages of Needham's *Science and Civilization in China* II (Cambridge, 1956), esp. in ch. 13 and 16.

Physicalism now treats the unity of the sciences in a materialist mode; the unification is a matter of experimental discovery of links between them, not the result of a decision to translate differing scientific statements into a common language.

[112]Carnap recently reiterated: "For a total (not only logical) theory and analysis of knowledge and science, it is certainly very important to take into account also activities, including (1) the practical behavior of scientists in their research work (this may include pragmatics but goes far beyond it), and (2) the ways in which science is of help in all fields of practical life. I have myself not made any investigations of these kinds; but this does not mean that I regard them as less important" (in a letter to R. S. C. dated 12 August 1954). But what is the *status* of a purely logical analysis of knowledge in a total theory of scientific knowledge, once pure syntactic and pure (formal) semantic reconstructions are left behind?

knowledge situation. So far, one might claim that empirical materialism and dialectical materialism differ in their factual account of the knowledge situation, that is to say in their appraisals of the relevance to philosophy of physiological psychology and the social history of science; thus the meaning and significance of *praxis* is at issue.[113] But such disagreement is not serious, since Carnap is intent primarily upon rational reconstruction of confirmed and confirmable theories; they are to be liberated from ambiguity (and perhaps from ideological clutter as well?) by explicit rules for the use and understanding of language.

Dialectic need not meet the theory of linguistic purification head-on. It should welcome the technique of rational analytic reconstruction on dialectical grounds, for this is a necessary scientific task of self-criticism in the spirit of Marx's aperçu: *language is practical consciousness.*[114]

VI. *Agreement and Difference*

1. Dialectic and empiricism now agree on an impressive range of propositions. They reject supernatural explanations as logically impervious to refutation. They reject such *a priori* substitutes for practical experience as metaphysical rationalism, pure conventionalism, unmitigated coherence theories, Platonic realism, and categorical atomism.[115] Both demand sensuously presented evidence as the means for validating empirical propositions, hypothetico-deductive and probabilistic reasoning as the technique for assessing evidence, practical activity (as in natural and social science) as the mode of proof. Each treats man as a creature of the natural and social worlds, and holds that the evolution of human nature in all its aspects, biological, emotional, intellectual, social, is a matter for scientific study. They agree, furthermore, that the total situation of each person, in his private, class, and cultural position, gives him a perspective upon nature and society which may, depending on circum-

113This disagreement is perhaps not as sharp as needed, since Carnap and Neurath frequently indicated their general agreement with an historical materialist theory of social history and with a socio-technological interpretation of the history of scientific knowledge. See, e.g. Otto Neurath, *Empirische Soziologie* (Vienna, 1931), *passim,* and *Lebensgestaltung und Klassenkampf* (Berlin, 1928), esp. ch. 9, "Marx und Epikur." Even in their most phenomenalist period, Neurath concluded a discussion of the sociological conditions of knowledge and illusion by stating that "Gerade das Proletariat würde zum Träger der Wissenschaft ohne Metaphysik" *(ibid.* 152). See also the volume of *Selected Works of Otto Neurath,* ed. R. S. Cohen (New York and London, forthcoming).

114Marx and Engels, *The German Ideology,* tr. Roy Pascal (London and New York, 1939), 19; see *Marx-Engels Gesamtausgabe* I/5 (Berlin, 1932), 20. Compare Wittgenstein's remark: "And to imagine a language means to imagine a form of life," *Philosophical Investigations* (Oxford, 1953), 8e.

115"Where speculation ends,—in real life—, there real, positive science begins . . . when reality is depicted, philosophy as an independent branch of activity loses its medium of existence." Marx and Engels, *ibid.,* 15.

stances, either clarify or obscure both given facts and potential developments; they also agree that these perspectives are themselves open to scientific investigation and, possibly, to control. They agree, finally, that personal and social liberation is dependent upon a freely developing scientific outlook as well as upon related material conditions. A free society would set its course logically, objectively and consciously; that is, in the light of rational analysis of empirical evidence about nature and about the material and esthetic characteristics of human beings; and by means of corrigible judgments of a scientifically literate citizenry.

2. The permanently unfinished business of scientific inquiry—Lenin speaks in this vein of "the inexhaustible electron"[116]— is accompanied by unresolved questions of scientific philosophy. Here dialectic and empiricism each have been too quick to reject problems, too slow to reconsider solutions other than their own. Both physicalist reconstruction and undogmatic dialectic should be applied to such issues as these:

(a) The status of subjective events, intrinsically closed to intersubjective acquaintance (as distinct from description), frequently open to introspective or self-conscious cognition. This is a peculiar case of the more general problem of inferred entities, in that there is an epistemologically unique observer, whether of the data of immediacy or, upon reflection and varying psychoanalyses, of subjective events whose existence was previously unknown to him. Can confirmation be intersubjective in this case? Yes, at least in principle, since the subject is a natural (objective) entity and since confirmation is distinct from meaning. Behaviorist and physiological (e.g. Pavlovian) theories on the one hand, and on the other hand Marx's hypothesis that man's subjective nature (consciousness) is "an ensemble of social relations" might be joined in a parallel-language account of the objective conditions and characteristics of the inner life.[117]

(b) The status of natural laws, inadequately explicated by purely adjunctive relations and extensional logic, and with this, the status of natural (physical) entailment in each law-like instance. Can a law of Nature have one instance? Is 'natural' explicable in terms

[116]Lenin, *op. cit.,* 319.

[117]See Sandor Ferenczi, "Freud's Influence on Medicine" (1933) reprinted in *op. cit.,* for a stimulating suggestion along these lines, and for the term 'utraquism,' coined to avoid the classic associations of epiphenomenalist parallelism and metaphysical dualism. See also his fragment of 1920 *(ibid.,* 190) on reliable utraquistic views of reality, and his discussion of the stages in development of cognitive objectivity, "The Acceptance of Unpleasant Ideas," in *Further Contributions (Sel. Papers* II, London and New York, 1955), 373. In this connection, see the incisive essay on "The 'Mental' and the 'Physical,'" by Herbert Feigl, *Minn. Studies Phil. Sci.* II (Minneapolis, 1958), 370-497, and the important treatise by S. L. Rubenstein, *Grundlagen der allgemeinen Psychologie* (Berlin, 1958; tr. from Russian by H. Hartmann; orig. Moscow, 1946).

of 'connective' or 'causal' implication?[118] Then what is the explanatory status of statistical regularities? Or must a wholly different explication be sought, as thought by Whitehead and Needham?

(c) The status of persistent entities, construed either as beings or as gen-identical events. The career of a persistent entity will be described jointly by natural laws which refer to its own spontaneous or normal potentialities, and by laws which refer to the external but causally relevant environment. The working inter-relation between external or mechanical causation and internal or dynamic self-development is the typical dialectical situation. But "internal" to what natural boundaries? Is a 'natural entity' one whose *normal* career is potentially unified and self-determined? For Marx this might explicate the sociological term 'alienation,' and the metaphorical use of 'rational.' What are the criteria, within each science, for identifying the abstracted or 'artificial' entities and the concrete or 'natural' entities?

(d) A naturalistic concept of emergence, whether of laws or of properties. Is this a concept which refers to relations between different sciences? or is it useful within a science? What is meant by 'causal explanation' of emergent properties? How can one distinguish (1) temporary explanatory emergence, (2) objective qualitative emergence, (3) coexisting and irreducibly distinct qualities? A causal interpretation of emergent properties would then have to be linked, in an attempt to show the unity of science, with the existing unification which is provided by the common methodology of the physicalist confirmation base.[119]

(e) The adequacy of systematic or 'pure' logical explication of philosophical or scientific views, when we consider that historically determined meanings may expand the significance of terms and theories beyond the explicit statements which have been rejected or affirmed. What are the relations of "context and content in the theory of ideas?"[120]

(f) The status of metaphysics and the meaning of reason. To the em-

[118]See H. Reichenbach's discussion of "connective," i.e. physical entailment in his *Nomological Statements and Admissible Operations* (Amsterdam, 1954). The importance of this task is underlined by the ambiguity of 'law' in earlier empiricism, e.g. Moritz Schlick, "Positivism and Realism," recently translated in *Synthese* VII (1949), 478-505, esp. 504.

[119]See note 111.

[120]The phrase is the title of Abraham Edel's distinguished essay in *Philosophy for the Future,* ed. Marvin Farber, *et al.* (New York, 1949), 419-452. See also Ernest Nagel's view in *Sovereign Reason* (Glencoe, 1954), 132, that the genetic method of analysis need not be used so as to commit the genetic fallacy.

The meaning of "reason" requires historical explication, and metaphysical terms generally deserve such expansive treatment. But so do scientific ones. See, e.g. Max Jammer, *Concepts of Force* (Cambridge, Mass., 1957), and B. M. Kedrow's discussion

piricist, metaphysics is nonsense, although of historical interest.[121] To the dialectician, metaphysics is philosophically interesting *because* of historical interest (although its sense and its social role may be far from what the metaphysician thought). Sharply separating the logic of knowledge from the psychology and sociology of knowledge, Carnap swept aside questions of the sources and functions of speculative philosophy. They were relegated to a branch of the science of history, namely to the history of philosophy, not to bother the pure philosopher again. In this way, a decidedly non-empirical approach was taken toward the problem of understanding the ideas of other philosophers. For it *is* a problem, which ought to have been dealt with, so far as possible, as are other problems. But rational reconstruction, in ideological matters, requires social theory as well as empirical criteria. Even the concept of reason, upon explication, would transcend its positivist imprisonment in deductive schema; can scientific sense be made of the frequent metaphysical use of 'reason' as fulfillment? Thus, a reasonable society or a reasonable life might be one that has not been deviated from its free (self-determined) nature by alienating, subjugating factors. This is an idealistic usage; in order to be naturalized, metaphysical 'reason,' as a criterion of human society, requires further specification, an objective definition in terms of human nature.[122]

3. These unsettled queries circle around differing conceptions of the task of philosophy. Without a concept of Reason which will permit

of the dialectical development of the concept of 'element' in *Ueber Inhalt und Umfang eines sich verändernden Begriffs* (trans. from Russian ed., Moscow, 1953; Berlin, 1956).

121Thus Carnap: "All philosophers in the old sense, beginning with Plato, Thomas, Kant, Schelling, or Hegel, whether they construct a new metaphysics of being or a 'geisteswissenschaftliche' philosophy, appear before the inexorable judgment of modern logic as not only false in content but as logically untenable, i.e. meaningless," "Die alte und die neue Logik," *Erkenntnis* I (1931), 13.

122Herbert Marcuse expressed the first step in this explication: "Vernunft ist die Grundkategorie philosophischen Denkens, die einzige, wodurch es sich mit dem Schicksal der Menschheit verbunden hält," in "Philosophie und kritische Theorie," *Z.f. Socialforschung* VI (1937), 632. A succinct exposition of the varying social content of 'reason' in Western metaphysics is to be found in Herbert Marcuse, *Reason and Revolution* (2nd ed., New York, 1954), esp. 16-28 and 253-257. The Marxian materialization of the idealists' a priori rational critique of man's estate may seem homocentrically trivial indeed: *the demand for genuine individual happiness is the content of the metaphysical demand for a rational world-order*. But, in fact, it signals the transformation of philosophy into the sciences of human nature on the one hand, and into critical social theory and practical activity on the other. That is, "the realization of reason is not a fact but a task" (Marcuse, *ibid.,* 26) for which knowledge, not Utopian analysis, is needed; and the rest of metaphysical speculation will ultimately require a similar respectful translation. See also Roger Garaudy, *Le Communisme et la Morale* (Paris, 1948), esp. ch. 5-8. Explication by reconstruction and interpretation is common, of course, in discussing religion; but the interpreters are not

realistic criticism of the world revealed by experience, positivistic empiricism constructs a world of empty and inhuman mechanisms, a cyclic flux, divorcing the human spirit from natural process. But, under intellectual circumstances of such poverty, ordinary men will turn to irrational and arbitrary accounts, unscientific accounts, of their daily life of action and feeling. Dialectic must conclude, then, that neo-positivism has so far abdicated from the chief task of philosophy, by abandoning the creative practical jobs to the *blind* unconscious determinism of social and historical necessities, and permitting our dealings with these necessities to be dominated by *un-critical,* and irrational ideological reflections of political economy, that is by uncontrolled passions and existing inhuman dominations.

Now the present and observed facts are surely true, even if not the whole truth. What then is meant by 'critical'? If we are to understand a criticism of positivist and empiricist social trends, we must be able to criticize the present and the observed, themselves part of reality.[123] It is when the factual statements, which describe the present, conceal what might be, and divert from what ought to be, that the social yield of positivism is transformed from enlightenment to obscurantism and even falsehood. The optimistic realism of Hegel's thought is contained in his idea that there could be a world which would, in his sense, be reasonable. Marx added that such a world must be made; in it, the facts would no longer conceal. It therefore made sense to say that the truth needs to be practiced; or, to put the same point negatively, that the nominal facts may be one-sided and (partly) false. The limitation imposed by Hume on his modern followers appears in that

> the positivist attack on universal concepts, on the ground that they cannot be reduced to observable facts, cancels from the domain of (genuine) knowledge everything that may not yet be a fact.

Moreover since Hegel's truth goes beyond the partiality of the immediately given or any catalogue of givens, it

> signifies in the concrete that the potentialities of men and things are not exhausted in the given forms and relations in which they actually appear; it means that men and things are all that they have been and actually are, and yet more than all this.[124]

Epistemologically, dialectic is a theory of concept formation, not distinctively a theory of verification. Neither logic nor reality rests with

always completely scientific; see e.g. Mircea Eliade, *The Myth of the Eternal Return* (trans. from French ed., Paris, 1949; New York, 1954).

[123]The neo-positivist view was sharply in contrast; e.g. Hans Hahn wrote that "the conception, that we have in thought a means at hand to know more about the world than is observed, . . . appears to us to be mysterious," *Logik, Mathematik und Naturerkennen* (Vienna, 1933), 9.

[124]Herbert Marcuse, *op. cit.,* 113.

conflict, so that dialectic furnishes the language of conceptual development to describe the drive for self-fulfillment of humanity. But only in social theory can this be formulated scientifically, and only in specific historical action can it be confirmed. It was no mere slogan that the Marxist conception of verification was revolutionary practice. According to Marx, the real object is to be understood as sensuous human activity, a subjective sort of phrase until we add that the activity, through objects, is practical invention of a world-for-us. In the material economic necessities of human existence until the mid-twentieth century lay the root causes of the hostile divorce between spiritual possibilities and practical reasoning, between sensual subjectivity and a repressive objective world, a divorce which was enlarged beyond earlier belief with the transition from craft to mass production. A successful reunion of pleasure and work, subjective experience and objective achievement, which natural science makes possible, requires that the hope of objective idealism be made real, that a rational union of subject and object *be known* by inner acquaintance and *be known about* intersubjectively. Then too control of nature would be joined by self-control. Therefore, from a science of work, so many centuries in the making, man might pass to a science of pleasure, the rational enjoyment of self-expression.

The aims of self-control, so radically different from the socio-technological purpose of rendering nature (including the human nature of other people) subservient, are evident in the paradoxical phrase 'science of pleasure.' The idealistic ethic of self-fulfillment would be re-constituted by a materialist esthetic, a theory of natural fulfillment, that is, by a theory of the characteristics of unalienated human nature.[125] How might such a program be feasible?

4. Can empiricists and naturalists comment on these questions? Fifteen years ago, when John Dewey wrote that "until naturalists have de-

[125]Beauty has its hidden "metaphysical" meaning, which historical and psychological explication may reveal; cf. the highly suggestive and apparently Kantian propositions of Schiller that "Beauty (is) a necessary condition of Humanity," and that "if we are to solve the political problem in practice, we must follow the path of esthetics, since it is through Beauty that we arrive at Freedom," *On the Aesthetic Education of Man,* 10th and 2nd letters as trans. by Reginald Snell (London and New Haven, 1954), 60 and 27. Alienation is the initial concept of Schiller's esthetic as it is of Marx's social theory. Describing modern machine society, Schiller wrote ". . . enjoyment was separated from labor, means from ends, effort from reward. Eternally chained to only one single little fragment of the whole, Man himself grew to be only a fragment; with the monotonous noise of the wheel he drives everlastingly in his ears, he never develops the harmony of his being, and instead of imprinting humanity upon his nature he becomes merely the imprint of his occupation, of his science," *ibid.*, 40. In order to compare the Marxist "alienation," see the precise exposition, with detailed references to Marx's writings, in Stanley W. Moore, *The Critique of Capitalist Democracy* (New York, 1957), ch. 4, esp. 4.5.1, and also Herbert Marcuse, *op. cit.*, "Marx: alienated labor," 273-287. For a Marxist exploration of esthetics and cognition, see Max Raphael, *op. cit.* For a moving account of the present educational task of

finitely applied their own principles, methods and procedures to formulation of such topics as mind, consciousness, self, person, value, and so forth, they will be at a serious and regrettable disadvantage,"[126] his dialectical critics soon retorted that "it is an empty promise that some day positivism (*sic*) will solve the essential problems it has been too busy to solve up to now."[127]

Whatever the correct appraisal of Horkheimer's judgment of its role in recent history, the logical positivism of the Vienna Circle was a deliberate and conscious revolt against an environment marked by obscurantist theology and verbose social science. Its immediate predecessors, Russell on the one side and Mach on the other, were themselves in revolt, seeking to extend the clarity of science to a new foundation for human knowledge and humane living. Taken as a matter of *conscious* motivation, and seen in its social context of intellectual mystification, Viennese positivism was a movement of brilliant illumination. Its goal was to reconstruct the philosophical understanding of scientific methods of inquiry so that an armory of weapons would be available for use against human errors and misunderstandings. Nor was it merely destructive in intent. It sought with equally strong conviction to help furnish a stocked toolhouse for those, socialists or others, who were trying to construct a world that would have the material and spiritual requisites for social justice and human freedom. Not all positivists were equally specific in their social and economic views, but it seems clear that all recognized that theirs was a radical movement, which ultimately would replace the emotional and intellectual foundations of the existing political and social order just as surely as it would banish the reigning system of philosophical thought to an exile of illegitimate nonsense.[128]

The Utopian optimism of neo-positivism was premature.[129] Undogmatic as positivism wished to be, it had an implicit and naive moral

overcoming alienated and isolated human situations see Anton Makarenko, *The Road to Life* (trans. from Russian ed. of 1938; Moscow, 1951).

126John Dewey, in *Naturalism and the Human Spirit,* ed. Y. H. Krikorian (New York, 1944), 4.

127Max Horkheimer, *op. cit.,* 80.

128Some, of course, were quite precise in joining their social with their philosophical views e.g. Carnap's close associate, the economist, sociologist and philosopher, Otto Neurath.

For a brief account of Neurath's view of the relation between the Marxist social-scientific hypothesis of historical materialism and philosophical outlooks in the classic sense, see his "Weltanschauung und Marxismus," *Der Kampf* XXIV (1931), 447-451, and *Empirische Soziologie* (Vienna, 1931), 40-45, 136-145. "Von allen Versuchen, eine streng wissenschaftliche unmetaphysische physikalistische Soziologie zu schaffen, ist der Marxismus der geschlossenste . . . nicht nur in der Theorie, sondern vor allem auch in der planmässigen Praxis." But he came to fear closed and dogmatic forms of the Marxist world-view, "metaphysical" forms as he termed them.

129This is not to maintain that wishful thinking has been any less operative in other philosophies.

faith: if we clarify empirical findings so that we and our fellow human beings can agree on them, we and they will be saved. In logical empiricism, the Baconian observation that knowledge is power became the Socratic belief that knowledge is virtue. So it is, but knowledge is as much the result, as the cause, of action and interaction. In a discussion of ethics, Feigl recently referred to "the constancy of the *human-social situation*,"[130] an empirical conclusion which restates the classic idealist demand for a universal content as well as grammar for ethical judgments and hence goes beyond neo-positivist ethics. Feigl went on to recognize that needs and values may be so attached to the differing situations of persons and groups that mutually incompatible aspirations exist, that "social justice is differently conceived." For this he offers regrets but no theory, whether of accommodation or of conflict. Thus both the social theory of empiricism and the dialectical conception of natural science may be considered sparse. If, as we have hoped to show, empiricism is now resistant to subjectivist restrictions upon concepts and theories, it may turn to historical, contextual, and comparative analysis of human affairs and the humane sciences. Dialectic, in its turn, (provided it is cured of the terrifying "disease of orthodoxy"[131]) might apply the great virtues of the scientific enlightenment to its job of social criticism: self-correction, testability, reliability, comprehensiveness, lucidity. *Philosophy is criticism.* Therefore it has these two tasks: to explicate human knowledge, and to dissect the human situation.[132] Each is a task for reason working with facts, and they are not independent, for the second depends upon the first. But danger, irritability, and controversy descend when philosophy discharges its second responsibility, that is, upon philosophy as social critique. Nor is this unexpected, for a dialectical criticism is constructive and prescriptive, an agent as well as an analyst. Philosophy has never been wholly assimilated to pure science; it has always maintained a core of conscience, even though repressed. Empirical humanism found no rational or other guide for conscience in the observational authority of science; and likewise rational idealism found no tools for action in pure thought. Beyond observations, and beyond logic, philosophy still has the social function of a persistent, historically concrete, and constructive analysis of human relations.

ROBERT S. COHEN

DEPARTMENT OF PHYSICS
BOSTON UNIVERSITY

130Herbert Feigl, "Aims of Education for our Age of Science: Reflections of a Logical Empiricist," *Modern Philosophies and Education,* ed. Nelson B. Henry (Chicago, 1955) 330.

131This phrase is Beatrice Webb's in Beatrice and Sidney Webb, *Soviet Communism* 3rd ed., (London, 1944) , xlv.

132Maurice Cornforth, "Philosophy, Criticism and Progress," *Marxism Today* I (1957), 22-28; Max Horkheimer, "Traditionelle und kritische Theorie," *op. cit.,* 625-647; M. M. Rosental, *op. cit.,* esp. ch. 5.

3

Philipp Frank

THE PRAGMATIC COMPONENTS IN CARNAP'S "ELIMINATION OF METAPHYSICS"

AMONG the numerous writings of Carnap probably none has had so great and wide effects as the paper on "The Elimination of Metaphysics through Logical Analysis of Language."[1] People who have always had an aversion against metaphysics felt an almost miraculous comfort by having their aversion justified by "logic." On the other hand, people for whom metaphysics had been the peak of human intellectual achievement have regarded Carnap's paper as a flagrant attack upon all "spiritual values" from the angle of a pedantical logic. Logical Positivism got the reputation of being cynical skepticism and, simultaneously, intolerant dogmatism.

These are certainly two facts which seem to be contradictory to each other. Firstly, the fact that metaphysics is meaningless and secondly the fact that metaphysical beliefs have always had a great effect upon human action and human behavior. Some philosophers and educators have accused Logical Positivism of having ignored completely all questions of moral behavior. This accusation was even advanced by a man like Bertrand Russell who was in general sympathetic to Positivism, but had been looking to philosophy for support of social improvement. Other authors again have claimed that Logical Positivism is itelf a kind of metaphysics and is giving advice for moral and political behavior in the same sense as idealistic or materialistic metaphysics does.

One has frequently held the doctrine of Logical Positivism and particularly this work of Carnap's as responsible for these apparent contradictions. From the strictly logical viewpoint, Canap's doctrine does not lead to these contradictions. In his basic papers on the *Logical Analysis*, he had consistently distinguished between the logical (syntactical), semantical, and pragmatical components. Every discourse on the Logical Analysis of Language contains these three components in different percentages. In his article "Foundations of Logic and Mathematics"[2] Carnap writes: "Three components have to be distinguished in a situation where lan-

[1] *Erkenntnis,* II (1931); reprinted in A. J. Ayer, *Logical Positivism* (Glencoe, Ill., 1959), 60-81.

[2] *International Encyclopedia of Unified Science* (University of Chicago Press), I, 139ff.

guage is used." Firstly, there is the action, state and environment of the man who speaks or hears this language. Secondly, there are the words as elements of a certain linguistic system, and thirdly, the properties of things to which the speaker refers when he uses a certain word, e.g., 'the man means this color by the word blue.' "The complete theory of language," Carnap writes,

> has to study all these three components. We shall call *pragmatics* the field of all these investigations which take into consideration the first component (the action, state and environment of the speaker) whether it be alone or in combination with the other components. Other inquiries are made in abstraction from the speaker.

The two fields of study which have only to do with the expressions of the language and their objects (designata) are called *semantics* and *logic.* "We see that pragmatics is an empirical discipline dealing with a special kind of human behavior and making use of the result of different branches of science (principally social science, but also physics, biology and psychology)." From these statements it follows clearly that the 'pragmatics of mathematical or physical science' has also to deal with social and psychological science. In this sense the doctrine of Carnap agrees with the doctrine of Positivism which was developed in the School of August Comte, the founder of Positivism.

Whereas August Comte originally formulated his hierarchy of the sciences as a linear series starting from logic and mathematics and winding up with biology and sociology, his disciple, E. Littré regarded this sequence as a closed circle. Originally, every science was only dependent upon the previous members of the series, e.g., sociology upon biology and mathematics, whereas the previous members like mathematics were independent of sociology. However, according to the later order of the sciences which was set up by Littré, but later also accepted by August Comte himself, the series became circular and mathematics became also dependent upon the later members of the series, e.g., sociology.

According to Carnap, every author can, according to his personal intentions, formulate his chosen problem by using any mixture of the three components. In his famous paper on "The Elimination of Metaphysics," Carnap has used almost exclusively the logical and semantical components and only very little of the pragmatical. It is interesting to consider how a man, who is predominantly interested in the pragmatic component would look at Carnap's paper. We reprint, for this reason, the review of Carnap's paper which appeared, immediately after its publication, in the official philosophical journal of Soviet Russia, "Under the Banner of Marxism,"[3] written by V. Brushlinsky.

> What does Carnap understand by the 'metaphysics' which he is trying to

[3]*Pod Znamenem Marksisma* (1932).

overcome? 'Metaphysics,' he declares, 'seeks to find and express the knowledge that is inaccessible to empirical science' [p. 236]. Carnap divides all propositions having a meaning into three classes: (1) Propositions that are true in virtue of their form alone (*tautological* or *analytical* judgments). These propositions, according to Carnap, say nothing of reality. Among these he counts the formulae of logic and mathematics. (2) Propositions containing a logical contradiction: these are false in virtue of their very form. (3) The remaining propositions are judgments of experience and belong to empirical science and may be either true or false. Now propositions that do not belong to any one of these classes are devoid of all sense. Such he declares metaphysical propositions to be, understanding by 'metaphysical' not only speculative metaphysics which claims knowledge on the basis of 'pure reason' and 'pure intuition' independent of experience, but also metaphysics' which is based on experience but, through special kinds of inferences, seeks to know what lies behind direct experience ('the thing in itself'). Carnap proceeds to enumerate the metaphysical trends which he is combating. These are 'realism (Carnap means 'materialism') and its opponents: subjectivism, idealism, solipsism, phenomenalism, positivism (in its old sense)' [p. 237].

Carnap's philosophical position is quite clear: it is that of 'shamed idealism' fancying itself as having risen above the radical contradiction between materialism and idealism. It is equally clear that Carnap's position is not very original. Long ago, Hume divided the objects of human knowledge into relations between ideas and what he called 'facts of experience.' Hume also thought that mathematics deals not with an aspect of the real material world but with the ideal relations independent of reality.

How then does Neo-Positivist Carnap overcome metaphysics? He thinks that, although the enemies of metaphysics have existed for a very long time, only the 'latest Logic' can give an accurate answer as to whether metaphysics is possible, this answer being provided by an analysis of language. This language analysis reveals that there are word combinations which look like propositions at first glance but which actually are not propositions at all. In the strict sense, these pseudo-propositions are meaningless. This is because either the words appearing in them are meaningless or, if they have a meaning, they are combined in such a way as to break the laws of logic.

In order that a word should have a meaning, it must, according to Carnap, satisfy the following conditions: (1) the form of the simplest proposition in which this word figures has to be determined (e.g. for the word 'stone' the form of an elementary proposition would be 'x is a stone'); (2) for this elementary proposition there must exist the answer to the questions 'from what propositions can it be deduced?' and 'what propositions can be deduced from it?'

With this criterion, Carnap proceeds to the analysis of 'metaphysical words' and discovers that these words are devoid of significance and meaning. As an example, he takes the word 'principle' in the metaphysical sense of 'the principle of being' or 'the universal principle,' etc., and the word 'god.' The word 'principle,' Carnap declares, had at first the empirical meaning of 'origin' ('that from which something derives'). The metaphysicians, however, use it in some different, super-empirical sense, which they cannot even define themselves. In the same way, 'god' used to have, once upon a time, an empirical meaning which it has since lost, and which used to denote certain beings inhabiting certain empirical places. According to Carnap, this word has lost its primary, naive meaning but failed to acquire any other. The concepts of 'essence,' 'thing *per se*,' 'infinite,' and 'absolute' are, according to Carnap, just as meaningless metaphysical words as the word 'god.'

Further, he gives some examples of meaningless combinations of meaningful words. The proposition 'Caesar is and' is meaningless because of its grammatical form, since 'and' cannot be a predicate. Now, the proposition 'Caesar is a prime number' is meaningless because it mixes logical categories, since 'prime number' cannot be either affirmable or deniable with respect to persons (or to things). Carnap holds that if language were built in accordance with strict logic, with arrangement of words into logical categories, meaningless propositions of the second type would be almost as impossible as meaningless propositions of the first type ('Caesar is and').

After these formalistic exercises in the 'logical analysis' of words and propositions, Carnap quotes from 'What is Metaphysics' (1929) by Martin Heidegger, one of the metaphysicians now in vogue in Germany. The quotation, true, enough, is almost nothing but an accumulation of words on the subject *Das Nichts nichted* ('Nothing nothings,' formed by an analogy with the proposition 'the rain rains'). By a lengthy 'logical analysis,' Carnap discovers the absurdity of this quotation. But even without this cumbersome analysis, it is quite evident that there is no positive scientific meaning in Heidegger's reasoning about 'nothing.' It does not follow however that this reasoning is devoid of social significance. It is quite typical of the decadent, degenerate philosophy of the modern bourgeoisie which, feeling the ground slipping from under its feet, is trying to escape into verbal mysticism, away from reality which no longer promises its lasting domination over the toiling masses. But Carnap is only interested in formal logic and is concerned with nothing but the scholastic analysis of individual words and propositions.

Summing up his 'analysis,' Carnap declares: "All metaphysics is meaningless' (p. 233). But, in his words, while metaphysics is devoid of all cognitive content, it is nevertheless useful as an expression of the 'feeling of life' of those individuals who create metaphysical systems. But even in this, Carnap tries to present himself as an irreconcilable opponent of metaphysics: he declares that whereas art (particularly music) is an adequate means of expressing the 'feeling of life,' metaphysics is a quite inadequate one since it lays claim to be something, namely a knowledge, which it cannot be. 'Metaphysicians,' Carnap says, 'are musicians without musical talent' (p. 240).

This is all of Neo-Positivist Carnap's 'overcoming' of metaphysics. It is obvious that there is no question here of an actual overcoming of metaphysics. There is not even any understanding of metaphysics. Carnap painstakingly elaborates mechanistic, formal-logic, scholastic schemes and criteria to determine the 'meaning' and the 'sense' of words and propositions without noticing that these very schemes and criteria are devoid of all concrete content and are therefore incapable of giving a correct idea of science or of metaphysics. Declaring war on all metaphysics, Carnap himself sinks into the phenomenalist type of metaphysics which asserts that the task of science is simply to provide the most convenient description of phenomena. 'Essence' for Carnap is a meaningless metaphysical word. He does not understand 'the essence is,' 'a phenomenon is essential,' 'human thought goes infinitely deeper, from phenomenon to essence, and from essence of, so-to-speak, the first order to the essence of the second order, and so on without end' (Lenin). But then Carnap, the logician and mechanist, is unable to understand either, the gnoseological or the social-economic roots of the idealism and metaphysics that he claims to combat. He does not understand that 'philosophical idealism is a one-sided, exaggerated development (blowing up, swelling) of one of the traits, aspects, facets of knowledge in the absolute, torn off from matter, from nature, deified' (Lenin), and that it is fed and strengthened by the 'class interest of the ruling classes' (Lenin). Failing to grasp all this, Carnap cannot climb out of the bog of mechanistic idealism with its positivist coloring, despite all his attacks on every form of 'metaphysics,' despite his aspirations toward a 'scientific philosophy.' His is not a scientific philosophy but a special kind of scholastics, in which he uses the whole arsenal of sterile formulae of formal logic, in order to give it a scientific appearance. We have here not the overcoming of metaphysics but a plea for idealism, mechanism and formalism—and this is what Carnap's Neo-Positivism is.

Bourgeois limitations appear at every step in Carnap's 'anti-metaphysical' philosophizing just as they do in the philosophizing of other staff members and contributors to the 'left'-wing bourgeois magazine *Erkenntnis.*

The emphasis on the pragmatic component is noticeable from the way in which the Soviet author understands the term "elimination of metaphysics." Before we "eliminate" metaphysics, we have to understand it as a means to support a certain way of life, a certain political or religious creed. The purpose of eliminating would be to destroy this undesirable ideology. Carnap, however, according to the Soviet reviewer, attempts to "separate theory from practice," ignoring the practical goal of metaphysics and declaring it as meaningless. In doing so he criticizes traditional metaphysics which contains terms like 'god,' 'principle,' 'real world,' etc. and replaces it by a new metaphysics, in which the 'real world' is eliminated and replaced by a "scientific" world, which is a system of symbols from which observable facts can be derived. This is the only function of this system of symbols; it is not a photo of the "true" or "real world." The official Soviet Philosophy summarizes its objections against the positivistic theory of knowledge approximately as follows: Carnap and the 'positivists' say that science is only a way of "organizing experience," not of finding objective truth. But, if this is so, there may also be other ways of "organizing experience," e.g. Thomistic Cosmology, which has been a support of traditional Christian Religion. By denying the objective truth of science, positivism provides a scientific support of traditional Religion. If one thinks as the Soviet Government does, that the belief in 'religion' in this sense is harmful to the attempts for social improvements one would, of course, regard the positivistic theory of science as harmful to the well-being of man. To the modern scientist this kind of argument against positivism will seem to be awkward. By calling science a way of organizing experience we regard it as legitimate to replace our science by different "organizations of experience." The scientist would say that the choice is arbitrary between these "organizations" provided they yield the same observable facts.

If we have to do with material obtained from physical experiments the choice is only arbitrary from the viewpoint of logic and of physical experience. This means roughly that it is arbitrary if we restrict ourselves to the logical and semantical components of language. If we add the pragmatic component, we have to ask by what factors the choice of the scientist is determined. To say that the choice is arbitrary in the domain of sociological and psychological factors would mean that one individual psycho-social fact, the choice of the scientist, is independent of all other facts in this area. This would be to believe in a metaphysical "freedom of choice" and quite a few adversaries of Logical Positivism have accused this doctrine of advocating indirectly a belief in "free choice."

Not only the Soviet philosophers but also Western philosophers who follow the Pragmatism of John Dewey would rather argue: If several choices are possible from the viewpoint of logic and physical experience, there are some of them which support desirable social effects and some support undesirable ones. The question whether and why hypotheses or principles like the existence of a god or the non-existence of the external world have desirable social effects can, of course, not be investigated without empirical research in psychology and sociology. If we consider the pragmatic component of scientific language we have to speak about the influence of his environment upon the builder of scientific theories, in other words, we have to investigate the reasons which have induced the scientist to introduce such formulations of principles in which words like 'god' or 'reality' enter. Carnap in his "eliminating of metaphysics" does not investigate elaborately the pragmatic component but does not, on the other hand, deny its existence and relevance.

However, the perusal of the above review which was published in a Journal that has followed the official line of Soviet Philosophy of 1932 will serve as a concrete example for the attitude of authors who give much attention to the pragmatic component of scientific language. According to this review, Carnap did not actually achieve an "elimination of metaphysics," because he restricted his universe of discourse to the logical component of language. In order to understand this objection from a broader background, we have to remember that Pragmatists with strong social interests raise similar objections. John Dewey, e.g. pointed out that one cannot overcome metaphysics fully by proving that it is meaningless but by understanding its meaning fully and exposing it. The word "fully" means: "Including the pragmatic component." The lack of attention given to the pragmatic component brings about, according to the Soviet Philosophy, a lack of co-ordination between theory and practice and, in connection with it, an exaggerated importance to the logical component. Since, according to the Soviet Philosophy, metaphysics consists in the exaggerated role ascribed to some concepts, the author of the review, as we have seen, claims that Carnap himself made use of three metaphysical creeds: idealism, formalism and mechanism.

PHILIPP FRANK

INSTITUTE FOR THE UNITY OF SCIENCE
AMERICAN ACADEMY OF ARTS AND SCIENCES
BOSTON, MASSACHUSETTS

4

Paul Henle

MEANING AND VERIFIABILITY

I

THE business of a theory of meaning is to present a criterion for distinguishing meaningful from meaningless expressions. Before presenting a criticism of Carnap's, or any other such theory, it would be well to characterize the theory and to notice the kind of ground claimed in the theory for awarding or withholding meaningfulness. Does the theory, for example, claim an empirical basis or does it perhaps claim to be a stipulation? There is at least one important advantage to be gained from such procedure—a characterization of the theory leads to a determination of the criteria to be used in its evaluation. Thus, if the theory is empirical, the usual criteria for scientific hypotheses must be applied; if a stipulation, the utility of the stipulation must be investigated, and so in other cases. This would not, of course, lead at once to agreement with regard to the theory; there would still be room for difference of opinion with regard to the application of the criteria, but at least there would be a general framework of agreement on which further agreements might be built.

It would seem that there are at least four types of reason which might be given in a theory of meaning for differentiating what is meaningful from what is meaningless. First, the theory might rest on empirical considerations surveying the sorts of combinations of sounds which are found meaningful and making distinctions on the basis of such findings. Second, a theory might differentiate what is meaningful from what is meaningless on the basis of normative considerations, finding desirable characteristics in certain types of discourse and then arguing that discourse should be limited to sorts having these traits. Again, a theory of meaning might be based on some synthetic a priori grounds, the range of possible meanings being determined by the conditions of experience or by some similar standard. Finally a theory of meaning might be considered a stipulation, resting on a nominal definition of 'meaningful in language L' or something of the sort. A theory of meaning need not, of course, rest on one of these grounds alone, but may represent a combination of two or more. There may also be other grounds on which meaningful expression could be differentiated from meaningless, but I do not know what they would be.

In considering any view of Carnap's it is safe to eliminate theories involving a synthetic a priori and no more need be said concerning theories of this type. One further alternative may be eliminated from the list of possibilities, though this is more controversial. Stipulation does not in itself constitute an independent basis for differentiating meaningful from meaningless expressions, but is always the reflection of some other type of theory. The point may be seen from the following considerations: suppose one is confronted with two formally developed language systems which differ only in their stipulations with regard to what is meaningful.[1] How is a choice to be made between them? When faced with the problem, Carnap suggests such criteria as conformity with actual practice[2] and avoidance of arbitrary distinctions.[3] He stresses the point that these are "not proofs for an assertion, but motives for a decision."[4] This may be granted, but one must also insist that the usages of actual practice, though they may motivate one to act in a certain way, may also be the basis of an empirical theory of meaning. If one wanted to establish inductive generalizations of what is meaningful and what is not one could, to a very large extent, appeal to these same usages. Similarly, if one were laying down norms for what is meaningful, the avoidance of hiatus by arbitrary rules might be such a norm. More generally, it would appear to be the case that any consideration to which one might appeal as a motive for making a stipulation might equally well appear as evidence for an empirical theory of meaning or else might be a factor weighed in developing a normative theory. The converse, I would think, is also the case and anything which might be used in an empirical theory or a normative one might also appear as a motive for a stipulation.

The reason for pointing out this sort of equivalence is to reduce the number of types of theory of meaning which are to be considered. One may either speak of empirical theories and normative theories or else of stipulation, but there is no point in a separate consideration of all three. Any finding in favor of a certain type of empirical theory would favor a certain stipulation, and *vice versa*. It is a matter of choice then whether, on the one hand, one speaks of stipulations as to meaning and allows empirical and normative motives for stipulations or whether, on the other hand, one speaks of empirical and normative theories of meaning. My own preference is for the latter form of expression and I shall

[1]Several systems of this kind are suggested by Carnap in "Testability and Meaning," *Philosophy of Science*, III (1936), 419-471 and IV (1936), 1-40. Reprinted without change of pagination by Graduate Philosophy Club, Yale University (New Haven, 1950).

[2]*Ibid.*, 26.

[3]*Ibid.*, 27.

[4]*Ibid.*, 26.

use it, though if any reader has the opposite choice, it is easy to transpose into the other manner of speaking.

The problems regarding a theory of meaning may thus be reduced to two: First, what are the empirical facts regarding actual use of expressions on which it rests; and, second, what are the ideals such as simplicity, clarity, and the like, which it embodies. Whether these considerations be taken as themselves constitutive of a theory or whether they are the motives of a stipulation need not be a matter of primary concern.

We may notice in passing that the problem as here outlined takes us from the type of problem which Carnap designates internal to the type which he stigmatizes as external.[5] This is unavoidable in any question, dealing with the comparative advantage of languages, involved in discussing alternative theories of meaning. Since, as we have just seen, there are features involving more than the elaboration of a given language, but rather questions of how people actually talk and what modes of talking are desirable, it seems impossible to confine discussion within the framework of a given language system. If such questions are excluded all that would be left to philosophy would be the development of formal languages without any way of reaching a choice between them. Yet the problems of choice remain, to be settled by one means or another, and to deny the name of philosophy to these attempts at solution seems captious.

II

To consider the empirical evidence relevant to a theory of meaning is to consider what people understand. If language is used and comprehended, then it must be meaningful, and any theory of meaning which claims empirical sanction may begin with a reference to what is understood. There would be no advantage to bringing in the notion of understanding if there were not empirical evidence of a definitely describable sort for a statement's being understood. There is, for example, a peculiar sort of feeling of comprehension and of being in control of the situation which most often accompanies understanding. This is in marked contrast to the feeling of blankness and being at a loss which is the usual concomitant of not understanding. The contrast is perhaps most marked when one comes upon an unintelligible sentence in a paragraph which otherwise is clear. For a while everything has been going along smoothly, one has been in complete control, suddenly he is faced with an obstacle. One re-reads the sentence to be sure he has not mis-read it, but, finding no error here, he stops to conjecture what possibly might be meant, then, perhaps, gives up this sentence as a bad job and goes on to others.

[5]Rudolf Carnap, "Empiricism, Semantics, and Ontology," *Revue Internationale de Philosophie,* IV (1950), 20-40.

There is quite the opposite feeling when the meaning of a passage which hitherto has been obscure suddenly dawns on one. The irresolution and confusion are replaced by mastery and one goes ahead serenely untroubled. It would be foolish, of course, to claim that this sense of understanding is infallible, for, certainly, there have been cases where a person thought he understood something which subsequent experience showed he had failed to. There have even been cases where persons have understood what they thought they had failed to, as when they expected something profound and heard something trivial. Granted all these exceptions, however, it would still be the case that this feeling of understanding is evidence and strong evidence that actually something has been understood.

Subjective feelings are not, of course, the only sort of evidence available. Any experienced lecturer can tell by watching his audience whether it is understanding him. The members of an audience which is perplexed twist and shuffle, they look at one another, they frown. In part, this conduct is similar to that of a bored audience, but the frowning and turning to neighbors are sufficiently distinctive to leave no doubt in the mind of the lecturer. Examinations, to take another case from the class-room, are often tests of comprehension. Once again, no one would claim them to be infallible, but on the whole they would generally be conceded to be a pretty fair index of understanding. Along the same lines also, even casual conversation may reveal understanding or lack of it. Ability to obey commands constitutes a similar criterion.

We may speak of all these occurrences, inter-personal as well as subjective, as the *phenomena of understanding*. The paragraphs above are by no means intended to be exhaustive of these phenomena but merely to suggest their range. The reason for calling attention to them, however, is to formulate more precisely the requirements for empirical justification of any meaning theory. We may say that a theory of meaning is empirically justified to the extent that the class of statements which it designates as meaningful coincides with the class of statements in conjunction with which all or most of the phenomena of meaning occur.

So far this discussion has been completely general, intended to indicate the considerations by which any theory of meaning is to be judged. Without narrowing the discussion more than is necessary, I should now like to restrict it to verifiability theories of meaning and for this purpose it is sufficient to characterize verifiability theories as those which make the meaningfulness of synthetic statements dependent on their being capable of some sort of empirical verification. This characterization is not precise but to make it more precise would be to restrict it to one type of verifiability theory rather than another. For the present, it is accurate enough; restrictions as to types of verifiability theories will be introduced later. Given verifiability theories characterized in this broad way, this section will consider the empirical evidence for and against them. The normative considerations which may favor or oppose such theories are reserved for another section.

One of the aspects of unformalized language to which the positivists have called violent attention is the occurrence of utterances called metaphysical. These utterances, allegedly characteristic of treatises on metaphysics, are claimed to be totally without possibility of verification. These claims must be investigated because, if they can be substantiated, they lead to the further question of whether the phenomena of meaning occur in connection with such statements. If so, any empirical basis would be destroyed for a verifiability theory of languages as a whole. There would still be the possibility, of course, that there were normative reasons for holding a verifiability theory or that a verifiability theory applied to some more restricted linguistic domain, such as a language for some science. Still the matter is of sufficient importance to be considered.

In what follows I shall argue that, on the whole, the positivist accusation against traditional metaphysics has been mistaken and that metaphysical hypotheses do have empirical content. This is not universally the case, however, and there are some metaphysical statements which seem to lack such content. Where this is the case, however, the statements none the less exhibit many phenomena of understanding and therefore on an empirical basis should be accounted meaningful.

On the first point, the empirical content of many metaphysical hypotheses, one of the more striking phenomena in the history of philosophy, is the way in which metaphysical theories are refuted by later scientific discovery. Critics of philosophy have, in fact, made much of the point. Thus, with whatever assurance we believe in contemporary physics, with that assurance, we must disbelieve in Lucretius's cosmology. According to modern physics, the atoms out of which Lucretius builds his universe simply do not exist. Again, with whatever assurance we believe in the conservation of momentum, we must disbelieve in the Cartesian theory of interaction of mind and body. Again, on one interpretation of Aristotle at least, everything would increase in perfection until it became identical with God, if it were not for absolute limitations imposed by the fixity of species. On this interpretation, one must either construe the term 'species' in some non-biological sense or else admit that Aristotle is flatly wrong. Again, there are certainly metaphysical implications to Kant's work, even though he did not consider himself a metaphysician, and notice how much harder it is to accept Kant's position since the physical employment of non-Euclidean geometries. All these are cases in which philosophers have maintained doctrines as important aspects of their metaphysical views which subsequent empirical investigations have shown to be false. And if empirical investigations can disprove them, they must have some empirical content.

We may trace the same sort of connections even where a philosophy accords with empirical investigations. Notice the reliance on the theory of evolution in such metaphysicians as Bergson and Alexander. If evolution were conclusively disproved, these philosophies would be as good as refuted. Again, there is no doubt as to what would be the fate of Whitehead's doctrine of the self-determination of each actual occasion if empirical investigations would give overwhelming support to a doctrine of universal determinism, extending even to the minutest particle. There is no doubt either as to what would be the fate of Santayana's materialism if strong arguments could be adduced for the existence of mental telepathy without any physical basis.

Here again are cases in which characteristic metaphysical doctrines have their probabilities affected by empirical investigations. These are not peripheral opinions, accidental accretions to the philosopher's central thought, but the characteristic and distinctive doctrines of the systems in question. I shall not here claim that all metaphysical statements are empirical in this sense, but it is clear that at least some are and important ones.

Granted that much of metaphysics has at least some verifiable content, it would still, I believe, have to be admitted that there are exceptions and some cases of unverifiable statements could be found. Consider, for example, such a statement as 'God exists' in a system in which a deity is thought of as a supremely perfect being and in which the ontological argument is rejected, so that the statement is synthetic. Suppose furthermore the statement is asserted without reference to response to prayer or to mystical communion and even without reference to any design in nature. It would seem in this case that we had here a metaphysician's assertion, held to be meaningful, for which, even ideally, no empirical verification could be given. I have not, I realize, thus far in this discussion taken up the question of how far the notion of verifiability can be stretched, how far "verifiability in principle" may extend, but if the requirement is intended to exclude anything, the statement in question must be excluded.

There is a further question, however, as to whether the phenomena of understanding occur in connection with the statement. Here I think the answer must be in the affirmative. With many people at least, there will be no feeling of bafflement on encountering the statement, an audience will not look blank when it hears it, and a group of students may even write a clear examination involving it. It may be that the people who evince these phenomena of understanding are not keeping in mind all the restrictions mentioned above which are necessary to make the statement synthetic and without empirically verifiable content. In many cases this might be admitted, but there is no evidence to show that it need be admitted in all cases and, particularly in the case of trained theologians, there is every reason to believe that the conditions would be kept in mind.

In this case then, and in others of a similar sort, the phenomena of understanding are the opposite of what one should expect if there is to be empirical confirmation of verifiability theories. The evidence all goes to show that metaphysical statements are understood, and if, according to the verifiability theories, they are said to be incapable of being understood, this is a defect of the theories. Depending on which formulation of the theories one uses, one must say either that they fail the empirical test as theories or else that they lack the motive of conformity to actual practice which might lead to adopting them as stipulations.

The point may be made in another way. Roughly, the positivistic argument against metaphysics might be expressed in the syllogism:

Unverifiable utterances are meaningless
Metaphysical utterances are unverifiable
∴ Metaphysical utterances are meaningless.

The minor premise is objectionable as not being universally true, but as being true only for a subclass of metaphysical utterances. Instead of drawing the stated conclusion for these cases, however, I have argued that it is false on empirical grounds. The denial of the conclusion taken together with the modified minor allows an inference of the falsity of the major, that is, of verifiability theories. Or the argument of this section is capable of still another alternative formulation. According to verifiability theories, theological discussions cannot be understood. Without pretending to understand all such discussions, I am more sure that I have understood some of them than I am that the verifiability theories are correct.

III

Even though, according to the argument of the last section, verifiability theories of meaning receive no empirical confirmation from the phenomena of understanding when taken as theories of language as a whole, it may be that they receive such confirmation from some part of language. In particular, it may be that verifiability theories account for meaning as it occurs in the sciences. Indeed, the theory is most often put forth as an account of scientific meaning and everyone would admit that there is a verifiability requirement for scientific theories. As has often been remarked, science is an inter-personal enterprise, not concerned with truths supported by insight alone, but requiring publicly available support for each assertion made. Given this requirement, there must be evidence for any scientific hypotheses and this evidence is the verifiable aspect of the theory.

The matter may be put in another way—a theory equally compatible with every conceivable state of affairs in the world would not be counted as a scientific theory at all. It might be a mathematical theorem or perhaps a metaphysical hypothesis, but it would not be science. Every scientific theory, then, is at least materially equivalent to the denial of some possible state of affairs. In principle at least, one must be able to investigate whether this state of affairs obtains, and a verifiability requirement is therefore implicit in any scientific theory.

Thus it may be admitted that scientific theories have a requirement of verifiability and it is doubtful if anyone would seriously deny the point. This is not the same, however, as saying that scientific laws are subject to a verifiability requirement of meaning. It must be admitted that a statement which is not verifiable is not worth discussing for scientific purposes, but this is not equivalent to saying that it is unintelligible. The scientific verifiability requirement is in fact a good deal more stringent than any positivist theory of meaning has imposed, for statements which are verifiable in principle only, while admitted to be intelligible, are relegated to a limbo of conjecture, not perhaps totally condemned, but certainly considered unworthy of the serious attention of a scientist in the practice of his profession. This is, however, a judgment as to what is a part of science and even perhaps as to what is worth discussing, not a judgment as to what is intelligible. Thus, while granting that there is a verifiability requirement of scientific laws and indeed a stringent one, this gives no reason to claim that this is a requirement for meaning.

An apparent exception to what I have been claiming is found in the doctrine of operationalism, the view that scientific concepts are to be defined in terms of physical operations, that mass is to be defined in terms of the operation of weighing, length in terms of the manipulation of measuring sticks, and the like. Once again no one would deny that these operational characteristics are desirable in a scientific concept, but the desirability, as before, may be explained in different ways. It may be that, apart from operational standards, concepts are not intelligible, or it may be that concepts, though intelligible if not meeting these standards, are lacking in a desirable sort of precision. From this latter point of view, though operational concepts possess certain advantages, other forms of concepts may also be intelligible. So construed, operationalism is not a theory of meaning but a demand for a certain sort of scientific practice. Even the author of the term 'operationalism' claims no more for it at present. He says:

> It is often supposed that the operational criterion of meaning demands

that the operations which give meaning to a physical concept *must* be instrumental operations. This is, I believe, palpably a mistaken point of view for simple observation shows that physicists do profitably employ concepts the meaning of which is not to be found in the instrumental operations of the laboratory, and which cannot be reduced to such operations without residue. Nearly all the concepts of theoretical or mathematical physics are of this character. . . .[6]

The correctness of this point of view is further substantiated by some developments in the social sciences. Psychoanalytic theory though rich and clinically productive, lacks the sort of precision and verifiability which is characteristic of the more advanced sciences. Recently there have been attempts to determine some sort of operational meanings for the Freudian concepts to translate them, or at least to turn part of their meaning into more rigourously formulated and experimentally applicable concepts. This may be regarded as an attempt to operationalize Freudian psychology. Similarly, I have heard discussions as to how Veblen's notion of conspicuous consumption could be reduced to operational concepts or how tests might be devised which would similarly transform some of Benjamin Lee Whorf's notions of the influence of language upon thought. This is not the place to comment on the utility of such attempts or their probable success, but one aspect of them is pertinent to the present discussion: If they represent the attempt to displace non-operational concepts by operational ones, the non-operational concepts must be meaningful. Without this assumption there could be no comprehension of what one was doing or of whether one had done it correctly. Thus the attempt to extend operationalism serves only to confirm the position that operationalism, like verifiability requirements in science generally, serves as an ideal of scientific discourse which is independent of meaningfulness.

Much of what has been claimed in the preceding discussion might be summarized by claiming that the verifiability theory has confused a requirement that scientific questions be decidable with a claim that unverifiable statements are meaningless. This confusion has been aided by an ambiguity characteristic of such terms as 'meaningful,' 'meaningless,' 'nonsense' and the like. In one sense, an event is meaningful if it signifies something important—if it portends something. There is a matching sense of 'significant' to go with it where 'significant' implies having an important meaning. A significant book in this sense is not merely one which is composed of comprehensible standard sentences, but it is one which is especially worth reading. In these senses 'meaningful' and 'significant' can be equated, roughly at least, and can be opposed to what is meaningless or insignificant. These latter terms com-

[6]P. W. Bridgman, *The Nature of Some of Our Physical Concepts* (New York, 1952), 8.

prehend not merely what is not a sign at all and so literally has no meaning or significance, but also what signifies something unimportant and which therefore may be neglected safely. Because of the emphasis on what is important the senses which have been discussed may be referred to as *evaluative* senses of 'meaningful,' 'significant' and kindred terms. It must, of course, be remembered that this evaluative use is relative and that what is meaningful from one point of view or assuming a given set of goals may be meaningless if the context is shifted.

In opposition to the evaluative sense of these terms is their *semantic* sense, their functioning to indicate what is intelligible and what not. There is no assertion of importance here, merely the claim that something can be understood. In this sense a statement is meaningful or significant—once more the terms are roughly synonymous—if it is comprehended, if it conveys intelligence to someone. There is no requirement that what is conveyed be vital or that any evaluation be made, but merely that something be understood. Similarly, in this sense, the meaningless is the unintelligible, what can't be grasped. In this sense, it is perhaps better to use 'non-significant' rather than 'insignificant' as an antonym of 'significant.' In the semantic use as well as the evaluative there is a relativism, but a relativism to a person rather than to a goal. Something is intelligible not in itself but to some one under some determinate conditions.

The term 'nonsense' likewise has its evaluative and semantic senses. In the former sense one accuses people of talking nonsense if they hold views with which one is in violent disagreement. Yet they cannot be talking nonsense in the semantic sense, otherwise there would be no view expressed with which to disagree.

In terms of this distinction, it is possible to summarize the objection to finding in science a basis for a verifiability theory of meaning. At most scientific practice shows that unverifiable statements are meaningless in the evaluative sense of 'meaningless.' If theory of meaning is to be something distinct from theory of value, it is necessary to establish meaninglessness in the semantic sense; and this has not been done. The existence of the two senses of the same words has made this confusion easier.

So far the argument has been largely negative; it has contended that one need not assume there are special sorts of scientific meanings subject to a verifiability requirement. It has suggested the alternative that the verifiability requirements of science are to be explained by the needs of scientific evidence rather than the demand of a peculiar sort of scientific intelligibility. It has not, however, offered any considerations decisive between these alternatives and in order to arrive at a decision a more detailed consideration of the verifiability theories is required. It is clear that in some respects scientific theories go beyond the immediately verifiable, but whether they go farther than would be allowed by a verifiability theory depends on the particular verifiability theory in question. One issue on which verifiability theories differ is the matter of verifiability in principle, and we shall begin with it. The problem arises because no one proposes to limit what is verifiable to what can be verified at the moment and under the given circumstances. Some extension is necessary so that one may say that the statement that an eclipse will occur at some future time is verifiable, though not verifiable now, and that the statement that there are mountains on the other side of the moon is verifiable even though no one at present can build the rocket necessary to carry out a direct verification. Just what extension shall be allowed beyond what is verifiable here and now constitutes the problem.

Schlick has given what is perhaps the most liberal answer[7] in distinguishing physical from logical possibility and arguing that any statement is verifiable so long as there is a logical possibility of its verification. By this standard, Schlick finds such problems meaningful as that of survival after death and of the persistence of the physical world in the absence of any living beings. It is difficult in fact to see what traditional metaphysical problems would be excluded by this criterion. Schlick, following Wittgenstein, finds fault with the dictum "I can feel only my pain," since it is maintained by idealists in a sense which does not admit of any empirical confirmation or disconfirmation. Even granting that the statement is a tautology, it hardly seems that any important traditional metaphysical problem would be excluded. Certainly Schlick's view would be broad enough to include any of the entities required in scientific theories.

If a more restrictive version of verifiability in principle be adopted, the field of the meaningful must be limited to what is verifiable according to certain scientific principles. This is to say that a physical possibility of verification rather than a logical one becomes the criterion of meaningfulness. This is open to two objections the first of which is admirably presented by Schlick:[8]

> Now since we cannot boast of a complete and sure knowledge of nature's laws, it is evident that we can never assert with certainty the empirical possibility of any fact, and here we may be permitted to speak of *degrees* of possibility. Is it possible for me to lift this book? Surely–This table? I think so!–This billard table? I don't think so! This automobile? Certainly not!–It is clear in these cases the answer is given by *experience*, as the result of experiments performed in the past. Any judgment about empirical possibility is based on experience

[7]Moritz Schlick, "Meaning and Verification," *Philosophical Review* XLV (1936), 339-368. Reprinted in Feigl, H. and Sellars, W. *Readings in Philosophical Analysis* (New York, 1949), 146-171. Page references are to this reprint.

[8]*Op. cit.*, 153.

and will often be rather uncertain; there will be no sharp boundary between possibility and impossibility.

The result of this shading off from physical possibility to physical impossibility, Schlick argues, is the lack of any clear-cut standard of what is meaningful. Instead of a sharp dichotomy between the meaningful and meaningless, there would be a continuum of degrees of meaning.

The other difficulty is related and pertains to the fact that there are changes with respect to what physical laws are accepted and these changes extend even to the laws which at a given period are best established. Physical possibility must be determined by reference to accepted physical laws and if it is made the criterion of meaningfulness, then an expression may gain or lose meaning as the result of an experiment. If the bestowal of meaning is considered merely as a fiat, this need cause no surprise; but if meaning is intended to be correlated with the phenomena of understanding, the conclusion is impossible to accept. The occurrence of a result in a way to upset an established theory is a contingent matter, determinable only a posteriori. The occurrence of the phenomena of understanding in a given person is also a empirical matter, determinable only a posteriori. That the two should be so related that the first occurrence inhibits the second is an empirical claim for which, so far as I know, there is not the slightest shred of evidence.

Any attempt to narrow verifiability in principle beyond the limits of logical possibility then runs into the difficulties which we have noticed. If, on the other hand, the full scope of logical possibility is allowed, it is not clear that anything of traditional metaphysics would be excluded. Faced with this dilemma, Carnap has, in disagreement with Schlick, accepted the first alternative[9] without, however, making at all clear how the difficulties we have noticed are to be met. Rather than working along such lines, Carnap has taken a more constructivist approach and attempted to build up the set of allowable concepts.

He begins with a group of predicates called "observable" and while the term has no formal definition within his system, it is explained as follows:

> A predicate 'P' of a language L is called *observable* for an organism (e.g. a person) N, if, for suitable arguments e.g. 'b', N is able under suitable circumstances to come to a decision with the help of few observations about a full sentence, say 'P(b),' *i.e.*, to a confirmation of either 'P(b)' or '∼P(b)' of such a high degree that he will either accept or reject 'P(b).'[10]

Clearly all the difficulties previously pointed out are inherent in the concept as so explained and Carnap himself admits that the explanation

[9]Cf. "Testability and Meaning," *loc. cit.*, 423.
[10]*Ibid.*, 455.

is vague. He proceeds, however, to introduce other predicates by means of *reduction sentences*. These are pairs of expressions of the form:

$$Q_1 (x) \supset \cdot Q_2 (x) \supset Q_3 (x) \text{ and}$$
$$Q_4 (x) \supset \cdot Q_5 (x) \supset \sim Q_3 (x)$$

Where Q_1 and Q_4 state experimental conditions or other conditions of observation; Q_2 and Q_5, results of observations; and Q_3 is a new predicate introduced by the reduction sentences. The procedure is intended to give meaning to a new concept in certain cases, i.e., those in which $Q_1 (x) \cdot Q_2 (x) \cdot \mathbf{v} \cdot Q_4 (x) \cdot Q_5 (x)$ holds, but not in any others. Thus, to quote one of Carnap's examples, if x is placed in water (Q_1), then if x dissolves (Q_2), x is soluble (Q_3). This explains the conditions under which the term 'soluble' is to be attributed to something. Similar conditions would explain when it is to be denied. In this particular case $Q_4 = Q_1$ and $Q_5 = \sim Q_2$. There is a *prima facie* difficulty here, namely, that this mode of introducing terms allows the term 'soluble' to be used meaningfully only in the case of objects which are immersed. This is precisely where the term is not needed; there is little point in saying that something is soluble when it is already dissolved; one needs, rather, a way of saying that something which has not been immersed is soluble. Carnap meets this difficulty as follows:

> In the case of the predicate 'soluble in water' we may perhaps add the law stating that two bodies of the same substance are either both soluble or both not soluble.[11]

This requires the introduction of the notion of a substance, though not of course in any metaphysical sense, and this notion is considerably more complex than that of predicate. Still, it does accomplish what was intended and allows a useful application of 'soluble' and other disposition predicates.

There is a question of just what can be accomplished by means of reduction sentences. Clearly, as is indicated above, the procedure will serve to introduce disposition predicates, though I am inclined to agree with Pap that this can better be done in terms of a connective of the sort required for counter-factual conditionals.[12] How much further one can go, however, is difficult to see; in particular it is difficult to see how inferred entities such as notions of atom, electron and the like can be introduced in this manner. There is a two-fold problem here: do such inferred entities belong to science and, if so, can they be introduced by Carnap's theory.

On the first point, it is necessary to distinguish two aspects of theories generally, what may be called their static as opposed to their dynamic

[11] *Ibid.*, 445.

[12] Arthur Pap, "Reduction-Sentences and Open Concepts," *Methodos* V (1953), 3-30.

aspects. The distinction is drawn by analogy to the contrast of hydrostatics to hydrodynamics. From the static point of view, one regards a theory as it is at a moment, without regard to how it developed or how it may change in the future. There can be no growth of concepts; for a concept to change its meaning would be for it to become a different concept. Ideally, at least, each statement in a scientific theory would be assigned its weight or probability and what one would have is the science frozen at a moment. The dynamic point of view, however, stresses continuity. Theories change but are recognizably the same theory, concepts have a history and probabilities change with the accretion of evidence. It may be that the dynamic aspect of theories is not considered within the scope of philosophy of science at all, and certainly it cannot be handled in terms of formal logic; but at the very least changing theories are understood and so provide material for a theory of meaning.

An example may make the distinction clearer and, for this purpose, the nineteenth century kinetic theory of gases will do as well as any. The theory assumed that gases are composed of elastic particles, small relative to the distances between them, with random distribution of velocities but with mean kinetic energy proportional to the absolute temperature. None of these assumptions could, of course, be substantiated by direct observation; still they gave rise to such results as the gas equation, explanations of deviation from the gas equations at high pressures, Dalton's law, and other laws all of which were subject to more immediate confirmation. If one raises the question of the purpose and justification of such inferred entities as the molecules of this theory, one is in the midst of a controversy which continues to the present time and where a variey of answers is possible. This much at least would be conceded on all sides: that the inferred entities provide a means of summarizing the entire theory and that they provide a way of developing the theory. By adding assumptions as to the degrees of freedom of the particles, for example, new phenomena could be brought within the scope of the theory. This is not to claim that these are the only uses of inferred entities—it may well be that the inferred entities give us a picture of reality, but this much is disputable and we shall confine our attention to the two stated claims.

Now granted the static point of view, the point of view which confines itself to the instantaneous view of the science, there is no interest in inferred entities as a matrix of growth. In many cases, moreover, it seems theoretically possible to enumerate the observable laws of the system or or at least a subset of these laws from which the others can be deduced. From this point of view the only indubitable advantages of the inferred entities disappear and it seems natural in an idealization of the science to eliminate them. Thus it becomes natural to limit the meaning of scientific statements to their verifiable content and so to arrive at a position like that of Mach. If, on the other hand, the dynamic aspects were kept in prominence, the function of inferred entities as providing a basis for change could not so easily be neglected. It would be necessary to give some place to statements involving inferred entities which recognized them as meaningful in their own right.

I do not wish here to object to the static view of science, for certainly it has its uses. It serves admirably to bring out the deductive element in science and to show something of its logical structure. Its influence,—for it has been quite wide-spread—has made for rigor, particularly in the social sciences. Some approximation to a consideration of scientific change may be obtained, moreover, by considering a series of instantaneous views of a theory. Still, it is fair to emphasize that this is only one aspect of the situation and that the other view of science is equally possible.

If one considers alterations and developments of the kinetic theory, these took place by varying the conception of the gas molecule, by allowing differing sizes and degrees of freedom to the molecules. There is a parallel situation in the development of the atomic theory where different models of the atom served as the basis of different views. Viewing the development of theory, it seems difficult to ignore the status of hypothetical constructs.

It is not part of the present argument that such hypothetical entities must exist or even that scientists working with them must believe that they exist. It may be that they are thought of merely as instruments of prediction; but the point is that, if they are to serve any useful purpose, statements about them must be understood. Such statements must be understood, moreover, as something different from their verifiable consequences, otherwise there would be no process of derivation of these consequences. Another reason pointing in the same direction is the constant complaint that the properties of hypothetical entities cannot be derived from observable laws. Since the converse derivation is possible, there must be an additional element in these statements not found in the former. I do not see how one can escape the conclusion that this represents something understood, but something which at the same time is unverifiable.

To claim that there is an unverifiable element in the theory of gases is not of course to claim that the theory itself, taken as a whole, is unverifiable. This would be silly. It is, however, to claim that the theory says something more than the sum-total of its verifications. We have seen that this element has a role in the development of theories. The question now is: Can it be introduced into a language by means of reduction sentences?

Quite clearly I think the answer is no. Reduction sentences give meaning to terms under certain conditions. Thus in the general schema of reduction sentences Q_3 (x) is meaningful only under conditions $Q_1 (x) \cdot Q_2 (x) \cdot \mathbf{v} \cdot Q_4 (x) \cdot Q_5 (x)$. Thus originally 'soluble' was meaningful only for something immersed in water which dissolved or something immersed which did not dissolve. The extension which Carnap suggested would extend the meaning to anything which was the same kind of substance as something which dissolved when immersed or which did not dissolve when immersed. Even with further extensions there would be some condition of meaningfulness of the introduced term. This condition may be treated as a presupposition; this is to say that to use a predicate introduced by reduction sentences is to presuppose a certain state of affairs in the absence of which the predicate is undefined. Granted the presupposition, moreover, the reduction sentences function as ordinary definitions with the introduced term eliminable in the usual fashion. We may substitute for the reduction sentences, then, a set of presuppositions and ordinary definitions. In this arrangement the predicates will be either observable or else introduced by reduction sentences. Since the series of introductions is finite, everything can be reduced to presuppositions stated exclusively in terms of observable predicates and definitions whose definientes are observable predicates. In these terms there seems to be no possibility of getting at the unverifiable and hence unobservable components of physical theory.

If this analysis is correct, it is not merely the case that a verifiability theory of meaning is not implied by an analysis of the language of science, but, more positively, there are aspects of it which preclude the adoption of any theory such as Carnap's, if the theory be viewed as a descriptive hypothesis concerning the language. The point may be stated alternatively that if one's motive is to follow scientific usage, he will not stipulate a verifiability theory.

IV

So far, the verifiability theory has been treated as a descriptive hypothesis without consideration of the norms which it might embody. This remains to be done. Fortunately, the normative and descriptive elements are related and this discussion can be brief.

One might hold a verifiability theory, not on grounds that meanings as actually used all conformed to it, but for the reason that the meanings which did conform were in some manner preferable to others. Such a feeling might lead to a suggestion for the reform of language in the direction of a verifiability theory or even to a stipulative definition of meaning. This sort of motive has, I think, been strong among the holders of the theory and it may be well to survey these advantages.

If one adheres to a verifiability criterion of meaning, all questions which he raises will be answerable in principle and discussions will be avoided which are incapable of solution. This certainly is an advantage and it is desirable to start a discussion with the assurance that it is not impossible to reach a conclusion. Again, concepts seem clearer to the extent to which they can be expressed in terms of observable characteristics. If this is coupled with some such device as a linguistic system admitting of a clear-cut set of stated descriptions, such as Carnap employs, the resulting feeling of clarity is even greater.

If I have stated these advantages briefly it is not because I under-estimate them or fail to feel their force. While admitting every advantage of concepts which conform to the verifiability requirement, the upshot of our previous discussion is that they are simply not sufficient to deal with the range of meanings actually employed. If one is to have any respect for the phenomena of meaning, other forms of meaning must be admitted. To call these other forms meaningless is to belie the facts of understanding.

Any sort of investigation must have as its goals both rigor and breadth, but one of these goals may momentarily be placed ahead of the other. Different groups may differ in their stress, as is illustrated in the field of psychology where academic psychology stresses rigor and psychoanalysis emphasizes scope, though in the end each hopes for a comprehensive theory both exact and broad. If the verifiability theories similarly were conceived as one approach to philosophy stressing rigor at the expense of broadness, but hoping ultimately to achieve greater scope, there could be no objection to them. They would be compatible with other attempts which place primary emphasis on breadth. In Kantian language this would be a regulative use of the theories and they would amount merely to an injunction to be as rigorous as possible. Instead, however, they have most often been used constitutively as definitive of meaning rather than a plea to use rigorous concepts wherever possible. This use does not seem justified.

PAUL HENLE

DEPARTMENT OF PHILOSOPHY
UNIVERSITY OF MICHIGAN
SEPTEMBER, 1954.

5

Karl R. Popper

THE DEMARCATION BETWEEN SCIENCE AND METAPHYSICS*

Summary

PUT in a nut-shell, my thesis amounts to this. The repeated attempts made by Carnap to show that the demarcation between science and metaphysics coincides with that between sense and nonsense have failed. The reason is that the positivistic concept of "meaning" or "sense" (or of verifiability, or of inductive confirmability, etc.) is inappropriate for achieving this demarcation—simply because metaphysics need not be meaningless even though it is not science. In all its variants demarcation by meaninglessness has tended to be *at the same time too narrow and too wide:* as against all intentions and all claims, it has tended to exclude scientific theories as meaningless, while failing to exclude even that part of metaphysics which is known as "rational theology."

I. *Introduction*

Writing about Carnap—and in criticism of Carnap—brings back to my mind the time when I first met him, at his Seminar, in 1928 or 1929. It brings back even more vividly a later occasion, in 1932, in the beautiful Tyrolese hills, when I had the opportunity of spending part of my holidays in prolonged critical discussions with Carnap and with Herbert Feigl, in the company of our wives. We had a happy time, with plenty of sunshine, and I think we all tremendously enjoyed these long and fascinating talks, interspersed with a little climbing but never interrupted by

*(Added in proofs.) This paper was begun in 1953 and was sent in its final form to the Editor of this volume in January 1955.

In view of the delay in the publication of this volume my contribution has been, with the permission of Professor Schilpp, distributed in a stencilled version since June 1956; it is also contained in my *Conjectures and Refutations,* 1962. Apart from small stylistic corrections, I have made no changes in the text although since my contribution was written I have further developed a number of points in various publications. See especially my "Probability Magic or Knowledge out of Ignorance," *Dialectica,* XI, 1957, 354-374; my *Logic of Scientific Discovery,* 1959, 1960, 1961, new appendix, especially p. 390f.; latter chapter; and a Note in *Mind,* LXXI, N.S., 1962, "On Carnap's Version of Laplace's Rule of Succession." See also a forthcoming note in *Mind:* "Demonstrable Irrelevance: A Reply to Professor Richard C. Jeffrey."

it. None of us will ever forget, I am sure, how Carnap once led us in a steep climb up a trackless hill, through a beautiful and almost impenetrable thicket of alpine rhododendrons; and how he led us, at the same time, through a beautiful and almost impenetrable thicket of arguments whose topic induced Feigl to christen our hill *"Semantische Schnuppe"* (something like "Semantical Shooting Star")—though several years had to elapse before Carnap, stimulated by Tarski's criticism, discovered the track which led him from Logical Syntax to Semantics.[1]

I found in Carnap not only one of the most captivating persons I had ever met, but also a thinker utterly absorbed in, and devoted to, his problems, and eager to listen to criticism. And indeed, among some other characteristics which Carnap shares with Bertrand Russell—whose influence upon Carnap and upon us all was greater than anyone else's—is his intellectual courage in changing his mind, under the influence of criticism, even on points of fundamental importance to his philosophy.

I had come to the Tyrol with the manuscript of a large book, entitled *Die beiden Grundprobleme der Erkenntnistheorie* ("The Two Fundamental Problems of Epistemology"). It is still unpublished, but an English translation may appear one day; parts of it were later incorporated, in a much abbreviated form, in my *Logik der Forschung (The Logic of Scientific Discovery).* The "two problems" were the problems of induction and demarcation—*the demarcation between science and metaphysics.* The book contained, among much else, a fairly detailed criticism of Wittgenstein's and Carnap's doctrine of the "elimination" or "overthrow" *(Ueberwindung*[2]*)* of metaphysics through meaning-analysis. I criticised this doctrine not from a metaphysical point of view, but from the point of view of one who, interested in science, feared that this doctrine, far from defeating the supposed enemy metaphysics, in effect presented the enemy with the keys of the beleaguered city.

My criticism was directed, largely, against two books of Carnap's, *Der logische Aufbau der Welt, "Aufbau,"* for short, and *Scheinprobleme in der Philosophie,* and some of his articles in *Erkenntnis.* Carnap accepted part of it,[3] although he felt, as it turned out,[4] that I had exaggerated the

[1]In 1932 Carnap used the term "Semantics" as a synonym for "logical syntax;" see *Erkenntnis,* III (1932), 177.

[2]See Carnap's "Ueberwindung der Metaphysik durch logische Analyse der Sprache" ("The Overthrow of Metaphysics through Logical Analysis of Language"), *Erkenntnis,* II (1932), 219ff.

[3]See Carnap's generously appreciative report on certain of my then still unpublished views in *Erkenntnis,* III (1932), 223-228 (and my discussion of it in my *Logik der Forschung* (1934), note 1 to § 29). (Added in proofs: my *Logik der Forschung* has now been published in English as *The Logic of Scientific Discovery,* with some new additions, in 1959.)

[4]See Carnap's review of my *Logik der Forschung* in *Erkenntnis,* V (1935), 290-294, esp. 293: "By his efforts to characterize his position clearly [Popper] is led to over-

differences between my views and those of the Vienna Circle of which he was a leading member.

This silenced me for many years,[5] especially as Carnap paid so much attention to my criticism in his *Testability and Meaning*. But I felt all the time that the differences between our views were far from being imaginary; and my feeling that they were important was much enhanced by Carnap's most recent papers and books on probability and induction.

The purpose of this paper is to discuss these differences, so far as they concern the problem of demarcation. It is with reluctance that I expose myself again to the charge of exaggerating differences. (But I hope that Professor Carnap won't be prevented from speaking his mind by an apprehension of silencing me for the rest of my days: I promise to be more reasonable this time.) I have, however, accepted the invitation to write this paper; and this leaves me no alternative but to try to characterize our differences as clearly and as sharply as possible. In other words, I must try to defend the thesis that these differences are real—as real as I have felt them to be for the last 25 years.

In § II of this paper I try to give a brief outline of some of my own views which form the basis of my criticism. In the later sections I try to trace the development—as I see it—of Carnap's views on the problem of the demarcation between science and metaphysics. My approach throughout is critical rather than historical; but I have aimed at historical accuracy, if not at historical completeness.

II. *My Own View of the Problem*

It was in 1919 that I first faced the problem of *drawing a line of demarcation* between those statements and systems of statements which could be properly described as belonging to empirical science, and others which might, perhaps, be described as "pseudo-scientific" or (in certain contexts) as "metaphysical," or which belonged, perhaps, to pure logic or to pure mathematics.

emphasize the differences between his views and those . . . which are most closely allied to his. . . . [Popper] is very close indeed to the point of view of the Vienna Circle. In his presentation, the differences appear much greater than they are in fact."

[5] I published nothing even alluding to these differences of opinion during the first ten years after the publication of my *Logik der Forschung* (although I alluded to them in some lectures); and next to nothing during the next ten years, i.e. until I started on the present paper—no more, at any rate, than a few critical remarks on Wittgenstein and Schlick. (Cf. my *Open Society,* first published in 1945; see notes 51f., 46, 26, and 48 to chapter 11; and in a paper "The Nature of Philosophical Problems," *British Journal for the Philosophy of Science,* III (1952) and two critical allusions to the theory of meaninglessness (in a paper in the *Proc. of the 11th Intern. Congress of Phil.,* Brussels, VII (1953); and in a little dialogue "Self-Reference and Meaning in Ordinary Language," *Mind* LXII (1954). These papers are now republished in *Conjectures and Refutations.*)

This is a problem which has agitated many philosophers since the time of Bacon although I have never found a very explicit formulation of it. The most widely accepted view was that science was characterized by its *observational basis,* or by its *inductive method,* while pseudo-sciences and metaphysics were characterized by their *speculative method;* or as Bacon said, by the fact that they operated with *"mental anticipations"*—something very similar to hypotheses.

This view I have never been able to accept. The modern theories of physics, especially Einstein's theory (widely discussed in the year 1919) were highly speculative and abstract, and very far removed from what might be called their "observational basis." All attempts to show that they were more or less directly "based on observations" were unconvincing. The same was true even of Newton's theory. Bacon had raised objections against the Copernican system on the ground that it "needlessly did violence to our senses"; and in general the best physical theories always resembled what Bacon had dismissed as "mental anticipations."

On the other hand, many superstitious beliefs, and many rule-of-thumb procedures (for planting, etc.) to be found in popular almanacs and dream books, have had much more to do with observations, and have no doubt often been based on something like induction. Astrologers, more especially, have always claimed that their "science" was based upon a great wealth of inductive material. This claim is, perhaps, unfounded; but I have never heard of any attempt to discredit astrology by a critical investigation of its alleged inductive material. Nevertheless, astrology was rejected by modern science because it did not fit accepted theories and methods.

Thus there clearly was a need for a different criterion of demarcation; and I proposed (though years elapsed before I published this proposal) that the *refutability or falsifiability or testability* of a theoretical system should be taken as the criterion of its demarcation. According to this view which I still uphold, a system is to be considered as scientific only if it makes assertions which may clash with observations; and a system is, in fact, tested by attempts to produce such clashes, that is to say, by attempts to refute it. Thus testability is the same as refutability, and can therefore likewise be taken as a criterion of demarcation.

This is a view of science which sees in its *critical approach* its most important characteristic. Thus a scientist should look upon a theory from the point of view of whether it can be critically discussed: whether it exposes itself to criticism of all kinds; and—if it does—whether it is able to stand up to it. Newton's theory, for example, predicted deviations from Kepler's laws (due to the interactions of the planets) which had not been observed at the time. It exposed itself thereby to attempted empirical refutations whose failure meant the success of the theory. Einstein's theory was tested in a similar way. And indeed, all real tests are attempted refutations. Only if a theory successfully withstands the pressure of these attempted refutations can we claim that it is confirmed or corroborated by experience.

There are, moreover (as I found later[6]), *degrees of testability:* some theories expose themselves to possible refutations more boldly than others. For example, a theory from which we can deduce precise numerical predictions about the splitting up of the spectral lines of light emitted by atoms in magnetic fields of varying strength will be more exposed to experimental refutation than one which merely predicts that a magnetic field influences the emission of light. A theory which is more precise and more easily refutable than another will also be the more interesting one. Since it is the more daring one, it will be the one which is *less probable.* But it is better testable, for *we can make our tests more precise and more severe.* And if it stands up to severe tests it will be better confirmed, or better attested, by these tests. *Thus confirmability (or attestability) must increase with testability.*

This indicates that the criterion of demarcation cannot be an absolutely sharp one but will itself have degrees. There will be well-testable theories, hardly testable theories, and non-testable theories. Those which are non-testable are of no interest to scientists. They may be described as metaphysical.

Here I must again stress a point which has often been misunderstood. Perhaps I can avoid these misunderstandings if I put my point now in this way. Take a square to represent the class of all statements of a language in which we intend to formulate a science; draw a broad horizontal line, dividing it into an upper and lower half; write "science" and "testable" into the upper half, and "metaphysics" and "non-testable" into the lower: then I hope, you will realize that I do *not* propose to draw the line of demarcation in such a way that it coincides with the limits of a language, leaving science inside, and banning metaphysics by excluding it from the class of meaningful statements. On the contrary: beginning with my first publication on this subject,[7] I stressed the fact that it would be *inadequate* to draw the line of demarcation between science and metaphysics so as to exclude metaphysics as nonsensical from a meaningful language.

I have indicated one of the reasons for this by saying that we must not try to draw the line too sharply. This becomes clear if we remember that most of our scientific theories originate in myths. The Copernican system, for example, was inspired by a Neo-Platonic worship of the light of the Sun who had to occupy the "centre" because of his nobility. This indi-

[6]See *Logik der Forschung,* §§ 31 to 46.

[7]See "Ein Kriterion des empirischen Charakters theoretischer Systeme," *Erkenntnis,* III (1933), 426ff., cf. *Logik der Forschung,* esp. §§ 4 and 10.

cates how myths may develop testable components. They may, in the course of discussion, become fruitful and important for science. In my *Logik der Forschung*[8] I gave several examples of myths which have become most important for science, among them atomism and the corpuscular theory of light. It would hardly contribute to clarity if we were to say that these theories are nonsensical gibberish in one stage of their development, and then suddenly become good sense in another.

Another argument is the following. It may happen—and it turns out to be an important case—that a certain statement belongs to science since it is testable, while *its negation* turns out not to be testable so that it must be placed below the line of demarcation. This is indeed the case with the most important and most severely testable statements—the *universal laws of science.* I recommended, in my *Logik der Forschung,* that they should be expressed, for certain purposes, in a form like "There does not exist any perpetual motion machine" (this is sometimes called "Planck's formulation of the First Law of Thermodynamics"); that is to say, in the form of a *negation of an existential statement.* The corresponding existential statement—"There exists a perpetual motion machine"—would belong, I suggested, together with "There exists a sea serpent" to those below the line of demarcation, as opposed to "There is a sea serpent now on view in the British Museum" which is well above the line since it can be easily tested. But we do not know how to test an isolated purely existential assertion.

I cannot in this place argue for the adequacy of the view that isolated purely existential statements should be classed as untestable and as falling outside the scientist's range of interest.[9] I only wish to make clear that *if* this view is accepted, then it would be strange to call metaphysical statements meaningless,[10] or to exclude them from our language. For if we accept the *negation* of an existential statement as meaningful, then we must accept the existential statement itself also as meaningful.

I have been forced to stress this point because my position has repeatedly been described as a proposal to take falsifiability or refutability as the criterion of *meaning* (rather than of demarcation), or as a proposal to exclude existential statements from our language, or perhaps from the

[8]*Logik der Forschung,* § 85, p. 206.

[9]*Ibid.,* § 15. I suppose that some people found it hard to accept the view that a pure or isolated existential statement ("There exists a sea-serpent") should be called "metaphysical," even though it might be deducible from a statement of an empirical character ("There is now a sea-serpent on view in the entrance hall of the British Museum"). But they overlooked the fact that (a) in so far as it was so deducible, it was no longer isolated, but belonged to a testable theory, and (b) if a statement is deducible from an empirical or a scientific statement then this fact need not make it empirical or scientific. (Any tautology is so deducible.)

[10]But one may perhaps find in Brouwer's theories a suggestion that a universal statement could be meaningful while its existential negation was meaningless.

language of science. Even Carnap, who discusses my position in considerable detail and reports it correctly, feels himself compelled to interpret it as a proposal to exclude metaphysical statements from some language or other.[11]

But it is a fact that beginning with my first publication on this subject (see note 7 above), I have always dismissed the problem of meaninglessness as a pseudo-problem; and I opposed the idea that it may be identified with the problem of demarcation. This is my view still.

III. *Carnap's First Theory of Meaninglessness*

One of the theories which I had criticized in my manuscript (and later, more briefly, in my *Logik der Forschung*) was the assertion that *metaphysics was meaningless, and consisted of nonsensical pseudo-propositions.* This theory[12] was supposed to bring about the "overthrow" of metaphysics, and to destroy it more radically and more effectively than any earlier anti-metaphysical philosophy. But as I pointed out in my criticism, the theory was based on a naive and "naturalistic"[13] view of the problem of meaningfulness; moreover, its propagators, in their anxiety to oust metaphysics, failed to notice that they were throwing all *scientific theories* on one same scrap-heap with the "meaningless" metaphysical theories. All this, I suggested, was a consequence of trying to destroy metaphysics instead of looking for a criterion of demarcation.

The "naturalistic" theory (as I called it) of meaningfulness and meaninglessness in Carnap's *Aufbau,* which here followed Wittgenstein's *Tractatus,* was abandoned by Carnap long ago; it has been replaced by the more sophisticated doctrine that a given expression is a meaning-

[11]See *Testability and Meaning,* § 25, p. 26: "We may take Popper's principle of falsifiability as an example of the choice of this language" (viz. of a language that excludes existential sentences as meaningless). Carnap continues: "Popper is however very cautious in the formulation of his . . . principle [of demarcation]; he does not call the [existential] sentences meaningless but only non-empirical or metaphysical." This second part of the quotation is perfectly correct, and seems quite clear to me; but Carnap continues: "Perhaps he [Popper] wishes to exclude existential sentences and other metaphysical sentences not from the language altogether, but only from the language of empirical science." But why does Carnap assume that I should wish to exclude them from *any* language, when I had repeatedly said the opposite?

[12]Carnap and the Vienna Circle attributed it to Wittgenstein, but it is much older. The theory goes back to Hobbes, at least; and in the form described below as "condition (a)"—asserting that words purporting to denote unobservable entities cannot have any meaning—it was clearly and forcefully used by Berkeley (and other nominalists). See my "Note on Berkeley as Precursor of Mach," *B.J.P.S.,* IV (1953), 26f; now in my *Conjectures and Refutations);* also my reference to Hume, *Logik der Forschung,* § 4.

[13]Although I called the theory "naturalistic" (I now also call it "absolutistic" and "essentialistic;" cf. note 18 below) for reasons which may perhaps emerge, I do not propose to argue these reasons here; for my criticism of the theory was not, and is not, that it is "naturalistic" etc., but that it is untenable. See also the passages referred to in note 7 above.

ful sentence of a certain (artificial) language if and only if it complies with the rules of formation for well-formed formulae or sentences of that language.

In my opinion, the development from the naive or naturalistic theory to the more sophisticated doctrine was a highly important and a highly desirable one. But its full significance has not been appreciated, as far as I can see; it has not been noticed, apparently, that it simply destroys the doctrine of the meaninglessness of metaphysics.

It is for this reason that I am now going to discuss this development in some detail.

By the naturalistic theory of meaninglessness I mean the doctrine that every linguistic expression purporting to be an assertion is either meaningful or meaningless; not by convention, or as a result of rules which have been laid down by convention, but as a matter of actual fact, or due to its nature, just as a plant is, or is not, green in fact, or by nature, and not by conventional rules.

According to Wittgenstein's famous verifiability criterion of meaning, which Carnap accepted, a sentence-like expression, or a string of words, was a meaningful sentence (or proposition) if, and only if, it satisfied the conditions (a) and (b)—or a condition (c) which will be stated later:

(a) all words which occurred in it had meaning, *and*

(b) all words which occurred in it fitted together properly.

According to condition (a) of the theory (which goes back to Hobbes and Berkeley) a string of words was meaningless if any word in it was meaningless. Wittgenstein formulated it in his *Tractatus* (6.53; italics mine): "The right method of philosophy is this: when someone . . . wished to say something *metaphysical,* to demonstrate to him that *he had given no meaning to certain signs* in his propositions." According to Hobbes and Berkeley the only way in which a meaning was given to a word was by linking (associating) the word with certain observable experiences or phenomena. Wittgenstein himself was not explicit on this point, but Carnap was. In his *Aufbau,* he tried to show that *all concepts used in the sciences could be defined on the basis of* ("my own") *observational or perceptional experience.* He called such a definition of a concept its "constitution," and the resulting system of concepts a *"constitution system."* And he asserted that *metaphysical concepts could not be constituted.*

Condition (b) of the theory goes back to Bertrand Russell who suggested[14] that certain "combinations of symbols," which looked like propositions, "must be absolutely meaningless, not simply false," if certain paradoxes were to be avoided. Russell did not mean to make a *proposal* —that we should *consider* these combinations as contrary to some (partly

[14]See, for example, *Principia Mathematica,* 2nd edition, p. 77.

conventional) rules for forming sentences, in order to avoid the paradoxes. Rather, he *thought that he had discovered the fact* that these apparently meaningful formulae expressed nothing; and that they were, in nature or in essence, meaningless pseudo-propositions. A formula like *"a* is an element of *a"* or *"a* is not an element of *a"* looked like a proposition (because it contained two subjects and a two-termed predicate); but it was not a genuine proposition (or sentence) because a formula of the form *"x* is an element of *y"* could be a proposition only if *x* was one type level lower than *y*—a condition which obviously could not be satisfied if the same symbol, *"a"*, was to be substituted for both, *"x"* and *"y"*.

This showed that a disregard of the type-level of words (or of the entities designated by them) could make sentence-like expressions meaningless; and according to Wittgenstein's *Tractatus* and more explicitly, Carnap's *Aufbau,* this confusion was a major source of metaphysical nonsense, i.e. of the offering of pseudo-propositions for propositions. It was called "confusion of spheres" in the *Aufbau;*[15] it is the same kind of confusion which nowadays is often called a "category mistake."[16] According to the *Aufbau,* for example, "my own" experiences *("das Eigenpsychische");* physical bodies; and the experiences of others *("das Fremdpsychische"),* all belong to different spheres or types or categories, and a confusion of these must lead to pseudo-propositions and to pseudo-problems. (Carnap describes the differences between physical and psychological entities as one between *"two types of order"*[17] subsisting within *one* kind or range of *ultimate entities,* which leads him to a solution of the body-mind problem on the lines of "neutral monism.")

The outline just given of the "naive" or "naturalistic" theory[18] of meaningful and meaningless linguistic expressions covers only one side of this theory. There is another side to the so-called *"verifiability criterion"* which may be formulated as the condition (c):

(c) an alleged proposition (or sentence) is genuine if and only if it is a truth function of, or reducible to, elementary (or atomic) propositions expressing observations or perceptions.

[15]*"Sphaerenvermengung"*; see *Aufbau,* § 30f; the *"Sphaere"* is identified with the *logical type* in § 180, p. 254.

[16]See G. Ryle, *The Concept of Mind* (1949). This use of the expression "category" may be traced back to Husserl's term "semantical category" *("Bedeutungskategorie");* see his *Logische Untersuchungen,* II, part 1 (second edition) 1913, pp. 13, 318. Examples of category mistakes given by Husserl are: *"green is or"* (p. 54); *"a round or"; "a man and is"* (p. 334). Compare Wittgenstein's example: *"Socrates is identical."* For a criticism of the theory of category mistakes, see my paper "Language and the Body-Mind Problem," *Proc. of the 11th Int. Congress of Philosophy,* Brussels, VII (1953). See also J. J. C. Smart's very striking "A Note on Categories, *B.J.P.S.,* IV, 227f.

[17]*"Ordnungsformen"*; see *Aufbau,* §162, p. 224; see also the bibliography, 225.

[18]At present, I should be inclined to call it an "essentialist" theory, in accordance with my *Poverty of Historicism,* § 10, and my *Open Society,* esp. chapter 11.

In other words, it is meaningful if and only if it is so related to some observation sentences that its truth follows from the truth of these observation sentences. "It is certain," Carnap writes,[19] "that a string of words has meaning only if its derivability relations from protocol-sentences [observation sentences] are given . . ."; that is to say, if "the way to [its] verification . . . is known."[20]

The conditions (a) and (b) on the one hand, and (c) on the other hand, were asserted by Carnap to be equivalent.[21]

A result of this theory was, in Carnap's words,[22] "that the alleged sentences of metaphysics stand revealed, by logical analysis, as pseudo-sentences."

Carnap's theory of the intrinsic meaningfulness or meaninglessness of strings of words was soon to be modified; but in order to prepare a basis for judging these modifications I must say a few words of criticism here.[23]

First, a word on (c), the verifiability criterion of meaning. This criterion excludes from the realm of meaning all scientific theories (or "laws of nature"); for these are no more reducible to observation reports than so-called metaphysical pseudo-propositions. *Thus the criterion of meaning leads to the wrong demarcation of science and metaphysics.* This criticism was accepted by Carnap in his *Logical Syntax of Language*[24] and in his *Testability and Meaning;*[25] but even his latest theories are still open to it, as I shall try to show in § VI, below.

[19]See his paper on the "Overthrow of Metaphysics," *Erkenntnis,* II (1932), 222f. The "Overthrow"-paper belongs, strictly speaking no longer to the period of the *first* theory of meaninglessness, owing to its recognition of the fact that meaninglessness *depends upon the language in question;* for Carnap writes (220): "Meaningless in a precise sense is a string of words which, within a certain given language, does not form a sentence." However, the obvious consequences of this remark are not yet drawn, and the theory is still asserted in an absolute sense: our conditions (a) and (b) are formulated on the bottom of 220, and (c) on 222f. (as quoted).

[20]*Ibid.,* 224.

[21]*Aufbau,* § 161, p. 222; and § 179 (top of 253). See also the important § 2 of Carnap's "Overthrow"-paper, *Erkenntnis,* II (1932), 221-224. (This passage in many ways anticipates, by its general method, the doctrine of reduction of Carnap's *Testability and Meaning,* except that the latter weakens the demand for verification.)

[22]*Erkenntnis,* II, 220. Cf. the foregoing note.

[23]See my *Logik der Forschung,* esp. §§ 4, 10, 14, 20, 25, and 26.

[24]See the end of the first paragraph and the second paragraph on p. 321, esp. the following remarks of Carnap's on the Vienna Circle: "It was originally maintained that every sentence, in order to be significant, must be *completely verifiable*. . . . On this view there was no place for the *laws of nature* amongst the sentences of the language. . . . A detailed criticism of the view according to which laws are not sentences is given by Popper." The continuation of this passage is quoted below, text to note 48. See also note 71, below.

[25]Cf. esp. notes 20 and 25 (and the text following note 25) to § 23 of *Testability and Meaning* with note 7 to § 4 (and text), and note 1 to § 78 of my *Logik der Forschung.*

Next we consider condition (a) of the doctrine, the (nominalistic) view that only empirically definable words or signs have meaning.

Here the situation is even worse, although it is very interesting.

For the sake of simplicity, I begin my criticism with a very simple form of *nominalism.* It is the doctrine that all non-logical (or, as I prefer to say, non-formative) words are names—either such as "Fido," of a single physical object, or as "dog," shared by several such objects. Thus "dog" may be the name shared by the objects Fido, Candy, and Tiffin; and so with all other words.

This view may be said to interpret the various words *extensionally* or *enumeratively;* their "meaning" is given by *a list or an enumeration of the things they name:* "this thing here, and that thing over there . . . ." We may call such an enumeration an "enumerative definition" of the meaning of a name; and a language in which all (non-logical or non-formative) words are supposed to be enumeratively defined may be called an "enumerative language," or a "purely nominalistic language."

Now we can easily show that such a purely nominalistic language is completely inadequate for any scientific purpose. This may be expressed by saying that all its sentences are analytic—either analytically true or contradictory—and that no synthetic sentences can be expressed in it. Or if we prefer a formulation which avoids the terms "analytic" and "synthetic" (which at present are under heavy fire from Professor Quine's guns), then we can put it in this way: in a purely nominalistic language no sentence can be formulated whose truth or falsity could not be decided by merely comparing the defining lists, or enumerations, of the things which are mentioned in the sentence. Thus the truth or falsity of any sentence is decided as soon as the words which occur in it have been given their meaning.

That this is so may be seen from our example. "Fido is a dog" is true because Fido was one of the things enumerated by us in defining "dog." As opposed to this "Chunky is a dog" must be false, simply because Chunky was not one of the things to which we pointed when drawing up our list defining "dog." Similarly, if I give the meaning "white" by listing (1) the paper on which I am now writing, (2) my handkerchief, (3) the cloud over there, and (4) our snowman, then the statement, "I have white hair" will be false, whatever the colour of my hair may be.

It is clear that in such a language hypotheses cannot be formulated. It cannot be a language of science. And conversely, every language adequate for science must contain words whose meaning is not given in an enumerative way. Or, as we may say, every scientific language must make use of *genuine universals,* i.e. of words, whether defined or undefined, with an indeterminate extension, though perhaps with a reasonably definite intensional "meaning": (For the intensional analysis of meaning see Carnap's excellent book *Meaning and Necessity*.)

Precisely the same criticism applies to more complicated languages, especially to languages which introduce their concepts by the method of extensional abstraction (used first by Frege and Russell) provided the class of the fundamental elements upon which this method is based, and the fundamental relations between these elements, are supposed to be given extensionally, by lists. Now this was the case in Carnap's *Aufbau:* he operated with one primitive relation, *"Er"* (Experience of remembering"), which was assumed to be given in the form of a *list of pairs.*[26]

All concepts belonging to his "constitution system" were supposed to be extensionally definable on the basis of this primitive relation *"Er,"* i.e. of the list of pairs which gave a meaning to this relation. Accordingly, all statements which could be expressed in his language were true or false simply according to the (extensional) meaning of the words which occurred in them: they were all either analytically true or contradictory,[27] owing to the absence of genuine universal[28] words.

To conclude this section, I turn to the condition (b) of the theory, and to the doctrine of meaninglessness due to "type mistakes" or "category mistakes." This doctrine was derived, as we have seen, from Russell's theory that an expression like *"a* is an element of the class *a"* must be meaningless—absolutely, or intrinsically or essentially, as it were.

Now this doctrine has long since turned out to be mistaken. Admittedly, it is true that we can, with Russell, construct a language (embodying a theory of types) in which the expression in question is not a well-formed formula. But we can also, with Zermelo, and his successors (Fraenkel, Behmann, von Neumann, Bernays, Lesniewski, Quine, Ackermann) construct languages in which the expression in question is well-formed and thus meaningful; and in some of them it is even a true statement (for certain values of *a*).

These are, of course, well known facts. But they completely destroy the idea of an "inherently" or "naturally" or "essentially" meaningless

26See esp. *Aufbau,* § 108. Carnap said there p. 150 of his *Theorem 1* which asserts the asymmetry of the primitive relation, *"Er,"* that it is an *empirical theorem,* since its asymmetry can be read off the list of (empirically given) pairs. But we must not forget that this is the same list of pairs which "constituted," or defined, *"Er";* moreover, a list of pairs which would lead to the negation of theorem 1, i.e. to the theorem that *"Er"* is symmetrical, could not have been interpreted as an adequate list for *"Er,"* as is particularly clear from §§ 153 to 155.

27This is the criticism of the *Aufbau* which I put to Feigl when we met first. It was a meeting which for me proved momentous for it was Feigl who arranged, a year or two later, the vacation meeting in the Tyrol.

28"The Difference Between Individual Concepts and Universal Concepts" was discussed in the *Aufbau* § 158; it was criticized briefly in my *Logik der Forschung,* §§ 14 and 25.

expression. For the expression "*a* is an element of the class *a*" turns out to be meaningless in one language but meaningful in another; and this establishes the fact that a proof that an expression is meaningless in some language, must not be mistaken for a proof of intrinsic meaninglessness.

In order to prove intrinsic meaninglessness we should have to prove a great deal. We should have to prove not merely that an alleged statement, asserted or submitted by some writer or speaker, is meaningless in *all* (consistent) languages, but also that there cannot exist a meaningful sentence (in any consistent language) which would be recognised by the writer or speaker in question as an alternative formulation of what he intended to say. And nobody has ever suggested how such a proof could possibly be given.

It is important to realize that a proof of intrinsic meaninglessness would have to be valid with respect to *every consistent language* and not merely with respect to *every language that suffices for empirical science.* Few metaphysicians assert that metaphysical statements belong to the field of the empirical sciences; and nobody would give up metaphysics because he is told that its statements cannot be formulated within these sciences (or within some language suitable for these sciences). After all, Wittgenstein's and Carnap's original thesis was that metaphysics is absolutely meaningless—that it is sheer gibberish and nothing else; that it is, perhaps, of the character of sighs or groans or tears (or of surrealist poetry), but not of articulate speech. In order to show this, it would be quite insufficient to produce a proof to the effect that it cannot be expressed in languages which suffice for the needs of science.

But even this insufficient proof has never been produced by anybody, in spite of the many attempts to construct metaphysics-free languages for science. Some of these attempts will be discussed in the next two sections.

IV. *Carnap and the Languages of Science*

Carnap's original "overthrow" of metaphysics was unsuccessful. The naturalistic theory of meaninglessness turned out to be baseless; and the total result was a doctrine which was just as destructive of science as it was of metaphysics. In my opinion this was merely the consequence of an ill-advised attempt to destroy metaphysics wholesale, instead of trying to eliminate, piecemeal as it were, metaphysical elements from the various sciences whenever we can do this without endangering scientific progress by misplaced criticism (such as had been directed by Bacon against Copernicus, or by Duhem and Mach against atomism).

But the naturalistic theory of meaning was abandoned by Carnap a long time ago, as I said before. It has been replaced by the theory that whether a linguistic expression is well-formed or not depends on the rules of the language to which the expression is supposed to belong; together with the theory that the rules of the language are often not precise enough to decide the issue, so that we have to introduce more precise rules—and with them, an *artificial language system.*

I wish to repeat that I regard this as a very important development, and as one that provides the key to a considerable number of interesting problems. *But it leaves the problem of demarcation between science and metaphysics exactly where it was.* This is my thesis.

To put it quite differently, the naive or naturalistic or essentialistic theory of meaningfulness discussed in the previous section is mistaken, and had to be replaced by a theory of well-formed formulae, and with it, of languages which are artificial in being subject to definite rules. This important task has since been carried out by Carnap with great success. *But this reformation of the concept of meaningfulness completely destroys the doctrine of the meaninglessness of metaphysics.* And it leaves us without a hope of ever reconstructing this doctrine on the basis of the reformed concept of meaninglessness.

Unfortunately, this seems to have been overlooked. For Carnap and his circle (Neurath was especially influential) tried to solve the problem by constructing a *"language of science,"* a language in which every legitimate statement of science would be a well-formed formula, while none of the metaphysical theories would be expressible in it—either because the terminology was not available, or because there was no well-formed formula to express it.

I consider the task of constructing artificial model languages for a language of science an interesting one; but I shall try to show that the attempt to combine this task with that of destroying metaphysics (by rendering it meaningless) has repeatedly led to disaster. The anti-metaphysical bias is a kind of philosophical (or metaphysical) prejudice which prevented the system builders from carrying out their work properly.

I shall try to show this briefly, in this section(for (a) the *Physicalistic Language,* (b) the *Language of Unified Science,* (c) the *languages of the "Logical Syntax,"* and *later,* in section 5, more fully for those proposed in *Testability and Meaning.*

(a) *The Physicalistic Language.* Carnap's *Aufbau* had sponsored what he called a *methodological solopsism*—taking one's own experiences as the basis upon which the concepts of science (and thus the language of science) have to be constructed. By 1931 Carnap had given this up, under Neurath's influence, and had adopted the *thesis of physicalism,* according to which there was *one* unified language which spoke about physical things and their movements in space and time. Everything was to be expressible in this language, or translatable into it, especially psychology in so far as it was scientific. Psychology was to become radically behaviouristic; every meaningful statement of psychology, whether human or animal, was to be translatable into a statement about the movements of physical bodies, human or animal, in space and time.

The tendency underlying this programme is clear: a statement about the human soul was to become as meaningless as a statement about God. Now it may be fair enough to put statements about the soul and about God on the same level. But it seems questionable whether anti-metaphysical and anti-theological tendencies were much furthered by placing all our subjective experiences, or rather all statements about them, on the same level of meaninglessness as the statements of metaphysics. (Theologians or metaphysicians might be very pleased to learn that statements such as "God exists" or "The Soul exists" are *on precisely the same level* as "I have conscious experiences" or "There exist feelings —such as love or hate—distinguishable from the bodily movements which often, though not always, accompany them.")

There is no need, therefore, to go into the merits or demerits of the behaviourist philosophy, or the translatability thesis (which, in my opinion, is nothing but materialist metaphysics in linguistic trappings— and I, for one, prefer to meet it without trappings): we see that as an attempt to kill metaphysics this philosophy was not very effective. As usual, the broom of the anti-metaphysicist sweeps away too much, and also too little. As a result we are left with an untidy and altogether untenable demarcation.

For an illustration of "too much and too little" I may perhaps cite the following passage from Carnap's "Psychology Within the Physical Language."[29] "Physics is, altogether, practically free from metaphysics, thanks to the efforts of Mach, Poincaré, and Einstein; in psychology, efforts to make it a science free from metaphysics have hardly begun." Now "free from metaphysics" means here, for Carnap, reducible to protocol-statements. But not even the simplest physical statements about the functioning of a potentiometer—the example is Carnap's[30]—are so reducible. Nor do I see any reason why we should not introduce mental states in our explanatory psychological theories if in physics (old or new) we are permitted to explain the properties of a conductor by the hypothesis of an "electric fluid" or of an "electronic gas."

The point is that all physical theories say much more than we can test. Whether this "more" belongs legitimately to physics, or whether it should be eliminated from the theory as a "metaphysical element" is not always easy to say. Carnap's reference to Mach, Poincaré, and Einstein was unfortunate, since Mach, more especially, looked forward to the final elimination of atomism which he considered (with many other

[29]See *Erkenntnis,* III (1932), p. 117.
[30]*Op. cit.,* 140.

positivists) to be a metaphysical element of physics. (He eliminated too much.) Poincaré tried to interpret physical theories as implicit definitions, a view which can hardly be more acceptable to Carnap; and Einstein has for a long time[30a] been a believer in metaphysics, operating freely with the concept of the "physically real"; although, no doubt, he dislikes pretentious metaphysical verbiage as much as any of us. Most of the concepts with which physics works, such as forces, fields, and even electrons and other particles are what Berkeley (for example) called *"qualitates occultae."* Carnap showed[31] that assuming conscious states in our psychological explanations was exactly analogous to assuming a force—*a qualita occulta*—in order to explain the "strength" of a wooden post; and he believed that "such a view commits the fallacy of hypostatization"[32] of which, he suggested, no physicist is guilty, although it is often committed by psychologists.[33] But the fact is that we cannot explain the strength of the post by its structure alone (as Carnap suggested[34]) but only by its structure together with laws which make ample use of "hidden forces" which Carnap, like Berkeley, condemned as occult.

Before concluding point (a) I wish to mention only briefly that this physicalism, although from my point of view too physicalistic in most respects, was not physicalistic enough in others. For I do believe, indeed, that whenever we wish to put a scientific statement to an observational test, *this test must in a sense be physicalistic;* that is to say, that we test our most abstract theories, psychological as well as physical, by deriving from them statements about the behaviour[35] of physical bodies.

I have called simple descriptive statements, describing easily observable states of physical bodies, *"basic statements,"* and I asserted that, in cases in which tests are needed, it is these basic statements[36]

[30a](Added in proofs.) When I wrote this, Albert Einstein was still alive.

[31]*Op. cit.*, 115.

[32]*Op. cit.*, 116.

[33]*Op. cit.*, 115.

[34]*Op. cit.*, 114.

[35]This behavior, however, is always *interpreted in the light of certain* theories (which creates a danger of circularity). I cannot discuss the problem fully here, but I may mention that the behavior of men, predicted by psychological theories, nearly always consists, not of purely physical movements, but of physical movements which, if interpreted in the light of theories, are "meaningful." (Thus if a psychologist predicts that a patient will have bad dreams, he will feel that he was right, whether the patient reports "I dreamt badly last night," or whether he reports "I want to tell you that I have had a shocking dream"; though the two "behaviors" i.e. the "movements of the lips" may differ *physically* more widely than the movements corresponding to a negation may differ from those corresponding to an affirmation.)

[36]The terms "basic statement" ("basic proposition" or "basic sentence": *"Basissatz"*) and "empirical basis" were introduced in *Logik der Forschung,* §§ 7 and 25 to 30; they have often been used since by other authors, in similar and in different senses.

which we try to compare with the "facts," and that we choose these statements, and these facts, because they are most easily comparable, and intersubjectively most easily testable.

Thus according to my own view, we do *not,* for the purpose of such basic tests, choose reports (which are difficult to test intersubjectively) about our own observational experiences, but rather reports (which are easy to check) about physical bodies—including potentiometers—which we have observed.

The point is important because this theory of mine concerning the "physicalist" character of test statements is radically opposed to all those widely accepted theories which hold that we are constructing the "external world of science" out of "our own experiences." I have always believed that this is a prejudice (it is still widely held); and that, quite properly, we never trust "our own experiences" unless we are confident that they conform with intersubjectively testable views.

Now on this point Carnap's and Neurath's views were much less "physicalistic" at that time. In fact, they still upheld a form of Carnap's original "methodological solipsism." For they taught that the sentences which formed the "empirical basis" (in my terminology) of all tests, and which they called "protocol-sentences," should be reports about *"our own" observational experiences,* although in a physical language, i.e. as reports about our own bodies. In Otto Neurath's formulation, such a protocol-sentence was to have, accordingly, a very queer form. He wrote[37] "A complete protocol-sentence might for example read: 'Otto's protocol at 3.17: [Otto's verbalized thinking was at 3.16: (In this room was at 3.15 a table observed by Otto)].' " One sees that the attempt is made here to incorporate the old starting point—the observer's own subjective experiences, i.e. "methodological solipsism."

Carnap later accepted my view; but in the article ("On Protocol-Sentences"[38]) in which he very kindly called this view of mine "the most adequate of the forms of scientific language at present advocated . . . in the . . . theory of knowledge,"[39] he did not quite appreciate the fact (which he saw clearly in *Testability and Meaning,* as we shall see) that the difference between my view and Neurath's concerned a fundamental point: whether or not to appeal in our tests to simple, observable, *physical facts* or to *"our own sense-experiences"* (methodological solipsism). He therefore said, in his otherwise admirable report of my views, that the testing subject *S* will, "in practice, often stop his tests" when he has arrived at the "observation statements of the protocolling subject *S;*" i.e.

[37]*Erkenntnis* III (1932), 207.

[38]"Ueber Protokollsätze", *Erkenntnis* III (1932), 223-228.

[39]*Op. cit.,* 228; cf. *Testability and Meaning* (see below, note 60, and the next footnote here).

at statements of *his own sense-experience;* whereas I held that he would stop only when he had arrived at a statement about some easily and intersubjectively observable *behaviour of a physical body* (which at the moment did not appear to be problematic).[40]

The point here mentioned is, of course, closely connected with the fact that I never believed in induction (for which it seems natural to start "from our own experiences") but in a *method of testing predictions* deducible from our theories, whereas Neurath did believe in induction. At that time I felt sure that, when reporting my views, Carnap had given up his belief in induction. If so, he has returned to it since.

(b) *The Language of Unified Science.* Closely connected with physicalism was the view that the physicalist language was a universal language in which everything meaningful could be said. *"The physicalist language is universal,"* Carnap wrote.[41] "If, because of its character as a universal language, we adopt the language of physics as the . . . language of science, then all science turns into physics. *Metaphysics is excluded as nonsensical.*[42] The various sciences become parts of the unified science."

It is clear that this *thesis of the one universal language of the one unified science* is closely connected with that of the elimination of metaphysics: if it were possible to express everything that a non-metaphysical scientist may wish to say in one language—one which, by its rules, makes it impossible to express metaphysical ideas—then something like a *prima facie* case would have been made out in favour of the conjecture that metaphysics cannot be expressed in any "reasonable" language. (Of course, the conjecture would still be very far from being established.)

Now the queer thing about this thesis of the *one* universal language is that before it was ever published (on the 30th of December 1932) it had been refuted by a fellow-member of Carnap's of the Vienna Circle. For Gödel, by his two famous incompleteness theorems, had proved that one unified language would not be sufficiently universal for even the purposes of elementary number theory; although we may construct a language in which all assertions of this theory can be *expressed,* no such language suffices for formalising all the proofs of those assertions which (in some other language) can be proved.

It would have been best, therefore, to scrap forthwith this doctrine of the one universal language of the one universal science (especially in view of Gödel's second theorem which showed that it was pointless to try to discuss the consistency of a language in that language itself).

40See also for a brief criticism of Carnap's report, notes 1 and 2 to § 29 of my *Logik der Forschung.* (The quotation in the text next to note 2 of § 29 is from Carnap's report.)

41*Erkenntnis,* III (1932), 108.

42*Loc. cit.,* italics mine.

But more has happened since to establish the impossibility of the thesis of the universal language. I have in mind, especially, Tarski's proof that every universal language is paradoxical (first published in 1933 in Polish, and in 1935 in German). But in spite of all this, the doctrine has survived; at least, I have nowhere seen a recantation.[43] And the so-called "International Encyclopedia of Unified Science," which was founded upon this doctrine (despite my opposition,[44] on the "First Congress for Scientific Philosophy," in Paris, 1935) is still being continued. It will remain a monument to a metaphysical doctrine, once passionately held by Neurath and brilliantly wielded by him as a major weapon in the anti-metaphysical crusade.

For no doubt the strong philosophical belief which inspired this forceful and lovable person was, by his own standards, purely "metaphysical." A unified science in a unified language is really nonsense, I am sorry to say; and demonstrably so, since it has been proved, by Tarski, that no consistent language of this kind can exist. Its logic is outside it. Why should not its metaphysics be outside too?

I do not, of course, suggest that Carnap did not know all this; but I suggest that he did not see its devastating effect upon the doctrine of the unified science in the unified language.

It may be objected, perhaps, that I am taking the doctrine of the unified language too seriously, and that a strictly *formalised* science was not intended. Neurath, for example, used to speak, especially in his later publications, of a "universal slang," which indicates that he

[43]The doctrine is still maintained, in all essentials (although in a more cautious mood) in *Testability and Meaning,* and not touched upon in the corrections and additions added to various passages in 1950; see below, note 50, and text. In an excellent and by now famous paragraph of his *Introduction to Semantics* (§ 39) Carnap indicated "how the views exhibited in [his] earlier book, *The Logical Syntax of Language,* have to be modified as a result, chiefly, of the new point of view, of semantics." But the *Syntax,* although it continues to subscribe to the doctrine of the unified science in a unified language (see esp. § 74, the bottom of 286, and 280ff.) did not investigate this doctrine more fully; which may be perhaps the reason why Carnap overlooked the need to modify this doctrine.

[44]In Paris, I opposed the foundation of the *Encyclopedia.* (Neurath used to call me "the official opposition" of the Circle, although I was never so fortunate as to belong to it.) I pointed out, among other things, that it would have no similarity whatever with an encyclopedia as Neurath conceived it, and that it would turn out to be another series of *Erkenntnis* articles. (For Neurath's ideal of an encyclopedia, see for example his critical article on my *Logik der Forschung, Erkenntnis,* V, 353-365, esp. § 2.) At the Copenhagen Congress, in 1936, which Carnap did not attend, I tried to show that the doctrine of the unity of science, and of the one universal language was incompatible with Tarski's theory of truth. Neurath thereupon suggested in the discussion which followed my lecture that Tarski's theories about the concept of truth must be untenable; and he inspired (if my memory does not deceive me) Arne Ness, who was also present, to undertake an empirical study of the usages of the word "truth," in the hope of thus refuting Tarski. See also Carnap's appropriate remark on Ness, in the *Introduction to Semantics,* 29.

did not think of a *formalised* universal language. I believe that this is true. But this view, again, destroys *the doctrine of the meaninglessness of metaphysics*. For if there are no strict *rules of formation* for the universal slang, then the assertion that we cannot express metaphysical statements in it is gratuitous; and it can only lead us back to the naive naturalistic view of meaninglessness, criticized above in § III.

It may be mentioned in this context that Gödel's (and Church's) discoveries also sealed the fate of another of the pet doctrines of positivism (and of one of my pet aversions[45]). I have in mind Wittgenstein's doctrine: "*The riddle* does not exist. If a question can be put at all, it *can* also be answered."[46]

This doctrine of Wittgenstein's, called by Carnap in the "*Aufbau*,"[47] "the proud thesis of the omnipotence of rational science," was hardly tenable even when it first appeared, if we remember Brouwer's ideas, published long before the *Tractatus* was written. With Gödel (especially with his second theorem of undecidability) and Church, its situation became even worse; for from them we learned that we could never complete even our *methods* of solving problems. Thus a well-formed mathematical question may become "meaningless" if we adopt a criterion of meaning according to which the meaning of a statement lies in the method by which it can be verified (in mathematics: proved or disproved). This shows that we may be able to formulate a question (and, similarly, the possible answers to it) without an inkling as to how we might find out which of the possible answers is true; which demonstrates the superficiality of Wittgenstein's "proud thesis."

Carnap was the first philosopher who recognized the immense importance of Gödel's discoveries, and he did his best to make them known to the philosophical world. It is the more surprising that Gödel's result did not produce that revision which it should have produced in the Vienna Circle's tenets (in my opinion, undoubtedly and obviously metaphysical tenets, all too tenaciously held) concerning the language and the scope of science.

(c) Carnap's *Logical Syntax* is one of the few philosophical books which can be described as of really first rate importance. Admittedly,

[45]Another is 6.1251 of the *Tractatus* (see also 6.1261): "Hence there can never be surprises in logic" which is either trivial (viz. if "logic" is confined to the two-valued propositional calculus) or obviously mistaken, and most misleading in view of 6.234: "Mathematics is a method of logic." I think that nearly every mathematical *proof* is surprising. "By God, this is impossible," Hobbes said when first encountering the theorem of "Pythagoras."

[46]*Tractatus*, 6.5. We also read there: "For an answer which cannot be expressed the question too cannot be expressed." But the question may be "Is this assertion (for example Goldbach's conjecture) demonstrable?" And the true answer may be, "We don't know; perhaps we may never know, and perhaps we can never know."

[47]See *Aufbau*, § 183, p. 261, under "Literature."

some of its arguments and doctrines are superseded, owing mainly to Tarski's discoveries, as Carnap himself explained frankly in that famous last paragraph of his *Introduction to Semantics*. Admittedly, the book is not easy to read (and even more difficult in English than in German). But it is my firm conviction that, if ever a history of the rational philosophy of the earlier half of this century should be written, this book ought to have a place in it second to none. I cannot even try here (wedged between critical analyses) to do justice to it. But one point at least I must mention. It was through this book that the philosophical world to the west of Poland was first introduced to the method of analysing languages in a "metalanguage," and of constructing "object-languages"—a method whose significance for logic and the foundations of mathematics cannot be overrated; and it was in this book that the claim was first made, and, I believe, completely substantiated, that this method was of the greatest importance for the philosophy of science. If I may speak personally, the book (which came out a few months before my *Logik der Forschung,* and which I read while my book was in the press) marks the beginning of a revolution in my own philosophical thinking, although I did not understand it fully (because of its real internal difficulties, I believe) before I had read Tarski's great paper on the Concept of Truth (in the German translation, 1935). Then I realized, of course, that a syntactic metalinguistic analysis was inadequate, and must be replaced by what Tarski called "semantics."

Of course I believe that, from the point of view of the problem of demarcation, a great step forward was made in the *Syntax*. I say "of course," since I am alluding to the fact that some of my criticism was accepted in this book. Part of the relevant passage is quoted above (in note 24). But what is most interesting from our present point of view is the passage immediately following the quotation; it shows, I believe, that Carnap did not accept enough of my criticism. "The view here presented," he writes[48] "allows great freedom in the introduction of new primitive concepts and new primitive sentences in the language of physics or of science in general; yet at the same time it retains the *possibility of differentiating pseudo-concepts and pseudo sentences* from real scientific concepts and sentences, *and thus of eliminating the former.*" Here we find, again, the old thesis of the meaninglessness of metaphysics. But it is mitigated, if only a little, by the immediate continuation of this passage (which Carnap places in square brackets, and which shows the influence of my criticism, mentioned by him on the preceding page). "This elimination, however, is not so simple as it appeared on the basis of the earlier position of the Vienna Circle, which was in essentials that of

[48]*Syntax,* § 82, 322 top. (The italics are Carnap's).

Wittgenstein. On that view it was a question of '*the* language' in an absolute sense; it was thought possible to reject both concepts and sentences if they did not fit into *the* language."

The position indicated by these passages (including the one quoted briefly in note 24 above) may be described as follows:

(1) Some difficulties, especially those of Wittgenstein's verifiability criterion of meaning, are recognized; also the inadequacy of what I have called the "naturalistic" theory of meaningfulness (which corresponds to the belief in "*the* language" in which things simply are, or are not, essentially meaningful by their nature).

(2) But the belief is still maintained that we can, by some feat of ingenuity, establish *one* language which does the trick of rendering meaningless precisely the "metaphysical" concepts and sentences and no others.

(3) Even the belief that we can construct one universal language of unified science is still upheld, in consequence of (2); but it is not stressed, and not examined in detail. (See point (b) in this section, above, and especially the passage from the *Syntax,* §74, p. 286 mentioned in note 43 above.)

This situation does not call for further criticism on my part: practically all that needs to be said I have said before, especially that this approach renders Tarski's Semantics meaningless, and with it most of the theory of logical inference, i.e. of logic. Only one further—and I believe important—comment has to be made.

One of the difficulties of this great and important book of Carnap's lies in its emphasis upon the fact that the syntax of a language *can* be formulated in that language itself. The difficulty is the greater because the reader has hardly learnt to distinguish between an object language and a metalanguage when he is told that, after all, the distinction is not quite as radical as he supposed it to be, since the metalanguage, it is now emphasized, may form part of the object language.

Carnap's emphasis is, undoubtedly, misplaced. It is a fact that part of the metalanguage (viz. its "syntax") can form part of the object language. But although this fact is very important, as we know from Gödel's work, its main use is in the construction of self-referring sentences, which is a highly specialized problem. From the point of view of promoting the understanding of the relation between object language and metalanguage, it would no doubt have been wiser to treat the metalanguage as distinct from the object language. It could, of course, have still been shown that at least a part of the metalanguage—and enough for Gödel's purposes—may be expressed in the object language, without stressing the mistaken thesis that the whole of the metalanguage can be so expressed.

Now there is little doubt that it was the doctrine of the one universal language in which the one unified science was to be expressed which led Carnap to this emphasis which contributes so much to the difficulties of his book; for he hoped to construct a unified language which would automatically eliminate metaphysics. It is a great pity to find this excellent book spoiled by an anti-metaphysical dogma—and by a wrong demarcation which eliminates, together with metaphysics, the most important parts of logic.

The *Syntax* continues the doctrine of the meaninglessness of metaphysics in the following form: All meaningful sentences either belong to the *language of science,* or (if philosophical) they can be expressed within the *syntax* of that language. This syntax comprises the whole of the philosophy and logic of science so far as these are translatable into the "formal mode of speech"; morever, this syntax can, if we wish, be formulated in the same universal ("object-") language in which all the sciences may be formulated.

Here then is not only the doctrine of the one universal language which I cannot accept: I also cannot accept the ruling that what I say must be translatable into the "formal mode of speech" in order to be meaningful (or to be understood by Carnap). No doubt one should express oneself as clearly as possible; and no doubt what Carnap calls the "formal mode of speech" is often preferable to what he calls "the material mode" (and I have often used it, in my *Logik der Forschung* and before, without having been told to do so). But it is not necessarily preferable. And why should it be necessarily preferable? Perhaps because the *essence* of philosophy is language analysis? But I am not a believer in essences. (Nor in Wittgenstein.) How to make oneself better understood can only be a matter of thought and experience.

And why should *all* philosophy be linguistic analysis? No doubt it may often help to put a question in terms of language-construction. But why should *all* philosophical questions be of this kind? Or is this the the one and only non-linguistic thesis of philosophy?

The positivist attack has put, if I may say so, the fear of God into all of us who wish to speak sense. We have all become more careful in what we say, and how we say it, and this is all to the good. But let us be clear that *the philosophical thesis that language analysis is everything in philosophy is paradoxical.* (I admit that this criticism of mine no longer applies in this form to *Testability and Meaning* which replaces the *thesis* by a *proposal* that is no longer paradoxical; no reasons, however, are offered in favour of the proposal, except that it is an improved version of the thesis; and this is no reason, it seems to me, for accepting it.)

V. *Testability and Meaning*

Carnap's *Testability and Meaning* is perhaps the most interesting and important of all the papers in the field of the philosophy of the empirical sciences which were written in the period between Wittgenstein's *Tractatus* and the German translation of Tarski's essay on the concept of truth. It was written in a period of crisis, and marks great changes in the author's views. At the same time, its claims are very modest. "The object of this essay is not to offer . . . solutions . . . It aims rather to stimulate further investigations." This aim was amply realized: the investigations which sprang from it must number in hundreds.

Replacing "verifiability" by "testability" (or by "confirmability"), *Testability and Meaning* is, as its title indicates, very largely a treatise on our central problem. It still attempts to exclude metaphysics from the language of science ". . . an attempt will be made to formulate the principle of empiricism in a more exact way, by stating a requirement of confirmability or testability as a criterion of meaning," we read in §1; and in §27 (p. 33) this hint is elaborated: "As empiricists, we require the language of science to be restricted in a certain way; we require that descriptive predicates and hence synthetic sentences are not to be admitted unless they have some connection with possible observations . . ." What is "not to be admitted" is, of course, metaphysics: " . . . even if L were to be a language adequate for all science . . . [we] should not wish for example to have [in L] . . . sentences [corresponding] to many or perhaps most of the sentences occuring in the books of metaphysicians."[49]

Thus the main idea—excluding metaphysics from the well-formed formulae of L, the language of science—is unchanged. Unchanged, too, is the idea of the *one* language of science: although Carnap now says, very clearly, that we can *choose* our language, and that various scientists can *choose* it in different ways, he proposes that we accept a universal language, and he even defends the *thesis of physicalism* in a modified form. He often speaks (as in the passage quoted) of *the* language of science, or of the possibility of having a language for *all* science, or of the *whole* or the *total* language of science:[50] the impossibility of such a language he still does not realize.

Carnap is however very careful in the formulation of his new ideas. He says that we have the choice between many languages of science, and he says that the "principle of empiricism"—which turns out to be another name for the principle of the meaninglessness of metaphysics—

[49] *Testability,* § 18, p. 5.

[50] See *Testability,* §§ 15, p. 467f., and 27, p. 33, 18, p. 5, as quoted, and 16, p. 469f.

should preferably be formulated not as an assertion, but as a "proposal or requirement"[51] for selecting a language of science.

One might think that, with this formulation, the idea of excluding metaphysics as meaningless has been in fact abandoned: for the metaphysician need not, and clearly would not, accept any such proposal; he would simply make another proposal in its place according to which metaphysics would become meaningful (in an appropriate language). But this is not how Carnap sees the situation. He sees it, rather, as the task or duty imposed upon the anti-metaphysician *to justify his view of the meaninglessness of metaphysics by constructing a language of science free from metaphysics.* And this is how the problem is still seen by many, I fear.

It is easy to show, using my old arguments, that no such language can be constructed.

My thesis is that a satisfactory language for science would have to contain, with any well-formed formula, its negation; and since it has to contain universal sentences, it has therefore to contain existential sentences also.

But this means that it must contain sentences which Carnap, Neurath, and all other anti-metaphysicians always considered to be metaphysical. In order to make this quite clear I choose, as an extreme example, what may be called *"the arch-metaphysical assertion"*:[52] "There exists an omnipotent, omnipresent, and omniscient personal spirit." I shall briefly show how this sentence can be constructed as a well-formed or meaningful sentence in a physicalistic language which is quite similar to those proposed in *Testability and Meaning.*

We can take as primitive the following four physicalistic predicates:

(1) "The thing *a* occupies a position *b*" or more precisely, "*a* occupies a position of which the (point or) region *b* is a part"; in symbols *"Pos (a, b)."*[53]

(2) "The thing (machine, or body, or person . . .) *a* can put the thing *b* into position *c*"; in symbols *"Put (a, b, c)."*[54]

(3) *"a* makes the utterance *b*"; in symbols *"Utt (a, b)."*

(4) *"a* is asked (i.e. adequately stimulated by an utterance combined, say, with a truth drug) whether or not *b*"; in symbols *"Ask (a, b)."*

[51] §27, p. 33.

[52] One need not believe in the "scientific" character of psycho-analysis (which, I think, is in a metaphysical phase) in order to diagnose the anti-metaphysical fervour of positivism as a form of a father killing.

[53] *"Pos(a,b)"* is used for the sake of simplicity; we should, really, operate with position *and* momentum, or with the "state" of *a*. The necessary amendments are trivial. I may remark that I do not presuppose that the variables *"a," "b,"* etc. all belong to the same type of semantical category.

[54] Or, as Carnap would put it, *"a* is able to make the full sentence *Pos(b,c)* 'true' "; see Carnap's explanation of his primitive *"realizable"* (a term of the metalanguage, however, in contradistinction to my "Put"), in *Testability* § 11, p. 455, Explanation 2.

We assume that we have in our language *names* at our disposal of all expressions of the form *"Pos (a, b)," "Put (a, b, c),"* etc., including some of those introduced below with their help. I shall use for simplicity's sake, *quotation names.* (I am aware, however, of the fact that this procedure is not exact, especially where variables in quotes are bound, as in (14).)

Now we can easily introduce, with the help of explicit definitions using (1) and (2):[55]

(5) *"a* is omnipresent," or *"Opos (a)."*

(6) *"a* is omnipotent," or *"Oput (a)."*

Moreover, with the help of (3) and (4), we can introduce, by Carnap's reduction method:

(7) *"a* thinks *b"* or *"Th (a, b)."*

Carnap recommends[56] that such a predicate should be admitted. With the help of (7) we can now define explicitly:

(8) *"a* is a thinking person," or *"Thp (a)."*

(9) *"a* is a (personal) spirit," or *"Sp (a)."*

(10) *"a* knows that *b* is in position *c,"* or *"Knpos (a, b, c)."*

(11) *"a* knows that *b* can put *c* into the position *d,"* or *"Knput (a, b, c, d)."*

(12) *"a* knows that *b* thinks *c,"* or *"Knth (a, b, c)."*

(13) *"a* is unfathomable," or *"Unkn (a)."*

(14) *"a* knows the fact *b,"* or *"Kn (a, b)."*

(15) *"a* is truthful," or *Verax* (a)."

(16) *"a* is omniscient," or *"Okn (a)."*

Nothing is now easier than to give an existential formula expressing *the arch-metaphysical assertion:* that a thinking person *a* exists, positioned everywhere; able to put anything anywhere; thinking all and only what is

[55]The definitions are: (5) *Opos (a)* ≡ *(b) Pos (a, b).*—(6) *Oput (a)* ≡ *(b) (c) Put (a, b, c),* Next we have the *"Bilateral reductions sentence"* (7) *Ask (a, b)* ⊃ *(Th (a, b)* ≡ *Utt (a, b)).* —The remaining definitions are: (8) *Thp (a)* ≡ *(Eb) Th (a, b).*—(9) *Sp (a)* ≡ *(Thp (a)* & *((b)* ~*Pos (a, b))* **v** *Opos (a)).*—An alternative (or an addition to the definiens) might be *"Sp (a)* ≡ *(Thp (a)* & *(b)* ~*Utt (a, b))".*—(10) *Knpos (a, b, c)* ≡ *(Pos (b, c)* & *Th (a, "Pos (b, c)")).*—(11) *Knput (a, b, c, d)* ≡ *(Put (b, c, d)* & *Th (a, "Put (b, c, d)")).*—(12) *Knth (a, b, c)* ≡ *Th (b, c)* & *Th (a, "Th (b, c)")).*—(13) *Unkn (a)* ≡ *((Eb) (c) Th (a, b)* & *(a* ≠ *c* ⊃ ~*Knth (c, a, b))).*—(14) *Kn (a, b)* ≡ *((c) (d) (e) ((b = "Pos (c, d)"* & *Knpos (a, c, d))* **v** *(b = "Put (c, d, e)"* & *Knput (a, c, d, e))* **v** *(b = "Th (c, d)"* & *Knth (a, c, d))).*—(15) *Verax (a)* ≡ *(b) Th (a, b)* ≡ *(Kn (a, b)).*—(16) *Okn (a)* ≡ *(b) (c) (d) (e) (f) (g) (h) (((a* ≠ *b)* ⊃ *(Knput (a, b, c, d)* ≡ *Put (b, c, d)))* & *((a* ≠ *e)* ⊃ *(Knpos (a, e, f)* ≡ *Pos (e, f)))* & *((a* ≠ *g)* ⊃ *(Knth (a, g, h)* ≡ *Th (g, h))))* & *Verax (a)).*—We can easily prove that *"Unkn (a)* & *Okn (a)"* implies the uniqueness of *a;* alternatively, we can prove uniqueness, along lines which might have appealed to Spinoza, from *"Opos (a),"* if we adopt the Cartesian axiom: *a* ≠ *b* ⊃ *(Ec) ((Pos (a, c)* & ~*Pos (b, c))* **v** *(*~*Pos (a, c)* & *Pos (b, c))).*

(Added in proofs.) Our definitions can be simplified by employing the Tarskian semantic predicate *'T(a)'*, meaning *'a* is a true statement'. Then (14) may be replaced by *Kn (a, b)* ≡ *Th (a, b)* & *T (b);* (15) by *Verax (a)* ≡ *(b) Th (a, b)* ⊃ *T (b);* and (16) by *Okn (a)* ≡ *(b) T (b)* ⊃ *Kn (a, b).*

[56]*Testability,* § 18, p. 5, S_1.

in fact true; and with nobody else knowing all about *a*'s thinking. (The uniqueness of an *a* of this kind is demonstrable from *a*'s properties. We cannot, however, identify *a* with the God of Christianity. There is a difficulty in defining "morally good" on a physicalistic basis. But questions of definability are anyway, in my opinion, supremely uninteresting —outside mathematics—except to essentialists: see below.)

It is clear that our purely existential arch-metaphysical formula cannot be submitted to any scientific test: there is no hope whatever of falsifying it—of finding out, if it is false, that it is false. For this reason I describe it as metaphysical—as falling outside the province of science.

But I do not think Carnap is entitled to say that it falls outside science, or outside the language of science, or that it is meaningless. (Its meaning seems to me perfectly clear; also the fact that some logical analysts must have mistaken its empirical incredibility for meaninglessness. But one could even conceive of experiments which might "confirm" it, in Carnap's sense, that is to say, "weakly verify" it; see note 66, below.) It helps us very little if we are told, in *Testability*,[57] that "the meaning of a sentence is in a certain sense identical with the way we determine its truth and falsehood; and a sentence has meaning only if such a determination is possible." One thing emerges clearly from this passage—that it is not Carnap's intention to allow meaning to a formula like the arch-metaphysical one. But the intention is not realized; it is not realized, I think, because it is not realizable.

I need hardly say that my only interest in constructing our arch-metaphysical existential formula is to show that there is no connection between well-formedness and scientific character. *The problem of how to construct a language of science which includes all we wish to say in science but excludes those sentences which have always been considered as metaphysical is a hopeless one. It is a typical pseudo-problem.* And nobody has ever explained *why it should be interesting to solve it (if it is soluble)*. Perhaps in order to be able to say, as before, that metaphysics is meaningless? But this would not mean anything like what it meant before.[57a]

[57] *Testability*, § 1, end of first paragraph.

[57a] (Added in proofs.) The reaction of my positivist friends to my "arch-metaphysical formula" (I have not yet seen Carnap's reaction, but I received a report from Bar-Hillel) was this. As this formula is well-formed, it is "meaningful" and also "scientific": of course not scientifically or empirically *true;* but rather scientifically or empirically *false;* or, more precisely, disconfirmed by experience. (Some of my positivist friends also denied that my name "arch-metaphysical" had any historical justification, and asserted that the anti-metaphysical tendencies of the Vienna Circle never had anything to do with anti-theological tendencies; and this in spite of Neurath's physicalism which was intended as a modern version of either classical or dialectical materialism.

Now should anyone go so far as to commit himself to the admission that my arch-metaphysical formula is well-formed and therefore empirically true or false then I think he

But, it may be said, it may still be possible to realize at least part of the old Wittgensteinian dream, and to make metaphysics meaningless. For perhaps Carnap was simply too generous in allowing us to use *dispositional predicates,* such as "*a* is able to put *b* into *c*" and "*a* thinks *b*" (the latter characterized as a disposition to utter *b*). I cannot hold out any hope to those who pursue this line of thought. As I tried to show when discussing the *Aufbau* in § III above, we need in science *genuine non-extensional universals.* But in my *Logik der Forschung* I indicated briefly—much too briefly, for I thought that the "reductionist"[58] ideas of the *Aufbau* had been given up by its author—*that all universals are dispositional;* not only a predicate like "soluble," but also "dissolving" or "dissolved."

I may quote from my *Logik der Forschung ("L.d.F,"* for short): "Every descriptive statement uses . . . universals; every statement has the character of a theory, of a hypothesis. The statement, 'Here is a glass of water' cannot be verified by any observational experience. The reason is that the *universals* which occur in it cannot be correlated with any particular observational experience. . . . By the word 'glass,' for example, we denote physical bodies which exhibit a certain *law-like behaviour;* and the same applies to the word 'water.' Universals . . . cannot be 'constituted.'" (That is, they canot be defined, in the manner of the *Aufbau.*)[59]

will encounter difficulties in extricating himself from this situation. For how could anybody defend the view that my arch-metaphysical formula is false, or disconfirmed? It is certainly unfalsifiable, and non-disconfirmable. In fact, it is expressible in the form

$$(Ex)\ G(x)$$

—in words: "there exists something that has the properties of God." And on the assumption that "$G(x)$" is an empirical predicate, we can *prove* that its probability must equal 1. (See Carnap's *Logical Foundations of Probability,* p. 571). I can prove, further, that this means that its probability cannot be diminished by any empirical information (that is, by any information whose logical probability differs from zero). But this means, according to Carnap's *Logical Foundations,* that its degree of confirmation equals 1, and that it *cannot* be disconfirmed—as I asserted above.

How then can my positivist friends assert that the empirical statement "$(Ex)\ G(x)$" is false? It is, at any rate, better confirmed than any scientific theory.

My own view is that it is non-testable and therefore non-empirical and non-scientific.

[58]The term *"reductionism"* is, it seems, Quine's. (It corresponds closely to my term "inductivism"; see, for example, Carnap's report in *Erkenntnis,* III (1932), 223f.) See also my remarks in *Logik der Forschung,* § 4, p. 8, where, in criticism of what Quine calls "reductionism," I wrote: "The older positivists accepted as scientific only such concepts (or terms) as . . . could be reduced to elementary experiences (sense-data, impressions, perceptions, experiences of remembrance [Carnap's term in the *Aufbau*], etc.)." See also *L.d.F.* § 14, esp. notes 4 and 6, and text.

[59]The passage is from *L.d.F.* (end of § 25; see *also* §§ 14 and 20). Although this passage, together with Carnap's related passage about the term "soluble" (*Testability,* § 7, p. 440) may perhaps have contributed to starting *the so-called "problem of counterfactual conditionals,"* I have never been able, in spite of strenuous efforts, to understand this problem; or more precisely, what remains of it—if one does not subscribe either to essentialism, or to phenomenalism, or to meaning-analysis.

What then, is the answer to the problem of defining, or introducing, a dispositional term like "soluble"? The answer is, simply, that the problem is insoluble. And there is no need whatever to regret this fact.

It is insoluble: for assume we have succeeded in "reducing" "*x* is soluble in water" by what Carnap calls a "reduction-sentence," describing an operational test, such as "if *x* is put into water then *x* is soluble in water if and only if it dissolves." What have we gained? We have still to reduce *"water"* and "dissolves"; and it is clear that, among the operational tests which characterize *water,* we should have to include: "if anything that is soluble in water is put into *x*, then if *x* is water, that thing dissolves." In other words, not only are we forced, in introducing "soluble," to fall back upon "water" which is dispositional in perhaps even a higher degree, but in addition, we are forced into a circular mode of introducing "soluble" with the help of a term ("water") which in its turn cannot be operationally introduced without "soluble."

The situation with "*x* is dissolving" or "*x* has dissolved" is very similar. We say that *x* has dissolved (rather than that it has disappeared) only if we expect to be able to show (say, by evaporating the water) that certain traces of this process can be found, and that we can, if necessary, even *identify* parts of the dissolved and later reclaimed substance with parts of *x* by tests which will have to establish, among other things, the fact that the reclaimed substance is, again, *soluble*.

There is a very good reason why this circle cannot be broken by establishing a definite order of reduction or introduction. It is this: our actual tests are never conclusive and always tentative. We never should agree to a ruling telling us to stop our tests at any particular point—say, when arriving at primitive predicates. All predicates are for the scientist equally dispositional, i.e. open to doubt, and to tests. This is one of the main ideas of the theory of the *empirical basis* in my *L.d.F.*[60]

[60]In *Testability,* Carnap accepts most of my theory of the empirical basis *(L.d.F.,* §§ 25 to 30) including most of my terminology ("empirical basis," "basic sentences," etc.; cf. also his introduction and use of the term "observable" with *L.d.F.,* § 28, p. 59). Even the slight but significant discrepancy (which I have here interpreted—see text to notes 38 to 40, above—as a survival from his days of "methodological solipsism," and which I criticized in *L.d.F.,* note 1 and text to note 2 to § 29) is now rectified (*Testability,* § 20; see esp. "Decision 2," p. 12, and text to note 7, p. 13). Some other points of agreement (apart from those to which Carnap himself refers) are: the thesis that there is a *"conventional component"* in the acceptance or rejection of any (synthetic) sentence (cf. *Testability* § 3, p. 426 with my *L.d.F.,* § 30, p. 64; and the rejection of the doctrine of atomic sentences which state ultimate facts (cf. *Testability* § 9, p. 448, with *L.d.F.,* § 38, p. 80). Yet in spite of this far-reaching agreement, a decisive difference remains; I stress a *negative view of* testability which, for me, is the same as refutability: and I accept confirmations only if they are the outcome of unsuccessful but genuine attempts at refutation. For Carnap, testability and refutability remain *weakened forms of verification.* The consequences of this difference will become clear in my discussion of probability and induction in § VI below.

So much about the fact that "soluble" cannot be "reduced" to something that is less dispositional. As to my contention that there is no need to regret this fact, I want only to say (again) that outside mathematics and logic problems of definability are mostly gratuitous. We need many undefined terms[61] whose meaning is only precariously fixed by usage—by the manner in which they are used in the context of theories, and by the procedures and practices of the laboratory. Thus the meaning of these concepts will be changeable. But this is so with all concepts, including defined ones, since a definition can only reduce the meaning of the defined term to that of undefined terms.

What then, is behind the demand for definitions? An old tradition, reaching back far beyond Locke to Aristotelian essentialism; and as a result of it, a belief that if a man is unable to explain the meaning of a word which he has used, then this shows that "he had given no meaning" to it (Wittgenstein), and has therefore been talking nonsense. But this Wittgensteinian belief is nonsense, since all definitions must ultimately go back to undefined terms. However, since I have discussed all this elsewhere,[62] I shall say here nothing further about it.

In concluding this section, I wish to stress again the point that testability, and confirmability, even if satisfactorily analysed, are in no way better fitted to serve as *criteria of meaning* than the older criterion of verifiability. But I must say that, in addition, I am unable to accept Carnap's analysis of either "test," "testable," etc. or of "confirmation." The reason is, again, that his terms are substitutes for "verification," "verifiable," etc. slightly weakened so as to escape the objection that laws are not verifiable. But this compromise is inadequate, as we shall see in the next and last section of this paper. *Acceptability in science depends, not upon anything like a truth-surrogate, but upon the severity of tests.*[63]

[61]In Testability, § 16, p. 470, Carnap hopes that we may introduce all terms on the basis of *one* undefined one-termed predicate (either "bright," or alternatively "solid"). But one cannot introduce any other term on this basis with the help of a reduction

[62]See for example my *Open Society,* chapter 11, § ii.

[63]As a consequence, the following "content condition" or "entailment condition" is invalid: "If x entails y (i.e. if the content of y is part of that of x), then y must be at least as well confirmed as x"; the invalidity of the content condition was pointed out in my *L.d.F.,* §§ 82 and 83 (cf. § 33f. where content is identified with degree of testability and [absolute] logical improbability, and where it was shown that the invalidity of the content condition destroys the identification of degree of confirmation with logical probability. In *Testability,* however, Carnap's whole theory of reduction rests upon this condition. (Cf. paragraph 1 of § 6, p. 434, and Definition *I.a.* on p. 435.) In *Probability,* p. 474 (cf. p. 397), Carnap notes the invalidity of the entailment condition (or "consequence condition"); but he does not draw from it the (I believe necessary) conclusion that degree of confirmation cannot coincide with probability. (I have re-affirmed this conclusion in my note "Degree of Confirmation," *B.J.P.S.,* V (1954), Cf. notes 74 and 77f. below, and text.)

VI. *Probability and Induction*

The full consequences of approaching confirmation as if it was a kind of weakened verification become manifest only in Carnap's two books on probability—the big volume entitled *Logical Foundations of Probability* (here referred to as *"Probability"*) and the smaller progress-report, *The Continuum of Inductive Methods* (here referred to as *"Methods"*).[64]

The topics of these two books are very closely related to our problem. They deal with the theory of induction, and induction has always been one of the most popular criteria of demarcation for science; for the empirical sciences are, as a rule, considered to be characterised by their methods; and these, in turn, are usually characterized as *inductive.*[65]

This is Carnap's view too: his new criterion of demarcation is, as we have seen, *confirmability*. And in these two books Carnap explains that the methods of confirming a sentence are identical with *the inductive method.* Thus we must conclude that the criterion of demarcation now becomes, more precisely, *confirmability by inductive methods.* In other words, a linguistic expression will belong to the empirical sciences if, and only if, it is logically possible to confirm it by inductive methods, or by inductive evidence.

As I have indicated in § II, this criterion of demarcation does not satisfy my requirements: all sorts of pseudo-sciences (such as astrology) are clearly not excluded. The answer to this would be, no doubt, that the criterion

[64]There is very little of relevance to the particular problem of demarcation in two of the three books published between *Syntax* and *Probability—Introduction to Semantics,* and *Meaning and Necessity* (and nothing, so far as I can see, in *Formalization of Logic* which comes between them). In the *Introduction,* I only find (a) what I take to be an allusion to Neurath's opposition to Tarski's concept of truth. (Carnap gives an excellent and tolerant reply to it, pp. vii f.), and (b) a just dismissal of the relevance of Arne Ness' questionnaire method (p. 29) see also my note 44 and text, above). In *Meaning and Necessity* which I for one believe to be the best of Carnap's books (it is also perhaps the one which has been most fiercely attacked), there are a few remarks on ontology and metaphysics (p. 43) which, together with a reference to Wittgenstein (p. 9f.), appear to indicate that Carnap still believes in the meaninglessness of metaphysics; for his reference reads: ". . . to know the meaning of a sentence is to know in which of the possible cases it would be true and in which not, as Wittgenstein has pointed out." This passage, however, seems to me to be in conflict with Carnap's main Conclusions which I find convincing. For the cited passage outlines, it is clear, what Carnap calls an *extensional* approach, as opposed to an *intensional* approach to meaning; on the other hand, "the main conclusions . . . are" that we must *distinguish* between "understanding the *meaning* of a given expression and investigating *whether and how it applies*" (p. 202, italics mine), and meaning is explained with the help of *intension, application* with the help of *extension.* Relevant to our problem is also Carnap's explication (to use his terminology) of his concept "explication," p. 8f; see below.

[65]Our problem of demarcation it not explicitly discussed in these two books except for a remark in *Probability,* p. 31 on the *"principle of empiricism"* (also mentioned on pp. 30 and 71), and a discussion of the *empirical character of the "principle of uniformity"* of nature, p. 179ff. Both passages will be mentioned below.

is not intended to exclude what I call "pseudo-sciences," and that these consist, simply, of false sentences, or perhaps of *disconfirmed* sentences, rather than of metaphysical *non-confirmable* ones. I am not satisfied by this answer (believing as I do that I have a criterion which excludes, for example, astrology, and which has proved extremely fruitful in connection with a host of problems) but I am prepared to accept it, for argument's sake, and to confine myself to showing, as before, that *the criterion produces the wrong demarcation.*

My criticism of the verifiability criterion has always been this: against the intention of its defenders, *it did not exclude obvious metaphysical statements; but it did exclude the most important and interesting of all scientific statements,* that is to say, the scientific theories, *the universal laws* of nature. Now let us see how these two groups of statements fare under the new criterion.

As to the first, it turns out that my arch-metaphysical existential formula obtains, in Carnap's system, a high confirmation value; for it belongs to the almost-tautological ("almost L-true") sentences whose confirmation value is 1 or, in a finite world of sufficient size, indistinguishable from 1. Moreover, it is a kind of statement for which even experimental confirmation is conceivable,[66] although *no tests in my sense:* there is no conceivable way of refuting it. Its lack of refutability puts it into the class of metaphysical sentences by *my* criterion of demarcation. Its high confirmation value in Carnap's sense, on the other hand, should make it vastly superior to, and more scientific than, *any scientific law.*

For *all universal laws have zero confirmation,* according to Carnap's theory, in a world which is in any sense infinite (temporal infinity suffices), as Carnap himself has shown;[67] and even in a finite world their value would be indistinguishable from zero if the number of events or things in this world is sufficiently large. All this is an obvious consequence of the fact that confirmability and confirmation, in Carnap's sense, are just slightly weakened versions of verifiability and verification. The reason why the universal laws are not verifiable is thus identical with the reason why they are not confirmable: they assert a great deal about the world—more than we can ever hope either to "verify" or to "confirm."

[66]There may, conceivably, be seers like Swedenborg who make accurate predictions of future events whenever they tell us (under the influence of truth drugs) that they are now inspired by that *a* for which our existential formula is true; and we may, conceivably, be able to build receivers to take their place—receivers which under certain circumstances turn out always to speak, and to predict, the truth.

[67]See *Probability,* § 110f., p. 571. For a similar result, see my *L.d.F.,* § 80, p. 191: "One might ascribe to a hypothesis [the hypotheses discussed are universal laws]. . . . a probability, calculated, say, by estimating the ratio between all the tests passed by it to all those [conceivable] tests which have not yet been attempted. But this way too, leads nowhere; for this estimate can be computed with precision, and the result is always that the probability is zero." (Another passage from this page is quoted in note 70, below.)

In face of the fact that natural laws turn out to be non-confirmable, according to his definition of "degree of confirmation," Carnap adopts two courses: (a) he introduces *ad hoc* a new concept, called the (qualified[68]) "instance confirmation of the law," which is so defined that we sometimes obtain, in place of zero, a confirmation value close to 1; (b) he explains that natural laws are not really needed in science, and that we can dispense with them. (Verificationism made them meaningless. Confirmationism merely makes them unnecessary: this is the gain which the weakening of the verifiability criterion achieves.)

I shall now discuss (a) and (b) a little more fully. (a) Carnap realizes, of course, that his zero-confirmation of all laws is counter-intuitive. He therefore suggests measuring the intuitive "reliability" of a law by the degree of confirmation of an instance of the law (see note 68 above). But he nowhere mentions that this new measure, introduced on p. 572 of *Probability,* satisfies practically none of the criteria of adequacy, and none of the theorems, which have been built up on the preceding 571 pages. This is so, however, and the reason is that the "instance confirmation" of a law l on the evidence e is simply *not a probability function* of l and e (not a "regular c-function" of l and e).

And it could hardly be otherwise. We are given, up to p. 570, a detailed theory of confirmation (in the sense of probability_1). On p. 571, we find that for a law this confirmation is zero. We are now faced with the following alternatives: either (i) we accept the result as correct, and consequently say that the degree of rational belief in a well-supported law cannot differ appreciably from zero—or from that of a refuted law, or even from that of a self-contradictory sentence; or (ii) we take the result as a refutation of the claim that our theory has supplied us with an adequate definition of "degree of confirmation." The *ad hoc* introduction of a new measure, in order to escape from an unintended result, is hardly an acceptable third possibility. But what is most unsatisfactory is to take this momentous step—a break with the method of "explication" (see note 69, below) used so far—without giving any warning to the reader. For this may result in the serious misconception that only a minor adjustment has been made.

[68]I confine my discussion to what Carnap calls (*Probability,* p. 572f.) the "qualified" instance confirmation; (a) because Carnap prefers it as representing "still more accurately" our intuitions; and (b) because in a sufficiently complex world (with sufficiently many predicates) the non-qualified instance confirmation leads in all interesting cases to extremely low confirmation values. On the other hand, the "qualified instance confirmation" (this I mention only in passing) is squarely hit by the so-called "paradox of confirmation" (see *Probability,* p. 469). But this is a defect which (I found) can always be repaired—in this case by making the two arguments of the definiens in (15), p. 573, symmetrical with respect to the two logically equivalent implicative formulations of l; they become respectively (after simplification), "$j \supset h'$" and "$e.(h' \supset j)$. This avoids the paradox.

For if we are to take probability, or confirmation, at all seriously, then the adjustment could not have been more radical; it replaces a confirmation function whose value is 0 by another whose value will be often close to 1. If we permit ourselves the freedom thus to introduce a new measure with no better justification than that the zero probability was counterintuitive while the probability near to 1 "seems to represent . . . still more accurately what is vaguely meant by the reliability of a law,"[69] then we can obtain for any sentence any probability (or degree of confirmation) we like.

Moreover, Carnap nowhere attempts to show that the newly introduced instance confirmation is adequate, or at least consistent (which it is not; see note 68 above). No attempt is made, for example, to show that every *refuted* law obtains a lower instance confirmation than any of those which have stood up to tests.

That this minimum requirement cannot be satisfied (even after repairing the inconsistency) may be shown with the help of Carnap's example, the law "all swans are white." This law ought to be considered as *falsified* if our evidence consists of a flock of one black and, say, 1000 white swans. But upon this evidence, the instance confirmation, instead of being zero, will be very near to 1. (The precise difference from 1 will depend upon the choice of the parameter discussed below.) More generally, if a theory is again and again falsified, on the average, in every nth instance, then its (qualified) "instance confirmation" approaches $1 - \frac{1}{n}$, instead of 0, as it ought to do, so that the law "All tossed pennies always show heads" has the instance confirmation $\frac{1}{2}$ instead of 0.

In discussing in my *L.d.F.* a theory of Reichenbach's which leads to mathematically equivalent results,[70] I described this unintended consequence of his theory as "devastating." After 20 years, I still think it is.

[69]*Probability*, p. 572. Cf. *Meaning and Necessity*, § 2, p. 7f.: "The task of making more exact a vague or not quite exact concept . . . belongs to the most important tasks of logical analysis. . . . We call this the task of . . . giving an *explication* for the earlier concept . . ." (See also *Probability*, § 2, p. 3.) I must say here (again only in passing) that I disagree with Carnap's views on explication. My main point is that I do not believe that one can speak about exactness, except in the relative sense of *exactness sufficient for a particular given purpose*—the purpose of solving a certain given problem. Accordingly, concepts cannot be "explicated" as such but only within the framework of a definite problem-situation. Or in other words, adequacy can only be judged if we are given a *genuine problem* (it must not in its turn be a problem of explication) for the solution of which the "explication" or "analysis" is undertaken.

[70]The confirmation values are identical if Carnap's λ (see below) is zero; and for any finite λ, the value of Carnap's instance confirmation approaches indefinitely, with accumulating evidence, the value criticized by me in my old discussion of Reichenbach's theory. I quote from my *L.d.F.*, § 80, p. 191, so far as it fits the present case: "The probability of this hypothesis [I am speaking quite generally of universal laws] would then be determined by the truth frequency of the [singular] statements which correspond to it [i.e. which are its instances]. A hypothesis would thus have a probability

(b) With his doctrine that laws may be dispensed with in science, Carnap in effect returns to a position very similar to the one he had held in the heyday of verificationism (viz. that the language of science is "molecular") and which he had given up in the *Syntax* and in *Testability*. Wittgenstein and Schlick, finding that natural laws are non-verifiable, concluded from this that they are not genuine sentences (overlooking that they were thus committed to call them "meaningless pseudo-sentences"). Not unlike Mill they described them as rules for the derivation of genuine (singular) sentences—the *instances* of the law—from other genuine sentences (the initial conditions). I criticized this doctrine in my *L.d.F.;* and when Carnap accepted my criticism in the *Syntax* and in *Testability*,[71] I thought that the doctrine was dead. But with Carnap's return to verificationism (in a weakened form), it has come to life again (in a weakened form: I do not think that the odds for its survival are great).

In one respect Carnap goes even further than Schlick. Schlick believed that without laws we could not make predictions. Carnap however asserts that "the use of laws is not indispensible for making predictions."[72] And he continues: "Nevertheless it is expedient, of course, to state universal laws in books on physics, biology, psychology, etc. Although these laws stated by scientists do not have a high degree of confirmation," he writes (but this is an understatement, since their degree of confirmation could not be lower), "they have a high qualified instance confirmation . . . ."

While reading through this section of my paper, Dr. J. Agassi has found a simple (and I believe new) *paradox of inductive confirmation* which he has permitted me to report here.[72a] It makes use of what I propose to call an "Agassi-predicate"—a factual predicate *"A(x)"* which is so chosen as to hold for *all* individuals (events, or perhaps things) occurring in the evidence at our disposal; but not for the majority of the others. For example, we may choose (at present) to define *"A(x)"* as *"x"* has occurred (or has been observed) before January 1st. 1965." (Another choice—"Berkeley's choice," as it were—would be *"x has been perceived."*) It then follows from Carnap's theory that, with growing evidence, the degree of confirmation of *"A(a)"* must become indistinguishable from 1 for any

of ½ if, on the average, it is contradicted by every second statement of this sequence [i.e. by every second of its instance]! In order to escape from this devastating conclusion, one might still try two more expedients." (One of these two leads to the zero probability of all universal laws: the passage is quoted in note 67, above.)

[71]See *L.d.F.*, notes 7 and 8 to §4, and 1 to §78; and *Testability*, note 20 to § 23, p. 19. See also notes 24f. above.

[72]*Probability*, p. 575.

[72a](Added in proofs.) Professor Nelson Goodman, to whom I sent a stencilled copy of this paper, has kindly informed me that he has anticipated Dr. Agassi in the discovery of this paradox and of what I have here called an "Agassi predicate."

individual *a* in the world (present, past, or future). And the same holds for the (qualified or unqualified) instance confirmation of the universal law, "$(x)A(x)$"—a law stating that all events in the world (present, past, or future) occur before 1965; which makes 1965 an upper bound for the duration of the world. Clearly, the famous cosmological problem of the approximate period of its creation can be equally easily dealt with. Nevertheless, it would hardly be "expedient, of course, to state universal laws" like those of Agassi "in books on physics" or cosmology—in spite of their "high qualified instance confirmation. . . ."

In the last pages of *Testability,* Carnap discussed the sentence "If all minds . . . should disappear from the universe, the stars would still go on in their courses." Lewis and Schlick asserted, correctly, that this sentence was not verifiable; and Carnap replied, equally correctly (in my opinion) that it was a perfectly legitimate scientific assertion, based as it was on well confirmed *universal laws.* Yet in *Probability, universal laws have become dispensible;* and without them, the sentence in question cannot possibly be upheld. Moreover, one sees easily from Agassi's argument that a sentence that contradicts it can be maximally confirmed.

But I do not intend to use this one case—the status of natural laws—as my main argument in support of my contention that Carnap's analyses of confirmation, *and with it his criterion of demarcation, are inadequate.* I therefore now proceed to offer in support of this contention arguments which are completely independent of the case of natural laws, although they may allow us to see more clearly why this inadequacy was bound to arise in Carnap's theory.

As motto for my criticism I take the following challenging passage of Carnap's:[73]

> . . . if it could be shown that another method, for instance a new definition for degree of confirmation, leads in certain cases to numerical values more adequate than those furnished by c^*, that would constitute an important criticism. Or, if someone . . . were to show that any adequate explicatum must fulfil a certain requirement and that c^* does not fulfil it, it might be a helpful first step towards a better solution.

I shall take up both alternatives of this challenge but reverse their order: (1) I shall show that an adequate concept of confirmation cannot satisfy the traditional rules of probability. (2) I shall give an alternative definition of degree of confirmation.

Ultimately, I shall show (3) that Carnap's theory of confirmation appears to involve (a) an infinite regress, and (b) an *a priori* theory of the mutual dependence of all atomic sentences with like predicates.

(1) To begin with, I suggest that we distinguish not only between *logical probability* (probability_1) and *relative frequency* (probability_2),

[73] *Probability,* § 110, p. 563.

as Carnap does, but between (at least) *three* different concepts—the third being *degree of confirmation.*

Surely, as a first suggestion this is unobjectionable: we could still decide, after due investigation, that *logical probability* can be used as the explicatum for *degree of confirmation.* Carnap, unfortunately, prejudges the issue. He assumes, without any further discussion, that his distinction between *two* probability concepts is sufficient, neglecting the warnings of my old book.[74]

It can be shown that confirmation, as Carnap himself understands this concept, cannot be logical probability. I offer three arguments.

(a) We can easily agree on the kind of thing we may both call, provisionally, "probability"; for we both call "probability" *something that satisfies the laws of the calculus of probability.*[75]

More specifically, Carnap says of the concept of logical probability_1 that it satisfies certain axiom systems, and in any case the (special) addition principle and (general) multiplication principle.[76] Now it is an elementary consequence of the latter that *the more a statement asserts, the less probable it is.* This may be expressed by saying that the logical probability of a sentence x on a given evidence y decreases when the informative content of x increases.[77]

But this is sufficient to show that a high probability cannot be one of the aims of science. For the scientist is most interested in theories with a high content. He does not care for highly probable trivialities but for

[74]See *L.d.F.*, before § 79, p. 186: "Instead of discussing the 'probability' of a hypothesis . . . we should try to assess how far it has been 'corroborated' [or 'confirmed']." Or § 82, p. 198f.: "This shows that it is not so much the number of corroborating instances which determines the degree of corroboration as *the severity of the various tests* . . . [which] in its turn depends upon the *degree of testability* . . . of the hypothesis." § 83, p. 200: "A theory can be the better corroborated, the better testable it is. Testability, however, is converse to . . . *logical probability."* (Cf. §§ 33-35.) And against Keynes (p. 202): "Keynes' theory implies that corroboration [or confirmation] *decreases* with testability [in contrast to my theory]." See also notes 63 above and 78 below.

[75]In a note in *Mind,* XLVII (1938), p. 275f., I said that it was "desirable to construct a system of axioms" for probability, "in such a way that it can be . . . interpreted by any of the different interpretations," of which "the three most discussed are: (1) the classical definition of probability as the ratio of the favourable to the equally possible cases, (2) the frequency theory . . . (3) the logical theory, defining probability as the degree of a logical relation between sentences. . . ." (I took this classification from *L.d.F.,* § 48, reversing the order of (2) and (3).) A similar classification can be found in *Probability,* p. 24. Contrast also the discussion of the *arguments* of the probability function in my *Mind* note with *Probability,* § 10, A & B, and § 52. In this note I gave an independent formal axiom system which, however, I have much simplified since. It has been published in the *B.J.P.S.,* VI (1955), p. 53.

[76]*Probability,* § 53, p. 285; see also § 62, pp. 337ff.

[77]This is equivalent with the "content condition" (see note 63 above). Since Carnap considers this condition to be invalid (*Probability* § 87, p. 474 "consequence condition"), he is, I believe, committed to agree that "degree of confirmation" cannot be a "regular confirmation function," i.e. a probability_1.

bold and severely testable (and severely tested) hypotheses. If (as Carnap tells us) a high degree of confirmation is one of the things we aim at in science, then degree of confirmation cannot be identified with probability.

This may sound paradoxical to some people. But if high probability were an aim of science, then scientists should say as little as possible, and preferably utter tautologies only. But their aim is to "advance" science, that is, to *add* to its content. Yet this means lowering its probability. And in view of the high content of universal laws, it is neither surprising to find that their probability is zero, nor that those philosophers who believe that science must aim at high probabilities cannot do justice to facts such as these: that the formulation (and testing) of *universal laws* is considered their most important aim by most scientists: or that the intersubjective testability of science depends upon these laws (as I pointed out in § 8 of my *L.d.F.)*.

From what has been said it should be clear that an adequately defined "degree of confirmation" cannot satisfy the general multiplication principle for probabilities.[78]

To sum up point (a): *Since we aim in science at a high content, we do not aim at a high probability*$_1$.

(b) The severity of possible tests of a statement or a theory depends (among other factors) on the precision of its assertions and upon its predictive power; or in other words, upon its informative content (which increases with these two factors). This may be expressed by saying that *the degree of testability of a statement increases with its content.* But the better a statement can be tested, the better it can be confirmed, i.e. attested by its tests. Thus we find that the opportunity of confirming a statement, and accordingly the degree of its confirmability or corroborability, or attestability, increases with its testability, and with its content.[79]

To sum up point (b). *Since we want a high degree of confirmation (or corroboration), we need a high content (and thus a low absolute probability).*

(c) Those who identify confirmation with probability must believe that a high degree of probability is desirable. They implicitly accept the rule: "Always choose the most probable hypothesis"!

Now it can be easily shown that this rule is equivalent to the following rule: "Always choose the hypothesis which goes as little beyond the evidence as possible!" And this, in turn, can be shown to be equivalent, not only to "Always accept the hypothesis with the lowest content

[78]See §§ 4-5 of my note "Degree of Confirmation," *B.J.P.S.* V. Dr. Y. Bar-Hillel has drawn my attention to the fact that some of my examples were anticipated by Carnap in *Probability*, § 71, 394f., case *3b*. Carnap infers from them that the content condition (see notes 63 and 77 above) is "invalid," but fails to infer that all "regular confirmation functions" are inadequate.

[79]For a fuller argument see *LdF.*, §§ 82f.

(within the limits of your task, for example, your task of predicting)!" but also to "Always choose the hypothesis which has the highest degree of *ad-hoc* character (within the limits of your task)!" This is an unintended consequence of the fact that a highly probable hypothesis is one which fits the known facts, going as little as possible beyond them.

But it is well known that *ad hoc* hypotheses are disliked by scientists: they are, at best, stop-gaps, not real aims. (Scientists prefer a bold hypothesis because it can be more severely tested, and *independently* tested.)

To sum up point (c). *Aiming at high probability entails a counter-intuitive rule favouring ad hoc hypotheses.*

These three arguments exemplify my own point of view, for I see in a *confirming instance* the result of a severe test, or of an attempted (but unsuccessful) refutation of the theory. Those, on the other hand, who do not look for severe tests but rather for "confirmation" in the sense of the old idea of "verification" (or a weakened version of it), come to a different idea of confirmability: a sentence will be the better confirmable the more nearly verifiable it is, or the more nearly deducible from observation sentences. It is clear that, in this case, universal laws are not (as in our analysis) highly confirmable, but that owing to their high content, their confirmability will be zero.

(2) In taking up the challenge to construct a better definition of confirmation, I wish to say first that I do not believe that it is possible to give a completely satisfactory definition. My reason is that a theory which has been tested with great ingenuity and with the sincere attempt to refute it will have a higher degree of confirmation than one which has been tested with laxity; and I do not think that we can completely formalise what we mean by an ingenious and sincere test.[80] Nor do I think that it is an important task to give an adequate definition of degree of confirmation. (In my view, the importance, if any, of giving the best possible definition lies in the fact that such a definition shows clearly the inadequacy of all probability theories posing as theories of induction.) I have given what I consider a reasonably adequate definition elsewhere.[81] I may give here a slightly simpler definition (which satisfies the same *desiderata* or conditions of adequacy):

$$C(x,y) = \frac{p(y,x) - p(y)}{p(y,x) - p(x.y) + p(y)}$$

Here "*C(x,y)*" means the degree of confirmation of *x* by *y*," while

[80]See the end of my note "Degree of Confirmation," *B.J.P.S.* V.

[81]"Degree of Confirmation," *B.J.P.S.*, V (1954), p. 147f. Cf. my remark p. 149: "The particular way in which *C(x,y)* is here defined I consider unimportant. What may be important are the *desiderata,* and the fact that they can be satisfied together."

"$p(x,y)$" and "$p(x)$" are relative and absolute probabilities, respectively. The definition can be relativized:

$$C(x,y,z) = \frac{p(y,x.z) - p(y,z)}{p(y,x.z) - p(x.y,z) + p(y,z)}$$

Here z should be taken as the general "background of knowledge" (old evidence, and old and new initial conditions) including, if we wish, accepted theories; while y should be taken as representing those (new) observational results (excluded from z) which may be claimed to confirm the (new explanatory hypothesis, x.[82]

My definition satisfies, among other conditions of adequacy,[83] the condition that the *confirmability* of a statement—its highest degree of confirmation—equals its content (i.e. the degree of its testability).

Another important property of this concept is that it satisfies the condition that the severity of a test (measured by the improbability of the test-instance) has an almost-additive influence upon the resultant degree of confirmation of the theory. This shows that some at least of the intuitive demands are satisfied.

My definition does not automatically exclude *ad hoc* hypotheses, but it can be shown to give most reasonable results if combined with a rule excluding *ad hoc* hypotheses.[84]

So much about my own present positive theory (which goes very considerably beyond my *L.d.F.*). But I must return to my critical task: I believe that my positive theory strongly suggests that the fault lies with the verificationist and inductivist approach which—in spite of the attention paid to my criticism—has never been completely abandoned by Carnap. *But inductive logic is impossible.* I shall try to show this (following my old *L.d.F.*) as my last critical point.

(3) I asserted, in my *L.d.F.*, that an inductive logic must involve either (a) an infinite regress (discovered by Hume), or (b) the acceptance (with Kant) of some synthetic principle as valid a priori. I have a strong

[82]That is to say, the total evidence e is to be partitioned into y and z; and y and z should be so chosen as to give $c(x, y, z)$ the highest value possible for x, on the available total evidence.

[83]Called *"desiderata"* in the note in question. Kemeny has rightly stressed that the conditions of adequacy should not be introduced to fit the explicatum. That this is not the case here is perhaps best proved by the fact that I have now improved my definition (by simplifying it) without changing my *desiderata*.

[84]The rule for the exclusion of *ad hoc* hypotheses may take the following form: the hypothesis *must not repeat* (except in a completely generalized form) the evidence, or any conjunctive component of it. That is to say $x =$ "This swan is white," is not acceptable as a hypothesis to explain the evidence $y =$ "This swan is white" although "All swans are white" would be acceptable; and no explanation x of y must be circular in this sense with respect to any (non-redundant) conjunctive component of y. This leads to an emphasis upon *universal laws as indispensable,* while Carnap believes as we have seen (see above, and *Probability* § 110, H. esp. 575) that universal laws can be dispensed with.

suspicion that Carnap's theory of induction can be criticized as involving both (a) and (b).

(a) If we need, in order to justify induction as probable, a (probable) *principle of induction,* such as a *principle of the uniformity of nature,* then we also need a second such principle in order to justify the induction of the first. Carnap, in his § 41 on the "Presuppositions of Induction"[85] introduces a principle of uniformity. He does not mention the objection of a regress, but a remark in his discussion seems to indicate that he has it in mind: "The opponents," he writes (p. 181), "would perhaps say that the statement of the probability of uniformity must be taken as a factual statement. . . . Our reply is: . . . this statement is itself analytic." I was far from convinced by Carnap's arguments; but since he indicates that "the whole problem of the justification and the presupposition of inductive method" will be treated in a later volume "in more exact, technical terms," it is perhaps better to suppress, at this stage, my inclination to offer a proof that no such principle of uniformity can be analytic (except in a Pickwickian sense of "analytic"); especially since my discussion of point (b) will perhaps indicate the lines on which a proof of this kind might proceed.

(b) Natural laws, or more generally, scientific theories, whether of a causal or a statistical character, are hypotheses about some *dependence.* They assert, roughly speaking, that certain events (or statements describing them) are *in fact not independent* of others, although so far as their purely logical relations go, they are independent. Let us take two possible facts which are, we first assume, completely unconnected (say "Chunky is clever" and "Sandy is clever"), described by the two statements x and y. Then somebody may conjecture—perhaps mistakenly—that they are connected (that Chunky is a relation of Sandy's); and that the information or evidence y increases the probability of x. If he is wrong, that is, if x and y are independent, then we have

(1) $$p(x,y) = p(x)$$

which is equivalent to

(2) $$p(x.y) = p(x)p(y)$$

This is the usual definition of independence.

If the conjecture that the events are connected or inter-dependent is correct, then we have

(3) $$p(x,y) > p(x)$$

that is, the information y raises the probability of x above its "absolute" or "initial" value $p(x)$.

I believe—as I think most empiricists do—that any such conjecture about the inter-dependence or correlation of events should be formulated

[85]*Probability,* § 41, F., p. 177ff., esp. pp. 179, 181. For the passages from *L.d.F.,* see § 1, p 3, and 81, p. 196.

as a separate hypothesis, or as a natural law ("Cleverness runs in families") to be submitted first to a process of careful formulation, with the aim of making it as highly testable as possible, and after that to severe empirical tests.

Carnap is of a different opinion. He proposes that we accept (as probable) a principle to the effect that the evidence "Sandy is clever" increases the probability of "*A* is clever" for any individual *A*—whether "*A*" is the name of a cat, a dog, an apple, a tennis ball, or a cathedral. This is a consequence of the definition of "degree of confirmation" which he proposes. According to this definition, any two sentences with the same predicate ("clever" or "sick") and different subjects are inter-dependent or positively correlated, whatever the subject may be, and wherever they may be situated in the world; this is the actual content of his principle of uniformity.

I am far from certain whether he has realized these consequences of his theory, for he nowhere mentions them explicitly. But he introduces a universal parameter which he calls λ; and $\lambda + 1$ turns out, on a simple mathematical calculation, to be the reciprocal of the "logical correlation coefficient"[86] for any two sentences with the same predicate and different subjects.[87] (The assumption that λ is infinite corresponds to the assumption of independence.)

According to Carnap, we are bound to choose a finite value of λ when we wish to choose our *definition* of the probability$_1$ function. The choice of λ, and with it of the degree of correlation between any two sentences with the same predicate, thus appears to be part of a "decision" or "convention": the choice of a definition of probability. It looks, therefore, as if no statement about the world was involved in the choice of λ. But it is a fact that our choice of λ is equivalent to the most sweeping assertion on dependence that one can imagine. It is equivalent to the acceptance of as many natural laws as there are predicates, each asserting the same degree of dependence of any two events with like predicates in

[86]The "logical correlation coefficient" of x and y can be defined as $(p(xy)-p(x)p(y))/(p(x)p(y)p(\bar{x})p(\bar{y}))^{1/2}$. Admitting this formula for all ("regular") probability functions means a slight generalization, of a suggestion which is made in Kemeny and Oppenheim, "Degree of Factual Support," *Philos. of Sc., XIX*, 314, formula (7), for a special probability function in which all atomic sentences are (absolutely) independent. (It so happens that I think that this special function is the only one which is adequate.)

[87]We can prove this for example, by taking *Methods*, p. 30, formula (9-8), putting $s = s_M = 1$; $w/\kappa = c(x) = c(y)$; and replacing "$c(h_M,e_M)$" by "$c(x,y)$." We obtain easily $\lambda = c(\bar{x}y)/(c(xy-c(x)c(y))$, which shows that λ is the reciprocal of a dependence-measure, and from this $1/(\lambda + I) = (c(xy)-c(x)c(y))/c(\bar{x})c(y)$, which, in view of $c(x) = c(y)$, is the logical correlation coefficient. I may perhaps say here that I prefer the term "dependence" to Keynes' and Carnap's term "relevance": looking (like Carnap) at probability as a generalized deductive logic, I take probabilistic dependence as a generalization of logical dependence.

the world. And since such an assumption about the world is made in the form of a non-testable act—the introduction of a definition—there seems to me an element of *apriorism* involved.

One might still say, perhaps, that there is no *apriorism* here since the dependencies mentioned are a consequence of a definition (that of probability or degree of confirmation), which rests on a convention or a "decision," and is therefore analytic. But Carnap gives two reasons for his choice of his confirmation function which do not seem to fit this view. The first of the two reasons I have in mind is that his confirmation function, as he remarks, is the only one (among those which suggest themselves) "which is not entirely inadequate."[88] Inadequate, that is, for explaining (or "explicating") the undoubted *fact that we can learn from experience*. Now this *fact* is empirical; and a theory whose adequacy is judged by its ability to explain, or cohere with, this fact does not quite look like being analytic. It is interesting to see that Carnap's argument in favour of his choice of λ (which I am suspecting of *apriorism)* is the same as Kant's or Russell's, or Jeffrey's, it is what Kant called a "transcendental" argument ("How is knowledge possible?"), the appeal to the fact that we possess empirical knowledge, i.e. that we can learn from experience. The second of the two reasons is Carnap's argument that the adoption of an appropriate λ (one which is neither infinite, for an infinite λ is equivalent to independence, nor zero) would be more successful in nearly all universes (except in the two extreme cases in which all individuals are independent or have like properties). All these reasons seem to me to suggest that the choice of λ, i.e. of a confirmation function, is to depend upon its success, or upon the probability of its success, in the world. But then it would not be analytic—in spite of the fact that it is also a "decision" concerning the adoption of a definition. I think that it can be explained how this may be so. We can, if we like, define the word "truth" so that it comprises some of those statements we usually call "false." Similarly we can define "probable" or "confirmed" so that absurd statements get a "high probability." All this is purely conventional or verbal, as long as we do not take these definitions as "adequate explications." But if we do, then the question is no longer conventional, or analytic. For to say of a contingent or factual statement *x* that it is true, *in an adequate sense of the word "true,"* is to make a factual statement; and so it is with "*x* is (now) highly probable." It is the same with "*x* is strongly dependent upon *y*" and "*x* is independent of *y*"—the statements whose fate is decided upon when we choose λ. The choice of λ is therefore indeed equivalent to that of adopting a sweeping though unformulated statement about the general interdependence or uniformity of the world.

[88]*Probability,* § 110, p. 565; cf. *Methods,* § 18, p. 53.

But this statement is adopted without any empirical evidence. Indeed, Carnap shows[89] that, without adopting it, we can never learn from empirical evidence (according to his theory of knowledge). Thus empirical evidence does not and cannot count *before* the adoption of a finite λ. This is why it has to be adopted a priori.

"The principle of empiricism," Carnap writes in another context,[90] "can be violated only by the assertion of a factual (synthetic) sentence without a sufficient empirical foundation, or by the thesis of *apriorism* when it contends that for knowledge with respect to certain factual sentences no empirical foundation is required." I believe that what we have observed here shows that there is a third way of violating the principle of empiricism. We have seen how it can be violated by constructing a theory of knowledge which cannot do without a principle of induction —a principle that tells us in effect that the world is (or very probably is) a place in which men can learn from experience; and that it will remain (or very probably remain) so in the future. I do not believe that a cosmological principle of this kind can be a principle of pure logic. But it is introduced in such a way that it cannot be based upon experience either. It therefore seems to me that it cannot be anything else but a principle of a priori metaphysics.

Nothing but the synthetic, the factual, character of λ seems to be able to explain Carnap's suggestion that we may try out which value of λ is most successful in a given world. But since empirical evidence does not count without the prior adoption of a finite λ, there can be no clear procedure for testing the λ chosen by the method of trial and error. My own feeling is that I prefer in any case to apply the method of trial and error to the *universal laws* which are indispensible for intersubjective science; which are clearly, and admittedly, factual; and which we may succeed in making severely testable, with the aim of eliminating all those theories that can be discovered to be erroneous.

I am glad to have been given an opportunity to get these matters off my mind—or off my chest, as physicalists might say. I do not doubt that, with another vacation in the Tyrol, and another climb up the *Semantische Schnuppe,* Carnap and I could reach agreement on most of these points; for we both, I trust, belong to the fraternity of rationalists—the fraternity of those who are eager to argue, and to learn from one another. But since the physical gap between us seems unbridgeable, I now send to him across the ocean—knowing that I shall soon be at the receiving end—these my best barbed arrows, with my best brotherly regards.

KARL R. POPPER

UNIVERSITY OF LONDON

[89]*Probability,* § 110, p. 556.
[90]*Probability,* § 10, p. 31.

6

Herbert Feigl

PHYSICALISM, UNITY OF SCIENCE AND THE FOUNDATIONS OF PSYCHOLOGY

The present essay attempts to analyze the meaning and to appraise the validity of the various theses of physicalism. Since I have had the privilege of discussing these issues with Carnap intensively and extensively on many occasions ever since 1926, I shall only rather briefly deal with some of his earlier views of this matter, and dwell more fully on recent modifications in his outlook—most of which do not exist in published form but are known to me from personal conversations. One of the purposes of the following observations then is to invite Carnap to react critically to my own suggestions and formulations on several basic points.

I shall begin by stating informally and relatively independently of Carnap's contributions what I consider to be the commonsense background of the doctrines of physicalism. After this introduction I shall go on to scrutinize some of the more strenuous and rigorous formulations of the theses of physicalism and of the unity of science. The first thesis of physicalism or the thesis of the unity of the language of science is essentially the proposal of a criterion of scientific meaningfulness in terms of intersubjective confirmability. "Unity of science" in this first thesis means essentially a unity of the confirmation basis of all factually cognitive (i.e., non-analytic) statements of the natural and the social sciences. A corollary to this thesis is the assertion of the unity of scientific method. Despite the tremendous variety of special scientific techniques in the various disciplines, there are basic common features of the inductive and the hypothetico-deductive methods of establishing knowledge claims in all sciences. Contrasted with this first thesis which Carnap always regarded as well established by logical analysis, is the second thesis of "unitary science" (as I shall call it for short) which Carnap considers only as a fruitful research program of the sciences, but by no means as sufficiently established by the progress of research to date. This second thesis of physicalism claims that the facts and laws of the natural and the social sciences can all be derived—at least in principle—from the theoretical assumptions of physics. We may formulate this second thesis as the belief in the possibility of a unitary explanatory system.

The first thesis of physicalism may in a preliminary and informal manner be construed as the principle of the primacy of sensory observation in the validation of the statements of empirical knowledge. Statements about the objects and events of the world—be they classified as physical, chemical, biological, psychological, sociological or historical—are generally confirmed (or disconfirmed) by means of sense perception. The data of observation can serve as confirming or disconfirming evidence, of course, only if certain principles of interpretation and of confirmation are presupposed. These principles, if explicitly stated, would tell us which data are evidence for which "facts" and how strongly the data support the assertions of "fact." Issues of inductive logic aside, the important point here is simply this: Knowledge claims in common life, and certainly in science, are disregarded if they are so conceived as to be absolutely incapable of intersubjective check. No matter how strong our own subjective conviction or the force of "self-evidence," we would not consider a judgment justified if it could not conceivably be tested by others. Suppose, by way of an extreme example, someone claimed telepathic or clairvoyant intuition of distant events which are inaccessible to him through the normal channels of sense perception. He might be subjectively convinced that, e.g., at this very moment his old friend N. in Vienna (from whom he has not heard for 25 years) is writing a letter to him. The "target" (object) of his telepathic or clairvoyant act is clearly something distinct from the act itself. The fact that the act itself occurred, he could report on the basis of introspection; and others could presumably confirm the occurrence of this act on the basis of their observations of his behavior (including, of course, his verbal utterances). But the very meaning of the target proposition, and not only its validation, involves reference to something beyond his direct experience and can be understood only within the frame of the customary commonsense conception of the spatio-temporal world. "The actions of the Viennese friend N." is a phrase whose meaning could never be explicated exclusively in terms of anybody's "telegnostic" insight. I am not here stressing the obvious need of a check on the reliability of telegnostic acts. I am rather concerned to point out the even more obvious fact that any tests of such reliabilities ineluctably require independent checks of the truth of the proposition about the target. And in the commonly accepted frame the target proposition requires confirmation by the usual evidence of sensory perception. This commonly accepted frame is precisely that of intersubjective confirmability. I doubt very strongly that we could even coherently imagine a *reversal* of this situation, i.e. that statements about "external" or "distant" events could be established on the basis of telegnostic insight alone, and that the validity of ordinary sense perception be checked by comparison with the "more basic" extrasensory perception. I do not wish to deny that among the logically conceivable universes there might be some in which this situation prevails. That is to say, I don't think that an outright logical inconsistency is involved in this however utterly fantastic conception. Nevertheless,—and this is all our little thought experiment was to demonstrate—the primacy of sense perception for the interpretation and the establishment of intersubjectively meaningful and valid knowledge claims is an extremely fundamental feature of *our*-world-as-we-are-accustomed-to-conceive-it. The old empiricism of Locke and the new empiricism of Carnap, ultimately rest on the conviction that sensory experiences are much more reliable indicators of "external" states of affairs than are thoughts, images, wishes, sentiments or other "non-sensory" data. Just as the reliability of intuition (normal "hunches" or alleged paranormal gnostic acts) would have to be ascertained by the *normal* inductive methods, so the very meaning of statements, even if they were paranormally *arrived at,* can be understood only within the *normal* frame of a spatio-temporal world in which the to-be-known objects can be causally related to the sense organs of the knowing subjects.

These remarks on the case of paranormal knowledge claims were made only in order to illuminate the idea of the intersubjective frame. The controversial issues of extrasensory perception are not part of our theme here. But the point of our remarks applies *mutatis mutandis* to the claims of normal introspective knowledge. It is now fairly generally admitted by psychologists even of predominantly behavioristic orientation that introspection or self-observation is not to be discarded or disregarded but to be used with caution, i.e., with the proper safeguards with respect to its reliability. But behaviorism conceived as a "psychology of the other one" has long been able to provide an account in intersubjective terms of "subjectivity," "privacy," "the phenomenally given," and its observation by "introspection,[1] while the precise logical form

[1]Cf. E. A. Singer, *Mind as Behavior* (Columbus, Ohio: Adams & Co., 1924). A. P. Weiss, *A Theoretical Basis of Human Behavior* (Columbus, Ohio: 1925); and with greater philosophical and scientific subtlety respectively: Gilbert Ryle, *The Concept of Mind* (London: Hutchinson's University Library, 1949); and B. F. Skinner, *Science and Human Behavior* (New York: Macmillan, 1953). It is to be noted that Carnap's first formulations of the unity of science thesis and of physicalism (or logical behaviorism) were made quite independently of E. A. Singer's and A. P. Weiss's contributions, and that he anticipated in the main points much that is essential in the basic outlook of Ryle and of Skinner. Carnap's own views had developed in this area as much as elsewhere under the predominant influence of Bertrand Russell. But the abandonment of the earlier Mach-Russell type phenomenalism in favor of physicalism was largely due to Karl Popper's critique of observation propositions (later published in Popper's *Logik der Forschung,* Vienna, 1935) and by Otto Neurath's enthusiastic, though logically

of such an account is still in dispute—and will be discussed in greater detail a little later—its main emphasis may again be construed in terms of the primacy of sensory perception as the confirmation basis of all intersubjective knowledge claims. Perhaps the best way to get clear about just what this emphasis implies, is to ask what this thesis excludes or denies. The answer seems very plain and simple to me: Physicalism thus understood excludes as scientifically meaningless sentences which could be confirmed *only* subjectively: Analytic philosophers, especially those practicing the methods of G. E. Moore and Wittgenstein,[2] have in various ways rather convincingly argued that the *absolute* privacy or subjectivity which for some philosophers constitutes *the* criterion of the

often defective, advocacy of the unity of science thesis. Carnap's most important pronouncements on the subject are:

1. *Scheinprobleme in der Philosophie.* Das Fremdpsychische und der Realismusstreit (Berlin: 1928, Leipzig: F. Meiner).
2. "Die physikalische Sprache als Universalsprache der Wissenschaft," *Erkenntnis,* II (1931), 432-465.
3. English Translation: *The Unity of Science.* (Psyche Miniatures) (London: Kegan Paul, 1934).
4. "Psychologie in physikalischer Sprache," *Erkenntnis,* III (1933), 107-142.
5. "Erwiderung auf die Aufsätze von E. Zilsel und K. Duncker," *Erkenntnis,* III (1933), 189-200.
6. "Ueber Protokollsätze," *Erkenntnis,* III (1933), 215-228.
7. *Logical Syntax of Language.* (Int. Library of Psych. and Philos.) (London: Kegan Paul; New York: Harcourt, Brace and Co., 1937).
8. "Les Concepts psychologiques et les concepts physiques sont-ils foncièrement differents?" *Revue de Synthese,* X (1935), 43-53.
9. "Existe-t-il des premisses de la science qui soient incontrolables?" *Scientia,* LVIII (1936), 129-135.
10. "Testability and Meaning," *Philos. of Science,* III (1936), 419-471; IV (1937) 1-40. (Reprinted and separately available from: Graduate Philosophy Club, Yale University, New Haven, Conn.: also in: H. Feigl and M. Brodbeck, *Readings in the Philosophy of Science* (New York: Appleton-Century-Crofts, 1953).
11. "Logical Foundations of the Unity of Science," *Intern. Encycl. of Unified Science,* I, No. 1 (Univ. of Chicago Press, 1938), 42-46; (also reprinted in H. Feigl and W. Sellars, *Readings in Philosophical Analysis* (New York: Appleton-Century-Crofts, 1949).

Cf. also C. G. Hempel, "The Logical Analysis of Psychology," in Feigl and Sellars, *Readings in Philosophical Analysis.*

[2]A. J. Ayer, *Language, Truth and Logic* (2nd edition; London: Gollancz, 1948).

A. J. Ayer, "One's Knowledge of Other Minds," *Theoria,* XIX (1953), 1-20.

A. J. Ayer, "Can there be a Private Language?" *Aristot. Soc. Suppl.* XXVIII (1954).

Max Black, "Linguistic Method in Philosophy," in his *Language and Philosophy* (Ithaca: Cornell University Press, 1940).

B. A. Farrell, "Experience," *Mind,* LIX (1950).

Stuart Hampshire, "The Analogy of Feeling," *Mind,* LXI (1952).

Gilbert Ryle, *The Concept of Mind* (London: Hutchinson's Univ. Library, 1949).

Michael Scriven, "The Mechanical Concept of Mind," *Mind,* LXII (1953).

John Wisdom, *Other Minds* (Oxford: Blackwell, 1952).

Ludwig Wittgenstein, *Philosophical Investigations* (New York: Macmillan, 1953).

mental is an idea begotten by confusions and pregnant with unresolvable perplexities. There are important passages in Carnap's formulations of 1932 which anticipate in very compact form much of what has been dialectically (and partly independently) elaborated by the British analytic philosophers. As an illustration of this point consider the problem of the silent thinker. We are inclined to say: What goes on in his mind is "private" to him, that is to say that *only he* knows what he is thinking about, and that the practical situation is such that no other person, no matter how closely he observes the behavior of the thinker could possibly find out. But practical impossibility of finding out was soon distinguished from absolute impossibility. It is generally admitted that the present state of scientific techniques (including kymographic registration of subvocal speech responses, electro-encephalograms, lie-detectors, etc.) does not enable us to obtain highly reliable information about the thought contents even of non-silent thinkers. By "transcending the limit," or illegitimately extending the ordinary usage of terms some philosophers have concluded that there are intersubjectively absolutely unknowable mental contents, qualia or "raw feels." These private states may be "had," "experienced," "enjoyed" (or "suffered"), "lived through" by the individual subject, but are distinct from and something over and above the intersubjectively observable or discoverable behavioral or physiological processes and could for this reason not themselves be the objects of intersubjective knowledge. This way of conceiving the problem of "other minds" leads notoriously to such unanswerable questions as: Are other persons' experienced raw feels (colors, sounds, smells, itches, tickles, etc.) quite similar to those with which I am familiar by direct acquaintance or could they be utterly different, i.e. systematically interchanged, such that the other person "privately" experiences *green* when looking at ripe cherries and *red* when looking at grass? (The puzzle of the "inverted spectrum.") Do other persons experience anything at all even if they behave in every respect as if they did? (One form of the solipsism puzzle.) Analytic philosophers have been alert to point out that these puzzles are quite similar to those that have been posed in connection with our knowledge of the past, or of physical objects. A historian might say: The present evidence is in every respect as if such and such had really happened in Egypt four thousand years ago. To which the skeptical philosopher responds with the query: Can you ever be sure that it really happened that way? Could not the laws of nature themselves have changed in the meantime, so that your inference might really be invalid? Or, might it not be that the world with all "traces," "remnants," "memories," etc. sprang into existence only five minutes ago, and that therefore all "history" is nothing but an illusion? Admittedly, no philosopher can raise such questions without shamefaced blushing. But the special hygiene or therapy for the prevention or elimination of these anomalies and perplexities needs to be made quite explicit by analytic philosophy. Since the resolution of these curious quandaries is by now fairly familiar, I shall state it here very succinctly and in my own way. Philosophers afflicted by extreme doubts (of the sort described) insist on direct verification as a means for the removal of such doubts. But in the nature of the case, as they themselves conceive it, direct verification is *ex hypothesi* excluded as either logically or physically (i.e. not just practically) impossible. The continued discussions of the "other minds" puzzle have shown, I think, that "having another person's experience" is a self-inconsistent phrase. Direct verification of knowledge-claims whose very conception allows only for indirect verification (confirmation) is thus to be recognized as a *logical* impossibility. But even logical impossibilities of this sort are inconsistencies within a special pre-supposed conceptual frame. Just because the very statement of the philosophical doubts inescapably (if even only implicitly or unwittingly) requires adoption of that frame, the puzzles posed can only be surreptitiously arrived at and thus reveal themselves as the gratuitous pseudoproblems as which they have always been diagnosed by positivists and analytic philosophers. To make this more specific, let us first consider the conceptual frame of historical knowledge. Common sense conceives of a sequence of events in temporal order which by and large (e.g., especially in the astronomical, geological, paleontological, and partly even in the human phases of history) is what it is, independently of whether it is or is not known. Embedded in this sequence of world events are cognizing human beings who make it their business to interpret evidence, i.e., to reconstruct past events or predict future ones, or to infer contemporaneous but not directly observed states of affairs. The philosophically uncorrupted historian does not deplore the impossibility of literally "going back to the past" (as with a "time machine" à la H. G. Wells). He knows implicitly that if he, the historian, was born in the twentieth century, he could not conceivably also have been born in the first century B.C., and thus might have been able to witness Caesar's assassination. What I am trying to point out is simply the fact that implicit in the ordinary conceptual frame of our cognitive activities is the distinction between direct and indirect verification. Although this distinction can be formulated more or less restrictively (down to an extremely limited notion of direct verification), and perhaps never quite sharply, it remains nevertheless a very clear and indispensable distinction.

Now, just as in the case of historical knowledge, we must distinguish between the evidence and that which is evidenced, so in the case of our knowledge of other minds it is imperative to distinguish between the behavioral symptoms and the mental states they symptomatize or indicate. Anxious to avoid pseudoproblems of the type mentioned before, Carnap, and with him many others in the early radical phase of logical positivism, maintained that psychological statements describe *nothing but* actual (or possible) behavior. Psychological concepts expressed by mentalistic terms were conceived as logical constructions erected on a basis of purely behavioral concepts. This was plausible enough in all cases except that of human introspection. If, for example, I report that I feel elated, grieved, or that I hear a ringing sound, there are—to be sure—a great number of behavioral symptoms which may indicate with varying degrees of reliability that I am actually in the mental state described by myself in introspective terms. The very utterance of sentences containing those introspective terms is an important symptom and may, depending on further circumstances, be taken as fairly reliable evidence for the presence of the corresponding mental state. But in experiencing or having (living through,*"erleben")* the mental state I am in the privileged position of being able directly to confront a statement (no matter whether uttered by myself or by some other person) with the pertinent mental state.[3] The asymmetry that this privilege involves is clearly borne out by the fact that while for everybody else it would be possible to have the usual (empirical) doubts as to whether I really hear a ringing in my left ear, or as to whether I merely behave as if I did, I myself could not without a special kind of absurdity say: "I am not sure whether I experienced a ringing sound." I might of course be in doubt as to whether it is just a buzzing in my ear or whether I hear a distant squad car siren or a telephone bell. I might also doubt as to whether "ringing" rather than "whistling," "hissing," or "tinkling" would best describe the sound. But I would not doubt that it is a sound rather than a smell that I am experiencing. I could not possibly doubt the occurence of the experience itself while it lasts. The questions "how do I know?" or "on the basis of what evidence do I believe" that I have that experience seem utterly inappropriate. But the question how some other person knows, i.e., on the grounds of what evidence he could infer that I hear a ringing sound, is perfectly appropriate.

So much then by way of a characterization of the difference between direct and indirect verification of knowledge claims. Directly verifiable introspective reports about immediately experienced states utilize phe-

[3] I am referring to such cases of introspection as, for example, one would undergo when asking oneself (or when asked by a psychotherapist) whether one feels anxiety when contemplating one's insufficiencies, whether one feels a glow of proud satisfaction when remembering a great achievement, etc., . . . Of course, even in the so-called "physical" examination of one's eyes by the oculist, or of one's ears by the otologist, some of the questions asked are answered on the basis of introspection: "I still see the last row of letters a bit too blurred to be able to read them," "the ringing is in my left ear, not in my right ear," etc.

nomenal predicates such as "hot," "cold," "loud," "soft," "red," "green," etc., i.e., without any attempt at interpretation as in the physical mode (did I hear a telephone bell?) or in the psychological mode (did I feel cold because I was "chilled" by fears or anxieties?)

What then is the position of physicalism regarding the directly verifiable knowledge claims of self-observation? The discussions of the last few decades should certainly tend to moderate and modify the originally rather "crass," "materialistic" pronouncements of behaviorists and physicalists. The epistemological arguments against classical materialism have been directed also against the more sophisticated versions of modern physicalism. It is urged that the very knowledge of the "physical" behavior of organisms rests on a basis of evidence which when analyzed sufficiently far down to the immediately certifiable must be expressed in phenomenal terms. A more defensible form of physicalism must therefore render account of the epistemic primacy of immediate experience and of the difference between direct verification (confrontation with immediate experience) and indirect verification (inference with the help of laws or statistical rules).

Before sketching some possible forms of such a more liberal physicalism, let us first ask once more just what the first thesis of physicalism opposes or excludes. Perhaps a good way to get to the heart of the matter is to consider Carnap's critique of the analogical inference of mental states in other persons (in "Psychologie in Physikalischer Sprache," p. 118 ff.). I shall put the illustration in my own way: Suppose we compare the entirely unproblematic inference of the presence of brains in as yet unopened skulls, with the (allegedly) quite different and philosophically problematic inference of mental states associated with the behavior and/or brain states of other persons. It is of course admitted that inductive or analogical inference is essential and indispensable in the establishment of empirical knowledge claims. Thus we might formulate the inference in simple symbols (S_1 = skull of a first person, S_2 = skull of a second person, B_1 and B_2 the corresponding brains):

$$S_1 : B_1 = S_2 : \mathrm{B}_2$$

The italicized symbols stand for observed facts, i.e., both the skull and the brain inside it have been observed in the case of the first person, but only the skull of the second person has been observed, it has not yet been examined as to its internal contents. The inference of B_2, i.e., the presence of a brain in S_2, is the more probable the more similarities are noted between S_1 and S_2, or the more cases of such similarities we have observed for a large number of skulls containing brains (as revealed by opening them). This is clearly the familiar case of empirical inference.[4]

[4]Doubts about it could be raised only by those who on philosophical grounds are perplexed with the legitimacy of induction. We are not concerned with these perplex-

Now consider by way of contrast the inference of mental states on the basis of observed behavior or brain states. Let B_I stand for *my* molar behavior and/or brain states; M_I for my mental states as I can describe them in phenomenal terms on the basis of introspection; B_{II}, and M_{II}, corresponding states of a second person. The analogical inference might again be symbolized by

$$B_I : M_I = B_{II} : M_{II}$$

Early physicalism as represented by Carnap in 1932 declared this inference as illegitimate for the reason that M_{II} (the mental state of the other person) is not independently certifiable as is B_2 (the brain of the other person) in the previous example. In other words, Carnap maintained that inductive inferences are legitimate, in the sense of meaningful or at all permissible (not necessarily in the sense of reliable) if and only if the inferred conclusion is capable of independent test. Obviously, much in this argument will hinge on just what one will admit as "independent test." If one insists on *direct* independent test, then a very large class of inferences would be ruled out. Carnap saw this clearly in a later phase of his physicalism (in "Logical Foundations of the Unity of Science," reprinted in Feigl and Sellars, *Readings in Philosophical Analysis,* p. 419 f.) The example of the electric charge on a raindrop which far away from any observer falls into the ocean demonstrates clearly that with a liberalized formulation of the meaning criterion, statements about such only *practically* unconfirmable but theoretically confirmable statements must be admitted as perfectly meaningful. Or, consider as another example the impossibility for *me* to verify directly the state of my own body when in total anaesthesia or after my death.[5]

Returning to the parallel of the impossibility of direct verification in history and in the psychology of "other minds" we might say: It is impossible directly to verify that the Grand Canyon was formed by erosion; but nobody, unless afflicted by philosophical doubt, would question the legitimacy (i.e., the meaningfulness, not necessarily the reliability) of the inference that at a time long before there were human beings present to observe the formation of the canyon, erosion was the main factor in the process.

Similarly, we might say that, while *I cannot* verify directly the presence of a feeling of elation in my friend, I can legitimately infer it on the basis of his "radiant" expression, lively behavior, speech, etc. or—more reliably—on the basis of various psychological tests; and this in-

ities here. I think they have been satisfactorily resolved, by the analytic philosophers as well as by Reichenbach and Carnap. For a general summary of these results and my own analysis of the problem of induction, see: "Scientific Method Without Metaphysical Presuppositions," and the references listed at the end of that article, in *Philos. Studies* V (1954), 17-29.

[5]This illustration was suggested by my friend, P. E. Meehl.

ference *is* legitimate precisely because there are a number of independent avenues for its confirmation. But in the case of the inference of the mental state, i.e., the feeling of elation, as something distinct from actual or possible behavior or brain processes, we could say that my friend himself is in a privileged position and can verify its presence directly, independently of any behavioral or neurophysiological evidence that *others* could marshall. The reason why physicalism in its early form did not pay any attention to direct verification by the person concerned was of course the supposedly "purely subjective" character of such verifications. Behavioral and physiological tests could presumably be carried out by any observer properly equipped with the instruments and techniques of observation and experimentation. But if there were a domain of immediate experience radically private and secluded, i.e., absolutely isolated and insulated, hence completely inaccessible even through the most indirect routes to test by other individuals, then by this very character such immediate experiences could never be or become a subject matter for *science*. This is of course merely an obvious analytic consequence of the definition of scientific knowledge which insists on intersubjective testability. Before we examine some of the philosophical implications of this definition of science, it may be well to remember that mental states which are absolutely private in the sense just indicated would also be precluded from behavioral manifestation of any sort. Neither facial expression, nor verbal report, nor even the intonation of verbal utterances could in any lawful way be connected with these private states; for if they were, these behavioral symptoms could be used as a confirmation base for statements about those (in this case not *'absolutely'*) private experiences.[6] Philosophers—some as early as the sophist Gorgias and the Cyrenaics, others as recent as C. I. Lewis[7]—who raised the issue of the inverted spectrum and pursued its consequences to the bitter end, must however, have had absolute, unmitigated privacy in mind. That is to say, their assertion that person B might see the grass "really" red while person A sees it "really" green, is understood in such a way, that neither color vision tests, nor any other behavioral, neuro-anatomical or neurophysiological evidence would reveal the discrepancy which is assumed to exist exclusively in the pure "qualia" of the direct experience of the two persons.

I would urge that these assertions, while extremely fanciful, if not absolutely groundless in the light of the normal principles of commonsense and scientific inference, are nevertheless, *not* absolutely meaningless. I am also inclined to think that the assertion of the survival of a

[6]For a suggestive discussion of a closely related point, see the brief article by P. E. Meehl, "A Most Peculiar Paradox," in *Philos. Studies,* I (1950), 47-48.

[7]Cf. *Mind and the World Order* (New York: Scribner's, 1929), 74f.

totally isolated stream of experience after bodily death[8] makes perfectly good sense—in a sense of "sense" which must then of course be classified as purely subjective, and which *ex hypothesi* could not be the sort of intersubjective meaning which must be attributed to typically occultist hypotheses according to which the "surviving mind" ("soul," "psychoid," etc.) can manifest itself in alleged mediumistic physical phenomena—such as, e.g., giving messages by plucking piano strings or speaking through a living human "medium." Now, while I am personally utterly skeptical about "survival" in either form, I have used these excursions into the domain of scientifically "taboo" ideas, simply to point out the difference between two proposals for the delimitation of factual meaningfulness. Subjective confirmability is clearly the wider and more tolerant proposal; intersubjective confirmability is more restrictive in that it excludes all those assertions which could be checked by only one subject and are "in principle" unconfirmable to others. When scientists repudiate what they call (often rather loosely) "mysticism" or "supernaturalism," I think they have primarily reference to assertions which are not open to public test. The positivist scientists and naturalistic philosophers of various types suspect that knowledge claims of this sort are illegitimate because (a) they may be no more than expressions of emotions, and thus only because of the grammatical form of the sentences confused with genuinely cognitive assertions, and/or (b) while they may have the modest cognitive content of autobiographical, introspective reports, they pretend to knowledge of something over and above the experience itself (religious, mystical, etc.); but this "something more," by its very conception is in principle removed from independent intersubjective check, and thus the suspicion remains that the "apprehension of an Absolute" in mystical experience—even if this mystical experience be similar for many individuals—may well be an illusion of the sort that can be produced by hypnosis or autosuggestion. Physicalism is the explicit formal expression of this scientific attitude.

In the interest of the very clarity advocated by analytic philosophers and logical empiricists we must now ask two searching questions: (1) What is the logical status and the justification for the physicalistic criterion of factual meaningfulness? (2) Is, as its critics often maintain, logical empiricism (and physicalism) merely one form of metaphysics—namely a rather negativistic one?

It is today generally agreed among logical empiricists that the criterion of factual meaningfulness is to be construed as a norm proposed for

[8]Suggestively discussed by V. C. Aldrich in "Messrs. Schlick and Ayer on Immortality," H. Feigl and W. Sellars, *Readings in Philosophical Analysis* (New York: Appleton-Century-Crofts, 1949) and by C. Lewy, "Is the Notion of Disembodied Existence Self-Contradictory?" *Proc. Aristot. Soc.*, N. S., XLIII.

the purpose of avoiding unanswerable questions. Just as certain purely syntactical rules, such as Russell's rule of types, are designed to eliminate logical antinomies, so the *additional* requirement of confirmability-in-principle eliminates pseudo-problems, i.e., problems which by their very construction can be recognized as absolutely insoluble. By regarding the meaning criterion as a proposal rather than as a proposition it becomes impossible to subject it to its own jurisdiction or to ask whether it is true or false. What *is* true is the tautology that in a language conforming to the meaning criterion, unanswerable questions (of pretended *factual intent*) can not even be asked, let alone answered responsibly. For example, if absolute space is so conceived as to permit not even incompletely or indirectly confirmable answers to questions regarding the positions or motions of observable bodies with respect to that absolute space, then sentences which embody attempted answers to such questions are absolutely meaningless on the proposed criterion. A conservative way of putting all this might be: The rules of logical syntax together with the requirements of confirmability-in-principle form at least a necessary (but possibly not sufficient) condition for the factual meaningfulness of linguistic sign combinations. I am inclined to think that even metaphysicians or theologians cannot pursue their own purposes without some such delimitation of sense from non-sense.[9]

The justification for the adoption of such criteria of meaning can of course be only a practical one. If we wish to avoid the agonies and perplexities of problems which through our own making are unresolvable, then a criterion in terms of confirmability will have the desired salutary effect.[10] This is to say that the vindication of the adoption of and adherence to, a meaning criterion must refer to the purposes one aims at in using the language of cognition. Now, since the aim of the *scientific* enterprise is generally so conceived as to provide knowledge which is susceptible to *inter-subjective* test, it is clear that *purely* private, only subjectively confirmable knowledge claims are to be ruled out, i.e., declared as scientifically meaningless. As we have tried to indicate by our illustration above, subjective confirmability may be fulfilled even where intersubjective confirmability is absent. I may be able to confirm a strange continuation of my own stream of thoughts and emotions in the complete absence of sense data concerning the extradermal or intradermal

[9]In fact, I believe that the continuing controversy could be considerably clarified if metaphysicians and theologians came forth with at least an outline of their own criteria of meaningfulness.

[10]I have dealt in some detail with the problem of the meaning and the limits of justification, not only of the meaning criterion, but also of the principles of deductive and inductive logic, and the moral principles, in my essay, "De Principiis non disputandum . . . ?" in M. Black (ed.) *Philosophical Analysis* (Ithaca, N. Y.: Cornell University Press, 1950).

world. This might lead me to think, once this sort of thing had happened, that this part of my self (constituted by thoughts, images, remembrances and sentiments) had survived my "bodily" death. And, *ex hypothesi,* no other person could possibly confirm this. Here then is a fork in the philosophical road: Which of the two meaning criteria—subjective or intersubjective—are we to adopt? Why is it that scientifically oriented thinkers strongly oppose adoption of a criterion of meaning on a purely subjective basis? Why is it that they insist on the *public* character of knowledge as a defining (necessary) condition of the scientific enterprise? This insistence of scientifically minded thinkers seems to rest on the belief that there is nothing in heaven or on earth (or even beyond both) that could not possibly be known, i.e., there are no assertions about reality which could not conceivably be confirmed or disconfirmed on the basis of sense perception. Translating from the epistemological into the cosmological idiom, this amounts to the thesis that whatever there is in any shape or form, things, events, states, anywhere, at any time, "inorganic," "organic," "mental," "social," etc. can be causally related—even if only very indirectly by complicated chains —to the sense organs of human organisms. In other words, there is nothing absolutely isolated, causally completely unrelated to those parts of the world which form the stimuli of sense perception. Put in this way, this appears like a very bold belief about the nature of the universe. It is this belief which metaphysicians, by turning the tables on the logical empiricists, have called the "metaphysics of positivism." Again and again have we heard the criticism that the positivists rule out extra-scientific knowledge by declaring the scientific method the *only* method by which knowledge claims can be established, and that by "arbitrary" decree any other sources or methods of knowledge are ruled out of court.

And yet, metaphysicians or theologians often defend the "rationality" of their beliefs in the existence of extra-natural or non-physical entities by arguments of a typically inductive or hypothetico-deductive flavor. Many have come to realize that appeal to logic (purely deductive or dialectical) or to self-evidence simply will not do. But if they base their arguments on empirical evidence—even if "empirical" covers for them a much wider range than sensory experience—they will have to face the question as to whether they can justify the positing of transcendent entities in the manner in which, for example, the assumptions of atomic physics can be justified by the hypothetico-deductive method as applied to the data of experimental physics and chemistry. In this day and age it is obvious that we have extremely "good reasons" for the assumptions of the atomic theory, and that these assumptions cannot possibly be interpreted as merely "shorthand expressions" for the regularities on the macrolevel of observed phenomena.[11] The case of the mystic (theologian or metaphysician) is plausible only as long as naturalistic explanations of religious and mystical experience are not available. "Naturalistic explanations" here refers to the type of account given in various psychologies of religion—Jamesian, Freudian, etc. Even if many of the striking features of religious and mystical experience have not been explained in detail, the majority of psychologists are quite confident that the available evidence on the whole points in the direction of explanations within the present frame of psychological (and cultural-social) regularities and will not require the introduction of fundamentally different categories. Whether one formulates the principles underlying this scientific confidence as an aspect of the policy of induction and theory construction, or as an aspect of the rules of simplicity or parsimony, or simply as norms of giving "good reasons," they are in any case characteristic of the sort of conservatism without which scientific research would be unprotected against the dangers of groundless and limitless speculation. There is, one may hope, less reason to fear the opposite danger, viz., that scientific conservatism may degenerate into a rigidly dogmatic retention of a given frame of explanation. The tremendous and often revolutionary advances of science since the Renaissance, and especially in our century, bear ample testimony to the flexibility and the highly imaginative and ingenious character of scientific theorizing. The notorious difficulties of an exact delimitation of the concepts of the "natural" or the "physical" reflect the often surprising expansions of scientific concept formation and theory construction.

Returning to the case of mystical experience, we may say that the present prevalent scientific attitude acknowledges the occurrence of these unusual experiences, but doubts the interpretation in terms of transcendent entities that the mystics themselves (or some theologians or metaphysicians) impose upon them. I am inclined to think that the scientific attitude should be very different (and perhaps will be very different in the near future) with respect to the phenomena of parapsychology. If it were fully established that the phenomena of extrasensory perception, i.e., clairvoyance and telepathy, and perhaps even precognition and psychokinesis, do not result from experimental or statistical errors (not to mention self-deception or outright fraud), then our conception of the basic laws of nature may well have to be revised at least in some essential aspects. Curious "actions at a distance"—spatial as well as tem-

[11]Cf. H. Feigl "Existential Hypotheses," *Philos. of Science,* XVII (1950); W. Kneale, "Induction, Explanation and Transcendent Hypotheses" in H. Feigl and M. Brodbeck, *Readings in the Philosophy of Science* (New York: Appleton-Century-Crofts, 1953); L. W. Beck, "Constructions and Inferred Entities," *ibid.;* R. B. Braithwaite, *Scientific Explanation* (Cambridge: Cambridge Univ. Press, 1953).

poral, and—conceivably though by no means necessarily—some alterations in our basic psychophysiological assumptions might have to be introduced. The only alternative would seem to be the assumption of some cosmically pre-established sets of "spurious" coincidences and correlations—an assumption which in any other field governed by statistical evidence would seem objectionably ad hoc and thus bound to obstruct scientific progress.

The foregoing considerations are to call attention to (1) the flexibility or "openness" of the concept of the "physical," and consequently (2) the need to re-examine the two theses of physicalism in their relations to one another. If "physical" means the sort of entities, no matter how inferential or hypothetical, whose assumption can be justified on the basis of *sensory* confirmation, then the first thesis of physicalism does imply the assertion of a certain generic feature of the universe and is thus clearly not a truth of pure logic (pure syntax or pure semantics). Carnap himself pointed out [12] the factual nature of intersubjectivity and its analogy to the intersensory character of ordinary perceptual objects. In the latter case it is a matter of empirical fact that certain objects are accessible tactually as well as visually, and that—epistemologically speaking—the existence of single objects is predicated upon the regular concomitance[13] of sensory data, or "appearances" in the various modalities. Similarly, the assertion that everything there is in our world is in principle susceptible to at least indirect confirmation by sensory experience of *any* human observer, not only amounts to an assumption about the universe, but also specifies at least very sketchily certain features of the laws of the universe. These general features consist in the assumption of a spatio-temporal-casual network in which the knowing subjects are embedded as genuine parts. This is a thesis common to most forms of philosophical naturalism—a thesis, which despite its vagueness, has certain implications for the second thesis of physicalism. This second thesis, it will be recalled, asserts that scientific theories attain progressively more and more unifying syntheses of their subject matter, and that they tend toward a unitary set of explanatory principles. The thesis furthermore asserts that these explanatory principles will be (note the unavoidable vagueness!) somewhat like the most comprehensive postulates of present-day theoretical physics. The progress of physics in the last few centuries, the great syntheses achieved successively by classical mechanics, classical electromagnet-

[12]It may be noticed however that these facts, though of empirical nature, are of far wider range than single empirical facts or even specific natural laws. We are concerned here with a perfectly general structural property *(ordnungshafter Zug)* of experience which is the basis of the possibility of [an intersensory as well as intersubjective] science." (From: Carnap, *The Unity of Science*, M. Black, transl., 65.)

[13]Or as we might say nowadays, the truth of certain lawful connections as expressed in subjunctive conditionals.

ics, the atomic theory, the theory of relativity and quantum mechanics, the prospect of incorporating the bio-psychological sciences (possibly with the help of cybernetics) into an ever more adequate grand scheme—these have been some of the encouraging factors in the various stages of monistic philosophies. The unitary-science thesis may be regarded as a twentieth century sequel and incisive revision of eighteenth century materialism. Some of the culturally understandable motivations may be similar, but present-day physicalism displays a much greater logical and epistemological sophistication.

The second thesis of physicalism, in asserting that the facts and laws of mental life can be given a "physical" explanation, while not strictly implied by the first thesis, is at least rendered rather plausible. If there is nothing in the realm of mental phenomena that is in principle excluded from sensory confirmation, then all mental phenomena must in some way be part of the nomological network (the causal, or at least statistical order) which alone makes indirect confirmation possible. The notions of *"physical$_c$,"* i.e., an object in principle connectible with the sensory confirmation basis, and *"physical$_e$,"* i.e., object of explanation in terms of the basic laws of nature, are thus seen to be much more closely related than Carnap's original sharp distinction of the two theses of physicalism suggested.

Before we return to the epistemological analysis of physicalism let us try to assess its cosmological aspects. If the term "physical" designates the objects of the laws and theoretical assumptions of physics, then obviously the first question to be asked is: of *which* physics? It should scarcely be necessary here to review the drastic and pervasive changes wrought by the successive revolutions in theory construction mentioned above. The concept *"physical$_e$"* has expanded tremendously beyond the original identification with the "mechanical" so characteristic of the natural philosophy of the seventeenth and eighteenth centuries. The field theories of the nineteenth century, the revisions due to the relativity and quantum theories in our century have affected profoundly our concepts of space, time, substance and causality. These alterations were required precisely because a larger range of observable phenomena was to be encompassed by increasingly comprehensive and increasingly unified systems of explanation. There are in present-day physics principles of continuity (fields), of discontinuity (quanta of energy, as in the interaction of fields with particles, and of particles with one another, etc.); important new relations of spatial and temporal magnitudes (involving an upper limit for the propagation of causal influences—according to the theory of relativity); the mutual transformability of radiation-energy and basic particles; and principles of organization, fundamental for the formation and structure of atoms and molecules (as formulated in W. Pauli's exclusion principle).[14] It would seem hazardous to assume that the concept of "physical$_e$" will in the future undergo no further radical alterations or expansions. The most cautious definition one might suggest would be a dated one ("physical" in terms of the respective scientific theories of, e.g., 1687, 1900, 1905, 1925, 1958, etc.). The only alternative to this sort of definition would be the much vaguer, but nevertheless more fruitful one of defining "physical$_e$" simply as the object of any more or less comprehensive explanatory system whose concepts are defined implicitly by a set of postulates, partially interpreted in terms of a sensory confirmation basis. This definition of "physical$_e$" in terms of the hypothetico-deductive procedure with a basis in intersubjectively testable observation propositions recommends itself in that it reflects (a) the elasticity and openness of the explanatory concepts of advancing science, and (b) the "objectivity" which has always been a prime desideratum (and often an achieved virtue) of the natural sciences.

The openness of the concept "physical$_e$" which frees the second thesis of physicalism from dogmatic dependence upon a given stage of physical theories allows for a non-metaphysical interpretation of emergent novelty and emergent evolution. The important point in the notion of emergence is not so much that there are in the course of the history of the universe completely new entities—qualities, relations, structures, events or processes—but rather that a certain set of concepts and laws sufficient for the explanation and prediction of a given range of phenomena may not be sufficient for the explanation of a wider range of phenomena. The triumphant achievements of the mechanistic world view—until about the middle of the nineteenth century—are responsible for the confidence (characteristic also of the much more speculative views of the ancient atomists, as well as of modern atomic theory at least since the days of Rutherford and Bohr) that the striking novelties connected with high complexity of structures are derivable with the help of mathematical-geometrical devices only. That is to say, that no special *physical* composition laws are required for the explanation of the behavior of structures of higher degrees of complexity. Geometry plays the role of a "silent partner," very much like logic and arithmetic do, in these derivations. This is of course not to deny the empirical character of applied geometry; it is merely to emphasize its subsidiary role of being "presupposed." Modern atomic theory has its own peculiar *physical* composition rules, especially the Pauli principle. The behavior of electrons in the context

[14]We might mention also some even more drastic, and hence more problematic, departures from classical conceptions, such as the Wheeler-Feynman theory of advanced potentials with its apparent time reversals); present theories of the role of mesons in nuclear structure (with its completely unvisualizable duality of particle and wave aspects, already introduced in earlier phases of quantum mechanics); and the Bondi-Gold theory of the continuous accretion of matter on a cosmic scale.

of atomic structure cannot be derived from the laws of motion of free electrons (as in cathode or β-rays); additional *physical* principles are needed. But again, once the basic laws of atomic structure and dynamics have been ascertained in the simpler cases of atoms like hydrogen, helium and lithium, the rest of the periodic table as well as the structure of molecules are found to be derivable from those laws *more geometrico*. Whitehead's suggestion that the behavior of electrons within living organisms may be fundamentally different from that in inorganic compounds can of course not be refuted a priori. It is entirely a matter of empirical research to find out how broad or complex a basis of evidence is needed in order to permit us to glean those laws which then applied by purely mathematical-geometrical computations, will also be sufficient for a range of phenomena of greater breadth or complexity. It must be admitted that it is conceivable that as we advance in the study of structures of higher and higher complexity, there might never be an end to the emendation of the laws of nature. In view of the difficulties of current theory perhaps something of this sort may even be expected as research penetrates to deeper levels of the structure of matter. Nevertheless, according to the prevalent—and perhaps somewhat sanguine—view of many scientists, nature while extremely complex is not hopelessly difficult to unravel into basic regularities. This is no doubt what Einstein means by the famous epigram (exhibited at Princeton): "God is sophisticated, but he is not malicious." Metaphysicians will insist that this optimism of the scientists is really an "act of faith," and as such as unjustifiable on empirical grounds as are transcendent theological beliefs. But empiricists need not be disturbed over this. "Belief in the ultimate simplicity of nature" is not a logical presupposition of science, except in the trivial and tautological sense that—to the extent to which science achieves, on some level of analysis (i.e., in terms of a certain set of variables) an adequate and unitary explanatory system, nature has—on that level—as much simplicity as is reflected in the given explanatory system. Empiricists are therefore perfectly justified in viewing the "principle of simplicity" as a guiding maxim of research, as part and parcel of the policy of the inductive and hypothetico-deductive procedures of science, rather than as a metaphysical postulate.[15] Any speculation regarding the "ultimate," "rock bottom" structure of nature is bound to be an utterly irresponsible piece of dogmatism. Elevating the best established laws of a given stage of science to

[15]Cf. Arthur Pap, *Elements of Analytic Philosophy* (New York: Macmillan, 1949). (Chapter "Does Science Have Metaphysical Presuppositions?" reprinted in H. Feigl and M. Brodbeck, *Readings in the Philosophy of Science* (New York: Appleton-Century-Crofts, 1953).

H. Feigl, "Scientific Method Without Metaphysical Presuppositions," *Philos. Studies*, IV (1954).

the rank of a rigid philosophical a priori—as, e.g., Kant did with the principles of Newtonian physics—is not only unjustifiable, it is also pernicious in that it is apt to impede the progress of research.

The implications of the preceding excursion for the two theses of physicalism will now be summarized and discussed:

The decision to rule out as scientifically meaningless statements which are not even indirectly confirmable intersubjectively on a sensory basis, and the confidence that this decision will not exclude anything in existence from the realm of science, reflects the conviction that whatever is subjectively verifiable is in principle also intersubjectively confirmable. This conviction—if it is not to be a "metaphysical presupposition"—must therefore be so construed as to fall under the jurisdiction of the principles of induction. In plain and ordinary words this means that naturalists claim to have good empirical reasons for their belief that nothing is inaccessible to study by the scientific method. If the first thesis of physicalism is to formulate more than a tautological consequence of a definition of "scientific method," it would indeed seem to be the expression of an inductively grounded assumption, and would thus be in principle subject to refutation.

Inductive validation of the first thesis of physicalism is, however, not the simple straightforward sort of thing with which we are so familiar in common life and in the empirical sciences. Ordinary inductive justification occurs within a frame of spatio-temporal-nomological structures which are usually unquestioningly assumed although they are not in principle unquestionable. The adoption of this frame can be practically justified (vindicated) by its entailed consequences. This vindication is in part deductive, in that the demonstration of the entailed consequences is a matter of purely logical derivation. But the adoption and retention of a certain frame contains an irreducibly inductive element, the "by their fruits ye shall know them" maxim. This maxim clearly refers to continued appraisal in the light of expected and forthcoming "fruits." This may be illustrated by a reflection upon the adoption of the traditional and customary spatio-temporal (4-dimensional) frame of physical description. In the usual concerns of everyday life and of the experimental sciences the employment of this frame is a matter of unquestioned practice. Innumerable factual questions of various degrees of specificity or generality are formulated as well settled within this frame. But there have been occasions when the frame itself was subjected to questions—as, e.g., in the topological modifications required for the Einsteinian cosmology, or in the suggestions regarding a genuinely spatial fifth dimension as in a now largely forgotten theory of Kaluza's.—I am concerned to point out that the "empirical method" is a matter of various levels. Simple questions on the level of observation are so convincingly decidable just because the frame[16] within which they are asked is accepted and not at all questioned in this context. When it comes to the acceptance of a certain set of natural laws or hypotheses, simple observations or measurements alone will not be decisive, because scientific laws and theoretical assumptions constitute confirmation rules and thus furnish the frame for the decision of more specific descriptive questions. But the acceptance or rejection of theoretical assumptions themselves is regulated by frame principles of still more fundamental and generic significance—such as the norms of factual meaningfulness and validation. While these norms are best construed as prescriptive proposals rather than as descriptive propositions, they differ from the rules of deductive logic in that they are not matters of merely formal or intralinguistic relevance, but do reflect certain basic and pervasive features of our world. It is, however, impossible to describe these features directly as one would describe specific facts or regularities within the world. Wittgenstein (at least in the mood of his *Tractatus*) would have said that these features "show forth" in the successful application of a language, in the adequacy of a certain type of conceptual system. To say of space that it is three-dimensional does not make sense in the same way in which it makes sense to say of a specific scrap of paper that it is triangular. Similarly, to say that whatever there is in the world is in principle (no matter how indirectly) causally connectible with human sense organs does not make sense in the same way in which it makes sense to say, e.g., that lights of a specified minimum luminosity and a specified maximum distance are visible to persons with normal vision. This becomes clear by reflection upon the conditions of confirmation or disconfirmation of the respective assertions. Specific empirical assertions (such as those about triangularity, visibility, or the like) may be confirmed or disconfirmed by clearly circumscribed types of evidence; whereas the categorical or generic statements about the tridimensionality of space or about the causal accessibility of everything in the world, while not a priori in the analytic manner, might nevertheless be regarded as a priori pragmatically or functionally.[17] That is to say, the adoption of certain norms of meaningfulness and of validation is not a matter of arbitrary decision, but is guided by the consequences of their adoption as these con-

[16]Cf. Carnap, "Empiricism, Semantics and Ontology," *Rev. Internat. de Philos.*, IV (1950), 11; also reprinted in L. Linsky (ed.), *Semantics and Philosophy of Language* (Urbana: University of Illinois Press, 1952); and in P. P. Wiener (ed.), *Readings in Philos. of Science* (New York: Scribner's, 1953).

[17]Cf. C. I. Lewis, *Mind and the World Order* (New York: Scribner's, 1929). Victor Lenzen, *Procedures of Empirical Science, Internat. Ency. of Unified Science,* I (1938), 5. Arthur Pap, *The A Priori in Physical Theory* (New York: Kings Crown Press, 1946). Wilfrid Sellars, "Is There a Synthetic a Priori?" *Phil. of Science,* XX (1953).

Corresponding to Carnap's notion of P-rules of inference ("P-transformation rules" in his *Logical Syntax of Language)* it may be suggested that the 3-dimensionality of space (or the 3 + 1-dimensionality of space-time) could be formulated as *P-formation*

sequences are disclosed in the management of cognition in a world "we never made."

The first thesis of physicalism may then be regarded as a new formulation of the principles of empiricism: (1) Statements are to be regarded as *scientifically meaningful* only if they are in principle intersubjectively confirmable or disconfirmable. If a statement, by the very interpretation imposed upon it, is in principle incapable even of the most indirect sort of intersubjective test, then though it may have meaning of a purely logical sort, or may be significant in that it carries pictorial, emotional or motivative appeals, or may even be testable in an *exclusively* subjective manner, it cannot be accepted as an answer to a *scientific* question. The phrase "in principle intersubjectively confirmable or disconfirmable" should be understood in the most liberal manner. The sort of indirect testing of assertions here allowed for includes of course the testing of only partially interpreted postulate systems. It countenances as scientifically meaningful, statements about the most remote, the most intricately concealed or difficult to disentangle states of affairs. It includes statements about unique and unrepeatable occurrences, if only they are of a type that places them within the spatio-temporal-nomological net which itself has an intersubjective confirmation base. (2) Statements are to be accepted as scientifically valid only if they are sufficiently highly confirmed by in principle intersubjectively available evidence. The precise meaning of "sufficiently highly confirmed," as well as the exact explication of "degree of confirmation," "inductive probability," or "evidential support" need not be discussed in the present context.

The preceding formulations render briefly but, I trust, sufficiently adequately Carnap's present liberal empiricist views. The early forms of rational reconstruction—both the phenomenalist reduction of the *Logischer Aufbau der Welt,* and the radical physicalist reduction of the "Unity of Science" phase of the early thirties have been completely abandoned. Epistemological analysis no longer consists in the retracing of logical constructions to elementary concepts on the phenomenal or on the macro-behavioral ground level. Statements concerning "physical events" are *not translatable* into statements about sense data (actual or possible). Statements about mental events are *not translatable* into statements about (actual or possible) overt behavior.[18] In both cases epistemological analysis consists in making explicit the conceptual structure

rules of the language of science. In field physics certain variables (electric, magnetic, gravitational, etc. magnitudes) are ascribed to space-time points. In a well formed formula (representing a singular proposition) a functor is assigned to a quadruple of numbers.

[18]In the *Aufbau* ideology "translatability" meant mutual logical deductibility. That this relation does not apply here is shown in some detail in my article "Existential Hypotheses," *Philos. of Science,* XVII (1950).

of the *nomological* relations between the data of observation and posited events or processes for which the data serve as evidence. The meaning of statements (at least in one very important sense of "meaning") is to be identified with their factual reference, and not with their evidential basis. The slogans of early logical positivism and of ultra-operationism about meaning and verification—while helpful in the repudiation of transcendent metaphysics—despite their imprecision were far too restrictive to do justice to the actual conceptual structure of knowledge. According to Carnap's present view the essential requirements of empiricism are fulfilled if the nomological net which implicitly defines the concepts of science is tied in a sufficient number of points to concepts of the observation base. While it is useful, and perhaps indispensable for a logical analysis of unfinished and developing science to distinguish between observation language and theoretical language, it is equally instructive to reflect the more stabilized parts of science or the tentatively anticipated parts of highly unified[19] science in a reconstruction in which all terms belong to the same language. In his important essay "Über Protokollsätze" (*Erkenntnis* III, 1932, pp. 215-228) Carnap discussed the relative advantages and disadvantages of each form of reconstruction. Even in a unitary-language reconstruction there will of course still be a distinction between observation terms (terms designating immediately experienceable qualities or relations) and other terms designating unobservables. It is fairly generally agreed[20] now that the unobservables (i.e., concepts designating unobservables) are implicitly defined by the partially interpreted postulate system which—together with its explicit definitions and derived theorems—formulates the nomological net. The observables usually occur only as highly derived terms of the system (although there is no a priori reason why some of them might not figure as primitives). The meaning of the unobservables (theoretical concepts of physics, for example) is thus specified through their place in the network; or—if a metaphor be permitted—the meaning of the unobservables is fixed by "triangulation in logical space" from points on the observation base. The richer the various connections in the net, the more fully and definitely can the meaning of each concept be specified with respect to other concepts of the net.

If the unitary language is strictly intersubjective, the characterization

[19]"Unified" in the sense of the unitary explanatory system to which the second thesis of physicalism refers.

[20]Cf. R. Carnap, *Foundations of Logic and Mathematics,* I, No. 3 of the *Internat. Ency. of Unified Science* (the relevant parts are reprinted in Feigl and Brodbeck, *Readings).*

C. G. Hempel, *Fundamentals of Concept Formation in the Empirical Sciences,* II, No. 7 of the *Internat. Ency. of Unified Science* (1952).

R. B. Braithwaite, *Scientific Explanation* (Cambridge: Cambridge University Press, 1953).

of the observables themselves can be achieved internally, i.e., by reference to their peculiar locations in the nomological net. The lessons of behaviorism point the way here. (We shall criticize certain behaviorist reductive fallacies a little later.) Subjectivistic and phenomenalistic epistemologies have traditionally employed some principle of acquaintance or the notion of ostensive definition in this connection. The terms for unobservables (universals or particulars) were to be understood through reference to aspects or items of direct experience or intuition. In the intersubjective reconstruction this analysis is supplanted (or, if you will, paralleled) by an account of the habitual regularities (acquired through learning processes) of the use of certain words in connection with various exteroceptive or interoceptive stimuli or stimulus configurations. Ostensive definitions had been something of a vexing anomaly anyway. They could not be written down—as any normal definition can be. They had therefore better be reinterpreted as rules for the use of symbols to be incorporated by drill in our linguistic habit system. The intersubjective description of the behavior of human organisms gives an account of the use of direct observation terms including the so-called "subjective" terms referring to "private" experience.[21] We acquire the use of such phrases as "I feel happy" (or "tired," "indignant," "elated," "depressed," etc., etc.) in a way not fundamentally different from the way we acquire the use of color, sound, taste or smell terms. In the process of education we learn to associate certain words with certain situations, things, feelings, etc. through the familiar processes of learning (conditioning, imitation), i.e., through reinforcement by our social environment. Once our linguistic abilities have matured more fully, we can also make up our own words for experienced qualities which are "private" in the two senses of: "not shared by anyone else" and "resulting from intradermal stimuli." Thus it would be possible for someone experiencing utterly strange qualities (as under the influence of drugs or Yoga practices) to label them with 'α,' 'β,' 'γ,' etc. and thus to develop a partly "private" language. But it is obvious that a perfectly intersubjective account of this private language can be given, as soon as the causal relations between the eliciting internal states and the associated verbal responses are ascertained. Returning to the more usual private experiences, such as headaches, memory images, dreams or the like, it is generally plausible that their introspections may be viewed intersubjectively as processes caused by co-present or immediately preceding central states, sometimes—but not necessarily—issuing in

[21]Cf. especially: B. F. Skinner, "The Operational Analysis of Psychological Terms," *Psych. Rev.*, LII (1945); also reprinted in Feigl and Brodbeck, *Readings*.
B. F. Skinner, *Science and Human Behavior* (New York: Macmillan, 1953).
W. Sellars, "Some Reflections on Language Games," *Philos. of Science*, XXI (1954).
Carnap anticipated the basic idea of Skinner's analysis in his article on "Psychologie in Physikalischer Sprache," *Erkenntnis*, III (1933).

overt verbal responses. Given a fuller development of neurophysiology the details of such a causal analysis of "private" experience and of introspection could presumably be filled in quite satisfactorily.

The controversial problem of the certainty of direct observation statements can perhaps be resolved by distinguishing between the subjectively felt *certitude* of statements made during their actual confrontation with the data they describe, and the *objective degree of certainty* (degree of confirmation) that can be ascribed to them on the basis of the best intersubjective evidence that can be marshalled for their support. Furthermore, it seems possible to account for the high degree of subjective certitude of direct observation statements within the intersubjective frame. The relatively short and usually smoothly functioning set of processes that connect a cerebral state with a learned verbal response assure on the whole a high objective probability for statements involving a minimum of inductive extrapolations.

At this point we have to deal with the notorious and perennial objections which will be raised by all those philosophers who maintain that behavioristic as well as neurophysiological accounts *necessarily leave out something essential,* namely a description of direct experience as we "have" it, "live it through," "enjoy" or "suffer" it; in short what they miss is an account of precisely the subjective awareness of, or acquaintance with, the "raw feels" of direct experience. Another equally notorious and insistent objection concerns the irreducibility of "meaning," "reference," "intentionality," "norms," etc. to physicalistic categories. Since I agree in a certain respect with this last line of objections and since there is no space for their detailed discussion here, I shall restrict myself to some extremely brief suggestions.[22] I do agree that physicalistic categories do not and could not possibly provide a basis for an adequate analysis of the normative aspects of meaning. But logical empiricists have admitted this throughout. What is under discussion here is the psycho-logical, not the psycho-physical problem. Ever since Frege's and Husserl's devastating critiques of psychologism, philosophers should know better than to attempt to reduce normative to factual categories. It is one thing to describe the actual regularities of thought or language; it is an entirely different sort of thing to state the rules to which thinking or speaking *ought* to conform. Whether we deal with rules of inference or rules of designation, the only aspect that a causal-descriptive, behavioristic account can possibly cover are those dealt with in *descriptive* syntax, semantics or pragmatics. The meaning-relation (reference, intentionality) of *pure* semantics—Carnap uses the term "designation"—is neither phenomenal nor

[22]For a fuller analysis of these issues cf. W. Sellars, "Mind, Meaning and Behavior," *Philos. Studies,* III (1952).

W. Sellars, "A Semantical Solution of the Mind-Body Problem," *Methodos,* V (1953).

behavioral. It is a concept in a purely formal discipline developed for the express purpose of reflecting the norms of designation and of inference by the construction of an ideal language model. But in the *descriptive* disciplines of semiotic we deal with linguistic behavior, and with the various aspects of the actual use of words—in connection with other words, with events inside or outside the communicator, etc. If "meaning," "reference," "intentionality," are understood psychologically, then these concepts belong to *descriptive* semiotic and no insuperable difficulties arise. But it is, and will always remain, a category mistake, to attempt to reduce *pure* to *descriptive* semiotic.

I turn now to the other problem which is much more germane to our general topic: Is the physicalistic reconstruction of mental life necessarily incomplete in that it cannot include an account of direct experience of the "raw feels?" This question constitutes perhaps the most perplexing central issue of the modern mind-body problem and is basic for an appraisal of the status of psychology in the system of the sciences. The contention of behaviorism that psychology is a natural science (continuous with biology) must now be more carefully scrutinized. Certain naive forms of behaviorism are easily repudiated. In the early phase of "logical behaviorism" Carnap[23] tended to regard statements in the mentalistic, subjectivistic language as logically equivalent with statements about overt behavior. But even in that early phase Carnap qualified this radical view, on the one hand, by pointing out the dispositional form of many psychological concepts, and on the other by reference to the possibility of neurophysiological explanations. The dispositional form of psychological concepts was especially emphasized later in "Testability and Meaning." To ascribe a psychological predicate to a certain organism was declared equivalent to (or shorthand for) a test condition→test result conditional, or to an open set of such conditionals (or equivalences) as formalized by means of unilateral or bilateral reduction sentences.[24] If psychological statements are to be intersubjectively confirmable, they must be established on a sensory confirmation basis. In the terminology previously sug-

[23]Cf. especially "Les concepts psychologiques et les concepts physiques sont-ils foncièrement differents?" *Revue de Synthese,* X (1953), 43-53. Also the closely related (now equally superseded) presentation by C. G. Hempel, "Logical Analysis of Psychology," in Feigl and Sellars, *Readings in Philos. Analysis.*

[24]It must be remembered that the term "reduction sentence" is used by Carnap for a formula which provides a partial and conditional definition of a dispositional concept. Dispositional concepts, Carnap emphasized, are not explicitly definable on the basis of observation predicates, they can only be introduced just through this sort of partial specification of meaning, on the basis of empirical regularities among observables. Reduction in this sense must therefore be sharply distinguished from the other, more customary methodological concept of reduction in the sense of explanatory derivation. "Reduction" in this latter sense is illustrated, for example, by the derivation of the laws of classical thermodynamics from the assumptions of the kinetic theory of heat (statistical mechanics).

gested this would make psychological concepts and statements physical$_c$, while their status as regards physical$_e$ is thereby not prejudged. The empirical regularities of behavior (which are compressed into dispositional statements) may however eventually become derivable from neurophysiological premises. Encouraging precedents of such derivations or explanatory reductions are plentiful in the history of physics, chemistry and biology. Countless macro-laws have been explained, i.e., logico-mathematically derived from assumptions about micro-structures and micro-processes in those disciplines. Even if psychological research at present may more fruitfully concentrate on macro-behavior, the progress of neurophysiology, especially since the advent of cybernetics, should be a sufficient warning to the protagonists of exclusively molar forms of behaviorism. They should not repeat in the field of psychology the sort of error committed in physics by the opponents of atomic theory (Mach, Ostwald, and other positivists some fifty years ago).[25]

Given this general outlook it becomes obvious that the naive peripheralistic forms of behaviorism must be repudiated and their shortcomings remedied by the admission of central states and processes as the genuine referents of psychological terms. Although at the current stage of neurophysiological research specific identifications of these states and processes are mostly quite problematic, this does not make the idea in principle objectionable. Many terms in physics, chemistry and biology were construed as having a surplus meaning (beyond the empirical dispositionals which "anchored" them in the confirmation basis) long before that surplus meaning could be more precisely specified in terms of micro-structures confirmed by new and independent sorts of evidence. This "promissory note" feature of many scientific concepts must therefore be regarded as an essential part of their meaning. Concepts such as memory trace, habit strength, unconscious wish, etc. may plausibly be taken to refer to (as yet very incompletely specified) central conditions. The philosophical puzzles of the mind-body problem become poignant only in the case of psychological terms which in the introspective situation have a direct reference to items of the phenomenal field, i.e., to "raw feels." Once the naive behavioristic identification of the referents of phenomenal terms with overt peripheral behavior is abandoned, the new identification with central states may be questioned on similar grounds. The liberal meaning criterion of physicalism$_c$ does not necessarily rule out dualistic interpretations of either the interactionistic or parallelist type. One would of course want to be very careful in explicating the precise meaning of such dualistic doctrines. But as long as mental events are at all located

[25]Cf. H. Feigl, "Principles and Problems of Theory Construction in Psychology," in *Current Trends in Psychological Theory* (Pittsburgh: University of Pittsburgh Press, 1951). (See also the references given at the end of that essay.)

in the intersubjectively anchored nomological net, they are thereby physical$_c$, even if there be some doubt as to their precise status in regard to physical$_e$. But if the application of the label "physical$_e$" is not limited to some given stage or style of explanatory theory, then whatever the place of mental events in the nomological net, no matter what type of laws are characteristic of them, they would be physical$_e$. This is surely too easy and too cheap a demonstration of a monistic physicalism. Contemporary naturalistic monists have often espoused so omnivorous a concept of "nature" that their thesis became unassailable—at the price of triviality. If physical$_e$" is understood in this extremely tolerant way, it becomes practically indistinguishable from the meaning of "physical$_c$." It is clear, however, that monistic physicalism, past and present, is conceived somewhat more narrowly. It excludes, at least and especially, the ascription of typically teleological features to "purely" mental factors or events in that it insists on explanations of teleological and purposive behavior on the basis of organic structures and processes. It rejects teleological explanations of the vitalistic type as anthropomorphic and mythological, and insists on the explanation even of conscious purposive behavior in terms of such neurophysiological mechanisms as, e.g., negative feedback. "Teleological explanation" is rejected, not necessarily as meaningless (it *could* be physical$_c$), but as presumably superfluous, i.e., because a scientific account of "teleological mechanisms" (no longer a contradiction in terms) by means of non-teleological concepts is becoming increasingly successful.[26]

Limitations of the meaning of "physical$_e$" of the sort just suggested would seem to exclude typically interactionistic theories of the relation of the mental to the physical. The essential core of such theories which always seemed extremely objectionable to physical monists was the assumption that an "immaterial" agent could in some way organize and direct the course of "material" processes toward certain ends or outcomes. The terms "material" and "immaterial" are, however, typical of the earlier, mechanistic phase of natural science. If we disregard the philosophically irrelevant pictorial connotations of the term "material" (e.g., hard little balls in perpetual motion), it means the sort of structures and processes describable and explainable by the principles of Newtonian mechanics. The fields and particles of modern physics are then clearly not material in *this* sense. They are, however, physical$_e$ (as well as, of course, physical$_c$). Now, the doctrine of immaterial agents directing the behavior of organisms was evidently suggested by the introspectively founded interpretation of voluntary action. Action carried out with an

26The only reservation here to be made concerns again the questionable and puzzling phenomena of extrasensory perception—especially precognition. The physical monist will have to await further developments in this field with an open mind.

end in view is one of the most familiar features of our experience. Many forms of pre-scientific thought adopted this sort of will-directed action as a paradigm of explanation. But with the advance of modern science we have learned that explanation does not necessarily or even usually coincide with familiarization. The vast majority of present-day psychologists still oppose in principle animistic explanations and insist on physical_e explanations. With the qualifications made above this is no longer the trivial all-embracing thesis of a vague naturalism but a testable hypothesis, or at least a research program whose success can be appraised in the light of empirical evidence. The introspectively impressive "efficacy" of intentions and volitions must then be explained in a manner compatible with physical_e principles.

Epiphenomenalistic parallelism was never a plausible doctrine. Voluntary action, the role of attention, as well as psychosomatic phenomena, such as hysterical symptoms, appeared as strong evidence against a doctrine which would make mental events a dispensable luxury a causally superfluous and inefficacious by-product of neurophysiological processes. For this reason various double aspect, double knowledge, double language or identity theories strongly recommended themselves to scientifically oriented thinkers. This sort of solution of the old puzzle has been very plausible also because it harmonized well with the familiar analytic clarification of the free-will problem.[27] Once the notorious confusions of the free-will perplexity were removed, it became clear that it makes perfectly good sense to say that our volitions are free to the extent that they are determined by our basic personality, i.e., to the extent our interests, knowledge and deliberations are causally effective in the actions we perform. A general account of mental phenomena in physical_e terms thus seems to face no overwhelming "metaphysical" objections. The available scientific evidence points on the whole strongly in the direction of a monistic solution. I shall now try to explicate it more precisely, and to test its strength against various criticisms. We thus return to the question: Is physicalism defective in that it omits or excludes from consideration anything essential to the science of psychology? Our answer, briefly is this: If by "physical" we mean, as specified, both physical_c and physical_e then a physicalism in the form of an identity theory of the mental and the physical can be formulated which though contingent in its validity upon certain pervasive features of empirical evidence, is nevertheless not neces-

[27]Cf. Alois Riehl, *Science and Metaphysics* (London: Kegan Paul, 1894).
M. Schlick, *Allgemeine Erkenntnislehre* (Berlin, 1918, 1925).
Durant Drake, *Mind and Its Place in Nature* (New York: Macmillan, 1925).
Durant Drake, *Invitation to Philosophy* (New York: Houghton Mifflin, 1933).
R. W. Sellars, *The Philosophy of Physical Realism* (New York: Macmillan, 1932).
R. E. Hobart, "Free Will as Involving Determinism and Inconceivable Without It," *Mind,* XLIII (1934).

sarily defective; and can be defended against a number of charges that have been traditionally levelled against psychophysical monism.

First then a more precise statement of the physicalistic identity theory:[28]

It claims that there is a synthetic (basically empirical) relation of systemic identity between the designata of the phenomenal predicates and the designata of certain neurophysiological terms. This sort of identity differs *in its mode of ascertainment* from accidental identities as well as from ordinary nomological identities. An accidental identity would be formulated, for example, by the statement: "The woman named Ann E. Hodges (32 years old) of Sylacauga, Alabama, is the person who was hit by a meteorite weighing nine pounds in December 1954." A nomological identity: "The metal which has a specific heat of 0.24 and a specific gravity of 2.7 has an electric resistivity of 2.8 microhms per cc." Systemic identity differs from nomological identity in that it requires a background of scientific theory and of semantical analysis. Systemic identity might also be called "theoretical identity" because it is only in the light of a

[28] In the development of my own formulation of the identity theory I was stimulated by the work of Schlick and by continued discussions and correspondence with Carnap. Readers will be interested in the following crucial passages (fairly literally translated by me from the German) contained in a letter Carnap wrote me from Prague, June 21, 1933, in response to some critical queries I had then submitted to him.

"Example:	B_1 "The organism of N. is in the state of house-imaging"
A "N. has a visual image of a house."	B_2 "In the organism of N. there is an electrochemical condition of such a kind" (described in terms of electrochemistry).

Both B_1 and B_2 are translations of A. According to my recently adopted terminology I assert: A is equivalent("gehaltgleich") with both statements on the right side; viz., L-equivalent (*logically* equivalent) with B_1; but P-equivalent (*physically* equivalent) with B_2, i.e., mutually translatable (derivable) using besides the logical laws also natural laws as rules of inference, incorporated as transformation rules in the scientific language. You are therefore right in saying that B_2 is only synthetically equivalent with A. This holds also of your example [quoted from Whitehead] about the relation of the tactual and the visual breakfast; and for the agreement between direct and indirect measurements of distance . . . "

"The difference between natural laws and logical laws is admitted, but it is not as enormous as we (with Wittgenstein) supposed it to be. Even the logical principles of language may be modified if this appears as expedient; and this not just on the basis of purely speculative considerations, but possibly prompted by the facts of experience."

. . . "The whole 'riddle of the universe' [Schopenhauer's 'Weltknoten,' i.e., the mind-body problem] seems finally to come to this: one will have to make clear to oneself in an appropriate manner that brain processes are, on the one hand, *objects* of scientific sentences, and on the other hand *causes* of the emission of sentences. This, in itself by no means mysterious, situation should then be so formulated that people with emotional (not to use the offensive word 'metaphysical') headaches can accept it more easily. As to whether these aches can be completely eliminated is a psychological question, or perhaps a practical task of psychoanalysis."

theory that this sort of identity can be recognized. In a complete theory of the atomic structure of matter the nomological identities (as well as other relations formulated by empirical laws) which our previous example illustrates would be deducible from the postulates of the theory. The systemic identity would then hold between the referent of the description of a certain metal in terms of its atomic (or molecular) structure and the referent of a description of a certain metal (in our example aluminum) in terms of its directly observable or measurable physical and chemical properties. Other examples: The macro-concept of temperature designates the same state of matter that is designated by (a disjunction of) micro-descriptions in terms of molecular motions; the macro-concept of electric current (as used in experimental physics) designates the same process, which in greater detail is described by the micro-account (again in disjunctive form) of the motion of electrons through a lattice of atoms. It should be noticed that in all the identities illustrated so far we deal with cases of empirically ascertainable synonoymy (or perhaps I had better call it co-reference?). This is as it should be. Logically it is improper, if not inconsistent, to say that two *things* are identical. If they were, they (?) would be *one*. Identity can legitimately be ascribed to the referent of two different names, of a name and an (individual) description, of a predicate and a (generic) description, two different descriptions (individual or generic), etc. Empirically valid synonymies[29] of the accidental, nomological or systemic types must of course be distinguished from purely logical synonymies, as for example, "$2^3 = + \sqrt[2]{64}$"; or "x is *earlier than* y = y is *later than* x."

The systemic identity of the referent of phenomenal terms with neurophysiological ones (such as, perhaps, "mounting anxiety = increasing hypothalamic activity") can consistently be maintained only if the phenomenal terms are used intersubjectively, i.e., if their referents are physical_c events. The application of the neourophysiological term (systemically synonymous with the phenomenal term) provides the setting for incorporation in the nomological net of physical_e concepts and laws. *Absolutely* private phenomenal terms would according to our earlier discussion not even be physical_c and would thus not fulfill the necessary condition for being physical_e.

[29]In order to forestall a possible misunderstanding, it should be noted that the phrase "empirically valid synonymy" as understood in the cases of accidental, nomological or systemic identities refers to something different from the sort of synonymies that a mere descriptive-semantical examination of a natural language can disclose. That "tepid" and "lukewarm" are used synonymously in English can be ascertained by observation of linguistic customs without a special study of the materials to which these predicates may be applied. That "temperature" refers to the state of material objects which is also the referent of micro-physical descriptions can be established only by special experimental research and theoretical interpretation.

A familiar objection[30] to the identity theory maintains that the "raw feels" of direct experience could not conceivably be the referents of neurophysiological terms. Neurophysiology deals with the processes in the sensory-neural-glandular-muscular structures, it has reference to the electrochemical aspects of the "firing" of neurons, etc.—and so it is argued, how could directly experienced qualities such as colors, sounds, smells, pains, emotions, or the like, be identical with neural processes whose properties are so fundamentally different? It is usually granted that these two types of processes may be lawfully related, so that to a given quality of experience there corresponds a certain neural state or process (or a disjunction thereof) either by way of simple concomitance or as a consequence of causal relations of interaction between "mind" and "brain." Since what is regarded as the decisive point in this objection depends on various emphases, we shall have to consider each of them.

First of all it must be pointed out that according to our epistemological point of view the designata of the concepts of physical science are by and large totally unfamiliar, i.e., unknown by acquaintance. Only phenomenal terms are directly associated with certain qualities and relations in the field of immediate experience. A Martian super-scientist who did not share any of our human repertory of immediate data could nevertheless (conceivably) attain a perfect behavioral and neurophysiological account of human life. He might not "know by acquaintance" what colors look like, what pains feel like, what it "means" to experience "pity," "reverence," "regret," etc. As has often been pointed out, a congenitally blind (human) scientist, equipped with the necessary instruments and intelligence could achieve not only an adequate knowledge of the *physics* of colors and radiations, he could also arrive at a (behavioristic and neurophysiological) account of color perception and imagination. Similarly a clinical psychologist completely deprived of certain sectors in the area of emotional experience would in principle be able to introduce the behavioral or neurophysiological equivalents of such (to him completely unfamiliar) emotions in his "psychology of the other one." Of course, it must be admitted, that (a) without *some* basis of immediate experience neither the Martian superscientist nor the emotionally "blind" clinical psychologist could ever get started in his cognition of anything in the world; and (b) that possession of a repertory of experience of a cer-

[30]For incisive (but in my opinion inconclusive) arguments against various forms of physicalistic monism cf. especially C. J. Ducasse, *Mind, Nature and Death* (LaSalle: Open Court Publ. Co., 1951); N. Jacobs, "Physicalism and Sensation Sentences," *Jl. of Philos.*, XXXIV (1937); C. I. Lewis, "Some Logical Considerations Concerning the Mental," *Jl. of Philos*, XXXVIII (1941) (also reprinted in Feigl and Sellars, *Readings*); Arthur Pap, "Other Minds and the Principle of Verifiability," *Revue Internat. de Philos.*, XVII-XVIII (1951); "Semantic Analysis and Psycho-Physical Dualism," *Mind*, LXI (1952).

tain breadth will be immensely helpful in a *heuristic* way for the projection of tentative hypotheses or laws concerning the regularities of human experience. In taking himself as an instance or sample of the type of object ("person" in this case) to be investigated, the psychologist will have a certain advantage if he finds in himself the kind of processes which he studies in others. On the other hand there are of course also certain dangers of error involved in overestimating the interpersonal similarities. But it is clear that direct acquaintance with, e.g., melancholia, or megalomania, is not an indispensable prerequisite for the psychiatric diagnosis or etiological explanation of these mental conditions. The Martian may be completely lacking experiences of the sort of human piety and solemnity, and hence unable to "understand" (empathize) what goes on in the commemoration of, e.g. the armistice—but this would not in principle make it impossible for him to give a perfectly adequate causal account of the behavior of certain human groups on a November 11th at 11 a.m.[31] Quite generally, the significance of intuition, insight, empathetic understanding consists in the power of these processes to *suggest* hypotheses or assumptions, which, however, could *not* be established, i.e. confirmed as scientific statements except by intersubjective methods.

Returning to the central issue, the distinction between "knowledge by acquaintance" and "knowledge by scientific description" can be drawn in such a way, that the first reduces strictly to familiarity in the sense of ability to recognize a quality immediately when experienced, i.e., the ability to affix the proper phenomenal label. Knowledge by acquaintance also involves in some areas, but not generally or necessarily, the ability to imagine certain qualities or configurations. One may rightly wonder whether the word "knowledge" should at all be applied to acquaintance or familiarity in the sense just explained. If it is the mere having *("erleben")* of certain contents of experience, no truth-claim is connected with it. If it is the ability of correct labeling, then it is perhaps "knowing how," but again not "knowing that" which alone makes a truth-claim.

The electrochemical concepts of neurophysiology, like all concepts of the natural sciences, have their epistemic roots in the area of sensory evidence. If one confuses evidence with reference, as positivists and phenomenalists stubbornly do, then of course it would seem that the meaning of physical concepts had to be indentified with the sensory data that serve as a confirmation basis. Very naturally when we hear of "cerebral processes" we think of a brain-as-seen-when-opening-the-skull, or of nervous-tissue-as-seen-under-the-microscope. It is this "root-flavor" which is so often mistaken for the factual meaning of our statements or concepts. More precisely, it is the pictorial appeals (usually the visual imagery)

[31]The example is taken from Eddington's *Science and the Unseen World* (New York: Macmillan, 1929.)

which masquerade as the "true meaning" of our concepts. But while, as empiricists, we insist on "rooting" our concepts in a sensory confirmation base, this does not imply that our concepts *refer* to it. The concept of the electromagnetic field, for example, must of course be introduced in such a manner that it is not completely disconnected from the data of sensory experience, but its referent is not visualizable at all. "Thou shalt not make graven images unto thyself" is a warning to be heeded in the philosophical interpretation of the concepts of physics; this notwithstanding the admittedly often great but always limited heuristic (or didactic) value of images and models. The prima facie implausibility of the identity thesis arises, I believe, mainly from the psychological incompatibility of images such as of nervous tissue or of molecular structures (as pictured by didactic tinker-toy models) with the qualities of some data of consciousness, such as sounds, smells or emotions. More fundamentally, perhaps the most perplexing difficulty of the mind-body problem can be avoided by distinguishing between phenomenal and physical space.[32] Visual, tactual, and kinaesthetic data contribute the "intuitive" character of phenomenal space (or spaces). The geometry employed in the description of physical space is a conceptual system which, though based upon the evidence of the sensory kind of spatiality, is itself not adequately intuitable (visualizable, etc.). This implies that the neurophysiological concepts which are used in the description of cerebral processes are not to be "visualized" in terms of the phenomenal data on whose basis they are confirmable. Some parts of direct experience (the visual, tactual, etc.) have *phenomenal* spatial extension, others (emotions, volitions, etc.) have at best a very vague and diffuse phenomenal localization. In opposition to Descartes I feel tempted to say that it is only the mental, i.e., the phenomenal data, which have (intuitable) spatial extension, whereas physical objects as conceived in physical science have only abstract conceptual (non-intuitable) topological and metrical relationships. Hence there is no conflict and no incompatibility in regard to the "location" of, e.g., a directly experienced patch of color. It is where we "see" it in phenomenal space. The systemically identical cerebral process is assigned a place in the abstract 3-dimensional manifold of physical space; and a detailed analysis of the central process in its relations to afferent and efferent impulses should be able to account for the behavior relevant in place learning, spatial orientation, optical illusions, etc.

The psychophysiological isomorphism assumed by the Gestalt psychologists may well be interpreted as the identity of certain items or aspects

[32]Cf. especially the chapters on qualitative and quantitative knowledge, and on the psychophysical problem in M. Schlick's *Allgemeine Erkenntnislehre* (Berlin, 1918, 1925) which contains a superb and undeservedly neglected clarification of these issues.

of the phenomenal field with certain global or configurational aspects of the (in dualistic terms: "correlated") neurophysiological processes. The criticism that the physical language necessarily omits reference to the experienced aspect may then be rejected because reference is here confused with the evocative appeal of certain terms of our language. Many psychological terms of the intersubjective language of ordinary communication carry such an evocative appeal. This comes simply from the way their use has been learned. If in the utopian future of a complete neurophysiology children could be taught to use the appropriate neurophysiological terms on the basis of introspection, these terms would then have the same sort of emotive (pictorial, emotional, motivative) appeals that psychological words have in common language; and there would be the additional advantage of getting rid of the spurious dualism that is essentially linguistic. The incorporation of words which fulfill a phenomenal-introspective function into the total terminology of scientific explanatory terms could thus be achieved.[33]

Philosophically more interesting is the closely related question whether the physical language is not bound to disregard the experienced *uniqueness* of particulars as well as of universals. There is, to be sure, a certain sense of "uniqueness which escapes all efforts of conceptual characterization. The "absolute" uniqueness of the "now" (*this* present moment, of the "I" (*this* present person), as it is experienced directly, and reflected in the expressions of poets and the anguished stammerings of existentialists, is indeed a matter of *acquaintance* and not of knowledge at all. The only way in which the uniqueness of particulars and of universals can be cognitively represented deprives it of its absolute character and assigns to individuals and to qualities the sort of singularity that they have in a total relational structure. In the scientific description of the world the "now," the "here," and the "I"—no matter how poignantly and uniquely experienced subjectively—are supplanted, respectively, by a moment in time (among a continuum of other moments), a point in space (in a continuum of other points) and a person (among other persons and things). Whatever can be conceptually formulated about the *empirical* singularity of certain moments, places or persons is so formulated with the help of definite descriptions (unambiguous characterizations) which owe their uniquences to either a sufficiently plausible (but always problematic) singleness of the qualitative or relational setting, or to a unique association of proper names with their designata. The attachment of

[33]Perhaps I should at this point reassure emotionally tender persons that I am using this fantasy merely as a thought experiment, and that I am not seriously proposing this sort of language reform. I too happen to have a certain romantic attachment to the homey, christmassy, or poetic appeals of many words of ordinary introspective language.

proper names (or of coordinates) to their designata is a pragmatic affair, presupposed in the semantical analysis of language.[34]

The question "Why am I I?" not only looks queer in print, but is apt to provoke needless perplexity. If it is not an empirical question as to the causal factors which contributed to the formation of my personality, it is probably a manifestation of deep bewilderment with "existence," the sort of emotional expression which Heidegger mistook for profound philosophy. The thought experiments regarding the inverted spectrum show clearly that the empirically assertible uniqueness of the qualities is inseparable from the nomological net in which they have their cognitive, conceptual place. In this way scientific knowledge does symbolize the qualities, they are not excluded, omitted or disregarded. The rules according to which the symbols are used reflect the total relational structure. Even the correctness of the affixing of a symbolic label to an experienced quality can be *checked*—subjectively or intersubjectively—only with reference to the conceptual structure. But the *use* of phenomenal terms, being a matter of *doing* rather than of a *knowledge claim* can be considered as a result of training or conditioning, and as such is not a conceptual affair. But as soon as we wish to give even the sketchiest *account* of such training and its results (habits of verbalization) then, of course, we are making a knowledge claim, and this can occur only within the frame of a conceptual structure, i.e., a nomological net.

Moritz Schlick, in his London lectures on "Form and Content"[35] had developed an analysis of cognition in terms of directly experienced content and conceptual structure. He was aware of the dangers of a metaphysics of "ineffable" contents, although in his somewhat metaphorical manner of writing he could perhaps not completely avoid gratuitous perplexities. But his doctrine jibes well with his original critical-realistic solution of the mind-body problem.[36] A purified doc-

[34]For an important recent analysis of the logic of egocentric particulars (or token-reflexive words) cf. Y. Bar-Hillel, "Indexical Expressions," *Mind.* LXIII (1954).

[35]Cf. *Gesammelte Aufsätze* (Vienna, 1938). (The lectures "Form and Content" are printed in the English language.)

[36]Schlick, in his *Allgemeine Erkenntnislehre* (Berlin, 1918, 1925) had expounded, perhaps with greater clarity than other monistic critcal realists of that period, a physicalistic identity theory which—due to the predominantly phenomenalist tendencies of the Vienna Circle—had later been suppressed (even by Schlick himself). If I am not altogether mistaken, it is precisely this theory which, properly formulated in modern semantical terms, deserves resuscitation and which impresses me as the sort of solution that should be especially acceptable to Carnap's present way of thinking.

For other largely independent older or more recent similar doctrines of various degrees of epistemological sophistication, cf. Alois Riehl, *Science and Metaphysics* (London: Kegan Paul, 1894); F. Gätschenberger, *Symbola* (Karlsruhe: G. Braun, 1920); and Durant Drake, *Mind and Its Place in Nature* (New York: Macmillan, 1925), R. W. Sellars, *The Philosophy of Physical Realism* (New York: Macmillan, 1932); Curt

trine of form and content would merely insist on distinguishing between (a) *having* a datum and its *description;* (b) the *evoking of data* (images, feelings) through the pictorial or emotional uses of language, and their symbolization by the representative, descriptive function of language; (c) the *activities* and *abilities* of affixing names *(or predicates)* to data or aspects of data), the *empirical description* of these activities and abilities (in descriptive pragmatics), and their metalinguistic formalization (in pure pragmatics); (d) descriptions of *data* and descriptions of *non-data* (inferred or posited on the basis of presupposed nomological relations). Once these distinctions are recognized, there is no occasion for a metaphysics of the inexpressible, ineffable or unknowable.[37] The qualitative features of the raw feels directly designated by phenomenal terms may also be indirectly but (empirically) uniquely characterized by their place in the nomological net of neurophysiological descriptions.

At this point it may be well to consider briefly another critical question. If raw feels are designated by certain neurophysiological concepts, how do we decide as to whether butterflies, earthworms—or amoebas, for that matter—are "sentient" beings? In keeping with the two theses of physicalism as interpreted thus far, this comes down to the question of the degree of similarity between the processes in these various organisms. Systemic identity presupposed, there is no additional cognitive significance in the ascription of raw feels over and above the identifiable physiological processes. Certain philosophers have adopted a panpsychistic position, but this doctrine is to be rejected not because it is unconfirmable but because it does not really make its predications, as it pretends, on the basis of considerations of analogy. The differences of organization between organisms are so tremendous that the sort of structure which is characteristic of human mental life is either extremely impoverished or completely absent in lower organisms. But wherever the similarities warrant it, the application of (human) phenomenal terms, preferably with proper qualifications and cautions will add the emotive appeals which give ethical and quasi-ethical questions their peculiar poignancy. Does my fellow man really suffer agonies when subjected to torture? Does the wriggling of the worm on the fishook manifest genuine pain? If these questions, though admittedly sometimes extremely difficult to answer, are not to be made absolutely unanswerable (by our own perverse intellectual devices), then proper attention to

Weinschenk, *Das Wirklichkeitsproblem der Erkenntnistheorie und das Verhältnis des Psychischen zum Physischen* (Leipzig: Reisland, 1936); H. Reichenbach, *Experience and Prediction* (Chicago: Univ. of Chicago Press, 1938), especially Chapter IV.

[37]Cf. Carnap's pertinent and trenchant replies to the criticisms of E. Zilsel and K. Duncker in *Erkenntnis,* III (1933). These were written, however, in his syntactical phase, i.e., before the indispensability of pure semantics and pure pragmatics were realized.

analogy is the only responsible way to settle them. Lately the same sort of puzzle has been posed in regard to man-made robots. Electronic computers ("thinking machines") might be equipped with additional devices which mimic responses to various "perceptual," "pain," etc., stimuli and which even display "manifestations of emotions."[38]

We do not *seriously* apply mentalistic terminology to such machines because their internal structure is so radically different. All response mechanisms are deliberately built into them, and it seems extremely unlikely that a machine consisting of inorganic parts could in *every* respect duplicate the complex, adaptable, docile, purposive behavior of human beings. If, on the other hand, a *homunculus* could be produced by synthesis and combination of essentially the sort of materials (proteins, etc.) of which human organisms consist, then only a theologian might be reluctant to ascribe mental life to it.

Two final crucial questions: How does the here proposed systemic identity theory differ from parallelistic dualism or from a physicalistic emergentism? Dualistic parallelism has for a long time been the implicit if not the explicit preference of cautious philosophers and psychologists. "The facts of psychophysiology indicate a *correlation* of the mental and the physical," this is the customary formulation. "Mental" means here at least the phenomenal, but usually also the much larger rest of the subject matter of psychology, including the unconscious processes and dispositions of psychoanalysis. "Physical" is usually understood as a rather unclarified combination of (picturized) materiality and subject matter of physical science (intersubjective, non-teleological, etc.). A little reflection shows that "correlations" of the "mental" and the "physical" taken in these senses cannot be interpreted consistently. There are empirical relations between the processes in the central nervous system and the peripheral sensory and motor processes. These are *causal* relations of a complex structure, scientifically analyzable into relatively more "micro" linkages, of neural and ultimately of molecular-atomic-electromagnetic nature. They do *not* have the character of an ultimate "parallel" concomitance. This sort of parallelism is indeed more usually asserted to hold between the phenomenal (directly given) states of consciousness and the "corresponding" neural processes. The experimental situation in which this kind of parallelism could presumably be ascertained, would be the observation of one's own brain processes along with some other directly given mental states. Let us assume a device, the "autocerebroscope," were available for this sort of observation. While one experiences, e.g., a sequence of musical tones (or of odors, tastes, feelings, emotions, etc.) one would simultaneously also

[38]Cf. especially A. M. Turing, "Computing Machinery and Intelligence," *Mind,* LIX (1950), and Michael Scriven, "The Mechanical Concept of Mind," *Mind,* LXII (1953).

be confronted in one's visual field with certain shape and color patterns, which according to plausible (realistic) interpretations, would indicate in great detail the configurations of neural processes in one's own brain. Now, it is easy to see that precisely on the basis of the parallelism hypothesis the relation between the visual patterns and the brain processes correlated with (parallel to) the sequence of tones would again be of a *causal* nature. That is, the visual patterns would be *effects* of immediately preceding brain states, made visible by the cerebroscope. In no conceivable experimental setup could one "observe" both a brain state *and* its so-called mental correlate *simultaneously*. The parallel correlation would therefore always be a matter of *interpretation* of the autocerebroscopic data. Now, it must be admitted, the liberal empiricist meaning criterion would not rule out as meaningless the assumption of two parallel series—the brain states on the one hand and the mental states on the other. But the positive assertion of their duality could be justified only by the sort of evidence (autocerebroscopic, parapsychological, occultist or otherwise) which, assuming the parallelistic hypothesis, could not be forthcoming. It is therefore much more in keeping with the usual procedures of inductive and theoretical science to identify the designata of certain phenomenal descriptions with the designata of certain neurophysiological descriptions. This avoids the introduction of superfluous hypotheses. This empirical core combined with the epistemological considerations concerning acquaintance and description, and the semantical analysis of systemic synonymy, constitutes the difference between the physicalistic identity (or double language) view of mind and body, and dualistic parallelism, i.e. the theory according to which the mind-body relation is analyzed in terms of a general empirical equivalence of mentalistic and physicalistic propositions. It must be emphasized again that the identity theory stands or falls with the empirical evidence, and can therefore never be regarded as justified by purely logical considerations alone. Evidence of the independent existence of "mind-like" agents as conceived by some vitalists or parapsychologists would indeed have to be scrutinized very seriously. As long as the scope of naturalistic ($physical_e$) explanations is uncertain, nothing more compelling can be offered than confidence in certain inductive generalization on the one side and a miscellaneous group of puzzling and recalcitrant phenomena on the other. While the analytic philosopher might well be completely neutral in such issues, philosophers of science are apt to express certain predilections. Physicalists (like myself), in any case, are so impressed with the triumphs of scientific explanation, that they would, if necessary, admit all sorts of revisions in the ($physical_e$) laws of the universe, rather than to abandon the identity view and thus to open the door for typically animistic doctrines.

The sort of revisions which physicalists should not too strenuously oppose are those (briefly touched upon before) of the doctrines of evolutionary emergence. Since emergence need not conflict with scientific determinism, or with the degree of determinism countenanced by modern physics, it is conceivable that the concepts and laws required for the explanation of biological or psychological processes will not be reducible to those sufficient for inorganic processes. Emergence understood in this way[39] would be entirely compatible with the first thesis of physicalism. But it would qualify the second thesis to the effect that certain concepts of biology and psychology would have to be implicitly defined by the nomological net, i.e. that they could not all be defined explicitly on the basis of the primitives sufficient for the physics and chemistry of inorganic phenomena. Or, even if the biological phenomena were completely reducible to physicochemical ones, it is conceivable, though (to me) not plausible, that the explanation and prediction of the "raw feels" of psychology may require genuinely irreducible (i.e., primitive) concepts connected by nomological rather than by merely logical relations with the primitives of (inorganic) physics.[40]

I conclude by a succinct statement of the philosophically most challenging points of our critical review of the theses of physicalism.

Both theses of physicalism reflect certain assumed basic features of our world. The first thesis, far from being a purely syntactical criterion of meaningfulness, asserts that subjective and intersubjective confirmability coincide in their extensions. This expresses one essential aspect of scientific optimism, namely the belief that there is nothing in the realm of existence which is in principle inaccessible to examination and exploration by the scientific method. Metaphysicians must however be cautioned not to feel triumphant about this. Given the methods—the only ones we can justifiably call "objective"—for the certification of knowledge claims, any speculations concerning realities beyond the reach of those methods remain as boundless and hence as irresponsible as they have always been regarded by empiricists. For all we know, and possibly may ever know, confirmability on a sensory basis is a necessary condition for the intersubjective meaningfulness of factual knowledge claims. As long as this is not regarded as an absolutely unquestionable a priori presupposition, but as a frame principle of human knowledge,

[39]Cf. P. Meehl and W. Sellars, "The Concept of Emergence," in H. Feigl and M. Scriven (eds.), *Minnesota Studies in the Philosophy of Science,* I (Minneapolis: Univ. of Minnesota Press, 1956). Also G. Bergmann, "Holism, Historicism and Emergence," *Philos. of Science,* XI (1944).

[40]In the terminology of Meehl and Sellars this would make all psychological concepts physical_1 (part of the intersubjectively confirmable nomological net) but not physical_2 (part of the intersubjective nomological net sufficient for the explanation of all inorganic and [most?] biological phenomena).

dovetailing with what commonsense and science tell us about the embeddedness of knowing organisms in the known or to-be-known world, there is no danger of relapsing into the rationalistic metaphysics which logical empiricists have consistently opposed. The "logical behaviorism" of some twenty years ago tended to assert that mentalistic terms are attached to behavior by sheer convention. This would make the first thesis of physicalism analytic. A more adequate appraisal of the total empirical and logical situation however forces us to formulate the basic psychophysical relation as one of synthetic, empirically grounded systemic (or theoretical) synonymy. But in being a relation of synonymy, rather than of mere empirical equivalence, the "identity" of the referents of introspective and certain physical terms, reflects—if it holds—a very fundamental trait of our world. As such it is much more fascinating, but of course also much more problematic than a purely analytic thesis could ever be.

The second thesis of physicalism expresses a related but even bolder belief characteristic of the optimistic attitude of scientists. In endorsing a program of theory construction which attempts to subsume a maximum of facts under a minimum of unitary basic postulates, and in conceiving these basic postulates according to the paradigm of modern physical theory, physicalism amounts to a monistic view of scientific explanation, and therefore—in a sense—also of the universe. Despite a certain unavoidable and even desirable vagueness in the conception of "physical explanation," the thesis is definite enough in what it rules out. Animistic or irreducibly teleological explanations are quite clearly excluded—if not as scientifically meaningless, than certainly as superfluous. Apart from the impressive success of the physicalistic mode of explanation, and apart from ideological (anti-obscurantist) motivations, there is perhaps a more trenchant and philosophically more significant argument in favor of the second thesis. Just as *testability* is a necessary condition for the *possibility* of scientific knowledge (first thesis of physicalism), so is *predictability* a necessary condition for the *success* of the scientific endeavor. Even if vitalistic or animistic hypotheses could be formulated in conformity with the liberalized meaning criterion, they would, if true, restrict predictability (and explainability) quite severely. Whether our universe will accommodate the scientific quest for more and more complete physicalistic reduction, will in principle always remain an open question.

The general philosophical lesson to be drawn from these conclusions would seem to be: A properly reformulated physicalism contributes greatly to our analysis of scientific method. But since both these involves assertions about the world, physicalism cannot and should not claim to settle by logical analysis any issues in the strife of the "Weltanschauungen." It will be helpful, if in the future, purely analytic philosophy, i.e. clarification without cosmological presuppositions or commitments, were even more sharply than heretofore separated from the advocacy and justification of such presuppositions.[41]

HERBERT FEIGL

DEPARTMENT OF PHILOSOPHY
UNIVERSITY OF MINNESOTA

[41]The present paper was completed and submitted to the editor, Professor Paul A. Schilpp, in December 1954. I have subsequently written a further and more elaborate essay on "The 'Mental' and the 'Physical'" which is contained in H. Feigl, M. Scriven, and G. Maxwell (eds.), *Minnesota Studies in the Philosophy of Science,* II: *Concepts, Theories and the Mind-Body Problem* (Minneapolis: Univ. of Minnesota Press, 1958), 370-497.

7

A. J. Ayer

CARNAP'S TREATMENT OF THE PROBLEM OF OTHER MINDS

IN the period between 1928 and 1935, when he was devoting much of his attention to the theory of knowledge, Carnap several times recurred to the problem of other minds. So far as I am aware, he first attacked it in a pamphlet which he entitled "Scheinprobleme in der Philosophie: das Fremdpsychische und der Realismusstreit."[1] This title is, however, misleading, at least as regards the problem of other minds; for, so far from showing it to be a pseudo-problem, to which there could be no solution, he himself offers a solution of it. The thesis which he claims to prove is that "in every concrete case in which one has knowledge of another's mind, the epistemological core of this knowledge consists in physical observations: or: other minds come in only as offshoots (epistemologically) of physical events."[2] From the way in which this thesis is formulated it is not at all easy to discover exactly what is being maintained; but the general tone of the pamphlet makes it fairly clear that Carnap was here adumbrating, in what he came to call the material mode of speech, a view which in later articles he expressed more formally by saying that statements about the minds of others are reducible to statements about physical events. This version of his thesis is still somewhat loose. A more accurate way of putting it would be that sentences containing expressions of a certain sort, namely such as ostensibly refer to the mental state of some person other than the speaker, are equivalent to sentences containing expressions of a different sort, namely such as refer to physical events, and specifically to the physical states of the other's body. So far as I know, this has remained Carnap's view: indeed I do not think that on this subject he has ever expressed any other. It is true that in *Der logische Aufbau der Welt* he asserts that "the whole course of an-

[1]Published in 1928. The other relevant texts are *Der logische Aufbau der Welt* (1928), 185-200; "Psychologie in physikalische Sprache," *Erkenntnis*, II (1932); "Die physikalische Sprache als Universalsprache der Wissenschaft," *Erkenntnis*, II (1932), which is better known in its English version "The Unity of Science" (1934); and "Concepts Psychologiques et Concepts Physiques," *Revue de Synthese*, X, 1 (1935).

[2]"Scheinprobleme in der Philosophie," 18.

other man's experience consists in a re-arrangement of my experiences and their components."[3] But the reason for this is that he then held what he has since regarded as the mistaken opinion that all other objects were to be constituted on the basis of the subject's private experiences. He even then allowed the possibility of constructing an equally comprehensive system with physical objects as the basic elements: but he preferred to take "my" experiences as his basis, because he thought that they were fundamental in the order of knowledge. But here too the experiences of others are "constituted" out of physical objects. If they are said to consist of "my" experiences, it is only because this is held to be true of physical objects also.

The thesis is, then, that to talk about the minds of others, that is, about their thoughts or feelings or experiences, in some way comes down to talking about their physical states, or behaviour, in connection perhaps with other physical events. But in what way? How is the reduction of one sort of statement to the other supposed to be effected? Here Carnap appears to waver between two different views. In the *Erkenntnis* articles he seeks to show that the reduction is a purely logical procedure. His arguments are designed to prove that if expressions which refer to the experiences of others are to have any meaning at all the sentences in which they occur must be logically equivalent to sentences which describe physical events. But elsewhere he seems to adopt a milder view, maintaining only that statements about other minds can always be derived from statements about the appropriate physical events with the help of certain universal statements, which themselves are not logically but only factually true. And this comes to little, if anything, more than an assertion of psycho-physical parallelism, or, perhaps only of the causal dependence of mental upon physical events.

It is this weaker position that seems to be taken in "Scheinprobleme in der Philosophie." Carnap there draws a distinction between what he calls the sufficient and the dispensable components of the situations in which knowledge is acquired. A component is said to be dispensable when its existence can be inferred from the existence of the other, the sufficient, component on the basis of previous knowledge. From the examples given it appears that the cases envisaged are those in which the two components are connected by some universal statement for which past experience has furnished good inductive evidence. But this makes it at least conceivable that one component should exist without the other. Although knowledge of their physical manifestations may in fact be sufficient for knowing the states of other minds, so that we need not trouble ourselves with getting to know what lies "behind" these physical displays, it would, on this showing , still remain logically possible that other people had experiences

[3] *Aufbau*, 86.

for which there were no physical correlates. Moreover, if psycho-physical parallelism holds, the inference can go either way; we could equally well maintain that knowledge of the non-physical component was sufficient in these cases, and knowledge of the physical component dispensable.

At this point, however, other considerations are brought in. As in the quotation given above, a distinction is drawn between the epistemological core of a cognitive process and its offshoot.[4] For *a* and *b* to stand in this relation of core to offshoot two conditions must be satisfied. First, observation of *a* must be necessary to establish the existence of *b*, whereas the observation of *b* must not be necessary to establish the existence of *a:* and secondly, while the observation of *a* must ordinarily be taken as sufficient for establishing the existence of *b*, it must leave room open for error: it must be possible that the inference from *a* to *b* should lead to a false conclusion. Now both the conditions are held to be fulfilled in the case where *a* is the observation of some physical event and *b* is the experience of some other person. It is, therefore, taken as proved that "in all cases in which knowledge is obtained of other people's minds, the epistemological core of the cognitive experience consists only in observations of physical events."[5]

But if the inference from these physical events to the corresponding mental states can lead to false results, if, indeed, it is not a deductive but only an inductive inference, its premises and conclusion are logically distinct. The mental experiences and their physical manifestations cannot be identical. How then did Carnap come to think that he had proved that "every assertion about a particular mental state of another person, e.g. 'A is now happy' could be translated into an assertion which referred only to physical occurrences, namely to expressive movements, actions, words etc."?[6] It may be that he was allowing for the possibility of error only in the sense that one might mistakenly infer from one such physical manifestation to another; but he offers no good reason for supposing that this is the only sort of mistake that could occur. On the contrary, the whole tenor of his argument lies the other way. The logical independence of the two "components" appears to be assumed throughout.

This assumption becomes explicit in the article on "Concepts Psychologiques et Concepts Physiques." We are there told that statements about mental processes, whether it be one's own or other people's, are, not logically, but physically equivalent to statements about their physical manifestations. Let us, says Carnap, use the expression "anger_{ps}" to

[4]The German words which I have translated by 'core' and 'offshoot' are 'Kern' and 'Nebenteil.'

[5]*Op. cit.*, 23.

[6]*Ibid.*, 37.

refer to "the mental state of anger, the feeling of anger, the state of consciousness called 'anger'": and let us use the expression "$anger_{ph}$" to refer to the physical state, or class of physical states, in which a person's body is when (and only when) he is in a mental state of "anger." Then, he maintains, the two statements "Mr. A is now in a state of $anger_{ps}$" and "Mr. A is now in a state of $anger_{ph}$" are "physically equipollent" inasmuch as each can be inferred from the other with the help of the true empirical generalization that "if, at any given moment, a person is in a state of $anger_{ps}$ he is at the same time in a state of $anger_{ph}$, and vice versa."[7] How Carnap knows that this empirical generalization is true he does not say. Neither does he discuss the philosophical difficulties which arise when one considers how it might be proved. He simply assumes, perhaps with reason, that it is empirically justifiable.

Suppose that this assumption be granted, not only with respect to anger but to all other "mental" states. It will thus follow that every indicative sentence of what Carnap calls the "psychological language" is physically equipollent to a sentence, or class of sentences, belonging to the "physical language." In other words, there are laws of nature which enable one to be inferred from the other. In itself, this conclusion is not very startling. What is astonishing is that Carnap thinks himself entitled to infer from it that these psychological and physical sentences have the same factual meaning. He does not deny that they may have different meanings, in the sense that they may evoke different associations, but he insists that, in the "logical" as opposed to the psychological sense of "meaning," their meaning is the same. To say that Mr. A is in a state of $anger_{ps}$ adds nothing factual to the observation that he is in a state of $anger_{ph}$.

The only argument which Carnap produces in defence of this view is that, both for Mr. A himself and for others, any observations which in any degree confirm either of the two statesments in question in some degree confirm the other. It follows, so he thinks, that the relation between the two concepts of $anger_{ps}$ and $anger_{ph}$ is analogous to the relation between different physical concepts which occur in the description of different methods of verifying a single physical statement. To bring out the analogy he takes as an example the statement: "A current of $intensity_5$ is now passing through this conductor." This statement may be verified in very different ways. "One may calculate the intensity (a) from the resistance of the conductor and the difference of potential at its two extremities (b) from the heating of a liquid in which the conductor is immersed (c) from the elongation of the conductor through heating (d) from the deflection of a magnetic needle (e) from the quantity of explosive gas engendered by the electrolysis of the water (f)

[7] *Revue de Synthese* X, 1, 45.

from the quantity of silver separated by electrolysis, and so forth." Suppose now that a physicist were to say, as he very well might if he believed that physical concepts were to be defined in terms of measuring operations, that strictly speaking the intensity which was measured by the different procedures was not in every case the same; not that the operations yielded different values for it, but that they were measuring different things. Carnap suggests that he might distinguish between intensity$_1$, which was measured in the ways a, b and c, and intensity$_2$, which was measured in the ways d, e and f. For such a physicist it would then become a law of nature that "In any conductor at any given time the values of intensity$_1$ and intensity$_2$ are equal." The most that could be objected to him would be that his distinction served no useful purpose. He would still be free to make it if he wished. But this is not to say that anyone is obliged to make it. The physicists who continued to say, as most of them would, that the different sets of operations measured the same intensity would not be wrong. And if a philosopher were to ask whether intensity$_1$ was "really" the same as intensity$_2$ he would be raising a fictitious problem. The best answer he could receive would be that one may say what one chooses. In the same way, Carnap argues, it is senseless to raise the question whether anger$_{ps}$ is really the same as anger$_{ph}$. The "psycho-physical problem of traditional philosophy" is spurious.

But the most that his example from physics proves is that one and the same statement may be verified in different ways without thereby altering its meaning. The statement that a current of intensity$_5$ is now passing through this conductor may be allowed to have the same meaning for A who has confirmed it only by the first three of the methods listed as it has for for B who has confirmed it only by the second three. It has the same meaning for them insofar as they both regard it as being confirmed by the result of any of these operations, whether they themselves have carried it out or not. They may even hold that under suitable conditions the statement about the intensity of the current entails the various statements in which the results of the operations are described. But from the fact that these statements about the heating of the liquid, the deflection of the needle, and so forth, are alike in confirming, and even perhaps in being entailed by, the statement about the current it by no means follows that they are equivalent to one another. You can say, if you must, that they are physically equivalent, but this is only a somewhat misleading way of expressing the belief in the truth of the synthetic proposition which connects them. The fact remains that it is perfectly conceivable that any one of them should be true and any of the others false.

Pursuing the analogy, we find that all that Carnap's argument goes to show in the example of A's anger is that the statement that A is angry may have the same meaning for another person B as it has for A himself. This point is indeed important inasmuch as it has sometimes been assumed, I think wrongly, that since A alone can verify the statement that A is angry_{ps} directly, the statement that he is angry must have a different meaning for him from any that it can have for anyone else. Against this Carnap appears to be maintaining that "A is angry" entails both "A is angry_{ps}" and "A is angry_{ph}"; and that it need not have a different meaning for B, who confirms the psychological component only through the physical, from that which it has for A who verifies the first directly; any more than the statement about the current has a different meaning for those who confirm it by different operations. The analogy is indeed imperfect since it is not logically impossible that someone who in fact only carries out the process of electrolysis should also have made the experiment with the magnetic needle, whereas it is logically impossible that B should have A's feeling: but for the moment we may let this pass. The point which I now wish to make is that from the fact, if it is a fact, that "A is angry_{ps}" and "A is angry_{ph}" are both entailed by "A is angry", it again by no means follows that they are equivalent to one another. To say that they are physically equivalent is merely to express a belief in psycho-physical parallelism. We are still left with the philosophical question whether there can be any reason to believe that other people have experiences, when these are distinguished from their physical manifestations; whether indeed there can be sense in saying of another person that he is having such and such an experience, unless it is merely a way of saying that he is in such and such a physical state. It would seem that Carnap thought he was disposing of this problem in the works which we have been considering. But so far from showing it to be spurious, the arguments so far examined can hardly be said to have dealt with it at all.

This objection cannot, however, be brought against the articles in *Erkenntnis* or against the English version of one of them which appeared in a booklet with the title of the "Unity of Science." For here, Carnap straightforwardly defends the much more interesting thesis that the psychological and physical statements in questions are not merely factually but logically equivalent.

His argument is simple. He takes his stand upon the principle that "a statement asserts no more than can be verified."[8] Now "an experience in the sense in which we are now using the word is always the experience of a definite person and cannot at the same time be the experience of another person."[9] I cannot have another person's expe-

[8] *The Unity of Science*, 79.
[9] *Ibid.*. 78.

riences. Consequently I cannot directly verify their existence, in the way that he can. The best that I can ever hope to do is to observe some physical state of his body, or some outward expression of his thoughts or feelings, from which I conclude that he is having such and such an experience. But if the only way in which I can possibly test my statement about the other man's experience is by observing such physical phenomena, then it is only to them that my statement can refer. No doubt when I assert that he is in a given mental state, on the basis of what are deemed to be its physical manifestations, I am doing something more than merely describing these physical events. I am making an inference from them: but the inference can only be to further actual, or possible, manifestations, not to the existence of anything 'behind' them. To construe my statement as referring to any such hidden entity would be, so far as I am concerned, to make it totally unverifiable, and consequently meaningless.

To this it may be objected that it is not impossible that one person should have direct access to the experiences of another: he may do so through intuition or telepathy. But Carnap's answer to this would be that the most that can be claimed for intuition, or telepathy, is that they are methods of obtaining knowledge. It is a matter of dispute how far they are useful or reliable. But however useful or reliable they may turn out to be, this cannot affect the meaning of the statements which they enable us to know. If I have a telepathic experience it is just as much as any other an experience of my own. On the basis of it I may correctly attribute a certain experience to another person. But the only way in which I can test the correctness of this attribution is by observing his behaviour, or other physical events. And it is the way in which a statement is tested, not the way in which it comes to be put forward, that determines what it means.

A similar answer would be given to the suggestion, which many philosophers have made, that belief in the existence of other people's experiences, as distinct from their physical manifestations, is to be justified by an argument from analogy. I know that certain features of my behaviour are associated with experiences of my own. When I observe similar behaviour in others I may reasonably infer that they are having similar experiences. But the objection to this is that no argument from analogy can justify me in accepting a conclusion to which I can attach no meaning. Arguments from analogy are, indeed, commonly used to support belief in the existence of events which no one has actually observed; but it is necessary that they should be, at least theoretically, observable: it is necessary that certain observations should be counted as verifying the statements which describe them, even if the observations are never actually made. But, so the argument runs, there is nothing that would count as observing the experiences of another, unless it were the observation of their physical manifestations. The word 'manifestation' is misleading in this context, because it suggests that there is something which is manifested, a reality which is not to be identified with the appearances it shows us. But while we can, in this as in other cases, distinguish appearance from reality, we can do so only in terms of the inter-connection of "appearances." To impute experiences to others can only be to describe the physical manifestations which are all that we can conceivably observe: accordingly, the only sort of inference with respect to these experiences that any inductive argument can justify is an inference from one such physical occurence to another.

It is to be noted that this line of reasoning is, on the face of it, inconsistent with the view, which Carnap also wishes to hold, that a statement such as 'A is angry' has the same meaning for A as it has for another person B. For A is not limited, as B is, to the observation of the physical expression of his anger: he actually feels it. And even if 'A is angry' entails both 'A is $angry_{ph}$' and 'A is $angry_{ps}$,' it would seem, if the foregoing argument is correct, that at least "A is $angry_{ps}$" must have a different meaning for A himself from any that it can have for B. But it seems strange to say that a statement has the same meaning for A and B when they attach different meanings to part of what it states. Carnap himself eventually removes this assymetry by abolishing the distinction between "A is $angry_{ph}$" and "A is $angry_{ps}$" altogether. He maintains that one must give a "physicalist" interpretation not only to the statements which one makes about the experiences of others but also to the statements which one makes about one's own. But for this he uses other arguments which we shall presently examine. So long however as this psycho-physical distinction is retained, his argument appears to lead to the conclusion that the analysis of psychological statements follows a different pattern according as they refer to other people or to oneself.

At one time I accepted this conclusion because I was convinced by the argument which seemed to me to lead to it. But I now think that the argument is invalid. It puts too narrow an interpretation upon the principle of verifiability. Let it be granted that a statement has factual content only in so far as it can be empirically tested. It does not follow that each of us is limited to speaking only of what he himself can be in a position to observe. Being where I am and living when I do it is impossible for me to observe events which occur at other places and times; it does not follow that statements which purport to refer to these events can have no meaning for me, or that in order to give them meaning I have to interpret them as referring to what I myself can verify here and now. We are not debarred from describing the past by the fact that the experiences by which we indirectly test the accuracy of our descriptions can themselves be located only in the present or future. The ways in which we can verify empirical statements are limited by our circumstances. In saying that such statements must be verifiable, we are not, however, committed to including any reference to these circumstances in our analyses of what they state.

Nevertheless it may be argued that there is a special difficulty about statements which refer to the experiences of others. It is not inconceivable that I should be at a different place from that at which I am; it is not inconceivable that I should have lived at a different time, though this is harder to envisage, especially if the time be remote: but it does seem inconceivable that I should be someone else. And if, as is commonly assumed, it is necessary that I should be another person in order to enjoy his experiences, then it is inconceivable that I should enjoy his experiences. But it is only if I can enjoy his experiences that I can directly verify the statements which describe them. Consequently, these statements are unverifiable, so far as I am concerned, in a way in which statements about events which are remote from me in space or time are not. For in their case, while my actual situation makes it impossible for me to have direct access to the events which they describe, it is not logically impossible that I should have had it; my situation might have been such as to allow it. But there is nothing that would count as my having direct access to the experiences of others. It follows that I cannot understand statements which refer to these experiences unless I construe them as referring to what is accessible to me, namely their so-called physical manifestations.

But even if the premises of this argument are accepted, I do not think that the conclusion holds. When I attribute a feeling, say a feeling of anger, to another, I do so on the basis of certain evidence, such evidence as Carnap summarizes in his expression "A is in a state of anger_{ph}." I then, as Carnap says, make use of the general hypothesis that states of anger_{ph} are accompanied by states of anger_{ps}. If I maintain this hypothesis without qualification, I assert that anger_{ph} is conjoined with anger_{ps}, irrespective of the presence or absence of any other properties. Otherwise I may put in the saving condition that these two are conjoined provided that certain other factors are not present. Thus, in ascribing anger_{ps} to A, on the basis of my observations that he is in a state of anger_{ph}, I imply that the other properties which he possesses are not such as to nullify my general hypothesis. I cannot directly test the truth of this assumption with respect to the totality of these properties; for that would require my being indentified with A. But I can directly test it with respect to a selection of them; and it is, I think, not inconceivable that I should have been able to test it with respect to any given selection of them, though of course I cannot do so in fact. But if this is so, the argument from analogy becomes legitimate. My attribution of experiences to others is the result of a permissible inductive inference.[10]

The mistake which philosophers have often made is to set out the analogy in the form: as my behaviour is to my experiences, so the behaviour of others is to their experiences. For not only do they then encounter the objection that the fourth term of the analogy, since it brings in something unobservable, is not on a par with the other three; but they make their inductive argument extremely weak; the inference from 'outer' manifestations to 'inner' experiences is made to rest upon a single instance. Against this I suggest that the process is not so much that of generalizing what I know to be true only of myself as that of inferring from a known conjunction of properties in various different contexts to their continued conjunction in further contexts. Having found in a number of different circumstances that $anger_{ph}$ and $anger_{ps}$ are connected, I may infer that when the circumstances are further varied the connection will still hold. And I do not think that it is an objection to this argument that, in the majority of cases, the further properties which I thus associate with $anger_{ps}$, namely such properties as constitute being a person of a certain sort in such and such a situation, are not among those that I myself possess.

There remains only to be examined the argument by which Carnap has tried to show that not only statements about the experiences of others but even statements about one's own experiences must be logically equivalent to statements about physical events. Assuming, as before, that "an experience . . . is always the experience of a definite person and cannot at the same time be the experience of another person,"[11] and also that "a statement asserts no more than can be verified," he argues that if a statement were to "express only what is immediately given" to a person S_1 it could not be understood by an other person S_2. If there were "protocol languages," which served not to describe physical events, but merely to give a 'direct record' of the subject's experiences, they "could be applied only solipsistically." It is only if the protocol language is part of the physical language, that is if the statements which are made in it can be translated into statements about physical occurrences, that it can be inter-subjective. And it must be inter-subjective if any experiences are to be communicable.

Furthermore, Carnap maintains, our understanding of the physical language itself requires that the protocol language be included in it.

[10]This argument is developed at a greater length in my paper on "One's Knowledge of Other Minds," *Theoria,* XIX (1953) 1-2.

[11]*The Unity of Science,* 78.

An inferential connection between the protocol statements and the singular physical statements must exist, for if, from the physical statements, nothing can be deduced as to the truth or falsity of the protocol statements there would be no connection between scientific knowledge and experience. Physical statements would float in a void disconnected, in principle, from all experience. If, however, an inferential connection between physical language and protocol language does exist there must also be a connection between the two kinds of facts. For one statement can be deduced from another if, and only if, the fact described by the first is contained in the fact described by the second. Our fictitious supposition that the protocol language and the physical language speak of completely different facts cannot therefore be reconciled with the fact that the physical descriptions can be verified empirically.[12]

It might be thought that we could meet this difficulty by following the opposite course of making physical statements refer to the contents of experience. But Carnap argues that that will not do either.

S_1's protocol language refers to the context of S_1's experience, S_2's protocol language to the context of S_2's experience. What can the intersubjective physical language refer to? It must refer to the context of the experiences of both S_1 and S_2. This is however impossible for the realms of experience of two persons do not overlap. There is no solution, [he concludes,] free from contradictions in this direction.

The whole of this argument seems to me fallacious. The initial mistake is to suppose that what makes a language public or private is its referring to public or private objects. Carnap seems to hold that there is a natural division of objects into public and private, and that it is only when a statement refers to a public object that it can be publicly understood. But there is no such natural division: there is only a linguistic distinction which we find it convenient to make: and the possibility of there being a public language does not depend upon it. I say that the distinction is linguistic because it depends upon the question whether a certain type of statement is meaningful. An object is public or private according as we do or do not attach a sense to saying that more than one person observes it. Physical objects are public because we allow it to be said that different persons observe the same physical object. Experiences are private, because we equate observing them with having them and then deny a sense to saying that different persons are having literally the same experience. But other ways of speaking are conceivable. We can introduce a notation in which two persons' perceiving the same physical object is represented as their each sensing their own sense-data; and conversely, if we found it useful, for example in dealing with para-normal phenomena, we could give a sense to saying that different persons were having, or observing, the

[12] *The Unity of Science*, 81.

same experiences. The point is that none of this affects the question whether our statements are publicly intelligible. A statement is publicly intelligible if it can be understood in the same sense by different people; and it is understood in the same sense by different people if they regard the same circumstances as making it true or false. If S_2 can entertain the conception of S_1's experiences, and we have argued that he can, he is in a position to understand the statements that S_1 makes about them. The fact that we may make it logically impossible for him to share S_1's experiences is nothing to the purpose.

Carnap's second mistake is to think that by making the protocol language into a section of the physical language he establishes a connection between scientific knowledge and experience. So far from establishing the connection by this means, he destroys it. The protocol statements which served to describe our experiences are transformed into statements about the condition of our bodies. The place which they filled in our language is left vacant; and the question how physical statements, including the statements of what is now misleadingly called the protocol language, can be empirically verified still remains.

Against this I hold that we can deal with the verification of physical statements by allowing protocol statements to keep the part originally assigned to them; for the contradictions, with which Carnap threatens us if we pursue this course, seem to me illusory. We verify a physical statement, or rather confirm or disconfirm it, by deriving a protocol statement from it; the protocol statement, which is verified directly, is a description of such and such an experience. It may then be said, though the propriety of this is disputable, that part of the meaning of the physical statement is that given such and such conditions an experience of the kind in question is obtained. But to say this is not to say that the physical statement refers to the experience of any one particular person. The experiences by which it is actually verified, or refuted, will always in fact be the experiences of some person or other; but there is nothing in the physical statement which requires that they be the experiences of this person rather than that. Insofar as physical statements refer to experiences at all, they refer to them neutrally. All that is demanded for their verification is that someone should have an experience of the relevant sort. Thus S_1 may verify a physical statement p by having an experience e_1 and S_2 may verify p by having an experience e_2. Both e_1 and e_2 are of the appropriate kind E, and the fact that they are not identical with one another does not lead to any contradiction at all. The answer to Carnap's question "What can the intersubjective physical language refer to"? is that it refers, in this sense, neither to the "private world" of S_1 or to that of S_2, but to the experiences of anyone you please.

I conclude that Carnap has produced no valid argument for saying that we must put a physicalist interpretation upon the statements that we make about the experiences of others, let alone those that we make about our own. Nor, in default of such argument, is this a plausible way of analysing statements about 'other minds.' Psychologists may indeed find it useful to adopt a behavioural terminology, or even to confine themselves to the study of what Carnap would classify as physical events. But whatever may be the practical advantages of this procedure, it cannot claim any special favour on philosophical grounds.

A. J. Ayer

Department of Philosophy
University College, London

8

Robert Feys

CARNAP ON MODALITIES

CARNAP'S contribution to the study of modalities consists mainly of two studies, one numbered here (I)—on "Modalities and Quantification" which has appeared in the *Journal of Symbolic Logic* XI (1946) pp. 33-64, the other—numbered here (II)—"On the Logic of Modalities" which is Chapter V of *Meaning and Necessity, a Study in Semantics and Modal Logic,* Chicago, 1947.

Our exposition may be considered as a somewhat informal exposition of the ideas contained in both works. Incidentally it will refer to "Introduction to Semantics" (Introduction) or to "Formalization of Logic" (Formalization). It will be followed by a Critique, or rather by remarks which call to mind other systems, which are not excluded by the author, but which seem somewhat alien to his point of view.

Carnap's work on Modalities hinges upon his Semantics: "It seems to me . . . that it is not possible to construct a satisfactory system before the meanings of the modalities are sufficiently clarified. I further believe that this clarification can best be achieved by correlating each of the modal concepts with a corresponding semantical concept (for example, necessity with L-truth). ((I), p. V.)

Our exposition will consider:

1. Non-Modal propositional logic (PL) and propositional calculus (PC),
2. As a transition to modalities, and informal justification of the interpretation of "S is necessary" as "S is L-true",
3. Modal propositional logic (MPL) and modal propositional calculus (MPC), corresponding to Lewis' S5,
4. (Non-Modal) functional logic (FL) and functional calculus (FC),
5. Modal functional logic (MFL) and modal functional calculus (MFC),
6. Considerations about the intensional character of modal logic,
7. Difficulties arising from the combination of quantification with modalities.

A certain familiarity with Carnap's terminology and symbolism is assumed subsequently, at the same level as in (I) or (II).

I. *Non-Modal Propositional Systems. Propositional Logic (PL) And Propositional Calculus (PC)*

Carnap does not develop PL and PC in (I) or (II) for their own sake, and does not even treat them as a separate logic or calculus. He only indicates on which conditions a given logic contains PL and a given calculus contains PC.

1.1. Systems will "contain PL" roughly speaking if they contain the ordinary connectives and semantical rules for them, corresponding to the ordinary truth-tables. We shall not dwell at length upon these, but only recall, according to (II), the definitions leading to the notion of "L-true".

All sentences (declarative sentences) in PL are closed (without free variables).

> A class of sentences . . . which contains for every atomic sentence either this sentence or its negation, but not both, and no other sentences, is called a *state-description* . . . , because it obviously gives a complete description of a possible state of the universe of individuals with respect to all properties and relations expressed by predicates of the systems. Thus the state-descriptions represent Leibniz' possible worlds or Wittgenstein's possible states of affairs.
>
> It is easy to lay down semantical rules which determine for every sentence . . . whether or not it *holds in* a given *state-description*. . . .
>
> The class of all those state-descriptions in which a given sentence S_i holds is called the range of S_i . . . All the rules together . . . determine the range of any sentence . . . therefore they are called *rules of ranges.*
>
> A sentence S_i is L-true . . . $=_{Df}$ S_i holds in every state-description. ((II), pp. 9-10).

In other words, the range of an L-true sentence is the universal range.

We say that S_i is L-false by PL, that S_i L-implies S_j by PL, or that S_i is L-equivalent to S_j if and only if '$\sim S_i$', '$S_i \supset S_j$', or '$S_i \equiv S_j$', respectively, is L-true by PL. (These simple definitions can be used here because all sentences are closed.) ((I), p. 38).

Although no use is made of the semantical definition of truth in the rules of ranges, there is an obvious relation between truth and L-truth.

> There is one and only one state-description which describes the actual state of the universe; it is that which contains all true atomic sentences and the negation of those which are false. Hence it contains only true sentences; therefore we call it the true state-description. A sentence of any form is true if and only if it holds in the true state-description.
>
> If S_i holds in every state-description, then the semantical rules of ranges suffice for establishing this result. . . . Therefore, the semantical rules establish also the truth of S_i because, if S_i holds in every state-description, then it holds also in the true state-description and hence is itself true. . . . If, on the other hand, S_i does not hold in every state-description . . . even if S_i is true, it is not possible to establish its truth without reference to facts. ((II), pp. 10-11).

1.2. The logic PL can be formalized in a propositional calculus PC according to one of the usual systems of rules and axioms. (The PC used here will not contain propositional variables). A "full formalization" of PL is not discussed in this context. The concept of C-true and the other concepts are defined in the well-known way.

A method of "P-reduction" is explained in I §3, amounting to the usual transformation in a conjunctive normal form, but simplified by the use of the symbol 't' for tautology; it leads to a decision-method.

1.3. There exist well-known relations of completeness between PL and PC (I, T2-1 and T 3-1).

(a) If S_i is C-true (C-false) by PC, it is L-true (L-false) by PL; hence PC is adequate. (b) If S_i is L-true (L-false) by PL, it is C-true (C-false) by PC.

II. *Introduction of Modality*

2.1. We now have to build up propositional modal logic (MPL), to be formalized in a propositional modal calculus (MPC).

> The guiding idea in our constructions of systems of modal logic is this: a proposition *p* is logically necessary if and only if a sentence expressing *p* is logically true. That is to say, the modal concept of the logical necessity of a proposition and the semantical concept of the logical truth or analyticity correspond to each other. Both concepts have been used, in logic and philosophy, mostly, however, without exact rules. If we succeed in explicating one of these concepts . . . then this leads . . . to an explication for the other concept. ((I), p. 34).

We herewith confine ourselves to the interpretation of necessity as logical necessity, and that of logical necessity as L-truth. "S is L-true" has been defined above as "S holds in every state-description" or "The range of S is the universal range." More precisely: the range of S_i is the universal range if that of S_i is the universal range, otherwise it is the null range.

2.2. "Now the following two questions remain: (1) if 'N (. . .)' is true, is it L-true? If so, 'NN (. . .)' is likewise true; in other words, 'Np ⊃ NNP' is always true. (2) If 'N (. . .)' is false, is it L-false? If so, '∼N (. . .)' is L-true and hence 'N∼N (. . .)' is true, in other words '∼Np ⊃ N∼Np' is always true." ((I), p. 34-35).

(1) "Suppose that 'N(C)' is true. Then . . . 'C' must be L-true. Hence the truth of 'C' is determined by certain semantical rules. Then these rules together with the rule for 'N' determine the truth of 'N(C)'. Therefore 'N(C)' is L-true, and hence 'NN(C)' is true. Thus our earlier question . . . is answered to the affirmative". ((I), p. 36).

(2) The answer to the second question may be summarized thus. Suppose that 'N(C)' is false, i.e. that 'C' is not L-true. Then it is L-false or it is neither L-false nor L- true.

If 'C' is L-false, the semantical rules determining the L-falsity of 'C' determine the falsity of 'N(C)'. Hence 'N(C)' is L-false, '~N(C)' L-true and 'N~N(C)' true.

If 'C' is neither L-true nor L-false, then factual data might be relevant for the truth value of 'C' but not for its L-character. The falsity of 'N(C)' must be determined by semantical rules, hence 'N(C)' is L-false, '~N(C)' L-true and 'N~N(C)' true.

As a consequence we are led to the strongest of Lewis' systems, S5, in which there are no irreducible "superposed" modalities such as "necessarily necessary", "possibly necessary".

III. *Modal Propositional Systems*

3.1. On the basis of the preceding paragraph a modal propositional logic (MPL) may be formulated by adding to PL the modal symbol 'N' for (logical) necessity, with a rule of ranges as in 2.1.

3.2 A modal propositional calculus is also constructed. It uses 'p', 'q', . . . only as auxiliary variables; '◇ p', 'p ⥽ q', 'p ≡ q' are short respectively for '~N ~p', 'N (p ⊃ q)', 'N (p ≡ q)'.

a. Rules and primitive sentences for MPC are those of the calculus of Wajsberg interpretable as S5. Familiar theorems of S5 are proved in MPC, and the number of functions of n propositions is computed.

b. A method of "MP-reduction" is framed for MPC. It uses two sets of rules. (1) Rules of the first kind are those of P-reduction, supplemented by rules of omission of 'N' according to 2.2 and by rules of distribution of 'N'. A sentence S_j obtained from S_i according to these rules is L-equivalent to S_i. (2) Rules of a second kind transform a sentence S_i into a sentence S_j such that, if S_i is is L-true, S_j is L-true.

No 'N' occurs in the scope of another 'N' in a "MP-reduction". The MP-reduction yields a decision method.

3.3. It may be proved that MPC is adequate and complete with respect to MPL.

a. MPC is adequate, i.e. any sentence which is C-true (C-false) by MPC is L-true (L-false) by MPL.

b. MPC is complete: if a sentence is L-true (L-false) by MPL, it is C-true (C-false) by MPC. This result is reached in two steps: (1) every L-true sentence is reducible to 't' by MP-reduction, (2) a sentence reducible to 't' is C-true.

IV. *Functional Non-Modal Systems*

In preparation for the construction of modal functional systems, which is the chief object of (I), rules for non-modal functional logic (FL) and functional calculus (FC) are outlined.

4.1. The system FL has several peculiarities. It is a first order logic and there are no predicates of predicates. It contains a denumerable infinity of constants for individuals (we have an infinite universe), as well as a denumerable infinity of variables. It is a system with identity and such that different individual constants denote different individuals.

The rules of ranges are complicated by the fact that, owing to the infinity of individual constants, class-products of ranges have to be considered.

4.2. The formalization of FL is a calculus FC, whose primitives are those of Quine's *Mathematical Logic* (as simplified by Berry) with additional axioms for identity, and with a rule of refutation.

As is well known, there exist methods of reduction to normal forms, but no general decision method.

4.3. As for the adequacy and completeness of FC with respect to FL:

a. FC can be shown to be adequate. Every C-true sentence in FC is L-true in FL.

b. The Gödel proof of completeness does not seem valid here. Some sentences may hold in an infinite universe, but not in a finite one, and hence not be provable by the ordinary functional calculus. Bernays however, maintains in his review that FC might still be proved complete.

V. *Modal Functional Systems*

Carnap was unaware of the existence of any modal functional system existing when he wrote his paper. Independently of him, Mrs. Barcan developed such a system (for ordinary functional calculus in S2).

5.1. The modal functional logic (MFL) starts from the convention ((I), p. 37) that " 'N' is to be interpreted in such a way that any sentence of the form '(x) [N (. . . x . . .)]', is regarded as L-equivalent to . . . the corresponding sentence 'N[(x)(. . x . .)].' " (A difficulty concerning the values of the variables will have to be considered later.)

5.2. MFC (Modal functional calculus) is built as a formalization of MFL, by the addition of 'N' to FC.

a. Its primitive sentences may roughly be described as consisting of the primitive sentences of MPC, those of FC, primitive sentences equivalent to the convention of 5.1, plus rules of substitution and rules concerning identity.

b. As 'N' is analogous to an universal quantifier and '$\Diamond$' to an existential quantifier the theorems peculiar to MPC are analogous to the few theorems of FC in which two quantifiers are occurring. E.g.:

((I) T10-2b) $(\ )\ [(\exists i_k)\ N\ (\mathbf{M}_k) \supseteq (i_k)\ \Diamond\ (\mathbf{M}_k)]$

c. Carnap delineates carefully a method of MF-reduction ((I), §11). This does not lead to a general decision method.

5.3 As for relations between MFL and MFC:

a. MFC is adequate. Every C-true (C-false) sentence in MFC is L-true (L-false) in MFL.

b. The question of completeness is not clear. A partial answer is ((I), T12-3):
"Let S_i be an MF-reduction in which no '=' and no sentence of the form '~N (. . .)' occurs. If S is L-true in MFL, it is C-true in MFC."

VI. *Intension and Extension*

The considerations developed in (II) are considered by Carnap as preliminary, as they do not lead to detailed semantical deductions or to a formalization of modal logic; in fact their interest becomes more apparent when modal logic has already been built up and when it has to meet the difficulties raised by its interpretation.

The leading idea in (I) was that the concept of logical necessity becomes clarified when equated to that of L-truth. In (II) the concept of sameness of intention becomes clarified when equated to that of L-equivalence.

a. The opposition of extension and intension was already familiar in traditional logic; but there remains some vagueness in it when it is taken intuitively as an opposition between the "content" and that to which a concept "applies". If with Carnap we rather try to analyze what is meant by *sameness* of extension we find that two concepts have the same extension if they apply factually to the same things, if the concepts yield materially equivalent statements when applied to the same things. More generally Carnap will say two sentences have the same extension if they are materially equivalent and two names for individuals have the same extension if they designate factually the same individual.

On the contrary L-equivalence corresponds to identity of intension, because two L-equivalent concepts or propositions may be transformed one into another by a pure application of logical rules, without any appeal to factual data. And designations of individuals have the same intension when one can pass from one to the other by virtue of purely logical rules. This is clear when these designations are descriptions—the more so when (as this is the case with Carnap) descriptions are defined in such a way that they always designate something definite.

In Carnaps terminology ((II), §11):

An expression occurring within a sentence is said to be interchangeable with another expression if the truth-value of the sentence remains unchanged when the first expression is replaced by the second. If, moreover, the intension of the sentence remains unchanged, the two expressions are said to be L-interchangeable. We say that a sentence is extensional with respect to an expression occurring in it, or that the expression occurs within an extensional context if the expression is interchangeable at this place with every other expression equivalent to it. We say that the sentence is intensional with respect to the expression, or that the expression occurs within an intensional context, if the context is not extensional and the expression is L-interchangeable at this place with every other expression L-equivalent to it.

Let us introduce similar definitions for other designators (predicate-symbols, symbols for individuals). Then a system of classical logic without modalities, is extensional, and a system with modalities (the 'N' being interpreted as denoting logical necessity) is intensional.

It has to be underlined that Carnap's use of the word "intensional" does not coincide with that in which "intensional" is taken somewhat loosely as synonymous with "non-extensional"; in Carnap's present terminology, a context as "I believe p" is neither extensional nor intensional with respect to p, as we are not allowed to substitute 'q' for 'p' in "I believe p", even if 'q' is L-equivalent to 'p'. Let us also underline that, in both an extensional and an intensional system, L-equivalent expressions are L-interchangeable; the difference is with expressions which are simply equivalent; these are interchangeable everywhere (in any context) if the system is extensional; if the system is intensional then (12-4) "equivalent expressions are interchangeable . . . except where they occur in an intensional context (for example in a system with modalities, in a context of the form 'N (. . .) ')."

b. Although Carnap's considerations about ((II), Chapter 5) modalities presuppose the whole theory of extensions and intensions explained in the first 4 chapters of the book, we shall have to content ourselves here with a bare outline of the critique of the "name-relation method" made by Carnap and of the principle of solution suggested by Carnap's theory of extension and intension. The method of the name-relation of Frege and others is summarized by Carnap ((II), 24-1, 2, 3) as resting upon three principles:

The principle of univocality. Every expression used as a name (in a certain context) is the name of exactly one entity; we call it the nominatum of the expression.

The principle of subject matter. A sentence is about (deals with, includes in its subject matter) the nominata of the names occurring in it.

The principle of interchangeability (or substitutivity). The principle occurs in either of two forms:

a. If two expressions name the same entity, then a true sentence remains true when the one is replaced in it by the other; in our terminology . . . the two expressions are interchangeable (everywhere).

b. If an identity sentence '. . . = ———' (or '. . . is identical with ———' or '. . .' is the same as '———') is true, then the two argument expressions '. . .' and '———' are interchangeable (everywhere).

Carnap does not claim that the name-relation method, even as used by Frege, is incorrect in any way, but he stresses that Frege's distinction between nominatum and sense and his own distinction between extension and intension do not coincide. He finds a serious inconvenience in the fact that several nominata have to be distinguished if, according to Frege, the nominatum in oblique contexts has to be identified with the sense. But even when this is excluded the method of the name relation has the inconvenience of multiplying entities—which seems to lead to the necessity of introducing different notations for them.

VII. *Modal Logical As Intensional Logic*

The preceding considerations lead us to a coherent interpretation of modal logic as a logic of intensional connections: but they raise several problems which seem inherent to any intensional logic whatever.

a. Let us recall Lewis' starting point in the field of modalities. Lewis is averse to taking the "If p then q" as a material implication, synonymous with the truth-function '$\sim p \vee q$' with such "paradoxical" consequences as '$\sim p \supset (p \supset q$' or '$\sim p \wedge \sim q \supset (p \equiv q)$'; more paradoxical even are '$(p \supset q) \vee (q \supset p)$' or '$(p \supset q) \vee (p \supset \sim q)$'. When we speak of "paradoxical" assertions this may not be taken in the sense—rather usual in modern logic—of antinomies arising from the fact that the use of apparently correct rules lead to a contradiction. The paradox lies only in this; some strange consequences of the principles show that the meaning to be attached to a function, here to the material implication, is not the meaning one had intended to translate into symbols.

Such a difficulty remains somewhat indefinite so long as the "meaning" intended remains some kind of intuitive meaning. But the advantage of a semantical interpretation is to make the question precise.

When Lewis claimed that his strict implication '$N(p \supset q)$ or $(p \bar{\supset} q)$' was the correct translation of the "If p then q" or at least a more correct translation than the material implication, his claim could not be justified peremptorily. If a semantical interpretation of the 'N' and of the '$N(p \supset q)$' is brought forward, a great step is made towards a precise posing of the problem.

Carnap's solution, as we have explained, is that $N(p \equiv q)$ if p and q are L-equivalent and that $N(p \supset q)$ if p L-implies q, i.e. if the range of 'p' is contained in that of 'q'. There is no method to prove that the range of a sentence is included in that of another, unless both ranges are universal or null.

As we know the paradoxical

statements are not valid if '$\bar{\supset}$' is substituted for '$\supset$' and '$\bar{\equiv}$' for '$\equiv$'; we only have $N \sim p \bar{\supset} (p \bar{\supset} q)$ and $Np \,\&\, Nq \bar{\supset} (p \bar{\supset} q)$ or $N \sim p \,\&\, N \sim p \bar{\supset} (p \bar{\supset} q)$,

b. As the truth-value of a sentence is its extension and as its range may be considered as its intension, the modal proposition may be said to be about the intensions of the sentences mentioned in it. But if sentences are to be interpreted intensionally, so must predicators (names of predicates) and names of individuals. In Carnap's terminology, predicators must not be interpreted as classes, but as properties; and names of individuals are not to be interpreted as individuals but as "individual" concepts.

This last has to be admitted, not only for descriptions but also for names of individuals which are not descriptions.

Now the duality of sense and denotation is not suggested distinctly (explicitly) by the ordinary language, nor is the distinction of extension and intension either; this has led to the so called antinomies of the name-relation, which reappear with extensions and intensions. It is not our task to discuss these antinomies and the proposed solutions, and we must refer for them to (II). We only point out that these antinomies reappear for modalities, quite distinctly if modalities are interpreted in terms of intensions. It is clear that (factually) the number of major planets is—let us say—7 and that (necessarily) $7 = 4+3$. Has it to be said that necessarily the number of planets is $4+3$? It is clear that necessarily Venus is Venus, and that (factually) the Evening star is the Morning star; it may not be said however that the Evening Star is necessarily Venus.

How can we escape these "antinomies?" How can we escape, in general, difficulties raised by "oblique reference", by "not-transparent" or "referentially opaque" reference? These difficulties may be compared with the difficulties arising from the sentences about beliefs; we shall not consider here how even these difficulties about beliefs might to some extent be solved by a reference to a stronger intensional equivalence (viz., the "intentional isomorphism,") than the sameness of ranges; it will suffice to consider here the difficulties involved in the L-interpretation of modalities.

c. Here again we may not enter into full details. The ambiguities of common language may be avoided by the use of a language with semantical rules.

The language involved in the solution of the antinomies akin to the name-relation antinomy has to distinguish between extensions and intensions.

Extensions and intensions are spoken of, not in the object-language, but in a metalanguage. Among other questions, has the metalanguage to use a different notation for extensions and intensions? Carnap claims he can avoid such a multiplication of symbols. The same

neutral symbols may be used as well in intensional as in extensional contexts; the contexts decide which interpretation has to be adopted. Neutral symbols are sentences, predicators, names for individuals. They are interpreted, according to the context, as truth-values or as propositions, as classes or as properties, as individuals or as individual concepts.

Even in intensional contexts it remains possible to define extensions (about the same way as classes are defined in the *Principia Mathematica*).

Carnap claims he can escape in this way the disadvantage contemplated by Quine, namely that in the intensional language of modalities extensions and factual truths could not be expressed. (The question whether intensions could be defined within extensional contexts is left open by Carnap.)

Some Critical Remarks

In the remarks we are about to make, we shall attempt to assess the significance of Carnap's contribution against the background of the ensemble of problems facing the modal logician. They will concern first the peculiar interpretation which Carnap has chosen for modalities: is there no other distinctly workable interpretation for necessity as L-truth, and even are there no other satisfactory interpretations of logical consequence as strict implication? On the other hand have all difficulties of an intensional system been considered? In both cases we are not in any way denying the value of Carnap's theory, but we should like to suggest constructively some points of view he has not excluded, but to which he does not seem to attach much importance.

VIII. *Has the Interpretation of Modality To Be Confined To L-Truth?*

a. Carnap makes necessity correspond exclusively to L-truth, in the sense of his semantics; of course he does not exclude other interpretations and he repeatedly expresses himself in that sense. But he stresses that L-truth-interpretation makes things clear and he seems very diffident of the possibility of making things clear another way.

We shall readily concede that Carnap's interpretation makes "things clear," as it is in agreement with one very fundamental intuitive meaning of necessity, as it gives also a neat criterion for a choice between S4 and S5, and as it leads to a satisfactory proof of completeness of the system. We shall concede that other existing interpretations have not these advantages. Modal logic of the past has been a realm of confusion; recent modal logic from Lewis on has been a striking example of precise syntax paired with unprecise interpretation or with no interpretation at all. Parry's deductions leading to the 42 modalities of S3 are beyond reproach, but nobody has put forward an idea of how to interpret the most complicated of them. It may be hoped that a well-built syntax must have somewhere a well-built semantical interpretation to match with it. But could that hope not be disappointed?

b. Many *intuitive* interpretations have been proposed for modalities, most of them normative or physical ones: many critics will stress these are tentative and confine themselves to the somewhat trival S5 (with or without non-modal statements) for which L-truth provides a better "logical" interpretation.

But much more precise interpretations, for S4, have been given by Gödel and by McKinsey.

Gödel, as is well known, has interpreted 'p is necessary' as 'p is provable' ('p ist beweisbar' translated by 'Bp'). And we may resumé as follows the result obtained by him: if instead of truth-functions we consider functions of necessary truths, if e.g. we write '∼Bp' instead of 'non-p' 'Bp v Bq' instead of 'p or q', 'Bp ⊃ Bq' instead of the material implication of q by p, and if we admit just the reductions provable in S4, then we are led to an interpretation deductively equivalent to intuitionistic logic.

Now provability in a given system is syntactically definable—and so is possibility definable in another interpretation by McKinsey (or in its revised form as suggested by Fitch's review). Even the concept of something constructively provable (in conformity with an intuition underlying Brouwer's ideas) is much clearer than the tentative interpretations recalled above, and might be made clearer by the use of an appropriate descriptive language.

In all these cases the choice of S4 is by no means arbitrary. Because if something is (constructively) provable, the fact that it is provable is provable. But on the other hand if something is not constructively provable (in fact) it is not evidently provable that it is not provable. Hence we have BBp if Bp, but we have not B∼Bp if we have ∼Bp.

Moreover: from an algebraical point of view, which is very general and interesting indeed, the postulates of S4 are those of a closure (or "aperture") as pointed out by McKinsey and Tarski and underlined by Curry.

c. We have just met several interesting and non-trivial interpretations for S4. One of the reasons for which Carnap prefers S5 is that this system leads to very determinate results. But the question may be put whether systems involving some indeterminacy (e.g., non-distributive lattices) are not interesting on their own account—perhaps to express some physical theories, certainly to translate theories, such as intuitionistic reasoning, in which a higher standard of rigor is maintained than in classical logic.

It might be objected at this moment that it does not seem to be possible to found an universal all-embracing logic upon anything other than the rock of a semantics—and of a semantics built up according to the model worked out by Carnap.

But first must there be an all-embracing logical calculus? Nobody will deny that some peculiar problems might require some peculiar ways of reasoning, embodied in some peculiar form of calculus. And nobody will deny Carnap's own principle of tolerance, admitting any calculus whose syntax is accurately formulated. If logical calculus were to merge itself more and more into abstract algebra, this tendency might even be stressed in the future.

But do not all calculi have to be founded upon a logic, and hence upon a semantics, which will then enjoy a separate and somewhat final position? It seems that just at that point may lie the root of a divergence between Carnap and others. Carnap himself underlines that in his semantics a sharp distinction between pure semantics and applied semantics (semantics of a descriptive language) has to be drawn, and that Tarski seems to go into the opposite direction. Tarski's point of view seems to be shared by Beth. And Quine is inclined to consider the existence of some absolute concept of analyticity as a "dogma of empiricism." Personally the author of these pages is inclined to share these points of view.

IX. *Strict Implication and Consequence*

a. We should like to make some reservations—although there is nothing quite new in them—to the claim of modal strict implication to represent adequately "the" relation of logical consequence. According to Lewis 'p implies q' has to be the equivalent of 'If p then q,' the material implication 'p⊃q' fails to do so, because of the paradoxical theorems of 7b, and fundamentally because of the equivalence of this 'p ⊃ q' with '∼p ∨ q'. We have 'p ⊃ q' if '∼p', because '∼p ∨ q' follows from '∼p'; 'q' however cannot be deduced from 'p' if 'p' is false; hence 'p ⊃ q' does not deserve to be called an implication. On the contrary, Lewis claims, as the paradoxical theorems are not provable with modal strict implication, this modal strict implication may definitely be called (logical) implication.

b. We think it may be said more modestly that some reasons against the denomination "logical implication" have disappeared if this denomination be applied to 'p ⥽ q', rather to 'p ⊃ q'.

Let us add that the paradoxical 'q ⥽ (p ⥽ q)' is absent from modal logic, where we have only 'Nq ⥽ (p ⥽ q)'; also from this point of view strict implication is more satisfactory.

But even, it must be conceded, the strict implication analogues of paradoxical theorems have not become free from any "paradox", as all necessary propositions remain strictly equivalent (and are strictly implied by everything), and all impossible propositions remain strictly equivalent (and imply strictly everything).

Let us recall that the unsatisfactory situation created by this last situation, especially as concerns "belief sentences", has not escaped Carnap. He suggests that in such sentences two propositions may not be substituted one for the other, unless they are "intensionally isomorphic", i.e., if they are "built in the same way out of designators" or designator matrices). But intensional isomorphism is a much stronger likeness than identity of intension; it introduces a quite new "structural" element, such that intensionally isomorphic expressions are synonymous in a nearly trivial sense.

c. Moreover, the real starting-point of Lewis seems at this point to have been somewhat forgotten. If there was something as "the" logical implication of 'q' by 'p', it seemed to be a relation, affirmable in the object language if and only if the syntactical relation of consequence exists between the assertion of p and the assertion of q. It has however been proved by Kleene that such a relation is the *intuitionistic* relation expressed by 'p ⊃ q'.

Curry goes a step further, and, in our opinion, legitimately. If we confine ourselves to logic without negation, there is no difference between intuitionistic, minimal or D-logic; in all three cases we have to do with Curry's absolute or A-logic. If negation is introduced, it seems better to avoid '∼p ⊃ (p ⊃ q)' as a theorem; hence we have to choose between minimal and D-logic. As it seems to conform to the usually intended meaning of negation to accept 'p **v** ∼p' as a theorem, we are led to the unexpected conclusion that the most adequate translation of 'If p then q' is the 'p ⊃ q' of D-logic.

Even then it remains somewhat odd that if 'q' is true then 'q' is implied by everything. A logical calculus escaping even this consequence can be constructed, as shown by Church and Sobocinski; but this calculus can hardly be considered as a normal translation of logical reasoning.

d. It may be a strange conclusion to arrive at, that possibly there be no adequate translation—and especially no ideal semantical translation of the "If —— then . . . ." It seems that the intuitive idea of a logical consequence cannot be freed from a certain psychological element by which somewhat confusedly two kinds of sentences would be excluded, on the one hand those which do not involve a real deduction, on the other hand sentences which are not somehow analytical in the sense of traditional logic. We might admit more simply that there is no such thing as an absolute concept of logical consequence, but only a syntactical concept of consequence with respect to various equally acceptable systems, involving more or less stringent conditions of logical rigor.

X. *Multiplication of Entities?*

Difficulties brought out in n. 7 may be centered about the question of the somewhat indefinite multiplication of entities arising when not only sentences as wholes, but also the elements of sentences, names for predicates and individuals, are to be interpreted from the intensional point of view, from which, with Carnap, we consider modal logic. Once again we shall not explain and discuss exhaustively the objections raised, but rather try to clarify the subject fragmentarily, from some points of view not brought habitually to the foreground.

a. Let us start from what we might call the statute of non-modal expressions in modal logic, and of its consequences concerning the analysis of these expressions in components.

In non-modal logic the expression "John is a man" which we may write 'Mj' is a sentence and expresses an unambiguous fact; it may be analyzed or split into an unambiguous predicator ('M' or 'man') applied to an unambiguous object-name ('j' or 'John'). For 'M' may be substituted '$\hat{x}Mx$' formed by abstraction; similarly '$\hat{X}(Xj)$' may be formed by abstraction and '$[\hat{X}(Xj)]\ M$' may be substituted for 'Mj'.

Now, in modal logic a non-modal expression such as 'Mj' is not an (unambiguous) sentence as it leaves unexpressed for which state of affairs it is said true. If we write '$(Mj)\ \delta$' or '$Mj\ \delta$' for 'Mj' is true in the (variable indetermined) state of affairs δ, we may translate '$[N(Mj)] \supset Mj$' as '$[(\delta)\ Mj\delta] \supset Mj\delta$'. One might be tempted to translate the modal 'Mj' as 'Mj' is true in fact but this is: 'Mj' is true in the real case, for which a special notation would be needed, let us say '$(Mj)\ \varrho$' or '$Mj\varrho$'.

Now, can the ambiguous 'Mj' be split into an unambiguous 'M' and an unambiguous 'j'?

Certainly 'Mj' is equivalent to '$(\hat{x}Mx)\ j$' and '$(\hat{X}Xj)\ M$'. The modal abstracts '$\hat{x}Mx$' and '$\hat{X}Xj$' correspond to Carnap's intensions, but with several differences; they are (ambiguous) expressions of the object-language, and intensions are defined (unambiguously) in the semantical metalanguage. Besides '$\hat{X}Xj$' denotes a set of predicates, whereas Carnap's "individual concepts" seem to be taken as a kind of individual.

b. Undoubtedly the interpretation of modal logic involves a reference to different "individual concepts" corresponding to one factual individual. We think that in appropriate contexts the distinction of such individual concepts is no mere subtlety: the Evening Star and the Morning Star should be distinguished in a system describing phenomena, and the distinction of various juridical personalities in one individual may have a precise technical sense from the point of view of law. Of course the possibility of accurate formalized reasoning upon phenomena and upon juridical concepts may be questioned. It may be worth stressing however that we have not to do here with pure "fiction". If a lawyer wants to explain some technicalities to his client, he may say: "Well, this amounts to considering a man in this situation and the same man in that other situation as several persons", but this is a rough explanation for persons lacking capacity for technical abstract thinking.

It may be added that in a modal system it is possible (as Carnap points out) to speak of extensions, using e.g., instead of the form 'x is an M' the form 'If P is equivalent to M, then x is a P'. Let us nevertheless point out that this factual equivalence may not be translated simply by the non-modal '$(x)\ (Px \equiv Mx) \supset Px$', because in modal logic this is not a sentence, not an unambiguous statement. The "If P is equivalent to M" has to be "P is factually, really, in the real case, equivalent to M", and this leads to something like '$[(x)\ (Px \equiv Mx)]\ \wp \supset Px$'.

c. Now we have alluded more than once to a theory in which the difficulties of modal logic appear distinctly, that is to the theory of description. As is well known a description designates (normally) an object as "the" unique object to which a given predicate has to be applied. Clearly the idea of uniqueness and hence that of identity enter into the explanation of what is meant by "the so and so". But in modal logic the theory of identity offers curious features, which have been brought out by Barcan and by Quine.

It is well known that

$$\text{'}Ax \supset (x = y \supset Ay)\text{'}$$

holds. Let us take for 'A' the predicate '$\hat{y}N\ (x = y)$'. Then we have:

$$\text{'}N\ (x = x) \supset [x = y \supset N\ (x = y)]\text{'}.$$

And as we have '$N\ (x = x)$' it follows that:

$$x = y \supset N\ (x = y).$$

Hence we should come to this paradoxical result that whenever factual identity exists, necessary identity must exist. Barcan even proves that both kinds of identity are strictly equivalent in S4 and hence in S5.

d. But this argumentation accepts as granted that both sentences 'N Ay' and 'y has the predicate "to be an x, which is necessarily an A,"' i.e., '$(\hat{x}NAx)\ y$', are logically equivalent.

But this is not the case. 'NAy' is a sentence expressing a necessary proposition, whereas '$(\hat{x}NAx)\ y$' is a modally ambiguous statement attributing a necessary predicate to y.

Abstract modal predicates and abstract modal (necessary) individual concepts seem to lie at the root of the (modal) name-relation paradoxes. If now the legitimacy of this abstraction be restricted—in the sense that a modal abstract applied to something may not be reduced to a usual sentence as 'NAy'—we must recognize that modal logic represents a greater departure from "logical common sense" than had been supposed hitherto. A modal logic is commonly considered as adding the consideration of modalities to the consideration of facts (of factual propositions); but it goes much farther indeed if the assertion of a fact becomes ambiguous and hence may no more be handled simply as "hard fact".

ROBERT FEYS

UNIVERSITY OF LOUVAIN.

9

John Myhill

AN ALTERNATIVE TO THE METHOD OF EXTENSION AND INTENSION*

THE purpose of this paper is to offer certain criticisms of the analysis of meaning and modalities made by Carnap in [1],[1] and to present an alternative analysis which seems to avoid these criticisms and to invite no new ones.

I. *Criticisms of Carnap's Analysis*

We will presuppose that the reader is familiar with Carnap's analysis, and will regard this analysis as given in definitive form by the system S_2 of modal logic (pp. 182-186) and its extension S'_2 (p. 198; referred to as S on pp. 181f.). Our criticisms are as follows:

(1) The variables of lowest type S_2 range over individual concepts rather than individuals. While this does not prevent us making all the statements about individuals which we could make in an extensional system (pp. 193-202), it nonetheless lends a certain air of artificiality to the system.

(2) It is not immediately apparent how S_2 could be extended so as to take care of belief- and assertion-sentences. The analysis of such sentences given by Carnap (pp. 53-64) is not formalizable within S_2, and even if it were it would still be open to the objections of Church [2].

(3) If S_2 is extended to S'_2 by admitting (proposition- and) property-variables (pp. 181f., 198) the rule of universal instantiation for property-variables (i.e. the rule that from $(f)(\ldots f \ldots)$ one can infer $\ldots(\lambda x)$ $($——x——$)\ldots$), and its dual, the rule of existential generalization for property-variables (the rule that from $\ldots(\lambda x)$ $($——x——$)\ldots$ one can infer $(\exists f)(\ldots f \ldots)$), cease to hold. I consider this feature of a system of logic so strange and counter-intuitive that one should be very reluctant

*I am very much indebted to Prof. Carnap for correspondence concerning this paper, in which he pointed out errors in an earlier version, and made many valuable suggestions.

[1]Numbers in square brackets refer to the bibliography at the end of the paper. Page references are to [1] unless otherwise stated.

to use such a system unless there is proof positive or at least very strong heuristic evidence that no other will do the job. Such is here apparently not the case; indeed we shall present in this paper a system not possessing this unnatural feature which seems to do as well as, or better than, the systems S_2 and S'_2, the job for which these latter systems were constructed.

The first two of the above criticisms are not new; see especially Quine [3] and his remarks quoted in [1], pp. 196f., Church [2]. But the third one is to my knowledge not to be found in the literature, and clearly Carnap himself at the time of writing [1] was unaware of it. (Cf. for example his uncritical use of existential generalization for property-variables on p. 191.) We shall therefore speak no more of our first two criticisms, and proceed immediately to develop the third.

The failure of universal instantiation (or existential generalization) for property-variables in S'_2 can be seen in the two following examples.

Example A. The formula[2]

$$(f)(x)(y)(x = y \supset (fx \equiv fy)) \qquad \text{I}$$

is L-true in S_1, or rather in an extension of S'_1 of S_1 (p. 198)[3] containing variables not of the lowest type. Therefore (p. 200, at top), the formula I is L-true in S'_2. If universal instantiation were permitted in S'_2 we could infer (taking f as $(\lambda z)\,N(z = x)$)

$$(x)(y)(x = y \supset (N(x = x) \equiv N(x = y))) \qquad \text{II}$$

and thence

$$(x)(y)(x = y \supset N(x = y)) \qquad \text{III}$$

which is L-false in S_2 (cf. C on p. 191) and therefore in S'_2.

This argument is not quite rigorous, because S_2 and S'_2 are not presented as deductive systems but by means of an interpretation. Nonetheless if we look at this interpretation (41-2 on pp. 183f. and the bracketed sentences on p. 182) we can verify by a simple but tedious computation that I is L-true, while II and III are L-false in S'_2. This established what we need, i.e. that universal instantiation for property-variables fails in S'_2 in the sense that it leads from an L-true to an L-false sentence and therefore cannot be used as a rule of inference.

Example B. The formula

$$(\lambda x)N(x = a) = (\lambda x)N(x = a) \qquad \text{IV}$$

is L-true in S_2, hence also in S'_2. The formula

$$(\exists f)(f = (\lambda x)N(x = a)) \qquad \text{V}$$

obtained from IV by existential generalization is L-false in S. For (elimi-

[2]In sections I-III we modify Carnap's notation by writing $=$ instead of $\equiv$ between individuals and properties.
[3]Called S in [1], 115.

nating the existential quantifier, and applying conversion) V is L-equivalent to

$$\sim(f) \sim(x)\,(fx \equiv N(x = a)) \qquad \text{VI}$$

i.e. to the negation of

$$(f)\,(\exists x) \sim(fx \equiv N(x = a)) \qquad \text{VII}$$

Now by the rules of interpretation of S'_2 (pp. 182-4), VII is L-true. (Outline of proof: if the value of '*f*' sends '*a*' into a range to which the actual state-description belongs, assign to '*x*' a value which sends the actual state-description into '*a*' and at least one other state-description into some individual constant other than '*a*'. Then '*fx*' holds in the actual state-description and '$N\,(x = a)$' does not. On the other hand if the value of '*f*' sends '*a*' into a range to which the actual state-description does not belong, assign to '*x*' a value which sends every state-description into '*a*'. Then '*fx*' does not hold in the actual state-description and '$N\,(x = a)$' does. Therefore VII is true. If we reflect either that VII, since it contains no descriptive signs, is L-determinate, or else that all reference to 'the actual state-description' in the above proof could be replaced by references to 'an arbitrary state-description', we see that VII is not only true but L-true.)

Hence VI and the L-equivalent formulation V are L-false. Hence existential generalization leads from the L-true statement IV to the L-false statement V, and so cannot be used as a rule of inference in S'_2.

The essence of both examples consists in showing that *the values of the variable 'f' in* S'_2 *do not include all the properties* (in the intuitive sense) *expressible in* S'_2. This could hardly be made clearer than by Example B; for the L-true statement

$$(f)\,(f \neq (\lambda x)\, N(x = a)$$

says simply that the 'property' $(\lambda x)\ N(x = a)$ is not amongst the values of the variable '*f*'.

II. *A Suggested Modification in Carnap's Analysis, and its Refutation*

We explore here an alternative which the reader may have thought of for himself. Could it be that 'individual constants' on p. 182, lines 3-4, is either a misprint or a slip for 'individual concepts?' It is easily checked that if we interpret the property-variables in S'_2 as ranging over mappings from individual *concepts* to ranges rather than as Carnap says over mappings from individuals *constants* to ranges, then every sentence of the form

$$(\exists f)\,(f = (\lambda x)\,(\ldots x \ldots))$$

is L-true is S'_2, so that after all we could by a slight modification of the rules of ranges for S'_2 ensure that all properties expressible in S'_2 were among the values of the property-variable of S'_2, and that L-truth was preserved by existential generalization and universal instantiation. This would accord with Carnap's uncritical use of the former mode of inference on p. 191.

But this emendation will clearly not do. For if we treat property-variables in this way the formula I turns out to be L-false in S'_2 while L-true and provable in the System S'_1 formed by adding higher-type variables to S_1; provable moreover without recourse to the principle of extensionality. And this contradicts a principle highly desirable in any system of modal logic, namely that any sentence provable in a non-modal system without recourse to the axiom of extensionality should likewise be provable or at least L-true in any modal extension of that system. Let us call this the *principle of modal extensions* (PME). Then Example A shows that *we cannot combine in the same system PME, the ordinary rules of the second-order functional calculus, and the negation of III,* i.e. the merely contingent identity of individuals. (This does not apply to systems like Church's in [4] of course, in which there are distinct variables for individuals and for individual concepts, at least not without some further argumentation. Nonetheless, cf. [4], p. 21, lines 18-19.)

As a matter of fact Carnap asserts (p. 200) something even stronger than PME, namely the principle that 'any designator in S'_1 and the same expression in S'_2 are L-equivalent to one another.' But this is clearly too strong, as Carnap pointed out in a letter to the author. For it implies that any sentence L-true in S'_1 is likewise L-true in S'_2 regardless of the fact that the range of bound predicate variables in the former is narrower than in the latter. In particular, it would make the axiom of extensionality L-true in S'_2.

We now proceed to give an account of a system S'_3 of modal type-theory which conforms to PME and which keeps an ordinary second-order functional calculus. This system is essentially a type-theory built on Carnap's own semantical system MFL and calculus MFC [5]. Familiarity with Carnap's paper [5] is presupposed in what follows.

III. *The System S_3*

We first adduce some heuristic considerations motivating our choice of MFL as a starting-point. Our final aim being to construct a calculus which serves the same purpose as S'_2 and avoids artificiality as much as possible, we see from the last paragraph of the preceding section that we must choose between

(1) Abandoning PME,

(2) Abandoning the ordinary nth-order calculus, and

(3) Abandoning the possibility of merely contingent identity of individuals.

Evidently (3) is by far the most natural course, if we can only find a way to carry it out. The difficulties in the way of (3) are of two kinds, technical and philosophical. (By philosophical difficulties we mean simply inadequacy to dispel the paradoxes of the name-relation and other paradoxes which arise from the use of modalities in ordinary language. We will concentrate for the present on the merely technical problem of constructing calculi and systems, and will defer all philosophical considerations to a later section.)

If we succeed in carrying out (3) while keeping PME and the ordinary *n*th-order functional calculus, we will have automatically rendered ourselves immune to criticism (3). Moreover, the idea that by taking MFL as a starting-point we can simultaneously avoid criticism (1) is suggested by the following consideration: According to Carnap ([1] p. 183, footnote 3) the variables (of lowest type) in MFL range not over all individual concepts but only over the L-determinate ones. But it is possible to identify L-determinate intensions in general with extensions (pp. 90-95), and L-determinate individual concepts in particular with individuals (p. 95). Hence we are led to consider the possibility of an interpretation of MFC as a calculus whose variables range over individuals; in this manner we might hope to overcome the need for individual concepts altogether. (We reemphasize that we are at present concerned only with the technical problem of constructing a system of modal logic whose individual variables range truly over individuals rather than over L-determinate or any other individual concepts. The question of the 'philosophical' arguments for individual concepts is deferred till later.)

The signs, matrices and sentences of S_3 are those of MFL (LL9-1, 2, 3 on p. 53 of [5]). [The sign $\imath$ will be introduced by definition in a manner to be explained immediately.] The ranges of the sentences of S_3 are the same as the ranges of the same sentences of MFL (D9-5 on p. 54 of [5]). A sentence of S_3 is *true* if the actual state-description belongs to its range, *L-true* if every state-description belongs to its range. Thus the only difference between S_3 and MFL is one which does not show up in the formalism at all; the individual constants are taken as denoting, and the individual variables as ranging over, individuals rather than L-determinate individual concepts. We now explain that any sentence containing $\imath$ is to be treated as short for some sentence resulting from applying $\imath$-elimination (8-2, p. 37) in some specified order until all descriptions have disappeared. The scope of $\imath$-operators has to be taken into account, since for example

$$N(a = (\imath x)(Fx))$$

could be taken as short for

$$(\exists x)(Fx \,\&\, (y)(Fy \supset y = x) \,\&\, N(a = x))$$

or for

$$N(\exists x)(Fx \,\&\, (y)(Fy \supset y = x) \,\&\, a = x)$$

according to how we fix the scope of the description-operator. In order to avoid ambiguity of this kind we make the convention that the scope of $\imath$ is to be as small as possible. This convention has the convenient consequence that a sentence *NS* is true just in case *S* is L-true, whether or not *S* contains descriptions. We do not lay any restriction on *N*'s appearing within descriptions (as Carnap does, p. 184).

IV. *The System* S'_3

The system S'_3 is formed by building a hierarchy of types on top of S_3. It was observed before that the variables of S_3 are construed as ranging over extensions, i.e. individuals; clearly we do not wish the higher types also to range over extensions, since we would then not have a modal logic at all. [Outline of proof: By a higher-type analogue of Example A, $f = g \supset N(f = g)$; hence $p \supset [(\lambda x)\ (x = x) = (\lambda x)\ (x = x \ \&\ p)] \supset N[(\lambda x)\ (x = x) = (\lambda x)\ (x = x \ \&\ p)] \supset Np$.] Since we wish to avoid the complexities of Church's system [4], we try to steer clear of having two styles of variables, one for extensions and one for intensions, in each type; for once this is done, there seems to be no way of avoiding an infinite number of styles ([1], pp. 129-136, [4], p. 12, footnote 13) or at any rate an uncomfortably large finite number of styles ([1], pp. 114f.) On the other hand, in I of this paper we have not found too much to hope for in Carnap's idea of variables which range over intensions and extensions simultaneously (p. 45). We therefore adopt the only remaining course, namely to *take the higher-type variables as ranging over intensions only, although the variables of the lowest type range over extensions only.* We present the resulting system as a calculus S'_3 with the following rules.

A. The signs of S'_3 are the same as those of S_3, with the addition of variables $f_n, g_n, \ldots$ for properties of the nth level, and $p, q, \ldots$ for propositions; also quantifiers for these additional kinds of variables; also λx and λf_n.

B. Matrices may have any of the forms listed in D9-2 ([5], p. 53). and also the following forms; p, $f_1(x)$, $f_{n+1}(f_n)$, $[(\lambda x)\ (\ldots x -)]y$, $[(\lambda f_n)\ (\ldots f_n -)]g_n$, where $\ldots x -$ and $\ldots f_n -$ are matrices. Sentences are closed matrices as usual.

C. The context $(\imath x)(\ldots x -)$ is introduced as it was for S_3 in the preceding section. The context $(\imath f_n)(\ldots f_n \ldots)$ is introduced either analogously or as in ([1], pp. 38f).

D. We give here no rules of ranges for S'_3. These rules naturally depend on the interpretation given to 'proposition' and 'property', and there appear to be a great many equally natural interpretations. I hope to investigate this question in a future paper; here I present only a calculus.

E. The primitive sentences of the calculus S'_3 are as follows:

(i) The primitive sentences of MFC (D10–1, [5], pp. 54f.V).

(ii) The closures with respect to all variables of the sentences a-n on p. 186 of [1].

(iii) All sentences of the forms

$$(\ )N((p)(\ldots p \ldots) \supset \ldots S \ldots)$$
$$(\ )N((f^1)(\ldots f^1 \ldots) \supset \ldots (\lambda\, x)(\text{---}x\text{---}) \ldots)$$
$$(\ )N((f_{n+1})(\ldots f_{n+1} \ldots) \supset \ldots (\lambda f_n)\ (\text{---}f_n\text{---}) \ldots)$$

where S, ---x--- and f_n--- are matrices.

(iv) The sentence $N(x)(y)(x = y \equiv (f)(fx \equiv fy))$

(v) The sentences

$$N(x)(\ldots x - \equiv [(\lambda y)(\ldots y -)]x)$$
$$N(f_n)(\ldots f_n - \equiv [(\lambda g_n)(\ldots g_n -)]f_n)$$

The only rules of inference of S'_3 are modus ponens and substitution.

F. The abbreviations following are convenient

$$(f_n = g_n) =_{Df} (f_{n+1})\,(f_{n+1}\ (f_n) \equiv f_{n+1}\ (g_n))$$
$$(f_{n+1} \simeq g_{n+1}) =_{Df} (f_n)\ (f_{n+1}\ (f_n) \equiv g_{n+1}\ (f_n))$$
$$(f_{n+1} \equiv g_{n+1}) =_{Df} N(f_{n+1} \simeq g_{n+1})$$

and similarly for $f_1 \simeq g_1$, $f_1 \equiv g_1$. We notice that $=$ is stronger than $\equiv$ and $\equiv$ than $\simeq$. Two properties stand in the relation $\simeq$ if they have the same extension and in the relation $\equiv$ if it is logically necessary that they have the same extension. They stand in the relation $=$ only if they are *the same property* in a sense which may be clarified in any way which seems convenient. (The relevance of this stronger notion to the analysis of belief-sentences is clear.) However, the notion $N\ (f = g)$ is no stronger than the notion $f = g$; for we have

$$f_n = g_n \supset [((\lambda h_n)N(h_n = f_n))f_n \equiv ((\lambda h_n)N(h_n = f_n))g_n]$$
$$\supset N\ (f_n = g_n)$$

The distinction between coextensiveness, logically necessary coextensiveness and sheer identity of properties certainly does not seem forced; indeed Carnap himself comes close to admitting the need of an analogous distinction in the case of propositions (p. 176). We thus have three equivalence relations between properties as against one between individuals (Example A above). We have also three equivalence relations between propositions: $p \equiv q$, $p \equiv q$ and again sheer identity, $p = q$. If we had variables ranging over properties of propositions, we could introduce this last by a definition

$$(p = q) =_{Df} (f)(f(p) \equiv f\ (q))$$

and perhaps this will turn out to be the best method. I do not see at present, however, any objection to the alternative definition[4]

$$(p = q) =_{Df} ((\lambda x)(x = x \,\&\, p) = (\lambda x)(x = x \,\&\, q))$$

V. *The Adequacy of* S'_3

It is easy to satisfy oneself that the system S'_3 is adequate to the development of at least all the mathematics in Principia. (Cf. [1], pp. 115-117). There is an apparently major difficulty in the way of extending S'_3 to transfinite types; but these are mainly used in order to get very large infinite ordinals, which could probably be obtained as (empty but distinct) properties of relations in S'_3 in some fairly low type. In any case, we are somewhat on the fringe of classical mathematics here, and the difficult technical problem of developing ordinal number theory in S'_3 is best deferred for separate consideration in a more technical paper. Certainly S'_3 is as adequate mathematically as is S'_2. We are therefore concerned here only with the philosophical adequacy of S'_3. We note first that we have adopted the method of the name-relation (p. 98); any closed well-formed expression denotes (is a name of) exactly one entity; the entity named by an individual constant is an extension, that named by a sentence or a closed λ-expression is an intension. We also can prove the principle of interchangeability in the form

$$(u = v) \supset (fu \equiv fv)$$

whether f is intensional or extensional or neither. We might therefore expect one or other of the antinomies of the name-relation to arise. We are thus left with the following topics to consider

A. The immunity of S'_3 to the criticisms (1)-(3);

B. Antinomies of the name-relation;

C. Philosophical adequacy of S'_3 in other respects; specifically in regard to the analysis of belief-sentences and the paradox of analysis.

Ad A. Criticism (2) (adequacy to the analysis of belief-sentences, etc.) will be discussed under C. It might be noted however that the difficulty over belief-sentences only arises in systems which identify L-equivalent propositions, and this our system was designed not to do. However I must confess to not yet having found a proof that

$$(p)(q)(p \equiv q \supset p = q) \qquad \text{VIII}$$

is independent.

Criticisms (1) and (3) are automatically taken care of by the con-

[4]Professor Carnap has suggested to me the possibility of defining λ contextually in S'_3 as follows:

$$\phi[(\lambda f_n)(\chi f_n)] = (f_{n+1})\,[(f_n)(f_{n+1}f_n = \chi f_n) \supset \phi f_{n+1}]$$

This implies $(\lambda f \chi f)f = \chi f$ and thus approximates Alternative (1) of [4]. It appears however that in view of the philosophical applications we intend to make of modal logics, *we should never identify intensions unless we are forced to;* for the fewer identifications we make the more flexible will be our analysis of belief-sentences.

struction of the system. However somebody might ask how we know the system to be consistent. This is a technical question whose detailed discussion would be out of place in the present paper. This much however can be said: I am morally certain that a model can be constructed in ordinary (theory-of-types) extensional logic, which satisfies all the primitive sentences of S'_3 *and also VIII.* I am not at all certain that such a model can be constructed *without satisfying VIII.* If this is so one can infer only a disjunction; *either* VIII is provable in S'_3 *or* the system of intensions is vastly more complex than the system of extensions. The latter alternative seems perfectly plausible, and my most devious attempts to prove VIII in S'_3 have been fortunately unsuccessful. We might also add the remark that even if VIII turns out to be provable in S'_3, S'_3 will still be an improvement on S'_2 in not being subject to criticism (1) or (3).

Ad B. The first of the antinomies of the name-relation is as follows. If '*a*' and '*b*' name the same entity, then they are interchangeable everywhere, i.e. for every context '. . . *a* . . .', '. . . *a* . . .' is equivalent to '. . . *b* . . . '. Consequently, if '*a*' and '*b*' denote the same entity, '*N*(. . . *a* . . .)' is equivalent to '*N*(. . . *b* . . .)'. Yet there seem to be many cases in which substitution of one name of an entity for another name of the same entity can transform a logical truth into an empirical one.

This form of the antinomy is resolved in two ways under our analysis, according as the entity named is or is not an individual. If the entity named is an individual, the '*a*' and '*b*' must be individual constants, hence the same individual constant; hence '. . . *a* . . .' and '. . . *b* . . .' must be the same expression, and their logical truth must stand or fall together. (We do not regard descriptions as names of individuals, but merely as convenient abbreviations eliminable in context; this does not mean however that we avoid by a verbal trick the Author-of-Waverley paradox (p. 134), but rather that we defer its consideration until we come to the second form of the antinomy of the name-relation.)

The first form of the antinomy of the name-relation disappears in a different way when the entity named in two ways is a proposition or a property. If it is a proposition, it will be recalled that two propositions are only considered identical on our analysis when they fulfill very stringent conditions. Indeed, it is hard to see how we could ever prove a statement of the form $S = T$, S and T being sentences, when S and T were not intentionally isomorphic. (Nonetheless

$$(\exists f)(\exists g)(f \neq g \cdot (p)(fp) = (p)(gp)) \qquad \text{IX}$$

is a theorem of the system formed by adding to S'_3 variables ranging over properties of propositions; so we had best be careful!) In any case, if there is *anything* that could be truly affirmed of the proposition denoted by T in S'_3 or any consistent extension thereof, we would dispose of the antinomy by asserting (truly) $S \neq T$ rather than $S = T$.

For an example of the first form of the antinomy of the name-relation using properties, we take Carnap's illustration on p. 135. Let F mean featherless, B biped and H human.

Then we have

$$N(x)((Fx \cdot Bx) \supset Bx)$$

and from this, if we assume that '$(\lambda x)\ (Fx \cdot Bx)$' designates the property H, we get the falsehood

$$N(x)(Hx \supset Bx).$$

But for us '$(\lambda x)(Fx \cdot Bx)$' does not designate H, but another property with (contingently) the same extension. (Notice that we do not here insist that λ-expressions be regarded as abbreviations, as we did with descriptions.)

The second form of the antinomy of the name-relation depends on the fact that we are very often inclined to assert $S = T$ for some designators S and T, and yet are unwilling to deduce $N(\ldots T \ldots)$ from $N(\ldots S \ldots)$. In the case where S and T designate properties or propositions, we handle this in S'_3 in the same way as the first form. (The premiss $S = T$ is replaced by one of the weaker statements $S \equiv T$, $S \equiv T$ for propositions; or $S \simeq T$, $S \equiv T$ for properties.) Where S and T are descriptions, or where one is a description and the other a proper name, we take a different course entirely. Thus, letting 's' denote Scott, 'w' the book Waverley, and 'A' the relation of authorship, the inference

$$s = (\imath x)(Axw) \qquad \text{X}$$

$$N(s = s) \qquad \text{XI}$$

$$N(s = (\imath x)(Axw)) \qquad \text{XII}$$

is usually presented as an illustration of the antinomy of the name-relation. We cannot make the inference from X and XI to XII however, since for us X is not (in primitive notation) a statement of identity at all, but a contingent existence-statement. For a like reason we cannot use universal instantiation with descriptions, otherwise we could make the invalid inference from

$$(x)\ (y)\ (x = y \supset N(x = y))$$

to

$$s = (\imath x)(Axw) \supset N(s = (\imath x)(Axw))$$

and thence (using X) to XII. But this failure of universal instantiation is a trifling matter compared with the corresponding failure in S'_2 expressed by criticism (3). The latter failure compels us to admit the existence of a designator in S'_2 which designates a property not in the range of values of the property-variables of S'_2, while our own failure in no way compels us to admit that the designator '$(\imath x)\ (Axw)$' designates an individual not in the range of values of the variables 'x'. It designates the entity Scott, which is a perfectly good value of 'x'.

Ad C. Belief-sentences seem to yield no trouble in S'_3. Let the sign B, denoting the relation of belief between a person and a proposition, be added to the primitive signs of S'_3 and let xBM be a matrix for any sentence M. Then (using the letters 'A', 's', 'w' as above, and 'g' to denote George IV), we are unable to make the inference from X and

$$\sim gB(s = (\iota x)\ (Axw))$$

to the ridiculous

$$\sim gB(s = s),$$

again for the reason that X is not a statement of identity. A more subtle device is needed to take care of example like that in [1], p. 54. George IV certainly believed *some* but not *all* L-true propositions. Let q be an L-true proposition which he did not believe. We have (presumably)

$$gB(g = g)$$

and we also have

$$N(g = g)$$
$$Nq$$

and therefore

$$(g = g) \equiv q.$$

But we do *not* have $(g = g) = q$, and so we see no way of inferring the falsehood

$$gBq.$$

We should not conceal, however, a difficulty which arises here. For the reasons given in [1], p. 53, we need for the analysis of belief-sentences a stronger equivalence relation between propositions than L-equivalence. (Such a relation is lacking in S'_2; this was essentially our criticism (2).) It appears that VIII is not provable in S'_3; therefore there is good reason to suppose that $p = q$ is the relation we are seeking. But by IX *the relation $p = q$ is weaker than intentional isomorphism* ([1], pp. 56-64) and the possibility that S'_3 does not provide "enough" propositions to serve as an adequate formal basis for an analysis of belief-sentences remains, I suppose, theoretically open. I can only report that having applied S'_3 to the most bizarre belief-sentences I could imagine, I could find no signs of trouble anywhere, and concluded that such a possibility was exceedingly remote.

We conclude with a discussion of the *paradox of analysis* ([1], pp. 63f.). I take it that this paradox lies in the apparent inferribility of the falsehood

(Brother = Brother) is non-trivial XIII

from the supposed truths

(Brother = Male Sibling) is non-trivial XIV

and

Brother = Male Sibling. XV

From our point of view, XIII *does* follow from XIV and XV, and therefore one or the other of XIV, XV is false. Let us suppose a clear definition of 'is analysable as' has been given; clearly this relation is no weaker than L-equivalence and may be stronger. All the above 'paradox' shows is *that it cannot be as strong as our* $\equiv$. Until somebody explains precisely what analysis is, I don't see that there is anything further to be said on the matter. But if it is a precise notion at all, I have little doubt that it can be incorporated into S'_3.

Indeed, the great strength of S'_3 as a tool of philosophical analysis is that it distinguishes three rather than two kinds of equivalence of concepts, and that there seems no obstacle to introducing a great many more (e.g. Lewis's 'synonymy' and 'equivalence in analytic meaning', [6], pp. 245f.), if the need should arise. An indefinitely extendible number of different gradations of equivalence appear more manageable than an infinite number of value-ranges of variables of one type, as in Church's [4]; while an indefinite number of *interpretations* of variables (corresponding to Carnap's value-extensions and value-intensions), which we claim would be necessary if Carnap's S'_2 is to be prepared for every philosophical contingency, seems unwieldly enough to paralyze the intellect.

John Myhill

Department of Philosophy
Stanford University

BIBLIOGRAPHY

A. *Articles and Books referred to explicitly.*

[1] Carnap, R. *Meaning and Necessity.* Chicago, 1947.

[2] Church, A. "Carnap's Analysis of Statements of Assertion and Belief," *Analysis,* X, 97-99.

[3] Quine, W. V. "Notes on Existence and Necessity," *Journal of Philosophy,* XL, 113-127.

[4] Church, A. "A Formulation of the Logic of Sense and Denotation," *Structure, Method and Meaning,* New York, 1951, 3-24.

[5] Carnap, R. "Modalities and Quantification," *Journal of Symbolic Logic,* II, 33-64.

[6] Lewis, C. I. "The Modes of Meaning," *Philosophy and Phenomenological Research,* XIV, 236-250.

B. *Articles and Books anticipating in various respects the views expressed in this paper.*

Fitch, F. B. "The Problem of the Morning Star and the Evening Star," *Philosophy of Science,* XVI, 137.

Fitch, F. B. *Symbolic Logic,* New York, 1952, especially pp. 64-83, 112-115, 164-166.

Smullyan, A. "Modality and Description," *Journal of Symbolic Logic,* XIII, 31.

10

Donald Davidson

THE METHOD OF EXTENSION AND INTENSION[1]

I

THE simplest seeming of all semantical concepts is that of naming. Naming is a function which to every expression of an appropriate kind (a *name*) assigns exactly one entity (the *nominatum*). Among the principles which would appear to govern the use of this concept are:[2]

P1. The nominata of the names in a sentence constitute the subject matter of the sentence.

P2. If two names $\mathbf{A}_i$ and $\mathbf{A}_j$ name the same entity then any true sentence remains true if $\mathbf{A}_i$ is replaced by $\mathbf{A}_j$.

P3. An identity sentence $\mathbf{A}_i = \mathbf{A}_j$ is true if and only if $\mathbf{A}_i$ and $\mathbf{A}_j$ name the same entity.

As Frege pointed out long ago, however, puzzles arise in the attempt to apply this theory to ordinary language. One such puzzle is: if an identity sentence 'a = b' is true if and only if 'a' and 'b' name the same entity, then how can the apparently informative sentence 'a = b' differ in meaning, when it is true, from the trivial sentence 'a = a'? (We may call this the *Paradox of Identity* in analogy with its sophisticated variant, the *Paradox of Analysis.*) Another such puzzle (called by Carnap the

[1]I am grateful to Professors Carl G. Hempel and Patrick Suppes for several helpful criticisms and suggestions. My indebtedness to the teachings of Professor W. V. Quine is too general and too obvious to permit or require detailed acknowledgment.

[2]Carnap, *Meaning and Necessity* (hereafter abbreviated [Meaning]) (Chicago, 1947), 98. Other books and papers by Carnap to which reference is made, with associated abbreviations, are: *Introduction to Semantics* ([Semantics]) (Cambridge, Mass., 1942); "Modalities and Quantification" ([Modalities]), *Journal of Symbolic Logic,* XI (1946), 33-64; "Empiricism, Semantics and Ontology" ([Empiricism]), *Revue Internationale de Philosophie,* XI (1950), 20-40; "Remarks on the Paradox of Analysis: A Reply to Leonard Linsky" ([Paradox]), *Philosophy of Science,* XVI (1949), 347-50. In general I have followed the notation of [Meaning], but for the printer's convenience bold Gothic letters have been substituted for Carnap's German capitals. Thus bold Gothic letters function as metalinguistic variables taking expressions in some object language as values; logical constants from the object language serve as names for themselves when combined with bold Gothic letters; and a string of such names of expressions is the name of the expression formed by concatenating the named expressions in the order named.

Antinomy of the Name-Relation) arises from the attempt to apply P2 to the sentence:

(1) Necessarily, the morning star is the morning star.

For since 'the morning star' names the same entity as 'the evening star,' (1) should remain true when the first occurrence of 'the morning star' is replaced by 'the evening star'; but it does not.

To solve the first puzzle, Frege augmented the simple theory of naming by providing that in addition to having a nominatum, every name also has a sense, or meaning. Since 'a' and 'b' may have different senses and the same nominatum, the interest of 'a = b' is explicable in terms of the difference in sense while its truth depends on the identity of nominata.

The second puzzle Frege met by specifying that in certain contexts within sentences (for example after the word 'necessarily' or the words 'John believes that') names acquire new nominata and new senses. Such contexts Frege called *oblique.* Thus expressions used as names are ambiguous, but systematically so since once the context is determined, sense and nominatum are fixed.

The solutions to the paradox of identity and the antinomy of the name-relation, taken together, demand that an expression used as a name have two senses and two nominata. But here an easy economy occurred to Frege: by taking the sense of a naming expression in an ordinary context as the nominatum of that expression in an oblique context, a reduction in the total machinery seems possible. The device recommends itself on other grounds than economy; for one thing, given the sense or meaning of a naming expression in an ordinary context, its nominatum in oblique contexts is determined.

The decision to interlock ordinary sense and oblique nominatum has far-reaching consequences. Failing this decision it remains an open question whether having a sense or meaning requires a meant entity in addition to a named entity; but once meanings are nominata, they are entities, and require names. Names for the senses of names in ordinary contexts are provided by the same expressions in oblique contexts; but now names are needed for the senses of names in oblique contexts, which in turn will have further nameable entities for *their* senses. The apparent economy is spurious; it leads straight to an infinite hierarchy of names and entities. Even if we consider a naming expression in its ordinary and oblique contexts only, identifying ordinary sense and oblique nominatum makes for an increase in the number of entities which must of necessity be postulated.

The assumption that meanings are entities which can be named also lends weight to the view that in addition to ordinary truth, there is a special kind of truth, that is, truth by virtue of meanings. Consider these two sentences:

(2) All rubelites are red tourmalines,

(3) Necessarily, all rubelites are red tourmalines.

Suppose for the moment we allow the appropriate expressions of (2) and (3) within the category of names. Then sentence (2) is, by virtue of what it says about its nominata, true. So, for that matter, is (3), although it has (on Frege's theory) an entirely different subject matter. But since (3) is about the meanings of the words in (2), we may say the truth of (3) implies that (2) is true by virtue of the meanings of the words. There are thus two entirely distinct sets of entities to which we may appeal in establishing the truth of (2): the nominata of (2); or the nominata of (3).

It is natural to ask whether, since it leads to such complications, Frege's system might not be modified in some way to restore part of the lost simplicity of the original theory of the name-relation. It appears obvious that Frege's entire theory is unnecessarily cumbersome if it is designed merely to resolve the antinomy of the name-relation. What is needed in order to explain away the antinomy is to show why, in oblique contexts, words which ordinarily name the same entity cannot be interchanged freely *salva veritate*. Two different solutions seem implicit in Frege, either of them simpler than his:

Course 1. Expressions name different entities in different contexts, hence two expressions which name the same entity in one context may not in another. This course makes no reference to the sense of naming expressions at all. But sense as distinguished from nominatum could be reintroduced without reinstating the infinite hierarchy of entities and names, provided having a sense is not construed as a relation between an expression and an entity.

Course 2. A name has a nominatum and a sense, and the rules of substitution are based upon the first in ordinary contexts and the second in oblique contexts. This course promises to eliminate the duplication of nominata and of names (if not expressions) required by Course 1, and it appears to offer the obvious solution to the paradox of identity.

Carnap's method of extension and intension may be regarded as a modification and generalization of Course 2. According to Carnap, the method of extension and intension differs fundamentally from all other modifications of the method of the name-relation, and has several important advantages. The present paper will be devoted primarily to the examination of these claims, not so much with the purpose of refutation as of clarification and evaluation. A brief exposition of some of the key concepts of the method of extension and intension brings out the fact that insofar as Carnap achieves a "reduction of entities," it is at the expense of extensions (II). The question is then raised how it is possible, according to Carnap's semantics, to deal with ordinary individuals and other extensional entities (III). It is argued that with respect to those problems which depend for their solution upon the distinction between intension and extension, Carnap's method has no clear advantage over various other modifications of the method of the name-relation (IV), while with respect to those problems which demand for their solution further distinctions, the method of extension and intension appears less consistent than other methods (V). At the end a point is raised which is political rather than technical, concerning the usefulness of Carnap's method as a *general* method for the analysis of meaning in language. Carnap's present semantic method, like that of Frege and others, seems dictated by the tacit acceptance of a strangely gerrymandered linguisic territory (VI).

II

Let us agree (whether or not with Frege) that two different expressions may have the same sense.[3] Then we may in particular distinguish two relations in which names may stand to one another: they may have the same nominatum but not the same sense, or they may have the same sense and the same nominatum. The first of these relations may equally well be expressed without direct reference to entities named: it is the relation in which 'a' and 'b' stand to one another if and only if 'a = b' is true. If the first relation can be expressed in terms of truth rather than *via* intermediate entities, then it seems natural to express the second in an analogous way, in terms of a special kind of truth. This is truth by virtue of meaning or analytic truth, what Carnap calls L-truth. The second relation may therefore be explained as the relation which holds between 'a' and 'b' and only if 'a = b' is L-true.

At this point it will be convenient to introduce fragments of Carnap's notation (in [Meaning]). Between individual expressions (individual constants or descriptions) '≡' will take the place of the identity sign used above. The expression formed by interposing '≡' between two n-place predicates (e.g. 'H ≡ F•B' where 'H' means 'is human' and 'F•B' means 'is featherless and is a biped') is defined as standing for the same expression with appropriate variables inserted in the predicate places, and the

[3]The comments throughout this paper on Frege's semantics apply properly (save where explicit exceptions are noted) not to Frege's views but to the Fregean semantics outlined by Alonzo Church, especially in "The Need for Abstract Entities in Semantic Analysis" ([Abstract Entities]), *Proceedings of the American Academy of Arts and Sciences,* LXXX-I (1951), 100-112; and "Carnap's Introduction to Semantics" ([Review Semantics]), *Philosophical Review,* LII (1943), 298-304.

whole closed with universal quantifiers (e.g. '$(x)[Hx \equiv Fx \cdot Bx]$'). Finally, the biconditional between sentences has its usual meaning. The two relations mentioned above for the names 'a' and 'b' may now be generalized to apply to many kinds of expressions. Suppose $\mathbf{A}_i$ and $\mathbf{A}_j$ are two expressions of the same type (individual expressions, predicates with the same number of places, or sentences). Then $\mathbf{A}_i$ and $\mathbf{A}_j$ will be said to be *equivalent* if and only if $\mathbf{A}_i \equiv \mathbf{A}_j$ is true, and *L-equivalent* if and only if $\mathbf{A}_i \equiv \mathbf{A}_j$ is L-true.

Employing the concepts of equivalence and L-equivalence Carnap distinguishes three kinds of context.[4] A context $\mathbf{A}_i$ is called *extensional* if every expression $\mathbf{A}_j$ which results from replacing an expression within $\mathbf{A}_i$ by an equivalent expression is equivalent to $\mathbf{A}_i$. Let us call a context $\mathbf{A}_i$ wholly intensional if it contains no extensional context and every expression which results from replacing an expression with $\mathbf{A}_i$ by an L-equivalent expression is L-equivalent to $\mathbf{A}_i$. Carnap then calls any context *intensional* which contains at least one wholly intensional context, and whose other contexts are extensional. As a third case, a context may be neither extensional nor intensional (for example the sentence 'John believes that the moon is made of green cheese').

Analogues of P2 follow immediately. In an extensional context, both equivalent and L-equivalent expressions may be interchanged *salva veritate*. In an intensional context, it is not generally true that equivalent expressions may be interchanged *salva veritate,* but L-equivalent expressions may be interchanged not only *salva veritate,* but *salva L-veritate.*

It will now be apparent that solutions to the paradox of identity and the antinomy of the name-relation are at hand without recourse to expressions of more than one kind. The paradox of identity is solved, for the simplest case, by remarking that in $\mathbf{A}_i \equiv \mathbf{A}_j$, $\mathbf{A}_i$ and $\mathbf{A}_j$ may be equivalent but not L-equivalent. And the failure of the true sentence (1) to remain true when 'the evening star' is put for the first occurrence of 'the morning star' is explained by pointing out that (1) is an intensional context, while 'the morning star' and 'the evening star' are, although equivalent, not L-equivalent.

So far we have seen how a metalanguage armed with the concepts of truth and L-truth could speak of various relations between the expressions of an object language. Now we turn to the problem of providing metalinguistic means for translating the sentences of an object-language. For illustration I shall use Carnap's metalanguage M′, the extensional object-language S_1, and the intensional object-language S_2.[5] A typical

[4] In this informal summary various restrictions and generalizations are suppressed which may be found in [Meaning], §§11, 12.

[5] [Meaning], §§1, 34, 41.

sentence of S_1 is the following, which says that all and only featherless-bipeds are human beings:

(4) $F{\cdot}B \equiv H$.

Since (4) is true, 'F·B' is equivalent to 'H.' The previous sentence (about (4)) is in M′, the metalanguage, and contains the word 'equivalent.' It will be noted that 'equivalent' in M′ in this case expresses a relation between expressions, while the biconditional of (4) stands between expressions whose reference is non-linguistic. Carnap adopts the harmless expedient of using 'equivalent' in M′ also as a translation for '$\equiv$' in S_1; its meaning may be unambiguously determined in a given context by noting whether it stands between expressions which refer to expressions or expressions whose reference is non-linguistic. The translation for 'F·B' in M′ is 'Featherless Biped' and the translation for 'H' is 'Human'; (4) therefore be translated into M′ as:

(5) Featherless Biped is equivalent to Human.

If, with Carnap, we let 'RA' mean 'is a rational animal' in S_1 (translated 'Rational Animal' in M′), then the following is an L-true sentence of S_1:

(6) $RA \equiv H$.

Because S_1 has none but extensional contexts, there is no way to express the analytic character of (6) in S_1. However the analyticity of (6) is explained in M′ by pointing out that 'RA' and 'H' are L-equivalent in S_1. S_2 contains in addition to the resources of S_1 the modal operator 'N' (read 'necessarily'). 'N' is defined on the basis of the notion of state-description; the definition is such that a sentence 'N(A)' of S_2 is true if and only if 'A' is L-true.[6] Since (6) is not only an L-true sentence of S_1 but also of S_2, the following is a true (and L-true) sentence of S_2:

(7) $N(RA \equiv H)$.

There is next the question how (7) is to be translated into M′. No translation of 'N' appears to be needed, for just as 'equivalent' was put to use in translating '$\equiv$' of S_1, so 'L-equivalent' may be put to a new use in translating (7):

(8) Rational Animal is L-equivalent to Human.

It will be observed that (8) is L-true in M′ not because of any fact about S_2 but rather because:

(9) Rational Animal is equivalent to Human

[6] [Meaning], §39. Compare [Modalities], 34.

is L-true in M′. And (9) is L-true in M′ because 'Rational Animal' and 'Human' are L-equivalent in M′.

What has been said of predicates like 'Human' and 'RA' can be applied also to sentences and individual expressions; and what has been shown for '$\equiv$', 'equivalence' and 'L-equivalence' as standing between sentences or expressions referring to sentences can be extended to the conditional, 'implies' and 'L-implies' in similar contexts. Variables have, in part, been surreptitiously dealt with by virtue of the abbreviation which resulted in expressions like '$H \equiv F{\cdot}B$.' Thus the broad outlines of the method of extension and intension have in one sense been sketched.

We have been accepting the concepts of truth and L-truth as undefined primitives; and indeed the reader of [Meaning] must in strictness do this, since neither concept is given a formal definition. If truth and L-truth are taken for granted, then no specific mention need be made of further semantical relations between expressions and the world. It is natural to enquire, however, what the sentences of S_1 and S_2 are true *of*. The following sentence, for example, is a true sentence of M′, and a translation of a true sentence of S_2:[7]

(10) There is an *x* such that *x* is equivalent but not
L-equivalent to the Author of Waverly.

What sort of an entity is it which must exist in order to verify (10)? To answer this question in a general way is just to specify the values of the individual variables of M′ and S_2: these at least are entities which irreducibly are required for sentences of M′ and S_2 to be true.[8] Carnap agrees with Quine's dictum on this point (although he balks at the word 'ontology'):[9] if we are to give an account of truth in terms of reference at all, then we must give an account of the values of variables.

Besides entities which serve as values of individual variables, Carnap also provides entities corresponding to predicates of all kinds (including relations) and entities corresponding to sentences. It is not altogether clear what Carnap's reasons are for postulating these further classes of

[7]Compare [Meaning], 43-4c, 192.

[8]Since Carnap admits type distinctions of variables in M′ but not in S_1 and S_2, these remarks apply only to those variables of M′ with the help of which M′ translates the sentences of S_1 and S_2. We may ignore the question whether a formal definition of 'true in S_1' or 'true in S_2' would require that the variables of the metalanguage range over values unknown to the variables of S_1 and S_2; any such increase in the stock of entities may be accounted to the technical requirements of M′ and not to the subject matter of S_1 and S_2.

[9][Meaning], 10, [Empiricism], 30ff. W. V. Quine, "Notes on Existence and Necessity," *Journal of Philosophy*, XL (1943), 113-127; "On What There Is," *Review of Metaphysics*, II (1948), 21-38. Subsequent references to these and other articles by Quine will, where possible, be made to their reprinted and revised form in *From a Logical Point of View* ([LPV]) (Cambridge, Mass., 1953).

entities; there are, it will turn out, compelling reasons, but these are not the reasons Carnap gives. Before discussing the entities stipulated or required by the method of extension and intension, we must therefore consider briefly what Carnap says about "semantical meaning analysis" in general.

Here it is necessary to depend rather heavily on hints found in Carnap's criticism of Russell's theory of descriptions as a contribution to semantical analysis. According to Russell's theory, most of what would generally count as proper names of individuals and classes, as well as ordinary descriptions, have no meaning in themselves although the sentences in which they occur are meaningful. The theory of descriptions provides (Carnap writes)

> . . . a rule for transforming a sentence containing a description into a sentence with the same meaning which no longer contains the description . . . What the sentence actually means is shown only in its expanded form. . . Although individual expressions and class expressions may, in a certain sense, be regarded as naming individuals or classes, they do not occur in the primitive notation but are incomplete symbols without independent meaning. As nominata in the strict sense, neither individuals nor classes nor truth values occur. . .[10]
>
> The disadvantage of Russell's method lies in the fact that meaning is denied to individual expressions and class expressions. That these kinds of expressions can be introduced by contextual definitions and hence that what is said with their help can also be said without them is certainly a result of greatest importance but does not seem a sufficient justification for excluding these expressions from the domain of semantical meaning analysis. It must be admitted, I think, that descriptions and class expressions do not possess a meaning of the highest degree of independence; but that holds also for all other kinds of expressions except sentences. And it certainly is useful for the semantical analysis of the meanings of sentences to apply that analysis also to the meanings, however derivative, of the other expressions, in order to show how out of them the independent meanings of the sentences are constituted.[11]

There are two points of importance to notice in this passage. The first is that given a semantical theory, such as Russell's, only those expressions can be said to receive semantical meaning analysis relative to that theory which can be *directly* analyzed by the theory. On Russell's theory, a sentence containing a description in unexpanded form cannot be directly analyzed because it does not show variables in the appropriate places. On Carnap's theory, for a different example, individual constants can be directly analyzed because there is always (by fiat) a corresponding individual; descriptions also can be directly analyzed because there is always one and only one individual described. In order to have a terminology, let us say that those sentences which can be semantically analyzed in a semantical theory without transformation are *directly* interpreted (by that

[10] [Meaning], 139.
[11] [Meaning], 140, 141.

theory), while those sentences which cannot be directly interpreted but can be transformed by rule into directly interpreted sentences are *indirectly* interpreted. Expressions which are proper parts of sentences will be considered as interpreted relative both to a theory and a context: expressions are directly or indirectly interpreted according to whether they appear in directly or indirectly interpreted sentences (thus the same expression may be directly interpreted in one context and indirectly interpreted in another).

The second inference we may draw from Carnap's criticism of Russell is this: relative to a given semantical theory, an expression receives a semantical meaning analysis only if the characteristic feature of the method is applied directly to the expression. According to Carnap, Russell's theory is an example of the method of the name-relation. Thus only those expressions are semantically analyzed in the full sense (within that theory) which are treated as names. The method of extension and intension requires that key expressions stand in two relations, designation and L-designation (to be explained), to certain "neutral entities." Within the method of extension and intension, therefore, only those expressions are considered by Carnap to be fully meaningful which have appropriate corresponding entities.

Just what expressions should be given a full semantical meaning analysis is, according to Carnap, "more or less a matter of convention."[12] He applies his method to predicates, individual constants, descriptions, sentences, functors and class expressions, but not to punctuation marks or sentential connectives. Thus the guiding principle is, perhaps, that the more expressions that can be treated as referring in some sense, the better. At any rate, it is clear that Carnap postulates entities for expressions not necessarily because the direct interpretation of the sentences in which they appear demands such entities, but because he considers it a virtue in a semantical theory that whatever basic semantic analysis is accepted for some expressions be applied to as many expressions as possible. No doubt Ryle is right in saying that Carnap, by insisting that every fully meaningful expression correspond to some entity, has accepted one of the most characteristic features of the method of the name-relation.[13] Whether this in itself constitutes a serious defect in Carnap's system is not so evident however. One may well ask what it adds to our understanding of an expression (or ability to "grasp its meaning"[14]) to be told it corresponds to an entity when all we are told of the entity, in effect, is that it is the meaning of the expression. When this is the only

[12] [Meaning], 7.

[13] Gilbert Ryle, "Discussion: Meaning and Necessity," *Philosophy*, XXIV (1949), 69-76. For Carnap's answer, see [Empiricism], §4.

[14] [Meaning], 202.

function served by an entity within the theory then those who wish to be parsimonious may simply reject the entity in question without serious consequences for Carnap's theory. In such a course they may find encouragement in Carnap's remark that sameness of meaning can be explained without any reference to "problematic entities,"[15] provided we understand the concept of truth and L-truth. Once the superfluous entities are weeded out (supposing there are such), the serious question will remain what entities *must* be presupposed in order to interpret the sentences of Carnap's languages.

Leaving aside for the moment the question what entities are indispensable, we may now give a brief account of the entities Carnap specifically postulates. Carnap classifies as *designators* individual constants, descriptions, predicates of all sorts, and sentences (we shall not discuss functors, which are also considered designators by Carnap). Although he denies that these expressions are "names of some entities,"[16] Carnap provides exactly one entity corresponding to each designator. Not every entity has a corresponding expression, but no expression has more than one corresponding entity. We shall call the entities corresponding to individual expressions *individual entities,* those corresponding to predicates *property entities,* and those corresponding to sentences *sentence entities.* In the languages to which Carnap's analysis can be applied, no two distinct individual constants correspond to the same entity. Individual descriptions may correspond to the same entities as individual constants, but many individual descriptions have corresponding entities to which no individual constant corresponds.[17] L-equivalent individual descriptions correspond to the same entity; but no two individual constants are L-equivalent. The range of the (individual) variables constitutes the totality of individual entities corresponding to possible descriptions in the language.[18] There is one sentence entity corresponding to each sentence, and one predicate entity corresponding to each predicate. There is a question, however, whether to two L-equivalent predicates (e.g. 'H' and 'RA') there correspond two, or only one, entities.

Curiously, it is not clear whether Carnap has provided a term to express the relation between a designator and its corresponding entity. Possibly in place of such a term he introduces (without formal definition) two expressions, 'designates' and 'L-designates,' into M′. Entities are equivalent if the corresponding designators are equivalent, L-equivalent

[15] [Meaning], 24, 49.

[16] [Meaning], 7.

[17] This can most clearly be seen from the account of descriptions for S_2 [Meaning], 180, 181. One may assume the same account applies to S_1.

[18] It may exceed this; the exception is unimportant for present purposes. See [Meaning], 181 and [Modalities], 37.

if the corresponding designators are L-equivalent. (Sentences (8) and (9) for example may be taken as saying the property entities Rational Animal and Human are L-equivalent, and equivalent.) The relation of designation is such that an expression designates all entities equivalent to the entity to which the expression corresponds; it follows that if an entity is designated by an expression it is also designated by all equivalent expressions. The relation of L-designation is such that an expression L-designates all entities L-equivalent to the entity to which the expression corresponds; it follows that if an entity is L-designated by an expression it is also L-designated by all L-equivalent expressions.[19] The reason it is uncertain whether L-designation expresses the relation between a designator and its corresponding entity is that unless there is only one entity corresponding to all L-equivalent designators, the same designator may L-designate several entities. Since there is no motive in Carnap's system for discriminating between L-equivalent entities, this complication could easily be eliminated by taking as L-designata classes of all L-equivalent entities.[20] If this is done, L-designation becomes a relation between a designator and exactly one entity.

It is obvious that no such simplification can be performed for designation without introducing new entities of an entirely different sort, e.g. classes of equivalent entities. On the other hand, given the notions of equivalence and L-designation, designation could be defined as follows:

D1. An expression $\mathbf{A}_i$ designates an entity u (of a certain type, in a given language) $=_{\mathrm{Df}}$ there exists an entity v such that $\mathbf{A}_i$ L-designates v, and v is equivalent to u.

Thus while it is easy to arrange that an expression shall L-designate just one entity, nothing short of the wholesale generation of new categories of entities will in general reduce the entities designated by an expression to one.

III

We saw how Frege was led to distinguish between the nominatum and sense of a name, and then to find a name for the sense. If we do not go on to consider the sense of the name which names the sense of the first name then we have, all told, two expressions (or one expression used as two names) and two entities. Let us, without any regard for historical accuracy, call the nominatum of the first name the *extension* of that name, and the sense of that name its *intension*. The second name (or the first in a new context) then has the intension of the first name as its extension.

19[Meaning], 163, 164.

20This suggestion is related to the idea of taking as the entity corresponding to a designator the class of all L-equivalent designators [Meaning], 16, 19, 152).

By analogy, one might distinguish the extension of a predicate (the class of objects to which it applies) from its intension (a property, perhaps), and then hunt for an expression to name the intension of the predicate. If sentences are taken to have truth values as extensions, then their intensions may be propositions. By some such line of reasoning, Carnap argues, adherents to the method of the name-relation have been led to assume at least a duplication of entities (intensions and extensions) in order to explain the semantics of single expressions; and this in turn has led to a duplication of expressions in order to give names to all the entities.

Carnap's method in [Meaning] is to reverse the process. First he shows that a single set of expressions is adequate to refer to two sets of entities; and then he proposes to get along with just the one set of entities which we discussed at the end of the previous section. This may sound like a long trip around Frege's barn only to end up with the naïve version of the name-concept: one entity for each expression. There is, however, one very important consequence of the detour. For while, on the simplest version of the name-relation, the entities named by expressions on the first level are extensions, the entities which correspond to expressions on Carnap's theory cannot be. To consider the case of sentences, sentences which are not L-equivalent correspond to different entities. Thus 'Hs' (meaning 'Scott is human') and '(F•B)s' (meaning 'Scott is a featherless biped'), since they are not L-equivalent, cannot correspond to the same entity. They do, however, have the same truth-value since both are true; consequently they have the same extension. It follows that the entities to which sentences correspond on Carnap's theory cannot be truth-values or extensions. The same reasoning may be applied to predicates and individual expressions. This may be illustrated with respect to individual expressions in the following way. The sentences:

(11) The Author of Waverly is equivalent to Scott

and:

(12) Scott is equivalent to Scott

are true sentences of M′. Sentence (12) is moreover L-true, while (11) is not. Hence:

(13) The Author of Waverly is not L-equivalent to Scott,

(14) Scott is L-equivalent to Scott

are also true sentences of M′. A comparison of (11) and (13) shows that while the entities which correspond to 'the Author of Waverly' and 'Scott' are equivalent, they are not L-equivalent, hence not the same entity.[21] But the extensions of 'Scott' and 'the Author of Waverly' are

[21]See Quine as quoted by Carnap, [Meaning], 196, 197.

supposed to be the same entity, namely the individual Scott, the author of Waverly. Apparently, then, Carnap's individual entities do not include the individual Scott. Since from (11) we may infer:

(15) There is an x such that x is equivalent to Scott,

it might be thought that the individual Scott is at least among the entities which the variables take as values. However, if there is any such value, there is only one, since there is only one individual Scott. But from (11) and (13) together we infer:

(16) There is an x such that x is equivalent but not L-equivalent to Scott.

(17) There is an x such that x is equivalent and also L-equivalent to Scott.

Since it would be contradictory for the same entity to satisfy both (16) and (17), at least two distinct entities are equivalent to Scott, and neither can be the individual Scott.

Sentences (11)–(17) belong to M′, but are translations of sentences in S_2; what has been said of the entities corresponding to the expressions of M′ may therefore also be said of the entities corresponding to the expressions of S_2 of which the expressions in (11)–(17) are translations. The extensional language S_1 contains no sentences corresponding to (13), (14), (16) and (17). It does, however, contain sentences corresponding to (11), (12), and (15), and since these sentences are correctly translated into M′, whatever holds for the variables and designators of M′ must hold for the expressions they translate in S_1. This may be seen directly from the fact that:

's' L-designates Scott

is a true semantical statement (in M′) both of S_1 and S_2, bearing in mind that it is L-designation which assigns to each expression the unique entity to which it corresponds.[22] Thus the entities which correspond to expressions even in an extensional language do not include extensions.

It would be a mistake to imagine that the entities designated by expressions are the extensions of those expressions. Designation differs from L-designation, not in introducing new entities, but in introducing a new relation between expressions and the same entities. The extension of 'Scott' is intended to be that one individual, Scott; but 'Scott' designates each of the entities equivalent to the entity L-designated by 'Scott' (and of these there are at least two). The extension of a predicate like 'Human' is the class of human beings. But 'Human' designates, not a class, but each of the entities equivalent to Human. 'Human' *does* have a class of designata, but this class contains neither the individual Scott, nor any

[22]It is assumed here and henceforth that L-equivalent entities are identified.

of the individual entities designated by 'Scott,' but consists rather of property entities.

We have shown that the entities which in Carnap's semantics correspond to designators can in no case be identified with the extensions of those designators, and that nowhere among those entities are the ordinary individuals of the world to be found. This is not surprising, however, since there is no reason not to identify the sentence entities, property entities and individual entities of which we have been speaking with the intensions of the expressions to which they correspond. This follows simply from the fact that sameness of intension and sameness of corresponding entity are determined for two expressions by precisely the same condition: L-equivalence of the expressions. Carnap avoids *calling* his entities intensions (he calls them 'neutral entities') because he does not wish to give the impression that his languages lack resources for speaking of extensions. But this is a mere matter of vocabulary; so henceforth we may as well use the terminology of intensions when convenient. (Thus individual entities become individual concepts, property entities become properties, and sentence entities become propositions.)[23]

One of the chief merits Carnap claims for the method of extension and intension is that it does not lead to an unnecessary duplication of entities, that is to a need both for intensions and extensions.[24] Since semantics does, according to Carnap, require *some* entities, and these are, as we have shown, not extensions but intensions (or precisely analogous to intensions), the question naturally arises how a language can, on Carnap's analysis, deal with extensions. Here we may concentrate our attention on the extensions of individual expressions, for it seems likely that neither classes nor truth-values are called for in semantics or elsewhere as entities, if properties and propositions are in stock.[25]

Carnap's answer is that although extensions are not among the neutral entities which he postulates, every sentence of S_1 and S_2 as well as of M′ may be interpreted as speaking of individuals, classes, and other extensional entities. He writes:

> In order to see correctly the functions of these languages, and generally of any languages, it is essential to abandon the old prejudice that a predicator must stand either for a class or for a property but cannot stand for both and that an individual expression must stand either for an individual or for an individual concept but cannot stand for both. To understand how language works, we must realize that every designator has both an intension and an extension.[26]

[23]The identification of the neutral entities with intensions is in effect endorsed by Carnap, [Meaning], 154, 157, 199.

[24][Meaning], 2, 17, 24, 91, 145, 146, 203, etc.

[25]Thus [Semantics] takes individual expressions, predicates and sentences as designating individuals, properties, and propositions respectively.

[26][Meaning], 202.

In this passage, Carnap appears to speak of two kinds of entities, for example, individuals and individual concepts. In fact, however, while such formulations

> . . . seem to refer to two kinds of entities . . . no such duplication of entities is presupposed by our method . . . those formulations involve only a convenient duplication of modes of speech. As it was shown to be unnecessary to use different expressions for classes and properties in a symbolic object language, it likewise turned out to be unnecessary to use those pairs of terms in the word language as metalanguage.[27]

The fact that separate expressions for intensions and extensions may be eliminated does not in itself, of course, prove that a similar reduction in entities has taken place, for it may be necessary, in interpreting the expressions which remain, to call upon both kinds of entities. If such a phrase as "an individual expression may stand both for an individual concept and for an individual" is to be understood in accord with Carnap's claims, what is essential is not that it should be rephrased to exclude certain expressions, but that it should be interpreted without reference to two kinds of entities. Since the "neutral" interpretation retains intensional entities, it is the apparent appeal to extensional entities which must be explained away.

Thus the outcome seems to be that although it is important to see that language may be interpreted as speaking about individuals and other extensional entities, this interpretation is unnecessary to our understanding of the language, and may be relegated to an unofficial role. The reason an extensional interpretation is unnecessary is that, according to Carnap, all the distinctions usually drawn by appeal to extensions and intensions may in fact be drawn by appeal to intensions alone. I think it should be agreed that in a certain sense this claim is justified by Carnap's results; let us see in what sense.

It has often been pointed out that many of the purposes served by postulating meanings or intensions could be as well served by appeal to a concept of sameness of meaning or intension.[28] Although this is not true for Carnap's purposes, something analogous does hold: given the notion of sameness of extension, it is possible to do without direct appeal to extensions as entities. Sameness of extension is, in turn, explicable in terms of equivalence; expressions have the same extension if and only if they are equivalent. Thus the problems of semantical interpretation come, in Carnap's method, to depend upon intensions as entities, and the concept of equivalence.

The technical elimination of extensions achieved in this way is a success, of course, only as long as no attempt is made to explain the no-

[27] [Meaning], 203.

[28] See Quine, [LPV], esp. Essays I and II.

tion of equivalence. The assertion that "individual expressions are equivalent if and only if they are expressions for the same individual" and the related "rule of truth" which introduces '≡' between individual expressions cannot be accepted since they depend on extensions as entities.[29] The bi-conditional sign between predicates and sentences is defined in terms of the rules of truth; but these include essentially a rule for atomic sentences which reads: "An atomic sentence in S_1 consisting of a predicate followed by an individual constant is true if and only if the individual to which the individual constant refers possesses the property to which the predicate refers."[30] This could be legitimatized, but to no avail for the analysis of equivalence, as: "An atomic sentence in S_1 . . . is true if and only if all individual concepts equivalent to the individual concept corresponding to the individual constant possess all the properties equivalent to the property corresponding to the predicate."

Since the distinction between extensions and intensions is reflected by the distinction between designation and L-designation, and designation does not, as we have seen, introduce extensions as entities, the extensional side of Carnap's method could be made to rest on the notion of designation. Equivalence between entities (intensions) would be explained as holding when the entities were designated by the same expressions, while those expressions would be equivalent which designated equivalent entities. Such a course, it is plain, would leave us in the dark if we wanted to state the conditions under which two entities were designated by the same expression. To take an example, consider what may be said about the extension of the expression 's' in S_1 or S_2. Neutrality rules out the statement 'The extension of 's' is the individual Scott'; we may however "translate" this into M′ as:[31]

(18) 's' designates Scott.

If we wish to know how to interpret (18), Carnap provides us with:[32]

(19) The extension of 'Scott' in M′ is the individual Scott.

In the light of (19) we may be tempted to suppose (18) tells us that the expression 's' in S_1 or S_2 designates the individual Scott; but this supposition is consistent neither with the neutrality of M′ nor with the interpretation of designation. For if 's' designates the individual Scott, it can designate no other individual wthout ambiguity, while if appeal to individuals as entities must be made to interpret (18), then M′ is not truly neutral. Either (18) or (19) therefore is misleading; either (18) tacitly

29[Meaning], 14, 15.
30[Meaning], 5.
31[Meaning], §37, 37-14.
32[Meaning], 154, 34-3.

refers to the individual Scott while purporting to be neutral, or (19) appears to refer to the individual Scott while in fact it does not. The character of (18) is better brought out by the logically equivalent sentence:[33]

(20) For every *x*, 's' designates *x* if and only if *x* is equivalent to Scott.

But (20), while it reveals what (18) does not (the conditions under which two entities are designated by the same expression), makes use of the notion of equivalence.

To summarize the foregoing discussion: the elimination of a duality of types of entities can be accomplished in Carnap's method if intensions and the notion of equivalence are taken as given. But in the final analysis, equivalence (or sameness of extension, or designation) can be understood only by appeal to such extensional entities as the individual Scott. This appeal may be left tacit by employing metalanguages which, like their object languages, are capable of neutral interpretation; but this only postpones the problem of explaining equivalence. Thus the official neutrality of the method of extension and intension may always be maintained by holding off explicit reference to extensions until the level of an unofficial metalanguage is reached. Once the reference to extensions is made, however, its force seeps back through every level *via* the concepts of equivalence and designation. Whether one wants to call this a genuine "reduction of entities" is a matter of terminology.

We have seen how, according to Carnap, every sentence, whether it appears to speak of intensions or of extensions, may be given an interpretation in terms of intensional entities. If this is done, the evidence that no important distinctions have been lost rests in part on the fact that those sentences which appear to speak of extensional entities may, if we want, be interpreted in the ordinary extensional way. In response to Quine's criticism that in Carnap's modal language the individual variables take intensions only as values and that therefore "the individuals of the concrete world have disappeared,"[34] Carnap answers that

> ... there is no objection against regarding designators in a modal language as names of intensions and regarding variables as having intensions as values, provided we are not misled by this formulation into the erroneous conception that the extensions have disappeared from the universe of discourse of the language. . . .[35]

All the sentences of S_1 (which is extensional) appear, unaltered, in S_2 (which is modal); since these sentences are clearly capable of interpreta-

[33] [Meaning], 164, 34-17.

[34] Quine, quoted in [Meaning], 197. Quine also comments on this point in [LPV], Essay VIII, and "Three Grades of Modal Involvement," *Actes du XI ème Congrès International de Philosophie,* XIV, 65-81.

[35] [Meaning], 199.

tion in terms of extensions in S_1, they remain so when they are transplanted to S_2: "nothing in the semantical analysis . . . needs to be different."[36] The dualism is, in fact, complete. Not only are extensional sentences, whether in an extensional or intensional language, capable of both an extensional and intensional interpretation; the same holds for intensional sentences.[37]

It is central to the method of extension and intension that a double interpretation of all designators (including sentences) be possible; and if extensions are to remain in the official ontology it is necessary. If extensions really have not "disappeared from the universe of discourse of the language," if it is correct to say (in any ordinary sense) that one expression can "speak about," "refer to," or "stand for" both its extension and its intension,[38] then both extensions and intensions must be admitted as entities. It is time to consider therefore what the method of extension and intension is like if extensions are given equal status with intensions.

Giving extensions equal status with intensions means showing how each sentence may be interpreted twice, once in terms of the extensions of the expressions in the sentence, and once in terms of the intensions in the sentence. It is not sufficient merely to demonstrate that sentences as a whole may be given two interpretations; both interpretations must be *direct* in the sense of showing how the meaning of the sentences as a whole follows from the meanings of the other designators. Otherwise the method of extension and intension fails to assign both an extensional and intensional meaning to every designator in accord with Carnap's criteria of semantical meaning analysis.

First let us consider some typical extensional sentences of S_1 and S_2 and see how they may be interpreted. '$RA \equiv H$' (sentence (6)) for example may be interpreted as saying that the class Rational Animal and the class Human are identical; or that the property Rational Animal and the property Human are equivalent. It is important to notice that the two interpretations demand two interpretations of the non-designator '$\equiv$'; as a consequence the two predicators must both be interpreted in the same way. The sentence as a whole must be interpreted extensionally or intensionally.

Similar considerations apply to:

(21) Hs.

This may be interpreted as saying that the individual Scott belongs to the class Human; or that the individual concept Scott is subsumable un-

36[Meaning], 201.

37Although the extensional interpretation of modal sentences is possible, Carnap believes it is 'dangerous.' [Meaning], 189.

38[Meaning], 2, 199, 202.

der the property Human.[39] In (21) juxtaposition expresses the relation between the entities referred to by 'H' and 's,' and this relation is different depending upon whether we give an extensional or intensional interpretation of the designators. Carnap contemplates the possibility of "mixed" interpretations for such sentences as (21), but as this would demand a further stock of odd relations between entities for which no explanation is offered, and there is no evidence such mixed interpretations could be systematically developed for other sentences (for example (6)), it seems best to ignore all but homogeneously extensional or intensional interpretations.

As it is, the relation expressed by the phrase 'subsumable under' is far from clear. It cannot be the relation between an entity and a property which that entity has, since the intension of 'H' is a property of individuals, not concepts. Indeed if the properties of individuals were also the properties of individual concepts, this would amount exactly to what Carnap calls hypostatization: "mistaking as things entities which are not things."[40] Despite this warning, Carnap does say that a description in S_2 "characterizes, not one individual concept, but mutually equivalent individual concepts–in other words, one individual" and speaks of an individual concept as "possessing the descriptional property."[41]

In any case, (21) cannot be taken as a statement about one individual concept, but must be interpreted as a statement about all individual concepts equivalent to the individual concept Scott. The point may be brought out by studying some definitions by means of which Carnap shows how apparently explicitly extensional words like 'individual' and 'class' can be introduced into (and hence eliminated from) a language previously lacking such terms.[42] His definitions are formulated for the translation part of M′, but may be applied as well to S_2 and, in some cases, to S_1. The definition for introducing the expression 'ind a' ('the individual a') would be:

D2. $\ldots \text{ind a} \ldots =_{Df} (x)\,[(x \equiv \text{a}) \supset \ldots x \ldots]$.

What is interesting about D2 is not its ability to introduce 'ind a' into a language which lacks it but its ability to transform sentences which do not contain 'ind a' into others which also do not, but which are of a different logical form. This may be shown as follows.

(22) $(x)\,[(x \equiv \text{a}) \supset (x \equiv \text{a})]$

is an obvious logical truth. Applying D2 to (22), we get:

(23) $\text{ind a} \equiv \text{a}$.

39Cf. [Meaning], 42.
40[Meaning], 22.
41[Meaning], 185.
42[Meaning], 159, 160, cf. 151.

Since (23) is transformed from a logical truth, it must be logically true; hence 'ind a' and 'a' are L-equivalent and have the same extension and intension. By the same token, 'ind s' and 's' are L-equivalent, and 'H ind s' is L-equivalent to 'Hs.' By D2, 'H ind s' becomes:

(24) $(x)\,[\,(x \equiv \text{s}) \supset \text{H}\,x\,].$

Comparing (21) with (24) we now see that (21), from the point of view of an intensional analysis, conceals its logical form: it is actually a universal sentence in disguise. Since it lacks the universal quantifier which in (24) provides explicit reference to every individual concept fulfilling a certain condition, (21) cannot be *directly* interpreted in terms of the intensions of the expressions which appear in it alone. (21) is *indirectly* interpreted by transforming it into the L-equivalent sentence (24) which is directly interpreted (in terms of intensions). Actually, (24) still does not "show" its intensional form completely: to achieve this, a further transformation is needed to care for 'H':

(25) $(x)\,(f)\,[(x \equiv \text{s}) \cdot (f \equiv \text{H}) \supset f\,x].$

Here *f* must be taken as ranging over properties. Therefore, the direct intensional interpretation of extensional sentences demands that among the entities available as values of variables we find, not merely individual concepts, but also properties. Similar reasoning would reveal the necessity for propositions as values of other variables. It cannot be considered an accidental feature of the method of extension and intension that it posits every brand of intensional entity.

Sentences like (6) must also be rewritten in the spirit of (25) before they can be directly interpreted in terms of intensional entities: (6) asserts a relation between the intensions of 'H' and 'RA' only by way of asserting that all properties equivalent to the property Human are also equivalent to the property Rational Animal. In general, sentences which lend themselves to direct extensional interpretation cannot be given a direct intensional interpretation; there exist L-equivalent sentences into which they may be transformed (given definitions like D2) which can be directly interpreted intensionally.

Now we may turn to the analysis of a typical intensional sentence. Let '$\equiv$' be a sign for L-equivalence of entities in S_2 and let 's_1' and 's_2' abbreviate two L-equivalent descriptions of Scott which are equivalent, but not L-equivalent, to 's.' Then we have as a true sentence:

(26) $s_1 \equiv s_2.$

This may be interpreted directly as saying that two individual concepts are identical. Can it be interpreted as saying the individuals which are the respective extensions of 's_1' and 's_2' are L-equivalent? The difficulty is, of course, that the individual which is the extension of 's_1' is identical with the individual which is the extension of 's'; but we cannot conclude '$s \equiv s_2$' without contradicting the assumption that 's' and 's_2' are not L-equivalent. Nor is the difficulty due merely to a provincialism in our ordinary way of thinking. Suppose we consider that 's_1' in (26) refers to an individual. Then (26) says of this individual that he is characterized by being L-equivalent to the entity to which 's_2' refers; in other words if 's_1' refers to an entity, the rest of (26) may be treated as a predicate. Following the reasoning which led from (21) to (24), we may now apply D2 to (26) to obtain:

(27) $(x)\ [\ (x \equiv s_1) \supset (x \equiv s_2)\ ].$

This is clearly false, however, as may be seen by taking 'x' as 's.' This shows we cannot give a direct interpretation of (26) in terms of extensions. Carnap prevents results like (27) by requiring that the transforming definitions be applied to the smallest sentence or matrix in the primitive notation in which the expression to be transformed occurs. (26) is not in primitive notation, since '$\equiv$' is defined in terms of the operator 'N.' If (26) is changed to:

(28) $N\ (s_1 \equiv s_2)$

then application of D2 leads harmlessly to:

(29) $N\ (x)\ [\ (x \equiv s_1) \supset (x \equiv s_2\ ].$

The necessity of eliminating modal connectives in favor of the modal operator 'N' before making transformations of the sort allowed by D2 indicates clearly why sentences like (26) which contain modal connectives cannot be directly interpreted in terms of extensions.

Since 'N' cannot in Carnap's theory be taken as a semantical predicate applicable to names of sentences, neither (28) nor (29) can be interpreted extensionally. In (29) the variables must take as values individual concepts; this holds for the variables in modal sentences generally.[43] Both (28) and (29) may be directly interpreted intensionally, the effect of the 'N' being to change the main connective into the corresponding modal connective. (Thus the direct intensional interpretation of (28) is identical with that of (26).)

We may now survey our findings with respect to the types of sentences we have considered. Ordinary extensional sentences like (4), (6) and (21) may be directly interpreted extensionally but not intensionally and may be transformed into sentences which are directly interpretable in terms of intensional entities. Intensional sentences on the other hand may be directly interpreted intensionally but have no genuine interpretation in

[43] [Meaning], 180.

terms of extensional entities. If we disregard such peculiar and dispensable sentences as (25) and consider only ordinary extensional sentences and ordinary extensional sentences preceded by one or more occurrences of 'N', then the situation is very simple: extensional sentences may be directly interpreted extensionally, and extensionally only; intensional sentences may be interpreted intensionally, and intensionally only. We here come back, in fact, to Frege. For now we are free to interpret '$\equiv$' uniformly as a sign for identity, identity of extensions in extensional sentences, identity of intensions in sentences ruled by 'N'. The force of the 'N' then becomes, as in Frege, to change the reference of the designating expressions which it governs. The only difference, so far, is this: for Carnap, iteration of the sign for logical necessity has no effect at all, while on Frege's theory each additional 'N' drives the entities to which the affected designating expressions refer a level higher in the realm of intensions.

This simple Fregean version of the method of extension and intension may be maintained only by excluding sentences which, unlike those we have been discussing, allow quantifiers outside to bind variables within modal contexts. For sentences like (10), (16), (17) and (27) (and the symbolic translations of the first three into S_2) there is no direct interpretation possible either in terms of extensions or intensions. The variables in such sentences must, in order to do their duty through the intensional part of their careers, take as values intensions; this rules out the possibility of extensional interpretations. But the extensional portions of such sentences, while spoiled for extensional interpretation by the presence of tainted variables,[44] cannot be directly interpreted intensionally. For example, the first segment of:

(30) $(\exists x)\ [(x \equiv s) \cdot \sim N\ (x \equiv s)]$.

says there exists an entity equivalent to Scott. Since in the light of the rest of (30) this entity cannot be the individual Scott, the first part of (30) must be read 'There exists an individual concept equivalent to the individual concept Scott.' And this, spelled out with the help of D2 into a form which reveals its intensional structure, becomes:

$$(\exists x)(y)\ [(y \equiv s) \supset (x \equiv y)].$$

The Fregean conception of 'N' as an operator which changes the reference of the referring expressions in the context it governs cannot be applied to sentences like (30), for in (30) 'N' influences the interpretation of the quantifier which precedes it and thereby of all the designators in the

[44] This argument does not apply to sentences in which all quantifiers standing outside, and binding variables within, modal contexts fail to bind variables outside the modal contexts.

sentence. A further consequence is that both occurrences of '≡' in (30) cannot be interpreted in the same way.

Much more serious is the fact that once modal operators are allowed, by way of antecedent quantifiers, to force an intensional interpretation on apparently extensional contexts, a doubt is cast on the propriety of an extensional interpretation for any sentence. Even a sentence like 'Hs' for example is always in danger of being used, in conjunction with '∼N(Hs)', as the basis of an inference to:

(31) $(\exists x)\ [Hx \cdot \sim N\ (Hx)]$.

But this inference is sustained only on the assumption that 's' in 'Hs' as in '∼N (Hs)' refers to an intensional entity.

The symmetry between extensions and intensions which the method of extension and intension seems to assume is thus incomplete. If 'Hs' is asked to support an inference to '$(\exists x)\ (Hx)$' we have, perhaps, a choice of intensional and extensional interpretations of 's.' But if 'Hs' is asked to help support an inference to (31) we have no such choice. Once quantification and the modalities are allowed to intermix, only an intensional interpretation can be consistently maintained even for apparently extensional sentences. Under these circumstances, Quine's law appears to hold: intensions drive out extensions.[45]

IV

We are now in a position to compare more narrowly the method of the name-relation and the method of extension and intension. In the previous section, we considered two alternative versions of Carnap's semantical method. These may be summarized as follows:

Version 1. According to this version (which was the second to be discussed) every designator refers both to an extensional entity and to an intensional entity. Carnap appears to claim that every sentence can be directly interpreted in terms of the intensions of the designators therein and also in terms of the extensions of the designators it contains, but this does not seem to be correct. Ordinary extensional sentences may be interpreted directly in terms of extensions but only indirectly in terms of intensional entities; intensional sentences may be directly interpreted intensionally but not extensionally. Sentences which quantify from outside into modal contexts must be given a uniformly intensional interpretation.

Version 2. According to the other version (which is not stressed in [Meaning] but apparently represents Carnap's final word) intensions

45 [LPV], 157.

alone are admitted as entities (they are called, in this version, "neutral entities"); extensions are retained, if at all, in the ontology of some unofficial metalanguage where they do service by explaining such official terms as 'equivalent,' 'designates,' and 'have the same extension.'

Since Version 1 and Version 2 correspond in a rough way to Course 1 and Course 2 which suggested themselves earlier as possible simplifications of Frege's theory, it is now reasonable to inquire in what sense the method of extension and intension is not itself an example of the method of the name-relation. Course 1 grants that the same expression may refer to different entities in different contexts, but it eliminates the need for an infinite hierarchy of entities and names by denying that intensions require any other names than the expressions which name them in intensional contexts. The kinds of entities may, in fact, be limited to just two by lumping all intensional contexts together. Version 1 of Carnap's method is similar in essential respects; indeed, as we saw in the last section, it may be considered as exactly the same as Course 1 up to the point where sentences are introduced in which quantifiers outside modal contexts bind variables within. Beyond this point there are certain differences, but the differences are not so great as to obscure the basic resemblance: like Course 1, Version 1 of the method of extension and intension abandons the notion that a referring expression always refers to the same entity. In consequence, principles P2 and P3 (or their analogues in Carnap's theory) assume a modified form. Related modifications are, of course, explicit in Frege's original theory, and Carnap considers that Frege's theory is an example of the method of the name relation.[46] If Carnap's method is to be interpreted along the lines of Version 1, therefore, it is difficult to see why it is not as good a representative of the method of the name-relation as Frege's theory.

Course 2, like Version 2 of Carnap's method, depends upon altering P2 and P3 to allow different rules of substitution in different contexts for certain expressions, while the entities to which those expressions correspond remain unchanged. This approach allows the distinction between intensions and extensions to be dropped entirely; expressions come unequivocally to refer to one entity. In one respect, therefore, Course 2 in Carnap's hands is even more like the unmodified method of the name-relation than Frege's system, for it retains the key notion that the same expression always refers to the same entity. On the other hand it will be granted that by retaining this notion, the alteration required in P2 and P3 is, in effect, more serious.

46[Meaning], 143. There is a slight puzzle here for the reader: Carnap implies that Frege's theory is consistent with the principles of the name-relation (143), and that Frege's theory avoids the antinomy of the name-relation (136); however, the principles of the name-relation permit the antinomy to arise (133).

So far no clear reason has emerged for not viewing the method of extension and intension as a variant of the method of the name-relation, as least as closely wedded to the principles of the name relation as Frege's method. Carnap is however exercised to demonstrate that anyone who adheres, even in a general way, to the method of the name-relation will be led into certain confusions and difficulties which his method avoids. We shall now examine briefly Carnap's three main arguments to this effect.

1. According to Carnap,[47] the method of the name-relation "involves an essential ambiguity." The ambiguity arises from the fact that the same expression, embedded in the same, interpreted, language can be analyzed in two ways, each in accord with the principles of the method of the name-relation, and yet such that the two analyses are mutually inconsistent. For example, in the sentence 'Joyce is jolly' 'jolly' may be taken either as the name of a class or as the name of a property. But an expression used as a name must, according to the theory, name exactly one entity (at least in a given context).

In 'Joyce is jolly,' the word 'jolly' may indeed be taken as naming a class provided 'is' means 'is a member of the class of those who are,' or as naming a property in case 'is' means 'has the property of being.' But the ambiguity of 'jolly' thus adduced depends on the accidental ambiguity of 'is'; once the latter ambiguity is eliminated, the former cannot arise.

Carnap tries to show how the ambiguity can exist even in an artificial language, taking as example a sentence like:

(32) $(x)\,(\mathrm{H}x \supset \mathrm{R}x)$.

A partisan of the method of the name-relation will find, Carnap argues, that he may interpret (32) either as saying something about properties ('everything that has the property of being human has the property of being rational') or as saying something about classes ('the class of humans is included in the class of rational beings'). The correctness of the second interpretation is brought out, Carnap believes, by observing that in an appropriately constructed language, (32) is L-equivalent to:

(33) $\hat{x}\,(\mathrm{H}x) \subset \hat{x}\,(\mathrm{R}x)$.

Thus, Carnap concludes, the method of the name-relation leads to the possibility of taking 'H' and 'R' either as names of properties or names of classes. But does this conclusion, which Carnap says follows, really follow from its premises?

There is no doubt that in an appropriately constructed language (33) is L-equivalent to (32) and therefore, in some sense, "says the same thing." Thus a correct interpretation of (32) is a correct interpretation of (33) and

47 [Meaning], §25.

vice versa. There are two identical pairs of correct interpretations for (32) and (33): one interpretation (of both sentences) has it that everything with the property Human has the property Rational; the other interpretation has it that the class of humans is included in the class of rational beings. Clearly the two interpretations are correct for each sentence simply *because* they are two ways of saying the same thing. But if both interpretations are correct for both sentences, we don't need both interpretations any more than we need both sentences; (32) alone says whatever we could say with (33), and one interpretation says, in other words, what the other does.

But the fact that (33) is logically equivalent to (32) has no tendency to show that 'R' stands for one thing in (32) and another in (33), nor that it stands for two things in either sentence. Indeed, the L-equivalence of the two sentences depends upon 'R' and 'H' each meaning in (33) what it meant in (32). If 'R' and 'H' refer to properties in (32), they still do in (33). The fact that (32) may be correctly interpreted as saying one class is included in another is not due to 'R' and 'H' coming to refer to classes, but to the fact, if we want to put it that way, that (32) is L-equivalent to (33). The two interpretations of (32) are not two interpretations of the individual expressions taken one by one, but two interpretations of the sentence *as a whole.* One interpretation (in terms of properties) is a direct interpretation of (32) and an indirect interpretation of (33); the other (in terms of classes) gives a direct interpretation of (33) and an indirect interpretation of (32); but the very fact that only contextual definition relates (32) to (33) shows that whatever simple semantic correlation is set up betwen expressions and classes will not work also for the same expressions and properties. There is, in eliminating sentences like (33) in favor of sentences like (32), a genuine economy of expression and conceptual apparatus. This is due, not to making the same expressions mean two *different* things, but to showing that two apparently different interpretations of the entire sentence mean the *same* thing.

It is possible, then, to give two interpretations of sentences like (32) and (33) as a whole without implying that inconsistent or even different interpretations are being given for the expressions which occur in those sentences. Carnap's case against the method of the name-relation must turn, therefore, on taking the *same* expressions as names of different entities while relying on no ambiguity in the text. In English eligible expressions might be such predicates as 'is red'; in Carnap's languages, predicates like 'H.' But now, is it possible to apply the method of the name-relation to these expressions in such a way that, in any given context, an ambiguity arises? It will be agreed, I imagine, that the fact that 'H' or 'is red' may be construed either as the name of a class or of a property represents no real ambiguity if there is no difference between classes and properties. The difficulty we noted before in English that the grammar of class expressions and property expressions differs, has now disappeared, since we are considering 'is red' as a potential name rather than 'red.' Carnap assumes that classes and properties differ in that classes are identical if their members are identical, while properties may apply to the same objects and yet be discrete. Where does this difference show itself? Suppose, for example, we take 'is red' as the name of a class in a given language S. Then, according to P2 any other name of the same class may be put for 'is red' in any sentence in S, *salva veritate*. If some such substitution fails, but none does if we take 'is red' as naming a property, then the ambiguity of interpretation is settled in favor of the property. Suppose, on the other hand, that every context in S containing 'is red' is extensional. Then no ambiguity results from saying 'is red' is either the name of a class or a property, since the class and the property may be identified. By excluding non-extensional contexts we exclude all contexts which might show a difference between the two interpretations. For the accusation of ambiguity to carry weight, there must be some possibility of error or confusion. We conclude that in contexts in which it makes a difference whether a predicate names a class or a property, two analyses are not possible on the basis of the method of the name-relation; while in contexts in which both analyses are possible, no genuine ambiguity arises.

2. A second disadvantage of the method of the name-relation, Carnap contends, is that it leads to an unnecessary duplication of names in the object-language.[48] Consider the two sentences (which cannot be formulated in this way in M′), S_1 or S_2:

(34) The class of human beings is identical with the class of featherless bipeds,

(35) The property of being a human is not identical with the property of being a featherless biped.

If we interpret identity in the same way in (34) and (35) and agree that both sentences are true, then it cannot be the case that the expressions 'the class of human beings' and 'the property of being a human' name the same thing and the expressions 'the class of featherless bipeds' and 'the property of being a featherless biped' name the same thing. Here we have, then, necessarily distinct names for classes and properties. The question is, in what sense is this duplication unnecessary? On some appropriate theory (34) and (35) can be expressed as:

(36) $(x)\ [(\mathrm{F}\cdot\mathrm{B})\ x \equiv \mathrm{H}x]$

(37) $\mathrm{N}\ (x)\ [(\mathrm{F}\cdot\mathrm{B})\ x \equiv \mathrm{Hx}]$

[48] [Meaning], §26.

And if these are interpreted in accord with the "neutral" version of the method of extension and intension, then (36) and (37) contain only two name-like expressions, 'F·B' and 'H,' which in both (36) and (37) refer to the same respective entities (properties). Since (36) and (37) do express whatever is expressed by (34) and (35), and the former pair of sentences may be interpreted as containing only two names while the latter pair contains four names, it may be urged that (34) and (35) require a duplication of names which is eliminated in (36) and (37).

While this is an economy, it may be questioned whether it is an *overall* economy. There remain two ways of speaking, and the economy in referring expressions is bought at the expense, in this case, of an addition to the basic logical vocabulary: and at the further expense of eliminating expressions which refer to extensions. It could be argued with equal justice, it seems, that the method of extension and intension leads to an unnecessary duplication of connectives.

If we interpret (36) and (37) as suggested by Version 1 of Carnap's method, the savings in referring expressions is only apparent, for 'F·B' and 'H' refer to classes in the direct interpretation of (36) and properties in the direct interpretation of (37). It is no great economy to make one expression do the work of two if there are really two kinds of work to be done. In the light of this consideration Church has proposed that in an artificial language it would be clearer to have different expressions for referring to intensions and extensions.[49] The elimination of duplication represented by letting (32) do the work of (33) is due to the fact that there was only one job that needed doing; but for the expressions which recur in (36) and (37) no such genuine elimination of dual interpretation is possible, for there are two sorts of jobs to be done.

Carnap shows, quite correctly, that there is an unnecessary duplication in *Principia Mathematica,* which contains names both of classes and of properties. But success in the elimination of *this* duplication is due, not to abandoning the method of the name-relation, but to the fact that mathematics as constructed in *Principia Mathematica* is in essence extensional, and hence there is no essential need for distinguishing properties from classes.

3. The third debility which Carnap considers intrinsic to the method of the name-relation is connected with the antinomy of the name-relation. If the principles of the name-relation are accepted without restriction, the antinomy arises once non-extensional contexts appear; while if the principles are modified along standard lines to do least violence to

[49] Alonzo Church, Review of Quine's "Notes on Existence and Necessity," *Journal of Symbolic Logic,* VIII (1943), 46, and "A Formulation of the Logic of Sense and Denotation" ([Formulation]) in *Structure, Method and Meaning: Essays in Honor of Henry M. Sheffer,* Henle, Kallen, Langer, eds. (New York, 1951).

P2 the complications of Frege and Church result. It is bootless to worry whether Carnap's or Frege's system (as interpreted by Church) has closer blood ties with the original name-concept, especially failing a definitive reading of the method of extension and intension. Both systems are a far cry from the simplest conception of the relations between words and their objects; both systems require what are really formidable alterations in the principles of the name-relation, as well as a totally revised view (for Church and Carnap) as to which expressions are to be considered referring expressions. Carnap will perhaps grant that the difficulties he raises for adherents to the method of the name-relation are not intrinsic to the method, but temptations in its practice.[50] At any rate it does not seem clear that the ambiguities, duplications and antinomies with which Carnap charges the method are not as well resolved by the Frege-Church approach as by his own.

V

But whether or not Carnap's method differs from the others in the ways he emphasizes, there can be no doubt it differs from the others in a very important respect. In order to bring out this respect, we need a rude classification of semantical systems.[51] Some systems accept no distinction between reference and meaning (or extension and intension, or sense and nominatum) at all. For such systems there is reference alone. Other systems admit a distinction, but deny that having a meaning or intension involves an entity, and therefore deny the existence of expressions which refer to such entities. Systems of both these types we may call first level semantical systems. Some systems, like those of Church and Frege, involve an infinite series of interlocking levels of expressions and entities, with the entities on each but the ground level serving as the senses of some (possible) expressions and the nominata of other (possible) expressions. Such systems we may say have an infinity of semantical levels. Finally, it would in theory be possible to stop the series at some point by denying to the expressions at some level either a sense or a nominatum, an extension or an intension. Such a system would be an n-level semantical system, where n is the number of levels of entities. It should be observed that this classification has nothing to do with the kinds of entities involved (except that some must be meanings or intensions when the system is more than first level); and that the attainment of levels above the second depends entirely on the fact that some entities serve both as extensions and as intensions.

50[Meaning], 110, 111, 127-129.

51For further discussion of this, or a closely related classification, see Church, [Abstract Entities], 111.

Carnap's method of extension and intension is, as its name perhaps suggests, a two-level semantical system. According to one interpretation, expressions refer, either simultaneously or on occasion, both to intensions and to extensions. According to the other interpretation, the expressions to which the semantical method is directly applied refer to one sort of entity only, and these entities are not on the ground level. But tacit reference is made to ground level entities (individuals, for example) in accounting for the basic notions of equivalence and truth; and it is essential that whole sentences may be construed as speaking of ground level entities. Thus on either interpretation, the method of extension and intension really admits entities on two semantic levels. The important difference between Carnap's system and Frege's is not that one is more like the unmitigated method of the name-relation than the other, but that Carnap's system has two levels while Frege's has infinitely many.

No doubt of two otherwise resembling semantical systems a two-level system is far simpler (since infinitely more parsimonious of expressions and entities) than a system with an infinity of levels, provided the two-level system can solve the relevant puzzles and problems equally well, and provided it does not introduce additional complications to outweigh its advantages. It is into such matters that we shall now make brief inquiry, taking as the relevant puzzle the paradox of analysis and as the relevant problem the analysis of belief sentences.

The method of extension and intension and Frege's method lead to closely related solutions of the paradox of identity. Thus if 'a' and 'b' are individual expressions, Frege explains the difference between 'a = b' when true and 'a = a' by pointing out that 'a' and 'b' may name the same thing but have different senses. Carnap explains the same difference by showing that while 'a = a' is L-true, 'a = b' may, although true, not be L-true; this happens if 'a' and 'b' are equivalent but not L-equivalent.

A paradox analogous to the paradox of identity is easily produced on the second level. Consider the two sentences:

(38) The concept Brother is identical with the concept Male Sibling,

(39) The concept Brother is identical with the concept Brother.

In terms of the theory of the name-relation, the paradox may be stated in this way: the phrases 'the concept Brother' and 'the concept Male Sibling' have as nominata the same entity (which is, perhaps, the common sense or intension of 'brother' and 'male sibling'). Since (38) is true, the two phrases name the same entity; therefore the meaning of (38) will remain unchanged if one phrase replaces the other to produce (39). But (38) is informative, while (39) is not. This is the paradox of analysis.[52] Within

[52]For references, see [Meaning], 63.

the general scope of Frege's system an obvious solution is available, in effect the same solution which met the paradox of identity. For while in (38) and (39) the expressions 'the concept Brother' and 'the concept Male Sibling' have the same nominatum, they may not have the same sense.[53]

The paradox of analysis may easily be set forth in Carnap's terms. We may translate (38) and (39) into:

(40) Brother is L-equivalent to Male Sibling

(41) Brother is L-equivalent to Brother.

Since (40) is true, 'Brother' and 'Male Sibling' are L-equivalent (i.e., have the same intension). But L-equivalent expressions can be substituted for one another in a context without changing its intension; (41) is thus L-equivalent to (40). How then can (40) and (41) differ in meaning since one results from the other merely by replacing an expression by another with the same intension? The method of extension and intension cannot meet this paradox as it did the paradox of identity, because 'Brother' and 'Male Sibling' have the same intensions in (40) and (41) and therefore not only are equivalent but also are L-equivalent. The solution to the paradox of identity was forthcoming, both for Frege and Carnap, by virtue of the distinction between first and second level entities; where third level entities are available as in the Frege-Church theory a perfectly analogous solution to the paradox of analysis is possible; but such an analogous solution is automatically forestalled in a system like Carnap's which lacks third level entities.

To deal with the paradox of analysis, Carnap defines a stronger relation between expressions than L-equivalence which he calls *intensional isomorphism*. Roughly speaking, two expressions $\mathbf{A}_i$ and $\mathbf{A}_j$ are intensionally isomorphic if $\mathbf{A}_j$ may be obtained from $\mathbf{A}_i$ by performing the following operations: (a) replacing a simple designator (a designator containing no variables and no designator as proper part) in $\mathbf{A}_i$ by another simple designator to which it is L-equivalent, and (b) replacing a predicate (or sentential connective) with an L-equivalent predicate, provided the order of the argument expressions is unchanged.[54] The following are examples of pairs of intensionally isomorphic expressions: 'Greater than (a,b)' and 'a > b'; 'Conj (Hs, (F•B)s)' and 'RAs • (F•Bs).' The following are examples of pairs of expressions which are L-equivalent but not intensionally isomorphic:

[53] The fact that "the paradox of analysis is a special case of Frege's puzzle [the paradox of identity] and is to be solved in the same way, on Frege's theory of meaning" was pointed out by Church in a review *Journal of Symbolic Logic,* XI (1946), 132, 133.

[54] Carnap's more precise and general characterization, [Meaning], p. 59, is intended to apply also to cases where the expressions $\mathbf{A}_i$ and $\mathbf{A}_j$ belong to different languages. For the purpose of this characterization sentential connectives may be considered as predicates with sentences or sentential matrices as their argument expressions.

'a > b' and 'b < a'; 'RAs · (F·B)s' and '(F·B)s · RAs'; '3 + 4 = 11' and '7 = 11.'

The paradox of analysis, as it arises with respect to (40) and (41), is now resolved according to Carnap's method by noting that 'Brother' and 'Male Sibling,' while L-equivalent, are not intensionally isomorphic. In general, Carnap feels that intensionally isomorphic expressions differ (from a cognitive point of view) only trivially while L-equivalent expressions which are not intensionally isomorphic differ significantly.

It is easy to find expressions which, while intensionally isomorphic, do seem to differ significantly, and pairs of non-intensionally isomorphic expressions which seem to differ only trivially.[55] Carnap does not consider such exceptions a strong argument against his method: he urges that one would hardly expect very hard and fast criteria of triviality and significance. In order to care for the cases with which intensional isomorphism does not appear suited to deal, Carnap therefore offers to define a whole array of semantic relations between expressions, ranging from identity of design to L-equivalence.[56]

A more central objection to intensional isomorphism and its ilk as conceptual tools for dealing with the paradox of analysis lies rather in the *ad hoc* nature of such devices. Equivalence is firmly based on sameness of extensional reference; L-equivalence is provided with a similarly impressive semantic ground, sameness of intensional reference. But intensional isomorphism has no such factual or theoretical justification. It seems to be an arbitrary fence set up in a likely place in the hope that the trivial and the significant will be found on opposite sides. Yet why should the solution to the paradox of analysis be any more arbitrary, or any less fundamental, than the solution to the paradox of identity? Once the distinction between first and second level entities is admitted, it is hard to deny the complete analogy between the two paradoxes; but in that case it is hard to see why the solutions should not be analogous. If it is reasonable to postulate intensional entities to solve the paradox of identity, it is as reasonable to postulate super-intensional (or third-level) entities to solve the paradox of analysis. Whatever arguments are good enough to vindicate second-level semantical systems seem equally valid in favor of each additional level; so at least present considerations indicate.

The problem of analysing sentences about belief resembles the problem posed by the paradox of analysis in this respect, that if sameness of meaning, sense or intension is based upon L-truth or L-equivalence, then a straightforward solution to either problem requires appeal to a stronger semantical relation than sameness of intension. Just as interchange of L-

[55]See L. Linsky, "Some Notes on Carnap's Concept of Intentional Isomorphism and the Paradox of Analysis," *Philosophy of Science,* XVI (1949), 343-47.

[56]Carnap, [Paradox].

equivalent expressions turns the interesting sentences (38) and (40) into the trivial sentences (39) and (41), so interchange of the L-equivalent expressions '$3 = 4$' and '$5^7 = 75125$' in:

(42) Simon believes that $5^7 = 75125$

may turn (42) from true to false. This also brings to our attention an important difference between the problems; for while sentences like (42) may change in truth-value when L-equivalent expressions are exchanged, sentences like (38) - (41) do not. Thus the problem of belief sentences is in this respect like the antinomy of the name-relation, and may be considered as related to it in the same way the paradox of analysis is related to the paradox of identity. The paradox of identity and the paradox of analysis arise when substitution of equivalent (L-equivalent) expressions in extensional (intensional) contexts alter the significance, although not the truth-value, of the sentences in which they appear. The antinomy of the name-relation and the problem of belief sentences arise when sentences occur in the object-language such that the substitution of equivalent (L-equivalent) expressions in those sentences may alter their truth-values. The sentences which give rise to the antinomy of the name-relation are those containing the modal operator for necessity and its derivatives; the sentences which give rise to the problem of belief sentences are those containing such phrases as 'Simon believes that.'[57]

We remarked that it seemed difficult to justify appeal to the concept of intensional isomorphism to solve the paradox of analysis once resort was had to such a fundamental distinction as that between extensional and intensional entities to solve the paradox of identity. On similar grounds one might now argue that if the semantical analysis of intensional contexts demands recourse to intensional entities, the semantical analysis of belief sentences, by precisely analogous reasoning, should lead to the postulation of further, perhaps superintensional (or third-level), entities. On Carnap's account intensional contexts and the contexts provided by belief sentences are not the same, since the former admit substitution of L-equivalent expressions while the latter do not; but no reason has been put forward for applying entirely different semantical techniques to the two, apparently analogous, situations.

Since the method of extension and intension is a two-level system of semantics, it cannot treat the problem of belief sentences on the analogy of modal sentences; instead, the concept of intensional isomorphism is used. But whereas in the case of the paradox of analysis the worst that could be argued against Carnap was that he attempted to deal with

[57]Presumably similar contexts are provided by such phrases as 'thinks that,' 'says that,' 'doubts that.' The relation between the paradox of analysis and the problem of belief sentences is emphasized by considering the sentence which would result by prefacing (38) with the words 'It is a true and interesting analysis that.'

similar problems in arbitrarily dissimilar ways, in the case of belief sentences, because the problem is put over into the object-language, it is possible to show that Carnap's solution based on the concept of intensional isomorphism is, according to Carnap's own view of semantical analysis, inadequate.

The character of Carnap's treatment of belief sentences will emerge if we consider some criticisms made by Church.[58] The following sentence:

(43) Plato believed that the realm of ideas is real

is interpreted by Carnap in this way:[59]

(44) There is a sentence $\mathbf{S}_i$ in a semantical system S′ such that (a) $\mathbf{S}_i$ is intensionally isomorphic to 'The realm of ideas is real' as an English sentence and (b) Plato was disposed to an affirmative response to $\mathbf{S}_i$ as a sentence of S′.

None of the force of Church's first objection to Carnap's analysis will be lost if we proceed to reason as follows: the meaning of (43) will be preserved if it is translated into another language, say German (let us call the resulting sentence (43′)); next we may apply Carnap's analysis to (43′) to produce an interpretation (in German) of (43′) (call this (44′)); finally, we translate (44′) back into English. The result will be:

(45) There is a sentence $\mathbf{S}_i$ in a semantical system S′ such that (a) $\mathbf{S}_i$ is intensionally isomorphic to 'Das Ideenreich ist wirklich' as a German sentence and (b) Plato was disposed to an affirmative response to $\mathbf{S}_i$ as a sentence of S′.

Church contends that if Carnap's method of analysis were correct, (45) would 'convey the same information' as (44). In particular he remarks that (44) and (45) are not intensionally isomorphic.[60]

The demand that (44) and (45) be intensionally isomorphic is unreasonable since (43) and (44) obviously are not intensionally isomorphic. According to Carnap's view of analysis, an analysis is true and interesting if and only if analysans and analysandum are L-equivalent but *not* intensionally isomorphic. Since (44) is intended as a analysis of (43), it is presumably not intended to be intensionally isomorphic to it. On the other hand, it is reasonable to demand that (44) and (45) be L-equiva-

[58] Alonzo Church, "On Carnap's Analysis of Statements of Assertion and Belief" ([Belief]), *Analysis,* X (1950), 97-99, and [Formulation], 5, 6.

[59] This interpretation is more explicit than Carnap's in including the words 'as an English sentence' and the final words 'as a sentence of S′.' The necessity for these additions was pointed out by Church, [Belief], 98 and [Formulation], 6.

[60] Church, [Belief], 99.

lent; Church is however willing to agree that they may be given sufficiently explicit meanings for the expressions in (44) and (45). The difficulty that (44) and (45) do not have the same content is not clear. L-equivalent sentences which are not intensionally isomorphic always differ in content in some respect; but if such differences invalidate analyses, most analyses are invalid (all, if we accept Carnap's criterion). Church remarks (in effect) that (44) and (45) would convey different meanings to someone who knew English but not German. But ' 'Das Ideenreich ist wirklich' ' must, if (45) is a grammatical sentence at all, be good English, and hence understood by anyone who knows English. It is possible to understand the meaning of ' 'Das Ideenreich ist wirklich' ' without understanding 'Das Ideenreich ist wirklich' since the first may, as an expression in English, refer to a German sentence, while the second is, of course, a sentence in German. By a similar token, it is possible to know that (44) is logically equivalent to (45) without (in any ordinary sense) knowing German. The fact that someone who understood (44) might not understand (45) is no more against Carnap's analysis than the fact that someone who understood (43) might not understand (44).

Church's second objection concerns such sentences as:

(46) Speusippus believed that Plato believed that the realm of ideas is real.

Let the numeral '44' be an abbreviation of (44). Then applying Carnap's analysis to the last nine words of (46) we obtain as a partial analysis of (46);

(47) Speusippus believed that 44.

It is not necessary to complete the analysis of (46) since it is easy to see that (47) may be false while (46) is true; Speusippus may have had no beliefs at all about semantical systems and intensional isomorphism, or those he had may have been mistaken.

The difficulty which has just arisen is a special case of the problem of belief sentences. Since (46) provides a context for (43) which is neither intensional nor extensional and Carnap's analysis guarantees merely that (43) and (44) are L-equivalent, there is no reason why replacement of (43) by (44) in (46) should leave the truth-value of (46) unaltered. The difficulty is not due to any particular inadequacy of Carnap's analysis; if it were, *any* analysis in which analysans and analysandum were not intensionally isomorphic could be shown inadequate by embedding the analysandum in an appropriate belief sentence and demonstrating how the truth-value of the belief sentence might be changed by replacing in it analysandum by analysans.

A simple and plausible convention would save Carnap's analysis of sentences like (46) from Church's second line of attack: in cases of iteration, the analysis is always to be applied to the larger context first. The analysis of (46) then begins:

(48) There is a sentence $\mathbf{S}_i$ in a semantical system S′ such that (a) $\mathbf{S}_i$ is intensionally isomorphic to 'Plato believed that the realm of ideas is real' as an English sentence and (b) Speusippus was disposed to an affirmative response to $\mathbf{S}_i$ as a sentence of S′.

The words enclosed in quotation marks in (48) are now ineligible for further analysis since they merely help form, with the aid of the quotation marks, the name of a sentence. (48) thus constitutes the complete analysis of (46) in accord with Carnap's method.

In the light of the foregoing considerations it seems that Church has presented no reasons for rejecting Carnap's analysis of belief sentences, provided Carnap's criteria of a successful and correct analysis are accepted. What Church has demonstrated is that Carnap has not given a semantical analysis of belief sentences in the sense in which he has given a semantical analysis of intensional contexts. For intensional contexts, Carnap lays down rules for the interchange of expressions based on the semantic relations between those expressions and entities; to paraphrase Carnap, he applies his method of meaning analysis to the designators within intensional sentences in order to show how out of the meanings of other expressions the meanings of sentences are constituted.[61] Although Carnap's analysis of belief sentences makes use of the semantical notion of intensional isomorphism, it does not provide a semantical analysis of sentences like (42), (43) and (46) in the sense of showing how out of the meanings of the expressions of less than sentential scope the meanings of the sentences are constituted. Rather the analysis translates such sentences as wholes into other sentences to which, *then,* Carnap's full semantical analysis (in terms of the method of extension and intension) may be applied.

The device of transforming sentences before submitting them to formal semantical analysis is certainly essential if semantical methods of any degree of rigor and simplicity are to be applied to ordinary language. What is surprising is not that Carnap makes use of such devices but that he denies them in some cases and not in others. Thus his criticism of Russell's analysis of descriptions and proper names rests, as we have seen, on the claim that 'meaning is denied' these expressions and that they are thus 'excluded . . . from the domain of semantical meaning and analysis.' Precisely the same may be said of Carnap's treatment of the expressions embedded in (42), (43) and (46).

[61] [Meaning], 141.

The analogy between intensional contexts and belief sentences thus once more raises the question: if only full-scale semantical analysis, with its apparatus of entities, is appropriate to intensional contexts, on what grounds is similar treatment denied belief sentences? If the Fregean duplication of entities is allowed as the proper solution for intensional contexts, it seems arbitrary to disallow triplication of entities as the proper solution for the contexts provided by belief sentences. Or, to reverse the argument, if it is good tactics to transform sentences containing 'believes that' before treating them to semantical analysis, why isn't the same handling indicated for contexts containing 'necessarily'?

The main results of the present section may now be summarized. The method of extension and intension does not appear to differ from other modified versions of the method of the name-relation in departing any more radically from the original concept and principles characteristic of that method. The chief distinguishing feature of Carnap's new semantical method seems rather to be the fact that unlike the simplest systems, which admit only extensional entities, and the Frege-Church systems, which admit infinite hierarchies of entities, Carnap's system admits just two varieties of entities. Despite the possibilty of several alternative interpretations, Carnap's system apparently appeals, either explicitly or implicitly, to extensions and intensions as discrete categories of entities; it may thus be regarded in essence as a truncated version of the Frege-Church system.

The simplicity which is gained for semantics in this way does not perhaps justify itself, since once duplication of kinds of entities is accepted as the appropriate solution to the paradox of identity and the antinomy of the name-relation there seems no valid point in withholding an analogous solution to the analogous problems raised by belief sentences and the paradox of analysis. Frege's "spurious economy" in interlocking senses and nominata of successive levels of expressions is thus seen to be, if not an economy, at least not spurious either—granted, of course, the need for more than one type of entity to begin with. The two courses which suggested themselves at the close of (I) as likely ways of simplifying Frege's theory now appear in a somewhat different light. Any theory based on Course 2, insofar as it explains the rules of substitution in intensional contexts in terms of intensional entities, and any theory based on Course 1, insofar as it rests on the supposition that expressions in intensional contexts refer to intensional entities, will be subject to the same criticisms we have brought against the method of extension and intension. If these criticisms have weight, only the extremes of single- or infinite-level methods can solve the problems and puzzles of semantics with any real consistency, while genuine simplicity is reserved for single-level methods alone.

VI

There seems to be nothing intrinsic to the nature of the problems to warrant an essentially different sort of analysis for belief sentences and what Carnap calls intensional contexts. In fact it might be contended not only that the analyses ought to be similar, but that they ought to be identical; this end could be achieved by rejecting altogether the distinction between the contexts created by belief sentences and the contexts created by the modal operators. There is no evidence Frege accepted such a distinction; but since he specified no conditions for sameness of intension it is impossible to tell what Frege's developed doctrine would have been.

The course of assimilating belief sentences to intensional contexts generally is not plausibly open to Carnap however for the reason that his treatment of intensional contexts is geared to the very special problem of interpreting a language in which modalities and quantification are intermixed. Indeed, since Carnap's intensional entities take on life only by virtue of whatever cogency attaches to the concept of L-truth, and L-truth depends in turn on the notion of state-descriptions, and state-descriptions finally are constructed largely with an eye to giving a semantical analysis for languages combining modalities and quantification, it is hard to overstate the degree to which the method of extension and intension as a whole hinges on the requirements of this special problem. It is, for example, due to the peculiar exigencies of state-descriptions that Carnap must in effect simply settle out of hand the difficult question of individual constants which do not refer; the same exigencies demand that sentences like 'The present king of France is bald' may turn out true in case some arbitrary individual in the universe is bald. The specialized pressures which lead to these consequences result also in a general dependence of vocabulary on fact. Not only must there be a one-to-one correspondence between ordinary individuals and individual constants, but there must be no logical interrelations between primitive predicates; further, primitive relations may possess no logical properties. The last two conditions can be removed, but only by writing into the language (or its metalanguage) axioms (or "meaning postulates") which make the language indistinguishable from a physical theory. It seems that in Carnap's view one must know a great deal about what is actual in order to say what is possible.

Yet the warping of general theory to accommodate the problems of the modalities cannot, from one point of view, be called capricious. If calculi which permit quantification into modal contexts are to be more than technical inventions, they must be given an interpretation within a comprehensive theory of language, a theory suitable also for something resembling the language of science and common sense. Without such an interpretation no one can pretend to know with any certainty what is meant by sentences like (10), (13), (16), and (17). Sentences such as these appear nowhere in science or in ordinary discourse; if they did, we should ask for an explanation. Carnap is right that if we want to understand and use language of this brand we need a theory to sustain it; and there is no compelling reason to believe that any more transparent or less intricate apparatus than his will do the job.

But in the end it would seem that a general question of policy must be raised. In attempting to achieve generality, any theory of language will have the task of deciding which problems, which sorts of sentences and contexts, are to be dealt with by head-on methods, and which are better handled by preliminary transformations, translations and analyses. Even the decision to transform 'John laughed and cried' into 'John laughed and John cried' before confiding it to the formal system represents, on a low level, such a decision. More serious are the decisions to accept whole classes of sentences (perhaps the simple modalities, or belief sentences) as appropriate for treatment *without* gross transformation. In systems in which intensional entities are enlisted as meanings, or non-garden varieties of truth are introduced, decisions directly to accommodate one or another area in the total linguistic territory become especially binding since they influence the interpretation not only of the contexts they were devised to explicate but also the interpretation of other contexts. When such accommodations are in favor of linguistic phenomena which are readily observed and for which intuition already has much to say, they are at least to that extent justified. But when, as in the case of quantified modal logic, there is neither recognized need nor recognized use, justification is harder to come by. The *primary* goal of systematic theory of language, it will perhaps be granted, is to interpret or rationally reconstruct the language we understand the best and need the most. Quantified modal logic can't be a candidate for rational reconstruction simply because it never has been constructed (as an interpreted system) in the first place. It would be pleasant, no doubt, to reward workers in the modalities by finding a reasonable interpretation for the results of their formal labors. But if the cost is unduly to obscure and complicate the analysis of ordinary and scientific discourse, it is a question whether the modal game was worth so many intensional candles.

Donald Davidson

Department of Philosophy
Stanford University

11

R. M. Martin

ON CARNAP'S CONCEPTION OF SEMANTICS

By a *semantical system,* Carnap understands a "system of rules, formulated in a metalanguage and referring to an object language, of such a kind that the rules determine a *truth-condition* for every sentence of the object language, i.e., a sufficient and necessary condition for its truth."[1] The notion of a semantical system is one of the fundamental notions of semantics. In this essay we shall try to characterize such systems explicitly and to exhibit very roughly their important role within the Carnap *corpus.*

The discussion here will center mainly upon *Introduction to Semantics* and *Foundations of Logic and Mathematics,*[2] which contain the foundations of Carnap's semantics. We shall also refer to the chapter "Deductive Logic" in *The Logical Foundations of Probability.*[3] Although this chapter contains nothing essentially new not contained in the other works mentioned, the treatment there is especially suitable for applications to empirical science. We shall *not,* however, be concerned in this paper with *Formalization of Logic*[4] or *Meaning and Necessity.*[5] Those books are concerned primarily with more special problems, some of which are being discussed elsewhere in this volume.

We shall not discuss Carnap's semantics in the chronological order in which it was developed. We shall rather concentrate upon the one procedure Carnap himself regards as the most satisfactory. (This is essentially the modification of procedure E of *I.S.* presented in Chapter III of *L.F.P.).* This semantical method is an extensional one and thus has

Note added in proof: Some few paragraphs of this paper have been used in the author's *Truth and Denotation, A Study in Semantical Theory* (Chicago: University of Chicago Press, 1958), with the kind permission of Professor Schilpp.

[1] *Introduction to Semantics* (Cambridge: Harvard University Press, 1944), 22. This book will subsequently be referred to as I.S.

[2] *Foundations of Logic and Mathematics, International Encyclopedia of Unified Science,* I, No. 3 (Chicago: University of Chicago Press, 1939).

[3] *The Logical Foundations of Probability* (Chicago: University of Chicago Press, 1950). This work will subsequently be referred to as L.F.P.

[4] *Formalization of Logic* (Cambridge: Harvard University Press, 1943).

[5] *Meaning and Necessity* (Chicago: University of Chicago Press, 1947).

certain important advantages. We shall subject this method to careful analysis, reformulate it in a rigorous way, and compare and contrast it with allied formulations. In passing, we shall also consider very briefly the non-extensional (and perhaps therefore less satisfactory) formulations. In this way we shall gain a clear conception of the most important features of Carnap's extensional semantics without wholly neglecting the non-extensional procedures.

We shall not always *literally* follow Carnap's formulations with regard to all matters of detail. We shall frequently diverge from his terminology, from his notation, and from other specialities of his presentation. We shall follow him, however, in all essential respects, giving therewith a kind of "rational reconstruction" of his extensional semantical views.

More specifically, § I is merely *introductory* and § II is devoted to the *syntactical preliminaries* needed. The fundamental notions of *designation* and *truth* are introduced in § III for a restricted class of systems. § IV is concerned with the so-called *L-concepts,* including the notions of *L-range* and *L-truth.* The theory of §§ III-IV is *generalized* in § V. In § VI two semantical metalanguages are formulated, closely akin to those of Carnap, as *axiomatic systems.* In § VII some of Carnap's *intensional* procedures in semantics are briefly indicated. § VIII is concerned with the notion of how one kind of system can provide an *interpretation* for another. In § IX the notion of a *meaning postulate* is considered briefly. Finally, in §X some concluding remarks are offered concerning the relationship of Carnap's semantics to other formulations, concerning its significance for philosophy and the methodology of science, and so on.

I. *Introduction*

By an *object-language* Carnap understands a language which is the object of our investigation or which is to be described or analyzed or formulated precisely for specific purposes. The *metalanguage* is the language in which the results of this investigation or description or analysis are couched. The metalanguage is used to talk *about* the object-language, whereas the object-language is used to talk about objects. On some occasions we might also wish to talk *about* the *metalanguage* itself. We should ordinarily do this within a meta-metalanguage. And so on. (The fundamental importance of the distinction between object- and metalanguage as a means of avoiding the semantical antinomies is now so well established as to require no further comment here.)

The notion of a *language,* in the preceding paragraph, is left somewhat vague. "A language," Carnap notes, "as it is usually understood, is a system of sounds, or rather of the habits of producing them by the speaking organs, for the purpose of communicating with other persons, i.e., of influencing their actions, decisions, thoughts, etc. Instead of speech sounds other movements or things are sometimes produced for the same purpose, e.g., gestures, written marks, signals by drums, flags, trumpets, rockets, etc. It seems convenient to take the term 'language' in such a wide sense as to cover all these kinds of systems of means of communication. . . ."[6] Of course Carnap does not intend this explanation as an exact definition, but only as a rough description. One of the crucial notions in this description is that of *system*. A language is a system of sounds (or whatever) organized according to certain patterns or *rules*. A heterogeneous conglomeration of sounds (or whatever) cannot constitute a language except as they bear explicit relations to each other. The rules of the language describe what these relations are, tell us which sounds bear such-and-such a relation to other sounds, tell us how certain sounds or sequences of sounds are combined to form longer phrases or sentences, etc.

Some languages are said to be *natural* and some are said to be *formalized*. However this may be, both kinds of languages are *language-systems*. The grammatical rules of a natural language are no doubt empirical generalizations describing actual linguistic usage or behavior. They are to be formulated no doubt by grammarians and other specialists in empirical linguistics. The natural language can then perhaps be identified in some way with the totality of its grammatical rules. The rules of a formalized language-system are not empirical generalizations of actual linguistic behavior, but rather stipulations laid down explicitly for specific purposes by the working logician or methodologist. Formalized language-systems are thus usually very much simpler than natural languages. Because their grammatical properties are determined by *fiat* rather than by empirical investigation, formalized language-systems are perhaps of greater interest for the philosophical logician than natural languages. They exhibit a certain logical structure because this structure has been imposed upon them more or less self-consciously for specific purposes. Carnap's object-languages are always formalized language-systems, whereas his metalanguages are usually couched in a natural language supplemented by symbols or special expressions for the sake of clarity and explicitness.

The rules of either a natural or formalized language-system divide conveniently into three kinds. There are *syntactical* or grammatical (in the narrow sense) rules, *semantical* rules, and rules of usage or *pragmatical* rules. Corresponding to these three kinds of rules we have three ways of approaching the study of a language, through syntax, semantics, or pragmatics. These three kinds of study in effect exhaust the formal study of language. Sometimes they are said to constitute the discipline of

[6] I.S., 3.

semiotic.[7] In syntax interest focusses exclusively upon the signs or expressions of the language and their interrelations. In semantics, which presupposes syntax, one is concerned not only with expressions and their interrelations but also with the objects which the signs or expressions denote or designate. Finally, in pragmatics there is reference not only to the signs and what they denote but also to the speaker or user of the language. Pragmatics thus contains semantics as a part, just as semantics contains syntax.

By *pure syntax* one means the syntactical analysis or description of a formalized language-system. *Descriptive* syntax is concerned with natural languages and is therefore, according to Carnap, an empirical science. In a similar way one distinguishes between pure and descriptive semantics, and also between pure and descriptive pragmatics. Because Carnap's object-languages are always formalized language-systems we shall have little to say hereafter concerning natural languages, and hence little to say concerning descriptive semiotic. Also we shall have very little to say concerning pure pragmatics. Very little work has yet been done in this subject, "an untilled field calling for workers." Perhaps pragmatical studies will prove to be of great importance for the exact philosophical investigation of the problems of meaning.

Within pure syntax or semantics one distinguishes also between *special* and *general* syntax or semantics. In special syntax or semantics one is concerned with a specific object-language. In general syntax or semantics one is concerned with the features of *all* object-languages or with all object-languages of such and such a kind. To date there has been intensive study of special syntax and semantics, whereas only a few steps have been taken toward formulating adequately a completely general theory.

II. *Syntactical Preliminaries*

Before going on to a discussion of semantical systems, let us glance briefly at some of the syntactical notions which will be presupposed.

The smallest units of a language-system Carnap calls *signs.* Sequences of signs are then *expressions.*

> A continuous utterance in a language, [Carnap notes,] e.g., a speech, a book, or a flag message, may be analyzed into smaller and smaller parts. Thus a speech may be divided into sentences, each sentence into words, each word into phonemes. . . . Where we stop the analysis is to some extent arbitrary, depending upon the purpose of our investigation. When interested in grammar, we may take (spoken or written) words or certain parts of words as ultimate units;

[7]See C. Morris, *Foundations of the Theory of Signs, International Encyclopedia of Unified Science,* I, No. 2 (Chicago: University of Chicago Press, 1938).

when interested in spelling, letters; when interested in the historical development of letter forms, the single form elements of the letters.[8]

Once the ultimate units or signs are decided upon, the expressions of the language are taken as any finite sequences of them. "Thus we treat all utterances in language as being of linear form. This is convenient because it enables us to specify the positions of signs in an expression by enumeration. A spoken utterance in one of the ordinary languages is a temporal series of sounds; a written utterance consists of marks ordered in lines. . . ." One of the fundamental notions of syntax is thus the operation of forming sequences of signs from the constituent signs or from the constituent sub-sequences. This operation is called *concatenation*. Suppose, for the moment, that 's_1', 's_2', . . . , 's_n,' are the (primitive) signs of some language-system. To form the expression 's_1s_2', e.g., the two signs 's_1' and 's_2' are concatenated (in that order). To form longer expressions, such as '$s_5s_1s_2$' we can concatenate first 's_1 with 's_2' and then 's_5' with this result, or we can first concatenate 's_5' with 's_1' and then concatenate this result with 's_2'. This operation is, obviously, associative in an appropriate sense.

There are several ways of handling concatenation within syntax. One is the method of Tarski, in which a symbol for concatenation is taken as a syntactical primitive.[9] Axioms are then laid down characterizing explicitly this notion. Another method is that of Gödel in which concatenation is handled as an arithemetical operation.[10] The syntactical axioms then become statements of arithmetic. Still another method is to regard concatenates as in some way definable in terms of *sequences* of the primitive signs. The syntax must then contain a method of handling sequences in such a way that the basic properties of concatenation are forthcoming as properties of sequences.

There are several different ways of formalizing syntax on the basis of any of these methods, depending upon the kind of logic presupposed. Now any formalized theory must contain a basic logic as a part. This may be a logic of *first order*, of *second order*, and so on, or it may even be a logic of a very different kind. In the present paper, we shall be concerned only with logics in the classical, two-valued sense, and hence only with logics of first, second, etc., order. A formulation of first-order logic contains symbols, e.g., 'and', 'or', 'not', and so on, for the so-called truth-functions as well as quantifiers, phrases of the form 'for all *x*' or 'there exists at least

8I.S., 4.

9See A. Tarski, *Der Wahrheitsbegriff in den Formalisierten Sprachen, Studia Philosophica,* I (1936), 263-405, esp. 291-303.

10See K. Gödel, "Über Formal Unentscheidbare Sätze der *Principia Mathematica* and Verwandtner Systeme I," *Monatshefte für Mathematik und Physik,* XXXVIII (1931), 173-198.

one *x* such that', where the variable '*x*' must be thought of as ranging over a well-specified domain of *individuals.* There is great freedom in the choice of individuals. Once they have been chosen, however, variables over *classes* of individuals or over *relations* between or among individuals are not admitted. For this we must go on to a system of *second* order. Systems of second order contain, in addition to variables and quantifiers over individuals, variables and quantifiers over classes of and relations between or among individuals. Systems of *third* order contain, in addition to variables and quantifiers of these kinds, variables and quantifiers over classes of and relations between or among classes and relations of individuals. Thus, systems of second, third, etc., order contain many modes of expression not contained in systems of first order.[11] Systems of higher order have proved to be of great interest for the foundations of mathematics, for the logical analysis of science, and for the formulation of various philosophical theories.

If we wish to formalize syntax on the basis of the Tarski method of concatenation, the underlying logic may be of second or even higher order. But there are also ways of formalizing Tarski's syntax on the basis of a first-order logic, utilizing the modifications of Chwistek and Quine.[12] If, on the other hand, the syntax is arithmetized or if one employs the sequence method one may use any of the many satisfactory ways of formalizing arithmetic or the theory of sequences respectively.

In Carnap's semantical writings it is never quite clear which method of handling concatenation is presupposed. It is presumably a form of the sequence method, because this is sketched informally in *I.S.*[13] The discussion there is, however, somewhat obscure. Sequences of objects are usually identified with one-many relations between the objects and the positive integers, as Carnap notes. To formalize the theory of such sequences, we should need not only variables over the signs of the object-language, but also variables over positive integers and over relations between signs and integers. Hence we should presuppose a basic logic of at least second, possibly third, order. In such a treatment symbols for sequences of signs would be of higher logical type than symbols for the signs themselves. This would seem to be somewhat awkward and unnatural. Further, in such a treatment positive integers are presupposed anyhow, and hence an arithmetized syntax is available. This would no doubt give a more economical way of handling syntax.

[11]Cf., however, A. Church, *Introduction to Mathematical Logic* (Princeton: Princeton University Press, 1956). Note that Church's classification of systems as of first, second etc., order differs from the one used here, which is essentially that of Carnap and Tarski.

[12]See L. Chwistek, *The Limits of Science* (London: Kegan Paul, 1948), 83-100 and 162-191, and W. V. Quine, *Mathematical Logic,* 1st ed. (New York: Norton, 1940), 291-305.

[13]I.S., 18f.

But this difficulty is by no means fundamental. Carnap's semantics may be thought of as presupposing syntax in any form which renders the axioms and theorems of concatenation as *laws of logic.* There is considerable latitude as to just what form of logic one can presuppose. For some purposes on may need only a simple logic of first order with or without identity. For other purposes one needs a logic of second or higher order, or perhaps the whole of the functional calculus of order ω, formalized so as to include as axioms a law of extensionality, a law of sub-class formation, an axiom of infinity, and an axiom of choice.[14] For still other purposes one may presuppose the whole of the Zermelo-Skolem or the von Neumann-Bernays-Gödel set theory regarded as a logic.[15] Thus, if we presuppose Tarski's method of handling concatenation, the axioms of concatenation are to be regarded as analytic or logically true or valid formulae of the metalanguage. If we presuppose Gödel's method of arithmetizing syntax, the theory of integers is to be presumed formalized as a branch of logic, possibly in terms of the Frege-Russell concept of number. And similarly for the sequence method.

Once the method of treating concatenation is decided upon, the remaining notions of syntax relativized to a given object-language are definable. Thus, one can define the notions of *term* and *variable* as any concatenates of such and such a kind. Likewise the notions of *formula* or *sentence* are definable by recursion or otherwise. By enumeration one defines the notion of *axiom* as formulae or sentences of such and such a form. Likewise an expression is a *logical consequence of* or *derivable from* or *provable from* other expressions if and only if it bears such and such a syntactical relationship to those expressions. Similarly one can define the notion of a *proof* and hence the notion of being a *theorem,* either by recursion or by some suitable alternative method. The various laws governing these notions are then provable from the underlying laws concerning concatenation. Thus the whole syntax of a language comes out of the concatenation theory presupposed. In Carnap's words, "pure syntax deals with syntactical systems. A *syntactical system* (or calculus) *K* consists

[14]Cf. Tarski, *Der Wahrheitsbegriff,* esp. 364-366.

[15]See E. Zermelo "Untersuchungen über die Grundlagen der Mengenlehre I," *Mathematische Annalen,* LXV (1908), 261-281; Th. Skolem, "Einige Bemerkungen zur Axiomatische Begründung der Mengenlehre," *Wissenschaftliche Vorträge auf den Fünften Kongress der Skandinavischen Mathematiker in Helsingfors vom. 4. bis 7. Juli 1922* (Helsingfors: 1923), 217-232; J. von Neumann, "Eine Axiomatisierung der Mengenlehre," *Journal für die Reine und die Angewandte Mathematik,* CLIV (1925), 219-240 (and *Berichtigung, ibid.,* LV (1926), 128), and "Die Axiomatisierung der Mengenlehre," *Mathematische Zeitschrift,* XXVII (1928), 669-752; P. Bernays, "A System of Axiomatic Set Theory," *The Journal of Symbolic Logic,* II (1937), 65-77, VI (1941), 1-17, VII (1942), 65-89 and 133-145, VIII (1943), 89-106, and XIII (1948), 65-79; and K. Gödel, *The Consistency of the Continuum Hypothesis* (Princeton: Princeton University Press, 1941).

of rules which define syntactical concepts, e.g., 'sentence in *K*', 'provable in *K*', 'derivable in *K*'. Pure syntax contains the analytic sentences of the metalanguage which follow from these definitions."[16]

Not only are the syntactical laws presupposed analytic, according to Carnap; all the laws of pure *semantics* likewise are "entirely analytic and without factual content."[16] In fact the rules of a semantical system *S*, Carnap says, "constitute, as we shall see, nothing else but a definition of certain semantical concepts with respect to *S*, e.g., 'designation in *S*' or 'true in *S*'. Pure semantics consists of definitions of this kind and their consequences. . . ."[16] Hence also, any axioms that may be needed for semantics must also be regarded as analytic. (See §VI below.)

One further preliminary remark is needed before we turn to a detailed discussion of Carnap's semantics. Heretofore we have spoken of the signs and expressions of a language but have not in any precise way specified what kind of objects these are supposed to be. In fact, 'sign' and 'expression' are ambiguous. Let us consider first 'sign'. A sign may be a particular occurrence in space-time, or it may be a class of such occurrences all sufficiently similar to each other. In the former case Carnap speaks of a *sign-event;* in the latter case, a *sign-design.* Sign-events are presumably actual occurrences of some kind within the spatio-temporal world. They are singular and particular in some sense, occupy a certain portion of space-time, and are no more. A sign-design, on the other hand, is an entity of an altogether different kind. It is an "abstract" entity in the sense of having instances. Thus, e.g., the sign-design '*a*' has as an instance a particular, concrete, perhaps visible chalk- or ink-mark in some specific spatio-temporal region. Sign-designs are presumably best construed as *classes* of sign-events. But of course not just *any* class of sign-events is to be thought of as comprising a sign-design. As already suggested, the members of a sign-design must all be sufficiently similar to one another, of similar shapes, sizes, etc.

Likewise expressions may be construed as complexes of sign-events taken in a certain order, in which case expressions then also occupy space-time, are particular occurrences, etc. Or expressions may be construed as abstract entities having instances. We can distinguish these two meanings of 'expression' by speaking of *expression-events* and *expression-designs.*

There are then two quite distinct views concerning the nature of signs or expressions. The view that expressions are best construed fundamentally as expression-designs may be called the *classical* view. This view is classical in two senses: syntax and semantics were first formulated on the basis of this view, and the view construes expressions as classes of objects. The view that expressions are best construed as expression-events may be called the *nominalist* view. This view appears to have originated with

[16] I.S., 12.

Leśniewski, but has received a systematic treatment only recently in the hands of Goodman and Quine.[17] Of course, one may wish to take a mixed view, regarding expressions for some purposes as the one, for other purposes as the other. In a syntax or semantics of this mixed kind, one would presumably have variables ranging over expression-events as well as class variables ranging over expression-designs. In this kind of a theory we should have two concatenation operations, one applying to expression-designs, one to expression-events.

Carnap's syntax and semantics are based almost entirely upon sign- and expression-designs. "In historical descriptions of particular acts of speaking or writing," he notes,

> expression-events are often dealt with. But they are usually characterized by the designs to which they belong. When we say "Caesar wrote 'vici'," then we are speaking about a certain word-event produced by Caesar's hand; but we describe it by its design; the sentence is meant to say: "Caesar wrote a word-event of the design 'vici'." When we are not concerned with the history of single acts but with the linguistic description of a certain language or the logical (syntactical or semantical) analysis of a certain language-system, then the features which we study are common to all events of a design. Therefore, in this kind of investigation, it is convenient to drop reference to expression-events entirely and to speak only about designs . . .[18]

It is true that many of the fundamental notions of syntax and semantics, if nominalized so as to be applicable to expression-events at all, are applicable uniformly to all expression-events of the same design. Thus, if a given expression-event is a sentence, say, of a given language, then every similar expression-event is a sentence likewise. Nonetheless Carnap has perhaps underestimated the importance of expression-events for pure syntax and semantics. To give a syntactical or semantical description of a language containing one or more of the so-called egocentric particulars, words such as 'I', 'here', 'this', etc., reference to sign- or expression-events seems essential. Also expression-events are of interest in connection with phenomenalist theories of knowledge and with attempts to construe syntax and semantics in purely finitistic terms. But these and other such topics need not concern us here. Henceforth we shall follow Carnap in construing expressions exclusively as expression-designs.

III. *Designation and Truth*

A semantical system, as we have already observed, is a system of rules determining a (necessary and sufficient) truth-condition for every sentence of the system.

[17]See N. Goodman and W. V. Quine, "Steps Toward a Constructive Nominalism," *Journal of Symbolic Logic,* XII (1947), 105-122. Cf. also R. M. M. and J. H. Woodger, "Toward an Inscriptional Semantics," *ibid.,* XVI (1951), 191-203.

[18]I.S., 6.

In this way the sentences are *interpreted* by the rules, i.e., made understandable, because to understand a sentence, to know what is asserted by it, is the same as to know under what conditions it would be true. To formulate it in still another way: the rules determine the *meaning* or *sense* of the sentences. Truth and falsity are called the *truth-values* of sentences. To know the truth-condition of a sentence is (in most cases) much less than to know its truth-value, but it is the necessary starting point for finding out its truth-value.[19]

Thus it is most important to distinguish clearly between the truth-value and the truth-condition of a sentence. Failure to do so seems to have generated confusion. (Cf. the discussion of *adequacy* below.)

A semantical system is completely determined by certain *rules*. Throughout his semantical writings Carnap uses 'rule' in essentially the sense of 'definitional abbreviation'. A rule thus stipulates precisely the conditions under which a given word is used. But 'rule' is also often used by logicians in the sense of a rule of inference or of a statement (sometimes called a meta-axiom) directly stipulating axioms. This seemingly ambiguous use of 'rule' may seem somewhat confusing. Upon closer inspection, however, we note that the rules of inference of a given language serve to define the syntactical notion of *logical consequence* for that language, and the meta-axioms serve to define the notion of *axiom* for that language. Thus such rules are in effect definitions in disguise. The semantical rules of a language are likewise definitions of semantical terms as applied to the expressions of that language. Carnap's usage of 'rule' in his semantical writings is thus clear-cut and defensible. Rather than to speak of semantical rules in the sequel, however, we shall use the more direct word 'definition'.

For the construction of a semantical system *S* we give

(1) a classification of the signs of *S*,

(2) definitions of 'term of *S*', 'formula of *S*', 'sentence of *S*', and perhaps of other syntactical notions,

(3) definitions of 'designation in *S*' and of allied semantical notions,

(4) a definition of 'true in *S*'.

In fact, the semantical system *S* itself may in effect be identified with (1) - (4).

In order to give an example of these definitions for a specific *S*, let us suppose that *S* is a *simple, applied* functional calculus of first order (without identity), in essentially the sense of Church.[20] This means simply that *S* contains the familiar classical, two-valued theory of truth-functions (involving notions expressed by 'and', 'or', 'if—then', etc.) and quantifiers upon individual variables ('for all *x*', 'for some *x*'). Also let *S* contain only a *finite* number of primitive individual constants and a finite num-

[19] I.S., 22.

[20] See A. Church, *op cit.*, 37.

ber of primitive predicate constants. (Some further restrictions on *S* will be given in §IV below.)

Let 'a_1',..., 'a_n' be the primitive individual constants and 'P_1',..., 'P_k' the primitive predicate constants, each of specified degree. For the present, we shall not admit *propositional variables* although this may of course be done if desired. (Cf. §VII below.) For definiteness, let us suppose also that all the truth-functional notions are defined in terms of negation and disjunction, i.e., in terms of 'not' and 'or'. (These last are usually symbolized, by '∼' and 'v' respectively.) Also, let '*x*', '*x*′', '*x*″', '*y*', '*y*′', etc., be the variables of *S*. Quantifiers may then be expressed as '(*x*)', '(*x*′)', etc., and the existential quantifier, '(∃*x*)', e.g., may be defined as '∼(*x*)∼'. Variables and quantifiers over attributes (or classes or properties) or relations are not admitted within this restricted kind of a language.

Because (1) - (4) are essentially definitional, the formulation of a semantical system *S* consists essentially of a sequence of definitions. Definitions will be given throughout as equivalences using 'if and only if'. Strictly definitions are mere abbreviations and use of 'if and only if' in such contexts has the effect of 'is an abbreviation for'.

The classification of signs (1) consists in defining several syntactical notions. E.g., we can say that an expression is a *primitive individual constant* if and only if it is an expression having such and such a shape. This definition may be given by enumeration because there is only a finite number of primitive individual constants. Similarly an expression is a primitive *predicate constant* if and only if it has such and such a shape. Finally an expression is a primitive *logical constant* if and only if it is of such and such a shape. Similarly for the (logical) *variables*. The primitive signs of *S* are thus classified syntactically into individual constants, predicate constants, and logical signs including variables, wholly in virtue of their shapes.

Now as to (2), in which we classify not just the primitive signs of *S* but also concatenates of such. (2) likewise consists of a sequence of definitions. First an expression of *S* is said to be a *term* of *S* if and only if it is either a variable or a primitive individual constant. An expression is a (well-formed) *atomic formula* of *S* if and only if it consists of a primitive predicate constant of degree *n* followed by *n* terms. An expression is then said to be a (well-formed) *formula* if and only if it

(i) is an atomic formula, or
(ii) is the negation of a formula, or
(iii) is the disjunction of two formulae, or
(iv) is the result of prefixing a quantifier to a formula.

This definition is of the recursive kind. Several other syntactical notions may also be defined either by recursion or otherwise. Among these are the notions of being a *free* or *bound variable* in a given expression, of being a *sentential function* (formula containing at least one free variable), and *sentence* (formula containing no free variables).

It should be noted in particular that we do not include amongst the syntactical definitions here under (2), the definitions of 'axiom' or 'provable' or 'derivable'. These notions are essential in *syntactical* systems, as we have seen. But strictly they play no role within a semantical system according to Carnap. This is a point upon which other formulations of semantics diverge from Carnap. (See §§IX-X below.)

We now turn to the *semantical* definitions under (3) and (4). Strictly under (3) it is not just 'designation in *S*' which we shall define but rather two closely allied semantical notions of designation. The first, *designation of individuals in S,* symbolized by 'DesInd_S', can be defined by enumeration because *S* contains only a finite number of primitive individual constants. Thus, we can say that a primitive predicate constant *b* bears DesInd_S to an individual *x* if and only if *b* is 'a_1' and *x* is the individual a_1 or *b* is 'a_2' and *x* is the individual a_2 or etc. Of course this definition by enumeration can be carried out only where *S* contains a fixed finite number of primitive individual constants.

In a similar way, one defines the notions of *designation of (primitive) attributes of degree n in* S. Thus, the primitive one-place predicates of *S* are said to bear $\mathrm{DesAttr}^1_S$ to their respective properties, the primitive two-place predicates of *S* bear $\mathrm{DesAttr}^2_S$ to the appropriate dyadic relations, etc. Suppose 'P_2' is the only two-place primitive predicate constant of *S*. We can then say that an expression *a* of *S* bears $\mathrm{DesAttr}^2_S$ to a dyadic relation *R* if and only if *a* is 'P_2' and *R* is P_2. In this way we define '$\mathrm{DesAttr}^1_S$', '$\mathrm{DesAttr}^2_S$', and so on. But because we have only a finite number of primitive predicate constants in *S,* we have only a finite number of relations $\mathrm{DesAttr}^1_S$, $\mathrm{DesAttr}^2_S$, and so on, to consider.

These various notions together with DesInd_S give us the only kinds of designation in *S* to be introduced. Note of course that we do not define the notion of *designation of propositions.* (Cf. §VII below.) Nor do we define what it means to say that a given truth-functional sign, say 'and', designates such and such an entity. One speaks of designation here only in the sense in which the *non-logical* primitive constants of *S* can be said to designate.[21]

Closely allied with the notions of designation of attributes is the semantical notion of *determination* in *S,* using which we can say that a given sentential function (containing just one free variable) or a given sentence determines a given property or attribute.[22] Suppose the primitives 'P_1' and 'P_2' are, respectively, one- and two-place predicate constants. We then wish to be able to say that the sentential function 'P_1x' deter-

[21] I.S., 25 and 49-55.

[22] I.S., 45f.

mines the property P_1, that '$(P_1 x \vee \sim P_2 a_1 x)$' determines the property of having P_1 or of not being borne P_2 by a_1, and so on. Likewise the sentence '$P_1 a_1$' is to determine the class (property) of all objects x such that a_1 has the property P_1, and thus determines the universal property if a_1 has the property P_1 and the null property if a_1 lacks the property P_1. And so on for more complicated cases. (The exact definition of determination involves some technical complications and hence will be omitted here. See, however, §VI below.) In terms of determination we can define an allied notion of *satisfaction*. We can say that an object x satisfies a given sentence or sentential function of one variable if and only if x has the property which that sentence or sentential function determines. (Also given a notion of satisfaction, determination is definable. Thus, a sentence or sentential function of one variable determines a property F if and only if F is the attribute (or class) applying to just those objects which satisfy that sentence or sentential function. See again §VI below.)

Another notion allied with those of designation and determination is that of the class or set of *values of variables* of S.[23] This notion we define directly by saying that the class of values for variables, which we can symbolize by 'ValVbl_S', is such and such a class of objects. E.g., ValVbl_S may be the class of positive integers, or the class of space-time points in such and such a kind of 4-dimensional space, or the class of cells of a certain biological species, etc., depending upon the purposes for which S is intended. Note that although S is assumed for the present to contain only a finite number of primitive individual constants, ValVbl_S may be either a finite or an infinite class. Of course the members of ValVbl_S will include all the individuals designated by the primitive individual constants of S, and may include other individuals as well. These other individuals are not needed at present, however, and for subsequent purposes (§IV) we shall wish definitely to exclude them.

Having given definitions of designation of individuals in S, determination in S, and of the class of values for variables in S, let us turn now to (4), the definition of 'true in S'. This may be given in two ways. First, we can say that an expression a of S is true in S if and only if it is a sentence and determines the universal class of objects. This gives an especially simple and straightforward definition.

We can give another, perhaps more intuitive, definition of truth in terms of a slightly narrower relation of determination. Suppose the domain of the determination-relation is taken as containing only sentential functions (of just one free variable) but no sentences. The truth-concept can be defined recursively in terms of this restricted determination-rela-

[23] I.S., 45.

tion as follows.[24] An expression *a* of *S* is true in *S* if and only if *a* is a sentence and

(i) *a* is atomic and there is an individual constant *b* contained in *a*, some individual *x*, some sentential function *c* of some one variable *d*, and some property *F* such that *b* bears DesInd_S to *x*, *c* differs from *a* only in containing (free) occurrences of *d* wherever *b* occurs in *a*, *c* determines *F* and *x* has the property *F*, or

(ii) *a* is of the form of the negation of a sentence *b* of *S* and *b* is not true, or

(iii) *a* is of the form of a disjunction of two sentences *b* and *c* of *S* and at least one of *b* and *c* is true, or

(iv) *a* is of the form:

left parenthesis concatenated with *b* concatenated with right parenthesis concatenated with *c*,

where *b* is a variable and either *c* is a sentential function of the one variable *b* and every member of the class ValVbl_S has the property determined by *c*, or *c* is a sentence and is true.

Note that because every sentence of *S* is of one of the forms covered in (i)–(iv) here, this definition introduces the phrase 'true in *S*' in full generality, i.e. the phrase is defined as applied to any sentence whatsoever of *S*. Note also that the definition is not an enumerative definition, defining first the truth of one sentence, then the truth of another, etc. The definition is rather of a recursive kind defining in effect the phrase

'*a* is true in *S*'

for variable '*a*'. Finally, note also the way in which the preceding semantical notions, designation of individuals in *S*, determination in *S*, and ValVbl_S, are used in the definiens, (i) using designation and determination, (iv) determination and ValVbl_S, (ii) and (iii) presupposing all of these recursively.

Given (1)–(4), we have then the semantical system *S* explicitly formulated. We may now ask whether in fact we have achieved the goal aimed at, namely, "a system of rules [definitions] . . . of such a kind that . . [they] . . determine a truth-condition for every sentence . . . , i.e., a sufficient and necessary condition for its truth." To answer this we must reflect a moment upon how 'true' is used in semantics. "We apply this term," Carnap says,

> chiefly to sentences (and later to classes of sentences also) . . . We use the term here in such a sense that *to assert that a sentence is true means the same as to assert the sentence itself;* e.g., the two statements "The sentence 'The moon is round' is true" and "The moon is round" are merely two different formu-

[24] Cf. I.S., 46.

lations of the same assertion. (The two statements mean the same in a logical or semantical sense; from the point of view of pragmatics, in this as in nearly every case, two different formulations have different features and different conditions of application; from this point of view we may, e.g., point to the difference between these two statements in emphasis and emotional function.)[25]

"The decision . . . ," Carnap goes on,

concerning the use of the term 'true' is itself not a definition for 'true'. It is rather a standard by which we judge whether a definition for truth is adequate, i.e., in accordance with our intention. If a definition . . . is proposed as a definition of truth, then we shall accept it as an adequate definition of truth if and only if, on the basis of this definition, . . . ['true'] fulfills the condition mentioned above, namely, that it yields sentences like " 'The moon is round' is [true] if and only if the moon is round."[26]

More precisely, we can say that a predicate 'true' is an *adequate* predicate for truth in *S* if and only if every sentence of the metalanguage of the form

(T) '*a* is true if and only if ——'

holds in the metalanguage, where in place of '——' we put in a sentence of *S* and in place of '*a*' the name (structural description) of that sentence.[27]

We may now ask whether the definition of 'true in *S*' is in fact adequate. The answer is in the affirmative, although an explicit proof of this important fact will not be given. To give the proof here would entail going too deeply into technical details. However, the existence of an adequacy proof for the definition given assures us that for every sentence of *S*, we have a necessary and sufficient condition for its truth.

The definition of adequacy must not itself be mistaken for a definition of truth. The two definitions cannot even be given in the same language.

[25]I.S., 26.

[26]I.S., 26.

[27]Cf. I.S., 26-28. The formulation given, however, is the author's, not that of Carnap. The phrase 'holds in the metalanguage' here is of course vague. It may mean 'is provable in the metalanguage', 'is true in the metalanguage', or 'is L-true in the metalanguage' (see §IV). Thus strictly we have here *three* adequacy concepts differing from one another in important respects. Carnap's definition of adequacy seems to be the third, that in terms of L-truth. According to him, every sentence of the form (T) must, for adequacy, "follow from the definition" of 'true'. Presumably this is to be construed as meaning that every sentence of the form (T) is L-true in the metalanguage.

Concerning the first and second of these concepts, see Church's review of the author's "Some Comments on Truth and Designation," *Analysis*, X (1950), 63-67, in *The Journal of Symbolic Logic*, XVII (1952), 70. Note that Church's objection does not hold where 'name' is construed only as 'structural-descriptive name'. The author, following Tarski, was using 'name' exclusively in this sense in that paper. Because Black, whose views were under consideration, was in turn discussing Tarski's work, it seemed natural to think that he (Black) was also using 'name' exclusively in this sense. However, the author may have been in error in attributing this usage to Black.

The definition of 'true in *S*' is given in a semantical metalanguage of *S*, that of 'adequate' in a meta-metalanguage of *S*. One might, however, regard any specific *instance* of the schema (T) as a kind of *partial* definition of truth. Thus,

'*a* is true in *S* if and only if ——',

where '——' is a specific sentence of *S* and '*a*' is taken as its (structural-descriptive) name, can in a sense be regarded as a partial definition of truth for the one sentence *a*. But the full definition must be more general, as has already been suggested, and must be given for *variable* '*a*'. The situation is similar to that in a formalized arithmetic, where, e.g., we might wish to define '+'. To give just partial definitions of '2 + 7', '2 + 3', '7 + 6', etc., *seriatim* would clearly not be satisfactory; we should rather need a general definition of '$x + y$' where 'x' and 'y' are numerical variables. So also in semantics, we require a general definition of '*a* is true in *S*' for variable '*a*'. Just as in arithmetic where the general definition of '$x + y$' is in a sense a logical sum of an infinite number of partial definitions, so also in semantics the general definition of truth must give the effect of an infinite logical conjunction of all partial definitions of the kind mentioned. This effect is gained in arithmetic by assuming recursion equations in some form or by presupposing a very powerful basic logic. So also in semantics, one must assume a powerful logical substructure or achieve the effect of such infinite conjunctions in some other way.

It should be emphasized again that a semantical definition of 'true in *S*' does not provide us with a *criterion* by means of which we can determine the truth-value of any given sentence. The semantical definition merely provides us with an *analysis* of or definition of what it means to say that a sentence is true. Further, an adequate definition gives us a necessary and sufficient *truth-condition* for each sentence. To decide, by observation or logical analysis or perhaps other means, whether a sentence is true or false is not strictly the affair of semantics. This is, broadly conceived, the task of the special sciences. The related distinctions between providing a criterion for applying the truth-concept and an analysis of its meaning and between giving the truth-value of a sentence and its truth-condition are obvious enough, but seem frequently to have been misunderstood.

It will thus simply not to do to dismiss the semantical truth-concept as philosophically irrelevant, as many philosophers have attempted to do. We have in modern semantics a full-fledged, successful explication of the concept of truth, a logical analysis of one of the historically most important philosophical concepts, as applied to the sentences of formalized language-systems of certain kinds. Those philosophers who work with formalized language-systems, rather than with perhaps inconsistent natural languages, are merely trying to do more carefully and with more secure intellectual tools what analytically minded philosophers have always been trying to do. In the case of the semantical truth-concept, the analysis or explication seems wholly successful. The age-old problem as to the meaning of the truth-predicate has been wholly clarified.

Once the truth-concept for *S* is available, several further notions in the semantics of *S* are definable more or less as a matter of routine. Carnap calls these the *radical* semantical concepts, to distinguish them from the L-concepts and F-concepts to be defined in a moment. Thus clearly a sentence *a* is said to be *false* in *S* if and only if it is not true in *S*. And a sentence *a* is said to be an *implicate* in *S* of a sentence *b* if and only if either *b* is false or *a* is true or both. A sentence *a* is said to be *equivalent* in *S* with a sentence *b* if and only if either both are true or both are false. A sentence *a* is *disjunct* in *S* with a sentence *b* if and only if at least one of them is true, and *a* is *exclusive* (in *S*) of *b* if and only if at least one of them is false.

IV. *L-Concepts*

We have sketched thus far the basic features of any semantical system *S* of first order, containing a finite number of primitive individual constants and a finite number of primitive predicate constants. In §V the treatment will be generalized in various respects. Let us consider now an important group of concepts as relativized to the restricted kind of *S* already considered. These are what Carnap calls the *L-concepts,* concepts which roughly speaking apply wholly *for logical reasons.* These concepts comprise such notions as that of *L-truth, L-falsity, L-implication, L-equivalence,* and the like. The theory of these concepts relativized to *S* gives, according to Carnap, the theory of logical deduction of *S*. The most important of these notions, and that in terms of which the others are definable, is that of L-truth, "truth for logical reasons in contradistinction to empirical, factual reasons."

Let us turn to the definition of L-truth for *S*. Carnap, in *I.S.*, sketches several alternative procedures for handling this concept. Here we shall follow the adaptation of procedure E (of *I.S.*) given in *L.F.P.* This procedure Carnap has also used elsewhere and regards as "the most convenient [method] among those known at present for the semantical construction of a system of deductive logic."[28] The formulation of *S* above is presupposed, so that 'DesInd_S' and 'true in *S*' are available.

For the definition of L-truth, a few preliminary notions are needed.[29] A sentence *a* of *S* is said to be a *basic sentence* if and only if *a* is either an atomic sentence or the negation of one. A *basic pair* is a class of sentences containing just two members, one of which is an atomic sentence

[28]See *Meaning and Necessity,* 9, footnote 9.
[29]Cf. L.F.P., 67-79.

and the other its negation. A sentence a is then said to be *state-description* if and only if a is a conjunction which contains as components one and only one sentence from each basic pair and no other sentences.[30] A sentence a is said to *belong to* a sentence b if and only if a is a basic sentence, b is a state-description, and a occurs in b as one of the (basic) conjunctive components of b. Finally, we define, recursively, that a *holds in* b if and only if a is a sentence, b is a state-description, and

(i) a is atomic and belongs to b, or

(ii) a is the negation of a sentence c which does not hold in b, or

(iii) a is a disjunction of two sentences at least one of which holds in b, or

(iv) a is of the form:

left parenthesis concatenated with b concatenated with right parenthesis concatenated with c,

where b is any variable, and c is a sentence or a sentential function of the one variable b, and every d holds in b, where d is a sentence formed from c by replacing the free occurrences of b in c (if any) by an individual constant.

In order to give examples of each of these notions, we suppose for the moment that S contains only two primitive predicate constants 'P_1' and 'P_2', that 'P_1' is of degree one and 'P_2' of degree two, and that S contains only three individual constants 'a_1', 'a_2', and 'a_3'. 'P_1a_1', '$\sim P_2a_1a_2$', '$\sim P_1a_3$', etc., are clearly basic sentences. The state-descriptions may be listed as follows, where '.' is the sign for logical conjunction:

(1) '$(P_1a_1 \cdot P_1a_2 \cdot P_1a_3 \cdot P_2a_1a_1 \cdot P_2a_1a_2 \cdot P_2a_1a_3 \cdot P_2a_2a_1 \cdot P_2a_2a_2 \cdot P_2a_3a_1 \cdot P_2a_3a_2 \cdot P_2a_3a_3)$',

(2) '$(\sim P_1a_1 \cdot P_1a_2 \cdot \ldots \cdot P_2a_3a_3)$',

(3) '$(P_1a_1 \cdot \sim P_1a_2 \cdot P_1a_3 \cdot \ldots \cdot P_2a_3a_3)$',

.

.

.

(4096) '$(\sim P_1a_1 \cdot \sim P_1a_2 \cdot \sim P_1a_3 \cdot \sim P_2a_1a_1 \cdot \sim P_2a_1a_2 \cdot \ldots \cdot \sim P_2a_3a_3)$'.

Note that (1) here contains just 12 atomic components and hence there are 2^{12} or 4096 possible ways of taking these components together as true or false. Thus there are here just 4096 state-descriptions.

Clearly the basic sentence 'P_1a_2' *belongs to* the state-descriptions (1) and (2) but not to (3) and (4096). Clearly also, the sentence '$(P_1a_1 \vee P_1a_2)$' *holds in* (1), (2), and in (3), but not in (4096).

The notion of a state-description is especially important in Carnap's semantics. It provides an explication of the concept of possible cases

[30] Strictly, an additional clause is needed here concerning the lexicographical order of the component conjunctions.

or states-of-affairs of the domain of individuals of *S* with respect to all the primitive properties or relations of *S*. If the state-descriptions as defined above are really to provide such an explication, certain restrictions upon the choice of primitive individual and predicate constants must be imposed. In fact, it must be assumed that the *atomic sentences* of *S* be logically *independent* of each other in the sense that no "class [*K*] containing some atomic sentences and the negations of other atomic sentences logically entails . . . another atomic sentence [*c*] or its negation." "If this requirement is not fulfilled," Carnap notes, "then some state-description will be self-contradictory and hence not describe a possible state. (This holds for any state-description containing the class [*K*] specified and, in addition, the negation of the other atomic sentence [*c*] or this sentence [*c*] itself, respectively.)"[31] Suppose, e.g., that *a* and *b* are atomic sentences of *S* such that *b* is derivable from *a*. Then any state-description containing both *a* and the negation of *b* would be contradictory and hence would not describe a possible state of affairs. In order to fulfill this requirement of independence for the atomic sentences, (1) the primitive individual constants of *S* must be taken as designating separate individuals (i.e., no two can designate the same individual), and (2) the primitive predicates must be taken in such a way that they designate properties or relations which are in some sense logically independent of each other. Also, in order for state-descriptions to describe all possible states, it is assumed that (3) the values for variables in *S*, i.e., the members of ValVbl_S, are just the individuals designated by the primitive individual constants. Otherwise there would be some possible states described by no state-description.

One more important notion is needed for the definition of L-truth in *S*, that of the *range* of a sentence. The range of a sentence *a* is defined as the class of all state-descriptions in which *a* holds. Ranges are then classes of sentences of certain kinds. The *universal range* is the class of all state-descriptions of *S*, the *null range,* the null class of state-descriptions of *S*. The range of the sentence '$\mathrm{P}_1\mathrm{a}_1$', e.g., consists of just those state-descriptions to which it belongs. That of '$(x)\mathrm{P}_1 x$', on the other hand, consists of just the state-descriptions to which '$\mathrm{P}_1\mathrm{a}_1$', '$\mathrm{P}_1\mathrm{a}_2$', '$\mathrm{P}_1\mathrm{a}_3$' all belong.

Using these preliminaries, we are now prepared for the definitions of L-truth and allied notions. A sentence is said to be *L-true* (logically true) or analytic in *S* if and only if its range is universal, and *L-false* (logically false) or contradictory in *S* if and only if its range is null. A sentence *a* is said to *L-imply* in *S* a sentence *b* if and only if the range of *a* is a subclass (is included in) the range of *b*, and *a* is said to be *L-equivalent* in *S*

[31] I.S., 61f.

with *b* if and only if their ranges are the same. Two sentences are said to be *L-disjunct* in *S* if and only if the (class) sum of their ranges is universal, and *L-exclusive* in *S* if and only if the product of their ranges is null.[32] A sentence is *L-determinate* in *S* if it is either L-true or L-false; otherwise, L-indeterminate or *factual* in *S*. Thus, e.g., '$(P_1a_1 \vee {\sim}P_1a_1)$' is L-true, and so is '${\sim}(x)P_1x \vee P_1a_1$'. '$(P_1a_2 \cdot {\sim}P_1a_2)$' is clearly L-false. '$P_1a_1$' L-implies '$(P_1a_1 \vee P_1a_2)$' because every state-description in which 'P_1a_1' holds is also a state-description in which '$(P_1a_1 \vee P_1a_2)$' holds. '${\sim}(P_1a_1 \vee P_1a_2)$' is L-equivalent with '$({\sim}P_1a_1 \cdot {\sim}P_1a_2)$'. '$P_1a_1$' and '${\sim}P_1a_1$' are L-disjunct as well as L-exclusive. And so on.

Note that these definitions are *purely syntactical* and involve no reference to *semantical* concepts in their definientia. Carnap calls these notions semantical and important semantical concepts are definable when we combine the L-concepts with the semantical truth-concept, as we shall see in a moment. Strictly, however, the definientia here involve reference only to the expressions and to classes of expressions of appropriate kinds. No reference is made to the entities which these expressions designate. The L-concepts as thus defined are strictly concepts of syntax.

The L-concepts are of great significance for the logical analysis of science.

> Suppose that a certain physical theory, formulated as a class of laws K_1, is investigated and compared with another theory K_2. There are many questions which are beyond the scope of a merely logical analysis and require factual observation; . . . . On the other hand, there are questions of another kind, usually called logical questions, whose answers are not dependent upon the result of observations and therefore can be given before any relevant observations are made. These questions involve L-concepts.[33]

E.g., a given statement in K_1 may be L-true and hence there would be no need to look for a method of verifying or testing that statement. Thus that statement could be omitted from K_1 without diminishing the power or usefulness of that theory. Likewise, a given statement in K_1 may perhaps be shown to be an L-implicate of another in which case it also may be omitted from K_1. Similarly, for logical reasons alone, two statements of K_1 may be shown to be L-exclusive or incompatible, in which case K_1 is inconsistent. And so on.

Philosophically also the L-concepts are of great interest. That of L-truth, e.g., seems to provide a clear-cut explication of the notion of *analytic* as over and against synthetic truth. What appears to be essentially this distinction has played an important role in the history of philosophy

[32]It will be recalled that the sum of the classes of sentences *K* and *L* is the class of all sentences which are members of either *K* or *L* or both, and the product is the class of sentences which are members of both.

[33]I.S., 61f.

and is in some form an essential distinction for many philosophical purposes.

If we combine the semantical truth-concept with the L-concepts, we can define several further semantical notions, the so-called *F-concepts.* Thus, a sentence *a* is *F-true* in *S* or true for *factual* reasons if any only if *a* is true in *S* but not L-true. Similarly a sentence *a* is *F-false* in *S* if and only if it is false but not L-false. A sentence *a* is said to be an *F-implicate* in *S* of *b* if and only if it is an implicate of *b* but not an L-implicate of *b*. And similarly for the notions of *F-equivalence* in *S, F-disjunction* in *S* and *F-exclusiveness* in *S.*[34]

Every term of Carnap's semantics is either (a) a radical concept, (b) an L-concept, or (c) an F-concept. (For the so-called *absolute* concepts, see § VII below.) In terms of concepts already available, therefore, all other semantical notions should be definable.

One further semantical notion should be mentioned, that of the *content* in *S* of a sentence *a*. This may be defined as the (class-) negation of the range of *a*. In other words, the content in *S* of a sentence *a* is the class of all state-descriptions in which *a* does not hold. This definition accords well with the intuitive notion that the assertive power of a sentence consists primarily in its excluding certain states of affairs. The more the sentence excludes, the more it asserts.[35]

V. *Toward a General Semantics*

The main characteristics of Carnap's conception of a semantical system *S* are now before us, where *S* is of first order, containing a finite number of primitive individual constants and a finite number of primitive predicate constants. Let us consider now the changes required in Carnap's treatment if *S* contains a denumerable infinity of primitive individual constants, but is otherwise as above. The preliminary syntactical concepts can then be given as in § II, but with certain slight changes. In particular, the notion of being an *individual constant* can no longer be defined by enumeration. Instead, this notion may be defined recursively, or in some other appropriate way.

Two methods of handling the semantics of *S* will now be sketched.

In the first method 'DesInd_S' is taken as a primitive in the semantical metalanguage. Its meaning is assumed to be known, and therefore no definition of it is required. But in order to fix this meaning, we shall need some semantical axioms stating explicitly its properties. (See § VI below.) The other semantical notions are then definable with only slight changes as above.

34I.S., 141-145.

35I.S., 148-154. Cf. K. Popper, *Logik der Forschung* (Vienna: Springer, 1935), 67.

The notion of a state-description must now be defined, not as a finitely long sentence of such and such a kind, but as an infinitely large class of sentences. (A *basic pair*, it will be recalled, is a class of just two sentences, one of which is an atomic sentence and the other of which is its negation.) Thus, a class of sentences *K* can be said now to be a *state-description* in *S* if and only if *K* contains as its only members one and only one sentence from every basic pair. Also a sentence *a* is now said to *belong* to a state-description *K* if and only if *a* is a member of *K*. Also one can now define '*a holds in* a state-description *K*' essentially as above, as well as the notions of *range* and hence *L-truth* in *S*.[36]

Note that here, where we have an infinity of primitive individual constants, the range of a sentence is a class of classes of sentences. The theory of ranges thus requires fundamentally variables and quantifiers over such classes and hence presupposes a basic logic of at least third order.

A second method of handling designation of individuals, for *S* containing an infinite number of primitive individual constants as primitive, is to assume that the individuals under consideration are *ordered* in an appropriate way. In particular we can assume that the individuals of *S* have the structure of a linear, discrete order with one initial but no terminal member. Suppose suc(x) is the successor of x in this order, and suppose a_1 is the one initial member. The individual constants of *S* are 'a_1', 'a_2', etc. But a_2 is to be identified with suc(a_1), a_3 with suc(suc (a_1)), etc., so that 'a_2', 'a_3', etc., may be dropped as primitives. We shall refer to 'a_1', 'suc(a_1)', 'suc(suc(a_1))', etc., as *individual terms*. The notion of 'DesInd_S' can then be defined recursively as follows. An expression *a* bears DesInd_S to an individual x if and only if

(i) *a* is 'a_1' and x is a_1, or

(ii) there is an individual term *b* and an individual y such that *b* DesInd_S y, *a* consists of 'suc' concatenated with '(' concatenated with *b* concatenated with ')' and x is a suc(y).

On the basis of this definition the semantics of *S* can be developed essentially as above. (For a more rigorous formulation of this theory see §VI.)

The significance of the method of assuming the individuals ordered may be seen as follows. If the object-language *S* is, e.g., intended to formalize certain elementary domains of physics, the individuals of *S* may be thought of as *positions* in a physical coordinate system. The individuals may then be identified outright with the natural numbers, a_1 being 0, suc(a_1) being 1, and so on. The numerical symbols may be construed ambiguously as standing either for natural numbers or for posi-

[36] L.F.P., 72ff.

tions in the fixed order. This ambiguity is, so to speak, packed into the meaning of the primitive predicate constants. Thus, e.g., if 'Prim' is a primitive predicate constant standing for the property of being a prime number, then 'Prim 3' may state that the *number* 3 is a prime number. Where 'Blue' is another one-place primitive predicate constant, 'Blue 3' on the other hand may state that the *position* whose coordinate is 3 is blue. The positions corresponding to the natural numbers may be within any discrete (presumably Euclidean) space of any finite number of dimensions.

In our considerations thus far *S* has been assumed to be of first order. It might appear therefore that Carnap's semantics, in being restricted to first-order systems, is too limited. The class of first-order systems, however, is an immensely wide class and includes many of the important languages which have been studied throughout the literature of modern logic. Further, systems which ordinarily are regarded as of higher order can be reinterpreted as first-order systems.[37] Therefore the class of systems which Carnap treats is actually a very wide and inclusive class. However, for the definition of *state-description* and *range*, as we have seen above, we assume that the fundamental domain of individuals of the language under consideration consists of just the individuals designated by the primitive individual constants. If there is only a finite number of such constants, there will be only a finite number of individuals; if an infinite number, an infinite number. But in no language can the fundamental domain consist of more than a denumerable totality.[38] For such languages would have to contain individuals not designated by a primitive individual constant, and hence there would be possible states not described by a state-description. Thus, in this important respect, Carnap's semantical method is limited. It cannot provide a semantics, e.g., for such important systems as those based upon the simplified theory of types or for systems based upon the Zermelo or von Neumann-Bernays set theories.

Thus Carnap does not achieve a *general* semantics applicable to all systems whatsoever. Nonetheless, especially in *I.S.*, the desirability of such a semantics is emphasized, and many tentative formulations are given. Here one or more semantical concepts, including at least one L-concept, are taken as primitives and specific axioms concerning them are laid down. We need not discuss these various formulations here, the kind of generality they achieve being somewhat limited.

37See, e.g., L. Löwenheim, "Ueber Möglichkeiten im Relativkalkül," *Mathematische Annalen,* LXXVI (1915), 447-470, and Th. Skolem, *op. cit.*

38We are presupposing here, as is customary, that *S* cannot contain more than a denumerable number of expressions.

VI. *Two Formalized Semantical Metalanguages*

Carnap's semantical metalanguages are always couched in ordinary language supplemented with logical and other symbols for clarity and explicitness. In this present section we shall formalize two of Carnap's semantical metalanguages, thereby exhibiting their precise logical structure. We shall thus be able to see clearly how the various parts of a semantical metalanguage are interrelated, what is presupposed by way of an underlying logic, what semantical axioms, if any, are needed, etc. etc. These formalizations will not be given here in rigorous detail, but only somewhat roughly.

The object-language *S* will be taken as above and as containing an infinite number of primitive individual constants. We can therefore presuppose the notation for *S* already given. The first metalanguage will incorporate the first method suggested in § V above. The second metalanguage will presuppose that the individuals of *S* are ordered according to the second method in § V.

Semantical metalanguages contain, roughly speaking, four tightly interwoven parts, a *logical* part, a *syntactical* part, a *translation* part, and a *semantical* part. The logical part contains the basic logical signs, including quantifiers over all the kinds of entities admitted as values for variables. The syntactical part must be such as to provide definitions of the basic notions discussed in § II. The semantical metalanguage must also contain a translation of the object-language to which it applies. The translation part may therefore consist of just the object-language itself, or of any language which corresponds appropriately with the object-language. The semantical part enables us to interrelate the expressions of the object-language with the objects for which, in one way or another, they stand.

The first semantical metalanguage we shall call SM_1. It will contain 'DesInd$_S$' as a primitive. The logical part of SM_1 contains the usual signs for the truth-functions, say 'v' and '~', as well as variables (together with quantifiers over them) of at least three logical levels or types. The variables of lowest type are to range over the *expressions* of *S* as well as over the *objects* about which *S* speaks. The variables of second type are to range over classes (or properties taken in extension) of and relations between or among the entities over which the variables of lowest type range. And finally, the variables of third type are to range over the classes and relations of or between or among the classes and relations over which the variables of second type range. As the underlying logic, one presupposes thus a functional calculus of third order. Identity of individuals and of these various kinds of classes and relations can easily be defined within such a logic.

The logical rules of SM_1 must provide for the familiar laws of truth-functions and quantifiers of third-order logic, for the rule of *modus ponens* and rules of generalization (for all kinds of variables admitted), as well as for axioms of extensionality. No axiom of infinity is needed, however, the effect of such being provided by the syntactical axioms. Also it seems likely that the axiom of choice is not needed.

The syntactical primitives of SM_1 include a symbol for concatenation, symbols for each of the primitive predicate and individual constants of *S*, as well as symbols for the basic logical signs of *S* including the variables of *S*. Some of the syntactical primitives of SM_1 are *structural descriptions* of the corresponding expressions of *S*. Concatenates of the structural-descriptive symbols of SM_1 are then also called the structural descriptions of the corresponding concatenates of symbols of *S*. In terms of concatenation the fundamental notions in the syntax of *S* are definable, as we have seen above.

As the syntactical axioms of SM_1 we can take the axioms of concatenation due essentially to Tarski. These include axioms to the effect that (1) no primitive symbol of *S* is identical with any other primitive symbol of *S*, (2) no primitive symbol of *S* is identical with any concatenate of expressions of *S*, and (3) the concatenate of two expressions *a* and *b* of *S* is identical with the concatenate of *c* and *d* if and only if either *a* is identical with *c* and *b* with *d* or there is an expression *e* of *S* such that *b* is the concatenate of *e* with *d* and *c* is the concatenate of *a* with *e* or else *a* is the concatenate of *c* with *e* and *d* is the concatenate of *e* with *b*. Also two rules of infinite induction (of the type sometimes called *Carnap's Rule* or *Hilbert's Rule*) are needed. The first is a syntactical rule to the effect that if one can prove within SM_1 that a certain property holds of each specific expression of *S* separately, then it is also provable that that property holds of all expressions of *S* whatsoever.[39] (Thus if one can prove that a certain property holds of 'a_1', 'a_2', etc., of '$\mathbf{P}_1$', '$\mathbf{P}_2$', etc., of '**v**', '~', '(', ')', '*x*', etc., and of all concatenates of such, of all concatenates of these concatenates, and so on, one can then infer that all expressions of *S* have that property.) Finally, a similar rule is presupposed with regard to the individuals of *S*. Thus, if one can prove that a certain property holds of the individual a_1, of a_2, of a_3, and so on, then it is also provable that all individuals of *S* have that property.

The translation part of SM_1 can be taken simply as *S* itself. Thus each primitive individual or predicate constant of *S* reappears as a primitive individual or predicate constant of SM_1. Note that the logical constants and variables of *S* are in effect already provided for in the underlying logic of SM_1. Recall that no axioms were laid down for *S*, and therefore there is no need for translation axioms within SM_1.

[39]Cf. Tarski, *op. cit.*, 289, 383.

The only specifically semantical primitive in SM_1 is 'DesInd$_S$', standing for the relation of designation of individuals. This being primitive, we need certain axioms to characterize the relation involved. The semantical axioms or rules needed are as follows:

(1) a DesInd$_S$ x,

where in place of 'x' we put in any primitive individual constant from the translation part of SM_1 and in place of 'a' the structural-descriptive name of that constant.

(2) If a DesInd$_S$ x and a DesInd$_S$ y, then $x = y$, for all a, x, and y.

(3) If a DesInd$_S$ x then a is a primitive individual constant of S, for all a and x. (It is presupposed that 'primitive individual constant of S' is appropriately defined within the syntactical part of SM_1.)

(1) tells us that 'a_1' designates in S the specific individual a_1, that 'a_2' designates a_2, etc. (1) thus helps to make explicit how we are using 'DesInd$_S$' *within* SM_1. (2) is in effect a *uniqueness principle.* It tells us that an expression designates in S at most one individual. (3) is a *limitation axiom,* stating that the only things which designate (in the sense of 'DesInd$_S$') are the individual constants of S.

The notion of 'ValVbl$_S$' may be defined very simply within SM_1 as the class of all objects designated (in the sense of DesInd$_S$) by some primitive individual constant or other.

We noted above that one must also assume, for the theory of state-descriptions, that no two primitive individual constants designate in S the same individual. It might be thought that this requirement should be made explicit by an additional semantical axiom. Rather than to make such an additional assumption in semantics we can in effect assume it as part of the underlying logic of identity. Thus the individual a_1 is to be distinct from the individual a_2, from a_3, etc.

In general we assume that

(4) $\sim \mathrm{a}_n = \mathrm{a}_m$,

for distinct m and n.

The second additional requirement needed for the theory of state-descriptions, concerning the logical independence of the primitive predicates, need not be discussed at this point, because it does not involve, directly at least, 'DesInd$_S$'.

The third assumption, that the members of ValVbl$_S$ are just the objects designated in S by the primitive individual constants of S, is now immediately provable, in view of the definition of 'ValVbl$_S$'.

As an example of a theorem within SM_1, we prove now another form of a uniqueness law, namely, that an individual of S is designated by at most one primitive individual constant. More precisely, we prove that

(5) If a DesInd$_S$ x and b DesInd$_S$ x then $a = b$, for all a, b, and x.

First, suppose either a or b or both are not primitive individual constants; then (5) holds, because by (3) either a or b or both do not bear DesInd_S to x. Thus, we have

(6) If a DesInd_S x and b DesInd_S x, then $a = b$,

where in place of 'a' or 'b' or both we put in any structural descriptions which do not name primitive individual constants. Next, suppose both a and b are primitive individual constants, say 'a_n' and 'a_m', respectively. If $m = n$, clearly the theorem holds. The formula (5) in this case we call (7). Next, suppose $m \neq n$. If in place of 'x' we put in 'a_n', (5) becomes

(8) If 'a_n' DesInd_S a_n and 'a_m' DesInd_S then 'a_n' = 'a_m'.

But from (1),

$$\text{'a}_m\text{' DesInd}_S\ \text{a}_m,$$

and by (2),

$$\text{If 'a}_m\text{' DesInd}_S\ \text{a}_n \text{ and 'a}_m\text{' DesInd}_S\ \text{a}_m, \text{ then a}_n = \text{a}_m.$$

But by the basic logic of identity,

$$\sim \text{a}_n = \text{a}_m,$$

for $m \neq n$. Therefore

$$\sim \text{'a}_m\text{' DesInd}_S\ \text{a}_n,$$

and hence (8) holds. A similar result follows if in place of 'x' we put in 'a_m' or 'a_k' for any $k \neq m$ and $\neq n$. Hence, using the second rule of infinite induction, we see that

(9) For all x, if 'a_n' DesInd_S x and 'a_m' DesInd_S x, then 'a_n' = 'a_m'.

But (9) holds for all choices of primitive individual constants in place of 'a_n', and by (6) for all structural descriptions other than of primitive individual constants. Therefore, using the first rule of infinite induction we gain

(10) For all a, for all x, if a DesInd_S x and 'a_m' DesInd_S x, then a = 'a_m'.

By a similar argument, we can generalize the 'a_m', thereby gaining (5). (Q.E.D.)

Many of the definitions in §§II-IV above are of the kind called recursive. Recursive definitions can always be eliminated in favor of direct ones, if the underlying logic is of sufficient power.[40] In order to show this by means of an example, let us return to the syntactical definition of 'formula of S' given in §III. There, it will be recalled, an expression a of S was said to be a formula, if and only if it is (i) an atomic formula, or (ii) is the negation of a formula, or (iii) is the disjunction of two formulae, or (iv) is the result of prefixing a quantifier to a formula. We can turn this recursive definition into an explicit one as follows, using a quantifier of higher logical type. We can say that an expression a of S is now a formula if and only if for every class K, if

(i) every atomic formula is a member of K, and

[40]Cf., e.g., D. Hilbert and P. Bernays, *Grundlagen der Mathematik,* I (Berlin: Springer, 1934), 286-382, and II (1939), 392ff. and 451ff.

(ii) for every b, if b is a member of K then the concatenate of '∼' with b is also, and

(iii) for every b and c, if b and c are separately members of K then the result of writing '(' concatenated with b concatenated with '**v**' concatenated with c concatenated with ')' is a member of K, and

(iv) for all b, if b is a member of K then any result of prefixing a quantifier to b is also a member of K;

then a also is a member of K.

All of the recursive definitions given above in §III can be transformed into explicit definitions in a similar way. For this transformation, note that the quantifier 'for all classes K' is essential. Such quantifiers are available in SM_1, the underlying logic of being of third order.

Within SM_1 we thus have a foundation for giving the semantics of S as outlined above. The various semantical notions defined informally in §§III-IV can now be rigorously defined within SM_1. The precise logical structure of one formulation of semantics is thus given.[41]

The second formalized semantical metalanguage, which will be called SM_2, presupposes that the individuals of S are ordered in the way described in §V. The syntax presupposed is essentially as in SM_1. Here we do not have 'DesInd_S' as a semantical primitive. The object-language S, however, contains the primitive 'suc'. Concerning this notion S presumably contains some axioms which reappear also within the translation part of SM_2. These axioms can, e.g., be taken essentially as the famous axioms of Peano, for the natural numbers. As above in §V, let a_1 be the one individual which is initial in the order. Thus as logical *order axioms* of S and hence of the metalanguage we have:

01. There is no x such that a_1 is suc(x).

02. If suc(x) and suc(y) are identical, then so also are x and y.

03. If some property F holds of a_1 and for all x, if it holds of x then it holds also of suc(x), then F holds of all objects.

Within SM_2, we can define 'DesInd_S', simply by transforming its recursive definition in §V into an explicit one. Thus, we can say that a bears DesInd_S to x if and only if for all dyadic relations R, if for all b, and for all y, b bears R to y if and only if

(i) b is 'a_1' and y is a_1, or

(ii) there as a c and a z such that c is an individual term (i.e., is 'a_1' or 'suc(a_1)' or 'suc(suc(a_1))', or etc.) which bears R to z, b consists of 'suc' concatenated with '(' concatenated with c concatenated with ')', and y is suc(z);

then a bears R to x.

The syntactical axioms of SM_2 are essentially those of SM_1. The axioms governing 'DesInd_S' in SM_1 are now provable in SM_2. There is

[41]Cf. however, Tarski, *op. cit.*, esp. 279-327.

no need here of the second rule of infinite induction nor of the supposition that

$$\sim a_n = a_m$$

for distinct m and n. (But in both metalanguages it is understood of course that the primtive predicate constants of the translation of S are logically independent of each other in the appropriate sense.) The further development of SM_2 is essentially like that of SM_1.

VII. *Propositions and Intensional Procedures*

All the metalanguages we have discussed thus far have been *extensional* metalanguages. Expressions standing for such intensional objects as propositions, e.g., have not been admitted. "I personally believe," Carnap notes,

> that there is no danger in speaking of propositions and classes of propositions provided it is done in a cautious way, ... However, there are advantages in avoiding propositions altogether and speaking instead about the sentences or classes of sentences expressing them, whenever this is possible. . . . There are chiefly two advantages to this method. First, we avoid a discussion of the controversial question whether the use of the concept of proposition would involve us in a kind of Platonic metaphysics and would violate the principles of empiricism. Second, there is the technical advantage that for this method a metalanguage of simpler structure suffices.[42]

These technical advantages have been exhibited in the various metalanguages considered above.

'Proposition' is used by Carnap

> neither for a linguistic expression nor for a subjective, mental occurrence, but rather for something objective that may or may not be exemplified in nature. . . . . We apply the term 'proposition' to any entities of a certain logical type, namely, those that may be expressed by (declarative) sentences in a language.[43]

For certain philosophical purposes, fundamental use of propositions may be essential. Further, as has been suggested above, Carnap has been very interested in semantical procedures which involve propositions.

If variables over propositions are admitted in a semantical metalanguage and propositions are regarded as entities designated by declarative sentences, it seems reasonable to admit also a further type of designation-relation. 'DesInd_S' and the various notions of attribute-designation in S are presupposed. But *sentences* now also are allowed to designate. Therefore, a new relation of proposition-designation is needed. This is symbolized by 'DesProp_S'.[44] Whether 'DesProp_S' is taken as a primitive or as a defined symbol depends upon special features of the semantical metalanguage that need not concern us here.

42L.F.P., 71.

43*Meaning and Necessity,* 27.

44See I.S., 49-55.

In terms of 'DesProp$_S$' the semantical concept of truth is immediately definable. Thus, a sentence a of the object-language S is true if and only if there is a proposition p such that a bears DesProp$_S$ to p and p.

Also now that propositions are available we can define the so-called *absolute* concepts. The absolute concepts do not belong strictly to syntax or semantics, because they apply to nonlinguistic entities. They do, however, correspond more or less roughly with some of the semantical notions introduced above. Thus, we can say that

A proposition p is *true* if and only if (by definition) p,

p is *false* if and only if $\sim p$,

q is an *implicate* of p if and only if $(\sim p \vee q)$, and so on.

Likewise we can introduce some absolute terms corresponding to the L-concepts. Thus,

p is *L-true* if and only if there is a sentence a which bears DesProp$_S$ to p and which is L-true in S.

Similarly,

p *L-implies* q if and only if $(\sim p \vee q)$ is L-true,

$p = q$ if and only if p L-implies q and also q L-implies p,

and so on. This last definition introduces *propositional identity* as mutual L-implication. L-equivalent sentences thus bear DesProp$_S$ to the same proposition.

In terms of propositions, various alternative procedures of handling the notions of state-description and range are available.[45] These are considerably more complicated than the extensional methods developed above. We need not sketch them here. Also it seems that everything of fundamental import in the intensional theories of state-descriptions and ranges can be accomplished more easily extensionally.

What is now needed, in the opinion of the author, is (1) a compelling argument as to why propositions are required in philosophical analysis, and then (2) an exact and meticulous formalization of a semantical metalanguage accommodating such entities. Carnap's work in this direction is no doubt of great value. But neither (1) nor (2) has yet, it would seem, been given in a wholly satisfactory way.

VIII. *Interpretation*

It will be recalled that a *syntactical* system includes a specification of *axioms* or primitive sentences together with an indication of the circumstances under which a formula is provable or derivable from another formula or other formulae. In a *semantical* system, on the other hand, as we have seen, definitions of such notions play no role. In a semantical system the notion of *truth* in effect supplants that of provability. There is, however, an important analogy between the roles these two notions

[45] I.S., 88-118.

play, respectively, within semantical and syntactical systems. The question as to how these two concepts are interrelated brings us to the question as to how syntactic and semantical systems are interrelated.

The most important way in which a syntactical and a semantical system are interrelated is when the latter can be said to be an *interpretation* for the former. More specifically, we can say that *S* is an interpretation for *K* if *K* is a syntactical system, *S* is a semantical system, and every sentence of *K* is a sentence of S.[46] There are several different kinds of interpretations to be distinguished, that of a *true* interpretation, of a *false* interpretation, of an *L-true* interpretation, an *L-false* one, and so on. Of these the notion of a true interpretation is of especial importance. *S* is said to be a true interpretation for *K* if and only if *S* is an interpretation for *K*, every primitive sentence of *K* is true in *S*, and for all *a* and *b*, if *b* is derivable from *a* in *K* then *b* is an implicate of *a* in *S*. On the other hand, *S* is an L-true interpretation for *K* if and only if *S* is an interpretation for *K*, every primitive sentence of *K* is L-true in *S*, and derivability in *K* becomes the converse of L-implication in *S*. And so on.

These definitions incorporate important intuitive ideas. Note that these definitions are given in some kind of a comparative semantical metalanguage of *K* and *S*. The exact features of this metalanguage remain to be worked out. Within such a metalanguage syntactical and semantical languages themselves would presumably be values for variables. For this we should need a more careful analysis as to precisely what such languages are.

IX. *Meaning Postulates*

We have just noted that Carnap's semantical systems do not contain *axioms*, nor hence *theorems*. Because the addition of axioms would in effect limit the number of actual states, the theory of state-descriptions must be considerably altered. In a recent paper Carnap has considered the changes in his semantics which the addition of a finite number of axioms necessitates.[47] Let us glance at this briefly.

The axioms which one adds to a semantical system are called *meaning postulates*, i.e., axioms which tell us how the *meanings* of the primitive predicate constants are interrelated. The meaning postulates are thus not to be confused with factual assertions. They are rather statements authenticated or warranted by an intent to use the primitive predicate constants in a certain way rather than by any appeal to facts or to observations. For example, let '*W*' be a primitive predicate constant of some semantical system *S* designating the relation of *being warmer than*. Then *W* is clearly

[46] I.S., 202ff.

[47] "Meaning Postulates," *Philosophical Studies*, III (1952), 65-73. See also the papers referred to there by Bar-Hillel and Kemeny.

transitive, irreflexive, and hence asymmetric wholly in virtue of its meaning. But in order to ascertain that *W* has these properties we need not make any observations or perform any experiments. That *W* has these properties results rather from our decision to use '*W*' in a certain way. Therefore the statements

(1) $`Wa_1\ a_2 \cdot Wa_2\ a_3 \cdot \sim Wa_1\ a_3`$,

(2) $`Wa_1\ a_2 \cdot Wa_2\ a_1`$,

(3) $`Wa_1\ a_1`$,

are false due to their meaning. Some of the state-descriptions, however, of *S* (assuming that *S* contains only a finite number of individual constants and hence that the state-descriptions of *S* are in fact statements) are statements containing the components of (1), (2), and (3) as subconjunctions. These state-descriptions would be false in view of the falsity of (1), (2), or (3), and hence could not represent possible states. Thus if meaning postulates are added, the theory of state-descriptions must be altered.

Let *P* be the conjunction of the finite number of meaning postulates adopted. Consider now just the state-descriptions of *S* in which *P* holds. Clearly these state-descriptions are just those compatible with the assumption of *P*. Hence this sub-class of the state-descriptions of *S* we may now think of as the actual state-descriptions of *S*. We can then say that an expression *a* is L-true in *S* if and only if it holds in each state-description of this sub-class. The other L-concepts can then be defined as before.

Of course this method does not apply if axioms other than meaning postulates are admitted, in particular, for axioms which are factual assertions or empirical generalizations of one kind or another. Hence to define 'L-true' for systems based on meaning postulates presupposes that the meaning postulates themselves are in some sense *directly* L-true. This latter term is then in effect taken as a semantical primitive. Thus the concept of L-truth for such systems is not really analyzed *ab initio,* but is merely reduced to that of direct L-truth.

X. *Some Concluding Remarks*

Leaving aside for the moment Carnap's comments concerning meaning postulates, let us recall again that Carnap's semantical systems do not contain axioms or theorems. This is in marked contrast to other treatments of semantics, especially those of Tarski and Church, in which an interpreted system is constructed from an underlying calculus in an appropriate way by the addition of semantical rules or definitions. Although *prima facie* this might appear an important differentia of Carnap's semantics, actually it seems to be a rather minor one. Carnap's notion of being an interpretation gives the necessary interrelation between syntactical and semantical systems. Further, for some philosophical purposes, it is desirable to have a notion of semantical system available independent of an underlying axiomatics. Thus, e.g., Carnap's illuminating discussion of the question as to whether logic is a matter of convention depends upon having syntactical and semantical systems available independently.[48] Only then can one discuss the question as to how a calculus can be constructed *in accord with* a given intended interpretation, or how, given a calculus, one can interpret it in this way or that. In discussing the problem of the conventional character of logic, one can then distinguish two different procedures. In one we start our inquiry with an interpretation and construct a calculus in accord with it. In the other, we construct first a calculus and then formulate a semantical system which interprets it. In the latter method there is greater freedom. The syntactical rules

> can be chosen arbitrarily and hence are conventional if they are taken as the basis of the construction of the language system and if the interpretation of the system is later superimposed. On the other hand, a system of logic is not a matter of choice, but either right or wrong, if an interpretation of the logical signs is given in advance. . . .[49]

In either method, Carnap notes, conventions are of fundamental importance, but they are of different kinds. Although Carnap's remarks on this topic are far from conclusive, they have helped enormously to clarify some of the problems involved.

This paper has contained in the main a sympathetic exposition and "rational reconstruction" of Carnap's extensional semantics. Here and there, however, certain criticisms have been hinted at or indicated, and it may be useful if we summarize here very briefly the more important of these. (1) Carnap's method of handling concatenation does not appear to be clearly described. (2) Many of Carnap's metalanguages are very loosely formulated. (3) Many of his object-languages are so weak as to be uninteresting. Such important languages as those incorporating a type theory or those based upon the Zermelo set-theory in one way or another are not considered. (4) Carnap's metalanguages are too powerful. Many of them contain virtually the whole of mathematics. To use very powerful metalinguistic procedures as applied to weak object-languages constitutes an inversion of Hilbert's original concept of *Beweistheorie,* which was to utilize narrow metalinguistic resources for examining powerful object-languages. In spite of the important set-back to Hilbert's program provided by the work of Gödel, Skolem, Tarski, and others, the original concept remains a vital ideal, perhaps still attainable in an appropriately modified sense. (5) L-truth as defined by Carnap is in fact a syntactical concept, and is thus not defined in terms of the semantical truth-concept. This procedure is in some sense counter-intuitive, if one feels that L-truth ought to be

[48]See *Foundations of Logic and Mathematics,* 24-29.
[49]*Ibid.,* 48.

defined as a special case of truth. (6) Carnap's intensional procedures require a more careful and meticulous formulation. (7) Carnap has underestimated the philosophical importance of sign-events.

In closing let us attempt to indicate briefly the significance which Carnap attaches to semantics. There are, it would seem, at least six compelling reasons for regarding semantics as philosophically or methodologically important. First, it has given a clear-cut explication of the age-old classical conception of truth. Second, it has given a clear-cut explication of the notion of analytic truth. Third, it has provided a basis for Carnap's analysis of intensions and modalities. Fourth, it has provided a basis for inductive logic. Fifth, it has provided a framework for some very fruitful discussions of topics in the philosophy of science, which is now preeminently concerned with the semantics of scientific language. Finally, the notion of *system,* which semantics helps to clarify, explicates fully the vague notion of system which has haunted the history of philosophy. A primary task of most kinds of philosophy from the earliest times has been to exhibit a system of concepts or principles adequate for some intended purpose. The notion of system involved here seems to be now fully explicated by modern semantics.

It is thus clear why many philosophers think that modern semantics provides a necessary prologomenon for philosophical analysis. This is not to suggest, however, that semantical studies exhaust the whole of the philosophical analysis of language. As we have seen above, semantics abstracts from pragmatics just as syntax abstracts from semantics. Thus in a full analysis of language pragmatical and perhaps other ingredients will also be seen to play an important role.

Carnap's eminence as a philosopher is not due alone to his many illuminating and important technical contributions. Perhaps more than any other contemporary he has reasserted the very central role of logic in the various areas of philosophy and methodology. Most of the great philosophers of the past have recognized this centrality in one way or another, and Carnap thus stands (in this respect) squarely in the traditions *inter alia* of Plato, Aristotle, St. Thomas, Descartes, Leibniz, Hume, Mill, Peirce, Whitehead, and Russell. In the face of the various heterodoxies of our time—some even led by professional logicians!—it is of great significance to have revitalized the role of philosophical logic to the extent that Carnap has done. In his hands logic has indeed become "the olive branch from the old to the young, the wand which in the hands of youth has the magic property of creating science."[50]

R. M. Martin

Department of Philosophy
New York University

[50] A. N. Whitehead, *The Aims of Education* (New York: Macmillan, 1929), 179.

12

W. V. Quine

CARNAP AND LOGICAL TRUTH

MY dissent from Carnap's philosophy of logical truth is hard to state and argue in Carnap's terms. This circumstance perhaps counts in favor of Carnap's position. At any rate, a practical consequence is that, though the present essay was written entirely for this occasion, the specific mentions of Carnap are few and fleeting until well past the middle. It was only by providing thus elaborately a background of my own choosing that I was able to manage the more focussed criticisms in the later pages. Actually, parts also of the earlier portions correspond to what I think to be Carnap's own orientation and reasoning; but such undocumented points are best left unattributed.

I

Kant's question "How are synthetic judgments a priori possible?" precipitated the *Critique of Pure Reason*. Question and answer notwithstanding, Mill and others persisted in doubting that such judgments were possible at all. At length some of Kant's own clearest purported instances, drawn from arithmetic, were sweepingly disqualified (or so it seemed; but see §II) by Frege's reduction of arithmetic to logic. Attention was thus forced upon the less tendentious and indeed logically prior question, "How is logical certainty possible?" It was largely this latter question that precipitated the form of empiricism which we associate with between-war Vienna—a movement which began with Wittgenstein's *Tractatus* and reached its maturity in the work of Carnap.

Mill's position on the second question had been that logic and mathematics were based on empirical generalizations, despite their superficial appearance to the contrary. This doctrine may well have been felt to do less than justice to the palpable surface differences between the deductive sciences of logic and mathematics, on the one hand, and the empirical sciences ordinarily so-called on the other. Worse, the doctrine derogated from the certainty of logic and mathematics; but Mill may not have been one to be excessively disturbed by such a consequence. Perhaps classical mathematics did lie closer to experience then than now; at any rate the infinitistic reaches of set theory, which are so fraught with speculation and so remote from any possible experience, were unexplored in his day. And it is against just these latter-day mathematical extravagances that empiricists outside the Vienna Circle have since been known to inveigh,[1] in much the spirit in which the empiricists of Vienna and elsewhere have inveighed against metaphysics.

What now of the empiricist who would grant certainty to logic, and to the whole of mathematics, and yet would make a clean sweep of other non-empirical theories under the name of metaphysics? The Viennese solution of this nice problem was predicated on language. Metaphysics was meaningless through misuse of language; logic was certain through tautologous use of language.

As an answer to the question "How is logical certainty possible?" this linguistic doctrine of logical truth has its attractions. For there can be no doubt that sheer verbal usage is in general a major determinant of truth. Even so factual a sentence as 'Brutus killed Caesar' owes its truth not only to the killing but equally to our using the component words as we do. Why then should a logically true sentence on the same topic, e.g. 'Brutus killed Caesar or did not kill Caesar', not be said to owe its truth *purely* to the fact that we use our words (in this case 'or' and 'not') as we do? — for it depends not at all for its truth upon the killing.

The suggestion is not, of course, that the logically true sentence is a contingent truth *about* verbal usage; but rather that it is a sentence which, *given* the language, automatically becomes true, whereas 'Brutus killed Caesar', given the language, becomes true only contingently on the alleged killing.

Further plausibility accrues to the linguistic doctrine of logical truth when we reflect on the question of alternative logics. Suppose someone puts forward and uses a consistent logic the principles of which are contrary to our own. We are then clearly free to say that he is merely using the familiar particles 'and', 'all', or whatever, in other than the familiar senses, and hence that no real contrariety is present after all. There may of course still be an important failure of intertranslatability, in that the behavior of certain of our logical particles is incapable of being duplicated by paraphrases in his system or vice versa. If translation in this sense is possible, from his system into ours, then we are pretty sure to protest that he was wantonly using the familiar particles 'and' and 'all' (say) where he might unmisleadingly have used such and such other familiar phrasing. This reflection goes to support the view that the truths of logic have no content over and above the meanings they confer on the logical vocabulary.

[1]An example is P. W. Bridgman, "A Physicist's Second Reaction to Mengenlehre," *Scripta Mathematica,* II (1933-34), 101-117, 224-234.

Much the same point can be brought out by a caricature of a doctrine of Levy-Bruhl, according to which there are prelogical peoples who accept certain simple self-contradictions as true. Over-simplifying, no doubt, let us suppose it claimed that these natives accept as true a certain sentence of the form '*p* and not *p*'. Or—not to over-simplify too much—that they accept as true a certain heathen sentence of the form '*q* ka bu *q*' the English translation of which has the form '*p* and not *p*'. But now just how good a translation is this, and what may the lexicographer's method have been? If any evidence can count against a lexicographer's adoption of 'and' and 'not' as translations of 'ka' and 'bu', certainly the natives' acceptance of '*q* ka bu *q*' as true counts overwhelmingly. We are left with the meaninglessness of the doctrine of there being prelogical peoples; prelogicality is a trait injected by bad translators. This is one more illustration of the inseparability of the truths of logic from the meanings of the logical vocabulary.

We thus see that there is something to be said for the naturalness of the linguistic doctrine of logical truth. But before we can get much further we shall have to become more explicit concerning our subject matter.

II

Without thought of any epistemological doctrine, either the linguistic doctrine or another, we may mark out the intended scope of the term 'logical truth', within that of the broader term 'truth', in the following way. First we suppose indicated, by enumeration if not otherwise, what words are to be called logical words; typical ones are 'or', 'not', 'if', 'then', 'and', 'all', 'every', 'only', 'some'. The logical truths, then, are those true sentences which involve only logical words *essentially*. What this means is that any other words, though they may also occur in a logical truth (as witness 'Brutus', 'kill', and 'Caesar' in 'Brutus killed or did not kill Caesar'), can be varied at will without engendering falsity.[2]

Though formulated with reference to language, the above clarification does not of itself hint that logical truths owe their truth to language.

[2]Substantially this formulation is traced back a century and a quarter by Yehoshua Bar-Hillel, "Bolzano's Definition of Analytic Propositions," *Methodos,* II (1950), 32-55 (= *Theoria,* XVI (1950), 91-117). But note that the formulation fails of its purpose unless the phrase "can be varied at will," above, is understood to provide for varying the words not only singly but also two or more at a time. E.g. the sentence 'If some men are angels some animals are angels' can be turned into a falsehood by simultaneous substitution for 'men' and 'angels', but not by any substitution for 'angels' alone, nor for 'men', nor for 'animals' (granted the non-existence of angels). For this observation and illustration I am indebted to John R. Myhill, who expresses some indebtedness in turn to Benson Mates.—The matters dealt with in these pages are currently undergoing such lively discussion that it may be well to record the date when this essay left my hands: May 15, 1954, apart from the present footnote.

What we have thus far is only a delimitation of the class, *per accidens* if you please. Afterward the linguistic doctrine of logical truth, which is an epistemological doctrine, goes on to say that logical truths are true by virtue purely of the intended meanings, or intended usage, of the logical words. Obviously if logical truths *are* true by virtue purely of language, the logical words are the only part of language that can be concerned in the matter; for these are the only ones that occur essentially.

Elementary logic, as commonly systematized nowadays, comprises truth-function theory, quantification theory, and identity theory. The logical vocabulary for this part, as commonly rendered for technical purposes, consists of truth-function signs (corresponding to 'or', 'and', 'not', etc.), quantifiers and their variables, and '='.

The further part of logic is set theory, which requires there to be classes among the values of its variables of quantificaton. The one sign needed in set theory, beyond those appropriate to elementary logic, is the connective 'ϵ' of membership. Additional signs, though commonly used for convenience, can be eliminated in well-known ways.

In this dichotomy I leave metatheory, or logical syntax, out of account. For, either it treats of special objects of an extra-logical kind, viz. notational expressions, or else, if these are made to give way to numbers by arithmetization, it is reducible via number theory to set theory.

I will not here review the important contrasts between elementary logic and set theory, except for the following one. Every truth of elementary logic is obvious (whatever this really means), or can be made so by some series of individually obvious steps. Set theory, in its present state anyway, is otherwise. I am not alluding here to Gödel's incompleteness principle, but to something right on the surface. Set theory was straining at the leash of intuition ever since Cantor discovered the higher infinites; and with the added impetus of the paradoxes of set theory the leash was snapped. Comparative set theory has now long been the trend; for, so far as is known, no consistent set theory is both adequate to the purposes envisaged for set theory and capable of substantiation by steps of obvious reasoning from obviously true principles. What we do is develop one or another set theory by obvious reasoning, or elementary logic, from unobvious first principles which are set down, whether for good or for the time being, by something very like convention.

Altogether, the contrasts between elementary logic and set theory are so fundamental that one might well limit the word 'logic' to the former (though I shall not), and speak of set theory as mathematics in a sense exclusive of logic. To adopt this course is merely to deprive 'ϵ' of the status of a logical word. Frege's derivation of arithmetic would then cease to count as a derivation from logic; for he used set theory. At any rate we should be prepared to find that the linguistic doctrine of logical truth holds for elementary logic and fails for set theory, or vice versa. Kant's readiness to see logic as analytic and arithmetic as synthetic, in particular, is not superseded by Frege's work (as Frege supposed[3]) if "logic" be taken as elementary logic. And for Kant logic certainly did not include set theory.

III

Where someone disagrees with us as to the truth of a sentence, it often happens that we can convince him by getting the sentence from other sentences, which he does accept, by a series of steps each of which he accepts. This of course is the common-sense notion of proof. Disagreement which cannot be thus resolved I shall call *deductively irresoluble.* Now if we try to warp the linguistic doctrine of logical truth around into something like an experimental thesis, perhaps a first approximation will run thus: *Deductively irresoluble disagreement as to a logical truth is evidence of deviation in usage (or meanings) of words.* This is not yet experimentally phrased, since one term of the affirmed relationship, viz. 'usage' (or 'meanings'), is in dire need of an independent criterion. However, the formulation would seem to be fair enough within its limits; so let us go ahead with it, not seeking more subtlety until need arises.

Already the obviousness (or potential obviousness) of elementary logic can be seen to present an insuperable obstacle to our assigning any experimental meaning to the linguistic doctrine of elementary logical truth. Deductively irresoluble dissent from an elementary logical truth *would* count as evidence of deviation over meanings if anything can, but simply because dissent from a logical truism is as extreme as dissent can get.

The philosopher, like the beginner in algebra, works in danger of finding that his solution-in-progress reduces to '$0 = 0$'. Such is the threat to the linguistic theory of elementary logical truth. For, that theory now seems to imply nothing that is not already implied by the fact that elementary logic is obvious or can be resolved into obvious steps.

The considerations which were adduced in §I, to show the naturalness of the linguistic doctrine, are likewise seen to be empty when scrutinized in the present spirit. One was the circumstance that alternative logics are inseparable practically from mere change in usage of logical words. Another was that illogical cultures are indistinguishable from ill-translated ones. But both of these circumstances are adequately accounted for by mere obviousness of logical principles, without help of a linguistic doctrine of logical truth. For, there can be no stronger evidence of a change

[3]See §§87f., 109 of Gottlob Frege, *Foundations of Arithmetic* (New York: Philosophical Library, and Oxford: Blackwell, 1950), a reprint of *Grundlagen der Arithmetik* (Breslau, 1884) with trans. by J. L. Austin.

in usage than the repudiation of what had been obvious, and no stronger evidence of bad translation than that it translates earnest affirmations into obvious falsehoods.

Another point in §I was that true sentences generally depend for their truth on the traits of their language in addition to the traits of their subject matter; and that logical truths then fit neatly in as the limiting case where the dependence on traits of the subject matter is nil. Consider, however, the logical truth 'Everything is self-identical', or '$(x)(x = x)$'. We *can* say that it depends for its truth on traits of the language (specifically on the usage of '$=$'), and not on traits of its subject matter; but we can also say, alternatively, that it depends on an *obvious* trait, viz. self-identity, of its subject matter, viz. everything. The tendency of our present reflections is that there is no difference.

I have been using the vaguely psychological word 'obvious' non-technically, assigning it no explanatory value. My suggestion is merely that the linguistic doctrine of elementary logical truth likewise leaves explanation unbegun. I do not suggest that the linguistic doctrine is false and some doctrine of ultimate and inexplicable insight into the obvious traits of reality is true, but only that there is no real difference between these two pseudo-doctrines.

Turning away now from elementary logic, let us see how the linguistic doctrine of logical truth fares in application to set theory. As noted in §II, we may think of 'ϵ' as the one sign for set theory in addition to those of elementary logic. Accordingly the version of the linguistic doctrine which was italicized at the beginning of the present section becomes, in application to set theory, this: Among persons already in agreement on elementary logic, deductively irresoluble disagreement as to a truth of set theory is evidence of deviation in usage (or meaning) of 'ϵ'.

This thesis is not trivial in quite the way in which the parallel thesis for elementary logic was seen to be. It is not indeed experimentally significant as it stands, simply because of the lack, noted earlier, of a separate criterion for usage or meaning. But it does seem reasonable, by the following reasoning.

Any acceptable evidence of usage or meaning of words must reside surely either in the observable circumstances under which the words are uttered (in the case of concrete terms referring to observable individuals) or in the affirmation and denial of sentences in which the words occur. Only the second alternative is relevant to 'ϵ'. Therefore any evidence of deviation in usage or meaning of 'ϵ' must reside in disagreement on sentences containing 'ϵ'. This is not, of course, to say of *every* sentence containing 'ϵ' that disagreement over it establishes deviation in usage or meaning of 'ϵ'. We have to assume in the first place that the speaker under investigation agrees with us on the meanings of words other than 'ϵ' in the sentences in question. And it might well be that, even from among the sentences containing only 'ϵ' and words on whose meanings he agrees with us, there is only a select species *S* which is so fundamental that he cannot dissent from them without betraying deviation in his usage or meaning of 'ϵ'. But *S* may be expected surely to include some (if not all) of the sentences which contains *nothing* but 'ϵ' and the elementary logical particles; for it is these sentences, insofar as true, that constitute (pure, or unapplied) set theory. But it is difficult to conceive of how to be other than democratic toward the truths of set theory. In exposition we may select some of these truths as so-called postulates and deduce others from them, but this is subjective discrimination, variable at will, expository and not set-theoretic. We do not change our meaning of 'ϵ' between the page where we show that one particular truth is deducible by elementary logic from another and the page where we show the converse. Given this democratic outlook, finally, the law of sufficient reason leads us to look upon *S* as including *all* the sentences which contain only 'ϵ' and the elementary logical particles. It then follows that anyone in agreement on elementary logic and in irresoluble disagreement on set theory is in deviation with respect to the usage or meaning of 'ϵ'; and this was the thesis.

The effect of our effort to inject content into the linguistic doctrine of logical truth has been, up to now, to suggest that the doctrine says nothing worth saying about elementary logical truth, but that when applied to set-theoretic truth it makes for a reasonable partial condensation of the otherwise vaporous notion of meaning as applied to 'ϵ'.

IV

The linguistic doctrine of logical truth is sometimes expressed by saying that logical truths are true by linguistic convention. Now if this be so, certainly the conventions are not in general explicit. Relatively few persons, before the time of Carnap, had ever seen any convention that engendered truths of elementary logic. Nor can this circumstance be ascribed merely to the slipshod ways of our predecessors. For it is impossible in principle, even in an ideal state, to get even the most elementary part of logic exclusively by the explicit application of conventions stated in advance. The difficulty is the vicious regress familiar from Lewis Carroll,[4] which I have elaborated elsewhere.[5] Briefly the point is that the logical truths, being infinite in number, must be given by general

[4]"What the Tortoise Said to Achilles," *Mind,* IV (1895), 278ff.

[5]"Truth by Convention," in O. H. Lee (ed.), *Philosophical Essays for A. N. Whitehead* (New York, 1936), 90-124. Reprinted in H. Feigl and W. Sellars (eds.), *Readings in Philosophical Analysis* (New York: Appleton, 1945).

conventions rather than singly; and logic is needed then to begin with, in the metatheory, in order to apply the general conventions to individual cases.

"In dropping the attributes of deliberateness and explicitness from the notion of linguistic convention," I went on to complain in the aforementioned paper, "we risk depriving the latter of any explanatory force and reducing it to an idle label." It would seem that to call elementary logic true by convention is to add nothing but a metaphor to the linguistic doctrine of logical truth which, as applied to elementary logic, has itself come to seem rather an empty figure (cf. §III).

The case of set theory, however, is different on both counts. For set theory the linguistic doctrine has seemed less empty (cf. §III); in set theory, moreover, convention in quite the ordinary sense seems to be pretty much what goes on (cf. §II). Conventionalism has a serious claim to attention in the philosophy of mathematics, if only because of set theory. Historically, though, conventionalism was encouraged in the philosophy of mathematics rather by the non-Euclidean geometries and abstract algebras, with little good reason. We can contribute to subsequent purposes by surveying this situation. Further talk of set theory is deferred to §V.

In the beginning there was Euclidean geometry, a compendium of truths about form and void; and its truths were not based on convention (except as a conventionalist might, begging the present question, apply this tag to everything mathematical.) Its truths were in practice presented by deduction from so-called postulates (including axioms; I shall not distinguish); and the selection of truths for this role of postulate, out of the totality of truths of Euclidean geometry, was indeed a matter of convention. But this is not *truth* by convention. The truths were there, and what was conventional was merely the separation of them into those to be taken as starting point (for purposes of the exposition at hand) and those to be deduced from them.

The non-Euclidean geometries came of artificial deviations from Euclid's postulates, without thought (to begin with) of true interpretation. These departures were doubly conventional; for Euclid's postulates were a conventional selection from among the truths of geometry, and then the departures were arbitrarily or conventionally devised in turn. But still there was no truth by convention, because there was no truth.

Playing within a non-Euclidean geometry, one might conveniently make believe that his theorems were interpreted and true; but even such conventional make-believe is not truth by convention. For it is not really truth at all; and what is conventionally pretended is that the theorems are true by non-convention.

Non-Euclidean geometries have, in the fullness of time, received serious interpretations. This means that ways have been found of so construing the hitherto unconstrued terms as to identify the at first conventionally chosen set of non-sentences with some genuine truths, and truths presumably not by convention. The status of an interpreted non-Euclidean geometry differs in no basic way from the original status of Euclidean geometry, noted above.

Uninterpreted systems became quite the fashion after the advent of non-Euclidean geometries. This fashion helped to cause, and was in turn encouraged by, an increasingly formal approach to mathematics. Methods had to become more formal to make up for the unavailability, in uninterpreted systems, of intuition. Conversely, disinterpretation served as a crude but useful device (until Frege's syntactical approach came to be appreciated) for achieving formal rigor uncorrupted by intuition.

The tendency to look upon non-Euclidean geometries as true by convention applied to uninterpreted systems generally, and then carried over from these to mathematical systems generally. A tendency indeed developed to look upon all mathematical systems as, qua mathematical, uninterpreted. This tendency can be accounted for by the increase of formality, together with the use of disinterpretation as a heuristic aid to formalization. Finally, in an effort to make some sense of mathematics thus drained of all interpretation, recourse was had to the shocking quibble of identifying mathematics merely with the elementary logic which leads from uninterpreted postulates to uninterpreted theorems.[6] What is shocking about this is that it puts arithmetic qua interpreted theory of number, and analysis qua interpreted theory of functions, and geometry qua interpreted theory of space, outside mathematics altogether.

The substantive reduction of mathematics to logic by Frege, Whitehead, and Russell is of course quite another thing. It is a reduction not to elementary logic but to set theory; and it is a reduction of genuine interpreted mathematics, from arithmetic onward.

V

Let us then put aside these confusions and get back to set theory. Set theory is pursued as interpreted mathematics, like arithmetic and analysis; indeed, it is to set theory that those further branches are reducible. In set theory we discourse about certain immaterial entities, real or erroneously alleged, viz. sets, or classes. And it is in the effort to make up our minds about genuine truth and falsity of sentences about these objects that we find ourselves engaged in something very like convention in an ordinary non-metaphorical sense of the word. We find ourselves

[6]Bertrand Russell, *Principles of Mathematics* (Cambridge, 1903), 429f; Heinrich Behmann, "Sind die mathematischen Urteile analytisch oder synthetisch?," *Erkenntnis*, IV (1934), 8ff; and others.

making deliberate choices and setting them forth unaccompanied by any attempt at justification other than in terms of elegance and convenience. These adoptions, called postulates, and their logical consequences (via elementary logic), are true until further notice.

So here is a case where postulation can plausibly be looked on as constituting truth by convention. But in §IV we have seen how the philosophy of mathematics can be corrupted by supposing that postulates always play that role. Insofar as we would epistemologize and not just mathematize, we might divide postulation as follows. Uninterpreted postulates may be put aside, as no longer concerning us; and on the interpreted side we may distinguish between *legislative* and *discursive* postulation. Legislative postulation institutes truth by convention, and seems plausibly illustrated in contemporary set theory. On the other hand discursive postulation is mere selection, from a preëxisting body of truths, of certain ones for use as a basis from which to derive others, initially known or unknown. What discursive postulation fixes is not truth, but only some particular ordering of the truths, for purposes perhaps of pedagogy or perhaps of inquiry into logical relationships ("logical" in the sense of elementary logic). All postulation is of course conventional, but only legislative postulation properly hints of *truth* by convention.

It is well to recognize, if only for its distinctness, yet a further way in which convention can enter; viz. in the adoption of new notations for old ones, without, as one tends to say, change of theory. Truths containing the new notation are conventional transcripts of sentences true apart from the convention in question. They depend for their truth partly on language, but then so did 'Brutus killed Caesar' (cf. §I). They come into being through a conventional adoption of a new sign, and they become true through conventional definition of that sign *together with* whatever made the corresponding sentences in the old notation true.

Definition, in a properly narrow sense of the word, is convention in a properly narrow sense of the word. But the phrase 'true by definition' must be taken cautiously; in its strictest usage it refers to a transcription, by the definition, of a truth of elementary logic. Whether such a sentence is true by convention depends on whether the logical truths themselves be reckoned as true by convention. Even an outright equation or biconditional connecting the definiens and the definiendum is a definitional transcription of a prior logical truth of the form '$x = x$' or '$p \equiv p$'.

Definition commonly so-called is not thus narrowly conceived, and must for present purposes be divided, as postulation was divided, into legislative and discursive. Legislative definition introduces a notation hitherto unused, or used only at variance with the practice proposed, or used also at variance, so that a convention is wanted to settle the ambiguity. Discursive definition, on the other hand, sets forth a preëxisting relation of interchangeability or coextensiveness between notations in already familiar usage. A frequent purpose of this activity is to show how some chosen part of language can be made to serve the purposes of a wider part. Another frequent purpose is language instruction.

It is only legislative definition, and not discursive definition nor discursive postulation, that makes a conventional contribution to the truth of sentences. Legislative postulation, finally, affords truth by convention unalloyed.

Increasingly the word 'definition' connotes the formulas of definition which appear in connection with formal systems, signalled by some extra-systematic sign such as '$=_{df}$'. Such definitions are best looked upon as correlating two systems, two notations, one of which is prized for its economical lexicon and the other for its brevity or familiarity of expression.[7] Definitions so used can be either legislative or discursive in their inception. But this distinction is in practice left unindicated, and wisely; for it is a distinction only between particular acts of definition, and not germane to the definition as an enduring channel of intertranslation.

The distinction between the legislative and the discursive refers thus to the act, and not to its enduring consequence, in the case of postulation as in the case of definition. This is because we are taking the notion of truth by convention fairly literally and simple-mindedly, for lack of an intelligible alternative. So conceived, conventionality is a passing trait, significant at the moving front of science but useless in classifying the sentences behind the lines. It is a trait of events and not of sentences.

Might we not still project a derivative trait upon the sentences themselves, thus speaking of a sentence as forever true by convention if its first adoption as true was a convention? No; this, if done seriously, involves us in the most unrewarding historical conjecture. Legislative postulation contributes truths which become integral to the corpus of truths; the artificiality of their origin does not linger as a localized quality, but suffuses the corpus. If a subsequent expositor singles out those once legislatively postulated truths again as postulates, that signifies nothing; he is engaged only in discursive postulation. He could as well choose his postulates from elsewhere in the corpus, and will if he thinks this serves his expository ends.

VI

Set theory, currently so caught up in legislative postulation, may some day gain a norm—even a strain of obviousness, perhaps—and lose all trace of the conventions in its history. A day could likewise have been

[7]See my *From a Logical Point of View* (Cambridge, Mass.: Harvard Univ. Press, 1953), 26f.

when our elementary logic was itself instituted as a deliberately conventional deviation from something earlier, instead of evolving, as it did, mainly by unplanned shifts of form and emphasis coupled with casual novelties of notation.

Today indeed there are dissident logicians even at the elementary level, propounding deviations from the law of the excluded middle. These deviations, insofar as meant for serious use and not just as uninterpreted systems, are as clear cases of legislative postulation as the ones in set theory. For here we have again, quite as in set theory, the propounding of a deliberate choice unaccompanied (conceivably) by any attempt at justification other than in terms of convenience.

This example from elementary logic controverts no conclusions we have reached. According to §§I and III, departure from the law of the excluded middle would count as evidence of revised usage of 'or' and 'not'. (This judgment was upheld in §III, though disqualified as evidence for the linguistic doctrine of logical truth.) For the deviating logician the words 'or' and 'not' are unfamiliar, or defamiliarized; and his decisions regarding truth values for their proposed contexts can then be just as genuinely a matter of deliberate convention as the decisions of the creative set-theorist regarding contexts of 'ϵ'.

The two cases are indeed much alike. Not only is departure from the classical logic of 'or' and 'not' evidence of revised usage of 'or' and 'not'; likewise, as argued at length in §III, divergences between set-theorists may reasonably be reckoned to revised usage of 'ϵ'. Any such revised usage is conspicuously a matter of convention, and can be declared by legislative postulation.

We have been at a loss to give substance to the linguistic doctrine, particularly of elementary logical truth, or to the doctrine that the familiar truths of logic are true by convention. We have found some sense in the notion of truth by convention, but only as attaching to a process of adoption, viz. legislation postulation, and not as a significant lingering trait of the legislatively postulated sentence. Surveying current events, we note legislative postulation in set theory and, at a more elementary level, in connection with the law of the excluded middle.

And do we not find the same continually in the theoretical hypotheses of natural science itself? What seemed to smack of convention in set theory (§V), at any rate, was "deliberate choice, set forth unaccompanied by any attempt at justification other than in terms of elegance and convenience"; and to what theoretical hypothesis of natural science might not this same character be attributed? For surely the justification of any theoretical hypothesis can, at the the time of hypothesis, consist in no more than the elegance or convenience which the hypothesis brings to the containing body of laws and data. How then are we to delimit the category of legislative postulation, short of including under it every new act of scientific hypothesis?

The situation may seem to be saved, for ordinary hypotheses in natural science, by there being some indirect but eventual confrontation with empirical data. However, this confrontation can be remote; and, conversely, some such remote confrontation with experience may be claimed even for pure mathematics and elementary logic. The semblance of a difference in this respect is largely due to over-emphasis of departmental boundaries. For, a self-contained theory which we can check with experience includes, in point of fact, not only its various theoretical hypotheses of so-called natural science but also such portions of logic and mathematics as it makes use of. Hence I do not see how a line is to be drawn between hypotheses which confer truth by convention and hypotheses which do not, short of reckoning *all* hypotheses to the former category save perhaps those actually derivable or refutable by elementary logic from what Carnap used to call protocol sentences. But this version, besides depending to an unwelcome degree on the debatable notion of protocol sentences, is far too inclusive to suit anyone.

Evidently our troubles are waxing. We had been trying to make sense of the role of convention in a priori knowledge. Now the very distinction between a priori and empirical begins to waver and dissolve, at least as a distinction between sentences. (It could of course, still hold as a distinction between factors in one's adoption of a sentence, but both factors might be operative everywhere.)

VII

Whatever our difficulties over the relevant distinctions, it must be conceded that logic and mathematics do seem qualitatively different from the rest of science. Logic and mathematics hold conspicuously aloof from any express appeal, certainly, to observation and experiment. Having thus nothing external to look to, logicians and mathematicians look closely to notation and explicit notational operations: to expressions, terms, substitution, transposition, cancellation, clearing of fractions, and the like. This concern of logicians and mathematicians with syntax (as Carnap calls it) is perennial, but in modern times it has become increasingly searching and explicit, and has even prompted, as we see, a linguistic philosophy of logical and mathematical truth.

On the other hand an effect of these same formal developments in modern logic, curiously, has been to show how to divorce mathematics (other than elementary logic) from any peculiarly notational considerations not equally relevant to natural science. By this I mean that mathematics can be handled (insofar as it can be handled at all) by axiomatization, outwardly quite like any system of hypotheses elsewhere in science; and elementary logic can then be left to extract the theorems.

The consequent affinity between mathematics and systematized natural science was recognized by Carnap when he propounded his P-rules alongside his L-rules or meaning postulates. Yet he did not look upon the P-rules as engendering analytic sentences, sentences true purely by language. How to sustain this distinction has been very much our problem in these pages, and one on which we have found little encouragement.

Carnap appreciated this problem, in *Logical Syntax,* as a problem of finding a difference in kind between the P-rules (or the truths thereby specified) and the L-rules (or the L-truths, analytic sentences, thereby specified). Moreover he proposed an ingenious solution.[8] In effect he characterized the logical (including mathematical) vocabulary as the largest vocabulary such that (1) there are sentences which contain only that vocabulary and (2) all such sentences are determinable as true or false by a purely syntactical condition—i.e. by a condition which speaks only of concatenation of marks. Then he limited the L-truths in effect to those involving just the logical vocabulary essentially.[9]

Truths given by P-rules were supposedly excluded from the category of logical truth under this criterion, because, though the rules specifying them are formally stated, the vocabulary involved can also be recombined to give sentences whose truth values are not determinate under any set of rules formally formulable in advance.

At this point one can object (pending a further expedient of Carnap's, which I shall next explain) that the criterion based on (1) and (2) fails of its purpose. For, consider to begin with the totality of those sentences which are expressed purely within what Carnap (or anyone) would want to count as logical (and mathematical) vocabulary. Suppose, in conformity with (2), that the division of the totality into the true and the false is reproducible in purely syntactical terms. Now surely the adding of one general term of an extra-logical kind, say 'heavier than', is not going to alter the situation. The truths which are expressible in terms of just 'heavier than', together with the logical vocabulary, will be truths of only the most general kind, such as '$(\exists x)(\exists y)(x$ is heavier than $y)$', '$(x){\sim}(x$ is heavier than $x)$', and '$(x)(y)(z)(x$ is heavier than $y \cdot y$ is heavier than $z \cdot\supset\cdot x$ is heavier than $z)$'. The division of the truths from the falsehoods in this supplementary domain can probably be reproduced in syntactical terms if the division of the original totality could. But then, under the criterion based on (1) and (2), 'heavier than' qualifies

[8] Carnap, *Logical Syntax of Language,* §50.

[9] Cf. §I above. Also, for certain reservations conveniently postponed at the moment, see §IX on "essential predication."

for the logical vocabulary. And it is hard to see what whole collection of general terms of natural science might not qualify likewise.

The further expedient, by which Carnap met this difficulty, was his use of Cartesian coördinates.[10] Under this procedure, each spatio-temporal particular c becomes associated with a class K of quadruples of real numbers, viz. the class of those quadruples which are the coördinates of component point-events of c. Further let us write $K[t]$ for the class of triples which with t appended belong to K; thus $K[t]$ is that class of triples of real numbers which is associated with the momentary state of object c at time t. Then, in order to say e.g. that c_1 is heavier than c_2 at time t, we say '$H(K_1[t], K_2[t])$', which might be translated as 'The momentary object associated with $K_1[t]$ is heavier than that associated with $K_2[t]$'. Now $K_1[t]$ and $K_2[t]$ are, in every particular case, purely mathematical objects; viz. classes of triples of real numbers. So let us consider all the true and false sentences of the form '$H(K_1[t], K_2[t])$' where, in place of '$K_1[t]$' and '$K_2[t]$', we have purely logico-mathematical designations of particular classes of triples of real numbers. There is no reason to suppose that all the truths of *this* domain can be exactly segregated in purely syntactical terms. Thus inclusion of '*H*' does violate (2), and therefore '*H*' fails to qualify as logical vocabulary. By adhering to the method of coördinates and thus reconstruing all predicates of natural science in the manner here illustrated by '*H*', Carnap overcomes the objection noted in the preceding paragraph.

To sum up very roughly, this theory characterizes logic (and mathematics) as the largest part of science within which the true-false dichotomy *can* be reproduced in syntactical terms. This version may seem rather thinner than the claim that logic and mathematics are somehow true by linguistic convention, but at any rate it is more intelligible, and, if true, perhaps interesting and important. To become sure of its truth, interest, and importance, however, we must look more closely at this term 'syntax'.

As used in the passage: "The terms 'sentence' and 'direct consequence' are the two primitive terms of logical syntax,"[11] the term 'syntax' is of course irrelevant to a thesis. The relevant sense is that rather in which it connotes discourse about marks and their succession. But here still we must distinguish degrees of inclusiveness; two different degrees are exemplified in *Logical Syntax,* according as the object language is Carnap's highly restricted Language I or his more powerful Language II. For the former, Carnap's formulation of logical truth is narrowly syntactical in the manner of familiar formalizations of logical systems by axioms and

[10]*Logical Syntax of Language,* §§3, 15.

[11]Carnap, *Philosophy and Logical Syntax,* 47.

rules of inference. But Gödel's proof of the incompletability of elementary number theory shows that no such approach can be adequate to mathematics in general, nor in particular to set theory, nor to Language II. For Language II, in consequence, Carnap's formulation of logical truth proceeded along the lines rather of Tarski's technique of truth-definition.[12] The result was still a purely syntactical specification of the logical truths, but only in this more liberal sense of 'syntactical': it was couched in a vocabulary consisting (in effect) of (a) names of signs, (b) an operator expressing concatenation of expressions, and (c), by way of auxiliary machinery, the whole logical (and mathematical) vocabulary itself.

So construed, however, the thesis that logico-mathematical truth is syntactically specifiable becomes uninteresting. For, what it says is that logico-mathematical truth is specifiable in a notation consisting solely of (a), (b), *and* the whole logico-mathematical vocabulary itself. But *this* thesis would hold equally if "logico-mathematical" were broadened (at *both* places in the thesis) to include physics, economics, and anything else under the sun; Tarski's routine of truth-definition would still carry through just as well. No special trait of logic and mathematics has been singled out after all.

Strictly speaking, the position is weaker still. The mathematics appealed to in (c) must, as Tarski shows, be a yet more inclusive mathematical theory in certain respects than that for which truth is being defined. It was largely because of his increasing concern over this self-stultifying situation that Carnap relaxed his stress on syntax, in the years following *Logical Syntax,* in favor of semantics.

VIII

Even if logical truth were specifiable in syntactical terms, this would not show that it was grounded in language. Any *finite* class of truths (to take an extreme example) is clearly reproducible by a membership condition couched in as narrowly syntactical terms as you please; yet we certainly cannot say of every finite class of truths that its members are true purely by language. Thus the ill-starred doctrine of syntactical specifiability of logical truth was always something other than the linguistic doctrine of logical truth, if this be conceived as the doctrine that logical truth is grounded in language. In any event the doctrine of syntactical

[12]*Logical Syntax,* esp. 34a-i, 60a-d, 71a-d. These sections had been omitted from the German edition, but only for lack of space; cf. p. xi of the English edition. Meanwhile they had appeared as articles: "Die Antinomien . . . " and "Ein Gültigkeitskriterium . . . . " At that time Carnap had had only partial access to Tarski's ideas (cf. "Gültigkeitskriterium," f.n. 3), the full details of which reached the non-Slavic world in 1936; Alfred Tarski, "Der Wahrheitsbegriff in den formalisierten Sprachen," *Studia Philosophica,* I, 261-405.

specifiability, which we found pleasure in being able to make comparatively clear sense of, has unhappily had to go by the board. The linguistic doctrine of logical truth, on the other hand, goes sturdily on.

The notion of logical truth is now counted by Carnap as semantical. This of course does not of itself mean that logical truth is grounded in language; for note that the general notion of truth is also semantical, though truth in general is not grounded purely in language. But the semantical attribute of logical truth, in particular, *is* one which, according to Carnap, is grounded in language: in convention, fiat, meaning. Such support as he hints for this doctrine, aside from ground covered in §§I-VI, seems to depend on an analogy with what goes on in the propounding of artificial languages; and I shall now try to show why I think the analogy mistaken.

I may best schematize the point by considering a case, not directly concerned with logical truth, where one might typically produce an artificial language as a step in an argument. This is the imaginary case of a logical positivist, say Ixmann, who is out to defend scientists against the demands of a metaphysician. The metaphysician argues that science presupposes metaphysical principles, or raises metaphysical problems, and that the scientists should therefore show due concern. Ixmann's answer consists in showing in detail how people (on Mars, say) might speak a language quite adequate to all of our science but, unlike our language, incapable of expressing the alleged metaphysical issues. (I applaud this answer, and think it embodies the most telling component of Carnap's own anti-metaphysical representations; but here I digress.) Now how does our hypothetical Ixmann specify that doubly hypothetical language? By telling us, at least to the extent needed for his argument, what these Martians are to be imagined as uttering and what they are thereby to be understood to mean. Here is Carnap's familiar duality of formation rules and transformation rules (or meaning postulates), as rules of language. But these rules are part only of Ixmann's narrative machinery, not part of what he is portraying. He is not representing his hypothetical Martians themselves as somehow explicit on formation and transformation rules. Nor is he representing there to be any intrinsic difference between those truths which happen to be disclosed to us by his partial specifications (his transformation rules) and those further truths, hypothetically likewise known to the Martians of his parable, which he did not trouble to sketch in.

The threat of fallacy lurks in the fact that Ixmann's rules are indeed arbitrary fiats, as is his whole Martian parable. The fallacy consists in confusing levels, projecting the conventional character of the rules into the story, and so misconstruing Ixmann's parable as attributing truth-legislation to his hypothetical Martians.

The case of a non-hypothetical artificial language is in principle the same. Being a new invention, the language has to be explained; and the explanation will proceed by what may certainly be called formation and transformation rules. These rules will hold by arbitrary fiat, the artifex being boss. But all we can reasonably ask of these rules is that they enable us to find corresponding to each of his sentences a sentence of like truth value in familiar ordinary language. There is no (to me) intelligible additional decree that we can demand of him as to the boundary between analytic and synthetic, logic and fact, among his truths. We may well decide to extend our word 'analytic' or 'logically true' to sentences of his language which he in his explanations has paired off fairly directly with English sentences so classified by us; but this is our decree, regarding our word 'analytic' or 'logically true'.

IX

We had in §II to form some rough idea of what logical truth was supposed to take in, before we could get on with the linguistic doctrine of logical truth. This we did, with help of the general notion of truth[13] together with a partial enumeration of the logical vocabulary of a particular language. In §VII we found hope of a less provincial and accidental characterization of logical vocabulary; but it failed. Still, the position is not intolerable. We well know from modern logic how to devise *a* technical notation which is admirably suited to the business of 'or', 'not', 'and', 'all', 'only', and such other particles as we would care to count as logical; and to enumerate the signs and constructions of that technical notation, or a theoretically adequate subset of them, is the work of a moment (cf. §II). Insofar as we are content to think of all science as fitted within that stereotyped logical framework—and there is no hardship in so doing—our notion of logical vocabulary is precise. And so, derivatively, is our notion of logical truth. But only in point of extent. There is no epistemological corollary as to the *ground* of logical truth (cf. §II).

Even this half-way tolerable situation obtains only for logical truth in a relatively narrow sense, omitting truths by "essential predication" (in Mill's phrase) such as 'No bachelor is married'.[14] I tend to reserve the term 'logically true' for the narrower domain, and to use the term 'analytic' for the more inclusive domain which includes truths by essen-

[13]In defense of this general notion, in invidious contrast to that of analyticity, see my *From a Logical Point of View,* 137f.

[14]Cf. Morton White, "The Analytic and the Synthetic: An Untenable Dualism," in Sidney Hook (ed.), *John Dewey: Philosopher of Science and Freedom* (New York: Dial, 1950), 316-330. Reprinted in Leonard Linsky (ed.), *Semantics and the Philosophy of Language* (Urbana: University of Illinois Press, 1952).

tial predication. Carnap on the contrary has used both terms in the broader sense. But the problems of the two subdivisions of the analytic class differ in such a way that it has been convenient up to now in this essay to treat mainly of logical truth in the narrower sense.

The truths by essential predication are sentences which can be turned into logical truths by supplanting certain simple predicates (e.g. 'bachelor') by complex synonyms (e.g. 'man not married'). This formulation is not inadequate to such further examples as 'If *A* is part of *B* and *B* is part of *C* then *A* is part of *C*'; this case can be managed by using for 'is part of' the synonym 'overlaps nothing save what overlaps'.[15] The relevant notion of synonymy is simply *analytic* coextensiveness (however circular this might be as a definition).

To count analyticity a genus of logical truth is to grant, it may seem, the linguistic doctrine of logical truth; for the term 'analytic' directly suggests truth by language. But this suggestion can be adjusted, in parallel to what was said of 'true by definition' in §V. 'Analytic' means true by synonymy and logic, hence no doubt true by language and logic, and simply true by language *if* the linguistic doctrine of logical truth is right. Logic itself, throughout these remarks, may be taken as including or excluding set theory (and hence mathematics), depending on further details of one's position.

What has made it so difficult for us to make satisfactory sense of the linguistic doctrine is the obscurity of 'true by language'. Now 'synonymous' lies within that same central obscurity; for, about the best we can say of synonymous predicates is that they are somehow "coextensive by language." The obscurity extends, of course, to 'analytic'.

One quickly identifies certain seemingly transparent cases of synonymy, such as 'bachelor' and 'man not married', and senses the triviality of associated sentences such as 'No bachelor is married'. Conceivably the mechanism of such recognition, when better understood, might be made the basis of a definition of synonymy and analyticity in terms of linguistic behavior. On the other hand such an approach might make sense only of something like degrees of synonymy and analyticity. I see no reason to expect that the full-width analyticity which Carnap and others make such heavy demands upon can be fitted to such a foundation in even an approximate way. In any event, we at present lack any tenable general suggestion, either rough and practical or remotely theoretical, as to what it is to be an analytic sentence. All we have are purported illustrations, and claims that the truths of elementary logic, with or without the rest of mathematics, should be counted in. Wherever there has been a sem-

[15]Cf. Nelson Goodman, *The Structure of Appearance* (Cambridge, Mass.: Harvard Univ. Press, 1951).

blance of a general criterion, to my knowledge, either there has been some drastic failure such as tended to admit all or no sentences as analytic, or there has been a circularity of the kind noted three paragraphs back, or there has been a dependence on terms like 'meaning', 'possible', 'conceivable', and the like, which are at least as mysterious (and in the same way) as what we want to define. I have expatiated on these troubles elsewhere, as has White.[16]

Logical truth (in my sense, excluding the additional category of essential predication) is, we saw, well enough definable (relative to a fixed logical notation). *Elementary* logical truth can even be given a narrowly syntactical formulation, such as Carnap once envisaged for logic and mathematics as a whole (cf. §VII); for the deductive system of elementary logic is known to be complete. But when we would supplement the logical truths by the rest of the so-called analytic truths, true by essential predication, then we are no longer able even to say what we are talking about. The distinction itself, and not merely an epistemological question concerning it, is what is then in question.

What of settling the limits of the broad class of analytic truths by fixing on a standard language as we did for logical truth? No, the matter is very different. Once given the logical vocabulary, we have a means of clearly marking off the species logical truth within the genus truth. But the intermediate genus analyticity is not parallel, for it does not consist of the truths which contain just a certain vocabulary essentially (in the sense of §II). To segregate analyticity we should need rather some sort of accounting of synonymies throughout a universal language. No regimented universal language is at hand, however, for adoption or consideration; what Carnap has propounded in this direction have of course been only illustrative samples, fragmentary in scope. And even if there were one, it is not clear by what standards we would care to settle questions of synonymy and analyticity within it.

X

Carnap's present position[17] is that one has specified a language quite rigorously only when he has fixed, by dint of so-called meaning postulates, what sentences are to count as analytic. The proponent is supposed to distinguish between those of his declarations which count as meaning postulates, and thus engender analyticity, and those which do not. This he does, presumably, by attaching the label 'meaning postulate'.

But the sense of this label is far less clear to me than four causes of its seeming to be clear. Which of these causes has worked on Carnap, if

[16]Quine, *From a Logical Point of View,* Essay II; White, *op. cit.*

[17]See particularly "Meaning Postulates."

any, I cannot say; but I have no doubt that all four have worked on his readers. One of these causes is misevaluation of the role of convention in connection with artificial language; thus note the unattributed fallacy described in §VIII. Another is misevaluation of the conventionality of postulates: failure to appreciate that postulates, though they are postulates always by fiat, are not *therefore* true by fiat; cf. §§IV-V. A third is over-estimation of the distinctive nature of postulates, and of definitions, because of conspicuous and peculiar roles which postulates and definitions have played in situations not really relevant to present concerns: postulates in uninterpreted systems (cf. §IV), and definitions in double systems of notation (cf. §V). A fourth is misevaluation of legislative postulation and legislative definition themselves, in two respects: failure to appreciate that this legislative trait is a trait of scientific hypothesis very generally (cf. §VI), and failure to appreciate that it is a trait of the passing event rather than of the truth which is thereby instituted (cf. end of §V).

Suppose a scientist introduces a new term, for a certain substance or force. He introduces it by an act either of legislative definition or of legislative postulation. Progressing, he evolves hypotheses regarding further traits of the named substance or force. Suppose now that some such eventual hypothesis, well attested, identifies this substance or force with one named by a complex term built up of other portions of his scientific vocabulary. We all know that this new identity will figure in the ensuing developments quite on a par with the identity which first came of the act of legislative definition, if any, or on a par with the law which first came of the act of legislative postulation. Revisions, in the course of further progress, can touch any of these affirmations equally. Now I urge that scientists, proceeding thus, are not thereby slurring over any meaningful distinction. Legislative acts occur again and again; on the other hand a dichotomy of the resulting truths themselves into analytic and synthetic, truths by meaning postulate and truths by force of nature, has been given no tolerably clear meaning even as a methodological ideal.

One conspicuous consequence of Carnap's belief in this dichotomy may be seen in his attitude toward philosophical issues, e.g. as to what there is. It is only by assuming the cleavage between analytic and synthetic truths that he is able e.g. to declare the problem of universals to be a matter not of theory but of linguistic decision.[18] Now I am as impressed as Carnap with the vastness of what language contributes to science and to one's whole view of the world; and in particular I grant that one's hypothesis as to what there is, e.g. as to there being universals, is at bottom just as arbitrary or pragmatic a matter as one's adoption of a new brand of set theory or even a new system of bookkeeping. Carnap

[18]See Carnap, "Empiricism, Semantics, and Ontology," esp. §3, longest footnote.

in turn recognizes that such decisions, however conventional, "will nevertheless usually be influenced by theoretical knowledge."[19] But what impresses me more than it does Carnap is how well this whole attitude is suited also to the theoretical hypotheses of natural science itself, and how little basis there is for a distinction.

The lore of our fathers is a fabric of sentences. In our hands it develops and changes, through more or less arbitrary and deliberate revisions and additions of our own, more or less directly occasioned by the continuing stimulation of our sense organs. It is a pale grey lore, black with fact and white with convention. But I have found no substantial reasons for concluding that there are any quite black threads in it, or any white ones.

W. V. QUINE

DEPARTMENT OF PHILOSOPHY
HARVARD UNIVERSITY

[19] *Op. cit.*, §2, fifth paragraph.

13

Herbert G. Bohnert

CARNAP'S THEORY OF DEFINITION AND ANALYTICITY

THE view that a sharp line can be drawn between analytic and synthetic sentences has been called one of the "two dogmas of empiricism." Whether or not the epithet is justified, there can be no denying that Carnap's development of the analytic-synthetic distinction has had a powerful influence on empiricist philosophers, providing, in the minds of many, a fundamental frame of reference for the organization of knowledge and thought. A profound reorientation would be called for if current charges[1] against the distinction were accepted as well founded.

In keeping with a policy, followed on other issues in this volume, of specifying a pro and a contra, this essay may be regarded as an exposition and defense of Carnap's position.

I

In order to appreciate the issues at stake, it may be well to review briefly the developments underlying Carnap's position.

The separating out of the concept of an analytic sentence from closely related concepts, and its growth in articulateness and generality, has been a steady development throughout almost the entire history of philosophic thought. But until the late nineteenth century it was a slow development because of a number of impediments. Often the motive for precision was not strong. The concept of analytic proposition was

[1]Surveys of the controversy since the flare-up initiated by M. G. White's "The Analytic and the Synthetic—an Untenable Dualism" in *John Dewey, Philosopher of Science and Freedom—A Symposium,* ed. S. Hook, (N.Y., 1950), and W. V. Quine, "Two Dogmas of Empiricism," *Philosophical Review* (1951), 20-41, together with ample bibliographical references may be found in the following: Mates, B. "Analytic Sentences," *Philosophical Review* (1952), 525-534, Peach, B., "A Non-descriptive Theory of the Analytic," *Philosophical Review* (1952) 349-367. Gewirth, A., "The Distinction Between Analytic and Synthetic Truths," *Journal of Philosophy* (1953), and R. Martin "On 'Analytic,'" *Philosophical Studies* (1952), among others, have already appeared. The present defense has been written as supplementary to theirs and the reader is recommended to these papers for discussion of important issues not taken up here.

often brought forward only to be unfavorably contrasted with that of "real" (empirical) proposition, and dismissed as "verbal" (Mill) or "frivolous" (Locke) or to be contrasted with more interesting kinds of necessary truth (Kant). It was cramped by the limited resources of formal logic. Even when the concept figured heavily, as in the doctrines of Leibniz and Kant, these formal lacks led to analyticity conceptions restricted to narrow classes of sentences, identities (Leibniz) or subject-predicate sentences (Kant), which were incapable of embracing more than limited portions of mathematics, leaving this great structure of knowledge a standing challenge to empiricists.

This shortcoming was aggravated by lack of rigorous analysis within the rapidly growing edifice of mathematics itself. Mathematics, unlike logic, seemed too resourceful. It spawned paradoxical and "imaginary" entities that seemed hard at times to reduce to reason in any sense, let alone analyticity. The traditional inclusion of geometry as a part of mathematics (adopted as a matter of course by Kant) posed a further obstacle to the disentanglement of analytic from synthetic, especially since its theorems often seemed more visualizably self-evident than the theorems of mathematical analysis.

Psychologism in logic—the view that propositions, properties, relations, are mental acts or dispositions and hence that "true", "valid", "analytic", and other logical terms must apply primarily to mental entities—furthered the confusion of self-evidence with analyticity and so helped obscure the possibility of mathematic's being analytic and, contrarily, favored the attempt to view geometry as resting on definitions. Psychologism furthermore discouraged hope for precise characterization of analyticity by making it appear to require a final knowledge of the mind and its workings. And, most important, it stood in the way of grasping the possibility of defending analyticity in terms of explicit linguistic convention, i.e. for sentences rather than for (mental) judgments.

This cloud began to lift with the developments in logic, mathematics, and physics in the later nineteenth and early twentieth centuries. Mathematical analysis was subjected to painstaking scrutiny, purified of paradoxical entities, and reduced by constructive stages to the Peano axiom system. Logic, in the hands of Frege, Russell, and others, grew up to meet it, and the reduction of mathematics to logic, long inconclusively debated, was seemingly carried out in large part. The Humean view, sometimes lost sight of during the Frege-Russell development, that mathematics did not involve matters of fact, was now reinforced; the reduction of mathematics to logic generated a logic so clear and explicit that Wittgenstein was able to make the tautological character of logic far more plausible than it had ever been before (though his proof was not complete). Geometry, on the other hand, was distinguished from the rest of mathematical analysis in two stages. First, the creation of non-Euclidean geometries gave rise to a sharp distinction between a postulate system and its interpretation—especially since these geometries were proved consistent by being given various purely mathematical interpretations. Secondly, the relativistic revolution in physics seemed to put previously self-evident truths of geometry to empirical test and to find them wanting. Consequently, the axiom systems of geometry had to be regarded as synthetic or analytic depending on their interpretation, i.e. as formalizations of competing, synthetic, physical theories when taken in their (normal) physical interpretations, but as analytic when given purely numerical (e.g. Cartesian) interpretations (and neither when left uninterpreted). This view, adumbrated by Helmholtz, was made explicit in the writings of the Vienna and Berlin philosophers during the twenties and thirties, and was taken by them to provide a basis for a complete resolution of Kant's synthetic a priori category. The basis for the escape from psychologism was laid when the postulate system was taken as a model and nucleus for the more inclusive and more significant concept of a *language*. This step was taken in principle by Frege in his inclusion of precise formation rules specifying the admissible sentence structures in the system of the *Grundgesetze*, and his drawing of a sharp line between sentences *in* the system (object language) and sentences *about* the system (in the metalanguage). It was made increasingly explicit by the Polish logicians but received its fullest formulation in Carnap. A language system with all its sentential forms precisely determined by recursive definitions strongly invited a definition of analyticity for sentences instead of judgments, especially since the rules of inference were so exact that validity of inference could be calculated. Furthermore the line between the contributions of linguistic convention and the contributions of fact to the formulation of empirical law seemed capable of being made sharp and clear with the help of a linguistic, as opposed to a mentalistic, analyticity concept, if only the empirical theory in question were adequately formalized. This was important, since Delboeuf and Poincaré, under the impact of the discovery of non-Euclidean geometries, had raised the role of convention in science almost to that of being as great a screen between the scientific observer and the *Ding-an-sich* as the Kantian transcendental contribution of the mind.

The line between analytic and synthetic, as mentioned above, was doubly marked by the Vienna and Berlin philosophers by being taken to coincide not only with that between mathematical knowledge and other scientific knowledge but also with that between a priori and a posteriori. This was made especially plausible by further aspects of the logico-mathematical development which tended to dissolve the aprioristic claims of metaphysics proper. First, the step from postulate systems to langauges via addition of formation rules revealed that sources of error may lie not only in inference but in sentence formation. Certain sentence forms, if admitted unconditionally, were shown to lead to paradoxes. Russell's theory of types guarded against these paradoxes by restricting sentence form. It thereby ruled out a class of near-sentences as nonsense or, more exactly, as non-sentences, and suggested that certain philosophically interesting sentences, such as "Beauty alone is beautiful," might rest on grammatical principles which, if made explicit, would lead to contradictions. Conversely, the process of formulating sentence formation rules suggested, especially to Carnap, that much of the language of traditional metaphysics could only be intelligibly interpreted as disguised formation rules, or, more generally, as analytic sentences about a (proposed) language, disguised as statements of fact. It seemed always possible to provide a syntactical parallel to every metaphysical sentence which seemed to contain all that was genuinely intelligible in the latter while pointing a way to the active development and use of this intelligible part in system building (language construction).[2] Carnap took the view that metaphysics was in fact based essentially on this confusion between object language and metalanguage and so, strictly speaking, constituted another category of nonsense. (He still holds this view though now he would use semantical parallels for some metaphysical "material mode" sentences.) For empiricists it was a short and tempting step to suppose that ways could be found to categorize all non-analytic language forms which were in principle immune to empirical confirmation as a third kind of nonsense.

These, then, make up the elements which were synthesized in the doctrines of the Unity of Science philosophers, especially Carnap. The realm of analyticity was held to be capable of being made, by appropriate formalization, to include all of logic, all of mathematics except physically interpreted geometry, and the entire definitional structure of the empirical sciences in so far as these were made explicit. The Comteian hierarchy of the sciences (in which mathematics stood at the top as the most general science) was rearranged. Mathematics, except geometry, was put in a class by itself, as without factual content, and all question of reducing science to mathematics (as suggested in different ways by Jeans and Eddington) was put aside. (Natural laws might, of course, be formulated mathematically, but not proven nor even completely interpreted by mathematics alone.)

The issues at stake, then, involve the boldest, yet most carefully articulated attempt so far made to lay the foundations for a consistent empirical outlook by accounting completely for the necessity of math-

[2]See Part V of *The Logical Syntax of Language* for detailed examples of such parallelisms.

ematics and delimiting explicitly the role of convention in empirical science.

With this in mind we may now turn to technical aspects of Carnap's development of the analyticity concept. This development may be divided into two main phases—the syntactical and the semantical—with the latter subdivided again into qualitative and quantitative (the latter being characterized by the use of range and measure concepts).

The first, syntactical, phase involved the attempt to characterize the analyticity concept in a purely formal way, in the context of an uninterpreted language or calculus. This approach was motivated by the increase in rigor made possible by the new treatment of systems in abstraction from interpretation, and by the fact that purely formal treatment had proved capable of representing forms of inference (especially those involving relations) which had previously been thought to rest on meanings alone. (In fact Carnap supposed this method so complete that he took as one of his objectives to show that nothing of the sort he now calls semantical was necessary.) Especially important was the asceticism made possible with respect to empirical knowledge and concepts. The entire syntactical system was capable of being built up by enumerative and recursive definitions[3] from a very small store of undefined descriptive predicates standing for the basic sign designs to be used in the system plus a sequence forming concept. And the empirical character even of these could be effectively ignored or even avoided.

[3]Roughly speaking, a recursive definition is one which proceeds in two steps. The first consists of an enumerative specification of certain entities (e.g., individuals, numbers, classes, couples) as being characterizable by the defined term. The second consists in specifying one or more relationships to any known member entity (or perhaps class of member entities) which will qualify an entity in its turn as characterizable by the defined predicate. The importance of this sort of definition lies in the fact that it permits the singling out of a (usually infinite) class of entities which have no (known) purely qualitative characteristic in common and so is ideally suited to the purposes of "arbitrary" or "non-natural" classifications and constructions. Since "abstract" entities have no purely qualitative characteristics in the first place and since this method of definition provides in itself an explicit method of proving universal sentences involving the defined class, recursive definition is a central constructive device of mathematics. A concept may be called recursive, even though explicitly defined itself, if it rests only on recursive concepts. Usually recursive concepts are logically determinate, but they need not be, if either the terms of the original enumeration or the generating relations are not purely denotative, but carry a descriptive or empirical sense. For example, "Member-of-Jones-Family", abbreviated "J", might be defined recursively by identifying individual *A* as a *J* ("A" being a denotative proper name) and adding that male parents of *J*'s are *J*'s and that any child, not both married and female, of a *J* is a *J*, and that all *J*'s satisfy one of these conditions. The class *J* so defined is not logically determinate. On the other hand, a recursive concept may involve descriptive terms in its basic enumeration and still be logically determinate. It will be maintained that Carnap's semantical concepts are of this last type and that this constitutes a significant difference from syntactical concepts, which must be taken into account in discussions of the independent meaningfulness of constructed language concepts.

Since their definition would evolve only a finite enumeration of physical shapes or events, they would raise no philosophical problems and so could be left undefined for purposes of discussion. In fact it would be possible in the light of Carnap's later semantical methods, to make the Gödelian process of arithmetization (correlating numbers to signs and to their combinations) by which Carnap reduced all the syntactical primitives to a single descriptive functor over the natural numbers, a basis for eliminating all non-logical signs, i.e. by allowing numbers themselves and number-theoretic functions to constitute, not merely designate, the signs of the syntactical metalanguage (though of course such a "language" would not be writable). One thing making this parsimony important was the desire to separate logical concepts from anything involving experience. Another was that Carnap was concerned to refute Wittgenstein's contention that discourse about language involved an attempt to convey something essentially unspeakable. By showing all logic to be syntactical and by showing that a syntactical system could formulate its own syntax, Carnap hoped to show that all philosophically significant sentences about a language could be made at least as precise as sentences in that language.

It was natural in this context to take provability as the essential trait of an analytic sentence. While self-evidence was to be discarded it seemed that an analytic sentence ought to be provable by means available to human minds. This encountered difficulties of a purely syntactical nature. While the barrier of an over-narrow conception of sentence structure was overcome, a new barrier of incompletableness arose, engendered by this very richness of means of expression. Gödel showed that languages with formation and transformation rules adequate to the construction of number theory contained "purely logical" sentences which were neither provable nor refutable by finite processes. This meant that there would be sentences true but unprovable if one maintained the law of excluded middle for the sentences of such a language. This situation has given rise to suggestions that either such sentences or the law of excluded middle itself, when stated in certain unrestricted ways, must be regarded as synthetic a priori. Carnap in his *Logical Syntax of Language* attempted to meet this difficulty by extending the concept of provability to admit transfinite processes (allowing deductions based on infinite classes of premises). In view of the extreme indefiniteness of the resulting concept of provability ("indefiniteness" is here a technical term roughly transcribable as impossibility of prescribing a general finite method) this approach has been criticized by Kleene as giving only "conceptual completeness", though inclusion of transfinite rules does effect a genuine extension of the realm of the technically and practically provable. However the methods used are so strong in principle that they give rise to doubts among intuitionists whether this provability concept does not go beyond what can be honestly accepted as humanly provable. On the other hand, even the boldest countenancing of infinities in system construction has not produced a system capable of reaching far into the upper reaches of Cantor's series of alephs.

Whatever the final judgment on these questions may be, Carnap's detailed syntactical constructions did much to reveal the potentialities of the methodology of metalogic. Under the influence of Tarski, however, Carnap came to believe that in addition to the above-mentioned difficulties his treatment was not adequate to the handling of the semantical dimension of the analyticity concept. An analytic sentence is conceived of not merely as provable in a purely formal sense. It must be distinguished from theorems provable on the basis of synthetic laws by being true "in virtue of meanings." Hence in his later works a language is no longer conceived as a bare syntactical structure but as a semantical system, i.e. roughly speaking, as a system in which signs of a syntactically constructed calculus are linked to objective realities by a designation relation, and truth is defined for sentences in terms of facts holding for the entities designated by the words in the sentences.

Such semantical systems are built up, like syntactical systems, by iterated enumerations and recursions. For example, a term like "designates-in-L_0" might be defined as what Russell would call a "relation-in-extension" simply by enumerating the term-entity pairs between which the relation is to be said to hold, e.g. by a list of sentences such as " 'Brue' designates-in-L_0 Blue", supposing "Brue" to be one of the symbols determinable by definition to be a term-of-L_0. This means that no peculiarly semantical term needs to be taken as primitive in order to construct a semantical system.

In the second, quantitative phase, Carnap has shown that by an approach based on concepts reminiscent of Leibniz' class of all possible worlds it becomes possible to define quantitative concepts including that of the strength of a sentence. Monotonically related to the strength concept is the amount of information in a sentence. Involved in these definitions also there is a qualitative concept of the content of a sentence (as a class of sentences of minimal positive strength). The definitions are articulated in such a way that it becomes provable that analytic sentences have null content, zero strength, and convey no information. Such concepts had often been appealed to in characterizing analyticity but had not been precisely formulated before.

Carnap has also proposed languages extended by the inclusion of the modal concepts of necessity, possibility, etc. in such a way that it becomes provable, for example, that the propositions (states-of-affairs) designated by analytic sentences are necessary.

This may serve as a short account of the approach I propose to defend.

II

Quine has claimed that any definition of "analytic" must either be circular, or must involve equally problematic terms such as "definition", "synonymous", or "necessary", or must be somehow arbitrary, providing at best only a reasonable extension of the term "analytic" without giving the real reason for singling out that particular class of sentences as *analytic.*

Since there is no formal circularity in Carnap's approach (though there is a certain sort of regress to be discussed presently), and since the terms "definition", "synonymous", and "necessary" do not appear in the definition chains of the corresponding terms being defined with respect to a given object language, it appears that only the last alternative is a direct challenge to Carnap's approach. In order to have this aspect of the argument before us as clearly as possible I shall quote at some length from Quine:[4]

> For artificial languages and semantical rules we look naturally to the writings of Carnap. His semantical rules take various forms, and to make my point I shall have to distingush certain of the forms. Let us suppose, to begin with, an artificial language L_0 whose semantical rules have the form of a specification, by recursion or otherwise, of all the analytic statements of L_0. The rules tell us that such and such statements, and only those, are the analytic statements of L_0. Now here the difficulty is simply that the rules contain the word "analytic" which we do not understand! We understand what expressions the rules attribute analyticity to, but we do not understand what the rules attribute to those expressions. In short, before we can understand a rule which begins 'A statement is analytic for language L_0 if and only if . . .', we must understand the general relative term 'analytic for'; we must understand 'S is analytic for L' where 'S' and 'L' are variables.
>
> Alternatively we may, indeed, view the so-called rule as a conventional definition of a new simple 'analytic-for-L_0', which might better be written untendentiously as 'K' so as not to seem to throw light on the interesting word 'analytic'. Obviously any number of classes K,M,N, etc. of statements of L_0 can be specified for various purposes or for no purpose; what does it mean to say that K, as against M, N, etc. is the class of "analytic" statements of L_0?

The first method described, in which "analytic" appears undefined in the rules of the language, is, as far as I know, a figment of Quine's imagination as regards Carnap's actual systems, though it would be a technical possibility (in cases where one's interest lay not in philosophical explication but in providing an interpretation for a newly axiomatized branch of science). It is the second method, in which the rules are to be taken as defining "analytic-for-L_0", which Carnap has always employed, with, of course, the express intention of throwing light on the

[4] W.V. Quine, *From a Logical Point of View* (Cambridge, Mass.: Harvard University Press, 1953), 33.

interesting analyticity concept. What is Quine's objection? The picture seems to be that Carnap's method of defining "analytic-for-L_0", is something like defining "Resident-of-Grey-Mountain" as the class consisting of Jedrow, Abbott, and Moss, instead of providing a criterion (in this case geographical) whereby these men could be "identified" as Grey Mountain Residents. This might appear to be an almost self-refuting analogy since one of the reasons for rejecting such a definition would be that one would want to leave it an empirical question as to whether Abbott, say, was a Grey Mountain Resident, while in the case of "analytic" we might want any true application of the term to be itself analytic. Nevertheless we should not want our definition of analyticity to be trivial; and it would be trivial if the only thing an application of the resulting analyticity predicate said was that the sentence involved belonged to a set whose definition specifically involved its membership. This picture of a Carnapian analyticity concept whose only predicative accomplishment, when ascribed to a sentence S_1 is something like "S_1 is identical with S_1 or with S_2 or with . . .", appears less apt when one takes adequate account of the sort of intricately contrived net of other concepts in which Carnap imbeds his analyticity concept and which works as a whole to provide a very full characterization of the concept. What, after all, are the essential characteristics that we expect an acceptable definition of analyticity to "attribute to" an expression characterized by it? Roughly speaking, I take it that we expect analytic sentences to be true but to have no content, to provide no genuine information, to hold in all possible worlds, to be provable without evidence or at least to be true independently of fact, and we expect a proposition designated by an analytic sentence to be necessary and one designated by the negation of an analytic sentence to be impossible. Now suppose we want to define an analyticity concept in terms of some or all of these traits and not in a way which simply spells out (structurally describes) the sentences to which the term is to apply. How shall we proceed? The terms mentioned are obscure. Some may mask circularities; others may rest on dubious "ontological commitments." Obviously somewhere along the line we must define them. And ultimately these definitions must form one integrated system with clearly marked starting points and explicit rules of procedure if the very obvious threat of circularity is to be squarely met. Now the point of these remarks is that this is precisely what Carnap does. And he does it in just such a way that the sentences above, or reasonable facsimiles, are obtainable by applying the definitions. The fact that the sentences to which the term is to apply are in fact spelled out by recursive procedures is necessary to the concept's being logically determinate, which, in turn, is one of the characteristics we expect.

If it is asked at this point whether Carnap in contriving his definitions to make these results provable is not tacitly utilizing the "real" definition of natural language's "analytic", we may readily grant that he is guided and motivated by presystematic conceptions, as must anyone who seeks to replace a vague concept by an exact one, but this does not have the consequence that the definitions, once created, *require* this previous linguistic background to be understood. All that is formally required is an understanding of the metalanguage (though not of any undefined semantical term of the metalanguage).

The question may yet be raised as to how this whole structure of recursive definitions acquires a meaning. Surely mere multiplicity and complexity can not create significance. If all the definitions involved are of the sort exemplified in the enumerative definition of "Grey-Mountain-Resident" is not the whole structure at best an abstract model of a system of meanings?

The answer is that they are not quite of this sort. While such a charge might justly be brought against the syntactical approach of the *Logical Syntax of Language,* it misses the full significance of the step from syntax to semantics. In semantics, as opposed to syntax, the recursive definitions involve more than mere enumerated sign designs. They provide, in the definition of the designation concept, upon which all subsequent semantical concepts for the language in question are based, a linkage between signs of the newly created calculus and *non-verbal* entities described in the metalanguage which is already presumed to be understood. This linkage fixes the interpretation of both the signs of the object language and that of the semantical terms defined for it.

There remains the question of regression. There is undeniably a regressive aspect to the hierarchy of metalanguages. For a metalanguage to provide a complete interpretation for an object language its empirical vocabulary must be at least as rich and its logical apparatus must, according to Tarski's results, be richer (in the sense of containing, for instance, more classes of variables). Vicious regression is avoided, however, at least as regards semantical concepts, by the fact that at each stage, L_n, all semantical concepts are built up afresh on the basis of recursive definitions which themselves involve no specifically semantical concept of L_{n+1}. To be sure, stating and proving theorems at each stage requires the logical apparatus of the metalanguage, which may involve its own analyticity concept but confusion will arise only if it is assumed that "analytic-for-L_n" and "analytic-for-L_{n+1}" are necessarily both instances of some more generic concept of analyticity. Whatever deliberate similarities there may be, each concept is autonomous and sufficiently defined in precisely the way that "sentence-in-L" must be for each language L. At any stage (and these stages might be regarded as stages in a purely formal "growth" of a single language, since no descriptive terms are added) there will be certain sentences for which no sufficiently comprehensive analyticity concept will have been defined. However even to raise explicitly the question of their status requires the step to the next stage of construction which allows these in turn to be taken as analytic in a slightly broadened sense. While there may be a problem in the finitude of human ability to describe a description of a description of a . . . etc., it does not seem to reflect upon the completeness of interpretation of any already defined analyticity concept.

This autonomy of meaning entirely within the framework of a given language is a feature of all the concepts of semantics. There need be, for example, no generic concept of *definition,* but only separate concepts, definition-of-L_0, definition-in-L_1, etc. similar in many ways, but each defined by separate recursions. Friedrich Waismann has persuasively pointed out the lack of a generic concept of definitionness by inquiring into how, in common sense and common language, we may distinguish definitional equivalences from other analytic equivalences.[5] He finds it, of course, impossible. However, he uses this fact to attack the analytic-synthetic distinction rather than to point out the obvious fact of lack of explicit convention in natural language. Definitions are not to be recognized by any intrinsic quality of definitionness simply because they are the very embodiment of linguistic convention. Ultimately (i.e. when a language is formalized) they can be identified only through the fact of their having been explicitly enumerated under this heading. This sort of answer has seemed to some a confession of meaninglessness. It has to Quine in the case of semantical rules. "Semantical rules are distinguishable, apparently, only by the fact of their appearing on a page under the heading "Semantical Rules; and this heading is itself then meaningless."[6] Much of the uneasiness seems to stem from a misunderstanding of the function of enumerative, recursive, and other "arbitrary", "extrinsic", or "artificial" definitions in human communication and affairs. It comes, I believe, from a confusion between the often complex use we intend a term so defined to have and the sharp, unambiguous meaning the term must have if it is to fulfill that use. Suppose a military commander defines "Arcadia", "Babylon", and "Chippewa" as certain small stretches of beach. These would be typical arbitrary definitions. No significant difference distinguishes these from neighboring stretches except that on the next day Force F will land upon one of them. But if "Arcadia" were defined not arbitrarily in terms of position but "significantly" in terms of this distinguishing fact (its use) as the Landing Place of Force F it would be useless for purposes of the intended military communication.

[5]F. Waismann, "Analytic-Synthetic", *Analysis,* X-XI.
[6]*Ibid.,* 34.

The matter may be made clearer by looking into the alleged prescriptive character of definitions. Waismann has made much of the prescriptive or normative function of definition pointing out how we speak of a definition's being observed or infringed, used to *justify* a deductive step, etc. He stresses their analogy to laws (in the legal sense). He finds it difficult to explain how analytic sentences, which he takes to be non-normative, are supposed to be derived from (normative) definitions. The answer is that analytic sentences are no more or less prescriptive than definitions. All are declarative sentences. All achieve a prescriptive aspect from the fact that each constitutes a part of the very concept of the language being spoken and there is usually a strong social compulsion to speak a given language consistently. The fact that definitions are often thrown into imperative form may be regarded as stemming from the closely associated command to interpret following remarks as belonging to the momentary artificial language there being created. Needless confusion has arisen from stressing the conventional character of definitions to such an extent that they are no longer regarded as sentences and hence as neither true nor false. Such a position would justify Waismann's qualms and would make all of declarative logic depend upon a non-declarative form of utterance whose semiotic status is obscure to say the least. We must distinguish between a term's meaning and the social role that can be assigned to it on the basis of that meaning. We may, if we wish, make stipulations or commands to "Speak English" or "Speak L_0" but these commands will contain a curious regression if what English *is* or what L_0 *is* cannot itself be specified by simple declaratives.

If we follow through the analogy between definitions and (legal) laws urged by Waismann, we will find it, I believe, to be a significant and revealing one. Attempts to define "law" by political philosophers have usually taken one of two paths. The first is taken by those who would define the concept in sociological terms to apply to the *de facto* norms that actually guide behavior in a society. Armed with such a concept they could, they suppose, enter a strange community and determine what its laws were in such a way that what was written in its statutory codes, if any, could constitute only a rough guide in this determination. The second path is taken by those who would define "law" in the *de jure* sense. Both paths are rocky. While the concept sought by the first group may be desirable it seems to miss the distinction between legal law and natural law. Law courts could not function on such a concept. The status of specific sociological norms would cause endless dispute. Moreover, courtroom justice seems to require, if not explicit contract, at least the possibility of definite foreknowledge as to the legal status of contemplated acts, without protracted sociological investigation. (Scientists and mathematicians would, I submit, suffer analogous embroilments if definitions were conceived as empirical descriptions of shifting speech habits instead of creating for communication a solid framework of truth-by-convention.) The second, *de jure,* group also encounters difficulties. The multitude of existing and *possible* legal arrangements seems to render impossible a definition so comprehensive yet so exact as to single out all and only the actual legal laws of all communities at all times. There is, however, a third group that deals with the problem, but not as political philosophers, namely the lawyers, judges, and law-makers. For these it seems essential only to be sure of the meaning of such phrases as "N.Y. State Statute No. 3873". Such phrases are defined enumeratively in exactly the way that "semantical rule" might be. In fact the laws themselves may, perhaps, best be regarded as enumerative definitions of classes of acts (e.g. New York State Traffic Offense). A law stating that an act of type A is a N.Y. Traffic Offense cannot be regarded as making an empirical assertion. The only empirical question before a court would be whether a defendant had committed an act of type A. Yet this "non-natural", extrinsic classification of acts makes much important social communication precise and unambiguous. Enumerative definition is, in fact, an essential ingredient in all systematic social activity from office filing to language construction and mathematics. I submit that both groups of political philosophers have failed to appreciate this essential point and that philosophers of logic are all too often in the same predicament. In fact one might say that behavioristic, semiotic sociologism has come to replace mentalistic, epistemological psychologism as the prevalent threat to the drawing of precise distinctions in logic. The sociology and psychology of language is of great scientific importance to be sure, but at any stage of scientific development we must have a language to speak and this language must be as unambiguous as possible. If we were to use a logic founded on an empirical concept of synonymy, as Quine seems sometimes to suggest, we should be as helpless in trying to prove a mathematical theorem as a court of law would be in trying to convict a defendant of transgressing a folkway.

It may further the appreciation of the role of enumerative definitions in language construction and mitigate the uneasiness that may be caused by the statement that full interpretation of the semantical terms defined for an object language requires a fully understood metalanguage whose descriptive vocabulary is equally rich and whose logical apparatus is stronger, if we consider the process by which a languageless beginner would learn a formalized language and the role of recursive metalinguistic constructions in this process. Suppose a society already speaks a language L_n containing a sublanguage L_0 adequate to the purpose of the natural sciences and that L_n contains enough metalinguistic hierarchical structure not only to give a complete syntactical and semantical characterization of L_0 but to permit a certain ease in speaking of definitions in various sublanguages, translations, synonymies, etc. A child could not, of course, learn the language from its definition, i.e. its syntactical and semantical rules, any more than he could, at first, learn the meaning of any word from its definition. He would learn to speak and understand by pointings, contexts, and trials in the way one learns any language initially. He would learn to use (the L_0 correlates of) "cow", "oatmeal", "father", without any regard for the fact that the definitions of these terms involved words he had not yet heard. And also the logical and semantical words corresponding to "or", "every", and "true" would be learned by context and trial. In the process of education he would be given definitions of words and would in turn form ever deeper notions of definitional procedure, just as his understanding of "father" would be deepened and corrected by the study of biology. He might well come to use semantical words, e.g. the correlate of "designates-in-L_0", without at first grasping its merely enumerative definition in the same way that children may come to believe there is a "natural" connection between a word and its designatum. This would be corrected by a process similar to, but far more explicit and literal than, that by which a student is persuaded of the purely conventional relation between word and meaning.

It is a well-known fact of axiomatics that as one adds postulates or other strictures to a system, the range of possible interpretations or realizations is, in general, progressively cut down, and this would be essentially the force at work here. The system of metalanguages, the tightly interwoven net of definitions of both empirical and logical terms makes misinterpretation increasingly unlikely the more the learner follows out its implications and interrelations.

There is a holistic or Gestalt aspect to the learning process, of course, and to the logical situation too. Interpretations given by a learner to any one word depend upon his interpretation of the whole, just as, non-psychologically, the cutting down of possible interpretations of an axiom system depends upon theorems derivable from conjunctions of new postulates with old. In this light, Quine is right in stressing the dependence of interpretation upon total context. However, it seems wrong to suppose that because exact psychological interpretation of the net of definitions depends upon its containing both empirical and logical terms that no distinction can be drawn. On the contrary it would appear that only by interpreting analytic sentences strictly as analytic (factually contentless, etc.) can such a narrowing of possible interpretations be achieved. In favor of his view that the basic unit of meaning is the total structure of science, Quine invokes the fact of the strong logical interdependence of all parts. But how else is logical interdependence to be made explicit except through definitional structure? Perhaps he would claim that by logical interdependence he means only that laws interlock by containing common terms. But how are even the various occurrences of a sign in different contexts to be known to be synonymous? Surely by referring to definitions which specify the rules of the language being used. The kind of synonymy to which we appeal to prove anything must be an "absolute" synonymy" created by fiat" and not a synonymy which must be tested for sociologically.

I should now like to touch briefly on the last aspect of Quine's remarks, quoted earlier, concerning the view that a term like "analytic-for-L_0", must presuppose an understanding of a relational predicate "S is analytic-for-L" where "S" and "L" are variables. As Quine pictures it, it would seem that this relational predicate would have, itself, to be a logically determinate concept since a logically determinate one place predicate is to be gotten from it by simple substitution of "L_0" for "L". This would require complete specificity as to the structures of all languages in the range of "L", obtainable, presumably, only by recursive methods, which would be hard to reconcile with Quine's desire for extreme generality. Presumably a better way of posing the metalogical problem would be to find a definition of "*x* is an analyticity concept for L" in terms of adequacy conditions to be met by the definition of x in the metalanguage of L.[7] Even here, however, the range of language would have to be exactly delimited by fixing certain general features essential to being a language and the cry would go up again that the philosophically essential features lay in the non-formally expressed reasons for specifying these features in just the way they were. Let me pose a more informal version of what I take to be the question. Why do we, in fact, use the English word "analytic" as a root in all these hyphenated analyticity terms constructed separately for separate languages if there is no generic concept? My answer would be: because of strong analogies between the languages involved and between the situations of the "analyticity" concepts within them. However, since all languages, natural or artificial, are, in a sense, human artifacts, I would say that no single feature of similarity is essential, so that dropping all inessential features would yield meaningless generality, while insisting on any one feature would unduly restrict and artificialize the whole. I would say that a locution like "*x* is an analyticity predicate for L" might be regarded as a recipe term usable by language builders for certain frequently employed ingredients in language building, not a technical term for any particular sort of built structure. Engineers work by studying in detail what has been done in previous

[7]R. Carnap, *Introduction to Semantics,* §16.

cases and then designing new structures which can only be said to be roughly analogous to preceding ones and which will differ in ways too unpredictable to permit useful compass by exact definition.

Let me illustrate my point. It would presumably be possible to define some such term as "Chevrolet-2-door-utility model-1931" very precisely with detailed specifications of form and materials, without employing the term "automobile". Similarly it would be possible to define its parts, designated, say, by General Motors catalogue numbers, without using such terms as "carburetor", "starter", etc. However, a writer on the design of automobiles might well want to use such general terms. But he would be hard put to it to define them in such a way as to apply exactly, for example, not only to all carburetors, past, present, and future, but to all possible carburetors. He has experience only with a large number of very definite appliances. Three alternatives seem open to him. He may define "carburetor" exactly and narrowly to cover this experienced class with a fair amount of specificity and on the basis of this make very explicit directions, leaving open the possibility that they may not apply to many closely analogous devices not strictly carburetors. Or he may define it exactly and broadly, whereupon all his generalizations would have to be heavily qualified, leaving the deliberate generality of his definition without useful function. Or he may decide to use the recipe term roughly and speak with varying degrees of generality and precision and to depend upon analogy and cxample to aid in communication, often concentrating on special ways of constructing special machines. Analogously, making metalogical recipe terms of varying levels of generality precise can be of great philosophical value but it is no more necessary to the understanding of terms defined for any specific system than is a definition of "automobile to the understanding of "Chevrolet-2-door-utility-model-1931".

The situation is parallel in many respects to the use of the term "work" in physics. Work-like concepts appear in several alternative physical theories, e.g. classical, relativistic, and quantum mechanics, but in each case, the meaning of the term is fixed by its definition in terms of the primitives of the theory involved, and their interpretation, and requires no prior understanding of a relational predicate such as "W is a work-like term of theory T" with "W" and "T" variables, nor any carry-over from a natural language concept in the form of an assertion that " 'Work' (as defined in theory T) explicates 'Work' (in natural language)."

III

I now move to a less formal but no less formidable area of controversy having to do with the meaningfulness of the analytic-synthetic distinction in the interplay of convention, invention, and confirmation in the natural sciences. It has increasingly been suggested that whatever the ultimate decision on purely logical or mathematical truth might be, descriptive scientific discourse might prove invulnerable to analysis in terms of a sharp analytic-synthetic distinction. The reasons put forward frequently center on the role of definition in the natural sciences.

It is said that definitions of non-logical terms in the sciences have repeatedly been revised under the impact of experience in ways hard to distinguish from those in which hypotheses are altered, and that basic laws appear to fluctuate in use or function between being synthetic hypotheses and being definitions or analytic meaning-postulates for the magnitudes involved in them. It is claimed, furthermore, that definitions in the natural sciences, especially those of the so-called reductive sort, embody knowledge and so can not be regarded as acting in a merely abbreviatory way.

Before examining these and related issues more closely, it may be well to reemphasize certain aspects of the view of definition which is here being defended.

The term "definition" is often used broadly to mean almost any indication of a word's meaning by using other words or even gestures (as in the phrase "ostensive definition"). The term will be used here in a stricter sense requiring complete identity of designation between verbal expressions of a given language. What that sense is will not be fully specified since "definition" is regarded as a recipe term in the sense of the preceding section, being definable with greater or less generality in different metalogics. But as an idealization we may picture "Definition of L", for a specific language L, as being defined, by enumeration, to denote a class of sentences of L of certain familiar forms, e.g. equivalences obeying certain limitations on the use of variable, and we may picture the term so defined appearing within the definitions of "designation", "synonomy", etc. in such a way that the sides of the equivalences are synonymous, designating the same entities, and so on, and appearing also within the definitions of "true" and "analytic" in such a way as to permit replacements *salva veritate* and *salva analyticitate*. Such a picture excludes other perfectly usable ones in which definitions belong to the metalanguage, the defined term being in the object language, metalanguage, or in some other more redundant object language, but it will save cumbersome locutions. The suggested formality of the idealized picture is intended, among other things, to make clear that I shall not be speaking of semantical rules, nor pointings, nor crude meaning indications of "the unfamiliar in terms of the familiar" —something impossible in an advanced science if the *salva veritate* and *salva analyticitate* tests are to be met — nor of various kinds of sentences *about* definitions which seem sometimes confused with definitions.

As an amplification of this last remark, I note that it has become a widespread and misleading practise to classify definitions in various ways and to attribute different status to the different classes with respect to the analytic-synthetic distinction. We are presented with lexicographical (or reportive), abbreviational (or nominal or stipulative), and explicative (or analytic or real) definitions; and we have real definitions in the old sense of setting forth the structural or causal nature of something—a sort that might be called *explanative* to contrast with explicative. Reportive and explanative definitions have been said to be synthetic. Abbreviational definitions are usually granted analytic status (outside those circles which hold that, being stipulations, they are not sentences). And the status of explicative definitions has been in debate. There seems no good reason, however, to suppose that the appellations singling out the various kinds point to differences of a logical nature. It seems sufficient to suppose that they refer only to differences of use or attitude. A single definition, e.g. of "aspirin" as acetyl salicylic acid, may be reportive for the lexicographer and abbreviational for the chemist; it may constitute an explanative definition for the student and may not "serve as a definition" at all for a child. If there appear to be changes in analytic-synthetic status among these various contexts, it seems more reasonable to suppose that they inhere in statements about these uses and attitudes rather than that they simultaneously apply to the single definition in question. This might be more easily seen if we occasionally avoided the convenient but overly categorizing adjectival formulation and admitted that it is not a *reportive definition* which is synthetic but rather a *report about a definition* (e.g. that a certain community accepts it) —a sentence of very different form from the definition itself; and that it is not an *explicative definition* whose analyticity is in question but the very different *assertion that a given definition constitutes an explication* (of another term formally outside the language in question); and so on for the other "kinds" of definition.

Carnap has said, in polemic moments, that he recognizes only one kind of definition, the abbreviational. (And for purposes of reference I shall call the view being defended the abbreviational view). Abbreviation is itself only a use to which definition is put and Carnap does not suppose that all definitions are sought, or ought to be sought, only for purposes of abbreviating longer locutions already in use. Rather what is meant is that all definitions, *qua* definitions, must share all of the logical features that we are ready to attribute to those definitions we use for abbreviatory purposes but which are often obscured by psychological factors in other circumstances, i.e. complete determination of the meaning of the defined term by the definiens without consideration of psychological residues from previous associations, establishment of synonymy "by fiat", eliminability in favor of defining terms with no loss of power of expression, and so on. Most of the philosophers who raise questions concerning the analytic-synthetic distinction in science seem ready to admit that there are purely abbreviational definitions in science (e.g. conductance defined as the reciprocal of resistance) and manifest no great qualms about the analytic status of sentences arising from their functioning, or even about using such otherwise shunned terms as "synonymy" in discussing them. Carnap would simply take these admittedly abbreviational definitions as a nucleus of agreement and would suppose that the analytic-synthetic status of more disputed sentences would be determined as the sciences become more explicitly formalized.

One of the things that seem to make this acceptance possible for abbreviational definitions is the lack of prior psychological associations for the word being defined. Quine sanctions synonymy when it is created by fiat, and fiat seems to act more easily on words previously unfamiliar. But meanings for Carnap are not mental. They cannot be if words are to be intersubjective. And enough has been said in the preceding section about the necessity of there being some central sense in which assertions about meanings are not assertions about behavioristic regularities either.

With this picture in mind (of definition as purely abbreviational with respect to designation but not necessarily with respect to purpose or understanding), we may now turn to the arguments against the analytic-synthetic distinction based on the role of definition in the non-analytic sciences. Let us take the revision argument first. Quine has said that since definitions act as premises in predictive inference, the decision to alter one of these in the face of conflict between prediction and observation differs in no fundamental respect from that of altering or rejecting an empirical hypothesis. It is, he says, merely a matter of degree. What it is a degree of, he does not clearly say, sometimes suggesting something like simple psychological or sociological inertia or recalcitrance to change, sometimes something like systematic economy or Hegelian coherence, and sometimes a sort of (non-Carnapian) degree of confirmation. In any case, the resulting view is the familiar one that no law can be tested alone but only in a context, and that ultimately it is only science as a whole that can be regarded as a self-contained meaning unit. In so far as a distinction is accepted between logical truths and analytic truths which become logical truths only through definitional substitution of descriptive terms, this attitude is felt to weigh especially heavily against the latter sort. However, once the principle of confirmation of total contexts only is accepted, the gradualism (as it has been called in slightly different senses by B. Peach[8] and A. Gewirth[9] seeps, with considerable reasonableness, into the realm of logical truth itself, affecting first the various existential aspects such as the infinity, multiplicative, and *Aussonderungs*–axioms,

[8]B. Peach, *Philosophical Review,* LXI, 52.

[9]A. Gewirth, *Journal of Philosophy,* L, 53.

and the use of variables, and then into all other parts down to the most "minimal" fragments of sentential logic.

While there seems a good deal to be said for the view that *synthetic* statements, especially those that mention physical entities not accessible to observation, may not be confirmable or even interpretable except in a context, the argument for extending contextualism to definitions because of their alleged empirical revision seems faulty. What can it be to disconfirm or revise a *definition* (on any grounds)? I submit that it can not be done. Every definition of a term in a language L figures indirectly in the basic formational and transformational rules constituting that language. To give a certain sign-design a different definition than that already given to it in language L is to move to a new language L′. Aside from the fact that this seems involved in what we mean by the recipe terms "definition" and "language", it is clear that if we attempted to introduce two nonequivalent definitions of the same sign-design into the same language L, i.e. without changing the replacement rules of L, we should be faced with non-analytic, perhaps even contradictory theorems. It may seem odd that the actual, widespread practise of giving the same sign-design different definitions in different contexts would have to be regarded as the creating of new languages, but this way of speaking seems at least as simple as any other consistent alternative. And of course to define a *different* sign-design to replace the old in synthetic statements which new evidence has shown to be false when formulated with the old terms is not to falsify the old definition but to abandon certain uses of the old term. (The addition of a new sign design also creates a "new" language, of course, if a language is thought of as determined, in part, by its vocabulary. It has, however, the advantage that the language so created still possesses the old term and, using it, can negate the old laws directly, while the other new language can do so only indirectly since it has no term for the old concept. The exact sciences tend to follow the second pattern, e.g. "Lebesgue integral" is not a redefined "integral" but a distinct term for a distinct concept.)

Now if it be granted that definition revision can not, strictly speaking, take place, what may we say about the empirical motivation of these other two processes? It still appears that, being faced with a new piece of evidence which according to the rules of language L, disconfirms law (law-like sentence) S involving term *t*, we may prefer to move to a language L′ in which *t* has a different definition and S, syntactically the same but semantically different, remains highly confirmed in L′ by *e* or to a language L″ containing both *t* with its original definition and *t* with a different one, in which we focus our attention on S′, syntactically like S except for the replacement of *t* by *t′*, which is highly confirmed in L″ by *e* (S being disconfirmed by *e* in L″). However, if the original language

L had the means of expression necessary to define the new term and hence to assert the revised law without the new term, the only thing "empirical" about the motivation for the language shift is the empirical fact that humans prefer shorter ways of speaking to longer. If L did not have the necessary means of expression then the new term is not introduced by definition but as a primitive and no definition has been disconfirmed or revised.

There is one other form the revision argument might take. It might be argued that apparent revisions or disconfirmations of definitions have, in function, really been disconfirmations of hypotheses which, because of their previously high confirmation had been confusedly spoken of as definitions, perhaps on the basis of a basically unsound analogy between mathematics and the factual sciences, and that all descriptive terms must be treated as independent, i.e. no sentence not purely logical should be treated as immune to empirical revision. All that needs to be said about this argument is that, if true, it in no way blurs the analytic-synthetic line. It simply moves it in the direction of making more sentences synthetic. In passing, however, it may be remarked that this view seems ill-advised on other grounds. Not only does there seem little to be gained by holding open the possibility of disconfirming the hypotheses that a meter is a hundred centimeters in length or that electric field strength is the gradient of electrical potential, but a serious loss of control in communication would result from the abandonment of definitions or other devices for producing analytic sentences other than logical truths. As mentioned in the preceding section, definitions provide the tight logical interdependences upon which interpretation of a total theory depends. It would be hard to see, for example, how any test for the presence of a certain chemical could be taken as stronger than any other or than any apparently irrelevant fact. All would appeal to observational evidence not involving the name of the chemical itself. If one appealed to "known" laws concerning the chemical the question would be simply turned to how such laws were confirmed, i.e. what evidence would one have that the substance mentioned in the pertinent observation statements was the chemical named?

I conclude from the preceding discussions that the revision argument is without consequence for the analytic-synthetic distinction.

As for the second argument mentioned at the beginning of section III, it hardly needs to be said in view of the foregoing that apparent fluctuations of status between analytic and synthetic in the treatment of various laws (e.g. Newton's law of motion, the conservation of energy law, Hooke's law) can only be regarded as fluctuations between various language systems which bestow different meanings upon the same syntactical sentence-designs. If the shifts are too informal or fragmentary we must simply remain in doubt as to the exact meanings of the terms and assertions and as to the analytic-synthetic status of the latter.

There seems to have developed, almost as a game, in recent discussions, the habit of adducing various "borderline" sentences, formulated in informal language, to which one is, so to speak, challenged to assign a single status as analytic or synthetic, e.g. "Space is three-dimensional" "The relation Precedes-in-Time is transitive", as if the fact that we understood the terms as clearly as informal language can be understood fixed a perfectly definite meaning to them. Yet it seems clear that within the limits of ordinary understanding there are fairly straightforward constructions which would make most of them clearly either analytic or synthetic. For example, I see no reason why "Space is three-dimensional" could not be taken as analytic if it be simultaneously granted that empirical facts may arise which could lead us to speak of our facts as arranged in some ampler continuum than space. It could, on the other hand be taken as empirical if dimensionality were definitionally involved in certain ways with physical terms, e.g. for light rays. Either way seems within the limits of our informal understanding of the terms. Similar remarks apply to "precedence" and other examples (with the exception of those which are held to involve observational primitives, e.g. "No area is simultaneously all-red and all-green" which require an additional discussion. Due to lack of space this discussion is only hinted at in connection with the issue next to be treated.)

I now turn to the last argument mentioned at the beginning of this section, namely that many definitions in science (especially so-called reductive definitions) embody knowledge and so can not be regarded as merely abbreviational. Speaking in terms of an example, when a "reduction" of elementary heat theory to classical mechanics is effected via the definition within kinetic theory of terms "identifiable with" the basic terms of heat theory (e.g. "temperature," "pressure") in the sense that the laws of mechanics suffice to prove theorems about these concepts which bear not only a formal similarity to the basic laws of heat theory but, on the basis of a hypothesis of the molecular constitution of matter, bear the far stronger correspondence of having the thermo-mechanical term-pairs apply to exactly the same space-time regions, it is often said that the terms of heat theory have been defined within mechanics. Such a definition would appear empirical because it would be felt that "temperature" say, had a prior meaning (perhaps though to be given or partially fixed by an "operational definition"). In truth, of course, the statement that heat theory temperature was defined in kinetic theory could only be made in a metalanguage common to both theories and only if the semantics of the two theories determined the designatum of the corresponding sign-designs to be identical. This failing, not only would there be no definition but laws linking thermo-mechanical term-pairs could not be formulated in either language alone. Let us, therefore, picture a language containing the primitives of both theories with the "bridge laws" formulated in it. Supposing the heat theory temperature, Temp_H, to be undefined and the kinetic theory temperature, Temp_K, to be defined, one such law would read "$\text{Temp}_H = \text{Temp}_K$." If we are quite sure that our interpretation provides an independent meaning for "Temp_H" then we have an empirical law and not a reductive or nomological or any other sort of definition, and no blurring of the analytic-synthetic line. However, it seems more likely that we should not be at all sure that we had an independent interpretation for "Temp_H". It was, to begin with, only a theoretical construct interpreted via none too explicit "operational definitions" (which are not strict definitions but at best reduction sentences which leave a term's application in doubt when test conditions are not met; and which, moreover, suffer from the dilemma that the more one tries to formulate them in an economical and non-circular vocabulary, the more abstract and "unoperational" they become). In so far as we are not sure of an interpretation, it seems reasonable that we should not be sure of the analyticity status of a sentence. But this is no more against the analytic-synthetic distinction than vagueness is an argument against the law of excluded middle. Now suppose, however, that any operational definition or method of measurement that we propose for Temp_H, when purified of extraneous references, e.g. to acts of human beings, to specific chemical substances, etc. (except in terms of their mechanical properties), can be formulated entirely in the vocabulary of the combined theory which speaks of physical objects and their mechanical and thermal properties. Each condition on Temp_H, according to our original assumption, has a purely mechanical correlate (in the strong sense mentioned) in which "Temp_K" appears in place of "Temp_H" and which is a theorem of mechanics or, for the special case of the bridge laws, tautologies. This means that it becomes impossible to find a situation which would distinguish Temp_H from Temp_K, since every measurement for Temp_H provides a parallel one for Temp_K. If Temp_H does not behave, the same evidence would show that either a law of mechanics or an assumption as to something's molecular constitution was false; i.e. Temp_K would also not behave. In such a case it becomes purely a matter of economy to move to a language without heat theory primitives. This does not mean that we might not later want to construct another theory with a temperature-like concept as primitive but only that there would be no grounds for identifying its meaning with that of the old Temp_H.

It is sometimes supposed that because Temp_H was used before there was a kinetic theory to reduce it to, we must have had an independent meaning for it. We had, of course, hot-feelings, but Temp_H was not a sense-data term but always a theoretical construct, representing, it was hoped, some objective aspect of the state of physical things, and there is no reason for not associating hot-feelings as intimately with $Temp_K$. What can it be to understand the theoretical construct $Temp_H$? Only, it would seem, to be able to use it correctly, the use being governed by test or measurement procedures which now, according to our assumption, have found mechanical interpretations but which were originally understood in a similar loose way. There is no reason why we should assume that practical understanding of a theoretical term (i.e. just about any term) requires the ability to define it or to know in any exact way its meaning, i.e. the "external" reality, if any, it is assumed to refer to. In using such words as "crystal", "cancer", "salt", we have the *words* in mind and are familiar with *them* and with many aspects of, and facts about, what they designate and this constitutes our understanding. It should come as no surprise if these terms are defined in terms unfamiliar to us. We must not assume that just because we use a word successfully we have some neat, fixed mental something that corresponds to it and that we merely need to sit down and analyze to arrive at a full definition. Professor Nagel has scoffed at the notion that the mechanical concept of temperature could be arrived at by analyzing the meaning of the thermodynamical concept of temperature but I say that this is because we have never fully known what that concept was.

This brief discussion indicates, I believe, an adequate answer to the view that reductive definitions constitute a challenge to the analytic-synthetic distinction. The position taken here is, to summarize, that reductive definitions are purely abbreviatory and analytic (though they may be instructive in the way that the analytic sentences of mathematics are instructive, or the definitions of family-relationship words are instructive to a child); they do not define the primitives of another theory but a set of terms whose designata are operationally indistinguishable, on the basis of laws independently established in the reducing theory and on the basis of vocabulary already included in, or needed for the interpretation of, the reduced theory. This allows a genuine reduction of primitive vocabulary (through disuse of the superfluous reduced theory).

Unsolved problems admittedly remain. I have dealt only with those charges which seem most clearly based on misunderstandings and which have not been treated elsewhere. Whatever the outcome, I can see no worthwhile alternative to the use of "Carnap-like" formalized constructions in the continued exploration of systematic ways of speaking about the world. It seems a permanent advance in philosophic method.

HERBERT G. BOHNERT

I.B.M. RESEARCH CENTER
YORKTOWN HEIGHTS, NEW YORK

14

Wilfrid Sellars

EMPIRICISM AND ABSTRACT ENTITIES

IF our language did not contain the words 'particular,' 'quality,' 'relation,' 'universal,' 'proposition,' and 'entity,' we could not make such statements as 'There are particulars,' 'There are universals,' and 'There are entities.' For that matter, if our language didn't contain the word 'river,' we couldn't say 'There are rivers.' In the latter case, however, we know that even if our language happened not to contain the word 'river,' it does contain resources which permit the formulation of *There are rivers* in other terms. The question thus arises, What are the resources which are tapped by the former, and philosophically more exciting, statements?

In his important essay. "Empiricism, Semantics and Ontology,"[1] Carnap poses essentially the same question when he asks (in effect) what resources would have to be added to a language which did not enable one to say, e.g. "There are propositions," in order for this to become possible. He writes (p. 25)

> New variables "p" "q", etc., are introduced with a rule to the effect that any (declarative) sentence may be substituted for a variable of this kind; . . . Further, the general term "proposition" is introduced. " p is a proposition" may be defined by "p or not p" (or by any other sentence form yielding only analytic sentences). Therefore, every sentence of the form ". . . is a proposition" (where any sentence may stand in place of the dots) is analytic . . . With the help of the new variables, general sentences may be formed, e.g. . . . "there is a p such that p is a proposition."

Carnap calls the introduction of these resources the "construction" of "the framework of propositions." It is essential, however, to note that the resources *introduced* (i.e. the variables and the term "proposition") can do their job only because the language already contains the sentential connectives with their characteristic syntax by virtue of which such sentences as "Either Chicago is large or Chicago is not large" are analytic. In other words, the introduced *nominal* resources mobilize existing *syntactical* resources of the language to make possible the statement "There are propositions."

[1]*Revue Internationale de Philosophie,* XI (1950), 20-40.

In a more general formulation of his thesis, Carnap writes (p. 30) that

> the acceptance of a framework of new entities is represented in the language by the introduction of new forms of expression to be used according to a new set of rules. . . . the two essential steps are. . . . First the introduction of a general term, a predicate of higher level, for the new kind of entities, permitting us to say of any particular entity that it belongs to this kind (e.g. "red is a *property*," "five is a *number*"). Second, the introduction of variables of the new type . . . With the help of the variables, general sentences concerning the new entities can be formulated.

Now it is indeed clear that unless a language contains nominal resources having the force of (a) the word "proposition" and (b) a variable—say "v"—for which sentences are substituends, the language does not permit the formulation of a sentence having the force of "(∃v) v is a proposition." But, as Quine has pointed out,[2] it is just a mistake to suppose that the variable in "(∃v) v is a proposition" must be one for which *only* sentences are substitutable. The use of differently designed sets of variables for syntactically different sets of substituends is indeed one way of avoiding logical nonsense. However, the same results can be achieved with a single set of variables by specifying the necessary restrictions in terms of context.[3] In such a language, individual constants, one-place predicates, multi-place predicates, class terms, class of classes terms, sentences, etc. would all be substitutable for, say, the familiar "x," "y," "z," etc. Given suitable conventions (which I shall not attempt to specify) "x is a proposition" might be defined as "either x or not x;" "x is a property" as "y is x or not (y is x);" "x is a dyadic relation" as "yz is x or not (yz is x)," etc. These omnivorous variables would enable us to give a simple sense to "There are universals," "There are abstract entities," and even "There are entities," the least informative answer to Quine's question "What is there?"[4] The first of these becomes "(∃x) x is a property or x is a relation;" the second, "(∃x) x is a universal or x is a proposition;" the third, "(∃x) x is a particular or x is an abstract entity."[5]

To accept a framework of entities, then, is to adopt a certain form of language. Within this language the question "Are there E's?" where

[2] "Carnap's Views on Ontology," *Philosophical Studies,* II (1951), 65-72.

[3] Of course, as Quine points out (p. 69), it would always be possible to introduce special variables into such a language as notational conveniences.

[4] It is interesting to note that Carnap, discussing as he is the problem of abstract entities, does not explore the linguistic framework required for saying "There are abstract entities," and hence for asking the question "Are there abstract entities?"

[5] These definitions are proposed by way of illustrations; the task of providing illuminating definitions of these terms is an enterprise of great difficulty, the most important part of which would be the philosophical commentary in which the definitions were justified.

"E" is the term for the relevant kind of entity, receives an analytic answer, while questions of the form "Are there E's conforming to such and such conditions?" receive answers which are "either factually true or analytic" (p. 31). Thus, in the appropriate linguistic framework, "Are there numbers?" is answered by the analytic sentence, "There are numbers;" "Are there numbers greater than 100?" is answered by the analytic sentence "There are numbers greater than 100;" while the question "Are there numbers less than 1,000,000 which have not turned up in the numbers game?" is answered (let us suppose) by the factually true sentence "There are numbers less than 1,000,000 which have not turned up in the numbers game." These questions, asked in the language of the framework, Carnap calls "internal questions."[6] From them, he tells us (p. 31)

> we must clearly distinguish external questions, i.e. philosophical questions concerning the existence or reality of the framework itself. Many philosophers regard a question of this kind as an ontological question which must be raised and answered before the introduction of the new language form. In contrast to this view, we take the position that the introduction of the new ways of speaking does not need any theoretical justification, because it does not imply any assertion of reality. . . To be sure we have to face . . . an important question; but it is a practical, not a theoretical question; it is the question whether or not to accept the new linguistic forms.

The external question, "Shall I accept such and such a form of language?" is, as Carnap points out, a practical question in that it calls for "decision rather than an assertion" (p. 29). But although a question of the form "Shall I . . .?" calls indeed for decision, it is generally sensible to ask of a decision "Is it reasonable?" or "Can it be justified?" and *these* questions call for assertion rather than a decision. Thus, the question inevitably arises, Is it proper to ask of a decision to accept a framework of entities, "Is it reasonable?" "Can this decision be justified, and if so, how?" This is the crux of the matter, and on this point, it must be remarked, Carnap's discussion is less incisive. At times, as in the passage quoted immediately above, he seems to tell us that the demand for a justification is improper. On the other hand, only a few sentences further on he writes that "the acceptance . . . can only be judged as being more or less expedient, fruitful, conducive to the aims for which the language is intended." Here, as on several other occasions, he implies that such a decision can be justified, that is, shown to be reasonable. As to the nature of such justification, however, he gives no more than a few obscure hints. One looks in vain for an unpacking of "expediency," "fruitfulness,"

[6]*Ibid.*, 21.

and "conduciveness to the aims for which the language is intended."[7]

Carnap, as one would expect, is particularly concerned to emphasize that "the acceptance of a framework must not be regarded as implying a metaphysical doctrine concerning the reality of the entities in question." (p. 32). But just *why* is the *internal* assertion "there are propositions," to which we are committed by the acceptance of the framework of propositions, not a metaphysical one? Carnap's answer, is, in effect, "because it is *analytic*." And, indeed, it is certainly true that if you mean by a metaphysical statement, a statement which is neither analytic nor empirical, then this internal statement is not a metaphysical one. I doubt, however, that many philosophers with a background in the history of the subject would take this to be an adequate analysis of the term 'metaphysics' as a working term in philosophy.

Carnap also tells us (p. 35) that metaphysicians

> believe that only after making sure that there really are entities of the kind in question, are we justified in accepting the framework by incorporating the linguistic forms into our language.

In other words, the metaphysician appeals to a *bogus* method of justifying the acceptance of a framework of entities. Carnap is, in effect, comparing the metaphysician to a scientist who tells us that before we adopt the language in which we can say "There are molecules," we should first make sure that there really are molecules. Here empirically oriented philosophers would all agree that the scientific justification of the acceptance of the language of molecules does not involve the premise *There are molecules.*

Now, I can conceive of two by no means foolish lines that Metaphysicus Platonicus might take by way of reply. In the first place, he might deny that he employs the above bogus method of justifying the acceptance of a framework of abstract entities. He might insist that the parallel of abstract entities with molecules is a good one, and that the framework of abstract entities is a sound theoretical language, the acceptance of which, like the acceptance of the framework of molecules, is justified by its power to "save the appearances." Abstract entities would be "metaphysical" not because experience provides no reason for putting them into our intellectual picture of the world, but because they are neither mental nor physical, nor, as is shown by their pervasive role, a third class of entities coordinate with these. A nominalistic metaphysician (pace Quine) on the other hand, would com-

[7]See Warner Wick's discussion of this point in "The 'Political' Philosophy of Logical Empiricism," *Philosophical Studies* (June, 1951). Herbert Feigl has made a detailed exploration of puzzles relating to the justifiability of conceptual frameworks in his essay "*De Principiis . . .*" which appeared in *Philosophical Analysis* (ed.) Max Black (New York: Cornell University Press, 1950).

pare the framework of abstract entities to the framework of caloric or phlogiston.

Is the Carnap of the semantical period a realistic metaphysician who introduces abstract entities as theoretical objects to "save the appearances"? One might think that to decide this question one way or the other, one would have to know more (as in any case we should like to) about the way in which, as he sees it, the acceptance of a framework of abstract entities is to be justified. But Carnap can be expected to reply that no such additional information is necessary as internal assertions of the existence of abstract entities spring from analytic sentence forms, and analytic sentence forms can never formulate a hypothesis which saves appearances. Our evaluation of this reply will be determined by the outcome of our discussion of Quine's critique of Carnap's "ontology."

The second line our metaphysician might take is to admit that, as he sees it, we are justified in adopting the language of abstract entities "because we know that *there really are* abstract entities." He might, in effect, deny that abstract entities are *theoretical* entities introduced to save appearances, and insist that we have an immediate awareness of abstract entities, an awareness which does not involve a covert use of the linguistic framework of abstract entities. Indeed, he might enter a *tu quoque;* for Metaphysicus is not alone in suspecting that if Carnap had once been asked, How is the acceptance of the framework of sense-data to be justified? he would, in effect, have replied "because colors, sounds, etc. are *given,*" where further questioning would have made it clear that this *givenness* did not involve a convert use of a (however rudimentary) symbolic framework of sense-data. I think it is obvious that many empiricists have taken this line. Whether or not Carnap still does (or has ever done) it is not easy to say. Certainly he has, on many occasions, availed himself of the philosophical jargon of givenness, and nowhere he has explicitly discussed and rejected the epistemological views it embodies.

I have spoken here of two lines that Metaphysicus Platonicus might take. Actually these two lines turn out to be different parts of one and the same line. For the appearances which M. P. believes to be saved by the 'hypothesis' of abstract entities, and the saving of which he believes to justify the acceptance of the framework of abstract entities. are such characteristically mental phenomena as thought and desire. He argues that to explain (indeed even to describe) these phenomena we need the concept of a relation of awareness which holds between minds and such abstract entities as universals and propositions. And its is to exactly such an awareness M.P. appeals when he takes the second of the two lines distinguished above. One is reminded of the view that sensations, images, etc. are data to the psychologist as self-observer, but also, in the psychology of the other one, theoretical objects necessary to save the behavioral appearances.

II

Is a framework of abstract entities to be justified as a device for saving appearances? We shall discuss this question on two levels. First, from a logical point of view, in terms of such abstract issues as the analytic-synthetic distinction, and (phoenix!) the comparative statuses of logico-mathematical propositions and the assertions of empirical science; later in terms of the more concrete issues raised by the persistent (if currently repressed) notion that relations between minds and abstract entities must be invoked by an adequate psychological theory of the 'higher processes.'

Is there a parallel between the manner in which the acceptance of the framework of, say, propositions and the acceptance of the framework of, say, molecules, is to be justified? One philosopher who thinks so is W. V. Quine. He writes

> Within natural science there is a continuum of gradations, from the statements which report observations to those which reflect basic features say of quantum theory or the theory or relativity. The view which I end up with . . . . is that statements of ontology or even of mathematics and logic form a continuation of this continuum, a continuation which is perhaps more remote from observation than are the central principles of quantum theory or relativity. The differences here are in my view differences only in degree and not in kind. Science is a unified structure, and in principle it is the structure as a whole, and not its component statements one by one that experience confirms or shows to be imperfect. Carnap maintains that ontological questions and likewise questions of logical or mathematical principle, are questions not of fact but of choosing a convenient conceptual scheme or framework for science; and with this I agree only if the same be conceded for every scientific hypothesis.[8]

In this passage Quine puts the question "Are there propositions?" in a continuum with "Are there molecules?" But his reason for doing so is not that there is a certain set of appearances which is saved by the 'propositional hypothesis' as another set is saved by the 'molecular hypothesis.' It springs rather from his rejection of a logical distinction, the dichotomy analytic-synthetic which lies at the heart of the traditional "dogma" of a chasm between *verités de fait* (factual science) and *verités de raison* (formal science).

I have already followed Quine's lead in emphasizing that the crux of Carnap's treatment of abstract entities is the distinction, within a form of language, between existence statements which are analytic, and those which are synthetic. As Quine points out, both kinds of

[8] *Op. cit.*, pp. 71-2.

existence statements are answers to what Carnap calls *internal* questions. Now, if a statement of the form "There are Φ's" in a certain language framework, is analytic, let us say that "Φ" is a category of that framework. Clearly, the categories of a framework would form a classificatory system. Thus, in the framework we were adumbrating above, "entity" would be the most inclusive category, "abstract entity" a proximate sub-category, and "universal" a sub-category of "abstract entity." Also, if the language form were of a familiar kind, "number" would be a sub-category under "class of classes," and "even number" under "number." Indeed, unless a reasonable way were found of restricting the term "category" to the more inclusive pigeon holes, there would be such categories as "Even number greater than 100." However this may be, the aspect of this conception of a category which is of primary concern to us is the fact that the categories of a given language stem from the analytic sentence forms of a language.

But just what *are* the analytic sentence forms of a language? And just how are they to be distinguished from its synthetic forms? These are crucial questions which must be faced by anyone who seeks to defend the above conception of a category—for, as Quine points out (p. 71),

> If there is no proper distinction between the analytic and the synthetic, then no basis at all remains for the contrast which Carnap urges between analytical and empirical statements of existence. Ontological questions then end up on a par with questions of natural science.

Now, a rounded and systematic discussion of the analytic-synthetic distinction would at the very least consume the space alloted to this essay, leaving none for other equally important aspects of the problem of abstract entities. I have, however, dealt extensively with this topic in other papers[9] to which the reader is referred for the broader background of the following remarks. The nub of the matter is that in the literature of modern philosophy, the *verbal* dichotomy 'analytic-synthetic' conceals two conceptual dichotomies, the lumping together of which has been, and continues to be, responsible for serious philosophical confusions. In other words, the term 'analytic' (and its correlative 'synthetic') have been used in two different—though related—senses. In one of these senses, which I shall represent by the subscript "1," the term 'analytic' has a much wider scope than in the other ("analytic$_2$"). In particular, all statements which are analytic$_2$ are also analytic$_1$, but by no means vice versa. For this reason "analytic$_2$" will be said to be the narrower, "analytic$_1$" the broader, sense.

Let us now turn to a brief explication of the two dichotomies. But first a general remark. I shall not argue the question whether the

[9]Most recently in "Is There a Synthetic A Priori?" *Philosophy of Science* (1953), and "Some Reflections on Language Games," *Philosophy of Science* (1954).

dichotomies analytic-synthetic apply to natural languages. I shall merely assume that they are no worse off in this respect than other distinctions which are acknowledged to have a proper place in the logician's tool box.[10] With this in mind, we shall say that a statement is analytic$_1$ —analytic in the broad sense—if it is "true (or false) *ex vi terminorum*," if, that is to say, *given that the reasonableness of using the language to which it belongs is not in question,* the statement does not require, indeed it would be a mistake to give, a justification in terms of observation. In this sense both "$2 + 2 = 4$" and the fundamental principles of, say, molecular theory are analytic. Correspondingly, a statement is synthetic$_1$ if—*again given that the reasonableness of using the language to which it belongs is not being challenged*—it is appropriate to justify the statement by an appeal to observational evidence. In this sense neither arithmetical statements nor the fundamental principles of molecular theory are synthetic. On the other hand, "There are 10^6 molecules on the point of this pin" is synthetic$_1$. I have italicized the qualifying clause in these explications, for while, *given that the reasonableness of using molecule language is not in question,* we can distinguish between those molecule statements which do, and those which do not, require (or permit of) observational backing, there is a distinguishable mode of 'observational backing' in which the decision to use molecule language at all, and hence the assertion of *any* molecule sentence, can be justified only by an appeal to observational backing.

Let us distinguish between the two modes of 'appeal to observation' as, respectively, the *internal* and the *external.*[11] And let us say, with a justification which will grow with our discussion, that a statement is an *empirical* statement if it requires (or permits of) justification by either an internal or an external appeal to observation. In this sense of the term, even the most fundamental principles relating to molecules are empirical; and since they are also analytic$_1$, it follows that a statement can be *both analytic$_1$ and empirical.*

The second, or narrow, sense of "analytic" can (for our purposes) be more briefly characterized. A statement is analytic$_2$ if it is analytic$_1$ and if the non-logical or descriptive terms it contains either occur vacuously,

[10] There are, indeed, statements to which the analytic-synthetic dichotomies with which we are concerned do not apply. These statements involve predicates for the application of which there is no neat set of separately necessary and jointly sufficient criteria. But while statements of this kind are much more prevalent than logicians have hitherto realized, it would be a mistake to suppose *either* that all statements in natural languages have this character, *or,* that the (more complex) logical properties of even these statements cannot be captured by a "formal reconstruction."

[11] For a sketch of the role of this distinction in an empiricist philosophy of inductive logic, see the concluding sentences of "Some Reflections on Language Games," *Philosophy of Science* (1954).

or if they occur vacuously in the statement one gets by replacing definable terms by their definitions.[12] In this second sense of "analytic," "$2 + 2 = 4$" is analytic, but the fundamental principles of molecular theory are not. Indeed, these principles (which are analytic$_1$) and "There are 10^6 molecules on the point of this pin" are alike synthetic$_2$. And surely the coincidence of the *empirical* with the *synthetic*$_2$ yields a sense of closure. For it is exactly those statements in which descriptive concepts have essential occurrence, and which therefore commit one to a distinction between this and other possible worlds, which one would expect to require justification by some form of appeal to experience.

It should be clear by now whither my argument is tending. For if we take seriously the idea that the analytic$_1$ sentence forms of the language of science (and of everyday life) include far more than the sentence forms studied by formal logicians, and, in particular, that they include sentence forms in which there is an essential occurrence of descriptive terms, *and* if we use the term "category" for expressions which could be introduced in terms of sentence forms which are analytic in the broad sense in ways analogous to that in which

v is a proposition

was introduced in terms of the analytic$_2$ sentence form

v or not v

then we should not be surprised if certain descriptive terms (in that broad—if unfortunate—use of "descriptive" which occurs in the technical literature of logic and is bound up with the dichotomy "descriptive-logical") both in theoretical languages and in everyday discourse turn out to be *in this sense* categories. As examples from ordinary language we may take "thing," "material object," "person,"[13] "event,"[14] "cause," "action" and perhaps even "color" and "shape;"[15] from theoretical discourse

[12]I am assuming, of course, that such terms as "definiens" and "definiendum" are applicable to natural languages. I am well aware that this assumption will be regarded by many as question-begging. I can only say that this paper as a whole is, in a sense, a justification of the assumptions which are operative in the present section. For it is my conviction that the current "nominalistic" campaign against "synonymy" and the "analytic-synthetic dichotomy" is motivated, at bottom, by a desire to avoid a metaphysics of meanings. If sound, however, my argument will show that one can avoid both Plato's beard and Quine's band-aids and yet make full use of these traditional categories, purged of philosophical misconceptions.

[13]An illuminating discussion of this category is to be found in P. F. Strawson's essay, "Persons," *Minnesota Studies in the Philosophy of Science* II *(Minneapolis:* University of Minnesota Press, forthcoming).

[14]For a defense of the idea that material things, Space and Time, rather than spatially and temporally related events (let alone sense-data) are, among other items, the particulars of the framework of ordinary discourse, see my essay "Empiricism and the Philosophy of Mind," *Minnesota Studies in the Philosophy of Science* I (Minneapolis: University of Minnesota Press, forthcoming).

[15]Cf. A. N. Prior, "Determinables and Determinates," *Mind,* LVIII (1949).

"particle," "stimulus," "field," "space-time interval," "force," "event."[16]

Now there is nothing outlandish in the idea that the above expressions stand for categories of entity. Indeed, this broad use of category is backed by a venerable tradition. And once it is recognized that an expression is a category by virtue of its status in a specific framework of discourse, there is nothing in this usage at which an empiricist need boggle.

But if in an alphabetized list of the categories—thus construed—of the language of science, "particle" might be cheek by jowl with "proposition" and "quantum" with "quality," we could nevertheless distinguish a subset which mobilizes sentence forms which are analytic$_2$ —analytic, that is, in the narrower sense. These might be called the "formal" or "logical"[17] in contrast to the "material" or "descriptive" categories which make up the remainder. This time "proposition" will be on one side of the ledger and "particle" on the other. Thus, when the necessary distinctions are drawn, the exciting idea that "There are propositions" belongs in a "continuum" with "There are particles" is seen to be a dangerous half-truth.[18]

But is the matter really so simple? No. The essential points have been made, but we must cut a bit deeper to defend the argument against a plausible counter-thrust. Let us take another look at a passage we have already quoted.

> . . . Science is a unified structure, and in principle it is the structure as a whole, and not its component statements one by one, that experience confirms or shows to be imperfect. Carnap maintains that ontological questions and like-

[16]Here I have in mind that use of "event" in which events are the particulars of a framework, and not the ordinary use of "event" in which discourse about events rests on discourse about things and persons. See Reichenbach's discussion of the relation between "George VI was crowned at Westminster Abbey" and "The Coronation of George VI took place at Westminster Abbey" in *Elements of Symbolic Logic*, 266 ff.

[17]As we have used the term "category" above, it is *expressions* which are categories; thus the expression "proposition" rather than the abstract entity *proposition* (the character of being a proposition). The issues involved in the question whether to speak of 'proposition' or *proposition* as the category echo at a higher level those involved in interpreting the difference between the use of such category words as proposition in connection with (a) quoted, and (b) unquoted, expressions. That category words used in connection with unquoted expressions (ontological categories) are the equivalents in the 'material mode' of category words used in connection with quoted expressions (syntactical categories) was argued by Carnap in *The Logical Syntax of Language*.

[18]I am well aware that ever so much more would have to be said to make the above analysis secure. The following remarks may serve to indicate certain additional distinctions which would have to be drawn in a more complete account. I pointed out above that the particulars of the commonsense framework include, among other items, material things, the Space in which they move and the Time by virtue of which their states are temporally related. Now material things are not particulars which, so to speak, *happen* to have the distinguishing traits of material thinghood. They are *essentially* material things. "Particular" is a category which transcends the specific conceptual frameworks in which it nevertheless rightly appears. In the material mode,

wise questions of logical and mathematical principle, are questions not of fact but of choosing a convenient conceptual scheme or framework for science; and with this I agree only if the same be conceded for every scientific hypothesis.

This passage is a distillation of many insights. But in the present context it blurs a vital distinction. It would be an over-simplification, however, to put this distinction by saying that the adoption of the analytic$_1$ sentences forms of scientific theory calls for observational justification, whereas observational justification is *irrelevant* to the adoption of analytic$_2$ sentence forms. For there is a sense in which even the adoption of analytic$_2$ sentence forms can be justified by an appeal to experience. This, however, is not as exciting as it seems, for it amounts to pointing out that scientific hypotheses cannot be formulated in a language unless that language has a certain formal richness in available analytic$_2$ sentence forms. And it would be a mistake to suppose that the use of the necessary analytic$_2$ sentence forms is subject to justification by experience in the sense in which the use of the analytic$_1$ (but not analytic$_2$) sentence forms of the theory is subject to justification. For a moment's reflection reveals that the justification of the scientific hypothesis involves syntactical relations between the descriptive terms of the hypothesis and the vocabulary of observation. And, of course, no *additional* machinery of this kind is involved in the justification of the use of the analytic$_2$ sentence forms. The latter are not, so to speak, theories within theories. Thus, the fact that there are, in a perfectly legitimate sense, scientific reasons for using certain analytic$_2$ sentence forms, when examined, lends no aid or comfort to Quine's continuum.

A framework of abstract entities is not a super theory to be justified (or the contrary) in terms of its power to save appearances. If we are justified in accepting certain resources in the way of analytic$_2$ sentence forms, then we can mobilize these resources, by purely nominal means,

things (substances, continuants) are the particulars of one framework; momentary-punctiform-events the particulars of another. And each of these categories ("thing," "event") is the category it is because of certain analytic$_1$-but-not-analytic$_2$ sentences in the framework to which it belongs. Otherwise put, "thing" is the category it is because of the "axiomatics" which connects thing words with such other fundamental terms as "Space," "Time," "process words," etc. And what is true of "particular" is true of the other categories which, as we have put it, mobilize the analytic$_2$ resources of a framework. In short, we must distinguish between those categories which are independent of the analytic$_1$-but-not-analytic$_2$ resources of a framework because they have their roots in a general syntactical theory of frameworks (e.g. "particular," "universal," "relation," "proposition") from these categories in whoch those more general distinctions find expression in the context of a specific framework (e.g., "thing" "dispositional property"). The latter are *not* independent of the analytic$_1$-but-not-analytic$_2$ resources of the framework to which they belong. The fact that general syntax, apart from Carnap's pioneering (and monumental) effort exists only in the material mode of speech of traditional metaphysics has made more difficult the task of coping with the philosophical perplexities which surround the topic of *categories*.

into a corresponding framework of abstract entities. It is the acceptance of the analytic$_2$ resources, rather than the acceptance of the framework, which requires justification. And, as we have seen, the acceptance of the resources is justified by pointing out that without them certain *empirical* statements cannot be made.

III

I have no reason to believe that Carnap would take serious exception to the main lines of the first two sections. They are intended to provide a background of agreement for the sections to follow. In the middle sections, my purpose will be to establish the following points: (1) The core of the Platonic tradition lies in a blurring of the distinction between empirical and ontological categories. It denies their mutual exclusiveness on the ground that the phenomena of *meaning* (aboutness or reference) involves some sort of commerce (usually spoken of in terms of 'intuition,' 'apprehension' or 'awareness') between persons and abstract entities. Platonism, therefore, is, in essence, a thesis in the psychology of the higher processes; and to reject it—which by no means involves a rejection of the linguistic framework of abstract entities—is to be what I shall call a 'psychological nominalist.' (2) The key to the clarification of the "relation between thought and its objects" (and hence of the Platonism issue) is the correct analysis of the semantical form " (in L) '—' means ***" (thus, "(in German) 'rot' means red.")

In the concluding sections, therefore, I shall be concerned with the light thrown on descriptive semantical statements in actual usage by Carnap's studies in pure semantics. Do they point to a conception of these statements which safeguards psychological nominalism? Or do they leave the door open to Platonistic metaphysics? My answer will be that they provide the essential materials for a non-metaphysical account of abstract entities, but that, by failing to examine in more detail the relation between pure and descriptive semantics, they leave dark corners where metaphysical views can find sanctuary.

We have seen that the ontological categories of a language spring from analytic$_2$ sentence forms of the language. We should therefore expect to find the ontological categories of a language paralleled by syntactical categories of the metalanguage in which the syntax of the language is formulated. And, of course, this is indeed the case, as Carnap pointed out some twenty years ago in his monumental *Logical Syntax of Language*. Thus, "*It is raining* is a proposition" said in L, corresponds to " 'It is raining' is a sentence of L" said in a syntactical metalanguage of L. Again, "There are propositions" said in L, corresponds to the syntactical sentence "L contains (in the appropriate sense) at least one sentence"; and similarly in the case of the pairs "quality" and "one-place predicate," "relation" and "multi-place predicate," "universal" and "predicate," and so on. Now, having called attention to this parallelism, Carnap coined a terminology ("pseudo-object sentence," "quasi-syntactical sentence," "material mode of speech") which gave expression to his philosophical conviction that this parallelism of quasi-syntactical (ontological) and syntactical categories reinforces and illuminates the contention of the Vienna Circle that the traditional problems of ontology are pseudo-problems. But clearly this parallelism seemed to Carnap to have this consequence only because he viewed it against the background of other commitments which were scarcely shared by his realistic opponents. And while his conclusions were, on the whole, welcomed by nominalistically minded philosophers, there were many who felt, with some justification, as we shall see, that there are genuine issues between nominalism and realism which Carnap did not adequately discuss, even though nominalists could feel confident that his heart was in the right place.

If we lay aside Carnap's terminology on the ground that it begs the questions in which we are interested, and ask Why did Carnap think that the parallelism of ontological and syntactical categories illuminates the traditional "problem" of universals: the answer is surely that he believed himself to have shown that ontological categories are the *shadows,* so to speak, of syntactical distinctions. But why not apply the metaphor in the opposite direction? Why not join the realist in claiming that ontological categories are the substance and syntactical distinctions the shadow? How is one to decide which way the sun lies, or even whether the metaphor is appropriate in either direction? The fact of the matter is that Carnap and his realistic opponents have approached this parallelism with different commitments concerning what is involved in learning and using a meaningful language. Thus, the next step in the clarification of the controversy over universals takes us to certain philosophical problems of psychology and semantics.

When the nominalist looks at Carnap's new account, he notices that even though "There are propositions" said in L does not *mention* a sentence of L, nevertheless all a user of L needs to know in order to assert "There are propositions" (given that his language has the machinery necessary to the formulation of this sentence) is that his language contains at least one sentence. This warms his nominalistic heart. The realist, however, counters with the claim that since a sentence isn't a sentence unless it is meaningful, and since it isn't meaningful unless there is a proposition which it means, one couldn't know that one's language contains a sentence without knowing that there is at least one proposition. Thus, whereas the nominalist moves the spotlight from "There are propositions" said *in* L to "There are sentences" said *about* L, the realist moves it right back. He argues that in order to give an account of what a language is, that is, to explain the meaningful use of counters, we *must* make use of such statements as "There are propositions," "There are qualities," "There are particulars," "There are abstract entities," and "There are entities." And clearly there is *something* to this claim.

We have already seen that as *internal* questions, "Are there qualities?" "Are there universals?" etc. if they can be asked at all, can be answered a priori. As *external* questions they are properly formulated as practical questions of the form "Shall we use a language framework the resources of which permit the introduction of such and such a category?" And we have found Carnap to be tantalizingly vague as to the circumstances in which it would be reasonable to decide such questions in the affirmative. But on this same point the realist is the opposite of vague. While he does not deny that there may be other reasons for adopting a given framework of entities, he insists that unless we adopt the traditional apparatus of abstract entities, we can neither characterize nor account for two (related) classes of facts: (a) *mental* facts, (b) *semantical* facts.

By "mental fact" I mean such facts as that *John believes that it is raining, John hopes to go downtown, John realizes that if it continues to rain, the busses will be late, John wishes it would stop raining.* Realists from the time of Plato on have claimed that facts such as these involve a mental "perception" of abstract entities, traditionally universals, more recently propositions as well. Thus, in a passage from the *Sophist* (248A) in which the stranger from Elea is summing up certain strands of the theory of Ideas as it is found in the earlier dialogues (e.g. the Phaedo), Plato writes

Stranger. Let us turn, then, to the opposite party, the friends of Forms. Once more you shall act as their spokesman.
Theaetetus. I will.
Stranger. We understand that you make a distinction between 'Becoming' and 'Real being' and speak of them as separate. Is that so?
Theaetetus. Yes.
Stranger. And you say that we have intercourse with Becoming by means of the body through sense, whereas we have intercourse with Real being by means of the soul through reflection.
. . . .
Theaetetus. We do.[19]

Diogenes of Sinope is reported (by Diogenes Laertius) to have reacted to such notions with the scoffing remark "Table and cup I see; but your tablehood and cuphood, Plato, I nowhere see."

"That's readily accounted for," said Plato, "for you have the eyes to see the visible table and cup; but not the understanding by which ideal tablehood and cuphood are discerned."[20]

[19]Quoted from F. M. Cornford's translation in *Plato's Theory of Knowledge,* 239.

[20]Diogenes Laertius, *Lives and Opinions of Eminent Philosophers,* trans. R. D. Hicks (Loeb Classical Library, 1925), 55.

And a recent formulation of the Platonic thesis which is the more valuable in that it is taken from a paper by one of the central figures in the current controversy over abstract entities, is as explicit as one could wish.

> The extreme demand for a simple prohibition of abstract entities under all circumstances perhaps arises from a desire to maintain the connection between theory and observation. But the preference of (say) *seeing* over *understanding* as a method of observation seems to me capricious. For just as an opaque body may be seen, so a concept may be understood or grasped. And the parallel between the two cases is indeed rather close. In both cases the observation is not direct but through intermediaries—light, lens of eye or optical instrument, and retina in the case of the visible body, linguistic expressions in the case of the concept.[21]

Now, it is certainly true that mentalistic discourse makes full and essential use of the framework of abstract entities. Only the most specific statements about what a person believes, desires, expects, etc. can be made without using the common sense equivalents of "There is a proposition such that . . . ," "There is a quality such that . . . ," etc. Does it follow that abstract entities must be evoked by psychological theory to account for mental phenomena?

I shall use the term "Psychological Nominalism" to stand for the denial of the claim, characteristic of the realistic tradition, that a "perception" or "awareness" of abstract entities is the root mental ingredient of mental acts and dispositions.[22] In other words, the psychological nominalist argues that it is in principle possible to describe and causally account for the episodes and dispositions singled out by such sentences as "John believes that it is raining," without positing a "perception" or "awareness" of abstract entities. Anyone who is at all familiar with modern academic psychology, particularly in the United States and Great Britain, will recognize that it is thoroughly committed to psychological nominalism. And it has not been without its proponents in philosophical circles. Unfortunately, the philosophers who have viewed this *scientific*

[21]Alonzo Church, in "The Need for Abstract Entities in Semantic Analysis," *Proceedings of the American Academy of Arts and Sciences,* LXXX (1951), 104.

[22]I use the phrase "psychological nominalism" to distinguish this dimension of the nominalistic tradition from (a) the peculiar idea that puzzles about abstract entities can be resolved by dispensing with *properties* in favor of *classes* and/or by taking "resemblance" to be the "ontological fundamentum of class and property talk"; (b) nominalism as the claim that everything we need to say can be said without quantifying predicate and class-term variables. Needless to say, I am contending that nominalists in the latter sense are desperately sharpening their razor because they (mistakenly) believe that if it *should* prove necessary to quantify predicate variables in order to say something that needs to be said, this fact would give aid and comfort to Plato's beard.

A more adequate conception of psychological nominalism as the rejection of any *factual relation,* indeed any *relation,* between minds and abstract entities will emerge at the final stage of our argument.

program with sympathy have tangled it up, at least in their own minds, with bad philosophy in one or both of the following ways. On the one hand, they have tended to confuse psychological nominalism with the claim that commonsense mentalistic discourse can be *translated* into a vocabulary congenial to the psychological nominalist. But while it is indeed the case that something which could without too much of a stretch be called a "translation" of mentalistic language is indeed the distant *goal* of empirical psychology, such a "translation" must not be confused with an *analysis* or *explication* of mentalistic discourse. Empirical psychology is scarcely an application of logical analysis. The latter is rather the method of what used to be called "rational psychology," or, more recently, the "phenomenology of mind." In short, it must not be supposed that the goal of the empirical psychologist is a list of defined terms which can be *equated in meaning* with mentalistic expressions in ordinary discourse.

Certainly, the psychologist hopes to end up with *equivalences* of the form

$$x \text{ believes } y \equiv \Phi x$$

where the left hand side is in ordinary mentalistic discourse, while the "Φ" of the right hand side is a function defined in terms of a basic vocabulary congenial to psychological nominalism. But these hoped for equivalences must not be confused with identities of meaning, even though, once these equivalences are secured, the psychologist may *borrow* mentalistic *words* and stipulate that *in his science* they are to have the sense of the right hand sides. This stipulated identity of meaning could not create an identity of meaning of these mentalistic words *in their ordinary usage* with expressions occurring on the right hand sides of the equivalences.

Yet the fact that these hoped-for equivalences would not be identities of meaning should not be taken to imply that psychological nominalism is committed to dualism in its epiphenomenalistic form. And the task of showing that it is not so committed is identical with the task of exploding the platonistic conception of abstract entities as *scientific* objects, that is to say, as playing an appearance-saving role in psychological theory.

Nor, on the other hand, would the success of the program of psychological nominalism entail that there was no point in saying "There are universals," "There are propositions," etc. The most one would be entitled to conclude is that psychology does not need universals and propositions as scientific objects, as objects belonging in Quine's continuum. Yet philosophers have tended to suppose that if psychological nominalism were successful, there would be no point in making these statements, and have even tended to suppose that on this assumption we could safely say, "There are no universals," etc. Why? Partly because "There are no universals," has come to be used by many philosophers as though it were just another formulation of psychological nominalism. But primarily because nominalists have tended to assume that, if it were true to say "There are universals," this fact would give aid and comfort to the denial of psychological nominalism. For presumably, as they see it these entities," unless they were quite superfluous, would play some role in the economy of the universe, and what role more plausible than that of being involved in the description and explanation of the facts singled out by mentalistic discourse. Consequently, to make the psychological nominalist happy about saying "There are universals," we must make clear to him just why the truth of this statement does not, indeed could not, have this consequence. And while we have made some progress in this direction, more remains to be done.

We saw above that only the most specific statements about what a person believes, desires, expects, etc., can be made without using the common sense equivalents of "There is a proposition such that . . ." "There is a quality such that . . .," etc.

Now the *mind*-body problem (as distinguished from such problems relating to sensory consciousness as (a) the *analytic* or *phenomenological* task of clarifying the logical grammar of ordinary talk about seeing colors and having images, and its relation to ordinary talk about the body; and (b) the *scientific* task of giving a theoretical account of what transpires in Jones when we can correctly say, at the common sense level that Jones saw a certain color, or has a certain image) is essentially the problem of clarifying the relation between what can be said about a person by the use of mentalistic language, and what can, in principle, be said about him without the use of this language.[23] I am not going to attempt to untie this venerable knot on the present occasion. Rather I am going to cut it by assuming the correctness of an approach the general lines of which can, I believe, be justified by careful argument. The effect of this approach will be to turn our attention directly to the second class of facts to which the realist or platonist appeals in his defense of abstract entities—namely *semantical facts.*

As we introduced the phrase "psychological nominalism," it is not quite an analytic proposition to say that psychological nominalists have

[23]I have offered what I believe to be the broad lines of such a clarification in "A Semantical Solution of the Mind-Body Problem," *Methodos* (1953).

For an abbreviated account, see "Mind, Meaning and Behavior," *Philosophical Studies,* III (1952). This clarification is carried one step further in my essay "Empiricism and the Philosophy of Mind" (see f.n. 14 above). It contains an interpretation of the relation between the framework of mental entities and the framework of semiotic discourse about linguistic entities which pins down the claim, central to the argument of these earlier papers, that mental entities are, *in an extended sense,* linguistic entities.

tended to interpret the processes singled out by mentalistic expressions as *linguistic* phenomena. Yet it must be admitted that where psychological nominalists have not built their account solely in terms of the use of *verbal* symbols, the other items they have introduced (e.g. images) have been attributed, explicitly or implicitly, roles characteristic of verbal symbols. And, for the purposes of the present argument, it is this thesis in its narrower form which I shall assume to be correct; the thesis, that is to say, that the conceptual element in all the phenomena singled out by mentalistic expressions is a matter of the use of verbal symbols.

The philosophical opponents of the claim that the processes singled out by mentalistic expressions can, in principle, be described and explained in accordance with the program of psychological nominalism, thus understood, immediately retort that unless we can correctly say of the counters of a language that they *mean* such and such, then it is not a *language*. They proceed to speak of the "meaning relation" and to argue that the analysis of this relation takes us back to minds and their "perceptions" of abstract entities. And indeed, realistically inclined philosophers are not alone in the conviction that the business of sentences of the form " '——' means ***" is to speak of a relation between "——" and ***, the analysis of which would require a mention of the users of the language to which "——" belongs. For this reason, philosophers of a nominalistic bent are notoriously reluctant to admit sentences of this form where the supposed relatum, †††, has the prima facie appearance of an abstract entity (e.g. " 'rot' means red" as opposed to " 'Fido' means Fido") unless they can show either that in these cases the form " '——' means ***" has a Pickwickian use, or that the relation in question can be analysed into relations between terms more congenial to nominalistic sentiments. If neither of the latter expedients were available, they would believe themselves forced to choose between the Scylla of refusing to talk semantically, that is, use the above sentence-form, about expressions which, in everyday life we find it quite proper to discuss in these terms, and the Charybdis of recognizing mental "perceptions" of abstract entities. Thus, in his paper on "Semantics and Abstract Objects," read at the same symposium as the paper by Church quoted above, Quine distinguishes between two "provinces" of semantics: *theory of reference,* which deals with semantical material of a kind which can be handled, as he sees it, without too seriously offending nominalistic sensibilities, and *theory of meaning* which, at least in its contemporary form, not only affronts nominalistic sensibilities, but raises all sorts of obscure and metaphysical perplexities. And if one examines his paper for clues as to *which* characteristics of this second "province," as currently expounded, offend nominalistic sensibilities, one finds that at bottom it is the fact that it takes seriously those semantical statements which, *given that one thinks* *of semantical statements as relational statements,* appear to assert a relation between expressions and abstract entities, and, therefore, between minds and abstract entities.

> The theory of meaning is not troubled by paradox, but it has troubles of a different order. The most conspicuous question is as to the nature of its objects: what sort of things are meanings? They are evidently intended to be ideas, somehow—mental ideas for some semanticists, Platonic ideas for others. Objects of either sort are so elusive, not to say debatable, that there seems to be little hope of erecting a significant science about them.[24]

And although for reasons some of which have already been given, while others are yet to come, I disagree radically with Quine's whole treatment of abstract entities, I must confess that when I juxtapose this statement with the passage previously quoted from Church, my sympathies lie with Quine.

Quine concludes that the future of the theory of meaning lies in the direction of a use of Ockham's Razor to cut away the distinctively semantical aspects of its apparent subject matter. For, in effect, he proposes that in approaching this subject matter, logicians limit themselves to what can be said in fundamentally syntactical terms, supplemented by the theory of reference, and, perhaps, by "pragmatic," (i.e. psychological) considerations.

> Once the theory of meaning is sharply separated from the theory of reference, it is a short step to recognizing as the business of theory of meaning simply the synonymy of expressions, and the analyticity and entailment of statements; meanings themselves, as obscure intermediary entities may well be abandoned . . . Predicates are synonymous if, when they are applied to variables, their universally quantified biconditional is analytic. An expression is meaningful if synonymous with itself. . . . But there is great difficulty in tying this well knit group of concepts to terms that we really understand. The theory of meaning, even with the elimination of the mysterious meant entities, strikes me as in a comparable state to theology—but with the difference that its notions are blithely used in the supposedly most scientific and hard-headed brands of philosophy.[25]

IV

What, then, is the sense of such statements as

(1) "Rot" (in German) means *red*
(2) "Es regnet" (in German) means *it is raining*

from which, availing ourselves of our framework of abstract entities, we can go smoothly to

(3) There is a quality which "Rot" (in German) means
(4) There is a proposition which "Es regnet" (in German) means.

[24]Semantics and Abstract Objects," *Proceedings of the American Academy of Arts and Sciences,* LXXX (1951), 91.
[25]*Ibid.,* 91-2.

Do these statements commit us to relations between minds and abstract entities? To answer this question we must clarify the role of meaning talk, in other words, we must turn to philosophical semantics.

Now, a careful distinction must be drawn between two aspects of "semantical theory." (1) There is the business of making explicit and systematizing the grammar of meaning and truth talk. This involves, among other things, distinguishing between various semantical concepts, and showing that some can be defined in terms of others. (2) There is the business of sizing up the point of meaning talk, of locating semantical discourse in the intellectual economy. And while the distinction between these tasks can be pressed too far, it is abundantly clear that a person may make significant contributions to the former, while bringing darkness rather than light to the latter. A similar situation obtains in the field of ethics. A person may achieve wonders in the way of disentangling the internal syntax of obligation talk, and yet be hopelessly confused when it comes to seeing what obligation talk is all about.

Before we can hope to cope successfully with the more characteristically philosophical aspects of semantical theory, we must first look at meaning talk through logician's eyes. And let us begin by examining the distinction Carnap draws between *descriptive* and *pure* semantics. His initial statement of this distinction, in his *Introduction to Semantics,* reads as follows:

> By descriptive semantics we mean the description and analysis of the semantical features either of some particular historically given language, e.g. French, or of all historically given languages in general. . . . Thus, descriptive semantics describes facts; it is an empirical science. On the other hand, we may set up a system of semantical rules, whether in close connection with a historically given language or freely invented; we call this a *semantical system.* The construction and analysis of semantical systems is called *pure semantics.* The rules of a semantical system S constitute, as we shall see, nothing else that a definition of certain semantical concepts with respect to S, e.g. 'designation in S' or 'true in S.' Pure semantics consists of definitions of this kind and their consequences; therefore in contradistinction to descriptive semantics, it is entirely analytic and without factual content.[26]

But before we attempt to interpret this conception of descriptive semantics, it is essential to draw a distinction between a broader and a narrower sense of "empirical." A statement is empirical in the broad sense if it is properly supported by reasons of an empirical, and, ultimately, of an observational character. A statement is empirical in the narrow sense, if it is empirical in the broad sense and, apart from logical terms in a suitably narrow sense, contains no concepts which could not, in principle, be constructed out of descriptive primitives. To illustrate:

> (5) In Borneo young men believe themselves obligated to hunt heads.

is empirical in the broad, but not the narrow sense.

Now the concept of a descriptive term is itself by no means intuitively clear. It is easier to specify kinds of terms which are *not* descriptive, than to single out what it is that descriptive terms have in common. Thus, I think it would be generally agreed that the class of non-descriptive terms includes, besides logical terms in a suitably narrow sense, *prescriptive* terms, and the logical and causal modalities.[27] Indeed, if we include in the class of non-descriptive terms those terms (they might be called "mixed") which even though they have a rich descriptive content require for their explication the use of at least one nondescriptive term other than the purely logical notions which are necessary to structure a complex meaning, then the class of non-descriptive terms is inclusive indeed. For, in this sense, such concepts as *pawn* and *Prime Minister* would be non-descriptive.

It might be thought that, in the last analysis, a descriptive term is one that is used, in its typical sentences, to describe. But what is to describe? Must one be describing an object if one says something about it that is either true or false? Scarcely, for modal and even prescriptive statements (e.g. "Jones ought to make amends") can be correctly said to be either true or false. Perhaps to describe an object is to specify some of its qualities and/or relations. Unfortunately, the terms "quality" and "relation" raise parallel difficulties. Is it absurd to speak of goodness as a *prescriptive quality?* Indeed, one use of the terms "property" and "relation" is such that it is correct to say of any meangingful expression which has the grammatical characteristics of a predicate that it means a quality or relation. And in this usage it is correct to say that "good" means a quality. On the other hand, there is a usage which ties the terms "quality" and "relation" to *describing* as opposed to *prescribing.*

We are back with the question, What is to describe? In my opinion, the key to the answer is the realization that *describing* is internally related to *explaining,* in that sense of "explanation" which comes to full flower in scientific explanation—in short, *casual* explanation. A descriptive term is one which, *in its basic use,* properly replaces one of the variables in the dialogue schema

> What brought it about that x is Φ?
> The fact that y is Ψ.

[27]Logicians, including Carnap, have used the phrase 'descriptive sign' in such a broad sense that 'descriptive sign' and 'logical sign' are jointly exhaustive as well as mutually exclusive. This usage reflects the Procrustean convictions of early logical positivism, when the modalities were in eclipse, and emotivism rampant.

where what is requested is a causal explanation. I say "in its basic use" to exclude the use of a term in mentalistic and semantical contexts. For since it is proper to ask "What brought it about that Jones believes he ought to go downtown?" and "What brought it about that the German word "gut" means good?" even prescriptive terms would be descriptive, on the above account, were we to admit these contexts.

But what about "believes" and "means" themselves? Are they descriptive terms? Our discussion of mentalistic discourse has placed the burden of this question on the term "means." What kind of a term is it? To ask this question is to ask what is the role of sentences of the form

(6) "——" (in German) means ***

It is also to ask, granted that the sentence

(7) "Rot" (in German) means *red*

is empirical in the broad sense, is it also empirical in the narrow sense? For to ask this is to ask whether "means" is a descriptive term.

With these (adumbrated) distinctions in mind let us examine Carnap's elaboration of the initial characterization of descriptive semantics quoted above.

> Sometimes the question is discussed whether semantics and syntax are dependent upon pragmatics or not. The answer is that in one sense they are but in another they are not. Descriptive semantics and syntax are indeed based on pragmatics. . . . Only after finding by observation the the pragmatical fact that [Eskimos] have the habit of using the word 'igloo' when they intend to refer to a house are we in a position to make the semantical statement " 'igloo' means (designates) house" and the syntactical statement " 'igloo' is a predicate." In this way all knowledge in the field of descriptive semantics and descriptive syntax is based upon previous knowledge in pragmatics. *Linguistics* . . . is the descriptive, empirical part of semiotic . . . hence it consists of pragmatics, descriptive semantics and descriptive syntax. But these three parts are not on the same level; *pragmatics is the basis for all of linguistics.* However, this does not mean that, within linguistics, we must always explicitly refer to the users of the language in question. Once the semantical and syntactical features of a language have been found by way of pragmatics, we may turn our attention away from the users and restrict it to those semantical and syntactical features. Thus, e.g. the two statements mentioned before no longer contain explicit pragmatical references. In this way, descriptive semantics and syntax are, strictly speaking, parts of pragmatics.[28]

Now, if one takes the pragmatical study of an historical language (L) to eventuate in statements which are empirical in the *narrow* sense—if, for example, one takes it to be the behavioristic socio-psychology of language habits in a certain community—then no process of 'abstraction' will result in semantical or syntactical statements about L, or

[28] *Op. cit.,* 12-13.

even in pragmatical statements about L in that sense of "pragmatical" in which

(8) "red" is an observation predicate of L

(9) "There is a unicorn in the garden" is an (empirically) confirmable sentence of L

are characteristically pragmatical sentences.[29] The point is most obvious in the case of syntactical statements about L, for even if these latter are not prescriptive statements, they involve prescriptive concepts. Analogy: although (5) above is not a prescriptive statement, it involves the prescriptive concept of obligation. And even if (5) can in principle be correlated with a gapless description and explanation of the Borneo social scene in behavioristic terms, and therefore in which no prescriptive term occurs, the latter would not constitute the *analysis* of (5). On the other hand, if one means by the pragmatical study of an historical language, the attempt to arrive at conclusions about it on the basis of empirical evidence, then, indeed, these conclusions will include syntactical statements, and may include semantical statements provided that the language is translatable into the language in which the study is made. The point at which I am driving is that the fact that empirical evidence is relevant to the statements of descriptive semantics no more entails that characteristically semantical concepts are *descriptive,* than the fact that empirical evidence is relevant to the statements of descriptive syntax entails that characteristically syntactical concepts are descriptive, or the fact that empirical evidence is relevant to the statements of comparative ethics entails that characteristically ethical concepts are descriptive.

V

Now, before we consider what light is thrown on the nature of semantical statements by Carnap's semantical writings, let us digress for a moment on a topic which *prima facie,* has little to do with the case. We have seen that statements of the form

(10) (In English) '——' is derivable from '***'

are clearly, in the broad sense, empirical. Now,

(11) In the most popular Russian game, each side has 16 pieces

is also an empirical statement. But here it could be argued that once I know that the most popular game in Russia is chess, the next step in

[29]In the remainder of this paper I shall drop this use of "pragmatical" (on which I have insisted in earlier publications) and, to avoid confusion, follow current practice by using the term "semantical" in a broad sense such that "observation predicate" and "confirmable" can be said to be *semantical predicates.*

verifying (11) is no longer empirical. Surely, it *might* be said, to know what chess is, is to know that it is played with 16 pieces on a side. After all, it is an empirical matter that the number of planets is nine, but once I know that the number of planets is nine, the next step in verifying the statement

(12) The number of planets is odd

is no longer empirical.

The success of this gambit clearly depends on just how the word "chess" is related to the rules of chess. For, if the word "chess" were shorthand for something like "the game which was invented in China, etc.,"[30] it would be an empirical fact that chess is played with 16 pieces on a side. It is only if the criterion for the applicability of the label "chess" to a performance is that the performance be governed by the rules of chess, that statements of the form

(13) (In chess) ——— may (or may not) be done in circumstances ***

are a priori. And it is clear that these a priori and non-prescriptive statements presuppose the prescriptive form

(14) ——— may (or may not) be done in circumstances ***.

Let us call the name of the game a "rule-bound name" if it functions as we have just supposed "chess" to do. And let us ask "What are the presuppositions of the truth-or-falsity of statements of the form

(15) (In G) ——— may (or may not) be done in circumstances ***

where 'G' is such a rule-bound name"?

The answer I wish to propose is that even though statements of this form *when true* are true *a priori* they are nevertheless neither-true-nor-false *unless there is such a game as G,* where the fact that there is such a game is an empirical fact. In short, I wish to argue that in such cases at least an *a priori statement* can have an *empirical* presupposition.

But what can it mean to say "G exists?" At this stage an analogy (which will turn out to be more than a mere analogy) will help. It *is* plausible to say that the statement

(16) Oliver Twist is a male

if true, is a priori. And it is surely sound doctrine to say that this statement is neither-true-nor-false unless there is (was) such a person as Oliver Twist. And that there is no such person as Oliver Twist is a matter of empirical fact. To say that there is such a person as Oliver Twist is, in effect, to claim that the masculine name "Oliver Twist" as

[30] I shall not explore the more plausible idea that it is a "vague" or "open" concept for the application of which there is a set of relevant criteria, but no neat, necessary and sufficient condition.

it occurs in Dickens' book refers to somebody in the world around us. This claim would, of course, be false. Dickens makes a *fictional* use of this name, and in this use, the presupposition of the truth-or-falsity of (16) does not obtain. We can indeed say that there *could be* such a person as Oliver Twist. This we should back up by pointing to the logical and nomological consistency of what Dickens tells us about Oliver Twist.

Now the situation is quite the same in the case of (15). There *could be* such a game as G if the system of prescriptive sentences to which "G" is bound is a consistent one (and if the performances they enjoin have a gamelike character). But to say that G exists is to say more than this. It is to say that the (rule-bound) name "G" applies to something in the actual world. And this something could only be the circumstance that G is played. (The *esse* of games is *ludi*.) More accurately, for G to exist is for there to be people who *know how* to play it.

VI

Let us now examine Carnap's account of the relation between pure and descriptive semantics, in the hope that it will throw light on the nature of semantical concepts, particularly the concept 'means' or 'designates.' Fortunately, however, we can simplify our task by first examining his distinction between pure and descriptive syntax, thus availing ourselves of the less problematic character of syntactical concepts. That the two cases are parallel is asserted by Carnap in a passage which immediately follows our first quotation from the Introduction to Semantics.

> We make an analogous distinction between *descriptive* and *pure* syntax. . . . Descriptive syntax is an empirical investigation of the syntactical features of given languages. Pure syntax deals with syntactical systems. A syntactical system (or calculus) K consists of rules which define syntactical concepts, e.g. 'sentence in K,' 'provable in K,' 'derivable in K.' Pure syntax contains the analytic sentences of the metalanguage which follows from these definitions.[31]

Carnap thus traces the *ex vi terminorum* character of the sentences of a pure syntactical system to the fact that the syntactical predicates of the system are defined in terms of the sign designs of the object calculus. Thus, the *ex vi terminorum* character of

(17) (in K) 'Φ' is a predicate

would be traced to the definition

(18) x is a predicate-of-K $=_{\text{Df}}$ x = 'Φ' or x = 'Ψ' or . . .

But clearly, without serious qualifications—to be discussed in a moment—such a definition won't do at all. 'Predicate' is a role word, and to

[31] *Op. cit.*, 12.

specify the counters which are to play a role is not to define the role word. Let me be quite clear about the point I am making. I am *not* saying that by defining syntactical words in terms of sign designs, Carnap has been led to mistaken syntactical theorems. The crux of a formally developed syntax of a calculus is, indeed, a matter of combinatorial mathematics. And to set it up, one must indeed specify various categories of expressions, pairs of expressions, and so on. But the same results could be attained by using *non-syntactical* words for these categories, e.g.

(19) x is a P-expression-of-K $=_{Df}$ x = 'Φ' or = 'Ψ' or . . .

and, after developing the formal structure in these terms, by *adding* a set of sentences of the form

(20-1) x is a predicate of K *if and only if* x is a P-expression-of-K

(20-2) x is a sentence of K *if and only if* x is an S-expression-of-K

(20-3) x is derivable from y in K *if and only if* x is an α-expression of K and y is a *β-expression-of-K*

and so on. But although this is what ought, *in principle*, to be done, in practice it is certainly convenient to use the syntactical role words for the defined categories of sign designs which play these roles in the calculus. And this need have no untoward consequences, provided that one realizes what is being done. The danger is that the uncritical reader may draw the inference that syntactical words in actual use ('sentence,' 'predicate,' etc.) are definable in terms of sign designs. And this, as we have seen, is just not the case.[32]

Carnap, on occasion, formulates the difference between descriptive and pure syntax as the difference between syntactical sentences about an historical language, and syntactical sentences about a "constructed" language—whether modeled on an historical language or "freely" invented.[33] We are now, however, in a position to make clear just how misleading this formulation is. For actually we have a four-fold classification based on *two* dichotomies: (1) the dichotomy historical-fictitious; (2) the dichotomy (in which the latter item is a proper part of the former) *syntactical characterization of a calculus—combinatorial analysis of categories of expressions belonging to the calculus.*

[32]One queer consequence of the supposition that such definitions can be given is that 'predicate' as applied to German words would not mean the same as 'predicate' applied to English words.

[33]See, for example, *Introduction to Semantics,* 11-12.

In effect, then, we must contrast (A) a system of syntactical statements claiming to be about an historical language *with* the combinatorial analysis of the categories of expressions playing a role in the language; (B) a system of syntactical statements *not* claiming to be about an historical language, but occurring within the rubric "Suppose a language L . . .," *with* the combinatorial analysis of the categories of expressions playing syntactical roles in the language. And what I have been trying to make clear is that a statement is not, properly speaking, a *syntactical* statement unless it uses syntactical predicates in their ordinary (though 'tidied up') sense, and is either about an historical language (past, present or future) or involves the fictional rubric. Or, to put the matter in the manner most pertinent to our purpose, if by 'pure syntactical system' is meant the combinatorial analysis of the expression-categories which play certain syntactical roles in an historical or fictitious language, but are not asserted by the system to do so, then syntactical predicates, properly so-called, do not occur in the system. If, however, by a 'pure syntactical system' is meant a mathematically elaborated set of syntactical statements governed by the rubric "Suppose a calculus K . . .," then syntactical predicates do occur in pure syntax, but as so occurring they have exactly the same sense as in descriptive syntactical statements about an historical language. In particular, they are not defined in *logical* terms, as they would be if it were correct to define the syntactical expression "predicate of K" in terms of *disjunction* and *identity* (as in (18) above), nor, a *fortiori,* would the non-empirical character of a 'pure syntactical system' in this sense, hinge on such definitions. Fictional statements are already, in a sense, non-empirical. And, which is more important, if 'K' is construed as a rule-bound name,

(21) x is a predicate of K if and only if x = 'Φ' or x = 'Ψ' or . . . .

would be true *ex vi terminorum*!

VII

My aim in the preceeding section has been to show that the status of pure syntax is obscured, and its philosophical fruitfulness jeopardized, when it is supposed that any of the technical manoeuvres which have revolutionized the formal study of calculi, in general, and of languages, in particular, rest on definitions of *syntactical* expressions, properly so called, in *logical* terms. I shall now argue that the same is true in the case of semantics.

The descriptive semantics of a language differs from its descriptive syntax by being more inclusive, and, in particular, by including statements of the form,

(22) (in L) '——' means ***

(23) (in L) '——' is true if and only if ***

These, of course, are only the more familiar of a long list of statement forms which involve semantical concepts. Now, just as we have subdivided descriptive syntax into (a) historical descriptive syntax, and (b) fictional or suppositional descriptive syntax, and contrasted both with pure syntax, so we must make a corresponding set of distinctions in the case of semantics. And just as the syntactical predicate 'predicate' which occurs in the descriptive syntactical statement

(24) 'Ψ' is a predicate of L

must be carefully distinguished from the defined expression 'predicate-of-L' belonging to the corresponding pure or mathematical syntactical system, the relation between them being that

(25) x is a predicate of L if and only if x is a predicate-of-L[34]

so the semantical term 'means' which occurs in the descriptive semantical statement

(26) (in German) 'Blau' designates blue

must be distinguished from the expression 'designates-in-G' as a defined expression in the corresponding pure semantical system. The definition of the latter expression will look somewhat as follows:[35]

(27) x designates-in-G y $=_{Df}$ x = 'Φ' and y = red
or x = 'Ψ' and y = blue
or....................

In setting up a system of descriptive semantical statements about the suppositional or fictitious language L, we may properly say

(28) (in L) x designates y *if and only if* x designates-in-L y

[34]Note that whereas the pure syntactical sentence " 'Ψ' is a predicate-of-L" is analytic as being true by definition, the descriptive syntactical sentence " 'Ψ' is a predicate of L" holds *ex vi terminorum,* though not "by definition" if 'L' is construed as a rule-bound name. The *ex vi terminorum* character of descriptive syntactical statements about a fictional language L, thus construed, makes it easy to confuse properly syntactical statements about a fictional language with the analytic statement of pure syntax which are, properly speaking, their correlates.

[35]Compare Carnap's definition of 'x designates t in S_2' on page 25 of *Introduction to Semantics.*

but it is essential to realize the radical difference in the role of the two occurrences of designates in this sentence. The pure semantical sentence

(29) 'Ψ' designates-in-L blue

is an analytic sentence which is true by definition. The corresponding properly semantical sentence about the supposed language L is *not* true by definition, though it holds *ex vi terminorum* if 'L' is construed as a rule-bound name. The specification of what (in L) designates what ('where 'designates' is a properly semantical concept) must no more be confused with the definition of 'designates-in-L,' the corresponding expression in pure semantics, in terms of a disjunction of conjunctions of identities, as in (27) above than the specification of what (in K) is derivable from what (where derivable is a properly syntactical concept) with a definition of 'derivable-in-K, as an expression in pure syntax.

To use an analogy, we can readily appreciate that it would be incorrect to propose the following definition of '(action) A ought to be done in (circumstances) C':

(30) A ought to be done in C	$=_{Df}$	A = paying n to y and C = having borrowed n from y or A = telling the truth to y and C = having been asked a question by y or ....

We see clearly that instead of '$=_{Df}$' we should put 'if and only if' even though we can appreciate that in making a logical analysis of a moral system (M) it might be useful to introduce a defined expresison for the disjunction of conjunctions of identities on the right hand side of (3), and convenient to use the expression 'x ought to be done in C (in M)' for this purpose.

Characteristically semantical words have a conceptual role which is no more reducible to non-semantical roles than the role of prescriptive terms is reducible to non-prescriptive roles. And just as the empirical (in the broad sense) character of statements in descriptive (historical) syntax was seen not to entail that syntactical concepts, properly so-called, are descriptive, so the empirical (in the broad sense) character of statements in descriptive (historical) semantics does not entail that semantical concepts, properly so-called, are descriptive. Reichenbach was just plain wrong, as will become clear shortly, if it is not so already, when he wrote

The ink marks "Kt c 3" stand in a certain relation to the pieces on the chess board; therefore these marks form a true sentence. *Truth therefore is a physical property of physical things, called symbols;* it consists in a relation between these things, the symbols, and other things, the objects.[36]

What, then, is the sense of "means" or its technical equivalent "designates" in semantical sentences properly so-called?[37] It is immediately clear that "means" is not a *prescriptive* term. Whereas

(31) (in German) '——' is derivable from '***'

is the form of a rule,

(32) (in German) '——' means ***

is not. But if "means" is not a *prescriptive* term, and if it is not a *logical* term, is it then a *descriptive* term? No! The Procrustean urge must be suppressed. It is none of these. It is a *semantical* term.

What, then, *is* the function of sentences of form (32) said about "——" as an expression belonging to a certain language L?[38] Surely it is to give information about the role played by "——" (in L.). One might try to put this by claiming that sentences of this form "are just another way of saying "what is said by sentences of the form

(33) '——' plays in German the role played in our language by'***'

And, indeed, sentences of form (32) would not be true unless of form (33) were also true. But it is a far cry from this to the claim that (32) is just another way of saying what is said by (33).

Suppose we were asked What *is* the role played in German by "rot" and in our language by "red"? Isn't it just the role of *meaning red?* of *standing in the meaning relation to red?* These questions bring us at once to the heart of the matter. For the expression "the role of '——' " is ambiguous. If it is being used in a context of interest in which *expressions* are *predicates,* which *logical constants,* etc. etc. then of

[36]*Experience and Prediction,* 32 (my italics).

[37]The distinction between various "designation relations" as drawn in the technical literature of semantics is not germane to our present discussion, although certain other distinctions, to be drawn towards the close of this paper, are, indeed, the essence of the matter. Compare Carnap, "Empiricism, Semantics and Ontology," 33, f.n.2.

[38]I do not wish to imply that the only everyday use of "means" is in sentences of the form " '—' means ***." I am deliberately focussing my attention on those elements of everyday usage which are reconstructed by the semantics of Carnap and Tarski, for it is the misunderstanding of these elements that has, over the centuries, generated the puzzles about abstract entities.

course *the role of* "——" cannot be specified without using the categories of syntax and semantics. A *semiotic* question is appropriately given a *semiotic answer;* just as *prescriptive* question is given a *prescriptive* answer. And part of the answer to the semiotic question "What is the role in German by 'rot,' and in our language by 'red'? is "They both mean *red.*"

But "the role of '——' " can also be understood in another sense. In this sense, to ask What is the role of "——"? is not to ask about the role of an *expression.* It is to ask about the *causes* and *effects* of a certain empirically definable stimulus configurations. Here the word "role" is used as in What is the role of HCL in the electrolysis of H_2O? And it is the thesis of psychological nominalism that the questions as to the role of "——" *thus understood* requires no use of *semantical* or *syntactical* terms in the answer.

We have already seen that many philosophers who are sympathetic to psychological nominalism find a stumbling block in statements of the form " '——' means ***" where "***" is a predicate or class term or sentence. As Carnap points out

> As long as physical things or events (e.g. Chicago or Caesar's) death are taken as designata . . . , no serious doubts arise. But strong objections have been raised, especially by some empiricists against abstract entities as designata, e.g. against semantical statements of the following kind:
>
> (1) "The word 'red' designates a property of things"
>
> . . . .
>
> (3) "The word 'five' designates a number"
>
> . . . .
>
> . . . they reject the belief, which they regard as implicitly presupposed by semantical statements, that to each expression of the types in question (adjectives like 'red', numerals like 'five', etc.) there is a particular real entity to which the expression in question stands in the relation of designation.[39]

In his reply, Carnap points out that if we accept a framework of abstract entities, so that we can say (analytically)

(34) Five is a number

and if we are prepared to say

(35) 'Fünf' designates five

then we are committed to

(36) 'Fünf' designates a number

He concludes (p. 35) that "the question of the admissability of entities as designata is reduced to the question of the acceptability of the en-

[39]"Empiricism, Semantics and Ontology," 33-4.

tities." Carnap is quite willing to say that the descriptive semantical statement " 'fünf' means a number" asserts that 'fünf' stands in the designation relation to a number. He emphasizes that the fact that a number stands in the designation relation no more implies that the number is a *datum* than facts about electrons imply that electrons are data (pp. 38-9). But he tells us little if anything positive about the status of this designation relation.

This brings me to the heart of the matter. The emphasis of Carnap's studies in semantics is on the formal manipulation of semantical words as defined expressions in pure semantical systems. He deals in much too cavalier a fashion with semantical words as they function in the assertions of descriptive semantics, that is to say, with semantical words functioning as such. The latter, however, is the essential concern of a *philosophical* semantics. For it, the primary value of formally elaborated semantical systems lies in their contribution to the analysis of semantical concepts in actual usage. Now Carnap is, of course, aware that a pure semantical theory is a *semantical* theory only if it relates its vocabulary to semantical expressions in actual usage. And he undoubtedly thinks of his semantical studies as providing an explication (in his sense) of semantical discourse. My complaint is that his treatment of the relation between pure and descriptive semantics is much too perfunctory. It leaves important and relevant things unsaid, and what he does say is, by its over-simplification, misleading where it is not downright mistaken.

The burden of Carnap's account rests on a comparison of descriptive semantics with physical geometry. Thus he writes,

> Both in semantics and in syntax, the relation between the descriptive and the pure field is perfectly analogous to the relation between pure or mathematical geometry, which is a part of mathematics and hence analytic, and physical geometry, which is a part of physics, and hence empirical.[40]

Let us examine this parallel. Are we to infer that just as the mathematician constructs calculi such that when their primitive signs, e.g. 'points,' 'line,' etc., are given a physical interpretation, the formulae of the calculus become propositions in physical geometry; so the mathematician as semanticist constructs calculi such that when their primitive signs are given a certain interpretation, the formulae of the calculi become descriptive semantical propositions? But notice that whereas a sub-set of the expressions which, when a pure geometrical calculus is interpreted become geometrical expressions in a physical geometry are primitive signs of the calculus, if one of Carnap's pure semantical systems is construed as a calculus, the expressions which, when the cal-

[40] *Introduction to Semantics*, 12.

culus is appropriately interpreted, would, as he apparently sees it, become semantical expressions of descriptive semantics, *are without exception defined expressions of the calculus.* The *undefined* expressions of the system construed as a calculus would be on the one hand, expressions, e.g. " 'Φ'," " 'Ψ'," " 'a' " etc., which, when interpreted become the names of sign designs, and on the other, expressions, e.g. 'red,' 'blue,' 'Chicago,' etc. which, interpreted, mention non-linguistic entities (individuals, properties and relations). Consequently, this account of the relation between pure and descriptive semantics presupposes that semantical expressions in actual usage are definable in terms of sign designs and non-linguistic entities, thus

(37) x means y
(in German) $=_{Df}$ x = 'Rot' and y = red *or*
x = 'Blau' and y = blue *or*
....

Nowhere, however, does Carnap give an *independent* defense of the idea that semantical expressions in ordinary usage are thus definable (or explicable). Indeed, it clearly has not occurred to him that the relation between the semantical words of a pure semantical system and the semantical words of the corresponding set of descriptive semantical sentences could be other than that of 'interpretation.' He rather *infers* the logical status of semantical words in descriptive semantics from the logical status of semantical words in pure semantics together with the premise that the relation between the two is one of interpretation.

Now, an interpretation of the expression 'straight line' as it occurs in a pure geometrical calculus can, indeed, be formulated by means of an 'if and only if' sentence, thus

(38) x is a straight line *if and only if* x is the path of a light ray.

And, in semantics, we can correctly assert such 'if and only if' sentences as

(39) x means y (in German) *if and only if* x Des-in-G y

where to the left of 'if and only if' is a sentential function in descriptive semantics, and to the right a sentential function in the combinatories of sign designs and non-linguistic entities. But here the resemblance ceases. For, as I have been arguing, (39) is to be compared, not with (38) but with

(40) x is right *if and only if* x maximizes general welfare

To make the same point in a somewhat different way, if we take the pure semantical function 'x Des-in-G y' to be an uninterpreted (though defined) expression in a pure semantical system construed as a calculus, then its interpretation would be, *not* the descriptive semantical function 'x means y (in German)' but rather a sentential function which simply expresses a *listing* of what designates what in German. And, of course, *this* sentential function *can* be defined—as in (37) —in terms of sign designs and non-linguistic entities.

Now the philosophical consequences of supposing that such a descriptive semantical term as 'means' as applied, say, to German, is definable in terms of a list of German sign designs and a list of things qualities and relations, are relatively innocuous. This supposition has the essential virtue of preserving the core of psychological nominalism; on the other hand, it generates a feeling of uneasiness concerning the whole semantical approach to meaning and truth. For it appears to commit semantical theory to "definitions by disappearance" of semantical words,[41] and makes it difficult to understand how semantical words can have the same meaning when applied to different languages, which they obviously do.[42])

We begin by thinking of *meaning* as a relation between signs and entities, and when we are offered such a definition as (37), we tend to react to it as we would to

(41) x is the uncle of y $=_{Df}$ x = Tom and y = Bill *or*
x = Dick and y = John *or*

x........................

But the magnitude of the philosophical stakes on the table—as we have seen, the problem of meaning is not only the problem of abstract entities, but the mind-body problem as well—makes us leery of first impressions. At this point there are, *prima facie,* two courses a naturalistic empiricist may follow. (a) He may seek to secure psychological nominalism at the expense of swallowing such definitions as (37). (b) He may insist that meaning is a relation over and above the logical correlation of two lists (thus replacing the '$=_{Df}$' in (37) by 'if and only if'), and seek to preserve psychological nominalism by restricting the non-linguistic *relata* to such nominalistically congenial entities as particulars. My aim in this paper has been to make it clear that (a) and (b) do not exhaust the alternatives open to the psychological nominalist, and, indeed, to establish that the correct alternative is to combine the thesis that the '$=_{Df}$' in (37) should be replaced by 'if and only if' with the denial that meaning is, in any but the the most superficial sense, a *relation.*

It is the idea that the 'means' or 'designates' of semantical sentences

41P. F. Strawson, "Truth," *Analysis,* XIX.

42Max Black, "The Semantical Definition of Truth," *Analysis* (1948).

in a framework of abstract entities is a descriptive or factual relation such that (39) is true, but (37) false, which leads the tender-minded to Platonism, and the tough-minded to a rejection (or attempted Pickwickian interpretation) of these sentences, of semantics or the 'theory of meaning,' and of the framework of abstract entities. It is this idea, rather than any simple identification of designation with *giveness*, which is the source of nominalistic anxieties. For if an adequate theory of language required us to hold that linguistic expressions stand in such a relation to abstract entities, how could psychological nominalism, the thesis that linguistic phenomena can, in principle, be described and causally accounted for without using semantical or prescriptive expressions, be true?

Thus, the nominalist balks, as we have seen, already at "'Fünf' means five," and would continue to do so even if he had succeeded in showing that not even classical mathematics requires us to quantify predicate or class-term variables, let alone sentential variables. He does so because, sensing the incorrectness of the *definition* (37), which, if sound, would preserve the discontinuity between protons and propositions, he infers that to take semantics (or the 'theory of meaning') seriously is to introduce abstract entities as a queer kind of pseudo-scientific object.

But why should it be thought that sentences of the form "'——' means ***" assert a relation between "——" and ***? Partly because these sentences have a grammatical form which puts one in mind of statements in which we *are* asserting that two items stand in a certain relation. And, indeed, if all that one meant by saying that a sentence asserts a relation between two items were that the sentence can be represented by the grammatical form '(a) R (b),' then both "(Jones) ought (to run)" and "('rot') means (red)" would assert relations. Yet philosophers today know how misleading such appearances can be, and the primary source of this error lies elsewhere. Consider the following three sentences:

(42) (In German) 'Aachen' means *Aix-la-Chapelle*
(43) (In German) 'rot' means *red*
(44) (In German) 'und' means *and*

Now (42) clearly wouldn't be true unless some empirically definable situation involving Germans, Aix-la-Chapelle and the vocable "Aachen" had taken place. To take a more familiar example, the previous occurrence of some situation involving my old dog, Rover, his new master and the vocable "Fido" makes it correct for me to say

(45) 'Fido' means *Rover*.

But we must beware of supposing that (42) *says* that a certain descriptive or factual relation[43] has been established between Germans the vocable "Aachen" and Aix-la-Chapelle. For if one does, then one is bound to suppose that other semantical statements, (e.g. (43) and (44)) assert that relations have been established between words and entities.

Again, unless certain empirically definable relations had been established between Germans, the vocable "rot" and red things (*not* redness!) it would not be true to say "(In German) 'rot' means *red*." But the latter does not assert these relations to obtain, let alone that as used by Germans, "rot" stands in a relation to *red* or *redness*. And it is only a person who was handcuffed by a theory who would suppose that "(in German) 'und' means *and*" asserts a descriptive or factual relation between "und" and *and* or *Conjunction*.

The term "means" as it occurs in (42), (43), and (44) communicates the information that the words "Aachen," "rot" and "und" respectively play the same roles in German that "Aix-la-Chapelle," "red" and "and" play in English. It does not, however, specify what this role is, *nor in particular, does it claim that it is the same role in the case of all* three pairs. Clearly in each case the role is a different one.

Now it is important to see that there are correct *semiotic* ways of distinguishing these roles. Thus, (42), (43) and (44) must be distinguished from

(42′) (In German) 'Aachen' is the *name* of Aix-la-Chapelle.
(43′) (In German) 'rot' means *the observable property* red
or
(In German 'rot' is an *observation predicate* meaning *red*
(44′) (In German) 'und' means *the propositional connective and*
or
(In German) 'und' is a *sentential connective* meaning *and.*

Clearly the notions of a *name* and of an *observation predicate* are "pragmatical" notions, in that their analysis requires a mention of relations between language users, the vocables in question, and objects. But, as was pointed out above, the relations by virtue of which "rot" is a German observation predicate involve not *red* or *redness*, but *red things*.

Thus, the root mistake of Platonism, that is, the idea that "(In

[43]In these concluding remarks, the phrase 'designates (in German) is a descriptive or factual relation' is shorthand for the idea that *x designates y* (in German) is a descriptive or factual relation such that (39) is true, but (37) false.

German) 'rot' means *red*" asserts a descriptive relation to obtain between "rot" and redness, is the assumption that the "man of all work" semantical term "means" always has the specialized sense of "names." For when correctly used, sentences of the form

(46) (In L '——' *names* ***

in addition to asserting that (in L) '——' means "***" and thus conveying the information that "——" is used in L as "***" is used in the speaker's language, do assert those factual relations to obtain the vocable '——' and the object *** which must be brought about for the vocable to serve the purpose of a name.

The same mistake also lies at the heart of traditional nominalism, leading nominalists to boggle at such an innocent sentence as "(In German) 'rot' means *red*." Thus, the distinctions we have been drawing undercut this venerable controversy, and make it clear that there is nothing in such sentences as

(43) (In German) 'rot' means *red*
(47) (In German 'rot' means *a quality*
(48) (In German) 'rot' means *a universal*
(49) (In German) 'rot' means *something*, and does not mean a particular
(50) (In German) 'rot' means *something*

which should disturb the scientific and empiricist sensibilities of the most tough-minded philosopher. Though, if (49) and (50) are formulated in a familiar jargon as

(49′) (In German) 'rot' means an *entity* which is not a particular—an *abstract entity*
(50′) (In German) 'rot' means an *entity*

we are, unless we are careful, likely to read "means" as "names" and be off on the old merry-go-round.

VIII

The linguistic framework of abstract entities, which is such an indispensable part of human discourse, not only semantical discourse, but mentalistic discourse and scientific discourse generally, as well, does not involve a commitment to Platonism. It is a misinterpretation of semantical sentences, a 'category mistake,' which has generated the contrary supposition. Let us be clearly understood that I am not attributing this misinterpretation to Carnap. My thesis, so far as it concerns him, amounts rather to the wish that he had devoted more of his time and energies to bringing out the full philosophical significance of his syntactical and semantical studies, and less to the technical elaboration of lemmas and corrolaries. Today, for the first time, the naturalistic-empiricist tradition has the fundamentals of an adequate philosophy of mind. To the creation of this truly revolutionary situation, which is just beginning to make itself felt, Carnap's *Logical Syntax of Language* and *Introduction to Semantics* have contributed at least as much as any other single source.

Wilfrid Sellars

Department of Philosophy
University of Minnesota

15

E. W. Beth

CARNAP'S VIEWS ON THE ADVANTAGES OF CONSTRUCTED SYSTEMS OVER NATURAL LANGUAGES IN THE PHILOSOPHY OF SCIENCE

I. *A Guide in Life*

I may be allowed to open this contribution with a few personal recollections from the later years of my life as a student. In 1932, I completed my studies in mathematics at the State University of Utrecht, and I started working in the fields of foundations of mathematics and philosophy of science, especially on the theory of space; these studies finally resulted in a thesis for the doctor's degree.[1] During this more or less uncertain period in my career—I was compelled to switch over from the Faculty of Science to the Faculty of Letters—, I had the good luck of becoming a member of a group of mostly younger philosophers in which, together with P. G. J. Vredenduin, I represented the philosophy of mathematics and physical science.[2] The preceding years had been particularly uneventful for philosophical life in the Netherlands. The influence of Bolland's Hegelianism was fading, that of Neo-Kantianism was past its culmination, while phenomenology was not yet in vogue. In addition, the Amsterdam Schools of Intuitionism and Significs were—temporarily—less active than they had been before, as was the case with the School of Groningen. Therefore, most of us were looking for new directives, and it will be understood that the new philosophy of the Vienna Circle was given great attention.[3] Especially Carnap's work, as far as it was available—and understandable—to us, met with keen interest, if not always with approval. This preference must be explained by reference to various factors; in the first place, Vredenduin and I found in his writings[4] on logic and

[1]*Rede en Aanschouwing in de Wiskunde* (Groningen, 1935).

[2]*Aspecten van de Tijd.* Een bundel wijsgerige studies, ter gelegenheid van zijn 25-jarig bestaan uitgegeven door het Genootschap voor Wetenschappelijke Philosophie, waaraan is toegevoegd een Overzicht van zijn Geschiedenis (Assen, 1950).

[3]There is sufficient evidence to show that interest in the work of the Vienna School and of related groups was also present outside Utrecht. But our contact with other groups in our country was slight.

[4]*Der Raum* (Berlin, 1922); *Abriss der Logistik* (Vienna, 1929).

mathematics exactly the kind of material which we needed; other members of the group must have been fascinated, or at least challenged, by Carnap's *Der logische Aufbau der Welt.*[5] But I feel the inherent qualities of Carnap's work: its solidity and lucidity and the author's obvious sincerity of purpose, must have been of even more importance. In addition, the emphasis on method and the moderate character of the views defended, if compared to the more sweeping statements of Hahn and Neurath, must have appealed to philosophers trained in a Neo-Kantian school. Vredenduin managed to incorporate into a neo-kantian synthesis views on logic which were strongly influenced by Carnap's doctrines.

In the course of the years, the "Genootschap"[2] gave up its exclusively neo-kantian character and its close connections with the University of Utrecht, and devoted itself to scientific philosophy in a broad sense. My own development followed a similar line. Already before the war, I became more and more critical towards all traditional philosophy and deeply interested in the formal methods applied in modern logic and research on foundations. During these years, I was strongly stimulated by Carnap's successive publications.[6] After the war, his influence became less exclusive. In the meantime, I had become more familiar with Brouwer's intuitionism; moreover, I had assimilated Hilbert and Bernays' "Beweistheorie" and Tarski's semantics and, by and by, I had started developing a conception of my own. But for about ten years, Carnap has been a guide for me, and the present essay may serve to witness my gratitude and admiration, feelings which, I am deeply convinced, are shared by numerous logicians, philosophers, mathematicians, and men of science all over the world.

II. *Carnap and Frege*

As a rule, Carnap is considered in the first place as a member of the Vienna Circle and hence as a typical representative of the logical empiricism which sprung from its activities; but I feel that, if Carnap's work is interpreted under this angle, its character cannot be fully understood and its importance cannot be rightly judged. His connection with the Vienna Circle[7] is certainly characteristic of his way of thinking, but by no means did it determine his philosophy. It seems to me that the influence of Frege's teaching[8] and published work has been much deeper. In fact, this influence must have been decisive, and the development of Carnap's

[5]Berlin, 1928.

[6]*Logische Syntax der Sprache* (Vienna, 1934); *Foundations of Logic and Mathematics* (Chicago, 1939).

[7]From 1926 to 1930, or perhaps to 1936; cf. Herbert Feigl, "Logical Empiricism," in Dagobert D. Runes (ed.), *Twentieth Century Philosophy* (New York, 1943), 407.

[8]Carnap heard Frege as a student in Jena; cf. Marcel Boll, "Introduction," in Rudolf Carnap, *L'ancienne et la nouvelle logique* (Paris, 1933), 3.

ideas may be considered as characteristic of Frege's philosophy as well. Carnap's *logicism,* for instance, is much closer related to Frege's than to Russell's and Couturat's, though Carnap, of course, has taken full advantage of the technical innovations embodied in *Principia Mathematica.* Therefore, it will be necessary to say a few words on Frege.

There is, in the fate of Frege's life-work, an undeniable touch of tragedy. The discovery of the Russell paradox, at the eve of the publication of *Grundgesetze der Arithmetik,*[9] was a heavy blow at that time, but it does not, as we know now, impair the importance of Frege's ideas or the value of his discoveries. It is, however, significant that at the same time the very doctrines which Frege had set out to combat emerged in entirely new forms and with arguments which Frege was sometimes unable to follow and more often unable to refute.

(i) Psychologism revived in Husserl's more subtle *phenomenology,* which paid lip-service to Frege but at the same time rejected his most valuable ideas.[10]

(ii) The Kantian conception of pure mathematics was taken up again by intuitionism, as developed by L. Kronecker, H. Poincaré, and, in particular, by L. E. J. Brouwer.[11] At the same time, Kant's thesis of the synthetic a priori character of geometry, accepted by Frege,[12] turned out to be untenable on account of criticism by Mach, Poincaré, Brouwer, and many others, and of the development of the theory of relativity.

[9] 2.Band, Jena 1903; the discovery is announced in an Appendix, dated October, 1902. Frege's correspondence with Russell on this subject (June 16, 1902-December 12, 1904) is now at the Berliner Staats-Bibliothek and at the Institut für Mathematische Logik und Grundlagenforschung (formerly Philosophisches Seminar B) of the University in Münster; cf. H. Scholz-F. Bachmann, "Der wissenschaftliche Nachlass von Gottlob Frege," *Actes du Congrès International de Philosophie Scientifique, Sorbonne,* [Paris, 1935] (published Paris, 1936), fasc. VIII, 25.

[10] It is true that Husserl's criticism of Frege's definition of the notion of a number ("Anzahl") appears in *Philosophie der Arithmetik,* I. Band (Halle, 1891), 134, a work belonging to his "psychologistic" period. But it was never withdrawn, and it has been used by Husserl's followers; cf. Albert Spaier, *La pensée et la quantité* (Paris, 1927), 186. In this connection, cf. the polemics between A. Koyre and J. Bar-Hillel in *Philosophy and Phenomenological Research,* VIII (1947/48). The reactionary tendency inherent in phenomenology is discussed by Marvin Farber in a paper on "Experience and Transcendence," same review, XII (1951/52). In his book on *The Foundation of Phenomenology* (Cambridge, Mass., 1943), the same author warns against over-estimation of Frege's influence on Husserl.

[11] *Over de grondslagen der wiskunde* (Amsterdam-Leipzig, 1907).

[12] *Die Grundlagen der Arithmetik* (Breslau, 1884), 101. In my opinion—as stated, for instance, in a paper on Kants Einteilung der Urteile in analytische und synthetische, *Alg. Ned. Tijdschr. v. Wijsbeg. en Psychol.* XLVI (1953/54)—the whole discussion on Kant's conception of pure mathematics rests upon an incorrect interpretation of his doctrine of analytic and synthetic statements, which originated with Bolzano. But this is of no importance in the present context, as this interpretation was adopted both by Kant's opponents (Bolzano, Frege, Russell, Couturat, Carnap) and by his defendants (Heymans, Poincaré, Brouwer).

(iii) Formalism, effectively attacked by Frege[13] in the crude form in which it appeared in Thomae's work, was given a completely new shape on account of Hilbert's work in axiomatics.

(iv) Cantor's theory of sets, though also menaced by the discovery of the paradoxes, derived a considerable prestige from its importance for mathematical research, to the detriment of Frege's constructions which were much more satisfactory from a logical point of view. Frege himself recognised the value of Cantor's work and the possibility of giving it a more satisfactory foundation,[14] but he did not carry out this program, probably on account of his failure to deal effectively with the paradoxes.

A new man was needed to take up the task which Frege did not complete. But this man did not appear too promptly, and the first world war caused a new delay. When Carnap finally started his research into the foundations of mathematics and physical science, the situation had again completely changed, though certainly not for the worse.

(v) The discussions on the theory of relativity had given rise to the development of a new brand of empiricism (M. Schlick, H. Reichenbach) in which there was no place for psychologism.

(vi) The work of Löwenheim and Wittgenstein had contributed, from opposite directions, to fill the gap between logicism and formalism.

(vii) Similarly, Whitehead and Russell and, somewhat later, Skolem, Fraenkel and von Neumann had prepared the ground for an understanding between cantorism and logicism.

Of course, I do not mean to say that these and other similar connections could be clearly seen in the first years after the first world war. To the contrary, they were only gradually realised and it was Carnap who, in a series of carefully written works, brought order and light into the situation and thereby helped to create an atmosphere in which the work of Frege could be taken up again. Hence, even though Carnap never presented himself as Frege's legitimate successor, his affinity with Frege has become more and more manifest.

III. *Carnap on Space*

Though we are not concerned now with Carnap's views on space, a few words should be said on this subject, as it has been treated in Carnap's first publication[15] which presents already many features which are characteristic of his later work. There are two points which I should like to stress.

In the first place, this booklet contains on pages 9-12 an extremely able

[13] *Grundlagen,* 38.
[14] *Grundlagen,* 98.
[15] *Der Raum, ein Beitrag zur Wissenschaftslehre* (Berlin, 1922).

summary of formal logic. Of course, no formalisation can be expected, but otherwise the main lines of Carnap's *Abriss* (1929) and *Symbolische Logik* (1954) are clearly visible. It is especially characteristic, that *use* and *mention* are clearly distinguished:

> Wir nennen alles das, was entweder wahr order falsch ist, ein *Urteil.* Eine Zusammenstellung von Zeichen, insbesondere Schriftzeichen, die ein Urteil bezeichnet, heisst (vollständiger) *Satz.*

Secondly, extreme empiricistic or even sensualistic conceptions as found, for instance, in Whitehead,[16] and which give rise to the well-known attempts to avoid the notion of a point, are not discussed nor even quoted, but simply brushed aside.

> Wir werden . . . einfach von "Punkten" im physischen Raume sprechen, ohne dabei zu berücksichtigen, dass jede irgendwie bezeichnete oder auch nur kenntliche Stelle im physischen Raum eine wenn auch noch so kleine, von der Genauigkeit unsrer Beobachtungsmittel abhängige Ausdehnung haben muss.
>
> Auch die Schwierigkeit, dass die Gebilde des physischen Raumes als stetig behandelt werden, während die Physik den unstetigen Aufbau der Körper aus getrennten Teilen lehrt, sei hier nicht erörtert, da sie die Lehre vom physischen Raum nach unsrer bisherigen Kenntnis nicht wesentlich beeinflusst.

In full agreement with this point of view, the axiom systems for certain parts of physics, which are discussed in Carnap's *Abriss*[17] and *Symbolische Logik,*[18] admit the concept of a world point as a primitive notion. It is true that, as an exercise, the last-mentioned book suggests the construction of an axiom system based upon the inclusion relation between events as its only primitive notion, the points being obtained by Whitehead's method of extensive abstraction, but even here no attention is given to the objections which must be made to such a construction from a radically empiricist point of view.

Hence there seems to be some evidence in favor of the supposition that Carnap is, basically, a logician who is interested in "Wissenschaftslogik" mainly on account of the logical problems which it involves. If considered under this angle—and, therefore, somewhat one-sidedly—his *Logischer Aufbau der Welt*[5] and related writings[19] may be interpreted as essays in applied logic, which derive their interest mainly from their logical form and not from their contents. This possibility, however, was hardly realised by most of Carnap's readers.

[16]A. Grünbaum, "Whitehead's Method of Extensive Abstraction," *British Journ. for the Philos. of Sc.*, IV (1952/53).

[17]*Abriss der Logistik* (Vienna, 1929).

[18]*Symbolische Logik* (Vienna, 1954).

[19]*Physikalische Bergriffsbildung* (Karlsruhe, 1926); *Scheinprobleme in der Philosophie* (Berlin, 1928).

IV. *The "Abriss"*

The intentions of this book were clearly, though modestly, expressed by the words in the title: "mit besonderer Berücksichtigung der Relations-Theorie und ihrer Anwendungen." No attempt is made to defend new doctrines; all that is given is a summary of symbolic logic in accordance with the logicist tradition of Frege, Russell and Couturat, in which, however, the technicial innovations introduced by Chwistek, Nicod, Ramsey, Sheffer, Wittgenstein, and many others were taken into account.

However, the adoption of new techniques had certain implications on the doctrinal level. In particular, the acceptance of the simple theory of types made it possible to adopt the "no class theory" which Russell had tentatively stated as early as 1903 but which he did not even accept in the second edition of *Principia Mathematica* (1925). This step naturally leads to the conception of an entirely extensional logic.

On the other hand, the acceptance of an extensional logic was hardly compatible with certain basic features in Frege's logicism; what Frege had always objected to in Thomae's, Korselt's, and Hilbert's formalism was its neglect of the necessity of an interpretation of formal mathematics:[20]

> Die formale Arithmetik setzt demnach die inhaltliche voraus; ihr Anspruch, diese zu ersetzen, fällt damit zu Boden.

And Frege's treatment of interpretation, in particular his distinction of "Sinn" and "Bedeutung" (sense and denotation), was dependent upon the introduction of intensional concepts.

The necessity of an interpretation was also stressed by Carnap in his well-known paper on "Die Mathematik als Zweig der Logik:"[21]

> Andererseits jedoch bemerkt der logizistische Beurteiler im System des Formalismus, wie es bisher vorliegt, eine Lücke. Wie wir an Freges Grundgedanken schon bemerkten, wendet der Logizismus seine Aufmerksamkeit besonders dem Umstand zu, dass die Mathematik auf Wirklichkeit anwendbar sein soll. Die Arithmetik muss uns in den Stand setzen, von einem Wirklichkeitssatz ohne mathematische Zeichen zu einem solchen mit mathematischen Zeichen überzugehen, z.B. von dem Satz "in diesem Zimmer sind nur die Personen Fritz und Karl" zu dem Satz "in diesem Zimmer sind zwei Personen". Der Formalismus müsste sein mathematisch-logisches Axiomensystem derartig ergänzen, dass solche Umformungen sich als logisch legitime Schlüsse ergeben. Dann aber wird durch die Axiome, die solches leisten, den Zahlzeichen, die zunächst als blosse Figuren aufgefasst werden, eine Bedeutung beigelegt, und zwar eine rein logische.

In connection with this remark, which is in full agreement with

[20] G. Frege, "Die Unmöglichkeit der Thomaeschen formalen Arithmetik aus neue nachgewiesen," *Jahresber. d. D.M.V.*, XVII (1908), in particular S. 55. According to Scholz and Bachmann, l. c. footnote 9), Löwenheim convinced Frege, in an extensive exchange of letters, of the possibility of a correct construction of formal arithmetic.

[21] *Bl. f. deutsche Philos.*, IV (1930/31), in particular S. 309.

Frege's views, Carnap then strongly suggests the possibility of an agreement between logicism and formalism;

Man darf vielleicht vermuten, dass diese Bedeutung der Zahlzeichen, auf die der Formalismus von seinem eigenen System aus geführt wird, sich als übereinstimmend herausstellen wird mit der, die der Logizismus den Zahlen beilegt, und dass die Formeln der formalistischen Mathematik sich dann als Tautologien herausstellen werden.

So bestehen, wenn auch noch keine Beweise, so doch einige Gründe für die Hoffnung, dass, sobald der Formalismus eine gewisse, für die Wissenschaft unentbehrliche Ergänzung seines Systems vornimmt, der jetzt bestehende Gegensatz der beiden Richtungen überbrückt werden wird. Die Einzelheiten in der endgültigen Lösung des Problems der Grundlegung der Mathematik lassen sich heute noch nicht übersehen. Angesichts der Tatsache aber, dass der Formalismus die wichtigsten Grundgedanken des Intuitionismus in seinem System zur Anerkennung gebracht hat, und der soeben gegebenen Andeutung über das Verhältnis zwischen Formalismus und Logizismus darf die Auffindung einer Problemlösung, die von den verschiedenen Gesichtspunkten aus als befriedigend erscheinen wird, gegenwärtig nicht mehr als so aussichtslos angesehen werden, wie es noch vor wenigen Jahren schien.

These few sentences seem to me of crucial importance for an understanding of Carnap's general attitude. It is obvious that Carnap starts from Frege's position. But he certainly lays considerably more stress upon the necessity of explaining the rôle of mathematics in the scientific analysis of reality, and much less on the opposition between logicism and formalism.

At the same time, he restores to a certain extent the connections with philosophical tradition, in particular with German speculative philosophy, in which this peculiar rôle of mathematics had always provided matter for discussion; this tendency is already clearly visible in *Der Raum*. But we also see the reason for his interest in modern empiricism, which mainly deviates from traditional empiricism by giving up the empiricist interpretation of logic and pure mathematics.

V. *Logical Syntax*

The programme of a fusion of logicism and formalism was carried out by Carnap in his famous *Logical Syntax of Language,*[22] which we shall have to discuss in more detail.

We distinguish in the book four main parts, namely:

[22](New York and London, 1937). This book is a translation, by Amethe Smeaton, of *Logische Syntax der Sprache* (Vienna, 1934), but also incorporates the main contents of two closely related papers: "Die Antinomien und die Unvollständigkeit der Mathematik," *Monatsh. f. Math. u. Physik* XLI (1934), and "Ein Gültigkeitskriterium für die Satze der klassischen Mathematik"; ibid., XLII (1935). A more popular exposition of the main ideas is found in *Die Aufgabe der Wissenschaftslogik* (Vienna, 1934), and *Philosophy and Logical Syntax* (London, 1935).

(i) The programme of a reconstruction of logic as part of a syntax for certain languages;

(ii) The construction of a syntax for two special languages, intended to answer the needs of intuitionistic and of classical mathematics respectively;

(iii) The construction of a general syntax;

(iv) The tranformation of philosophy into a logic of science, and, thereby, into a part of syntax.

Rather than a fusion of logic and formalism or an incorporation of formalism into logicism, *Logical Syntax* appears to advocate a surrender of logicism to formalism, though this surrender is not unconditional; it depends upon the acceptance of non-constructive methods, which had turned out to be unavoidable on account of Gödel's results on the incompleteness of certain formal systems; it is mainly by the introduction of non-constructive, though purely formal, rules that Carnap's syntax deviates from proof theory as originally conceived by Hilbert.

This attitude is understandable in view of the development of logic between 1930 and 1934, which was inconsistent with certain doctrines current during the previous decade. The conception of the propositional calculus as a set of *tautologies,* set forth by Wittgenstein in his *Tractatus,* had been extended by F. P. Ramsey[23] to the entire system of *Principia Mathematica,* with the exception of the axiom of infinity. This tautological character of logic and, hence—on account of its logicistic reconstruction—of pure mathematics, seemed to provide a full explanation of the possibility to construct pure mathematics in a completely formal manner, independent of an appeal to experience or intuition; therefore, it appeared to be possible to incorporate formalism into logicism, and this was certainly Carnap's intention when he wrote his paper on "Die Mathematik als Zweig der Logik."[24] But in 1931, Gödel published his famous incompleteness theorem, which implied the indefinite (undecidable) character of the notion of a tautology.

It is obvious and well-known that Gödel's results directly affect Hilbert's formalism. One may doubt whether logicism is affected to the same extent. But from *Logical Syntax* it is clear that, at any rate in Carnap's opinion, logicism was indeed affected no less than formalism. This opinion is based upon an argument which may be summed up as follows: according to logicism, it is possible to derive all theorems of pure mathematics starting from the principles of logic; however, on account of Gödel's result it is impossible to find a set of principles from which all theorems of arithmetic can be derived.

Hence, instead of weakening Carnap's conviction of a certain sol-

[23]"Foundations of Mathematics," *Proc. London Math. Soc.,* XXV (1926).

[24]In this paper, Ramsey's article is quoted and discussed on S. 307.

idarity between logicism and formalism, Gödel's results appear to have strengthened it; and instead of trying to develop logicism beyond the too narrow boundaries which Hilbert had imposed upon formalism, Carnap was induced to trying to develop formalism in such a way as to evade the disturbing implications of Gödel's results and thereby to provide a new and larger formal frame-work in which logicism could find a place.

There are, of course, also technical reasons for Carnap's choice in favor of a formal approach. The necessity for formal rigor had already been realised by Frege, but Frege's strain after formal rigor had been always counter-balanced by his stress on content; when Carnap adopted and developed Hilbert's device of a distinction between *object language* and *syntax language,* it was necessary to give considerably more attention to the demands of formal rigor.

A third, and powerful, reason is found, of course, in the adoption of the *Principle of Tolerance;* this step was, presumably, intended to enable Carnap to extend his investigations to "heterodox" systems of logic and mathematics—in particular to Brouwer's intuitionism—and to avoid difficulties in the establishment of connections between the formal systems of logic and mathematics and the language of the empirical sciences.

The formalistic inspiration of *Logical Syntax* reveals itself quite strikingly in Carnap's treatment of the concept of *interpretation.* An interpretation is defined to be a *translation.*

On the other hand, we find in *Logical Syntax* also concepts which, though defined in a purely formal fashion, are clearly inspired by a non-formal interpretation which, if made manifest, would imply a return to Frege's logicism.[25] I think that it is even possible to show that, in the absence of such a non-formal, intuitive, interpretation, the whole edifice of *Logical Syntax* would miss its purpose.

Following the lines of Gödel's argument, Carnap constructs a certain sentence W_{II} which belong to his Language II and which constitutes the arithmetisation of a certain sentence in the syntax of Language II expressing the consistency of Language II. It can be shown that, if Language II happens to be consistent—which will be assumed throughout the following argument—then W_{II} cannot be proved in Language II, though, according to the intended intuitive interpretation of Language II, W_{II} must, of course, be true.

Hence if non-W_{II}, the negation of W_{II}, is introduced as a new axiom, so as to extend Language II into a stronger system II*, then II* is still consistent. On account of Henkin's completeness theorem for the theory

[25]Cf. S. C. Kleene's review, *J. Symbolic Logic,* IV (1939).

of types,[26] which can be proved within II, II admits a certain model M*, which, of course, must be different from the intuitive "standard" model M for II.

In order to avoid the use of an elaborate terminological apparatus, let us now introduce a hypothetical logician, Carnap*, whose logical and mathematical intuitions are in accordance with model M*. Let us try to construct Carnap*'s view on the situation.

It seems reasonable to suppose that, for Carnap*, all theorems of II are intuitively true. Now these theorems include the arithmetisations of the theorems of a certain extension S* of the Syntax S of II; arithmetisation is an interpretation, hence a translation; it follows that, for Carnap*, the theorems of S* must be intuitively true. As II* contains *non*-W_{II}, it follows that for Carnap* Language II is inconsistent. On the other hand, S* contains Henkin's theorem, hence, for Carnap*, Language II, and a fortiori II*, cannot admit a model. However, Carnap* was supposed to be endowed with the intuitive model M*!

The solution of this paradox is as follows. We made an error in supposing that, for Carnap*, all theorems of II* are intuitively true; for Carnap's* set of all theorems of II* does not coincide with *our* set of all theorems of II*.[27] Roughly speaking, Carnap*'s set contains *more* theorems than ours, and for some of these additional theorems M* is not a model.

It is easy to see, that for Carnap* *non*-W_{II} is a theorem of language II; hence, for him, II* coincides with II and S* coincides with S. This remark implies at once a positive solution to a problem which I stated once[28] in connection with a critical analysis of *Logical Syntax:* do the syntactical properties of a given object language O depend on the choice of a syntax language S? For, from our point of view, the choice of S allows us to believe in the inconsistency of II, the choice of S* allows us to prove the inconsistency of II, whereas the choice of a suitable extension of II allows us to prove the consistency of II.

The above considerations, which are only variants of the Skolem-Löwenheim paradox, suggest strongly that, if arguments as contained in *Logical Syntax* serve a certain purpose, this can only be the case on account of the fact that they are interpreted by reference to a certain

26L. Henkin, "Completeness in the Theory of Types," *J. Symbolic* Logic, XV (1950).

27As for Carnap* as well as for us, each model for all axioms is a model for all theorems, it follows that already the set of all axioms of II* is different for Carnap. As for each finite set, however, Carnap*'s and our intuitions coincide, it follows that the set of all axioms of II* (and hence the set of all axioms of II, and of all related systems) must be infinite. For more elaborate proofs of theorems of this kind, cf. papers by A. Mostowski and C. Ryll-Nardzewski in *Fund. Math.* XXXIX (1952).

28L'évidence intuitive dans les mathématiques modernes," *Travaux du IXe Congrès International de Philosophie* (Congrès Descartes) (Paris, 1937).

presupposed intuitive model M[29]). Carnap avoids an appeal to such an intuitive model in the discussion of Language II itself, but he could not avoid it in the discussion of its syntax; for the conclusions belonging to this syntax would not be acceptable to Carnap*, though Carnap and Carnap* would, of course, always agree with respect to those conclusions which depend exclusively on formal considerations.

It should be noted that we also meet here with a limitation regarding the Principle of Tolerance. Indeed, Carnap could be tolerant with respect to Carnap*, for Carnap would be able to understand why Carnap* adopting for certain personal reasons additional axioms for Language II is compelled to accept additional theorems and to reject certain (and indeed all) models for language II. But Carnap* would never be able to understand why Carnap, having accepted certain axioms and certain rules of inference, as stated in *Logical Syntax,* stubbornly refuses to accept *non*-W_{II} as a theorem and believes Language II to have a model.

VI. *Constructed Systems and Natural Language*

I have tried to show, in Section V, that arguments, as set forth in *Logical Syntax,* cannot serve any purpose, unless they are interpreted by reference to a certain presupposed intuitive model M. However, this fact is nowhere mentioned in *Logical Syntax,* and indeed an overt appeal to intuition could hardly be expected from Carnap. Nevertheless, an implicit appeal to intuition is present, namely in the way in which natural language is used.

In a treatise such as *Logical Syntax,* natural language can be used in two different ways, which I should like to denote as *strict usage* and *amplified usage,* respectively. In strict usage of natural language, we refer to a definite model of the theory to which our statements belong; it is this model which has been called the *intuitive model.*[30] In amplified

[29]Cf. R. McNaughton, "Axiomatic Systems, Conceptual Schemes, and the Consistency of Mathematical Theories," *Philosophy of Science* XXIV (1957).

[30]For instance, we may safely assume that, in Euclid's *Elements,* we find strict usage of geometrical terms such as "*point*" and "*straight line.*" These terms are meant to refer to entities in "the" space, no distinction being made between intuitive space, mathematical space, physical space, and so on. In Hilbert's *Grundlagen,* however, we find amplified usage of the same terms, as all possible models of the axioms are admitted on the same footing. In contemporary mathematics, we still find very often strict usage of the term "*natural number.*"—It would clearly make no sense whatsoever here to discusss the ontological question whether there exists such a thing as an intuitive model. In strict usage of natural language, however, the existence of an intuitive (in the sense of: privileged by nature) model is, explicitly or implicitly, presupposed. This point will become clearer in the course of this Section.—I understand that Carnap prefers to avoid the term "*model*" and, in order to prevent confusion with the meaning currently given to it by physicists, it may be useful to say here that I use this term to denote a mathematical *structure,* that is, a set in which certain predicates or operations are defined. Also, as we shall see, I use the term "*semantics*" in a sense which differs somewhat from Carnap's.

usage of natural language—and in *all* usage of formalised languages—on the other hand, we refer to *any* model of this theory. Hence amplified usage of natural language may be equivalently replaced by usage of a formalised language, but strict usage cannot; in fact, amplified usage of natural language takes place nearly exclusively in situations where, for reasons of convenience, we wish to avoid the use of a formalised language.

So I have now to show that, in *Logical Syntax,* we can find strict usage of natural language.[31] And this is not a difficult task.[32] For instance, we find strict usage of natural language on page 13, where Carnap introduces the symbols:

$$0,\quad 0',\quad 0'', \ldots$$

as a notation for natural numbers. For it is (implicitly) understood that there is *only one* correct manner of completing the sequence of symbols only the first numbers of which have been explicitly written down. Or, to put it in another way: The term *"etc.,"* which appears in Carnap's text, is supposed to be univocal.[33]

I have now to show that strict usage of natural language plays an *essential* rôle in *Logical Syntax*. In order to do so, I introduce once more our hypothetical logician Carnap*. It has already been pointed out that certain statements in *Logical Syntax* cannot be accepted by Carnap*, for instance, Theorem 36.6 on page 133. Now suppose Carnap* sets out to read *Logical Syntax;* at which point will he have to stop?

Not yet, certainly, on page 13. Indeed, for Carnap* as well, there is only one correct manner of completing the above-mentioned sequence of symbols; it is true that this is not the manner which Carnap wishes to suggest, but there is nothing in the text to warn Carnap* off. So he will continue reading without noticing any essential difficulties, though always consistently understanding certain statements the wrong way. The first place where real trouble arises is indicated by Carnap himself on page 113.

Carnap there points out that a certain point in the given definition of 'analytic in II' may appear dubious. This definition contains certain phrases meaning "for all syntactical properties of accented expressions. . . ." Now the meaning of such phrases for Carnap and for Carnap*

[31]More precisely: I have to show that strict usage plays an essential role in *Logical Syntax.*

[32]It would, of course, be much more difficult to point out exactly where usage of natural language is strict and where it is amplified.

[33]This implicit presupposition was once strikingly pointed out by G. Mannoury by means of the following anecdote. A gives B a certain instruction, winding up with the words: "1, 2, 3, and so on." To which B replies: "But *how* on?" Much has been made of this point by intuitionists and significists. But Skolem has been the first to prove that it is relevant from a mathematical point of view.

is different, as for Carnap* the set of all accented expressions is larger than it is for Carnap. It follows that Carnap will make (or accept) certain statements concerning the set of all syntactical properties of accented expressions which Carnap* must reject.

Hence, from this point onward, Carnap* will no longer be able to follow Carnap's argument, the conclusion of which—the consistency of language II—he cannot accept; indeed, as we have seen, for Carnap* Language II is inconsistent.

Now Carnap* could settle the dispute at once in his favor by exhibiting the inconsistency which, according to him, exists in Language II, that is, by actually deriving a contradiction. But this he is unable to perform.[34] So he is compelled to proceed entirely by indirect argument, guided by his intuitive model M*. But in doing so, he will again and again resort to assertions which Carnap cannot accept and for which no basis can be found in *Logical Syntax*. Therefore, he will not be able to convince Carnap of an error.

On the other hand, Carnap will no more be able to convince Carnap* for the statements to which Carnap* appeals are consistent with every statement made in *Logical Syntax;* if Carnap is to refute Carnap*'s assertions, he must resort to his "sufficiently rich syntax language" for Language II, and some statements provable in this syntax language are, for Carnap*, either false or devoid of meaning.

The step from which all these complications derive is, to state the same point in a different manner, the *"translation"* of the Syntax of Language II into a formalised language. For this syntax was first stated by means of strict usage of natural language, and hence was meant to refer to only one model. To this model, the term "Language II" was meant to refer; but once syntax has been "translated" into a formalised language, we have—according to well-established customs in modern logic—to accept all possible models on equal terms. Hence it is misleading in this connection to speak of a translation.

The above observations are not intended to support a certain tendency of ascribing to natural language a "mystical" quality not inherent in formalised languages. They are only meant to clarify the manner in which these various languages are currently used in considerations as found in *Logical Syntax*. It would be quite possible to introduce a special formalised language for strict usage in addition to the various formalised languages already in existence.[35]

But I feel that, even though this would be quite contrary to Carnap's own intentions, his *Logical Syntax,* in the absence of some distinc-

[34]As stated in Section V, we assume Language II to be consistent.

[35]It is, of course, possible to resort to other devices to obtain the same practical effect.

tion as to the manner in which languages can be (and are) used, might conceivably countenance "mystical" attitudes with regard to natural language; in fact, it might encourage such attitudes in still various other connections.

For instance, it is stated in Carnap's Introduction, page 2, that, but for the practical difficulties deriving from the unsystematic and logically imperfect structure of natural language, it would be possible to state the rules of its syntax in much the same way as this is done for formalised languages. Statements to this effect tend, I am afraid, to encourage investigations as to the logical structure of natural language, and in fact attempts in this direction are by no means rare in the literature of recent years. In my opinion, investigations along these lines are bound to remain futile; but, moreover, there is an acute danger that their negative results are used in such a manner as to depreciate the positive results which are obtained with respect to certain formalised languages and to support "mystical" attitudes toward natural language.

I am aware that the preceding discussion of part of the contents of *Logical Syntax* has been rather critical, and that some readers may feel that I have been unfair to Carnap by taking advantage of results which, when the book was written and published, were either not available or at least not generally understood, the more so, as in later years Carnap has given ample proof of his willingness and ability to draw from these results the conclusions which were relevant from his point of view.

Therefore, I should like to say, in defense of my observations, that I expect Carnap's *Logical Syntax* to remain one of the classics in logical literature and hence to be read and studied by many generations of future logicians. For this reason, it seems better frankly to point out those doctrines in the book which, in my opinion, do not sustain a critical examination in the light of other investigations, even if in subsequent publications such doctrines have been revised by Carnap himself. Moreover, my critical observations are intended to prepare the discussion of some of Carnap's later work in the following sections of this contribution.

VII. *Foundations of Logic and Mathematics*

We now pass on to consider a small but valuable contribution, which witnesses an important development with respect to *Logical Syntax*.[36] This development consists in the adoption of Tarski's semantical method which involves a rupture with the formalistic tendency in *Logical Syntax* and the possibility of a return to Frege's logicism.

It will be convenient to make a few comments on the semantical

[36] *Foundations of Logic and Mathematics, Int. Enc. of Unified Science,* I, no. 3 (Chicago, Ill., 1939).

method in general, as an introduction to my discussion of Carnap's treatment of it. According to Tarski[37] the semantical method is meant to fill the gaps which Skolem's, Gödel's and his own results have revealed in the edifice of deductive science.

The first to point out such gaps and to realise their serious character has been Thoralf Skolem,[38] but no general attention was given them previously to the publication of Gödel's famous incompleteness theorem in 1931. The reason of this neglect was, presumably, the fact that Skolem's result, the so-called Skolem-Löwenheim paradox, concerned axiomatic set theory, and therefore could be ascribed to the peculiar character of Cantor's set theory rather than to a general deficiency of a large group of deductive systems; Gödel's result, however, is concerned with arithmetic, and therefore his discovery could exert an enormous influence.[39]

The results of Skolem, Gödel, and Tarski point in the first place to the restrictions imposed upon the means of expression of any formalised language.[40] We have already met with a striking example of this phenomenon: our hypothetical logician Carnap* was able to follow the greater part of Carnap's discussions on Language II—in fact, the part which could be "translated" into Language II—though, almost from the very beginning, he understood these discussions the wrong way; this shows that, without the tacit understanding of strict usage—an understanding which Carnap* fails to grasp—the language used by Carnap does not provide sufficient means of expression to warn Carnap* off.

It would be completely consistent with current word usage to denote Carnap*'s way of understanding Carnap's discussion as an interpretation; we could even construe our description of Carnap*'s way of understanding in such a manner as to provide an interpretation in the sense of Carnap's definition of this notion. We can ascribe to Carnap* a language which "typographically" is exactly like the language in which *Logical Syntax* is written but which differs from it by the fact that certain expressions have a different *denotation,* refer to different *designata;* this is, for instance, the case with the term *"etc."* as it appears in Carnap's text.

Now Carnap* may be said to have translated—without realising this

37"Grundlegung der wissenschaftlichen Semantik,"*Actes du Congrès International de Philosophie Scientifique* (Paris: Sorbonne, 1935).

38"Einige Bemerkungen zur axiomatischen Begründung der Mengenlehre," *Math.-kongressen i Helsingfors* (1922).

39Carnap discussed the Skolem-Löwenheim paradox in his paper on "Die Antinomien,"[22] apparently without fully realising its implications with respect to syntax.

40and also upon the means of expression of natural language in amplified usage. Natural language in strict usage is not affected with such restrictions, but only on account of the understanding implicit in this usage.

—Carnap's text (up to page 113) into his own language, with the bad results which have already been discussed. Let L and L* be Carnap's and Carnap*'s languages respectively. Is it possible, within the conceptual framework of *Logical Syntax,* to describe the difference between L and L*?

Though at first sight the reply to this question may appear to be negative—on account of the fact that L and L* are typographically, and hence syntactically, similar—we find in *Logical Syntax* a basis for an affimative answer as well. For it has been shown that Carnap extends his language L into a "richer syntax language" L_1, for which Carnap* has no equivalent. Hence we could distinguish L and L* by pointing to the fact that L is part of L_1 whereas L* is not.

But this conception is far from satisfactory, as it does not account for the reasons of Carnap*'s inability to extend L* into an equivalent of L_1. Of course, one might feel very happy for not being compelled to discuss the psychological—or psychopathic—disposition of Carnap*, but in point of fact the above-mentioned reasons have nothing to do with the mental abilities of Carnap*; they derive exclusively from the different properties of the models M and M*, and there is no reason whatever to avoid a discussion of these models and of their respective properties.

It follows that if we wish to discuss the differences between L and L* in a satisfactory manner, it will be convenient to enlarge the conceptual framework of syntax in such a manner as to enable us to discuss, besides the formal properties of L and L*, the mathematical properties of the models M and M*. By doing so, *we pass from syntax to semantics.*

It hardly needs saying that this step, without demanding any digression into the domains of psychology or psychiatry, provides for a considerable amplification of our horizon. For instance, it enables us to investigate, in addition to interpretation in the sense of logical syntax—interpretation by translation—a different kind of interpretation, namely, interpretation by reference to models. Implicitly, we have already used this notion, but the conceptual apparatus of semantics enables us to define it in an accurate manner. Other important notions for which semantics provides a definition are the notions of truth, of fulfillment, of definition, of logical consequence.

In *Foundations,*[36] Carnap takes as *object-language* a language B, which is a rudimentary part of the German language; the English language is used as a *metalanguage* which includes the languages of both syntax and semantics. By stating a system B-F of syntactical rules, we reconstruct B as a *formal calculus,* and by stating a system B–I of semantical rules, we reconstruct B as an *interpreted calculus.*[41] In

[41]For reasons to be explained in Section 9, I adopt a vocabulary which is slightly different from Carnap's.

such a case, we are not free in the construction of B–F and B–I as we wish the syntactical and semantical rules for our calculus to be in accordance with our previous knowledge of the language B.

The situation will be different if we wish to construct a new language system Z. We then are free in constructing the corresponding syntactical and semantical systems Z–F and Z–I. Even in this case, however, we will be anxious to establish a certain degree of harmony between the systems Z–F and Z–I. For instance, Z–F will contain, among others, certain formal rules of inference; likewise, Z–I will contain, among others, certain truth conditions for sentences belonging to Z. It will be clear that these rules of inference and these truth conditions ought to be chosen in such a manner that, by applying the rules of inference to true sentences, we always obtain true sentences.

This conception provides the basis for an interesting discussion on the connections between logicism and formalism.[42]

(i) *Logicism* constructs a language system L for classical logic, involving both syntactical system L—F and a semantical system L—I; now classical mathematics is interpreted by translation into L; it follows that L—I provides automatically for an interpretation by reference to the usual model of classical logic.[43]

(ii) *Formalism,* on the other hand, constructs a language system T for certain mathematical theories—in particular for arithmetic and for the theory of sets—involving a syntactical system T—F but not, in general, a corresponding semantical system T—I; formalists are particularly interested in finding a consistency proof for T.

According to Carnap, it does not make much difference which of the two methods is adopted. For if T is constructed as part of L, then we have automatically a consistency proof for T,[44] and, moreover, we obtain an interpretation T—I and thereby a basis for the application of T in empirical science. On the other hand, if T is proved or assumed to be consistent, then it is always possible to find for T an interpretation by translation into L.[45]

[42]*Foundations,* 48-49.

[43]On the question of the existence of such a model, cf.[30] and Section X below. I do not agree with Carnap's tendency, as displayed in "Empiricism"[46] to dismiss this question as a pseudo-problem; but at present it is scarcely my task to give an elaborate discussion of this matter; cf. P. Bernays, "Mathematische Existenz und Widerspruchsfreiheit," in *Etudes de Philosophie des Sciences en Hommage à F. Gonseth* (Neuchâtel, 1950).

[44]Though not, in general, a *finitist* consistency proof as demanded by Hilbert; a proof of this kind, however, on account of Gödel's result cannot be expected in those cases in which it would be most helpful.

[45]This assertion is not justified in the general form in which it is stated by Carnap. If T belongs to the lower predicate calculus, then the assertion is justified on account of Gödel's completeness theorem (1930), and if T belongs to the theory

In spite of Carnap's words, it seems pretty obvious that he is now again fully convinced of the superiority of the logicist approach, and that he feels confident of being able to incorporate the formalist construction of mathematics into the logicist system. His preference of the logicist approach is, in *Foundations,* mainly based on the fact that it provides at once a suitable background for the application of logic and mathematics in empirical science.

The ideas which *Foundations* presents in outline were developed by Carnap in a series of books and papers.[46] The contents of these various writings will be discussed in a systematic order which happens to agree with their relative order of publication, as follows:

(i) Construction of semantics, as compared with the construction of syntax; connections between the two fields;
(ii) Method of semantics; antinomies in semantics;
(iii) Ontological commitments.

However, before I pass on to carrying out this programme, a few words must be said on the connections of Carnap's work in semantics to Tarski's. Though, in his Preface to *Introduction,* Carnap duly stresses his indebtedness to Tarski, he also points to certain divergences; he wishes to give more attention to the distinction between semantics and syntax and to the distinction between logical truth and factual truth; he submits that the root of this divergence is a different conception about the distinction between *logical* and *descriptive signs.*[47]

Personally I feel that, at bottom, the divergences derive from the fact that Carnap attempts to construct semantics as a general theory, covering a large class of language systems—including language systems adequate for expressing empirical science or part of it—whereas Tarski rather tends to investigate specific language systems which for some

of types, then it is justified by Henkin's result; cf.[26]. In fact, a general completeness theorem can be stated in such a manner as to apply to every language system T which incorporates the classical sentential calculus and the classical theory of quantifiers; the interpretations which exist on account of this theorem will, however, often turn out to be non-normal; cf. Section 8 below.

[46]*Introduction to Semantics,* "Studies in Semantics," I (Cambridge, Mass., 1942); *Formalization of Logic,* "Studies in Semantics," II (Cambridge, Mass., 1943); "Modalities and Quantification," *J. Symbolic Logic* (1946); *Meaning and Necessity* (Chicago, Ill., 1947); "Empiricism, Semantics and Ontology," *Revue Int. de Philosophie* IV (1950).

[47]Or between *logical* and *extralogical terms.* In his paper "Ueber den Begriff der logischen Folgerung," *Actes du Congrès International de Philosophie Scientifique* (Paris: Sorbonne, 1935). (Paris, 1936), Tarski pointed to the importance of this distinction, but seems to doubt the possibility of giving an objective and non-arbitrary criterion for it. In *Logical Syntax,* Carnap tried to give a syntactical criterion but this idea was given up cf. *Introduction,* 247). In *Foundations,* the distinction is mentioned, but no precise criterion is stated; this point was criticised by M. Kokoszynska in her review of the book, *J. Symbolic* Logic, IV, 117. Cf. *Introduction,* 87.

reason appear to be especially interesting, and in particular language systems for certain theories of logic and mathematics.

Now if a specific language system is investigated, it is sometimes extremely difficult to draw the line between logical and descriptive signs. Take, for instance, the identity sign. It is well-known that in a logical system, based upon Russell's theory of types, it is possible to define identity in terms nobody will hesitate to qualify as logical signs. On the other hand, in the elementary theory of simple order, that is, in the theory formalised within the lower predicate calculus and based upon the axioms:

$$(x = y . \mathbf{v} . x < y) \rightarrow \overline{y < x}.$$
$$x \neq y . \rightarrow (x < y . \mathbf{v} . y < x),$$
$$(x < y . \&. \; y < z) \rightarrow x < z,$$

it is possible to define identity by stating:

$$x = y =_{Df} \overline{x < y} . \&. \; \overline{y < x}.$$

In the first case, one will be compelled to classify identity as a logical sign, but in the second case many people will be inclined to classify it, with the sign for the order relation, as a descriptive sign.

Again, if we investigate one single language, call it Z, it will sometimes be possible to define certain semantical notions in syntactical terms. This possibility depends on the choice of a syntax language and, in particular, on the character of the logical system incorporated into it. As pointed out by A. Church,[48] if we understand syntax as a body of directives for the concrete manipulation of certain physical objects, namely, the signs of the object language,[49] then it makes no sense to use as syntax language, a language involving a logic of higher order; it may be added that, if natural language is used as a means of expression for elementary syntax, then we have to take natural language in strict usage.

On the other hand, it has been repeatedly pointed out by Tarski that, in order to be of any use, a language for semantics must involve a logic of higher order. Moreover, it is often convenient to extend elementary syntax into *theoretical syntax* by the introduction of a logic of higher order.[48] It becomes then convenient to introduce one single *metalanguage* as a means of expression for both syntax (elementary and theoretical) and semantics. On account of the fact that the metalanguage is used as a means of expression for elementary syntax, it must be understood in accordance with its strict usage.

However, if we are mainly interested in theoretical syntax and in semantics as deductive theories, then we will be inclined to forget about strict usage and to indulge in amplified usage; at this moment, the cleav-

[48]In his review of *Formalization, Philos. Review,* LIII (1944).

[49]This part of syntax is called *elementary syntax.*

age between syntax and semantics will vanish, and the two theories merge into one theory which may be called the *metatheory* for Z. Exactly the same step is made when, forgetting about the strict usage of arithmetical and geometrical terms, one constructs *analytic geometry* as a synthesis of the algebra of real numbers and of geometry.

In the present case, however, there is a feature in the metatheory which gives the situation a certain piquancy; suppose the language Z to serve as a means of expression for a certain deductive theory T. Then the semantics of Z must include a certain translation of T, and the same can be said of the metatheory M. Hence we find in M three kinds of notions: those which stem from T, those which stem from the syntax of Z, and those which stem from the semantics of Z. In M, all these notions are treated on equal terms; so there can be no objection to looking for a possibility of defining notions of one kind in terms of notions of other kinds. This possibility depends in particular on the special character of T; it presents itself, for instance, if T includes the arithmetic of natural numbers. In this case, it may be possible to define the notions which stem from syntax and from semantics in terms of notions which stem from T and of purely logical notions, provided M involves logical types which surpass those which are available in T. An analysis of situations of this kind leads to highly interesting results, regarding, for instance, the undecidability of certain theories.

Though obtained by an analysis of specific languages rather than by a theory covering a large class of language systems, such results may nevertheless have implications affecting many other languages as well.[50] But this is a topic with which we are at present not concerned. I have only tried to point out why, from Tarski's point of view, it would not be convenient to lay too much stress upon the distinction between syntax and semantics.

We may, perhaps, say that, while Tarski is mainly interested in deductive theories, Carnap is primarily concerned with language systems. This explains at once why Carnap consistently takes the notions of syntax and semantics in accordance with their strict usage, whereas Tarski is inclined to switch over from strict to amplified usage. I do not think there is any other or even more profound divergence between Carnap's and Tarski's approach.

VIII. *Construction of Semantic Systems*

In order to obtain a clear conception of the problems of semantics, let us consider the problem of constructing an interpretation for a given formal calculus; we consider some version of the sentential calculus, for

[50]A. Tarski, A. Mostowski, and R. M. Robinson, *Undecidable Theories* (Amsterdam, 1953).

instance, the following one. Let $U_1, U_2, \ldots, U_k$ and V be expressions constructed, in the usual manner, starting from atoms p, q, r, . . . and by means of the sentential connectives $^-$(negation) and $\rightarrow$ (implication). Then V will be said to be *derivable* from $U_1, U_2, \ldots, U_k$, whenever V can be obtained by applying again and again the modus ponens to some set of expressions obtaining, besides $U_1, U_2, \ldots, U_k$, any number of expressions of one of the forms:

$$(P \rightarrow Q) \rightarrow [(Q \rightarrow R) \rightarrow (P \rightarrow R)],$$
$$(\overline{P} \rightarrow P) \rightarrow P,$$
$$P \rightarrow (\overline{P} \rightarrow Q).$$

Suppose this and no more is explained to a logician Carnap°, who is supposed to use a language involving "ordinary logic" and to be familiar with many-valued logic; he just happens—strange though it may appear—not to have come across the above-mentioned version of the sentential calculus. Now Carnap° wishes to make sure which interpretations would fit to the given calculus. To start with, he makes two suppositions (which we are not going to question), namely: (1) the given calculus is meant to provide a formalisation of some kind of (possibly many-valued) sentential logic, and (2) if V is derivable from true expressions $U_1, U_2, \ldots, U_k$, then V itself is also true.

Now one solution of this problem would, of course, correspond to the customary interpretation of the calculus. But, as Carnap observes this is not the only solution which would be consistent with suppositions (1) and (2).[51] Infinitely many other solutions are possible, of which two will be mentioned as examples.

(i) The given calculus is supposed to have no negation sign. $\overline{U}$ is supposed to have the same meaning as U, U→V is supposed to be the conjunction of U and V.[52]

(ii) The given calculus is supposed to correspond to part of a logic with four truth values: true, nearly-true, nearly false, and false. $\overline{U}$ is supposed to be true, nearly-true, nearly-false, or false, according as U is false, nearly-false, nearly-true, or true. U→V is true whenever V is true, whenever U and V are both nearly-true, both nearly-false, or both false, and whenever U is false; U→V is nearly true, whenever U is either true or nearly-false, while V is nearly-true, and

[51]This observation of Carnap had been anticipated by B. A. Bernstein, "Relation of Whitehead and Russell's Theory of Deduction to the Boolean Logic of Propositions," *Bull. A. M. S.* XXXVIII (1932); cf. E. V. Huntington, "New Sets of Independent Postulates for The Algebra of Logic," with special reference to Whitehead and Russell's "Principia Mathematica," *Trans. A. M. S.* XXXV (1933); E. J. Nelson, "Whitehead and Russell's Theory of Deduction as a Non-Mathematical Science," *Bull. A. M. S.* XL (1934); and Church's review of *Formalization.*[48]

[52]This reminds me of a conversation reported by Mannoury. A tries to explain to B the meaning of negation. Finally A gives up, saying: "You don't understand what I mean, and I am not going to explain any longer," to which B replies: "Yes, I see what you mean, and I am glad you are willing to continue your explanations."

whenever U is nearly-false while V is false; U→V is nearly-false, whenever U is true while V is nearly-false, and whenever U is nearly-true, while V is nearly-false or false; U→V is false whenever U is true and V is false.

Generally speaking, there are two kinds of such "non-normal" interpretations, namely:

(i) Every expression of the calculus is supposed to be true;

(ii) U → V may be true even though neither U is false nor V is true.

On account of the fact that, in addition to the normal interpretation, non-normal interpretations of the calculus are available, Carnap considers that the usual sentential calculus is not a satisfactory formalisation of sentential logic. Hence the question arises to construct a more suitable formalisation; we shall not give here Carnap's answer to this question.[53]

But I think that to the whole procedure some objections can be made. I do not agree with Church's objection that it is arbitrary for Carnap° to demand that the notion of derivability should receive a given semantical interpretation. I feel, to the contrary, that supposition (2) should be somewhat reinforced. For instance, it is natural to suppose that not all expressions are meant to be true; this takes at once care of the non-normal interpretations of the first kind. Other more or less natural suppositions would be: (3) every deductive system can be extended into a maximal deductive system, and (4) the calculus is exhaustive with respect to its interpretation.

As the lower predicate calculus is an extension of the sentential calculus, it admits interpretations which are non-normal even though the interpretation of the sentential connectives is normal. In this case an interpretation involves a certain domain M the elements of which are the values of the individual variables x, y, z, ... In addition to the individual variables, the calculus may contain individual constants (it appears more appropriate to denote symbols of this kind as individual parameters). Then the following cases of non-normality may arise:

(i) The values of the individual constants are not (or not all) contained in M;

(ii) (∃x) U (x) may be true though no element in M fulfills U (x);

(iii) (x) U (x) may be true though some elements in M do not fulfill U (x).

In cases (i) and (ii), normality may be restored by enlarging the domain; in case (iii), the domain should rather be restricted. But it does not follow that the choice of M is uniquely determined by the conditions of normality.

[53]It is, as Church[48] points out, different from Bernstein's but similar to Huntington's answer. H. Hermes and H. Scholz, *Mathematische Logik, Enzyklopädie der Math. Wiss.*, 2. Aufl., Band I 1, Heft 1, Teil 1, S. 35, footnote 45, observe that already Gentzen's formalisation of sentential logic provides an answer to Carnap's question; cf. G. Gentzen, "Untersuchungen über das logische Schliessen," *Math. Zeitschr.* XXXIX (1934).

For the lower calculus with identity, it may happen, in addition, that the identity sign "=" in the calculus is not interpreted as identity in M.

Even more involved situations arise with respect to calculi which are supposed to be intended as formalisations of arithmetic, of a logic of higher order, or of the theory of sets; they are connected with the so-called Skolem-Löwenheim paradox, and in these cases it is not possible to impose upon the calculus syntactical conditions so as to exclude non-normal interpretations. For some important calculi of this kind it is known that, to the contrary, they admit no normal interpretation.[54]

But there are no reasons to dwell upon this point, as so far it has not been taken up by Carnap.

IX. *The Method of Semantics*

While the syntax of a language Z restricts itself to describing the formal structure of the expressions of Z, without reference to their meaning or their truth-value, its semantics defines an interpretation of Z, in the first place by way of stating truth-conditions for the sentences of Z. Therefore, both syntax and semantics are part of the metatheory which goes with Z, so to speak, as a set of directions for use.

This point must be made fully clear, as Carnap's terminology is not always helpful in this respect. For instance, in *Introduction,* page 155, we read:

> A syntactical system or *calculus* K is a system of formal rules.

Such a statement strongly suggests that K is meant to be part of the metatheory (which, by the way, is undoubtedly *not* the case). On the other hand, we find on page 187 a definition of the phrase:

> The calculus K is C-inconsistent,

and here Carnap certainly does not intend to state a condition for (a certain kind of) inconsistency in the above-mentioned formal rules.

In a systematic treatment, as given by Carnap, this queer terminology will not be too troublesome, once the reader has become acquainted with it. But in these critical comments, I cannot suppose the reader to be familiar with all the details of Carnap's work; and I am afraid that, if I should adopt Carnap's terminology as it stands, these comments could easily give rise to a misunderstanding of Carnap's and of my own conceptions; therefore, it seems better to agree on a slightly different vocabulary.

Let us denote as a *calculus,* any formalised object-language Z. The deductive theory which is based upon the formal (or syntactical) rules for the language Z will then be called the *syntactical system* Z–F for Z; and the deductive theory which is based on the rules of interpretation

[54] J. Barkley Rosser and Hao Wang, "Non-standard Models for Formal Logics," *J. Symbolic Logic,* XV (1950); L. Henkin.[26]

(or semantical rules) for Z will be called the *semantical system* Z–I for Z. The deductive theory obtained by merging Z–F and Z–I into one system will be called the *metatheory* Z–M for Z. The language in which Z–M is expressed is called a *metalanguage* for Z. In order to express Z–F, we need, in general, only part of the metalanguage for Z; this part is called a *syntax language* for Z.

If, for an object-language or calculus Z, we only have a syntactical system, then Z will be called a *formal calculus;* if, besides Z–F, we also have a semantical system (or an interpretation) Z–I, then Z will be called an *interpreted calculus.* In Section VIII, we have discussed the connections between the systems Z–F and Z–I, and in particular the question, to which extent the system Z–I is determined by the system Z–F. In many respects it would be convenient, if Z–F could be chosen in such a way as to determine in a unique manner the corresponding system Z–I.[55] But we found that for formalised languages Z adequate for expressing current theories of logic and mathematics, every choice of Z–F would leave open the choice between various interpretations Z–I.

Syntax, in general, will not restrict itself to stating formal rules for one single object language Z, but will also deal with the formal properties of classes of object languages Z; likewise, *semantics* may deal with the possible interpretations of classes of object languages Z.

At present, we are not so much concerned with the problem of constructing general semantics as with the problem of constructing a suitable conceptual apparatus—in other words: a suitable language—for semantics. In general, if a certain formalised object language Z is given for which we are to construct syntactical and semantical systems Z–F and Z–I, our first step will be to use natural language as a metalanguage. However, as stated above, both Z–F and Z–I are intended to be deductive sciences,[56] and it is well-known that, as a means of expression for deductive sciences, natural language has certain deficiencies. Therefore, it seems convenient to replace natural language, as a metalanguage, by a formalised language, say, M(Z). The problem is now to state the con-

[55]In other words: if formal calculi could be constructed which would admit only one single interpretation.

[56]It is one of the main advantages of formalised languages as compared to natural language that their syntax and semantics can be constructed as deductive sciences. Thus numerous questions which cannot be settled satisfactorily with regard to natural language can be answered in a completely rigorous manner for formalised languages. For this reason, it is most regrettable that British analytic philosophy has recently turned away from using and investigating formalised languages and now develops what I have described in Section VI as a "mystical" attitude with regard to natural language. This tendency has been most effectively discussed by Bertrand Russell in his brilliant essay on "The Cult of 'Common Usage,'" *British Journ. for the Philos. of Sc.,* III (1952/53). Compare W. V. Quine, "Mr. Strawson on Logical Theory," *Mind,* n.s., LXII (1953).

ditions to be fulfilled by a suitable metalanguage M(Z). This problem is discussed in Carnap's *Meaning,* which defends a new method for semantics, the *method of extension and intension;* this method is intended to supersede the *method of the name-relation,* on which previous work, including Carnap's own investigations, were based. The arguments in favor of this new method are closely connected with Carnap's discussion of the so-called *antinomy of the name-relation* and of the various solutions which have been presented for it; therefore, it seems better to give first a statement of this antinomy.[57]

Let us consider the following dialogue between Eubulides and Aristotle:

E. Do you know the numerals by which the natural numbers up to hundred are denoted?

A. Yes!

E. How is that possible? Suppose I take the smallest number k such that the decimal representation of π presents a sequence of 100–k equal digits, and ask: 'Do you know the numeral by which the natural number k is denoted?' —what will be your answer?

A. That I don't know it, of course!

E. But now the number k happens to be twenty-three![58] So, if you don't know the numeral by which the natural number k is denoted, you don't know the numeral by which the natural number twenty-three is denoted.

It will be clear that indeed this argument is concerned with the natural number twenty-three and the numeral "$\overline{\kappa\gamma}$" by which, presumably, Aristotle and Eubulides were accustomed to denote it. Aristotle is supposed to be ready to concede Eubulides that:

(a) $k = 23$;

(b) A. knows that "$\overline{\kappa\gamma}$" has the name relation to 23.

(c) A. does not know that "$\kappa\gamma$" has the name-relation to k. But from (a) and (c), Eubulides draws the conclusion that:

(d) A. does not know that "$\overline{\kappa\gamma}$" has the name-relation to 23.

According to Carnap, the method of the name-relation is based upon the following principles:

(i) Every expression used as a name in a certain context is a name of

[57]The first to notice the difficulties inherent in a treatment of the name-relation has been Frege, "Ueber Sinn und Bedeutung," *Zeitschr r.f. Philos. u. philos. Kritik,* C (1892); however, its antinomical character was for the first time fully realised by Russell, "On Denoting," *Mind,* XIV (1905); an English translation of Frege's paper and a reprint of Russell's are found, with other interesting material on semantics, in: H. Feigl and W. Sellars, *Readings in Philosophical Analysis* (New York, 1949). —An anticipation may be found in Eubulides' Larvatus Paradox: "Do you know your father? Yes! How is that possible? Suppose I show you a masked man and ask: 'Do you know this man?'—what will be your answer? That I don't know him, of course! But now that man happens to be your father! So, if you don't know that man, you don't know your own father."

[58]The responsibility for this assertion is left, of course, to Eubulides.

exactly one entity, which is called the *nominatum* of the expression in that context (principle of univocality);

(ij) A sentence is about the nominata of the names occurring in it (principle of subject matter);

(iij) If two expressions have the same nominatum, then a true sentence remains true when one expression is replaced by the other (principle of interchangeability).

Now Eubulides's conclusion is based upon the presupposition that the expression "k" in (c) has the same nominatum as the expression "k" in (a), even though the contexts in which it appears are quite different. Hence, on the basis of the method of the name-relation, various solutions of the antinomy are possible.

(1) The expression "k" in (a) and (c) has different nominata; so (a) does not provide a basis for replacing "k" by "23" in (c). This is, in substance, Frege's solution. According to Frege, in those contexts in which replacement is possible, the nominatum of "k" is its *denotation;* in other contexts, it is its *sense.*

(2) The expression "k" or, rather, "the smallest number k such that . . ." is not a name. A sentence in which such a "pseudo-name" or *description* occurs is an abbreviation of another sentence in which it does not present itself. Again, there is no basis for the application of the principle of interchangeability.

(3) The expression "k" may sometimes occur without being used as a name. This solution, given by Quine,[59] is related to Frege's, as it stresses the importance of the context in which an expression happens to occur; but it avoids the introduction of a multitude of nominata for one and the same expression.

(4) Church[60] accepts Frege's analysis as a correct description of the situation as it presents itself with regard to expressions in natural language. But he does not consider this situation as acceptable and demands the construction of a language in which a name would always stand for its denotation, and which would also provide a name for the corresponding sense.[61]

(5) The antinomy of the name-relation presents itself exclusively when names occur in non-extensional contexts. Hence, the antinomy

[59]W. V. Quine. "Notes on Existence and Necessity," *J. of Philosophy,* XL (1943), reprinted in *From a Logical Point of View* (Cambridge, Mass., 1953), and in Feigl-Sellars, 57.

[60]In his review of Quine's Notes, *J. Symbolic Logic,* VIII (1943).

[61]Such a language has been constructed by Church in "A Formulation of the Logic of Sense and Denotation," *Structure, Method and Meaning.* Essays in Honor of Henry M. Sheffer (New York: 1951); cf. "On Carnap's Analysis of Statements of Assertion and Belief," *Analysis,* X (1950), and "The Need for Abstract Entities in Semantic Analysis," *Proceedings Amer. Acad. of Arts and Sciences,* LXXX (1951). However, the construction leads to considerable complications.

would be avoided if semantics could be expressed in an extensional metalanguage. In *Meaning*, Carnap sets out to prove that such a metalanguage can be constructed if previously the method of the name-relation is replaced by the *method of extension and intension.*

I will attempt to give an independent but equivalent statement of the principles of this method. Let Z be the language by which a certain deductive theory T is expressed, in accordance with the syntactical rules for the lower predicate calculus with identity. We suppose that in Z there are predicate parameters F, G, H, . . . and individual parameters, a, b, c, . . .—those parameters correspond to the primitive notions of T—and, moreover, individual variables x, y, z, . . . as well as corresponding quantifiers.

In order to construct an interpretation of Z, we introduce a certain non-empty set S of individual constants u, v, w, ... We then construct state-descriptions T′ satisfying the following conditions[62]

(i) T′ includes T and is expressed by means of the language Z′ obtained from Z by the introduction of the above-mentioned individual constants;

(ii) T′ is consistent and complete with regard to the lower predicate calculus with identity;

(iii) If (x)U(x) is in T′, then all expressions U(u) are in T′;

(iv) If (∃ x)U(x) is in T′, then some expression U(u) is in T′;

(v) All expressions u ≠ v, for different elements u and v of S, are in T′.

Let K be an index set, such that $T\mu$ ranges over all state-descriptions T′ if μ ranges over K. Let K* be some subset of K, and let μ° be an element of K*. We denote by T*, the intersection of all $T\mu$ such that μ is in K*, and by T°, the state-description $T\mu^\circ$. We have, of course, $T \subseteq T^* \subseteq T^\circ$.

Now we can define Carnap's radical concepts by reference to T°, and his L-concepts by reference to T*. For instance, the expressions U $(x_1, x_2, \ldots, x_k)$ and V $(x_1, x_2, \ldots, x_k)$ will be called *equivalent,* if the sentence:

$$(x_1)\,(x_2)\ldots(x_k)\,[U\,(x_1, x_2, \ldots, x_k) \longleftrightarrow V\,(x_1, x_2, \ldots, x_k)] \quad (A)$$

[62]The conditions for the existence of such state-descriptions are given by the theorem of Löwenheim-Skolem-Gödel.—It seems only fair to mention a certain discrepancy between Carnap's approach and mine. Carnap assumes that the above F, G, H, . . . and a, b, c, . . . are not *parameters* but *constants;* that is, F, G, H, . . . denote certain specific predicates and a, b, c, . . . denote certain specific individual objects. In other words, Carnap assumes *strict usage* for the symbols of the language Z, whereas I assume *amplified usage,* as explained in Section VI. However, I do not believe that this difference can be of any importance with a view to the conclusions in this Section. This follows from the results by Lindenbaum and Tarski on the limitations of the means of expression of deductive theories; cf. A. Tarski, *Logic, Semantics, Metamathematics* (Oxford, 1956).

is in T°; they will be called L-*equivalent,* if sentence (A) is in T^*. It should be noted that these and similar semantical concepts are only applied to these expressions which belong to Z, that is, which contain no individual constants.

We say that the above-mentioned expressions *have the same extension,* if they are equivalent; we say that they *have the same intension,* if they are L-equivalent.

On the other hand, we may represent extensions and intensions by classes (or sets), as follows. We consider(k+1)-tuples $< \mu, u_1 u_2, \ldots, u_k >$, where μ is in K and $u_1, u_2, \ldots, u_k$ are in S. Let us say that $<\mu, u_1, u_2, \ldots, u_k >$ *fulfills* $U(x_1, x_2, \ldots, x_k)$, if $U(u_1 u_2, \ldots, u_k)$ is in $T\mu$.

Now the *extension* of $U(x_1, x_2, \ldots, x_k)$ will be the class of all (k+1)-tuples $<\mu, u_1, u_2, \ldots, u_k$ such that $<\mu_0, u_1, u_2, \ldots, u_k >$ fulfills $U(x_1, x_2, \ldots, x_k)$; and the *intension* of $U(x_1, x_2, \ldots, x_k)$ will be the class of all (k+1)-tuples $<\mu, u_1, u_2, \ldots, u_k >$ which fulfill $U(x_1, x_2, \ldots, x_k)$, if μ is in K^*.

In order to justify these definitions, it will be necessary to prove that:

(i) The respective extensions of $U(x_1, x_2, \ldots, x_k)$ and of $V(x_1, x_2, \ldots, x_k)$ coincide, if and only if sentence (A) is in T°;

(ii) The respective intensions of the above-mentioned expressions coincide, if and only if sentence (A) is in T^*.

I will restrict myself to proving assertion (ii).

(a) Suppose sentence (A) is in T^*. Then sentence (A) is in $T\mu$ for every μ in K^*. Hence, $U(u_1, u_2, \ldots, u_k) \longleftrightarrow V(u_1, u_2, \ldots, u_k)$ is in $T\mu$ for every μ in K^*. And, if μ is in K^*, then $<\mu, u_1, u_2, \ldots, u_k >$ fulfills $U(x_1, x_2, \ldots, x_k)$ if and only if it fulfills $V(x_1, x_2, \ldots, x_k)$. It follows that the intensions of the last-mentioned expressions coincide.

(b) Suppose sentence (A) is not in T^*. Then, for some μ in K^*, sentence (A) is not in $T\mu$. So we can find some $u_1, u_2, \ldots, u_k$ such that $\overline{U(u_1, u_2, \ldots, u_k) \longleftrightarrow V(u_1, u_2, \ldots, u_k)}$ is in $T\mu$. Therefore, $<\mu, u_1, u_2, \ldots, u_k >$ either fulfills $U(x_1, x_2, \ldots, x_k)$ without fulfilling $V(x_1, x_2, \ldots, x_k)$, or conversely. It follows that the last-mentioned expressions have different intensions.

It is easy to see that assertion (i) can be proved in the same manner, and that the intension of an expression is always included in its extension.

We now return to the problem of constructing an extensional metalanguage M as a means of expression for the semantics of Z (or T). It will be clear by now, that the construction of such a metalanguage M is possible, and also, how such a construction should be carried out. We may start from a language N which is adequate for the (non-elementary) syntax of Z (or T) to such an extent that a proof for the theorem of Löwenheim-Skolem-Gödel-Tarski can be carried out. Then we must introduce such devices as are required for defining the various classes (or sets) which play an essential rôle in the method of extension and intension. There seems to be no reason whatever for the metalanguage M to be non-extensional.

It seems that the method at once carries over to all logical systems for which there is an analogue to the theorem of Löwenheim-Skolem-Gödel-Tarski; these systems include the logic of higher order, based on the theory of types, intuitionistic logic, and modal logic with quantifiication.[63]

X. *Ontological Commitments*

The problem of ontological commitments was discussed by Carnap in *Logical Syntax,*[64] in connection with his definition of analyticity, which contained the phrase "for all syntactical properties".

> . . . the definition must not be limited to the syntactical properties which are definable in S, but must refer to all syntactical properties whatsoever. But do we not by this means arrive at a Platonistic absolutism of ideas, that is, at the conception that the totality of all properties, which is non-denumerable and therefore cannot be exhausted by definitions, is something which subsists in itself, independent of all construction and definition? From our point of view, this metaphysical conception—as it is maintained by Ramsey for instance . . . —is definitely excluded. We have here absolutely nothing to do with the metaphysical question as to whether properties exist in themselves or whether they are created by definition. The question must rather be put as follows: can the phrase "for all properties . . ." (interpreted as "for all properties whatsoever" and not "for all properties which are definable in S") be formulated in the symbolic syntax-language S? This question may be answered in the affirmative.

From the formalist point of view defended in *Logical Syntax,* this is a quite acceptable position, though even from this point of view objections could be raised. But, strangely enough, a closely related position is still defended in *Meaning.*[65]

> Suppose somebody constructs a language not only as a subject matter of theoretical investigations but for the purpose of communication. Suppose, further, that he decides to use in this language variables '*m*', '*n*', etc., for which all (natural) numerical expressions (e.g., '0', '3', '2+3', etc.) and only those are substitutable. We see from this decision that he recognizes natural numbers in this sense: he is willing to speak not only about particular numbers (e.g., '7 is a prime number') but also—and this is the decisive point—about numbers in general. He will, for example, make statements like: 'for every *m* and *n*,

[63]L. Henkin,[26] H. Rasiowa, "Algebraic Treatment of the Functional Calculi of Heyting and Lewis," *Fund. Math.,* XXXVIII (1952).

[64]Page 114. This discussion first appeared in "Ein Gültigkeitskriterium;" cf. [22].

[65]P. 42 ff.; cf. "Empiricism, Semantics, and Ontology," *Revue Int. de Philos.,* IV (1950).

$m + n = n + m$' and 'there is an m between 7 and 13 which is prime'. The latter sentence speaks of the existence of a prime number. However, the concept of existence here has nothing to do with the ontological concept of existence or reality. The sentence mentioned means just the same as 'it is not the case that for every m between 7 and 13, m is not prime'. By the same token, we see, furthermore, that the user of the language is willing to recognize the concept of Number. . . . It is important to emphasize the point just made that, once you admit certain variables, you are bound to admit the corresponding universal concept. It seems to me that some philosophers (not Quine) overlook this fact; they do not hesitate to admit into the language of science variables of the customary kinds . . . ; at the same time, however, they feel strong misgivings against words like 'proposition', 'number', 'property' (or 'class') 'function', etc., because they suspect in these words the danger of an absolutist metaphysics. In my view, however, the accusation of an absolutist metaphysics or of illegitimate hypostatizations with respect to a certain kind of entities, say propositions, cannot be made against an author, merely on the basis of the fact that he uses variables of the type in question (e.g., '*p*', etc.) and the corresponding universal word ('proposition'); it must be based, instead, on an analysis of the statements or pseudo-statements which he makes with the help of those signs.

Therefore, Carnap objects to Quine's usage of certain traditional terms in discussions on this subject.

I should prefer not to use the word '*ontology*' for the recognition of entities by the admission of variables. This use seems to me at least misleading; it might be understood as implying that the decision to use certain kinds of variables must be based on ontological, metaphysical convictions. In my view, however, the choice of a certain language structure and, in particular, the decision to use certain types of variables is a practical decision. . . .I agree, of course, with Quine that the problem of "Nominalism" as he interprets it is a meaningful problem; it is the question of whether all natural sciences can be expressed in a "nominalistic" language, that is, one containing only individual variables whose values are concrete objects, not classes, properties, and the like. However, I am doubtful whether it is advisable to transfer to this new problem in logic or semantics the label 'nominalism' which stems from an old metaphysical problem.

There is in these words much to remind one of Tarski's "impression that the term 'metaphysical' has lost any objective meaning, and is merely used as a kind of professional philosophical invective."[66] It may be said in defence of the terminology, adopted by Quine,[67] that many notions and problems of traditional metaphysics were, in their original form, closely connected with questions which, in our times, are usually considered as belonging to semantics.[68] It is true that traditional philosophy, in the first place, did not, as a rule, understand the specific character of

[66]"The Semantic Conception of Truth and the Foundations of Semantics," *Philos. and Phenomenol. Research,* IV (1944); reprinted in Feigl-Sellars.[57]

[67]Cf. [59]

[68]E. W. Beth, "The Prehistory of Research into Foundations," *British Journ. for the Philos. of Sc.,* IV (1951/52).

these sorts of questions and often mixed them up with problems of speculative anthropology and theology and, secondly, did scarcely have any methods to deal with them in an effective manner. But it was only in German Philosophy since the later part of the 18 century[69] that the treatment of these questions took the peculiar anti-scientific forms which have so justly been denounced by Carnap and other members of the movement of Logical Empiricism.

One might feel that the adoption or rejection of terms like 'ontology' and 'nominalism' is merely a matter of terminology. But in my opinion much more is at stake: modern scientific philosophy will only gain general acceptance if it succeeds in establishing its connections with philosophical traditions in a more positive sense than has been done so far.

I now come to the main point in this discussion, namely, the question as to *whether the choice of a certain language structure not only as a subject matter of theoretical investigations, but for the purpose of communication,* is really nothing more than *a practical decision,* in which no ontological commitments are involved. Carnap's answer to this question, as quoted above, is, of course, in full agreement with his Principle of Tolerance.[70]

Before stating my objections to Carnap's doctrine, I should like to emphasize that, in my opinion as well, one must allow for a considerable amount of freedom—more considerable, in fact, than is usually realised by most philosophers and mathematicians—in the choice of a language structure, even in those cases in which a language is intended actually to serve as a means of communication. But there are, in my opinion, certain natural limitations which go farther than those which Carnap would be ready to accept. And this is in particular the case, if the language under consideration is to be used as a metalanguage.

In the first place, such a language, which may be called M, should enable us, as pointed out by Church,[48] to state the necessary directives for the concrete manipulation of certain physical objects, namely, the signs of the object language. This implies that M must contain the means of expression for a certain version of elementary arithmetic or of a suitable general arithmetic.[71] Moreover, this part of M, which will be called M_1, must be *understood in accordance with strict usage.*

[69]Even here there are noteworthy exceptions, for instance, Bolzano, Herbart, Trendelenburg, and Brentano. It is characteristic that the ideas of such men were usually described as old-fashioned and even reactionary by contemporary philosophers.

[70]Stated in *Logical Syntax*, 51 f., and maintained explicitly, though with some qualifications, in *Introduction*, 247.

[71]A. Tarski, "Einige Betrachtungen über die Begriffe der ω-Widerspruchsfreiheit und der ω-Vollständigkeit," *Mon. Math. Phys.* XL (1933); E. W. Beth[1]; H. Hermes, *Semiotik*, Forschungen zur Logik, N. F. VI (1935); S. C. Kleene, *Introduction to Metamathematics*, Amsterdam-Groningen (1952).

This demand, however, strongly restricts the development of M_1, the language of elementary syntax, into a means of expression, called M_2, for theoretical syntax; this follows from our discussion in Section 6. The final step, which leads from M_2 to M_3, a means of expression for the corresponding semantical system, based on the method of extension and intension, will not demand a considerable amplification, provided M_2 is already sufficiently rich.

It is at the passage from M_1 to M_2 that ontological commitments come in. In order to make this point fully clear, I introduce again our hypothetical logician Carnap*. This logician was characterised in Section 5 as one who is endowed with non-normal mathematical intuitions; we may characterise him now, perhaps more accurately, as one who is inclined to stand for non-normal ontological commitments. In particular, Carnap* will not accept the existence of *our* set of symbols:

$$0, \quad 0', \quad 0', \ . \ . \ . \ \text{etc.}$$

by which we mean, the *real* set, without the additional elements which Carnap* *wrongly* supposes to be contained in it. On the other hand, *we* accept the existence of Carnap*'s so-called set of numerals, but we know that, in addition to all numerals it must contain still other elements. We even understand why Carnap*, because of his fatal inclination for non-normal ontological commitments, is unable to see his own errors. As Spinoza[72] said: *veritas norma sui et falsi est.*

If we do not wish to be caught in the same trap as Carnap*, and, for instance, to be compelled to conclude that certain consistent theories are inconsistent, then we ought to be cautious in carrying out the passage from M_1 to M_2. Hence the question arises as to which precautions we could take in this connection. Unfortunately, it is impossible to point out precautions which are fully adequate.

In the first place, we shall demand that M_2 be consistent; but we cannot convince ourselves of the consistency of M_2 by means of a formal proof, as, by Gödel's incompleteness theorem, such a proof could only be carried out in a language richer than M_2 and, therefore, even more suspect. And a consistency proof for M_2 would by no means exclude the possibility of proving in M_2 sentences which, if understood in accordance with strict usage, would be false.

In order to exclude this possibility one could try to prove, for instance, that M_2 admits standard models. But here, new difficulties arise. In the first place, an existence proof for standard models involves all dfficulties inherent in a proof of consistency, and in addition it presents new difficulties of its own.[73] Secondly, it is by no means the case that a system M_2 which looks reasonable always admits a standard model; to the con-

[72]*Ethica* I, prop. XLIII, schol.

[73]L. Henkin.[26]

trary, it is rather likely that many systems which play an important rôle in modern logic do not admit a standard model.[74] And finally the notion of a standard model, if understood in accordance with strict usage, involves an appeal to certain ontological commitments.

Therefore, in connection with the problem of the method of semantics, a discussion on the acceptance or rejection of certain ontological commitments cannot be avoided. And such a discussion cannot be restricted, as *Logical Syntax* suggests, to the question whether a certain phrase "for all properties . . ." can be formulated in S (or M_2); for it remains to be seen whether this phrase "for all properties . . ." can be interpreted as "for all properties whatsoever," and, if understood in accordance with strict usage, such an interpretation is impossible without an appeal to certain ontological commitments.

In my opinion, the acceptance or rejection of ontological commitments will be influenced by certain intuitive considerations. But this does not imply that a discussion on logical commitments is condemned to remain on the level where only subjective convictions are exchanged without any attempt at a rational foundation.[75]

XI. *Conclusions*

The above considerations should not be interpreted as a more or less systematic criticism of Carnap's philosophical doctrines. To the contrary, not only have I a great admiration for Carnap's work, which has strongly influenced the development of my own ideas; I also agree to a considerable extent with his doctrines; more specifically:

(i) I agree with Carnap's conceptions in the theory of space (cf. Section III);

(ii) I agree with Carnap's ideas on the connections between logic, mathematics, and physical science; there was no reason for discussing these ideas in the present contribution;

(iii) I agree, with certain qualifications, with Carnap's doctrines in the domain of logic, syntax, and semantics; in particular, I share his views on the advantages of constructed systems over natural language, both as means of expression and as subject-matter of

[74] Rosser-Wang.[54]

[75] How fruitful such a discussion can be was demonstrated at a meeting which took place in Amersfoort on August 31 and September 1, 1953, and in which the nominalistic point of view was defended by W. V. Quine and A. Tarski; *cf.* E. W. Beth, *L'existence en mathématiques* (Paris, 1955).—Our readiness to accept ontological commitments will reflect itself, for instance, in the acceptance or the rejection of entities which are introduced by means of impredicative definitions; the acceptance of such entities is required, among others, for proving the theorem of the least upper bound in the theory of real numbers. Thus a discussion on ontological commitments clearly raises serious issues of a scientific nature and cannot be dismissed as vacuous.

theoretical investigation; for the philosophy of (exact) science, in particular, there is no reason to investigate certain subtleties which present themselves in natural language and which are usually avoided in the construction of formalised languages.

I feel these points of agreement should be explicitly stated, as, naturally, in the above considerations they did not receive the stress which they deserve. I now come to the issues on which Carnap's views and mine seem to diverge.

(iv) In discussions on the foundations of logic, natural language plays a special role in those cases, where strict usage is desired; though there is no reason to exclude strict usage of formalised languages, strict usage is actually restricted to natural language; this is also the case in Carnap's writings;

(v) His neglect of the distinction between strict usage and amplified usage of a language has induced Carnap to defend assertions—and, in particular, the Principle of Tolerance—which cannot be accepted without restrictions; moreover, Carnap has not been able to avoid every appeal to logical or mathematical intuitions, or, what amounts to the same, to ontological commitments.

This criticism leaves the main body of Carnap's doctrines fully intact. It only calls for modifications and restrictions at its ultimate boundaries, which at the same time are the boundaries of our knowledge.

E. W. Beth

Instituut Voor Grondslagenonderzoek en
Philosophie der Exacte Wetenschappen,
Universiteit van Amsterdam

16

P. F. Strawson

CARNAP'S VIEWS ON CONSTRUCTED SYSTEMS VERSUS NATURAL LANGUAGES IN ANALYTIC PHILOSOPHY

The Two Methods

I understand that the question on which I am to discuss Carnap's views is that of the comparative merits of two methods of philosophical clarification. To follow one method is to construct a formal system, which uses, generally, the ordinary apparatus of modern logic and in which the concepts forming the subject-matter of the system are introduced by means of axioms and definitions. The construction of the system will generally be accompanied by extra-systematic remarks in some way relating the concepts of the system to concepts which we already use in an unsystematic way. This is the method of 'rational reconstruction'; and indeed the system of elementary logic itself can be regarded as just such a reconstruction of the set of concepts expressed by the logical constants of daily life. Following the other method seems very different. For it consists in the attempt to describe the complex patterns of logical behaviour which the concepts of daily life exhibit. It is not a matter of prescribing the model conduct of model words, but of describing the actual conduct of actual words; not a matter of making rules, but of noting customs. Obviously the first method has certain advantages. The nature and powers of the apparatus to be used are clear. Its users know in advance what *sort* of thing they are going to make with it. The practitioner of the second method is not so well placed. Unless he is to be content with the production and juxtaposition of particular examples, he needs some metavocabulary in which to describe the features he finds. Ex hypothesi, the well-regulated metavocabulary of the first method is inadequate for his purposes. So he has to make his own tools; and, too often, hastily improvised, overweighted with analogy and association, they prove clumsy, lose their edge after one operation and serve only to mutilate where they should dissect.

Clarification and Science

The issue, or apparent issue, between the two methods is only too easily trivialised or made uninteresting. I spoke of them both as methods of *clarification,* and one could understand this word in such a way that there was no interesting question as to which of the two methods was better for this purpose. Such a result would ensue, for example, from taking 'clarification' in the sense which Carnap seems to give to it in the first chapter of 'Logical Foundations of Probability'.[1] A pre-scientific concept C is clarified in this sense if it is *for certain purposes* replaced (or supplanted or succeeded) by a concept C′ which is unlike C in being both *exact* and *fruitful.* The criterion of exactness is that the rules of use of the concept should be such as to give it a clear place 'in a well-connected system of scientific concepts'. The criterion of fruitfulness is that the concept should be useful in the formulation of many logical theorems or empirical scientific laws. An indication of the sense in which the new concept is said to *correspond to* and to *replace* the old may be given by examples. One example which Carnap gives is the replacement of the sensory quality concept of warmth by the quantitative concept of temperature. An example analogous to another which he gives would be the use by the entomologist of the word 'insect' in a way more restrictive and more exactly defined than the way (or ways) in which it is used by children and nursemaids. There is a further suggestion (though not an explicit assertion) in this chapter, to the effect that introducing a concept into a well-connected system of scientific concepts and constructing a formal axiom system which incorporates both it and them, are really just different names for the same thing.[2] And if 'clarification' is so understood as to include 'rendering exact', and 'rendering exact' is understood to include incorporation in a formal system, then clearly the thesis that clarification can be best achieved by system-construction appears as an understatement.

Even if we abjure this last step and think of clarification more vaguely as the introduction, for scientific purposes, of scientifically exact and fruitful concepts in the place of (some of) those we use for all the other ordinary and extraordinary purposes of life, the issue between the two methods remains less than exciting. I am not competent to discuss the extent to which theoretical scientists, in framing new concepts or refurbishing old ones, either examine minutely the behaviour of words in ordinary language or construct axiom systems. It seems to me extremely improbable that they do much of the first; and I suspect (but may be quite wrong) that logicians exaggerate the extent to which they do, or ought to do, the second. But my incompetence in this matter troubles me not at all. For however much or little the constructionist technique is the right means of getting an idea into shape for use in the

[1]Cf. *op. cit.,* 3-15.
[2]See 15.

formal or empirical sciences, it seems prima facie evident that to offer formal explanations of key terms of scientific theories to one who seeks philosophical illumination of essential concepts of non-scientific discourse, is to do something utterly irrelevant—is a sheer misunderstanding, like offering a text-book on physiology to someone who says (with a sigh) that he wished he understood the workings of the human heart.

The scientific uses of language, whether formal or empirical, are extremely highly specialized uses. Language has many other employments. We use it in pleading in the law courts; in appraising people's characters and actions; in criticising works of art; in recounting our states of mind; in getting people to fetch things; in narrating histories; in describing what things look and sound and feel like; in entering into engagements with one another; in identifying people—and so on. It is quite certain that such ways of using language as these may give rise to philosophical problems; that the concepts employed in these activities may generate perplexity, may call for philosophical clarification. How do we conceive of *responsibility?* What is the difference between describing states of mind and describing physical objects? What does it mean to say that the person now before us is *the very man who* did such-and-such a thing? This is a minute and random selection of typical questions concerning concepts employed in non-scientific discourse. Moreover the language used outside the research institutes has its general and structural features, running through quite disparate realms of subject-matter and purpose. These too have seemed to demand philosophical investigation. Thus we wish to know what it is to say that one thing is conditional upon another, is a case or instance of another, is real, is good, is the same. And it seems in general evident that the concepts used in non-scientific kinds of discourse could not literally be *replaced* by scientific concepts serving just the same purposes; that the language of science could not in this way *supplant* the language of the drawing-room, the kitchen, the law courts and the novel. It might at this point be objected that while it is trivially true that doing science is not doing not science, it does not follow that the employment of scientific concepts for the purposes for which non-scientific concepts are at present employed is impossible; i.e. that from the necessary truth that scientific uses of language are different from non-scientific uses of language, it does not follow that use of scientific language could not replace the use of non-scientific language for non-scientific purposes. And of course it does not follow; and, in certain cases, for certain descriptive purposes, the replacement might be effected. But it seems to require no argument to show that, in most cases, either the operation would not be practically feasible or the result of attempting it would be something so radically different from the original that it could no longer be said to be fulfilling the same purpose, doing the same thing. More of the types of linguistic activity in which we constantly engage would succumb to such an attempt than would survive it; and there are many such types on which we should not know how to start. The kinds of concept we employ are not independent of the kinds of purpose for which we employ them; even though some concepts can fulfil more than one kind of purpose.

If these things are true, it follows that typical philosophical problems about the concepts used in non-scientific discourse cannot be solved by laying down the rules of use of exact and fruitful concepts in science. To do this last is not to solve the typical philosophical problem, but to change the subject. In the case of many a philosophically troubling concept, indeed, it is hard to know in what direction to look for a scientifically satisfactory concept which stands to it in the required relation of correspondence or similarity. But the general conclusion holds even for those cases where there is a clear correlation. I may mention again Carnap's own example of the clarification of the prescientific concept of warmth by the introduction of the exact and scientifically fruitful concept of temperature. Sensory concepts in general have been a rich source of philosophical perplexity. How are the look, the sound, the feel of a material object related to each other and to the object itself? Does it follow from the fact that the same object can feel warm to one man and cold to another that the object really is neither cold or warm nor cool nor has any such property? These questions can be answered, or the facts and difficulties that lead to our asking them can be made plain; but not by means of formal exercises in the scientific use of the related concepts of temperature, wavelength, frequency. Indeed, the introduction of the scientific concepts may itself produce a further crop of puzzles, arising from an unclarity over the relations between two ways of using language to talk about the physical world, the relations between the quantitative and the sensory vocabularies. This unclarity is another which will scarcely be removed by exhibiting the formal workings of the quantitative concepts.

So, then, since the clarification of philosophically puzzling concepts is not achieved by the introduction of related scientific concepts, it is not important for our purpose to discuss whether this introduction is best performed by the method of formalisation. Nor is it very important to discuss this, even if 'clarification of philosophically puzzling concepts' is taken to be *synonymous* with 'introduction of related scientific concepts'. For the answer is trivially 'Yes' for formalised sciences and trivially 'No' for others. If it is objected that the real question is whether all sciences would not be the better for axiomatisation, then the real question is one which I must leave, thankfully, to those equipped to answer it.

Clarification and 'Pseudo-questions'

It is possible, however, to understand the idea of clarification, and of the contribution which system-construction may make to it, in a different and more philosophical way; in such a way, in fact, that the issue stated at the outset remains open, requires to be argued further. But before I turn to this other approach, I want to consider a possible source of the uncompromising position I have just discussed. I think it arises partly from the view that philosophical questions and perplexities cannot really be taken seriously; that the only serious questions are *either* questions to be answered within the conceptual framework of a scientific theory or of some non-scientific mode of empirical discourse *or* pragmatic questions about the desirability of adopting such a framework. This view is strongly suggested by certain passages in Carnap's 'Empiricism, Semantics and Ontology'.[3] It is worth while to consider in detail some of the things which Carnap says in this article, since to do so will both illuminate our general question, and show how thin (despite appearances) may be the barrier which divides the philosopher who constructs systems from the philosopher who describes the workings of ordinary language. Carnap declares that the 'framework of propositions' (i.e. a use of language in which propositions appear as entities having such properties as truth, necessity, etc.) may be introduced by means of a set of rules, of which he indicates a few. Then he continues as follows:[4]

(i) It is important to notice that the system of rules for the linguistic expressions of the propositional framework (of which only a few rules have here been briefly indicated) is sufficient for the introduction of the framework. Any further explanations as to the nature of the propositions (i.e. the elements of the framework indicated, the values of the variables "*p*", "*q*", etc.) are theoretically unnecessary because, if correct, they follow from the rules.

(ii) For example, are propositions mental events (as in Russell's theory)? A look at the rules shows us that they are not, because otherwise existential statements would be of the form: "If the mental state of the person in question fulfils such-and-such conditions, then there is a *p* such that . . .". The fact that no references to mental conditions occur in existential statements [of the framework] shows that propositions are not mental entities. Further, a statement of the existence of linguistic entities (e.g. expressions, classes of expressions, etc.) must contain a reference to a language. The fact that no such reference occurs in the existential statements here, shows that propositions are

[3]*Revue Internationale de Philosophie,* XI (1950), 20-40. But the article is itself a brilliant informal contribution to the philosophical clarification of the concept of existence. How would Carnap characterise what he himself is mainly concerned to do in the article?

[4]*Op. cit.,* 26-27. I quote a continuous paragraph, which I have broken up into numbered sections for ease of reference.

not linguistic entities. The fact that in these statements no reference to a subject (an observer or knower) occurs (nothing like "There is a *p* which is necessary for Mr. *X*"), shows that the propositions (and their properties, like necessity, etc.) are not subjective.

(iii) Although characterisations of these or similar kinds are, strictly speaking, unnecessary, they may nevertheless be practically useful. If they are given, they should be understood, not as ingredient parts of the system, but merely as marginal notes with the purpose of supplying to the reader helpful hints or convenient pictorial associations which may make his learning of the use of the expressions easier than the bare system of rules would do.

(iv) Such a characterization is analogous to an extra-systematic explanation which a physicist sometimes gives to a beginner. He might, for example, tell him to imagine the atoms of a gas as small balls rushing around with great speed, or the electro-magnetic field and its oscillations as quasi-elastic tensions and vibrations in an ether. In fact, however, all that can accurately be said about atoms or the field is implicitly contained in the physical laws of the theories in question.

It will be noticed that the existence of typical philosophers' questions about propositions is acknowledged (in (ii)); and it is said that answers to the questions mentioned follow from a consideration of the rules of use of the linguistic expressions concerned. But it is also said (in (i)) that, given the rules of use, 'further explanations of the nature of propositions . . . are theoretically unnecessary', just because 'they follow from the rules.' Further, it is said (in (iii)) 'that such further (extra-systematic) explanations, though 'strictly unnecessary', may be 'practically useful' in making it easier to learn the use of the expressions. Finally (in (iv)) such extra-systematic explanations are said to be analogous to the quasi-pictorial models which a physicist might use in introducing his theoretical concepts to a beginner. Several points in this deserve comment.

(1) The fact that answers to (some) philosophers' questions in some sense follow from the rules of use of the expressions concerned does not have the consequence that it is 'strictly speaking, unnecessary' to give these further explanations, unless one assumes that it is, strictly speaking, unnecessary to take philosophers' questions seriously. For one thing may well follow from another and yet someone may fail to see that it does, unless it is pointed out to him by means of 'further explanations'; and if this is the situation in this case, then the further explanations are, strictly speaking, necessary if the aim is to be achieved of resolving the puzzles, of showing how the answers to the conceptual questions are implicit in the rules of use of the expressions concerned.

(2) Carnap admits that extra-systematic explanations may nevertheless be useful: he says they may be *practically* useful in helping someone to *learn the use* of the expressions concerned. But of course it is characteristic of philosophers' perplexities and questions that they are felt and raised by people who know very well how to use the expressions

concerned, who have no practical difficulties at all in operating with the concepts in question. To the extent to which Carnap regards the role of extra-systematic conceptual explanation as simply that of resolving such practical difficulties, he ignores the role of conceptual explanation in resolving philosophical difficulties; and this perhaps springs again from the view that the latter are not real difficulties. And of course they are *not* (in general) real difficulties, if by 'real difficulty' is meant a difficulty in actually operating with the concepts in question in the course of framing and answering 'real questions', i.e. questions which arise within the framework to which the concepts belong.

(3) Carnap says that the extra-systematic explanations are analogous, to the pictorial models by means of which scientists may introduce theoretical concepts to a beginner (and, he might have added, which they may themselves make use of in extending and applying their theories). But it is easy to see that they are not analogous, just in so far as the conceptual explanations 'follow from', or are implicit in, the rules of use of the expressions concerned. For it does not appear to be the case, indeed it is not clear what would be meant by saying, that the scientists' pictorial models 'follow from' any 'rules of use' of the relevant scientific expressions. Another respect in which the two things are not analogous is that the scientists' models *do* seem to be of practical use in helping the beginner to learn to use the theoretical concepts in question and, perhaps, in helping the scientist to frame and extend theories; whereas the explanations which are of help to the philosopher do not in general have, or need, this power.

It seems not unreasonable, then, to find in this passage, as in others, evidence of a lack of sympathy with, and even of understanding of, that need for the elucidation of concepts which can coexist with perfect mastery of their practical employment. Now this is precisely the need for their philosophical elucidation. But if the idea of this kind of clarification is rejected, or not even entertained, then it does become intelligible that the title of 'clarification' should be reserved for some other activity. And this is why I said that a certain extreme view of the nature of clarification is perhaps traceable in part to the belief that philosophical questions and difficulties are non-serious and unreal. This was the extreme view that to clarify a concept used for non-scientific purposes consisted in looking away from it at a different, though in some way related, concept which was unlike the first in being scientifically exact and fruitful. It is true that we may be diverted from the wish to understand what we are doing, by encouragement to do something else; and that if the wish seems futile, the diversion may seem desirable; and then the complaint that the wish is not thereby satisfied will, no doubt, seem futile too.

Formal Constructions and Philosophical Understanding

Now I want to consider once again, but this time with a different purpose, the earlier part of the passage I quoted. I have tried to show how the passage can be used to explain in part how a certain extreme conception of clarification might come to be held. I now wish to show how it also points to a less extreme conception, and thereby to a still open issue between constructionism and the analysis of ordinary language. I noted that Carnap acknowledges the existence of typical philosophical questions about, in this case, propositions; and claims that they could be answered[5] by attention to 'the system of rules for the linguistic expressions of the propositional framework', the system of rules, that is, whereby the framework was 'introduced'. Now it may strike us that in advance of the explicit framing of a system of linguistic *rules,* there already exists in unformalised discourse an ordinary linguistic *practice* which might itself be said to constitute a propositional framework. That is to say, we commonly use quite a large range of substantival expressions which can occur as grammatical subjects of such grammatical predicates as 'is true', 'is incompatible with so-and-so', etc. These expressions will include clauses beginning with the word 'that'; and also expressions beginning 'the statement that . . .', 'the suggestion that . . . ,' 'the belief that . . .'; and also descriptive phrases which do not incorporate a 'that'—clause, like 'what you said just now', 'what X believes' and so on. Moreover, a comparison of the typical uses of these expressions with those of expressions used to refer to (designate) mental occurrences or linguistic entities or states of a person will show that the expressions in question are in fact used differently from expressions of any of these other classes; or, in other words, that the entities which the expressions in question are used to refer to cannot be identified with entities of any of these other classes. So we have, in ordinary unformalised discourse, something very like Carnap's framework of propositions. (We could not conveniently get on without it. And it is merely to echo the main thesis of Carnap's article to add that this is no reason either for despondency or for elation). Here, then, we have a (perhaps untypically) simple instance of an apparent choice of methods. Carnap claims that we can very easily read off answers to (some) typically philosophical questions from a study of the rules of the constructed system. On the other hand, it seems that the same or similar questions can be answered by the examination of the linguistic practice which precedes construction. Why should either method be preferred to the other?

I do not propose to debate the general issue on this narrow ground.

[5]Notice that to deal with the philosophical worry which makes the questions seem so urgent, more is required than the answers. Carnap provides something on the necessary lines in the article as a whole.

I use the case only to bring out (what has not hitherto appeared) that, after all, the two methods can, up to a point, be represented as different ways of attaining the same or similar ends. Only if this is so can there be an issue between them as methods. But it is important to see how differently we must now conceive of the formalist programme of clarification. It is no longer a matter of replacing an unclear concept used for one (non-scientific) purpose with a clear, though related, concept used for a different (scientific) purpose. The constructed propositional framework may indeed be used by Carnap in attacking other problems; but this further use is irrelevant to its success or failure in the task of clarifying *this* problem. Unformalised concepts are to be clarified by formal construction; and the fact (if it is a fact) that the formal construction may then be put to work in new ways, is not now to be taken as germane to the purpose of clarification (of *this* piece of clarification) at all, but as an extra gift of fortune.

Even if agreement can be reached on a common aim of *understanding* ordinary concepts, however, the danger of trivialising the issue is not altogether averted. Let me state a little more fully the position the constructionist is now assumed to occupy. He is now to be seen not as offering his construction on the ground of its value for other purposes, nor as one who seriously maintains that his system of well-regulated expressions could actually displace ordinary usage for ordinary purposes. He offers his system as an object of contemplation which has the following features: first, it is intrinisically clear, in that its key concepts are related in precise and determinate ways (which the system exhibits), whereas, *ex hypothesi,* the ordinary concepts to be clarified do not have such precise and determinate relations to each other or to other ordinary concepts in terms of which one might seek to explain them; and, second, at least some of the key concepts of the system are, in important respects, very close to the ordinary concepts which are to be clarified. (The qualification 'at least some' is introduced to allow for the fact that the constructed system may legitimately accord a central place to new concepts which do not have any ordinary correlates, but which possess considerable power of unifying or systematising those elements of the system which do have ordinary correlates.) The system as a whole then appears as a precise and rigid structure to which our ordinary conceptual equipment is a loose and untidy approximation. The way in which the debate could once more reach an uninteresting deadlock is the following. It could be maintained dogmatically on the one hand that nothing but the mastery of such a system would really *be* understanding, in a philosophical sense, the concepts to be clarified; and to one who maintained this, phrases like 'the underlying logical structure of our concepts' might seem to carry the weight of his conviction. Or it might be maintained dogmatically on the other hand that since, *ex hypothesi,* the ordinary concepts to be examined do not behave in the well-regulated way in which the model concepts of the system are made to behave, there can be no real understanding of the former except such as may be gained by a detailed consideration of the way they do behave, i.e. by an investigation of the ordinary uses of the linguistic expressions concerned. Here the deadlock is reached by each party refusing to count as *understanding,* a condition which is not reached by the method he advocates.

There may be something final about this deadlock. For there may here be something which is in part a matter simply of preference, of choice. Nevertheless, there are considerations which may influence choice. For surely, in deciding what to count as philosophical understanding, it is reasonable to remind ourselves what philosophical problems and *un*clarities are *like.* Such a reminder I shall briefly attempt in the next section. But I shall partly anticipate it now, in mentioning some general difficulties which arise for the constructionist in the position he is now assumed to occupy.

The constructionist would of course agree that it is necessary to supply an interpretation for the linguistic expressions of his theory. This is not secured merely by the formal relationships between the constructed concepts which the theory exhibits. At some point it is necessary also to explain the meaning of the linguistic expressions for the constructed concepts in terms which do not belong to the theory and the meaning of which is taken as already known. So *some* extra-systematic remarks are essential. This point need not in itself raise any particular difficulty. So long as a small number of extra-systematic points of contact are clearly made, the meaning of the remaining elements follows from their clearly defined relationships within the system to those to which life has been given by the extra-systematic remarks. (To give a simple instance: it is enough to explain, say, '·' and '∼' in extra-systematic terms—and this is not a hard task—for the interpretation of the remaining constants of the propositional calculus to be fixed.) But if the constructionist claim to achieve clarification is to be vindicated, it is not sufficient, though it is necessary, that the interpretation of the linguistic expressions of his theory should be determined. For the claim to clarify will seem empty, unless the results achieved have some bearing on the typical philosophical problems and difficulties which arise concerning the concepts to be clarified. Now these problems and difficulties (it will be admitted) have their roots in ordinary, unconstructed concepts, in the elusive, deceptive modes of functioning of unformalised linguistic expressions. It is precisely the purpose of the reconstruction (we are now supposing) to solve or dispel problems and difficulties so rooted. But how can this purpose be achieved unless extra-systematic points of contact are made, not just at the one or two points necessary to fix the interpretation of the constructed concepts, but at *every* point where the relevant problems and difficulties concerning the unconstructed concepts arise? That is to say, if the clear mode of functioning of the constructed concepts is to cast light on problems and difficulties rooted in the unclear mode of functioning of the unconstructed concepts, then precisely the ways in which the constructed concepts are connected with and depart from the unconstructed concepts must be plainly shown. And how can *this* result be achieved without accurately describing the modes of functioning of the unconstructed concepts? But this task is precisely the task of describing the logical behaviour of the linguistic expressions of natural languages; and may *by itself* achieve the sought-for resolution of the problems and difficulties rooted in the elusive, deceptive mode of functioning of unconstructed concepts. I should not want to deny that in the discharge of this task, the construction of a model object of linguistic comparison may sometimes be of great help. But I do want to deny that the construction and contemplation of such a model object can *take the place* of the discharge of this task; and I want also to suggest that one thinks that it can, only if one is led away from the purpose of achieving philosophical understanding by the fascination of other purposes, such as that of getting on with science. The point I am making is twofold. First, in so far as the purpose of a constructed system is philosophical clarification, the extra-systematic remarks, so far from being—apart from the minimum necessary to fixing the interpretation—comparatively unimportant trimmings, are just what give life and meaning to the whole enterprise. Second, these extra-systematic remarks must include exercises in just that method to which system-construction appeared as a rival.

Moreover, the general usefulness of systems of constructed concepts as objects of comparison with the unconstructed concepts in which our problems are rooted is necessarily limited. For the types or modes of logical behaviour which ordinary concepts exhibit are extremely diverse. To detect and distinguish them is a task in which one may well be hindered rather than helped by fixing one's eye too firmly on the limited range of types of logical behaviour which the concepts occuring in a formal system can there be shown to display. This is not to say that the metavocabulary of description and classification should not itself be made as systematic as possible. (*This* aim, it need hardly be said, is entirely independent of formal systematisation of the concepts which the metavocabulary is used to discuss.) But (1) an adequate set of metaconcepts for the dissection of the expressions of a natural language will scarcely be found by attending primarily to artificial languages; and (2) clarity about the metaconcepts themselves will be achieved only by attention to the use that is made of them and hence, ultimately, by attention to the actual functioning of the concepts they are used to discuss. It is the same with the improvement and refinement of such metaconcepts. Classifications are found to be crude and misleading, to obliterate logical features, to blur distinctions; and these discoveries, too, are made by attention to the actual modes of functioning of actually used linguistic expressions.

Finally, I may suggest that the very success of logicians in developing techniques of formalisation has itself generated philosophical problems which cannot, in their very nature, be solved by further essays in the use of these techniques. This is not, of course, a reproach to the logicians. It is characteristic of major scientific advances that the effective use of the new concepts and methods introduced in making them may precede the adequate philosophical understanding of that use, and hence of the relation of these concepts and methods to others belonging to different, though perhaps overlapping, fields. Descartes' mathematical ideal of knowledge has such a source, and so have the recurrent perplexities about perception which the work of physicists and psysiologists engenders. Nor is it in any way to be regretted that these problems should arise; for their resolution results in a clearer, more self-conscious understanding of what we are doing both with new concepts and with old. But it is necessarily not within the field of the puzzle-generating advance that such problems as these can be solved. For these problems are defined as those which result from the attempt to make inappropriate applications of the concepts of the field. So may we see in the barely sketched but grandiose plan of logical atomism the outlines of an attempt to find in ordinary empirical discourse the real formal structure which the planners were encouraged by the advances of logic to believe must be there to be found. And so, to set a small thing beside a large one, we may see in the attempts to analyse the ordinary conditional in terms exclusively of the constants of modern elementary logic, the force of the conviction that concepts successful for some purposes must be adequate for others. From such attempts we may learn much; but not by their succeeding. Part of what we have to explain and free ourselves from, in dealing with them, is the undue fascination exercised by formal systems.

Philosophy and Ordinary Language[6]

It is, no doubt, rash to attempt to describe in general the nature of

[6]See Professor Ryle's article, "Ordinary Language," *The Philosophical Review* (April, 1953), for a discussion of this topic, and, in particular, for the removal of some misunderstandings about the phrase "ordinary language."

philosophical problems, difficulties and questions. But at any rate this much will be broadly agreed: that they are problems, difficulties and questions *about* the concepts we use in various fields, and not problems, difficulties and questions which arise *within* the fields of their use. (A philosophical problem about mathematics is not a mathematical problem.) To say more is to risk the loss of general agreement. Nevertheless, I think it is possible roughly to distinguish, though not to separate, certain strands or elements in the treatment of this diverse mass of conceptual questions. First, and very centrally, we find the necessity of dealing with paradox and perplexity. For it often happens that someone reflecting on a certain set of concepts finds himself driven to adopt views which seem to others paradoxical or unacceptably strange, or to have consequences which are paradoxical or unacceptably strange. (He may or may not himself embrace these conclusions with complacency.) Or—the obverse of this—it may happen that someone so reflecting becomes unable to see how something that he knows very well to be the case can *possibly* be the case. In this situation the critical philosopher must not only restore the conceptual balance which has somehow been upset; he must also diagnose the particular sources of the loss of balance, show just how it has been upset. And these achievements are not independent of each other. It also seems to me possible to say in general what kind of thing the source of conceptual unbalance is. Such unbalance results from a kind of temporary one-sidedness of vision, a kind of selective blindness which cuts out most of the field, but leaves one part of it standing out with a peculiar brilliance. This condition may take many different, though interconnected, forms. The producer of philosophical paradox, or the sufferer from philosophical perplexity, is temporarily dominated by one logical mode of operation of expressions, or by one way of using language, or by one logical type or category of objects, or by one sort of explanation, or by one set of cases of the application of a given concept; and attempts to see, to explain, something which is different, in terms of, or on analogy with, his favoured model. The distortions which result from such attempts are of equally many kinds. To correct the distortions, one must make plain the actual modes of operation of the distorted concepts or types of discourse; and, in doing this, one must make plain the differences between their modes of operation and those of the model concepts or types of discourse; and, in doing this, one must, if one can, make plain the sources of the blinding obsession with the model cases.

This, then, is one strand in the treatment of philosophical problems; and I call it central, partly because the need for it has in fact provided so strong an impetus to the whole activity. From it can be distinguished, though not separated, two other strands. One is the attempt to explain, not just how our concepts and types of discourse operate, but why it is that we have such concepts and types of discourse as we do; and what alternatives there might be. This is not an historical enquiry. It attempts to show the natural foundations of our logical, conceptual apparatus, in the way things happen in the world, and in our own natures. A form which propositions exemplifying this strand in philosophy may often take, is the following: if things (or we) were different in such-and-such ways, then we might lack such-and-such concepts or types of discourse; or have such-and-such others; or might accord a subordinate place to some which are now central, and a central place to others; or the concepts we have might be different in such-and-such ways. It might reasonably be maintained, or ruled, that full understanding of a concept is not achieved until this kind of enquiry is added to the activities of comparing, contrasting and distinguishing which I mentioned first. Of course speculations of this kind are restricted in certain ways: they are limited by the kinds of experience and the conceptual apparatus we in fact have. But this is only the restriction to intelligibility; it leaves a wide field open to philosophical imagination. The distinction I used above between the way things happen in the world, and our own natures, is here, though vague, important. For it is a part of our nature that, things other than ourselves being as they are, it is natural for us to have the conceptual apparatus that we do have. But human nature is diverse enough to allow of another, though related, use of philosophical imagination. This consists in imagining ways in which, without things other than ourselves being different from what they are, we might view them through the medium of a different conceptual apparatus. Some metaphysics is best, or most charitably, seen as consisting in part in exercises of this sort. Of course, even when it can be so interpreted, it is not *presented* as a conceptual or structural revision by means of which we might see things differently; it is presented as a picture of things as they *really* are, instead of as they delusively seem. And this presentation, with its contrast between esoteric reality and daily delusion, involves, and is the consequence of, the unconscious distortion of ordinary concepts, i.e. of the ordinary use of linguistic expressions. So metaphysics, though it can sometimes be charitably interpreted in the way I suggest, in fact always involves paradox and perplexities of the kind I first mentioned; and sometimes embodies no rudimentary vision, but merely rudimentary mistakes.[7]

There is a third strand to be distinguished; something soberer than

[7]It might seem that in the foregoing I have committed myself to an unintelligible notion of *things as they are* as opposed to things as we see them through the medium of a conceptual apparatus. But to think this is to forget that I have made use of a rough distinction between things other than ourselves and our own natures, interests and needs. Features of each can intelligibly be imagined to vary—with varying conceptual consequences—while the other remains constant.

the second. That examination of current concepts and types of discourse to which paradox and perplexity so commonly give the initial impulse, can be pursued with no particular therapeutic purpose, but for its own sake. This is not to say that puzzlement is not in question here. One can, without feeling any particular temptation to mistaken assimilations, simply be aware that one does not clearly understand how some type of expression functions, in comparison with others. Or, having noticed, or had one's attention drawn to, a certain logico-linguistic feature appearing in one particular area of discourse, one may simply wish to discover how extensive is the range of this feature, and what other comparable features are to be found. Of course, the resulting enquiries may well pay therapeutic dividends. But this need not be the purpose for which they are undertaken.

In relation to the first and third of these three types of philosophical aim, the roles of the two apparently contrasted methods of philosophical clarification should already be clear. The description of the modes of functioning of actually employed linguistic expressions is of the essence of the third aim; and it is simply the least clouded form of a procedure which is essential to the achievement of the first. Here the arguments of the previous section apply. To observe our concepts in action is necessarily the only way of finding out what they can and cannot do. The right kind of attention to the ordinary use of expressions provides a means of refutation of theories founded on mistaken assimilations; it provides a description of the actual functioning of the problematic concepts, to take the place of the mistaken theory; and, finally, it helps, or may help, with the diagnosis of the temptations to the mistakes. This last it may do because the analogies which seduce the philosopher are not, in general, private fantasies; they have their roots in our ordinary thinking, and show themselves in practically harmless, but detectable ways, in ordinary language—both in its syntactical structure and in the buried figures which individual words and phrases contain. I have already acknowledged that system-construction may have an ancillary role in achieving these two types of aim, and given reasons for thinking that it must remain ancillary—and limited. Model objects of linguistic comparison may help us to understand the given objects; but it is dogmatism to maintain that the construction of model objects is the best or the only means of achieving such understanding.[8]

With the second philosophical strand I distinguished, the case is somewhat different. To understand the foundation of our concepts in natural facts, and to envisage alternative possibilities, it is not enough to have a sharp eye for linguistic actualities. Nor is system-construction a direct contribution to the achievement of the first of these two, i.e. to

[8]Cf. *The Logical Syntax of Language,* Introduction, 8.

seeing why we talk as we do. But it may be the second, i.e. to imagining how else we might talk. The constructionist may perhaps be seen as an enlightened metaphysician—one who, perhaps wistfully, envisages the possibility of our situation and our need for communication so changed and simplified that such a well-regulated system of concepts as he supplies is well adapted to both. It is only when the claim to exclusiveness is made on behalf of the constructionist method, and of particular constructions, that one must begin to query the enlightenment. For behind these claims may lie a formalizing mystique: the belief that the model systems embody the *real* structure of our concepts, hidden from us by the untidiness of our actual practice. But, again, this claim may be softened to the expression of a preference—which leaves one no more to say.

To conclude, then. There is not just one thing which is legitimately required of the philosopher who would increase our conceptual understanding. In particular, it is certainly not *enough* to say that he should describe the functioning of actually employed linguistic expressions. For simply to say this would not be to give any indication of the sort of decription he should provide. That indication is given when it is shown how description of the right sort may bear upon our conceptual confusions and problems. Next we see how more may be required of him than the resolution of these confusions with the help of those descriptions; how a more systematic classification and ordering of the types of discourse and concept we employ may be sought; how a fuller understanding of both may be gained by enquiring into their foundation in natural facts; and how room may here be found for the envisaging of other possibilities. If the philosopher is to do all or only some of these things, it is true that he cannot stop short at the literal description, and illustration, of the behaviour of actually used linguistic expressions. Nevertheless, the actual use of linguistic expressions remains his sole and essential point of contact with reality; for this is the only point from which the actual mode of operation of concepts can be observed. If he severs this vital connexion, all his ingenuity and imagination will not save him from lapses into the arid or the absurd.

P. F. STRAWSON

UNIVERSITY COLLEGE
OXFORD UNIVERSITY

17

Yehoshua Bar-Hillel

REMARKS ON CARNAP'S LOGICAL SYNTAX OF LANGUAGE

AFTER I had accepted the task of evaluating Carnap's *Logical Syntax of Language*[1] for the present volume, I cherished for some time the thought of both presenting the main ideas of the *Logical Syntax* and of criticizing them in the light of the progress made in logic and methodology during the last twenty years. But one more careful reading of the book made me realize the absurdity of my original intention. How could one possibly summarize, and critically evaluate, the contents of a book in a few dozen pages, when every single one of its sections contains such a wealth of ideas, painstakingly elaborated, carefully explained and illuminatingly illustrated? Not all of these ideas were original with the author, but even when he adopted somebody else's flashes of genius—his debts to Frege, Russell, Wittgenstein, Hilbert, Gödel and Tarski are acknowledgedly great—he made them change their character and often gain in importance by incorporating them into his own general framework. How would one go about condensing a book when he is convinced that often not a single word can be omitted, not a single illustration discarded, not a single historical aside passed over, without becoming involved in some serious loss, and when he has, moreover, every few pages the impression that the author could and should have said much more on a certain subject and that only lack of space prevented him from giving us the enlightenment for which we now have to struggle all by ourselves. There are many pages containing short remarks that carry convincing proof that Carnap must have deeply thought about the problem treated there but would have needed many more pages to expand

[1]The following abbreviations will henceforth be employed: *LSL* for *The Logical Syntax of Language* (London and New York, 1937), being an expanded and corrected translation of the German original *Die logische Syntax der Sprache* (Vienna, 1934); TM for "Testability and Meaning," *Philosophy of Science,* III (1936), 419-471, and IV (1937), 1-40, reprinted by Graduate Philosophy Club, Yale University, New Haven, Connecticut (1950); ESO for "Empiricism, Semantics, and Ontology," *Revue Internationale de Philosophie,* IV (1950), 20-40, reprinted in *Readings in Philosophy of Science,* ed. P. P. Wiener (New York, 1953), 509-522 (and quoted according to this reprint).

his ideas. (As a matter of fact, I myself have already had twice the opportunity of publishing papers whose content is essentially nothing more than a series of footnotes to pp. 168-170 of *LSL*.) [2]

The only rational way, that was left open to me, of discussing Carnap's masterwork within the frame of this volume could therefore consist of choosing, almost at random, a couple of what I regard as the most important insights gained by Carnap and evaluating their impact as of today. I would like to show, on the one hand, that in spite of the intense study which *LSL* has undergone in the hands of many competent students much has been left that still awaits understanding, elaboration and application, and that, on the other hand, in order to encourage this application, certain revisions in some formulations might be indicated.

I

The *Logical Syntax of Language* should have exercised a decisive influence on modern linguistic research. It didn't. Part of the fault was Carnap's. Not because what he had to say was couched in a language no linguist without many years of logico-mathematical training could understand; this could not be helped. But because he left them with the impression that the content and methods of *LSL* were of little relevance for their issues, so that it was not worthwhile for them to undergo this kind of training. I believe this to be the only case in Carnap's teaching where his cautiousness betrayed him. He did not write *LSL* in order to provide a framework in which to discuss ordinary languages. He wrote it in order to create a tool, at least the outlines of a tool, with which one could efficiently handle constructed language-systems of science. But he did not forcefully enough drive home the point that the tool he created was almost equally efficient for the treatment of the vernacular. He discussed this application many times throughout the book, but the conclusions at which he arrived were somewhat ambivalent. In the introduction he says:

> In consequence of the unsystematic and logically imperfect structure of the natural word-languages (such as German or Latin), the statement of their formal rules of formation and transformation would be so complicated that it would hardly be feasible in practice (2).

A few pages later he makes the following claim which, though not exactly contradicting the former passage, still shifts the emphasis considerably:

[2]These papers are "On Syntactical Categories," *The Journal of Symbolic Logic,* XV (1950), 1-16, which belabors pp. 169-170 of *LSL* and "Indexical Expressions," *Mind,* LXIII (1954), 359-379, in which Carnap's tantalizingly condensed remarks on p. 168 of *LSL* are expanded.

The method of syntax . . . will also help in the *logical analysis of the word-languages*. Although here . . . we shall be dealing with symbolic languages, the syntactical concepts and rules—not in detail but in their general character—may also be applied to the analysis of the incredibly complicated word-languages (6).

The reconciliation of these two slightly antithetic views is then effected as follows:

The direct analysis of these [word-languages], which has been prevalent hitherto, must inevitably fail, just as a physicist would be frustrated were he from the outset to attempt to relate his laws to natural things—trees, stones, and so on. In the first place, the physicist relates his laws to the simplest of constructed forms; to a thin straight lever, to a simple pendulum, to punctiform masses, etc. Then, with the help of the laws relating to these constructed forms, he is later in a position to analyze into suitable elements the complicated behaviour of real bodies, and thus to control them. One more comparison: the complicated configurations of mountain chains, river frontiers, and the like are most easily represented and investigated by the help of geographical co-ordinates—or, in other words, by constructed lines not given in nature. In the same way, the syntactical property of a particular word-language, such as English, or of particular classes of word-languages, or of a particular sub-language of a word-language, is best represented and investigated by comparison with a constructed language which serves as a system of reference (8).

That this reconciliation is still not unambiguously clear can be seen from the fact that one of the leading American structural linguists, Zellig Harris, derived from it a conflict of attitudes between logicians and linguists. After quoting from the last-mentioned passage of Carnap's he continues:

Linguists meet this problem differently than do Carnap and his school. Whereas the logicians have avoided the analysis of existing languages, linguists study them.[3]

One sees clearly how a nice little and completely superfluous and unwarranted controversy of logicians versus linguists is in the making. It is true that logicians, i.e. Carnap, avoided large-scale analysis of existing languages, but they did this very deliberately, not because they wanted to meet this problem differently than do linguists, but quite simply out of a certain division of labor. Carnap finishes the last-quoted passage with the following characteristic sentence: "Such a task, however, lies beyond the scope of this book (8)." But from a division of labor neither a difference in belief nor even a difference in attitude should be derived. I admit that Carnap's formulations lack here their usual clean-cut pregnance and I complained myself about this fact before. I imagine that many a linguist who, attracted by the title of the book, was looking through its preface and introduction in order to determine whether it

[3]*Methods in Structural Linguistics* (Chicago, 1951), 16, n. 17.

might not contain some new tools for linguistic analysis closed it in desperation when, after the stirring remarks of p.1 of the introduction (which we shall quote presently), he read, on p. 2, the discouraging sentence we quoted first. After that he might well have decided that reading and trying to understand the whole book with its strange symbolism was not worth the trouble. He did not care whether logic and mathematics were to be constructed simultaneously or the one on the basis of the other. He was not at all impressed by the differences of two language-systems, consisting in the fact that the one allowed for limited operators only whereas the other admitted also unlimited operators. It must be understood, though still deeply deplored, that the *Logical Syntax of Language,* after this discouraging opening, did not touch the heart of the linguists.

This is the more deplorable since at approximately the same time at which Carnap conceived his book and tried to incorporate in it his deep conviction that it is worthwhile, nay necessary, to deal with languages qua *calculi,* i.e. uninterpreted formal systems, and to disregard, for the investigation of their syntax, the meaning of their expressions, their connections with actions and perceptions, and their sociological status in communication, many linguists arrived at the very same conviction utterly independently and out of a quite different historical development. Logical syntax originated with the efforts of the Hilbert school to prove the consistency of mathematics by treating it as a calculus and the partly simultaneous, partly subsequent generalizations of this approach by the Polish logicians, especially by Leśniewski and his pupils, to language-systems in general. Not a single professional linguist is mentioned by Carnap in his extensive bibliography to *LSL* (with the exception of Bréal and Bühler, who are mentioned once, on p. 9, in connection with a minor terminological discussion). American structural linguistics, on the other hand, started off as a revolt against mentalistic linguistics but arrived at the conviction that it is worthwhile to study the regularities in the distributional relations among the elements of speech, in abstraction from the various other observable regularities. In Leonard Bloomfield's book *Language,* that appeared in 1933, no mention is made of any work by Carnap or the Polish logicians.[4]

In spite of this entirely different background, there might still have been a complete convergence of linguists and logicians towards a new approach to linguistics (a partial rapprochement took indeed place in the late Thirties), were it not that Carnap's attitude did little to encourage linguists to study his work, leaving them without the benefit of a

[4]Later on, however, there was a considerable rapprochement between Carnap and Bloomfield. In 1939, Bloomfield published *Linguistic Aspects of Science* for the International Encyclopedia of Unified Science, of which Carnap was an Associate Editor.

major insight of his, the lack of which caused them, and is still causing them, many quite superfluous troubles.

The irony of this failure of convergence is the greater since that insight of Carnap's which would have, in my opinion, helped the structural linguists immensely, is to be found on the very first page of the introduction:

> The prevalent opinion is that syntax and logic, in spite of some points of contact between them, are fundamentally theories of a very different type. The syntax of a language is supposed to lay down rules according to which the linguistic structures (e.g. sentences) are to be built up from the elements (such as words or parts of words). The chief task of logic, on the other hand, is supposed to be that of formulating rules according to which judgments may be inferred from other judgments; in other words, according to which conclusions may be drawn from premisses. . . . In the following pages, the view that logic, too, is concerned with the *formal* treatment of sentences will be presented and developed. We shall see that the logical characteristics of sentences (for instance, whether a sentence is analytic, synthetic, or contradictory; whether it is an existential sentence or not; and so on) and the logical relations between them (for instance, whether two sentences contradict one another or are compatible with one another; whether one is logically deducible from the other or not; and so on) are solely dependent upon the syntactical structure of the sentences. In this way, logic will become a part of syntax, provided that the latter is conceived in a sufficiently wide sense and formulated with exactitude. The difference between syntactical rules in the narrower sense and the logical rules of deduction is only the difference between *formation rules* and *transformation rules*, both of which are completely formulable in syntactical terms (1-2).

The thesis that rules of transformation are as much syntactical as rules of formation has been completely missed by all structural linguists and, to my knowledge, not even been mentioned if only to be refuted. That it is up to English syntax to tell us that any sequence of two English statements 'a' and 'b' with 'and' or 'or' in between is a statement, was, of course, perfectly recognized by all linguists. But that it is up to the same English syntax to tell us that 'a' is derivable from 'a and b' but not from 'a or b,' escaped their attention. Since it is only by this and similar rules of transformation that the difference in functioning between 'and' and 'or' can be formally described, structural linguists were either obliged to relegate the treatment of this difference in function to some non-formal part of linguistics or else to embark on the *prima facie* utterly hopeless task of explaining this difference in terms of rules of formation. A similar situation prevails with respect to the relationship between say, 'loves' and 'is loved by.' In terms of rules of transformation, this relationship is easily determined: 'A loves B' and 'B is loved by A' are mutually interderivable. It should be rather obvious that it is beyond the rules of formation to provide for an equivalent determination. Leaving for some other occasion the detailed criticism of one such heroic attempt by a distinguished structural linguist[5] to get along with rules of formation alone, let us be satisfied to state here that it is at least highly plausible that the neglect of the rules of transformation has led structural linguists either to restrict unduly the field of application of their methods or to embark on futile attempts to achieve the impossible with inadequate tools.

That the vital importance of the rules of transformation in formal linguistic description was overlooked is, of course, due to the fact that for structural linguists, not appreciably less than for linguists of other brands, "the prevalent opinion is that syntax and logic, in spite of some points of contact between them, are fundamentally theories of a very different type (1)." This opinion is prevalent among linguists in 1954 no less than in 1934, and Carnap's work, for reasons stated above, did not succeed in changing it. There existed, of course, quite valid motives for linguists to want to uphold this cleavage. The brand of logic which was taught at the universities in the Twenties or early Thirties was surely not something a self-respecting structural linguist would have wanted to have to do much with. Psychologism and introspectionistic insistence on "meaning" was exactly what they tried to avoid in their own work. It was Carnap's brand of logic, his *LSL,* which was congenial to their approach—but they missed it.

I have no intention to claim that every logician should undergo an extensive linguistic training or vice versa. Even when the fundamental unity of syntax and logic is recognized, there still remain large parts in linguistics, such as phonology, for which logical training would be of little practical value, and large parts in logic, for which linguistic field training would be of no help whatsoever. I do however believe that a straightforward claim by Carnap that his work should serve as a methodological and terminological basis for structural linguists and a similarly straightforward recognition by structural linguists that Carnap's investigations, in spite of their so completely different background and motivation, are of immediate importance for their work, especially the recognition of the vital part played by the rules of transformation in language description, should have a healthy impact. Another artificial barrier, this time between logic and linguistics, would be brought down, and a few more linguistically trained logicians, a few more logically trained linguists, a few more logicians and linguists cooperating, should be able to arrive in the near future at many interesting new results.

Logical syntacticians and structural linguists have in common the aim of providing for a structural description of ordinary languages (in addition to other aims which are specific for each group). The achievement of this aim requires both the development of efficient and reliable techniques of elicitation in order to get the data, and the development of a concep-

[5]Zellig S. Harris, "Discourse Analysis," *Language,* XXVIII (1952), 1-30, see esp. p. 19.

tual and terminological framework in which can be analyzed those constructed language-systems from which in ever increasing approximation those data can be derived. Since rather different qualifications seem to be required for practical work in these two branches, the existing division of labor between linguists and logicians may well be justified. It would surely be detrimental to the common aim to transform this division of labor into an antagonism.

In developing his General Syntax, Carnap's major aim in *LSL* was definitely and admittedly not the construction of language-systems that could serve as systems of reference with which to compare particular ordinary languages. "Such a task lies beyond the scope of this book (8)." Therefore, though he claims in the first section of chapter B of part IV, where he opens the discussion of "the syntax of any language"—this is the title of this chapter—that

> in this section we shall attempt to construct a *syntax for languages in general,* that is to say, a system of definitions of syntactical terms which are so comprehensive as to be applicable to any language whatsoever (167),

he immediately qualifies this somewhat sweeping claim in three ways. Firstly,

> We have, it is true, had chiefly in mind as examples languages similar in their principal features to the usual symbolic languages, and, in many cases, the choice of the definitions has been influenced by this fact. Nevertheless, the terms defined are also applicable to languages of quite different kinds (167).

Secondly,

> The outline of a general syntax which follows is to be regarded as no more than a first attempt. The definitions framed will certainly need improvement and completion in many respects (167).

Thirdly,

> In what follows, we shall deal only with languages which contain *no expressions dependent upon extra-linguistic factors.* The logical character of all the sentences of these languages is then invariant in relation to spatio-temporal displacements; two sentences of the same wording will have the same character independently of where, when, and by whom they are spoken. In the case of sentences having extra-syntactical dependence, this invariance can be attained by means of the addition of person-, place-, and time-designations (168).

It must be perfectly clear that especially the last qualification restricts highly the immediate applicability of Carnap's General Syntax to ordinary languages. The overwhelming majority of the sentences in these languages are *indexical,* i.e. dependent upon extra-linguistic factors, and their transformation into a context-invariant form poses formidable problems, which are only touched upon in the last-quoted sentence. These problems, moreover, cannot be solved any more within the framework of

LSL, their solution lying clearly within what became known as *pragmatics* a short time after the appearance of *LSL.*[6]

Though Carnap himself did little to apply his General Syntax to ordinary languages, there were a few logicians who did some work along this line. Among them are some British analyticists, though doubtless from a somewhat different angle and from certain particular motives. Many analyses in Gilbert Ryle's *Concept of Mind,*[7] to mention just one recent influential book emanating from this school, should have very straightforward linguistic value—in addition to its philosophical significance—and his notion of category mistakes (which could still stand some refinements) is based on the observation that two expressions may have some linguistic environments in common without thereby necessitating that their total distributions should be identical.[8] This is a piece of distributional analysis, and distributional analysis is at the heart of present structural linguistics.

Hans Reichenbach was very definitely of the opinion that the incredible complication of ordinary languages was no sufficient obstacle to the search for regularities in these languages. His *Elements of Symbolic Logic*[9] already contained a chapter, wholly devoted to the application of the techniques and terminology of modern logic to the analysis of ordinary languages, and in his posthumous work, *Nomological Statements and Admissible Operations,*[10] he makes a strong plea for the possibility and necessity of such applications.[11] Though he does not mention Carnap by name in this context, it is fairly obvious that his remarks were, at least partly, directed against Carnap's attitude. I think that Reichenbach was basically right and I would be glad to learn that Carnap would not fundamentally disagree with him.

W. V. O. Quine's excursions into the analysis of ordinary languages have become more and more frequent recently, and his last volume of essays *From a Logical Point of View*[12] contains many incisive remarks, revealing both a mastery of the fundamental teachings of structural linguistics and a clear insight into the role logic is dedicated to play in the future linguistics.

Now, however, it is time to notice that with the last-mentioned logi-

[6]Some of the problems posed by the indexical character of most ordinary discourse were discussed in the second paper mentioned in footnote 2.

[7]*The Concept of Mind* (London, 1949).

[8]This point touched upon in *LSL,* 169-170, is extensively analyzed in the first paper mentioned in footnote 2.

[9]*Elements of Symbolic Logic* (New York, 1947).

[10]*Nomological Statements and Admissible Operations* (Amsterdam, 1954).

[11]*Ibid.,* 14.

[12]*From a Logical Point of View* (Cambridge, 1953); see esp. essay III on "The Problem of Meaning in Linguistics."

cians it is, in general, no more Logical Syntax whose techniques, terms and methods are invoked for the analysis of ordinary languages, but rather Logical Semantics, if I am allowed to coin this term, the adjective 'logical' serving to distinguish this science from the various other occupations that are also known under the name 'Semantics'. There can, of course, be no doubt that Carnap would approve of this development. This would mean not a repudiation of the teachings of *LSL* but rather an implementation. It was Carnap himself who reintroduced semantical considerations into the logic of science, even before the ink of the English edition of *LSL* was dry. The reasons for this development will probably be discussed in other contributions to this volume. Let me notice here only the fact that no parallel development has taken place in structural linguistics to such a degree of overtness, though there are many indications that the high tide of anti-semantic feeling is slowly but surely subsiding. The return of semantics into modern, scientific linguistics will not be a capitulation before the good, old ways of thinking, but a recognition of the fact that this branch of the theory of signs has come of age and has finally turned from an introspectionistic art into a publicly controllable science, whose basic concepts are about as rigidly definable as those of any other science, including syntax. But since I dealt with this aspect at some length elsewhere,[13] no more will be said here.

II

During the first half of the twentieth century, more and more thinkers became increasingly aware of the fact that certain types of linguistic behavior tended to be misevaluated by many people who were professionally engaged in putting this behavior under rules through the customary scientific procedures of abstraction and generalization. As a result, paradoxes and antinomies were generated, whose resolution required much mental energy that might otherwise have been put to more fruitful and creative work, and pseudo-problems formulated that would continue to be discussed without end unless their baselessness could be convincingly pointed out, thereby causing their dissolution rather than their solution.

For lack of space, we shall not deal with the interpretation of Russell's and Wittgenstein's teachings under this aspect but turn immediately to the discussion of what Carnap had to say on this topic in *LSL* and some later works and compare it with Gilbert Ryle's approach as expressed in "Systematically Misleading Expressions."[14]

The term Carnap used for characterizing some of this misevaluated

[13]"Logical Syntax and Semantics," *Language,* XXX (1954), 230-237.

[14]I shall quote from the version printed as chapter II in *Logic and Language,* First series, ed. by A. G. N. Flew (Oxford, 1951), 11-36. The paper originally appeared in the *Proceedings of the Aristotelian Society* for 1931-2. It will hereafter be quoted as SME.

linguistic behavior was *'the material mode of speech'*. This term has become widely known and applied, and the method of resolving certain philosophical problems by showing that they were based on formulations in this mode of speech but disappeared when the underlying issue was reformulated in *the formal mode of speech* has since been repeatedly discussed and criticized. It was less noticed that Carnap himself regarded the material mode of speech only as a special kind of *transposed mode of speech (LSL* 308*)*. Though Carnap deals, both prior to this passage and afterwards, mainly with the material mode of speech and its dangers, and in the systematic treatment of this topic in Part IV of *LSL* with this mode and the autonymous mode of speech exclusively as the only possible interpretations of *quasi-syntactical sentences,* there can be no doubt that he was aware of the possibility of running into obscurities, inconsistencies, pseudo-questions and the other undesirable by-products of the material mode of speech also through the use of other kinds of transposed mode of speech.

I am quite ready to accept the thesis that many philosophical troubles are due to a failure of recognizing the transposed character of a certain formulation, but I am in some cases hesitant to accept Carnap's specific suggestions that the responsibility for these troubles rests in the fact that the transposed mode of speech takes the specific form of the material mode of speech rather than some other form. However, even if I am right, this does not reduce the value of Carnap's method but, in my opinion, rather enhances it, since it suffices to show, in order to exhibit the "pseudo"-character of a given formulation, that this formulation is *transposed,* though not necessarily *material.*

But before we proceed to the exposition of Carnap's views on this topic and our criticism of them, it is neccesary to be somewhat more precise than we were so far. First, the term 'transposed mode of speech' has to be explained. Carnap's own explanation–which, he insists, is not meant to be an exact definition–is:

> By a transposed mode of speech we mean one in which, in order to assert something about an object *a*, something corresponding is asserted about an object *b* which stands in a certain relation to the object *a* (*LSL* 308).

It is obvious why Carnap is so cautious about this characterization. Too many expressions that occur in it are either vague or indefinite (or both) to a rather high degree. This holds not only for the deliberately vague 'corresponding' and the deliberately indefinite 'certain' but also, perhaps less deliberately so, for 'to assert something about an object'. (I am not even sure whether the term 'assert' is to be taken very seriously. It is surely worthwhile to extend the analysis of transposed modes of speech also to speech-acts other than assertions, e.g. to questions, commands, etc. Carnap's choice of 'assert' is due, of course, to his customary self-restriction to the treatment of the assertive aspects of language.) But, even taking all this into account, I find it difficult to interpret these terms in such a way that every metaphor will turn out to be an expression in the transposed mode of speech, as Carnap claims in the sentence immediately following the quoted characterization. I think that the sentence 'I am dead' (for 'I am very tired') would commonly be regarded as a metaphor. I cannot see what is the object *b* about which something is asserted in this sentence, when I am using it, in order to assert something about the object *a,* which is, in this case, obviously myself. Or is perhaps identity included in the range of indefiniteness of 'certain'? This, I must say, seems to me extremely unlikely.

Let us then start afresh. What Carnap wants to put his fingers on is clearly the fact that not all expressions are always used by all people in a way which is standard, by some criterion, for a certain class to which these expressions belong. To illustrate: Most English sentences of the form '. . . is ——' (with a proper name instead of '. . .' and an adjective instead of '——') are used most of the time by most people so as to convey to the receiver (listener or reader) that the object denoted by the proper name substituting ' . . . ' has the property (or quality, or character) denoted by the adjective substituting '——'. If we are ready to regard this usage as *standard,* then divergent usages are *non-standard.* When using 'John is clever' in order to convey that John is dull—for instance, when speaking "ironically"—this usage is non-standard. When using 'John is dead' in order to convey that John is beyond his apex in creative work—i.e., when speaking "metaphorically"—this usage is non-standard. (This is true, of course, only if we consider being-dead as *the* (only) character denoted by 'dead'. To be a metaphor is relative to a set of semantic rules. This needs further expansion, which will, however, not be undertaken here.)

On the other hand, when someone is using 'John is popular' in order to convey that John is popular or, more cumbrously, that John has the property of being popular, his usage is standard. But is it? Is being-popular a property (or quality, or character) at all? This question, of course, is itself a likely candidate for turning out to be a pseudo-question or, at least, a "verbal issue." I do not know of any sufficiently standard usage of 'property' for which this question could be decided one way or the other. The point is, however, that being-popular and being-clever are sufficiently different to necessitate some difference in terminology, perhaps best by adding some qualifying adjective to 'property'. This difference can be roughly put in the following way: If someone is clever at t_0, he will be so at t_1, with $t_1 > t_0$, unless some "changes" occurred in him, whereas someone may be popular at t_0 and cease to be so at t_1, with no changes having occurred in him. (That the term 'changes' begs the question, at least partly, is obvious. It is believed, however, that enough meat is left in the preceding statement to justify the introduction of a discriminating terminology—leaving a fuller justification for deeper investigation.) One might perhaps decide to use the qualifier 'categorical' for properties of the "clever"-type and 'relational' for properties of the "popular"-type.— The situation can be described also, and perhaps better, in the following way: 'John is popular' and 'Many people like John, and many more like him than either dislike or are indifferent to him' (cf. SME 33) can be anticipated to be sufficiently pragmatically equivalent; this anticipation could be checked, in principle, through a study of the linguistic behavior of English-speaking people. If this anticipation is right, the overtly relational form of the expanded statement can be taken to be a hint for the hidden relational character of the adjective 'popular'. No such reformulation is in view for 'John is clever' (at least not on an unsophisticated level—on a more sophisticated level, 'John is clever' may be taken to be pragmatically equivalent to 'John is more clever than most other people (in his community),' hence being-clever to be a relational property, too; indeed one could envisage John ceasing to be clever at t_1 through a sudden rise in the intelligence of the other people in his community between t_0 and t_1, without there having occurred any "interior" changes in John himself).

Should now careful observation of linguistic behavior lead to the establishment of the fact that most people are strongly disposed to expect that a sentence starting with 'John is' and ending with an adjective will end with an adjective denoting a categorical property—the psychological analysis of this disposition will again be dodged here—then the ordinary usages of 'John is popular' will be non-standard. This formulation sounds somewhat paradoxical. It seems as if at least a misuse of terminology is involved, when an "ordinary" usage is treated as "non-standard." But the pseudo-problem created here is, of course, nothing more than another illustration of the issue under discussion. A sentence of the form 'A certain ordinary usage is non-standard' looks as if by it the property of non-standardness is assigned to usages that have already the property of ordinariness, creating thereby the feeling of self-contradiction. But the term 'non-standard' is a relational term involving a certain class of sentences to which the treated sentence belongs. And no contradiction is involved in saying that an ordinary usage of a given sentence is extraordinary (or non-standard) for the members of a given sentence-class, to which this sentence belongs.

Non-standard usages serve as a constant and obvious source for failures in communication (though they may, and indeed often do, serve as a source for especially successful communication, if this peculiar effect is judiciously anticipated), but it seems that only non-standard usages of the second kind are philosophically dangerous. The fact that a given sentence may, within a specific context, be used differently from its standard usage is too well known to create any theoretical troubles. But the fact that even the *ordinary* usages of some sentences should be non-standard does not seem to be as generally recognized by the language theoreticians and, consequently, constitutes a fertile breeding ground for pseudo-problems.

I now propose to christen those sentences whose ordinary usage is non-standard (with respect to a certain sentence-class, to be determined on a pragmatic basis) *sentences in the transposed mode of speech.* This is still not an exact definition but is, I hope, more exact and helpful than Carnap's characterization. I also hope that Carnap will agree that my characterization is an adequate expansion of his intention. Should this hope turn out to be unwarranted, some other definiendum for the above-given definiens will have to be found. Tentatively, I shall proceed as if my proposed usage is adequate to Carnap's intentions.

But whether this characterization is adequate for Carnap's intentions or not, it seems to me that it coincides almost completely with the intentions of Gilbert Ryle when he introduced his term 'systematically misleading expressions'. This does not mean that I agree with the way Ryle himself characterizes these expressions. On the contrary, I think that his own characterization is not very helpful and is itself misleading to a degree, though not systematically so.

Let us first notice that Ryle talks about 'systematically misleading *expressions*', where 'expression' is used "to cover single words, phrases, and sentences" (SME 14). However, when Ryle gets to characterize these expressions, he talks in terms of being "couched in a syntactical form improper to the facts recorded" (SME 14), a formulation which is proper only for statements, i.e. sentences in the indicative, and even only for true statements. It seems therefore that what Ryle was up to was primarily a characterization of systematically misleading sentences (or perhaps statements) and only on this basis also of other kinds of expressions that are systematically misleading, though he nowhere gives us this secondary characterization. At any rate, I shall deal only with systematically misleading *sentences,* and the claim I made before that my characterization of sentences in the transposed mode of speech is more or less identical, in spirit if not in words, with the one given by Ryle is meant to hold with this restriction.

Let me quote in full the passages, in which Ryle introduces his conception of systematically misleading expressions:

The gist of what I want to establish is this. There are many expressions which occur in non-philosophical discourse which, though they are perfectly clearly understood by those who use them and those who hear or see them, are nevertheless couched in grammatical or syntactical forms which are in a demonstrable way *improper* to the states of affairs which they record (or the alleged states of affairs which they profess to record). Such expressions can be reformulated and for philosophy but not for non-philosophical discourse must be reformulated into expressions of which the syntactical form is proper to the facts recorded (or the facts alleged to be recorded) . . . When an expression is of such a syntactical form that it is improper to the fact recorded, it is systematically misleading in that it naturally suggests to some people—though not to 'ordinary' people—that the state of affairs recorded is quite a different sort of state of affairs from what it in fact is.

. . . expressions . . . which occur and occur perfectly satisfactorily in ordinary discourse, but which are, I argue, *systematically misleading,* that is to say, that they are couched in a syntactical form improper to the facts recorded and proper to facts of quite another logical form than the facts recorded (. . . And when I call a statement 'systematically misleading' I shall not mean that it is false, and certainly not that it is senseless. By 'systematically' I mean that all expressions of that grammatical form would be misleading in the same way and for the same reason.) (SME 13-15)

Ryle's talk of the "logical form" of facts and of syntactical forms being proper and improper to the facts might cause the impression that being systematically misleading is for him a semantical property of certain classes of sentences, and therefore quite different from our conception of sentences in the transposed mode of speech. But Ryle himself voices some misgivings about "what makes an expression formally proper to a fact" (SME 34). In spite of his scruples, Ryle was not ready at that time—though he might be so today—to repudiate the whole notion of the logical form of facts and was satisfied with stating his view

that the propriety of grammatical to logical forms is more nearly conventional than natural though I do not suppose it to be the effect of whim or of deliberate plan (SME 34).

That the semantic characterization of systematic misleadingness is not to be taken too seriously seems also to follow from the passage, already quoted, in which the term 'systematically misleading' is justified

in that it naturally suggests to some people—though not to 'ordinary' people—that the state of affairs recorded is quite a different sort of state of affairs from that which it in fact is (SME 14).

If we take *this* passage seriously—and I would prefer to do just that—then it seems that the whole talk about "logical form of fact" and "propriety" to these forms should better be completely forgotten and systematic misleadingness directly and non-misleadingly characterized in terms of what expressions exhibiting this feature "naturally suggest" to people, as I tried to do with respect to sentences in the transposed mode of speech. Should Ryle be ready to accept this interpretation, then my claim that there is an essential coincidence between these two terms would be vindicated.

There are still a few more minor points where I would disagree with

Ryle. I think that sentences in the transposed mode of speech do sometimes mislead also "ordinary" people, hence do not always "occur perfectly satisfactorily in ordinary discourse" —the child looking for the equator, having probably been misled by sentences of this type—though the problems created by such misunderstandings will usually be of a rather harmless character. (This much, however, seems to be admitted by Ryle himself when he qualifies his contention, that the non-philosophical author of systematically misleading expressions is not ignorant or doubtful of the nature of the state of affairs which his expression recorded, by a parenthesized "save in a special class of cases" (SME 17).) Ryle is still essentially right when he claims that only people professionally engaged with theorizing and generalizing about language are apt to be seriously misled by these sentences to a degree that whole theories might be created by them in order to solve pseudo-problems generated by their own shortsighted generalizations.

Carnap and Ryle both clearly see the important role played by sentences in the transposed mode of speech, or systematically misleading expressions, in the creation of philosophical pseudo-problems. But though Ryle displayed great ingenuity and acute insight into the workings of ordinary language in his classification of systematically misleading expressions into quasi-ontological statements, quasi-platonic statements, quasi-descriptive sentences, quasi-referential 'the'-sentences, etc., and in providing convincing illustrations of these various transposed modes of speech, he did not succeed in crystalizing what seems to be the philosophically most interesting class of sentences in this mode of speech, i.e. the sentences in *the material mode of speech*, though he came on occasion (SME 19) very close to this discovery.

If I had to point out what I regard as the greatest single achievement of Logical Empiricism (and of Analytical Philosophy in general), I would not hesitate to declare that this greatest achievement consists in establishing and corroborating the thesis that many, if not most, philosophical controversies are not, as they are commonly regarded by participants and onlookers alike, theoretical disagreements on questions of fact (of a scientific, or ethical, or aesthetical, or . . . nature) but rather disagreements (whose exact nature will be discussed later on) on the kind of linguistic framework to be preferably used in a certain context and for a certain purpose. That it took so long to develop this thesis and that so many thinkers are still so reluctant to accept it, is easily explained by the fact that philosophers, like scientists, ordinarily use the indicative mood in their sentences and that the standard use of this mood—and the one adopted almost unexceptionally by scientists in their scientific writings—is that of making statements about the entities denoted by their subjects, or so at least one was accustomed to assume unquestioningly until very recently.

If one philosopher of mathematics writes that

(1) Numbers are classes of classes of things

and another that

(2) Numbers belong to a special primitive kind of objects (cf. *LSL* 300), then these sentences look very much like contrary statements of which at most one can be true. But looking upon the controversy of these philosophers in this way is perhaps unkind to them. No scientifically acceptable method is in view by which this controversy could be decided, if the dispute is taken to be about the ontological status of numbers. It might perhaps be kinder to interpret their intentions, when using these sentences, not as making assertions but rather as making proposals to look upon numbers as classes of classes of things or as objects of a special primitive kind, respectively. Putting the situation this way would, however, be of little help, since the reader's reaction would probably be: "What do you mean by *proposing to regard* numbers as classes of classes? Either this is what they are, then your proposal is superfluous, or they are something else, then your proposal is preposterous." In any case, one would be led back to an investigation of what numbers "really" are, an attempt of whose futility we convinced ourselves before.

It is at this stage that Carnap's great insight comes to our help. Uses of the sentences (1) and (2) are still interpreted as proposals and not as assertions, but not as proposals to regard certain entities as belonging to the one or the other category of entities, but rather as proposals to construct (or use) a language in which certain expressions belong to the one or the other category of expressions. More specifically, (1) is interpreted as being used for proposing to construct (or for suggesting to use) a language-system in which numerical expressions are class-expressions of the second level, (2) for proposing to construct a language-system in which numerical expressions are expressions of the zero-level and of a special sort. Under this interpretation, sentences (1) and (2) are treated as being formulated in a special kind of transposed mode of speech, namely in the *material mode of speech.* Though they look like ordinary sentences dealing with certain objects treated in the object-language, Carnap insists that it is more profitable to regard them as *pseudo-object sentences.* Their "true" character is revealed by putting them into the *formal mode of speech.*

(1a) Numerical expressions are class-expressions of the second level

and

(2a) Numerical expressions are expressions of the zero-level

are nice syntactical sentences in the metalanguage of . . . Well, of what object-language exactly? Here we come to the major point of the reformulation: it forces us to relativize these formulations with respect to some object-language, already in existence or to be constructed. Without such a relativization, formulations (1a) and (2a) are just incomplete, whether their uses are interpreted as assertions or suggestions. What looked before as a grim disagreement about facts, the grimmer since no way of coming to terms on these "facts" was in view, becomes now a disagreement about which language-system is to be preferably used. This disagreement need not be less intense for that shift, but the outlook for coming to terms is not so hopeless any more.

So far, we described Carnap's insight as involving a double reinterpretation of certain sentences: their apparent use for *making assertions* is reinterpreted as being one for *making suggestions,* and their apparent subject-matter is shifted from that of the objects belonging to the universe of discourse of the object-language, their properties and relations, to that of the designations of these objects, properties, and relations, and *their* properties and relations. So far, we stressed rather the first shift, involving the reinterpretation of many philosophical disagreements as being of a practical rather than of a theoretical nature. This point should, however, not be overstressed. Though a sentence like (1), whose use, if standard, would have been that of making assertions about certain objects, might be used for making suggestions about the construction of a certain language-system in which numerical expressions will belong with a certain syntactical category, this is by no means the only obvious interpretation, under which the character of this sentence will be changed from a philosophical pseudo-thesis to something more interesting. At least two other interpretations are in view. Under both, the sentence is assumed to be used for making assertions; the asserted statements, however, are rather different. The first interpretation, already mentioned in *LSL,* would transform (1) and (1a) into

(1b) There is a language-system in which numerical expressions are class-expressions of the second level,

the second interpretation would result in

(1c) It is fruitful and expedient to construct a language-system in which numerical expressions are class-expressions of the second level

or perhaps rather in

(1d) It is more fruitful and expedient (for certain purposes) to work with a language-system in which numerical expressions are class-expressions of the second level than with differently constructed language-systems.

There is of course an enormous difference between these interpretations.

(1b) is an innocuous and almost trivial statement that nobody would want to dispute. Its rival statement

(2b) There is a language-system in which numerical expressions are expressions of the zero level and of a special sort

would turn out to be equally innocuous and trivial, completely blunting the point of the original dispute. Under the second interpretaion, however, and especially for its second variant, we would get as the counterpart of (1d) the statement

(2d) It is more fruitful and expedient (for certain purposes) to work with a language-system in which numerical expressions are expressions of the zero level and of a special sort than with differently constructed language-systems,

a statement that may or may not contradict (1d), depending upon the exact meaning of the parenthesized clause 'for certain purposes'. Should the proponents of (1d) and (2d) agree that the purposes are the same, a genuine theoretical disagreement would exist between them, though *toto coelo* different from the theoretical disagreement that seemed to exist between them before this analysis. Instead of a dispute about the intrinsic character of certain spurious entities, with no indication in view on the kind of scientifically acceptable evidence that might be relevant for deciding between the rival theses, we now have a dispute about the relative merits of two language-systems, an interesting affair, difficult but certainly not hopeless. Though there exist no generally accepted criteria for the comparison of two language-systems—and here lies an important task for present-day methodology—one can easily imagine conditions under which a dispute of this kind could be definitely settled.

For our illustrative sentences (1) and (2), three interpretations have been discussed here altogether. As a matter of fact, Carnap himself mentioned in *LSL* (299) *eight* different interpretations of sentences in the material mode of speech. As these are only variants of the first two interpretations discussed here, there is no need to go into further details, for our purposes. It should, however, be noticed that our third interpretation, in either of its variants (c) and (d), is not mentioned in *LSL* though it appears in essence in the much later publication ESO. In a sense, this interpretation is only a variant of that in terms of proposals and one may insist—rightfully, I think—that discussing the utility of a proposal is essentially the same as discussing the truth of the assertion that this proposal is useful. This would confirm my contention, at which I hinted above, that out of the various advantages, which Carnap claims for the translation of controversial philosophical theses from the material into the formal mode of speech, that of forcing the participants to clarify whether they intended to make an assertion or a suggestion is probably of minor importance. The decisive advantage is in the transition from "ontological" disputes to methodological controversies.

When I mentioned just now the formal mode of speech, I was still talking the language of *LSL*. It should be noticed, however, that the translation of (1) into (1c) or (1d) is not, strictly speaking, a translation into the formal mode of speech, since (1c) and (1d) do not deal with purely syntactical properties of linguistic entities but rather with their pragmatical properties. Under this interpretation, (1) is not a *quasi-syntactical* but rather a *quasi-pragmatical sentence*.[15] This way of putting the situation transcends, of course, the lines of thinking adopted by Carnap in *LSL*. There, it is well known, Carnap made great efforts to show that it is not necessary, for philosophical discussions, to go beyond syntax. This attitude makes it understandable why our third interpretation does not occur as such in *LSL*. As soon, however, as one is ready to accept semantics and pragmatics as fields standing on a par with logical syntax —and Carnap was ready to do this at the time the English edition of *LSL* was published—we have much greater freedom in the interpretation of pseudo-object sentences, and there can be no doubt that our third interpretation, for instance, is rhetorically superior to the others; it does neither transform a seemingly theoretical controversy into a pair of theoretical assertions which do not contradict each other at all—an interpretation that might well look as an affront to the intelligence of the disputants—nor into a disagreement on a practical issue—an interpretation which involves a loss of prestige, in another sense—but rather into a different theoretical controversy, which is both real and interesting.

I am again pretty much convinced that Carnap would now agree to all this. I also think that he would now be ready to reformulate some of the statements he made in *LSL* on traditional philosophical controversies in a way which would be both less offensive and more correct. I believe, for instance, that he would no longer want to regard

> the controversy between positivism and realism . . . [as] an idle dispute about pseudo-theses which owes its origin entirely to the use of the material mode of speech (*LSL* 301).

Though certain theses maintained by positivists, such as

(3) A *thing* is a complex of sense-data,

and the corresponding theses maintained by realists, such as

(4) A *thing* is a complex of atoms,

are systematically misleading, being formulated as pseudo-object sentences, and may hence be characterized, in a sense, as pseudo-theses, they

[15]Cf. Charles W. Morris, *Foundations of the Theory of Signs, International Encyclopedia of Unified Science,* I, no. 2 (Chicago, 1938), esp. 40-41.

can be transformed, by translation into what we might call the *pragmatical mode of speech,* to the following antithetical statements

(3d) It is preferable to use as a language of science a phenomenological language (in which sentences containing thing-designations are reducible to a class of sentences containing only sense-data descriptions)

and

(4d) It is preferable to use as a language of science a physicalistic language (in which sentences about things are reducible to a class of sentences containing space-time coordinates and certain descriptive functors),

creating thereby a dispute which is by no means idle and in which, as a matter of fact, Carnap himself actively participated (TM).

It is worthwhile to see how the method of pseudo-object sentences fared in Carnap's later publications, especially in ESO. The distinction there made between *internal* and *external questions* is somewhat related to that between the material and the formal (or pragmatical) mode of speech. Internal existence questions, such as questions as to the existence of numbers in general, of prime numbers, of prime numbers greater than one trillion, of prime number twins greater than one trillion, or of elephants, are in any case philosophically uninteresting, since the answers to such questions are to be obtained either by ordinary scientific methods, as used in the empirical sciences, or by logical proof—trivial in the case of numbers, less trivial in the case of prime numbers, and far from trivial in the case of prime number twins. Of philosophical interest is only the external question of the acceptability of the linguistic framework for, say, natural numbers. The traditional opinion seems to have been that this framework is acceptable if and only if natural numbers "exist," above and beyond any linguistic framework. Since this traditional approach leads nowhere, the only way out of this impasse is, according to Carnap, to interpret the seemingly theoretical external question of the existence of numbers as a practical question of the acceptance of certain linguistic forms to be solved by decision, which "is not in need of a theoretical justification (except with respect to expedience and fruitfulness)" (ESO 519).

Later on (ESO 521), Carnap proposes to replace alleged ontological questions of the existence of abstract entities in general by the question whether the use of certain abstract linguistic forms is expedient and fruitful for certain purposes. He does not state, however, that he proposes the latter question as a possible interpretation or reformulation of the original ontological question. The difference is, of course, very slight and probably no more than a matter of politeness and skill in controversy. I still believe that Carnap's position would be practically greatly strengthened if he were to express his readiness to interpret some or all ontological theses as theoretical theses about the expediency of the corresponding linguistic frameworks. It would, of course, be unduly optimistic to assume that many adherents of the original ontological theses would accept Carnap's reinterpretation as congenial.

III

So far, the two topics I selected from *LSL* for evaluation in this paper have been completely unrelated. I propose to discuss now an issue which is perhaps basic for Carnap's philosophy in general and which combines these topics, i.e., the applicability to natural languages of a terminological framework originally designed for language-systems and the method of transposed modes of speech.

The question that will be raised here is very simple and straightforward: Granted that for a given pair of language-systems, L_1 and L_2, such that L_2 is the syntax-language of L_1, each sentence of the object-language L_1 is either a real object-sentence or a pseudo-object-sentence (though these properties need not be definite so that there might not exist a method by which the specific character of any given sentence could be decided), what is the exact balance of gains and losses that results from a direct application of this dichotomy to ordinary languages?

It is well known that analogous questions arise with respect to other dichotomies such as object-language versus metalanguage, descriptive versus logical, synthetic versus analytic,[16] etc., and it is obvious that all these questions are methodologically strongly interconnected. To these one may add the pair introduced by Carnap in ESO, viz. internal versus external. All these dichotomies may be regarded, loosely speaking, as ramifications of the age-old dichotomy, *reality versus language*.

That adherence to this dichotomic conceptual framework is valuable at least as a first approximation is clear from the simple fact that common sense adheres to it and fares pretty well with it. The point is, therefore, whether this attitude will fare well enough in matters where a first approximation is not sufficient, e.g. in philosophical discussions. Should one even there insist on applying these dichotomies and explaining obvious non-conformities as residual effects due to mixtures, impurities, or noise (in the communication-theoretical sense), or should one, for this purpose, replace the whole methodological framework by a new and probably very complex one?

Assume, to give a rather simple-minded illustration, that John hears Bill utter the sentence, "All ravens are black," and that circumstances are such that there are good reasons to believe that this utterance was meant

[16] Since this will be discussed elsewhere in this volume, no references will be given here.

to be an assertion. Is it now fruitful for John to require from Bill to make clear whether his statement was meant to be analytic or synthetic by explicitly stating whether in his, i.e. in Bill's, usage the meaning of 'raven', which in the everday language in general is rather vague, is such that it entails 'black' or not and, if he did not think of it before in this light, to make up his mind on this point?[17] And should Bill regard John's request as a really helpful one and try to comply with it? Will communication be improved by such procedures? (It is clear that the request "State your meaning-postulates!"—which is, of course, nothing but a highly refined version of the old "Define your terms!"—will be made and taken seriously only if the issue is serious enough; extending this request to everyday situations would annihilate communication.)

Assume, now, that Bill replies to John's suggestion as follows: "Well, I understand your point completely. I know from my studies in the semantics of language-systems how important the distinction is between statements whose truth is analytic and those whose truth is synthetic. However, with regard to the statement, "All ravens are black," I made just now I cannot see why I should commit myself. You see, I made this statement because you asked me a minute ago whether the bird we both saw sitting on the nearby tree was not a raven. You will probably recall that the bird had some red plumage on its neck. My statement was meant to indicate that the bird we saw could not have been a raven. I assume that the aim of this statement has been achieved. What point is there now in committing myself as to the *character* of this statement? And what would you gain even if I committed myself? You are hardly interested in the character of the sentence, "All ravens are black," according to *my* usage, but rather in its character according to the *general* usage and if this usage is vague as to whether 'black' is entailed by 'raven', then this is all there is to be said about it and the analytic-synthetic dichotomy is simply inapplicable. The ordinary meaning of 'raven' is vague and being-black lies within its region of vagueness, though being-a-bird does not lie within that region, or at most only at its fringes so that the sentence, "All ravens are birds," is analytic according to the general usage, at any rate much more analytic than the sentence, "All ravens are black," if you allow me to express myself this way. A better way of expressing this situation would avoid the semantical term 'analytic' altogether and make use of some corresponding pragmatical term, say Quine's 'central'. We could then say that the sentence, "All ravens are birds," occupies a much more central position in the system of sentences which are generally believed to be true

[17]For the following discussion, see R. Carnap, "Meaning Postulates," *Philosophical Studies* III (1952), 65-73, esp. 68.

than the sentence, "All ravens are black," though this sentence is itself pretty central, too. The partial indefiniteness of meaning of the predicate 'raven', notice well, does not interfere at all, for almost all practical purposes, with successful communication in which this predicate is used. My conclusion is, then, that though the customary analytic-synthetic dualism is helpful enough as a first approximation even for the treatment of ordinary languages, this instrument is not fine enough for a higher degree of approximation. To leave it at the stage I mentioned, i.e. to say that common usage is too vague to allow for an application of this dichotomy, is surely not very fruitful, and to state one's meaning postulates is beside the point. What we need is a more elaborate methodological framework in which positive things can be said even of only partially meaning-determined expressions. I admit that no such framework exists so that for the time being we shall have to go along with the usual one as far as it goes, but I am afraid that it does not go far enough for a really interesting discussion of philosophically important questions. By the way, whatever I said so far for the analytic-synthetic dichotomy holds also, and for exactly the same reasons, for the logical-descriptive, external-internal, object-language-metalanguage dichotomies and for the determination of the synonymy of two expressions in ordinary language. When I say "Five is a prime number," I am not only talking about the number five, and when I say "Five is a number," I am not only talking, though in a transposed way, about the number-word 'five'. To put it this way may be good enough as a first approximation but it is far from an exact description of the whole situation. In whatever I say, both reality and language are involved, though sometimes the one and sometimes the other component may be practically neglected. To be more exact: the communicational process is a unity whose separation into a reality and a language component is an artifice which is immensely helpful in almost all practical situations but which nevertheless may break down under certain critical circumstances. Any attempt to enforce this separation beyond certain limits must lead to unsatisfactory formulations. I admit, however, that I have no conceptual framework ready in which to treat these critical situations."

I am afraid that Carnap would regard Bill's long speech—with which I am in considerable sympathy, as the reader has probably guessed—as just another embodiment of philosophical obscurantism. Indeed, this attitude is, at least for the time being, wholly negative. The fruitful applicability of the customary dichotomic methodological terminology to sophisticated theoretical issues is denied beyond a first approximation but nothing is proposed instead. There is even a flair of paradoxality in this denial itself since it is formulated in ordinary language, in which the reality-language dualism is so firmly rooted. By refusing to commit yourself, Carnap might argue, you simply put yourself outside of rational argumentation altogether. Ordinary logic, as you admit, is not applicable to expressions whose meaning is only partly determined, but there is no other logic in existence. On which basis shall we then go along discussing these issues?

It is very difficult to answer these objections. I shall not try to do it here, if only for lack of space. Let me then remark only this. Carnap put his method of the material mode of speech to a most powerful use in pointing out the pseudo-character of many traditional philosophical disputes. I do not think that it would do much good to the adherents of the philosophical theses under discussion to seek refuge from this criticism by claiming that this method is too crude to handle their theses. If they are right, then their theses lie already in that region where the separation of reality from language is no longer operational. But in this case the significance of these theses becomes totally blurred, since no tools are known of rationally manipulating statements in this region. Ontology might be saved from becoming either a collection of platitudinous pseudo-object statements or a set of theses about the expediency of certain linguistic frameworks (or a set of proposals to use certain linguistic frameworks) but only to become a self-defeating attempt to say something significant about pure reality at a level of sophistication where this simply cannot be done any more.

This last section might contain too much loose talk for Carnap to want to react to it. But he still owes us a general statement about the methods of explicating philosophically important concepts for ordinary languages. I hope that my last remarks, with all their crudeness and indecisiveness, will induce him to give us this statement.

YEHOSHUA BAR-HILLEL

HEBREW UNIVERSITY
JERUSALEM, ISRAEL

* (Added in January, 1962) In view of the fact that close to eight years have passed since the present paper was submitted to the editor, the following supplementary remarks, which, for obvious reasons, have been kept at a minimum, should be of help:

1. In the meantime, I saw an early version of Carnap's Reply and tend to agree almost completely with its content. However, in order not to detract from its value, no changes were made in the paper.

2. The promise I made in the text (pp. 523-524) to which Footnote 5 belongs was fulfilled in the paper mentioned in Footnote 13. I would like to acknowledge that a good part of Noam Chomsky's defence of Harris' position, undertaken in "Logical Syntax and Semantics: Their Linguistic Relevance," *Language* XXXI (1955), 36-45, was well taken and that many more linguistic facts than I had originally thought of can be adequately described with the help of rules of formation. Among these facts belong, e.g., also those relating to the active-passive relationship. However, those formation rules which can handle these facts

are of a type which has only recently been analyzed and understood, a development in which my critique might have played some slight role. It is interesting that this novel type of formation rules has been called by Harris and Chomsky (and is now being called by everybody else) "rules of transformation," and the reader should beware of confusion. Cf. Zellig Harris, "Co-occurrence and Transformations in Linguistic Structure," *Language* XXXIII (1957), 283-340, and Noam Chomsky, *Syntactic Structures* ('s-Gravenhage, 1957). The last book is a living corroboration of the fact that the incredible complications of ordinary languages are no sufficient obstacle to the search for formal regularities in these languages (cf. above, p. 521).

3. For refreshingly new light on the issues discussed on pp. 526-527, above, see Paul Ziff, *Semantic Analysis* (Ithaca, N.Y., 1960).

4. For the issue discussed above under II, cf. also my recent paper, "A Prerequisite for Rational Philosophical Discussion," *Synthese* XII (1960), 328-332.

18

Nelson Goodman

THE SIGNIFICANCE OF *DER LOGISCHE AUFBAU DER WELT*

I. *Evil Days for the* Aufbau

THE *Aufbau* is a crystallization of much that is widely regarded as worst in 20th century philosophy. It is an anathema to anti-empirical metaphysicians and to alogical empiricists, to analytic Oxonians and to anti-analytic Bergsonians, to those who would exalt philosophy above the sciences and to those who would abolish philosophy in favor of the sciences. A good part of current polemical writing in philosophical journals is directed against views found in virulent form in the *Aufbau*. The *Aufbau* stands preëminent as a horrible example.

My purpose here is to survey and appraise the charges against the *Aufbau*, and to set forth some convictions concerning the significance of the work. This virtually amounts to the unpromising, but welcome, task of defending the *Aufbau* against almost everybody, including Carnap himself—indeed, including a succession of Carnaps who have belittled this early work for different reasons at different times in the twenty-six years since it was published. But I am more interested in the current atmosphere of opinion concerning the *Aufbau* than in what particular people have said at particular times; and my adversary, except where specifically named, is a composite figure encountered as often in conversation as in the journals.

II. *Phenomenalism and the* Aufbau

In place of the 'impressions' or "simple ideas' of 18th century British philosophy, Carnap based his system on total moments of experience—the *Elementarerlebnisse*—in order to begin as early as possible with what he regards as unanalyzed and unprocessed experience. The system is plainly phenomenalistic, and phenomenalism has been under heavy and incessant attack.

The most popular objection is that phenomenalism is *incompletable*. No full and adequate account of the objective and intersubjective world of the sciences can be given, it is contended, upon a purely phenomenalistic basis. Carnap's own first disavowal[1] of the *Aufbau* expressed the conviction that a phenomenalistic system, unlike a physicalistic one, could not be all-embracing for science; and perhaps nothing else he has ever written has found such widespread agreement.

The arguments commonly adduced to support the charge of the incompletability of phenomenalism cannot, in the nature of the case, be very cogent by themselves; for the thesis they are designed to prove is not precise enough, and there is available no developed body of theory within which a sound proof might be given. Proof that a complete system cannot be constructed on any phenomenalistic basis prerequires some precise delimitation of the class of phenomenalistic bases, a full statement of admissible methods of construction, and a clear conception of what constitutes completeness of the kind in question; and none of these requirements is easy to meet. Thus, for example, the argument that phenomenalism is incompletable because the infinite world of mathematics and the sciences cannot be accounted for upon a finite basis has at first sight the simple force of the statement that an infinite number of things cannot be made out of a finite number. But if we understand that the question is rather whether we can interpret in terms of statements about a finite number of entities all indispensable statements that *prima facie* refer to an infinite number of entities, the matter cannot be settled so easily.

On the other hand, the thesis that phenomenalism is incompletable hardly needs proof. Surely no complete system will be offered within any foreseeable length of time; and no other means of proving the possibility of completion is in prospect. The task of construction is so formidable, and the tendency to regard it as hopeless is so strong, that the presumption is all against the claim that any phenomenalistic system—or for that matter any system with a very narrow basis—is completable. Even without proof or clarification of the thesis that phenomenalism is incompletable, one is justified in accepting this thesis at least until the opposite is rendered more credible.

But if the thesis—proven or unproven—is accepted, what conclusion can be drawn from it? Usually phenomenalism is taken to be utterly discredited once its incompletability is acknowledged. It is just this step in the argument—a step commonly passed over as obvious—that I want to challenge. I am ready to maintain that the value of efforts to construct a system on a phenomenalistic or any other narrow basis is very little affected by whether or not the system can be completed. Euclid's geometry is not robbed of value by the fact that the circle cannot be squared

[1]In "Die physikalische Sprache als Universalsprache der Wissenschaft," *Erkenntnis*, II (1931), 432-465.

by Euclidean means. Indeed, acceptance prior to Euclid of the impossibility of squaring the circle with compass and straight-edge would not in the least have diminished the importance of developing Euclidean geometry; and it would not, I think, have been ground for turning attention solely to the discussion of the adequacy of various bases or to the development of geometry on a basis broader than Euclid's. Moreover, propositions affirming the Euclidean insolubility of certain problems could hardly have been precisely formulated or have been capable of proof except against the background of elaborated, even if incompletable, mathematical systems. But my point is not just that it was psychologically necessary or helpful to work in this way. What is accomplished in the incompletable system has permanent value when incorporated into a fuller system. Indeed after a system like Euclid's has been developed as far as possible, questions concerning what can be accomplished with even fewer means (e.g. without a straight edge or without a given postulate) often still have interest.

The analogy, I take, is transparent. Incompletability by itself is no decisive objection against the attempt to build a system on a phenomenalistic basis. Only by positive efforts with severely restricted means can we make any progress in construction; only so can we discern the exact limitations of a basis and the exact supplementation needed. And what we achieve may be retained in an expanded system, and will help solve parallel problems in alternative systems. Carnap's suggestion that his single chosen primitive might be enough for a complete system was indeed rash and untenable. But his mistake here was no worse than that of people who thought Euclid's basis enough for a complete plane geometry. The incompletability of the system of the *Aufbau* or of phenomenalism in general is not a very damaging charge.

Incompletability is not the only count urged against phenomenalism. Sometimes the objection is rather that a phenomenalistic system, whether completable or not, is epistemologically false: that it misrepresents the cognitive process. Phenomenal events or qualities, it is held, are not the original elements of knowledge but are products of an artificial and highly sophisticated analysis, so that a phenomenalistic system gives a highly distorted picture of actual cognition.

Any such view rests on the premise that the question "What are the original elements in knowledge?" is a clear and answerable one. And the assumption remains uncontested so long as we are dominated by the tradition that there is a sharp dichotomy between the given and the interpretation put upon it—so long as we picture the knower as a machine that is fed experience in certain lumps and proceeds to grind these up and reunite them in various ways. But I do not think this view of the matter will stand very close scrutiny. For the question in what units experience is actually given seems to amount to the question what is the real organization of experience before any cognitive organization takes place; and this, in turn, seems to ask for a description of cognitively unorganized experience. But any description itself effects, so to speak, a cognitive organization; and apart from a description, it is hard to see what organization can be. The search for the original given is sometimes envisaged as an interrogation in which I am first asked what I just saw. I reply "I saw the worst criminal alive today," but my questioner complains that I am making too many judgments about what I saw; he wants me to tell him exactly what I could see and nothing more. As he continues to press me, I reply successively: "I saw a man", "I saw a human-looking animal", "I saw a moving object", "I saw such-and-such a configuration of color patches". But if my questioner is consistent and persistent, none of these replies—or any other I can give him—will satisfy him; for all answers describe my experience in words and so impose on it some organization or interpretation. What he is covertly demanding is that I describe what I saw without describing it. All my answers may be true descriptions of what I saw, but no description can be a satisfactory answer to the question what I *merely* saw;[2] for the question is a bogus one.

But obviously I cannot discuss the whole question of epistemological priority very thoroughly here. And there is no need. For the value and validity of a constructional system do not depend upon the epistemological primacy of the elements it starts from, however one may conceive such primacy to be determined. The old idea that philosophy aims at writing the story of the cognitive process had already been abandoned in the *Aufbau.* Carnap warned that his constructions are intended to preserve only the 'logical value' not the 'epistemological value' of the terms defined, and stated expressly that his system is not to be regarded as a portrayal of the process of acquiring knowledge. Nevertheless, he considered the system to be a 'rational reconstruction' of that process, a demonstration of how the ideas dealt with 'could have been' derived from the original given; and for that reason, he bases his system on elements that are as close as possible to what he regards as the given. But it becomes almost immediately obvious that if we do not care whether steps in the system picture corresponding steps in cognition, neither do we care whether the system starts from what is originally given. The function of the system is not to portray the genesis—either actual or hypothetical—of ideas, but to exhibit interconnections between them. The consideration relevant in choosing elements for a

[2]The snares in the question whether some description describes an experience *just as* it is experienced have been discussed in my book *The Structure of Appearance,* hereinafter referred to as SA, Cambridge, Mass.: Harvard University Press, (1951), 103-106, and in Wittgenstein's *Philosophical Investigations* (Oxford: Basil Blackwell, 1953), 193-214.

system is thus not primacy in the cognitive process but serviceability as a basis for an economical, perspicuous and integrated system.

I shall have more to say on the nature and purpose of constructional systems as we proceed, especially in the following section; but the brief answer to the charge that phenomenalistic systems are false as pictures of the cognitive process is simply that such systems need not be true in this way. Carnap claims a diluted truth of this sort for his system, as he tentatively claims completability for it; but the system is not to be judged in terms of these needless and misleading claims.

A third and more considered line of attack upon phenomenalism is directed towards showing not that phenomenalistic systems are incompletable or false, but that they are disadvantageous—that the important purposes at hand can be better served by starting from a physicalistic basis. It is pointed out that even the most commonplace objects of daily experience are extraordinarily difficult to construct upon a phenomenalistic basis; that the *Elementarerlebnisse* or qualities or appearance-events from which a phenomenalistic system proceeds are unfamiliar units of discourse, elusive if not illusive, difficult to catch and identify; and that a system based upon such elements is an ingrown development of technical philosophy, remote from practical concerns or scientific discourse. In contrast, it is held, a physicalistic system begins with familiar and well-understood elements, is able to deal at once with the world of everyday experience, and much more readily yields the objects of the sciences.

This argument, with its appeal to the familiar, the practical, and the scientific is so overwhelming that those who spend time on phenomenalistic constructions are regarded as stubborn and old-fashioned crackpots who shut their eyes to the facts of life and science. Nevertheless, let us look at the argument more closely.

In the first place, one great advantage claimed for a physicalistic system is that it does not face the difficult and perhaps insoluble problem of constructing physical objects on the basis of phenomena. This is quite true. Likewise, it is true that if you simply use a double compass (a compass with another mounted on one leg) you can trisect any angle. And since a double compass is easy to obtain, and since the goal is to get angles trisected, isn't it impractical and quixotic to deny ourselves use of this instrument? If physical objects are hard to construct in terms of phenomena, why not begin with physical objects? Let's be clear, though, that in both cases we are not solving a problem but evading one. The difference, it will be claimed, is that in the case of geometry the choice is between two equally simple and ordinary bases, while in the shift from a phenomenalistic to a physicalistic system we are dropping an abstruse and elusive basis in favor of a plainly more comprehensible and familiar one. Thus the argument for physicalism here cannot be that it solves a problem that phenomenalism does not, but rather that it begins with a more acceptable basis and frees us of the need for bothering with a difficult and unimportant problem before we come to grips with the realm of everyday life and of science.

The comfortable, homey character of the physicalist's basis lasts only so long as he is arguing for his basis rather than trying to use it. Once he makes any serious beginning towards systematic construction, he quickly finds that ordinary things like tables, and chairs are much too gross, complicated, ill-assorted and scattered to serve his purpose; and while we are looking the other way, he slips in substitutes. In "Testability and Meaning," (hereafter referred to as T. & M.) for example, Carnap at first speaks of a 'thing-language' in which atomic sentences consist of observable predicates applied to ordinary things (III, p. 466). But a few pages later (IV, p. 9) he is speaking of "observable predicates of the thing-language attributed to perceived things of any kind or to space-time points". This last phrase makes a radical addition. Whether the space-time points in question are those of physics or are minimal perceptible regions, they are by no means the familiar things of everyday experience. What the physicalist and the phenomenalist both do is this: they begin informally with ordinary discourse and indicate in terms of it a set of entities that are quite different from ordinary things but possess a uniformity, simplicity and joint exhaustiveness that makes them serviceable as elements for a system. The physicalist does not, any more than the phenomenalist, take the usual objects of daily life as the basic elements of his system.

Moreover, there is a good deal of equivocation about the space-time points taken as elements by the physicalist. When he maintains that he is in a better position to construct the objects of science, the supposition is that his elements are the space-time points of mathematics and physics. But this cannot be the case; for he retains 'observable predicates'. Carnap gives (T. & M., IV, p. 9) as examples of admissible atomic statements: "This space-time point is warm" and "at this space-time point, is a solid object". Obviously no mathematical space-time point is warm, and at no such point is there any object that is solid or red or that has any other observable quality; observable qualities belong to objects of perceptible size. But if the elements called space-time points are perceptible regions, then we are faced with a good many of the problems—for example, the explication of imperceptible differences—that the physicalist sought to avoid. And his claim that his basis is adequate for constructing the objects of science no longer looks so plausible. The problem of deriving the objects of physics from such a basis is hardly less formidable than, and is in many ways not very different from, the problem of constructing ordinary objects from a strictly phenomenal basis; and there is no *prima facie* reason to suppose that the one is soluble if the other is not. The physicalist offers the argument that (T. & M., III, p. 467) "For every term in the physical language physicists know how to use it on the basis of their observations. Thus every such term is reducible to observable predicates . . . ;" but the phenomenalist has characteristically argued in exactly parallel fashion that "for every term that is used at all competently, the user knows how to use it on the basis of what appears to him, and thus every term is reducible to phenomenal predicates." If the former argument is good so is the latter; if the latter is bad so is the former. The serviceability of ordinary thing-language for constructing the realm of physics remains a totally unsupported claim.

If the problem of constructing the entities of physics from observable things is so troublesome, one might expect the physicalist to skip it as inessential—as he has already skipped the problem of constructing ordinary objects from phenomena—and to achieve a language adequate for physics by starting from the particles and predicates of physics itself. This would be consistent with the currently popular idea that the goal of all investigation is the prediction and control of nature;[3] but he never quite takes this step, for to do so would be to drop philosophy for physics. The physicalist and other constructionalists are trying to serve some purpose not served by physics and the other sciences; but they cannot formulate the difference very clearly, and often seem unaware of it.

Here a major and delicate question emerges. A good part of the dispute over the relative merits of different systematic bases arises from confusion as to pertinent standards. The criteria most often appealed to —such as epistemological primacy, and utility for the sciences—are clearly inappropriate; and just what are the requirements upon an acceptable basis for a philosophical system, as distinguished from a system of psychology or physics, is a neglected, important and exasperating problem. Luckily, it is beyond the scope of this paper.

In summary, then, the argument that phenomenalism is incompletable has no more weight against the system of the *Aufbau* than the argument that angles cannot be trisected with straight-edge and compass has against Euclidean geometry; and the argument that phenomenalism is epistemologically false has no more weight than the argument that Euclid's postulates are not fundamental self-evident truths. Moreover, the popular arguments for a physicalistic versus phenomenalistic system involve vacillation as to the physicalistic basis to be used, unsup-

[3]The recent dominance of this idea seems to me to have blocked any clear understanding of either philosophy or the sciences. But some relief is in sight. Psychologists have lately produced experimental evidence that monkeys will exert more effort out of sheer curiosity than for food. Satisfaction of curiosity may in time become almost as respectable a goal as satisfaction of hunger; and then we shall no longer have to justify astrophysics by what it may eventually do for the wheat crop.

ported claims concerning possible constructions, and tacit appeal to criteria that, applied consistently, would rule out physicalistic as well as phenomenalistic systems and reject all philosophical investigation in favor of the special sciences.

My aim, let me emphasize, is not to advocate phenomenalism as against physicalism, but only to show the weakness of the case against phenomenalism. Systems of both types may well prove to be valuable.

III. *Constructionalism and the* Aufbau

So far, I have considered only the opposition to phenomenalism in particular as distinct from the opposition to constructionalism in general. But there is also active opposition to constructionalism (or 'reductionism' as its enemies call it) of all varieties—not just to a certain choice of basis but to the very program of a systematic logical construction from any set of primitives.

The root of such opposition is, of course, the anti-intellectualism that finds forthright expression in Bergson. The complaint against all definition, analysis, and systematic description is that it employs static, abstract, and Procrustean concepts to construct a bloodless caricature of the rich and pulsating world of experience. Conceptualization, abstraction, symbolization are instruments of excision and dessication. This appears to be an attack less against one kind of philosophy than against philosophy in general as compared with poetry. Or, since poetry uses words and symbols and selects aspects, perhaps the protest is rather against all verbalization as contrasted with non-verbal living. In this extreme form, the position need not much concern us here; for we are considering the *Aufbau* as compared to other philosophical efforts, not as compared to a moonlight walk or a drunken brawl. Yet the basic anti-intellectualistic complaint that philosophy does not duplicate experience is worth noting; for it underlies many another objection to attempts at precision and systematization in philosophy.

The function of a constructional system is not to recreate experience but rather to map it. Though a map is derived from observations of a territory, the map lacks the contours, colors, sounds, smells, and life of the territory, and in size, shape, weight, temperature and most other respects may be about as much unlike what it maps as can well be imagined. It may even be very little like other equally good maps of the same territory. A map is schematic, selective, conventional, condensed, and uniform. And these characteristics are virtues rather than defects. The map not only summarizes, clarifies, and systematizes; it often discloses facts we could hardly learn immediately from our explorations. We may make larger, fuller, and more complicated maps or even three-dimensional models in order to record more information; but this is not always to the good. For when our map becomes as large and in all other respects the same as the territory mapped—and indeed long before this stage is reached—the purposes of a map are no longer served. There is no such thing as a completely unabridged map; for abridgment is intrinsic to mapmaking.

This, I think, suggests the answer not only to rampant anti-intellectualism but to many another objection against the abstractness, poverty, artificiality, and general unfaithfulness of constructional systems. Let no one complain that the turnpike is not red like the line on the map, that the dotted state boundaries on the map are not visible in the fields, or that the city we arrive at is not a round black dot. Let no one suppose that if a map made according to one scheme of projection is accurate then maps made according to alternative schemes are wrong. And let no one accuse the cartographer of merciless reductionism if his map fails to turn green in the spring.

The anti-intellectualist confronts us with a spurious dilemma. The choice is not between misrepresentation and meticulous reproduction. The relevant question about a system or a map is whether it is serviceable and accurate in the way intended.

Many contemporary philosophers are opposed not to analysis as such but to the use of logic and artificial terminology and to step-by-step construction. A system of formal definitions, the objection runs, raises irrelevant problems, is too rigid and precise, and is too insensitive to the subtle variations of ordinary use. A philosophic problem is considered to arise from lack of care in the use of ordinary language, and the recommended treatment consists simply of explaining in ordinary language the nature of the misuse or misunderstanding of use. The analyses offered as examples of this method are often much needed and highly illuminating. They are like directions that tell us how to go from the post office to the park without taking a wrong turn at the red barn. In general, we need ask such directions only when we are lost or puzzled, since we do most of our daily travelling quite efficiently without them. And good verbal directions, as compared with a map, have obvious virtues: they are in the vernacular, mention recognizable landmarks, and tell us without waste just what we immediately need to know.

But a map has its advantages, too. It is, indeed, in an artificial language, and has to be read and related to the terrain; but it is consistent, comprehensive, and connected. It may needlessly give us a good deal of information we already have well in mind; but it may also reveal unsuspected routes and lead us to rectify misconceptions that might otherwise have gone unquestioned. It gives an organized overall view that no set of verbal directions and no experience in travelling can provide unaided. Verbal directions may often be useful even when we have a map;

they may help us interpret the map or save us the trouble. But they do not supplant the map.

There are dangers in maps, of course. A map may be taken too literally or otherwise misread. But the map is not at fault if the user supposes that the numbering of the lines of longitude reflects a scale of metaphysical priority, or if disputes arise over whether a marking off by square miles or by minutes is more in keeping with reality.

We are still, admittedly, in a rather primitive stage of philosophical mapmaking; and no one is to be blamed for an inclination to trust skilled verbal directions as against new and imperfect maps. Nor is the reputation of cartography improved by elaborate maps drawn too hastily on the basis of too little exploration. Yet the opposition to the principles of constructionalism by the practitioners of verbal analysis has always surprised me; for I think there is no irreconcilable conflict of objectives or even of methods. Verbal analysis is a necessary preliminary and accompaniment of systematic construction, and deals with the same sphere of problems. For example, the verbal analyst may well concern himself with explaining the vague locution we use when we say that several things are 'all alike'; and he may well examine the difference between saying that a color is at a given place at a given time and saying that a color is at a given place *and* at a given time. The constructionalist dealing with qualities and particulars will likewise have to be clear on these points. The analyst, treating these as separate problems, may well miss the intriguing relationship between the two, while a systematic treatment shows them to be two cases of a single logical problem.[4] But verbal analysis and logical construction are complementary rather than incompatible. The constructionalist recognizes the anti-intellectualist as an arch enemy, but looks upon the verbal analyst as a valued and respected, if inexplicably hostile, ally.

Apart from entrenched philosophical positions, the opposition to constructionalism degenerates into greeting each proposed definition of a so-and-so as a such-and-such with the naive protest that a so-and-so is Not Merely a such-and-such but Something More. This betrays a simple failure to grasp what the constructionalist is doing. In defining a so-and-so as a such-and-such, he is not declaring that a so-and-so is nothing but a such-and-such. Carnap disclaimed any such idea by insisting that his definientia need have only the same extension as his definienda; and as my discussion above suggests, "$=_{Df}$" in a constructional definition is not to be read "is nothing more than" but rather in some such fashion as "is here to be mapped as." But the nature and import of a constructional definition now need to be examined more closely.

[4]For further explanation, see SA, 161-169.

IV. *Extensionalism, Definition, and the* Aufbau

Some critics of the *Aufbau* take issue primarily neither with its phenomenalistic orientation nor with constructionalism in general but with the particular conception of constructional method that the *Aufbau* sets forth and exemplifies.

The first such objection is against the extensionalism of the *Aufbau.* The only non-formal requirement there placed upon a constructional definition is that the definiendum and the definiens apply to exactly the same things, so that replacement of the one by the other in admissible contexts preserves truth value.[5] Against this, many critics—including the Carnap of today—argue that since such extensional identity does not guarantee sameness of meaning, some more stringent criterion must be adopted.

Let us grant the premise that extensional identity is not a sufficient condition for synonymy. This alone does not settle the main question. For what is at issue here is not a theory of meaning but a theory of constructional definition; and acceptance of a non-extensional criterion of synonymy does not carry with it adoption of a non-extensional criterion of constructional definition.

From what I have said in the preceding section it will be clear why I sharply disagree with contentions that a stronger requirement than extensional identity should be imposed on constructional definitions. This would mistake and defeat the primary function of a constructional system. That function, as I see it, is to exhibit a network of relationships obtaining in the subject-matter; and what is wanted therefore is simply a certain structural correspondence between the world of the system and the world of presystematic language.

Only in this way, as a 'structural description'[6] rather than as a book of synonyms or as a full-color portrait of reality, can we understand a system like that of the *Aufbau.* The extensional criterion for constructional definition, far from being too weak, is too strong. To require that the definientia be extensionally identical with the definienda is in effect to claim a literal and exclusive truth for the chosen definitions; for if a quality is in fact identical with a certain class of *Elementarerlebnisse,* then it is not identical with a class of some other experiential elements that might be chosen as basic for a different system. Any such claim of exclusive truth is utterly foreign to the spirit and purpose of constructionalism. If we conscientiously try to elicit the criteria we actually em-

[5]The avowed extensionalism of so outstanding a monument of phenomenalism and constructionalism as the *Aufbau* would seem to confute Quine's recent charge (*Mind,* LXII (1953), 434) that the notion of analyticity is a 'holdover of phenomenalistic reductionism.'

[6]Carnap's own term *(Strukturbeschreibung);* see Section 12 of the *Aufbau.*

ploy in discussing and judging the correctness of particular constructions, I think we find that the pertinent requirement is not that each definiens be extensionally identical with its definiendum but rather that the entire system of definientia be *isomorphic,* in a certain specifiable way,[7] to the entire system of definienda. This clears away extraneous and unsatisfiable demands, and leaves room for many different but equally valid alternative systems.

The second common objection against the conception of method embodied in the *Aufbau* is almost the opposite of the first. Carnap himself has taken the lead in maintaining that the restriction to definition as a sole method of construction is much too confining. Not only have we small hope of achieving full definition for all the terms we want to introduce, but there is—he argues—another equally legitimate method of introducing new terms into a system. He claims, indeed, that the introduction of terms through what he calls 'reduction sentences' has the advantage of reflecting a common actual procedure of the scientist.

The latter argument is quite beside the point; but the chief trouble is that this supposedly new method of introducing terms adds nothing to the means that were already at our disposal. Reduction sentences are merely postulates; and terms introduced through postulates are introduced simply as primitives. The introduction of primitives requires no new method, and there is some danger in concealing it under a new name. For the suggestion that reduction sentences are fundamentally comparable to definitions obscures the fact that each addition of a new and ineliminable primitive (whether by reduction postulate or otherwise) constitutes a sacrifice in the economy of basis and the resultant integration of our system. The difference between frankly adopting a term as primitive and introducing it by reduction sentences is the euphemistic difference between a loss of ground and a strategic retreat.

We may indeed have to add new primitives from time to time in building a system, and we may want to use new syntactical or semantical techniques; but the adoption of new primitives is not a new technique.

The standard criticisms of the *Aufbau's* concept of constructional method, then, seems to me wrong in two ways. First, the extensional criteria for constructional definition needs weakening rather than strengthening. Second, the proposed supplementation of the method of definition by the so-called method of 'reduction' adds nothing whatever.

V. *Faults of Construction*

If we set aside all consideration of general principles and examine in detail the actual constructions in the *Aufbau,* we find a great many

[7]See SA, Chapter I.

faults.[8] A number of these are pointed out in the book itself, for Carnap did not profess to offer more than an imperfect sketch of a system. But there are other difficulties, too; and the cumulative effect is that hardly any construction is free of fault. Moreover, not all these defects are minor slips or mere matters of detail still to be worked out. Some of them are so basic and material that nothing short of rather drastic revision of the whole system is likely to correct them.

Nothing that can be said will explain away these faults or make them less serious; but they should be seen in perspective. They are the faults of an honest and early venture in a new direction. Such troubles can always be avoided by attempting nothing or by keeping cautiously vague; the likelihood of error increases with the earnestness and originality of the effort to attain precision. But the making of errors, the discovery of faults, is the first step towards correcting them. Something has already been accomplished when what is being done and what is being attempted have been clarified far enough to make possible a sound accusation of error. If we compare the *Aufbau* not with what we hope for but with what we had before, we may still not condone its errors—but we can appreciate their significance.

Furthermore, some of the most important errors in the *Aufbau* were not invented by Carnap. They had been made repeatedly and unsuspectingly by generations of earlier philosophers, and are still made today. If Carnap did not correct or even notice them all, the rigorous logical articulation he demanded and began brought them much nearer the surface and made their early discovery inevitable. To take just one example, in discussions of the status of qualities it is often assumed that if we take likeness as the relation obtaining between two things that have a common quality, then we can define a class of things having a common quality as a class of things that are all alike. But if to say that all are alike is to say merely that each two are alike, this does not guarantee that there is a quality common to all; and in fact no sufficient condition can be given solely in terms of the dyadic likeness of things. This difficulty is customarily camouflaged by the easy locution "all alike." Even Russell has fallen into a similar logical trap.[9] But one can hardly study the *Aufbau* intensively without becoming acutely aware of this problem.

What the opponents of the *Aufbau* usually offer us is not something to replace it, but discussions of methods and programs, arguments for one basis as against another, debates over what can and cannot be done. Altogether too much philosophy these days is, like the present article, merely

[8]For a detailed exposition of many of these, see SA, Chapter V.

[9]The passages on compresence and complexes in *An Inquiry into Meaning and Truth* (New York: Norton, 1940), 289-290, and *Human Knowledge* (New York: Simon and Schuster, 1948), 294, suffer from a parallel equivocation concerning the compresence of qualities.

philosophy about philosophy; the characteristic contemporary philosophical refuge is not metaphysics but metaphilosophy. The admission that the *Aufbau* is full of faults has to be coupled with the observation that the player on the field always gets caught in more mistakes than the player on the bench. And concerning many of the constructional errors in the *Aufbau* we may perhaps say, in summary, that they were serious, unoriginal, and worthwhile.

VI. *The significance of the* Aufbau

I am by no means suggesting, however, that the *Aufbau* is valuable only or primarily for its errors. Once misconceptions and groundless objections have been cleared away, the positive significance of the work becomes very evident.

The *Aufbau* brings to philosophy the powerful techniques of modern logic, along with unprecedented standards of explicitness, coherence, and rigor. It applies to basic philosophical problems the new methods and principles that only a few years before had thrown fresh and brilliant light upon mathematics. The potential importance to philosophy is comparable to the importance of the introduction of Euclidean deductive method into geometry. The *Aufbau,* for all its fragmentary character, and for all its defects, is still one of the fullest examples we have of the logical treatment of problems in non-mathematical philosophy. But its significance in the long run will be measured less by how far it goes than by how far it is superseded.

In stressing the novelty of its contribution, we must not be misled into regarding the *Aufbau* as an aboriginal work, unrelated to the course of thought preceding it. It belongs very much in the main tradition of modern philosophy, and carries forward a little the effort of the British Empiricists of the 18th Century. Although these philosophers thought of themselves as devoted to a 'historical, plain method' of dealing with knowledge, their chief contribution is to the geography rather than the history of our ideas. What were ostensibly inquiries into the question how certain ideas (e.g. of qualities) are psychologically derived from certain others (e.g. of particulars) were more often than not, I think, simply inquiries into the question how the former ideas may be defined in terms of the latter. And it is just such questions that the *Aufbau* deals with and clarifies. The language may be new but the ancestry of the problems is venerable.

The *Aufbau* cannot yet, however, be relegated to the status of a monument having purely historical interest. Its lessons have not been fully enough learned.

Nelson Goodman

Department of Philosophy
University of Pennsylvania

19

Arthur Pap

REDUCTION SENTENCES AND DISPOSITION CONCEPTS*

I. Reduction-Sentences, Causal Implication, and Material Implication

THERE is a close connection between theory of reduction-sentences (or "conditional definitions") which Carnap developed in his classical essay *Testability and Meaning,* and the problem of producing a satisfactory analysis within an extensional logic of the concept of causal implication, a problem which deservedly occupies a prominent position in contemporary analytic philosophy. The connection is simply this. Carnap succeeded in proving (in section 7 of part II of TM) that an important class of predicates indispensable to empirical science, viz. disposition-predicates, cannot be explicitly defined, by construing the connective "if-then" in such contexts as "if this piece of sugar is immersed in the liquid, then it will dissolve" in the sense of the truth-functional connective symbolized in PM by " ⊃". It was this reflection which led him to propose reduction-sentences as alternative means of introducing such predicates on the basis of "observable" predicates. It follows that, insofar as *this* argument against the possibility of explicit definition of disposition-predicates is concerned (which I propose to call "the argument from material implication"), one who believes in the analyzability of causal implication within an extensional logic might regard the technique of reduction-sentences as no more than a *temporary* device. I shall, indeed, show in a later section of this essay that Carnap advances further on in TM a second argument for the indispensability of reduction-sentences (to be referred to as "the argument from the openness of concepts") which is valid and wholly independent of the first argument. But let us begin with an examination of the question whether an escape from the first argument is possible even for one who shares Carnap's preference for an extensional language of logical reconstruction.

If a scientist who is ignorant of (some may add: and accordingly un-

*The following abbreviations will be used: "TM" for "Testability and Meaning," "PM" for "Principia Mathematica," "FUS" for "Foundations of the Unity of Science," "FLM" for "Foundations of Logic and Mathematics," "LFP" for "Logical Foundations of Probability."

corrupted by) formal logic were asked what he means by sentences of the form "*x* is soluble in *L*" he would no doubt reply "if at any time *x* were immersed in *L* it would dissolve"[1], and it would not occur to him that such a definition could give rise to paradoxical consequences. And, indeed, it does not. If Carnap succeeds in deriving from it the paradoxical consequence that any substance is soluble in any liquid in which it is never immersed, this is due to his formalizing the definiens, which is ordinarily meant as a *causal* implication, as a material conditional. And he is to be criticized for not mentioning, in the relevant passage, that his formalization thus involves a radical departure from ordinary usage. It is, indeed, easy to see that, e.g., "fragile $(x) \equiv (t)$ (dropped with sufficient force $(x,t) \supset$ breaks (x,t))" together with the singular premise "$\sim(\exists t)$ (dropped with sufficient force (a,t))" entails "fragile (a)", where a may be, for example, an extremely hard stone. In order to preclude such paradoxes Carnap proposes to replace explicit definitions of the form

(1) "$Q_3(x) \equiv [(t)(Q_1(x,t) \supset Q_2(x,t))]$"

by reduction-sentences of the form

"$(x)(t)[Q_1(x,t) \supset (Q_3(x) \equiv Q_2(x,t))]$".

These "conditional" definitions—so called because "Q_3" is defined only relatively to the experimental condition "Q_1" (like immersing, or dropping)—have the disadvantage that they do not enable elimination of the dispositional predicates. And this may be a serious disadvantage from the point of view of a "Konstitutionstheorie" (see Carnap's "Der logische Aufbau der Welt") or a program of "logical construction" (see Russell's theory of "incomplete symbols") which holds that only observation-predicates, designating directly given qualities, are theoretically indispensable for a complete description of the world.

But apart from this disadvantage, such a reduction-sentence suffers from another defect which must be recognized as such whether or not one still adheres to the ideal of a "logical construction of the world". A reduction-sentence for "Q_3" attributes a meaning to "Q_3" only within the class determined by the predicate "Q_1"; for individuals outside this class the question whether or not they have the dispositional property is *undecidable*, and since this undecidability is due to the dispositional predicate's not being defined (as mathematicians say) for non-members of that class, it is a theoretical, not just a practical, undecidability. In other words, with respect to such individuals it is meaningless to say that they either have or do not have the disposition in question, just as it would be meaningless to say of the fraction ⅔ (and, indeed, of any fraction)

[1]If he is cautious, he may say "If . . . , then, *others being equal,* — — —". This immunization of the dispositional statement against strict falsifiability reflects the "openness" of disposition concepts. This feature of disposition concepts will be discussed pp. 571ff., but may be overlooked in the present context.

that it is odd, and also meaningless to say of it that it is not odd.[2] But then it seems that Carnap's device throws us from Syclla into Charibdis: explicit definitions were discarded because they entail that any individual upon which the relevant experiment is never performed *has* the disposition, but now we seem to be faced with the no more palatable result that it is *meaningless* to attribute the disposition to such an individual. That Carnap was likewise aware of this difficulty, may be seen from the following passage in TM (p.445):

> We may diminish this region of indeterminateness of the predicate by adding one or several more laws which contain the predicate and connect it with other terms available in our language. . . . In the case of the predicate 'soluble' we may perhaps add the law stating that two bodies of the same substance are either both soluble or both not soluble. This law would help in the instance of the match; it would, in accordance with common usage, lead to the result 'the match *c* is not soluble', because other pieces of wood are found to be insoluble on the basis of the first reduction-sentence. Nevertheless, a region of indeterminateness remains, though a smaller one. If a body *b* consists of such a substance that for no body of this substance has the test-condition—in the above example: 'being placed in water'—ever been fulfilled, then neither the predicate nor its negation can be attributed to *b*—

and there is no doubt that Carnap means "can be meaningfully attributed to *b*", since it is not ignorance of facts which prevents a decision in that case. But it seems that even so disposition-predicates retain too large a "region of indeterminateness". One might ask, for example, whether on some uninhabited planet there exists a species of metal non-existent on this planet which, like the metal species the human race has experimented with, has the disposition called "electrical conductivity". This question seems to be perfectly meaningful, yet it seems to be condemned to meaninglessness by Carnap's theory. Carnap might deny this on the ground that our hypothetical bodies are, after all, metals, and that we can avail ourselves of the law "all metals are electrical conductors" in order to make the question whether they also have this disposition significant, just as he availed himself of the law "all wood is insoluble in water" in order to make the question "is this match, which has never been placed in water, soluble in water" significant. But then he would still be open to two lines of attack. First, assume a disposition which is unique to a particular individual. For example, a particular human being might have

[2]The class determined by "Q_1" may indeed be construed as the *range of significance* of the dispositional predicate, just the way the class of natural numbers is the range of significance of the contradictory predicates "odd" and "even". This analogy, which suggests applicability of conditional definitions far beyond dispositional predicates, has recently been noted by Bar-Hillel, in his article "On Syntactical Categories," *Journal of Symbolic Logic* (March, 1950), 11. I shall return to this point in the concluding section of the paper.

the disposition of feeling nauseated when exposed to the smell of an orange, and it is logically possible (whatever the probability of the supposition may be) that no other organism has that disposition and that the disposition is never actualized for the simple reason that this individual is never exposed to the fatal smell. To be sure, as long as the class determined by Q_1 (in this example, the class of organisms exposed at some time to the smell of an orange) is not empty, confirming or disconfirming evidence with respect to the statement "if this individual were exposed to the smell of an orange, he would feel nauseated" is still obtainable. But what if no oranges existed? Then the class Q_1 would be empty and hence the above statement would definitely be meaningless by Carnap's theory. And this is strange, since intuitively the truth, and *a fortiori* the significance, of the non-existential conditional "for any x and y, if x were an orange and y smelled x, then y would feel nauseated" is compatible with "there is no x such that x is an orange".

Secondly, Carnap's reduction-sentence for "soluble" implies that solubility is a *permanent* disposition, as evidenced by the omission of the time-variable as argument of the disposition predicate. But there are of course also transient dispositions, like electrical charge. Suppose, now, that x is the very first body whose electrical charge has been ascertained by a human observer. Then the statement that x is electrically charged at t_1 (where t_1 is the time of our supposed first experiment) would be meaningful, yet the statement that x is electrically charged at t_0 (where t_0 is prior to t_1) would be meaningless.

It seems, therefore, that Carnap's device for introducing disposition-predicates has the unacceptable consequence that the meaningfulness of predications of dispositions depends on contingencies of verification. This is no doubt a main source of dissatisfaction with conditional definitions which has led some philosophers to look for explicit definitions of disposition-predicates which are sufficiently sophisticated to avoid the difficulty already discussed.[3] An adequate explicit definition of a dispositional predicate D should have the advantage (a) over a conditional definition that it rescues the significance of the statement "$D(b)$", where b is an object upon which the test-operation has never been performed and possibly belongs to a kind K such that the test-operation has not been performed upon any member of K; (b) over the simple explicit definition criticized by Carnap that it does not allow *vacuous* predication of D. Of course, it would not do to amend (1) by adding to the definiens the condition that the test-operation has been performed at some time upon x, thus:

(2) $Q_3(x) \equiv (\exists t)[Q_1(x,t)] \cdot [(t)Q_1(x,t) \supset Q_2(x,t))]$,

[3]See, e.g., R. Chisholm, "The Contrary-to-Fact Conditional," in Feigl and Sellars, *Readings in Philosophical Analysis,* 488.

for then it would, though meaningful, be *false* to ascribe D to b.[4] Further, this definition does not even express the intended idea that the test-operation *has been* performed upon x, for "$(\exists t)\ (Q_1(x,t))$" is itself tenseless, meaning only "Q_1 is performed upon x at some—possibly future—time". Should one try to express this idea of pastness formally, this could be accomplished only by means of indicator-terms, like "now" in the context "at some time before now", or "this token" in the context "at some time before the occurrence of this token".[5] But then it would follow that no dispositional predicate can be used with the same meaning twice—an altogether shocking concession to the Heracleitean semantics of Hayakawa and associates.

If we want to allow for the possibility that D is truly but not vacuously predicable upon b even though the test-operation[6] has not been performed, and perhaps never will be performed, upon any instance of the proximate natural kind to which b belongs, we are likely to construct a relatively involved definition like the following:[7]

$$(3)\ Q_3(x) =_{\mathrm{Df}} (\exists f)[f(x) \cdot (\exists y)(f(y) \cdot Q_1(y)) \cdot (y)(f(y) \cdot Q_1(y) \supset Q_2(y))].$$

It cannot be denied that such a definition has considerable *prima facie* plausibility. For, it seems that if we have any grounds for predicating a disposition upon an object with which the relevant experiment has not been performed, it is that the object belongs to a class such that the experiment has been performed upon some of its members and that the constant outcome of these experiments led to a generalization which is now applied to the given object. And this is precisely the idea expressed by the above definition. Nevertheless, this type of explicit definition is open to three serious objections, though only the first of these has, to my knowledge, received attention in the extensive literature on the problem of

[4]This unacceptable consequence of (2) is pointed out by Kaila, in "Wenn-So," *Theoria* (1945), Part II. Unfortunately, though, his formulation of this unacceptable definition, viz. $Q(x) \equiv (\exists x)P(x) \cdot (x)\ (P(x) \rightarrow R(x))$, is syntactically meaningless since the free individual variable of the definiendum does not appear in the definiens.

[5]For this reason Reichenbach has aptly called tensed verbs, like "was dissolved", "token-reflexive symbols". See § 51 of *Elements of Symbolic Logic*.

[6]The term "test-operation" is here used broadly for any process designated by "Q_1" even if "Q_1" is not, in the terminology of TM, a *realizable* predicate. Thus the "test-operations" by which such dispositions as electric potential are defined in theoretical physics are sometimes such "unrealizable" processes as approaching a certain point with a test particle from infinity.

[7]This definition is copied from Anders Wedberg's "The Logical Construction of the World," *Theoria* (1944), Part III, 237, who cites it, for purposes of criticism, from Kaila's "Den maenskliga kunskapen." Kaila later improved the definition, in his book "Der physikalische Realitaetsbegriff" (in answer to an objection by Carnap), and finally, by the time he wrote "Wenn-So" *(loc. cit.)*, abandoned altogether this method of definition.

analyzing contrary-to-fact conditionals: (1) it is easy to produce values of the predicate-variable "*f*" which lead to the same sort of undesirable results as were to be avoided by the definition; (2) the definition entails that from a contrary-to-fact conditional one can logically deduce the existence of inductive evidence in its favor; and this is equivalent to confusing the concepts *truth* and *confirmation;* (3) the definition presupposes that all inductive evidence for contrary-to-fact conditionals is, either directly or indirectly, *instantial;* this, however, is to overlook the use of *idealized* disposition-concepts and the connected method of extrapolation to limiting cases in theoretical science.

(1) Assuming that *a* is the match that was burnt up before ever making contact with water, it can still be proved on the basis of (3) that *a* is soluble in water, by taking as the verifying value of "*f*" the function "$x = a \vee x = b$" where *b* is an object on which the relevant experiment was successfully performed (as reported by Kaila, Carnap pointed this difficulty out to him). To avoid this undesirable consequence, one will have to restrict the range of "*f*" to *general* properties, i.e., properties whose expression involves no individual constants.[8] However, as Wedberg points out (*loc.cit.*), it is unfortunately still possible to prove that the burnt up match was soluble, by taking "$Q_1 \supset Q_2$" as verifying value of "*f*", for then the third conjunct is tautologically satisfied, the first conjunct is vacuously true of *a,* and the second conjunct is easily satisfied by performance of Q_1 upon some object. Wedberg remarks correctly that proponents of such an explicit definition intend "*f*" to be restricted to what are vaguely called *intrinsic* properties, such as "wooden", "metallic". But there seems to be little hope that the desired end could be reached through such a restriction. For, in the first place, the concept of "intrinsic" properties is surely no clearer than the concept of "disposition" which is to be clarified. Secondly, I suspect that for the explication of "intrinsic property" semantic concepts would be needed, along one or the other of the following lines: (a) "*P* is an intrinsic property of *x*" is meaningless; a meaning can be attached only to "*P* is an intrinsic property of *x* qua instance of kind *K*", and this is to be defined as "'$x \in K$' *entails* '*Px*' ". (b) "*P* is an intrinsic property of *x*" if and only if it is *meaningless*

[8]In his paper "On Defining 'Soluble,'" *Analysis* (June, 1951), Thomas Storer constructs an explicit definition strikingly similar to Kaila's: $WD(x) \vee (\exists F)\ [F(x) \cdot (\exists y)(F(y) \cdot WD(y)) \cdot \sim(\exists y)(F(y) \cdot \sim WD(y))]$, where "$WD(x)$" means "there is a time at which *x* is put into water and dissolves," and seems to think that the above mentioned restriction of the predicate-variable suffices to make the definition fully adequate. But apart from the fact that, as shown in the text, the function of *f* to which "$(\exists f)$" refers can be trivially satisfied even if non-general properties are excluded, Storer's definition is open to an additional objection which will receive due attention in the sequel: it follows from the definition that the positive outcome of a single experiment upon an object *entails* that the object has the corresponding disposition, whereas this inference ought to be an inductive generalization.

to suppose that the same individual x has P at one time and does not have P at another time (e.g. that the same object is wooden at one time but, say, golden at another time; if x is a wooden object observed at t_0, and y a golden object observed—possibly at the same place—at t_1, one would have to say that x is distinct from y in spite of their strong similarity in other respects.)[9] If so, the definiens for "soluble" and other disposition-terms would contain metalinguistic terms. Apart from the consideration that thus disposition-terms would be, contrary to intent, relegated to the metalanguage of an empirical science, the original purpose of explicitly defining disposition-terms on the basis of observable predicates within an extensional language would then surely have been defeated.

(2) It must be kept in mind that, insofar as dispositional properties are regarded as explicitly definable, predications of such properties, i.e. statements of the form "$Q_3(x)$", are conceived as condensed statements of causal implications. An example of such a causal implication is "immersion in water causes *a* to dissolve". Now, the analysis we have been considering is a formalization of the Humean idea that, although a causal statement may *ex*plicitly refer only to a single case, it *im*plicitly refers to a class of similar cases; anything which is *similar* to *a* (an idea the vagueness of which is formally reflected by the indefinite "$(\exists f)$ . . .") dissolves if it is immersed in water. Hence the fact that something similar to *a* is actually immersed in water and dissolves therein is confirming evidence, but not conclusive, for the causal implication. And a look at the analysis (3) shows that according to it the causal implication entails the existence of such evidence. In this respect the analysis in question simply involves a confusion of the evidence which causes us to believe that a given object has a given disposition with the meaning of the statement believed to be true. Just suppose, for example, a universe with temperatures so high that the existence of liquids of any kinds in it is physically impossible. Then "$(\exists y)\ (Q_1(y))$" would be false, yet are we really prepared to deny that even in such a universe sugar would be soluble? It is apparent that the attempt to define disposition-concepts in an extensional language, a language devoid of intensional (or "modal") connectives, has entangled us in a dilemma: in order to prevent predication of dispositions from being vacuously true we have to include an existential clause in the definiens; but thus amended the analysis claims that in predicating a disposition we not only assert the existence of a law L in accordance with which one event may be inferred from another, but moreover that there exists confirming evidence for L. Were we permitted to re-

[9]According to this analysis of "intrinsic", sudden transmutation of a particular, such as the alchemists hoped for, would be logically absurd. Perhaps this speaks against the analysis. It is obvious that the problem of analyzing "intrinsic property" is closely connected with the problem of analyzing "genidentity".

place the extensional "$\supset$" in the definiens by a modal connective, there would be no further reason for retaining the existential clause.[10]

It might be replied that our objection rests on a misinterpretation of the existential quantifier; that the latter is tenseless, and that the extensional analysis, therefore, does not have the unacceptable consequence that dispositional statements assert that there exists a relevant law which *has already* (at the time of assertion) been confirmed. But, in the first place, it does not seem self-contradictory to suppose that a is soluble even though there is no instantial evidence whatever, neither past *nor future,* for a law of the form "for any x, if $f(x)$ and x is immersed in a liquid, then x dissolves". Secondly there is the difficulty, pointed out by Lewis (*An Analysis of Knowledge and Valuation*, ch. 8., s.9) but ignored by these who still believe that an extensional logic is adequate for the reconstruction of empirical science, that a formal implication in Russell's sense has no predictive content. If the range of "x" in "(x) $(F\ x \supset G\ x)$" consists of the designata of *logically proper names "a", "b" . . . "n",* and logically proper names designate actual existents (cf. the remarks in section 5, p. 54), then the formal implication makes no assertion about future instances of the property F: it is a contradiction to suppose that there exists *now* a logically proper name of a *future* crow, say (though there might exist now a *description* of a crow still to be born). It follows that the existential quantifier cannot be as tenseless as one would like it to be.[11]

(3) Apart from the consideration that no analysis of an empirical proposition can be correct if it entails that the proposition cannot be true without being confirmed at some time or other (it is, incidentally, Carnap himself who has lucidly warned us against this confusion, in "Truth and Confirmation"),[12] the schema of explicit definition of disposition-concepts under scrutiny suffers from an inadequate conception of inductive evidence. What is overlooked is the method of approximation to limiting cases which terminates in the assertion of conditionals whose antecedents are not just, as a matter of accidental fact, unfulfilled, but

[10]A modal definiens analogous to the definiens of (3) except for its intensional character and the absence of the existential clause will be discussed on pp. 584ff.

[11]I do not wish to maintain with finality that tenseless existential quantification over the individual variables of a physicalistic language is impossible unless one permit oneself to include *possible* existents in the range of the individual variables. The answer to this question depends on the answers to such difficult questions as whether names are eliminable in favor of descriptions, or whether descriptions, on the contrary, are to be treated, as by Russell, as contextually eliminable, and what existence assumptions are presupposed by the significance of statements involving variables of quantification. But at any rate one should suspend judgment on the question of translatability of causal statements into an extensional language until one thoroughly examines these questions, far removed though they may seem at first glance.

[12]Feigl and Sellars, *Readings in Philosophical Analysis,* 119ff.

could not be fulfilled. It so happens that the test-operation Q_1 has not been performed upon *a*, but *a* can be described by a predicate "*F*" which determines a class other members of which have been subjected to Q_1; and this kind of indirect evidence for a dispositional statement like "Q_3 (a)" may be called *instantial.* Clearly, the evidence for such statements of mechanics as "if this body were subject to no other force than a constant gravitational attraction, it would move with constant acceleration", "if all the mass of this pendulum were concentrated in its bob and its vibrations were uninfluenced by friction, it would oscillate at a constant period", "if the earth's revolution around the sun were exclusively determined by the sun's gravitational attraction it would describe a perfect ellipse", is not, and could not be, instantial. It is, of course, a mere linguistic accident whether there exist disposition-terms corresponding to such contrary-to-fact conditionals which are, as we might put it, *nomologically contrary-to-fact,* i.e., such that it follows from a law of nature that their antecedents cannot be fulfilled.[13]

In the terminology of TM, we may say that the test-operations here are described in terms of "unrealisable" predicates, and that therefore the evidence actually available in favor of such conditionals cannot be of the instantial kind contemplated by the extensional analysis. For this reason, I must likewise reject Reichenbach's analysis of "nomological" statements (*Elements of Symbolic Logic,* §61). According to Reichenbach, a nomological statement whose antecedent is never fulfilled must be derivable from an "original" nomological statement whose antecedent *is* fulfilled; thus he says that the statement "all iron which is lighter than water floats on water" is nomological, in spite of its unfulfilled antecedent, because it is derivable from the more general statement for which there is instantial evidence "all bodies lighter than water float on water". But if the nomological statement is nomologically contrary-to-fact, the evidence on which it is accepted is not in general that it is subsumable as a special case under a more general statement for which there is instantial evidence. That is, the process of confirmation cannot be represented by the schema: *E* confirms directly "$A \subset C$"; "$A \cdot B \subset C$" is derivable from "$A \subset C$"; therefore *E* confirms indirectly "$A \cdot B \subset C$". One may be tempted to suppose that the process of extrapolation to the limit which leads to assertion of such contrary-to-fact conditionals is really no different from the schematized process of confirmation, since it is logically necessary that a functional relationship which holds for *all* values of two variables also holds for their limiting values. For example, if the smaller the density of a medium, the smaller the difference of the accelerations of bodies of differing weights dropped therein, it follows

[13]Thus it follows from the law of gravitation that the antecedent of the first law of motion cannot be fulfilled.

that for the medium of smallest density, viz. the vacuum, that difference of acceleration is the smallest possible, viz. zero. But if the general functional law that supports the contrary-to-fact conditional is to be expressible in terms of observable predicates exclusively, then the range of its variables must be limited to observable values, and then the transition to the unobservable limit is not deductive after all. From the law that, for all finite distances of x from surrounding matter, the larger these distances, the smaller the acceleration of x (however it be measured), it does not follow deductively that the latter would be zero if x were at *no* finite distance from surrounding matter.

The approach to the analysis of nomological statements within an extensional language which is here criticized is the following: if a universal conditional whose antecedent-class is empty (like Reichenbach's example "all iron bodies specifically lighter than water are capable of floating on water") expresses a law, rather than an accidental concomitance of properties, then it is deducible from a universal conditional for which there is instantial evidence; only the latter kind of conditionals, then, express *fundamental* laws. But this analysis is in *prima facie* conflict with the fact that almost any fundamental law of physics that one can think of is a contrary-to-fact conditional, since it asserts what would happen if certain causal factors which are in actuality operative, were not operative. Is there a strictly "closed" system short of the entire universe? Even if there were, the physicist surely does not commit himself to this assumption in asserting that the sum of the energies in a closed system is constant in time. His evidence for the law is not "instantial". Now, what I call the "extensional analysis" (so called because it is motivated by the desire to avoid intensional connectives in the logical reconstruction of scientific language) might be reconciled with the apparent contrary-to-fact character of what may well be fundamental laws, by interpreting the latter as *limit-statements*. What does it mean to say "If *A* were at an infinite distance from other bodies, then the acceleration of *A* would be reduced to zero?" Guided by the principle "to find the meaning of a statement, reflect on the method of its verification (or confirmation)", an operationist may answer: "This only means that the larger *A*'s distance from other bodies, the smaller *A*'s acceleration, where only *finite* distances and accelerations are referred to. If, having obtained by measurement a set of values of two connected variables x and y which fit a law "$y = f(x)$", you extrapolate to an unobservable limit, say "if x were infinite, y would be zero," you merely use the law to predict further observable (i.e. measurable) values of the variables. Graphically speaking, what appears as a "logical jump" to a merely ideal limit, is nothing but a prolongation of the curve in accordance with the same equation which has already been confirmed".

Let us illustrate this method of interpretation in terms of Boyle's law. An ideal gas is often defined as a gas whose molecules exert no forces on each other. This definition is connected with the characterization of an ideal gas as a gas whose molecules are "point-particles" as follows: the larger the average distances between the molecules (the smaller the density of the gas, in other words), the smaller the intermolecular forces. And to say that the distances are large as compared with the diameter of a molecule, is equivalent to saying that the diameter of a molecule is infinitesimal as compared to the average distance between two molecules. We thus get the limit statement that the forces would vanish if the diameter vanished.[14] Now, in order to be justified in thus neglecting intermolecular forces, one must make sure that the gas density is sufficiently small, and this requires a certain minimal temperature and maximal pressure. Hence the physicist says that a real gas approximates the character of an ideal gas all the more closely, the closer the temperature and pressure of the gas are to those "critical" values. If "y" represents the degree of ideality of a gas and "x" the relative size of its molecules, we may formulate the limit-statement that as x approaches 0, y approaches asymptotically a maximum, viz. that value at which the behavior of the gas would exactly satisfy Boyle's law. The operationist interpretation of the law, which avoids even *hypothetical* assumptions of unobservables (i.e. contrary- to-fact conditionals about unobservables), consists in a restriction of the range of "x" to finite values, and extrusion of the limiting value "complete ideality" from the range of "y". Speaking of the completely ideal gas, the operationist might say, is to engage in a mere "facon de parler", like speaking of the point at infinity where the hyperbola meets the axis.

This interpretation certainly has the virtue of explaining how such limit-statements about unobservable situations are inductively arrived at. But does it really explicate what such statements *mean*? Is it not logically possible that "$y = f(x)$" (here "$f(x)$" is meant as an undetermined constant, i.e. as designation of a specific, though unspecified, function) holds for all finite values of x yet fails to hold for the unobservable limiting value? For example, even if Galileo had, *per impossibile,* verified that the deviation from constant gravitational acceleration for a given pair of bodies decreases with decreasing density of the medium *for all finite values* of the variables, it would have remained logically possible that as the independent variable assumes the unrealizable value 0 the function "jumps" contrary to expectation. It seems, therefore, that the "opera-

[14]There are other considerations in the kinetic theory which lead to the postulation of point-like molecules: the smaller the molecules, the smaller the chance of molecular collisions, and the smaller the average kinetic energy of rotation of a molecule. Hence the idealization of molecules as points reflects other simplifying assumptions, such as absence of molecular collisions (the only change of momentum occurs at the walls of the container) and the absence of energy of rotation, as well.

tionist" interpretation assumes a principle of continuity which is logically contingent (though it may be methodologically necessary) and for this very reason should not be assumed in the context of a *meaning analysis.* The references to ideal, experimentally unrealisable situations in physics are not so easily disposed of as "facons de parler" as the reference to a meeting point "at infinity", which is just a positive way of asserting the negative proposition that there is no meeting point at any finite distance from the origin.

The discussion so far has aimed at revealing the difficulties facing the task of explicitly defining disposition-predicates in an extensional language of "observables" and of thus dispensing with reduction-sentences. But I believe that such a language is not only inadequate for the introduction of such predicates by explicit definitions, but likewise for their introduction by reduction-sentences. Indeed, this is so obvious that only a strong prejudice in favor of the extensional language of PM can explain why it passed entirely unnoticed in TM. Consider Carnap's reduction-sentence for "soluble":

$$(x)(t)[Q_1(x,t) \supset (Q_3(x) \equiv Q_2(x,t))].$$

Carnap here treats the disposition-predicate as time-independent, as though it were meaningless to suppose that an object is soluble at one time but insoluble at another time. But even if solubility were a permanent disposition which is never acquired nor lost by a substance, this would be a contingent fact, not something implicit in the "logical grammar" of disposition-predicates. Such dispositions as electric charge, elasticity, irritability clearly are time-dependent (cf. later, p. 574), which is to be formally expressed by the use of a relational predicate with a time-argument along with the thing-argument. Let "$Q_3\ (x,t)$" represent such a non-permanent disposition, and let "$(x)(t)[Q_1(x,t) \supset (Q_3(x,t) \equiv Q_2(x,t))]$" be the bilateral reduction sentence by which this predicate is introduced. Now, Carnap argues that this sentence is analytic if the disposition-predicate has no independent meaning, specified by other reduction-sentences. If so, then the singular sentence "$Q_3(a,t_0)$" can be analytically inferred from the singular sentences "$Q_1(a,t_0)$" and "$Q_2(a,t_0)$". But this result is completely irreconcilable with the view that to predicate a disposition is to make an implicitly general statement, an assertion of causal connection which goes beyond a purely descriptive "post hoc" report. If I say of a given wire, e.g., that it was elastic at time t_0, I refer not just to the one specific test-operation which happened to produce the observed display of this disposition, but to an entire class of similar yet distinguishable test-operations (stretchings) which *would* have led to a similar result (reversal of the deformation). If, however, we recognize that the inference from "$Q_1(a,t_0) \cdot Q_2(a,t_0)$" to the dispositional statement "$Q_3(a,t_0)$" is an *inductive* inference to an implicitly general counterfactual conditional, then we cannot formulate the reduction-sentence as a material conditional which can be used only as a rule of *deductive* inference. It thus appears that the choice of the extensional language of PM as language of logical reconstruction makes it impossible to introduce disposition-predicates, no matter whether explicit definitions or reduction sentences be used.

II. *Probabilistic Meaning-Specification and the Collapse of the Analytic-Factual Dualism*

As noted above, Carnap maintains that every bilateral reduction sentence is analytic, which surprising theorem he proves as follows: the factual content of a reduction pair "$Q_1 \supset (Q_2 \supset Q_3)$; $Q_4 \supset (Q_5 \supset \sim Q_3)$", by which the term "$Q_3$" is introduced into a scientific language, must be expressible by a consequence of the pair which does not contain "Q_3". Indeed, "$\sim(Q_1 \cdot Q_2 \cdot Q_4 \cdot Q_5)$" is such a consequence. But a bilateral reduction sentence is simply the special case of a reduction pair which arises if $Q_4 = Q_1$ and $Q_5 = \sim Q_2$; in which case the mentioned consequence of the pair reduces to the tautology "$\sim(Q_1 \cdot Q_2 \cdot Q_1 \cdot \sim Q_2)$" (p.444). This result, obtained by apparently flawless demonstration, is surprising because on the usual conception of analyticity a conjunction of analytic sentences is itself an analytic sentence, yet any conjunction of distinct bilateral reduction sentences for the same term will have the same sort of factual consequence as is implicitly asserted by a reduction pair. Carnap would probably reply that this is no valid argument against his theorem since an essential premise entering into his proof was that "Q_3" has no antecedent meaning, which excludes the existence of a *system* of reduction sentences for this term. In other words, a bilateral reduction sentence for "Q_3" is analytic relatively to a language L which contains no other reduction sentences for "Q_3"; and this proposition is compatible with the proposition that the bilateral reduction sentence is synthetic relatively to a language L' which does contain such additional reduction-sentences. But I do not think that this relativization of analyticity to a language is a successful solution of the difficulty. For now we must admit that relatively to language L' which contains "$Q_1 \supset (Q_2 \equiv Q_3)$" and "$Q_4 \supset (Q_5 \equiv Q_3)$" as rules, and as the *only* rules, specifying the meaning of "Q_3", both of these reduction-sentences are synthetic; the evidence "$Q_1 \cdot Q_2 \cdot \sim Q_3$" could conceivably refute the first reduction sentence since "$\sim Q_3$" might be inferred, with the help of the second reduction sentence, from the evidence "$Q_4 \cdot \sim Q_5$"; and for a perfectly symmetrical reason, the second reduction sentence is to be regarded as an empirically refutable synthetic sentence. Yet, these reduction-sentences *also* serve to specify the meaning of "Q_3". Indeed, the conclusion that every reduction-sentence which is associated in the same language with other reduction-sentences for the same term is a meaning-rule and also an empirically disconfirmable statement, could be arrived at without particular consideration of *bilateral* reduction sentences; the above argument remains valid if for the two bilateral reduction sentences we substitute the two members of a reduction pair.

The just diagnosed dual nature of the sort of partial definitions by means of which Carnap hoped to be able to introduce disposition-terms into extensional descriptive languages cannot be reconciled with the tenet of logical empiricism that every non-contradictory sentence of an interpreted language is either analytic or factual but not both. What seems to be called for is a reconstruction of the process of partial specification of meaning, commendably called attention to by Carnap, in terms of a continuous concept of *probability-implication.* It is obvious anyway that any scientific illustration of a reduction sentence that one might offer would be treated as a probability-implication by scientists; this, however, is a feature of reduction-sentences which their formulation as material conditionals conceals. The inference from experimental evidence E_1 to a hypothesis about a "construct", like temperature or electrical current or, in psychology, another person's anger, is probable roughly in proportion to the improbability of E_1 on the assumption of the falsity of the hypothesis. Verification of further relevant evidence $E_2 \ldots E_n$ will increase the probability of the hypothesis, but the possibility remains that unfavorable evidence would turn up and that thus the probability of the hypothesis be diminished. This is no more than a commonplace of scientific methodology, but the lesson to be learnt from it is that if the connections between observation-statements and statements about constructs (such as dispositions are supposed to be) are to be represented by reduction sentences, then the latter must be given the form of probability-implications. One might think that probabilistic reduction-pairs can be cast into the simple form: $Q_1 \cdot Q_2 \mathrel{\ni\!\!-}_x Q_3$; $Q_4 \cdot Q_5 \mathrel{\ni\!\!-}_y \sim Q_3$. But according to this form, the hypothesis that a given object has a given disposition could be established as highly probable by a single experiment, which conflicts with the idea that in ascribing dispositions one expresses the expectation that a correlation which was observed to hold with a high frequency will also hold in not yet observed cases. Hence the following form seems more appropriate: $(Q_1 \mathrel{\ni\!\!-}_x Q_2) \mathrel{\ni\!\!\!-\!\!\!\ni}_y Q_3$. A negative reduction-sentence might be obtained simply by taking the converse of the positive reduction-sentence, where the weight, i.e. the degree of probability-implication from the correlation to the disposition, may or may not be the same: Q_3 ∋⥽$_z$ (Q_1 ∋-$_x$ Q_2).[15] If the correlation fails, it is improbable that the object has the disposition. What would correspond to the special case of the bilateral reduction-sentence in this probabilistic scheme is an equality of the forward and reverse weights. If the disposition is tied to several correlations, then it is presupposed that the correlations themselves inter-correlate: this corresponds to the "synthetic" presupposition of the Carnapian reduction-pairs: $\sim(Q_1 \cdot Q_2 \cdot Q_4 \cdot Q_5)$.

If reduction-sentences are thus reconstructed as probability-implications, their relevance to scientific concept-formation will become much clearer. The difference between explicit definition and conditional definition (or reduction) which Carnap placed the chief emphasis on was that explicit definitions state a necessary and sufficient condition for applicability of a term, while the latter state *separate* sufficient conditions for applicability of a term and for applicability of the negate of the term: in the case of a bilateral reduction sentence, $Q_1 \cdot Q_2$ is a sufficient condition for Q_3 · and $Q_1 \cdot \sim Q_2$ a sufficient condition for $\sim Q_3$, but no truth-functional compound of Q_1 and Q_2 is a *necessary and sufficient* condition for Q_3. That this difference was indeed foremost in Carnap's mind may be gathered especially from an important passage in "Foundations of the Unity of Science" in which it is argued that psychological terms, like "angry", are at the present stage of scientific knowledge not *definable* by means of physicalistic (physiological and/or behavioristic) terms *because* we do not know "a sufficient and necessary criterion to be found by a physiological analysis of the nervous system or other organs", and *because* "the peripheral symptoms known are presumably not necessary criteria because it might be that a person of strong self-control is able to suppress these symptoms". Since Carnap proceeds to maintain that a *reduction* of "anger" to behavioristic terms is nonetheless possible, he evidently holds that a sufficient condition, at least, can be described in behavioristic terms. But here one might counter that if Carnap's acknowledgement of the possibility of "strong self-control" led him to admit that no necessary condition can be formulated in behavioristic terms, then he should consistently admit that the formulation of a sufficient condition is impossible also, because of the possibility of putting on an act. All we can say is that such and such observations make the psychological hypothesis "he is angry now" *probable;* the inference from the observational basis to the predication of the reducible term is inductive. In-

[15]In order to get an application of epistemological interest, take as Q_3 any "objective" property of a physical object, as "Q_1 a character of a perceptual act, and as Q_2 the character of the sense-data that normally result if the object really has the property Q_3." "Q_1 ∋-$_x$ Q_2", then, is what Lewis calls a "terminating judgment", asserting a nomological probability-connection of sense-data. "∋⥽" is a symbol I have concocted out of Reichenbach's "∋-" and Lewis' "⥽"; it may be read as *degree of entailment.*

deed, we have already seen that this must be so if the reduced terms are disposition-terms with their usual connotation of inductive generality.

That the theorem of the analyticity of bilateral reduction sentences is paradoxical becomes further evident if we take a close look at the famous reduction sentence for "soluble" (TM, p. 440) which, unlike the examples of reduction sentences for "electrically charged" and "elastic" given in FUS, treats the dispositional property as time-independent. Consider its substitution-instance: $(t)\ [Q_1(a,t) \supset (Q_3(a) \equiv Q_2(a,t))]$. Since this conditional is allegedly analytic (any logical consequence of an analytic statement is itself analytic), "$Q_3(a)$" is a logical consequence, not a "*P*-consequence", of the conjunction of observation-statements "$Q_1\ (a,t_0) \cdot Q_2(a,t_0)$", likewise "$\sim Q_3\ (a)$" is a logical consequence of "$Q_1(a,t_1) \cdot \sim Q_2(a,t_1)$". Now, it would seem to be logically possible that both conjunctions are true; yet since in that case both "$Q_3(a)$" and "$\sim Q_3(a)$" would be true, the assumption that they are logical consequences of those conjunctions compels the conclusion that "$Q_1(a,t_0) \cdot Q_2(a,t_0) \cdot Q_1(a,t_1) \cdot \sim Q_2(a,t_1)$" is *not* logically possible.[16] This conclusion, however, would not follow if the implications from the observation-statements to the dispositional statements were probability-implications. One might reply that "$Q_1(a,t_0) \cdot Q_2(a,t_0) \cdot Q_1(a,t) \cdot \sim Q_2(a,t_1)$" is *indeed* impossible, since an object once dissolved cannot be made solid again in order to be tested for solubility once more, that from "$Q_2(a,t_0)$" it simply follows that at t_1 *a* does not exist any more. This reply, however, is not convincing because, even if solubility happens to be a time-independent disposition which a thing cannot manifest twice, it surely does not follow from the meaning of "time-independent disposition" that this is the case. Thus, "having mass *M*" might be regarded as a time-independent disposition of a body (at least if we disregard the dependence of mass on velocity), i.e. "*a* has mass *M*" is complete, does not require expansion to "*a* has mass *M* at *t*." The test-operation Q_1 might be the application of a definite force and the test-result a definite acceleration of *a*. The same body, however, may well undergo, upon repeated application of the same force, the same acceleration twice; thus its mass is a disposition which, though time-independent, is capable of manifesting itself more than once.[17]

[16] *Tollendo tollens,* since the conjunction evidently *is* logically possible, the universal conditional (the reduction sentence) which allows us to derive a contradiction from it must be synthetic. Or, we might argue directly that the synthetic statement "$\sim Q_1(a,\ t_0) \cdot Q_2(a,\ t_0) \cdot Q_1(a,\ t_1) \cdot \sim Q_2(a,\ t_1))$" is a logical consequence of the reduction sentence, since its negation is logically incompatible with it.

[17] As noted on p. 560, the bilateral reduction sentences which Carnap formulates in FUS, treat the dispositional properties as time-dependent. Against them the above argument cannot therefore, be used. Nevertheless, the argument from the inductive generality of dispositional statements remains applicable.

If reduction sentences are thus construed as probability implications, the contrast between explicit definition and reduction appears in a different light. We find ourselves maintaining something which goes against the orthodox position of logical empiricism, viz. that an empirical statement, specifically a statement of an assumed law, can serve as a semantic rule without losing its empirical content. I think that the definitions of class-terms which are given in empirical sciences, and which unlike definitions in the formal sciences are constantly replaced by more suitable ones as a result of new discoveries about the members of the respective classes, are best interpreted as reduction-sentences of probabilistic character. The point may be explained in terms of one of Carnap's favorite examples of a synthetic universal sentence of the thing-language: all swans are white. Was it analytic or synthetic at the time when European zoologists knew nothing of the black swans in Australia? If we contend the former, then we must interpret the statement "there are black swans in Australia" as a redefinition of the term "swan"; if we contend the latter, then the acknowledgement of the existence of black swans is interpreted as abandonment of a law, recognition of a new species of the same old genus "swan". But zoologists would find it difficult to answer the question which of these interpretations expressed their intention. For the class-term "swan" is *intensionally vague* in their usage, i.e. no fixed boundary has been drawn between the defining and the accidental characteristics of swans. As Carnap himself points out in TM, scientists tend to leave the rules of application of a term to some extent indefinite; there are conceivable situations *S* such that the question whether *T* is applicable in *S* is undecidable in terms of the rules fixed so far. With respect to our example, zoologists had no fixed rule of application that covered the eventuality of there being found animals exactly like swans except for their color. But it is even doubtful whether *any* of the properties whose perception induces application of a class-term *T* could be considered as *definitory* in the sense in which, say, divisibility by two is a definitory property of even numbers. For even if we are now inclined to withhold *T* from objects that do not exhibit a certain property *P*, a future discovery of many objects which are just like objects to which *T* is normally applied except that they lack *P* might induce us to apply *T* to such objects also, speaking perhaps of "anomalous specimens" of the class in question.

Once this flexibility of rules of application is recognized, the following interpretation of *definitions* of empirical class-terms may appear as the most adequate: a subset, say, $P_1 \cdot P_2 \cdot P_3$, of an open set of usually compresent qualities are selected as highly reliable indicators of the rest of the set, and the classificatory statement "$a \in K$" based on the observation statements "$P_1(a)$", "$P_2(a)$" and "$P_3(a)$" express the expectation of finding the indicated set compresent with the indicating set. The inference from "$P_1(a) \cdot P_2(a) \cdot P_3(a)$" to "$a \epsilon K$" is then inductive even though the corresponding probability-implication serves at the same time to specify the (open) meaning of "*K*".[18] When such a subset is chosen by scientists as a necessary and sufficient condition for membership of *K*, this is to be interpreted as an expression of high confidence that the remainder of the set will be instantiated wherever and whenever this subset is instantiated and also that the remainder will not be instantiated at a place and time at which the subset is not instantiated. But then "$\sim P_1(a) \cdot a \epsilon K$" cannot be regarded as a formal contradiction, as it would have to be regarded if "*K*" were introduced, by explicit definition, as an abbreviation for a finite conjunction of predicates of which P_1 is a member. All we can say is that the scientist has a strong reluctance to classify this object as a member of *K* because he strongly expects it to lack the other members of the correlation. (By the "correlation" connoted by "*K*" is meant the totality of properties compresent with those properties on the basis of which "*K*" is introduced. Inasmuch as many elements of such a totality are unknown, the meaning of "*K*" is relatively indeterminate; it becomes more determinate as more elements of the totality are empirically discovered). If, on the other hand, this expectation is revealed as unfounded, and such "anomalous" specimens turn up frequently, they will be classified as a new species of *K*. Yet, we cannot describe this decision as the decision to change the previous meaning of "*K*" if we interpret the connections between the observation-predicates and the construct "*K*" as probability-connections; for P_1 was never a defining property of members of *K* in the same sense in which, say, rectangularity is a defining property of squares. The analogy to introduction of terms by reduction-pairs is striking; when we specify the meaning of "Q_3", partially, by the pair "$Q_1 \cdot Q_2 \supset Q_3; Q_4 \cdot Q_5 \cdot \supset \sim Q_3$", we assume that $\sim(Q_1 \cdot Q_2 \cdot Q_4 \cdot Q_5)$, in other words that Q_1 and Q_2 will never be accompanied by Q_4 and Q_5. Analogously, the "definition" of, say, oxygen by its atomic weight presupposes that the atomic weight 16 will never be found in a substance that is uncapable of sustaining combustion. Should we nevertheless find cases of the conjunction $Q_1 \cdot Q_2 \cdot Q_4 \cdot Q_5$, we would have the choice between applying "Q_3" to those cases and abandoning the second reduction-sentence (which corresponds to classifying the anomalous specimen as oxygen on the basis of its atomic weight and abandoning the statement that all oxygen is capable of sustaining combustion), or applying "$\sim Q_3$" to them and abandoning the first reduction sentence (which corresponds to refusing

[18]On such "probabilistic" specification of the meanings of empirical class-terms, cf. Kaplan and Schott, "A Calculus for Empirical Classes," *Methodos* (1951).

the term "oxygen" to the anomalous specimen, thereby saving the empirical law but abandoning the definition in terms of atomic weight).

Now, what I call the "dualistic" interpretation of such choices is the view that the choice lies between abandoning a *law* (inductively derived universal proposition) and abandoning a *definition*. But this disjunction does not make sense if the concepts in question are partially defined by sets of reduction sentences, since to split such a set into definitions and laws, analytic and synthetic statements, is to miss the very nature of this kind of specification of meaning. For similar reasons the analytic-synthetic dichotomy is inapplicable to partially interpreted scientific theories whose primitive constructs are "implicitly" defined by the postulates of the theory—whether or not they be also empirically *interpreted* or only connected by theoretical statements to other constructs of the theory for which there is an empirical ("operational") interpretation.[19] To illustrate, suppose that two criteria of equality of time-intervals are given, viz. (a) $t_1 = t_2$ if the arc described by standard pendulum *P* during t_1 equals the arc described by *P* during t_2, (b) $t_1 = t_2$ if the distance moved by a light ray in t_1 equals the distance moved by a light ray in t_2. According to the meaning of the word "definition" in the formal sciences, it would be impermissible to regard (a) and (b) as two definitions of the same concept, for they are not logically equivalent. For this reason philosophers of science whose primary training is in formal logic and mathematics and who want to reconstruct physics as a system with *uniquely defined* terms, will understandably say: "You can't have your cake and eat it too. You may choose between (a) and (b) as definitions of time congruence, but you have to make a choice. If you choose (a) as definition, (b) becomes a synthetic, empirically refutable statement, and if you choose

[19]Carnap first suggested in FLM (p. 65) that it might be best to reconstruct a physical theory in such a way that the primitive theoretical terms in the postulates are left without direct interpretation and semantical rules, providing an interpretation by means of the "observation language", are applied to the "bottom" of the theory only. While Carnap at that time confined himself to the remark that this method of merely indirect and partial interpretation of theoretical terms like "electron", "magnetic field" etc. has its advantages, C. G. Hempel went further and argued that it is even in principle impossible to introduce such terms by means of reduction sentences: "Fundamentals of Concept Formation in Empirical Science," *Int. Encyclopedia of Unified Science*, II, 7; also in "The Concept of Cognitive Significance: A Reconsideration," *Proceedings of American Academy of Arts and Sciences*, LXXX, no. 1. Carnap's more recent views on what he calls the "theoretical language" of science and its relation to the "observation language" are to be found in "The Methodological Character of Theoretical Concepts," in H. Feigl and M. Scriven (eds.), *Minnesota Studies in the Philosophy of Science*, I. Taking as my point of departure the distinction theoretical-observational language as elaborated in the latter paper, I have argued in detail that the analytic-synthetic distinction is not applicable to partially interpreted theories of mathematical physics, in "Are Physical Magnitudes Operationally Definable?"

See also my book *Semantics and Necessary Truth* (New Haven: Yale University Press, 1957) ch. 11.

(b) as the definition, (a) becomes a synthetic, empirically refutable statement". Yet, if (a) and (b) are meant as partial definitions, whether theoretical postulates or reduction sentences, for the same term, then this rebuke to those who maintain that the physical laws themselves define the physical concepts—which position presupposes multiplicity of criteria of application for the same concept—is beside the point.

One of the perennial questions in the philosophy of science is whether the statements connecting theoretical constructs (like "electrical field") with observables (like "divergence of the leaves of an electroscope") are to be regarded as definitions (phenomenalism) *or* as synthetic statements of a causal character (realism).[20] The first alternative is unsatisfactory because it entails that at least one conjunction of the form "$C \cdot \sim O$", where "C" represents an existential statement in theoretical language) "there is an electrical field in this space-time region") and "O" an evidential statement about observables, is self-contradictory; whereas it is always conceivable that the negative evidence "$\sim O$" be outweighed by other evidence that favors "C" sufficiently to lead to its tentative assertion and tentative abandonment of the conditional "if C, then O". And the second alternative is likewise unsatisfactory, because it is impossible to describe conceivable evidence that would support a theoretical existence assertion except in terms of observables, and hence one is inclined to say that such existential statements must mean obscrvable phenomena though their meaning may be inexhaustible. But insofar as the theoretical concepts are at all interpreted in terms of observables, the semantical rules (in Carnap's terminology) or coordinative definitions (in Reichenbach's terminology) cannot take the form of an analytical equivalence; they are partial definitions of a probabilistic character. From this point of view it is misleading to reconstruct a partially interpreted physical theory "dualistically" as a set of object-linguistic postulates that "refer to reality" ("Tatsachenaussagen," in the language of the Vienna Circle) and a set of coordinative definitions in the metalanguage that are not *assertions* at all, let alone empirical assertions. It is but the conjunction of theoretical postulates and coordinative definitions that yields testable observation statements, hence a discrepancy between the interpreted theory and observations can be resolved either by modifying the theoretical postulates or by changing the coordinative definitions. An example which ought to clarify this point is the physical interpretation of a formal geometry by means of coordinative definitions. As a possible physical interpretation of the primitive "straight line" in Euclidean formal goemetry, one often mentions "path of a light ray". At the same time,

[20]For a comprehensive discussion of this problem, see H. Feigl, "Existential Hypotheses," *Philosophy of Science* (January, 1950).

however, one concedes that, should the resulting propositions of physical geometry, like the proposition that the sum of the interior angles of a triangle, no matter how large, equals 180°, turn out to be false, it would not be logically necessary to abandon Euclidean goemetry as a description of physical space; one might just as well question the *law of optics* that light rays are propagated rectilinearly. One thus admits that the coordinative "definition" has itself an inductive character, and there is nothing paradoxical about it if one construes this optical definition of straightness as a partial definition, a postulate. As Poincaré pointed out, the desire to continue using the simpler concepts of Euclidean geometry for the description of physical space may lead the physicist to reject the hypothesis that light rays are straight and to postulate deflecting forces. Now, suppose the question were raised whether in denying that light rays in gravitational fields travel in straight lines—in the Euclidean sense of "straight"—one is simply changing the physical meaning of "straight", i.e. changing the coordinative definition, or is rejecting an empirical hypothesis in order to restore agreement between the total system of empirical hypotheses and the results of observation. This question, I submit, is a pseudoquestion prompted by an untenably rigid analytic-synthetic dualism. For there is no criterion for distinguishing rejection of an empirical hypothesis formulated by means of a theoretical term T and reinterpretation of T. The meaning of "straight line" is determined by both the geometrical postulates and the coordinative definitions, and neither of them have a factual content in isolation from the other.

What does "probability" mean in the context of probabilistic reduction sentences? It is easy to see that the meaning cannot be "relative frequency". For according to the frequency interpretation a probability implication is a statement of an empirical correlation of *logically independent* properties, a statement, therefore, which cannot be established by logical analysis; and this very conception involves the dualism which appears problematic when one examines the logical relations between constructs and observation predicates. Consider, for example, a statement about the relative frequency of blue-eyed children within the class of children of blue-eyed parents. Such a statement presupposes that one can determine—as, indeed, one can—whether a child is blue-eyed independently of determining whether it has blue-eyed parents. On the other hand, when one says "on the evidence that animals breathing this gas in pure form get killed, it is probable to degree x that the gas is nitrogen," no such logical independence of properties is presupposed, for this very probability-implication serves as a partial definition of "nitrogen". To be sure, it is just because of the existence of other partial definitions for the same term, such as the definition of "nitrogen" as a gas in which flames get extinguished, that it is possible for the term "nitrogen" to be withheld from a gas satisfying the mentioned condition. But each of these partial definitions contributes its share to the meaning of the term and cannot be regarded as a synthetic statement about an independently identifiable entity. For similar reasons, the concept of probability here involved cannot be the logical concept which Carnap calls "degree of confirmation", unless essential changes are introduced into the kind of language-system to which it is relative. For a degree of confirmation depends on the *ranges* of the sentences involved, and a range is definable as a class of statement-descriptions which *entail* a given sentence. But the rules by which Carnap defines entailment refer to a language-system in which all non-primitive predicates are eliminable through complete definitions until sentences in primitive notation are reached whose logical relations to one another are purely formal. Such rules, however, are useless for deciding such questions as whether predications of a given construct, a term reducible to observation-predicates yet ineliminable, are true if such and such observation-statements are true. It is striking that there is no mention whatever of reduction-sentences in LFP. On the other hand, a brief remark on the possibility of introducing reduction-sentences into descriptive language-systems as "meaning-postulates" may be found in the recent paper "Meaning-Postulates" (*Philosophical Studies,* III, No. 5). Perhaps probabilistic reduction-sentences could be regarded as "meaning-postulates" postulating weights of dispositional statements relative to statistical evidence. But I suspect that if disposition-predicates, introduced by this method, are to be incorporated into the language relative to which "degree of confirmation" is defined (and if Carnap's inductive logic is to be relevant to science, such an innovation will sooner or later have to be countenanced), the concepts of "state-description" and "range" will have to be modified. For the function of meaning-postulates as originally proposed by Kemeny and Bar-Hillel[21] (and welcomed by Carnap) was to restrict the class of state-descriptions. For example, if "(x)(y) (warmer (x,y) $\supset$ $\sim$warmer (y,x))" is a meaning-postulate in L, then L does not contain state-descriptions incompatible with it, i.e. containing subconjunctions of the form "warmer (x,y) $\cdot$ warmer (y,x)". But no conjunction of atomic statements and negations of atomic statements involving Q_1, Q_2 and Q_3 is incompatible with: $(Q_1 \ni\!\!-_x Q_2) \ni\!\!-\!\!3_y Q_3$. Hence such a "meaning-postulate" does not restrict the class of state-descriptions. That a concept of "degree of entailment" cannot easily be incorporated into Carnapian semantics is, indeed, no surprise, since the latter rests on a sharp dichotomy between the logically possible and the logically impossible.

[21]See the reference given in "Meaning Postulates", *loc. cit.*

It was stated earlier in this section that the "dualistic" reconstruction of scientific language is inadequate because it presupposes that scientists operate with *complete* rules of application, while their frequent wavering between redefinition and recognition of a new species when certain discoveries are made rather indicates the contrary. Further, I have attempted to show that Carnap's theory of reduction sentences is indeed incompatible with such a dualistic reconstruction though Carnap himself inconsistently tried to divide reduction-sentences into "L-valid" and "P-valid" ones (holding that bilateral reduction-sentences are L-valid, in contrast to reduction pairs). Returning now to the initial question whether it is just the, rational or irrational, choice of an extensional language of reconstruction that forces reduction sentences upon the philosopher of science, we see that the answer is definitely negative. For the argument from incompleteness of rules of application (or from intensional vagueness, or from openness of meanings—whatever be the preferred terminology) would retain its force, if the concept of causal implication were used as an irreducible "logical constant" in defining disposition-concepts. One can find support for this contention in TM itself, as the following quotation will show:

> Thus, if we wish to introduce a new term into the language of science, we have to distinguish two cases. If the situation is such that we wish to fix the meaning of the new term once for all, then a definition is the appropriate form. On the other hand, if we wish to determine the meaning of the term at the present time for some cases only, leaving its further determination for other cases to decisions which we intend to make step by step, on the basis of empirical knowledge which we expect to obtain in the future, then the method of reduction is the appropriate one rather than that of definition. (p. 449)

However, Carnap did not clearly separate this argument from the "argument from material implication". The latter argument led, as we have seen, to the conception of reduction-pairs in the first place. Luckily, Carnap then finds that the technique of reduction is not something simply imposed upon the scientists in order that an extensional logic be applicable to scientific language; it corresponds to the openness of constructs. But if we take a close look at the reasons which Carnap thereupon imputes to the scientist for desisting from explicit definitions of constructs, we find ourselves simply returning to the argument from material implication. For such explicit definitions, says Carnap, would either have the form "$Q_3 \equiv (Q_1 \cdot Q_2)$" or the form "$Q_3 \equiv (\sim Q_1 \vee Q_2)$"; that is, they would either entail that pieces of sugar that are never immersed are insoluble, or that matches that are kept dry until they burn up are soluble. Yet, what needs proving in order to prove that the technique of reduction is actually operating in empirical science and has not just been invented in order to render extensional logic applicable to empirical science, is that even explicit definition of constructs in terms of *causal* implication would not correspond to the scientists' use of constructs. I believe that this, which Carnap failed to show in TM, can indeed be proved, as follows.

In the first place, such explicit definitions,[22] like "there is an electric field at place P at time $t \equiv$ if an electroscope were at P at t, then its leaves would diverge at t", or "the weight of $A =$ the weight of $B \equiv$ if A and B were suspended at equal distances from the fulcrum of a beam balance, then the balance would be in equilibrium", entail that if the test described by the definiens is positive, then an eventual derivation of contradictory statements about the constructs on the basis of physical laws involving them would be no cause for revoking the statements about the constructs; it would be cause for abandoning the physical laws. But if, e.g. A and B produced a state of equilibrium in perfect experimental conditions, yet produced unequal strains in a spring-scale and behaved in a variety of other situations as though they had different weights, it would not be unreasonable to suspect that they really differ in weight; and it seems exceedingly far-fetched to suppose that a scientist who finally decided to accept this hypothesis had decided to change the meaning of the expression "equal weight". It is of course possible to call such an operation "redefinition motivated by empirical discoveries", but such a description presupposes that the term in question has in any given context of usage a *fixed* meaning, which is just the question at issue. At any rate, if we cannot state an effective criterion for deciding whether a given adjustment of scientific theory to new observational data is a *change of meanings* or *a change of empirical laws,* it is doubtful whether the issue is more than terminological.

However, an analysis of the logical relations between statements of experimental physics and statements of theoretical physics may reveal that the "dualistic" reconstruction is not only arbitrary but definitely inadequate. Let us assume that what Bridgman and others call an "operational definition" of a construct, like the definition of temperature as what is measured by the mercury thermometer, is an explicit definition of a closed concept rather than a reduction sentence for an open concept. It is clear that this definition would not fit the meaning of "temperature" in such contexts of extrapolation beyond the experimental range of physical variables as statements about the temperature of the sun: whatever such a statement may mean, it is not a prediction of what coincidence would be observed on a gigantic mercury thermometer filled with non-vaporizable mercury if it were brought into contact with the sun. One

[22]"Explicit definition," is here used broadly to cover explicit definition in the narrower sense and definitions in use as special cases. The above examples are of course definitions in use.

who adheres to Bridgman's dictum that different operations of verification define different concepts would therefore have to say that "temperature" has different meanings, designates different concepts, accordingly as we substitute in the sentential function "$Te(x,t) = y° C$" "this room" *for* "x" and "20" for "y", or "the sun" for "x" and "5000" for "y". Now, in order to deduce the temperature of the sun we require as premises propositions of measurement about the average temperature at the surface of the earth and numerical laws involving the same functor "*Te*", like the Stefan-Boltzmann law of the relation between intensity of heat-radiation (*I*) and absolute temperature. More explicitly, the steps of the deduction are: (1) calculation of *I* for the earth's surface from the measured temperature of the earth and the Stefan-Boltzmann law, (2) calculation of *I* for the sun's surface from data yielding the sun's (average) distance from the earth and from the inverse square law of heat radiation, (3) calculation of the sun's temperature from the result of (2) and renewed application of the Stefan-Boltzmann law. But if the same functor "*Te*" has different meanings in the conclusion and in the experimental premise (used in step 1) of the deduction, the deduction cannot be valid. The argument could be repeated with reference to, say, calculations of atomic weights, or of the mass of an electron. It does not make sense to suppose that the operations of measuring *molar* weights, which according to the criticized naive form of "operationism" *define* "weight", be applied to atoms or electrons. Yet the scientists calculate such constants by using the same laws (additivity of weight, conservation of mechanical energy) which have already been verified on the molar level, and assuming that their variables *retain their physical meanings* when values so small as to be experimentally insignificant are substituted for them. It appears therefore, that an operationist "closure", so to speak, of the meanings of physical functors like "weight", "temp", "length" through explicit definitions in terms of observables, would destroy the logical bridge on which physicists move from measured values of those functors to calculated values which it is in principle impossible to check by similar measurements. To add one more illustration: if Mach's operational definition of mass in terms of mutually induced accelerations were an explicit definition of a closed concept, rather than a reduction sentence or a postulate for an open concept, then "mass" in the context "mass of the earth" could hardly mean the same determinable property as it means in the context "mass of a billiard ball". Yet, when the mass of the earth is calculated from the measurable acceleration of gravity, the *same law* "$F = m.a$" is used (in conjunction with the law of gravitation) which has been antecedently confirmed in experiments with such manipulable bodies as billiard balls. And such a calculational use of the law leads to a grounded conclusion only if the factor "mass" occurs in the latter with the same meaning as in the premises.[23]

III. Explicit Definability: Another Attempt

Let us return to the question whether disposition concepts are explicitly definable in terms of *causal* implication. An argument against this possibility which is independent of the argument from "openness of constructs" runs as follows:[24] Suppose we define "$Dx = Ox \rightarrow Rx$", where the arrow represents causal implication, implicitly defined by a set of postulates including the postulate that for self-consistent p, "$p \rightarrow q$" is incompatible with "$p \rightarrow \sim q$",[25] "O" refers to an operation of testing x for D, and "R" to a positive test-result, i.e. manifestation of D. Since one property causally implies another only if *anything* which has the first also has the second, this definition entails that everything within the range of "x" has the disposition—an undesirable consequence, since we want to define "soluble", e.g. in such a way that it remains false to say that a wooden object is soluble. The following ways of amending the definition suggest themselves:

(a) We should conjunctively add to the antecedent of the definiens a condition, other than the defined disposition itself, which only objects that have the disposition satisfy. The definiens then becomes "$Fx \cdot (Fx \cdot Ox \rightarrow Rx)$", where $(x)(Fx \rightarrow Dx)$. But the weakness of this amendment should be obvious. In order to know whether F is the property we want, we have to confirm the causal law "$(x)(Fx \rightarrow Dx)$", which presupposes that we can test an object for D independently of testing it for F. If we can do this, then an operational definition of "D" need not refer to F at all; and if we cannot do it, then we have no way of finding out whether F serves the purpose of narrowing the definiens so as to make it coextensive with the definiendum. But two more objections may be added: first, if we knew that an object a has F, we would already know that it has D, and so performance of O upon a would be unnecessary; and if we did not know that a has F, performance of O would not enable us to come to a decision whether a has D. Secondly, since it would at any rate be *logically* possible that an object which has F lacks D, it would

23As to the question of the criterion of identity of meaning for theoretical terms that are not definable on the basis of observation-predicates, see my more recent paper, "Are Physical Magnitudes Operationally Definable?" cited in footnote 19. The question is also discussed in H. Feigl, "Operationism and Scientific Method," in Feigl and Sellars, *Readings in Philosophical Analysis,* 504f; H. Margenau, *The Nature of Physical Reality,* ch. 12.

24This argument was first suggested to me by Wilfrid Sellars. It is implicitly stated also in the recent paper "On Defining Disposition Predicates," by Jan Berg, in *Analysis* (March, 1955).

25For an axiomatic treatment of causal implication, see A. Burks, "The Logic of Causal Propositions," *Mind* (July, 1951).

remain logically possible that the definiendum and definiens fail to be coextensive. Therefore the amended definition would not express an *intensional* equivalence. But I realize that this latter objection would not be taken seriously by those who, like perhaps Carnap himself find an absolute concept of necessity obscure.

(b) Perhaps we would fare better if, instead of mentioning a specific property F, we merely assert, in the definiens, the existence of some such property: $Dx = (Ef)(fx \cdot (y)(fy \cdot Oy \rightarrow Rx))$. This definition is exactly like Kaila's definition (see (3), p. 563), except that causal implication is used and therefore the existential clause, precluding vacuous truth of the universal conditional, is not needed. But even if the range of "f" is restricted to general properties (in order to escape Carnap's objection to Kaila), Wedberg's objection remains applicable: if we take as value of "fx" "$Ox \supset Rx$", an object a on which O is never performed satisfies the first conjunct, and it satisfies the second conjunct tautologically.[26] However, this objection is valid only if we so use "causal implication" that all logical ("strict") implications are counted as causal. And since one ordinarily means by a causal implication an implication which, though stronger than material implication, is not logically true, I do not consider this as a serious objection. And I do not see that there are values of "f" which satisfy all of the following conditions: (1) they are purely general, (2) "fa" follows from "$\sim(Oa)$", (3) "$(y)(fy \cdot Oy \rightarrow Ry)$" is true but not logically true.

Have we found, then, the explicit definition we were looking for? In order to decide, we must review our adequacy criteria for explicit definitions of disposition concepts. Perhaps so much attention has been paid to the obvious criterion which (1) so grossly violates, viz. that disposition concepts should not be vacuously predicable, that an equally obvious criterion has been forgotten: that dispositional statements should be in principle disconfirmable, indeed, that such dispositional statements as "wood is soluble in water", "water is an inflammable liquid", should be false. How could one refute the hypothesis that a wooden object has *some* property such that anything which has that property dissolves, by causal necessity, if it is immersed? But this objection again is not serious, if only we distinguish conclusive refutation from disconfirmation. Since in practice only a surveyable number of values of "f" would be considered as conceivably relevant to the question whether O would invariably lead to R for a given kind of object,[27] a dispositional statement may be said

[26] This is pointed out by Jan Berg, *loc cit.*

[27] Notice that one does, indeed, assume in ordinary dispositional talk that if a given object a has disposition D then a has some property F such that any other object which has F also has D. It is for this reason that I speak above of a "given *kind* of object".

to be disconfirmable to the degree that it is probable that no relevant value of "f" has been overlooked. As far as testability is concerned, our new definition, made possible by obstinate (and, I should say, commendable) determination to transcend both the straightjacket of a nominalistic language and the straightjacket of an extensional language, has no more alarming consequence than that dispositional statements are mixed general statements and therefore are neither conclusively verifiable nor conclusively refutable. In this respect, at any rate, it fares no worse than the kind of probabilistic reduction-sentence sketched on p. 572.

On the other hand, the definition is incompatible with the view that to ascribe a disposition to an object is to assert, though implicitly only, a law. For according to our definition a dispositional statement *asserts the existence of a law,* which is different from *asserting a law.* The difference may be illustrated by the following example. Suppose we define "elasticity", as a dispositional property of such materials as metal wires, as follows: x is elastic if and only if for all values of stress and strain, the stress upon x is equal to a constant times the strain produced in x. According to this definition, to assert that something is elastic is to assert a law. The statement that a is elastic would be refuted if for some values of stress and strain imposed on a the specified relation did not hold. In fact, since this is bound to happen no matter what material a is, there would be no elastic objects according to this definition. On the other hand, if the definition of "elastic" (considered here as a classificatory, not a comparative nor a metrical concept) follows the explored schema, it might read: . . . . if and only if there is a property f such that Fx and such that for all values. . . . If we now come upon a set of values of stress and strain which do not fit into the specified formula, we need not abandon the hypothesis that the object is elastic. On the contrary, guided by the belief that the object is elastic in the specified sense, we shall look for a property of the object which is such that only objects that do not have it behave in accordance with the specified formula. The property we are looking for may be the property of being subject to a stress exceeding a certain upper limit, called the "elastic limit".

Putting it in general terms: if the dispositional statement asserts the existence of a law, then satisfaction of the function "$(y)(fy \cdot Oy \rightarrow Ry)$"("$f$" being the free variable) is the *criterion* for determining whether a given property F is the "right" property, and therefore the dispositional statement enjoys an immunity from strict refutation which a causal law, according to usual conception of "causal law", does not enjoy. Notice that if by the "openness" of disposition concepts we mean this sort of thing, viz. the occurrence of a predicate *variable* in the definientia, then explicit definability is compatible with openness.

However, while the analysis of dispositional statements without predicate-variable is pregnant with the unsatisfactory consequence that many objects to which we wish to ascribe the defined disposition do not have the disposition—as we might put it, this type of analysis amounts to premature "closure" of disposition concepts—the analysis *with* predicate-variable faces the opposite danger of enlarging unduely the extensions of disposition-predicates. Consider, to illustrate, those dispositions whose manifestations consist in sense-data, e.g., colors as properties of physical objects. If "x is blue at time t" means "there is a property f which x has at t and which is such that any object which has f at t and is looked at by a visually normal organism at t, appears blue at t",[28] then many objects which we do not regard as being blue at any time would turn out to be blue at some time. Suppose, e.g., that a red physical surface was looked at through blue spectacles at some time. If we take as f just this property which the surface had at some time, we can prove by the definition that the surface was blue at that time. To be sure, if we crowd enough "normality conditions" into the constant part of the antecedent, i.e. into "O" (normal conditions of visual perception, we might stipulate, include absense of a discoloring medium), such consequences can be avoided. But then, on the other hand, the very purpose of the predicate-variable would be defeated: the predicate-variable, as we saw, just serves the purpose of turning the dispositional statement into a "guiding principle", a principle guiding the search for conditions necessary for the strict regularity of the sequence $O \rightarrow R$.

In conclusion I would suggest that to the extent that it is both possible and desirable to define disposition concepts explicitly, the definition schema involving a predicate-variable is correct, but that my application of the schema involves a mediation between the extremes of closure and openness for which no rules can be laid down a priori. That is, one should avoid the impasse of crowding so many conditions into the constant part of the antecedent that the variable part becomes redundant and the disposition concept gets closed once and for all, and should also avoid the impasse of leaving the constant part so thin (in intensional content) and wide (in extensional content), that the disposition concept receives a larger extension than it should.[29]

[28]The definiens can be less ambiguously expressed in symbolic logic: $(\exists f)\,(fx,t \cdot (y)\,(t)\,(fy,t \cdot Oy,t \rightarrow Ry,t))$.

[29]The distinction between "asserting a law" and "asserting the existence of a law" is emphasized by Herbert Bohnert in his acute article "Lewis' Attribution of Value to Objects," *Phil. Studies* (June, 1950). He proposes the term "potentiality" for properties explicated by means of a predicate-variable and "disposition" for properties that are "closed" in the sense above explained. But I think the distinction is not as sharp as he makes it out. I do not think "x is soluble" only means "there are conditions under which x dissolves", it rather means "there are conditions, such that if x were immersed in a liquid under those conditions, then x would dissolve". The conditions

IV. *Dispositions, Observables, and Physicalism*

Carnap's theory of reduction sentences involves the contrast between disposition-predicates and *observation*-predicates; for this reason I have referred to the former as designating *constructs*. As observation-predicates Carnap lists such primitive predicates of the thing-language as "hard", "red", "heavy". However, one might object that if what marks a predicate as dispositional is the fact that in order to explicate, partially or completely, its meaning one must use universal conditionals, then no predicate of the physical language (of which the thing-language is a part) can be other than dispositional: "*x is* red" (where "*x*" is a thing-variable) differs from "*x appears* red" in that it asserts that *x would* appear red if specified normal conditions (perceptual and environmental) were realised; and, of course, this explicit definition would, in an extensional language, have to give way to the corresponding reduction-sentence for exactly the same reason as has already been discussed in connection with "soluble". Are we not driven to the conclusion, then, that the only observation-predicates are sense-data predicates? This position, indeed, would correspond to the theme of the "Logische Aufbau der Welt" that all entities, of whatever type, are logical constructions out of the immediately given, and that the proper reduction-basis therefore is the "positivistic" basis (i.e. the basis consisting of sense-data predicates)—except that reduction sentences take the place of explicit definitions (or definitions in use).

Now, the idea that the positivistic basis is "proper", rather than the physicalistic basis, is repudiated by Carnap. He emphasizes in section 16 of TM that "there can be several and even mutually exclusive bases". Indeed, it is obvious that instead of reducing the thing-predicate "red^t" to the sense-data predicate "red^s" (with the help of an additional predicate, call it "L", designating a perceptual operation such as looking in a definite direction), one could just as well reduce "red^s" to "red^t". To get the latter, the physicalistic reduction, all we need to do is to exchange these predicates in the reduction sentence: $(y)(t)(L_{y,t} \supset red^t_x \equiv red^s_{y,t}))$ y,t)).[30] This formal feature of bilateral reduction-sentences connecting

thus summarily referred to without being individually enumerated are the "normality conditions" (frequently referred to by the safety-clause "others being equal"). But then objective colors or temperature degrees (Bohnert's examples of "dispositions" in his sense) are not significantly more "closed" than solubility: we claim that a thing is blue though we are ignorant of some of the, organic and environmental, normality conditions which must be realised if looking at the thing is to be followed invariably by a blue sensation, just as we claim that sugar is soluble though we do not know some of the conditions which must be realised if the sequence "sugar being immersed → sugar dissolving" is to be strictly exceptionless.

[30] The variable "*y*" here ranges over observers; hence "red^s" characterizes a perceptual state of an observer. Alternatively, one could let "*y*" range over sense-data and replace "L" by something like Lewis' "seeming to look". But then one would get into such difficult questions as whether the *same* sense-datum could be character-

thing-predicates and sense-data predicates has also an epistemological significance. It is conceivable that a human being be first taught, by the kind of conditioning called "ostensive definition", the use of perception-terms (the teacher points at a red thing and says, not "this is red", but "now you see red"), and be subsequently introduced to the corresponding thing-predicates by means of the "anybody would . . . , if . . ." idiom. And the very same idiom could be used to introduce one who was first made to feel at home in the thing-language, into the language of perception-terms. In other words, just as we can define "red^t" as the disposition of a thing to produce, under suitable conditions, perceptions characterized by "red^s", so we can define "red^s" as the kind of perception produced, under suitable conditions, by red things. It is therefore obscure what could be meant by the statement that "red^s", not "red^t", is *epistemologically primitive* although either of these terms may be taken as "primitive" in the syntactic sense. And this, one would expect, is the position of neutrality that Carnap would adopt in the controversy over which reduction-basis is the right one, the physicalistic or the positivistic (nowadays more commonly called "phemonenalistic") one.

However, a consistent adherence to this position necessitates, I believe, a *relativization* of the distinction between constructs and observables, disposition-predicates and observation-predicates, which is lacking in TM as well as in FUS. Carnap's definition of the term "observable predicate", which is so central in his scientific methodology, is vague:

A predicate '*P*' of a language *L* is called *observable* for an organism (e.g. a person) *N*, if, for suitable arguments, e.g. '*b*', *N* is able under suitable circumstances to come to a decision with the help of few observations about a full sentence, say '*P* (*b*)', i.e., to a confirmation of either '*P* (*b*)' or ~'*P*(*b*)' of such a high degree that he will either accept or reject '*P* (*b*)'. (pp.454-55).

Although Carnap promptly acknowledges the vagueness of this definition ("There is no sharp line between observable and non-observable predicates because a person will be more or less able to decide a certain sentence quickly . . .") he seems subsequently to have forgotten it. For he decides, in section 20, against the choice of perception-terms as primitive terms of an intersubjective, scientific language on the ground that they (more accurately: the states they designate) are only *subjectively observable*. Carnap means, of course, that I can observe *my* state of seeing red but not anyone else's, whereas red things are open to public obser-

ized as "seeming to look" and as "seeing red", or whether two sense-data variables "*y*" and "*z*" should be used, also whether "*t*" should not in that case range over perceptual, not physical, times. It should further be noted that the above reduction sentence is certainly false unless various normality conditions are specified in the antecedent. To immunize it against empirical disconfirmation by a single case of non-fulfillment of such conditions one would have to formulate it as a probability-implication (cf. section 2).

vation. Yet, how could Carnap defend the claim, entailed by his definition of "observable", that the sentence "the thing before me is red" can be confirmed to a high degree by a few observations, but that this is not possible for the sentence "John, who is now looking at the thing before me, sees red"? By virtue of the discussed bilateral reduction sentence—which, to put it cautiously, is at least as plausible as the reduction sentence for "soluble"—the evidence that the thing which John now looks at is red, confirms the hypothesis that John now sees red to just the same degree as the evidence that John, in looking at *x*, sees red, confirms the hypothesis that *x* is red. Carnap's justification of the choice of a physicalistic reduction-basis overlooks that a few observations induce an observer to pronounce a thing as red, or hard, or heavy, only because he expects on the basis of past experience that similar observations would produce similar perceptions in other observers; hence, if an inductive inference is involved in the judgment "he now sees red", it is likewise involved in the judgment "*x* is red"—and *tollendo tollens.* Therefore, Carnap's claim that thing-predicates are intersubjectively observable while perception-predicates are not, is untenable.

Now, remember that Carnap's criterion for the dispositional character of a predicate *"P"* was that a sentence of the form *"Px"* could not be directly confirmed but had to be inferred from sentences which could be directly confirmed with the help of a universal conditional (the reduction sentence). But then one might argue that even perception-predicates are dispositional, at least when they are applied to other minds. In the sentence "John now sees red", one might say, "sees red" designates a disposition, because the sentence is but indirectly confirmable, through inference from physical stimuli and responses. While there is no hint of this strange consequence in TM, it is indeed explicitly drawn in FUS. There Carnap tells us: "The logical nature of the psychological terms becomes clear by an analogy with those physical terms which are introduced by reduction statements of the conditional form. Terms of both kinds designate a state characterized by the disposition to certain reactions" (p.420). And he proceeds to illustrate the analogy in terms of "electrically charged" and "angry". The illustration he chose favors the analogy somewhat since "angry" is actually used in a dispositional sense quite often (e.g. "you'd better not speak to him now: he is still angry at you")—though it is *also* used in a non-dispositional sense (e.g. "that rude remark got me angry"). But had he chosen instead "seeing red", which is just as good a psychological term, one's suspicion would inevitably be aroused: what a strange use of the word "disposition", to say that seeing red is a disposition! Isn't there a big difference between saying *"X* has a disposition to see red when he looks at object *y*" and saying *"X* just now, while looking at *y*, saw red"? Does the latter statement simply amount to a dispositional statement of lowest order? But is there anything non-dispositional below this order of statements, then? Secondly, as Carnap explicitly admits, there is at least one observer who *can* directly confirm the sentence 'John is angry now", viz. John himself. It follows that Carnap's statement that psychological terms—as terms of an intersubjective physicalistic language —*designate dispositions* is inaccurate by his own criterion of dispositionality. At most he would be entitled to say that psychological terms are dispositional as applied to other minds (or other organisms, as he would prefer to say); in their autobiographical use, as when a human guinea-pig reports his sensations to an experimental psychologist, they would not be dispositional. It may be added that once so much is conceded, one ought to concede even more, viz. that terms like "seeing red" or "feeling excited" or "thinking of the Vienna City Hall" are *never* used dispositionally, no matter whether the sentences begin with "I" or with "he". For otherwise "I see red" could never be an answer to "do you see red?", and the language of psychology would have to forego just that intersubjectivity which the physicalists want to secure for it.

There seem to be two ways in which these difficulties might be overcome. One might, following a line which no philosopher is more ready to take than Carnap himself, relativize the concept "disposition-predicate" to a language, such that it makes no sense to say categorically " 'red' is an observation-predicate, not a disposition-predicate; 'soluble' is a disposition-predicate, not an observation-predicate". In effect, this would be turning "dispositional-predicate" into a synonym for "predicate *introduced* into *L* by reduction *sentences*" and "observation-predicate" into a synonym for "primitive predicate in *L*" (where *L* is a descriptive language). To say that it is the disposition-predicates which are introduced, and the observation-predicates which are taken as primitive, would then amount to a tautology. On this alternative, it would be meaningless to ask whether it is the thing-predicates or the perception-predicates which are *really* observation-predicates. The thing-predicates are observation-predicates relatively to the physical language, where they occur as primitives, and the perception-predicates are observation-predicates relatively to the phenomenalistic language, in which the thing-predicates are the "introduced" predicates. One might then graduate the dispositional-observable distinction, in addition to relativizing it. Within the language of physics (a sublanguage of the physicalistic language of science, as Carnap conceives the ideal scientific language), e.g., temperature-states would be low dispositions relatively to coincidences indicated by thermometers, but would be "observables" relatively to thermal conductivity which is a higher disposition (construct). Indeed, what is here called *degree* of dispositionality is the same as what Carnap calls degree of "abstractness" of scientific terms. (see FLM).

However, this formalization of the distinction—a method of analysis which many enemies of Carnap brand as escape from philosophical problems (report without commitment)—raises a question which leads straight to the second solution. The question is simply whether it does not, after all, make sense to say that "soluble" *as used in natural language,* not as introduced into a language-system, designates a disposition (whether of low or of high order), while "seeing red", again as used in natural language, does not? Undoubtedly, the answer is affirmative. But thus we have to face the task of defining the distinction as an *absolute* one and yet avoiding the difficulties that have been called attention to. We cannot say, it will be recalled, that a predicate is dispositional if it is reducible by universal conditionals to other predicates, for the reason that such reducibility is perfectly symmetrical (at least if the reduction sentence is bilateral). What, then, do we mean when we say that "soluble" is dispositional but that "dissolving" is not? We have already seen that it would not do to characterize the first predicate as dispositional on the ground that its atomic sentences involve no definite date (cf.p.562). I think what we mean, obscure as it is, is that the meaning of "soluble" is explicable on the basis of "dissolving", but not the other way around; that "dissolving" is the simpler predicate. At any rate, we would infer to the dispositional character of *"A"* from the reducibility of *"A"* to *"B"* and *"C"* only if the reduction-sentence seems to us to explicate what *"A"* means. For this reason, most of us would deny that seeing red is a disposition, like being electrically charged, even though "seeing red" is reducible to physical predicates; in the same obscure sense in which "dissolving" is simpler than "soluble", "red^{s}" is simpler than "red^{t}".

For the problem at hand, we may as well forget reduction sentences, and consider an intensional language in which the disposition-predicates are characterized by being introduced through definitions in use whose definiens is a causal implication. Then we may say that a predicate designates a disposition in the *absolute* sense if such a definition expresses an *analysis.* But then it follows that an observation-predicate is nothing else than a predicate designating a *simple* property, or more accurately, a *molecular property,* i.e. if *"P"* is an observation-predicate then *"P(a)"* is a factual statement which is not an inductive generalization. If this, however, is the sense of "observation-predicate", then the division of *physical* predicates into dispositional and observational ones is highly dubious. We seem to be left rather with the division of predicates into physical predicates and sense-data predicates. And the atomic sentences, which play such a fundamental role in Carnap's "Grundlegung" of deductive and inductive logic, would, as in Russell's "Philosophy of Logical Atomism", be sentences about sense-data, not about things, nor about space-time points. Since it is just the notorious difficulties setting this *epistemolog-*

ical concept of "atomic sentence" which led Carnap to the choice of a physicalistic basis for the language of science, I anticipate that he would prefer to relativize the concept of dispositionality to a language. At any rate, I hope I have made the problem sufficiently clear to make it possible for Carnap to tackle it in his usual lucid manner.

V. *Conditional Definitions, and Significance-Conditions*

Let us, in this concluding section, turn our attention to a feature of conditional definitions which was emphasized in section 1): whether a predicate introduced by such definitions is *significantly* (not just "truly") applicable in a given situation depends on contingent facts. If "Q_3" is introduced by a reduction-pair whose representative sentence is "$\sim(Q_1 \cdot Q_2 \cdot Q_4 \cdot Q_5)$", then it is significantly predicable of an individual *a* only if either "$Q_1(a)$" or "$Q_4(a)$" is true. Consequently the law of the excluded middle holds only conditionally with respect to such predicates, i.e., we cannot assert "$(x)\,(Q_3(x) \vee \sim Q_3(x))$", but only "$(x)[(Q_1(x) \vee Q_4\,(x) \supset Q_3(x) \vee \sim Q_3(x)]$". Or more accurately, in order to apply the law of the excluded middle to "Q_3" we must restrict the range of the variable bound by the universal quantifier to individuals within the class $Q_1 \vee Q_4$. A statement of the form "$\sim Q_1(x) \cdot \sim Q_4(x) \cdot Q_3(x) \cdot \sim Q_3(x)$" would be meaningless rather than contradictory; likewise, statements of the form "$\sim Q_1(x) \cdot \sim Q_4\,(x) \cdot (Q_3(x) \vee \sim Q_3(x))$" would be meaningless rather than tautologous. These considerations might lead to the following objections against conditional definitions: (a) a language containing predicates introduced by such definitions suffers from the defect that its *L*-true and *L*-false sentences are not formally characterizable. We cannot say that any sentence of the form "$Px \vee \sim Px$", and any sentence of the form "$(x)\,(Px \vee \sim Px)$", is *L*-true; for, if neither "$Q_1\,(a)$" nor "$Q_4\,(a)$" are true, then "$Q_3\,(a) \vee \sim Q_3(a)$" is meaningless, and consequently "$(x)(Q_3(x) \vee \sim Q_3(x))$" is meaningless; similarly, their negations would be, not *L*-false, but meaningless.[31] Whether or not a sentence containing a conditionally defined predicate is *L*-true or *L*-false would depend, as a matter of fact, on empirical circumstances; and thus such a language would not satisfy the requirement that the logical character of its sentences is logically decidable. Implicit in (a) is already objection (b): it would be impossible to formalize the notion of "significant sentence" with respect to such a language, i.e. segregate significant from insignificant sentences on the basis of formation-rules. For whether or not a sentence involving a conditionally defined descriptive predicate is significant, depends on empirical

[31]In this discussion it is assumed that a molecular sentence is meaningless if at least one component sentence is meaningless, and meaningful if all component sentences are meaningful.

facts. Now, these objections raise problems that require careful consideration. In the few pages that remain at my disposal I can but briefly suggest rebuttals to the stated objections.

(a) Is the sentence "$2/3$ is a prime number or $2/3$ is not a prime number", and the corresponding universal sentence "$(x)(PN(x) \vee \sim PN(x))$", *L*-true? No, for the predicate "prime number" is defined only for natural numbers, in other words, the significance-range of the function "*x* is a prime number" consists of the natural numbers, therefore the sentence "$2/3$ is a prime number" as well as its negation is meaningless. To be sure, the *L*-truth of "$(x)(PN(x) \vee \sim PN(x))$" could be preserved by restricting the variable "*x*" to natural numbers, for then "$2/3$ is prime or $2/3$ is not prime" would be an illegitimate substitution-instance. However, should one operate with wholly unrestricted variables, as some logicians who, following Zermelo's set-theory, work without type-theory prefer, one would be led to something analogous to the above conditional assertion of the law of the excluded middle: "(x) [natural number $(x) \supset (PN(x) \vee \sim PN(x))$]", for instance. Moreover, in order to make it immediately clear that the definition of "*PN*" refers to a limited domain of entities, or assigns to "*PN*" a meaning only within a limited domain of entities, one had best cast it in the form of a bilateral reduction-sentence: (x) [natural number $(x) \supset (PN(x) \equiv D(x))$], where "*D*" is the familiar definiens.[32] This kind of definition makes it clear that "$PN(a)$" is a decidable sentence only if *a* is a natural number. But then "$\sim$natural number $(a) \cdot (PN(a) \vee \sim PN(a))$" would be the same sort of meaningless sentence—and hence not an *L*-true sentence—as "$\sim Q_1(b) \cdot \sim Q_4(b) \cdot (Q_3(b) \vee \sim Q_3(b))$".

Objection (b) is more serious. That the meaningfulness of a statement should depend on contingent facts is at any rate a consequence which is distasteful to builders of formalized languages, like Carnap himself, since it is equivalent to the bankruptcy of the enterprise of *formalizing* the concept of meaningfulness (defining it recursively in terms of a set of formation-rules). Specifically, the occurrence of conditional definitions of descriptive terms makes it impossible to state the conditions of sentential significance formally because we cannot say any more that a sentence is significant if its descriptive terms are significant and if it has a specified form. For example, if "$Q_1(a) \cdot \sim Q_1(b) \cdot \sim Q_4(b)$" is a true factual sentence, then "$Q_3(a)$" is meaningful and "$Q_3(b)$" meaningless even though they are sentences of the same form. It is noteworthy, however, that the program of constructing an ideal syntax relatively to which questions of the meaningfulness of sentences become syntactically decid-

[32] My attention was first called to this possibility of extending the concept of "conditional definition" to formal sciences, by a penetrating paper by Erik Stenius: "Natural Implication and Material Implication," *Theoria* (1947), 151. See also the article by Bar-Hillel, already cited.

able runs into difficulties already in a different context, viz. the context of definite description.[33] According to Russell's theory of descriptions any sentence of the form "$g((\iota x)fx)$" is either true or false, provided its predicates are significant and of the appropriate type: specifically, it is false if the description does not denote. Hence the statements made by a bachelor, "my wife wants a child" and "my wife does not want a child"[34] are both false, according to that analysis; they are contraries, not contradictories. This consequence is highly counterintuitive; if A is known to be unmarried, nobody would say "it is not true that A's wife wants a child"; one just would not attach a truth-value at all to the statement in question, and in that sense would treat it as meaningless. As Strawson has put it, in making such a statement one "presupposes" that A has a wife (in other words, the speaker"s belief that A has a wife causes him to use the description "A's wife"), and if this presupposition is false, then the question of truth with regard to that statement "does not arise". A formal logician may reply that logical theory abstracts from the "pragmatic" dimension of language, the causal context of statement-utterances, and that Strawson's criticism of the theory of description is for that reason irrelevant. The best way to counter this reply is to show that the theory of descriptions exposes deductive logic to difficulties which surely are not the result of confusing logic with psychology. If we allow substitution of definite descriptions for individual variables, then the following equivalence is, on the basis of the theory of descriptions, not logically valid: $(x)(A)(\sim(x \in A) \equiv (x \in \bar{A}))$. That is, from the negative statement that x does not belong to class A one would not be entitled to infer logically that x belongs to the complement of A, because if a description is substituted for "x", then the latter statement has an existential consequence which the former statement does not have. Similarly, one would have to distinguish non-possession of a property P from possession of the negative property non-P. The law of the excluded middle would be valid in the form "$(x)(A)\ (x \in A \vee \sim(x \in A))$", yet invalid in the form "$(x)(A)\ (x \in A \vee x \in \bar{A})$". It follows that the notion of the complement of a class could not be defined by the usual contextual definition:
$x \in \bar{A} = \sim(x \in A)$.

Now, in PM descriptions are treated as "incomplete symbols", i.e., symbols which are not *names* of values of variables and thus are not substitutable for variables of quantification unless the condition $E!\ (\iota x)\ \Phi x$ is satisfied. And in this way, it seems, the mentioned difficulty is easily

[33]See on the problem briefly discussed in the following, A. Pap, "Logic, Existence, and the Theory of Descriptions," *Analysis* (April, 1953); also P. F. Strawson, "On Referring," *Mind* (July, 1950).

[34]In order to recognize this sentence as an instance of the form "$g((\iota x)fx)$", *take* "does not want a child" as "g", and "is my wife" as "f".

circumvented: For example, the above contextual definition of "$\bar{A}$"[35] remains unobjectionable since we are not allowed to derive from the tautology corresponding to it, viz. "$(x)(A)(x \epsilon \bar{A} \equiv \sim(x \epsilon A))$", an equivalence like "his wife is one of those who do not want a child if and only if his wife is not one of those who want a child" if he has no wife. It seems, then, that Russell's distinction between incomplete symbols and genuine names makes the decision to treat all well-formed sentences containing definite descriptions as either true or false innocuous. We cannot logically deduce from the law of the excluded middle the false sentence "the king of Austria in 1954 is anti-semitic or the king of Austria in 1954 is not antisemitic" since "the king of Austria" may not be substituted for a variable of quantification. However, this is a dodge rather than a solution of the problem. For, let "*a*" be a genuine name (Russell speaks of "logically proper" names), and consider the atomic sentences "$P(a)$" and "$\sim P(a)$". By the assumption that "*a*" is a genuine name, not a description, "$P(a) \vee \sim P(a)$" is—so we are told—a logically valid consequence of the law of the excluded middle, regardless of whether "$\sim P(a)$" be construed in the sense of "it is not the case that *a* has *P*" or in the sense of "*a* has non-*P*" —indeed, these sentences are supposed to be synonymous. But "*a*" is a genuine name only if it denotes an existing entity; this is its distinguishing feature as compared with descriptions. It follows that "$P(a)$", and any truth-function of it, is a significant, true-or-false, sentence only if "*a*" denotes an existing entity. Further, if as assumed by Russell, any sentence of the form "$E!\,(\imath x)f(x)$" is true-or-false provided "*f*" is a significant predicate of appropriate type, then this holds in particular of the singular existential sentence obtained by taking as "*f*" the semantic predicate "being denoted by '*a*' ". If this sentence, however, is false, "$P(a)$" and $\sim P(a)$" (in the sense: *a* has non-*P*) must be declared as *meaningless;* for if they were declared *false,* as they would be by Russell's theory of descriptions if "*a*" were a description, then they could not be regarded as contradictories.[36] But thus we have to acknowledge anyway that whether or not a sentence is significant (true-or-false) may depend on contingent facts: the proposition that something denoted by '*a*' exists is contingent, even though the hypothetical proposition "something denoted by '*a*' exists if '*a*' is a genuine name" is of course necessary.

What led to this excursion was the reflection that the use of conditional definitions is in apparent conflict with the possibility of formalizing the notions of "significant sentence", since it depends on contingent facts whether an atomic sentence whose predicate is conditionally defined

[35]The fact that class-symbols are in PM likewise incomplete—indeed, a special case of descriptive phrases—is here disregarded since it is irrelevant to the point under discussion.

[36]Cf. "Logic, Existence and the Theory of Descriptions," *loc. cit.,* 106-108.

is significant. We see now that the program of such a formalization, via the construction of an ideal language relatively to which "significant sentence" is syntactically defined encounters difficulties that are wholly independent of the question of conditional definitions: it seems that the significance of every atomic sentence presupposes the truth of some contingent statement. It may be expected that Carnap would dispose of the latter difficulty by urging that "*S* is a significant sentence" be replaced by "*S* is a sentence relatively to *L*" (cf. TM IV, 17). That the atomic sentences of *L* are significant is, indeed, a purely analytic statement if ". . . is significant" is construed in the sense of ". . . is a sentence in *L*". On the other hand, the dependence of questions of significance on questions of contingent existence would reappear once we ask whether such a syntactic definition of significance is adequate. What if the expressions introduced as "individual constants" of zero level (the arguments of the atomic sentences) are such logically improper names as "Pegasus", "Cerberus", "Hamlet?" Since "Pegasus is white" and "Pegasus is non-white", being sentences of *L*, would have to be accepted as both significant, and the non-existence of Pegasus precludes the ascription of truth to either one of them, one would have to say that they are both false and hence not contradictories. So, we cannot get around the requirement that the individual constants of *L* be names of existing entities. Unless this requirement is fulfilled, the syntactic definition of "significant sentence" which entails that all atomic sentences of *L* are significant will be inadequate; hence it is still true that the signficance of the atomic sentences depends, indirectly, on contingencies of existence. But be this as it may, the presence of conditionally defined predicates in a language *L* makes it impossible to give a general syntactic criterion for "sentence in *L*" (cf.p.593). One might, indeed, divide the *L*-indeterminate sentences of such a language into *decidable* and *undecidable* sentences, classifying "Q_3 (*b*) (where *b* does not belong to the class $Q_1 \vee Q_4$ not as a non-sentence, but as an undecidable sentence. And conceivably it may be fruitful to work with such a division of L-indeterminate (factual) sentences into decidable and undecidable ones. Yet, the question would then arise whether such a language containing undecidable factual sentences would not violate the confirmability criterion of meaning: if "meaningful factual sentence" is defined as "factual sentence constructible in *L*", and undecidable factual sentences can be constructed in *L*, then we can hardly maintain that all meaningful factual sentences are confirmable.

Here, then, is another difficulty implicit in TM. And we cannot accept TM, all its suggestiveness and precision notwithstanding, as a consistent and adequate theory of scientific language unless it can be solved.

Arthur Pap

Department of Philosophy
Yale University

20

Adolf Grünbaum

CARNAP'S VIEWS ON THE FOUNDATIONS OF GEOMETRY*

I. *Introduction*

THE causal theory of time, which had occupied an important place in the thought of Leibniz and of Kant, again became a subject of central philosophic interest during the current century after its detailed elaboration and logical refinement at the hands of G. Lechalas,[1] H. Reichenbach,[2] K. Lewin,[3] R. Carnap,[4] and H. Mehlberg.[5] Specifically, it earned its new prominence in recent decades by its role in the magisterial and beautiful construction of the relativistic topology of both time and space by Reichenbach[6] and Carnap.[7] More recently, the writer used the causal theory of time to show semantically that, with respect to the relation *"later than,"* the events of physics can meaningfully possess the seemingly counter-intuitive denseness property of the linear Cantorean con-

*The author is indebted to the National Science Foundation of the U.S.A. for the support of research.

[1]G. Lechalas, *Étude sur l'espace et le temps* (Paris, 1896).

[2]H. Reichenbach, *Axiomatik der relativistischen Raum-Zeit-Lehre* (Braunschweig, 1924).

[3]K. Lewin, "Die zeitliche Geneseordnung", *Zeitschrift für Physik* XIII, 16 (1923).

[4]R. Carnap, "Über die Abhängigkeit der Eigenschaften des Raumes von denen der Zeit," *Kantstudien* XXX, 331 (1925).

[5]H. Mehlberg, "Essai sur la théorie causale du temps," *Studia Philosophica* I (1935), and II (1937).

[6]H. Reichenbach, *Philosophie der Raum-Zeit-Lehre* (Berlin: 1928), esp. 307-308. An English translation entitled *The Philosophy of Space and Time* was published by Dover in 1958. Hereafter this translation will be cited as "PST."

[7]R. Carnap, *Abriss der Logistik* (Vienna, 1929), Section 36, 80-85. Cf. also his *Symbolische Logik* (Vienna, 1954), Sections 48-50, 169-181; an English translation, *Introduction to Symbolic Logic and its Applications* was published in 1958 by Dover. For an interesting comparison of Kant's version of the theory with the conceptions propounded by Carnap, Reichenbach, and Mehlberg, see H. Scholz, "Eine Topologie der Zeit im Kantischen Sinne," *Dialectica* IX, 66 (1955). A reduction of the space-time metric to a quantized time is offered by A. Markoff's article "Über die Ableitbarkeit der Weltmetrik aus der 'Früher als' Beziehung," *Physikalische Zeitschrift der Sowjetunion* I (1932), 387-406.

tinuum. And, in this way, he was able to supply the semantical *nervus probandi* which had been lacking in Russell's mathematical refutation of Zeno's paradoxes of motion.[8]

Although Carnap has shown, in three ways, that the topology of space is reducible to that of time and that the latter, in turn, is reducible to the topology of causal chains, his axiomatization does not, as such, commit him to an espousal of the causal theory of time. But it is of *epistemological* interest to inquire whether the physical meaning of the primitive asymmetric causal relation[9] of his space-time construction can be understood without possessing a *prior* understanding of the *temporal* terms which it is intended to define. And if Carnap's reduction was intended to exhibit the space-time order as the expression of a causal order whose nature can be understood independently, then the explanatory success of his reduction must be judged in the light of the causal theory's ability to weather critical scrutiny.

In an endeavor to elicit Carnap's views on the epistemological viability of that theory of time, whose deductive fertility he has established so skillfully, I shall devote the first part of this essay to an examination of the major defenses and criticisms of the theory. Although I once endorsed the Reichenbachian version of the theory which is based on the mark method,[10] my aim will be to show that (i) his mark method fails to define a serial temporal order within the class of physical events, being vitiated by circularity in its attempt to define the required asymmetric relation; (ii) although the classical Leibniz-Reichenbach version of the causal theory of time is vulnerable to these criticisms, it is possible to define *temporal betweenness* on the basis of the postulate of causal continuity for reversible mechanical processes; but nomologically contingent boundary conditions must prevail, if the betweenness defined by causal continuity is to have the formal properties of the triadic relation ordering the points on an *open* (straight) *undirected* line, hereafter called "o-betweenness"; alternatively, the boundary conditions may issue in a temporal order exhibiting the formal properties possessed by the order of points on a *closed* (circular) *undirected* line with respect to a tetradic relation of separation, hereafter called "separation closure"; (iii) as distinct from Reichenbach's mark method, his most recent account of the *anisotropy* of time as a statistical property of the *entropic*

8A. Grünbaum, "Relativity and the Atomicity of Becoming," *The Review of Metaphysics* IV, 143 (1950), esp. 168-169. Much material concerning time in this article is superseded by the present essay. In addition, there are distorting misprints.

9Formally, "causal relation" is the primitive term of only one of Carnap's three versions, but the formal differences among them in regard to their respective primitives are inessential for our purposes.

10H. Reichenbach, *Philosophie der Raum-Zeit-Lehre*, *op. cit.*, 161-163 or PST, 135-138, and A. Grünbaum, as cited in no. 8 above.

behavior of *space ensembles of* "branch"-systems,[11] is successful though only in a significantly *modified* form. But his conception of becoming as a forward march of a physically-distinguished "now" along the privileged direction of time is untenable.

In the second part of this essay, I shall discuss some neglected criticisms of the empiricist conception of the foundations of geometry in the context of Carnap's writings, Russell's philosophy of geometry and Poincaré's widely-misunderstood conventionalism. And while upholding the soundness of the empiricist conception with reference to these various issues, I shall argue that neither the relational conception of the topology of space and time in modern geometry and physics nor the recognition by these disciplines of the conventional element in the metrical concepts "rigid," "congruent," and "simultaneous"[12] lend support to phenomenalistic positivism or homocentric operationism.

> In conformity to the scientific ideal of physics, which *excludes* [reference to human] consciousness, the subjective sequence of percepts may not be invoked; wherever it is invoked, it is a sign of retarded development.
>
> Hugo Bergmann
>
> *Der Kampf um das Kausalgesetz in der jüngsten Physik.*

II. *Critique of the Causal Theory of Time*

Reichenbach introduces his mark method by giving the following topological coordinative definition of temporal sequence:[13] "If E_2 is the effect of E_1, then E_2 is said to be later than E_1." To show that causality defines an asymmetric temporal relation without circularity, he invites attention to the fact that when E_1 is the cause of E_2, small variations in E_1 in the form of the addition of a marking event

[11]H. Reichenbach, "Les fondements logiques de la mécanique des quanta," *Annales de l'Institut Henri Poincaré* XIII (1953), 140-158, and "La signification philosophique du dualisme ondes-corpuscules," in A. George (ed.), *Louis de Broglie, Physicien et Penseur* (Paris, 1953), 126-134. The most detailed account is given in his book *The Direction of Time* which was published posthumously in 1956 by the University of California Press after my essay was first written. Hereafter this book will be cited as "DT."

[12]In characterizing the concept of the simultaneity of spatially separated events as a metrical concept having a conventional ingredient, I do not intend to overlook that such simultaneity also has a purely non-conventional topological aspect deriving from the physical impossibility that simultaneous events be the termini of any causal chain: cf. A. Grünbaum, "Logical and Philosophical Foundations of the Special Theory of Relativity," in: A. Danto and S. Morgenbesser (eds.), *Philosophy of Science* (New York, 1960), 399-434, esp. §2.

[13]H. Reichenbach, *Phil. d. Raum-Zeit-Lehre, op. cit.*, 161 or PST, 136. Cf. also G. W. Leibniz, "Initia rerum mathematicorum metaphysica," *Math. Schriften*, ed. Gerhardt (Berlin, 1863), VII, 18; H. Weyl, *Philosophy of Mathematics and Natural Science* (Princeton, 1949), 101, 204, and "50 Jahre Relativitätstheorie," *Naturwissenschaften* XXXVIII, 74 (1951); H. Poincaré, *Letzte Gedanken*, tr. Lichtenecker (Leipzig, 1913), 54.

e to E_1 will be connected with corresponding variations in E_2, but *not* conversely. Thus, if we denote an event E that is slightly varied (marked) by "E^e", we shall find, he tells us, that we observe only the combinations

$$E_1E_2 \qquad E^e{}_1E^e{}_2 \qquad E_1E^e{}_2$$

but *never* the combination

$$E^e{}_1E_2.$$

In the observed combinations, the events E_1 and E_2 play an asymmetric role, thereby defining an order, and it is clear that this order would be unaffected by interchanging the subscripts in the symbols naming the events involved. The event whose name does not have an "e" in the *non-occurring* combination is called the effect and the later event.[14]

Reichenbach's formulation of his principle contains no restriction to causal chains which are either materially *genidentical,* such as stones, or possess the quasi-material genidentity of individual light rays. Thus, although the *illustrations* he gives of the principle do involve stones and light rays, it has been widely interpreted as *not* requiring this kind of restriction. Moreover, it is not clear even from his illustration of the stone whether the members of his three observed pairs of events are to belong to *three* rather than to only one or two different genidentical causal chains, a specification which is of decisive importance if such a restriction is to obviate certain of the criticisms of his method which are about to follow. Accordingly, those objections which might thus have been obviated will also be stated.

An illustration of the use of Reichenbach's method given by W. B. Taylor in an attempt to demonstrate its independence of prior knowledge of temporal order[15] will serve to let me set forth the objections to it.

An otherwise dark room has two holes in opposite walls such that a single light ray traverses the room. Since the light source is hidden in the wall behind one of the two holes, we are not able to tell, as we face the light ray from a perpendicular direction, whether it travels across the room from left to right or right to left and thus do not know the location of the light source. In order to ascertain the direction of this causal process, let us isolate three events E_L in it which occur at the left end of the beam and also three events E_R of the process occurring at the right end. And now suppose that *one* of the three events at *each* end is *marked,* say, by means of the presence of transparent color glass at the point and instant of its occurrence. The crux of the matter lies

[14]H. Reichenbach, *Phil. d. Raum-Zeit-Lehre, op. cit.,* 162-63, and PST, 137.

[15]W. B. Taylor, *The Meaning of Time in Science and Daily Life,* doctoral dissertation (1953), University of California at L.A., 37-39.

in Reichenbach's claim that if the events E_L are the respective (partial) causes of the events E_R, we shall observe only the combinations

$$E_L E_R \qquad E^e{}_L E^e{}_R \qquad E_L E^e{}_R$$

and *never* the combination

$$E^e{}_L E_R.$$

It can now be shown[16] that in order to obtain these particular kinds and pairs of events, on which the method relies to define an asymmetric relation, Reichenbach must either make tacit and inadmissible use of prior temporal knowledge or invoke the special requirement of irreversible marking processes. For in the absence of information concerning the temporal order within either triplet of events at the left end or at the right end, all that we can say is that our observations at the two ends can be represented by *temporally neutral* triangular arrays:

$$\begin{array}{ccc} & E_L & \\ E_L & & E^e{}_L \end{array} \qquad\qquad \begin{array}{ccc} & E^e{}_R & \\ E_R & & E^e{}_R \end{array}$$

And, again not presupposing temporal information, we are entitled to *interpret* our data to the effect that we observed the three combinations

$$E_L E^e{}_R \qquad E_L E^e{}_R \qquad E^e{}_L E_R$$

but *not* $E^e{}_L E^e{}_R$.

In the context of Reichenbach's program, this latter interpretation seems to be fully as legitimate as the formation of his own particular grouping, which likewise constitutes a mere interpretation. But the legitimacy of this alternate interpretation is fatal to Reichenbach's claim that E_L and E_R play an asymmetric role, since the alternate interpretation contains the combination $E^e{}_L E_R$, which is the very combination that he had to rule out in order to show that E_R is later than E_L!

Even if we know the temporal sequence *within* each of the two triplets of events to be, say,

$$\begin{array}{c} E_L \\ E^e{}_L \\ E_L \end{array} \qquad \text{and} \qquad \begin{array}{c} E_R \\ E^e{}_R \\ E^e{}_R \end{array}$$

where the downward direction is the direction of increasing time, it is still not clear which particular event at the right end is to be associated with a particular event at the left end to form a pair. Hence, Reichenbach's causal theory allows us to form event-pairs so as to obtain both his own asymmetric interpretation *and* the alternate interpretation above even from the two internally *ordered* triplets of events. The alternate interpretation is obtainable by combining the first event in the

[16]In the first of the objections which are to follow, the point of departure was suggested to me in general terms by Mr. Chester Schuler.

E_L column with the second in the E_R column, the respective third events in the two columns and the second in the E_L column with the first in the E_R column.

Nor is this legitimate alternate interpretation the only source of difficulties for the mark-method. For without a criterion for uniting the spatially separated events under consideration in pairs, we might unwittingly mark the pulse that actually emanated from $E^e{}_L$ upon its arrival at the right, instead of marking one of the other two pulses, which emanate from *unmarked* events at the left. Since the pulse coming from $E^e{}_L$ will already be bearing a mark, the marking of that particular pulse upon arrival at the right will be *redundant*. We could then interpret our data as forming the combinations

$$E_L E_R \qquad E^e{}_L E^e{}_R \qquad E_L E_R$$

in which E_L and E_R occur with complete *symmetry*.[17] The proponent of the mark method cannot, of course, avert this embarrassing consequence by requiring that we mark at the right end only a pulse not already bearing a mark from *before*.[18]

Equally unavailing is the following attempt by W. B. Taylor to justify the mark method:

> In the example concerning the light ray, it was said that we first mark E_L and *then* (a moment later) see if the mark appears on E_R. As it stands, this procedure employs time order, which would be undesirable for the purposes at hand. But this way of stating the procedure can be eliminated by saying that we mark E_L and observe (tenseless form of the verb "observe") whether that same mark appears (again tenseless) on the E_R which is causally connected with E_L. The reason that time order appears to be presupposed is perhaps that we must use verbs (e.g. observe, appear) to describe the procedure of marking and because English verbs in their usual usage are in a tensed, and hence time-referent form. If the observer does not himself mark the events, but instead relies on other agencies to provide the marks, then this apparent circularity does not arise. He, in this case, simply observes the event-pairs $E_L E_R$ to see in what arrangement e appears.[19]

This argument will not do, since we saw that it is not possible, without knowledge of the temporal order, to "simply observe" particular, observationally-*given* event-pairs $E_L E_R$ to see in what arrangement the mark e

[17]Using the term "partial cause" so as to allow its designata to be *non*-simultaneous, Hugo Bergmann offers another argument for the variational *symmetry* of cause and effect [*Der Kampf um das Kausalgesetz in der jüngsten Physik* (Braunschweig, 1929), 16-19] by showing that Reichenbach succeeds merely in proving that the variation of one of the *partial* causes does not vary the other, but *not* that the effect can be varied without varying the cause. Reichenbach's retort ["Das Kausalproblem in der Physik," *Naturwissenschaften* XIX (1931), 719] to Bergmann is superseded by his subsequent acknowledgment [DT, 198-199] of an inadequacy here which we shall soon consider.

[18]For a similar objection, cf. Mehlberg, *op. cit.*, I, 214-215.

[19]W. B. Taylor, *op. cit.*, 38-39.

appears. The issue is *not* that time is presupposed in having to mention in temporal succession the names of the members of already-given event-pairs or in stating first the result of our observation on one event in such a pair and then on the other. Instead, the difficulty is that time order is presupposed in assuring and singling out the membership of Reichenbach's specific three event-pairs to begin with, though not in the internal arrangement of their members after the pairs themselves are already chosen. Once we grant the uniqueness of the Reichenbachian choice of event-pairs, it is quite true that temporal order is only apparently presupposed in the description of the experiment, since E_L and E_R do occur asymmetrically in those pairs, independently of the order in which they are named within the pairs.

A further difficulty, which will turn out to have an important bearing on the relation of causality to the anisotropy of time, lies in the fact that in the case of reversible marking processes (if there be such), the mark method must make illicit use of temporal betweenness to preclude failure of its experiments. For, as Mehlberg has rightly observed in his searching paper on the causal theory of time,[20] if the mark c were removed, in some way or other, from a signal originating at E^e_L *while that signal is in transit,* the experiment would yield the combination $E^e_L E_R$, which is precisely the one disallowed by Reichenbach. To prevent such an eventuality, the mark-method must either incur failure by requiring that the physical system under consideration be *closed* during the *time interval between* E^e_L and E^e_R[21] or it must have recourse to an *irreversible* marking process such as passing white light through a color filter.

The question arises, therefore, whether the requirement that the marking processes be *irreversible* does not constitute an invocation of a *new criterion* of temporal order, since it is based on a much more restricted class of kinds of occurrences than the one to which causality is held to apply, the latter including *reversible* processes. Indeed, if the meaning of causality is correctly explicated by the mark method, and if that method—its other difficulties aside—can hope to be successful in defining a serial temporal order via an *asymmetric* causal relation for

20Mehlberg, *op. cit.,* I, 214; also 207 and 257.

21In another connection, Reichenbach defines a closed system as a system "not subject to differential forces" [*Phil. d. Raum-Zeit-Lehre, op. cit.,* 141, 33 or PST, 118, 22-23], differential forces being forces whose presence is correlated with *changes* of varying degree in different kinds of materials. But the absence of a change at any given instant t means the constancy of a certain value (or values) *between* the termini of a time interval containing the instant t (no *anisotropy* of time being assumed). Thus Reichenbach recognizes that the concept of closed system presupposes the ordinal concept of temporal betweenness. We see incidentally that the meaning of temporal betweenness is presupposed by the statement of the second law of thermodynamics, which concerns *closed* systems.

only those causal processes which are irreversible or which are rendered irreversible by its application, then it follows that causality as such is *not sufficient* to define those topological properties which are conferred on physical time by irreversible processes, and that Reichenbach's causal criterion cannot be logically *independent* of a criterion grounded on such processes. Though declining to discuss the issue in his book of 1924, Reichenbach admitted that the independence of these two criteria is open to question while nevertheless affirming the autonomy of the causal criterion and characterizing the concordance of the temporal orders based on causality, on the one hand, and irreversibility, on the other, as an empirical fact.[22] In his last paper on the subject, published just before his death, and in his posthumous book, he abandoned the ambitious program of the mark method to define an anisotropic serial time at one stroke. Instead, he offered a construction in which he relied on a certain kind of thermodynamic irreversibility and not merely on causality in an attempt to achieve this purpose.[23] In the next section we shall examine this construction critically and see in what specific sense irreversible processes can be held to define the anisotropy of time.

Before proceeding to a consideration of these issues, one additional criticism of the causal theory of time merits being stated.

On the causal theory of time, the existence of an *actual* causal chain linking two events is only a sufficient and not a necessary condition for their sustaining a relation of being temporally apart. Such a relation is likewise held to obtain between any two events for which it is merely physically *possible* to be the termini of a causal chain even if no actual chain connects them. Thus, causal connectibility rather than actual causal connectedness is the defining relation of being temporally apart. And causal non-connectibility rather than non-connectedness is the defining relation of topological simultaneity. But as Mehlberg has noted,[24] physical possibility, in turn, must then be definable or understood in such a manner as *not* to presuppose the ordinal concepts of time which enter into the laws that tell us what causal processes are physically possible. Carnap did not take cognizance of this difficulty in his construc-

[22]H. Reichenbach, *Axiomatik der relativistischen Raum-Zeit-Lehre, op. cit.,* 21-22. For critical comments on Reichenbach's early views concerning this issue, see E. Zilsel, "Über die Asymmetrie der Kausalität und die Einsinnigkeit der Zeit," *Naturwissenschaften* XV, 282 (1927).

[23]H. Reichenbach, "Les Fondements Logiques de la Mécanique des Quanta," *op. cit.,* 137-138; DT, 198n; for his earlier views, see *Phil. d. Raum-Zeit-Lehre, op. cit.,* 164-165 or PST, 138-139, "The Philosophical Significance of the Theory of Relativity," in P. A. Schilpp (ed.), *Albert Einstein: Philosopher-Scientist,* 304-306, and "Ziele und Wege der physikalischen Erkenntnis," *Handbuch der Physik* IV (1929), 53, 59-60, 64, 65.

[24]Mehlberg, *op. cit.,* I, 191, 195, and II, 143.

tion.[25] It would therefore be of considerable interest to learn in what way, if any, he now believes this particular circularity can be avoided by his own explication of the concept of physical possibility or by the recent proposals of others. Perhaps Mehlberg's theory of causal decompositions[26] provides a basis on which the difficulty might be circumvented. Maintaining that not-E must be held to be a physical event if E is such an event, Mehlberg thinks that any two events which are the termini of physically possible causal chains must therefore be held to be actually causally connected. Mehlberg thus proposes to guarantee the actual rather than merely potential existence of all the required causal chains by asserting[27] that for any event not belonging to a class of simultaneous events, there is at least one event in that class with which the first event is causally connected.

We saw that the mark method is vitiated by circularity, because it explicates the causal relation in such a manner that (1) the method is then required to provide a criterion for designating, within a pair of causally-connected events, the *one* event which is *the* cause of the other, thereby also being the earlier of the two in anisotropic time, and (2) the method leaves itself vulnerable to the charge of having tacitly employed temporal criteria to secure the particular pairs of events which are essential to its success. Despite the failure of the variational conception of causality offered by the mark method, the kind of causality exhibited by reversible processes *is* competent to define *some* of the topological features of time. Much as Leibniz and more recent proponents of his causal definition of the relation "later than"[28] were mistaken concerning the character and extent of the logical connection between the topology of time and the structure of causal chains, their affirmation of the existence of such a connection was sound. We shall see now that reversible genidentical causal processes do indeed define an order of temporal *betweenness* (albeit only in part) and also relations of *simultaneity* in the class of physical events.

By contrast to the mark method, our construction will have the following features: (1) we consider a kind of causal relation between two different events which is *symmetric* and involves no reference at all to one of the two events being *the* cause of the other, the criterion for the latter

[25]Carnap, "Über die Abhängigkeit der Eigenschaften des Raumes von denen der Zeit," *op. cit.*, 339 and *Symbolische Logik*, *op. cit.*, Section 48c.

[26]Mehlberg, *op. cit.*, I, 165-166, 240-241, and II, 145-146, 169-172.

[27]*Ibid.*, II, 169.

[28]For a discussion of the ancestral role of the Leibnizian conception, see H. Reichenbach, "Die Bewegungslehre bei Newton, Leibniz und Huyghens," *Kantstudien* XXIX, 416 (1924). An English translation by Maria Reichenbach has appeared in a volume of Reichenbach's selected essays entitled *Modern Philosophy of Science* (New York, 1959).

characterization to be supplied subsequently by *entropy* in the case of closed systems of finite size, and by non-entropic irreversibility in the case of systems which have no enclosing walls and are immersed in infinite space ("open" systems),[29] (2) we shall eschew resting the asymmetry, and, thereby, the seriality of the relation of "earlier than" on the causal relation itself; in fact, the latter relation will be seen to be neutral with respect to whether the temporal order has the formal properties of the "o-betweenness" exhibited by the points on an undirected straight line or those of "separation-closure" relating the points on an undirected circle;[30] instead of being made to depend on causality itself, the o-betweenness of time will depend for its existence on the *boundary conditions,* which determine the relations of the various causal chains to one another, (3) instead of construing causality variationally in the manner of the mark method, we shall begin with genidentical material objects whose behavior provides us with genidentical causal chains and then consider the causal relation between any pair of events belonging to a genidentical causal chain.

Consider any (ideally) *reversible* genidentical causal process such as the rolling of a ball on the floor of a room along a path connecting points P and P′ of the floor. And suppose that we do not know whether the ball rolls from P to P′ or in the opposite direction, because we have eliminated from our description of this causal process all reliance on the anisotropy of time. This renunciation of reference to all attributes depending on the anisotropy of time leaves intact all but one of the *causal* properties of the motion. Since it has no meaning in a temporally isotropic world to speak of *one* of two causally-connected events which belong to a genidentical reversible causal chain as *the* cause of the other (except as a matter of mere fiat), the rudimentary causal relation uniting

[29]For closed, finite systems, it will turn out that of two causally connected events, *the* cause (or earlier with respect to a positive time-direction) will be defined as the one lying in the direction of the *lower* entropy states of the majority of "branch"-systems, *the* effect lying in the direction of the correspondingly higher entropy states of these systems. For open systems, the appropriate definition will become evident in the light of our analysis of the kind of irreversibility exhibited by such systems.

[30]The order of points on an undirected circle which we have called "separation-closure" here is generally called "separation of point pairs" in the literature. It is the order of the points on a *closed,* undirected line with respect to a tetradic relation *ABCD* obtaining between points *A, B, C, D* in virtue of the separation of the pair *BD* by the pair *AC*. Axioms for separation of point pairs and for o-betweenness are given in E. V. Huntington, "Inter-Relations Among the Four Principal Types of Order," *Trans. Am. Math. Soc.* XXXVIII (1935), 1-9. Cf. also E. V. Huntington and K. E. Rosinger, "Postulates for Separation of Point-Pairs (Reversible Order on a Closed Line)," *Proc. Amer. Acad. Arts and Sciences* LXVII (Boston, 1932), 61-145, and J. A. H. Shepperd, "Transitivities of Betweenness and Separation and the Definitions of Betweenness and Separation Groups," *J. London Math. Soc.* XXXI (1956), 240-248.

the events of that chain is *symmetric.*[31] And the properties of that symmetric relation would exhaust all the properties of causality in a strictly reversible world like the Laplacean one of Newtonian mechanics.

Is it possible to provide an explicit definition of our symmetric causal relation *without* using any of the temporal concepts which that relation is intended to define? Every attempt to do so known to or made by the writer has encountered insurmountable difficulties which are closely related to those familiar from the study of law-like subjunctive conditionals by N. Goodman and others.[32] Suppose, for example, that we were to define the symmetric causal relation between two genidentically-related events E and E′ by asserting that either of these two events is *existentially a sufficient* and a *necessary* condition for the other's occurrence in the following sense: if the set U of events constituting the universe contains an event of the kind E, then it also contains an event of the kind E′, and if U does *not* contain an E-like event, then it also will *not* contain an E′-like occurrence, *no* assumptions being made *at all* as to one of these two events being *earlier* than the other in the sense of presupposing the anisotropy of time. But this attempt at definition won't do for several reasons as follows: (i) the statement of the existential sufficiency of E is either tautological or self-contradictory, depending upon whether it is understood in its antecedent that the set U does or does not contain E′, (ii) the corresponding statement of existential necessity is either self-contradictory or tautological depending on whether in its antecedent, U is or is not construed as having E′ among its members, and (iii) attempting to turn these tautological or self-contradictory statements into true synthetic ones by making these assertions *not* about U itself but about appropriate proper *subsets* of U founders on (a) the need to utilize *temporal* criteria to circumscribe the membership of these subsets and (b) our inability to specify *all* of the *relevant conditions* which must be included in the antecedent, if the statement of the existential sufficiency of E is to be *true.* The numerous difficulties besetting the specification of the relevant conditions[33] are not removed but only baptized by giving them a name—to borrow a locution from Poincaré—by the physicist's reference to the total state of a *closed system* in the antecedents of his

[31]In §3, we shall give reasons for rejecting the objections to this conclusion set forth by Reichenbach in DT, 32.

[32]Cf. N. Goodman, *Fact, Fiction and Forecast* (Cambridge: Harvard University Press, 1955), esp. 13-31.

It is noteworthy that even in a context which, unlike ours, does presuppose the temporal concept of "later," C. I. Lewis reaches the conclusion [cf. his *Analysis of Knowledge and Valuation* (LaSalle, Illinois: Open Court, 1946), 226-7] that the "if . . . then" encountered in causal statements does not yield to analysis, and therefore he speaks of the *undefined* "if . . . then of real connection."

[33]Many of these difficulties are discussed searchingly by Goodman, *op. cit.,* 17-24.

causal descriptions of physical processes. Instead of enlightening us concerning the content of the *ceteris paribus* assumption, the invocation of the concept of closed system merely shifts the problem over to ascertaining the *cetera* which must materialize throughout the vast Minkowski light cones *outside* the system in order that the system be *closed.*

These considerations suggest that we introduce the symmetric causal relation under discussion as a *primitive* relation for the purpose of then defining temporal betweenness and simultaneity. The reader will ask at once why the reduction of these ordinal concepts of time to such a primitive is not to be rejected as demanding too high a price epistemologically. Several weighty replies can be given to this question as follows:

(1) The various versions of the causal theory of time beginning with Leibniz's and including the Einstein-Minkowski formulation of special relativity as elaborated by Reichenbach, Carnap and Mehlberg have reduced the temporal order of the physical world to its causal order. Although the theory of relativity, like any geometry or other scientific theory, can be axiomatized in several different ways (at least in principle) by the use of different sets of primitives, the axiomatization of the relativistic topology of time on the basis of signal or causal chains gives telling testimony of the explanatory capabilities of the causal theory of time;

(2) The very explanation of the temporal features of the physical world on the basis of its causal features and the embeddedness of man's organism in this causal physical world lead us to expect that the causal acts of intervention (even insofar as they are reversible) which enter into man's *testing* of the Einstein-Minkowski theory will be part of the temporal order and will require for their practical execution by us *conscious* organisms recourse to the deliverances of our *psychological* sense of temporal order;

(3) my motivation for advancing below a particular version of the causal theory of time in which the attempt is made to dispense entirely with these psychological deliverances in the axiomatic foundations[34] derives from the following two premises: (a) the thesis of astro-physics (cosmogony) and of the biological theory of human evolution that temporality is a significant feature of the physical world independently of the

[34] This non-phenomenalistic approach was championed by Reichenbach in 1928, when he wrote [*Phil. d. Raum-Zeit-Lehre,* 161; cf. also 327-328 or PST, 136, and also 285-86]: "it is in principle impossible to use subjective feelings for the determination of the order of external events. We must therefore establish a different criterion." But in his last publication [DT, 33-35] he invokes *direct observation* of nearby quasi-coincidences as a basis for giving meaning to the local order of temporal betweenness of such coincidences. If this observational criterion is intended to involve man's subjective time sense, then one wonders what considerations persuaded Reichenbach to abandon his earlier opposition to it. And it is not clear how he would justify having recourse to

presence of man's conscious organism and hence ought to be explainable as a purely physical attribute of those preponderant regions of space-time which are not inhabited by conscious organisms, and (b) the view of philosophical naturalism that man is part of nature and that those features of his conscious awareness which are held to be isomorphic with or likewise ascribable to the inanimate physical world must therefore be explained by the laws and attributes possessed by that world independently of human consciousness. When coupled with certain results of statistical thermodynamics and information theory, the version of the causal theory of temporal order to be advanced below provides a *unified* account of certain basic features of physical *and* psychological time. Since man's body participates in those purely physical processes which confer temporality on the inanimate sector of the world and which are elucidated in part by the causal theory of time, that theory contributes to our understanding of some of the traits of psychological time.

So much for the justification of our use of the causal relation as a primitive.

Now if we are confronted with a situation in which two actual events E and E′ are *genidentical* and hence causally connected in our rudimentary *symmetric* sense—or "k-connected" as we shall say for brevity—then we are able to use the properties of genidentical chains, which include causal continuity, to define both temporal betweenness and simultaneity.

For reasons which will become apparent, the causal definition of temporal betweenness to be offered will be given, pending the introduction of further requirements, so as to *allow* that time be topologically *either* open in the sense of being a system of o-betweenness like a Euclidean straight line, *or* closed in the sense of being a system of separation closure like an undirected circle. In order to make the statement of the definition correspondingly general, we require the following preliminaries[35] in which we use the abbreviation "iff" for "if and only if":

(i) We shall call the quadruplet of events E L E′ M (where E≠E′) an "n-quadruplet," iff given the actual occurrence of E and E′, it is necessary that either L or M occur in order that E and E′ be k-connected, L and M being genidentical with E and E′, and "or" being used in the inclusive sense. It is *essential* to note that "it is

it in the very context in which he claims to be providing a "causal definition" of the order of temporal betweenness "by means of reversible processes" [DT, 32]. On the other hand, if he is making reference here not to the temporal deliverances of consciousness but rather to the directly observable indications of a material clock, then he has merely displaced the difficulty by posing but not solving the problem of showing how the causal features of a reversible clock furnish the definition of temporal betweenness.

[35] I wish to acknowledge the valuable assistance of my mathematical colleague Professor Albert Wilansky in the formulation of the particulars of the definition.

necessary that either L or M occur" does *not* entail "either the occurrence of L is necessary or the occurrence of M is necessary." The sentence "E L E′ M are an n-quadruplet" will be abbreviated to "n (E L E′ M)."

(ii) We utilize the property of causal continuity possessed by genidentical causal chains and assert: for any two genidentically-related (and hence k-connected) distinct events E and E′, there exist sets $\hat{X}$ and $\hat{F}$ of events genidentical with them, each of which has the cardinality ℵ of the continuum and such that for each X belonging to X and each F belonging to $\hat{F}$, we have n(E X E′ F). Thus, there are ℵ n-quadruplets.

(iii) Given E and E′, we shall call a set α an "n-chain" connecting E and E′, iff the members X of α are given by the following condition:

$X \varepsilon \alpha$ iff $(\exists F)$ [n(E X E′ F) · ~n(E F E′ F)].

All the members of n-chains connecting a given pair of genidentical events E and E′ are thus genidentical with E and E′.

We are now able to define temporal betweenness as follows: any event belonging to an n-chain connecting a pair of genidentical events E and E′ is said to be *temporally between* E and E′.[36] Once a definition of topological simultaneity becomes available, this definition admits of a generalization so as to allow that events which are *not* genidentical with E and E′ but which are *simultaneous* with any event both between and genidentical with them will likewise be temporally between E and E′. These topological definitions can then be particularized by the *metrical* definitions of simultaneity used in particular reference frames.

A very important feature of our definition of temporal betweenness is that it *leaves open* the question as to which one of the following alternatives prevails:

(1) The n-quadruplets which E and E′ form with pairs of members of the n-chains connecting E and E′ have the formal properties of the

[36]It might be objected that there is a difficulty in applying this definition to our earlier paradigmatic example of the rolling ball, for it would be possible to have someone place the ball at point P at the appropriate time even though that ball never was and never will be at point P′ and to have a different ball placed appropriately at the latter point. Or a critic might say that even if the original ball were to be at one of the points P or P′, it could always be prevented from reaching the other point by being suitably intercepted while in transit. The aim of such objections would be to show that in order to rule out these alleged counter-examples, our construction would become circular by having to invoke temporal concepts which it is avowedly not entitled to presuppose. But the irrelevance of these objections becomes clear, when cognizance is taken of the fact that instead of exhibiting a circularity in our causal definition of temporal betweenness, they merely call attention to the existence of pairs of events which do not fulfill the conditions for the applicability of our definition, because they are *not* causally connected (or connectible) *in the requisite genidentical way.*

tetradic relation of separation, thus yielding a system of separation closure as the temporal order, or

(2) The membership of the n-chains connecting E and E′ is such as to yield a system of o-betweenness as the temporal order.

In order to articulate this *neutrality* of the definition, we note, for purposes of comparison, the following *partial* sets of properties of the two alternative types of order in question. Letting "ABC" denote the triadic relation of betweenness, "ABCD" the tetradic relation of separation and "→" the relation of logical entailment, we have

o-betweenness

1. ABC→CBA (symmetry in the end-points or "undirectedness")
2. ABC→∼BCA (preclusion of closure)

separation-closure

If all four elements A, B, C, and D are distinct, then

1. ABCD→DCBA ("undirectedness")
2. ABCD→BCDA ("closure")

The corresponding *partial* properties of *cyclic* betweenness, as exemplified by the class of points on a *directed* closed line, are:

cyclic betweenness

1. ABC→∼CBA (preclusion of symmetry in the end-points or "directedness")
2. ABC→BCA (closure)

But we are not concerned with the species of closed order represented by cyclic betweenness, since we shall argue that it is not relevant to *temporal* betweenness.

The neutrality which we have claimed for our definition of temporal betweenness in regard to both o-betweenness and separation closure will be clarified by dealing with an objection which Dr. Abner Shimony has suggested to me for consideration.

If the definition is to allow time to be a system of o-betweenness and the subsequent introduction of a serial temporal order in which the members E, X, Y, E′, F and G of a genidentical causal chain are ordered as shown by the order of their names, then our definition ought *not* to *entail* that events like F, which are *outside* the time interval bounded by E and E′ are temporally between E and E′. Nor should it entail that *inside* events like X and Y turn out *not* to be temporally between E and E′. Now, our definition of the membership of n-chains α was designed to preclude precisely such entailments as well as to allow the order of separation closure, in which every event is temporally between every other pair of events. The question is whether it could not be objected that we have failed nonetheless on the following grounds: events such as F and G, which are outside the interval EE′, are each necessary for the respective occurrences of E and of E′, just as much as inside events like X and Y are thus necessary; and does it not follow then that every "outside" event like F does enter into an n-quadruplet n(E F E′ F), thereby qualifying no less than do "inside" events in this case, as necessary for the k-connectedness of E and E′? If this conclusion did in fact follow, then our definition would indeed preclude o-betweenness by making the n-chains α empty. For in that case, there would be no genidentical event whatever satisfying the requirement of *not* being necessary for the k-connectedness of E and E′, as demanded by our definition of α. But the reasoning of the objection breaks down at the point of inferring that outside events like F and G do form n-quadruplets with E and E′. For although all events genidentical with E and E′—be they inside ones or outside ones—are necessary for the respective occurrences of E and of E′, only the *inside* ones have the *further* property of being necessary for the *k-connectedness* of E and E′, *given* that the latter do occur. By noting the distinction between the properties of (i) being necessary for the respective occurrences of E and E′ and (ii) being necessary for the k-connectedness of events E and E′ whose occurrence is otherwise granted, we see that the objection to our definition derived its plausibility but also its lack of cogency from inferring the second property from the first.

The fact that our definition of temporal betweenness does not itself discriminate between closed and open time becomes further evident upon considering universes to each of which it applies but which have topologically different kinds of time:

1. Closed Time.

Let there be a universe consisting of a platform and one particle constantly moving in a circular path without friction. And be sure *not* to introduce surreptitiously into this universe either a conscious human observer or light enabling him to *see* the motion of the particle. Then the motion might be such that the temporal betweenness which it defines would exhibit closedness rather than openness, because there would be no physical *difference* whatever between a given passage of the particle through a fixed point A and its socalled "return" to the same state at A: instead of appearing periodically at the same *place* A at *different* instants in open time, the particle would be "returning"—in a highly Pickwickian sense of that term—to the *selfsame event* at the *same instant* in closed time. This conclusion rests on Leibniz's thesis that if two states of the world have precisely the same attributes, then we are not confronted by distinct states at different times but merely by two different *names* for the *same* state at *one* time. And it is this Leibnizian consideration which renders the following interpretation inadmissible as an alternative characterization of the time of our model universe: the same *kind* of set of events (circular motion) keeps on *recurring* eternally, and the time is topologically open and infinite in both directions. The latter interpretation is illegitimate since a difference in identity is assumed among events for which their attributes and relations provide no basis whatever. Hence that interpretation cannot qualify as a legitimate rival to our assertion that the events of our model world form an array which is topologically closed both spatially and temporally.

Ordinary temporal language is infested with the assumption that time is open, and a description of the closed time of our model world in *that* language would take the *misleading* form saying that the same sequence of states keeps *recurring* all the time. This description can generate pseudo-contradictions or puzzles in this context, because it suggests the following structure.

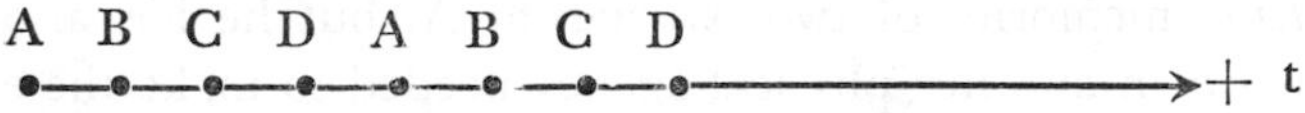

Here are *distinct* sets of events ABCD which are merely the same in *kind* with respect to one or more of their properties. But this is *not* the structure of closed time. A closed time is very counterintuitive psychologically for reasons which will emerge later on. And hence the assumption of the closedness of time is a much stranger one intuitively than is a cyclic theory of history. In a cyclic theory of history, one envisions the periodic recurrence of the same kind of state at *different* times. And this conception of cyclic recurrence affirms the openness of time. Perhaps the lack of *psychological* imaginability as distinct from theoretical intelligibility of a closed time accounts for the fact that its logical possibility is usually overlooked in theological discussions of creation. This failure of imagination is unfortunate, however, since there could be no problem of a beginning or creation, if time were to be cosmically closed.

Three kinds of objections might be raised to my claim that our model universe does provide a realization of a topologically closed kind of time: (i) It might be argued that my earlier *caveat* concerning the need for a highly Pickwickian construal of the term "returning" actually begs the question in the following sense: the mere contemplation of the model universe under consideration compels the conclusion that the particle does indeed return in the proper sense of that term to the same point A at *different* instants of *open* time. And it might be charged that to think otherwise is to disregard a plain fact of our contemplative experience, (ii) The complete circular motion could be subdivided into a finite number n of (equal) parts or submotions (episodes). And this has been claimed to show that instead of being topologically closed, the time of our model universe has the open topology of a *finite* segment of a straight line which is bounded by distinct end-points, the first and n^{th} submotions allegedly being the ones which contain the two terminal events, (iii) It has been said that it is of the essence of time to be open. Noting that my characterization of the model universe at issue as having a closed time depends on the invocation of Leibniz's principle of the identity of indiscernibles, a critic has maintained that instead of showing that a closed time is logically possible, this model shows that Leibniz's principle must be false!

As to the first of these objections, which rests on the deliverances of our contemplation of the model universe, my reply is that the objector has tacitly altered the conditions that I had postulated for that model universe, thereby tampering with the very features on which my affirmation of the closure of its time had been predicated. For the objector has not only introduced a conscious organism such as himself, whom he presumes to have *distinct* memories of two passages at A, but he has also surreptitiously brought in another physical agency needed to make these distinct memories possible: a light source such as a candle which enables him to *see* and which distinguishes an earlier and a later passage at A by being more dissipated or burnt-out at the time of the later passage. Thus, the objection is untenable, because the objector assumes a universe *differing* from my hypothetical one so as *not* to have a closed time.

The second objection, which adduces the n submotions, is vitiated by the following gratuitous projection of the ordinal properties of numerical *names* onto the events (or submotions) to which they are assigned in a counting procedure: the divisibility of the motion of the particle on the platform into n subintervals of events—where n is a *cardinal* number —does *not* make for the possession of any objective property of being *temporal termini* by the particular subintervals which were assigned the numbers 1 and n respectively. For no two of the n subintervals of events—whatever the particular numbers that happened to have been assigned to them in the counting—are *ordinally* distinguished objectively from any of the others. If therefore we count them by *arbitrarily* assigning the number 1 to some one of them and by then assigning the remaining n-1 numbers, this cannot serve to establish that temporally the ordinal properties of the particular subintervals thus accidentally named 1 and n respectively are any different from those of the subintervals which are thereby assigned natural numbers *between* 1 and n.

The justification for this rebuttal can be thrown into still bolder relief by noting the objective differences between our model universe of the particle moving "perpetually" in a circular path and the following different model universe whose time does indeed have the open topology of a finite segment of a straight line bounded by two end-points: a platform universe differing from the first one only by exchanging the particle moving in a closed (circular) path for a simple pendulum oscillating "perpetually" and frictionlessly over the platform as if under the action of terrestrial gravity. Let the oscillation be through a fixed small amplitude $\theta = 2\,\alpha$ between *two fixed points* whose angular separation from the vertical is $+\alpha$ and $-\alpha$ respectively. Then the *finitude* of the time of this pendulum universe is assured by the fact that the "perpetual periodic returns" of the pendulum bob to the same points over the platform are, in fact, identical events by Leibniz's principle. For this identity prevents this latter model universe from qualifying as an infinitely periodic universe whose time is open. But the two fixed points at angular distances $-\alpha$ and $+\alpha$ respectively from the vertical uniquely confine the motion spatially to the points *between* them. And hence the events constituted by the presence of the pendulum bob at $-\alpha$ and $+\alpha$ are objectively distinguished as *termini* from all other events belonging to the motion of the pendulum, although no one of these two events is distinguished from the other as the first rather than the last, since the motion is reversible. Accordingly, the time of the pendulum universe has the topology of an undirected finite segment of a straight line bounded by two termini. But there is no foundation for the objection that our first model universe of the particle in the circular path has the latter kind of time.

The third objection, which has the spirit of an argument based on Kant's presuppositional method, suffers from precisely the same well-known logical defects as does the claim that we know a priori that the universe must be *spatially* infinite (topologically open) rather than finite (closed but unbounded). For the defender of the a priori assertibility of the infinite Euclidean topology would offer the following corresponding argument regarding space: if it appeared that a spatial geodesic of our universe were traversable in a finite number of equal steps terminating at the *same* spatial point, the certification of the sameness of that point via Leibniz's principle would have to be rejected. And the a priori proponent of the Euclidean as opposed to the spherical topology of space would then adduce these circumstances to show that Leibniz's principle is false. Although the rise of the non-Euclidean geometries has issued in the displacement of the Kantian conception of the topology of physical *space* by an empiricist one in most quarters, a vestigial Kantianism persists in many quarters with respect to the topology of *time*. And this lingering topological apriorism seems to be nurtured by the following failure of imagination: the neglect to envision having to divest the topology of the time of a model universe—or the cosmic time of our actual universe—of some of the topological properties of the cosmically-local time of our everyday experience. That such divesture may be necessary has been emphasized by Gödel's discovery that Einstein's field equations allow solutions yielding a temporally closed universe.[37] And Gödel's result would seem to indicate that a cosmically closed time can also be possessed by a deterministic universe containing sentient beings like ourselves.

There is a rather simple way of seeing how man-like beings might discover that the cosmic time of their universe is closed, despite the *seriality* of the local segment of cosmic time accessible to their daily experience. Suppose that all the equations governing the temporal evolution of the states of physical and biological systems are deterministic with respect to the properties of events and that these equations are formulated in terms of a time variable t ranging over the real numbers, it thereby being assumed *to begin with* that time is topologically *open*. Now postulate further that the boundary conditions of this deterministic world are such that *all* of the variables of state pertaining to it (including those variables whose values characterize the thoughts of scientists living in it) assume precisely the *same* values at what are prima facie the time t and a very much *later* time $t + T$. Then upon discovering this result by calculations, these scientists would have to conclude that the two different values of the time variable for which this sameness of state obtains do *not* denote two objectively *distinct* states but are only two different numerical names for what is identically the same state. In this way, they would discover that their universe is temporally closed, much as a scientist who begins by assuming that the universe is *spatially* infinite may then find that, in the large, it is spatially closed. But there is an important difference between the *psychological* intuitability of a closed space and that of a closed time: a cosmically closed time could *not everywhere* be locally serial with respect to "earlier than."

As previously emphasized, it is of crucial importance in this context, if pseudo-puzzles and contradictions are to be avoided, that the term "returning" and all of the prëempted temporal language which we tend to use in describing a world whose time (in the large) is closed be divested of all of its tacit reference to an external *serial super-time.* Awareness of the latter pitfall now enables us to see that as between the two kinds of

[37]In recent papers ["An Example of a New Type of Cosmological Solutions of Einstein's Field Equations of Gravitation," *Reviews of Modern Physics* XXI, 447 (1949) and "A Remark about the Relationship of Relativity Theory and Idealistic Philosophy," in P. A. Schilpp (ed.), *Albert Einstein: Philosopher-Scientist* (Evanston, 1949), 560-562], Gödel has pointed out that there exist solutions of Einstein's field equations which assert the existence of *closed* time-like world-lines. Einstein says (*ibid.*, 688) that "It will be interesting to weigh whether these [solutions] are not to be excluded on physical grounds." Reichenbach himself points out [*Phil. d. Raum-Zeit-Lehre, op. cit.*, 166, 312-313 or PST, 141, 272-273] that in a world of closed time-like world lines, his causal criterion of temporal order becomes self-contradictory in the large [*Axiomatik der rel. Raum-Zeit-Lehre, op. cit.*, 22]. And, as Einstein remarks *(ibid.)*, in such a world, irreversibility also fails to hold in the large.

closed order which we have mentioned, separation closure and *not* cyclicity must be held to be the order of a closed *time*. For in the context of physical states, cyclic betweenness depends for its directional anisotropy on an appeal to a serial and hence *open time* and derives its closure only from a *spatial periodicity*. Thus, a closed physical time must exhibit separation-closure and cannot meaningfully be cyclic. And if we are to give a concise characterization of a physically plausible closed time, it should read: every state of the world is temporally between every other pair of states of the universe in a sense of "between" given by our definition for the case of separation closure. It might be asked why we have been assuming that the structure of a closed time would have to be that of a knot-free circle rather than that given by the self-intersecting closed line in the numeral 8. The reply is that the framework of our models of a closed time is deterministic and that the course of the phase curve representing a finite (closed) mechanical or other deterministic system is uniquely determined by *any one* of its phase points.

Our characterization of a closed time is to apply not only to a thoroughly uninteresting model world like that of the solitary particle moving in a circular path on a platform but to a cosmos whose total states are *not* elementary events but large classes of coincidences of many genidentical objects. It is therefore essential that we specify the meaning of topological *simultaneity*, which is presupposed by the concept of a state of the world. Reserving comment until we discuss *open* time and, in particular, the species of open time affirmed by the special theory of relativity, on the serviceability of the following definition in that context, we define: two events are topologically simultaneous, iff it is not physically *possible* that they be connected by genidential causal chains. It is to be noted in connection with this definition that a light ray directly connecting a pair of macroscopic events is held to qualify as an entity possessing genidentity, although this assumption no longer holds in contexts in which the Bose-Einstein statistics applies to photons.

2. Open Time.

Since our definition of topological simultaneity is completely neutral as to the closedness or openness of time, it is apparent that we can also utilize the definition of topological simultaneity for the description of a universe whose time is characterized by o-betweenness, such as that of Newton or of special relativity. In the latter Einsteinian world, the limiting role played by electromagnetic causal chains makes for the fact that the topological definition of simultaneity leaves a good deal of latitude for the synchronization rule and thereby for the *metrical* definition of simultaneity. And hence in that case, our purely ordinal definition would have to be particularized in each Galilean frame so as to render *metrically* simultaneous in any given frame only those pairs of causally non-connectible events which conform to the criterion of that particular frame.[38]

To appreciate the role of boundary conditions in conferring openness on time, we first recall our pendulum world model of a *finite* open time and now proceed to provide models of an *infinite* open time as follows: first a very simple kind of world and then a world having far greater relevance to the actual world in which we live.

Let there be a universe consisting of a platform, material clocks and at least two simple pendulums X and Y which have *incommensurable* periods of oscillation so that after once being in the same phase they are permanently out-of-phase with each other. Then these motions would define an infinite open time in virtue of Leibniz's non-identity of discernibles: in this case, a given passage E_p of the bob of pendulum X through a fixed point P would be physically *different* from any other such passage E_q in virtue of E_p's being simultaneous with a *different* phase of pendulum Y from the one with which E_q is simultaneous, thereby giving rise to an order of o-betweenness for time. In the overall light of the construction of physical time presented in this essay, this assertion involves a philosophical commitment to a *Leibnizian* criterion for the individuality of the *events* belonging to the causal chains formed by genidentical classical material particles or *macro*-objects, along with a *non*-Leibnizian primitive concept of material genidentity for the entities whose relations generate these events. I do not see any inconsistency or circularity in this feature of the construction. In particular it seems to me that only a confusion of the context of justification with the context of discovery (in Reichenbachian terminology) or of the factual reference with the evidential base (in Feigl's parlance) can inspire the charge that it is circular to use the concept of (material) genidentity as a primitive in a reconstruction of the temporal order of physical events, on the alleged grounds that the meaning of the temporal order is already presupposed in our *re*cognitions of objects as the *same* upon encountering them in different places at different times.

Now consider a finite universe or a large finite quasi-closed portion of our actual universe, if the latter be spatially infinite, to which the Maxwell-Boltzmann gas statistics is roughly applicable. The concept of what constitutes an individual micro-state ("arrangement" or "complexion") in the Maxwell-Boltzmann statistics depends crucially on the assumption that material genidentity can be ascribed to particles (molecules) and involves the very Leibnizian conception of the individuality of events which we set forth by reference to our illustrative examples of the simple model universes. An individual instant of time is thus

[38]For details, cf. A. Grünbaum, "Logical and Philosophical Foundations of the Special Theory of Relativity." *op. cit.*, §2.

defined for this universe by one of its particular micro-states. And, on this criterion, it will therefore be quite meaningful to speak, as I shall later on, of the occurrence of the *same macro*-state ("distribution") and hence of the same entropy at *different* times, *provided* that the respective underlying *micro*-states are different. But whether or not a universe constituted by a Maxwell-Boltzmann gas will exhibit a set of micro-states which define an *open* time rather than a time which, in the large, is closed depends *not* on the causal character of the motions of the constituent molecules but on the *boundary conditions* governing their motions! And whether the time thus defined will, if *open,* also be *infinite,* depends on the microstates having the degree of specificity represented by *points* in phase space rather than by the mere *cells* used to compute the probabilities of various macro-states. For a finite closed mechanical system of constant energy is at least quasi-periodic and can possibly qualify as aperiodic only with respect to a *punctal* characterization of its micro-states.

Hence, the symmetric kind of causality affirmed by the equations of mechanics themselves, as distinct from prevailing nomologically-contingent boundary conditions to which they apply, *allows* but does *not assure* that the temporal betweenness (and simultaneity) defined by genidentical causal chains is that of an open rather than a closed ordering.[39]

This analysis of the physical basis of open time requires the addition of a comment on the meaning of the "reversibility" of mechanical motions. We observed that the *total states* of our pendulums X and Y whose periods are incommensurable define an *infinite open* time by *not* exhibiting any *"reversals."* What is meant, therefore, when we attribute *reversibility* to the motions of either of the individual pendulums is that either *elementary* constituent of the total system can (under suitable boundary conditions of its own) give rise to the same *kind* of event at different times. We do *not* mean that the pendulum in question has "returned" to the selfsame event, since the total states of the complete physical system assure via the Leibnizian *non*-identity of discernibles that the events belonging to the individual pendulum form an infinite open order of time. Thus, the reversibility of the laws of mechanics has

[39]Mehlberg (*op. cit.,* I, 240) correctly calls attention to the fact that the principle of causal continuity is independent of whether physical processes are *reversible* or not. But then, affirming the complete reversibility of the physical world and thereby the isotropy of physical time (*ibid.,* 184), he takes it for granted that the principle of causal continuity as such always defines an open betweenness (*op. cit.,* I, 239-240, II, 179, 156-7, 168-9). But, as we just saw, in a completely reversible world, it can happen that the betweenness defined by the principle of causal continuity for genidentical chains is that of the closed variety associated with separation closure. Thus, instead of being isotropic while being open, time would then be both isotropic and closed.

a clear meaning in the context of an infinite open time. And the reversibility of the *elementary* processes in our Maxwell-Boltzmann universe, which is affirmed by these laws, is therefore entirely compatible with the infinite openness of the time defined by the total micro-states of that universe. We shall soon see, however, that the mere *non-reversal* of the total micro-states, which assures the infinite openness of time merely on the strength of the requisite boundary conditions, is a much weaker property of these states than the *irreversibility* that is a *sufficient* condition for the *anisotropy* of time.

We have emphasized the neutrality of our definition of temporal betweenness on the basis of causal continuity in regard to the rival possibilities of open and closed betweenness for time. The *second* feature of our definition of temporal betweenness which needs to be noted is that it is not exempt from the aforementioned threat of circularity inherent in the concept of physical possibility, if we expect it to order B as temporally between A and C even in those cases where B would be between A and C if A and C *were* genidentically connected but are not. This risk also applies to our definition of (topological) simultaneity for noncoincident events.

In the theories of pair-production due to Wheeler, Feynman, and Stückelberg (cf. footnote 92), some of the phenomena under investigation may be described in the usual macro-language by saying that a "particle" can "travel" both "forward" and "backward" in macro-time. Thus, in that description a "particle" can violate the necessary condition for simultaneity given in our definition here by being at two different places at instants which are macroscopically simultaneous. But this fact does not disqualify our definition of simultaneity. For the topology of the time whose physical bases our analysis is designed to uncover is defined by (statistical) *macro*-properties for which these difficulties do not arise. The macro-character of our concept of simultaneity is evident from the fact that it depends on the concept of material or quasi-material genidentity. Precisely this concept and the associated classical concept of a particle trajectory are generally no longer applicable to micro-entities, so that the consequences of their inapplicability in the Wheeler-Feynman theory and in the Bose-Einstein statistics need not occasion any surprise. Furthermore, the macro-character of the anisotropy of time will emerge from the analysis to be given later in this essay.

We see that since our definitions of temporal betweenness and simultaneity employed a concept of causal connection joining two events which made no reference to *one* of the events being *the* cause of the other by being *earlier,* these definitions do not presuppose in any way the anisotropy of time. On the other hand, they do exhaust the contribution which the causality of reversible processes can make to the elucidation of the structure of time. If physical time is to be anisotropic, then we must look to features of the physical world other than the causality of reversible processes as the source. In particular, since it has been shown[40] that if the micro-statistical analogue of entropy fails to confer anisotropy on time, all other micro-statistical properties of *closed systems for which an entropy is defined* will fail as well, we must turn to an examination of entropy to see in what sense, if any, it can supply attributes of physical time not furnished by causality.

Before doing so, however, a brief concluding remark concerning the bearing of the causal theory of time on the modern mathematical resolution of Zeno's paradoxes of motion is indicated.

Having no recourse to the anisotropy or even to the openness of time, our definitions of temporal betweenness and simultaneity established a *dense* temporal order. For our construction entails that between any two events, there is always another. Now, as I have explained elsewhere,[41] it was the ascription of this denseness property to the temporal order by the modern mathematical theory of motion which prompted the Zenonian charge by W. James, A. N. Whitehead, and P. Weiss that that theory of motion is neither physically meaningful nor consistent. Resting their case on the immediate deliverances of consciousness, *which include "becoming,"* these philosophers maintained that the temporal order is *discrete* rather than dense, the events of nature occurring *seriatim* or "pulsationally." We see that the causal theory of time as here presented refutes their polemic on the issue of the denseness of the temporal order of the physical world and that this refutation is not dependent on the logical viability of the unsatisfactory mark method, which I employed in my earlier paper, when giving a critique of their arguments on the basis of the causal theory of time.[42]

III. *Time and Irreversible Processes*

We shall have to determine what properties of the physical world, if any, confer anisotropy on the time of nature. After solving this problem, we shall be ready to see whether over and above structurally *distinguishing* two directions of time from one another, any features of the universe such as the hypothetical one of indeterminism can give a

[40] Cf. A. S. Eddington, *The Nature of the Physical World* (New York, 1928), 79-80. For details on the "principle of detailed balancing" relevant here, cf. R. C. Tolman, *The Principles of Statistical Mechanics* (Oxford, 1938), 165, 521.

[41] A. Grünbaum, "Relativity and the Atomicity of Becoming," *The Review of Metaphysics, op. cit.,* 143-160.

[42] The analysis on the basis of the mark method is given on pp. 160-186 of the paper cited in the preceding footnote. For a treatment not encumbered by the weaknesses of the mark method, cf. A. Grünbaum, "Modern Science and Refutation of the Paradoxes of Zeno," *The Scientific Monthly* LXXXI (1955), 234-239.

physical meaning to becoming as a forward march or "taking place" of events in *one* of the two distinguished directions via defining the transient "now" or specious present.

It will be essential to begin by giving an analysis of the concept of anisotropy in its application to time.

To begin with, it must be noted that while it is readily possible to define a triadic relation having all of the formal properties of o-betweenness in terms of a particular dyadic serial relation, the converse deduction is not possible, since in a given system of serial order, we can distinguish one "direction" from its opposite, whereas the system of o-betweenness does not, by itself, enable us to make such a differentiation. The case of the straight line will illustrate this fact. The points of the straight line form a system of o-betweenness. This order is intrinsic to the straight line in the sense that its specification involves no essential reference to an external viewer and his particular perspective. The serial ordering of the points with respect to a concrete relation "to the left of" is extrinsic in the sense of requiring reference to an external viewer, at least for the establishment of an asymmetric dyadic relation "to the left of" between two given arbitrarily-selected reference points U and V. Once we thus introduce an asymmetric dyadic relation between two such points, then, to be sure, we can indeed use the intrinsic system of o-betweenness on the line to define a serial order throughout the line.[43] To say that a given serial order with respect to the relation "to the left of" is conventional is another way of saying that it is extrinsic in our sense. For a particular external perspective, it is of course *not* arbitrary whether a given point *x* is to the left of another point *y* or conversely. In contrast to the "extrinsic" character of the serial ordering of the points on the line with respect to the relation "to the left of," the serial ordering of the real numbers with respect to "smaller than" is intrinsic in our sense, since for any two real numbers, the ordering with respect to magnitude requires no reference to entities outside the domain. It is essential *not* to overlook, as Reichenbach did and as the writer did in an earlier publication,[44] that a serial ordering *always* establishes a *difference* in direction independently of whether it is intrinsic or extrinsic! Confusing extrinsicality of a serial relation with *undirectedness,* Reichenbach maintains that the relation "to the left of" on the line is *not* unidirectional, i.e., fails to distinguish two opposite directions from

[43]The relevant details on these formal matters can be found in Lewis and Langford, *Symbolic Logic* (New York, 1932), 381-387 and in E. V. Huntington, "Inter-Relations Among the Four Principal Types of Order," *op. cit.,* 7, Section 3.1.

[44]H. Reichenbach, "The Philosophical Significance of the Theory of Relativity," *op. cit.,* 304-305 and DT, 26-27; A. Grünbaum, "Time and Entropy," *American Scientist* XLII (1955), 551.

one another, whereas the relation "smaller than" is both serial and unidirectional. But he found himself driven to this contention only because he failed to note that a serial relation is automatically a directed one by being asymmetric even when the seriality has an extrinsic basis, an oversight which led him to distinguish relations which are serial while allegedly being undirected from directed serial relations. And this error issued in his false distinction between the supposed mere seriality of time, which he called "order," and its "direction," a distinction which he attempted to buttress by pointing to the seriality of the time of Newton's mechanics and of special relativity in the face of the total neglect of irreversible processes by the fundamental equations of these theories. Reichenbach's distinction should be replaced by the distinction between intrinsically isotropic and anisotropic kinds of time, which we shall now explain.

The symmetric causal relation of reversible processes *intrinsically* defines a temporal order of mere o-betweenness under suitable boundary conditions but not a serial order. Just as it was possible, however, in the case of the line to introduce a serial ordering in its system of o-betweenness by means of an extrinsically-grounded asymmetric dyadic relation between two chosen reference points U and V, so also it is possible to choose two reference *states* in a time that is intrinsically merely open, and extrinsically render this time *serial* by making one of these two states *later* than the other through the assignment of suitable real numbers as temporal names. It is in this sense that worlds containing only reversible processes such as the worlds of Newtonian mechanics and of the Lorentz-transformations of special relativity can be legitimately and significantly described by a serial time. Historically, of course, the serial times of these theories derive simply from the fact that their propounders lived in a world also containing irreversible processes, processes which intrinsically define a serial time in a manner to be discussed below. We see that if the serial time of classical mechanics and of the Lorentz-transformations is denuded of its extrinsic component, then a world possessing suitable boundary conditions which is exhaustively described by one of these theories will *intrinsically* define only a temporal order of o-betweenness. And this order is *isotropic* in the following two-fold sense: (i) all elementary processes are reversible and (ii) there is no one property, possessed by each of the total states of the world, which *intrinsically* defines a dyadic relation between every pair of states such that the class of states forms a serial order with respect to that relation. But in a world like that of the *non*-statistical second law of classical thermodynamics, precisely the latter kind of property does exist in the form of the entropy, and hence such a world is temporally *anisotropic:* its time exhibits a special kind of *difference in direction* arising from the directed, *intrinsically*-grounded serial relation of "later than." It is apparent that to speak of the states of such a world as "irreversible" is to assert more than the mere nonreversal which we encountered in the intrinsically isotropic infinite open time of the universe of classical mechanics: the classical entropy law precludes the occurrence of the same (nonequilibrium) *macro*-state at different times rather than merely asserting that the micro-states define an *open* order of time in virtue of the *de facto* boundary conditions; furthermore, that law makes a specific assertion about the way in which macro-states occuring at different times do differ with respect to a single property.

Although the serial relation "later than" itself does have *a* direction in an obvious sense, the set of states ordered by it does *not* have *a* direction but rather exhibits a special *difference* of structure between the *two opposite directions*. Thus, when we speak of the anisotropy of time, this must *not* be construed as equivalent to making assertions about *"the"* direction of time. J. J. C. Smart and Max Black have correctly pointed out (cf. fn. 110 in Section IV below) that reference to "the" direction of time is inspired by the notion that time "flows." In particular, as we shall see in Section IV, Reichenbach's use of this term rests on his incorrect supposition that there is a physical basis for *becoming* in the sense of the shifting of a physically-defined "now" along *one* of the two physically-distinguished directions of time. In speaking of the anisotropy of physical time, we intend to refer only to the static directional difference between earlier and later and thus make no commitment whatever to a transient division of time into the past and the future by a present whose "advance" would define *"the"* direction of time. In fact, we shall argue in Section IV that the concept of becoming has no significant application outside human conscious awareness. Nevertheless, we shall find it desirable, after having entered this explicit *caveat,* to use the locution "the direction of time" as a synonym not only for "the future direction" in *psychological* time but also for "the one of two physically distinguished directions of time which our theory calls 'positive'."

Our analysis of the logical relations between symmetric causality, open time, extrinsic vs. intrinsic seriality of time, and anisotropy of time requires us to reject the following statement by Reichenbach (DT, p. 32):

> In the usual discussions of problems of time it has become customary to argue that only irreversible processes supply an asymmetrical relation of causality, while reversible processes allegedly lead to a symmetrical causal relation. This conception is incorrect. Irreversible processes alone can define a direction of time; but reversible processes define at least an [serial] order of time, and thereby supply an asymmetrical relation of causality. The reader is referred to the discussion of the relation *to the left of* (. . .). The correct formulation is that only irreversible processes define a *unidirectional* causality.

Reichenbach notes that while the causal processes of classical mechanics and special relativity are reversible, the temporal order affirmed by these "reversible" theories is serial. He then infers that (a) the causal relation in a reversible world must be asymmetric, and (b) in an irreversible world, we require a temporal relation which is not "merely" serial but also "unidirectional," as well as a causal relation which is both asymmetric and unidirectional. But he overlooks that in the reversible worlds, the seriality of time is extrinsic and that the assignment of the lower of two real numbers as the temporal name to *one* of two causally-connected events therefore does *not* express any objective asymmetry on the part of the causal relation itself.

We are now ready to examine in detail the physical basis of the anisotropy of time.

Our problem now is whether entropy, whose values are given by real numbers, succeeds, unlike the causality of reversible processes, in conferring anisotropy on open time by intrinsically defining a serial ordering in the class of states of a closed system.

In its original, non-statistical form, the second law of thermodynamics tells us that the entropy of a *closed* system, not already in thermodynamic equilibrium, always increases with time. This statement is synthetic in an obvious sense, *if* the direction of increasing time is defined independently of the entropy-increase either by reference to the continuous matter-energy accretion (as distinct from energy *dispersion*) postulated by the "new cosmology"[45] or—in the spatially-limited and cosmically brief career of man—by reliance on the subjective sense of time flow in human consciousness. We shall see, however, that contemporary information theory and thermodynamics *explain* several important features of man's subjective sense of time on the basis of the participation of his organism in the entropic lawfulness of physical nature. And, being unwilling to base the empirical content of so earthy a law as that of Clausius on a highly speculative cosmology, we reject both of these criteria. Instead, while postponing statistical considerations, we can follow Eddington[46] and use the second law of thermodynamics itself to give a coordinative definition of the positive direction of time, thereby inviting the query, often raised in the literature, how that law then avoids being a mere tautology. If we restrict ourselves to a *single* closed system and say that of two given entropy states, the state of greater entropy will be said to be "later than" the state of smaller entropy, then indeed we have merely given a coordinative definition. But just as other co-

[45]For details on the "new cosmology," see H. Bondi, *Cosmology* (Cambridge, 1952); a brief digest is given in A. Grünbaum, "Some Highlights of Modern Cosmology and Cosmogony," *The Review of Metaphysics* V (1952), 493-498.

[46]Eddington, *The Nature of the Physical World,* op. cit., 69ff.

ordinative definitions of empirical science,[47] this definition is prompted by the empirical fact that it does not give rise to ambiguities or contradictions, when *different* closed systems are used. For—statistical modifications being temporarily ignored—there is concordance in the behavior of all closed systems: given any two such systems A and B, but not in thermodynamic equilibrium, if an entropy state S_{A_j} of A is simultaneous with a state S_{B_j} of B, then there is no case of a state S_{A_k} being simultaneous with a state S_{B_i}, such that $S_{A_k} > S_{A_j}$ while $S_{B_i} \leq S_{B_j}$.[48]

Since the relation "larger than" for real numbers is serial, the entropic definition of "later than" just given renders the seriality of time, once its openness is assured by suitable boundary conditions, openness and seriality being attributes concerning which the causal theory of time had to be non-committal. But, as Eddington neglected to point out, that theory of time played an essential role in our entropic definition of "later than" by furnishing coordinative definitions for the concepts of "temporally between" and "simultaneous," which are needed to give meaning to the second law of thermodynamics. For this law uses the concept of "closed system," which, as we saw (cf. footnote 21), presupposes the concept of "temporal betweenness," and makes reference to the entropy of an *extended* system *at a certain time*, and implicitly, to the *simultaneous* entropy states of several systems.

Our recognition of the auxiliary role of the causal theory of time in Eddington's definition of the positive time-direction enables us to reply to a criticism of that definition by P. W. Bridgman.[49] As against Eddington's attempt to give a physical coordinative definition of time direction, Bridgman claims, on operational grounds, that this definition is circular

47Examples are the definition of the metric of time on the basis of the empirical law of inertia, and the definition of congruence for spatially separated bodies on the basis of the fact that two bodies which are congruent at a given place will be so everywhere, independently of the respective paths along which they are transported individually. Cf. M. Schlick, "Are Natural Laws Conventions," in Feigl and Brodbeck (eds.), *Readings in the Philosophy of Science* (New York, 1953), 184; H. Reichenbach, "Ziele und Wege der physikalischen Erkenntnis," *op. cit.*, 52-3 and *Phil. d. Raum-Zeit-Lehre, op. cit.*, 25-6, 331-2 or PST, 16-17.

48Cf. K. G. Denbigh, "Thermodynamics and the Subjective Sense of Time," *British Journal for the Phil. of Science* IV (1953), 183-186 and E. Zilsel, "Über die Asymmetrie der Kausalität und die Einsinnigkeit der Zeit," *Naturwissenschaften* XV, 282 (1927).

49P. W. Bridgman, *Reflections of a Physicist* (New York, 1950), 162-167. The rebuttal about to be offered to Bridgman's critique of Eddington's definition also applies to L. Susan Stebbing's arguments against it, as set forth in her *Philosophy and the Physicists* (London, 1937), Ch. XI, esp. 262-3. Furthermore, it will become clear later in this essay that Eddington has also been vindicated by the entropic account of the anisotropy of *psychological* time furnished by recent information theory.

I should emphasize, however, that my endorsement of Eddington's views on this particular issue must *not* be construed as agreement with either his general philosophy of science or his view [cf. *The Nature of the Physical World, op. cit.*, 84-85] that the universe's supposed past state of *minimum* entropy constitutes a conundrum to which

and that reliance on the *psychological* sense of time direction is indispensable. Says he:[50] "in any operational view of the meaning of natural concepts the notion of time must be used as a primitive concept, which cannot be analyzed, and which can only be accepted, . . . I see no way of formulating the underlying operations without assuming as understood the notion of earlier or later in time." In an endeavor to show that the specification of the entropy of a closed system at a given instant presupposes the use of the psychological sense of time *direction,* Bridgman says: "[Consider what] is involved in specifying a thermodynamic system. One of the variables is the temperature; it is not sufficient merely to read at a given instant of time an instrument called a thermometer, but there are various precautions to be observed in the use of a thermometer, the most important of which is that one must be sure that the thermometer has come to equilibrium with its surroundings and so records the true temperature. *In order to establish this, one has to observe how the readings of the thermometer change as time increases."*[51] Bridgman claims more than is warranted on precisely the point at issue. For to certify the existence of equilibrium at a certain instant t, we must assure ourselves of the absence of a change in the thermometer's reading during a time interval containing the instant t. But does the procurement of that assurance require a knowledge as to which of the two termini of such an interval is the *earlier* of the two with respect to a positive time direction? Is it not sufficient to ascertain the constancy of the reading *between* the terminal instants of the time-interval in question? Indeed, what is presupposed is merely temporal betweenness, which, as we saw, is defined by causal processes, independently of time *direction.* But this is hardly damaging to Eddington's definition of time direction. And it is irrelevant that, in practice, the experimenter may note *also* which one of the termini of the time-interval containing the instant t is the earlier of the two. For what is at issue is the *semantical* as distinct from the *pragmatic* anchorage of concepts, our inquiry being one in the context of justification and not in the context of discovery.[52] The complete dis-

theological ideas are relevant. For I not only deem theological considerations wholly unilluminating in any case [cf. my "Some Highlights of Modern Cosmology and Cosmogony," *The Review of Metaphysics* V, 481 (1952), esp. 497-498 and my "Science and Ideology," *The Scientific Monthly* LXXIX, 13 (1954)] but also believe that the statistical conception of entropy to be discussed below cuts the ground from under the assumptions implicit in Eddington's puzzlement.

[50]*Ibid.,* 165.

[51]*Ibid.,* 167, *my italics.*

[52]For a discussion of Bridgman's unwarranted absorption of semantics within pragmatics, which is a new version of the Sophist doctrine that man is the measure of all things, see A. Grünbaum, "Operationism and Relativity," *The Scientific Monthly* LXXIX (1954), 228-231 [reprinted in P. Frank (ed.) *The Validation of Scientific Theories,* (Boston, 1957)], where it is also argued that the conceptual innovations of the special

pensability of the experimenter's subjective sense of time *direction* is further apparent from the fact that the experimenter could certify equilibrium at the instant t, if he were given a film strip showing the constancy of the reading during a time interval between t_1 and t_2 which contains t, *without* being told which end of the film strip corresponds to the earlier moment t_1. A similar reply can be given to Bridgman's argument[53] that the *physical* meaning of "velocity" presupposes the psychological direction of time. For we shall see that entropic processes in physical nature define a difference in time-direction quite independently of human consciousness. And thus, for any given choice of the positive space-direction, physical processes themselves define the meanings of both the signs (directions) and magnitudes of velocities independently of man's psychological time-direction. Here again, Bridgman falsely equates and confuses two *different* meaning components of terms in physics: the physical or semantical with the psychological or pragmatic. The semantical component concerns the properties and relations of purely physical entities which are denoted (named) by terms like "velocity." On the other hand, the pragmatic component concerns the activities, both manual and mental, of scientists in *discovering* or coming to *know* the existence of physical entities exhibiting the properties and relations involved in having a certain velocity. That statements about the velocities of masses do *not* derive their physical meaning from our psychological time-direction is shown by the fact that cosmogonic hypotheses make reference to the velocities of masses during a stage in the formation of our solar system which *preceded* the evolution of man and his psychological time sense. In fact, even in a completely *reversible* world devoid of beings possessing a time sense, velocity would be a significant attribute of a body despite that hypothetical world's temporal isotropy. But this isotropy would have the consequence that the velocities in such a world—unlike those of our actual, temporally anisotropic world—would *not* involve a physically distinguished time-direction, any more

theory of relativity cannot be legitimately invoked as support for operationism in Bridgman's homocentric sense. The same absorption of semantics within pragmatics is found in the following statement by Bridgman ["Reflections on Thermodynamics," *American Scientist* XLI (1953), 554]: "In general, the meaning of our concepts on the microscopic level is ultimately to be sought in operations on the macroscopic level. The reason is simply that we, for whom the meanings exist, operate on the macroscopic level. The reduction of the meanings of quantum mechanics to the macroscopic level has, I believe, not yet been successfully accomplished and is one of the major tasks ahead of quantum theory."

For a critique of the use of Bridgman's homocentrism in the interpretation of quantum mechanics, see H. Reichenbach, DT, 224 and A. Grünbaum "Complementarity in Quantum Physics and Its Philosophical Generalization," *The Journal of Philosophy* LIV (1957), 719.

[53]Bridgman, *Reflections of a Physicist, op. cit.,* 167.

than the positive and negative directions in the isotropic *space* of our actual world involve a physically distinguished space-direction.

Bridgman raises an additional objection to Eddington's definition of time direction: "how would one go to work in any concrete case to decide whether time were flowing forward or backward? If it were found that the entropy of the universe were decreasing, would one say that time was flowing backward, or would one say that it was a law of nature that entropy decreases with time?"[54] But under what circumstances would it be found that the entropy of the universe "is decreasing"? Remembering that we are concerned with a non-statistical study of closed systems, this situation would arise in the purely hypothetical case in which the direction of increasing entropy among physical systems is not *also* the direction of memory or information increase among biological organisms, "higher" memory states corresponding to *lower* entropy states of physical systems. In other words, the direction of entropy increase and the future direction of psychological time would then be *counter-directed.* Since in our actual world the production of memory traces depends on an entropy increase in the overall external environment, as we shall see, Bridgman's hypothetical situation is hardly an argument against Eddington, who was concerned with the physical basis of the temporal anisotropy of our *actual* world and not of other logically possible worlds. But even if the situation depicted by Bridgman were to arise, it would certainly not invalidate Eddington's claim that (i) the behavior of the class of closed physical systems defines a structural *difference* in time direction via the difference in material content between the relation "y is a higher entropy state than x" and its converse, and (ii) the direction of increasing entropy can be called the direction of time increase. Eddington did not contend that entropically characterized time "is flowing forward" in the sense of a transiency or becoming, since he makes a special point of emphasizing that the shifting "now," so familiar from psychological time, eludes conceptual rendition as an attribute of physical processes.[55] But by his very unfortunate choice of the name "time's arrow" for the anisotropy of physical time, he ironically invited the very misunderstanding which he had been at pains to prevent, viz., that he was intending to offer a thermodynamic basis for the "unidirectional flow" of psychological time. There can be no problem of physical time flowing backward rather than forward, since it does *not* do any flowing at all. And in the context of *psychological* time, the locution "flow backward" is self-contradictory. Hence if Bridgman's hypothetical situation of counterdirectedness could actually materialize, then we would say that the entropy is

[54] *Ibid.*, 165.

[55] Eddington, *The Nature of the Physical World, op. cit.*, 68, 87-110.

decreasing with increasing psychological time and *not* that time is flowing backward.

More fundamentally, if the situation envisioned by Bridgman did arise, we would hardly survive long enough to be troubled by it. Poincaré and Costa de Beauregard[56] have explained, in a qualitative way, why prediction and action would become impossible under the circumstances posited by Bridgman: two bodies initially at the same temperature would acquire different temperatures, while we would be unable to anticipate which of these bodies will become the warmer one. Friction would no longer be a retarding influence but would set stationary bodies into motion in unpredictable directions. The most carefully conceived plan of action would precipitate enormous catastrophes, since unstable equilibria would now be the rule rather than the exception.

We can see, therefore, that in our *actual* world, the *inverse* temporal asymmetry must obtain under analogous initial conditions: there are physical conditions under which we *cannot* infer the past but can predict the future. The existence of this particular temporal asymmetry has been obscured by a preoccupation with both reversible processes whose past is as readily determinable as their future, and with *open non*-equilibrium systems for which the past can often be inferred from the present, as we shall see presently, whereas the future generally cannot.

Let us clarify the conditions which allow the prediction of the future while precluding the retrodiction of the past by reference to the equation describing a diffusion process, a process in which the entropy increases. This equation is of the form

$$\frac{\partial^2\psi}{\partial x^2} + \frac{\partial^2\psi}{\partial y^2} + \frac{\partial^2\psi}{\partial z^2} = a^2\frac{\partial\psi}{\partial t},$$

where a^2 is a real constant. This diffusion equation differs from the wave equation for a reversible process by having a first time derivative instead of a second. In the one-dimensional case of, say, heat-flow, the general solution of the equation governing the temperature ψ is given by

$$\psi(x,t) = \sum_{n=1}^{\infty} b_n \sin nx \, e^{-\frac{n^2}{a^2}t},$$

where the b_n are constants. The behavior of this equation is temporally asymmetric in the following two-fold sense: (i) if the physical system is in equilibrium at time $t = 0$, then we *cannot* infer what particular sequence of non-equilibrium states issued in the present equilibrium

[56]H. Poincaré, *The Foundations of Science*, tr. Halsted (Lancaster, 1913), 399-400. Costa de Beauregard, "L'Irréversibilité Quantique, Phénomène Macroscopique," in A. George (ed.), *Louis de Broglie, Physicien et Penseur*, *op. cit.*, 403, and *Théorie Synthétique de la Relativité Restreinte et des Quanta* (Paris, 1957), Ch. XIII, esp. 167-171.

state, since no such sequence is unique,[57] (ii) if the physical system is found in a *non*-equilibrium temperature state at t = 0, then it could *not* have been undergoing diffusion for *all past* values of t, although it can theoretically do so for all future values. Specifically, if external agencies impinge on the system and produce a non-equilibrium state of low entropy at time t = 0, then there is no basis for supposing that the system has been undergoing diffusion before t = 0 and then the diffusion equation cannot be invoked to infer the "prenatal" past of the system on the basis of its state at t = 0, although that equation can be used to predict its future as a closed system undergoing diffusion.

This possibility of prophesying the future states of an irreversible process in a closed system in the face of the enigmatic darkness shrouding the non-equilibrium states of the past under the stipulated conditions is so important that E. Hille, following J. Hadamard's analysis of Huyghens' principle in optics, has formulated the fundamental principle of scientific determinism as follows: "From the state of a [closed] physical system at the time t_0 we may deduce its state at a later [but not at an earlier] instant t."[58]

If this be the case, then it is natural to ask why it is that in so many cases involving irreversible processes, we seem to be far more reliably informed concerning the past than concerning the future. This question is raised by Schlick, who points out that human footprints on a beach enable us to infer that a person was there in the past but not that someone will walk there in the future. His answer is that "the structure of the past is inferred not from the extent to which energy has been dispersed but from the spatial arrangement of objects."[59] And he adds that the spatial traces, broadly conceived, are always produced in accord with the entropy principle. Thus, in the case of the beach, the kinetic energy of the person's feet became dispersed in the process of arranging the

[57]This is *not* to say that there are not *other* initial conditions under which at least a finite portion of the system's past *can* be inferred. For a discussion of this case, see J. C. Maxwell, *Theory of Heat,* 6th edition (New York, 1880), 264, and F. John, "Numerical Solution of the Equation of Heat Conduction for Preceding Times," *Annali di Matematica Pura ed Applicata* XL, 129 (1955). See also J. Crank, *The Mathematics of Diffusion* (Oxford, 1956).

[58]E. Hille, *Functional Analysis and Semi-Groups,* Am. Math. Soc. Publ. (New York, 1948), 388. Mathematically, the difference between the temporal symmetry of determination in the case of reversible processes and the corresponding asymmetry for irreversible processes expresses itself in the fact that the equations of the former give rise to associated groups of linear transformations while the latter lead to *semi*-groups instead.

[59]M. Schlick, *Grundzüge der Naturphilosophie* (Vienna, 1948), 106-7. J. J. C. Smart ["The Temporal Asymmetry of the World," *Analysis* XIV, 80 (1954)] also discusses the significance of traces but reaches the following unwarrantedly agnostic conclusion: "So the asymmetry of the concept of trace has something to do with the idea of formlessness or chaos. But it is not easy to see what." See also his paper in *Australasian Journal of Philosophy* XXXIII, 124 (1955).

grains of sand into the form of an imprint, which owes its (relative) persistence to the fact that the pedal kinetic energy lost its organization in the course of being imparted to the sand. To be sure, Schlick's claim that the process of leaving a trace occurs in accord with the entropy principle is quite true, but he fails to stress the crucial point at which the entropy principle is invoked in the retrodictive inference. Initially considering the beach itself as a closed system not far from equilibrium, we are informed by the discovery of footprints that the degree of order possessed by the grains of sand is higher and hence the entropy is lower than it should be, if the beach had actually been an isolated system. The *non*-statistical entropy principle, which precludes the beach's having evolved isolatedly from an earlier state of randomness to its present state of greater organization, therefore enables us to infer that the beach must have been an *open* system whose increase in order was acquired at the expense of an at least equivalent decrease of organization in the system with which it interacted (the stroller, who is metabolically depleted).

Our *statistical* analysis below will show, however, that the true conclusion of this inference *cannot* be made to rest on the statistically untenable premise that the entropy increase with time is monotonic in a permanently-closed system. It will turn out that the justification for this inference derives from the fact that (i) most systems which we now encounter in an isolated state of low entropy, behaving as if they might remain isolated, were not in fact permanently closed in the past, and (ii) in the case of such *temporarily* isolated or "branch" systems we *can* reliably infer a portion of the past from a present ordered state, an inference which is *not* feasible, as we shall see in detail, on the basis of the statistical version of the second law of thermodynamics as applied to a single, *permanently*-closed system, and (iii) the assumption that a transition from an earlier high entropy state to a present low one is overwhelmingly *im*probable, which is the basis for this inference, refers to the frequency of such transitions within a space-ensemble of branch systems, each of which is considered at *two* different times; this improbability does *not* refer to the time-sequence of entropy states of a single, permanently-closed system.

Hence, in the case of the beach whose sand forms a smooth surface except for one place where it is in the shape of a human footprint, we know with high probability that instead of having evolved *isolatedly* from a prior state of uniform smoothness into its present uneven configuration according to the *statistical* entropy principle for a permanently-closed system, the beach was an *open* system in *interaction* with a stroller. And we are aware furthermore that if there is some quasi-closed wider system containing the beach and the stroller, as there often is, the beach achieved its ordered low entropy state of bearing the imprint or interaction-indicator at the expense of an at least compensatory entropy increase in that wider system comprising the stroller: the stroller increased the entropy of the wider system by scattering his energy reserves in making the footprint.

We see that the sandy footprint shape is a genuine indicator and not a randomly-achieved form resulting from the unperturbed chance concatenations of the grains of sand. The imprint thus contains information in the sense of being a veridical indicator of an interaction. Now, in all probability the entropy of the imprint-bearing beach-system increases after the interaction with the stroller through the smoothing action of the wind. And this entropy increase is parallel, in all probability, to the direction of entropy increase of the majority of branch systems. Moreover, we saw that the production of the indicator by the interaction is likely to have involved an entropy increase in some wider system of which the indicator is a part. Hence, *in all probability the states of the interacting systems which do contain the indicators of the interaction are the relatively higher entropy states of the majority of branch systems as compared to the interaction state. Hence the indicator states are the relatively later states.* And by being both *later* and indicators, these states have *retrodictive* significance, thereby being traces, records or memories. And due to the high degree of retrodictive univocity of the low entropy states constituting the indicators, the latter are veridical to a high degree of *specificity*.

Confining our attention for the present to indicators whose *production* requires only the occurrence of the interaction which they attest, we therefore obtain the following conclusion, which holds except for two classes of *advance*-indicators requiring very special conditions for their production: *With overwhelming probability, low entropy indicator-states can exist in systems whose interactions they attest only after and not before these interactions.* If this conclusion is true (assuming that there are either no cases or not enough cases of *bona fide* precognition to disconfirm it), then, of course, it is not an a priori truth. And it would be very shallow indeed to seek to construe it as a trivial a priori truth in the following way: calling the indicator states "traces," "records" or "memories" and noting that it then becomes tautological to assert that traces and the like have only retrodictive and no predictive significance. But this transparent verbal gambit cannot make it true a priori that—apart from the exceptions to be dealt with below—interacting systems bear indicators attesting veridically only their *earlier* and *not* their later interactions with outside agencies.

Hence, the two exceptions apart, we arrive at the fundamental asymmetry of recordability: *reliable indicators in interacting systems permit only retrodictive inferences concerning the interactions for which they vouch but no predictive inferences pertaining to corresponding later interactions.*

And the logical schema of these inductive inferences is roughly as follows: The premisses assert (i) the presence of a certain relatively low entropy state in the system, and (ii) a quasi-universal statistical law stating that most low entropy states are interaction-indicators *and* were *preceded* by the interactions for which they vouch. The conclusion from these premises is then the inductive retrodictive one that there was an earlier interaction of a certain kind.

As already mentioned, our affirmation of the temporal asymmetry of recordability of interactions must be qualified by dealing first with the exceptional case of pre-recordability of those interactions which are veridically predicted by human beings (or computers). For any event which could be predicted by a scientist could also be "pre-recorded" by that scientist in various forms such as a written entry on paper asserting its occurrence at a certain later time, an advance drawing, or even an advance photograph based on the pre-drawing. By the same token, artifacts like computers can pre-record events which they can predict. A comparison between the written, drawn or photographic pre-record (i.e., recorded prediction) of, say, the crash of a plane into a house and its post-record in the form of a caved-in house, and a like comparison of the corresponding pre- and post-records of the interaction of a foot with a beach will now enable us to formulate the essential differences in the conditions requisite to the respective production of pre-records and post-records as well as the usual differences in make-up between them.

The production of at least one retrodictive indicator or post-record of an interaction such as the plane's crash into the house requires only the occurrence of that interaction (as well as a moderate degree of durability of the record). The retrodictive indicator states in the system which interacted with an outside agency must, of course, be distinguished from the *epistemic use* which human beings may make of these physical indicator states. And our assertion of the sufficiency of the interaction for the production of a post-record allows, of course, that the *interpretation* of actual post-records by humans as bona fide documents of the past requires their use of theory and not just the occurrence of the interaction. In contrast to the sufficiency of an interaction itself for its (at least short-lived) post-recordability, no such sufficiency obtains in the case of the pre-recordability of an interaction: save for an overwhelmingly improbable freak occurrence, the production of even a single pre-record of the coupling of a system with an agency external to it requires, as a necessary condition, *either* (a) the use of an appropriate theory by symbol-using entities (humans, computers) having suitable information, *or* (b) the pre-record's being a partial effect of a cause that also produces the pre-recorded interaction, as in the barometric case to be dealt with below. And in contexts in which (a) is a necessary condition, we find the following: since pre-records are, by definition, veridical, this necessary condition cannot *generally* also be sufficient, unless the predictive theory employed is deterministic *and* the information available to the theory-using organism pertains to a closed system.

In addition to differing in regard to the conditions of their production, pre-records generally differ from post-records in the following further respect: unless the pre-record prepared by a human being (or computer) *happens* to be part of the interacting system to which it pertains, the pre-record will not be contained in states of the interacting system which it concerns but will be in some other system. Thus, a pre-record of the crash of a plane into a house in a heavy fog would generally *not* be a part of either the house or the plane, although it can happen to be. But in the case of *post*-recording, there will always be at least one post-record, however short-lived, in the interacting system itself to which that post-record pertains.

Our earlier example of the footprint on the beach will serve to illustrate more fully the asymmetry between the requirements for the production of a pre-record and of a post-record. The pre-recording of a *later* incursion of the beach by a stroller would require extensive information about the motivations and habits of people not now at the beach and also knowledge of the accessibility of the beach to prospective strollers. This is tantamount to knowledge of a large system which is *closed,* so that all relevant agencies can safely be presumed to have been included in it. For otherwise, we would be unable to guarantee, for example, that the *future* stroller will *not* be stopped enroute to the beach by some agency not included in the system, an eventuality whose occurrence would deprive our pre-record of its referent, thereby destroying its status as a veridical indicator. In short, in the case of the footprint, which is a post-record and *not* a pre-record of the interaction of a human foot with the beach, the interaction itself is *sufficient* for its post-recording (though not for the extended *durability* of the record once it exists) but *not* for its pre-recording and prediction. Since a future interaction of a potentially open system like the beach is *not* itself sufficient for its pre-recordability, open systems like beaches therefore do not themselves exhibit pre-records of their own future interactions. Instead,—apart from the second species of pre-recordability to be considered presently—pre-recordability of interactions of potentially open systems requires the mediation of symbol and theory-using organisms or the operation of appropriate artifacts like computers. And such pre-recordability can obtain successfully only if the theory available to the pre-recording organism is deterministic and sufficiently comprehensive to include all the relevant laws and boundary conditions governing the pertinent closed systems.

The second species of exceptions to the asymmetry of recordability is exemplified by the fact that a sudden drop in the pressure reading of a barometer can be an advance-indicator or "pre-record" of a subsequent storm. To be sure, it is the immediately *prior* pressure change in the spatial vicinity of the barometer and only that particular prior change (i.e., the *past* interaction through pressure) which is recorded numerically by a given drop in the barometric reading, and *not* the pressure change that *will* exist as that same place at a *later* time: To make the predictions required for a *pre*-recording of the pressure changes which will exist at a given space point at later times (i.e., of the corresponding future interactions), comprehensive meteorological data pertaining to a large region would be essential. *But* it *is* possible in this case to base a rather reliable prediction of a future storm on the present sudden barometric drop. The latter drop, however, is, in fact, a *bona fide* advance indicator *only because* it is a partial effect of the very comprehensive cause which also produces (assures) the storm. Thus, it is the fulfillment of the *necessary condition* of having a causal ancestry that overlaps with that of the storm which is needed to confer the status of an advance indicator on the barometric drop. In contrast to the situation prevailing in the case of *post*-recordability, the existence of this necessary condition makes for the fact that the future occurrence of a storm is *not sufficient* for the existence of an advance indicator of that storm in the form of a sudden barometric drop at an earlier time.

An analogous account can be given of the following cases, which Mr. F. Brian Skyrms has suggested to me for consideration: situations in which *human intentions* are highly reliable advance indicators of the events envisaged by these intentions. Thus, the desire for a glass of beer, coupled with the supposed presence of the conditions under which beer and a glass are obtainable produces as a partial effect the intent to get it. And, *if* external conditions permit (the beer is available and accessible), and, furthermore, if the required internal conditions materialize (the person desiring the beer remains able to go and get it), then the intent will issue in the obtaining and drinking of the beer. But in contrast to the situation prevailing in the case of retrodictive indicators (post-records), the future consumption of the beer is *not* a *sufficient condition* for the existence of its probabilistic advance indicator in the form of an intention.[60]

The connection between low entropy states and retrodictive informa-

[60]For a refutation of purported counterexamples to the temporal asymmetry of the recordability of interactions as set forth here, cf. A. Grünbaum, "Temporally-Asymmetric Principles, Parity Between Explanation and Prediction, and Mechanism versus Teleology," *Philosophy of Science* XXIX (April, 1962), 155.

tion which emerged in our discussion of the asymmetry of recordability throws light on the reason for the failure of Maxwell's well-known sorting demon: in substance, Maxwell's demon cannot violate the second law of thermodynamics, since the entropy decrease produced in the gas is more than balanced by the entropy increase in the mechanism procuring the informational data concerning individual gas molecules which are needed by the demon for making the sorting successful.[61]

We saw earlier how reliance on entropy enables us to ascertain which one of two causally connected events is *the* cause of the other because it is the earlier of the two. Our present entropic account of the circumstances under which the past can be inferred from the present while the future cannot, as well as of the circumstances when only the converse determination is possible enables us to specify the conditions of validity for the following statements by Reichenbach: "Only the totality of all causes permits an inference concerning the future, but the past is inferrable from a partial effect alone" and "one can infer the total cause from a partial effect, but one cannot infer the total effect from a partial cause."[62] A partial effect produced in a system while it is open permits, on entropic grounds, an inference concerning the earlier *interaction* event which was its cause: even though we do not know the *total* present effect, we know that the part of it which is an ordered, low entropy state was (most probably) preceded by a still lower entropy state and that the *diversity* of the interactions associated with such a very *low* interaction entropy state is relatively *small,* thereby permitting a rather specific assertion about the past.

Thus, the asymmetry of inferability arises on the macro-level in the *absence* of knowledge of the microscopic state of the *total* (closed) system at a given time and is made possible by the relative retrodictive univocity of local low entropy states which result from interactions. We are therefore in possession of the answer to the question posed by J. J. C. Smart when he wrote (see p. 81 of the first of his two publications cited

[61]Cf. L. Brillouin, *Science and Information Theory* (New York, 1956); E. C. Cherry, "The Communication of Information," *Am. Scientist* XL, 640 (1952); J. Rothstein, "Information, Measurement and Quantum Mechanics," *Science* CXIV, 171 (1951), and S. Watanabe, "Über die Anwendung Thermodynamischer Begriffe auf den Normalzustand des Atomkerns," *Zeitschr. f. Physik* CXIII (1939), 482-513.

[62]H. Reichenbach, "Die Kausalstruktur der Welt und der Unterschied von Vergangenheit und Zukunft," *Ber. d. Bayer. Akad. München, Math.-Naturwiss. Abt.,* 1925, 157, and "Les Fondements Logiques de la Mécanique des Quanta," *op. cit.,* 146. Cf. also C. F. von Weizsäcker, "Der Zweite Hauptsatz und der Unterschied von Vergangenheit und Zukunft," *Annalen d. Physik* XXXVI, 279 (1939). By noting in his later publications (especially in DT, 157-167) that the temporal asymmetry involved here has an entropic basis, Reichenbach abandoned his earlier view that it provides an *independent* criterion for the anisotropy of time. Thus, he has essentially admitted the validity of H. Bergmann' s telling criticisms [*Der Kampf um das Kausalgesetz in der jüngsten Physik, op. cit.,* 19-24] of his earlier view.

in footnote 59): "Even on a Laplacian view, then, we still have the puzzling question 'Why from a limited region of space can we deduce a great deal of the history of the past, whereas to predict similar facts about the future even a superhuman intelligence would have to consider initial conditions over a very wide region of space?' " Moreover, it is clear now why and in what sense the *past* enjoys explanatory primacy over the future (mechanism in the *broad* sense): we explain present marks *a tergo* on the basis of interactions and do not invoke future ends, as the teleologist would have us do. But in the context of knowledge of the total micro-state of a closed physical system whose evolution is governed by time-symmetric laws, such as those of Newton's mechanics, the given state of the system at a time t can be inferred from a state *later* than t (i.e., *retrodicted*) no less than the given state can be inferred from a state *earlier* than t (i.e., *predicted*). Instead of furnishing the prototype for mechanistic explanation in the philosophical sense, the phenomena described by the time-symmetric laws of Newton's mechanics constitute a domain with respect to which both mechanism and teleology are false, thereby making the controversy between them a *pseudo-issue*. For mechanism and teleology are contraries and not contradictories: the mechanist maintains that occurrences at a time *t* can be explained *only* by reference to *earlier* occurrences and *not* also by reference to later ones, while the teleologist would allow *only later* occurrences as a basis for providing understanding. More generally, their controversy is a pseudo-issue with respect to any domain of phenomena constituted by the evolution of closed systems obeying *time-symmetric laws,* be they deterministic or statistical.

But there is indeed a wide class of phenomena with respect to which mechanism is true. And one may presume that tacit reference to this particular class of phenomena has conferred plausibility on the thesis of the *unrestricted* validity of mechanism: traces or marks of interaction existing in a system which is essentially closed at a time t are accounted for scientifically by *earlier interactions* or *perturbations* of that system— which are called "causes"— and *not* by later interactions of the system.

Our analysis of entropy so far has been in the macroscopic context of thermodynamics and has taken no adequate account of the important questions which arise concerning the serviceability of the entropy criterion for the definition of a time direction, when the entropy law is seen in the statistical light of both classical and quantum mechanics. These questions, which we must now face, derive from the attempt to deduce the phenomenological irreversibility of classical thermodynamics from principles of statistical mechanics asserting that the motions of the microscopic constituents of thermodynamic systems are completely reversible.

As is well-known, in the form of Boltzmann's H-theorem, the statistical version of the phenomenological entropy law affirms that the increase of entropy with time is overwhelmingly probable by virtue of the approach of the particles to their equilibrium distribution.[63] But soon after Boltzmann's enunciation of his theorem, it was felt that there is a logical hiatus in a deduction which derives the overwhelming probability of macroscopic irreversibility from premisses attributing complete reversibility to micro-processes. For according to the principle of dynamical reversibility, which is integral to these premisses, there is, corresponding to any possible motion of a system, an equally possible reverse motion in which the same values of the coordinates would be reached in the reverse order with reversed values for the velocities.[64] Thus, since the probability that a molecule has a given velocity is independent of the sign of that velocity, separation processes will occur just as frequently in the course of time as mixing processes. J. Loschmidt therefore raised the *reversibility objection* to the effect that for any behavior of a system issuing in an increase of the entropy S with time, it would be equally possible to have an entropy decrease.[65] A similar criticism was presented in the *periodicity objection,* based on a theorem by Poincaré[66] and formulated by Zermelo.[67] Poincaré's theorem had led to the conclusion that the long-range behavior of an isolated system consists of a succession of fluctuations in which the value of S will decrease as often as it increases. And Zermelo asked how this result is to be reconciled with Boltzmann's contention that if an isolated system is in a state of low entropy, there is an overwhelming probability that the system is actually in a microscopic state from which changes in the direction of higher values of S will ensue.[68]

These logical difficulties were resolved by the Ehrenfests.[69] They

[63]The entropy S is related to the thermodynamic probability W representing the corresponding number of microscopic complexions by the equation $S = k \log W$. And the quantity H of Boltzmann's theorem is connected with S by the relation $S = -kH$. Thus, an increase in the entropy is equivalent to a decrease in H.

[64]Cf. R. C. Tolman, *op. cit.,* 102-104.

[65]J. Loschmidt, "Über das Wärmegleichgewicht eines Systems von Körpern mit Rücksicht auf die Schwere," *Sitzungsber. Akad. Wiss. Wien* LXXIII, 139 (1876), and LXXV, 67 (1877).

[66]H. Poincaré, "Sur le problème des trois corps et les équations de la dynamique," *Acta mathem.* XIII, 67 (1890).

[67]E. Zermelo, "Über einen Satz der Dynamik und der mechanischen Wärmetheorie," *Wied. Ann. (Ann. d. Phys. u. Chem.)* LVII, 485 (1896).

[68]For additional details on these objections and references to Boltzmann's replies, see P. Epstein, "Critical Appreciation of Gibbs' Statistical Mechanics," in A. Haas (ed.) *A Commentary on the Scientific Writings of J. Willard Gibbs,* II (New Haven, 1936), 515-519.

[69]P. and T. Ehrenfest, "Begriffliche Grundlagen der statistischen Auffassung in der Mechanik," *Encykl. d. math. Wiss.* IV, 2, II, 41-51. See also, R. C. Tolman, *op. cit.,* 152-

explained that there is no incompatibility between (i) the assertion that *if* the system is in a low entropy state, then, *relative* to that state, it is highly probable that the system will soon be in a higher entropy state, and (ii) the contention that the system plunges down from a state of high entropy to one of lower entropy as frequently as it ascends entropically in the opposite direction, thereby making the *absolute* probability for these two opposite kinds of transition *equal.* The compatibility of the equality of these two absolute probabilities with a *high* relative probability for a future transition to a higher entropy becomes quite plausible, when it is remembered that (i) the low entropy states to which the high relative probabilities of subsequent increase are referred, are usually at the low point of a trajectory at which changes back to higher values are initiated, and (ii) the Boltzmann H-theorem therefore does not preclude such a system's exhibiting decreases and increases of S with equal frequency. The time variation of the entropy, embodying these two claims compatibly, can be visualized as an entropy staircase curve.[70]

Boltzmann's H-theorem can thus be upheld in the face of the reversibility and periodicity objections, but only if coupled with a very important *proviso*: the affirmation of a high probability of a future entropy increase must *not* be construed to assert a high probability that present low entropy values were *preceded* by *still lower* entropies *in the past.* For the relative probability that a *low* entropy state was *preceded* by a state of *higher* entropy is just as great as the relative probability that a low state will be *followed* by a higher state. And we saw that the absolute probability of an entropy decrease is equal to the absolute probability of an entropy increase. The fulfillment of the proviso demanded by these results has *two* consequences of fundamental importance which we shall now consider in turn and whose validity is *confined* to the behavior of *permanently* closed systems:

1. It destroys the thermodynamic foundation for the hypothesis that present ordered states may be regarded as *veridical traces* of past interactions from which the character and actual occurrence of past events may be reasonably inferred. Von Weizsäcker has rightly pointed out[71] that there is far more reason to regard present ordered states as *randomly achieved* low entropy states, rather than as veridical traces of actual past

158, esp. 156; R. Fürth, "Prinzipien der Statistik," in H. Geiger and K. Scheel (eds.), *Handbuch der Physik* IV (Berlin, 1929), 270-272 and H. Reichenbach, "Ziele und Wege der physikalischen Erkenntnis," *op. cit.*, 62-63.

The classical investigations by the Ehrenfests have recently been refined and extended to include quantum theory in D. Ter Haar's important paper "Foundations of Statistical Mechanics," *Reviews of Modern Physics* XXVII (1955), 289-338.

70Cf. R. Fürth, *op. cit.*, 272.

71C. F. von Weizsäcker, "Der zweite Hauptsatz und der Unterschied von Vergangenheit und Zukunft," *op. cit.*, 281.

interactions: it is statistically far more probable that present low entropy states are mere chance fluctuations rather than the continuous successors of actual earlier states of still lower entropy. But present low entropy states cannot serve as articulate documents of the past, unless we may assume that they evolved from and hence render veridical testimony of specifiable past states. And precisely this assumption is rendered untenable by the verdict of the H-theorem that the entropic behavior of a single, permanently-closed system is time-symmetric! Must we then abandon our ordinary practice of inferring the past from present ordered states and no longer interpret these to be traces? No. For we do have a reason *other than* the untenable conception of a monotonic entropic behavior of a permanently-closed system for supposing that a low entropy state in which we encounter a system is due to its past openness or interaction with the outside for which its present low state can vouch. In fact, we shall see that the statistics of the space ensembles of branch systems, which were merely mentioned in passing before, provide a sound empirical basis for our inferences concerning the past. This empirical basis, as well as difficulties of its own, undercut the subjectivistic a priori justification of our inferences concerning the past offered by von Weizsäcker on the basis of the alleged transcendental conditions of all possible experience, disclosed in this context by the application of Kant's presuppositional method.

2. Of crucial importance to one of the major concerns of this paper is the fact that the indicated statistical excisions in the monotonicity of the entropy function do *not* preserve sufficient irreversibility for an entropic definition of time direction: Reichenbach has argued convincingly[72] that although there is no contradiction between the high relative probabilities of Boltzmann's H-theorem and the equality among the absolute probabilities of the reversibility and periodicity objections, the aforementioned time-symmetry of the statistical results on which these objections are based shows decisively that the entropic behavior of a single, permanently-closed system does not confer anisotropy on time. For this time-symmetry precludes the inference that the *lower* of two given entropy states is the *earlier* of the two: a low entropy state is *preceded* by a high state no less frequently than it is *followed* by a high state. And we recall from our discussion of open kinds of time in Section II above that it is entirely meaningful to assert that the system is in the *same macro*-state and has the *same* entropy S_k at *different* times t and t′, since a difference in the underlying *micro*-states assures the non-identity of the states of the system at times t and t′.

[72]DT, 116-117.

Thus, the H-theorem fails to provide a basis for the anisotropy ("arrow") of time.

A way out of the problem was recently proposed by Max Born on the basis of a refusal to affirm the reversibility of elementary processes.[73] Noting that Boltzmann's averaging is the expression of our ignorance of the actual microscopic situation, he maintains that the reversibility of mechanics is supplanted by the irreversibility of thermodynamics as a result of "a deliberate renunciation of the demand that in principle the fate of every single particle be determined. You must violate mechanics in order to obtain a result in obvious contradiction to it." He therefore finds that "the statistical foundation of thermodynamics is quite satisfactory even on the basis of classical mechanics."[74] But it is precisely in the domain of elementary processes that classical mechanics must be superseded by quantum theory. Born therefore attempts to solve the problem by asserting that the new theory "has accepted partial ignorance already on a lower level and need not doctor the final laws" and then offers a derivation of Boltzmann's H-theorem from quantum mechanical principles.[75]

Since we shall be considering the status of irreversibility in quantum mechanics below, we first note yet another solution of the problem of phenomenological irreversibility recently proposed by Schrödinger.[76] We shall then be able to assess the capabilities of entropy to define a time-direction in the light of these two solutions.

Referring to Born's account of irreversibility, Schrödinger says: "to

[73]M. Born, *Natural Philosophy of Cause and Chance* (Oxford, 1949), 59, 71-73 and 109-114. In his review of this work (*Phil. of Science* XVII, 1950), G. Bergmann remarks (p. 198) that Born's point can be rendered more clearly by the statement that "in a very relevant sense of the terms statistical mechanics is not mechanics. If, in applying it to, say, the gas, one predicts from a distribution the probability of other distributions, one abandons the idea of orbits and, therefore, deals with "particles" only in the attenuated sense of using a theory whose fundamental entities have the formal properties of position-momentum coordinates."

In a different vein, L. L. Whyte has since suggested that the reversibility of elementary processes may have to be abandoned in future physical theory. Says he: "We should give up the long struggle with the question: 'How does irreversibility arise if the basic laws are reversible?', and ask instead: 'If the laws are of a one-way character, under what . . . conditions can reversible expressions provide a useful approximation' ". ["One-way Processes in Physics and Biophysics," *British J. Phil. of Science* VI, 110 (1955)]. The successful implementation of Whyte's proposal would readily provide a solution to the problem of time's arrow. But it must not be overlooked that there is such confirmation for fundamental reversibility as the fact that the experimentally substantiated reciprocity law is deducible, as Onsager showed, from the reversibility of elementary collisions. Cf. J. M. Blatt, "Time Reversal," *Scientific American* (August, 1956), 107-114.

[74]Born, *ibid.*, 72-73.

[75]***Ibid.*, 110, 113-114.**

[76]E. Schrödinger, "Irreversibility," *Proc. Royal Irish Acad.* LIII, Sect. A, 189 (1950) and "The Spirit of Science," in *Spirit and Nature* (New York, 1954), 337-341.

my mind, in this case, as in a few others, the 'new doctrine' which sprang up in 1925/26 has obscured minds more than it has enlightened them."[77] His proposal to deal with the issue without a "philosophical loan from quantum mechanics" does *not* take the form of deriving the increase of entropy with time from some kind of general reversible model. He rejects that approach on the grounds that he is unable to devise a model sufficiently general to cover all physical situations and also suitable for incorporation in all future theories. Neither does he wish to confine himself to a refutation of the arguments directed against Boltzmann's particular reversible model of a gas whose macro-behavior is irreversible.[78] Instead of *deriving* irreversibility, Schrödinger offers to "reformulate the laws of phenomenological irreversibility, thus certain statements of thermodynamics, in such a way, that the logical contradiction *any* derivation of these laws from reversible models seems to involve is removed once and for ever."[79]

To implement this program, he makes use of the fact that if, during a period of overall entropy increase or decrease, a system has separated into two subsystems that are isolated from one another, then the respective entropies of the latter will either increase monotonically in *both* of them (apart from small fluctuations) or will so decrease in both of them. And, instead of considering merely a single isolated system, he envisages at least two systems, called "1" and "2," temporarily isolated from the remaining universe for a period not greatly exceeding the age of our present galactic system. Specifically, using a time variable t whose relation to phenomenological time will soon be clear, he assumes that systems 1 and 2 are isolated from one another between the moments t_A and t_B, where $t_B > t_A$, but in contact for $t < t_A$ and $t > t_B$. Denoting the entropy of system 1 at time t_A by "S_{1A}" and similarly for the other entropy states, Schrödinger then formulates the entropy law as

$$(S_{1B} - S_{1A})\,(S_{2B} - S_{2A}) \geq O.$$

The ordinary version of the entropy law for a single closed system is seen to be a special case of this formulation, if we let system 2 be the part of the universe outside the closed system under consideration. Since the law is always applied to those *pairs* of systems having a common branching origin, the product of the entropy differences in it will yield the arithmetical "arrow" of the inequality even in the case of negative entropy differences.

Can Born's quantum mechanical approach or Schrödinger's alternative to it provide a criterion of time-direction? We saw that Born is

[77] *Ibid.*, 189.

[78] Born points out *(op. cit.,* 59) that it was not until recently that the H-theorem was proven for cases other than Boltzman's model of a gas.

[79] Schrödinger, "Irreversibility," *op. cit.*, 191.

guided by the view that since probability enters in quantum mechanics in a fundamental way *ab initio,* the derivation of the probabilistic macroscopic irreversibility affirmed by the H-theorem is feasible in that discipline and not liable to the charge, leveled against Boltzmann's classical derivation, that the deduction depended upon the addition of extraneous probability assumptions to the reversible dynamical equations. But Born's argument is open to important criticisms. To state these, we note first the requirements constituting the quantum mechanical analogue of the classical conditions for the *reversal* of the motion of a closed system: a system N can be said to behave in a manner reverse to that of a system M, if at any time t it exhibits the same probability for specified values of the coordinates, the same probability for specified values of the momenta taken with reversed sign, and the same expectation value for any function of the coordinates and reversed momenta as would be exhibited by system M at time —t. Now, it has been shown by reference to the Schrödinger equation governing the change of isolated (conservative) quantum mechanical systems with time that all three of these conditions are satisfied by such systems.[80] The Schrödinger equation for a single free particle relevant here is of the form

$$\frac{\partial^2\psi}{\partial x^2} + \frac{\partial^2\psi}{\partial y^2} + \frac{\partial^2\psi}{\partial z^2} = \frac{4\pi m}{ih}\frac{\partial\psi}{\partial t}, \text{ where } i \equiv \sqrt{-1},$$

and thus belongs formally to the same class as the diffusion equation, which we considered earlier. Due to the presence, however, of an imaginary constant in the Schrödinger equation in place of the real constant in the diffusion equation, the Schrödinger equation describes a *reversible* oscillation while the diffusion equation describes an *irreversible* equalization.[81]

What is the physical meaning of this purely *formal* reversibility? Instead of being confronted with the classical reversibility of the elementary processes themselves, we now have a *two-wayness* of the transitions between two *sets* of *probability distributions* of measurable quantities as follows: if nature permits a system which is characterized by the state function ψ' and the associated set s′ of probability distributions at time t_1 to evolve so as to acquire the state function ψ'' and the associated set s″ of probability distributions at time t_2, then it also permits the inverse transition from s″ at time t_1 to s′ at time t_2.[82] S. Watanabe was therefore able to demonstrate that Born's deduction of a monotonic en-

[80]Cf. R. C. Tolman, *The Principles of Statistical Mechanics, op. cit.,* 396-399; H. Reichenbach, DT, 207-211.

[81]See A. Sommerfeld, *Partial Differential Equations in Physics,* tr. E. G. Straus (New York, 1949), 34-35.

[82]Cf. O. Costa de Beauregard, "Complémentarité et Relativité," *Revue Philosophique* CXLV (1955), 397-400.

tropy increase with time from the basic principles of quantum mechanics is just as vulnerable to Loschmidt's reversibility objection as the corresponding classical derivation.[83] And the resulting irrelevance of Born's invocation of the non-deterministic character of the fundamental principles of quantum mechanics is now apparent from the following lucid statement by L. Rosenfeld, who writes:[84]

> The introduction of the quantal description of the elementary constituents as a basic assumption instead of the classical picture does not make the least difference to the fundamental structure of statistical thermodynamics; for the quantal laws, just as the classical ones, are reversible with respect to time, and the problem of establishing the macroscopic irreversibility by taking account of the statistical element involved in the concept of macroscopic observation remains unchanged and is again solved by ergodic theorems. The issue has been obscured by the fact that quantum theory itself, in contrast to classical theory, introduces a statistical element at the microscopic level; and it has sometimes been confusedly argued that it is this elementary quantal statistics which provides the basis of macroscopic irreversibility. In reality, we have here two completely distinct statistical features, which are not only logically independent of each other, but also without physical influence upon each other. The question whether the elementary law of change is deterministic (as in classical physics) or statistical (as in quantum theory) is entirely irrelevant for the validity of the ergodic theorems.

It will be noted that in articulating the physical meaning of the formal reversibility of the Schrödinger time-equation, we spoke only of two way transitions from present to *future* states and made no statement concerning inferences from a present state regarding the values we would have obtained in hypothetical *past* measurements, if we had carried them out earlier. There is a very important reason for this deliberate omission, and this reason is the source of a lack of isomorphism between classical reversibility and its quantum mechanical analogue: in quantum mechanics, the interaction between the system under observation and the measuring device *changes* the ψ-function characterizing the system before the measurement by imposing a random phase factor on that earlier ψ-function.[85] Thus, when the quantum mechanical system is subjected

[83]S. Watanabe, "Réversibilité contre Irréversibilité en Physique Quantique," in *Louis de Broglie, Physicien et Penseur, op. cit.*, 393. Cf. also that author's earlier *Le Deuxième Théorème de la Thermodynamique et la Mécanique Ondulatoire* (Paris, 1935), esp. Ch. IV, §3, where he shows that, like Newtonian mechanics, quantum mechanics can furnish an irreversible thermodynamics only by adding a distinctly statistical supplementary postulate to its fundamental dynamical principles.

[84]L. Rosenfeld, "On the Foundations of Statistical Thermodynamics," *Acta Physica Polonica* XIV (1955), 9. Cf. also G. Ludwig, "Zum Ergodensatz und zum Begriff der makroskopischen Observablen, I," *Zeitschrift für Physik* CL, 346 (1958).

[85]Details on metrogenic irreversibility in quantum mechanics are given in J. von Neumann, *Mathematische Grundlagen der Quantenmechanik* (Berlin, 1932), and New York, 1943, 191, 202-212 (English translation by R. T. Beyer, published by the Prince-

to observation by being coupled indivisibly to a *classically-describable* macroscopic system, a *present* state function obtained by a measurement of one of the eigenvalues of an observable may be utilized in Schrödinger's equation to determine future but *not* past values of ψ. Now, the alteration of the ψ-function prevailing before the measurement by the act of measurement is essential to the consistency of the quantum theory. Accordingly, the *irreversible* changes which take place both in the observed physical system and in the macroscopic measuring apparatus while the latter secures observational information enter integrally into the quantum theory in marked contrast to classical mechanics and electrodynamics.

We can now see the basis for A. Landé's argument that if we construe reversibility to mean that there are temporal "mirror-images" of physical processes such that the original process and its inverse each comprise an initial state, intermediate states, and a final state, then it is *incorrect* to suppose that the Schrödinger time-equation warrants the ascription of reversibility to elementary quantum mechanical processes. He maintains that (i) actual states are ascertained by particular tests (e.g., states of energy or position), whereas ψ is not a state but a statistical link between two states, and (ii) the Schrödinger time equation "does not describe processes from an initial to a final state via intermediate states actually passed through." And, having rejected all efforts to base a time-direction on the results of classical statistical mechanics as specious, he therefore contended that "A direction of time *is* defined within the framework of quantum theory" by its metrogenic irreversibility and only within *that* theory.[86]

A brief comment concerning the epistemological status of this metro-

ton University Press, 1955). Cf. also S. Watanabe "Prediction and Retrodiction," *Reviews of Mod. Phys.* XXVII, 179 (1955), Watanabe's essay for the de Broglie Festschrift (footnote 83), 389; D. Bohm, *Quantum Theory* (New York, 1951), ch. 22, and S. Watanabe, "Le Concept de Temps en Physique Moderne et la Durée Pure de Bergson," *Revue de Mét. et de Morale* LVI (1951), 134-135. Reichenbach does *not* take cognizance of quantum mechanical metrogenic irreversibility in his theory of the direction of time (cf. DT, ch. 24 and "Les Fondements Logiques de la Mécanique des Quanta," *op. cit.*, 148-154).

In an article "Philosophical Problems Concerning the Meaning of Measurement in Physics" [*Phil. of Science* XXV, 23 (1958)], H. Margenau has contested the "orthodox" conception of the process of measurement as the reduction of a wave packet. And thus he rejects the necessity of associating with the process of measurement a discontinuous change in the Ψ-function that is not governed by the Schrödinger equation. On this "unorthodox" view, the "orthodox" claim of temporal asymmetry would have to be revised accordingly.

86A. Landé, "The Logic of Quanta," *British J. Phil. of Science* VI, 300 (1956), esp. 305-307 and 311. More recently, he has abandoned that view, claiming that the metrogenic entropy increase is only statistical in the sense that "In reality, the entropy values yielded by successive tests will oscillate up and down just as the classical entropy values

genic irreversibility of quantum mechanics must precede our assessment of its capabilities to account for the anisotropy of our macro-time.

Guided by the precepts of philosophical idealism, Watanabe erroneously equates the observer qua recorder of physically-registered observational data with the observer qua *conscious* organism. He then infers that the metrogenic irreversibility of quantum mechanics shows "decisively" that "there is no privileged direction in the time of physics, and that, if one finds a unique direction in the evolution of physical phenomena, this is merely the projection of the flow of our psychic time. . . . the increase in entropy is not a property of the external world left to itself, but is the result of the union of the subject and the object."[87] Treating the seriality inherent in psychological time as autonomous and *sui generis,* he nevertheless admits that the uniformity of psychological time-directions as between different living organisms requires explanation, being too remarkable to be contingent. But he seeks the explanation along the lines of Bergson's very questionable conception that living processes obey autonomous principles.[88] In his mentalistic interpretation of metrogenic irreversibility in quantum mechanics, Watanabe requires, as a crucial premise in his argument, the traditional idealist characterization of the status of such material common sense objects as the classically describable pieces of apparatus used, in one way or another, in all quantum mechanical measurements. But this idealist premise is altogether unconvincing, and without it, there is every reason to regard the interaction between physical systems and the observational devices used in quantum mechanics as an entirely physical matter devoid of psychological ingredients of any kind. For, as has been explained by von Neumann[89] and, more recently, by Ludwig,[90] the demand that cog-

of the Ehrenfest curve." [Landé, "Wellenmechanik und Irreversibilität," *Physikalische Blätter,* XIII (1957), 312-314].

For a general discussion of these issues, see M. M. Yanase, "Reversibilität und Irreversibilität in der Physik," *Annals of the Japan Association for Philosophy of Science* I (1957), 131-149.

87Watanabe, "Le Concept de Temps en Physique Moderne et la Durée Pure de Bergson," *op. cit.,* 134-136. Cf. also that author's contribution to the de Broglie *Festschrift* cited above, 385, 392, 394.

88For a detailed discussion of the role of *physical* irreversibility in biological processes, see H. F. Blum, *Time's Arrow and Evolution* (2nd edition; Princeton, 1955); E. Schrödinger, *What is Life?* (Cambridge and New York, 1945), Ch. VI; R. O. Davies, "Irreversible Changes: New Thermodynamics from Old," *Science News* No. 28 (May, 1953). Attempts to prove the autonomy of living processes can draw no support from instances of entropy decrease in the human body. For, being an open system, that body's entropy can decrease or increase in complete conformity even with the non-statistical second law of thermodynamics.

89von Neumann, *op. cit.,* 187, 223-237, esp. 223-4. Cf. also Bohm, *op. cit.,* 584-5, 587-590, 600-609.

90G. Ludwig, "Der Messprozess," *Zeitschrift für Physik* CXXXV, 483 (1953), esp.

nizance be taken of the disturbances produced by measurements and observation can be adequately met in quantum mechanics without including the human observer's retina or body in the analysis, let alone his stream of consciousness. In regard to the macroscopic system which undergoes irreversible changes in the course of registering the results of microphysical measurements, Ludwig points out that, in principle, the perception of its readings by a conscious subject is irrelevant. Says he: "in principle it is not necessary that it was a physicist [i.e. human observer] who built the apparatus for the purpose of measurement. It can also be a system on which the microscopic object impinges, entirely in the natural course of events." Thus, as far as the role of the human observer qua conscious organism is concerned, there is no epistemological difference between quantum mechanics and classical physics.

Although quantum irreversibility is an entirely physical matter and a quantum world precludes our speaking of the physical properties of systems which are not in interaction with measuring devices, the irreversibility of our ordinary environment cannot be held to be attributable to metrogenic quantum irreversibility alone. Bohr's principle of complementarity must be taken in conjunction with his own emphasis in the correspondence principle that the measuring devices which constitute the epistemological basis of quantum mechanics are themselves describable by the principles of classical physics. The actual irreversibility of our macro-environment is set in a context in which Planck's constant h may be considered negligibly small and in which the classical view that the physical system can be said to have definite physical properties independently of any measurement is legitimately applicable.[91]

We can therefore endorse Schrödinger's *rejection* of the use of quantum mechanical metrogenic irreversibility as a basis for explaining phenomenological (macro-) irreversibility. Says he: "Surely the system continues to exist and to behave, to undergo irreversible changes and to increase its entropy in the interval between two observations. The observations we might have made in between cannot be essential in determining its course."[92]

486; see also his *Die Grundlagen der Quantenmechanik* (Berlin, 1954), 142-159, 178-182, and his "Die Stellung des Subjekts in der Quantentheorie," in *Veritas, Justitia, Libertas,* Festschrift zur 200—Jahr Feier der Columbia University (Berlin: Colloquium Verlag, 1954). See also H. Reichenbach, DT, 223-224 and *Philosophic Foundations of Quantum Mechanics* (Berkeley, 1948), 15ff.

91For an interesting discussion of the conditions governing such applicability, see L. Brillouin, *Science and Information Theory, op. cit.*, 229-232.

92Schrödinger, "Irreversibility," *op. cit.*, 190. Even less helpful than quantum irreversibility as a basis for defining time direction is the Wheeler-Feynman-Stückelberg analysis of pair production in quantum electrodynamics [cf. H. Margenau, "Can Time Flow Backwards?" *Phil. of Science* **XXI**, 79 (1954)] since it involves indeterminacies

Granted then that quantum mechanics does not furnish the required account of the time-direction for our macrocosm in its "current" non-equilibrium state, does Schrödinger's own classical account succeed in doing so? He avowedly made no attempt to *deduce* irreversibility. But he does explain that if at least one of the entropy differences in his formulation of Clausius' principle is positive, then it is the parametric time t which corresponds to phenomenological time and that, *alternatively,* if at least one such difference is negative, it is -t that corresponds to phenomenological time. Schrödinger's perceptive guiding idea that the attempt to characterize phenomenological time entropically without running afoul of the reversibility and periodicity objections can succeed only if we regard the entropy law as an assertion about *at least two temporarily* closed systems was developed independently by Reichenbach. And the *valid core*—but only the valid core—of Reichenbach's version of this idea seems to me to provide a basis for an entropic criterion of a statistical anisotropy of physical time. Believing that Reichenbach's account requires modification in order to be satisfactory, I shall now set forth what I consider to be a correct elaboration of his principal conception.

We must first describe certain features of the physical world having the character of initial or boundary conditions within the framework of the theory of statistical mechanics. The sought-after basis of a statistical anisotropy of time will then emerge from principles of statistical mechanics relevant to these *de facto* conditions.

The universe around us exhibits striking disequilibria of temperature and other inhomogeneities. In fact, we live in virtue of the nuclear conversion of the sun's reserves of hydrogen into helium, which issues in our reception of solar radiation. As the sun dissipates its reserves of hydrogen via the emission of solar radiation, it may heat a terrestrial rock embedded in snow during the day time. At night, the rock is no longer exposed to the sun but is left with a considerably higher temperature than the snow surrounding it. Hence, at night, the warm rock and the cold snow form a quasi-isolated subsystem of either our galactic or solar system. And the relatively low entropy of that subsystem was purchased at the expense of the dissipation of the sun's reserves of hydrogen. Hence, *if* there is some quasi-closed system comprising the sun and the earth, the branching off of our subsystem from this wider system in a state of low entropy at sunset involved an entropy increase in the wider system. During the night, the heat of the rock melts the snow, and thus the

even in regard to those order properties of time which are defined by reversible macroprocesses [cf. Reichenbach, DT, 262-9 and "Les Fondements Logiques de la Mécanique des Quanta," *op. cit.,* 150-153]. See also C. W. Berenda, "Determination of Past by Future Events," *Phil. of Science* XIV, 13 (1947).

entropy of the rock-snow system increases. The next morning at sunrise, the rock-snow subsystem merges again with the wider solar system. Thus, there are subsystems which branch off from the wider solar or galactic system in a state of relatively low entropy, remain quasi-closed for a *limited* period of time, and then merge again with the wider system from which they had been separated. Following Reichenbach,[93] we have been using the term "branch system" to designate this kind of subsystem.

Branch systems are formed not only in the natural course of things, but also through human intervention: when an ice cube is placed into a glass of warm gingerale by a waiter and then covered for hygienic purposes, a subsystem has been formed. The prior freezing of the ice cube had involved an entropy increase through the dissipation of electrical energy in some larger quasi-closed system of which the electrically-run refrigerator is a part. While the ice cube melts in the covered glass subsystem, that quasi-closed system increases its entropy. But it merges again with another system when the then chilled gingerale is consumed by a person. Similarly for a closed room that is closed off and then heated by burning logs.

Thus, our environment abounds in branch-systems whose initial relatively low entropies are the products of their earlier coupling or interaction with outside agencies of one kind or another. This rather constant and ubiquitous formation of a branch-system in a relatively low entropy state resulting from interaction often proceeds at the expense of an entropy increase in some wider quasi-closed system from which it originated. And the *de facto,* nomologically-contingent occurrence of these branch systems has the following *fundamental consequence,* at least for our region of the universe and during the current epoch: among the quasi-closed systems whose entropy is relatively low and which behave as if they might remain isolated, the vast majority have not been and will not remain permanently-closed systems, being branch systems instead.

Hence, upon encountering a quasi-closed system in a state of fairly low entropy, we know the following to be overwhelmingly probable: the system has *not* been isolated for millions and millions of years and does *not* just *happen* to be in one of the infrequent but ever-recurring low entropy states exhibited by a permanently-isolated system. Instead, our system was formed not too long ago by branching off after an interaction with an outside agency. For example, suppose that an American geologist is wandering in an isolated portion of the Sahara desert in search of an oasis and encounters a portion of the sand in the shape of "Coca Cola." He would then infer that, with overwhelming probability, a kindred person had interacted with the sand in the recent past by tracing "Coca

[93]Cf. H. Reichenbach, *The Direction of Time* (Berkeley, 1956), 118-143.

Cola" in it. The geologist would not suppose that he was in the presence of one of those relatively low entropy configurations which are assumed by the sand particles spontaneously but very rarely, if beaten about by winds for millions upon millions of years in a state of effective isolation from the remainder of the world.

There is a further *de facto* property of branch systems that concerns us. For it will turn out to enter into the temporally asymmetrical statistical regularities which we shall find to be exhibited in the entropic behavior of these systems. This property consists in the following *randomness* obtaining *as a matter of nomologically-contingent fact* in the distribution of the W_1 micro-states belonging to the initial macro-states of a *space*-ensemble of branch-systems each of which has the same initial entropy $S_1 = k \log W_1$: For each class of *like* branch-systems having the *same* initial entropy value S_1, the micro-states constituting the identical initial macro-states of entropy S_1 are *random samples* of the set of all W_1 micro-states yielding a macro-state of entropy S_1.[94] This attribute of randomness of micro-states on the part of the initial states of the members of the *space*-ensemble will be recognized as the counterpart of the following attribute of the micro-states of one single, permanently-closed system: there is equi-probability of occurrence among the W_1 micro-states belonging to the *time*-ensemble of states of equal entropy $S_1 = k \log W_1$ exhibited by one single, permanently-closed system.

We can now state the statistical regularities which obtain as a consequence of the *de facto* properties of branch systems just set forth, when coupled with the principles of statistical mechanics. These regularities, which will be seen to yield a temporally-asymmetric behavior of the entropy of *branch*-systems, fall into two main groups as follows.[95]

Group 1. In most space-ensembles of quasi-closed branch-systems each of which is initially in a state of non-equilibrium or relatively *low* entropy, the majority of branch systems in the ensemble will have *higher* entropies *after* a given time t. But these branch systems simply did not exist as quasi-closed, distinct systems at a time t *prior to* the occurrence of their initial, branching off states. Hence, not existing then as such, the branch systems did in fact *not* also exhibit the same higher entropy states at the *earlier* times t, which they would indeed have done then had they existed as closed systems all along. In this way, the space-ensembles of branch-systems do *not* reproduce the entropic time-symmetry of the single, permanently-closed system. And whatever the behavior of the components of the branch systems prior to the latter's "birth," that

[94]Cf. R. C. Tolman, *The Principles of Statistical Mechanics, op. cit.*, 149.

[95]Cf. R. Fürth, "Prinzipien der Statistik," *Handbuch der Physik, op. cit.*, 270 and 192-193. The next-to-the-last sentence on p. 270 is to be discounted, however, since it is self-contradictory as it stands and incompatible with the remainder of the page.

behavior is irrelevant to the entropic properties of branch systems as such.

The increase after a time t in the entropy of the overwhelming majority of branch systems of initially low entropy—as confirmed abundantly by observation—can be made fully intelligible. To do so, we note the following property of the *time*-ensemble of entropy values belonging to a single, permanently-closed system and then affirm that property of the space-ensembles of branch systems: since *large* entropic downgrades or decreases are *far less* probable (frequent) than moderate ones, the *vast majority* of *non*-equilibrium entropy states of a permanently-closed system are located either at or in the immediate temporal vicinity of the *bottom* of a *dip* of the one-system entropy curve. In short, the vast majority of the *sub*-maximum entropy states are on or temporally very near the *upgrades* of the one-system curve. The application of this result to the space-ensemble of branch-systems whose initial states exhibit the aforementioned *de facto* property of *randomness* then yields the following: among the initial low entropy states of these systems, the vast majority lie at or in the immediate temporal vicinity of the bottoms of the one-system entropy curve at which an upgrade begins.

Group 2. A decisive *temporal asymmetry* in the statistics of the temporal evolution of branch-systems arises from the further result that in most space ensembles of branch systems each of whose members is initially in a state of *equilibrium* or very *high* entropy, the vast majority of these systems in the ensemble will *not* have *lower* entropies *after* a finite time t, but will still be in equilibrium. For the aforementioned randomness property assures that the vast majority of those branch systems whose initial states are equilibrium states have maximum entropy values lying somewhere *well within* the plateau of the one-system entropy curve, rather than at the extremity of the plateau at which an entropy *decrease* is initiated.[96]

[96]Although the decisive asymmetry just noted was admitted by H. Mehlberg ["Physical Laws and Time's Arrow," in: *Current Issues in the Philosophy of Science,* ed. Feigl & Maxwell (New York, 1961), 129], he dismisses it as expressing "merely the factual difference between the two relevant values of probability." But an asymmetry is no less an asymmetry for depending on *de facto,* nomologically-contingent boundary conditions rather than being assured by a *law* alone. Since our verification of laws generally has the same partial and indirect character as that of our confirmation of the existence of certain complicated *de facto* boundary conditions, the assertion of an asymmetry depending on *de facto* conditions is generally no less reliable than one wholly grounded on a law. Hence when Mehlberg [*op. cit.,* 117, n. 30] urges against Schrödinger's claim of asymmetry that for every pair of branch systems which change their entropy in one direction, "there is nothing to prevent" another pair of closed subsystems from changing their entropy in the opposite direction, the reply is: Mehlberg's criticism can be upheld only by gratuitously neglecting the statistical asymmetry admitted but then dismissed by him as "merely" factual.

We see therefore that in the vast majority of branch systems, either one end of their finite entropy curves is a point of low entropy and the other a point of high entropy, or they are in equilibrium states at both ends as well as during the intervening interval. And it is likewise apparent that the statistical distribution of these entropy values on the time axis is such that the vast majority of branch systems have the *same direction of entropy increase* and hence also the same opposite direction of entropy decrease. Thus, the statistics of entropy increase among branch systems assure that in most space ensembles the vast majority of branch systems will increase their entropy in *one* of the two opposite time directions and decrease it in the other: in contradistinction to the entropic time-symmetry of a single, permanently-closed system, the probability within the space-ensemble that a low entropy state s at some given instant be *followed* by a higher entropy state S at some given later instant is much *greater* than the probability that s be *preceded* by S. In this way the entropic behavior of branch systems confers the *same* statistical anisotropy on the vast majority of all those cosmic epochs of time during which the universe exhibits the requisite disequilibrium and contains branch systems satisfying initial conditions of "randomness."[97]

[97]This conclusion departs significantly from Reichenbach's "hypothesis of the branch structure" (DT, 136) by (1) *not* assuming that the entropy is defined for the entire universe such that the universe as a whole can be presumed to exhibit the entropic evolution of the statistical entropy curve for a permanently closed, *finite* system, an assumption which leads Reichenbach to affirm the parallelism of the direction of entropy increase of the universe and of the branch systems, and therefore, (2) *not* concluding that cosmically the statistical anisotropy of time "fluctuates" in the following sense: the alternations of epochs of entropy increase and decrease of the universe go hand-in-hand with the alternations of the direction of entropy increase of the ensembles of branch systems associated with these respective epochs.

In view of the reservations which Reichenbach himself expressed (DT, 132-133) concerning the reliability of assumptions regarding the universe as a whole in the present state of cosmology, one wonders why he invoked the *entropy* of the universe at all instead of confining himself, as we have done, to the much weaker assumption of the existence of states of disequilibrium in the universe. More fundamentally, it is unclear how Reichenbach thought he can reconcile the assumption that the branch systems satisfy initial conditions of randomness during whatever cosmic epoch they may form—an assumption which, as we saw, makes for the *same* statistical anisotropy on the part of most disequilibrium epochs of the universe—with the following claim of alternation: "When we come to the downgrade [of the entropy curve of the entire universe], always proceeding in the same direction [along the time-axis], the branches begin at states of high entropy, . . . and they end at points of low entropy" (DT, 126). For we saw in our statement of the consequences of the postulate of randomness under Group 2 above that in the vast majority of cases, branch systems beginning in a state of equilibrium (high entropy) will *remain* in equilibrium for the duration of their finite careers instead of decreasing their entropies!

An inherent limitation on the applicability of the Maxwell-Boltzmann entropy concept to the entire universe lies in the fact that it has no applicability at all to a *spatially infinite* universe for the following reasons. If the infinite universe contains a denumerable *infinity* of atoms, molecules or stars, the number of complexions W becomes infinite, so

Let us now call the direction of entropy increase of a *typical representative* of these epochs the direction of "later," as indeed we have done from the outset by the mere assignment of higher time numbers in that direction but *without* prejudice to our findings concerning the issue of the anisotropy of time. Then our results pertaining to the entropic behavior of branch systems show that the directions of "earlier than" and "later than" are not merely opposite directions bearing decreasing and increasing time coordinates respectively but are statistically *anisotropic* in an objective physical sense.

The achievements of this entropic criterion of temporal anisotropy are as follows: (i) it provides an empirical justification for interpreting present ordered states as veridical traces of actual past interaction events, a justification which the entropic behavior of a single, permanently-closed system was incompetent to furnish, as we saw, and (ii) it explains why the subjective (psychological) and objective (physical) directions of positive time are parallel to one another by noting that man's own body participates in the entropic lawfulness of space ensembles of physical branch systems in the following sense: man's memory, just as much as all purely physical recording devices, accumulates "traces," records or information. And as we saw earlier, the direction of that accumulation is dictated by the statistics of branch systems. Thus, Spinoza was in error when he wrote Oldenburg that *"tempus non est affectio rerum sed merus modus cogitandi."* Contrary to Watanabe's conception of man's psychological time sense as *sui generis,* we see that the future direction of psychological time is parallel to that of the accumulation of traces (increasing information) in interacting systems, and hence parallel to the direction defined by the positive entropy increase in the branch systems.

But processes characterized by temporally asymmetric entropy changes are not the sole source of the anisotropy of time. Reichenbach's account took no cognizance of processes in nature which are *irreversible* yet do *not* involve any entropy increase. That there are such processes has

that the entropy is not defined and *a fortiori* no increase or decrease thereof [cf. K. P. Stanyukovic "On the Increase of Entropy in an Infinite Universe," *Doklady, Akad. Nauk.* SSSR, N. S. LXIX, 793 (1949), in Russian, as summarized by L. Tisza in *Math. Reviews* XII, 787 (1951)]. And if the number of particles in the infinite universe is only finite, then (a) the equilibrium state of maximum entropy cannot be realized by a *finite* number of particles in a phase-space of *infinitely* many cells, since these particles would have to be *uniformly* distributed among these cells, and (b) the quasi-ergodic hypothesis, which provides the essential basis for the probability metric ingredient in the Maxwell-Boltzmann entropy concept, is presumably false for an infinite phase space. For additional doubts concerning the cosmological relevance of the entropy concept, cf. E. A. Milne, *Sir James Jeans* (Cambridge, 1952), 164-165, and *Modern Cosmology and the Christian Idea of God* (Oxford, 1952), 146-150; also L. Landau and E. Lifshitz, *Statistical Physics* (2nd ed.; New York, 1958), 22-27.

recently been emphasized by K. R. Popper who cites a suggestion to this effect made by Einstein in 1910.

Popper considers a large surface of water[98] initially at rest into which a stone is dropped, thereby producing an outgoing concentric wave of decreasing amplitude. And he argues that the irreversibility of this process is attributable to the physical impossibility of the *uncoordinated* concatenation on all points of a circle of the initial conditions requisite to the occurrence of a *contracting* wave. Now, one might wish to object to this argument by pointing out that the entropy law is *not irrelevant* to the irreversibility of the outgoing wave propagation, pointing out that the diminution in the amplitude of this wave is due to the superposition of *two* independent effects: (1) the requirements of the law of conservation of energy (*first* law of thermodynamics), and (2) an entropy increase as a result of dissipative viscosity in an essentially closed system. While this retort is right to the extent that the entropy increase is a *sufficient* condition for the statistical irreversibility of this process, Popper's case is nonetheless sound in the sense that another, *independent sufficient condition* for irreversibility is provided by the physical impossibility of realizing the initial conditions required for the occurrence of a contracting wave process which was *not* set off by a prior *outgoing* wave motion or by any other influence first emanating from a *central source.* He admits that in a closed system of finite size, there is an entropy increase here as a result of viscous losses. But he goes on to strengthen his argument decisively by explaining that if a thin gas, for example, expands from a center in a system having no bounding walls (presumably in an infinite universe), then the expansion constitutes an irreversible process *without* entropy increase.

The existence of processes whose irreversibility is *not* entropic (cf. n.97) but derives solely from the fact that their temporal inverses would require a *deus ex machina* has been affirmed as a generalization of Popper's examples in the form of a general principle of nature by reference to a *spatially infinite* universe.[99] This claim concerning non-entropic irreversibility can be made more precise by considering illustratively a light wave emitted at a center and going out into *infinite* space. Its temporal inverse would be a light wave which has been *contracting* for *all* infinite past time. Now, in claiming that the latter would require a

[98]K. R. Popper, "The Arrow of Time," *Nature* CLXXVII, 538 (1956) and CLXXVIII, 382 (1956).

[99]E. L. Hill and A. Grünbaum, "Irreversible Processes in Physical Theory," *Nature* CLXXIX, (1957), 1296-1297. For a rebuttal of Popper's purported counterexample to this general principle [Popper, *Nature* CLXXIX (1957), 1297-1299], cf. A. Grünbaum, "Popper on Irreversibility," in M. Bunge (ed.), *The Critical Approach:* Essays in Honor of Karl Popper, to be published by the Free Press, Glencoe, 1963.

deus ex machina for its occurrence, the principle of non-entropic irreversibility is not laying down the self-contradictory condition (akin to Kant's fallacious procedure in his First Antinomy) that a process which has been going on for all infinite past time must have a finite beginning (production by past *initial* conditions) after all. What this principle does assert, however, is the *de facto* physical *non*-occurence of contracting wave processes which have been in progress through an infinite space for all past eternity, and therefore the assumption of their existence would involve a *deus ex machina* in that sense.

The temporal anisotropy defined by this non-entropic irreversibility is more pervasive than either the anisotropy depending on the formation of branch systems or any purely cosmological anisotropy of time such as is defined by the speculative expansion of a spherical space whose radius increases monotonically beginning with a singular state in the finite past having no temporal predecessor. For the irreversibility assured by the *deus ex machina* principle assures uniform temporal anisotropy both for local intervals in the time continuum and in the large.[100]

IV. *The Physical Status of "Becoming"*

The distinction between earlier and later dealt with so far in the context of the anisotropy of time makes no reference to a transient present. But the time of human conscious awareness exhibits not only the earlier-later distinction but also a flow, passage or becoming in the sense of a transiency of the "Now." And this apparent flux of events gives rise to the constantly *shifting* division of the time continuum into the *past* and the *future,* a division which involves more than the *"static"* one into earlier and later. It must be strongly emphasized that what is a factual property of psychological time is the existence and transiency of the "Now" in the sense of the diversity and order of the Now-contents. But the shifting of the "Now" *in the future direction cannot* be deemed a factual property, since this *directional* affirmation of shifting is *a mere tautology.*

Having found a physical basis for the anisotropy of time, our final concern in the consideration of the time problem is the physical status, *if any,* of "becoming." Our earlier characterization of the difference between the two directions of time does not, as such, affirm the existence of a *transient,* threefold division of events into those that have already "spent their existence," as it were, those which actually exist, and those

100For an interesting proposed cosmological explanation on the basis of the "steady state" theory of why it is "that the universe is a non-reflecting sink for radiation," cf. T. Gold's "The Arrow of Time" in: R. Stoops (ed.), *La Structure et l'Évolution de l'Univers* (Brussels, 1958), 81-91.

which are yet to "come *into* being." And the relativistic picture of the world makes no allowance for such a division.[101] It conceives of events not as "coming into existence" but as simply being and thus allowing us to "come across" them and produce "the formality of their taking place" by our "entering" into their absolute future. This view, which some writers *mistakenly* believe to depend on determinism, as we shall see, has been expressed by H. Weyl in the following partly metaphorical way: "the objective world simply *is,* it does not *happen.* Only to the gaze of my consciousness crawling upward along the life [world-] line of my body does a section of this world come to life as a fleeting image."[102]

Recognizing that deterministic physics generally and the theory of relativity in particular grant only a difference between earlier and later but not between past and future, Reichenbach, who thought he could show that an indeterministic physics does otherwise, deemed the Minkowskian world picture incomplete. And he attempted to find an ob-

101Cf. E. Cassirer, *Zur Einsteinschen Relativitätstheorie* (Berlin, 1921), 120-121.

102Weyl, *Philosophy of Mathematics and Natural Science, op. cit.,* 116. This metaphor involving "crawling" must *not,* of course, be taken to suggest the "metaphysical error" charged against it by J. J. C. Smart ["Spatializing Time," *Mind* CXIV, 240 (1955)] that psychologically time itself "flows" spatially at a certain rate measured in some non-existent hypertime. We shall see presently that the concept of "becoming" does *not* involve *this* logical blunder.

On the other hand, defenders of the objectivity of becoming such as M. Capek have been guilty of other misunderstandings of Weyl's metaphor on which they have then sought to erect a *reductio ad absurdum* of Weyl's thesis. Thus, Capek [cf. *The Philosophical Impact of Contemporary Physics* (New York, 1961), 165] writes: "although the world scheme of Minkowski eliminates succession in the physical world, it recognizes at least the *movement of our consciousness* to the future. Thus arises an absurd dualism of the timeless physical world and temporal consciousness, that is, a dualism of two altogether disparate realms whose correlation becomes completely unintelligible. ... in such a view ... we are already dead without realizing it now; but our consciousness creeping along the world line of its own body will certainly reach any pre-existing and nominally future event which in its completeness *waits* to be finally reached by our awareness. ... To such strange consequences do both spatialization of time and strict determinism lead." But it is a careless and question-begging falsehood to declare that on Weyl's view the physical world is "timeless." For what Weyl is contending is only that the physical world is devoid of becoming, while fully granting that the states of physical systems are ordered by an "earlier than" relation which is isomorphic, in important respects, with its counterpart in consciousness. Capek's claim of the unintelligibility of the correlation between physical and psychological time within Weyl's framework is therefore untenable, especially in the absence of an articulation of the kind (degree) of correlation which Capek requires and also of a justification of that requirement. More unfortunate still is the grievous mishandling of the meaning of Weyl's metaphor in Capek's attempt at a *reductio ad absurdum* of Weyl's view, when Capek speaks of our "already" being dead without realizing it now and of our completed future death *waiting* to be finally "reached" by our awareness. This gross distortion of Weyl's metaphorical rendition of the thesis that coming *into* being is only coming into present awareness rests on an abuse of the temporal and/or kinematic components of the meanings of the words "already," "completed," "wait," "reach," etc.

jective physical basis for the present in his paper of 1925[103] by means of a probabilistic interpretation of causality according to which the past is "objectively determined" while the future is "objectively undetermined" in virtue of the non-existence of a complete set of partial causes, a knowledge of which would render our predictions certain. The present is conceived, without the inadmissible use of absolute simultaneity, as the class of events not causally connectible with the particular "now." It is because Reichenbach maintained that on the basis of determinism, "the morrow has already occurred today in the same sense as yesterday has," thus making nonsense of all our planning, that he rejected determinism and sought a physical basis for the present and thereby for becoming. Most recently, he argued[104] that the micro-indeterminism of quantum mechanics is not an ephemeral *pis-aller* of present-day physical theory and extended his early views by attempting to utilize the indeterminacies of quantum mechanics. He writes:[105]

> Let us suppose that consecutive measurements are made alternately of two noncommuting [i.e., complementary] quantities. One will obtain a series of macroscopic events which one cannot predict, but which one can record. This series provides us with a clear distinction between the past and the future: the past is determined, but the future is not. . . .
>
> . . . The analysis of classical physics has shown us that one can record the past but not the future. The combination of this result with Heisenberg's uncertainty leads us to the consequence that one can know the past but that one cannot predict the future. . . .
>
> . . . Modern science . . . furnishes us with precisely the difference between the past and the future, which Laplace's physics could not recognize.
>
> To be sure, Boltzmann's physics, if coupled with the hypothesis of the branch structure, yields a certain structural difference between the past and the future, ... But while this difference enabled us to distinguish between the past and the future, it was not associated with a difference in determination: although one cannot record the future, one could predict it on the basis of the totality of causes. Thus, one cannot call the future undetermined. . . .
>
> It is no longer that way in quantum physics. . . . Here is the difference: there are future facts which cannot possibly be predicted, whereas there are no past facts which it would be impossible to know. In principle, they can always be recorded. . . .
>
> The distinction between the indeterminateness ("l'indéterminisme") of the future and of the determinateness ("détermination") of the past has, in the final analysis, found expression in the laws of physics. . . . The concept of "becoming" acquires significance in physics: the present, which separates the future from the past, is the moment at which that which was undetermined becomes

[103] Reichenbach, "Die Kausalstruktur der Welt und der Unterschied von Vergangenheit und Zukunft, " *op. cit.,* 141-143.

[104] Reichenbach, DT, 211-224 and "Les Fondements Logiques de la Mécanique des Quanta," *op. cit.,* 154-157.

[105] Reichenbach, "Les Fondements Logiques de la Mécanique des Quanta," *op. cit.,* 154-157.

determined, and "becoming" has the same meaning as "becoming determined." . . .

. . . It is not the [sole] privilege of man to define a flux of time; every recording instrument does likewise. What we call direction of time, direction of becoming, is a relation between a recording instrument and its environment. . . .

. . . The term "determination" denotes a relation between two situations A and B; the situation A does or does not determine the situation B. It is meaningless to say that the situation B, considered by itself, is determined. If we say that the past is determined or that the future is undetermined, it is tacitly understood that we are relating this to the present situation; it is with respect to "now" that the past is determined and that the future is not.

In the same vein, the astronomer H. Bondi contends that "In a theory with indeterminacy, . . . the passage of time transforms statistical expectation into real events."[106]

I believe that the issue of determinism vs. indeterminism is totally irrelevant to whether becoming is a significant attribute of the time of physical nature independently of human consciousness. And I wish to explain now why I regard the Reichenbach-Bondi thesis that indeterminism confers flux onto physical time as untenable. My reasons for likewise rejecting Reichenbach's further claim that "The paradox of determinism and planned action is a genuine one" [DT, p. 12] are given in other publications.[107]

In the indeterministic quantum world, the relations between the sets of measurable values of the state variables characterizing a physical system at different times are, in principle, *not* the one-to-one relations linking the states of classically behaving closed systems. But this holds for a given state of a physical system and its absolute future quite independently of whether that state occurs at midnight on December 31, 1800 or at noon on the day of publication of this volume. Moreover, if we consider *any one* of the temporally successive regions of space-time, we can assert the following: the events belonging to its particular absolute past could be (more or less) uniquely specified in records which are a part of that region, whereas its particular absolute future is thence quantum mechanically unpredictable. Accordingly, *every* "now", be it the "now" of Plato's birth or that of Carnap's, always constitutes a divide in Reichen-

[106]H. Bondi, "Relativity and Indeterminacy," *Nature* CLXIX, 660 (1952). Similarly, G. J. Whitrow tells us [*The Natural Philosophy of Time* (London, 1961), 295] that "There is indeed a profound connection between the reality of time and the existence of an incalculable element in the universe."

[107]Cf. A. Grünbaum, "Causality and the Science of Human Behavior," *American Scientist* XL (1952), 665-676 [reprinted in H. Feigl and M. Brodbeck (eds.), *Readings in the Philosophy of Science* (New York, 1953), 766-778]; "Das Zeitproblem," *Archiv für Philosophie* VII (1957), 203-206; "Historical Determinism, Social Activism and Predictions in the Social Sciences," *British J. Phil. Sci.* VII (1956), 236-240; "Complementarity in Quantum Physics and its Philosophical Generalization," *The Journal of Philosophy* LIV (1957), 724-727.

bach's sense between its own recordable past and its unpredictable future, thereby satisfying his definition of the "present." But this fact is fatal to his aim of providing a physical basis for a *unique*, transient "now" and thus for "becoming." Reichenbach's recent characterization of the determinacy of the past as recordability as opposed to the quantum mechanical indeterminacy of the future can therefore not serve to vindicate his conception of becoming any more than did his paper of 1925, which was penetratingly criticized by Hugo Bergmann as follows:[108]

> Thus, according to Reichenbach, a cross-section in the state of the world is distinguished from all others; the now has an objective significance. Even when no man is alive any longer, there is a now. "The present state of the planetary system" would even then be just as precise a descriptive phrase as "the state of the planetary system in the year 1000."
>
> Concerning this definition one must ask: Which now is intended, if one says: the present state of the planetary system? That of the year 1800 or 2000 or which other one? Reichenbach's reply is: the now is the threshold of the transition from the state of indeterminacy to that of determinacy. But (if Reichenbach's indeterminism holds) this transition has *always* occurred and will always occur. And if the rejoinder would be: the indeterminacy of the year 1800 has already been transformed into a determinacy, then one must ask: For whom? Evidently for us, for the present, for our now. Accordingly, this definition by Reichenbach seems to refer after all to a now which it must first define. What is the objective difference between the now of the year 1800 and the now of the present instant? The answer must be: now is the instant of the transition from indeterminacy to determinacy, that is, one explains the present now . . . by reference to itself.
>
> . . . Reichenbach writes: The problem can be formulated as the question concerning the difference between the past and the future. For determinism, there is no such difference. . . . But the reproach which Reichenbach directs at determinism here should be aimed not at it but at the world view of physics, which does not take cognizance of any psychological categories, for which there is no "I", . . . a concept which is inextricably intertwined with the concept "now". Even those who regard the supplanting of determinism by indeterminism as admissible, as we do, will not be willing to admit that the concept of "now" can be assigned a legitimate place within indeterministic physics. Even if one assumes—as we wish to do along with Reichenbach—that the future is not uniquely determined by a temporal cross-section, one can say only that this indeterminacy prevails just as much for Plato as for myself and that I cannot decide by physical means who is living "now". For the difference is a psychological one.
>
> . . . "Now" is the temporal mode of the experiencing ego.

Bergmann's demonstration here that an indeterminist universe fails to define an objective (non-psychological) transient now can be extended

[108]H. Bergmann, *Der Kampf um das Kausalgesetz in der jüngsten Physik, op. cit.*, 27-28. Wilfrid Sellars has independently developed the basis for similar criticisms as part of his penetrating study of a complex of related issues: cf. his "Time and the World Order," in: *Minnesota Studies in the Philosophy of Science* III (Minneapolis, 1962).

in the following sense to justify his contention that the concept "now" involves features peculiar to consciousness: the "flux of time" or transiency of the "now" has a meaning only in the context of the egocentric perspectives of *sentient* organisms and does *not also* have relevance to the relations between purely inanimate individual recording instruments and the environmental physical events they register, as Reichenbach claims. For what can be said of every state of the universe can also be said, *mutatis mutandis*, of every state of a given inanimate recorder. Moreover, the dependence of the meaning of now on the presence of properties peculiar to consciousness emerges from William James' and Hans Driesch's correct observations that a simple isomorphism between a succession of *brain traces* and a succession of states of awareness *does* not explain the temporal features of such psychological phenomena as melody awareness. For the hypothesis of isomorphism renders only the succession of states of awareness but not the *instantaneous awareness of succession*.[109] But the *latter* awareness is an essential ingredient of the meaning of "now": The flux of time consists in the *instantaneous awarenesses* of *both* the temporal order *and* the *diversity* of the membership of the set of remembered (recorded) or forgotten events, awarenesses in each of which the instant of its own occurrence constitutes a *distinguished element*.

I cannot see, therefore, that the accretion of time-tagged marks or traces on an inanimate recording tape so as to form an expanding spatial series can also be held to define a flux of time. Thus, Bergmann's exclusively psychologistic conception of this flux or becoming must be upheld against Reichenbach.

A brief comment needs to be added concerning an *unjustified* criticism of the concept of the flux of time. We see from our characterization that this idea is a *qualitative* concept without any metrical ingredients. It therefore will not do to offer a *metrical* refutation via a *reductio ad absurdum* in an endeavor to show that metaphorical discourse involving reference to "the flow of time" or to "the direction of time" commits a breach of logical grammar. Such a *reductio* was recently offered by J.J.C. Smart, who writes:[110] "The concept of the flow of time or of the advance

[109]Cf. W. James, *The Principles of Psychology* (New York, 1890 and 1950), 628-629 and H. Driesch, *Philosophische Gegenwartsfragen* (Leipzig, 1933), 96-103.

[110]J. J. C. Smart, "The Temporal Asymmetry of the World," *Analysis* XIV, 81 (1954). A similar *reductio* is presented by Max Black in "The 'Direction' of Time," *Analysis* XIX, 54 (1959). On the other hand, Smart has offered valid criticisms of Reichenbach's contention that we can "change the future" but not the past in *Phil. Quarterly* VIII (1958), esp. 76. And H. Mehlberg ["Physical Laws and Time's Arrow," *op. cit.*, 109-111] has given a telling refutation of Reichenbach's attempt to characterize "the" direction of time or becoming on the basis of his concept of a "undirectional" relation.

of consciousness is, however, an illusion. How fast does time flow or consciousness advance? In what units is the rate of flow or advance to be measured? Seconds per - ?"

V. *Empiricism and the Foundations of Geometry*

Ce qui est admirable, ce n'est pas que le champ des étoiles soit si vaste, c'est que l'homme l'ait mesuré.

Anatole France

In the course of the current century, mathematically competent criticisms of the contemporary empiricist conception of geometry fell into three main groups: (i) the phenomenological (psychologistic) neo-Kantian a priori of Husserl's *Wesensschau,* which Carnap espoused in his doctoral dissertation,[111] (ii) unmitigated *conventionalism,* which is widely though mistakenly associated with Henri Poincaré, (iii) B. Russell's thesis, set forth in his early *The Foundations of Geometry,*[112] that there are logical conditions—disclosed by the application of Kant's presuppositional method—which must be certifiable a priori to assure the very possibility of any science of exteriority in general and of metric geometry in particular, although these conditions are a good deal less restrictive than Kant's own requirement of Euclideanism.

An examination of some neglected aspects of these three positions will serve to justify the current empiricist view of the status of geometry and thereby place into bolder relief Carnap's more recent conception of which he has given us only a very brief statement.[113]

(i) Distinguishing the space of physical objects from the space of visual experience ("Anschauungsraum"), Carnap sided with empiricism even in his first work to the extent of maintaining that the topology of physical space is known a posteriori and that the coincidence relations among points disclosed by experience yield a unique metrization for that space once a specific coordinative definition of congruence has been chosen freely.[114] But the neo-Kantian *parti pris* of that period enters in his epistemological interpretation of the axioms governing the topology of *visual* space:

> Experience does not provide the justification for them, the axioms are . . . independent of the "quantity of experience", i.e., knowledge of them does not, as in the case of a posteriori propositions, become ever more reliable through multiply repeated experience. For, as Husserl has shown, we are dealing here

[111]R. Carnap, *Der Raum* (Berlin, 1922), [*Kantstudien,* Ergänzungsheft No. 56].

[112]Cambridge, 1897 and New York, 1957. A revised version, annotated by both Russell and L. Couturat, appeared in French translation (tr. A. Cadenat) as *Essai sur les Fondements de la Géométrie* (Paris, 1901).

[113]R. Carnap, *Foundations of Logic and Mathematics* (Chicago, 1939), 51-56.

[114]Carnap, *Der Raum, op. cit.*, 39, 45, 54, 63.

not with facts in the sense of empirically ascertained realities but rather with the essence ("eidos") of certain presentations whose special nature can be grasped in a single immediate experience.[115]

Reminding us of Kant's distinction between knowledge acquired "with" experience, on the one hand, and "from" experience, on the other, Carnap classifies these axioms as synthetic a priori propositions in that philosopher's sense.

This theory of the phenomenological a priori is a stronger version of Helmholtz' claim that "space can be transcendental [a priori] while its axioms are not."[116] For Helmholtz' concession to Kantianism merely was to regard an *amorphous* visual extendedness as an a priori condition of spatial experience[117] while proclaiming the a posteriori character of the topological and metrical articulations of that extendedness on the basis of his pioneering method of imagining ("sich ausmalen") the specific sensory contents we would have in worlds having alternative spatial structures.[118]

In his more recent publication on mathematics, Carnap denies the existence of synthetic a priori knowledge in general without mentioning his reason for no longer regarding the topological axioms of *visual* space as a species of such propositions.[119] Perhaps he will therefore wish to endorse the following argument against the phenomenological a priori in the context of his reactions to recent doubts concerning the tenability of the dualism between analytic and synthetic statements: it is an *empirical* fact that the experiences resulting from ocular activity have the indefinable attribute which is characteristic of visual extendedness rather than that belonging to tactile explorations or to those experiences that

[115] *Ibid.*, 22. Cf. also p. 62. For a more recent defense of the thesis that "there are synthetic a priori judgments of spatial intuition," cf. K. Reidemeister, "Zur Logik der Lehre vom Raum," *Dialectica* VI (1952), 342. For a discussion of related questions, see P. Bernays, "Die Grundbegriffe der reinen Geometrie in ihrem Verhältnis zur Anschauung," *Naturwiss.* XVI, 197 (1928).

[116] H. von Helmholtz, *Schriften zur Erkenntnistheorie,* ed. P. Hertz and M. Schlick (Berlin, 1921), 140.

[117] *Ibid.*, 2, 70, 121-2, 140-2, 144-5, 147-8, 152, 158, 161-2, 163, 168, 172, 174. Helmholtz attempts to characterize the distinctive attribute of space, not possessed by other tridimensional manifolds, in the following way: "in space, the distance between two points on a vertical can be compared to the horizontal distance between two points on the floor, because a measuring device can be applied successively to these two pairs of points. But we cannot compare the distance between two tones of equal pitch and differing intensity with that between two tones of equal intensity and differing pitch" (*ibid.*, 12). Schlick, however, properly notes in his commentary (*ibid.*, 28) that this attribute is necessary but not sufficient to render the distinctive character of space.

[118] *Ibid.*, 5, 22, 164-5. Cf. also K. Gerhards' papers "Nichteuklidische Kinematographie," *Naturwissenschaften* XX, 925 (1932) and "Nichteuklidische Anschauung und optische Täuschungen," *Naturwissenschaften* XXIV, 437 (1936).

[119] Carnap, *Foundations of Logic and Mathematics, op. cit.*, 55-6.

would issue from our possession of a sense organ responding to magnetic disturbances. In the class of all logically possible experiences, the "Wesensschau" provided by our ocular activity must be held to give rise to synthetic a posteriori knowledge. For the only way to assure a priori that all future deliverances of our eyes will possess the characteristic attribute which Husserl would have us ascertain in a single *coup d'oeil* is by resorting to a covert tautology via refusing to *call* the resulting knowledge "knowledge of visual space," unless it possesses that attribute!

Reichenbach made a particularly telling contribution to the disintegration of the Kantian *metrical* a priori of *visual* space by showing that such intuitive compulsion as inheres in the Euclideanism of that space derives from facts of logic in which the Kantian interpretation cannot find a last refuge and that the counter-intuitiveness of non-Euclidean relations is merely the result of both ontogenetic and phylogenetic adaptation to the Euclidicity of the physical space of ordinary life.[120] In recent years, experimental mathematico-optical researches by R. K. Luneburg[121] and A. A. Blank[122] have even led these authors to contend that although the *physical* space in which sensory depth perception by binocular vision is effective is Euclidean, the binocular *visual* space resulting from psychometric coordination possesses a Lobatchevskian *hyperbolic* metric of constant curvature. This contention suggests several questions.

The first of these is how human beings manage to get about so easily in a Euclidean physical environment even though the metric of visual space is presumably hyperbolic. Blank suggests the following as a possible answer to this question: (1) man's motor adjustment to his physical environment does not draw on *visual* data alone; moreover, these do contribute physically true information, since they supply a good approximation to the relative directions of objects and since the mapping of physical onto visual space preserves the topology (though not the metric) of physical space, thereby enabling man to control his motor responses

[120]Reichenbach, *Philosophie d. Raum-Zeit-Lehre, op. cit.*, 43-46 and 50-57 or PST, 32-34 and 37-44. In this connection, cf., also Poincaré's explanation of why geometry can be "the art of reasoning soundly concerning badly-drawn figures" in *Letzte Gedanken, op. cit.*, 57-59 and 94-99.

[121]R. K. Luneburg, *Mathematical Analysis of Binocular Vision* (Princeton, 1947); "Metric Methods in Binocular Visual Perception," in *Studies and Essays,* Courant Anniversary Volume (New York, 1948), 215-239.

[122]A. A. Blank, "The Luneburg Theory of Binocular Visual Space," *J. Opt. Soc. Am.* XLIII, 717 (1953); "The non-Euclidean Geometry of Binocular Visual Space," *Bull. Am. Math. Soc.* LX, 376 (1954); "The Geometry of Vision," *The British J. of Physiological Optics* XIV, 154 (1957); "The Luneberg Theory of Binocular Perception," in: S. Koch (ed.), *Psychology, A Study of a Science,* Study I, vol. 1 (New York, 1958), Part III, Sec. A. 2.; "Axiomatics of Binocular Vision. The Foundations of Metric Geometry in Relation to Space Perception," *J. Opt. Soc. Am.* XLVIII, 328 (1958); "Analysis of Experiments in Binocular Space Perception," *J. Opt. Soc. Am.* XLVIII, 911 (1958).

by feedback, as in the parking of a car or threading the eye of a needle, and (2) the thesis of the hyperbolicity of visual space rests on data obtained under experimental conditions which are far more restrictive than those accompanying ordinary visual experience. Under ordinary conditions, we secure depth perception by relying on the coordination of our two ocular images, which we have learned in the past in the usual contexts. But in order to ascertain the laws of merely *one* of the sources of spatial information—stereoscopic depth perception alone—the experimenters of the Luneburg-Blank theory endeavored to deny their subjects precisely that contextual reliance: there were no guideposts of perspectives and familiar objects whose positions the subject had determined by tactile means, the only visible objects being isolated point lights in an otherwise completely dark room; in fact, the subject was not even allowed to move his head to make judgments by parallax. Since these contextual guideposts are also available in monocular vision, the experimenters assumed that they play no part in the innate physiological processes governing the distinctive sensations of three-dimensional space which are obtained binocularly.

Several additional questions arise in regard to the Luneburg theory upon going beyond its own restricted objectives of furnishing an account of binocular visual perception and attempting to incorporate its thesis of the non-Euclidean structure of visual space in a comprehensive theory of spatial *learning:* (i) how is man able to arrive at a rather correct apprehension of the Euclidean metric relations of his environment by the use of a physiological instrument whose deliverances are non-Euclidean? (ii) how can students be taught *Euclidean* geometry by *visual* methods, methods which certainly convey more than the topology of Euclidean space and whose success is therefore not explained by the fact that the purportedly hyperbolic visual space preserves the topology of Euclidean physical space? (iii) if we have literally been seeing one of the non-Euclidean geometries of constant negative Gaussian curvature all along, why did it require two thousand years of research in axiomatics even to *conceive* these geometries, the Euclideanism of physical space being affirmed throughout this period? (iv) why did such thinkers as Helmholtz and Poincaré first have to retrain their *Anschauung* conceptually in a counter-intuitive direction before achieving a ready pictorialization of the Lobatchevski-Bolyai world, a feat which very few can duplicate even now? (v) if we took two groups of school children of equal intelligence and without prior formal geometrical education and taught Euclid to one group while teaching Lobatchevski-Bolyai to the other, why is it the case (if indeed that is the case!) that, in all probability, the first group would exhibit a far better mastery of their material?

The need to answer these questions becomes even greater, if we assume that our ideas concerning the geometry of our immediate physical environment are formed, in the first instance, *not* by the physical geometry of yardsticks or by the formal study of Euclidean geometry but rather by the psychometry of our visual sense data.

A. A. Blank, to whom the writer submitted these questions, has suggested that these questions may have answers which lie in part along the following lines: (1) man has to learn the significance of ever-changing patterns of visual sensations for the metric of *physical* space by *discounting* much of the psychometry of visual sensation, thereby developing the habit of *not* being very perceptive of the metrical details of his visual experiences. Thus, we learn before adulthood to associate with the non-rigid sequence of visual sensations corresponding to viewing a chair in various positions and contexts the attribute of physical rigidity, generally ignoring all but those aspects of the changing appearances that can serve as a basis for action. In fact, laboratory findings show that for any physical configuration whatever, there are an infinity of others which give the same binocular clues.[123] Since we retain those aspects of visual experience which enable us to place objects in the contexts useful for action, Euclidean relations can be more readily pictured (though not actually seen or made visible) than those of Lobatchevski; (2) those geometrical judgments disclosed by binocular perception which are *common* to both Euclidean and hyperbolic geometry[124] will be true physically as well. Moreover, there are certain small two-dimensional elements of visual space which are essentially isometric with the corresponding elements of the Euclidean space of physical stimuli. For example, in a plane parallel to the line joining the rotation centers of the eyes, physical metric relations are seen undistorted in the vicinity of a point at the base of the perpendicular to the plane from a point located half way between the eyes. We can therefore obtain first-order visual approximations to the physical Euclidean metric from viewing small diagrams frontally in this way. In a like manner, we can understand how the concept of similar figures, which is uniquely characteristic of Euclidean geometry among spaces of *constant* curvature, can be conveyed in the context of a non-Euclidean visual geometry: all Riemannian geometries are locally Euclidean, thus possessing a group of similarity transformations in the small; (3) the presumed greater ease with which students would master

[123]Cf. A. A. Blank, "The Luneburg Theory of Binocular Visual Space," *op. cit.*, 721-722 and Hardy, Rand, Rittler, Blank and Boeder, *The Geometry of Binocular Space Perception,* Columbia University College of Physicians and Surgeons (New York, 1953), 15ff. and 39ff.

[124]For the axioms of the so called "absolute" geometry relevant here, see R. Baldus, *Nichteuklidische Geometrie* (3rd revised edition, ed. by F. Löbell) (Berlin: Sammlung Göschen, 1953), vol. 970, Ch. II.

Euclid than Lobatchevski is due to the greater analytical simplicity of the numerical relations of the Euclidean geometry.

As for the metric of physical space, we saw that Carnap explained in *Der Raum* that once we have specified the coordinative definition of congruence which we wish to employ, then the topological facts of observation determine a unique metric geometry. He adds that, alternatively, we can begin by freely choosing a metric space of particular curvature to be our physical space, and he asserts incorrectly that the topology then determines a *unique* coordinative definition of congruence appropriate to that choice.[125] Carnap adroitly illustrates the first of these two latter contentions by having us consider a metrization of three dimensional physical space in which the surface of the earth is a Euclidean plane. The change in the congruence definition (remetrization) associated with a change in the geometry must *not* be identified with a mere recoordinatization (choice of new coordinates), which *preserves* the definition of congruence for both line segments and angles, thus leaving the geometry invariant. Such paths as the trajectories of light rays, which are straight lines (geodesics) in the customary metrization, will no longer be straight in the context of his new metric. Carnap argues, therefore, that the very facts which we customarily construe as evidence for the (approximate) sphericity of the earth (e.g. the appearance of objects at the horizon, the circular shadow cast by the earth during lunar eclipses) will also be fully consonant with the new metrization. In general, this contention is both true and illuminating, but it requires an important qualification omitted by him.[126] For the customary account of the earth's metrical properties and the alternate description suggested here by Carnap are not merely alternative metrizations of the same topology but involve a transformation from the "closed" space of the sphere to the topologically non-equivalent space of the Euclidean plane, which is "open" in both directions.[127]

[125]Carnap, *Der Raum, op. cit.*, 46-54. A proof has been given elsewhere [Cf. A. Grünbaum, "Conventionalism in Geometry" in: L. Henkin, P. Suppes and A. Tarski (eds.), *The Axiomatic Method in Geometry and Physics* (Amsterdam, 1959), 214-216] that the stipulation of a particular desired metric geometry does not yield a unique definition of congruence but allows infinitely many different criteria of congruence. Thus, contrary to Carnap's statement, there are infinitely many ways in which measuring rods could squirm under transport as compared to their actual ordinary behavior while still yielding the same geometry. For a much fuller discussion of these and related matters, cf. A. Grünbaum, "Geometry, Chronometry and Empiricism," *Minnesota Studies in the Philosophy of Science* III (Minneapolis, 1962), Section 3, part (iii).

[126]Cf. Reichenbach, *Phil. d. Raum-Zeit-Lehre, op. cit.*, 81-2, and especially 98, or PST, 65-66, and especially 80.

[127]Dimensionality is a topological invariant, but a sphere and a Euclidean plane are both 2-dimensional while being topologically non-equivalent. There is no inconsistency here, however, since the topological invariance of dimensionality merely assures that all topologically equivalent structures are equidimensional but *not* the converse.

The consequences of the impossibility of obtaining a Euclidean plane from a sphere by a homeomorphism are made evident by stereographic projection: the Euclidean plane is topologically equivalent to a sphere "torn" by the absence of a single point. Now Carnap mentions that if the earth is to be a Euclidean plane, there will need to be a point-singularity somewhere on the earth.[128] Presumably, this would take the form of the earth's having a point which cannot be traversed by a causal chain in any way, thus guaranteeing through the absence of causal continuity that opposite directions of the plane do not meet and leave the space "open". But Carnap treats the question of whether such a point exists as a matter subject to regulation by our desires.[129] Yet it would certainly seem that, at least in principle, the existence of such a point is a matter of empirical fact and that we know inductively that there is no such point, whatever our desires in regard to the global topology. I conclude, therefore, that our freedom to choose the geometry of the earth is objectively confined by the empirical facts of *causal continuity* to within the class of homeomorphic surfaces having a positive Gaussian curvature, which excludes the Euclidean plane.

Thus, the topology of space is a matter for *empirical* determination, once the existence of causal continuity has been established inductively.[130] Significantly, Carnap has proven in another paper[131] that the connection between causality and the number of spatial dimensions, which is only *one* of the invariants of the topology, is still more intimate in the following sense: the affirmation of causality *entails* logically that space has *at least three* dimensions. It should be added that, also for *logical* reasons, only some *one* number of spatial dimensions in the range of three or higher can characterize the physical world alongside causal continuity. For if causal continuity prevails in a world of events having k space dimensions, it cannot also prevail when this class of events

128Carnap, *Der Raum, op. cit.*, 48.

129*Ibid.*

130Reichenbach reached this empiricist conclusion when he wrote [PST, §12, 80]: *"Topology is an empirical matter as soon as we introduce the requirement that no causal relations must be violated;* whether there occur causal anomalies can be decided by the usual inductive methods of physics." [Italics in original]. But, surprisingly, a few pages earlier, he had maintained [*ibid.*, 63-67] that empirical findings showing that 3-dimensional physical space has the non-Euclidean topology of a torus space *in the context of the assumption of causal continuity* could also be adduced as evidence that the topology is Euclidean within the framework of assuming causal anomalies. And he had declared in that connection [*ibid.*, 66] that "no one can prevent us from believing in a preestablished harmony [i.e., causal anomalies in the sense of lack of causal continuity]."

131Carnap, "Dreidimensionalität des Raumes und Kausalität," *Annalen d. Phil.* IV, 105 (1924).

is arrayed so as to have a different number of dimensions, since redimensioning involves a destruction of continuity. As I see it, the determination of the actual particular value of k in the range of 3 or higher, which characterizes the space of our causal universe, is an empirical matter of fact not subject to being chosen arbitrarily by us. Here again, Carnap seems to have affirmed freedom to choose rather than empirical determinateness, because the constructionism of the thoroughgoing phenomenalistic positivism which he espoused at that time led him to consider the hypothesis of causality in the physical world as a matter of arbitrary stipulation and not as empirically necessitated in the inductive sense.[132] Since a discussion of the issue between phenomenalistic positivism and critical realism in regard to the concept of existence is entirely beyond the scope of this essay, I merely wish to record my puzzlement over Carnap's not having been swayed during the 1920's by the defense of realism given by Schlick in the second edition of his splendid *Allgemeine Erkenntnislehre*[133] and by Reichenbach.[134] Still more difficult to determine are the reasons for Schlick's own later abandonment of realism. I know of no successful refutation or even adequate treatment of these arguments for the realistic epistemology by phenomenalistic positivists, and I regard the phenomenalist version of logical empiricism as a profound error. In fact, it seems to me that rather than having been warranted by developments in the natural sciences, contemporary positivism's phenomenalist conception of the existence of inferred entities rests on logical grounds which, despite linguistic refinements of great ingenuity, are neither essentially different nor better than those which provided the basis for less skillfully formulated versions of that doctrine throughout the history of traditional philosophy.

We now turn to the second major rival of the empiricist conception of the foundations of geometry: *conventionalism*.

(ii) According to a widely-accepted interpretation of the writings of Henri Poincaré, he is said to have maintained that even *after* a system of abstract geometry is given a semantical interpretation via a particular coordinative definition of congruence, no experiment can verify or falsify the resulting system of physical geometry, the choice of a metrical

[132] *Ibid.*, 109-110, 117, 129-130. Cf. also *Der logische Aufbau der Welt* (Berlin, 1928), where he writes (p.6): "the concept and its object are identical. This identity does not signify a hypostatization (substantialization) of the concept, but rather conversely a 'functionalization' of the object."

[133] Berlin, 1925. For more recent arguments along these lines, see H. Feigl, *Phil. of Science* XVII, 35 and 186 (1950) and F. Kaufmann in *Phil. Thought in France and the U. S.*, ed. M. Farber (Buffalo, 1950), 565-588.

[134] "Ziele und Wege der physikalischen Erkenntnis," *op. cit.*, Section 6, 16-24.

geometry being entirely a matter of convention.[135] This anti-empiricist version of conventionalism is clearly incompatible with Carnap's view. Carnap recognizes the stipulational character of coordinative definitions of congruence and the associated possibilities of giving a variety of equivalent descriptions of the same set of objective (topological) facts by means of different metric geometries. But he emphasizes that once a system of abstract geometry has been given a physical interpretation, the resulting interpreted system is indeed verifiable or falsifiable by experiment.[136]

The principal basis for the belief that Poincaré took a stand in opposition to the kind of metrical empiricism upheld by Carnap seems to be Poincaré's treatment of "Experience and Geometry" in chapter V of his *Science and Hypothesis*.[137] The fifth section of this chapter culminates in the statement that "whichever way we look at it, it is impossible to discover in geometric empiricism a rational meaning."[138] But there seems to be general unawareness of the fact that Poincaré lifted Sections 4 and 5 of this chapter verbatim out of the *wider* context of his earlier paper "Des Fondements de la Géométrie, à propos d'un Livre de M. Russell,"[139] which was followed by his important rejoinder "Sur les Principes de la Géométrie, Réponse à M. Russell."[140] These neglected papers together with his posthumous *Dernières Pensées*[141] seem to me to show convincingly that Poincaré was *not* an opponent of the empiricist position taken by Carnap. And I explain his *apparent* endorsement of unmitigated, anti-empiricist conventionalism in his more publicized writings on the basis of the historical context in which he wrote. For at the turn of the century, the Riemannian kind of empiricist conception

135This interpretation of Poincaré is found, for example, in E. Nagel, "Einstein's Philosophy of Science." *The Kenyon Review* XII (1950), 525, and "The Formation of Modern Conceptions of Formal Logic in the Development of Geometry," *Osiris* VII (1939), 212-216; H. Weyl, *Phil. of Math. and Natural Science, op. cit.*, 34; H. Reichenbach, *Phil. d. Raum-Zeit-Lehre, op. cit.*, 49, 313 or PST, 36, 274 and "The Philosophical Significance of the Theory of Relativity," *op. cit.*, 297, and O. Hölder, *Die mathematische Methode* (Berlin, 1924), 400, n. 2.

136Thus, in his *Physikalische Bergriffsbildung* (Karlsruhe, 1926), he discusses the problem of deciding between Euclidean and non-Euclidean geometry, saying (p. 31): "Once the concept of length is made definite [physically], then the question concerning the structure of the space of the real world is an empirical one."

137Cf. Poincaré, *The Foundations of Science*, tr. G. B. Halstead (Lancaster, 1946), 81-86.

138*Ibid.*, 86.

139This critique of Russell's *Foundations of Geometry* appeared in *Revue de Mét. et de Mor.* VII (1899), 251-279; the transplanted excerpt is given in §12, 265-267 of this paper.

140*Revue de Mét. et de Mor.* VIII (1900), 73-86; the relevant paper by Russell is "Sur les Axiomes de la Géométrie," VII (1899), 684-707 of that same journal.

141Paris, 1913, German transl. *Letzte Gedanken, op. cit.*

of physical geometry, which we now associate with writers like Carnap and Reichenbach and which takes full cognizance of the stipulational status of congruence, had hardly secured a sufficient philosophical following to provide a stimulus and furnish a target for Poincaré's polemic. Instead, the then dominant philosophical interpretations of geometry were such aprioristic neo-Kantian ones as Couturat's and Russell's, on the one hand, and Helmholtz's type of empiricist interpretation, which made inadequate allowance for the stipulational character of congruence, on the other.[142] No wonder, therefore, that Poincaré's conventionalist emphasis in his better known writings seems *in the contemporary context* to place him into the ranks of such extreme conventionalists as H. Dingler.[143] It would therefore be a great service to philosophical posterity, if the neglected papers I have mentioned were republished, lest, by permitting them to sink into further oblivion, we incur from a future

[142]Helmholtz, *op. cit.,* 15-20. H. Freudenthal has maintained [*Mathematical Reviews* XXII (1961), 107] that instead of being a supporter of Riemann against Helmholtz, Poincaré was an exponent of Helmholtz's anti-Riemannian view that metric geometry presupposes a *three*-dimensional rather than a merely *one*-dimensional solid body as a congruence standard. Freudenthal backs that interpretation of Poincaré by the latter's declaration that "if then there were no solid bodies in nature, there would be no geometry" ["L'Espace et la Géométrie," *Revue de Métaphysique et de Morale* III (1895), 638]. According to Freudenthal ["Zur Geschichte der Grundlagen der Geometrie," *Nieuw Archief voor Wiskunde* (4), V (1957), 115] this declaration shows that "Poincaré still thinks quite in the empiricist spirit of Helmholtz's space problem and has not even penetrated to Riemann's conception, which is aware of a metric without rigid bodies." But, contrary to Freudenthal, it seems clear from the context of Poincaré's declaration that his mention of the role of solid bodies pertains *not at all* to a Helmholtzian insistence on a three-dimensional congruence standard as against Riemann's one-dimensional one; instead it concerns the role of solids in the *genesis* of the notion of mere change of position as against other changes of state, solids being distinguished from liquids and gases by the fact that their displacements lend themselves to compensation by a corresponding movement of our own bodies, which issues in the restoration of the set of sense impressions we had of the solids prior to their displacement.

But this view is, of course, entirely consonant both with Riemann's conception of the congruence standard as one-dimensional and with his claim that, being continuous, physical space has no intrinsic metric, the latter having to be brought in from elsewhere, as is done by the use of the rigid body. In fact, how except by embracing precisely this view could Poincaré have espoused the conventionality of congruence and the resulting alternative metrizability of physical space on which he founded his thesis of the feasibility of either a Euclidean or a non-Euclidean description? For a detailed demonstration that, contrary to Freudenthal, Poincaré's entire conventionalism in regard to metric geometry is a straightforward *epistemological* elaboration of Riemann's conception of the metric amorphousness of the spatial manifold, see A. Grünbaum, "Geometry, Chronometry and Empiricism" in: *Minnesota Studies in the Philosophy of Science* III (Minneapolis, 1962), Sections 2, 5 and 6.

[143]Poincaré himself deplored the widespread misunderstandings of his philosophical work and its misappropriation by "all the reactionary French journals." Cf. his *La Mécanique Nouvelle,* cited in R. Dugas, "Henri Poincaré devant les Principes de la Mécanique," *Revue Scientifique* LXXXIX (1951), 81.

rediscoverer of them Ribot's reproach: "Les métaphysiciens ne lisent rien; ils ne se lisent même pas entre eux."[144]

As evidence for my doubly "unconventional" Poincaré-interpretation to the effect that there is no disagreement between Carnap's and Poincaré's philosophies of geometry, I cite the following crucial and unequivocal concluding passage from Poincaré's rejoinder to Russell, who had maintained that the "axiom of free mobility" furnishes a uniquely *true* criterion of congruence as an a priori condition for the possibility of metric geometry in the Kantian sense and *not* in the sense of a coordinative definition. Poincaré writes:

> Finally, I have never said that one can *ascertain by experiment whether certain bodies preserve their form.* I have said just the contrary. The term "to preserve one's form" has no meaning by itself. But I confer a meaning on it by *stipulating* that certain bodies will be said to preserve their form. These bodies, thus chosen, can henceforth serve as instruments of measurement. But if I say that these bodies preserve their form, it is because *I choose to do so* and not because experience obliges me to do so.
>
> In the present context I choose to do so, because by a series of *observations* ("constatations") analogous to those which were under discussion in the previous section [i.e., observations showing the coincidence of certain points with others in the course of the movements achieving metrical congruence] *experience has proven* to me that their movements form a Euclidean group. I have been able to makes these observations in the manner just indicated *without having any preconceived idea concerning metric geometry.* And, having made them, I judge that the convention will be convenient and I adopt it.[145]

It must also be remembered that Poincaré's declaration that "no geometry is either true or false"[146] was made by him as part of a discussion in which he contrasted his endorsement of this proposition with his complete rejection of the following two others: (i) the truth of Euclidean geometry is known to us a priori independently of all experience, and (ii) one of the geometries is true and the others false, but we can never know which one is true. The entire tenor of this discussion makes it clear that Poincaré is concerned there with abstract uninterpreted geometries whose relations to physical facts are as yet indeter-

[144]Unfortunately, these papers will not be contained in any of the volumes of the scientific *Oeuvres de Henri Poincaré,* published under the auspices of the *Académie des Sciences.*

[145]Poincaré "Sur les Principes de la Géométrie, Réponse à M. Russell," *op. cit.,* 85-6, italics in the *latter* paragraph are mine. (For a similar statement by him, see his *Letzte Gedanken, op. cit.,* 49.) Cf. A. Grünbaum "Geometry, Chronometry and Empiricism," *Minnesota Studies in the Philosophy of Science* III, *op. cit.,* for a consistent empiricist interpretation of those passages in Poincaré's writings [e.g., *Foundations of Science, op. cit.,* 64-65, 79 and 240] which seem to conflict with his forthright statement here that once a definition of congruence has been chosen conventionally, the metric geometry is determined *empirically.*

[146]Cf. 73-74 of the first reference in the preceding footnote.

minate by virtue of the absence of coordinative definitions. It is because he is directing his critiquc against those who fail to grasp that the identification of the *equality* predicate "congruent" with its denotata is not a matter of factual truth but of coordinative definition that he asks in *Science and Hypothesis:* "how shall one know [without circularity] that any concrete magnitude which I have measured with my material instrument really represents the abstract distance?"[147] And his aim in giving a Euclidean interpretation to any seemingly non-Euclidean data obtained from stellar parallax measurements,[148] apparently was to show, just as Carnap endeavored to do by his example of treating the earth as a Euclidean plane, that we can always choose the resulting geometry to be Euclidean by first making a suitable adjustment in our coordinative definition of congruence. This adjustment consists in choosing a new definition of congruence whose associated geodesics will be Euclideanly related. And this new choice may effect a *renaming* of optical and other paths, thus issuing in a mere recasting of the same factual content in Euclidean language but *not* in a revision of the extra-linguistic content of optical and other physical laws. Reichenbach recently illustrated this general point by reference to Poincaré's particular astronomical example, showing clearly that it does *not* lend itself at all to the support of anti-empiricist, unqualified conventionalism (which he seems to attribute to Poincaré, however).[149] And he had shown earlier that Hugo Dingler's attempt to prove the inescapable Euclideanism of the physical world on the grounds that Euclidean geometry is presupposed in the very manufacture of our measuring instruments founders on the fact that Euclideanism

147Poincaré, *Foundations of Science,* op. cit., 82. Cf. also the paper cited in footnote 145, where he writes (p.77): "One would thus have to define distance by measurement" and (p. 78): "The geometric [abstract] distance is thus in need of being defined; and it can be defined only by means of measurement."

148Poincaré, *Found. of Science, op. cit.* 81. A much more lucid statement of the point which Poincaré endeavored to illustrate by reference to the interpretation of parallax measurements was given by him on p. 235 of the same work: cf. A. Grünbaum, "Conventionalism in Geometry," *op. cit.,* 211-212.

149Reichenbach, *The Rise of Scientific Philosophy* (Berkeley, 1951), 133-137; cf. also A. Grünbaum, "Conventionalism in Geometry," *op. cit.,* and "Geometry, Chronometry and Empiricism," *op. cit.,* Section 6 part (i). For a very useful discussion of the actual astronomical methods used to determine the geometry of physical space in the large, see H. P. Robertson, "Geometry as a Branch of Physics," in P. A. Schilpp (ed.), *Albert Einstein: Phil.-Scientist, op. cit.,* 323-325, 330-332 and Max Jammer's historical work *Concepts of Space* (Cambridge, Mass.), 1954, 147-148 as well as O. Struve, "The First Stellar Parallax Determination," in H. M. Evans (ed.), *Men and Moments in the History of Science* (Seattle, 1959), 177-206.

Contrary to the widespread belief that Gauss measured the triangle Brocken, Inselberg and Hohenhagen with a view to testing Euclidean geometry empirically, G. W. Dunnington adduces historical evidence [*Scripta Math.* XX (1954), 108-9] that this is a legend but that Gauss did envision such a test on the much larger scale of a stellar triangle.

holds infinitesimally anyway (Riemann), with the result that the Euclidean construction of our instruments does not preclude their disclosing non-Euclideanism in the large.[150]

Einstein[151] has impugned the qualified kind of empiricist conception of metric geometry espoused by Carnap and Reichenbach by offering a particular version of conventionalism which he attributes to Poincaré. The substance of Einstein's argument is the following:

Physical geometry is usually conceived as the system of metric relations exhibited by transported solid bodies *independently* of their particular chemical composition. On this conception, the criterion of congruence can be furnished by a transported solid body for the purpose of determining the geometry by measurement, only if the computational application of suitable "corrections" (or, ideally, appropriate shielding) has essentially eliminated inhomogeneous thermal, elastic, electric and other influences, which produce changes of *varying degree* ("distortions") in different kinds of materials. Einstein considers the case in which congruence has been defined by the diverse kinds of transported solid measuring rods *as corrected for their respective idiosyncratic distortions* with a view to *then* making an empirical determination of the prevailing geometry. His thesis is that the very logic of computing these corrections precludes that the geometry itself still be open to experimental ascertainment in this sense, since the rigid body is not even defined without *first decreeing* the validity of Euclidean geometry: *before* the *corrected* rod can be used to make an empirical determination of the *de facto* geometry, the required corrections must be computed via laws, such as those of elasticity, which involve *Euclideanly-calculated* areas and volumes. Yet the warrant for thus introducing Euclidean geometry *at this stage* cannot be empirical.

Since I can refer to a detailed empiricist rebuttal of this argument which I have given elsewhere,[152] it will suffice here to provide a documentary reason for questioning Einstein's claim that Poincaré was an exponent of this particular form of conventionalism. In speaking of the variations which solids exhibit under distorting influences, Poincaré says[153]: "we neglect these variations in laying the foundations of geome-

[150]Reichenbach, *Physik. Zeitschr.* XXII (1921), 379; *Erkenntnis* IV (1934), 77, and The Preface of H. Dingler's *Die Grundlagen der Geometrie* (Stuttgart, 1933), Cf. also P. Frank, *Das Kausalgesetz und seine Grenzen* (Vienna, 1932), 25, O. Hölder, *op. cit.*, 399.
Recently, Dingler has advanced slightly modified arguments for the alleged inevitability of Euclideanism [cf. "Was ist Konventionalismus?" *Proc. 11th Intern. Congr. Phil.* V, 199 (1953)]. But these arguments are vulnerable to essentially the same telling objections as his earlier contentions of a few decades ago.

[151]A. Einstein, "Reply to Criticisms," in *Albert Einstein: Philosopher-Scientist, op. cit.*, 676-678.

[152]See A. Grünbaum, "Geometry, Chronometry and Empiricism" *op. cit.*, §7, part (ii).

[153]Poincaré, *Foundations of Science, op. cit.*, 76.

try, because, besides their being very slight, they are irregular and consequently seem to us accidental."

Poincaré's account of the status of the tridimensionality of space is—again contrary to a widely-held interpretation—*not* incompatible with the empirico-realistic conception of that attribute of the physical world set forth above. In his rejoinder to Russell, we find him saying without elaboration: "I consider the axiom of three dimensions as conventional in the same way as those of Euclid."[154] But in his posthumous book,[155] he tells us that since his earlier treatment of this axiom was "very compressed", he now wishes to clarify it. Then, after explaining that in classifying the elements of a manifold as the same in some respect, we use the "basic convention" of abstracting from other qualitative differences among them, he notes that the three-dimensionality of the perceptual localizations of physical events is obtained upon abstracting from a variety of qualitative *non*-positional differences between them. This sense of "convention", however, hardly renders three-dimensionality non-objective any more than the reference to *kinds* of events makes particular causal statements true by convention. That Poincaré was entirely clear on this is apparent from the following assertion by him:

> We see on the basis of this brief explanation what experimental facts lead us to ascribe three dimensions to space. As a consequence of these facts, it would be more convenient for us to attribute three dimensions to it than four or two; but the term "convenient" is perhaps not strong enough; a being which had attributed two or four dimensions to space would be handicapped in a world like ours in the struggle for existence.[156]

After exhibiting how that handicap would arise from an interpretation of space as 2- or 4-dimensional, he shows on the basis of group-theoretical arguments[157] that in the context of causality, physical facts lead to the tri-dimensionality of physical space just as the structure of perceptual data had. And he concludes by saying that since we have the capacity to construct mathematically a continuum of an arbitrary number of dimensions, "this capacity would . . . permit us to construct a space of four dimensions just as well as one of [only] three dimensions. *It is the external world, experience,* which determines our developing ideas more in one of these directions than in the other."[158]

The success of empiricism in accounting for our knowledge of the tridimensionality of the physical world is intimately connected with its ability to refute Kant's claim that the existence of such *similar* but *in-*

[154] Poincaré, "Sur les Principes de la Géométrie," *op. cit.,* 73.

[155] *Letzte Gedanken, op. cit.,* 59.

[156] *Ibid.,* 86.

[157] *Ibid.,* ch. 3, §5, 87-94.

[158] *Ibid.,* 99, my italics. Cf. also O. Hölder, *op. cit.,* 393.

congruent counterparts as the left and right hands constitutes evidence for his transcendental a priori of space.[159] Since the reasons for the untenability of *this particular* Kantian contention are not given even in Reichenbach's definitive empiricist critique of the transcendental idealist theory of space and are not sufficiently known to the philosophical public, a brief statement of them may be useful.

If we take two arbitrarily (irregularly) shaped objects in a plane, which are metrically symmetric or "reflected" about a straight line in that plane, it will be seen that so long as we confine these two objects to that plane, they cannot be brought into congruence such that the points of one coincide with their respective image points in the other. But such congruence *can* be achieved, if we are allowed to rotate one of these reflected 2-dimensional objects about the axis of symmetry, thereby making use of the next higher (third) dimension. G. Lechalas credits Delboeuf with discovering that, in general, given two (n-1)-dimensional objects, metrically symmetric about some (n-2)-dimensional object, then to achieve congruence such that the points of the one coincide with their respective image points in the other, a continuous rotation in n-dimensional space is necessary.[160] Accordingly, the three-dimensional right-hand cannot be brought into this sort of congruence with the three-dimensional left-hand by a continuous rigid motion because of the *empirical* fact that the 4-dimensional space needed for the required kind of rotation is physically unavailable! This same fact enables us to infer the *three*-dimensionality as opposed to the two-dimensionality of optically active molecules from their dextro-rotary or levo-rotary behavior. For if they were only two-dimensional, then it would be possible to convert a dextro-rotary molecule into a levo-rotary one by merely flipping it over. But this cannot be done.[161]

Contrary to Kant, the specific structural difference between the right and left hands can be given a conceptual rather than *only* a denotatively-intuitive characterization as follows:[162] the group of Euclidean rigid motions is only a *proper* sub-group of the group of length-preserving ("non-enlarging") similarity mappings. For the determinant of the coeffi-

159Kant, *Werke,* ed. E. Cassirer (Berlin, 1912), II, 393-400 and IV, §13, 34-36.

160G. Lechalas, "L'Axiome de libre Mobilité," *Rev. de Mét. et de Mor.* VI (1898), 754. This property of reflections had already been pointed out by Möbius in his *Der Barycentrische Calcul* (Leipzig, 1827), 184.

The requirement of rotation through a hyper-space given here holds for spaces whose topology is Euclidean or spherical but does *not* hold unrestrictedly. Thus, it fails to hold for a surface such as the Möbius strip or for a one-dimensional space whose topology is that of the numeral 8.

161Cf. John Read, *A Direct Entry to Organic Chemistry* (London, 1948), ch. vii.

162Cf. F. Klein, *Elementary Mathematics from an Advanced Standpoint,* II (New York, 1939), 39-42; H. Weyl, *Phil. of Math. and Nat. Science, op. cit.,* 79-85. For a more elementary account, see O. Hölder, *op. cit.,* 387-9.

cients of the particular linear transformations constituting the latter type of similarity mappings must have *either* the value +1 or the value —1. But only those similarity transformations whose determinant ("Jacobian") is +1 form the group of Euclidean rigid motions, the remainder being the *reflections* whose Jacobian is —1 and which include the case of Kant's left and right hands.

Now the definition of a determinant is based on the distinction between even and odd permutations. And Weyl sees the combinatorial root of the distinction between left and right in the fact that the arrangement of the axes in a left-handed set of axes is obtained from the corresponding right-handed set by an *odd* permutation, whereas a set of axes (linearly independent vectors) fix the *same* 'sense', if they arise from each other by an even permutation.

What then is the relation, if any, between the Möbius-Delboeuf *dimensional* account of the source of the incongruence of the left and right hands, on the one hand, and Weyl's combinatorial account on the other? The answer is that since the behavior of the Jacobian is decisive both for the topological invariance of dimensionality and for the preservation of "sense", the Möbius-Delboeuf and Weyl explanations have a common basis. And just as the tridimensionality (rather than four-dimensionality) of space, which is invoked by Möbius and Delboeuf, is a matter of *empirical* fact, so also is the existence of pairs of physical objects in our physical 3-space which realize a formal transformation whose Jacobian is —1.[163]

[163]Since the tridimensionality of physical space has turned out to be a logically contingent empirical fact, one naturally wonders whether it is an autonomous, irreducible empirical fact or not. Huyghens' principle in optics tells us that if a single spherical light wave is produced by a disturbance at a point which lasts for a very short time between $t = t_0 - \varepsilon$ and $t = t_0$, then the effect at a point P at a distance cT (where c = the velocity of light) is null until the instant $t = t_0 - \varepsilon + T$ *and* is null again *after* the instant $t = t_0 + T$. And thus, according to Huyghens' principle, a single spherical wave would leave no residual after-effect at a point P. Now, J. Hadamard has shown [*Lectures on Cauchy's Problem in Linear Partial Differential Equations* (New Haven, 1923), 53-4, 175-177, and 235-236] that this requirement of Huyghens' principle is satisfied only by wave equations having an *even* number of independent variables. Since the time variable in conjunction with the space variables constitute the independent variables of these equations, Hadamard's result shows that Huyghens' principle holds only for cases in which the number of *space* dimensions is *odd,* as in the case of the 3-dimensional physical space of our world. [For an explanation of this result by reference to the special cases of 3 and 2 dimensions, cf. B. Baker and E. T. Copson, *The Mathematical Theory of Huyghens' Principle* (Oxford, 1939), 46-47]. Sharing the view of Aristotle and Galileo that the tridimensionality of physical space might be explainable as a consequence of other, more comprehensive empirical principles, H. Weyl suggests [*Phil. of Math. and Nat. Science, op. cit.,* 136] that the difference between spaces of even and odd numbers of dimensions in regard to the transmission of waves may be one clue to the required explanation. Cf. also P. Ehrenfest "Welche Rolle spielt die Dreidimensionalität des Raumes in den Grundgesetzen der Physik," *Annalen der Physik* LXI (1920), 440-446.

Finally, we turn to the third of the major rivals of our geometric empiricism: B. Russell's early views on geometry.

(iii) Half a century has elapsed since the publication of Russell's *Foundations of Geometry,* and the work has become dated mathematically and philosophically, notably because of the development of topology, beginning with the decade following its appearance.[164] In particular, the existence in the literature of Poincaré's definitive critique of Russell's book—a critique which is offered, I have argued, from the standpoint of empiricism—makes it possible to confine myself to two issues then raised by Russell which still invite comment.[165]

Under the influence of Riemann, Poincaré and Einstein, contemporary philosophy of geometry has evolved the conception that the length of a body is *not* a measure of any intrinsic amount of space between its end points or a relation between these by themselves, but rather an attribute involving the *relation* between *two* pairs of points: the body, on the one hand, and the stipulated standard of congruence on the other. This thesis goes beyond the undisputed, obvious one that the length of a body is arbitrary to within a constant factor depending on the choice of unit: it affirms that it is a matter of convention whether the transported rod used to effect length measurements is assigned the *same* length in different positions of space or not. When this conception of length is challenged by more traditionally-oriented thinkers, philosophers of science who are under the influence of operationism justify it on the grounds that all length *determinations* involve a comparison in the form of the (iterative) transport and application of the unit rod to the body whose length is desired and that there is nothing in the operations of transport and iterative application to require that the transported rod furnishing the standard of comparison be assigned the same length in different positions in space. But critics like Russell are not persuaded by this at all, since they maintain that it is absurd to suppose that our operations in determining or discovering the properties of things first confer these properties on them. Says he:

> It remains to be known what it is that one measures. . . . For if it is distances

[164] For a survey of some of these developments, see T.Y. Thomas, "Recent Trends in Geometry," in *Am. Math. Soc. Semicent. Publ.* II, Addresses (New York, 1938), 98-135; also, L. M. Blumenthal, *Theory and Applications of Distance Geometry* (Oxford, 1953).

[165] Russell deals with the question of how spatial extension can be held to be resolvable into points devoid of extension *(The Found. of Geometry, op. cit.,* §§196, 194, 129, 207). I can omit consideration of this problem here, since I have shown elsewhere [*Phil. of Science* XIX, 288 (1952)] how contemporary Cantorean mathematics makes it possible to uphold this conception of space successfully. If it should turn out that it is possible to construct a viable intuitionistic measure theory in which the measure of a denumerable point set need *not* be zero, then the Cantorean basis of my argument there will cease to be indispensable to its success.

that one has to measure, then these must exist prior to measurement. . . . It seems to be believed that since measurement is necessary to *discover* equality or inequality, these cannot exist without measurement. Now the proper conclusion is exactly the opposite. Whatever one can discover by means of an operation must exist independently of that operation: America existed before Christopher Columbus, and two quantities of the same kind must *be* equal or unequal before being measured. Any method of measurement is good or bad according as it yields a result which is true or false. Mr. Poincaré, on the other hand, holds that measurement *creates* equality and inequality. It follows [then] . . . that there is nothing left to measure and that equality and inequality are terms devoid of meaning.[166]

In the face of this reply, a person defending the relational theory of length *on the basis of operationism*—which, as we shall see presently, is not at all the *sole* basis on which it can be defended—is led by that very theory of meaning to fail to elucidate the crucial difference between the logical status of length and of the non-metrical properties of the Western Hemisphere ascertained by Columbus. The result is then that the critic holding Russell's view remains convinced—quite mistakenly, to be sure, but entirely understandably—that the relational theory of length rests on a subjectivism and homocentrism which is at best gratuitous if not palpably absurd and that he must therefore reject that conception of length.

The key to the defense of the relational theory of length must be sought, in the first instance, *not* in how we measure it, as the operationists would have it, but in the *failure* of the *continuum* of physical space to possess an intrinsic metric, a failure which is quite independent of our measuring procedures. For if we ask in virtue of what *intrinsic* attribute of the space between the end-points of a body AB or of what relation between these two points, taken by themselves, a certain amount of space can be said to lie between them, the continuity of physical space provides a *sufficient* condition for there not being any such attribute or relation. We know from Cantor that there are just as many points between the end-points A and B of a short segment AB as between the termini of a long segment CD which is located elsewhere. Hence the cardinality of intervals does not provide any basis for an intrinsic metric. Neither do any of the other topological properties of the respective spaces between the pairs of points AB and CD endow each of them with a distinctive metrical characteristic which is different in these two cases. That is what Riemann had in mind when he declared that "in the case of a discrete manifold the criterion of length is already contained in the concept of this manifold but in a continuous manifold, it must be brought in from

166 Russell, "Sur les Axiomes de la Géométrie," *op. cit.*, 687-8; cf. also, P. Weiss, "The Contemporary World," *The Review of Metaphysics* VI, 525 (1953).

elsewhere."[167] Thus it is the contingent fact, if indeed it is a fact, that physical space is continuous rather than discrete,[168] which makes reference to an external standard of congruence *constitutive* of the length of a body AB and renders length a *relational* property involving AB, on the one hand, and that external standard on the other. To be sure, inasmuch as the relation of congruence is reflexive, symmetrical and transitive in the set of all line segments, we can use a Peanoean "definition by abstraction"[169] to say that the entities sustaining such a relation have the same property of length. But the possibility of ascribing length individually in this manner does *not* provide a basis for impugning the relational conception of length. For it would still not be meaningful to speak of the length of a *single* solid object as an intrinsic factual property, if the latter were the only solid object in a world of gases and liquids. Two solids do not sustain the relation of having the same length because each of them, taken individually, has a certain length *ab initio.* Instead, the possession of length by either of them, taken individually, derives from a definition by abstraction. And the starting point of such a definition is the reflexive, symmetrical and transitive two-termed relation of congruence. It is the bodies or segments themselves, but not their individual lengths, which exist individually prior to any metrical relations which these segments sustain to one another. Their *lengths,* however, are inevitably ratios by being only the measures of their relations to one another.

If, on the other hand, space were discrete in some specified sense, then the "distance" between two elements could be defined *intrinsically* in a rather natural way by the *cardinality* of the least number of intervening elements. And in that case the logic of the discovery of length would be analogous to that of Columbus' discovery of America in Russell's example. For, on that assumption, a *separate* theoretical determination of the number of chunks or space-atoms contained in *each* of two bodies would yield the intrinsic amount of space in each of them before any comparison of them would need to be effected. Russell overlooked that

167B. Riemann, "Über die Hypothesen welche der Geometrie zu Grunde liegen," in *Gesammelte mathematische Werke,* ed. Dedekind and Weber (Leipzig, 1876), 268. For the qualification that must be introduced in Riemann's statement as it stands in order to assure its truth, see the criticisms given by B. Russell in *Foundations of Geometry, op. cit.,* 66-67 and A. Grünbaum in "Geometry, Chronometry and Empiricism," *op. cit.,* Section 2, part (iii).

168For the serious difficulties besetting the mathematical atomism of a theory of genuine space quantization, see H. Weyl, *Phil. of Math. and Nat. Science, op. cit.,* 43 and A. d'Abro, *The Evolution of Scientific Thought From Newton to Einstein* (New York), 1950, 40n.

169Cf. G. Peano, *Notations de Logique Mathématique* (Turin, 1894), 45; A. Tarski, *Introduction to Logic* (2nd ed., New York, 1946), 95, and R. Carnap, *Symbolische Logik, op. cit.,* 119.

in our actual *continuous* space, the congruence of two line segments cannot derive from their respective possession of an intrinsic metric attribute and that their congruence depends for its very obtaining and not merely for its human ascertainment on a relation to an *extrinsic* standard whose "rigidity" under transport is *decreed* conventionally. Accordingly, what makes the property of length in our actual continuous space different from those discovered by Columbus in Russell's example is *not* first generated by the difference in the respective operational procedures used by us in their discovery. Instead, it is the pre-existing difference in the properties to be discovered that determines and regulates the operational procedures appropriate to their discovery: simple properties in the one case, and relational attributes in the other. And it is because the continuity of physical space makes length a *relational* property of bodies that nothing is asserted by saying that everything in the universe expanded in the same ratio overnight. The failure of *our* measuring operations to disclose such an "expansion" is a consequence of its non-existence and is evidence for the latter but is not constitutive of its not obtaining. As Reichenbach has noted:[170] "The objective character of the physical assertion [concerning the geometry of physical space] is thus put into a relational assertion. . . . It is an assertion about a relation between the universe and rigid measuring rods." Operations are indispensable for *knowing* or discovering the properties of independently existing things, be they their simple properties or relational properties of them. But we do not confer either of these properties on things by our operations, since they have them independently of our presence in the cosmos.

I hope that I have shown, therefore, that the endorsement of the relational theory of length does *not* entail either operationism or phenomenalistic positivism. Proponents of these two philosophical movements are grievously mistaken when they claim that a rejection of their theory of meaning and of their ontology is tantamount to a repudiation of the profound mathematical and physical discoveries of Riemann, Poincaré and Einstein. In fact, I believe that it is now clear that if such positivists are to attempt to establish their case, they must adduce epistemological considerations independent of the particular mathematical and physical discoveries of modern science and thus deriving no support from these discoveries. The required epistemological considerations are the same, it seems to me, as have been advanced unsuccessfully throughout the history of traditional philosophy.

In concluding, I should like to cite a poignant counter-example to Russell's contention that the axiom of free mobility is a synthetic a priori

170*Phil. d. Raum-Zeit-Lehre, op. cit.*, 50 or PST, 37; I have omitted the italics of the original.

truth. Poincaré asks[171] on what grounds Russell supposes that in a space of three dimensions, there must necessarily be six degrees of freedom, i.e., three of translation and three of rotation, and that, in general, the number of degrees of freedom in n-space must be $\frac{n(n+1)}{2}$. Is it not conceivable that there be a three-dimensional space with only three degrees of freedom and in which measurement and thus metric geometry of a kind is still possible? Indeed it is. For, suppose that any figure can be transported such that one of its points coincides with an arbitrary point in space but that, once that coincidence is effected, the figure cannot rotate, thus having only *three* degrees of freedom while being a three-dimensional object. Poincaré asserts that, in that case, lengths, surfaces and angles will generally *not* be comparable but "the measurement of volumes will still be possible".[172] Although Poincaré does not at all explain further what he has in mind here, it seems that he is thinking of affine geometry. In that geometry, only *parallel* line segments can be measured against one another, but a socalled "unimodular affine transformation" is *volume-preserving*.[173] It is therefore a contingent empirical fact that our familiar solids realize the group of Euclidean rigid transformations instead of the unimodular affine geometry. And it is purely tautological to say that the axiom of free mobility in Russell's sense is an a priori condition of all metric experience of exteriority. For Russell is merely reserving the term "metric experience" for cases in which free mobility in his sense obtains and denying that label to the case of affine geometry in which it does *not* hold.

ADOLF GRÜNBAUM

DEPARTMENT OF PHILOSOPHY
UNIVERSITY OF PITTSBURGH

171Poincaré, "Les Fondements de la Géométrie," *op. cit.*, 259.

172*Ibid.*, 260.

173Cf. Birkhoff and MacLane, *A Survey of Modern Algebra* (2nd. ed., New York, 1953), 310, and F. Klein, *op. cit.*, 73.

21

Carl G. Hempel

IMPLICATIONS OF CARNAP'S WORK FOR THE PHILOSOPHY OF SCIENCE

I. *Reduction Vs. Definition*

IN the present essay, I intend to discuss some of Carnap's contributions to the philosophy of science, with special emphasis upon his inquiries into the status and function of scientific concepts and theories.

Carnap's theory of reduction sentences[1] offers a convenient access to our topic. That theory, it will be recalled, rejects the earlier view of the Vienna Circle, previously held also by Carnap himself,[2] that all extra-logical terms in the language of empirical science are capable of explicit definition on the basis of observation terms referring to directly observable aspects either of immediate phenomenal experience or of physical objects or events. This idea is replaced by the conception that, in general, the meaning of a scientific term permits of only partial specification by reference to observables; or, more precisely, that scientific terms have to be thought of as introducible, on the basis of an observational vocabulary that is antecedently understood, not by means of explicit definitions alone, but rather by a more general method called reduction. Just as definition is effected by means of definition sentences so reduction is achieved by sentences of a special kind, called reduction sentences; these have to meet certain formal and material requirements specified in Carnap's theory. For later reference, I give here a brief summary of those requirements.

The standard instrument of reduction is the reduction pair. A reduction pair introducing a one-place predicate '*Q*' consists of two sentences of the form

(1.1)
$$P_1x \supset (P_2x \supset Qx)$$
$$P_3x \supset (P_4x \supset -Qx)$$

If '*Q*' is to be introduced on the basis of a given vocabulary *V*, then the

[1]This theory is developed in detail in TM; its central idea is outlined already in ES, and a brief elementary survey is included in LFUS.

Abbreviated titles used throughout the footnotes refer to the bibliography at the end of this essay.

[2]Especially in *Aufbau;* cf. Carnap's own reference to this fact in TM, §15.

predicates other than 'Q' which appear in these sentences must either belong to V or must have been previously introduced by other reduction sentences which ultimately use only the vocabulary V. The appropriately ordered set of those reduction sentences is then said to form an introductive chain based on V.

In the special case where 'P_3' is equivalent with 'P_1' and 'P_4' with '$-P_2$', the reduction pair (1.1) may be cast into the form of a so-called bilateral reduction sentence:

(1.2) $$P_1x \supset (Qx \equiv P_2x)$$

and in the even more special case where 'P_1x' is universally satisfied, (1.2) may be replaced by an explicit definition sentence:

(1.3) $$Qx \equiv P_2x$$

A fundamental difference between definition and reduction is this: A definition sentence for 'Q' provides a condition, in terms of the given vocabulary, which is both necessary and sufficient for Q and thus makes it possible to eliminate 'Q' from any sentence in favor of its definiens. A reduction pair or a bilateral reduction sentence provides a sufficient condition and a necessary condition for Q; but the two do not coincide; thus the meaning of 'Q' is specified only incompletely, and the specifying sentences do not permit the elimination of 'Q' from all contexts in which it may occur.

The reduction pair (1.1) for example, provides the following conditions for Q:

(1.4) $$(P_1x \cdot P_2x) \supset Qx$$
$$Qx \supset -(P_3x \cdot P_4x)$$

These sentences specify only that the extension of 'Q' must fall between those of '$P_1 \cdot P_2$' and '$-(P_3 \cdot P_4)$' in the sense of including the former and being included in the latter; and unless those two extensions coincide, this determines the range of application of 'Q' only in part. In other words, (1.4) directs us to apply 'Q' to all instances of '$P_1 \cdot P_2$' and '$-Q$' to all instances of '$P_3 \cdot P_4$'; for all other cases, the question whether 'Q' or its negate applies is left open.

Suppose now that by virtue of some laws of nature, no object can be an instance of either of the two expressions just stated; in other words, suppose that

(1.5) $$(x)-((P_1x \cdot P_2x) \vee (P_3x \cdot P_4x))$$

holds by virtue of laws of nature. Then the criteria provided by (1.1) for the attribution of 'Q' can never be applied, and not even a partial specification of the meaning of 'Q' has been effected. Now, this possibility cannot be avoided altogether, simply because we do not know all the laws of nature. But surely it would be unreasonable to accept (1.1) as a reduction pair for 'Q' if (1.5) is a consequence of the scientific theory into which

'*Q*' is to be introduced. Carnap therefore lays down a restrictive condition which may be stated as follows:

(C) The sentences (1.1) form a reduction pair only if (1.5) is not valid,[3] i.e., is not true solely by virtue of the L-rules and P-rules governing the language in which (1.1) is formulated.

By L-rules, Carnap here understands the purely logical rules of inference; by P-rules, any additional rules that may be established by adopting certain physical statements, especially statements presumed to express universal laws, as primitive sentences of the language.[4] At the time when he set forth these ideas, Carnap considered it as a mere question of expedience which, if any, empirical statements should be given this privileged status;[5] but as the preceding argument shows, restriction (C) will serve its purpose only if it implies the following condition:

(C′) The sentences (1.1) form a reduction pair only if it is not the case that (1.5) holds by virtue of the statements which the theory at hand asserts as laws, irrespective of whether they have the status of P-rules.

One more point remains to be noted. The pair (1.4), and consequently also (1.1), evidently implies the sentence

(1.6) $(x)\,(P_1x \cdot P_2x \supset -(P_3x \cdot P_4x))$, or, equivalently, $(x)-(P_1x \cdot P_2x \cdot P_3x \cdot P_4x)$

Carnap calls this the representative sentence of the reduction pair (1.1); it "represents, so to speak, the factual content" of the latter.[6]

The method of reduction outlined in this section can readily be extended to the cases where the term to be introduced is a predicate with more than one argument or a functor representing a quantitative characteristic, such as length.

II. *Reduction and the Problem of Nomological Statements*

Carnap's thesis that not all scientific terms are definable by means of observational predicates was based on his well-known analysis of disposition terms. Thus, he argued that the predicate 'soluble in water' cannot be introduced by what might appear to be the obvious definition, namely,

(2.1) $Sx \equiv (t)\,(Wxt \supset Dxt)$

where '*Sx*' stands for '*x* is soluble in water', '*Wxt*' for '*x* is put in water

[3] TM, 442.

[4] TM, 432 and LSL, sec. 51.

[5] LSL, 180.

[6] TM, 451; see also *ibid.*, 444. It would seem, incidentally, that the following further requirement should be laid down for reduction sentences: An introductive chain is permissible only if its representative sentence is compatible with the theory into which it is to introduce a new term. Otherwise, the introduction of a new term might make a theory inconsistent.

at time t', and 'Dxt' for 'x dissolves at t'; for on this definition, any object that is never placed in water would have to be pronounced soluble; clearly, this is one aspect of the "paradoxes" of material implication. The difficulty is avoided if 'S' is introduced by a bilateral reduction sentence:[7]

(2.2) $$(x)\,(t)\,(Wxt \supset (Sx \equiv Dxt))$$

Now, underlying the attempt to define 'S' by (2.1) is the idea that to attribute solubility, or any other disposition, to a given object is to assert that under specifiable conditions, the object will, as a matter of general law, respond in a certain characteristic manner. The attribution of dispositions is thus intimately bound up with the assertion of laws, as has been made increasingly clear by recent studies, especially those dealing with counterfactual conditionals. An explicit definition of 'S' could be given if, in stating the intent of (2.1), we had some satisfactory way of specifying that 'S' is to apply to just those cases x for which the definiens in (2.1) is not simply true, but true by virtue of general laws. The "paradox" just mentioned would then be avoided because the mere information that a given object, say c, is at no time put in water would suffice to establish

$$(t)\,(Wct \supset Dct)$$

as an empirical truth only, but not as true by virtue of general laws. The use of causal modalities[8] has been contemplated for the assertion of truth by virtue of general law; but no matter what symbolic techniques might be used for the purpose, they will be satisfactory only if it is possible to clarify the meaning of the locution "such and such is the case by virtue of general laws". To attain such clarification, it will be necessary to explicate the concept of general law or the concept of lawlike, or nomological, sentence, i.e., of a sentence which has the character of a general law except for possibly being false. So far, these concepts have proved highly resistant to analytic efforts.[9] And even if this problem is solved, there remains the further task of explicating the phrase "by virtue of general laws"; and this presents considerable further difficulties because the phrase refers not only to some suitable set of laws, but tacitly also to a set of initial and boundary conditions which, together with the laws, imply the statement said to be true by virtue of general laws.

At first glance, Carnap's method of using reduction sentences instead of definitions seems to avoid all these obstacles. Actually, however, I think that method, too, involves reference to the nomological concepts just con-

[7] TM, 440-441.

[8] See, for example, Burks, CP.

[9] On this problem, see Braithwaite SE, ch. 9; Goodman, Cf; Hempel and Oppenheim LE, Part III; Reichenbach, NS. A promising novel approach to the problem of nomologicals is propounded in Goodman's FFF.

sidered. For, first of all, as was argued above, Carnap's requirement (C) must be construed so as to imply condition (C′), which clearly makes use of those concepts; and, in addition, Carnap would no doubt agree that a reduction pair can be admissible only if its representative sentence has the character of a statement that holds by virtue of general laws; it would be this lawlike character of its "factual content" that would justify the acceptance of the reduction pair.

For these reasons I think that the method of reduction neither resolves nor avoids the basic problem which gives rise to the difficulty pointed out by Carnap in regard to the definition of disposition terms; for that basic problem concerns the explication of the concepts of nomological statement and of truth by virtue of general laws.

III. *Reduction Vs. Operational Definition*

The great significance of Carnap's theory of reduction seems to me to lie in the fact that it initiated, and developed in considerable logical detail, a decisive departure from the earlier logical positivist insistence on the full verifiability or falsifiability of every "cognitively significant" empirical statement by some suitable finite set of observation statements, and on the full definability of all scientific terms by means of an observational vocabulary.

That the definability requirement may be too restrictive is suggested not only by the difficulties encountered in an attempt to define disposition terms: Even if we had a satisfactory way of dealing with nomologicals—a proviso which will no longer be mentioned from here on—there would be other considerations indicating that most scientific terms should be construed as only partly defined by means of observables.

First of all, as has often been stressed in the operationist literature, an operational "definition" determines the meaning of a scientific term only with respect to the class of those cases to which the specified operational criteria are applicable; thus, e.g., the interpretation of length by reference to rigid measuring rods cannot be applied directly to microscopic or to interstellar distances. Carnap's reduction sentences offer a convenient schema for such partial operational specification of meaning.

Furthermore, for a given scientific term, there usually are available a variety of alternative "operational" criteria of application, and advances in scientific research tend to add to their number. This consideration suggests that the various criteria available for a term may be combined into one introductive chain, and that, as a rule, such a chain, however rich, will still leave room for additional partial interpretations of the term at hand. Scientific terms exhibit, in this sense, an openness of content, which is well represented if their introduction is construed as being effected by chains of reduction sentences.

Thus, Carnap's theory of reduction takes into account, and affords a logical analysis of, certain aspects of scientific concept formation which have been thrown into relief also by operationism. In doing so, it yields an explication and generalization of the suggestive but extremely vague operationist conception of definition in terms of "symbolic" and "instrumental" operations. This is achieved by Carnap's precise characterization of the sentence chains effecting the introduction of scientific terms. Reference to "mental", "paper-and-pencil", and other "symbolic" operations is here replaced by specification of the logical form of reduction sentences, and of the logical and mathematical principles governing their use. And the demand that operational definition must ultimately refer to "instrumental" operations is restated in a more general manner which avoids the suggestion that operational criteria must make reference to physical manipulation. This is done by specifying that the basic vocabulary to which scientific terms are reduced consists of observational predicates, which can be applied on the basis of direct observation, and with good intersubjective agreement, by different observers.

In one respect, however, this explication of operationist ideas deviates essentially from the conceptions advanced by P. W. Bridgman, the originator of the idea of operational analysis. Bridgman has repeatedly insisted that every scientific term should be introduced by one single operational criterion of application. Even when two different procedures (e.g., optical and tactual methods of measuring length) have been found to yield the same results, they should be regarded, according to Bridgman, as specifying different concepts (e.g., optical and tactual length); and these should be distinguished terminologically, for the presumption that both methods yield the same results is based inductively on past evidence, and it is "not safe" to forget that new, and perhaps more precise, experimental findings may prove it spurious.[10]

Now, acceptance of two different criteria of application for one term does indeed commit us to a universal generalization which later findings may induce us to abandon. In the case of a reduction pair, that generalization is given by its representative sentence. But the inductive risk incurred in accepting it does not constitute sufficient grounds to accept Bridgman's position. For even when a term is used on the basis of just one operational criterion, its application to any one particular case already amounts to asserting a generalization. Thus, e.g., one of the operational criteria of application for the phrase "piece of mineral *x* is harder than piece of mineral *y*" is given by the scratch test: A sharp point of *x* must scratch a surface of *y*, but not conversely. But this criterion has universal form: *Any* sharp point that exists or might be produced on *x*

[10]Cf. Bridgman, LMP, 6 and 23-24; OA, 121-22; PC, 255.

must scratch *any* flat surface that exists or might be produced on y. Therefore, to assert of just one particular piece of mineral that it is harder than a certain other piece of mineral is to assert a generalization and thus to incur an inductive risk. Hence, the standard invoked in Bridgman's argument would disqualify as "not safe" even the application, to just one single instance, of a concept introduced by just one single operational criterion of application.[11]

Thus, the promise of inductive safety which Bridgman's procedure holds out in return for an enormous proliferation of terms proves specious, and it appears to be both more economical and more in keeping with scientific procedure to allow a scientific term several criteria of application. This is precisely the conception systematically developed in Carnap's theory of reduction.

Accordingly, introductive chains fuse two functions of language which have often been considered totally distinct: the specification of meanings and the description of facts. And indeed, the introduction of fruitful new concepts in science is always intimately bound up with the establishment of new laws, as is shown quite clearly already in Carnap's early little work, *Physikalische Begriffsbildung,* which presents a lucid elementary analysis of the operational and the logical aspects of concept formation in physics.

IV. *Interpretative Systems*

But once we grant the conception of a partial experiential interpretation of scientific terms through a combination of stipulation and empirical law, it appears natural to remove the limitations imposed by Carnap upon the form of reduction sentences and introductive chains. Suppose, for example, that the predicate 'Q' has been introduced by the sentence (1.2), and that then, in view of supporting empirical evidence, the general sentence

$$(x)(Qx \supset P_3x)$$

is added to the theory at hand. This broadens the range of interpretation for 'Q'; for while (1.2) enables us to apply 'Q' or its negate only to objects which have the property P_1, the new sentence makes the negate of 'Q' applicable to any object with the characteristic '$-P_3$', no matter whether it also possesses P_1. Thus, though the new sentence does not have the form of a bilateral reduction sentence or of a reduction pair, it provides an additional criterion of application for 'Q'. And generally, addition of a new sentence to a given theory will usually affect the possibilities of (affirmative or negative) application of some of the theoretical terms.

[11] A fuller statement of the observations here outlined on operationism is given in Hempel, AO, secs. 1, 2, 3.

This reflection militates in favor of broadening the conception of introductive or interpretative sentences, and indeed, Carnap's own writings contain several specific suggestions to this effect. Already in *The Logical Syntax of Language,* Carnap mentions the possibility of introducing "a new descriptive symbol . . . as a primitive symbol by means of new P-primitive sentences,"[12] i.e. by the specification of extra-logical postulates involving the term in question. In a later study of the logic of physical theories, Carnap specifically describes an alternative to the introduction of "abstract", i.e., theoretical, terms on the basis of "elementary" or observational ones; namely, the formulation of a physical theory as an axiomatized system whose primitive terms are highly abstract, and in which less abstract terms, and finally elementary terms amounting to an observational vocabulary, are then introduced by explicit definition.[13] —And more recently, Kemeny and Carnap have proposed a method of partly determining the meaning of a set of terms by the specification of suitable "meaning postulates", which limit the range of the possible interpretations of the terms in question.[14]

The following, more general, conception of interpretation is constructed in such a way as to include all these procedures, as well as the use of introductive chains, as special cases.

(D 4.1) Within a specified framework, let T be a theory characterized by a set of postulates in terms of some finite set of primitives, V_T, which will be called the *theoretical vocabulary;* and let V_B be a second set of terms, to be called the *basic vocabulary,* which shares no term with V_T. A finite set J of sentences will then be said to constitute an *interpretative system* for T with the basis V_B if (a) J is logically compatible with T; (b) J contains no extra-logical term that is not an element of V_B or V_T; (c) J contains every element of V_B and V_T essentially, i.e., J is not logically equivalent to some set of sentences in which at least one term of V_B or of V_T does not occur at all.

For example, the logical framework might be that of the first-order functional calculus with identity; all the theoretical terms, predicates of various degrees; the basic terms, predicates which are antecedently understood, and which refer to directly observable physical properties and relations. This is, in fact, one of the principal cases with which Carnap's theory of reduction is concerned.

As a rule, an interpretative system will not be purely stipulative in character; it will usually imply sentences in terms of V_B alone which are not logical truths within the given frame. The representative sentences of introductive chains illustrate this possibility.

12 LSL, 319.
13 FLM, sec. 24.
14 Kemeny, Rev and EM; Carnap, MP.

In what sense, and to what extent, does an interpretative system specify an interpretation of T? We will consider first the interpretation of the *terms* in V_T and then that of the *sentences* expressible by means of them.

For a given theoretical term, an interpretative system J may establish a necessary and sufficient condition in terms of V_B. For a one-place theoretical predicate 'Q', for example, this is the case if J logically implies a sentence of the form

(4.2) $$(x)(Qx \equiv Kx)$$

where 'Kx' is short for a schema containing 'x' as the only free variable, and containing no extra-logical constants other than those in V_B. One might be inclined, in this case, to say that (4.2) provides a translation, or even a definition, of 'Q' in terms of V_B; but it should be borne in mind that for the same predicate 'Q', the system J may well provide several sentences of the form (4.2), with "translations" or "definientia" which are not logically equivalent, but only equivalent relative to J, in the sense that any one of them is deducible from any of the others conjoined with J.

But it may be the case that for a given theoretical term, J establishes only a necessary and a different sufficient condition in terms of V_B, or just one of these kinds of condition; and finally, for some or even all of the theoretical terms, J may establish neither a necessary nor a sufficient condition in terms of the basic vocabulary.

We now turn to the interpretation given by J to those sentences which are expressible in terms of V_T alone, no matter whether they belong to T or not; any such sentence will be called a V_T-sentence.

For a sentence S of this kind, J may yield an "equivalent" in terms of V_B; i.e., there may be a sentence S' in terms of V_B alone such that J logically implies the biconditional[15]

(4.3) $$S \equiv S'$$

This will be the case, for example, whenever J provides an "equiva lent", in the sense of (4.2), for each of the extra-logical terms in S.

A biconditional of type (4.3) might be viewed as affording a translation of S into the basic vocabulary; but again it must be remembered that in this sense, a V_T-sentence may have several translations which are not logically equivalent.

In some cases, J will provide, for a given V_T-sentence, a necessary condition and a different sufficient condition in terms of V_B, or just one of these, or neither a necessary nor a sufficient condition.

We must now consider certain objections which have been raised

[15]Here as well as in a few other places in this essay, connective signs are used autonymously.

against the introduction of theoretical terms by means of reduction sentences, and which can be extended to the more general conception of interpretation here suggested.

In reference to introductive chains, the criticism may be put as follows: Let '*Q*' be a predicate introduced solely by the bilateral reduction sentence (1.2), and let *c* be some particular object. Consider the expression '*Qc*'. If *c* happens not to have the property P_1 then *c* belongs to the class of objects within which no meaning has been assigned to '*Q*'. Hence '*Qc*' is not a meaningful sentence; nor, as a consequence, is its negation. Therefore, also '$Qc \vee -Qc$' is meaningless rather than a truth of logic, and in a similar way other principles of logic break down when applied to sentence-like expressions containing '*Qc*' as a constituent. If, on the other hand, *c* does have the property P_1, none of these dire consequences arise. But whether *c* does or does not have the property P_1 is a factual question; hence, the admission of predicates introduced by reduction sentences seems to make the significance of sentences and the applicability of the principles of logic contingent upon matters of empirical fact. Now, it is by no means impossible for a language to have this characteristic; in fact, it appears to be quite a normal aspect of everyday discourse, where significance often depends upon empirical aspects of the given context. Yet, in a formalized language for the use of science, this feature would be very awkward indeed.

This awkwardness can be avoided, however, by specifying, for the language system at hand, purely syntactical rules of sentence formation and logical inference. These rules may be chosen in the familiar manner so as to qualify both '*Qc*' and '$-Qc$' as well-formed formulas, or sentences, and to countenance the applicability of all the usual rules of inference to sentences containing them—irrespective of any semantical questions, such as whether '$P_1 c$' is true or not.

But can those sentences be considered not only as properly constructed formulas of what Carnap would call the calculus underlying the theory, but also as significant statements each of which is either true or false? If for a given V_T-sentence *S*, the interpretative system *J* yields no equivalent V_B-sentence, then we cannot state a truth criterion for *S* (i.e., a necessary and sufficient condition for the truth of *S*) in terms of that part of the scientific vocabulary which was assumed to be antecedently understood. But in that event, is it possible at all to understand the sentence *S* and significantly to assert or to deny it?

In considering the issue of the "significance" of partially interpreted theoretical sentences, we will have to distinguish three concepts of significance, which may be roughly characterized as (a) pragmatic intelligibility; (b) empirical significance in the vague sense of relevance to potential empirical evidence expressible by means of V_B; (c) semantical significance in the sense of being true or false. We will now briefly examine theoretical sentences in these three respects.

A scientist understands the language of the theories in his field even though he is not able to give, for each theoretical expression, an equivalent in, say, the "observational" terms used in laboratory reports. He knows how to use the terms and sentences of the theory and how to connect them with expressions in terms of the observational vocabulary. In a formal reconstruction, the proper "how to" is expressed by the rules governing the use of the various expressions. In the case of the expressions that can be formed by means of V_T, those rules include the rules of the logical framework within which T is formulated, and the inferences made possible by the interpretative system J. These rules, we noted earlier, will not in general provide every V_T-expression with an equivalent in terms of V_B, but they may convey upon a V_T-sentence S empirical significance in the sense of enabling S to establish deductive connections among certain V_B-sentences. And the establishment of such connections, which permit the prediction of new empirical phenomena on the basis of given ones, is one of the principal functions of scientific theories. As a brief reflection shows, S will have this characteristic just in case S in conjunction with J logically implies at least one V_B-sentence which is not implied by J alone. It would be quite ill-advised, however, to require of a scientific theory that every one of its sentences which is not a purely logical truth must individually possess empirical significance in this sense; what matters is the capacity of the whole theory to establish connections, by virtue of J, among the empirical V_B-sentences, and this capacity may be high even when many sentences of T lack individual empirical import.

To turn, finally, to the question of semantic significance: Let T be interpreted by a system J which does not furnish for every V_T-sentence an equivalent in terms of V_B. Then it is nevertheless quite possible to provide a necessary and sufficient condition of truth for every sentence expressible in terms of the theoretical vocabulary. All that is needed for the purpose is a suitable metalanguage. If we are willing to use a metalanguage which contains V_B, V_T, and J, or translations thereof, then indeed each V_T-sentence has a truth criterion in it, namely simply its restatement in, or its translation into, that metalanguage. Carnap has made essentially the same point in regard to the possibility of stating semantical rules of designation for the terms of a theory with only partial observational interpretation.[16] Incidentally, this observation bears upon a controversial issue in recent methodological discussion: It reveals as futile the attempt to base a distinction between genuine theoretical

[16]FLM, 62.

constructs and mere intervening or auxiliary terms on the idea that the former but not the latter have "factual reference", or designata in the semantical sense.[17]

Let us note here with Carnap[18] that the semantical criteria of truth and reference which can be given for the sentences and for the terms, or "constructs", of a partially interpreted theory offer little help towards an understanding of those expressions. For the criteria will be intelligible only to those who understand the metalanguage in which they are expressed; and the metalanguage must contain either the theoretical expressions themselves or their translations; hence, the latter must be antecedently understood if the semantical criteria are to be intelligible. Fortunately, however, a partially interpreted theory may be understood even when full semantical criteria of truth and reference are not available in a language which we previously understand. For if we know how to use the terms of V_B we may then come to understand the expressions in terms of V_T by grasping the rules which govern their use and which, in particular, establish connections between the "new" theoretical vocabulary and the "familiar" basic one.

V. *On the Avoidability of Theoretical Terms in Science*

If scientific theories establish predictive connections between the data of experience, and if it is only by reference to such data that their soundness can be appraised, why could not the formulation of theories be limited to the vocabulary which is used to state the pertinent empirical data? Might not the use of theoretical terms be entirely avoided without prejudice to the objectives of science?

The idea of avoidability here invoked requires clarification. We will distinguish three conceptions of avoidability which have received attention in recent methodological research. They are arranged in order of increasing inclusiveness: Whenever (a) applies then so does (b), and whenever (b) applies then so does (c), whereas the converses of these statements do not hold.

(a) *Definability*. The terms of a theory T might be said to be avoidable if they are all definable in terms of a specified observational vocabulary, V_B.

(b) *Translatability*. The terms of T might be said to be avoidable if every V_T-sentence is translatable into a V_B-sentence.

(c) *Functional replaceability*. The terms of T might be said to be

[17] For presentations and critical discussions of this idea, see, for example, MacCorquodale and Meehl, HC; Feigl, EH; and the discussion of the latter article, with reply by Feigl, in the symposium "Existential Hypotheses" in *Philosophy of Science*, XVII (1950), 164-195.

[18] FLM, 62.

avoidable if there exists another theory, T_B, couched in terms of V_B, which is "functionally equivalent" to T in the sense of establishing exactly the same deductive connections between V_B-sentences as does T.

The ideas of positivism and physicalism as dealt with in Carnap's writings are directly pertinent to the questions of definability and translatability. The earlier form of the positivistic thesis, espoused by Carnap in *Der logische Aufbau der Welt,* asserted that every extra-logical term of empirical science is definable by means of perception terms and that, as a consequence, every sentence in the language of science is translatable into a sentence in terms of perception predicates. When Carnap developed his theory of reduction, he replaced this conception by the weaker one that all scientific terms are reducible to perception terms; as a consequence, the translatability thesis was abandoned.[19] Concomitantly, Carnap propounded an analogous revision of the earlier version of the physicalistic thesis, which asserted the definability of all terms of empirical science by means of the observational and theoretical vocabulary of physics, and which implied a corresponding thesis of translatability. The revised version maintains instead that all extra-logical terms in the language of empirical science are reducible to the physical vocabulary, and thence in turn to those terms in the language of physics which stand for directly observable properties or relations of physical objects.[20]

But to what extent "definitions", "translations", and reductions of the kind here contemplated are possible can be ascertained, in general, only by means of empirical research and not by logical analysis alone. In the case of definability, for example, the question at stake is not whether all scientific terms are in fact introduced by explicit definition in terms of observables; patently, they are not. The question is rather whether suitable definitions could be constructed. And this is a matter of extending the system of accepted scientific statements in such a way that it will imply, for every theoretical term t, a universal statement analogous to (4.2) which provides a necessary and sufficient condition for t in terms of observables; for the extended system of accepted scientific statements could then be reformulated in such a way as to give to those statements the status of definitions for the theoretical terms. And whether or to what extent the requisite extension of current scientific knowledge can be achieved will have to be determined on the basis of empirical research. In regard to translatability, the empirical aspect of the problem is reflected in Carnap's own emphasis that a theoretical sentence and its "translation" need be only physically, rather than logically, "equipollent"; i.e., the two sentences may be mutually deducible,

[19]See, for example, ES, sec. 3; TM, sec. 15.

[20]For the narrower version, see PhSp; CPs; LSL, 320. For the revised form, see ES, sec. 3; TM, sec. 15; LFUS, Part IV; FLM, sec. 24.

not by virtue of the rules of logic alone, but relatively to a system of physical laws which serves as an additional premise for the deduction.[21] And, as was noted earlier, even the establishment of introductive chains presupposes the availability of supporting laws, namely of the corresponding representative sentences.

In sum, then, the questions with which the narrower and wider theses of positivism and physicalism are concerned are partly empirical in character, and they cannot, therefore, be answered with finality on purely analytic grounds.

In a somewhat more recent publication,[22] Carnap raises the issue of the avoidability of theoretical terms in a slightly different form. "Would be possible," he asks, "to formulate all laws of physics in elementary terms, admitting more abstract terms only as abbreviations?"[23] The first part of this question suggests the third of the conceptions of avoidability which were mentioned above. Carnap answers in the negative, and, interestingly, on empirical grounds: It turns out—and "this is an empirical fact, not a logical necessity"[24]—that the use of elementary, i.e., observational, terms does not lead to a powerful and efficacious system of laws; for virtually every law stated in a concrete vocabulary is found to have exceptions, whereas with the help of abstract terms, it has been possible to formulate increasingly comprehensive and exact laws.

However, as has been shown by Craig,[25] it can be proved on purely logical grounds alone that in a very comprehensive class of cases, theoretical terms are avoidable in sense (c). As far as it bears upon our problem, Craig's result may conveniently be stated with the help of some of the concepts introduced in the preceding section. For the purpose at hand, it will be useful to consider the postulates of a theory T together with the sentences of an associated interpretative system J as constituting the postulates for a system T', which we will call an interpreted theory; the union of V_T and V_B will be called V_T'.

Craig's result may now be formulated as follows: Suppose that within the logical framework of the first-order functional calculus with identity, a system T' has been formulated by an effective (constructive) specification of a finite or infinite set of postulates in terms of an effectively specified extra-logical vocabulary, V_T' which may contain a finite or an infinite number of individual constants and a finite or infinite number of predicate constants. Let V_T' be divided, by means of some effective, but other-

21See, f, ex., CPs, 43-46.

22FLM, sec. 24.

23*Loc. cit.*, 64.

24*Ibid.*

25See Th and RAE. A highly condensed and considerably generalized statement of the principal results of Th has been published by Craig in AS.

wise arbitrary, criterion, into two mutually exclusive subsets, V_T and V_B. Then there exists a general method (i.e., one applicable to *all* cases of the kind just characterized) of constructing a new system, T_B, whose postulates are expressed in terms of V_B alone, and whose theorems are exactly those theorems of T' which contain no extra-logical constants other than those contained in V_B.

As a consequence, the new system is functionally equivalent to T' in the sense specified earlier. For let some V_B-sentence, say S_1, imply another, S_2, by virtue of T', i.e., let T' together with S_1 logically imply S_2. Then T' implies the conditional $S_1 \supset S_2$, and since the latter is a V_B-sentence, it is implied also by T'_B, by virtue of the theorem just stated. Hence, T'_B together with S_1 logically implies S_2. Thus, T'_B establishes all those deductive connections between V_B-sentences that T' can establish. The converse follows similarly. Hence, T' and the "new" system are functionally equivalent.

Thus, Craig's result shows that no matter how we select from the total vocabulary V_T' of an interpreted theory T' a subset V_B of experiential or observational terms, the balance of V_T', constituting the "theoretical terms", can always be avoided in sense (c).

Craig has shown that this result can be extended to a great variety of logical frameworks, including functional calculi of higher order.[26]

There are at least two reasons, however, which would make it distinctly inadvisable for science to avail itself of this possibility of avoiding theoretical terms. One of these was provided by Craig himself: He showed (1) that the "new" theoretical system constructed by his method always has an infinite set of postulates, irrespective of whether the postulate set of the original theory is finite or infinite, and (2) that his result cannot be essentially improved in this respect, for there is no general method which will yield, for any given system T', and any choice of V_B, a corresponding T'_B with a finite postulate set whenever a functionally equivalent theory with a finite postulate set exists. This means that the scientist would be able to avoid theoretical terms only at the price of forsaking the comparative simplicity of a theoretical system with a finite postulational basis, and of giving up a system of theoretical concepts and hypotheses which are heuristically fruitful and suggestive—in return for a practically unmanageable system based upon an infinite, though effectively specified, set of postulates in observational terms. Needless to say that this price is too high for the scientist, no matter how welcome the possibility of such replacement may be to the epistemologist.

But I think there is yet another reason why science cannot dispense with theoretical terms in this fashion. Briefly, it is this: The application

[26] See AS.

of scientific theories in the predication and explanation of empirical findings involves not only deductive inference, i.e., the exploitation of whatever deductive connections the theory establishes among statements representing potential empirical data, but it also requires procedures of an inductive character, and some of these would become impossible if the theoretical terms were avoided. Under this broader conception of the function of a scientific theory, then, T'_B is *not* functionally equivalent to T'.

To amplify and illustrate: It is an oversimplification to conceive of scientific theories as establishing deductive connections between "observational sentences" if the latter are thought of as statements which describe potential results of direct observation, and which have the form of singular (i.e., non-quantified) sentences in terms of a basic observational vocabulary, V_B. To be sure, a hypothesis expressible in the simple form of a universal generalization in terms of observational predicates does establish deductive connections of that sort; for example, the hypothesis '$(x)(P_1x \supset P_2x)$', where 'P_1' and 'P_2' both belong to V_B, permits the deduction of the observational sentence 'P_2c' from the observational sentence 'P_1c'. But in general, the connections which theoretical principles establish among observational sentences are of a more complex kind. By way of a somewhat oversimplified illustration, consider the hypothesis

(5.1) The parts obtained by breaking a rod-shaped magnet in two are again magnets.

Let us assume that the predicate 'Magnet', being a disposition term, is not included in V_B, but is connected with certain V_B-terms by sentences which reflect its dispositional character. To avoid inessential complications, we will suppose that there is just one such sentence, to the effect that if an object x is a magnet (if Mx) then whenever a small piece y of iron filing is brought into contact with x (whenever Fxy) then y clings to x (then Cxy). In symbols:

(5.2) $$Mx \supset (y)(Fxy \supset Cxy)$$

Here, the relational predicates 'F' and 'C' will be assumed to belong to V_B.

Under these conditions, does the hypothesis (5.1) establish any logical connections among observational sentences? From the initial information:

(5.3) Objects b and c were obtained by breaking object a in two, and a was a magnet and rod-shaped

we are clearly able to deduce, with help of (5.1), such observational sentences as

(5.4) If d is a piece of iron filing that is brought into contact with b then d will cling to b.

However, the premise, (5.3), of this deduction is not a V_B-sentence since it contains the non-observational sentence 'a was a magnet', or 'Ma'. Nor is (5.3) deducible from other V_B-sentences, for (5.2) specifies only a necessary, but not a sufficient, condition for 'M' in terms of V_B. Thus, if the deduction of (5.4) from (5.3) is to be utilized in establishing logical connections strictly among observational sentences, then we must first perform an inductive step leading to (5.3) from a suitable set of observational sentences. The essentially inductive part of this procedure is the establishment of 'Ma', i.e., the acceptance of this sentence on the basis of some confirmatory set of observational sentences. For example, 'Ma' might be accepted if the given set of accepted observation statements includes or implies a considerable number of instances of the statement form '$Fay \supset Cay$', and none of the form '$Fay \cdot \sim Cay$'; for these lend inductive support to '$(y)(Fay \supset Cay)$', which, in turn, by virtue of (5.2), partially supports 'Ma'. Thus, the hypothesis (5.1) may be said to lead us, in virtue of (5.2), from certain observational sentences—the instances of '$Fay \supset Cay$'—to predictions of the type (5.4), which again are observational sentences; but the transition requires, apart from deduction, also certain inductive steps. But this deductive-inductive connection becomes unavailable if our "theory", which here consists of (5.1) and (5.2) only, is replaced by its functional equivalent in terms of V_B; for that equivalent, as can be seen without much difficulty, consists of analytic sentences only.

To restate the basic idea in more general terms: The sentences among which scientific theories establish purely deductive relationships normally have the status, not of singular, but of generalized sentences in terms of the observational vocabulary. Hence the transition, by means of the theory, from strictly observational to strictly observational sentences usually requires inductive steps, namely, the transition, from some set of observational sentences to some non-observational sentence which they support inductively, and which in turn can serve as a premise in the strictly deductive application of the given theory. And, as our example suggests, the inductive-deductive connections mediated by a theory T' may be lost when T' is abandoned in favor of T'_B: this point provides, I think, a further systematic argument in favor of the use of theoretical terms in empirical science.

VI. *The Experiential "Basis" of Science*

Observational sentences, which serve to state the empirical evidence by which scientific theories are tested, have sometimes been conceived as referring to the most immediate and entirely incontrovertible deliveries of our experience, and as being capable, in consequence of this character, of being either affirmed or denied irrevocably, with definite certainty. The system of observational sentences which have been accepted on the basis of immediate experience would then constitute a bed-rock foundation for the edifice of scientific theory.

This conception, however, is a fiction. The language of actual science contains no statements of this kind; and, what is more important, it would be unwise to allow for such sentences even in a logical reconstruction, a theoretical model, of the language of science. For, given any observational sentence *S*, it is possible to describe potential observational findings whose actual occurrence would indirectly disconfirm *S* and might indeed make it reasonable to reject *S* even if that sentence should previously have been accepted as stating some actual datum of immediate experience.

Carnap, espousing certain ideas propounded by Popper,[27] early rejected the idea of a privileged class of "protocol sentences" conceived as terminal statements in the process of empirical verification, as final arbiters in the test of all scientific theories. Any evidence statement is capable of further test, and statements serving as evidence, just like all other scientific statements, are established, i.e., incorporated into the total system of accepted statements, only "until further notice", with the proviso that they may be reappraised, and indeed rejected, in the light of additonal evidence. On pain of an infinite regress in the process of confirmation, it is indeed inevitable that at any time, some statements must be accepted immediately, i.e., without the mediation of other, supporting, statements; but this does not imply that some statements are such that at any time, they must be accepted immediately. Thus, in the construction of the system of statements that constitutes the *corpus* of scientific knowledge, there are no absolutely primary sentences. Popper has expressed this idea in a suggestive metaphor: "The empirical basis of objective science has thus nothing 'absolute' about it. Science does not rest upon rock-bottom. The bold structure of its theories rises, as it were, above a swamp. It is like a building erected on piles. The piles are driven down from above into the swamp, but not down to any natural or 'given' base; and when we cease our attempts to drive our piles into a deeper layer, it is not because we have reached firm ground. We simply stop when we are satisfied that they are firm enough to carry the structure, at least for the time being."[28]

It is sometimes argued that empirical knowledge must ultimately be based upon a system of statements which are certain because otherwise no empirical statement could even be probable.[29] However, the attribution of probabilities to scientific hypotheses does not require that the senten-

[27]Cf. Carnap's acknowledgment and summary, in PS, sec. 2, of certain ideas which Popper had suggested to him on the subject, and which were subsequently presented and developed by Popper in LF and LSD (cf. especially secs. 1-8, and 25-30 of either book).

[28]LSD, 111.

[29]For an instructive discussion of this issue, see the symposium, "The Experiential Element in Knowledge," which consists of the following papers: Reichenbach, PR; Goodman, SC; Lewis, GE.

ces on which the attribution is based should be certain or irrevocable: it suffices that they be at least temporarily accepted as presumably true. Then—to the extent that the theory of logical probability makes possible the ascription of numerical values—each hypothesis can be assigned a definite probability relative to the system of accepted statements; if the latter is changed, the hypotheses will still have probabilities, though possibly of different numerical value.

VII. *A Remark on Analyticity and Testability*

As we have noted, Carnap denies the privileged status of irrevocability even to those sentences which purport to convey the results of direct observation or immediate experience; no statement accepted in empirical science is taken to be immune from reconsideration and possible rejection. Referring also to Duhem and Poincaré, Carnap emphasizes in addition that strictly speaking a statement in a scientific theory cannot be tested in isolation, for it will yield consequences capable of confrontation with experimental or observational findings only when conjoined with a variety of other accepted statements of the theory; thus, basically, it is always an entire theoretical system that is under test.[30]

In regard to our earlier characterization of a scientific theory, this observation may serve as a reminder that the distinction between the theory proper, T, and its interpretative system *J* is a somewhat arbitrary matter since the sentences of both sets have essentially the same function and the same status. For (1) it is only in conjunction with *J* that *T* implies consequences in terms of V_B; (2) *J* no less than *T* may contain sentences expressed in terms of V_T alone, such as the "meaning postulates" mentioned earlier; and (3) when discrepancies between predictions and experiential data call for a modification of the predictive apparatus, suitable adjustments may be effected not solely by changing *T*, but alternatively also by changing *J*. This suggests that we assign to the sentences of *J* a status analogous to that of the postulates of *T*: they are postulates in terms of a primitive vocabulary which is the union, V_T', of V_T and V_B; and together with the postulates of *T*, they determine what was called above an interpreted theory, *T'*.[31]

This conception, which seems to me a natural extension of Carnap's own, makes it increasingly difficult, however, to single out, as Carnap has endeavored to do, a special class of sentences which are analytic in the

[30] LSL, 318.

[31] In particular, reduction sentences thus come to be conceived as postulates. The possibility of construing them in this manner was pointed out quite early by Leonard in Rev.—More recently, Carnap has suggested a method of assimilating reduction sentences to meaning postulates; this idea is discussed at a later place in the present essay.

wider sense of including, in addition to the truths of formal logic, also certain other sentences, namely those which are true by virtue of the meanings of their extra-logical constituents. Sentences of either kind would be certain in the sense of being incapable of disconfirmation by empirical evidence; they would be devoid of factual content. Without entering into a detailed discussion of the various complex issues here involved, I wish to present here but one consideration, which grows out of the preceding discussion, and which exhibits a difficulty in preserving the idea of analyticity with respect to the theoretical sentences of science.

In *Testability and Meaning*, after countenancing the use of only partially defined terms, Carnap faces the problem of setting up a criterion of analyticity for sentences containing such terms. His criterion is, in effect, as follows: Let S be a sentence containing an essential occurrence of one non-basic predicate, 'Q'; and let this predicate have been introduced by a set R of reduction pairs, which may include bilateral reduction sentences. Then S is analytic just in case (1) S is logically implied by R, and (2) the representative sentence S' of R is analytic. Sentences which, like S', contain only basic extra-logical terms are qualified as analytic in effect if they are truths of formal logic.[32]

In more intuitive terms: S is said to be analytic if it can be deduced from the sentences specifying the meaning of 'Q', and if the latter have no factual content. This criterion of analyticity is unavailing, however, once the conception of an interpreted theory has been generalized in the manner suggested earlier. For the idea underlying the criterion would then direct us to say that a V_T'-sentence S is analytic if (1) S is logically implied by T', and (2) T' has no factual content, i.e., logically implies no V_B-sentences which are not analytic. But, as was noted in section 5, if T' establishes any deductive connections among V_B-sentences at all, then it does not meet the second of these conditions. Hence, in this case, a V_T-sentence can be analytic only if it contains all its V_T-terms inessentially, i.e., if it is a truth of formal logic. Thus, the only sense in which the concept of analyticity remains applicable to the sentences of a scientific theory is the nar-

[32]TM, sec. 10, especially 451-453. Note that if S is a bilateral reduction sentence for 'Q'—and is thus an element of R—then the first condition will be trivially satisfied, and therefore S will be analytic just in case the representative sentence of R is analytic. Carnap by an oversight asserts instead that "every bilateral reduction sentence is analytic, because its representative sentence is analytic." (*loc. cit.*, 452.) If this did follow from his criterion then it would vitiate the latter; for if R consists of the two bilateral reduction sentences '$P_1x \supset (Qx \equiv P_2x)$' and '$P_3x \supset (Qx \equiv P_4x)$', each of them would qualify as analytic, and yet they jointly imply the sentence

(S′) $(x) - (P_1x \cdot P_2x \cdot P_3x \cdot -P_4x \vee P_1x \cdot -P_2x \cdot P_3x \cdot P_4x)$

which is in terms of basic predicates solely and not a truth of logic, hence not analytic. (See also my discussion of this point in CS, pp. 71-72.) Actually, Carnap's general criterion implies only that each of the two reduction sentences for 'Q' is analytic just in case S' is analytic; for S' is the representative sentence expressing the factual content of R.

row one of truth by virtue of being an instance of a logically valid schema.

Recently, Carnap has suggested[33] an interesting variant of the method of introducing predicates by reduction sentences. Suppose that a predicate 'Q' has been introduced by a set R of reduction sentences whose conjunction is R'. Let S' be the representative sentence of R. Then clearly R' is logically equivalent to S'. ($S' \supset R'$). While S' expresses the factual content of R, the sentences $S' \supset R'$ is non-factual in this sense: all those of its logical consequences which are expressible in terms of basic predicates alone are truths of formal logic. Carnap's new method consists in introducing 'Q', not by R, but by $S' \supset R'$ alone, i.e., by making the latter sentence a meaning postulate of the language at hand. This procedure has two advantages, from Carnap's point of view: (i) It separates the two functions of language which are fused in reduction sentences, namely, the assertion of empirical fact and the specification of meaning; and (ii) it permits a neat and quite general characterization of analyticity: the analytic statements of a language are those which are logically implied by the meaning postulates.

This new procedure gives rise, however, to the question as to the meaning and the rationale of the distinction that is made here between meaning postulates and empirical postulates. Suppose for example, that in axiomatizing a given scientific theory a certain sentence is declared to be a meaning postulate. What peculiar characteristic is attributed to it by that characterization? What distinctive status is being conferred upon it? Inviolable truth in any conflict that might arise between the theory and pertinent experiential data suggests itself as an essential characteristic of meaning postulates; for presumably, such postulates are intended to specify, in part or in full, the meanings of their constituent extra-logical terms by the stipulation that those terms are to be used in such a way as to safeguard the truth of the meaning postulates under all circumstances. But, as was pointed out earlier, there are good reasons to think that—with the possible exception of the formal truths of logic and mathematics—any statement once accepted in empirical science may conceivably be abandoned for the sake of resolving a conflict between the theory and the total body of evidence available. Hence it would seem that, apart from purely logical or mathematical truths, there can be no scientific statements that satisfy the condition here contemplated for meaning postulates. And is it questionable, therefore, whether there is any aspect of scientific method or of scientific knowledge that would constitute an explicandum for the analytic-synthetic dichotomy in regard to the statements of empirical science.[34]

33MP, 71.

34For a fuller critical discussion of that dichotomy, see Quine, DE; White, AS; Pap, RS.

Similar considerations apply to the notions of testability and empirical significance. As long as theoretical terms are conceived as being introduced by chains of reduction sentences based upon an observational vocabulary V_B, it is possible to speak of individual sentences containing theoretical terms as being confirmable by reference to V_B-sentences. And the experiential import or significance of a sentence *S* of this kind may be taken to be represented by the class of all non-analytic V_B-sentences which are implied by *S* in conjunction with the reduction sentences for the theoretical terms in *S*; the sentence *S* would then be devoid of empirical meaning if that class was empty.

In the broadened conception of an interpreted theory, this idea has no useful counterpart. We would have to say that the experiential import of *S*, relative to a given interpreted theory *T'*, is expressed by the class of all non-analytic V_B-sentences implied by *S* in conjunction with *T'*. But this would render the notions of testability and experiential significance relative to a given scientific theory, and it would assign to all sentences of *T'* the same experiential import, represented by the class of all V_B-sentences implied by *T'*. These peculiarities are symptomatic of the fact, which was mentioned earlier, that testability and empirical significance are attributable, not to scientific statements in isolation, but only to interpreted theoretical systems.

An empiricist interested in preserving the notion of empirical significance as testability by experiential findings could not derive much comfort from the circumstance that the testability requirement is still applicable at least to entire theoretical systems. For thus applied, the requirement is extremely weak. For example, an "empirically significant" theory would remain so under enlargement by any set of sentences which leaves its deductive import in regard to V_B-sentences unchanged. Thus, a significant theory *T'* would remain significant if to its postulates we added a set of further postulates couched exclusively in terms of additional theoretical predicates, none of them contained in either the basic or the theoretical vocabulary of *T'*. An example of this procedure would consist in adding, to contemporary physical theory, an axiomatized metaphysics of Being and Essence; the outcome would be an empirically significant system.

Nor can we forestall this consequence by requiring that an empirically significant theory must contain no sentence—other than purely logical or mathematical truths—whose elimination would leave the experiential import of the theory (i.e., the set of all its consequences in terms of V_B) unchanged. For this requirement would prohibit the use of theoretical terms altogether, since as long as *T'* has not been reduced to an equivalent of T'_B it still contains statements which violate the requirement under discussion.

As these considerations suggest, the value of a scientific theory is not determined solely by the *range* of the connections it establishes among the data of our experience, but very importantly also by the *simplicity* of those connections. The problem of giving a precise explication of this aspect of scientific theories presents a new and challenging task for the philosophy of science.[35]

The neat and clean-cut conceptions of cognitive significance and of analyticity which were held in the early days of the Vienna Circle have thus been gradually refined and liberalized to such an extent that it appears quite doubtful whether the basic tenets of positivism and empiricism can be formulated in a clear and precise way.[36] This doubt applies with equal force, of course, to the various rival doctrines of empiricism; for what analytic research in recent decades has made increasingly clear is precisely that the conflicting theses and programs at issue involve concepts and assumptions which are found wanting upon closer logical scrutiny.

Carnap's ingenious and illuminating methods of logical analysis and reconstruction, and the example he has set in his own work of rigorous but open-minded and undogmatic philosophic inquiry, have provided a powerful stimulus for a precise analytic approach to philosophic problems; and if in the light of recent analytic studies the objective of clearly explicating the concepts of cognitive significance and of analyticity appears as elusive, the research that suggested this conclusion has yielded a rich harvest of insights into the logic and methodology of science. Thus, the quest for an ever more adequate statement and defense of some of the basic conceptions of empiricism has come to play the role of the treasure hunt in the tale of the old winegrower who on his death-bed enjoins his sons to dig for a treasure hidden in the family vineyard. In untiring search, his sons turn over the soil and thus stimulate the growth of the vines: the rich harvest they reap proves to be the true and only treasure in the vineyard.

CARL G. HEMPEL

DEPARTMENT OF PHILOSOPHY
PRINCETON UNIVERSITY

[35]In recent years, a number of authors have made contributions to the explication of various aspects of the notion of theoretical simplicity; among these, see especially Popper, LF, secs. 41-46; Reichenbach EP, sec. 42 and TP, 447; Goodman, SA, ch. 3 and RDS; Kemeny, US; and chapter 9 of Barker, IH.

[36]On this point, cf., in addition to the references given in note 34, Carnap, MP and Hempel, CS.

BIBLIOGRAPHY AND ABBREVIATIONS

Barker, S.F. *Induction and Hypothesis.* Cornell University Press, 1957. [IH]

Braithwaite, R. B. *Scientific Explanation.* Cambridge, England, 1953. [SE]

Bridgman, P. W. *The Logic of Modern Physics.* New York, 1927. [LMP]

"Operational Analysis." *Philosophy of Science,* V, 1938, 114-131. [OA]

"The Nature of Some of Our Physical Concepts." *Brit. J. for the Philos. of Science,* I, 1950-51, 257-272 and II, 1951-52, 25-44 and 142-160. [PC]

Burks, Arthur W. "The Logic of Causal Propositions." Mind, LX, 1951, 363-382. [CP]

Carnap, Rudolf. *Physikalische Begriffsbildung.* Karlsruhe, 1926. [PB]

Der logische Aufbau der Welt. Berlin, 1928. [Aufbau]

"Ueber Protokollsaetze." *Erkenntnis,* III, 1932, 215-228. [PS]

"Die physikalische Sprache als Universalsprache der Wissenschaft." *Erkenntnis,* III, 1932, 432-465. English translation published in book form under the title *The Unity of Science.* London, 1934. [PhSp]

"Les concepts psychologiques et les concepts physiques sont-ils foncièrement différents?" *Revue de Synthese,* X, 1935, 43-53. [CPs]

"Ueber die Einheitssprache der Wissenschaft." *Actes du Congrès International de Philosophie Scientifique,* Paris, 1935. II. "Unité de la Science." *Actualités Scientifiques et Industrielles,* no. 389, 60-70. Paris, 1936 [ES]

"Testability and Meaning." *Philosophy of Science,* III, 1936, 419-471, and IV, 1937, 1-40. [TM]

The Logical Syntax of Language. London, 1937. [LSL]

"Logical Foundations of the Unity of Science." In: *International Encyclopedia of Unified Science,* I, no. 1, 42-62. Chicago, 1938 [LFUS]

Foundations of Logic and Mathematics (Internat. Encyclopedia of Unified Science, I, no. 3, Chicago, 1939. [FLM]

"Meaning Postulates." *Philosophical Studies,* III, 1952, 65-73. [MP]

Craig, William. *A Theorem about First Order Functional Calculus with Identity, and Two Applications.* Ph.D. thesis, Harvard Univ., 1951. [Th]

"On Axiomatizability Within a System." *Journal of Symbolic Logic,* XVIII, 1953, 30-32. [AS]

"Replacement of Auxiliary Expressions." *Philosophical Review,* LXV, 1956, 38-55. [RAE]

Feigl, Herbert. "Existential Hypotheses." *Philosophy of Science,* XVII, 1950, 35-62. [EH]

Goodman, Nelson. "The Problem of Counterfactual Conditionals." *Journal of Philosophy,* XLIV, 1947, 113-128. [Cf]

The Structure of Appearance. Cambridge, Mass., 1951. [SA]

"Sense and Certainty." *Philosophical Review,* LXI, 1952, 160-167. [SC]

Fact, Fiction, and Forecast. Cambridge, Mass., 1955. [FFF]

"Recent Developments in the Theory of Simplicity". *Philosophy and Phenomenological Research,* XIX, 1958-59, 429-446. [RDS]

Hempel, Carl C. "The Concept of Cognitive Significance: A Reconsideration." *Proc. Amer. Acad. of Arts and Sciences,* LXXX, no. 1, 1951, 61-77. [CS]

"A Logical Appraisal of Operationism." *The Scientific Monthly,* LXXIX, 1954, 215-220. [AO]

Hempel, Carl G. and Oppenheim, Paul. "Studies in the Logic of Explanation." *Philosophy of Science,* XV, 1948, 135-175. [LE]

Kemeny, John G. Review of Carnap, *Logical Foundations of Probability. Journal of Symbolic Logic,* XVI, 1951, 205-207. [Rev]
"Extension of the Methods of Inductive Logic." *Philosophical Studies,* III, 1952, 38-42. [EM]
"The Use of Simplicity in Induction." *Philosophical Review,* LXII, 1953, 391-408. [US]
Leonard, Henry S. Review of Carnap, "Testability and Meaning," *Journal of Symbolic Logic,* II, 1937, 49-50. [Rev]
Lewis, C. I. "The Given Element in Empirical Knowledge." *Philosophical Review,* LXI, 1952, 168-175. [GE]
MacCorquodale, K., and Meehl, P. E. "On a Distinction Between Hypothetical Constructs and Intervening Variables." *Psychological Review,* LV, 1948, 95-107. [HC]
Pap, Arthur. "Reduction-sentences and Open Concepts." *Methodos,* V, 1953, 3-28. [RS]
Popper, Karl. *Logik der Forschung.* Wien, 1935. [LF]
The Logic of Scientific Discovery. London, 1959. [LSD]
Quine, W. V. "Two Dogmas of Empiricism." *Philosophical Review,* LX, 1951, 20-43. [DE]
Reichenbach, Hans. *Experience and Prediction.* Chicago, 1938. [EP]
The Theory of Probability. Berkeley and Los Angeles, 1949. [TP]
"Are Phenomenal Reports Absolutely Certain?" *Philosophical Review,* LXI, 1952, 147-159. [PR]
Nomological Statements and Admissible Operations. Amsterdam, 1954. [NS]
White, Morton G. "The Analytic and the Synthetic: An Untenable Dualism." In S. Hook (ed.), *John Dewey, Philosopher of Science and of Freedom.* New York, 1950, 316-330. [AS]

22

John G. Kemeny

CARNAP'S THEORY OF PROBABILITY AND INDUCTION*

I. *The Problem*

THE problem of induction is one of the most hotly debated issues of modern philosophy. It is certainly the central issue in any philosophy of science.

The problem has stimulated two different but complementary types of research. First of all there is the problem of how one can justify the inductive inferences that we do as a matter of fact make, a problem whose solution seems impossible since the days of Hume. The other approach is that of Bacon, Mill, and Laplace, who analyse the way we make inductive inferences. They try to find reasonable methods of inference, without necessarily giving a justification that would go counter to Hume's arguments. It is this latter problem that was so successfully attacked by Carnap.

Few, if any, modern philosophers still expect fool-proof rules for making inductive inferences. Indeed, with the help of such rules we could acquire infallible knowledge of the future, contrary to all our empiricist beliefs. So it will be well to clarify just how far we can hope to progress with Carnap's methods.

Let us consider a typical inductive inference. A scientist is confronted with certain data collected through careful observations. His task is the formulation of a hypothesis that is scientifically acceptable, and that will serve to explain the facts, or more usually it serves to explain most of the facts with the help of the remaining few. The selection of such a hypothesis can be analysed into three stages: (1) The choice of a language in terms of which the hypothesis is to be expressed. This usually involves the selection of a branch of mathematics, and the establishing of rules for its empirical interpretation. (2) The choice of a given statement from this language, which is to serve as the hypothesis. (3) The determination of whether we are scientifically justified to accept the hypothesis on the given evidence. It is, of course, not necessary that these be psychologically

*Received April 1954.

distinguishable steps, but they are logically distinct features of any inductive inference.

An example will serve to illustrate the three steps. Let us consider schematically Einstein's formulation of the General Theory of Relativity. The language chosen was a system of generalized geometry. It was given an empirical interpretation (at least in part) by specifying that certain complex formulas express the results of actual physical measurements. The statement selected is expressed by a complicated mathematical formula, known as the Einstein Field Equation. Finally, after investigating the content of this formula, Einstein decided that the available evidence made it sufficiently probable to accept it. In this case there were actually time-lags between the various stages.

It is the last step that Carnap is interested in. Just how does the expert decide that the given evidence makes the hypothesis sufficiently probable for acceptance? It is here that we find the close connection between the problem of induction and probability theory.

Before we can proceed with Carnap's approach to our basic problem, we must summarize his views as to the two concepts of probability.[1] One is the frequency concept, and the other is that of degree of confirmation. They are both functions of two variables (the frequency of a certain type of event in a given series, and the confirmation of a certain hypothesis by given evidence), and they obey certain fundamental mathematical laws in common. These features have caused considerable confusion, but here the similarity ends. The former concept is used within scientific theories and expresses an empirical connection between its two arguments. It states how frequently, in the long run, a certain type of event will *as a matter of fact* occur. The latter concept is used meta-scientifically, it is applied to theories, and it expresses a purely logical connection between its arguments. Once we accept a definition of "degree of confirmation", pure mathematics suffices for the calculation of the confirmation of a given hypothesis by given evidence. The arguments in favour of precisely this dichotomy are carried out by Carnap in complete detail, and in the opinion of the author they are unanswerable.

It is the second concept, that of inductive probability or degree of confirmation, that plays the role described above in induction. It is the attempt to clarify this concept that lies at the base of all Carnap's work in this field.

There is no doubt that scientists, and laymen, do use vague evaluations of the probability of a given hypothesis; an evaluation based on the evidence available to them. Certainly we find them choosing between hypotheses, demanding more evidence for acceptance, and finally agreeing

[1]Carnap, [2] and [7], ch. I. (See the bibliography at the end of the paper.)

that they have reached "sufficient certainty". These are at least evidence for comparative judgments. But there are just as many instances where our actions are based on intuitive quantitative judgments. The best example of this is a bet. If we assume that the only aim of a bet is the maximization of the expected gain, then from the odds a man is willing to accept one can tell how likely he considers his hypothesis (that he will win) on the basis of the evidence available to him. It is no great coincidence, therefore, that classical probability theory—which certainly deals with a logical concept of probability—grew out of a desire to place reasonable bets. Indeed this connection between degree of confirmation and fair bets will be fundamental for the following arguments. But Carnap also lists many other instances where someone who is "not a betting man" must, in effect, make a quantitative evaluation of the probability of a given hypothesis. Perhaps the best example of this is taking out an insurance policy. Here we consider (at least) two alternatives whose utility we know, and we must estimate whether the expected outcome is more favorable if we place the policy, or if we save our money. Such an estimate necessarily involves a numerical estimate of the relative probabilities of the two events. Again, the examples cited by Carnap are so numerous that there is no doubt that all of us have at least a vague method for estimating inductive probabilities.[2]

The task confronting us is one of making precise these vague and often semi-conscious methods. In short it is a problem of explication.

Present-day philosophy of science very often centers around an explication. Besides degree of confirmation there are dozens of very important concepts whose explication has occupied some of our leading philosophers. "Cause", "purpose", "law", "explanation", and "simplicity" are but a few typical examples. In each case certain terms expressing this concept are in common use, with more or less agreement as to where it applies, and the philosopher must find a single, precise definition to take the place of vague, intuitive notions. This task runs into many difficulties: Often there is no consensus of opinion as to the applicability of a term, at other times the term is used ambiguously, and again it may only be used in very special contexts. The philosopher starts with this vague, ambiguous, incomplete explicandum, and must find a precise, unambiguous, complete, simple, and fruitful explicatum.[3]

How is such a task possible? First of all we must assure that our final definition really reproduces the original meaning. To accomplish this it is best to set down all that our intuition tells us about the explicandum. These conditions will be our conditions of adequacy for the explicatum.

[2]Carnap, [7], §§ 48-51.
[3]Cf. Carnap, [7], ch. 1.

It is perhaps the most difficult part of an explication to set down all that we can. We must see through the vagueness, and we must make a choice in case of ambiguity (as we have chosen one of the two meanings of "probability"). These still leave us with a great deal of freedom. Some of this can be settled by the adoption of conventions, which do not affect the content of the definition. But we are still left with (infinitely) many ways of forming a precise concept satisfying the conditions of adequacy. Here our only guidance is simplicity and fruitfulness. We must select the simplest possible fruitful explicatum. Or if there is no unique one, at least find the class of simplest fruitful explicata, and then make an arbitrary choice.

A good illustration is the explication of our vague notions of "hot" and "cold", the explicatum being the concept of temperature. The conditions of adequacy concern circumstances under which qualitative or comparative judgments are made. Certain decisions as to the elimination of ambiguities were necessary, e.g. to eliminate cases where an object feels hot, but this turns out to be an illusion. Finally conventions were adopted, e.g. that we use a real-valued functor, with larger numbers corresponding to "hotter". The final concepts which turned out to be the simplest fruitful ones were the centigrade scale and its linear functions (several of which are still in use). Fruitfulness was demonstrated by the use of "temperature" in scientific theories.

Similarly we hope to explicate "degree of confirmation". The first steps in this process, due to Carnap, are summarized in the remainder of this paper.

Before undertaking this task, however, let us ask just what role a good explicatum would play in inductions. Let us recall our division of inductive inferences into three steps. The direct application of degree of confirmation occurs in the last stage. Given a hypothesis and the evidence, it serves to evaluate how probable the hypothesis is, and hence whether it is acceptable. So our explicatum provides an answer to (3), at least in principle; in an actual example we may find it impossible to carry out the calculation. But the answer to (2) is also provided, in principle, by our explicatum. Given the language, we can consider any meaningful statement of it as a potential theory. Then "the best confirmed hypothesis relative to the given evidence" is well defined, and may be selected. (Uniqueness is assumed for convenience only; it is easy to modify the argument by the addition of an arbitrary selection among equally confirmed hypotheses.) Of course, being best confirmed is not the only criterion for the selection of a hypothesis. We want it to explain as great a part of the evidence as possible, to be simple, etc. But any one of the other conditions appears to be easier to explicate than degree of confirmation, and hence at least our explicatum would solve the most difficult problem underlying step (2). But even if all these concepts are explicated step (1) would remain as the truly creative step. So our explicatum would provide the scientist with a powerful tool; it would not put him out of business.

And above all we must reemphasize that the explicatum is offered only as a simple, fruitful rational reconstruction of the way an "expert" evaluates inductive probabilities. It does not "justify" the making of inductions. Indeed any such justification would run counter to Hume's famous argument.[4]

II. *Preliminary Considerations*

Let us consider a typical situation in which we are asked to evaluate how well a hypothesis is confirmed. As is clear from the previous section, three ingredients must be present. A definite scientific language must have been chosen, call it *L;* a hypothesis, *h,* must have been selected; and we must be clear as to what the evidence, *e,* under consideration is.

If we are to hope for a rigorous logical definition, we must assume that *L* is a fully formalized logistic system. Without any great loss of generality we may assume that it is either a version of the lower predicate calculus, or that it is an extension of such a system. Since it is a scientific language, we must assume that it is fully or in part empirically interpreted. For the purpose of this discussion we need not consider the structure of *L,* or even what form it is presented in. It suffices to know two things: We must know what the meaningful statements or well formed formulas (*wffs*) are, and we must have a rule—necessarily non-effective—for the recognition of the analytic *wffs.*

Clearly, *h* and *e* must be *wffs.* But just what *wffs* are to be admitted to these roles? The only non-aprioristic approach is the admission of any meaningful statement as a hypothesis or as evidence. In the case of *h* this is especially clear. No statement, no matter how trivial or unlikely, is inadmissible as a hypothesis. And even if a certain *wff e* expresses a state of the world that could never occur, or could never actually be part of our factual knowledge, it still is meaningful to ask how likely we would consider *h* if contrary to fact we knew that *e* is the case. So any self-consistent *wff* is admitted as possible evidence. The question of what *wffs* will actually occur as hypotheses or as evidence is a pragmatic one, and irrelevant for a purely logical investigation.

It is nevertheless of interest to know what *wffs* would occur as *h* or *e* in an actual application. Einstein's Field Equation, a tip on tomorrow's race, and speculation about the existence of flying saucers illustrate the

[4]The word 'justification' is used here in the sense of giving certainty. It is of course not incompatible with Hume's argument that the reasonableness of a method should "justify" it in our eyes. Indeed, we *will* attempt to justify (in this weaker sense) a certain inductive method.

wide variety of hypotheses; these hypotheses can be most naturally formalized as purely universal, singular, and existential respectively. Any statement under consideration at all can serve as the hypothesis. One must, however, exercise more caution with the evidence. It is true that if one is only asking a hypothetical question, then *e* can be any logically possible *wff*. But in the type of investigations that gave rise to our problem it is most important to take as *e* a statement of all our factual knowledge.[5] Needless to say that while this is in principle indispensable, in practice one must make compromises. One does this the way a student rushed before an important test decides to read only the summaries at the end of each chapter, hoping that this will not affect his grade. We are forced to restrict ourselves to what we consider relevant evidence, hoping to get the same degree of confirmation as if we really took all the facts known to us into account. Of course, on occasion we make mistakes and ignore some relevant piece, the result being an answer as unsatisfactory as our student's resulting grade. But our principle of total evidence is not any less important because in practice we have to compromise.

Sometimes we are confronted with statements of inductive probability which seem to depend on only one variable, e.g. "I think that there is an even chance of rain tomorrow". But in this case it is quite clear that the evidence is the total factual knowledge of the speaker. Indeed, since we have required that the evidence be as complete as possible, in an application it is most reasonable to speak of "the probability of h", understanding by this that all available evidence was taken as *e*.

But we must be careful to distinguish questions of application from our logical problem. As far as our task is concerned, we have before us a logistic system *L*, and two *wffs* *h* and *e*. Our task is to calculate the degree of confirmation of *h* with respect to *e*, or $c(h,e)$.

We have recognized our task as an explication, which requires that we supply a definition of *c*. If we complete our task, then for any *L*, *h*, and *e*, the truth or falsity of a statement $c(h,e) = r$ will be a consequence of the given definition. It is in this sense of the word that we asserted above that a statement of inductive probability is an analytic statement.

We will soon find that the most general problem is far too difficult for the time being, and we must restrict ourselves to simple *L's*, always in the hope of extending the definition to more and more complex systems. But, with the entire problem in front of our eyes, we must at least try to formulate the conditions of adequacy in completely general terms. This will be the content of the following section.

The reader may be puzzled by the fact that we have asked nothing about the structure of *L*, and yet we hope to state fairly strong conditions

[5] Cf. Carnap, [7], 211-213.

applicable to it. It may be helpful to discuss briefly the logical tools that will enable us to do so.

The concept of a model, or interpretation, of a logistic system has been defined for any system.[6] We may conveniently suppose that analyticity has been specified by stating what the admissible models are. A *wff* is then analytically true if it is true under all permissible interpretations, i.e., true in all models. Complete knowledge of all models of L supplies us with all the needed semantic information. Models are also most useful for the definition of semantic measure-functions. Weights can be assigned to individual models, and the measure of a *wff* is simply the sum of the weights of all the models in which it is true. This procedure will prove most useful in the following. But if this procedure is to be applicable, without the greatest difficulties, we must assume that the number of models of L is finite. This assumption will be made until we reconsider this issue in section 5. It is important to show, however, that this is not too drastic a restriction on L.

A model is determined by its individual domain(s), and by the elements assigned to the various extra-logical constants. The former determines what the variables are supposed to range over, while the latter interpret the subject-matter constants. We will assume that in the determination of the models one definite domain (or one domain of each individual type) has been selected, and that the models vary only as to the various assignments to constants. The necessary and sufficient condition for the finiteness of the set of models is that the domain of individuals be finite (or the sum of domains be finite), and that there be only a finite number of extra-logical constants, each of a finite type.[7] We will see in the next section that we may require, without loss of generality, that the number of extra-logical constants be finite. Hence our only two restrictions are the requirement of a finite number of individuals, and the finiteness of the type of each constant. If L is a type-theory, this may, for example, be achieved by restricting L to a type not greater than ω, and requiring that no statement of infinity be provable. Such a system is quite weak as far as mathematics is concerned, but quite strong as far as descriptive science's requirements go. At any rate, at the moment we are very far from being able to define c for all these systems, so it is premature to inquire how these restrictions could be removed.

We are thus characterizing the semantic properties of L by having a finite number of permissible models specified, with a given domain (or domains) of individuals, and permitting various assignments to the extra-logical constants, in accordance with the structure of L. In particular it

[6]Kemeny, [1], [9].
[7]Cf. Kemeny, [7].

must be emphasized that many restrictions hitherto imposed have been removed. It is not necessary that *L* be a first order calculus, it is not necessary that all individuals have names, it is not necessary that the constants be logically independent of each other, and it is not necessary that every qualitative attribute be expressible in *L*. These are four considerable steps in the direction of widening the applicability of our general conditions of adequacy, steps taken since the publication of Carnap's book.[8]

Before we proceed to the conditions of adequacy, we must raise one further question that may trouble the reader. Is there really any hope of getting a numerical concept that is simple and fruitful in place of this terribly vague notion? We have even been presented with a priori arguments to show the impossibility of success. First, and perhaps most important to realize, is that a strong feeling that this is not a "numerical concept" is very poor evidence. Perhaps no concept sounds as unnumerical as being hot or cold, and yet it was most successfully explicated as the numerical concept temperature. Secondly, we must realize that the precise definition of any fairly complex concept can be considered a mathematical definition. Therefore, to say that we can give a mathematical definition is no more than to say that the concept can be rigorously defined. But a general mathematical definition need by no means be numerical. But if we take "number" in the broadest mathematical sense, we may expect that an experienced mathematician will be able to replace our definition by a numerical one. However, when by "number" we mean a real number, there is certainly no a priori argument to assure that *c* can be identified with a real-valued function. (Indeed, later we will discuss a proposal to let the values of *c* be more general than just real numbers.) Yet, knowing the vast wealth of the continuum of real numbers, it does not seem too optimistic to hope for at least some reasonably good explicata (e.g., giving equal weights to all the models). So the question is really not whether real-valued explicata exist, but how good they can possibly be. It is seriously to be doubted that anyone's intuition is good enough to answer that question a priori. It does seem more reasonable to seek out the best available explicatum and see whether it is a fruitful concept.

While a priori arguments seem pointless, we must still admit that the weight of proof rests on our shoulders. It is, however, sincerely hoped that the skeptic won't refuse to study the forth-coming definitions on the ground that he knows a priori that they cannot exist.

[8]The first three improvements resulted from ideas first mentioned in Kemeny, [2] and worked out in Kemeny, [4] and [7]. The fourth improvement was pointed out in Kemeny, [5], though the result of that paper is already contained in Carnap, [8].

III. *The Conditions of Adequacy*[9]

We must now state as completely as possible what our intuition tells us about $c(h,e)$. We have noted already that we come closest to having a numerical intuition in cases where we place bets. Our first condition will incorporate this intuition. Suppose we believe that the probability of the Democratic candidate's victory in the forthcoming election is ⅔. That means that he has a ⅔ chance of winning, and a ⅓ chance of losing. Hence we would be willing to give odds up to (and including) 2:1. Or we would be willing to bet on his losing if we get at least 2:1 odds. In particular, if the odds are fixed at exactly 2:1, it should be a matter of indifference to us which side of the bet we have. Thus we note that our assertion that $c(h,e) = r$ means that with the odds fixed at r: $(1\text{-}r)$ we are willing either to give the odds, or to take them.

Of course, in any particular situation we may lose our bet. What makes the bet interesting is that we have presumably evened out the expectation of the two bettors by fixing the odds correctly. Of course, the odds may not be correctly fixed, but just how to fix odds correctly is precisely our problem. But there is one thing our intuition clearly tells us: Unless the odds give us a sporting chance of winning, they are not fair.[10] Suppose that we have described our method of fixing odds, i.e. our definition of c, and that a shrewd gambler can study these and discover a way of placing a series of bets in such a way that no matter what happens he will profit, then the odds are not fair. Indeed, we can take as a definition of a *fair betting system* that this should not be possible.

An illustration may help. Suppose that for some hypothesis h and its negation $\sim h$ we fixed the odds by saying that $c(h,e) = ⅔$ and $c(\sim h,e) = ⅔$. Then the gambler need only place a dollar on h, and also a dollar on its non-occurrence or on $\sim h$. He will lose his dollar on one bet, but win two dollars on the other. By a well known theorem of elementary arithmetic, he will profit no matter whether h takes place or not. It is not difficult to see that there always is such a guaranteed profit possible, unless $c(h,e) = 1 - c(\sim h,e)$. Thus we see that the requirement of making the betting system fair imposes a restriction on the definition of c.

There is another version of this requirement, which we must also consider. It may happen that although the gambler cannot assure himself of a profit, he can at least make sure that he cannot possibly lose and

[9]The conditions of adequacy are taken from Carnap, [7], [8] and Kemeny [5]; but they have been somewhat modified, and they are here given a much more general formulation.

[10]This requirement originated in Ramsey, [1] and De Finetti, [1], [2]. DeFinetti's term 'coherent' is much less open to objections than our 'fair,' but the latter is more suggestive. There is no danger in our terminology as long as we keep in mind that 'fair' is used in a quite weak, precisely defined sense.

that he may win. E.g., he may be able to bet on each of three possible alternatives, in such a way that he would break even in two of these cases, and make a net profit in the third. This would also appear to be unfair to the people offering the bets. Hence we may require fairness not only in the previous sense, but also that the just described procedure should be impossible. This we may call the requirement of *strict fairness.*[11]

It certainly appears that even strict fairness must be required. But we will state it optionally, because certain definitions of c in the literature violate this condition. We are now ready to formulate our first general condition of adequacy.

CA 1. c must define a system of betting that is [strictly] fair.[12]

We have already indicated that this condition imposes restrictions on the definition of c. It has been shown that *CA* 1 is equivalent to the following restrictions:[13]

(1) $0 \leqq c(h,e) \leqq 1$.

(2) If h and e are logically equivalent to h' and e' respectively, then $c(h,e) = c(h',e')$.

(3) If e logically implies h, then $c(h,e) = 1$.

(4) If e logically implies $\sim(h\&h')$, then $c(h\mathbf{v}h',e) = c(h,e) + c(h',e)$.

(5) $c(h\&e',e) = c(e',e) \times c(h,e\&e')$.

Where e, e', $e\&e'$ arc not self-contradictory.

[In case we require strict fairness, we must strengthen (3) into:

(3′) $c(h,e) = 1$ if and only if e logically implies h.]

We must now try to see what use we can make of these conditions. Consider first (5). Let t be a tautology. (By (2) it does not matter which tautology. Uses of (2) won't be specifically indicated from now on.) One instance of (5) is

$c(h\&e,t) = c(e,t) \times c(h,t\&e) = c(e,t) \times c(h,e)$, or

$c(h,e) = c(h\&e,t) \,/\, c(e,t)$.

We note that the right side is a ratio of quantities $c(w,t)$. Since the exact form of t does not matter, this is a quantity depending on the *wff* w alone, and we denote it by $m(w)$. Then

(6) $c(h,e) = m(h\&e) \,/\, m(e)$.

We need only find the function of *one* variable m, which simplifies our task considerably.

11This condition was brought to the author's attention by Shimony. Cf. Shimony, [1].

12Modifications necessitated by requiring not only fairness but strict fairness will be indicated within square brackets.

13DeFinetti proved that (1)-(5) follow from the requirement of fairness. The converse of this, and the connection between strict fairness and (3′) are established in Kemeny [8].

Our task is the assignment of a measure to each *wff*. Since equivalent *wffs* will have the same measure, we may identify each *wff* with the set of models in which it is true. Thus we must assign measures to certain, though not necessarily all, sets of models. What can we say about this measure? From (4) we see that if h and h' are mutually exclusive, then

$c(h\mathbf{v}h',t) = c(h,t) + c(h',t)$ or $m(h\mathbf{v}h') = m(h) + m(h')$.

The sets of models in which h and h' respectively are true are clearly disjoint, and the set of $h\mathbf{v}h'$ is the sum of these. Hence we see that our measure is additive, wherever it is defined. From (3) we see that

$c(t,t) = 1$, or $\mathrm{m}(t) = 1$.

Hence the measure of the set of all models is 1. Again from (4),

$$c(t\mathbf{v} \sim t,t) = c(t,t) + c(\sim t,t) \text{ or } m(t) = m(t) + m(\sim t) \text{ or } m(\sim t) = 0.$$

Hence the measure of the empty set is 0. From (1) we see that each measure is non-negative. We must now show that such a measure can always be extended to all sets of models.

Lemma 1. Given a finite set, and a measure defined over some of its subsets, such that (a) it is additive where defined, (b) the measure of the universal set is 1, of the empty set 0, (c) each measure is non-negative, and (d) if defined over two subsets, then also defined over their complements, sum, and product; then we can extend the measure to all subsets, maintaining the above conditions.

Proof: Let us call a set minimal, if the measure is defined over it, but over no non-empty proper subset of it. If the measure is not defined over all sets, it must have a minimal set with more than one element. Choose one, let its measure be m_0, and let it have n elements. We, so to speak, assign weight m_0/n to each element. Let us call "old sets" those over which the measure is already defined. An old set has either nothing in common with our selected set or contains it (this follows from the fact that it is minimal). Consider now those new sets which are the sum of an old set and a set of k of the n elements. We assign to this the measure of the old set, plus (k x m_0/n). It is easy to check that this is an extension of the required kind. By a finite number of repetitions we must arrive at a measure defined over all subsets. Q.E.D.

We have already shown that our measure satisfies (a), (b), and (c). And since complements, sums, and products of sets of models correspond to the negations, disjunctions, and conjunctions respectively of their *wffs*, it also has the closure property (d). Our lemma assures us that we may require the measure to be defined over all sets of models, without loss of generality.

But if the measure is defined over all sets of models, and if it is additive, then it suffices to know what the measure of the unit-sets is; we get the other measures by addition of these. Or, more simply, we may conceive of the measure of a unit set as a weight assigned to its sole element. Then the measure of a set of models is the sum of the weights of its elements. $m(h)$ is the sum of the weights of the models in which h is true.

Our task has now been reduced to the assignment of weights to the models. From (b) and (c) we see that the weights are non-negative, and add up to 1. Any such assignment of weights will satisfy (1)-(5).

[What modification is necessary if we require strict fairness? From (3′) we see that $c(h,t) = 1$ only if $t \supset h$ or $m(h) = 1$ only if h is analytic.

Using (4) as once before, we see that $m(\sim h)$ is 0 only if h is analytic, hence only a contradictory *wff* has 0 measure. Hence (c) can be strengthened to require that that all non-empty sets have positive measure. The lemma still holds, and we can require measures for all sets of models. Hence we again arrive at weights for models, but this time they must be positive. Any such assignment of weights will satisfy (1), (2), (3′), (4), and (5). The condition of strict fairness can again be seen to be stronger than that of fairness, in that 0-weights are prohibited.]

We have now arrived at a necessary and sufficient condition for the satisfaction of *CA* 1. A non-negative [positive] weight must be assigned to each model, the sum of the weights being 1. $m(h)$ is the sum of the weights of the models in which h is true, and c is defined by (6). Our condition has been translated into a numerical requirement, which is universally applicable since it is formulated entirely in terms of models.

CA 2. $c(h,e)$ is to depend only on the proposition expressed by h and e.

This seems so obvious, that one would suspect that the condition is useless. Actually it has a two-fold purpose. It justifies us in restricting our attention when we search for relevant factors, and it justifies us in ignoring accidental features of L. It is the second role that is particularly useful.

Suppose that there are two systems, each of which is capable of expressing the hypothesis and the evidence, then the c-value must turn out to be the same in both. Considerable use will be made of this requirement.

It also tells us that we are justified in selecting any of these languages, in particular a minimal language. We may, e.g., assume that L has no other extra-logical constants than those occurring in h and e (and those, if any, of which the given ones are logically dependent). It was this requirement that enabled us to say earlier that we may always assume that L has only a finite number of extra-logical constants.

Again, if h and e are singular, we may assume that L has no more individuals in its models than those mentioned in h and e. This again will be useful. It also shows that the requirement of having a finite number of individuals is a real restriction only when we deal with generalized propositions.

It is thanks to the fact that we can choose L as a small fragment of a scientific language that we can proceed from simpler to more complex problems, step by step.

CA 3. Constants which are logically alike must be treated a priori alike.

This may be considered as the requirement of empiricism. "Logically alike" will be interpreted to mean that interchanging the elements assigned to the two constants by a model always gives us a model again. It is easy to translate this condition into a numerical requirement: Two models which can be gotten from each other by the above procedure must have the same weight assigned to them. In this formulation we recognize a version of the principle of indifference.

These are the three conditions on which our intuition is clearest. We will add two more, but it will not be attempted to show their significance in general. They will have to be applied, according to our intuition, problem by problem.

Before proceeding to the other two conditions, we must ask whether our three general conditions, which are quite strong, are consistent. We affirm this by giving a definition of c, for *any* h and e, satisfying *CA* 1-3: Form the minimal language, according to *CA* 2. Then assign equal weights (adding up to 1) to its models. Then define c as in the discussion of *CA* 1. This satisfies all three conditions. (We will see, however, that this is too simple to be satisfactory even in the easiest problems.)

CA 4. The definition of c must enable us to "learn from experience".

As we have already indicated, we are not as yet in a position to give a full mathematical translation of this condition. But that does not mean that it is utterly useless. E.g., we would say that if we have a series of evidences, consisting of more and more confirming instances, then the c-values should be monotone increasing. Another type of example is one in which the more things have turned out to have a certain property, the more probable we consider it that the next thing will have this property as well.

CA 5. We need consider only that part of e which is relevant to h.

While this condition is practically begging the issue, it is listed here to call our attention to the fact that in a particular type of problem our intuition may be quite clear as to what part of the evidence is relevant. Indeed this will be the case in the problem to be discussed in full detail below.

We have now listed all that our intuition tells us about degree of confirmation. The list is not entirely satisfactory. The last two conditions are too vague, and we are by no means certain that the list is exhaustive. Nevertheless it suffices for certain important problems. As an illustration we will give a full definition of *c* for a classical problem. This will be the subject-matter of the following section.

IV. *A Classical Problem*[14]

Since the early days of the theory of probability, throwing dice has been one of the favorite problems. We propose to show that *CA* 1-5 (with the last two properly interpreted for this problem) suffice to determine *c*, but for the choice of a parameter.

To make our problem more specific, let us suppose that we have a definite die in mind.[15] We will concern ourselves with the outcome of various throws of this die. Our only interest is whether a given throw is an ace, a deuce, etc. denoted by the predicates $P_1, \ldots, P_6$, respectively. They are mutually exclusive, and exhaustive. The individuals are throws of the die. In accordance with *CA* 2 we choose a minimal language, which is a first order predicate calculus whose only predicates are the above mentioned family of 6 constants. We need not fix the number of individual constants at the moment. In order to define analyticity, we must only specify how many individuals there are in the models, say n. This number can be chosen to be the number of throws specifically mentioned, or it can be the number of all throws with this die since its manufacture to the day it burns in the Great Fire of 1995, or any number in between. Let us refer to our language as $L_n{}^6$.

A model of $L_n{}^6$ assigns to each of the n individuals one and only one of the 6 predicates, i.e. it tells just what happens in each throw. Thus there are 6^n models. Our task is to assign weights to these, which will satisfy *CA* 1-5. We already know what the first three conditions require; we must try, however, to make the last two more specific. We can do this by specifying clear instances where they apply.

Suppose that throws keep coming up aces, then the more often this happens, the surer we will be that the die is "loaded", and hence that the next throw will also be an ace. In accordance with *CA* 4 we will make this a requirement.

CA 5 seems to be clearest when the hypothesis states simply that the

[14]The main result of this section was first found by Carnap, [8], and later independently by the author (Kemeny, [5]). The proof here given is due to the author, but it is based on a proof (unpublished) due to Carnap.

[15]The reader must not assume that it is a "perfect" die. Indeed, this assumption is usually made in order to avoid the inductive problem. We must also "forget" any information we may have as to the symmetry properties of the die, and as to the past behavior or similar objects. We are to consider it simply as a device which under given circumstances always presents us with one of six possible results.

next throw will be P_i. All that we would consider relevant in e is how many other throws were P_i, and how many were not. This will be required in accordance with *CA* 5.

We can now proceed to the step-by-step narrowing of the possibilities for c.

Let us for the moment consider a special case of the die-problem. Suppose the hypothesis h_i states that the next throw will be P_i, and suppose the evidence e^k states the outcome of k previous throws. Then $c(h_i,e^k)$ will be called a *special value*. We will show that if we know all the special values, then we know all the weights, and hence have the required definition.

This proof can be considerably simplified by use of *CA* 2. Since the c-values are not to depend on accidental features of the language, the weights will not change if we add a few individual constants to $L_n{}^6$. Let us call $\overline{L}_n{}^6$ the language differing from the previous one only by having n individual names, a_i (with analyticity so defined that these are really names of n different individuals). This language has the advantage that for each model there is a *wff* true only in this model. Namely, if the model assigns the property designated by P_{i_j} to the jth individual, then the *wff* in question is $P_{i_1}(a_1)\& \ldots \& P_{i_n}(a_n)$. Such a *wff* is known as a state-description (*sd*). Since it is true only in one model, its measure is simply the weight of this model. Let s be an arbitrary *sd*, our problem is the finding of $m(s)$, i.e. of $c(s,t)$. Let us denote by e^k the conjunction of the first k terms of s, with e^0 being analytic and e^n being s itself. By repeated applications of (5) we have:

$$c(s,t) = c(e^n,e^0) = c(h_{i1},e^0) \times c(h_{i2},e^1) \times \ldots \times c(h_{i_n},e^{n-1}).$$

Hence the required value is expressed as a product of special values. Thus we see that knowledge of the special values enables us to get all the weights of the models of $\overline{L}_n{}^6$, which are the same as those of $L_n{}^6$.

Our problem thus reduces to the finding of special values. What can $c(h_i,e^k)$ depend on? It is a ratio of 2 m-values, and an m-value is the sum of weights. So it is a ratio of sums of weights. If we replace the individuals named by others, this will leave the weights unchanged, and hence c cannot change, by *CA* 3. By the same condition we see that a permutation of the predicates must leave c unchanged. Hence it is immaterial what individual is named by the hypothesis, and which predicate P_i is, except insofar as it connects with the evidence. What is relevant in the evidence? We have noted above that we will interpret *CA* 5 to state that what is relevant is how many of the k previous throws were "favorable", say k', and how many were not P_i, namely k-k'. So the special value can depend only on k' and k-k', or equivalently on k and k'. So we let

$$c(h_i,e^k) = f(k,k'). \qquad k = 0,1,2, \ldots ; k' = 0, \ldots , k.$$

We will now determine the function f.[16] It may help the reader, however, if we explain more intuitively what has been done so far. A model expresses what happens in all n throws. We formed a language where this can actually be expressed within L. This statement is a long conjunction, and we apply the rule for computing the probability of a conjunction. It tells us to take the probability of the first throw, times the probability of the second given the outcome of the first, etc. Each factor is of the form: Given the outcome of k throws, what is the probability that the next will be so and so. These are our special values, and it suffices to find them. Then we demonstrated that the special values depend only on how many throws were observed (k) and how many of them were "favorable" (k'). We are now searching for the exact dependence of the special values on k and k'.

Lemma 2. Given six numbers k_i, adding up to k, then the sum of the six $f(k,k_i)$ is 1.

Proof: Form e^k stating that k_i of the k throws were P_i.

Then $f(k,k_i) = c(h_i,e^k)$.

$$f(k,k_1) + \ldots + f(k,k_6) = c(h_1,e^k) + \ldots + c(h_6,e^k) = c(h_1 \mathbf{v} \ldots \mathbf{v} h_6,e^k)$$
$$= c(t,e^k) = 1.$$

Q.E.D.

Consider some special cases of this lemma: Let $k = 0$, and each $k_i = 0$. Then $6 \times f(0,0) = 1$ or

(A) $f(0,0) = 1/6$.

This says in effect that if we have no information at all, we must assign probability $1/6$ to each possible outcome.

Next: $k = 1$, $k_1 = 1$, the other $k_i = 0$.

Then $f(1,1) + 5 \text{x} f(1,0) = 1$.

Let $f(1,0) = p$ (to be determined later, if possible).

(B) $f(1,1) = 1 - 5p$.

Lemma 3. $f(k+1,k')/f(k+1,0) = f(k,k')/f(k,0) \qquad k' = 1, \ldots, k$.

Proof:

Let e^k assert that of the k throws k' were P_1 and the rest P_3.

Let e^{k+1} assert that of the $k+1$ throws $k'+1$ were P_1 and the rest P_3.

Let $e_1{}^{k+1}$ assert that of the $k+1$ throws k' were P_1, 1 P_2, the rest P_3.

Let e^{k+2} assert that of the $k+2$ throws $k'+1$ were P_1, 1 P_2, the rest P_3.

We assert the identity:

$$[m(e^{k+2})/m(e_1{}^{k+1})] \times [m(e_1{}^{k+1})/m(e^k)] =$$
$$[m(e^{k+2})/m(e^{k+1})] \times [m(e^{k+1})/m(e^k)].$$

But this is the same as saying that

[16] f corresponds to the *characteristic function* of Carnap, [8]. Since the present argument is for a given type of problem, the argument k drops out.

$f(k+1,k')\mathrm{x}f(k,0) = f(k+1,0)\mathrm{x}f(k,k')$. The lemma follows immediately.
Q.E.D.

From this lemma we have

(C) $f(k + 1,k') = [f(k,k')/f(k,0)] \times f(k + 1,0) \qquad k' = 1, \ldots, k$

We need two more values of lemma 2. We put $k+1$ for k, and once the division is $k+1$ with five 0's, the other time k, 1, with four 0's. These give cursion equations, determining the $f(k,k')$ values for $k \geq 2$ in terms of us the two equations:

(D) $f(k+1,k+1) + 5\mathrm{x}f(k+1,0) = 1$.

Replace the first two terms of (E) from (C), and we can solve for $f(k+1,0)$ in terms of $f(k,k')$ values. Then (C) gives us similar solutions for the $f(k+1,k')$, and (D) for $f(k+1,k+1)$. The three together are re-

(E) $f(k+1,k) + f(k+1,1) + 4\mathrm{x}f(k+1,0) = 1$.

those with $k = 0$, 1. But these in turn are determined by (A) and (B), except for the constant p. So f is uniquely determined in terms of p. It is easy to verify that the equations are satisfied by

(F) $f(k,k') = [k' + p/1{-}6p] \;/\; [k + 6p/1{-}6p]$.

Hence (F) represents the unique solution. The equation is simplified if in place of p we choose the parameter

(G) $\lambda = 6p/1{-}6p$.

(H) $f(k,k') = [k' + \lambda/6] \;/\; [k + \lambda]$.

This determines f, which fixes the special values, which determine the measures of the *sd*'s which in turn determine our weights. So the weights are determined but for the choice of λ.

What are the range of values of our parameter? Let us examine its definition, (G). We must determine the range of $6p$. Since p is a *c*-value, it must be between 0 and 1. We get a better limitation by making use of our last remaining *CA*, namely *CA* 4. By our formulation of it we require that if we have already observed that the first throw was an ace we make the probability of another ace somewhat greater than it was to start with. Hence $f(1,1)>f(0,0)$. Or, by (A) and (B), $1\text{-}5p > 1/6$, or $p<1/6$. Hence we have

(I) $0 \leqq 6p < 1$ hence λ is any non-negative real number.

It is now seen by a routine check that all our conditions are satisfied. [But if we require strict fairness, we must assure that all the weights are positive. The weights are expressed as products of f-values, so all these must be positive. Hence $k' + \lambda/6$ must always be positive. The necessary and sufficient condition for this is, clearly, that λ be positive.]

To summarize: The c-definition for dice has been reduced in the described manner to the determination of certain special values. These are given by:

(J) $c(h_i,e^k) = [k' + \lambda/6] \ / \ [k + \lambda]$,

where λ is any non-negative [positive] real number. So the entire classical problem has been solved, except for the choice of a single number.

It is of considerable interest to discuss the basis on which λ is to be chosen. Let us consider the case where aces keep turning up on the die. We become surer with each throw that the next one will also be an ace. While on the first throw the probability of an ace is 1/6, sooner or later we have to make this probability as high as ½. How soon will this be? When $[k + \lambda /6] \ / \ [k + \lambda] = ½$, or $k = ⅔ \lambda$.

This shows that the number of throws required to assign a probability of ½ is directly proportional to λ. So a value of 3 would mean that after two consecutive aces we would be willing to bet even money that the next throw will be an ace. While a value of 300 means that we would wait for two hundred consecutive aces till we accepted an even money bet. One would be inclined to say that the former value is too small and the latter too large, but one's intuition is pretty vague on this point. It is clear however that a large value of λ makes it more difficult to generalize. Hence the name "index of caution" has been suggested. One possible interpretation is that this is a purely psychological factor, and that all values of λ are reasonable. Yet one would feel that neither extreme caution nor extreme daringness should be permitted by a truly rational method.

Secondly, it is important to note that for large values of k the choice of λ is unimportant. It is the case of a small sample that is strongly influenced by this choice. Hence we could say that the various methods are equivalent in the long run. But it is interesting to note that it is precisely in the case of small samples, where our intuitive evaluations are least precise, that our definition leaves us too much freedom.

Thirdly, we must consider a most ingenious computation carried out by Carnap.[17] He asked himself the question of how we would choose an optimal λ if we knew the distribution of things in the world. He shows that the less homogeneous the world is, the larger the optimal value. I.e., the more evenly the various throws are distributed among the six alternatives, the larger the optimal choice of λ. From this point of view we would incline to the interpretation that λ is a measure of how evenly we think we chose our alternatives. In the problem of dice we may expect considerable evenness. But with the usual way of enum-

[17]Carnap, [8], part II.

erating alternatives (e.g. "gold", "silver", "other") we expect unevenness, which may explain our inclination to low values of λ.

It is important to note that the derivation here given is by no means restricted to the problem of dice, or even to a problem with 6 alternatives. Given any problem in which individuals are classified according to a family of κ exclusive and exhaustive alternatives, we arrive at the formula

$$(K)\ c(h_i, e^k) = [k + \lambda / \kappa] / [k + \lambda],$$

of which (J) is a special case. (The derivation is somewhat more complex for the extreme case $\kappa = 2$.) Considerable time has been spent discussing whether λ is a universal constant or a function of κ. The author now inclines to reject both points of view, and feels that λ depends on the problem, or more precisely on the way the alternatives are selected.[18]

It is of special interest to discuss the extreme values of 0 and ∞. Carnap has demonstrated that $\lambda = 0$ is the only one of the so-called unbiased methods left open by our definition.[19] It is ideal in a completely homogeneous world, and it is highly conducive to the formation of strong generalizations. After the first k throws, all aces, probability 1 is assigned to the next throw being an ace—no matter how small k is, even if only one throw was observed. This choice of λ is forbidden by the requirement of strict fairness, which fact is connected with the above counterintuitive result. Nevertheless, unbiased methods are very popular, and one of the main rivals of Carnap's definition implies the above quoted result (of assigning probability 1).[20] In all fairness to these methods it must be noted that although $\lambda = 0$ is not acceptable, we can choose λ as a very small number, in which case our answers differ negligibly from the unbiased method's. So the latter may be regarded as a simplifying approximation.

$\lambda = \infty$ is the upper bound of permissible values. It corresponds to the choice of $p = 1/6$, and as it is easy to see from (F) upon multiplying through by $1—6p$, it makes all the f-values (and hence all the weights) equal. This corresponds to the so-called Wittgenstein probability func-

[18]This was first suggested in Kemeny, [6]. Compare the problem of the die, e.g., with one in which two dice are thrown and we are faced with the six alternatives of throwing 2, 3, 4, 5, 6, more than 6. Out intuition would certainly tell us that the alternatives were more evenly chosen in the former case (though it is difficult to separate this intuition from prior knowledge). If we assume for the moment that the dice in question are "perfect" and calculate the optimal values of λ by Carnap's method, we find a large value for the former problem (see below) and a small one (about 3) for the latter.

[19]Cf. Carnap, [8], §§ 19, 20, and 23.

[20]Helmer, Hempel, and Oppenheim, [1], [2].

tion.[21] It has the effect that the probability of an ace is 1/6 no matter what we have observed. It is no wonder that this value was eliminated by *CA* 4. But this choice would be optimal in a world in which individuals are distributed evenly among the κ alternatives. In such a world any short-range generalization would be misleading, and $\lambda = \infty$ discourages all such generalizations. While neither of the two extreme values seems acceptable, their study gives us a "feeling" for what the choice of a value for λ implies.

It is interesting to ask what the optimal λ is if we assume that our universe of discourse is a sample from an infinite random distribution. Let us take $\kappa = 2$ for simplicity. We make the plausible assumption that $\frac{1}{2}[n+\sqrt{n}]$ of the n objects are P's and the other $\frac{1}{2}[n-\sqrt{n}]$ are $\sim$*P's*. If we calculate the optimal λ according to Carnap's formula, we arrive at the value $\lambda = n-1$. Of course our assumption was only correct in its order of magnitude, but this shows that in such a "random" universe λ ought to be of the order of magnitude of n. By a previous calculation we know that this means that no appreciable change in the a priori probability can be introduced, unless the sample is an appreciable fraction of the total number of things; or conversely, that samples of the usual order of magnitude *will* affect the *c*-values, but only negligibly.

Let us next consider Reichenbach's *posits*. Reichenbach, who frequently expressed disapproval of Carnap's approach, based his inductive methods on the following rule (paraphrased quite freely): " If k' out of k events were of type *A*, then posit the hypothesis that a ratio k'/k of all events will be of this type." Let us see whether any connection can be established between these posits and our definition. If one accepts the most natural rule that we ought to posit the most probable hypothesis on any given evidence, then the above rule implies that on the evidence e^k, of all the hypotheses asserting that a ratio r of all throws will be aces, the hypothesis with $r = k'/k$ must have the highest *c*-value. We may at least ask whether any value of λ would give us this result. To adapt this rule to our more general approach we must require that if there are κ alternatives, with e^k as usual, we posit the hypothesis stating that for each i the ratio of P_i*'s* is k_i/k. If we consider the set of all hypotheses assigning some ratio r_i to each of the P_i, and ask which hypothesis is best confirmed by e^k, we can show (by a computation too lengthy to be included in this paper) that the hypothesis is determined by

$$\text{(L)} \qquad r_i = [k' + \lambda/\kappa - 1]/[k + \lambda - \kappa].$$

This gives us the Reichenbach posits if $\lambda = \kappa$. So if we decide for any problem with κ alternatives to choose the value κ for λ, a choice favored

[21] Wittgenstein, [1], *5.15.

by Carnap, then Reichenbach's rule is a consequence of our definition. Reichenbach also points out that any rule agreeing with his asymptotically would be just as good. Hence it is significant that any permissible λ leads to a rule asymptotically equivalent to Reichenbach's, as can be seen from (L).[22]

Another famous inductive rule is Laplace's *rule of succession.* It gives in place of (K):

(M) $$c(h_i,e^k) = [k' + 1]/[k + 2].$$

As Carnap shows, this leads to contradictions if applied to an arbitrary language. We must assume that there only two alternatives, if we are to get consistent results. Thus, if we interpret this rule to apply to the case $\kappa = 2$ only, then we see that it is a special case of (K) with $\lambda = 2$; incidentally, this is the same value that Reichenbach's posits lead us to in this special case. Carnap presents a most plausible argument that the natural generalization of Laplace's rule is the formula (K) with λ having the constant value 2.

We conclude this section with a table of numerical values, intended to give the reader some intuitive feeling for numerical inductive probabilities, and for the influence of λ. The example concerns throws with a given die. The values are $c(h_1,e^{60})$, that is the probability of throwing an ace, based on a sample of 60 throws. The chosen values of λ are the two extreme ones, Laplace's, Reichenbach's, an intermediate 60, which is the size of the sample, and a large 600 which we may suppose to be of the order of magnitude of n. The number of favorable instances varies from none to all. The values have been rounded to 2 decimals.

κ' \ λ	0	2	6	60	600	∞
0	.00	.01	.02	.08	.15	.17
10	.17	.17	.17	.17	.17	.17
20	.33	.33	.32	.25	.18	.17
30	.50	.49	.47	.33	.20	.17
40	.67	.65	.62	.42	.21	.17
50	.83	.81	.77	.50	.23	.17
60	1.00	.97	.92	.58	.24	.17

Table of $c(h,e^{60})$.

[22]Cf. Reichenbach, [1]. In Carnap, [8], pp. 44, 52, 53, we find a different interpretation. Reichenbach's posits are interpreted as estimates. This interpretation leads to the value $\lambda = 0$.

V. *Where the Problem Stands*[23]

The treatment given to the classical problem in the previous section sets a standard for future work. At the moment we are not able to give such complete treatment to any other type of problem. But as long as there is serious doubt as to the fruitfulness of numerical degrees of confirmation, it is most significant that at least one type of problem can be satisfactorily treated.

We must now consider the prospects for future progress. The next more complex problem is one in which more than one family of predicates enters. We might think of drawing balls out of an urn which are of various sizes, colors, and have various patterns on them. This would be a problem with 3 families of predicates. Considerable work has already been done on this type of problem, though the results are by no means as conclusive as for one family.

A single predicate presents us with two alternatives, either an individual has the property expressed by the predicate, or it does not. The case of a single family is just a generalization of the case of a single predicate. The case of many families generalizes the case of many one-place predicates. It turns out that the difficult step is going from one family to more than one farmily, their number does not present essential difficulties. In this work the solution presented in the last section plays a central role. Even if our language has several families of predicates in it, we can express in it hypotheses and evidences formulated in terms of a single family. In this case the *c*-value must agree with the one calculated according to (K), by *CA* 2. This is a considerable restriction on the weights assignable to the models of the extended language.

The difficulty in extending our results can be analyzed as follows: While in stating our version of *CA* 4 for one family we could simply refer to the "favorable instances", in the case of several families there are many types of more or less favorable instances (in the occupation of special values), agreeing with the predicted outcome in one, two, . . ., all families. More specifically, while we can still reduce the problem to the finding of the special values "the chance of drawing a large, blue ball with a star on it, given the outcome of *k* draws"; we must now consider as favorable not only large, blue, star-marked balls, but also balls having one or two of these attributes. But we are helped by knowing the solution of the one family problem, and we can strengthen our version of *CA* 5 by requiring that arguments by analogy be admitted. Tentative results based on these conditions indicate that in the case of several families besides λ (or a λ for each family) only one parameter is left open. While λ measures

[23]The discussion in this section is based on work done jointly by Carnap and the author in '52-'53. Publication of detailed results is planned for the near future.

how ready we are to learn from experience, the new parameter measures how ready we are to learn from arguments by analogy.

In connection with these problems we must consider Nagel's well-known argument (published in 1939) to justify his skepticism concerning the possibility of a numerical measure for degree of confirmation.[24] While his argument concerns a problem of several families, we will instead discuss an analogous problem for one family. Nagel admits that certain comparative judgments of confirmation are highly intuitive. E.g., if our hypothesis is that the next throw of our die will be an ace, then the more aces we have observed in a row the more probable our hypothesis becomes. Thus, with all the evidence favorable, $c(h_1,e^6) > c(h_1,e^2)$. Or again, if h_1' is the hypothesis that the next two throws will be aces, then on either given evidence h_1 is more probable than h_1'. But what about the comparison of $c(h_1,e^2)$ and $c(h_1',e^6)$? What is more probable, that two aces will be followed by an ace, or that six consecutive aces will be followed by two more? It certainly appears that our intuition fails us. But, granted our solution of the previous section, we can give a definite answer to the question. There is a certain real number (about 3.4) such that for any λ lower than that $c(h_1,e^2)$ is less probable, while for any λ above that it is more probable than $c(h_1',e^6)$. So if we have once chosen λ all these puzzling questions are answered.

It now appears why Nagel's argument carried so much weight. He is perfectly correct in asserting that in any such problem our intuition provides no answer, since we have no certain way of choosing λ. But this is not due to the fact that there is no numerical solution to the classical problem, but that there are infinitely many! And once any one of these is adopted, all the answers follow. Of course Nagel's argument (about the variety of instances) concerns a problem of several families. But here too there are infinitely many solutions. Once a definite one is selected (by determining the λ's of the families and the analogy-constant), one has a definite answer to all of Nagel's truly puzzling questions.

Let us suppose for the moment that the problem of several families of predicates has been solved. We must then consider relational predicates, and here dependences become much more complex. Yet the procedure is no different in principle. Let us take as an example a single equivalence relation (that is a two-place predicate which is reflexive, symmetric, and transitive). The models of a language having this sole predicate are determined by stating for each of the n^2 pairs of individuals whether they satisfy the relation or not. But this does not lead to 2^{n^2} models, because of the restrictions on the relation. E.g., any proposed model in which some individual does not bear the relation to itself must be omitted as

[24] Nagel, [1], § 8.

self-contradictory. We must then assign non-negative [positive] weights to the actual models. Here again the problem can be reduced to the determination of special values. We must be able to state what part of the evidence is relevant to the hypothesis $R(a,b)$, as our formulation of *CA* 4. Presumably we will have to take into account how many individuals are known to bear the relation to either *a* or *b* and how many are known not to bear it to *a* or to *b* or to bear it to neither. Perhaps these give us five different parameters on which our special values may depend. And then what new types of arguments must be admitted in *CA* 5? All these questions strain our intuition somewhat, and the solution taxes our mathematical talents to the limit. But they are in principle no different from the classical problem already solved.

After relations of the first order we must consider predicates of higher order. Again the demands are of the same kind, further intuitive clarification of *CA* 4-5, and vastly more difficult mathematical work. But the problems are not new in principle.

An entirely different type of difficulty is raised by generalized propositions. With singular sentences we could always restrict ourselves to models with a finite number of individuals (since we could assume that only individuals actually named occur in the models), but no such procedure is possible with generalized sentences. If the quantifiers range over a finite domain with known cardinal number, then no new difficulty arises. These are the so-called pseudo-generalizations, which are equivalent to singular sentences (except that we may not have a name for each individual in our language). The difficulty arises when the domain of discourse is infinite or even if its cardinal is a large unknown number. In the latter case we could simply introduce n as an unknown, but since we know no more about it than that it is large, this may not enable us even to make comparative judgments.

There is a well-known argument to show that no real-valued measure of degree of confirmation can be satisfactory for a language with an infinite domain of individuals. Let h^n be the hypothesis that n successive individuals will have the property P. It is easy to see from the solution of the classical problem that $c(h^n,t)$ tends to 0 with increasing n. $c((x)Px,t)$ must be smaller than any of the previous (since the hypothesis implies all of them), so it must be 0. But this violates the condition of strict fairness. Some authors, Carnap himself in his earlier publications, accepted this as inevitable and advocated theories violating the principle of strict fairness. But whatever we may think of the principle, $c((x)Px,t) = 0$ is strongly counter-intuitive. The present author has reached the conclusion that for such languages a measure more general than that of real numbers must be introduced.

The clue to these more general measures lies in our consideration that if we are ignorant of n, we get a c-value which is a function of n. The author has suggested that this function be taken as the c-value, and that the functions be compared by their asymptotic properties. In the case of singular *wffs* the function is a constant function with all the properties of a real number. In this sense the functions are a generalization of the real numbers. These real-valued functions of an integer argument may be thought of as a generalization of numbers. Or if this does not appeal to the reader, he may at least recognize the significance of the comparative judgments so obtained. These ideas are worked out in detail elsewhere.[25]

And we must admit that even if all these problems are solved it is still a large step to a full scientific language. But we will not be able to tell how difficult any of these problems are till the easier ones are solved. We must not lose sight of the fact that the first step, which seemed impossible to most philosophers of science, has already been taken.

If all these problems are solved, we will in principle be able to tell how well any given hypothesis is confirmed by the available evidence. Let us close our discussion by looking into this "in principle".

The first step in any application must be the formalization of h and e. The former causes less difficulty; we do require our authors to state their hypotheses in precise form, and the formalization is then just a routine (though quite possibly laborious) exercise. It is important to realize that no restriction has been placed on the nature of the hypothesis. It may be a weak prediction or postdiction, or it may be a strong general law, or it may even consist of all the laws of present-day Physics. (Clearly, if we can formalize each law, their conjunction can also be taken as a single hypothesis.) But the author was recently engaged in a long debate as to whether "all the available evidence" can be thought of as a single *wff*. It is perhaps one of the most significant features of human endeavour that all the work of any one man or of all humanity up to a given date *must* be finite. Some of the famous proofs of the unsolvability of certain mathematical problems rest on this fact. If by available evidence we mean, e.g., only what has actually appeared in print, then it is obvious that at any point in human history the totality of all written sentences (let alone that part admitted as scientific evidence) must be finite. Each sentence can be formalized, and their conjunction forms e.

In practice this procedure would be somewhat expensive, even for the U.S. Government. But then no scientist ever considers all the available evidence when he makes an intuitive judgment. He selects those facts

[25]Kemeny, [7].

which he judges relevant, and takes these as his evidence. Insofar as his judgment of relevance is correct his result will be good.

But there is a second equally difficult problem in applications. The scientific language in question (or its minimal segment required for the formalization of h and e) may be too complex for treatment by the available methods. This may take many forms: (1) The explication of inductive probability may not have reached this advance stage as yet. (2) While the explication is available, no general formula has been found. (3) While even a general formula exists, its application in this special case exceeds our mathematical ability.

It is important to realize that all these difficulties exist (or existed) in so sound a branch of science as Mechanics. As far as collecting all the evidence is concerned, one must always make a selection of initial conditions. It is not even too infrequent that some significant fact is overlooked in this selection. Till the formulation of the General Theory of Relativity many mechanical phenomena could not be adequately treated. Even after the publication of this theory there are many problems for which no general formulas have been deduced, so that we are forced to use Newton's Laws—i.e. approximations. And even granted Newton's Laws, just give the theoretical physicist three bodies moving around and he will throw his hands up—or make use of further approximations, which amounts to the same thing.

Let us not apply to the Philosophy of Science standards more strict than those we are prepared to apply to the practicing scientist. Let us rejoice if a philosophical problem can at least in principle be solved rigorously. And in the very unlikely eventuality that the scientist really turns to us for a practical measure of the degree of confirmation, we can trust the mathematician to find him suitable approximations. That such approximations exist we already know. $\lambda = 0$ is a good approximation if λ is low, or the sample is large. And so is $\lambda = \kappa$, which leads to very simple formulas.[26]

As philosophers we must concentrate our attention on the only purely philosophical problem, the complete explication of our fundamental concept.

VI. *Conclusion*

Carnap's work may be thought of as an extension and improvement of the pioneer work done by Laplace. His work has the great merit that he immediately saw the full problem, and appreciated the fact that the progress so far is only a small first beginning.

The author cannot help but feel that the crucial philosophical issue

[26]Carnap, [8], 46.

is whether a numerical measure of inductive probability is at all fruitful. It was this issue that was so hotly debated for so long. And this issue seems settled once and for all. One can define a concept of probability different from the frequency concept, one that is mathematically precise and intuitively convincing. It was only necessary to demonstrate this in one type of example.

How far we will be able to extend this explication is now a function of our philosophical and mathematical ingenuity, and of the amount of effort we are willing to devote to this task. There is no doubt that an entirely new branch of Mathematics will have to evolve before the explication is completed. But this very fact may attract more first class minds to philosophical problems.

Carnap has taken this fundamental problem, of the method by which inductions are reasonably performed, out of the stage of fruitless debate, and he has shown us the way to constructive research. He himself achieved the first important result in this research. Therefore, we must class Carnap's contribution to the problem of induction among the greatest achievements of modern Philosophy.

JOHN G. KEMENY

DEPARTMENT OF MATHEMATICS
DARTMOUTH COLLEGE

BIBLIOGRAPHY

CARNAP, Rudolf.

[1] "On Inductive Logic," *Philosophy of Science,* XII (1945), 72-97.

[2] The Two Concepts of Probability," *Philosophy and Phenomenological Research,* V (1945), 513-32.

[3] "Probability as a Guide to Life," *Journal of Philosophy,* XLIV (1947), 141-148.

[4] "On the Application of Inductive Logic," *Philosophy and Phenomenological Research,* VIII (1947-8), 133-148.

[5] "Reply to Nelson Goodman," ibid., 461-462.

[6] "Truth and Confirmation," *Readings in Philosophical Analysis* (edited by Feigl and Sellars), (New York 1949).

[7] *Logical Foundations of Probability.* Chicago: University of Chicago Press, 1950.

[8] *The Continuum of Inductive Methods.* Chicago: University of Chicago Press, 1952.

DE FINETTI, Bruno.

[1] "Sul significate soggettivo della probabilità," *Fundamenta Mathematica,* XVII (1931), 298-329.

[2] "La Prévision: ses lois logiques, ses sources subjectives," *Annales de l'Institut Henri Poincaré,* VII (1937), 1-68.

HELMER, Olaf *and* HEMPEL, C. G. *and* OPPENHEIM, Paul.

[1] "A Definition of Degree of Confirmation," *Philosophy of Science,* XII (1945), no. 2. By Hempel and Oppenheim.

[2] "Degree of Confirmation," *The Journal of Symbolic Logic,* X (1945), no. 2. By Helmer and Oppenheim.

KEMENY, John G.

[1] "Models of Logical Systems," *ibid.,* XIII (1948), 16-30.

[2] Review of Carnap [7], *ibid.,* XVI (1951), 205-207.

[3] "Carnap on Probability," *The Review of Metaphysics,* V (1951), 145-156.

[4] "Extension of the Methods of Inductive Logic," *Philosophical Studies,* III (1952), 38-42.

[5] "A Contribution to Inductive Logic," *Philosophy and Phenomenological Research,* XIII (1953), 371-374.

[6] Review of Carnap [8], *The Journal of Symbolic Logic,* XVIII (1953), 168-169.

[7] "A Logical Measure Function," *ibid.,* XVIII (1953), no. 4.

[8] "Fair Bets and Degree of Confirmation," *ibid.,* XX (1955), 263-273.

[9] "A New Approach to Semantics," *ibid.,* XXI (1956), 1-27 and 149-161.

NAGEL, Ernest

[1] "Principles of the Theory of Probability," *International Encyclopedia of Unified Science,* I, no. 6. Chicago: University of Chicago Press, 1939.

RAMSEY, F.

[1] *The Foundations of Mathematics, and Other Logical Essays.* London, 1931.

REICHENBACH, Hans.

[1] *The Theory of Probability.* California: University of California Press, 1949.

SHIMONY, Abner.

[1] "Coherence and the Axioms of Confirmation," *The Journal of Symbolic Logic,* XX (1955), 1-28.

WITTGENSTEIN, Ludwig.

[1] *Tractatus Logico-Philosophicus.* London, 1922.

23

Arthur W. Burks

ON THE SIGNIFICANCE OF CARNAP'S SYSTEM OF INDUCTIVE LOGIC FOR THE PHILOSOPHY OF INDUCTION[1]

I. Introduction

IT is philosophically important to distinguish a *logical system of probability*[2] from a *philosophy of induction*. The former is an abstract, logical or mathematical system or construction, while the latter is an epistemological theory of the nature of human knowledge of factual statements. The distinction may be illustrated from the work of J. M. Keynes.[3] Keynes' logical system of probability consisted essentially of the traditional calculus of probability modified so that 'the probability of q on p is one' implies 'p logically implies q.' Keynes' philosophy of induction consisted chiefly of the following theses about elementary statements of probability: that they are a priori, that the true ones determine rational degrees of belief, and that they are related in certain ways to a revised principle of indifference, a principle of limited variety, and a law of the uniformity of nature.

I think Carnap's system of *inductive logic* is the most important logical system of probability created since Keynes'. Carnap's main contribution here can be roughly characterized by saying that he supplements the traditional calculus of probability by an assignment of a priori probabilities (c_0-values) to Leibnitzian logically possible universes (more technically, to state-descriptions). In particular, Carnap has discovered how to do this (by means of his function c^*) in such a way that the traditional rules of induction by simple enumeration, analogy, etc., result.

[1]This paper was written while the author was a John Simon Guggenheim Memorial Fellow. Most of our references will be to Carnap's *Logical Foundations of Probability* (1950), and *The Continuum of Inductive Methods* (1952), hereafter referred to as *LFP* and *Continuum* respectively.

[2]We will use 'probability' in the sense of inductive probability unless otherwise noted; this sense is the same as that of Carnap's 'probability$_1$' provided it is left open at this stage whether or not an elementary statement of probability$_1$ is L-determinate. Cf. *LFP* 30 and Section V 2 below.

[3]*A Treatise on Probability*.

Thus by means of his inductive logic Carnap gives a more precise characterization of the inductive method of science than has ever been given before.

In this paper we shall examine the bearings of Carnap's inductive logic on three quite basic questions of the philosophy of induction: the first concerns the meaning of 'probability', the second is the traditional question about the justification of induction, and the third is a question about the presuppositions of induction. We will formulate these questions (in Sections III 4, IV 2, and VI 1, respectively) in the light of Carnap's system of inductive logic and show that while adequate solutions of them must take account of this logic, it does not in itself provide solutions to them. It will turn out that Carnap has said little on these three questions[4] and part of our motive is to invite him to give some indication of his answers to them. Finally, in the course of our discussion of these three fundamental issues we are led to raise a number of questions concerning the interpretation of Carnap's writings on the philosophy of induction (Sections III 2, III 5, V 1, V 2, and V 3).

Carnap's description of the inductive method of science is in itself an important result for the philosophy of induction, and since it is closely related to the three main questions we will discuss, we need first to formulate it in our own terms (Section II).

II. On the Inductive Method of Science

1. The key concept needed for the description is that of *inductive method,* which we will define[5] as follows. An inductive method is defined for a formal language.[6] To each pair of sentences h, e of this language such that e is non-contradictory, the inductive method assigns a unique numerical value, called the degree of confirmation (or c-value) of h on e, or $c(h,e)$. It is required, moreover, that the degrees of confirmation assigned satisfy the rules of the traditional calculus of probability.[7]

2. An inductive method as just defined is a highly abstract entity, nothing but a syntactic measure function defined over a language. Its relevance to induction is brought out only by considering a particular way in which it may be used.

The particular use we shall consider is in connection with the inductive arguments employed by a scientist and the elementary statements of

[4]Also, the summaries of the forthcoming Vol. II given in *LFP* ix-xi, 562-577 make little reference to them.

[5]Somewhat differently from Carnap; cf. *Continuum* 4.

[6]We will consider only languages having a finite number of individual constants.

[7]E.g., those given by J. Hosiasson, described at *LFP* 339.

probability[8] asserted and believed by him. Let e be the conjunction of the premises and h the conclusion of an inductive argument, and x the probability value attached to this conclusion. Then that inductive argument is in conformity with a given inductive method if x is the degree of confirmation assigned to the pair h, e by that method. The definition for an elementary statement of probability is similar. Finally, a scientist *uses an inductive method,* roughly speaking, when most of the probability values he assigns to inductive arguments and elementary statements of probability are approximately in conformity with that method.

The preceding definition needs amplification in two basic respects. In the first place, it omits the normative element present in inductive argumentation. For example, a person may try to make his probability assignments conform to the calculus of probability but sometimes fail, and we would not on this account say that he was not using the inductive method involved, just as we would not deny that a person was using deductive logic because he committed a deductive fallacy. Second, there is a pragmatic element in the concept being defined: the fact that using an inductive method implies having dispositions to act in specific ways in specific circumstances. Thus to say that a person assigns the probability x to the pair h, e is to imply that he is willing to bet on h with odds x to $1 - x$ (assuming he has no moral objection to betting, etc.) under certain conditions (e.g., e satisfies the requirement of total evidence—*LFP* 211). The general connections between degrees of belief, probabilities, utilities, expectations, and rational behavior under conditions of uncertainty are sufficiently known that we do not need to spell out the assumptions and conditions involved here in any greater detail.

It should be noted that while the concept of an inductive method is very precise, that of using an inductive method is quite vague and approximate. This imprecision has a number of sources. Scientists do not assign exact probability values to the conclusions of inductive arguments, and in many cases they are unwilling to assign any values whatsoever (cf. footnote[16]). The normative and behavioristic features of using an inductive method increase the difficulty of deciding whether or not a given method is being used. Finally, inductive methods have so far been defined only for formal languages of certain limited kinds which are far removed in many important respects from natural and scientific languages. Hence to apply the concept of an inductive method to an ordinary language we must regard the formal language as an idealization or model of the given language, and it is often difficult to determine whether or not the model embodies the relevant features of the language being modeled.

[8]Statements of the form 'the probability of h on e is x' (*LFP* 30), which we will abbreviate by '$P(h,e) = x$'.

3. One of Carnap's most significant contributions is to have shown rigorously that there are many possible inductive methods that could theoretically be used. We will discuss some philosophical implications of this result later; for the present we are interested in the question: Do all scientists use essentially the same inductive method, and if so, what is it?

Because of the vagueness just noted in the concept of using an inductive method this question does not admit of a simple answer but rather involves a matter of degree. We are interested here in gross differences rather than small variations, and for this case the answer is yes. Let us call the method based on Carnap's function c^* (*LFP* 564) the *star-method.* Then we assert

> Thesis I: All scientists use approximately the same inductive method, and this is close to the star-method.

Thesis I is at least part (cf. Section III 5 below) of what Carnap intends by his claim that c^* is a good explicatum of the concept of probability (*LFP* 563), and I have no doubt the evidence he has advanced and will advance for that claim will suffice to establish Thesis I.

III. On the Meaning of Elementary Probability Statements

1. The much debated question of the meaning of 'probability' can be fruitfully reexamined by means of Carnap's system of inductive logic. For, having the precise concept of c^* on the one hand, we can compare it with the vague concept of probability on the other, to determine the extent to which they agree and the extent to which they differ in meaning.

2. I will first state a certain thesis about the meaning of 'probability' which seems to me true, but which is of philosophical interest even if false.

This thesis is a specific application of the pragmatic doctrine that genuine belief in a proposition involves dispositions to act in various ways and to expect certain results. Thus if a person believes that there is a table in front of him he will expect it to support a book, and if he wishes to get to the other side of it he will in general walk around the place it occupies, etc. And if a person believes that 19 times 41 equals 779 he will expect to obtain a group of 779 objects when he combines 19 disjoint groups of 41 objects each under circumstances that preclude disappearance of the objects, etc. In general, then, the pragmatist holds that sentences of the form '*A* believes that *p*' imply that *A* has dispositions to act and expect in various ways which are intimately related to the meaning of the statement '*p*'. This general pattern of the analysis of belief sentences seems to me correct, whatever the truth status of the stronger pragmatic doctrine that practical consequences of the sort illustrated exhaust and serve to clarify the meaning of a proposition.[9]

Let us now apply this pragmatic pattern of analysis to[10] '*A* believes $P(h,e) = x$' ('*A* believes that the probability of *h* on *e* is *x*'). The result is already implicit in our definition of the concept of using an inductive method; for this definition contained a pragmatic element, which is connected to the word 'probability' since using an inductive method involves using 'probability' (and associated words) in certain ways. Thus it was stated that whenever a scientist, in the course of using an inductive method, assigns the probability *x* to the pair *h, e,* he has dispositions to bet, to act, and to expect under conditions of uncertainty in specifiable ways. Translating this in terms of beliefs we get that 'A believes $P(h,e) = x$' implies that when certain conditions are satisfied (e.g., *e* expresses *A*'s total non-probabilistic beliefs) *A*'s choices and expectation involving *h* are governed in a certain way by the quantity *x*. The kind of belief involved here is often called 'partial belief' or 'degree of belief', in contrast to 'total belief', illustrated in the preceding paragraph. In both cases the pragmatist holds that believing a proposition involves having dispositions to act in various ways and to have certain expectations.

The concept of partial belief stands in need of further analysis; in particular, it must be related to the normative aspect of using an inductive method.[11] Let us say that when *A* has dispositions to behave related to *h, e,* and *x* in the ways just described, *A* has an actual degree of belief in the pair *h, e* of amount *x*. Now the import of the previous paragraph is that '*A* believes $P(h,e) = x$' implies that *A* has an actual degree of belief in *h, e* of *x;* while the import of the assertion that 'probability' has a normative element is that there is more implied by the belief statement than that *A* has a certain actual degree of belief. It is difficult to state precisely what this additional element is; but roughly speaking it is some kind of claim or belief that this actual degree of belief is in conformity with a norm (i.e., an inductive method, though what method is being used need not be made explicit), together with a dispositional willingness to change this actual degree of belief if it is learned that it does not in fact approximately correspond with this norm

[9]*Collected Papers of Charles Sanders Peirce,* V, par. 9.

[10]Strictly speaking the qualification 'sentences of the form' is needed here. However, in the interest of brevity we will often speak loosely in this and similar cases (as in our use of "*p*" two sentences back and our subsequent references to the word 'probability' where a reference to its meaning is intended).

[11]Cf. Section II 2. The normative aspect of the use of an inductive method applies primarily to a person's total system of probabilistic beliefs and only derivatively to a single such belief taken in isolation. Hence it would be better to analyze '*A* believes $P(h_1e_1) = x_1, \ldots, P(h_n,e_n) = x_n$' rather than '*A* believes $P(h,e) = x$', but in the interest of brevity we will work with this latter (simpler) form.

(if, e.g., a fallacy is discovered in the reasoning process that led to the probability belief).

We shall say that *A believes h on e to degree x* whenever *A* has an actual degree of belief in *h, e* of approximately amount *x* and the normative element just described is also present.[12] Then the results of the foregoing analysis of probability may be summarized by the statement that '*A* believes $P(h,e) = x$' implies '*A* believes *h* on *e* to degree *x*', which we will call the *Pragmatic Thesis.*

Something similar to this thesis has been held by a number of careful thinkers,[13] and it seems to me correct. It is not entirely clear from what Carnap has so far said whether he would accept it or not. His emphasis on probability as a guide to life *(LFP* 247) implies that he would, and presumably he would accept Thesis I in which (or at least so it seems to me) the Pragmatic Thesis is implicit. But on the other hand an argument we will give in Section V 2 shows that a literal interpretation of Carnap's doctrine that elementary statements of probability are L-determinate is incompatible with the Pragmatic Thesis. Since this thesis asserts a basic point about the meaning of the concept (probability) Carnap has taken as an explicandum, it would be of interest to know whether he holds it to be true, false, or undecidable in principle because of the vagueness of ordinary usage.

Whatever the truth-status of the Pragmatic Thesis it represents a point of view concerning probability which is both plausible and important. Hence it is worthwhile for us to compare the concept of probability and Carnap's proposed explicatum (c^*) for it from this point of view.

[12]This normative feature of 'probability' is often covered by the phrase 'rational degree of belief', which we have avoided for two reasons. First, the ordinary use of 'rational' may connote that the norm is in fact approximately the star-method, whereas at this stage we wish to permit it to be any inductive method. Second, 'rational degree of belief' is ambiguous: it may mean either an actual degree of belief accompanied by this normative element or the degree of belief the person would have if in fact his actual degree of belief was in conformity with his norm.

[13]F. P. Ramsey, *The Foundations of Mathematics and Other Logical Essays* (1931), 156-198, was the first to apply the pragmatic doctrine to probability statements in the general way done above. A similar line of thought was more fully developed by Bruno de Finetti (see *LFP* 586-587 for references). Neither writer formulated the result in terms of the meaning of 'probability' in the context of belief sentences as we have done.

It is important that Ramsey did not state anything like Thesis I (the same is true of de Finetti); for while presumably he would have accepted the validity of induction by simple enumeration, etc., and so would have accepted this thesis, his discussion is in terms of the rules of the traditional calculus of probability and hence he never considered the matter. For this reason we have formulated the Pragmatic Thesis so that it states that the use of 'probability' in belief contexts implies only the use of some inductive method; that this method is in fact the star-method follows from the Pragmatic Thesis and Thesis I taken together. Cf. Section III 4.

3. We shall discuss first the question of whether the thesis derived from the Pragmatic Thesis by substituting 'c^*' for 'P' is truc.

We have already named the inductive method based on c^* the 'star-method'; let the method based on $c^\dagger$ (*LFP* 565) be called the *dagger-method.* Consider a typical scientist, who by Thesis I uses the star-method, and call him 'Mr. Star.' Imagine, now, a person who uses the dagger-method but who in all other relevant respects is the same in thought and behavior as Mr. Star, and call him 'Mr. Dagger'.[14] In particular, both Mr. Star and Mr. Dagger are well-trained in mathematics and logic, are fully acquainted with Carnap's system of inductive logic, and accept the rules of the traditional calculus of probability. It follows from Thesis I that Mr. Dagger is fictional, but we can easily form a conception of him.

Consider further a particular h' and e' such that $c^*(h',e') = .8$ and $c^\dagger(h',e') = .5$ (in the languages used by both Mr. Star and Mr. Dagger) and a situation in which both parties are aware of these equations and neither party commits an inductive fallacy. It follows from the above facts that Mr. Star believes h' on e' to degree *.8;* similarly, Mr. Dagger believes h' on e' to degree *.5*. Assume finally that e' satisfies the requirement of total evidence for both Mr. Star and Mr. Dagger in the given situation. This assumption enables us to describe more specifically the action and expectation dispositions of the two men; we can say now, for example, that Mr. Star would regard a ticket that is to pay $10 if h' is true (nothing otherwise) a bargain at $6 but Mr. Dagger would not (we here ignore various well-known refinements of the concept of utility). The kind of dispositions involved here can be conveniently stated in terms of non-relative degrees of belief,[15] i.e., by saying that in the given situation Mr. Star believes h' to degree *.8* while Mr. Dagger believes it only to degree *.5*.

Now notice that though Mr. Dagger believes h' on e' to degree *.5* he also believes '$c^*(h',e') = .8$'. The point of the example is that Mr. Dagger's belief in '$c^*(h',e') = .8$' does not involve a commitment to use the star-method in this instance. Similarly, Mr. Star's acceptance of '$c^\dagger(h',e') = .5$' does not constitute sufficient grounds for his betting even odds on h'. Of course Mr. Dagger's belief in '$c^*(h',e') = .8$' implies some action and expectation dispositions, but the point is that the use of the star-method in this instance is not one of these. This point may be obscured by the fact that there is a close relation between a belief in '$c^*(h',e') = .8$'

[14]Whether or not Mr. Dagger uses the word 'probability' does not matter for our purposes, though it would seem desirable for him to use some word which differs from '$c^\dagger$' in that it expresses the fact that this particular c-function is being used inductively. If it is the same word, then of course it may well have a different meaning for him than for Mr. Star; cf. footnote 32.

[15]Cf. footnote 12.

and the use of the star-method, so it is worthwhile to analyze this relation in some detail. Since Mr. Dagger believes '$c^*(h',e') = .8$' he has a conditional commitment to the star-method: if for each state-description Z he believed Z to degree $c^*_0(Z)$ then he would believe h' to degree $.8$ in the present situation. But it is clear that if he had degrees of belief in logically possible universes these would be of amount $c^\dagger_0(Z)$ for each Z, so that the antecedent of this conditional commitment would not be satisfied.[16] In contrast, Mr. Dagger has a non-conditional or categorical commitment to use the dagger-method. A similar argument, mutatis mutandis, holds for Mr. Star's belief in '$c^\dagger(h',e') = .5$'.

We conclude from this

(α) '*A* believes $c^*(h,e) = x$' does not imply[17] '*A* believes h on e to degree x'.

Thus if the Pragmatic Thesis is correct, there is an important difference in meaning between 'probability' and 'c^*' in belief contexts. It will be convenient to have a brief way of stating this alleged difference.

The Pragmatic Thesis implies that the ordinary scientific use of 'probability' involves (in a way made explicit in the Thesis) a commitment to use an inductive method; in contrast, 'c^*' does not involve this kind of commitment to an inductive method, as we have just shown. Since the alleged difference between these two terms concerns a commitment or lack of commitment to use an inductive method we will employ the phrase 'inductive-method committive' in our brief statement of this difference: we define a term to be *inductive-method committive* whenever the result of substituting it for '*P*' in the Pragmatic Thesis is a true statement. The Pragmatic Thesis may then be alternatively stated as: 'probability' as ordinarily used in science is inductive-method committive, while (α) is equivalent to: 'c^*' is not inductive-method committive.

4. Let us now combine the results of the Pragmatic Thesis and Thesis I. To this end we define a term to be *star-method committive* whenever it satisfies the following two conditions. First, it is inductive-method committive. Second, the inductive method to which commitment is in fact made is approximately the star-method; i.e., the inductive

16We are assuming that Mr. Dagger would make no mistakes in his reasoning about logically possible universes.

Objection might be taken to the concept of a degree of belief in a possible universe, since in every actual case of a person believing h on e to degree x, e expresses considerable factual information (even though all of it may be general in nature). However, the fact that these actual cases are sufficient to determine (in some sense) commitment to the star-method (cf. Thesis I) shows that our point could be made without using this concept, but there is not space so to formulate it here.

17The implication involved here, as in the Pragmatic Thesis, is a logical implication, holding or not holding by virtue of the meanings of the terms used.

method which is in fact used in connection with the term assigns approximately the same values to pairs of sentences as does the star-method. The Pragmatic Thesis implies that the ordinary scientific use of 'probability' satisfies the first condition; and Thesis I (together with the fact that scientists do use the word 'probability' in connection with their inductive arguments and elementary statements of probability) implies that this usage satisfies the second condition; so the two together imply that 'probability' as used by the typical scientist is star-method committive. In contrast, it follows from (α) that 'c^*' is not star-method committive.

We can now formulate a basic philosophical question concerning induction: Are there one or more probability concepts that are star-method committive, and if so, what are their analyses?[18] Though this question was formulated on the basis of the Pragmatic Thesis, its philosophical interest transcends that of the thesis. The Pragmatic Thesis is a statement about ordinary scientific usage, and even if it is false and probability is not star-method committive, there may still be concepts, closely related to the ordinary meaning of probability, which are star-method committive. It is this possibility that the above question is concerned with, and I think that the general pragmatic position is of sufficient importance that, whatever the verdict about ordinary usage, the question is of philosophical interest. (Cf. further Section V 3.)

5. It is evident from the foregoing that the Pragmatic Thesis has a bearing on Carnap's *Explication Thesis* that c^* is a good explicatum of probability (*LFP* 563). For if the latter concept is star-method committive and the former is not there is an important aspect of the meaning of the explicandum which is not preserved in the explicatum. Hence the Pragmatic Thesis is incompatible with a *stronger version* of Carnap's Explication Thesis according to which the explicatum preserves this particular feature of the meaning of the explicandum. On the other hand, the Pragmatic Thesis is compatible with a *weaker version* of Carnap's Explication Thesis which permits this difference in meaning between explicatum and explicandum. Since it is not clear from Carnap's writings whether he would accept the Pragmatic Thesis, and since he has not yet stated in detail what he means by saying that c^* is a good explicatum of probability, I am not sure which of these two versions he intends by his Explication Thesis. However, all that he has said concerning explication in general is compatible with the weaker version. We shall show this in some detail, spelling out the weaker version more explicitly in the process.

Carnap's requirements for a good explicatum are four in number: it must be (1) *"similar to the explicandum"* (though "considerable differ-

[18]See Section V 3 for the difference between our 'analysis' and 'analysans' and Carnap's 'explication' and 'explicatum' respectively.

ences are permitted"), (2) exactly formulated, (3) fruitful, and (4) simple (*LFP* 7). Now even if c^* differs from probability with regard to the property of being star-method committive, these concepts are quite similar in meaning. Thesis I implies this, for it states that the systematic relations of statements of the form '$P(h,e) = x$' are approximately the same as those of the form '$c^*(h,e) = x$', with regard to the actual values assigned as well as the relations covered by the traditional calculus of probability; and it would seem that this similarity is sufficient to justify holding that requirement (1) is satisfied by c^*.[19] Further, Carnap allows "considerable differences" between the explicatum and explicandum. He would undoubtedly agree that differences in meaning closely related to the imprecision and vagueness of the explicandum are essential to a good explication, for if the explicatum were fully synonymous with the explicandum it would have all the defects of the latter and the explication would have no point. Thus c^* and probability differ in that one can in principle always determine a precise value for $c^*(h,e)$, whereas one can rarely if ever determine a precise value for $P(h,e)$ and in some cases perhaps can determine no value at all; and in order for c^* to be a good explicatum of probability it is necessary that there be this difference between the two concepts. Now it is tenable to hold that the difference between c^* and probability with regard to star-method committiveness is a similar difference. An argument for this position is as follows: The notion of star-method committiveness is too vague and unclear to be formalized,[20] and since a good explicatum must be governed by exact rules (requirement 2), this notion should not be included in a good explicatum of probability. Hence the fact that c^* is not star-method committive while probability is, is quite compatible with the former's being a good explicatum of the latter. Finally, since c^* is fruitful and simple (requirements 3 and 4), it satisfies all the requirements for being a good explicatum of probability.

IV. On the Justification of Induction

1. There are three related philosophical questions concerning induction which need to be sharply distinguished. The first, to which

[19] It is worth noting that the only kind of evidence Carnap has so far advanced for his Explication Thesis supports merely Thesis I, and hence just the degree of similarity between c^* and probability mentioned above, and not the closer similarity between these two concepts required by the stronger version of the Explication Thesis.

[20] One could maintain that this notion may someday be sufficiently clarified to permit of formalization, or alternatively that it is non-cognitive and hence in principle non-formalizable (cf. Section V 3).

It is relevant to note here that instead of accepting or rejecting the Pragmatic Thesis one might hold that it is undecidable in principle because of the vagueness of ordinary usage, and that this is a further reason for not incorporating the property of star-method committiveness in the explicandum.

Thesis I constitutes an answer, is the question: What inductive method do scientists actually use? The second, discussed in the preceding section (III), is: To what extent are 'probability' and 'c^*' similar in meaning? The third is difficult to state, but it may be provisionally formulated as: What justification, if any, is there for using the star-method?

These questions have been stated in order of difficulty. The first is straightforward and admits of a definite answer, though further work is needed because of the gap between ordinary languages and the languages for which *c*-functions have hitherto been defined. The second question concerns intensions, and hence is more difficult, especially since 'probability' is undoubtedly vague. But with regard to the third question there is debate as to whether there is any question here at all, and if so, exactly what it is. In the present section we shall first try to clarify it somewhat and then discuss the bearing of Carnap's logical system of probability on it.

2. Let us consider the usual process of justifying the selection of one from a number of alternative courses of action. There are in general two kinds of judgments involved in the justification of such a choice: those concerning the factual properties of each alternative and those concerning the values associated with these properties. Using this distinction, we may give the following preliminary[21] description of the process of justification: one assesses the values realized by each alternative on the basis of its factual characteristics and the value criteria employed and then argues that the course of action chosen is at least as valuable as any alternative. As an example consider a man who journeys to a distant city by plane rather than by train. He could justify this choice by showing that the comparative costs, time required, etc., are such that, on the basis of the relative importance he attaches to his time, money, safety, etc., the plane alternative is better.

To use an inductive method is to behave in a certain way, and since there are alternative inductive methods there are, theoretically at least, alternative modes of inductive behavior. Now the crucial question is: Can the use of one inductive method (in particular, the star-method) be justified (as the best course of action among available alternatives) in a way analogous to the justification of the choice of a course of action described in the preceding paragraph?[22]

One important difference between the justification situation in in-

[21]At this stage our account of justification can be only preliminary, because part of the issue concerns the nature of justification. Of course our value-fact distinction already assumes something controversial, but since Carnap has never said that he would reject it there is no point in arguing this question here.

[22]We are considering in both cases the kind of justification that may be given before the course of action is embarked upon. Hence the alternative modes of inductive behavior referred to are those of using different inductive methods in the future.

duction and the ordinary kind of justification situation should be noted immediately. Though the inductive justification question is about practice it is not practical in the sense that anyone who has ever asked this question has seriously considered using any inductive method other than the star-method or something like it. But note that one can ask about the relative merits of alternative behavior patterns even where there is no thought of the deliberation affecting the outcome. E.g., suppose the man took the plane out of habit and didn't consider the train; another person can nevertheless ask whether the train choice would not have been better for this man. Similarly, one can contemplate the possibility of using different inductive methods even though he has no practical interest in the outcome of the discussion.

However, whenever the question is not a practical one it is perhaps better to avoid the word 'justification' in formulating it and to speak rather of showing that one behavior pattern is at least as beneficial to the parties concerned as any of a given set of courses of action. The crucial question concerning the justification of induction then becomes: Can it be shown that the use of the star-method is at least as beneficial as the use of any other inductive method in a way similar to the way it is usually shown that one behavior pattern is at least as beneficial as some other?

One further refinement is required before we have completely formulated the traditional justification-of-induction question. We must distinguish between slightly different inductive methods (e.g., the star-method and a slight variant of it) and grossly different methods (e.g., the star-method and the dagger-method); cf. Section II 3. It follows from the very nature of the explication process that there is a practical choice with regard to fine differences: 'probability' being vaguer than any *c*-function concept, there are many *c*-functions which fall within the range of indefiniteness of 'probability', and it is a practical question to decide which of these to use as an explicatum (and hence we will call this *the practical question of the choice of an explicatum for probability*). But the *traditional question about the justification of induction* concerned grosser differences, and this is the question we are dealing with in this section.

It seems to me that Carnap's inductive logic has a significant bearing on two important answers to this question.

3. The first is the pragmatic answer of Hans Reichenbach:[23] that the use of the straight rule of induction (which is similar to the star-method) can be justified as the best policy to follow.

Reichenbach conducts his argument in terms of the frequency concept

[23] *The Theory of Probability*. C. S. Peirce gave a similar answer.

of probability (Carnap's probability$_2$) and makes essential use of the limit properties of this concept, attempting to justify the use of the straight rule in the long run or infinite case.[24] Hence if we raise the traditional question about the justification of induction with regard to a finite case (e.g., a person's life span) instead of the indefinite future, Reichenbach's argument does not directly apply to it. To formulate this question we must use the concept of inductive probability, and Reichenbach would have objected that there is no exact, scientific non-frequency concept of probability, but Carnap's inductive logic shows that there is (e.g. c^*).

One might think one could construct a valid argument similar to Reichenbach's but in terms of c^* rather than a frequency concept of probability. This has not, however, been done, and I think the following considerations show that it cannot be done.

4. A second answer to the justification problem is that of Hume: any inductive argument to show that the use of the star-method (or a similar inductive method) is as beneficial as the use of alternative methods (e.g., the dagger-method) is necessarily question-begging. This answer seems to me essentially correct, but it needs to be restated in terms of Carnap's inductive logic.

Let us return to the usual process of justifying the choice of a pattern of action. This involves ascertaining various factual properties of the alternatives available and evaluating them by certain value criteria. Now we are supposing that the justification process takes place before an alternative is selected, so that each behaviour pattern lies completely in the future. It is clear that in this situation the relevant factual characteristics of the alternatives cannot be known with certainty or by direct observation, but only with probability and by means of an inductive method. In the plane-train case, for example, the man would not know whether the plane would have an accident on this trip, though he can judge (only roughly, to be sure) on the basis of past evidence what the chances of an accident are.

Thus an inductive method is used in the ordinary case of showing that one behavior pattern is more beneficial than another. Now consider the alternative behavior patterns of using the star-method in the future and of using some other method (e.g., the dagger-method). As before one cannot know what the actual success of each of these will be and is reduced to estimating the probable success of each in terms of an inductive method. But here the situation is very different from the usual case of

[24]Reichenbach also gives a form of the argument based on a finite frequency concept of probability, but the general considerations advanced here hold (with appropriate modifications) for that form too. See my review of his book, *The Review of Metaphysics* IV (1951), 377-393.

choosing between behavior patterns, for in the inductive case both the judge and the judged are, so to speak, inductive methods. Hence any attempt to show that the use of the star-method is at least as beneficial as the use of an alternative such as the dagger-method is question-begging because it requires the use of some inductive method. For example, if Mr. Star, in trying to persuade Mr. Dagger to adopt the star-method, used a similar method in the metalanguage,[25] Mr. Dagger could properly retort that whatever doubts he had concerning the star-method would apply to the analogue as well.

5. Carnap has not yet given any clear-cut answer to the traditional question about the justification of induction. Some of his remarks show sympathy for the attempt to justify the use of the star-method or a variant of it,[26] while others are in line with the Humean point of view (*Continuum* 59-60). He also makes, in connection with semantics, some remarks[27] that are relevant to the justification question, so let us now turn to a consideration of these.

V. External Questions and Induction

1. At *Ontology* 510 Carnap distinguishes *internal questions,* or questions concerning the existence of entities within a linguistic framework, from *external questions,* or questions concerning the reality of the system of entities mentioned by the linguistic framework. Carnap draws his distinction only with reference to semantics and deductive logic, and he has not said explicitly anywhere that it or a similar distinction is applicable to induction. It will nevertheless be instructive to consider his writings on induction from the point of view of such a distinction.

The distinction for induction could not be exactly the same as the one Carnap has drawn in *Ontology,* since no question concerning the existence of abstract entities is at issue here. But compare the questions:

(1) What is the c^*-value that the degree of actual statistical uniformity in nature is high relative to the available evidence? (Cf. *LFP* 180)

[25]Actually, the method would be in the meta-metalanguage, since the arguments of degree of confirmation are sentences. The point is that in discussing the use of an inductive method one is discussing the use of a language and hence must discourse in a language which is of higher level in the language hierarchy.

[26]"On Inductive Logic," *Philosophy of Science* XII (April, 1945), 96-97, and *LFP* v, 163, 177-182: concerning the latter references see also Section VI 1 below.

[27]"Empiricism, Semantics, and Ontology," *Revue Internationale de Philosophie* IV (January, 1950), 20-40. Reprinted with revisions in *Readings in Philosophy of Science,* edited by Philip P. Wiener, 509-522. Hereafter this title will be abbreviated *Ontology,* and page references will be made to the revised edition.

(2) The practical question of the choice of an explicatum for probability stated in Section IV 2.

with the questions:

(1′) Is there a prime number greater than one hundred?

(2′) Shall we accept a linguistic framework with natural numbers?

It seems clear that (1) is the same kind of question as (1′) (both are settled by logical techniques), which Carnap calls an internal question *(Ontology* 512), and that (2) is similar to (2′), which he calls an external question *(Ontology* 513).

Though Carnap does not talk of external and internal questions of induction his treatment of the problem of choosing an inductive method in *Continuum* seems to reflect such a distinction. For the most part he discusses the purely logical (and internal) question of measuring the success of an inductive method relative to a specified state-description. In a number of places (pp. 7, 53-55, etc.), however, he considers briefly an external question of choice and treats it in the same pragmatic way he regards external questions in *Ontology*. Though he is not very explicit as to what question of choice he is considering here (and in particular does not say that it is the question of choosing a good explicatum for probability) apparently it is question (2) above; at any rate question (2) is a "practical question [of] whether or not to accept [certain] linguistic forms" *(Ontology* 519). And though he never explicitly relates external questions to explications, what he says about external questions (in particular, their practical nature) clearly applies to questions concerning what explicatum should be used or what reconstruction of language should be adopted for a proposed formalization of science.

The possibility that there are external questions concerning induction is very significant from the point of view of this paper. The questions mentioned in the preceding paragraph are, of course, legitimate external questions, and they are indeed practical in nature. But once the existence of external questions is admitted the following queries must be faced: Are there not legitimate non-practical (theoretical) external questions of induction? In particular, are not the three main questions discussed in this paper (the question formulated in Section III 4, the traditional question about the justification of induction, and the question about the presuppositions of induction stated in Section VI 2) of this kind?[28] It would clarify Carnap's position for him to state whether or not he does admit the existence of external questions of induction; and if he does, for him to indicate their nature, specifically, to give grounds for his answers to the two queries just stated. To illustrate the difference the ad-

[28]It should be noted, in this connection, that our distinction between a logical system of probability and a philosophy of induction is similar to the distinction between internal and external questions of induction.

mission of external questions of induction would make to his philosophy of induction we shall (assuming for this purpose that he accepts such questions) examine the sense in which Carnap advocates an a priori theory of probability.

2. Consider the theory that there is an analysans of 'probability' which has both of these properties: (a) it is star-method committive, and (b) elementary probability statements framed in terms of it are non-factual or a priori.[29]

It seems to me that this theory is a reasonable extension of what is implicit in the writings of the advocates of the traditional a priori theory of probability, as represented, e.g., by Keynes. Point (b) is connoted by the very name of the school. The situation with regard to (a) is more involved. I think that in his pragmatic analysis of probability Ramsey was making explicit part of what Keynes[30] meant by his claim that a basic feature of the probability relation is that it justifies a rational degree of belief. Of course a priorists have heretofore thought in terms of the traditional calculus of probability, so it is an extension to pass from the Pragmatic Thesis and inductive-method committiveness to the star-method committiveness required by (a); but the a priorist can hardly deny Thesis I and therefore must accept the extension.

Once this extension of the a priori view is made explicit the inadequacy of this view becomes apparent. We saw in Section III that c^* does not satisfy both (a) and (b), and the kind of considerations advanced there tend to show that no concept can satisfy both of them. Thus it seems to me an important philosophical implication of Carnap's inductive logic that the traditional a priori theory of probability is wrong.

Since no analysans of probability can satisfy both (a) and (b), a fortiori the analysandum probability cannot do so. Hence the Pragmatic Thesis is incompatible with a literal interpretation of Carnap's claim that elementary statements of probability are L-determinate (and hence non-factual and a priori). However, Carnap could mean by this claim only that a good explicatum of 'probability' gives L-determinate statements, as indeed c^* does. That is, he could mean that the formalizable part of the meaning of 'probability' has the property in question; cf. in this connection our remarks on the weaker version of Carnap's Explication Thesis (Section III 4). This interpretation is especially plausible in the light of the internal-external question discussion of the preceding section. For it would seem to follow from the internal-external question distinction that the concept of probability would have external as well as internal aspects. Carnap could hold that the notion of star-method

[29](b) is stated so as to leave it open whether these statements are synthetic a priori or analytic a priori (L-determinate).

[30]*Op. cit.*, 4.

committiveness has to do with the use of an inductive method or linguistic framework and hence that (a) above deals[31] with an external aspect of probability; and on the other hand that L-determinacy concerns an internal matter, so that (b) deals with an internal aspect of probability. On this interpretation his claim that elementary statements of probability are L-determinate applies only to the internal aspect of the meaning of 'probability'. (See also the next Section (V 3).)

If this is a correct interpretation of Carnap's position it is quite misleading to classify him as an a priorist in probability. He would not seem to be claiming that there is one concept which satisfies both (a) and (b), but rather that different kinds of questions are involved here. As far as internal questions about probability are concerned he does indeed treat them in an a priori way, but there remain the external questions about probability, and Carnap gives no indication that he regards these as a priori in character (rather, he tends to treat them pragmatically). Such a position is clearly different from traditional a priorism in an important respect.

3. Consider the following analysis of probability. '$P(h,e) = x$' has two components, one cognitive (declarative), the other non-cognitive. The cognitive component is '$c^*(h,e) = x$'. The non-cognitive component is an expression of a commitment to use the star-method in this particular case.[32]

Though I don't maintain that this analysans is fully adequate, it does seem to me that it comes closer to ordinary scientific usage than does the first component alone. The main reason for mentioning it here, however, is that it throws some light on the internal and external aspects of probability.

An advantage of this analysis is that it makes explicit the external aspect of probability. Granted the Pragmatic Thesis, an important difference between probability and c^* is that the former is star-method committive and the latter is not; and granted the external-internal question distinction, it can be plausibly argued that this difference is an external one. On this view the proposed analysans differs from Carnap's explicatum only in that this external feature is added as a separate (non-cognitive) component. Since this added component is about the first component, there is a sense in which it belongs to a different language

[31]Perhaps confusedly — i.e., it could be argued that condition (a) involves a confusion of theoretical and practical external questions; cf. Carnap's treatment of Platonism, *Ontology*, 512-513.

[32]If Mr. Dagger employed the word 'probability' in connection with his use of the dagger-method (cf. footnote 14) this employment could be given a corresponding analysis: his '$P(h,e) = x$' would connote '$c^\dagger(h,e) = x$' and express his commitment to the dagger-method. Note that according to this analysis Mr. Dagger's 'probability' would be inductive-method committive but not star-method committive.

of the hierarchy of languages than does the first component. But in this respect the proposed analysans is probably closer to ordinary language than Carnap's explicatum. As the semantical paradoxes show, ordinary language is not confined to the object language to the exclusion of the metalanguage, and similarly one would not expect statements of ordinary language to be exclusively about internal matters.

As we suggested earlier (Section III 5) Carnap could accept the statements of the previous paragraph and still consistently hold that c^* is a good explicatum of probability. Indeed, it is quite possible that he intends it to be a criterion of a good explication that the explicatum should preserve only the internal aspect of the meaning of the explicandum (cf. particularly requirement (2) of *LFP* 7); in this case it would follow directly from the assertion that star-method committiveness is external that it should not be included in the explicatum. But if this aspect of probability is external it is nevertheless philosophically important, and hence it is desirable that it be analyzed. For this reason we have sometimes used (Sections III 4 and V 2) 'analysis' and its derivatives rather than 'explication', etc., where we intend it as a requirement of a good analysis that insofar as the analysandum has important external and/or non-cognitive aspects these should appear in the analysans.

While the analysans proposed above does not satisfy both (a) and (b) of the previous Section (V 2), it comes very close to it. It satisfies (a),[33] and its declarative component is L-determinate and hence satisfies (b). It would, however, be misleading to call the analysans L-determinate, because an important aspect of its meaning is non-declarative. Note finally that since the proposed concept is star-method committive, we have given an answer to the question of Section III 4.

VI. Presuppositions of Induction and External Questions

1. The extended a priori theory of probability formulated in Section V 2 implies that there is a justification of induction of the kind referred to in the traditional question about the justification of induction. Carnap himself talks as if there were such a justification of induction (*LFP* v,163,177-182). He points out that to justify the use of the star-method it is not necessary to show that this course of action will succeed better than the alternatives but only that it will probably do so, and then remarks that the explication of

[33] I am inclined to think that it follows from the ordinary meaning of 'belief' that beliefs are directed towards the non-cognitive as well as the cognitive meaning of a statement; but if it does not, I wish to stipulate that it does for my use of 'belief'. Thus if a person asserted the proposed analysans and hence expressed a commitment to the star-method, but was in fact not so committed, he could not truly be said to believe the analysans, even though he believed the cognitive component '$c^*(h,e) = x$'.

(3) On the basis of the available evidence it is very *probable* that the degree of uniformity of the world is high. (*LFP* 180)

is analytically true. He seems to argue that this and similar results constitute a justification of induction and show that the validity of inductive reasoning does not depend upon synthetic presuppositions.

Since probability is to be explicated by c^* (3) will become

(3′) The c^* value of 'the degree of unifomity of the world is high' relative to f is high,

where f states the total available evidence. That (3′) is analytically true is not surprising when it is realized that higher c^*_0 values are assigned to more statistically uniform state-descriptions than to less uniform ones. Correspondingly, the statistical uniformity of a state-description does not affect its $c^\dagger_0$-value, so that if the original statement were explicated by Mr. Dagger in terms of $c^\dagger$ the result would be analytically false (assuming that 'high' means the same in both cases). Hence knowledge of the truth of (3′) would not influence Mr. Dagger to use the star-method. This is a special instance of our general result that c^* is not star-method committive (Section III 3).

These considerations, together with those of Sections III, IV, and V, should make it clear why such results as the analyticity of (3′) do not constitute a justification of induction of the kind referred to in the traditional question about the justification of induction: (3′) is an answer to an internal question,[34] whereas the justification issue concerns primarily an external question.[35] Let us discuss now the bearing of this result on the following *question about the presuppositions of induction*: Does the validity of an inductive argument depend in a significant sense[36] on factual presuppositions.

The presupposition and justification questions are related in these ways: (i) the existence of a justification of induction implies the dispensability of presuppositions, but (ii) the non-existence of a justification of induction leaves the presupposition question open. Since results like the analyticity of (3′) do not suffice to justify induction, one cannot legitimately argue via (i) that they are sufficient to settle the presup-

[34] Of course the statement that (3′) is analytic is external to the framework, but it is about an internal property of the framework. In contrast, what are called external questions concern the relation of the linguistic framework to something outside it (the world or human users of it).

[35] In the terminology of Section I: (3′) is a theorem in Carnap's inductive logic, while the justification question belongs to the philosophy of induction.

[36] The exact sense in which factual statements are presupposed is one of the questions at issue: see further the following section. It should perhaps be mentioned that it is not adequate to speak of presuppositions as additional premises needed to convert inductive arguments into deductive arguments; because inductive arguments have 'probability' preceding the conclusion they could not be converted into deductive arguments in this way.

position question. But because of (ii) it might be thought that one could show in some other way that such results about internal matters are sufficient to settle the presupposition question in the negative. This is not the case, however, for, as we shall show, the presupposition question, like the justification question, concerns primarily external matters.

2. There is on the one hand, so to speak, the universe;[37] it is this that we get information about, make predictions about, adjust to, etc. There is, on the other hand, the star-method which we use in learning about and adapting to the universe. Now the presupposition view about the relation of these two is roughly as follows. There are some quite general synthetic propositions about the universe which the use of the star-method presupposes in the sense that if these propositions are in fact false the star-method is not correctly applicable to the universe.[38] There is space here to elaborate this characterization with regard to only one presupposition.

An inductive method is defined for a particular language, and the methods under consideration are defined only for languages with a finite number of primitive predicates. Thus one basic, general property of the star-method is that of finitude of primitive predicates. (That the method has this property is determinable by logical analysis.) Next let us consider a general property which the universe might have and which corresponds to the finitude of predicates of the star-method. It can be formulated with sufficient precision for present purposes as follows: There are a finite number of properties such that all properties exemplifiable in the universe are finite compounds of these. We shall call this the *Principle of Limited Variety*.[39]

The presupposition view about the Principle of Limited Variety is that it is a synthetic, factual proposition which is presupposed by the use of the star-method. This Principle is a factual, non-logical statement, for there is no logical impossiblity in a universe which exhibits an infinite number of irreducible properties (or their negations). It is presupposed by the use of the star-method in the sense that if it is in fact false there are an infinite number of properties which are not taken account of by the star-method, but which should be taken account of be-

[37]Language is of course a part of the universe; for present purposes we need to abstract from this part and consider only the non-linguistic entities of the universe.

[38]The presupposition theory described here is more general than that of my "The Presupposition Theory of Induction," *Philosophy of Science* XX (July, 1953), 177-197; the former states only that there are some presuppositions on which the use of the star-method rests, the latter that there are sufficient presuppositions to determine in some sense this method; the latter entails the former, but not vice-versa. We discuss the more general theory here because it is sufficient for present purposes, it seems to be the theory Carnap has in mind, and it would be acceptable to some who would reject the specific form of it of *ibid*.

[39]Cf. Keynes, *op. cit.*, 256ff, 427.

cause they may enter into causal relations with the properties to which the star-method is applied. The anti-presuppositionist may object that as a presupposition the Principle of Limited Variety is unverifiable, and hence not a theoretical cognitive sentence; but to invoke the verifiability theory of meaning at this point is to beg the very question at issue, since the presuppositionist would argue that the existence of a factual presupposition refutes the verifiability theory of meaning.

It is worth noting that Carnap himself seems to treat the Principle of Limited Variety as a factual, cognitive statement about the universe (*LFP* 74-76; cf. also *Continuum* 48-49). He even adduces factual evidence for it, which procedure seems to presuppose that it is a factual statement. Indeed, inasmuch as he says that one must assume the principle before using an inductive method, it seems circular for him to argue inductively for it, as any presuppositionist would quickly point out. But since the Principle of Limited Variety cannot be stated within any language for which the star-method has been rigorously defined, Carnap may intend such remarks to be merely motivational in function. In any event, he could withdraw such remarks and take a Humean type view to the effect that finitude of primitive predicates is a characteristic of the inductive method people actually use, and that's the end of the matter in the sense that it is impossible to speak meaningfully of a finitude property of the universe which corresponds to this finitude property of the star-method.

Such a view has its difficulties, since it must dispose of the prima facie factuality of the Principle of Limited Variety. Of course the presupposition view also has its problems of formulating precisely the presuppositions of the star-method and making clear the precise sense in which they are presupposed.[40] We need not, however, argue the pros and cons of this issue here, for our aim was not to defend either view, but to show that the question about the presuppositions of induction concerns primarily external matters, and we have said enough to establish this point. It follows that to refute the view that the validity of inductive reasoning is relative to presuppositions it is not sufficient to establish certain internal results about the star-method.[41]

ARTHUR W. BURKS

DEPARTMENT OF PHILOSOPHY
UNIVERSITY OF MICHIGAN

40E.g., the phrases 'not correctly applicable' and 'should be taken account of' in the first and third paragraphs of this section (VI 2) certainly need analysis.

41It could be argued that the presupposition view involves a confusion of theoretical and practical external questions (cf. footnote 31) on the ground that when one tries to formulate the presuppositions (e.g., the uniformity of nature) precisely they turn out to be answers to internal rather than external questions. But even so, the internal results themselves do not suffice to show that the presupposition view rests on such a confusion.

24

Hilary Putnam

"DEGREE OF CONFIRMATION" AND INDUCTIVE LOGIC

I

CARNAP'S attempt to construct a *symbolic inductive logic,* fits into two major concerns of empiricist philosophy. On the one hand, there is the traditional concern with the formulation of Canons of Induction; on the other hand, there is the distinctively Carnapian concern with providing a formal reconstruction of the language of science as a whole, and with providing precise meanings for the basic terms used in methodology.

Of the importance of continuing to search for a more precise statement of the inductive techniques used in science, I do not need to be convinced; this is a problem which today occupies mathematical statisticians at least as much as philosophers.

But this general search need not be identified with the particular project of defining a *quantitative* concept of "degree of confirmation". I shall argue that this last project is misguided.

Such a negative conclusion needs more to support it than "intuition"; or even than plausible arguments based on the methodology of the developed sciences (as the major features of that method may appear evident to one). Intuitive considerations and plausible argument might lead one to the conclusion that it would not be a good investment to spend ones *own* time trying to "extend the definition of degree of confirmation"; it could hardly justify trying to, say, convince Carnap that this particular project should be abandoned. But that is what I shall try to do here: I shall argue that one can *show* that no definition of degree of confirmation can be adequate or can attain what any reasonably good inductive judge might attain *without* using such a concept. To do this it will be necessary (a) to state precisely the condition of adequacy that will be in question; (b) to show that no inductive method based on a "measure function"[1] can satisfy it; and (c) to show that *some* methods (which can be precisely stated) *can* satisfy it.

From this we have a significant corollary: not every (reasonable) inductive method can be represented by a "measure function". Thus, we might also state what is to be proved here in the following form: the actual inductive procedure of science has features which are incompatible with being represented by a "measure function" (or, what is the same thing, a quantitative concept of "degree of confirmation").

II

Let us begin with the statement of the condition of adequacy. The first problem is the *kind of language* we have in mind.

What we are going to suppose is a language rich enough to take account of the *space-time-arrangement* of the individuals. Languages for which d.c. (degree of confirmation) has so far been defined are not this rich: we can express the hypothesis that five individuals are black and five red, but not the hypothesis that ten *successive* individuals are *alternately* black and red. Extension of d.c. to such a language is evidently one of the next steps on the agenda; it would still be far short of the final goal (definition of d.c. for a language rich enough for the formalization of empirical science as a whole).

In addition to supposing that our language, L, is rich enough to describe spatial relations, we shall suppose that it possesses a second sort of richness; we shall suppose that L contains elementary number theory. The problem of defining d.c. for a language which is rich enough for elementary number theory (or more broadly, for classical mathematics) might seem an insuperable one, or, at any rate, much more difficult than defining d.c. for a language in which the individuals have an "order". But such is not the case. I have shown elsewhere[2] that any measure function defined for an (applied) first order functional calculus can be extended to a language rich enough for Cantorian set theory; hence certainly rich enough for number theory, and indeed far richer than needful for the purposes of empirical science. The difficult (I claim: *impossible*) task is not the "extension to richer languages" in the *formal* sense (i.e. to languages adequate for larger parts of logic and mathematics) but the

[1]This is Carnap's term for an a priori probability distribution. Cf. Carnap's book *Logical Foundations of Probability* (Chicago: Univ. of Chicago Press, 1950); and for an excellent explanation of leading ideas, *vide* also the paper by Kemeny in this volume.

[2]"A Definition of Degree of Confirmation for Very Rich Languages," *Philosophy of Science,* XXIII, 58-62.

extension to languages richer in a *physical* sense (i.e. adequate for taking account of the fact of *order*).

In short, we consider a language rich enough for
(a) the description of space-time order.
(b) elementary number theory.

The purpose of the argument is to show that d.c. *cannot* be adequately defined for such a language. This is independent of whether or not the particular method of "extending to richer languages" used in the paper mentioned is employed. But by combining the argument of that paper with the present argument we could get a stronger result: it is not possible to define d.c. adequately in a language satisfying just (a).

To state our condition of adequacy, we will also need the notion of an *effective hypothesis* (a deterministic law).

Informally, an effective hypothesis is one which says of each individual whether or not it has a certain molecular property M; and which does so effectively in the sense that it is possible to *deduce* from the hypothesis what the character of any individual will be. Thus an effective hypothesis is one that we can *confront* with the data: one can deduce what the character of the individuals will be, and then see whether our prediction agrees with the facts as more and more individuals are observed. Formally, an hypothesis h will be called an effective hypothesis if it has the following properties:

(i) h is expressible in L.

(ii) if it is a consequence of h that $M(x_i)$ is true[3] (where M is a molecular predicate of L and x_i is an individual constant), then $h \supset M(x_i)$ is *provable* in L.

(iii) h is equivalent to a set of sentences of the forms $M(x_i)$ and $\sim M(x_i)$; where M is some molecular predicate of L, and x_i runs through the names of all the individuals.

The notion of an effective hypothesis is designed to include the hypotheses normally regarded as expressing putative universal laws. For example, if a hypothesis implies that each individual satisfies the molecular predicate[4] $P_1(x) \supset P_2(x)$, we require that (for each i) $(P_1(x_i) \supset P_2(x_i))$ should be deducible from h in L, for h to count as effective.

We can now state our condition of adequacy:

I. If h is an effective hypothesis and h is true, then the *instance confirmation* of h (as more and more successive individuals are examined) approaches 1 as limit.

[3]Logical formulas are used in this paper only as names of themselves; never in their object-language use.

[4]I.e., the predicate $P_1(\ldots) \supset P_2(\ldots)$; we use the corresponding open sentence to represent it.

We may also consider *weaker* conditions as follows:

I′. If h is an effective hypothesis and h is true, then the *instance confirmation* of h eventually becomes and remains greater than .9 (as more and more successive individuals are examined).

I″. (Same as I′, with '.5' in place of '.9'.)

Even the weakest of these conditions is violated—*must* be violated—by every measure function of the kind considered by Carnap.

III

In I and its variants we have used the term "instance confirmation"[5] introduced by Carnap. The instance confirmation of a universal hypothesis is, roughly speaking, the degree of confirmation that the next individual to be examined will conform to the hypothesis.

It would be more natural to have "degree of confirmation" in place of "instance confirmation" in I, I′, and I″. However, on Carnap's theory, the degree of confirmation of a universal statement is always zero. Carnap does not regard this as a defect; he argues[6] that when we refer to a universal statement as amply confirmed all we really mean is that the instance confirmation is very high. I shall make two remarks about this contention:

(1) This proposal is substantially the same as one first advanced by Reichenbach[7] and criticized by Nagel.[8] The criticism is simply that a very high confirmation in this sense (instance confirmation) is *compatible with any number of exceptions.*

(2) The whole project is to define a concept of degree of confirmation which underlies the scientist's "qualitative" judgments of "confirmed", "disconfirmed", "accepted", "rejected", etc. much in the way that the quantitative magnitude of *temperature* may be said to underlie the qualitative distinctions between "hot" and "cold", "warm" and "cool", etc. But a universal statement *may* be highly confirmed (or even "accepted") as those terms are actually used in science. Therefore it must have a high degree of confirmation, if the relation of "degree of confirmation" to "confirmed" is as just described. To say that it only has a high *instance* confirmation is to abandon the analogy "degree of confirmation is to confirmed as temperature is to hot". But this analogy explains what it *is* to try to "define degree of confirmation".

[5]*Logical Foundations of Probability,* 571ff.

[6]*Ibid.,* 572.

[7]*The Theory of Probability* (Berkeley, 1949). See the work cited in n. 8 for an exposition.

[8]*Principles of the Theory of Probability, International Encyclopedia of Unified Science,* I, no. 6 (Chicago: Univ. of Chicago Press, 1939), 63f.

(Carnap's reply is to maintain the analogy, and deny that a universal statement is ever really confirmed; what is really confirmed, on his view, is that no exceptions will be found in, say, our lifetime, or the lifetime of the human race, or *some* specifiable space-time region (which must be finite).)

IV

Before we proceed to the main argument, let us consider the possibility of obviating the entire discussion by *rejecting* I (and its weaker versions). To do this is to be willing to occupy the following position: (a) one accepts a certain system of inductive logic, based on a function c for "degree of confirmation", as *wholly adequate*; (b) one simultaneously admits that a certain effective hypothesis h is such that if it be true, we will never discover this fact by our system.

Such a position might indeed be defended by maintaining that certain effective hypotheses are *unconfirmable in principle.* For instance, suppose that we have an ordered series of individuals of the same order-type as the positive integers. Let h be the hypothesis that every individual in the series with a prime-numbered position is red and every individual with a composite position is black (count x_1 as "composite").

In other words, x_1,x_4,x_6,x_8,x_9,x_{10}, etc. are all black; x_2,x_3,x_5,x_7,x_{11}, etc. are all red.

Someone might reason as follows:

The arithmetic predicates "prime" and "composite" do not appear in a single known scientific law; therefore such a "hypothesis" is not a legitimate scientific theory, and it is only these that we require to be confirmable. In short, it is not a defect of the system if the hypothesis h just described cannot be confirmed (if its instance confirmation does not eventually exceed, and remain greater than, .9 or even .5).

But this reasoning does not appear particularly plausible; one has only to say—

"Of course the situation described by h has not so far occurred in our experience (as far as we know) ; but *could we find it out* if it did occur"?

I think the answer is clearly "yes"; existing inductive methods are capable of establishing the correctness of such a hypothesis (provided someone is bright enough to suggest it), and so must be any adequate "reconstruction" of those methods.

Thus, suppose McBannister says:

"You know, I think this is the rule: the prime numbers are occupied by red!"

We would first check the data already available for consistency with McBannister's hypothesis. If McBannister's hypothesis fit the first thousand or so objects, we might be impressed, though perhaps not enough to "accept". But if we examined another thousand, and then a million, and then ten million objects and McBannister's suggestion "held-up"— does anyone want to suggest that a reasonable man would *never* accept it?

A similar argument may be advanced if instead of the predicate "prime" we have any recursive predicate of positive integers. It may take a genius, an Einstein or a Newton, to *suggest* such a hypothesis (to "guess the rule", as one says) ; but once it has been suggested any reasonably good inductive judge can verify that it is true. One simply has to keep examining new individuals until any other, antecedently more plausible, hypotheses that may have been suggested have all been ruled out.

In short, if someone rejects I (and its several versions) he must be prepared to offer one of the following "defenses":

(a) I know that if h is true I won't find it out; but I am "gambling" that h is false.

(b) If h turns out to be true, I will *change my inductive method.*

Against the first "defense" I reply that such a "gamble" would be justifiable only if we could show that *no* inductive method will find it out if h is true (or at least, the *standard* inductive methods will not enable me to accomplish this). But in the case of McBannister's hypothesis about the prime-numbered objects and similar hypotheses, this cannot be urged. Against the second "defense" I reply that this defense *presupposes that one can find out* if h "turns out to be true." But, from the nature of h, the only way to find out would be *inductively*. And if one has an inductive method that will accomplish this, then one's definition of degree of confirmation is evidently not an adequate reconstruction of that inductive method.

V

To simplify the further discussion, we shall suppose that there is only *one* dimension, and not four, and that the series of positions is discrete and has a beginning. Thus we may name the positions $x_1, x_2, x_3, \ldots$ etc. (Following a suggestion of Carnap's we will identify the positions and the individuals. Thus "x_1 is red" will mean "the position x_1 is occupied by something red" or "red occurs at x_1"). The modification of our argument for the actual case (of a four-dimensional space-time continuum) is simple.[9]

[9]Thus we may suppose that $x_1, x_2, \ldots$ are a subsequence of observed positions from the whole four-dimensional continuum; and that the hypotheses under consideration differ only with respect to these.

Next we suppose a function c for degree of confirmation to be given. Technically, c is a function whose arguments are sentences h and e, and whose values are real numbers, $0 \leq c(h,e) \leq 1$. The numerical value of c(h,e) is supposed to measure the extent to which the statement expressed by h is confirmed by the statement expressed by e; thus c(h,e) may conveniently be read "the degree of confirmation of h on evidence e".

Admissible functions c for degree of confirmation are required by Carnap to fulfill several conditions. One of these conditions is that the degree of confirmation of $M(x_i)$ should converge to the relative frequency of M in the sample, as more and more individuals other than x_i are examined. This requirement can no longer be maintained in this form in the case of an *ordered* set of individuals; but the following weaker version must still be required:

II. For every n (and every molecular property M) it must be possible to find an m such that, if the next m individuals (the individuals $x_{n+1}, x_{n+2}, \ldots, x_{n+m}$) are all M, then the d.c. of the hypothesis $M(x_{n+m+1})$[10] is greater than .5, regardless of the character of the first n individuals.

If n is 10, this means that there must be an m, say 10,000,000 such that we can say: if the individuals $x_{11}, x_{12}, \ldots, x_{10,000,000}$ are all red, then the probability is more than one-half that $x_{10,000,001}$ will be red (whether or not some of $x_1, x_2, \ldots, x_{10}$ are non-red).

What is the justification of II? Let us suppose that II were violated. Then there must be an n (say, 10) and a property M (say, "red") such that, for some assignment of "red" and "non-red" to $x_1, x_2 \ldots, x_{10}$ (say, x_1,x_2,x_3 are red; $x_4,x_5,\ldots,x_{10}$ are non-red) it holds that no matter how many of $x_{11}, x_{12}, \ldots,$ are red, the d.c. that the *next* individual will be red does not exceed .5. Therefore the hypothesis h: x_1,x_2,x_3 are red; $x_4,x_5, \ldots x_{10}$ are non-red; x_{11} and all subsequent individuals are red—violates I (and in fact, even I″). For no matter how many successive individuals are examined, it is not the case that the instance confirmation of h (this is just the probability that the *next* individual will be red) becomes and remains greater than .5.

Thus I entails II. But II is independently justifiable: if II were violated, then there would be a hypothesis of an exceptionally simple kind such that we could never find it out if it were true; namely a hypothesis which says *all* the individuals (with a specified finite number of exceptions) are M. For we would know that h above is true if we knew that "all the individuals with seven exceptions are red", once we had observed $x_1,x_2, \ldots, x_{10}$. Thus if we want hypotheses of the simple form

[10]Relative to a complete description with respect to M of the individuals $x_1, x_2, \ldots x_{n+m}$. A similar "evidence" will be understood in similar cases.

"all individuals, with just n exceptions, are M" to be confirmable (to have an instance confirmation which eventually exceeds .5), we must accept II.

One more point: c cannot be an *arbitrary* mathematical function. For example, if the value of c were *never* computable, it would be no use to anybody. All the c-functions so far considered by Carnap and other workers in this field have very strong properties of computability. For instance, the d.c. of a singular hypothesis relative to singular evidence is always computable. However this will not be assumed here (although it would materially simplify the argument); all I will assume is the very weak condition: the "it must be possible to find" in II means *by an effective process*. In other words,[11] for each n (say, 10) there is some m (say, 10,000,000) such that one can *prove* (in an appropriate metalanguage M_L) that if $x_{11}, x_{12}, \ldots, x_{10,000,000}$ are "red", then the d.c. that the *next* individual will be "red" is greater than one-half.

If this is not satisfied, then (by an argument parallel to the above) there is some hypothesis of the simple form "all the individuals, with just n exceptions, are M" such that we *cannot prove* at any point (with a few exceptions "at the beginning") that it is more likely than not that the next individual will conform.

E.g. even if we have seen only "red" things for a very long time (except for the seven "non-red" things "at the beginning"), we cannot prove that the d.c. is more than .5 that the next individual will be red.

We can now state our result:

Theorem: there is no definition of d.c. which satisfies II (with the effective interpretation of "it is possible to find") and also satisfies I.

The following proof of this theorem proceeds *via* what mathematical logicians call a "diagonal argument".

Let C be an infinite class of integers $n_1, n_2, n_3, \ldots$ with the following property: the d.c. of Red(x_{n_1}) is greater than .5 if all the preceding individuals are red; the d.c. of Red(x_{n_2}) is greater than .5 if all the preceding individuals *after* x_{n_1} are red; and, in general, the d.c. of Red(x_{n_j}) is greater than .5 if all the preceding individuals *after* $x_{n_{j-1}}$ are red.

The existence of a class C with this property is a consequence of II. For (taking $n = 0$) there must be an n_1 such that if the first $n_1 - 1$ individuals are red, the d.c. is greater than one-half that x_{n_1} is red. Choose such an n_1: then there must be an m such that if the individuals x_{n_1+1}, $x_{n_1+2}, \ldots, x_{n_1+m}$ are all red, the d.c. is more than one-half that x_{n_1+m+1} is red; call n_{1+m+1} "n_2": . . . . etc.

Moreover, if we assume the "effective" interpretation of "it must be possible to find" in II, there exists a *recursive* class C with this property.

11 What follows "in other words" entails the existence of such an effective process, because it is effectively possible to enumerate the *proofs* in M_L.

(A class is "recursive" if there exists a mechanical procedure for determining whether or not an integer is in the class.) We shall therefore asume that our chosen class C is "recursive".

A predicate is called "arithmetic" if it can be defined in terms of polynominals and quantifiers.[12] For instance, the predicate "n is square" can be defined by the formula $(\exists m)$ $(n = m^2)$, and is therefore arithmetic.

Now, Gödel has shown that every recursive class is the extension of an arithmetic predicate.[13] In particular, our class C is the extension of some arithmetic predicate P. So we may consider the following hypothesis:

(1) An individual x_n is red if and only if $\sim P(n)$.

Comparing this with McBannister's hypothesis:

(2) An individual x_n is red if and only if n is prime.

We see that (1) and (2) are of the same form. In fact, the predicate "is prime" is merely a particular example of a recursive predicate of integers.

Thus the hypothesis (1) is *effective.* It is expressible in L, because P is arithmetic; it satisfies condition (ii) in the definition of "effective" (see above), because P is recursive; and (iii) is satisfied, since (1) says for each x_i either that Red(x_i) or $\sim$Red(x_i).

But the hypothesis (1) violates I. In other words, a scientist who uses c would never discover that (1) is true, even if he were to live forever (and go on collecting data forever). This can be argued as follows: However we interpret "discover that (1) is true", a scientist who has discovered that (1) is true should reflect this in his behavior to this extent: he should be willing to bet at even money that the next individual will be non-red whenever (1) *says* that the next individual will be non-red (the more inasmuch as the a priori probability of "non-red" is greater than "red"). But, by the definition of C, the scientist will bet at *more* than even money (when he has examined the preceding individuals) that each of the individuals $x_{n_1}, x_{n_2}, x_{n_3}, \ldots$, is *red.* Thus he will make infinitely many mistakes, and his mistakes will show that he has never learned that (1) is true.

Finally, it is no good replying that the scientist will be right more often than not. The aim of science is not merely to be right about particular events, but to discover general laws. And a method that will not *allow* the scientist to accept the law (1), even if someone *suggest*s it, and even if no exception has been discovered in ten billion years, is unacceptable.

[12]This usage is due to Gödel.

[13]"Über formal unentscheidbare Sätze der Principia Mathematica und verwandter Systeme I" *Monatshefte für Mathematik und Physik,* XXXVIII, 173-198. Cf. Kleene's *Introduction to Mathematics,* (New York: Van Nostrand, 1952), Theorem X., 292, and Theorem I, 241.

VI

One might suspect that things are not so black as they have just been painted; perhaps it is the case that *every* formalized system of inductive logic suffers from the difficulty just pointed out, much as every formalized system of arithmetic suffers from the incompleteness pointed out by Gödel. It is important to show that this is not so; and that other approaches to induction—e.g. that of Goodman,[14] or that of Kemeny[15] are not necessarily subject to this drawback.

Many factors enter into the actual inductive technique of science. Let us consider a technique in which as few as possible of these factors play a part: to be specific, only the direct factual support[16] (agreement of the hypothesis with the data) and the previous acceptance of the hypothesis.[17] Because of the highly over-simplified character of this technique, it is easily formalized. The following rules define the resulting inductive method (M):

1. Let $P_{t,M}$ be the set of hypotheses considered at time t with respect to a molecular property M. I.e. $P_{t,M}$ is a finite set of effective hypotheses, each of which specifies, for each individual, whether or not it is M.
2. Let $h_{t,M}$ be the effective hypothesis on M *accepted* at time t (if any). I.e. we suppose that, at any given time, various incompatible hypotheses have been actually suggested with respect to a given M, and have not yet been ruled out (we require that these should be consistent with the data, and with accepted hypotheses concerning other predicates). In addition, one hypothesis may have been accepted at some time prior to t, and may not yet have been abandoned. This hypothesis is called the "accepted hypothesis at the time t". So designating it is not meant to suggest that the other hypotheses are not considered as serious candidates for the post of accepted hypotheses on M" at some later t.
3. (Rule I:) At certain times t_1 t_2 t_3 . . . initiate an *inductive test with respect to M.* This proceeds as follows: the hypotheses in P_{t_i},M at this time t_i are called the *alternatives.* Calculate the character (M or not-M) of the next individual on the basis of each alternative. See which alternatives succeed in predicting this. Rule out those that fail. Continue until (a) all alternatives but one have failed; or (b) all alternatives have failed; (one or the other must

[14]*Fact, Fiction & Forecast* (Cambridge, Mass.: Harvard Univ. Press, 1955).

[15]"The Use of Simplicity in Induction," *Philosophical Review,* LXII, 391-408.

[16]This term has been used in a related sense by Kemeny and Oppenheim, "Degree of Factual Support," *Philosophy of Science,* XIX, 307-324.

[17]This factor has been emphasized by Conant, *On Understanding Science* (New Haven, Conn.: Yale Univ. Press, 1947).

eventually happen). In case (a) *accept* the alternative that does not fail. In case (b) reject all alternatives.

4. (Rule II:) hypotheses suggested in the course of the inductive test are taken as alternatives (unless they have become inconsistent with the data) in the *next* test. I.e. if h is proposed in the course of the test begun at t_3, then h belongs to $P_{t_4,M}$ and not to $P_{t_3,M}$.
5. (Rule III:) if $h_{t,M}$ is accepted at the conclusion of any inductive test, then $h_{t,M}$ continues to be accepted as long as it remains consistent with the data. (In particular, while an inductive test is still going on, the previously accepted hypothesis continues to be accepted, for all practical purposes.)

Ridiculously simple as this method M is, it has some good features which are not shared by any inductive method based on a "measure function". In particular:

III. If h is an effective hypothesis, and h is true; then, using method M, one will eventually accept h if h is ever proposed.

The method M differs from Carnap's methods, of course, in that the acceptance of a hypothesis depends on which hypotheses are actually proposed, and also on the *order* in which they are proposed. But this does not make the method informal. Given a certain sequence of sentences, (representing the suggested hypotheses and the order in which they are suggested), and given the "time" at which each hypothesis is put forward (i.e. given the *evidence* at that stage: this consisting, we may suppose, of a complete description of individuals $x_1, x_2, \ldots, x_t$ for some t); and given, finally, the "points" (or evidential situations) at which inductive tests are begun; the "accepted" hypothesis at any stage is well defined.

That the results a scientist gets, using method M, depend on (a) what hypotheses he considers at any given stage, and even (b) at what points he chooses to inaugurate observational sequences ("inductive tests") is far from being a *defect* of M: these are precisely features that M shares with ordinary experimental and statistical practice. (Carnap sometimes seems to say[18] that he is looking for something *better* than ordinary experimental practice in these respects. But this is undertaking a task far more ambitious, and far more doubtful, than "reconstruction".)

In comparing the method M with Carnap's methods, the problem arises of correlating the essentially qualitative notion of "acceptance" with the purely quantitative notion of "degree of confirmation". One method is this (we have already used it): say that a hypothesis is *accepted* if the instance confirmation is greater than .5 (if one is willing to bet

[18] *Logical Foundations of Probability,* 515-520; see esp. the amazing paragraph at the bottom of p. 518!

at more than even money that the next individual will conform). In these terms, we may say: using Carnap's methods one will, in general, accept an effective hypothesis sooner or later if it is true, and in fact one will accept it infinitely often. But one won't *stick* to it. Thus these methods lack *tenacity*.

Indeed, we might say that the two essential features of M are

i) *corrigibility:* if h is inconsistent with the data, it is abandoned; and

ii) *tenacity*: if h is once accepted, it is not subsequently abandoned *unless* it becomes inconsistent with the data.

It is the first feature that guarantees that any effective hypothesis will eventually be accepted if true; for the other alternatives in the set $P_{t_i,M}$ to which it belongs must all be false and, for this reason, they will all eventually be ruled out while the true hypothesis remains. And it is the second feature that guarantees that a true hypothesis, once accepted, is not subsequently rejected.[19]

It would, of course, be highly undesirable if, in a system based on "degree of confirmation" one had "tenacity" in quite the same sense. If we are willing to bet at more than even money that the next individual will conform to h, it does not follow that if it *does* conform we should *then* be willing to bet that the next individual in turn will conform. For instance, if we are willing to bet that the next individual will be red, this means that we are betting that it will conform to the hypothesis that all individuals are red; and also that it will conform to the hypothesis that all individuals up to and including it are red, and all those thereafter green.[20] If it *does* conform to both these hypotheses, we cannot go on to bet that the next individual in turn will conform to both, for this would involve betting that it will be both red and green.[21] But we can say this: for any effective hypothesis h, there should come a point (if h continues to be consistent with the data) at which we shall be willing to bet that the next individual will conform; and if the next individual conforms, we shall be willing to bet that the next in turn will conform; and so on. To say this is merely to say again: if it is true we ought *eventually* to accept it. And it is to this simple principle that M conforms, while the Carnapian methods do not.

[19]It is of interest to compare III with the "pragmatic justification of induction" given by Feigl, "De Principiis non Disputandum . . . ?" in *Philosophical Analysis,* ed. by M. Black (Ithaca, 1950).

[20]The difficulty occasioned by pairs of hypotheses related in this way was first pointed out by Goodman. *Vide* "A Query on Confirmation," *Journal of Philosophy,* XLIII, 383-385.

[21]This raises a difficulty for Reichenbach's "Rule of Induction"; the use of the rule to estimate the relative frequency of "green" and "grue" (see below) is another case in which contradictory results are obtained.

Moreover, that the method M has the desirable property III is closely connected with a feature which is in radical disagreement with the way of thinking embodied in the "logical probability" concept: the acceptance of a hypothesis depends on *which* hypotheses are actually proposed. The reader can readily verify that it is this feature (which, I believe, M shares with the actual procedure of scientists) that blocks a "diagonal argument" of the kind we used in the preceding section. In short, M is *effective,* and M is able to discover any true law (of a certain simple kind); but this is because what we will predict "next", using M, does not depend *just* on the evidence. On the other hand, it is easily seen that any method that shares with Carnap's the feature: what one will predict "next" depends *only* on what has so far been observed, will also share the defect: either what one should predict will not in practice be *computable,*[22] or some law will elude the method altogether (one is *in principle* forbidden to accept it, no matter how long it has succeeded).

This completes the case for the statement made at the beginning of this paper: namely, that a good inductive judge can do things, provided he does *not* use "degree of confirmation", that he could not *in principle* accomplish if he *did* use "degree of confirmation". As soon as a scientist announces that he is going to use a method based on a certain "c-function", we can exhibit a hypothesis (in fact, one consistent with the data so far obtained, and hence possibly true) such that we can say: if this is true *we* shall find it out; but you (unless you abandon your method) will never find it out.

Also, we can now criticize the suggested analogy between the "incompleteness" of Carnap's systems, and the Godelian incompleteness of formal logics. A more correct analogy would be this: the process of *discovery* in induction is the process of suggesting the correct hypothesis (and, sometimes, a suitable language for its expression and a mathematical technique that facilitates the relevant computation).

But once it has been suggested, the inductive checking, leading to its eventual acceptance, is relatively straightforward. Thus the suggestion of a hypothesis in induction is analogous to the *discovery of a proof* in formal logic; the inductive verification (however protracted, and however many "simpler" hypotheses must first be ruled out) is analogous to the *checking* of a formal proof (however tedious). Thus one might say: the incompleteness we have discovered in Carnap's system is analogous to the "incompleteness" that would obtain if there were no mechanical way of *checking* a proof, once discovered, in a formal logic. (Most logi-

22Even in the case of induction by simple enumeration; i.e., there will be hypotheses of the simple form "all individuals from x_n on are red," such that one will not be able to prove that one should accept them, no matter how many "red" things one sees.

cians[23] would hesitate at applying the word "proof" in such a case.) On the other hand, in the system M, it may take a genius to *suggest* the correct hypothesis; but if it *is* suggested, we can verify it.

VII

The oversimplified method M ignores a great many important factors in induction. Some of these, like the reliability of the evidence, are also ignored by Carnap's methods. In addition there is the simplicity of the hypothesis (e.g. the data may be consistent with McBannister's hypothesis, and also with the simpler hypothesis "no individual is red"); the "entrenchment" of the various predicates and laws in the language of science;[24] etc.

Also, the method M is only a method for selecting among deterministic hypotheses. But we are often interested in selecting from a set of statistical hypotheses, or in choosing between a deterministic hypothesis and a statistical hypothesis (the use of the "null hypothesis"[25] is a case in point). This is, in fact, the normal case: a scientist who considers the hypothesis "all crows are black" is not likely to have in mind an alternative deterministic hypothesis, though he might (i.e. all the crows in such-and-such regions are black; all those in such-and-such other regions are white, etc.); he is far more likely to choose between this hypothesis and a statistical hypothesis that differs reasonably from it (e.g. "at most 90% of all crows are black").

It is not difficult to adapt the method M to the consideration of statistical hypotheses. A statistical hypothesis is ruled out when it becomes statistically inconsistent with the data at a pre-assigned confidence level. (A statistical hypothesis, once ruled out, may later "rule itself back in"; but a deterministic hypothesis, as before, is ruled out for good if it is ruled out at all). This involves combining the method M with the standard method of "confidence intervals". If a statistical hypothesis is true, we cannot guarantee that we shall "stick to it": this is the case because a statistical regularity is compatible with arbitrarily long finite stretches of any character whatsoever. But the *probability* that one will stick to the true hypothesis, once it has been accepted, converges to 1. And if a deterministic hypothesis is true, we will eventually accept it and "stick to it" (if someone suggests it).[26]

[23] E.g. Quine, in *Methods of Logic,* 245.

[24] *Fact, Fiction & Forecast,* 95.

[25] (The hypothesis that the character in question is randomly distributed in the population.)

[26] The above is only a sketch of the method employed in extending M to statistical hypotheses. For statistical hypotheses of the usual forms, this method can be fully elaborated.

Another approach, with a feature very similar to III above, has been suggested by Kemeny.[27] This method rests on the following idea: the hypotheses under consideration are assigned a *simplicity order*. This may even be arbitrary; but of course we would like it to correspond as well as possible to our intuitive concept of simplicity. Then one selects the simplest hypothesis consistent with the data (at a pre-assigned confidence level).

Thus, if we have three incompatible hypotheses h_1, h_2, h_3, we have to wait until at most one remains consistent with the data, if we use the method M. And this may take a very long time. Using Kemeny's method, one will, in general, make a selection much more quickly.

On the other hand, Kemeny's method does not make it unnecessary to take into account *the hypotheses that have in fact been proposed,* as one might imagine. (E.g. one might be tempted to say: choose the simplest hypothesis *of all those in the language.)* For one cannot effectively enumerate all the effective hypotheses on a given M in the language.[28] However, we may suppose that a scientist who suggests a hypothesis shows that it is effective (that it does effectively predict the relevant characteristic); and shows that it does lead to different predications than the other hypotheses. Then with respect to the class $P_{t_i,M}$ of hypotheses belonging to the inductive test we may apply the Kemeny method; since every hypothesis in the class is effective, and no two are equivalent. For instance, one might simply take the hypothesis with the fewest symbols as the simplest (i.e. a 10-letter hypothesis is simpler than a 20-letter); but this would be somewhat crude. But even a *very* crude method such as this represents an improvement on the method M above, and a closer approximation to actual scientific practice.

It is instructive to consider the situation in connection with an over-simplified example. The following excellent example is due to Goodman:[29]

(1) All emeralds are green.

(2) All emeralds are green prior to time t; and blue subsequently.

We might object to (2) on the ground that it contains the name of a specific time-point (t). This does not appear to me to be a good objection. The hypothesis that the first 100 objects produced by a certain machine will be red; the next 200 green; the next 400 red; etc. mentions a particular individual (the machine) and a particular time-point (the point at which the machine starts producing objects). But a scientist who is forbidden to open the machine or investigate its internal construction

[27] "The Use of Simplicity in Induction," *Philosophical Review,* LXII, 391-408.

[28] This is a consequence of Gödel's theorem.

[29] *Fact, Fiction & Forecast,* 74.

might "behavioristically" acquire a considerable inductive confidence in this hypothesis.

Moreover, Goodman has shown how to rephrase (2) so that this objection is avoided. Define "grue" as applying to green objects prior to t; and to blue objects subsequently. Then (2) becomes:

(2′) All emeralds are grue.

What interests us about the hypotheses (1) and (2) (or (1) and (2′)) is this: if time t is in the future and all emeralds so far observed are green, both are consistent with the data. But in some sense (2) is less simple than (1). Indeed, if the language does not contain "grue", (1) is simpler than (2) by the "symbol count" criterion of simplicity proposed above. How do these hypotheses fare under the inductive methods so far discussed?

Under the method M, there are three relevant possibilities: (2) may be suggested at a time when no one has thought of (1) (highly implausible); or (1) and (2) may be suggested at the same time (slightly more plausible); or (1) may be advanced long before anyone even thinks of (2) (much more plausible, and historically accurate). In the last (and actual) case what happens is this: (1) is compared with, say

(3) All emeralds are red.

and (1) is accepted. Much later someone (Goodman, in fact) suggests (2). Then (1) is *still* accepted, in accordance with the principle of "tenacity", until and unless at time t (2) turns out to be correct.

In the case that (2) is suggested first we would, of course, accept (2) and refuse to abandon it in favor of the simpler hypothesis (1) until experimental evidence is provided in favor of (1) over (2) at time t. As Conant has pointed out[30] this is an important and essential part of the actual procedure of science: a hypothesis once accepted is not easily abandoned, even if a "better" hypothesis appears to be on the market. When we appreciate the connection between tenacity and the feature III of our inductive method, we may see one reason for this being so.

In the remaining case, in which (1) and (2) are proposed at the same time, *neither* would be accepted before time t. This is certainly a defect of method M.

Now let us consider how these hypotheses fare under Kemeny's method (as here combined with some features of method M). If (1) is suggested first, everything proceeds as it did above, as we would wish. If (2) is suggested first, there are two possibilities: we may have a rule of tenacity, according to which a hypothesis once adopted should not be abandoned until it proves inconsistent with the data. In this case things

[30]*On Understanding Science,* chap. 3.

will proceed as with the method M. Or, we may adopt the rule that we shift to a simpler hypothesis if one is suggested, provided it is consistent with the data. In this case we must be careful that only a finite number of hypotheses are simpler than a given hypothesis under our simplicity-ordering; otherwise we may sacrifice the advantages of the principle of tenacity (i.e. one might go on "shifting" forever). Then we would adopt (1) when it is suggested, even if we have previously accepted (2) and (2) is still consistent with the data. Lastly, if (1) and (2) are suggested at the same time, we will accept (1) (as soon as the "null hypothesis" is excluded at the chosen confidence level).[31]

Thus the method incorporating Kemeny's proposal has a considerable advantage over M; it permits us to accept (1) long before t even if (2) and (2′) are also available. In general, this method places a premium on simplicity, as M does not.

Another suggestion has been made by Goodman. Goodman rejects (2) as an inductive hypothesis as *explicitly* mentioning a particular time-point. This leaves the version (2′), however. So the notion of *entrenchment* is introduced. A predicate is better entrenched the more often it (or any predicate coextensive with it) has been used in inductive inferences. Under this criterion it is clear that "green" is a vastly better-entrenched predicate than the weird predicate "grue". So in any conflict of this kind, the data are regarded as confirming (1) and not (2′).

Goodman's proposal might be regarded as a special case of Kemeny's. Namely, we might regard the ordering of hypotheses according to "entrenchment" as but one of Kemeny's simplicity-orders. On the other hand, we may desire to have a measure of simplicity as distinct from entrenchment. (Under most conceptions, simplicity would be a *formal* characteristic of hypotheses, whereas entrenchment is a *factual* characteristic.) In this case we might order hypotheses according to some weighted combination of simplicity and entrenchment (assuming we can decide on appropriate "weights" for each parameter).

What has been illustrated is that the aspects of simplicity and entrenchment emphasized by Kemeny and Goodman (and any number of further characteristics of scientific hypotheses) can be taken into consideration in an inductive method without sacrificing the essential characteristics of *corrigibility* and *tenacity* which make even the method M, bare skeleton of an inductive method though it may be, superior as an inductive instrument to any method based on an a priori probability distribution.

[31]It is desirable always to count the null hypothesis as simplest; i.e., not to accept another until this is ruled out.

VIII

At the beginning of this paper I announced the intention to present a precise and formal argument of a kind that I hope may convince Carnap. I did this because I believe (and I am certain that Carnap believes as well) that one should never abandon a constructive logical venture because of *merely* philosophical arguments. Even if the philosophical arguments are well taken they are likely to prove *at most* that the scope or significance of the logical venture has been misunderstood. Once the logical venture has succeeded (if it does succeed), it may become important to examine it philosophically and eliminate conceptual confusions; but the analytical philosopher misconstrues his job when he advises the logician (or any scientist) to stop what he is doing.

On the other hand, it is not the part of wisdom to continue what one is doing no matter what relevant considerations may be advanced against it.

If the venture is logical, so must the considerations be. And in the foregoing sections we have had to provide strict proof that there are features of ordinary scientific method which cannot be captured by any "measure function". (Unless one wants to try the doubtful project of investigating measure functions which are not effectively computable, *even for a finite universe.*[32] And then one sacrifices other aspects of the scientific method as represented by M; its *effectiveness* with respect to what hypothesis one should select, and hence what prediction one should make.)

In short, degree of confirmation is supposed to represent (quantitatively) the judgments an ideal inductive judge would make. But the judgments an ideal inductive judge would make would presumably have this character: if a deterministic law (i.e. an effective hypothesis) h is true, and someone suggests it, and our "ideal judge" observes for a *very* long time that h yields only successful prediction, he will eventually base his predictions on it (and continue to do so, as long as it does not fail). But this very simple feature of the inductive judgments he makes is represented by no measure function whatsoever. Therefore, *the aim of representing the inductive policy of such a "judge" by a measure function represents a formal impossibility.*

Now that the formal considerations have been advanced, however, it becomes of interest to see what can be said on less formal grounds about the various approaches to induction. In the present section, let us see what can be said about the *indispensibility of theories* as instruments of prediction on the basis of the inductive methods we have considered.

[32] If a particular measure-function is computable for finite universes, the d.c. of a singular prediction on singular evidence is computable for *any* universe.

We shall find that the method M and the method incorporating Kemeny's idea "make sense" of this; the Carnapian methods give a diametrically opposite result.

To fix our ideas, let us consider the following situation: prior to the first large scale nuclear explosion various directly and indirectly relevant observations had been made. Let all these be expressed in a single sentence in the observation vocabulary, e. Let h be the prediction that, when the two subcritical masses of uranium 235 are "slammed together" to produce a single super-critical mass, there will be an explosion. It may be formulated without the theoretical expression "uranium 235", namely as a statement that when two particular "rocks" are quickly "slammed together" there will be "a big bang". Then h is also in the observation vocabulary. Clearly, good inductive judges, given e, did in fact expect h. And they were right. But let us ask the question: is there any *mechanical rule* whereby given e one could have found out that one should predict h?

The example cited is interesting because there was not (or, at any rate, we may imagine there was not) any *direct* inductive evidence from the standpoint of induction by simple enumeration, to support h. No rock of this kind had ever blown up (let us suppose). Nor had "slamming" two such rocks together ever had any effect (critical mass had never been attained). Thus the direct inductive inference *a la* Mill would be: "slamming two rocks of this kind (or any kind) together does not make them explode." But a *theory* was present; the theory had been accepted on the basis of *other* experiments; and the theory *entailed* that the rocks would explode if critical mass were attained quickly enough (assuming a coordinating definition according to which "these rocks" are U-235). Therefore the scientists were willing to make this prediction in the face of an utter lack of direct experiential confirmation.[33]

(Incidentally, this is also a refutation—if any were needed—of Bridgman's view of scientific method. According to Bridgman, a theory is a summary of experimental laws; these laws should be explicitly formulated, and should be accepted only insofar as they are directly confirmed (apparently, by simple enumerative induction). Only in this way shall we avoid unpleasant "surprises".[34])

But, if this view is accepted, then the scientists in the experiment described above were behaving most irrationally; they were willing to accept, at least tentatively (and advise the expenditure of billions of dollars on the basis of) an experimental law that had never been tested

33The physics in this example is slightly falsified, of course; but not essentially so.

34This seems the only possible reading of a good many passages in *The Logic of Modern Physics* (New York, 1927).

once, simply because it was deduced from a theory which entailed *other* experimental laws which had been verified.

I believe that we should all want to say that even the most "ideal inductive judge" could not have predicted h on the basis of e unless someone had suggested the relevant theories. The theories (in particular, quantum mechanics) are what connect the various facts in e (e.g. the fact that one gets badly burned if he remains near one of the "rocks") with h. Certainly it appears implausible to say that there is a *rule* whereby one can go from the observational facts (if one only had them all written out) to the observational prediction without any "detour" into the realm of theory. But this is a consequence of the supposition that degree of confirmation can be "adequately defined"; i.e. defined in such a way as to agree with the actual inductive judgments of good and careful scientists.

Of course, I am not accusing Carnap of believing or stating that such a rule exists; the existence of such a rule is a *disguised* consequence of the assumption that d.c. can be "adequately defined", and what I hope is that establishing this consequence will induce Carnap, as it has induced me, to seek other approaches to the problem of inductive logic.

Thus let O be the observational language of science, and let T be a formalization of the full-fledged language of science, including both observational and theoretical terms. O we may supppose to be an applied First Order Functional Calculus; and we may suppose it contains only (qualitative) predicates like "Red" and no functors. T, on the other hand, must be very rich, both physically and mathematically. Then we state: *if d.c. can be adequately defined for the language O, then there exists a rule of the kind described.*

Incidentally, it is clear that the possibility of defining d.c. for T entails the existence of a rule which does what we have described (since all the relevant theories can be expressed in T). But this is not as disturbing, for the creative step is precisely the invention of the theoretical language T.[35] What one has to show is that the possibility of defining d.c. just for O has the same consequence.

Carnap divides all inductive methods into two kinds. For those of the first kind, *the d.c. of h on e must not depend on the presence or absence in the language of predicates not occurring in either h or e.* Since h and e do not mention any theoretical terms, the d.c. of h on e must be the same, in such a method, whether the computation is carried out in T or O! In short, if we have a definition of d.c. in O, what we have is nothing less than a definition of *the best possible prediction in any evidential situation,* regardless of what laws scientists of the future may

[35]This has been remarked by Kemeny, in his paper in the present volume.

discover. For if the degree of confirmation of h on e is, say, .9 in the complete language T, then it must be .9 in the sub-language O.

For inductive methods of the second kind, the d.c. of h on e depends, in general on K (the number of strongest factual properties). But, with respect to the actual universe, each method of the second kind coincides with some method of the first kind (as Carnap points out).[36] Thus, if there is any adequate method of the second kind (for the complete language T) there is also some adequate method of the first kind.

If we recall that the degree of confirmation of a singular prediction is effectively computable relative to singular evidence, we get the further consequence that it is possible in principle to build an electronic computer such that, if it could somehow be given all the observational facts, it would always make the best prediction—i.e. the prediction that would be made by the best possible scientist if he had the best possible theories. *Science could in principle be done by a moron* (or an electronic computer).[37]

From the standpoint of method M, however, the situation is entirely different. The prediction one makes will depend on what laws one accepts. And what laws one accepts will depend on what laws are proposed. Thus M does not have the counter-intuitive consequence just described. If two "ideally rational" scientists both use M, and one thinks of quantum mechanics and the other not, the first may predict h given e while the second does not. Thus theories play an indispensible role.

This feature is intrinsic to M. We cannot take the class $P_{t_i,M}$ to be infinite; for the proof that each inductive test will terminate depends on it being finite. Also there is no *effective* way to divide all hypotheses into successive finite classes $P_{t_1,M}$, $P_{t_2,M}$, $P_{t_3,M}$, . . . in such a way that a) every class contains a finite number of mutually incompatible effective hypotheses, and b) every effective hypothesis is in some class.[38] M cannot be transformed into an effective method for selecting the best hypothesis from the class of *all* hypotheses expressible in the language (as opposed to the hypotheses in a given finite class). Thus science *cannot* be done by a moron; or not if the moron relies on the method M, at any rate.

The situation is even more interesting if one uses the Kemeny method. For the simplicity of hypotheses with the same observational consequences may vary greatly (even by the "symbol count" criterion).

36 *The Continuum of Inductive Methods* (Chicago: Univ. of Chicago Press, 1952), 48. For a lengthier discussion of the plausibility of making d.c. dependent on κ, see "On the Application of Inductive Logic," *Philosophy and Phenomenological Research,* VIII, 133-148; particularly 144.

37 Readers familiar with Rosenbloom's *Elements of Mathematical Logic* (Dover, 1950), will recognize the identification of the computer with the "moron".

38 This is a consequence of Gödel's theorem, as remarked above (n. 28).

A way of putting it is this: call two hypotheses "essentially the same" if they have the same observational consequences. Then the relative simplicity of hypotheses that are "essentially the same" may vary greatly depending on the language in which they are couched. (For instance, Craig has shown[39] that every hypothesis can be "essentially" expressed in O, in this sense; but the axiomatization required is infinite if the original hypothesis contains theoretical terms, so there would be infinite complexity.) Thus the hypothesis a scientist will accept, using a method which includes a simplicity order, will depend not only on what hypotheses he has been able to think of, but on the theoretical language he has constructed for the expression of those hypotheses. Skill in constructing theories within a language and skill in constructing theoretical languages both make a difference in prediction.

IX

There are respects in which all the methods we have considered are radically oversimplified: for instance, none takes account of the reliability of the data. Thus, Rule I of method M is unreasonable unless we suppose that instrumental error can be neglected.[40] It would be foolish, in actual practice, to reject a hypothesis because it leads to exactly one false prediction; we would rather be inclined to suppose that the prediction might not really have been false, and that our instruments may have deceived us. Again there is the problem of assigning a proper weight to *variety* of evidence, which has been emphasized by Nagel. But my purpose here has not been to consider all the problems which might be raised. Rather the intention has been to follow through one line of inquiry: namely, to see what features of the scientific method can be represented by the method M and related methods, and to show that crucial features cannot be represented by any "measure function".

Again, I have not attempted to do any philosophic "therapy"; to say what, in my opinion, are the mistaken conceptions lying at the base of the attempt to resuscitate the "logical probability" concept. But one such should be clear from the foregoing discussion. The assumption is made, in all work on "degree of confirmation", that there is such a thing as a "fair betting quotient", that is, the odds that an ideal judge would assign if he were asked to make a fair bet on a given prediction. More precisely, the assumption is that *fair odds* must exist in any evidential situation, and *depend only on the evidence*. That they must depend on the evidence is clear; the odds we should assign to the prediction "the next thing will be red" would intuitively be quite different (in the

[39] "Replacement of Auxiliary Expressions," *Philosophical Review*, LXV, 38-53.

[40] I am indebted to E. Putnam for pointing this out.

absence of theory!) if 50% of the individuals examined have been red, and if all have been. But, I do not believe that there exists an abstract "fairness of odds" independent of *the theories available to the bettors.* To suppose that there does is to suppose that one can define the best bet *assuming that the bettors consider the best possible theory;* or (what amounts to the same thing) assuming they consider all possible theories.

Such a concept appears to be utterly fantastic from the standpoint of the actual inductive situation; hence it is not surprising that any definition would have to be so non-effective as not to be of any use to anybody.

Since this assumption underlies the work of De Finetti,[41] and the "subjective probability" approach of Savage,[42] I am inclined to reject all of these approaches. Instead of considering science as a monstrous plan for "making book", depending on what one experiences, I suggest that we should take the view that science is a method or possibly a collection of methods for *selecting a hypothesis,* assuming languages to be given and hypotheses to be proposed. Such a view seems better to accord with the importance of the hypothetico-deductive method in science, which all investigators have come to stress more and more in recent years.

HILARY PUTNAM

DEPARTMENT OF PHILOSOPHY
PRINCETON UNIVERSITY

41"Sul significato suggestivo della probabilita," *Fundamenta mathematicae,* XVII, 298-329.

42*The Foundations of Statistics* (New York: Wiley, 1954).

25

Ernest Nagel

CARNAP'S THEORY OF INDUCTION

C. D. BROAD once remarked that though inductive reasoning is the glory of science, it is the scandal of philosophy. Whether or not this characterization of philosophy is a merited one, there is no doubt that despite substantial advances made by logicians and philosophical scientists in the analysis of inductive arguments, even competent students continue to disagree on many fundamental issues encountered in the subject. These issues include not only the notorious general problem of "justifying" principles of inductive reasoning, but also special questions concerning the formal logic and the methodology of inductive inference. They run the gamut from doubts about the relevance of the mathematical calculus of probability to the task of codifying the tacit rules governing habitual inductive reasoning, through questions about the conditions under which inductive arguments are valid and about the correct analysis of the central notion of "the weight of evidence", to problems concerning the epistemic status of generally accepted principles of inductive inference. If it is a scandal to have unresolved issues, then the present state of philosophic discussion on induction is indeed scandalous.

What is perhaps Carnap's most ambitious contribution to logical analysis is his monumental but still incompleted attempt to put an end to much of this scandal, if scandal it is. He has set himself the important task of codifying the logic of induction, in a manner analogous to modern systematizations of deductive logic, and of doing this within the unitary framework provided by a precise quantitative explication of the basic idea of "the strength of evidential support". The foundations for his system have been laid deep and in a characteristically meticulous fashion; and though the structure is far from complete, its present outlines already exhibit the magnificent architectonic qualities of the completed design. Carnap employs his basic conceptions with brilliant ingenuity, and he discusses mooted questions in the philosophy of induction with flexible insight and with his usual candor. No students of the problems of inductive inference, whether or not they find themselves in agreement with Carnap's approach, can fail to be instructed by the comprehensive analyses that support his system.

In this essay I propose to evaluate Carnap's theory of induction, even though such an evaluation is perhaps premature. It may be premature, because the published form of the theory is still but a fragment, and develops in detail only a relatively small portion of its intended content. Indeed, except for some preliminary outlines, a full explication of the notion of evidential support which Carnap apparently favors is not yet available; and it is not even entirely clear which, if any, of the infinitely many inductive methods that he presents as possible ones he will eventually recommend as the most promising. Comments on the theory at the present stage of its development may therefore turn out to be quite pointless in the light of the subsequent elaborations the theory will doubtless receive. Moreover, Carnap has reserved for later discussion a number of basic questions affecting the applicability of his theory. He has in fact been primarily engaged thus far in constructing a *logic* of inductive inference—in developing deductively relations between statements, each of which ascribes a degree of "confirmation" (or evidential support) to a given hypothesis by given evidence, and each of which is logically certifiable in the light of the postulates and definitions adopted. He has thus far not given comparable attention (at least not in published form) to what he calls the "methodological" problems that are generated when the *applicability* of the logic to actual scientific procedure is considered. Carnap's *logic* of induction, like any branch of pure mathematics, can of course be developed and examined without reference to its possible uses in empirical inquiry; but its worth as a *theory* of induction—as an explication and refined extension of ideas and principles employed in the search for empirical truth—cannot be judged independently of such reference. As Carnap makes clear, his definition of "degree of confirmation" and his theorems in inductive logic are intended to be reconstructions of familiar though vague notions and types of arguments implicit in the practice of science; and his logic is essentially a *proposal* that evidence for hypotheses be weighed in accordance with the rules which the logic postulates. But such a proposal cannot be evaluated exclusively in terms of the internal coherence of the system. Carnap himself notes that a deductive system "may be a theory which is wonderful to look at in its exactness, symmetry, and formal elegance, and yet woefully inadequate for the task of application for which it is intended."[1] Partly because of the unfinished state of Carnap's system, however, there have been no serious attempts to employ it in the conduct of inquiry; and objective data are therefore largely lacking for judging the adequacy of his inductive logic for its ostensible purpose.

[1]Rudolf Carnap, *Logical Foundations of Probability* (Chicago, 1950), 218. This work will be cited in the sequel as LFP. Carnap's *The Continuum of Inductive Methods* (Chicago, 1952), will be cited as CIM.

Despite these obstacles, there is nevertheless some basis for venturing a critique of Carnap's theory. He has developed enough of it to make clear the main lines of his approach; and though there is a scarcity of fully reliable evidence as to its potential effectiveness, there is much competent information concerning inductive practice, even if the use of such information for evaluating the theory must be somewhat impressionistic. It is perhaps unnecessary to add, however, that in view of the obstacles mentioned, a critique of Carnap's ideas on induction can at present be only a tentative one.

I

The stimulus for constructing an inductive logic is supplied by familiar facts such as the following: statements are frequently accepted in empirical inquiry as well-founded, even though the evidence for a given conclusion does not formally imply the latter; again, though the evidence for a hypothesis may not be regarded as sufficient to warrant its acceptance, the hypothesis may be judged to receive better (or stronger) support from one set of evidential premises than from another set; moreover, one hypothesis is sometimes taken to be better supported by given evidence than is some other hypothesis by the same or by different evidence. In such inductive arguments, the hypothesis (or conclusion) may be either general (strictly universal, existential, or statistical) or singular in form; they may employ only such notions which refer to matters accessible to direct observation, or they may use "theoretical" notions not applicable to directly observable things; and the evidential statements (or premises) may differ among themselves in a similar fashion. But a common feature of inductive arguments, setting them off from deductive ones, is that they may be "valid" or possess various degrees of "probative force", even though their conclusions are discovered to be false while their premises are assumed to be true.

It continues to be a matter of dispute whether in current practice numerical measures are *ever* assigned to the degree of support that available evidence lends to a hypothesis. For in those cases where such measures are apparently assigned (as in bets placed on the outcome of games of chance), students are in disagreement on the question whether the numerical values adopted are to be construed as measures of the weight of the evidence for a given hypothesis, or whether on the contrary those numerical values are to be understood as measures of the relative frequency with which *similar* hypotheses are true in classes of *similar* cases. On the other hand, no one seriously disputes the fact that in *most* cases current procedures in the sciences as well as in the practical affairs of life do not estimate the strength of evidential support in quantitative terms. It would be generally conceded, moreover, that there are many situations in which *no* degree of weight whatever is commonly associated with purported evidence for a given hypothesis, or in which the evidential support for one hypothesis is judged to be simply incomparable with the evidential support for another hypothesis. For example, if we assume that the captain of a certain ship was born in 1900, the hypothesis that he is to-day 40 years old is disconfirmed by this evidence; and if we were to contemplate introducing numerical measures, we might conceivably assign a zero degree of support to the evidence for that hypothesis. On the other hand, since information about the ship's position at sea on a certain day is irrelevant to the hypothesis about the captain's age, I do not believe *any* degree of support whatever (and certainly neither zero nor even one-half) would be assigned, in conformity with established habits of estimating evidence, to that "evidence" for the stated hypothesis. And *a fortiori,* we would not assign any measure of support for that hypothesis to "evidence" which is of the nature of a purely logical truth (e.g. the truth that the ship is either a coal-burner or not a coal-burner)—that is, we would attribute no numerical degree of probative force to an argument for a factual hypothesis, when the premises cite no empirical evidence for it. Similarly, it seems plausible to say, within the framework of established habits of inductive inference, that the mortality rate of man is better supported by the present biological evidence than is the hypothesis of telekinesis by the available para-psychological data. But I do not think that the tacit rules embodied in those established habits enable us to compare the support given by available evidence for the assumption that the earth was once part of the sun, with the support given by extant evidence for the hypothesis that Richelieu once loved Anne of Austria. In short, actual estimates of evidential weight are in general not quantitative, they are not made with respect to every consistent set of statements which may conceivably be introduced as evidential premises, and they are not always comparable.

Now Carnap's system of inductive logic not only aims to analyze and to bring into a coherent order inductive arguments which are commonly considered to be sound. His system also seeks to generalize the principles underlying those arguments, so as to bring within the scope of the broadened principles questions of inductive inference upon which common practice is usually silent. Carnap believes, in particular, that quantitative determinations of evidential support are not beyond the bounds of possibility; and he in fact devotes his major effort to the construction of systems of quantitative inductive logic.[2] There are therefore

[2]Carnap's attempt to develop a purely comparative logic of induction, in which only relations of order are assumed between degrees of confirmation but no numerical measures are assigned to them, has not been entirely successful thus far. Carnap has himself recognized that the comparative logic presented in Chap. VII of LFP leads to counter-

some obvious respects in which Carnap's proposed "rational reconstruction" of induction deviates from actual inductive practice.

The mere circumstance that such differences exist does not, of course, constitute a difficulty for his system. Customary standards of inductive reasoning are not beyond criticism and correction; and just as recent statistical theory has developed improved methods for the conduct of inductive inference, so Carnap's theory may also indicate ways for improving habitual modes of assessing inductive arguments. Moreover, no serious objection to his theory can be based on the fact that there are differences between his theory and customary conceptions, if the deviations occur at points at which habitual notions are vague or noncommittal, or if the innovations are simply "auxiliary" devices (introduced perhaps for the sake of achieving a uniform and formally satisfactory method for analyzing inductive arguments) which do not enter constitutively into the final assessment of the evidence for a given hypothesis. The picture is radically altered, however, if Carnap's approach requires the adoption of methods for weighing evidence that appear to be incompatible with ostensibly reliable inductive procedures, or if his methods rest on stipulations that are either question-begging or practically unrealizable. In the former case, some proof is required that the proposed innovations are more effective for achieving the objectives of empirical inquiry than are the customary methods; in the latter case, little if anything has been accomplished in the way of a viable theory of inductive inference. It is perhaps arguable, for example, that the assumption in Carnap's theory, according to which a hypothesis receives a measurable degree of support from any consistent set of empirical premises, is in general only an innocent formal requirement, and though it deviates from established procedures the assumption has only a negligible import for the normal task of assessing empirical evidence. On the other hand, the further assumption in Carnap's system, that even purely logical truths lend a degree of support to empirical hypotheses, does not appear to be quite so innocuous. For as it turns out, this a priori degree of support for a hypothesis enters fundamentally into the determination of the degree of support that *empirical* evidence gives to the hypothesis. The assumption seems therefore to be entirely in disaccord with the way in which the weight of evidence is normally assessed. There are, moreover, good reasons for maintaining that modern science has achieved its successes in part because it has rejected the mode of evaluating its hypotheses which is based on that assumption. This feature of Carnap's inductive logic, taken by itself, does not necessarily deprive the system

intuitive results—cf. his article "On the Comparative Concept of Confirmation," *British Journal for the Philosophy of Science*, III (1952-3). I shall therefore omit in this essay all discussion of Carnap's comparative inductive logic.

of all value, and it is certainly not unacceptable to many distinguished analysts of inductive procedure. There are, however, further assumptions underlying the system that appear to me no less debatable, and in what follows I propose to examine them.

II

Carnap bases his quantitative inductive logic on a definition of the notion of the degree of confirmation (or probability$_1$) of a hypothesis *h* relative to (non-contradictory) evidence *e*—written for short as '*c(h, e)*', and even more briefly when no confusion arises as '*c*'. A fundamental condition Carnap imposes upon *c* is that it satisfies a set of postulates, essentially the postulates usually assumed for the mathematical calculus of probability. These postulates require, among other things, that *c* be associated with a real number in the interval from 0 to 1 inclusive, for every pair of statements *h* and *e*—provided only that *e* is not self-contradictory. On the other hand, these postulates define *c* only implicitly, so that there is a non-denumerable infinity of ways in which *c* can be *explicitly* defined so as to conform with the postulates. Carnap therefore indicates how, for a certain class of specially constructed languages, explicit definitions for the *c* can be given, each definition corresponding to what he calls an "inductive method". These languages possess a relatively simple syntactical structure, adequate for formulating certain parts of scientific discourse, though not the whole of it. Carnap's problem then reduces to that of selecting from these infinitely numerous inductive methods, just those (possibly just one) which promise to be adequate for actual inductive practice and which are in reasonably good agreement with our habitual (or "intuitive") notions concerning the assessment of inductive evidence.

It turns out, however, that the infinitely numerous possible definitions fall into one or the other of two classes. The *c*'s falling into the first class are functions of the number of primitive predicates in the language for which they are defined; the *c*'s belonging to the second class are not functions of this number, but depend on a parameter whose value is assigned in some other way. Carnap appears to believe, though whether he really does so is not quite certain on the basis of his published statements, that a certain *c* belonging to the former class and designated as 'c^*' is particularly appropriate as the foundation for an inductive logic which can serve to clarify, systematize and extend actual inductive practice. I shall therefore first discuss c^*, and postpone comment on other definitions in Carnap's repertory of inductive methods.

Every language for which *c* (and therefore c^*) is defined has a finite number of primitive predicates, and a finite or denumerably infinite number of individual constants. Although the predicates may be of any degree, Carnap develops his system in detail mainly for the case that the predicates are all monadic. Moreover, although the individuals named by the individual constants may be of any sort (e.g., physical objects, events, etc.), he suggests that for technical reasons it is preferable to take them to be spatio-temporal positions.[3] In any case, the only characteristics that are to be ascribed to the individuals mentioned in a given language are those expressible in terms of its primitive predicates and the explicit definitions constructed out of these. Accordingly, there is one indispensible condition which the primitive predicates must satisfy, if the language in which they occur and the inductive logic based on c^* are to be adequate for the aims of science: the set of primitives must be *complete,* in the sense that they must suffice to express every "qualitative attribute" we may ever have the occasion to predicate of the individuals in our universe.

The reason for this requirement of completeness is that c^* is so defined that its numerical value for a given h and e is in general a function of the number of primitive predicates in the language. Thus, suppose a language is adopted containing π independent monadic primitive predicates. Then there will be k ($= 2^\pi$) "narrowest classes" specifiable with the help of these predicates and their negations. Suppose, moreover, that 'M' is a predicate which is expressible as the disjunct of w of these narrowest classes, w being the "logical width" of M. If now the evidence e asserts that in a sample of s individuals, s_1 have the property M, and h is the hypothesis that an individual not mentioned in e also has the property M, then $c^*(h, e) = \frac{s_1 + w}{s + k}$. However, if the language is not complete, and if new primitive predicates must be added to express some feature of the universe, the logical width of M in the new language will be increased, even though the *relative* logical width w/k of M will be unaltered. It follows immediately that $c^*(h, e)$ in the first language will differ from $c^*(h, e)$ in the second enlarged language. To be sure, as Carnap has explicitly noted, the values of the c^*'s will remain in the interval with the end-points s_1/s and w/k, where s_1/s is the observed relative frequency of M in the sample of size s and w/k is the constant relative width of M. He has also pointed out that if the sample size s is increased but the relative frequency s_1/s of M remains the same, then even though the number of primitive predicates is augmented, the relative frequency s_1/s will swamp the influence of π (the number of primitive predicates) upon the value of c^*, and that as s increases without limit $c^*(h, e)$ will approach s_1/s as the limit. Nevertheless, the fact that c^* varies at all with the number of primitive predicates in the language

[3] LFP, 62.

appears to be strongly counter-intuitive. Certainly no biologist, for example, would be inclined to alter his estimate of the support given by the available evidence to the hypothesis that the next crow to be hatched will be black, merely because the language of science becomes enriched through the introduction in some branch of sociology of a new primitive predicate. Nor is there any prima facie good reason why such an altered estimate should be made. On the other hand, if the set of primitive predicates is complete, their number cannot be augmented, and the difficulty disappears.

But is the proposed cure an improvement on the disease? Unless we do have good reasons for fixing the number of primitive predicates in a complete set, we cannot, even in principle, calculate the value of c^* for non-trivial cases, so that the inductive logic based on c^* is simply inapplicable. But the assumption that a complete set of primitives contains a given number π of predicates is not a truth of logic; it is at best a logically contingent hypothesis which can be accepted only on the basis of empirical evidence. The assumption is not a logical truth, for it in effect asserts that the universe exhibits exactly π elementary and irreducible qualitative traits, into which all other traits found in nature are analyzable without remainder. It is an assumption which would be contradicted by the discovery of some hitherto unnoted property of things (e.g. an odor or distinct type of physical force) that is not explicitly analyzable in terms of the assumed set of basic traits. Since the assumption must therefore be evaluated in the light of available empirical evidence, the obvious question arises as to how the weight of this evidence is to be estimated. It cannot be measured by way of c^* defined for the language with π primitive predicates. For in that language the assumption is an analytic truth, and its c^* has the maximum value of 1, contrary to the supposition that the assumption is a contingent hypothesis. Nor can the weight of the evidence for the assumption be measured in terms of a c^* defined for some different language. For this latter language would then have to have a complete set of primitive predicates, and we would thus be faced with an infinite regress. Perhaps a c, different from c^*, is needed, one for which the condition of completeness is not essential? But if so, there are no clues as to which alternative to c^* is to be employed; and in any event, if a c different from c^* is required in order to select a language in which c^* is to be defined, then c^* would not be the *uniquely* and *universally* adequate measure of evidential support—contrary to the supposition underlying the present discussion that c^* is such a measure.

However this may be, it is difficult to avoid the conclusion that the assumption that we have, or some day shall have, a complete set of primitive predicates is thoroughly unrealistic, and that in consequence an inductive logic based on that assumption is a form of science fiction.

Although in certain areas of experience we are fairly confident that all the directly observable traits have already been noted, there are no good reasons for believing that we have already catalogued such traits occurring in all parts of the universe. All possible experiments upon all individuals spread through time have not been, and are not likely to be, performed; and the ancient discovery of the previously unknown magnetic property of loadstones has had its analogue frequently repeated in the past and may continue to be repeated in the future. Moreover, though this point perhaps bears only on eventual developments of Carnap's system so as to make it potentially applicable to the whole of the language of science and not only to a fragment of it as is the case at present, even a presumptively complete catalogue of predicates referring to *directly observable* traits would not exhaust the primitive predicates actually required in *theoretical science*. The theoretical predicates which enter into modern systems of natural science (e.g. such predicates as 'entropy', 'gene' or 'electron') are not explicitly definable in terms of directly observable things, though without them scientific research as we know it would be impossible. Such theoretical predicates are usually the products of great feats of scientific imagination; and the introduction of new theoretical predicates into a branch of science is often accompanied by the elimination of older ones—this has been the fate of such terms as 'phlogiston' and 'caloric'. The theoretical parts of the language of science, at any rate, undergo frequent changes, and the direction of change does not appear to be converging towards a limit. The supposition that some day we shall have a complete list of theoretical predicates is thus tantamount to the assumption that after a certain date, no further intellectual revolutions in science will occur. But this is an assumption that is incredible on the available evidence.

As Carnap recognizes, the requirement of completeness is related to John Maynard Keynes's principle of limited variety (and incidentally, also to Francis Bacon's doctrine of "forms"), according to which the amount of variety in the universe is so limited that no one object possesses an infinite number of independent properties. Carnap does not find this principle implausible, and cites in its support the success of modern physics in "reducing" the great variety of phenomena to a small number of fundamental theoretical magnitudes.[4] But this evidence does not seem to be compelling, if only because it is at least debatable whether the phenomenal qualities of things are *explicitly definable* in terms of the theoretical concepts of physics; and if they are not so definable, the total number of primitive predicates has not in fact been diminished. Moreover, though no a priori limits can be set to the scope of physical

[4] LFP, 75.

theory, and it may well be that the physics of the future will account for larger areas of our phenomenal experience than it does at present, two points should be noted. In the first place, current physical theory does not in fact embrace all that experience, and it may never do so. In the second place, the evidence of history seems to show that as the scope of physics is enlarged, the number of its primitive theoretical predicates does not converge to any fixed value, and no plausible upper bound can be assigned to such a number, if indeed there is one. But without a reliable estimate of the value of such an upper bound (to say nothing of offering a reasonably based conjecture as to what will be the actual primitive predicates that a possibly complete physical theory of the future will require), a fully satisfactory inductive logic based on c^* cannot be constructed. The fulfillment of the requirement of completeness depends on our possessing more knowledge than we possess at present, or are likely to possess in the foreseeable future. And if the requirement should ever be fulfilled, we would, by hypothesis, have acquired so much knowledge about the universe that much of our present need for an inductive logic will no longer be actual.

III

There is a further difficulty (which may, however, be only an apparent one) that faces an inductive logic based on c^*—and more generally, on a c that is a function of the number of primitive predicates in the language. It is a familiar fact that two deductive systems may be logically equivalent, so that statements in one are translatable into statements in the other and conversely, even though each system is based on a distinctive set of primitive predicates and a distinct set of axioms. Thus, Euclidean geometry can be developed in the manner of Veblen (who employs, among others, the terms 'point' and 'between' as primitives), or in the fashion of Huntington (who uses 'sphere' and 'includes' as primitive predicates); and there is no statement in the Veblen system which cannot be matched in the Huntington codification, and vice versa. If two languages, each containing only monadic primitive predicates, are intertranslatable, then it can be shown that the number of primitives in one must be equal to the number in the other. But in general, if at least one of two intertranslatable languages has polyadic primitives, then it seems that the number of primitives in one may be different from the number in the other. But if this is so, the consequences are serious. For suppose that a hypothesis h and the evidence e for it can be formulated in two intertranslatable languages L_1 and L_2, where the number of polyadic primitives in the former is unequal to the number of primitives in the latter. It then follows that since c^* is a function of the number of primitive predicates in the language for which it is defined, the value of $c^*(h, e)$ calculated for

L_1 will be unequal to the value of c^* (h, e) calculated for L_2. Accordingly, the degree of support which the same evidence provides for a given hypothesis will depend on which of two equivalent languages is used for codifying the evidence and the hypothesis. This result is strongly counterintuitive. If the premise of this argument is sound (and I frankly do not know whether it is or not), then the degree of support which a hypothesis receives from given evidence on the basis of Carnap's approach is contingent on the arbitrary choice of one among several logically equivalent languages. But such a conception of evidential weight seems of dubious value as the basis for the practice of induction.

Two considerations occur to me, however, which may make this difficulty only a spurious one. One of them is Carnap's suggestion that in addition to satisfying the requirement of completeness, the primitive predicates of a language for which c^* is defined must also satisfy the requirement of simplicity. As Carnap once formulated this requirement, "the qualities and relations designated by the primitive predicates must not be analyzable into simpler components."[5] The required simplicity of primitive predicates must, on this stipulation, be an "absolute" one, and not merely relative to some given language or mode of analysis. If this notion of simplicity could be assumed to be sufficiently clear, the difficulty under discussion would presumably vanish. For if two intertranslatable languages are constructed on the basis of two sets of unequally numerous primitive predicates, it might be possible to show in general that one of the sets of primitives is simpler than the other, and that therefore the value of c^* must be calculated for the simpler of the two languages. Nevertheless, the notion of absolute simplicity is far from clear. If we do not employ psychological criteria such as familiarity, what rules are to be used in deciding whether, for example, the Veblen set of primitives for geometry are simpler than the Huntington set? When Carnap first proposed the requirement of simplicity he himself admitted his inability to give an exact explication of the notion; and the obscurity of the notion perhaps accounts for the fact that he has not mentioned this requirement in more recent publications. But in any event, the use of the notion of absolute simplicity for outflanking the above difficulty in c^* generates difficulties that are no less grave.

The second consideration mentioned above is of a more technical sort. The value of c^* is in fact an explicit function of the number of *state-descriptions* constructable in the language adopted, and only indirectly of the number of primitive predicates in it. Now a state-description states for every individual, and for every property or relation designated by the primitives, whether or not the individual has the property or relation.

[5]Rudolf Carnap "On the Application of Inductive Logic," *Philosophy and Phenomenological Research,* VIII (1947), 137.

Accordingly, a state-description is a non-contradictory conjunction of atomic statements or of their negations (or, in case of languages with an infinity of individual constants, it is an infinite class of such statements) —where an atomic statement ascribes a property (or relation) designated by a primitive predicate to an individual (or individuals) named by an individual constant (or constants). It follows that if the primitive predicates of a langauge are not totally logically independent of each other, not every conjunction of atomic statements or of their negations will be a state-description—since in that case some of the conjunctions will be self-contradictory in virtue of the logical relations between the predicates, and must therefore be omitted from the count of all possible state-descriptions. But if two intertranslatable languages L_1 and L_2 are based on two unequally numerous sets of primitive predicates, there will presumably be relations of logical dependence between the primitives in each set, so that the number of state-descriptions in L_1 will be the same as the number of state-descriptions in L_2. It will then follow that for given h and e, the values of $c^*(h, e)$ will also be the same for the two languages, so that the objection to c^* under present discussion loses its point.

There are, however, two comments on this solution of the difficulty which seem to me in order. The solution assumes that it is possible to give, for each of two intertranslatable languages, an exhaustive catalogue of the rules or postulates which specify the relations of logical dependence between its primitives. Such a catalogue can of course be offered for "artificial" languages, since artificial languages are actually constructed by explicitly stipulating what are the relations of logical dependence between the primitives and what are the logically contingent connections between them. But this is not so readily accomplished for the so-called "natural" languages (including much of the language of science), for in such languages it is not always clear which statements are logically necessary and which have the status of logically contingent hypotheses. Indeed, as is well-known, the same *sentence* may alter its status in this respect with the progress of inquiry or with alternate codifications of a scientific system. (For example, the sentence expressing the ostensibly contingent second law of motion in Newton's system of mechanics, appears as a statement of a logical truth in Mach's reformulation of the system.) On the other hand, though this problem of codifying a natural language is in practice often a difficult one, it is not a problem that is distinctive to Carnap's system of inductive logic.

The second comment is this. Carnap has thus far defined the notion of logical width only for languages with monadic predicates. But it seems plausible to assume that when he does develop his system for more complex languages, he will require an analogous notion for the latter. I have no idea how he will define the notion for the general case. However, it seems to me a reasonable conjecture that for languages with polyadic predicates, as for languages with exclusively monadic ones, the logical width of a predicate must also be some function of the number of primitive predicates in the system. But if this conjecture is sound, an important question immediately arises, one which bears directly on the adequacy of the suggested solution to the difficulty under discussion. Given two intertranslatable languages based on two sets of unequally numerous primitives, and granted that the number of state-descriptions in each is the same, will corresponding predicates in the two languages (i.e., predicates that designate the same property) also have the same logical width? If not, and since the logical width presumably enters into the value of c^*, then for given h and e the value of c^* (h, e) in the two languages will not be the same. In that eventuality, however, the difficulty under discussion will not have been put to final rest.

IV

I wish next to raise an issue that concerns not only c^* but also the whole continuum of inductive methods Carnap regards as possible candidates for explicating the notion of evidential support. Among the conditions he lays down which any reasonable c must satisfy, there are two that bear considerable resemblance to the notorious Principle of Indifference, often regarded as the Achilles heel of the classical theory of probability. The first of these stipulates that all the individuals are to be treated on par, the second introduces a similar requirement for the primitive predicates. According to the first, for example, if the evidence e asserts that the individuals a_1 and a_2 have the property M, while the hypothesis h declares that the individual a_3 has M, then $c(h, e)$ must be equal to $c(h', e')$, where e' asserts that the individuals a_4 and a_5 have M and h' declares that the individual a_6 has M. According to the second requirement, if 'P_1' and 'P_2' are primitive predicates, e asserts that a_1 and a_2 have the property P_1, and h asserts that a_3 has P_1, then $c(h, e)$ must equal $c(h', e')$—where e' declares that a_1 and a_2 have the property P_2 and h' declares that a_3 has P_2. In short, $c(h, e)$ must be invariant with respect to any permutation of individual constants as well as with respect to any permutation of the primitive predicates.

These requirements are initially plausible, and as Carnap points out assumptions very much like them are tacitly employed in deductive logic. Taken in context, they formulate a feature of actual inductive practice; and in generalizing sciences like physics they are unavoidable, on pain of putting an end to the use of repeated experiments for establishing universal hypotheses. For example, it obviously makes no difference to the evaluation of the evidence for the generalization that water expands on freezing, whether the evidence is obtained from one sample lot of water rather than another sample—*provided* that the samples are taken from a reservoir of the substance that is homogeneous in certain respects. Similarly, it makes no difference to the credibility of a generalization, whether the generalization under inquiry is that copper expands on heating or whether the generalization is that copper is a good electrical conductor—*provided* again that the instances used as evidence are the same in both cases, and *provided* also that the hypothetical relations between the properties under investigation are assumed to be dependent only on the traits of things explicitly mentioned.

On the other hand, as the examples just mentioned suggest, such judgments of indifference are made within contexts controlled by *empirical assumptions* as to what are the relevant properties of individuals that must be noted in using the individuals for evidential purposes, and as to the relevant factors that must be introduced into general statements concerning the concomitances of properties. Thus, different samples of water must be sufficiently homogeneous in their chemical composition, though not in their historical origins, if they are to be on par as evidence for the generalization concerning the expansion of water when cooled. Again, if given instantial evidence is to carry the same weight for the generalization that copper expands when heated as it does for the generalization that copper is a good conductor, the concomitances asserted must be assumed to be independent of variations in other properties exhibited by the instances—for example, of differences in the shapes or the weights of the individuals upon which observation is being made. It is clear, however, that these judgments of relevance and irrelevance are based on *prior experience,* and cannot be justified by purely a priori reasoning.

Within the framework of Carnap's construction, however, the status of the requirements concerning the indicated invariance of c is different. For in his system, the invariance is absolute, not relative to special contexts involving special empirical assumptions. Indeed, the invariance is postulated antecedently to any empirical evidence which might make the postulation a reasonably plausible one. It is not easy to see, therefore, what grounds—other than purely arbitrary and a priori ones—can be adduced for such a requirement of absolute invariance. Carnap defends the requirement by arguing in effect that since the primitive predicates are stipulated to be logically independent, there is no reason for assigning unequal c's to two hypotheses relative to the evidence for them, when the respective hypotheses and evidential statements are isomorphic under a permutation of individual constants or primitive predicates. But though there is no a priori reason for assigning unequal c's in such a case, neither is there a compelling a priori reason for assigning *equal* ones. There is surely the alternative, suggested by actual scientific practice, that the matter is not to be decided once for all by fiat, but settled differently for different classes of cases in the light of available empirical knowledge. In any event, the value of the Principle of Indifference is as debatable when it is used, as Carnap uses it, to specify in inductive logic which pairs of hypotheses and evidential statements are significantly isomorphic, as when the principle is employed in the classical manner to determine the magnitudes of empirical probabilities.

V

Some of the consequences which follow from the adoption of c^* as the measure of evidential support must now be examined. One of these consequences is that for a language with an infinity of individual constants (i.e. in a universe with a non-finite number of individuals), the value of c^* for any universal empirical hypothesis, relative to any finite number of confirming instances for it, is always zero. For example, despite the great number of known corroborative instances for the generalization that water expands on freezing, the evidential support provided by those instances for this ostensible law is zero when measured by c^* in an infinite universe, and is no better than the evidential support given by those instances to the contrary hypothesis that water contracts on freezing. Moreover, even if the number of individuals in the universe is assumed to be finite but very large, the c^* for the generalization relative to the available instantial evidence will normally differ from zero only by a negligible amount.

Accordingly, if c^* were a proper measure of what ought to be our degree of reasonable belief in hypotheses, none of the generalizations proclaimed by various sciences as laws of nature merits our rational confidence. The search by scientists for critical evidence to support such claims is then pointless, for however much evidence is accumulated in favor of universal laws, increments in the degree of that support remain at best inappreciable. This outcome of adopting c^*, however, is patently in disharmony with our customary way of judging such matters.

There are several ways, nevertheless, in which this apparently fatal consequence entailed by c^* may be made more palatable. It might be argued, in the first place, that it is gratuitous to assume the universe to contain an infinity of individuals, so that the theorem concerning the value of c^* for universal hypotheses in infinite languages simply does not apply to the actual world. It must of course be admitted that we have no certain knowledge that our universe does indeed contain an infinity of empirically specifiable individuals, even if the universe is taken to be extended in time without limit. On the other hand, neither do we know with certainty that the individuals in the universe are only finite in number. If the use of c^* is defensible only on condition that this number really is finite, its use must be postponed indefinitely until that fact is established; and we shall have to carry on our inductive studies (including the inquiry into the number of individuals in the universe) without the help of an inductive logic based on c^*. Moreover, as has already been noted, even if the universe contains only a very large finite number of individuals—and there surely is competent evidence that this number is very large indeed—for all practical purposes such a number entails the same undesirable consequences as if it were non-finite.

It might be claimed, in the second place, that it is just a mistake to raise questions about the "probability" of universal hypotheses, and thereby to view them as statements on par with instantial ones, concerning which it is significant to ask what measure of support they receive from given evidence. For universal hypotheses, so it is often said, function as guides to the conduct of inquiry, as instruments for predicting concrete events, or as means for organizing systematically the outcome of previous investigations. Universal hypotheses, on this view, are intellectual devices concerning which it is appropriate to ask whether they are adequate for achieving the ends for which they have been designed, but not whether they are true or false. Accordingly, the circumstance that for universal hypotheses the value of c^* is uniformly zero, simply calls attention to the absurdity of treating them as factual statements for which evidence is to be assessed. However, whatever the merits or limitations of this intellectual gambit may be, it is not one which Carnap can employ. For on his approach, universal hypotheses are considered to be on par with instantial ones in respect to their status as empirical statements. It is indeed a central feature of his system that for *any* hypothesis h and (non-contradictory) evidence e, $c^*(h, e)$ must have a determinate value.

Carnap's own proposed resolution of the difficulty bears a certain resemblance to the one just mentioned. But he offers a technically different answer, by way of the notion of the "instance confirmation" of universal laws. He introduces his discussion (though a full account by him is still not available) with the following general explanation:

> Suppose we ask an engineer who is building a bridge why he has chosen the particular design. He will refer to certain physical laws and tell us that he regards them as 'very reliable', 'well founded', 'amply confirmed by numerous experiences'. What do these phrases mean? It is clear that they are intended to say something about probability$_1$ or degree of confirmation. Hence, what is meant could be formulated more explicitly in a statement of the form '$c(h, e)$ is high' or the like. Here the evidence e is obviously the relevant observational knowledge. But what is to serve as the hypothesis h? One might perhaps think at first that h is the law in question, hence a universal sentence l of the form: 'For every space-time point x, if such and such conditions are fulfilled at x, then such and such is the case at x'. I think, however, that the engineer is chiefly interested not in this sentence l, which speaks about an immense number, perhaps an infinite number, of instances dispersed through all time and space, but

rather in one instance of l or a relatively small number of instances. When he says that the law is very reliable, he does not mean to say that he is willing to bet that among the billion of billions, or an infinite number, of instances to which the law applies there is not one counterinstance, but merely that this bridge will not be a counterinstance, or that among all bridges which he will construct during his lifetime there will be no counterinstance. Thus h is not the law l itself but only a prediction concerning one instance or a relatively small number of instances. Therefore, what is vaguely called the reliability of a law is measured not by the degree of confirmation of the law itself but by that of one or several instances.[6]

Carnap thereupon defines the instance confirmation of a law l on evidence e as the c^* value of the support given by e for the hypothesis that an individual not mentioned in e fulfills l. Furthermore, he defines the qualified-instance confirmation of the law l as the c^* value of the support given by e to the hypothesis that an individual not mentioned in e, but possessing the property mentioned in the antecedent clause of the universal conditional l, also has the property mentioned in the consequent clause of l.

Carnap then argues that contrary to usual opinion, the use of laws is not essential for making predictions, since the inference to a new case can be made *directly* from the instantial evidence, rather than through the mediating office of the law. Thus, suppose the hypothesis h under discussion is whether some given individual a has the property B, and that the evidence e asserts that all of the many other individuals which have been observed to possess the property A also possess B. Suppose further that j is the instantial datum that a has A. The usual account, as Carnap formulates it, is that from e we first inductively infer the law l: All A's are B's; and from l together with j we deductively infer h. However, since $c^*(l, e)$ is zero or very close to it, this argument is unsatisfactory. But according to Carnap we really do not need a high value for $c^*(l, e)$ in order to obtain a high value for $c^*(h, e.j)$—that is, for a qualified-instance confirmation of the law. On his view, on the contrary, the person X conducting the inquiry

need not take the roundabout way through the law l at all, as is usually believed; he can instead go from his observational knowledge $e.j$ directly to the singular prediction h. That is to say, our inductive logic makes it possible to determine $c^*(h, e.j)$ directly and to find that it has a high value, without making use of any law. Customary thinking in everyday life likewise often takes this short cut, which is now justified by inductive logic. For instance, suppose somebody asks X what he expects to be the color of the next swan he will see. Then X may reason like this: he has seen many white swans and no non-white swans; therefore he presumes, admittedly not with certainty, that the next swan will likewise be white; and he is willing to bet on it. Perhaps he does not even con-

[6] LFP 571f.

sider the question whether all swans in the universe without a single exception are white; and, if he did, he would not be willing to bet on the affirmative answer.

We see that the use of laws is not indispensable for making predictions. Nevertheless it is expedient, of course, to state universal laws in books on physics, biology, psychology, etc. Although these laws stated by scientists do not have a high degree of confirmation, they have a high qualified-instance confirmation and thus serve as efficient instruments for finding those highly confirmed singular predictions which are needed in practical life.[7]

In short, Carnap appears to be in substantial agreement with J. S. Mill's view that the fundamental type of inductive reasoning is "from particulars to particulars."

Carnap's proposed solution of the difficulty is brilliantly ingenious. But is it satisfactory? Several considerations make this doubtful to me. i) His solution is predicated on the assumption that the evidence in the qualified-instance confirmation of a law can in general be identified and established without even the tacit acceptance and use of laws, since otherwise a regress would be generated that would defeat the objective of his analysis. The assumption is illustrated by his own example, in which the instantial statement '*a* is a swan', constituting part of the evidence for the hypothesis that *a* is white, can presumably be affirmed on the strength of a direct observation of the individual *a* without the implicit use of any universal laws. I shall not dispute this particular claim, even though legitimate doubts may be expressed as to whether the assertion that *a* is a swan does not "go beyond" what is directly present to observation, and does not carry with it implicit assumptions about invariable connections between anatomical structure, physiological function, and other biological properties—connections which are assumed when an organism is characterized as a swan. But I do dispute the ostensible claim that this example is typical of the way laws are in general confirmed, and that the instances which confirm many scientific theories are quite so simply obtained. To be sure, most of these theories cannot be formulated in the restricted languages for which Carnap has thus far constructed his system of inductive logic; but I do not believe the point under discussion is affected by this fact. Consider, therefore, some of the confirming instances for the Newtonian theories of mechanics and gravitation. One of them is the obloid shape of the earth. The fact that it is obloid, however, can be established only through the use of a system of geometry and of optical instruments for making geodetic measurements—all of which involve at least the tacit acceptance of universal laws as well-founded. Could we inductively infer this fact from the instantial evidence alone, without including in the evidence

[7] LFP, 574f.

for it any general laws? It would not advance the solution of the problem, were we to construct an inductive argument, to parallel the schema suggested by Carnap, to read as follows: The qualified-instance confirmation of the Newtonian laws, where the instance is the obloid shape of the earth, is high relative to the instantial evidence that all of the many rotating solids which have been observed in the past have an equatorial bulge, supplemented by the additional evidence that the earth is a rotating solid. For how can the fact that the earth is a rotating solid be established, except by way of assuming an astronomical theory? But unless this fact (or an analogous one) is granted, it is difficult to see how Newtonian theory is relevant to ascertaining the earth's shape, or to understand why the earth's obloid shape is to be counted as a confirming instance for that theory. I do not believe, therefore, that Carnap has successfully defended c^* against the objection that it leads to grave difficulties when it is applied to universal hypotheses.

ii) There is a further point bearing on the present issue, which is suggested by Carnap's discussion of Laplace's Rule of Succession. As is well known, Laplace derived a theorem from the assumptions of his theory of probability, which asserts that if a property is known to be present in each member of a sample of s events, the probability that the next event will also have this property is $\frac{s+1}{s+2}$. Using the evidence available to him concerning the past risings of the sun, Laplace then calculated the probability of another sunrise to be $\frac{1{,}826{,}214}{1{,}826{,}215}$. This result has been severely criticized by many authors for a variety of reasons. Carnap also finds Laplace's conclusion unsatisfactory, because Laplace allegedly violated the "requirement of total evidence". According to this requirement, "the total evidence available must be taken as basis for determining the degree of confirmation" [or probability$_1$] in the application of the theorems of inductive logic to actual situations.[8] Carnap points out that Laplace assumed the available evidence to consist merely of the known past sunrises, and that he thereby neglected other evidence for the hypothesis that the sun would rise again—in particular, the evidence involved in his knowledge of mechanics. As Carnap puts the matter,

> the requirement of total evidence is here violated because there are many other known facts which are relevant for the probability of the sun's rising tomorrow. Among them are all those facts which function as confirming instances for the laws of mechanics. They are relevant because the prediction of the sunrise for tomorrow is a prediction of an instance of these laws.[9]

[8]LFP, 211.
[9]LFP, 212f.

Although I do not believe, as Carnap does, that there is no analogue to the requirement of total evidence in deductive logic,[10] I shall not pursue this side issue, and will assume that Carnap's diagnosis of Laplace's error is well taken. The question I do wish to raise is whether it is the *confirming instances* of the laws of mechanics, or the *laws of mechanics* themselves, which are to be included in the evidence when tomorrow's sunrise is predicted. Carnap appears to adopt the former alternative. It is not clear, however, why in that case most of the evidence—taken simply as so many *independent* instantial statements—is *relevant* to the prediction of another sunrise, and why it should raise the c* for the predictive hypothesis. For example, the confirming instances of the laws of mechanics include observations on tidal behavior, on the motions of double stars, on the rise of liquids in thin tubes, on the shapes of rotating liquids, and much else, in addition to observations on the rising of the sun. There is, however, no purely logical dependence between instantial statements about the height of the tides or instantial statements about phenomena of capillarity, on the one hand, and instantial statements on the rising of the sun on the other hand. Apart from the laws of mechanics, these statements express just so many disparate facts, no more related to each other than they are related to other statements which do *not* formulate confirming instances of these laws—for example, statements about the magnetic properties of a given metal bar, or about the color of a man's eyes. Why should the inclusion of the former instantial data increase the evidential support for the prediction of another sunrise, but the inclusion of the latter ones not do so? To make the point more fully, consider a language with three logically independent monadic primitive predicates 'P_1', 'P_2' and 'P_3'. Then according to the definition of c^*, $c^*(P_1 a_1, P_1 a_2) = 5/9$; and if the evidence is enlarged to include $P_1 a_3$, $c^*(P_1 a_1, P_1 a_2 \cdot P_1 a_3) = 6/10$, so that the c* for the hypothesis is increased. But if the evidence is further enlarged by including $P_2 a_4$, then $c^*(P_1 a_1, P_1 a_2 \cdot P_1 a_3 \cdot P_2 a_4) = 6/10$, so that this additional evidence is irrelevant; and the situation remains the same when the evidence is further augmented by adding to it $P_3 a_5$, or $P_2 a_6$, or in fact any number of instantial statements which ascribe properties to individuals other than the property designated by the predicate 'P_1'. Now most of the predicates occurring in the formulation of confirming instances for the laws of mechanics are *prima facie* quite analogous to the predictive predicates in this example in respect to their being logically independent of each other. Indeed, there are cases in the history of science when, on the basis of

[10] Thus, if we assume that only gravitational forces are present, we can deduce from Newtonian theory certain conclusions about the orbit of a given body. But if there are also magnetic forces in operation which enter into the determination of the orbit and which we have unwittingly ignored, our original conclusions are clearly wrong.

some well established theory, an event has been predicted which had rarely if ever been observed previously. In such cases, though the predictive hypothesis receives a considerable measure of support from the theory, the predicates in the instantial evidence for the theory are for the most part different from, and logically independent of, the predicates occurring in the hypothesis. To cite a notorious example, William R. Hamilton predicted the phenomenon of conical refraction from theoretical considerations, though this phenomenon had not been previously observed, so that instances of the phenomenon did not constitute a part of the evidence for the theory Hamilton employed. In consequence of all this, it does not appear plausible that, in conformity with the requirement of total evidence, it is the *instantial evidence* for the laws of mechanics, but rather the *laws of mechanics* themselves, which must be included in the evidence for the hypothesis of another sunrise.

But if this is so, I am also compelled to conclude that the use of general laws in inductive inference is not eliminable, in the manner proposed by Carnap. Accordingly, the notion of instance confirmation (or qualified-instance confirmation) of a law as a measure of the law's "reliability" does not achieve what he thinks this notion can accomplish. In short, I do not believe he has succeeded in outflanking the difficulty which arises from the counter-intuitive consequences of adopting c^* as a measure of evidential support in infinite languages.

VI

I must now raise an issue that affects not only an inductive logic based on c^*, but nearly all of the inductive methods Carnap has outlined.

It is commonly assumed that the evidential support for a hypothesis (whether singular or universal) is generally increased by increasing the sheer number of its confirming instances. For example, it is usually claimed that the hypothesis that the next marble to be drawn from an urn will be white is better supported by evidence consisting of 100 previous drawings each of which yielded a white marble, than by evidence consisting of only 50 such drawings; and many accounts of inductive logic attribute this difference in evidential weight entirely to the difference in the relative size of the two samples. Again, it is often supposed that simply by repeating an experiment on the period of a pendulum, where each experiment shows this period to be proportional to the square-root of the pendulum's length, the weight of the evidence for the generalization that the period of any pendulum follows this law is augmented. In any event, this assumption is implicit in most of the inductive methods (including the one based on c^*) which Carnap discusses. But although the assumption appears to be eminently plausible, I think it is a reasonable one only when it is employed under certain conditions, so that the assumption is acceptable only in a qualified form. I want to show, however, that most of Carnap's inductive methods in effect adopt it without such qualifications.

Consider first a language with two monadic primitive predicates 'R' and 'S' and N individual constants, so that if 'Q' is defined as 'R · S,' 'Q' specifies one of the four narrowest classes of individuals which is formulable in this language. The relative logical width of 'Q' is then $w/k = 1/4$. Suppose now that a sample of size s is drawn from the population, that just s_i individuals in the sample have the property Q, and that h is the hypothesis asserting that an individual a not contained in the sample also has Q. Carnap shows that for all the measures c satisfying the conditions he regards as minimal for a measure of evidential support, $c(h, Qa_1 \ldots Qa_{s_i} \cdot - Qa_{s_{i+1}} \ldots - Qa_s) = \frac{s_i + \lambda/4}{s + \lambda}$, with $0 \leq \lambda \leq \infty$, where the value of the parameter λ depends on the inductive method adopted and thus fixes the measure c of evidential support. For c^*, this parameter is equal to k (the total number of narrowest classes specifiable in the language), and in the present example is equal to 4. When all the individuals in the sample have the property Q, $s_i = s$ and $c(h, Qa_1 \ldots Qa_s = \frac{s + \lambda/4}{s + \lambda} = \frac{4s + \lambda}{4(s + \lambda)}$. Suppose now the size of the sample is increased by n, so that it contains $s + n$ individuals, and that every member of the sample has Q. Then $c(h, Qa_1 \ldots Qa_{s+n}) = \frac{4(s + n) + \lambda}{4(s + n + \lambda)}$. Since for $\lambda > 0$ and $n > 0$ $\frac{4(s + n) + \lambda}{4(s + n + \lambda)} > \frac{4s + \lambda}{4(s + \lambda)}$, it follows that $c(h, Qa_1 \ldots Qa_{s+n}) >$ $c(h, Qa_1 \ldots Qa_s)$. Accordingly, when all the individuals in a sample belong to the class Q (so that, since Q determines one of the narrowest classes specifiable in the language, the individuals are indistinguishable in respect to the properties they exhibit) and the sample size is increased, the measure of evidential support for the hypothesis is also increased. Indeed, in an infinite language if all the individuals in progressively more inclusive samples belong to Q and if the sample size is increased without limit, the degree of confirmation for the hypothesis approaches the maximum value of 1.

Suppose, next, that 'All A is B' is the formulation of a law in a language having only monadic predicates and N individual constants. where 'A' and 'B' are any molecular predicates defined in terms of the primitives, and where the predicate 'A· –B' has the logical width w. (It is clear that the law is logically equivalent to 'Nothing is A· –B'). Suppose, further, that the evidence e for the law asserts that s distinct individuals do not have the property A· –B and that all the individuals fall into *one* of the k narrowest classes specifiable in the language. (e is then the conjunction of s instantial statements, each of which asserts that some individual has the property determining this class—the property in question being incompatible with A· –B.) Carnap then shows that when s is very large in relation to k, c^* (All A is B, e) is approximately equal to $(s/N)^w$.[11] Accordingly, if the evidence for the law is increased by the addition of further instances all of which continue to fall into the same narrowest class, the degree of confirmation for the law is also increased. For infinite languages (i.e. when $N = \infty$) this degree of confirmation is of course zero, as has already been noted. On the other hand, if the logical width of the predicate 'A·B' is w', and if the evidence consists of a sample of s individuals all of which have the property A·B and all of which, moreover, fall into the same narrowest class, Carnap proves that for the measure c^* the qualified-instance confirmation of the law is equal to

$$1 - \frac{w}{s + w + w'}.$$

This latter is the value of the degree of confirmation of the hypothesis that an individual, known to have the property A, also has the property B, on the evidence that s other individuals all falling into one of the narrowest classes have both A and B. Since the value of the qualified-instance confirmation of the law is independent of the number of individual constants in the language, it will differ from zero even for infinite languages, and it will be close to 1 when s is made sufficiently large.

In my judgment, however, these results are incongruous with the normal practice of scientific induction, as well as with any plausible rationale of controlled experimentation. For according to the formulas Carnap obtains for his system, the degree of confirmation for a hypothesis is in general increased if the confirming instances for the hypothesis are multiplied—*even when the individuals mentioned in the evidence cannot be distinguished from each other by any property expressible in the language for which the inductive logic is constructed.* But it seems to me most doubtful whether under these conditions we would in fact regard the evidential support for a hypothesis to be strengthened. Suppose we undertook to test a proposed law, say the law that all crows are black, by making a number of observations or experiments on individuals; and suppose further that the individuals we examined were *known to be completely alike* in respect to all the properties which we can formulate. Would there be any virtue in repeating the observations or experiments in such a case? Would we not be inclined to say that under the imagined circumstances *one* observation carries as much weight as an *indefinite number* of observations?

[11] LFP, 571.

We do, of course, repeat observations and experiments intended to test proposed laws. But apart from our desire to make allowances for and to correct personal carelessness and "random" errors of observation, we do so only when we have some grounds for believing that the individuals are *not* completely alike in the properties they possess. In fact, we generally *select* the individuals upon which tests are to be performed so that they are *unlike* in as large a variety of features as possible, compatible with the requirement that the individuals exhibit the properties mentioned in the antecedent clause of the law we are testing. The rationale for this standard procedure is to show that the connections between properties asserted by the proposed law do hold in just the way the proposed law asserts them to hold, and that the hypothetical connections are not contingent upon the occurrence of some other property not mentioned by the proposed law. Accordingly, test-cases for the law that all crows are black will be drawn from a wide assortment of geographic regions, climatic conditions, and other variable circumstances under which crows may be found, in the hope that despite variations in these circumstances the color of the plumage is indeed uniformly associated with the anatomical structure that identifies crows, and in the desire to show that the color does not depend on the occurrence of some other properties which crows may have. In short, the sheer repetition of confirming instances does not, by itself, appear to carry much weight in the support given by the evidence to a hypothesis. But if this point is well taken, all those inductive methods considered by Carnap (including c^*) in which a contrary result is obtained (the only method for which such a contrary result does not hold is the one for which $\lambda = \infty$) are inadequate rational reconstructions of generally accepted canons of scientific inquiry.

The point just argued also has some bearing on the notion of the instance confirmation of a law. For if, as is required by Carnap's analysis, increasing the number of otherwise indistinguishable confirming instances for a law augments the degree of confirmation for a still unobserved additional instance of the law, why should not the degree of confirmation also be augmented by an equal amount for an *indefinite* number of further instances of the law—or even for the law itself? Under the conditions supposed, is there really a better reason for expecting that a *single* hitherto untested individual will conform to the law than for the hypothesis that many such individuals will do so? Thus, if all observed instances of crows are black, and if these instances are *known* to be alike in all respects formulable in the (hypothetically complete) language we employ (e.g. the crows observed come from the same locality, they have the same genetic constitution, their diet is the same, etc.), why should this evidence give stronger support to the prediction that the next crow to be observed will be black, than for the hypothesis that the next ten crows to be observed will be black, or for the hypothesis that all crows are black? The contrary view seems to me to reflect sound inductive practice.

To see the point more clearly, consider the following schematic example constructed in conformity with Carnap's procedure. Assume a language with four monadic primitive predicates 'P_1', 'P_2', 'P_3' and 'P_4'. The law 'Anything that is both P_1 and P_2 is also P_3' is proposed for testing. A sample consisting of $2s$ individuals is now examined, and each individual is found to possess the property $P_1 \cdot P_2 \cdot P_3$. Two possible cases will be considered: i) All the $2s$ individuals belong to the narrowest class determined by $P_1 \cdot P_2 \cdot P_3 \cdot P_4$, and are therefore otherwise indistinguishable; ii) only s individuals in the sample belong to this class, while the remaining half belong to the narrowest class determined by $P_1 \cdot P_2 \cdot P_3 \sim P_4$. Now the evidence in the first case leaves it unsettled whether P_3 is always present when the property $P_1 \cdot P_2$ alone is present, or whether the occurrence of P_3 is contingent not only on the presence of this property but also on the presence of P_4 as well. In the second case, however, the evidence shows that P_3 is dependent only on $P_1 \cdot P_2$, irrespective of the presence or absence of P_4. It therefore appears reasonable to maintain that the evidence in the second case is better than in the first as a support for the hypothesis that an individual not included in the sample, but known to possess $P_1 \cdot P_2$, also possesses P_3—and if I judge the matter aright, such a claim is in agreement with standard scientific practice. Now this point is also recognized by Carnap, since the value of c^* in the second case is higher than the value in the first case. It is clear, therefore (that the variety of instances contributes to the strength of evidence for a hypothesis. On Carnap's analysis, however, complete absence of variety in the instances is compatible with a high degree of confirmation, provided that the sheer number of instances is large; and this seems to me a defect in his system. Accordingly, if my argument holds water, his system fails to take into consideration an essential feature of sound inductive reasoning.

Moreover, I have not been able to persuade myself that the evidence in the first case supports to a lower degree the hypothesis that an *indefinite* number of further individuals possessing $P_1 \cdot P_2$ also possess P_3, than it supports the hypothesis that just one further individual is so characterized. It might be retorted that to deny this is counter-intuitive—since we normally do say, for example, that on the evidence of having drawn 100 white marbles from an urn, the "probability" of getting a white marble on the next trial is greater than the "probability" of getting two white marbles on the next two trials. But I do not find this rejoinder convincing. If we *know* that the 100 white marbles constituting the evidence are fully alike *in all relevant respects* upon which obtaining a white marble from the urn depends, then it seems to me that the evidence supports the hypothesis that any further marbles, resembling in those respects the marbles already drawn, will also be white—irrespective of how many further marbles will be drawn from the urn. It is because we generally do *not* know what are the complete set of properties in respect to which marbles may differ, and because we therefore do *not* know whether the marbles in the sample lot are alike in all relevant respects, that the evidence offers better support for the hypothesis concerning a single additional marble than it does for the hypothesis concerning two or more additional marbles. I cannot therefore evade the conclusion that because of the consequences noted, c^* as the measure of evidential support runs counter to sound inductive practice.

VII

I have been concerned thus far mainly with those inductive methods (chiefly with c^*) in the continuum of methods constructed by Carnap, in which the degree of confirmation depends on the number of primitive predicates in the language adopted. I wish now to discuss some of the assumptions underlying Carnap's construction of his continuum of methods, some features of those methods in which the degree of confirmation is not a function of the number of primitive predicates, and some of the considerations Carnap advances for adopting one method rather than another.

A fundamental assumption entering into the construction of Carnap's continuum of inductive methods is the following. If 'M' is a monadic predicate whose relative logical width is w/k, e_M is the evidence that in a sample of s individuals s_M possess the property M, and h_M is the hypothesis that an individual not included in the sample also possesses M, then the degree of confirmation of h_M on the evidence e_M must lie in the interval whose end-points are the relative frequency s_M/s and the relative logical width w/k. In fact, the value of $c(h_M, e_M)$ is set equal to a weighted mean of the "empirical factor" s_M/s and the "logical factor" w/k—so that eventually this value is taken to be equal to $\frac{s_M + \lambda(w/k)}{s + \lambda}$, where λ is a parameter which may have any value from 0 to infinity.

But why should the values of $c(h_M, e_M)$ be assumed to fall into the interval determined by these end-points? Carnap argues, in the first place, that

> Other things (including s) being equal, those values [of c^*] are higher, the greater s_M/s. This has often been stated explicitly and may be regarded as one of the fundamental and generally accepted characteristics of inductive reasoning. Moreover, all known methods of confirmation or estimation for rf [relative

frequency] agree that in any case of a sufficiently large sample the value of c or E [estimate function], respectively, is either equal to or close to s_M/s.[12]

I do not think, however, that this reasoning is entirely convincing. Carnap is doubtless correct in holding that "other things being equal", *estimates* of the relative frequency of some property in a population are often assumed to be close to the observed relative frequency in the samples drawn. But this is not always the case; and we do not, in general, measure the evidential support for a singular hypothesis by the relative frequency found to occur in a sample. Thus, in estimating a relative frequency in a population, much depends not only on the observed value of the relative frequency in the sample, but also on the way the sample has been obtained, and therefore upon the *general method* of sampling employed. For example, the mere fact that there is a high proportion of French-speaking individuals in a sample of 10,000 selected, say, form the residents in border town in northern Vermont, does not, by itself, provide competent support for the hypothesis that there is a correspondingly high relative frequency of French-speaking residents in the U.S.

Even more dubious, however, is the assumption that the degree of evidential support for the hypothesis that a still unexamined individual has some property M bears any determinate relation to the relative frequency with which M occurs in a sample. To take an extreme case first, if in a sample consisting of just *one* bird of a given species the bird is found to have a yellow plumage, so that the relative frequency of this property in the sample is 1, no one but a tyro in inductive procedure would assign a high degree of support to that evidence for the hypothesis that the next individual of that species will also have that property. In such a case, barring the use of some well-established theory, we would, I think, be inclined to regard the evidence as insufficient to warrant any conclusion; and if we did assign a degree of support to it, it would, I suspect, be vanishingly small. But consider a less fanciful example, and suppose we found that in 10,000 observed cases of human births 53 percent are male. Is it plausible to say that the degree of support this evidence gives to the hypothesis that the next human birth will be male is even approximately equal to .53? Since we do not, in actual practice, assign numerical measures to degrees of evidential support, it is not obvious how to answer this question. But it seems to me that here too much would depend on what method of sampling has been employed in obtaining the evidence, on whether we have any reason to believe that the sample is representative of the population, and on the care with which the data have been collected and recorded. The mere fact that the rela-

[12]CIM, 24.

tive frequency of male births in a sample is .53 does not necessarily indicate how cogent is the evidence of that sample for the hypothesis in question. It is certainly not absurd to believe that though the relative frequency of male births in two samples of 10,000 each is the same, the evidential support for the hypothesis given by one sample may be much higher than the support supplied by the other.

Carnap seeks to show, however, that the degree of confirmation for a hypothesis can be construed as the "fair betting quotient" on that hypothesis, and also as an estimate, based on the evidence, of the relative frequency with which a property occurs in the population. He defines a "bet" as a contract between two parties X_1 and X_2, which stipulates that X_1 will confer a benefit u_1 on X_2 if a certain prediction *h* is fulfilled, while X_2 will confer a benefit u_2 on X_1 if not-*h* is realized. The ratio $q = u_1/(u_1 + u_2)$ is called the betting quotient; and a betting quotient *q* is said to be "fair" if it does not favor either party—if, that is, given the evidence *e*, betting on *h* with odds *q* is as good a choice as betting on not-*h* with the odds $(1 - q)$. Carnap then reasons as follows. Suppose X_1 and X_2 make *n* similar bets, with the betting quotient *q*, on each of the *n* individuals in a class K having the property M. Let *h* be the hypothesis that a certain individual *a* in K has M; and assume that the evidence *e*, available to both parties, asserts the ratio of individuals in K with the property M to be *r*. Since X_1 will obviously win *rn* bets with a gain of rnu_2, and will lose $(1 - r)$ *n* bets with a loss of $(1 - r)nu_1$, his total gain or loss will be $n(u_1 + u_2)(r - q)$; and since he will break even if $q = r$, the betting quotient will be fair when $q = r$. Carnap therefore suggests that the statement "The probability$_1$ (or degree of confirmation) of *h* with respect to the evidence *e* has the value *q*", can be interpreted to say that a bet on *h* with a betting quotient *q*, is a fair bet when the bets are placed on the basis of the information contained in *e*. And he concludes that "If the relative frequency of M in a class to which *a* belongs is known to be *r*, then the fair betting quotient for the hypothesis that *a* is M, and hence the probability$_1$ of this hypothesis, is *r*."[13]

It is nevertheless not at all clear why the evidence *e*, which asserts that the relative frequency of M in K is *r*, should be assigned a probative force of degree *r*, for the hypothesis that an arbitrary member of K has M. Such an assignment is plausible when K is finite and *r* is 1 or 0; but for other values of *r*, it is only on the ground of some obscure continuity assumptions that *r* can be taken as the measure of evidential support which *e* gives to *h*. Moreover, it seems to me that it is only on the basis of a tenuous analogy that Carnap's reasoning in this context can be extended to the interpretation of his probability$_1$ when the hypothesis is

[13]LFP, 168.

a *universal* statement—for in this latter case the bets would have to be placed on possible universes. What does appear plausible is that r is a measure, not of the degree of support given to h by e *simpliciter,* but of the effectiveness in the long run of the *method of placing bets* on evidence such as e. On this interpretation, however, the degree of confirmation which the evidence e lends to h becomes identical with the relative frequency with which a certain method of inference yields true conclusions of a certain form from premises of a certain type. But such an interpretation is not congruous with Carnap's outlook, since the interpretation seriously compromises the purely logical (or analytical) character that statements about degrees of confirmation must have on his view.

Carnap also argues, however, that the degree of confirmation can be construed as the *estimate* of a relative frequency. Thus, suppose that in the above betting situation the evidence e does not contain information about the relative frequency of M in K. He then maintains that "Since the probability$_1$ of h on e is intended to represent a fair betting quotient, it will not seem implausible to require that the probability$_1$ of h on e determines an *estimate of the relative frequency* of M in K."[14] But the estimate based on e of the unknown value of a magnitude u is defined as the mathematical expectation of u—i.e. as the sum of the products formed by multiplying each possible value of u with the probability$_1$ of this value on the evidence e. Since K contains n individuals, there are $n + 1$ possible values for the unknown relative frequency r of M in K. Let r' be the estimate of r. Then the estimated gain or loss g' to the bettor X_1, were he to place n simultaneous bets with X_2, is $n(u_1 + u_2)(r' - q)$, where q is the betting quotient. And the bets will be fair when the estimated gain or loss is 0, so that r' must be equal to q.[15]

But here again the proposed identification of c with an estimate of relative frequency is made on assumptions that cannot be plausibly extended to all the cases to which Carnap's notion of probability$_1$ is intended to apply. One of these assumptions is that, provided the evidence e supplies no information about the individual members of K, it makes no difference which class K is under consideration when placing bets or how many individuals K contains.[16] Another assumption is that *simultaneous* bets are placed on all the members of K, so that e need contain no information about the way in which K is sampled—indeed, Carnap allows for the possibility of forming an estimate of relative frequency even when e is a purely logical truth and no sampling whatever has been made. But does an estimated relative frequency, when it is formed on such

[14] *Ibid.,* 168.

[15] *Ibid.,* 170.

[16] *Ibid.,* 171.

assumptions, constitute a reasonable measure for the support provided by the evidence for the hypothesis that a given member of the class has a given property? Suppose, for example, the hypothesis to assert that the next human birth will be a male, and the evidence to consist in the information that in a certain town with a population of 500 mothers 300 gave birth to boys. We may of course form an estimate of the relative frequency of male births. I do not think, however, that if we do so we would accept this estimate as the measure of the support which the evidence gives to the hypothesis. For the degree of support seems to me negligible, while the numerical value of the estimate is conceivably a fairly high ratio. Again, the assumption that simultaneous bets are placed on all members of a class is a bit of fiction that has verisimilitude in certain contexts, but appears to be quite unrealistic for most situations in which we form estimates of relative frequencies and weigh the evidential support for hypotheses. Moreover, Carnap requires his c to be capable of a completely general application, so that the hypothesis h might, in principle, be a state-description (i.e. a complete description of a "possible world"); and in such a case, at any rate, to place bets on h would be to bet on something concerning which we could in fact not know whether or not it is realized, so that the analogy to ordinary betting would be stretched to the breaking point.

Thus far, my comments have been addressed to that part of Carnap's assumption which makes the empirical factors s_M/s one of the end-points of the interval into which the value of $c(h_M, e_M)$ is postulated to fall. What about the remaining part of the assumption, that the other end-point is the logical factor w/k? Carnap maintains that "Other things (including k) being equal, if w/k is greater in one case, the value of c is higher or equal . . . . I believe that the stronger statement with 'higher' instead of 'higher or equal' also holds."[17] He defends this stronger condition by showing that otherwise a logical possibility would be ignored that the evidence e does not exclude.

The central issue which this part of the assumption raises is whether, in the absence of any factual evidence for a hypothesis, it is nevertheless reasonable to assign a degree of support for it on the "evidence" of a purely logical truth. For if $c(h_M, e_M)$ is in general equal to $\frac{s_M + \lambda\,(w/k)}{s + \lambda}$, then when $s = 0$, c is equal to w/k. The rationale for assigning such a value to c in this case appears to be the following. Since the logical width of M is w, then if an arbitrary individual a is to possess M, a must fall into one of the w narrowest classes specifiable in the language adopted. There are, however, k such classes. In the absence of any empirical

[17] CIM, 25.

evidence, is it not therefore plausible to take w/k as the measure of c for the hypothesis that a is M? Indeed, such reasoning appears to underlie assumptions commonly made in inductive reasoning. Consider, for example, three empirical generalizations having the forms G_1: All A is B; G_2: All AC is B; and G_3: All A is BD, where 'A', 'B', 'C' and 'D' are independent primitive predicates. It is sometimes said that even before empirical evidence is available for any of these generalizations, G_2 is initially "more likely" than G_1, and G_1 is initially "more likely" than G_3. The reason usually given for this claim is that G_1 asserts B to belong to everything that is A, while G_2 asserts B to belong only to the things that are both A and C—so that G_2 asserts less than what is asserted by G_1, and in consequence we are risking error to a lesser degree in accepting G_2 than in adopting G_1. Similarly, G_3 asserts that both B and D belong to everything that is A, while G_1 asserts only that the property B alone belongs to the A's, so that again less is being asserted by G_1 than by G_3. All this is in agreement with Carnap's stipulations, for if we calculate the relative logical widths of the predicates in these generalizations in the manner he describes, G_1 has the relative logical width $3/4$, G_2 has $7/8$, and G_3 has $5/8$. For G_1 to be true, $1/4$ of all the narrowest classes formulable in the language must be empty, for G_2 to be true $1/8$ must be empty, and for G_3 to be true $3/8$ must be empty. Accordingly, antecedent to any empirical evidence, there appears to be a "better chance" that G_2 is true than that G_1 is, and a "better chance" that G_1 is true than that G_3 is.

Nevertheless, however persuasive these considerations may seem, one must not ignore the fact that in all this we are simply counting logical possibilities. Unless there are some reasons for supposing that some of these possibilities are actually realized, their mere number does not constitute a relevant factor in estimating the evidential support for a hypothesis. For example, if in the case of G_2 there are in fact no individuals which are both A and not-C, the class determined by A· C coincides with the class determined by A alone; and in that eventuality it would be hard to imagine a good reason for regarding G_2 as "more likely" than G_1. But if we know neither that the class of things which are A· –C has any members nor that the class is empty, it is only on the most far-fetched assumption that it is plausible to assign a greater antecedent degree of confirmation to G_2 than to G_1—on such assumption, for example, as that our actual universe is a random instance of possible universes, each of which is generated by filling in various proportions the narrowest logically determinable classes that are formulable in our language.

To make this point for Carnap's actual assumption about w/k as one end-point of the interval into which $c(h_M, e_M)$ must fall, suppose that M is the property of possessing brown eyes, black hair and a light complexion, and that its relative logical width is 3/4. Then antecedent to any factual information as to whether M is physically realizable, or if so realizable whether there are any individuals with M, $c(h_M, e_M)$ must equal 3/4. How can this value be justified? It would be justified if we had some reason for supposing that, in Charles Peirce's words, universes are as plentiful as blackberries, and that were we to bet on the occurrence of an individual with M in each of the universes (though without possessing any factual information about any of them) we would win in approximately 3/4 of the time. Since, however, such a supposition is at best fanciful, it cannot really serve to justify the value assigned to *c*. But let us modify the example somewhat, and assume that in a sample of 100 individuals 80 are found to have M. Then $c(h_M, e_M)$ must, on Carnap's stipulations, be not less than 3/4, irrespective of the way in which the sample has been obtained—even if a sampling procedure is used which does not in general yield representative samples, so that the ratio 4/5 of M in the actual sample might happen to be far greater than the ratio of M in the population. It does not seem to me, however, that under the circumstances a value for *c* equal to or greater than 3/4 is either a plausible or a usable measure for the support which the evidence lends to the hypothesis. And I do not believe, therefore, that a good case has been made out for stipulating that in general the value of $c(h_M, e_M)$ must fall into the interval determined by the empirical and logical factors.

VIII

But even if Carnap's stipulations for constructing a continuum of inductive methods are granted, the problem still remains of choosing one of the methods as in some sense "the best." Carnap himself rejects the method specified by taking the parameter $\lambda = \infty$, on the ground that since this method gives an "infinite weight" to the logical factor, no amount of factual knowledge could alter the a priori degree of confirmation for a hypothesis, a result which is clearly incompatible with scientific practice. Carnap nevertheless maintains that the choice of a method is not a "theoretical" question, because the selection of a method involves a practical decision into whose determination a variety of non-factual considerations will enter. Thus, he maintains,

> A possible answer to a theoretical question is an assertion; as such it can be judged as true or false, and, if it is true, demands the assent of all. Here, however, the answer consists in a practical decision to be made by X. A decision cannot be judged as true or false but only as more or less adequate, that is, suitable for given purposes. However, the adequacy of the choice depends, of course, on many theoretical results concerning the properties of the various inductive methods; and therefore the theoretical results may influence the decision. Never-

theless, the decision itself still remains a practical matter, a matter of X making up his mind, like choosing an instrument for a certain kind of work.[18]

It will be clear, however, that the choice of a method is not a theoretical question, only as long as the objectives which an inductive logic is to achieve are not specified. Once these objectives are made explicit, there surely are factual grounds for preferring one method (or group of methods) over others. Indeed, Carnap himself recognizes this implicitly when he rejects the method $\lambda = \infty$, and explicitly when he declares:

> Suppose that X has chosen a certain inductive method and used it during a certain period for the inductive problems which occurred. If, in view of the services this method has given him, he is not satisfied with it, he may at any time abandon it and adopt another method which seems to him preferable. . . . How can X go over from one inductive method to another? It is not easy to change a belief at will; good theoretical reasons are required. It is psychologically difficult to change a faith supported by strong emotional factors (e.g., a religious or political creed). The adoption of an inductive method is neither an expression of belief nor an act of faith, though either or both may come in as motivating factors. An inductive method is rather an instrument for the task of constructing a picture of the world on the basis of observational data and especially of forming expectations of future events as a guidance for practical conduct. X may change this instrument just as he changes a saw or an automobile, and for similar reasons. . . . After working with a particular inductive method for a time, he may not be quite satisfied and therefore look around for another method. He will take into consideration the performance of a method, that is, the values it supplies and their relation to later empirical results, e.g., the truth-frequency of predictions and the error of estimates; further, the economy in use, measured by the simplicity of the calculations required; maybe also aesthetic features, like the logical elegance of the definitions and rules involved. The λ-system makes it easy to look for another inductive method because it offers an inexhaustible stock of ready-made methods systematically ordered on a scale. . . . Here, as anywhere else, life is a process of never ending adjustment; there are no absolutes, neither absolutely certain knowledge about the world nor absolutely perfect methods of working in the world.[19]

The crucial point to be noted in these comments is that if we wish to choose an inductive method which will be consonant with the aims of empirical science, we must take into consideration "the performance of a method, that is, the values it supplies and their relation to later empirical results, e.g. the truth-frequency of predictions and the error of estimates." For the question now arises in what way "later empirical results" and the truth-frequency of predictions are relevant for judging a method's "performance". On the basis of what has been said thus far, however, it is difficult to see that these things *are* relevant in the slightest degree. For in Carnap's system, if $c(h, e) = p$ is true, it is an analytic truth, invul-

[18] *Ibid.*, 53.
[19] *Ibid.*, 54f.

nerable to the facts of experience; and even though h should turn out to be false while p is high, nothing in this circumstance can affect the validity of the statement that p is the value of $c(h, e)$. Evidently, then, some further postulates are required—for example, a postulate such as that if h is a singular prediction and $c(h, e) = p$, then in a class of similar predictions made on the basis of analogous evidence the predictions turn out to be true with a relative frequency close to p. If such additional postulates are introduced, however, an inductive logic is in effect converted into an *empirical theory* about the success-ratios of predictions concerning the course of events. Though the logical structure of the predictive mechanism can be analyzed without reference to such events, the system which includes these additional postulates is no longer simply a branch of pure mathematics.

Carnap appears to recognize this in so many words. In his preliminary comments on the choice of an inductive method, he imagines a system of repeated simultaneous bets by two persons on the hypothesis that an individual not in the sample has some property M, where each person bases his wager on the evidence supplied by a sample of fixed size s but each uses a different c-function. (It is assumed that the number of successful bets each person makes can be ascertained.) Carnap supposes, furthermore, that such bets are made for all other properties as well, and that samples of all other (finite) sizes are employed as evidence. He then suggests that the over-all balance of gains or losses for the total system of bets based on one c-function, could be taken as the measure of the relative success of that inductive method, as compared with the analogous measure of success when a different c-function is used for placing such a system of bets. This is a daring though not immediately promising suggestion, for it proposes a measure for the merit of an inductive method that could be evaluated only if we had complete knowledge of the contents of our universe. Nevertheless, the suggestion does indicate that in Carnap's view, *theoretical* and not merely practical questions do enter into the choice of a satisfactory inductive method. The problem remains, however, whether Carnap can indicate an effective basis for choosing between the different alternatives in his continuum of inductive methods.

In point of fact, Carnap works out in a technically impressive way the central idea contained in these preliminary suggestions. On the assumption that the actual universe has a certain given constitution (i.e. on the assumption that a given state-description U is the true one), he develops a formula for the optimum value of the parameter λ. This formula is obtained as follows. Suppose that the k narrowest classes distinguishable in the language adopted are determined by the properties Q_i ($i = 1, 2, \ldots, k$), and that the relative frequency with which Q_i occurs in the universe is r_i. Suppose, further, that estimates are made of the r_i on the basis of all possible samples of fixed size s drawn from the universe, where the estimating function itself is given in terms of some definition of c (and therefore in terms of some value of the parameter λ). Now it is customary to regard an estimating function as the more successful, the smaller is the mean-square of the deviations of the estimates from the true value of the magnitude being estimated. It turns out that this mean-square for all the r_i's, where the estimates are based on samples of fixed size s, is equal to $\frac{s - (\lambda^2/k) + (\lambda^2 - s)\Sigma r_i^2}{k(s + \lambda)^2}$, which can therefore be taken as the measure of the effectiveness of the inductive method λ. In this formula, the sum Σr_i^2 is taken by Carnap to measure the degree of "order" or "uniformity" in the universe. This sum has the maximum value 1, when all the individuals in the universe fall into one of the narrowest classes (i.e. when they all possess just one of the Q-properties); it has the minimum value $1/k$, when the individuals are distributed equally among those classes. It immediately follows that when Σr_i^2 has neither the maximum nor the minimum value, the optimum inductive method for a given state-description U is given by

$$\lambda\Delta = \frac{1 - \Sigma r_i^2}{\Sigma r_i^2 - 1/k}.$$

But this result is of no value for actually choosing an inductive method, since even if we can persuade ourselves that we know the value of k (which is a function of the number of primitive predicates required for describing the universe), we certainly do not know the value of Σr_i^2 for our actual universe. As Carnap notes, "The practical knowledge situation for any human being at any time is such that he knows only a relatively small part of the universe, never the whole of it; it is just this fact that makes the use of inductive methods necessary."[20] Nevertheless, although Carnap leaves unanswered the question how then we are to choose the optimum inductive method, he believes it is possible to fix a lower bound for $\lambda\Delta$, and so eliminate certain inductive methods as not optimal. He reasons as follows. Let U_T be the unknown true state-description, and $r_{iT} = N_{iT}/N$ be the unknown relative frequencies with which the k Q-properties occur in it. Suppose a sample of size s is drawn, and that it is non-homogeneous—i.e. at least two distinct Q-properties occur in it. Then the universe itself cannot be homogeneous. If the sample contains s_i individuals which are Q_i, clearly $r_{iT} \geq s_i/N$. Suppose now that the property Q_m occurs most frequently in the sample, so that s_m/s is greater than any other relative frequency in the sample. Now construct a state-description U which will agree with the information in the sample, but which assigns to all individuals not included in the sample the property Q_m. According-

[20] *Ibid.*, 71.

ingly, if N'_i is the number of individuals in U with the property Q_i, the relative frequency of Q_i in U is given by $r_i = N'_i/N$. For $i \neq m$, $N'_i = s_i$; while for $i = m$, $N'_m = N - s + s_m$. It follows that $\Sigma r_i{}^2 < 1$. But the unknown true U_T cannot be nearer to homogeneity than U; hence $\Sigma r_{iT}{}^2 \leq \Sigma r_i{}^2 < 1$, and $\Sigma r_i{}^2$ is an upper bound for $\Sigma r_{iT}{}^2$. Carnap therefore declares than $\Sigma r_i{}^2$ is "a *known* upper bound" for the unknown $\Sigma r_{iT}{}^2$, so that the unknown optimum method $\lambda \underset{T}{\triangleq}$ must be not less than $(1 - \Sigma r_i{}^2)/(\Sigma r_i{}^2 - 1/k)$ and must therefore be greater than 0.

But it is clear that the value of $\Sigma r_i{}^2$ can be obtained only if N is known, and that the value of $\Sigma r_i{}^2 - 1/k$ is known only if both N and k are known. In point of fact, however, neither N nor k is known, and to assume that they are is to assume something about "the practical knowledge situation for any human being at any time" which Carnap himself would doubtless admit is contrary to the facts. Moreover, if N is very large when compared with s (the size of the sample), $r_m = N'_m/N = 1 - (s - s_m)/N$, which is close to one; in consequence, $\Sigma r_i{}^2$ itself will approach 1 with increasing N. Accordingly, for very large N (and there is good reason to believe that N is quite large when compared with the size of samples drawn from our actual universe), $1 - \Sigma r_i{}^2$ will be close to 0. It follows that even if the optimum method $\lambda \underset{T}{\triangleq}$ for the actual universe is admitted to have a lower bound greater than zero, this lower bound is for all practical purposes indistinguishable from 0. It does not seem, therefore, that Carnap has provided any usable clues for choosing between the inductive methods in his continuum. Indeed, so many fundamental questions are left unanswered in his system, so many appear impervious to a reasonable resolution, that I am forced to regard with grave scepticism its significance as a potential clarification of inductive practice.

IX

Carnap does not dismiss the problem of "justifying" induction as a spurious one. Though he touches on the question only briefly, the reasons he gives for requiring such a justification, as well as the way he thinks it can be supplied, throw further light on his general philosophy of inductive inference. I wish now to comment on these matters.

Carnap notes that we cannot know with certainty whether a prediction (e.g. it will rain to-morrow), based on given evidence, is true before the event. Lacking such certainty, we must, according to him, adopt an appropriate course of action in the light of statements like "With respect to the available evidence, the probability$_1$ that it will rain to-morrow is high." On Carnap's view, however, the latter statement expresses a truth of logic; and if this is so, the obvious question is why we should base our actions on it. Now we may have some ground for believing that though this single prediction may be falsified by the events, similar predictions will in the long run have a high success-ratio. Accordingly, the issue reduces itself to finding good reasons for a thesis such as the following: "If X makes a sufficiently long series of bets, where the betting quotient is never higher than the probability$_1$ for the prediction in question, then the total balance for X will not be a loss"—and more generally, if X makes his decisions by taking into acount the values of probability$_1$, "he will be successful in the long run."[21]

As Carnap is careful to point out, however, this thesis is not a truth of logic, and is warranted only "if the world as a whole had a certain character of uniformity to the effect, roughly speaking, that a kind of events which have occurred in the past very frequently under certain conditions will under the same conditions occur very frequently in the future." He thus accepts the orthodox view that a "presupposition" of induction (i.e. of basing our actions on the values of probability$_1$) is the familiar doctrine of the uniformity of nature—a doctrine which he renders as "The degree of uniformity of the world is high."[22] But since this doctrine is in turn a factual hypothesis, and ostensibly underlies all inductive inference, many thinkers have argued that the doctrine cannot be established by inductive reasoning, on pain of circularity or an infinite regress; and they have felt compelled to advocate either scepticism or the abandonment of empiricism. Carnap, on the other hand, does not believe this argument to be sound or the alternatives it presents to be exhaustive. For he maintains that it is not essential for the justification of induction that we know *with certainty* the truth of the doctrine of the uniformity of nature. All that is needed, according to him, is that we establish the claim that "On the basis of the available evidence it is very *probable* [in the sense of probability$_1$] that the degree of uniformity of the world is high."[23] This claim, then, is the presupposition sufficient for establishing the validity of induction. But this presupposition is no longer a factual hypothesis; and if it is true then, like all probability$_1$ statements on Carnap's view, it is a truth certifiable by logic alone—though the proof of this logical truth is reserved by Carnap for a later publication. He therefore concludes that we cannot obtain a reasoned assurance that we will be successful in the long run by using inductive methods; but we can have demonstrated assurance that it is *probable* that we will be successful, since the assertion that the success is probable is analytically true.

Is it not a puzzle, however, how an allegedly analytic truth, which asserts nothing about the constitution of the actual world, can serve

[21] LFP, 178.
[22] *Ibid.*, 179.
[23] *Ibid.*, 180.

as the basis for practical decisions about the actual course of events? Carnap's reply to this natural query is that the analytic truth in question simply *makes explicit* the inductive logical relations between the available evidence and the hypothesis of nature's uniformity: the analytic truth merely shows the high probability of the hypothesis relative to the evidence, and thereby makes evident that it is reasonable for us to act on high probabilities. And Carnap concludes:

> A practical decision is reasonable if it is made according to the probabilities with respect to the available evidence, even if it turns out to be not successful. . . . It is reasonable for X to take the general decision of determining all his specific decisions with the help of the inductive method, because the uniformity of the world is probable and therefore his success in the long run is probable on the basis of his evidence, even though he may find at the end of his life that he actually was not successful and that his competitor who made his decisions in accordance not with probabilities but with arbitrary whims was actually successful.[24]

I now turn to my comments. Carnap adopts what is in effect a species of deductive justification of induction, one in which all the premises and therefore the conclusion are allegedly analytic truths. I shall not question his claim that within his system, the high degree of uniformity of the world is probable on the evidence, is analytic, for in the absence of a published proof it would be pointless to do so.[25] But I do question whether his proposed justification can dispense with some factual assumptions, however disguised these assumptions may be by having them appear as conventions built into the structure of the language which is adopted. Thus, I have already noted the similarity between the Baconian doctrine of forms and Keynes's principle of limited independent variety, on the one hand, and Carnap's assumption that a finite number of primitive predicates is sufficient to describe the world completely. This assumption, like those of Bacon and Keynes, is surely a factual one; and though there may be good evidence for it, the degree of support which the evidence gives to it cannot be estimated, on pain of circularity, in terms of the inductive logic based on that assumption. If this point is well-taken, however, Carnap is faced with the problem, traditional to all attempts at a deductive justification of induction, of validating what is ostensibly the supreme factual major premise in all inductive reasoning. But as far as I am aware, none of the tools thus far included in his armory of logical devices is adequate to this task.

[24] *Ibid.*, 181.

[25] I suspect, however, that though a formally valid proof may be given, the proof requires premises which are question-begging, in the sense that the assumption of the world's uniformity is presumably built-in antecedently into the *c*-function used for determining the probability_1 of that assumption.

It is pertinent to ask, therefore, whether in fact a supreme factual major premise is needed for justifying induction—or alternatively, whether a deductive justification of induction in a wholesale fashion is a reasonable undertaking. As Carnap tacitly recognizes, no major premise of the required generality can be specified which would permit the deduction of an inductive conclusion from such a premise, even when the latter is combined with instantial evidence. The most one can hope to achieve in this connection is to deduce from the combined premises, not the inductive conclusion itself, but the statement that the inductive conclusion is probable to some degree on the evidence. Such a deduction will be effected, however, by way of the application of some *rule of inductive inference,* in accordance to which the deduction must be made; and presumably different rules will be required for different types of conclusions and evidential premises. The validity of inductive arguments is then reduced to the question as to the warrant for assigning, in accordance with such rules, stated degrees of probability to inductive conclusions based on given premises. But in any event, since a variety of rules are needed, the inductive conclusions may just as well be inferred from the specific evidential premises alone, in accordance with the rules referring to such premises exclusively, instead of being inferred from premises that include an otiose additional "major" assumption. For these reasons a wholesale deductive justification of induction seems entirely gratutitous.

But to return to Carnap. According to him, every statement which assigns a degree of confirmation to a hypothesis on given evidence is analytic; and the analytic character of such statements is indeed a consequent of the fact that the assignment of degrees of confirmation is made in accordance with stated definitions and rules. Once such rules are granted, the claim that statements about degrees of evidential weight are analytic, seems to me to hold not only for Carnap's precisely articulated system, but also for the looser evaluations of evidence we actually make in science and ordinary affairs of life. If we judge, for example, that the evidence consisting of a rolling gait, a bronzed complexion, and calloused hands confirms to a high degree the hypothesis that a certain person is a sailor, the judgment involves the application to the case at hand of some conception, however vague it may be, of what constitutes good evidence. Should two individuals disagree on the cogency of this evidence, the disagreement seems to follow either from the fact that one of the individuals possesses unmentioned items of evidence which the other lacks, or from the fact that the individuals are employing different standards of what constitutes good evidence. In the former case, the dispute can be settled by making explicit the full range of evidence upon which the differing judgments are made. In the latter case, the dispute can be settled only by making explicit the different standards employed, and so recognizing that evaluations of the same evidence in terms of differing standards cannot but be different. If, however, the available evidence and the standards of evaluation are common to the individuals, then, except for possible blunders in applying the standards, their judgments on the merit of the evidence for the given hypothesis will coincide—and no appeal to empirical data other than that which is mentioned in the evidence seems relevant in making the judgments. Under these conditions, accordingly, statements about degrees of evidential support are undoubtedly analytic.

The question remains, however, whether the standards employed in evaluating evidence—i.e. the rules used in assigning degrees of confirmation to hypotheses relative to stated evidence—are not themselves based on factual assumptions, and do not themselves require to be defended by some appeal to empirical data. The answer, in my opinion, is strongly affirmative, at any rate for the rules explicitly or tacitly employed in weighing evidence in actual inductive practice. For example, many inductive inferences proceed in accordance with the rule (induction by simple enumeration) that a conclusion about the composition of a class of elements may be asserted on the basis of the composition of samples drawn in a certain manner from that class. This rule cannot be defended on a priori grounds. It can be justified only on the ground that the ratio of successful inferences drawn in the past in accordance with the rule is actually high. More generally, while I do not believe that induction can be justified in a wholesale and once-for-all fashion, I think that individual inductive policies can be justified—and indeed justified without vicious circularity—in terms of the *de facto* success-ratios that are associated with the inductive rules underlying those policies.

Where does Carnap stand on this issue? I do not find his published writings entirely clear on the point. As some of the quotations cited above indicate, he does say that an inductive method is sound if, in making our decisions in the light of the degrees of confirmation the method specifies, we are "successful in the long run." Such remarks certainly suggest that Carnap subscribes to the conception of the justification of induction I have just outlined. But on the other hand, he also maintains that a man is acting "rationally" in basing his decisions on the degrees of confirmation prescribed by an inductive method, "even though he may find at the end of his life that he was not successful." If it is safe to assume that Carnap intends this dictum to cover not only the arbitrary period of one man's life, but also the longer period of the life of the human race (and perhaps an even more extended stretch of time), he is then committed to what is surely a curious notion of "rationality"—and he must then be understood as rejecting an interpretation of his views such as the one just mentioned. But in any event, I do not believe that a man would ordinarily be judged to be acting in a rational manner, provided only he conducts his affairs consistently in accordance with some fixed set of rules and irrespective of the consequences such action brings forth. Consistency is undoubtedly an ingredient in our conception of rationality; but while it may be a necessary requirement for rational behavior, it is hardly a sufficient one. If rationality is conceived in the manner in which Carnap appears to conceive it, probability ought surely not to be taken as the guide to life.

This is, I must admit, a most ungracious essay. For if the major criticisms advanced in it hold water, it shows that despite the remarkable constructive power and ingenuity Carnap has brought to the reconstruction of inductive logic, he has not resolved the outstanding issues in the philosophy of induction, and his general approach to the problems is not a promising one. My excuse for writing this essay is not only that a forthright critique of his work in this domain is itself a testimony to my profound admiration for the intellectual power his work exhibits. My excuse is, further, that Carnap may perhaps find useful for the completion of his magnificent system a statement of some of the difficulties which a sympathetic reader encounters in the fragments already published, and that he may perhaps be stimulated to show how those difficulties can be outflanked.

Ernest Nagel

Department of Philosophy
Columbia University

26

Abraham Kaplan

LOGICAL EMPIRICISM AND VALUE JUDGMENTS

PROPERLY speaking, logical empiricism has no theory of value; such a theory belongs in its view, not to philosophy, but to science. Even its theory of value judgments, however, has been only sketchily developed. Its inspection of the language of valuation has so far yielded mainly only the negative result that this language is radically different from the language of science. What has been presented is not so much a full-blown philosophical theory as a formulation of an expected outcome. A position has been stated without that working out of details so characteristic of logical empiricism, and especially of the work of Rudolf Carnap and Hans Reichenbach in logic, semantics, and philosophy of science. This is the state of affairs in which philosophical polemic flourishes, and in this area there has been a most luxuriant and chaotic growth.

This essay is written in the belief that the position on value judgments taken by logical empiricism is not required by either its logic or its empiricism. The objections to the position are brought forward here yet once more, not in the spirit of continuing a futile polemic, but in the hope of pointing to an increased range of possibilities for the work of logical empiricism in this area.

I

The position to be considered was stated by Carnap some twenty years ago as follows:[1]

The rule, "Do not kill," has grammatically the imperative form and will therefore not be regarded as an assertion. But the value statement, "Killing is evil," although like the rule, it is merely an expression of a certain wish, has the grammatical form of an assertive proposition. Most philosophers have been deceived by this form into thinking that a value statement is really an assertive proposition and must be either true or false. Therefore, they give reasons for their own value statements and try to disprove those of their opponents. But actually a value statement is nothing else than a command in a misleading grammatical form. It may have effects upon the actions of men, and these effects

[1] R. Carnap, *Philosophy and Logical Syntax* (1935), 24.

may either be in accordance with our wishes or not; but it is neither true nor false. It does not assert anything and can neither be proved nor disproved.

What is essential is that "true" and "false" are held to be inapplicable to value judgments, a point usually expressed by denying them "cognitive meaning." Within logical empiricism and related philosophical standpoints there is general agreement only on this denial. In the positive statement of the content of value judgments there are variants: they express imperatives (Carnap), volitions (Reichenbach), emotions (Ayer), or attitudes (Stevenson); or they are to be explicated in terms of these and a variety of other uses (the Oxford analysts). Following the usage now unfortunately established, we shall designate the general position as *emotivist,* recognizing the inappropriateness of so narrow a term; and the contrary position, holding that value judgments may be either true or false, as *cognitivist.*

The negative emphasis in emotivism is perhaps understandable in historical terms as a reaction to the dogmatic absolutisms of *fin de siecle* philosophy, notably the theologicial and idealistic ethics of neo-Hegelianism in Germany and England. It is tempting to interpret the virulence of some of the attacks on emotivism as in turn a reaction to the exposure of the groundlessness of cherished dogmas. At any rate, emotivism has been attacked as implying a cynical, immoral nihilism. There cannot, of course, be any question for one moment of any personal application of such charges; though it seems to be the rule in the history of western philosophy for those who depart from prevailing ethical theories to be branded as scoundrels. At worst, one could only say that the moral conduct of emotivists is inconsistent with the amorality of their philosophical standpoint. It is both practically and philosophically unwise to confuse the logical implications of a theory with its psychological consequences for action.

But there is serious ground for doubting whether even the alleged logical implication of amorality actually holds. As Reichenbach has pointed out in some detail, "It is a misunderstanding of the nature of moral directives to conclude that if ethics is not objectively demonstrable everybody may do what he wants."[2] A morality may be no less strongly felt or willed, no less conscientiously followed and courageously defended, for resting on a non-cognitive base. To think otherwise is, ironically, to accept that "scientism" which is supposedly being attacked. The tacit premise on which the criticism seems to depend is the identification of cognitive meaning with "significance" in the sense of importance and value, so that a denial of the first term of the identity would imply a

[2]H. Reichenbach, *The Rise of Scientific Philosophy* (1951), 287 ff. All further references to Reichenbach are to this book.

denial of the second. But since logical empiricism, and emotivism in particular, explicitly rejects this identity, it is difficult to see how the alleged amoral consequence is deduced.

On the contrary, the consequences of emotivism—both logical and psychological—have been to weaken both cynicism and coercive dogma. The matter has been very well put in a recent paper on the subject worth quoting at length:[3]

> . . . Amidst all the present philosophical and political hypochondria about "moral skepticism," it may be worthwhile to be reminded that the emotive theory, even in its more unsubtle formulations, has promoted the classic moral objectives of empirical philosophies. It has helped loosen the hold of the untestable absolutes by which so much otherwise avoidable human suffering is perennially legitimated, and it has cut through the pretensions of those philosophies which, on "metaphysical" or "theological" or "scientific" grounds, claim to know what is good for men without ever consulting the men concerned. In affirming that meaningful argument in the sphere of values is always argument about facts, it has helped, if only indirectly, in promoting a responsible type of discourse in this sphere—and this despite the fact that its protagonists have frequently chosen, somewhat arbitrarily, not to call such responsible discourse "moral." Furthermore, along with other empiricisms, the emotive theory has focused attention on the primacy for social control of material factors, such as the reconstruction of psychological attitudes and social institutions, as against the ancient dream that the world can be made over simply by changing men's philosophies. And its emphasis on the continuing possibility of disagreements in attitude is, after all, not only a reminder that coercion may be necessary in any society; it is also a reminder, again if only indirectly, of the desirability of institutions which promote chances of compromise.

The objections to emotivism, then, which we shall examine here do not raise any question of the morality of the position, but ask whether emotivism provides an adequate explication of value terms and of the logic of value judgments. The question is not how to "save morality" from a philosophical skepticism; it is rather whether justice has been done to the philosophical problem. The difficulties in the position so often brought forward will be summarized as falling into four groups. In accord with Carnap's conception of philosophic method, we may take these as pointing to four areas where more precise and detailed formulations are called for, so that alternative explications may be weighed against one another. It is to emphasize this need, rather than to support a particular alternative, that the arguments are here restated, in what I hope will be a useful summary of two decades of controversy.

II

The first area of difficulty in emotivism centers about the conception of a distinctive kind of meaning which belongs to value judgments, on

[3] C. Frankel, "Empiricism and Moral Imperatives," *J. of Philosophy* L (1953), 261-2.

the basis of which they are to be differentiated from the statements occurring in the language of science. Specifically, two kinds of meanings are distinguished, the first variously called "emotive," "persuasive," "instrumental," the second "factual," "descriptive," "cognitive." (As before, the term *emotive* will be used in a wide sense to cover any of the conceptions of the first kind of meaning.) Now the standpoint of emotivism is that emotive meaning is essential to value judgments. Any set of words in a natural language is extremely likely, of course, to be ambiguous, so that what *looks* like a value judgment may in fact, in a particular utterance, belong to the language of science. For it actually to *be* a value judgment in a characteristic sense, its meaning must be such as to give it a "prescriptive or quasi-imperative force." In so far as its meaning is declarative, it is not a value judgment. And since it makes no sense to ascribe truth or falsity to a prescription or imperative, value judgments, when understood and used as such, are non-cognitive.

The position thus involves two parts: (1) Any utterance must function normatively in order to be a value judgment, and (2) The normative function can be performed only if the utterance has, in that use, some sort of emotive meaning. Thus Reichenbach declares (pp. 276, 277), "If ethics were a form of knowledge it would not be what moral philosophers want it to be; that is, it would not supply moral directives. . . . The modern analysis of knowledge makes a cognitive ethics impossible: knowledge does not include any normative parts and therefore [sic] does not lend itself to an interpretation of ethics." The difficulties focus on the second of these theses: granted that value judgments characteristically have a normative function; does it follow that they must therefore be analysed as having a distinctive kind of meaning, and in particular, a non-cognitive meaning?

On the face of it, this appears to be a *non-sequitur*. To start with, doubts have been cast on the conception of a special sort of meaning at all. As Max Black and others have pointed out, what is sometimes called "emotive meaning" is more accurately designated emotive *influence*. The shock effect of certain words, for instance, is not meant by them, but is produced by what is meant—or, more accurately, is produced by the utterance of words with a certain meaning. That a statement is shocking, and even habitually and characteristically so, does not compel the analysis that it somehow "means" the shock. The effect of an utterance is in part a product of its meaning, but is not to be identified with the latter.

The issue here is not whether what Stevenson calls "independent emotive meaning" exists. Suppose it be granted that the occurrence of effects not traceable to meaning of the second kind ("descriptive meaning") points to the existence of a purely emotive meaning. The question still remains whether the normative effect of value judgments is of this sort. For only if a normative *use* of language requires a special non-cognitive *meaning* can emotivism ground its claim in the normative use which value judgments undeniably have.

Suppose, indeed, it be granted that value judgments have the same function as imperatives. (We shall consider below the argument that they have in fact a different function: not only to direct action, but to give a *reason* for acting in the manner directed.) It would not follow that value judgments therefore have the same kind of meaning as do imperatives. To the charge that cognitivism has been misled by sameness of *form* to treat value judgments like scientific propositions, it may be countered that emotivism has been misled by sameness of *function* to treat them like imperatives. Meaning is different from both form and function. Because of its recognition of the inadequacy of an analysis based on only syntactical characteristics, logical empiricism may have moved too hastily to a pragmatical analysis, passing over completely the problems on the level of semantics.

Cognitivism agrees that value judgments have a normative function; it denies only that this function requires that their meaning be only emotive. The position that truth and falsity *are* applicable to value judgments does not imply what has been called *ethical descriptivism*—the view that "ethical predicate terms function in the same way as ordinary descriptive predicates, e.g., round, red. . . ."[4] Such empirical cognitivists as Mill, Perry, Dewey, and Lewis have all recognized, and indeed insisted on, the normative function of value judgments.[5] Emotivists like Stevenson and the British analysts have rendered an important service in exploring the subtleties of this and related functions of value judgments. But the fact that value judgments do perform such functions does not of itself warrant emotivism. Value judgments *are* used as norms, and in that use are not serving merely as contributions to knowledge. The question whether they have cognitive meaning still remains; indeed, the possibility is even open that they can perform the normative function well *only* if they have a cognitive meaning, and if in that meaning they are true, or somehow "presuppose" true propositions.

The issue, then, turns on the relation between meaning and function and, in particular, between emotive meaning and normative function. For pragmatists and logical empiricists meaning is *somehow* derivative from function. This is only to say that words mean because people mean

[4]A. I. Melden, "On the Method of Ethics," *J. of Philosophy* XLV (1948), 179. Melden does not himself accept that view.

[5]Philip Blair Rice is not, I think, injudicious in charging that "when a critic asserts that empiricists have ignored or denied the non-cognitive *functions* of value judgments he has read them with inexcusable carelessness."—"Ethical Empiricism and Its Critics," *Philosophical R.* LXII (1953), 364 (emphasis mine).

something by them and that *what* words mean must be explicated ultimately by reference to what is done with them. In the familiar idiom, semantics is an abstraction from pragmatics, an abstraction which can be concretized only by relating it to the facts of linguistic behavior. But though every meaning must thus be analysable in terms of the effects produced by the sign having the meaning, the converse does not follow that every effect produced by language points to a corresponding kind of meaning. To assume this without question would be to make of such kinds only hypostatised functions. The rhythm of poetry contributes in a distinctive way to the poetic effect; surely, no special "motor meaning" need be invoked to account for it. Is there better justification for ascribing only emotive meaning to value judgments in order to account for their normative function?

Part of the difficulty here may be traceable to an important ambiguity in the notion of the "function" of an utterance, which is resolved by drawing some such distinction as C. W. Morris makes between a *mode* of signification and a *use* of what signifies. The former refers to the function of the sign in the process of semiosis, the kind of interpretation given the sign; the latter, to the function of the process of semiosis in the stream of behavior which it is a part, the kind of application given to the interpretation. "Function" in the sense of mode *does* correspond to a kind of meaning; in the sense of use it does not. These two are the more easily confused when the concrete context of an utterance is ignored. For the use is localized only in such a context; and when the context is abstracted from, the use must be absorbed into the mode if it is not to be lost sight of altogether. Thus the motives and consequences of an utterance may be confused with its content. And though in the last analysis the latter must be reducible to the former, a vast distance must be traversed before the last analysis is reached. The reduction is statistical and highly indirect, like that which relates usage to a particular use. It cannot be pretended that the matter is at all clear; but it is clear enough, perhaps, to throw grave doubt on the emotivist identification of normative function with the effect of an emotive meaning.

The upshot of this line of objection to emotivism is that statements which, like value judgments, undeniably have a normative use, may nevertheless be signifying in a cognitive mode.[6] There is no necessary connection between mode and use, unless a particular mode (or, alternatively, a particular logical form) is ascribed to an utterance simply because of the particular use it has.

The objection, however, goes further than pointing to a possibility.

[6]See, for instance, H. Fingarette, "How Normativeness Can Be Cognitive But Not Descriptive in Dewey's Theory of Valuation," *J. of Philosophy* XLVIII (1951), 625-35.

For once meaning and function are conceptually distinguished, it becomes very plausible that the normative function is *best* served by a cognitive meaning, and a true one. ("Best" here need be construed only as meaning: fulfilling the purposes which are agreed by emotivists and cognitivists alike to be operative in the normative function.) "If virtue were knowledge," Reichenbach argues, "ethical rules would be deprived of their imperative character" (p. 277). Surely not, if "imperative *character*" is not identified with "imperative meaning"! Could one say: "If medicine were knowledge, the rules of hygiene would be deprived of their imperative character"? Surely the contrary is closer to the truth. Such rules owe their imperative force precisely to the cognitive character of medicine, unless indeed the rules are followed blindly as magical rituals or neurotic compulsions.

To be sure, one might wish to say: The rule itself is not cognitive in character, but there exists a proposition *about* the rule—a metatheorem, as it were—which *is* cognitive, and whose truth provides the justification for the rule. Only those who have knowledge of this proposition may be said to be following the rule "rationally" (and others, "blindly"). In this sense, it must be conceded to emotivism that the normative force of value judgments may be blind as well as rational (and, alas! quite frequently *is* blind). But this makes the cognitive element no less relevant to value judgments than to propositions which are indubitably about matters of fact, but which may be (and often *are*) believed for reasons quite other than the possession of evidence in their favor.

Whenever an utterance purports to provide a justification of this sort for its own normative function, we may say that its meaning is *cognitive in the derived sense*. This is to be contrasted with the *directly cognitive meaning* of a straightforwardly descriptive proposition. Value judgments would be directly cognitive if they could be analyzed as ascribing value attributes to their subjects. Now, the intuitionist conception of the existence and mode of apprehension of distinctive value qualities is incompatible with empiricism. But a cognitivist theory of value judgments, if empirical, is not thereby driven to identify such attributes with some complex relational property, after the manner of the utilitarianism of such empiricists as Mill and Schlick. Cognitivism need not postulate the existence of value properties at all. Truth and falsity may be relevant to value judgments even though it is an *indirect* relevance, by way of certain facts concerning the normative functions of such judgments.

But a normative statement has derived cognitive meaning only if those facts, or rather, the claim that they *are* facts, enters into its meaning. Every imperative has a normative use, but the facts about its use are not always involved in its mode of signifying. When A makes a request of B, his utterance functions normatively; it may also be the case that A would punish B if the request were not acceded to. But only if the request signifies in part that something of this sort would occur does it have derived cognitive meaning. A derived cognitive meaning of an utterance U may be said to consist in the directly cognitive meaning of a proposition correlated to U, *provided* that the existence of this correlation is understood in the process of interpreting U itself. In this conception, the declarative grammatical form of value judgments is not a linguistic accident; it is partly determinative of the mode of signifying of such judgments. It helps direct attention to the derived cognitive meaning of a statement whose use, like that of a "pure" imperative, is normative.

Perhaps there are no "pure" imperatives; it may be that every imperative has derived cognitive meaning at least in so far as understanding it *as* an imperative requires its apprehension as expressing the fact that the speaker wishes or commands something. But it is not the correlated proposition stating *this* fact which gives to value judgments their derived cognitive meaning. The relevant facts are not about the speaker, but about the hearer and the behavior for which the judgment is to serve as norm. Cognitivism, however, need not hold that only value judgments have derived cognitive meaning, while imperatives do not. It is committed merely to holding that value judgments have *some* cognitive meaning, and that *what* meaning they have enters into their differentiation from other utterances which also have a normative use. If, in fact, there are no "pure" imperatives—i.e., utterances with normative use which do not at least partially signify in a cognitive mode, value judgments *a fortiori* would not be wholly non-cognitive in meaning.

There is another argument advanced against the emotivist position that *because* value judgments are normative their characteristic meaning is non-cognitive. It is that statements which undeniably have cognitive meaning must be recognized to have also a normative function: "Stevenson analyzes sentences of the form 'x is good' into what he considers a more articulate form: 'I approve of x; do so as well'. According to this plan, why should not sentences of the form 'x is true' find their logical articulation in sentences like 'I affirm x; do so as well'? Certainly *true* is as 'persuasive' as *good* is; and it is probably used even more often by politicians than the latter term is."[7] Russell and others have frequently pointed out that there is an imperative element in assertions, enjoining belief. In addition to the direct cognitive meaning of the proposition asserted, there is the derived cognitive meaning of the existence of good reasons for asserting and believing it. And this derived meaning relates to the normative function of the assertion. Overlooking this function in

[7]S. Cavell and A. Sesonske, "Moral Theory, Ethical Judgments, and Empiricism," *Mind* LXI (1952), 557.

assertions is the complementary error of overlooking the cognitive meaning in statements of norms. We mistake the restricted interest of our analysis for a limitation in what is being analyzed.[8] In short, if ethics were a form of knowledge, it might still supply moral directives; knowledge *does* include "normative parts," and might still lend itself to an interpretation of value judgments.

III

Now the emotivist position is that the preceding line of analysis could be carried through if value judgments functioned normatively as *hypothetical* imperatives. To these, a derived cognitive meaning can admittedly be assigned. To every hypothetical imperative we can correlate a cognitive proposition—not that which the value judgment, with its misleading grammatical form, appears to formulate (a value predicate applied to the subject of the judgment), but one which asserts that conduct in accord with the enjoined norm will serve as means to some given end. This, to be sure, is cognitive; if a value judgment had *this* content, the emotivist would not hesitate to ascribe truth or falsity to it. But in fact, the emotivist insists, value judgments typically formulate norms concerning ends, not means; their normative function must be rendered by categorical imperatives, not hypothetical ones. And to these, derived cognitive meaning can no longer be assigned.

This, then, is the locus of a second area of difficulty in the emotivist position: its conception of the way in which appraisals of means and ends enter into judgments of value. The objections raised in this connection reduce to the charge that emotivism persists in treating ends as absolute or categorical (although subject to change), whereas, in fact, in all genuine judgments of value (as distinguished from dogmatic affirmations of value) they are treated as conditioned and hypothetical. And in this latter case, value judgments are as capable of truth and falsity as are straightforward propositions about the conditions and consequences of action.

The emotivist argues to start with that the ends of action are not always determinate prior to the formulation of the judgments of value which are to provide the relevant norms. Solving a moral problem or even settling a moral disagreement is often a matter of making morality more definite, and not merely of applying a moral code already specified and accepted. In such cases, the value judgment proposes what is *to be* taken as end, and does not merely point to what Reichenbach has called

[8] H. Aiken, "Evaluation and Obligation," *J. of Philosophy* XLVII (1950), 20: "So long as you direct analysis to the purely descriptive content of a given statement, its obligatoriness will escape you, and this regardless of the particular type of obligation involved. On this point, the difference between the obligations of rational inquiry and those of morality are quite irrelevant."

the "entailed decisions" of ends previously adopted. It is "hypothetical" only in the sense of constituting a proposal, not in the sense of asserting a conditional proposition. And proposals themselves are neither true nor false.

But it is just here that the concept of derived cognitive meaning finds application. For though a proposal itself is not a conditional proposition, it may be justified with the help of a conditional proposition about the consequences of its adoption. And a proposal, in being made, purports to have such justification, just as an assertion, in being asserted, purports to be true. Thus a rule, say a rule for a formalized language, is a proposal, and as such, has no directly cognitive meaning. But it has derived cognitive meaning in so far as its proposal is understood as purporting to satisfy certain tacitly accepted metatheorems concerning the rule (e.g., the truth-preserving character of a rule of inference). In denying such derived cognitive meaning to a proposal, the emotivist is in the position of the White King, who pretends that his remark, "There's nothing like eating hay when you're faint!" means only that there's nothing *like* it, not that doing so would have desired consequences.

It may be worth noting that the concept of derived cognitive meaning of proposals is not introduced *ad hoc* for the analysis of value judgments, but is required also for the explication of the nature of definition in science. The definition of a scientific concept is neither directly cognitive, as reporting a fact of usage (save in the science of lexicography), nor wholly non-cognitive, as a purely notational stipulation to which knowledge about matters of fact is quite irrelevant. For knowledge about something other than usage unmistakably *is* relevant to the definitions arrived at in science. The definitions of a science have the derived cognitive meaning of the usefulness for the science of articulating its subject matter in the particular way proposed in its definitions.

To all this, emotivism replies that the cognitive analysis assumes that certain ends have already been given—preserving truth, in the case of the inference rules for a logic, or helping achieve it, in the case of the definitional proposals made in the process of inquiry. To make this assumption in the case of judgments of value is to secure a cognitive status for them only by smuggling in other values whose proposal as ends is not cognitive.

But it is not so much a matter of the cognitivist smuggling values in as of the emotivist smuggling them out. Ends are not isolated and atomistically projected. Every judgment, as a concrete utterance, is made in a context in which some ends are given. Only when the judgment is analyzed in abstraction from its context can the end which it enjoins be regarded as categorical. For if we abstract this one end from other ends, it is trivially true that we cannot consider its relations to other ends.

But the relations are there whether the analyst chooses to consider them or not. The question is whether the relations are not always considered by those making the judgment, whether, that is, the judgment has meaning *as* a judgment only in terms of such relations.

"From the statement 'Killing is evil' we cannot deduce any proposition about future experiences," Carnap argues *(op. cit.* 24-5). "Thus this statement is not verifiable and has no theoretical sense, and the same thing is true of all other value statements." To be sure, no proposition about future experiences can be deduced from the value judgment *alone;* but we *can* make such deductions if we are given also propositions about the values already operative in the context in which the judgment is made. What is deducible is that these values will not be realized by killing. Carnap considers the alleged deduction of such propositions as that remorse will be felt, but holds that such consequences belong only to psychology, not to a "philosophical or normative ethics." But if value judgments are cognitive, yet not directly cognitive *(a la* intuitionism), they *do* belong to psychology. The present point is that the proposition about remorse is deducible provided, as Carnap points out, that our premises include statements about "the character and the emotional reactions of the person"—and specifically, the cognitivist would say, about his values.

The emotivist, however, continues his objection as follows. The assignment of cognitive meaning to a value judgment by relating the end it proposes to other ends already given, only postpones the difficulty. We must either come eventually to final ends on which the whole sequence of valuations depends, and to which the cognitivist line of analysis could not apply, or involve ourselves in an endless regress. The situation is that which Rice *(op. cit.,* 358) has aptly termed "the Mountain Range Effect in ethics":

> Just as the mountain climber . . . struggles to the top of a ridge only to see another and higher range looming before him, and conquers that only in order to be confronted by still another range, and so on indefinitely, so with the empiricist in trying to subdue normative expressions. Behind every factual meaning to which he claims to have reduced the meaning of a value term there looms up a new value to be accounted for; after every resolution of the 'ought' into an 'is,' the empiricist seems to be confronted by a new 'ought,' and so he appears to be enmeshed in a hopeless regress.

Yet the regress is not a vicious one (as Rice himself points out). Cognitivism requires only that we can conquer each range in turn; we need not have climbed the whole series to be able to climb the next one. In the verification of a proposition with direct cognitive meaning a similar harmless regress can be instituted. A proposition P_1 is confirmed by evidence formulable in another proposition P_2; but to know P_2 we must have evidence for *it,* to be stated in another proposition P_3; and so on endlessly. But we need not traverse this endless series in order to be able to say that P_2 confirms P_1. At any rate, this is the position of the probabilistic empiricism of Carnap and Reichenbach, as contrasted with the neo-Humian epistemologies which require an absolute starting-point for the evidential chain in indubitable sense-data. The regress is seen to be harmless when we distinguish between *knowing* a proposition and *having* evidence for it. Whenever we know something, we must have evidence; to know *that,* we must have still other evidence. But so long as we *have* adequate evidence for a proposition, that proposition *is* known.

A similar situation arises also in the hierarchy of languages. The parallel argument would be: The relation of logical consequence (say) must be simply intuited, and cannot be explicated by reference to rules of language. For, that the relation holds in a language L_1 can indeed be proved in a metalanguage L_2; but then this proof conforms to rules to be formulated in a meta-metalanguage L_3, and so on. Here the relevant distinction is that between talking about a language and using it (knowing a proposition and having evidence for it, judging with respect to an end and having that end). The use of a language does not require that we first formulate its rules, even if we use the language to prove propositions about another one.

There is no need, therefore, to escape the regress by assuming the existence of final ends which allow cognitive meaning to subsidiary value judgments but not to judgments of their own value. On the cognitivist view no ends *are* terminal, so that no value judgments are exempt from cognitive appraisal. (This does not prevent some values from being inherent rather than instrumental.)

The absolutism of final ends involves a reversal of the order of a universal and existential quantifier. The situation is that, for every value judgment, there exist ends in relation to which the judgment has (derived) cognitive meaning; the position of a transcendental or intuitionist ethics is rather that there exist ends which give (direct) cognitive meaning to all value judgments. Empiricism, in rejecting this latter claim, is not thereby rejecting the former; it does not exclude all cognitivism but only the absolutistic sort. If the emotivist adopts the absolutistic premise of the existence of final ends, he is driven by his empiricism to deny cognitive meaning to value judgments. But if ends are not final, cognitivism can be made consistent with empiricism.

The denial of absolute ends is not only a matter of the existence always of *further* ends to be taken into account. It also involves what Dewey has unceasingly emphasized, the *reciprocal* determination of ends and means. Ends are subject to appraisal in terms of the means they require as much as means in terms of the ends to which they lead. There is no fixed order of priority, either temporal or logical. "When decisions are to be made," Reichenbach argues (p. 279), "implications between ends and means are not sufficient to determine our choice. We must first [sic] decide for the end." But this decision in fact need not be made "first"; the end may be (and in sound judgment *is)* only hypothetically projected. It is itself subject to appraisal by means-end implications. (Of course, as before, it is other ends, and not means as such, which cognitively ground this appraisal.) The circularity involved is no more vicious than is the regress considered above. The value judgment is arrived at, so to say, by successive approximation, a stepwise adaption of means and ends to one another. Which is problematic shifts from step to step. Nothing in the situation is forever unproblematic, needing no cognitive validation. But not everything is problematic at once; were this so, nothing would be capable of validation for lack of data, of givens, on the basis of which validation could be arrived at. The emotivist could as well argue against empiricism that empirical facts are not sufficient to determine our choice of scientific theories, because we must "first" decide on a theory in order to be able to establish what *are* the facts of the case. The theory helps establish this, yet is confirmed—without circularity—by those very facts.

It is possible that the absolutistic conception of ends is reinforced, in the emotivism of some logical empiricists, by their interest in an axiomatic analysis of value discourse. Reichenbach writes (pp. 280, 58):

> There must be at least one moral premise for an ethical argument, that is, one ethical rule which is not derived by this argument. This premise may be the conclusion of another argument; but going farther up this way, we remain at every step with a certain set of moral premises. If we succeed in ordering the totality of our ethical rules in one consistent system, we thus arrive at the axioms of our ethics. . . . In order to prove that virtue is knowledge, that ethical judgments are of a cognitive type, we would have to prove that the axioms of ethics are of a cognitive nature.

And this cannot be done, for as axioms they are not themselves deducible, and there are no further moral premises from which they might be inductively inferred. But do we not have here an "illegitimate totality" of ethical rules? We remain at *every* step with a certain set of moral premises, including the step of constructing an axiomatic system of ethics. This system is to serve certain purposes, and can be appraised in the light of those purposes. In purporting to serve them, the axioms have a derived cognitive meaning in terms of which they may be validated.[9] (What is in question, of course, is the purpose of the ethics, not of its axiomatic form—the latter purposes may be served equally well by any

[9]See H. Feigl, "De Principiis Disputandum . . .?" in M. Black (ed.), *Philosophical Analysis* (1950), 119-57, where the "vindication" of "supreme justifying principles" is held to consist in showing that the system for which the principles are "supreme" fulfils certain given purposes.

set of axioms satisfying certain purely formal requirements.) To speak of the totality of ethical rules is another way of speaking of final ends. If there were such a totality, by definition there would be no values outside it in relation to which the rules within it could be appraised, just as if there were a final end it could not have the derived cognitive meaning of a means-end implication.

All this is not to say that an axiomatic ethics cannot in principle be constructed, any more than we cannot construct an axiomatic logic because in order to do so we must always *use* a metalanguage with a logic of its own. The issue turns on the status assigned to axioms—rationalist incorrigibles or certitudes on the one hand, or empirical postulates subject to appraisal and correction on the other. Would we not face the same difficulties in attempting to construct an axiomatic system for "the totality of all knowledge"? For there would then be no knowledge outside the system by which the axioms could be either inductively or deductively grounded. Their validation would be a matter of immediate certitude, either of sense data or of rational insight. But both these alternatives in the theory of knowledge have been rejected by Reichenbach and Carnap; should they not also be rejected in the theory of value?

In sum, logical empiricism has recognized—indeed, insisted on—the cognitive character of value judgments, in so far as they affirm, at least in the derived sense, means-end implications. But its emotivism has stemmed in part from the supposition that some ends are absolute—isolated, unconditional, and final, and that value judgments are characteristically concerned with these. If this conception of ends is abandoned by logical empiricism, an important basis of its emotivism will have vanished.

IV

A third area of difficulty in emotivism is centered about its contrasts of reason and emotion, belief and attitude. Such contrasts have a long and tortuous history, from Plato and Pauline Christianity (where they were not only distinguished from but opposed to one another) to the faculty psychology of the eighteenth and nineteenth centuries. It is anomalous that they should be perpetuated today in logical empiricism, which elsewhere has brought philosophy into such close and fruitful relationship with modern science. Faculty psychology is of only historical interest; in contemporary philosophy it is equally anachronistic. To be sure, emotivism has stated often and with emphasis its desire to avoid the compartmentalization of psychological processes. But the statement of the desire does not itself constitute the avoidance. The objections to emotivism now to be considered may be summarized in the charge that such compartmentalization has in fact not been avoided, but is intrinsic to the emotivist analysis. However intimate and complex are the relations acknowledged to hold between belief and attitude, reason and emotion, an objectionable dualism remains. The situation is like that of the attempts to soften the mind-body dualism by introducing subtle interactions. The objection is not to the failure to recognize causal relations between the two, but rather to conceiving of them as relata in a causal complex. Beliefs and attitudes, reason and emotion are not to be analyzed as events standing in causal connection with one another, but as abstracta reducible to a single complex concretum.

Surely it is a psychological commonplace and not a matter of subtle philosophical doctrine that emotions may *be* rational. The antithesis of reason and emotion is a generalization from the occurrence of conflicts which are not only unnecessary but which we may succeed in resolving. If with Hume we recognize that reason owes both drive and direction to the "passions," we must recognize also that it repays the debt by adapting environmental stimuli and emotional responses to one another. Fear is a fitting response to real danger, in preparing us for flight or cautious advance. The basic error of emotivism in this connection lies in the supposition that such "fittingness" is not analyzable in cognitive terms, where reason has a part to play, but only by reference to other emotions. In *The Meaning of Meaning,* the source of much subsequent application of the emotive dualism to the analysis of discourse, the incredible statement is made (p. 159) that "it is not necessary to know what things are in order to take up fitting attitudes towards them. . . ." It is a question only of concordance with the other attitudes of the personality, somewhat after the manner of coherence theories of truth.

But the objective world must somewhere be taken into account in our explication: the emotional life is neither valuationally nor causally autonomous. Emotions, volitions, attitudes reach out to the world—they are not self-contained, objectless and encapsulated. It is in terms of this relation to the world that reason or belief, the cognitive element in short, must be assigned a role. Attitudes are not somehow adjoined to beliefs, or emotions to rational considerations, but are in part constituted by them. Even the rare and pathological "free-floating anxieties" involve beliefs and expectations about the real world which simply have not entered awareness. Emotions or attitudes are "rooted in" beliefs, in Stevenson's phrase, not in the sense of being caused by the latter (we are then tempted to consider their being produced by other causes), but, as the metaphor properly suggests, in the sense of growing out of beliefs. Beliefs and attitudes are root and flower of the same psychological plant. Emotivism rests its case on the supposed occurrence of attitudes not "rooted in" belief, and it takes these to provide the characteristic content of judgments of value. The objection of cognitivism here is not the empirical one that such attitudes simply do not exist, so that value judgments do not involve them. It is rather the logical or philosophical one that the proposed explication of value judgments cannot give an adequate account of the role of belief in validating value judgments even where the attitudes involved *are* "rooted in" belief.

Stevenson, like other emotivists, is very much concerned to provide a place for cognitive processes in arriving at a judgment of value. "To say that ethical judgments are 'neither true nor false,'" he writes, "is not to maintain . . . that they are to be made capriciously, in ignorance of one's self or the nature and consequences of the object judged." And elsewhere, "Whatever else the emotive conception of ethics may do, it does not imply that evaluative decisions must be thoughtless."[10] But what is the place assigned to cognition? It is that of a causal agency, "strengthening, weakening, or redirecting" attitudes. Cognition is important as establishing beliefs, which help resolve value conflicts by their effect on the attitudes in which such conflicts are to be localized. It is only in the causal sense, Stevenson points out *(ibid.)*, that beliefs provide 'reasons' for attitudes:

> His reasons do not 'entail' his expression of approval, of course, or make it 'probable.' An expression of attitude cannot stand in these logical relationships to descriptive statements, but only in causal relationships. But the reasons do make a difference: they help to determine whether the man will continue to make his judgment, or qualify it, or replace it by an unfavorable one. So they can be called 'reasons' in a perfectly familiar sense of that term.

But if the only sense in which we can speak of "reasons" for our attitudes is a causal one, how shall we distinguish between good and bad reasons? In particular, why *should* the beliefs causing attitudes be true ones, since false ones may be equally efficacious causally? Surely, only because the truth of the belief makes a difference in the attitude itself, giving it a characteristic which it would not have if produced by a false belief. But this is precisely what is involved in the cognitivist claim that the belief is a constituent of the attitude, and not an external causal agent. Truth is better than falsehood because it allows a certain relationship to the objective world; unless attitudes are capable of standing in such a relationship, it cannot matter what are the beliefs by which they are produced.

According to emotivism, "disagreements in attitude" or "volitional differences" are resolved by a process of persuasion, or as Reichenbach says (p. 296), "through the clash of opinions, through the friction between the individual and his environment, through controversy and the compulsion of the situation." This is, indeed, what produces a *de facto* settle-

[10] Ethics and Language (1944), 266; "The Emotive Conception of Ethics and Its Cognitive Implications," *Philosophical R.* LIX (1950), 302.

ment; but is it not a *de jure* settlement which is to be accounted for? "There can be no doubt," Richenbach continues, "that this process, to a great extent, is the learning of cognitive relations." But why should this be preferred to other ways of resolving conflict, unless cognitive questions are logically and not merely causally involved in the conflict? Stevenson recognizes that it is "cognitively nonsensical to speak either of 'valid' or of 'invalid' persuasion" as though this were a matter of logical argument. Then why introduce cognitive considerations in the process at all? Granted that such considerations will change attitudes; drink will also change them: "Malt does more than Milton can/ To justify God's ways to man!" Reason has more than a merely causal role, for what is involved is not merely a change in attitude, but an improvement. And the truth of relevant beliefs constitutes this improvement rather than just producing it.

The difficulty is not just that of distinguishing between good and bad reasons but even of relevant and irrelevant ones, as has been urged by Richard Brandt and others.[11] If relevance has only a causal sense, then whatever does in fact influence a value judgment is thereby a relevant consideration. Stevenson's reply to Brandt is basically that relevance is a matter of accordance with second-level attitudes, i.e., attitudes about the way of dealing with disagreements in attitude.[12] Such second level attitudes—let us call them procedural norms—are needed also to account for improvement in attitudes. Improvement in attitudes of other persons, or of my own past self, might be explicated by emotivism as increased conformity with my own present attitudes; but plainly this will not do for the future improvement of my own present attitudes, which every theory of value judgments must surely allow to be at least logically possible. The emotivist can say that the relevance and merit of reasons for our attitudes, and the corresponding improvement in them, is a matter of closer conformity to procedural norms.

But these same norms operate in the process of arriving at beliefs. Disagreements in belief also are resolved "through the clash of opinions, through the friction between the individual and his environment, through controversy and the compulsion of the situation." And disagreements may concern not only questions of fact but also of whether one procedural norm or another is to govern—the norms characterizing scientific method, for instance, or those deriving from a religious or political dogma.[13] If such norms are themselves only expressions of attitude, beliefs themselves become only matters of attitude, and the whole distinction

[11]R. Brandt, "The Emotive Theory of Ethics," *Philosophical R.* LIX (1950), 312-3.

[12]C. L. Stevenson, "Brandt's Questions About Emotive Ethics," *ibid.*, 528-9.

[13]The point is elaborated in V. Tomas, "Ethical Disagreements and the Emotive Theory of Values," *Mind* LX (1951), 209 ff.

collapses. But if the norms have cognitive meaning, and so provide cognitive justification for the beliefs to which they lead, why should they not do so for the attitudes which they determine? If conformity with procedural norms provides a *de jure* and not a merely *de facto* resolution in the one case, why not in the other?

Emotivists and cognitivists alike recognize the importance of cognitive considerations in arriving at judgments of value. The difference is only that, since the former deny cognitive meaning to such judgments, these considerations cannot be admitted by them to provide "reasons" in a logical sense. The British school has attempted to explicate a sense of "reasons" which is neither inductive nor deductive nor yet merely causal.[14] Such a conception is perplexing and scarcely congenial to the logic of scientific empiricism. The difficulty is that a purely causal relation between cognition and value judgments won't do. And if the relation is recognized to be a logical one, the essential position of emotivism is abandoned. It seems pointless to deny cognitive content to value judgments, introduce cognition by way of causal relations, then somehow give such relations a logical force.

This is perhaps done because the emotivists recognize the tautology that change in attitudes can only be causally produced, but fail to consider that the tautology holds also for change in beliefs. Belief is also enmeshed in a causal network, but this does not make it impossible to appraise belief in logical terms; no more does the causal involvement of attitudes exclude *their* logical appraisal.[15] It is paradoxical that here emotivism is more pragmatist than Peirce, as though inquiry aimed merely at securing agreement in belief, rather than only such agreement as results from the correspondence between belief and fact. Of course, logical empiricism rejects this position in the theory of knowledge; but it is apparently willing to accept it in the theory of value.

The emotivist claim is that correspondence with the objective world cannot always be invoked because an element of disagreement in attitude is irreducible to one in belief. "It is logically possible, at least," Stevenson insists, "that two men should continue to disagree in attitude even though they had all their beliefs in common, and even though neither had made

[14] S. Toulmin, *The Place of Reason in Ethics* (1950); R. M. Hare, *The Language of Morals* (1952); and numerous papers in *Mind* and elsewhere.

[15] Tomas, *op. cit.*, 214: "The relation between the epistemic attitude of belief and its supporting reasons is not logical, but psychological, in precisely the same sense that, according to Stevenson, the relation between reasons and attitudes is not logical, but psychological. It does not, however, permit us to conclude that there is no difference between a mere cause of belief and a reason for belief, nor between a rational man, whose beliefs are caused by his consideration of reasons, and an irrational man, whose beliefs are determined not by consideration of reasons, but by other causes. Nor, on analogous grounds, can we conclude that there is no difference between mere causes of attitudes and reasons for attitudes."

any logical or inductive error, or omitted any relevant evidence."[16] He is quite right that in such a case there would be no possibility of any cognitive resolution of the disagreement. But *is* such a case logically possible? Of course, as he points out, "differences in temperament, or in early training, or in social status, might make the men retain different attitudes." There is no question of that but only of whether in that case we can still say that neither is in error. In particular, the case required must not be one of a mere difference in attitude which is not a disagreement: the doctrine of "one man's meat" is unassailable, but need not give rise to disagreement if the judgment specifies the eater.

The issue, then, is whether having an attitude does not *entail* having certain beliefs, rather than merely causally presupposing them. It is to this point that the cognitivist directs his charge of compartmentalization. To have an attitude towards *x* is not to do something other than holding certain beliefs about *x*, but is to hold such beliefs in a certain way. Feeling is not a way of relating to things distinct from knowing them or doing something with them, but a quality of the experience of knowing and doing. The idiom of faculty psychology, according to which we say we feel a certain way *because* of what we know, is useful for everyday discourse, but should not be taken as the basis of a logical analysis of value judgments, any more than the idiom of mind-body interaction should provide the unanalyzed basis of a logic of psychology.

To be sure, in the dualistic idiom "a commonly accepted body of scientific beliefs" does not always "cause us to have a commonly accepted set of attitudes," as Stevenson rightly insists. The cognitivist does not make the opposite claim but points out that a commonly accepted set of premises does not always cause us to draw a commonly accepted set of conclusions either. This does not mean that inference is non-cognitive. The cognitivist's conception of belief as a constituent of attitude entails that in the case described either *additional* beliefs are in fact involved, or at least one of the disagreeing parties is guilty of illogicality. Either our alleged set of "all beliefs" conceived as in causal connection with an attitude is not really all of them, since it excludes the beliefs incorporated in the attitude itself, or a logical error has been committed by at least one of the parties to the disagreement in relating the attitudinal beliefs to the remainder of the set.

Thus, there is no denial in cognitivism that value judgments are expressive of attitudes, but only that this expression excludes their having cognitive meaning. If "emotive meaning" is conceived as such expression, then all language is emotive, expressing in one mode an attitude to what

[16] C. L. Stevenson, "The Nature of Ethical Disagreement," in H. Feigl & W. Sellars (eds.), *Reading in Philosophical Analysis* (1949), 591.

it signifies in another mode, even if the attitude be one of detachment or neutrality. More to the point is the converse, that the expression of attitude presupposes a signification of what the attitude is toward, and a claim that the attitude has a basis. Rejection of the dualism of reason and emotion carries with it an abandonment of the dualistic theory of discourse, according to which emotive and cognitive meanings are logically (though not always causally) independent.

An expression of attitude may be said to have a *cognitive meaning in the extended sense* in so far as it is understood as claiming that the attitude expressed is fitting or appropriate to its object, i.e., as signifying that its object has characters warranting the response. As in the case of derived cognitive meaning, this is a matter of a correlated proposition understood as indirectly signified. This proposition makes explicit the predication to the object of attributes to which the expressed attitude answers. Derived cognitive meaning applies to the normative mode, extended cognitive meaning to any expression of attitude. The former states the consequences of conformity to the norm signified, the latter states the conditions claimed to produce the attitude expressed. A single utterance, of course, may have both derived and extended cognitive meaning, as well as emotive meaning: it may express an attitude, purport to have justification for the attitude in the attributes of its object, enjoin a norm in accord with the attitude, and purport to have justification for the norm in terms of the consequences to which it would lead because of the attributes of the object.

The method of correlated statements has been employed by Reichenbach to assign cognitive meaning to imperatives, but only in terms of what is expressed concerning the will of the speaker (p. 281). We may call this *reflexive cognitive meaning:* the correlated proposition asserts that the speaker wills or feels such and such. But this by no means exhausts the cognitive content of imperatives or other statements with emotive meaning. Reflexive cognitive content is determinative of sincerity or hypocrisy, but does not differentiate between truth and error which may be equally sincere. The shout "Help!" has the reflexive meaning: "I want help"; but it has also the extended cognitive meaning: "I need help, i.e., my situation is dangerous." The first proposition may be true even though the second proposition is false. And there is in addition the derived cognitive meaning: "If you help me, your ends will be furthered"—which may be true if the call for help is made by the victim of a murderous attack but not if made by his attackers.

The relation of belief to attitude, then, can be explicated in terms of extended cognitive meaning. Because expressions of attitude may have such meaning, beliefs may be logically and not merely causally relevant to them. Attitudes "rooted in" true beliefs are better than those "rooted in" false ones, and methods of resolving disagreement which involve cognitive considerations better than other methods, for the reasons which in general make truth better than falsehood and rationality than irrationality: they enable us to come to terms—as we must—with the world as it really is. And only on the basis of such cognitive meaning can beliefs be given anything other than a causal relevance to attitudes.

The proposal has been made to allow a logical relevance of belief to attitudes while yet retaining the emotivist thesis:[17]

> Matters of fact are relevant to statements which are *not* descriptive statements about matters of fact; the former can be adduced to support or reject the latter. . . . The utterance of an emotive statement *presupposes* certain matters of fact that are as relevant to its favorable response as the fact that a man is in danger of his life when he calls for help is relevant to and provides a reasonable basis for an attempt to rescue him.

But if this relation of "presupposing" is a logical one, as it must be to do the work demanded of it, how is it to be explicated unless we grant to the emotive statement some sort of cognitive meaning? The alternative suggested amounts to the insistence that there is a "practical reason" which is not confined to "those relations of implication and probability which hold only between descriptive statements." Cognitivism here has at least the advantages of parsimony.

Emotivists like Stevenson are willing to grant a cognitive *function* to emotive meaning, while withholding cognitive content. Stevenson, with his usual perceptiveness and candour, recognizes cases "where nondescriptive language either takes up the lag between altered beliefs and altered attitudes, or stimulates people to consider new beliefs, or facilitates the communication of beliefs by promoting *einfühlung*. In these cases the nondescriptive aspects of language not only provide a supplement to knowledge, but actually help to extend it. . . ."[18] But may not emotive meaning also contribute to the content of what is to be known, not only facilitate learning but also help determine what is to be learned? May not a value judgment tell us something about what is judged, even though it do so indirectly by way of the attitudes it expresses? An affirmative answer to this question must be given, if we regard the appropriateness of a response to a situation as a matter of fact, not of mere think-so or feel-so on the part of the person judging it to be appropriate. In this matter of fact, feelings, volitions and attitudes will play a part; but they will not be decisive; and in any case they are not those of the judger, but of the men to whom the judgment tacitly refers.

[17]A. I. Melden, *op. cit.*, 176.
[18]*Ethics and Language*, 334.

V

The final area of difficulty in emotivism to be considered here is that centered about the relation between the experience of value and value judgments. The charge is that the emotivist position results from confusing judgments of value with sheer expressions of the experience of valuing something.

When we prize something, we may make utterances which are expressive of our prizing, in the sense of making that prizing explicit and overt. Let us call such utterances *value expressions.* They are not assertions that something has value but part of what we do in valuing it, as whispering sweet nothings is part of making love. Value expressions are cognitive in the reflexive sense but in no other. They may be appraised as hypocritical or sincere, but not, in their usual occurrence, as having or lacking justification in the object. They are the "Hurrah!" and "Ouch!" of hoary illustration, inseparable from immediate experience, and not so much reporting as reflecting it.

Now emotivism is unassailable as a theory of value expressions. Not being judgments at all, they are neither true nor false. What they embody is the *having* of an experience of value, but not the *knowing* that something is valuable (not even the experience itself). Uttering the value expression does not wait upon knowledge, but is a spontaneous response to what we experience; nor does the expression purport to rest upon knowledge. We either share the feeling expressed or we do not, succeed or not in changing the feeling in ourselves or others. The whole situation, in short, is in accord with the emotivist position. The question is whether value judgments are indistinguishable from value expressions in this sense.

The cognitivist argues for the negative, on the grounds that a value judgment is the outcome of an appraisal, for which the prizing embodied in a value expression is only a datum or subject matter. The value judgment itself may express such a prizing (though it need not). Cognitivism does not insist that the meaning of value judgments is exhaustively analyzable in cognitive terms, as though they have no emotive meaning at all, and are thus wholly unlike value expressions. It holds that value judgments can be justified and that cognitions suffice for this purpose. It insists, that is to say, on a cognitive analysis of the meaning of "justification of a value judgment" and not necessarily of the meaning of the judgment.[19] A value judgment may express a prizing, but it does something more. In addition to the emotive meaning and reflexive cognitive mean-

19Cf. the distinction between the "ground" of a judgment and its "normative force" in Cavell & Sesonske, *op. cit.,* 550.

ing of value expressions, a value judgment may have extended or derived cognitive meaning, or indeed, be directly cognitive.

Emotivism may be denying these meanings of value judgments because it focuses on the social functions of the judgments. Now these functions may be performed regardless of the truth-value of the judgment, and thus in disregard of their cognitive meaning; though how well they are performed is another matter, just as belief might be induced by the sheer emphasis with which a proposition is asserted, though it might be better if this were not so. Plainly, the analysis of assertion is inadequate if it confines itself to this inducing of belief, without regard to what is involved in the judgment of the truth of what is to be asserted. The claim to truth is part of the meaning of the assertion. Similarly, the utterance of a value judgment has an effect on behavior, but the meaning of the judgment cannot be exhaustively analyzed in terms of this effect and of the intention to produce it. The utterance of a value judgment follows an *act* of judgment, and this does not consist in having the intention but in determining what specifically the intention is to be. The cognitivist insistence here is not on a mentalistic antecedent of utterance—there is no reason why the making of a value judgment cannot be analyzed as behavioristically as the making of any other sort of judgment—but on the existence of an appraisal which purports to provide a justification for the utterance of the judgment. "We would not make statements regarding the value of things unless we had first made the judgments. One recommends something that one has judged to be worthy of recommendation; and to judge something to be worthy of recommendation is not actually to recommend it."[20]

Moreover, emotivism's attention to the social functions of value judgments seems to have prevented it from doing justice to their functions for the judger himself. Inquiry into value problems aims not only at being able to tell others how to act but also at being able to decide value questions arising in our own conduct. Emotivism, it has been pointed out, analyzes value judgments in the perspective of the moral critic rather than the moral agent.[21] The emotive meaning of a value judgment does not suffice to explain its working for the moral agent who has a decision to arrive at, even if we grant that its work for the moral critic consists in inducing conformity to the critic's prior decision, without regard to the grounds for urging such conformity. A value judgment, unlike a value expression, does not merely give voice to a desire, volition, or the like, but marks the terminus of an inquiry in the course of which the desire is made determinate. It is a familiar fact of everyday experi-

[20]Tomas, *op. cit.*, 220.

[21]S. Hampshire, "Moral Fallacies," *Mind* LVIII (1949); W. Wick, "Moral Problems, Moral Philosophy, and Metaethics," *Philosophical R.* LXII (1953).

ence and not just of psychoanalytic clinical data that often we do not know *what* we want. The judgment that x is valuable helps us settle this question, and does not merely record the settlement by expressing the fact that we do want x.[22]

Emotivism restricts the cognitive meaning of value judgments to the statement of this fact. This is what we have called reflexive cognitive meaning. It is a meaning of the value judgment as uttered by a particular person, i.e., a meaning of a particular utterance, and so is "token-reflexive" in Reichenbach's terms, like the meaning of the word "I" or "this." "The recognition that the phrase 'he should' in its moral meaning is a token-reflexive term," Reichenbach holds (p. 290), "is the indispensable basis of a scientific analysis of ethics." That is, its content, according to him, depends essentially on who uses it; the formulation of a "should" conveys something about the speaker, not about the action enjoined. There are no extended cognitive meanings; and even the derived cognitive meaning of imperatives—the statement of implications—does not belong to them in their moral sense. In this sense, moral imperatives, like the judgments of value in which they may be concealed, are indistinguishable from what we have called value expressions. Their only cognitive meaning is the reflexive one that the speaker has a certain attitude or volition.

Now all judgments, including judgments of valuc, have reflexive cognitive meaning—there is no disagreement on this point. What the cognitivist questions is the analysis of this reflexive meaning. Does it consist in the proposition that the speaker has the attitude embodied in the emotive meaning of the judgment? Were this the case, it is hard to see how self-criticism would be possible. A man may judge that something is worthy of approval even though he himself does not approve it. In that case the judgment that it is worthy of approval cannot have the reflexive meaning that in fact he does approve it, but only that in fact he recognizes its worth. And he may condemn himself for not acting or feeling in accord with this recognition. The reflexive meaning of his judgment is his belief that something is the case; and this requires that the judgment have some other cognitive meaning, a belief in which is being expressed.

This cognitivist line of analysis is equivalently formulated as an insistence on the impersonality of the value judgment. "The moral judge or critic acts as the voice of an impersonal system of prescriptions and procedures which are impersonally regulative of our deliberations."[23]

22The point is elaborated in J. Katz, "How to Resolve Disagreement in 'Attitude,'" *J. of Philosophy* XLXIII (1951), 723 ff.

23Henry Aiken, "Moral Reasoning," *Ethics* LXIV (1953), 35.

It is the value expression which is tied to the person of the speaker, but not the value judgment. To be sure, there are cases where this impersonality is a kind of moral ventriloquism, a personal desire speaking with the voice of extra-personal authority. And it may even be recognized that value discourse in general serves various social functions, embodied in what M. MacDonald has called the "ceremonial use" of value terms, so that the impersonal voice is that of society or some subculture. But beyond this is a reference to matters of fact whose being-so is distinct from their being-thought-so, even by the whole society. Social needs and interests undeniably enter into the judgment of value, but for the cognitivist they do so as part of what the judgment is about, and not as finding expression in an utterance which is not, strictly speaking, about anything.

The question whether value judgments are indistinguishable from mere value expressions reduces, then, to the question whether values are constituted by desires. If a desire for *x* is a sufficient condition for *x* to be valuable, the judgment that *x* is valuable might be regarded simply as expressing a desire for *x*. Such a judgment would be personal—*my* desire makes it valuable for *me*; and it could not be falsified (save in terms of the sincerity of its reflexive meaning), so it could not be verified either, and in short would be non-cognitive. But if desire is not a sufficient condition for value—even though it be a *necessary* one—the judgment that *x* is valuable would have the sense that *x* satisfies the sufficient conditions. And even though the judgment expressed a personal desire for *x* as part of its meaning, this would not be its whole meaning. The meaning of a value judgment would then be not only emotive but also cognitive. Logical empiricism may have committed itself to emotivism by treating a necessary condition of value—attitude, desire, volition—as though it were a sufficient condition, under the assumption that this treatment is required by its empiricism.

Empiricism requires, to be sure, that values be granted no existence apart from the process, act, or attitude of valuation. The locus of all value is ultimately in human experience, when this experience has a characteristic positive affect—what Lewis calls *intrinsic value,* or "directly experienced goodness." But empiricism does not require that value judgments be interpreted as marking the occurrence of such immediate experiences of value. It is value expressions, not value judgments, which do this; and because every experience tautologically has the qualities which it does have, such expressions are incorrigible, and so (for the empiricism of Carnap and Reichenbach, at any rate) non-cognitive. In the same way, empiricism holds that all knowledge must ultimately be brought into relation with immediate experience of sensory qualities, but not (for logical empiricism) that judgments about matters of fact be interpreted only as marking the occurrence of such immediate experiences. For here, too, the experienced quality is just what it is, and an utterance marking its occurrence is cognitive only if its reference transcends the immediately given. Emotivism accords with Russell's epistemology, perhaps, but not that of logical empiricism. Setting aside the epistemological question, we may say that empiricism is incompatible with a cognitivist position of the intuitionist type (and certainly with a position for which values are transcendent of human experience altogether), but not with all cognitivism—provided that value judgments are analyzed on the one hand as related to immediate experience of value but on the other hand as distinct from sheer expressions of such experience.

In insisting on this latter distinction, cognitivism is extending into the realm of value the categories of appearance and reality applied in the analysis of any cognitive statement. Something may appear to have a certain property and not really have it, though by hypothesis it really appears to. Something may appear to be valuable without really being so, though it really appears to. A statement which reports such an appearance we may call a *statement of taste,* as contrasted with a judgment of value, which purports to convey what is really the case. A statement of taste is either a value expression—marking, but not asserting, the occurrence of such an appearance—or a proposition asserting that something is being desired, for to be desired and to appear valuable are indistinguishable. But by the same token, to be desired and to *be* (and not merely appear to be) valuable are, alas, very different indeed.

This difference, as in the general case, need not be construed ontologically; what has all the appearances of such-and-such, really *is* such-and-such. But it must be *all* the appearances. Emotivism has continued the empiricist tradition in value theory by insisting that value is that which is experienced as valuable. But no single experience suffices. The difference between a statement of taste and a judgment of value is that the latter goes beyond immediate experience to predict the quality of other experiences. It goes, as Dewey has it, from the expression of our finding something satisfying to the judgment that it is satisfactory—that it will remain satisfying when its conditions and consequences are taken into account. And it may make this prediction even without the immediate experience, as we can judge that something is a tree even though it looks to us like a man. So far is a value judgment from being only an expression of the attitudes of the judger that it may even contradict the attitudes actually had: we may judge that our own taste is bad.

At bottom, logical empiricism may have been drawn to emotivism—rather than, like such empiricists as Dewey and Lewis, to cognitivism—because of its fear that a cognitivist theory of value judgments would require the introduction of "unique and peculiar" value properties, a notion repugnant to empiricism of all varieties. But cognitivism is wholly compatible with the insistence that value predicates can be completely explicated in terms of the predicates of the language of science. Emotivism secures this result by the heroic measure of holding that a value judgment asserts nothing and so does not make a predication at all—there are value exclamations and interjections but no value predicates. In cognitivism, the same result is achieved by the position that something is judged to be of value because of certain properties it has, while being of value is not an additional property over and above these. That an object has value is analyzable in terms of empirical characters of man and the world which are not in themselves—without regard to their status and function in behavior—valuational.

VI

Partisans of both the emotivist and cognitivist conceptions of value judgments cannot fail to recognize how lacking on both sides is a precisely formulated theory of the sort which distinguishes Carnap's philosophical writings. Thus what disagreements there are cannot easily be localized and precisely stated; and the appearance of disagreement, intensified by the vigor of polemic, may hide an underlying agreement on many important points.

There can be little doubt, for instance, that much of the divergence between the two views is no more than a matter of emphasis. The cognitivist focusses attention on the content of the value judgment, the emotivist on its function; the former is interested in the matters of fact entering into this content, the latter in the relation of these matters of fact to desire and volition, which alone gives the facts a value relevance. Paradoxically, the critics of the logical empiricist's position are concerned with the logical analysis of meanings, while he himself directs attention to the social and psychological role of meanings. The difference in emphasis might be summarized as follows:[24]

> The emotivist says, 'you can look at all the facts you like, but you will have to choose.' And the cognitivist says, 'You will have to choose, of course, but you must first look at all the facts you can.' For any ethical situation, the positivist insists that the best solution possible is a reasoned *choice*; the pragmatist insists the best possible solution is a *reasoned* choice.

Between *these* two viewpoints, it is scarcely necessary for a choice to be made.

Whatever differences there are that are not merely matters of emphasis are considerably lessened by the provision in emotivism of devices by which attitudes, and ways of changing them, can be rationally criticized.

[24]S. Cavell and A. Sesonske, "Logical Empiricism and Pragmatism in Ethics," *J. of Philosophy* XLVIII (1951), 16.

An emotivism which formulates criteria (like the procedural norms discussed earlier) for the appraisal of attitudes—as impartial or biased, rooted in comprehensive and true beliefs or in incomplete and misleading ones, expressing arbitrary caprice or resulting from careful reflection—such an emotivism is very little different in substance from cognitivism.[25] It is not an issue of great moment whether value judgments be held only to express attitudes or also to formulate propositions about matters of fact, if it is agreed that, whatever their content, they are subject to appraisal and criticism on the basis of what we know or can find out.

Still further differences must be construed as concerning the interpretation of "value judgment" not of value judgments. If there are absolute ends, attitudes not rooted in belief, liking to which further conditions and consequences are extraneous, the cognitivist does not regard them as the subject matters of judgments of value, but only of statements of taste—value expressions and reports of immediate satisfactions. Conversely, propositions affirming means-end connections, or ascribing to objects characteristics already accepted as justifying certain emotions or volitions, are not regarded by the emotivist as judgments of value in the characteristic sense. The two views differ on how they interpret "judgment of value" rather than in the conception of what each of them understands by this phrase. "On either view," it has been pointed out, "the following types of propositions are regarded as cognitively meaningful: (1) statements about the desires, attitudes, or interests of individuals; (2) statements about the powers of things to satisfy or frustrate, including all statements of costs and consequences. On both views, such assertions exhaust the cognitive elements of valuation."[26]

It is perhaps premature to attempt to discern the outlines of the theory of value to which the various currents in contemporary empiricism and pragmatism—emotivist as well as cognitivist—appear to be converging. But certain needs are clearly apparent, and may be specified as areas where polemic might give way to constructive effort.

1. The relation between the functions of an utterance and its meaning requires examination, whether in terms of the distinction between modes of signification and uses of what signifies, or on some other basis. Logical empiricism has already made much progress in the treatment of semantical problems. It may be unreasonable to demand of it an extension of precisely formulated semantic theory to other types of discourse than that of exact science and mathematics. But one *can* ask of it as serious and careful attention to the semantics of value discourse, within the

[25]See R. Brandt, "The Status of Empirical Assertion Theories in Ethics," *Mind* LXI (1952), 458-79.

[26]C. Schuster, "Rapprochement in Value Theory," *J. of Philosophy* L (1953), 658.

limits of precision that the subject matter allows, as has been given in the past few decades to the language of science.

2. The actual content of norms having derived cognitive meaning must be made concrete by a specification of their truth conditions. It is not enough for pragmatism to insist over and over again that the relation between means and ends gives value judgments cognitive content. The alleged content requires detailed specification in terms which will relate it to the empirical sciences that actually contain the cognitions to which such an important role is being assigned.

3. The extended cognitive meaning of expressions of attitude similarly requires elaboration in ways making plain what part beliefs play in attitudes. Stevenson's contribution here is unquestionably considerable, whether or not one adheres to his emotivist standpoint. But the general theory must be applied to the specific areas of ethics, esthetics, social philosophy, etc., with their distinctive concepts and problems. The status of judgments of value no more exhausts the philosophical theory of value than the problem of induction does the philosophy of science.

4. The relation between value expressions and judgments of value is as obscure as it is crucial. What this relation is can be discerned only by attention to the actual workings of language in concrete situations where problems or conflicts of valuation arise. This has been the dominant interest of the British analysts; such an approach, while not the only one possible, must surely be pursued. There may well be more promise in proceeding to the general questions on the basis of analyses of specific value expressions and judgments than in the continuance of the direct attack on the problem in a necessarily abstract and schematic fashion.

VII

Since the impetus of Wittgenstein's *Tractatus* logical empiricism has undergone a considerable development. Much of this development has consisted in the transformation of what Wittgenstein held to be "inexpressible" into clear and explicit statement in logic, foundations of mathematics, semantics, and philosophy of science. But the doctrine that "there can be no ethical propositions," that "ethics cannot be expressed," in short, that "ethics are transcendental" seems still to have been preserved, though to be sure without the aura of mysticism, in the emotivist commitment of logical empiricism. Because of this commitment, logical empiricism has seemed to some to present the ironic spectacle of insisting on the importance of logic everywhere save in the important problems of life. Others, on the contrary, have seen in it that exaggerated respect for logic that expresses itself in a cold disregard for mere matters of human feeling. Both viewpoints seem to me equally unjust. "The very nature of reason," Freud once remarked, "is a guarantee that it would not fail to concede to human emotions and to all that is determined by them, the position to which they are entitled." In Carnap's life and work, both personal feeling and impersonal logic find an embodiment in accord with the highest philosophical ideals.

ABRAHAM KAPLAN

DEPARTMENT OF PHILOSOPHY
UNIVERSITY OF CALIFORNIA, LOS ANGELES

THE PHILOSOPHER REPLIES

Rudolf Carnap

REPLIES AND SYSTEMATIC EXPOSITIONS

Introductory Remarks

EACH volume of the *Library of Living Philosophers* is designed to confront a philosopher with discussions, interpretations, and criticisms of various aspects of his philosophy by contemporary authors, and to give him an opportunity to clarify or defend his views in his replies to their essays. It seems to me that the philosopher's replies would not fulfill their purpose if he were to meet every critical argument which he finds unacceptable merely by a counter-argument. His answer will be intelligible only in the wider context of his general views on the problem discussed. Therefore I have frequently found it advisable to summarize my position on a particular problem, with special regard to those aspects which were sometimes not clearly understood or to those points on which I have modified my views. Sometimes I have given a summary of this kind at the beginning of a section in which I reply to a philosopher, at other times I have inserted the summary in the discussion. Philosophers usually shy away from condensing their views on a problem into a brief survey or a few concise theses. They feel that it is impossible in a few words to do justice to the great complexities of a given problem, and they fear that a reader might believe he has obtained from the summary alone full understanding of the philosopher's views and that he might think himself qualified to make critical judgments about them. I share these feelings; but I also remember how many times I found it illuminating and helpful when an author, at the end of a book or of a chapter, recapitulated its substance. Therefore I have decided to give this aid to my readers, even at the risk of possible misuse.

In some cases, it seemed advisable to give a more comprehensive exposition of my views in a special section which serves as a basis for my discussions of a number of essays in subsequent sections. Thus in §4 I have explained my views on ontological problems, the realism controversy, and the question of the admissibility of abstract entities. In §9 I have outlined my present ideas on many problems connected with modalities, including the problem of statements of beliefs. In connection with these issues, I have sketched in §10 my present conception of semantics, outlining and comparing two metalanguages one of which is extensional, the other intensional. In §25, I have explained my fundamental conceptions of logical probability, regarded as a conceptual tool for determining rational decisions, and of the task of inductive logic; on this basis, I have offered a new axiom system for inductive logic (§26) and have discussed some problems connected with it, including the problem of the reasons for choosing specific axioms. Except for §4, the sections mentioned contain a good deal of material not previously published; there are new points of view and, in brief outline, new results that I have worked out in recent years. Several of these new considerations were stimulated by incisive questions or objections raised in the essays published in this volume. But even some sections in which I reply to particular essays contain new ideas. For instance, in the context of the problem of physicalism (§7), I have made some remarks on continuity and emergentism and (§8) on the inference by analogy concerning other minds. Furthermore, there are discussions of causal modalities (§22C), of explications of experiential import and of analyticity with respect to a theoretical language (§24C and D), and of the distinction between cognitive and non-cognitive components of value statements (§32).

Notations like "[1921]" and "[1955-6]" refer to items in the Bibliography at the end of this volume.

I wish to thank the contributors and the editor, Professor Paul A. Schilpp, for their forbearance with the long delay in the completion of my contributions. The reader should keep in mind while reading the other authors' essays, that most of them were finished by 1954 or 1955, thus prior to my own publications in recent years.

Sometimes my reply to an author is rather brief because I find myself so much in agreement with his views that there is no need for long arguments.

I. Relations between Logical Empiricism and Other Philosophical Movements

1. Charles Morris on Pragmatism and Logical Empiricism

Logical empiricists from Berlin and from the Vienna Circle came into closer contact with pragmatism chiefly after they had come to the United States. A mutual understanding between the two schools was mainly fostered by Charles Morris and Ernest Nagel. Both attended the International Congress of Philosophy in Prague in 1934, where I became acquainted with them, and where they met their colleagues from Vienna and Berlin. Nagel was influenced by both movements, but avoided the application of any school label to his own view. Morris had the explicit aim of merging the two philosophical movements into one to which he sometimes applied the term "scientific empiricism".

Morris is certainly right in pointing out that, since I came to America, my philosophical views have clearly been influenced by pragmatist ideas, if not so much theoretically then with regard to the approach to certain problems. For instance, I put now more emphasis than previously upon the social factor in both the acquisition and application of knowledge, be it common sense knowledge or science; furthermore, upon points where the development of a conceptual system or of a theory involves practical decisions; and upon the fact that all knowledge begins with and serves the relations between a living organism and its environment. It is certainly important to keep these aspects in view in order to fully understand such social phenomena as language and science. The influence of the pragmatist ideas has been very fruitful for the development of my conceptions. It did not derive so much from the works of the founders of pragmatism (whose formulations I could often not easily accept, e.g., Peirce's metaphysics and Dewey's discussions of logical and epistemological problems), but from later representatives such as C. I. Lewis, Charles Morris, Ernest Nagel, and Sidney Hook, whose formulations seemed clearer and closer to those customary in science.

Morris stresses the importance of pragmatics, the theory of the use of language by human beings, as a field of semiotics on a par with logical syntax and semantics. I think he is right in saying that, although I have recognized all three fields of semiotics, I have dealt with them in different ways. In syntax and semantics, my main interest and practically all my constructive work was directed toward the non-empirical, purely logical side, called "pure syntax" and "pure semantics". In the case of pragmatics, I was mainly thinking of empirical investigations. Today I would agree with Morris that there is an urgent need to develop pure pragmatics, which would supply a framework for descriptive pragmatics. It seems that this idea is now in many minds, and is ready for realization. At about the same time, and independently of each other, Morris and I said almost literally the same thing; Morris writes: "An explicit concern with pure pragmatics becomes an urgent task", and I said: "There is an urgent need for a system of theoretical pragmatics" (in [1955-6]). In the paper just mentioned, I briefly indicated some concepts (belief, intension, assertion) which, together with related concepts, might serve as a basis for theoretical pragmatics. A study of the logical relations between concepts of this kind, relations which would be expressed by meaning postulates, would constitute a theory of pure pragmatics. Numerous recent articles deal with the logical analysis of belief sentences.[1] These articles are not chiefly concerned with psychological criteria for the confirmation of belief sentences or the like, but rather with the logi-

[1]In the first place, articles by Alonzo Church; further by Carnap (in [1947-2] §13), Benson Mates, Hilary Putnam, R. M. Chisholm, Arthur Pap, Wilfrid Sellars, and many others.

cal relations between such sentences. Therefore these investigations may be regarded as preliminary work for the construction of a system of pure pragmatics.[2]

Morris points out two main areas where there are greater differences between pragmatists and logical empiricists, viz. the problem of the nature of value judgments, and that of the nature of philosophy. I shall discuss the former problem in §32 in connection with Kaplan's essay. I am inclined to agree with Morris that the difference between my view and that of the pragmatists is not as large as it might appear at first glance.

In earlier periods, I sometimes made attempts to give an explication of the term "philosophy". The domain of those problems which I proposed to call "philosophical" became step by step more comprehensive, as Morris indicates. Yet actually none of my explications seemed fully satisfactory to me even when I proposed them; and I did not like the explications proposed by others any better. Finally, I gave up the search. I agree with Morris that it is unwise to attempt such an explication because each of them is more or less artificial. It seems better to leave the term "philosophy" without any sharp boundary lines, and merely to propose the inclusion or the exclusion of certain kinds of problems.

In particular, many problems concerning conceptual frameworks seem to me to belong to the most important problems of philosophy. I am thinking here both of theoretical investigations and of practical deliberations and decisions with respect to an acceptance or a change of frameworks, especially of the most general frameworks containing categorial concepts which are fundamental for the representation of all knowledge.

Morris thinks that the traditional metaphysical problems could be interpreted as problems of this kind. This may be the case for many metaphysical problems. But in the case of others, I doubt whether an interpretation of this kind would be historically correct, that is to say, whether the metaphysicians would have accepted such interpretations of their writings. In cases of this kind, I prefer, from a systematic point of view, not to take the framework problem as an interpretation of traditional metaphysics, but rather to abandon the latter and discuss the former. From a historical point of view, many metaphysical theses and discussions can certainly be regarded as more or less conscious preparatory stages on the way to a systematic logic and science, and as preliminary to framework analyses. I think this holds, in particular, for the metaphysical theories of Aristotle, Leibniz, Charles S. Peirce, and Whitehead.

[2]A book by Richard Martin is in preparation, in which a system of pragmatics is developed in a formalized metalanguage.—(Note added in 1962): The title is: *Toward a Systematic Pragmatics* (Amsterdam, 1959).

2. Robert S. Cohen on Dialectical Materialism vs. Empiricism

Cohen, influenced by both of these philosophical movements and himself taking an intermediate position, explains in his essay the main objections which have been raised by dialectical materialism against positivism and empiricism. These objections are, however, directed mainly against positivistic tendencies either of earlier philosophical thinkers like Hume, Comte, Kirchhoff, and others, or against neopositivism as represented mainly by Ernst Mach, by Bertrand Russell in some of his earlier publications, and to some extent by the Vienna Circle in the initial phase of the empiricist movement. Cohen himself states that many of the criticisms are no longer applicable to the views which we have developed since the Vienna period. And I shall attempt to show that some of the objections did not hold even for the conceptions of the Vienna Circle.

Cohen objects most strongly to the phenomenalist tendencies which he counts among the most important characteristics of positivism and neopositivism. In his discussion, however, he fails, like most critics of positivism and empiricism, to distinguish with sufficient clarity between two fundamentally different meanings of the term "phenomenalism". Sometimes, and perhaps in most instances, this term refers to a certain *ontological* thesis which asserts, roughly speaking, the primary reality (in the metaphysical sense) of phenomena, e.g., sense-data, in contrast to material objects. I do not wish to decide at this point whether Mach's conception and the earlier phase of Russell's philosophy may correctly be regarded as examples for this thesis. It is true that some of their formulations might be interpreted in this way; but they might also be understood in the second sense, to be explained presently. It seems to me that there cannot be any doubt that both Mach and Russell took a fundamentally scientific, anti-metaphysical position. Phenomenalism in the second, methodological or linguistic sense, may be understood as the proposal of a phenomenalistic language as the basis of the total language. Even before I came to Vienna, I emphasized in my book *Der logische Aufbau* [1928-1] that, although I constructed the language on a phenomenalistic basis, taking sense-data or experiences as starting points, this construction did not imply an acceptance of the metaphysical thesis of phenomenalism. In the Vienna Circle, under the influence of Wittgenstein, we made the distinction in an even more radical way by declaring the metaphysical theses of phenomenalism, solipsism, and idealism, together with the counter-thesis, viz., metaphysical materialism, as pseudotheses, i.e., as devoid of cognitive content (comp. § 4A). Cohen seems also to regard *methodological* phenomenalism as questionable and dangerous in its theoretical and even more in its practical implications. A similar view was held by Neurath and was for him one of the main motives for his efforts toward physicalism or "methodological materialism". I prefer those arguments against methodological phenomenalism which show that a language constructed on a physicalistic basis is more suitable for the purposes of science than a language constructed on a phenomenalistic basis. These arguments against a phenomenalistic method seem to me much clearer and more convincing than those brought forward by dialecticians, be it Hegel or Lenin or contemporary Marxists; but this may be a subjective bias on my part.

I think I need hardly say much concerning the charge of solipsism. I do not know of any neopositivist or empiricist who maintains solipsism (in the customary metaphysical sense of the term). In [1928-1] I used the term "methodological solipsism" in the sense of "methodological individual phenomenalism", but abandoned this term as soon as I found that it was misunderstood in the sense of the metaphysical theses, in spite of my explicit warnings.

To Cohen's criticism of *conventionalism* I should like to say that a pure conventionalism (like that of Hugo Dingler, for example) was never maintained by any adherent of logical empiricism, nor by Mach or Poincaré. (The latter was often regarded as a conventionalist; but Cohen now agrees with Grünbaum's explanation that this interpretation was based on misunderstandings.) Cohen believes that my so-called principle of tolerance in the logical syntax contains a "doctrine of conventionally-chosen basic-truths". But this is not the case. The principle referred only to the free choice of the structure of the language, and not to the content of synthetic sentences. I emphasized the non-conventional, objective component in the knowledge of facts, e.g., in [1936-5]. There I also pointed out that the first operation in the testing of synthetic statements is the confrontation of the statement with observed facts. Thereby I took a position clearly opposed to a pure conventionalism and to any coherence theory of truth. My discussion was implicitly meant to correct some formulations by Neurath, but not his actual views. He used to say that statements should be compared only with statements and not with facts. These formulations were misleading because they seemed, contrary to Neurath's intention, to represent a coherence conception of truth. They were indeed repeatedly interpreted in this sense, not only by outsiders like Russell and Ayer, but also by Schlick. Neurath vehemently rejected this interpretation in the discussions of the Vienna Circle, and also in a remark in his report on the Paris Congress of 1935 (*Erkenntnis,* V, 1936, 400). At any rate, there cannot be any doubt that Neurath never held this conception. Still less can it be attributed to me or to "the physicalists" in general, as critics have sometimes done.

Some of Cohen's main arguments are intended to point out the dangers of *subjectivism* (in § 4). According to him, subjectivist tendencies are strongly incorporated in neopositivism; they are somewhat weaker in present-day empiricism, yet still effective and dangerous. The term "subjectivism", as used in this context, seems to me even more ambiguous than the other terms, "phenomenalism", "conventionalism", etc. In the epistemological field, Cohen seems to mean by "subjectivism" primarily phenomenalism, either of the metaphysical or of the methodological variety, or an excessive emphasis on the rôle of subjective experiences. But in his present section, he points out the dangers of subjectivism in an entirely different field, that of social and industrial organization. I certainly agree with Cohen with respect to the dehumanizing effects of the contemporary forms of social and economic organization. But I see no basis for the view, frequently maintained by Marxists (since Lenin's criticism of Mach) and apparently also held to a certain extent by Cohen, that there is a close, perhaps causal connection between the harmful effects of the social and economic order surrounding us, on the one hand, and a way of thinking labelled subjectivist and allegedly represented by positivists, empiricists, and pragmatists (these terms understood here in a wide sense of these terms), on the other. However, we must concede one point in Cohen's criticism of logical empiricism in this context; this is the fact that our movement has not given sufficient attention to the foundations of the social sciences, but has restricted its work mainly to the foundations of physics and mathematics. This fact seems historically understandable, because physics and mathematics were most advanced and therefore the tradition of clear, exact, and responsible thinking was best developed in these sciences. As a result, the great majority of empiricists came from these fields. But it should be pointed out, as Cohen has done, that since the time of the Vienna Circle all of us have always agreed on the desirability, expressed especially by Neurath, of investigating, purifying, and clarifying the methods of the social sciences in the same empiricist spirit. In this direction much work remains to be done, and this is an urgent task. Some work has recently been done on the foundations of psychology, especially by the group working at the Minneapolis Center for the Philosophy of Science, and by others associated with it in various forms of co-operation. The dialecticians should also note the fact that comprehensive work in the fields of sociology, political theory, and theory of education has been done by empiricist thinkers working in directions closely related to logical empiricism, for example, by Russell on the one hand, and by Dewey and his followers on the other. The theoretical theses of logical empiricism, based on analyses of procedures of knowledge and of the structure of languages and conceptual frameworks, are as such neutral with respect to possible forms of organization of society and economics. Nevertheless, even these theoretical theses have an indirect social effect. They give support to the view that strictly scientific methods are applicable also to the investigation of men, groups, and societies, and thereby they help to strengthen that attitude which is a precondition for the development of more reasonable forms of the social order, forms in which the dehumanizing effects of the present organization of industrialization can be overcome. Furthermore, although the theoretical theses of logical empiricism are themselves neutral, it is nevertheless apparent, as Cohen himself has repeatedly emphasized, that the adherents of this philosophy are by no means neutral but strive, just like Russell, Dewey, and their followers, for a realization of their social and political aims.

Cohen believes that it is subjectivist positivism rather than dialectical materialism which would be the totalitarian philosophy of Big Brother (in Orwell's sense). Let us examine Cohen's view with regard to two illustrations which he himself uses to characterize this dangerous positivism which is supposed to lead to totalitarianism. The first is a certain change made in a new edition of the *Large Soviet Encyclopedia,* the second is Hans Kelsen's legal theory. The latter theory is correctly classified by Cohen as positivistic (in a wide sense). But to what kind of totalitarianism did Kelsen's thinking lead? Cohen says of him only that he adhered to relativism; therefore he mentions him in the same breath with Mussolini, because the latter also maintained relativism in his essay, "Relativismo e fascismo". Leaving aside the ambiguity of the term "relativism", I think this association of Kelsen with Mussolini will appear amazing to those who remember Kelsen as one of the main creators of the constitution of the Austrian Republic in 1919, a constitution which is regarded by many throughout the world as the model of a democratic constitution. And that the Soviet regime is here taken as representative of positivism in contrast to dialectical materialism will surprise most readers, even if they do not know that, since Lenin's book against Mach's philosophy, no author in the Soviet Union has dared to discuss neopositivism with sympathy or even only with an attitude of objective, unbiased criticism.

In section 5, Cohen gives a survey of the historical development of my conceptions. I appreciate his serious and careful study and scrutiny of my views and his attempt at their fair evaluation. But I am afraid it is inevitable that an author is never entirely satisfied by a representation of his views in which they are translated into terminology foreign to him, and are judged by standards grown in a different soil.

In his last section, Cohen explains the agreements and differences between logical positivism and dialectical materialism. Here he is not arguing the question which of the two sides is right, but is only trying to give a summarizing description of the disagreements which exist, in spite of the agreements on many points. I would agree with some of his descriptions of the divergencies. But some features in the picture of empiricism which he draws seem to me questionable. For example, in discussing the different conceptions of the task of philosophy in the two movements, he says: "Without a concept of Reason which will permit realistic criticism of the world revealed by experience, positivistic empiricism constructs a world of empty and inhuman mechanisms, a cyclic flux, divorcing the human spirit from natural process". I find it difficult to reconcile this picture with what Cohen himself has said at other places about our attitudes and conceptions. He has repeatedly explained that since Vienna, many of us, especially Neurath and I, have criticized the existing order of society as unreasonable and have demanded that it should be reformed on the basis of scientific insights and careful planning in such a way that the needs and aspirations of all would be satisfied as far as possible; this attitude is the core of our scientific humanism. Furthermore, Cohen himself has explained our physicalistic and naturalistic conceptions which are diametrically opposed to any dualism that divorces human spirit from natural process, and which emphasizes that man with all his experiences in the various spheres of life, not excluding those of philosophical thinking, is just a part of the one all-embracing nature.

Cohen indicates that at a later time he plans to give an exposition of the achievements of dialectical philosophy. Since he is one of the few who possess a comprehensive knowledge of both movements and is willing to examine them impartially, a work of this kind could be very fruitful. For us empiricists it would be especially desirable if he would think of his representation of dialectical philosophy as a counterpart to his present essay, and combine the exposition with a critical appraisal by empiricist standards.

3. Philipp Frank and V. Brushlinsky on Positivism, Metaphysics, and Marxism

Brushlinsky reviews my paper on metaphysics [1932-1] from a Marxist point of view. His main criticism, contained in the two last paragraphs, consists of two points. First, he asserts that I myself sink into a metaphysics, namely, phenomenalism. In other sections of these Replies, I have explained that even in the early phenomenalist phase of our movement and, in particular, of my thinking, we did not accept a metaphysical phenomenalism, but only a "methodological phenomenalism" (if we may use this term), which means the preference for a language constructed on a phenomenalistic basis.

Brushlinsky's second objection is that I, as a logician and mechanist, and the movement of neopositivism in general, are incapable of understanding the social-economic roots of idealism and of metaphysics which we wish to eliminate. As I have pointed out elsewhere, the Vienna Circle, essentially because of Otto Neurath, did recognize the importance of a sociological analysis of the roots of philosophical movements. But unfortunately a division of labor is necessary, and therefore I am compelled to leave the detailed work in this direction to philosophically interested sociologists and sociologically trained philosophers.

As is pointed out in the contributions by Frank and Morris, the movement of pragmatism, which logical empiricists regard as an ally in their fight against traditional metaphysics, has stressed the importance of a sociological analysis of metaphysics, and has devoted much more detailed work to it, in particular, in connection with investigations concerning the pragmatic component in language. This work began with Charles S. Peirce, and is especially prominent in the work of John Dewey. I agree with both Frank and Morris that the pragmatic component has so far not been sufficiently investigated by our movement, although its importance has been acknowledged theoretically by me and by empiricists in general.

II. Metaphysics, Realism, and Physicalism

4. My Views on Ontological Problems of Existence

A. The realism controversy. My friends and I have maintained the following theses (see [1928-2]):

(1) The statement asserting the reality of the external world (realism) as well as its negation in various forms, e.g., solipsism and several forms of idealism, in the traditional controversy are *pseudo-statements,* i.e., devoid of cognitive content.

(2) The same holds for the statements about the reality or irreality of *other minds,*

(3) and for the statements of the reality or irreality of *abstract entities* (realism of universals or Platonism, vs. nominalism).

At the time of the Vienna Circle, the views just stated were sometimes misunderstood. For example, our rejection of the thesis of realism was interpreted as indicating an idealistic position. This interpretation overlooks the important point that we rejected the thesis of realism not as false but as being without cognitive meaning ("meaningless", as we usually said at that time, following Wittgenstein). If the thesis is meaningless, so is its negation. Therefore we also rejected solipsism and idealism. In later years, we assumed that our conception with respect to this question was generally known, although, of course, not generally accepted. Therefore, we did not restate it frequently in recent years, but referred to it incidentally. To my surprise I see that some empiricists still misunderstand our view.

Although the three controversies referred to cannot be regarded as theoretically meaningful, we still can give to them a meaning by reinterpreting them or, more exactly, by replacing them with the practical questions concerning the choice of certain language forms. I shall later indicate this procedure more specifically.

Since the terms employed as names for the various languages under discussion are often used with different meanings, I propose the following terminology for my present discussion:

The *phenomenal* or *phenomenalistic language* speaks only about sense-data, raw feels, and the like. This language can neither refer to material objects nor to other minds. Sometimes this fact is expressed by saying that this language describes "my" sense-data, and by formulating sentences in this language of the form "now I have a toothache". However, the words "my" and "I" are redundant in this language; the correct sentence form is rather something like "now toothache", or "now a red spot in the visual field", and the like.

The *thing language* or *reistic language*. (The latter term is derived from Kotarbinski's term "reism" for the philosophical thesis that every meaningful sentence says something about observable, material things.) This language describes intersubjectively observable, spatio-temporally localized things or events.

The *physical language* is the language of physics. Its primitive terms designate fundamental particles (e.g., electrons) and fundamental magnitudes. Macro-terms for the description of observable events are defined on the basis of these primitives.

It is an essential characteristic of the phenomenal language that it is an absolutely private language which can only be used for soliloquy, but not for common communication between two persons. In contrast, the reistic and the physical languages are intersubjective.

The *dualistic language* may be mentioned here only incidentally because it is hardly used or proposed any longer by empiricists. This language consists of two interconnected parts: a reistic language for speaking about material things, and a mentalistic language for speaking about a second, autonomous, kind of basic entities, namely minds. A mind is usually assumed to be connected with a certain thing, the body of a human being or a higher animal. In the following discussions, I shall usually assume that we agree in rejecting the dualistic language.

We now replace the ontological theses about the reality or irreality of certain entities, theses which we regard as pseudo-theses, by proposals or decisions concerning the use of certain languages. Thus realism is replaced by the practical decision to use the reistic language, phenomenalism by the decision to use only the phenomenal language, and traditional psycho-physical dualism by the decision to use a dualistic language; and so on.

Grünbaum (§5) believes that in the controversy between phenomenal positivism and realism the Vienna Circle stood on the side of the former. From what I have just explained, it is clear that this is a misunderstanding of our position. Grünbaum is puzzled by the fact that we were not influenced by Schlick's realism, and he finds it difficult to understand the reasons for Schlick's later abandonment of realism. The explanation is that our discussions in the Circle led Schlick to the insight that the thesis of realism goes beyond the boundaries of the scientifically meaningful. However, this does not mean that he accepted the position of phenomenalism; he rejected this position, of course, for the same reasons. Grünbaum regards phenomenalism as a "profound error"; we are entirely in agreement with him in this rejection, but we should prefer to say "pseudo-statement" instead of "error". Furthermore, Grünbaum says that he does not know of any refutation or even an adequate treatment of the arguments for realism. If "realism" is understood as preference for the reistic language over the phenomenal language, then I am also a realist. However, if "realism" is understood, in the customary sense, as an ontological thesis, then the arguments against it were given in my monograph [1928-2]; I do not know of any refutation or even a thorough critical discussion of my arguments.

Later, Reichenbach gave to the thesis of realism an interpretation in scientific terms, as asserting the possibility of induction and prediction; a similar interpretation was proposed by Feigl. On the basis of these interpretations, the thesis is, of course, meaningful; in this version, it is a synthetic, empirical statement about a certain structural property of the world. I am doubtful, however, whether it is advisable to give to old theses and controversies a meaning by reinterpretation; I have similar doubts about Quine's reinterpretation of the term "nominalism".

To which language do psychological statements belong? If I make a statement about the so-called mental state of another person, e.g., "John has a toothache", then this statement is really a sentence of the reistic language (inasmuch as we have agreed to reject the dualistic language), namely a sentence about the human organism called "John". The question as to whether the property of having a toothache is a physical property, in other words, the question of physicalism, is hereby not yet decided.

Let us now consider a statement which I make about my own state on the basis of a so-called act of introspection, e.g., "Now I have a toothache". Many philosophical discussions about so-called mental states are quite unclear, because sentences of the form just mentioned are ambiguous. For any sentence of this form we must specify whether it is meant as a sentence of the phenomenal language or as a sentence of the reistic language (again disregarding the dualistic language). If it is meant as a sentence of the phenomenal language, then the formulation is misleading; as indicated earlier, the form "now toothache" would be more adequate. If, on the other hand, it is meant as a sentence of the reistic language, thus for use in intersubjective communication, then it would be better for the purposes of our discussion to avoid the indexical word "I" and to use instead an intersubjective name, e.g., "Now Carnap has a toothache". For myself this sentence is directly confirmable by observation, more specifically by introspection. But for other persons it is only indirectly confirmable, on the basis of their observations of my behavior. It seems useful for the subsequent discussion on physicalism, to distinguish between two forms of the reistic language: first, the *simple reistic language,* whose primitive predicates designate properties of observable things that are intersubjectively directly confirmable, like "blue", "warm", "hard", etc.; second, the *psychologically supplemented reistic language,* which, in addition, contains psychological predicates such as "having a toothache", "seeing green", and the like, which designate properties of things that can be directly observed only by the speaker himself, while they are merely indirectly confirmable by other persons.

B. The problem of abstract entities. As I have explained in greater detail in the paper on ontology [1950-1], the conception indicated above, if applied to the traditional controversy about the reality of abstract entities, says the following. An existential statement which asserts that there are entities of a specified kind can be formulated as a simple existential statement in a language containing variables for these entities. I have called existential statements of this kind, formulated *within* a given language, *internal* existential statements. They are usually analytic and trivial. Therefore, we may presume that the theses involved in the traditional philosophical controversies are not meant as internal statements, but rather as external existential statements; they purport to assert the existence of entities of the kind in question not merely within a given language, but, so to speak, before a language has been constructed. It seems to me that external existential sentences do not have cognitive content; therefore, I regard them as pseudo-statements if they claim to be theoretical statements. I think this holds for both the thesis of *realism* (in the medieval sense), asserting the ontological reality of abstract entities ("universals"; e.g., classes, properties, numbers, propositions, etc.), and for the thesis of *nominalism* asserting their irreality.

According to my earlier remarks we may similarly give meaning to these theses by interpreting them not as theoretical statements, but as proposals for the acceptance of certain language forms. Therefore, I suggest that we refrain from discussing the pseudo-theoretical ontological questions and instead discuss a non-nominalistic language, i.e., one containing variables whose values are abstract entities such as class variables, number variables, etc., or a nominalistic language. In a discussion of this kind, intended to lead to a practical decision concerning the form of a language to be accepted, some theoretical considerations are certainly relevant. For example, it would be important to investigate what can and what cannot be expressed in a nominalistic language of a specified form and, in particular, whether and how sentences of certain kinds containing abstract variables are translatable into sentences of the nominalistic language. Interesting results have emerged from investigations by Quine, Tarski, Goodman, Richard Martin, and others.

In recent years I have emphasized the point just mentioned, that theoretical questions too play an essential role in the philosophical discussions which are to take the place of the traditional ontological controversies. In view of this position, some philosophers, e.g., Beth (in §10 of his essay, see my §18), have wondered what kinds of questions I still wish to exclude. I shall try to explain my view by an example. Let us suppose that two logicians, X_1 and X_2, discuss, in the non-formalized everyday language, the properties of two constructed object languages, L_1 and L_2, of the following kind. Each of these languages contains the ordinary connectives, a sign of identity, and one kind of variable, which are not type-restricted, with universal and existential quantifiers; but the universe of discourse D_1 of L_1, i.e., the range of values of the variables, is more comprehensive than the universe of discourse D_2 of L_2. D_1 contains observable material objects as individuals, furthermore, classes of individuals and classes of classes of individuals (among them cardinal numbers defined according to the Frege-Russell method); by contrast, D_2 contains only entities of the first two kinds, but not classes of classes. Consequently, the syntactical rules of transformation and the semantical rules for L-concepts are of such a kind that the following sentence (or its corresponding symbolic formulation) is provable and L-true in L_1:

(4) For some x and some y, x is an element of an element of y.

In L_2, on the other hand, not this sentence but its negation and therefore the following universal sentence is provable and L-true:

(5) For every x and every y, x is not an element of an element of y.

On the basis of the semantical rules for L_1, a certain description (with iota-operator) designates the cardinal number three, whereas the same description in L_2 designates the null class (assuming Quine's convention for descriptions). The two logicians agree that language L_2 is simpler than L_1, and that, on the basis of the syntactical rules of transformation, there is less danger of an inconsistency for L_2 than for L_1. They proceed to communicate to each other their preferences and practical decisions concerning the acceptance of the two languages and their reasons for the decisions. X_2 accepts L_2 and rejects L_1, because he does not understand certain sentences of L_1. X_1 understands both languages and the semantical rules for both. He deliberates whether he should choose L_2 because of its greater simplicity and greater safety; but then he comes to the decision to accept language L_1 because of its greater wealth in means of expression and means of deduction. Both logicians understand the syntactical rules for both languages. Both are in agreement with respect to many results concerning the two languages, in particular, with respect to syntactical results. Although X_2 understands neither language L_1 nor its semantical rules, he can nevertheless learn to manipulate the sentences of this language according to the syntactical rules, and even to manipulate the semantical rules and semantical statements about L_1, if they are stated in the form of a semantical axiom system whose syntactical metalanguage he understands. Up to this point, I have no objection to anything that either X_1 or X_2 has said about the two languages, either in the form of theoretical statements or of declarations of preference and decision. I would object only if X_2 were to say to X_1: "In contrast to you, there is no possibility for me to choose between the two languages. On the basis of careful considerations, I have arrived at the following two ontological results:

(6) There are classes of objects.

(7) There are no classes of classes of objects.

What you regard as semantical rules for L_1 contains the phrase 'classes of classes of objects', which does not refer to anything. Therefore, no semantical rules for L_1 have actually been stated; thus L_1 is not an interpreted language but merely a calculus".

I would maintain that (6) and (7) are not genuine statements but pseudo-statements. I assume that (6) and (7) are meant absolutely and objectively, i.e., not relative to this or that language, or relative to this or that person; in other words, that they are meant as external statements. However, if they were meant as merely internal statements, and thus (7) was meant in the sense of the sentence (5) of L_2, then they would be cognitively meaningful sentences. Understood in the latter way, sentence (7), like (5), would merely say that in D_2 there are no classes of classes. But this statement is not incompatible with the sentence (4) in L_1 because (4) says that in a different universe of discourse, D_1, there are classes of classes. Thus we see that the difference between X_1 and X_2 is *not* a difference in *theoretical* beliefs, as X_2 seems to think when he makes the pseudo-assertion (7); it is merely a *practical* difference in preferences and decisions concerning the acceptance of languages. If X_2 were to believe that he made an assertion by his utterance of (7), I would challenge him to specify a method by which he and X_1 together could ascertain whether the alleged assertion is or is not true.

5. Paul Henle on Meaning and Verifiability

As a basis for my discussion, I shall formulate *two theses of empiricism,* and then make comments to elucidate them and to reply to Henle's arguments.

> *T1. Principle of confirmability.* If it is in principle impossible for any conceivable observational result to be either confirming or disconfirming evidence for a linguistic expression *A*, then expression *A* is devoid of cognitive meaning.

Note that what is denied here is only cognitive (theoretical, referential, descriptive) meaning. The thesis implies that the expression *A* is neither true nor false, in other words, that *A* does not express a proposition. *A* may still have meaning components of other kinds, e.g., pictorial, emotive, or motivative meaning.

> *Definition.* We say that an expression *A* is a *pseudo-statement* if *A* is devoid of cognitive meaning, but has the grammatical form of a declarative sentence and may therefore lead to psychological effects which are similar to those of a genuine statement.

Among the psychological effects of a pseudo-statement may be associations that resemble the genuine understanding of a propositional statement. This possibility explains why not only the listener but even the speaker sometimes mistakes a pseudo-statement for a genuine one. It follows from these explanations that the occurrence of the psychological phenomenon of subjective "understanding" of an expression *A* cannot be taken as a proof that *A* is a cognitive statement.

Henle regards a theory of significance (meaningfulness) as empirically justified to the extent that the class of statements which it takes as significant coincides with the class of those statements which lead to the psychological phenomenon of understanding. This criterion may often be useful in simple cases; but it can only be accepted as a crude approximation. The subjective impression of the existence of a material object may be taken as evidence for the actual existence of that object; but it is clear that this evidence is not conclusive, as is shown by sensory illusions. Analogously, the subjective phenomenon of understanding may be taken as evidence for significance, as Henle says; but this evidence cannot be regarded as necessarily conclusive.

> *T2.* Some of the main theses in certain systems of traditional metaphysics are incapable of confirmation or disconfirmation by any conceivable observational data, and are therefore pseudo-statements.

Note that the characterization as pseudo-statements does not refer to all systems or theses in the field of metaphysics. At the time of the Vienna Circle, the characterization was applied mainly to those metaphysical systems which had exerted the greatest influence upon continental philosophy during the last century, viz., the post-Kantian systems of German idealism and, among contemporary ones, those of Bergson and Heidegger. On the basis of later, more cautious analyses, the judgment was not applied to the main theses of those philosophers whose thinking had been in close contact with the science of their times, as in the cases of Aristotle and of Kant; the latter's epistemological theses about the synthetic a priori character of certain judgments were regarded by us as false, not as meaningless. Nor was it applied to those philosophers who tried to explain the world by audacious generalizations on the basis of experience, though perhaps on insufficient observational evidence. They might be regarded as the precursors of science taking the first tentative steps towards a scientific explanation of the world. Furthermore, the judgment is not meant to apply to those systems which are sometimes called "metaphysical", but which start explicitly from empirical knowledge and inductively infer from it a system of cosmology. Henle (in §II) gives examples of metaphysical statements which were refuted, or in some cases confirmed, by the later development of science. Theses of this kind, at least in the interpretation given to them by Henle, which may be historically correct, are confirmable and therefore are not regarded by us as pseudo-statements.

Henle discusses certain statements of theology which, in his view, are not confirmable but are nevertheless understood. As an example, he gives the statement "God exists". (Incidentally, I think it would be clearer to use a formulation like "there is at least one god" or "there is exactly one god", containing the predicate "god" instead of the alleged proper name "God".) In this context, it is important to distinguish between the mythical (or magical) and the metaphysical uses of the word "God" or "god". Neurath[3] emphasized the difference between the magic of primeval periods and later metaphysics. Magic was this-worldly and empirical; metaphysics, on the other hand, was transcendent and nonempirical. Neurath regarded theology as a transition phenomenon; in its primitive form it was magical, but later it became more and more metaphysical, although it preserved some of its original formulations. I made the same distinction in [1932-1] §3. I pointed out that the word "God", in its mythical use, has a clear, empirical meaning. In its metaphysical use, on the other hand, its old empirical meaning vanishes; since no new meaning is supplied, the term "God" becomes meaningless. I added that in theology the use of the word "God" is sometimes mythical and thus empirical, sometimes metaphysical, and sometimes ambiguous. In order to classify a theological statement, we have to take its interpretation or its context into consideration. The psychological phenomenon of the subjective understanding of theological statements, even in the

[3]Otto Neurath, *Empirische Soziologie* (Wien, 1931), ch. 1: "From Magic to Unified Science."

later metaphysical phase, can easily be explained by those associations connected with the word "God" which are remnants of the earlier mythical phase.

The hypotheses of telepathy and other forms of extra-sensory perception, of psychokinesis, and the like, are certainly empirical hypotheses, not fundamentally different from other hypotheses in science. If the evidence for a hypothesis of this kind should finally be so strong that the hypothesis would be regarded as scientifically acceptable, this result might possibly, though not necessarily, lead to a fundamental change in the system of science. It seems to me, however, that some analytic philosophers ascribe to hypotheses of this kind a greater importance for analytic-philosophical problems than is warranted; they would expect them, for example, to decide the issue between physicalism and dualistic emergentism. Henle seems to think that the acceptance of "mental telepathy without any physical basis" would constitute a refutation of Santayana's materialism. (Incidentally, it is not quite clear to me what is meant by "without any physical basis". In all telepathic experiments made so far, two human organisms have been involved in the situation.) In a similar sense, Rhine has asserted that the hypothesis of extra-sensory perception, which he accepts, constitutes a proof for idealism. In contrast to these views, I do not think that the thesis of materialism or idealism could be confirmed or disconfirmed by any observational evidence (compare my discussion of the realism controversy in §4A). I think that, in general, a representative of a metaphysical thesis of this kind is not willing to specify possible observational results which he would regard as confirming or disconfirming evidence for his thesis if they were to occur. But if he should be willing to do so, his specifications would make his thesis cognitive. Henle seems to think that if our criterion of significance is taken in the liberalized form as "confirmability in principle", then there are hardly any metaphysical theses left which would be excluded. I think, however, that our principle excludes not only a great number of assertions in systems like those of Hegel and Heidegger, especially since the latter says explicitly that logic is not applicable to statements in metaphysics, but also in contemporary discussions, e.g., those concerning the reality of space or of time.

Henle mentions also the important problem of unobservable entities like atoms and electrons. I think today, as he does, that concepts of this kind cannot be introduced by reduction sentences. I would prefer to introduce them as theoretical terms by postulates, but connected with observation terms by so-called rules of correspondence. I have discussed these questions in detail in the article [1956-4], which had not been published when Henle wrote his essay. There I propose a criterion of significance for theoretical terms of this kind; the criterion represents an explication of the requirement of confirmability in a modified form. In the same article (p. 53), I comment on the question of whether confirmability in this requirement is to be understood as logical or as physical possibility. In contrast to Schlick's view, I reaffirm my earlier conception that we should take physical possibility, although in a new form which refers to the theoretical language. For further discussions of the theoretical language, compare Hempel's essay and my reply (§24).

The purpose of my discussion in this section was rather to clarify the empiricist meaning criterion and its application to metaphysics than to offer arguments for our view. Such arguments can be found in the relevant publications, e.g., Wittgenstein's *Tractatus*, my [1928-2], and [1932-1], Ayer's *Language, Truth and Logic,* and numerous other books and papers in the field of analytic philosophy.

6. K. R. Popper on the Demarcation between Science and Metaphysics

Since the beginning of my acquaintance with Popper's work[4] I have regarded his investigations into the foundations of knowledge and into the character of the scientific method as generally interesting and valuable, and especially those about the formation, testing and confirmation of hypotheses, even though I could not agree in all details. On the other hand, as Popper remarks, even at that time I thought he tended to exaggerate our differences. Today I am more than ever convinced that this is the case.

A. The two problems of demarcation. The main problem in Popper's essay is that of the demarcation between science and metaphysics, which he discusses in §§1 through 4. (In §5 he discusses the problem of induction and probability; to this I reply in §31.) Popper's conception of this demarcation is not as fundamentally opposed to my conception and that of logical empiricists in general as he thinks. His main thesis is not incompatible with our conception because our respective theses concern entirely different problems. Previously, I was not aware of this difference, because Popper always claimed his thesis to be opposed to the views on metaphysics maintained by Wittgenstein and developed in the Vienna Circle. But a study of his present essay and of his [Report] makes the difference between the two problems quite obvious. I shall now explain the difference.

[4]Popper's main work on the theory of knowledge and methodology is his book *Logik der Forschung: Zur Erkenntnistheorie der modernen Naturwissenschaft* (Wien, 1935), to which I shall refer as "[*Logik*]". An English translation with additions is soon to appear under the title *The Logic of Scientific Discovery.* Popper has given a clear and concise survey of his main views and their development in his article "Philosophy of Science: A Personal Report," in: C. A. Mace (ed.), *British Philosophy in the Mid-Century* (London, 1957), 155-191. I shall refer to this article as "[Report]".

Let us first make a rough distinction between three kinds of statements, i.e., declarative sentences. (For the sake of simplicity, I shall omit statements of logic and pure mathematics.) Let *kind I* comprise genuine scientific statements, i.e., those which, in view of their form, would be regarded by scientists as of sound, scientific, empirical character, irrespective of whether the available evidence is sufficient for their acceptance or rejection. Under *kind II*, we shall classify those statements which we might call, with Popper, "pseudo-scientific". Statements of astrology, myths, ancient magic, and popular superstitions are examples of the second kind. Such statements are comprehensible and concern empirical matters, but they cannot be taken seriously from a scientific point of view. To *kind III* we delegate what we called "pseudo-statements" in Vienna, i.e., declarative sentences which are devoid of cognitive meaning (see §§ 4 and 5). Examples of this kind are "the cardinal number five is blue" and "the Nothing nothingeth" (Heidegger).

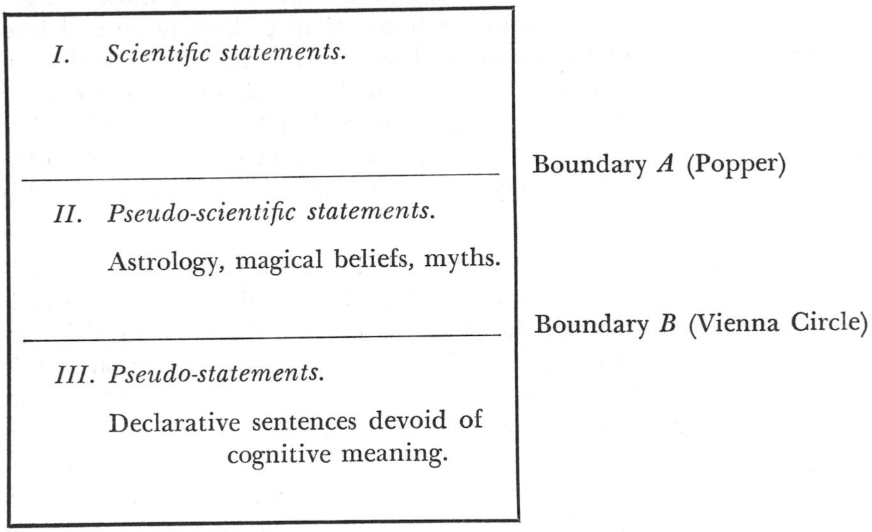

Figure 1. Comparison of Demarcation Problem in Popper and Carnap.

The difference between Popper's and our problem can now easily be specified. As indicated in figure 1, Popper's problem of demarcation consists in the task of explicating the boundary *A* between science and pseudo-science. Our aim, on the other hand, is to explicate the boundary *B* between the empirical realm, which comprises both science and pseudo-science, and the realm of meaningless pseudo-statements. Obviously, these problems concern two entirely different questions, and should be investigated independently of each other.

Popper classifies metaphysics under kind II, whereas we classify it under III. But this difference is not as sharp as it may appear. It is more a difference in emphasis than a fundamental difference in views. It seems to me that the books which are customarily called "metaphysical" contain statements of both kinds, II and III. To us those of kind III seem to be especially characteristic of metaphysics; therefore, in a generalizing way, we often called all statements of the kind III "metaphysical", even when they belonged not to the field usually called "metaphysics", but to epistemology or to the philosophy of science. In a similar way, Popper regarded statements of kind II as typical of metaphysics, and therefore used the term "metaphysics" sometimes as a collective label for class II. And so it happened that both Popper's formulation of his problem and our formulation of our problem referred to "the distinction between science (or: the empirical) and metaphysics". This fact was partly the reason why we believed erroneously with Popper that we all talked about the same problem and that we were engaged in a genuine controversy since he gave an answer different from ours. It remains to be seen whether, from our side, there are any objections left to Popper's solution of question *A*, and whether, from his side, there remain any objections to our solution of question *B*.

B. Popper's solution. Popper proposes the criterion of refutability by observational results (or testability, or falsifiability) as a solution for his problem *A*. He emphasizes that the distinction between scientific and pseudo-scientific statements is a matter of degree, and that there is no sharp line of demarcation. Popper's analysis of the problem and his detailed discussions are valuable contributions to methodology. Furthermore, it seems to me that the basic idea of his solution is correct: a statement or a theory is the stronger in content, the more precisely it is formulated and thus the more it is exposed to refutation. I am inclined to think, however, that his requirement is too narrow. As I showed in the article on testability ([1936-10] §§25f.), there are some sentence forms which are generally acknowledged to be scientific in the strictest sense, but which do not satisfy the condition of falsifiability. At that time I gave as examples sentences of the form "$(x)(\exists y)(..x..y..)$". In order to refute a sentence of this form, its negation "$(\exists x)(y)\sim(..x..y..)$" must be verified. Thus one would have to find an instance *a* for *x* such that "$(y)\sim(..a..y..)$" can be verified. But, of course, a universal sentence cannot be verified in the strict sense by observation; it can at best be confirmed to some degree. All sentences containing the mathematical concept of limit have the form specified above; most laws of theoretical physics belong to this class, since they involve velocity, acceleration, or other differential coëfficients. Therefore Popper's requirement must be modified. One might consider replacing falsifiability by refutability in a weaker, inductive sense. However, in his present essay, Popper seems to have retained the original version of his criterion.

C. Popper's discussion of my earlier conceptions. Popper discusses at length (in §§2 and 3) my earlier views on the demarcation between science and metaphysics (prior to my article [1936-10]). Since these views were later modified, as Popper mentions, I shall not go into details but shall comment only briefly on two points. Popper implies (in §3 (a)) that I considered all statements about subjective experiences to be as meaningless as metaphysical statements. In fact, I regarded statements about subjective experiences as meaningful, but insisted on a physicalistic interpretation of them (see [1932-5]). A detailed analysis of our physicalist thesis is given by Feigl in his contribution to the present volume; compare also my replies to Feigl and Ayer in §§7 and 8.

Popper asserts (in §3 (c)) that our thesis of the possibility of a unified language of science has been refuted by the results of Gödel and Tarski. These results are certainly of the greatest importance. But they show only that no fixed language can be logically and semantically complete; every language can be further strengthened by the addition of new logical forms of expression and new logical means of deduction. The thesis of the unity of science, as Neurath and I maintained it, has nothing to do with the question of logical completeness. Rather, it was meant as a rejection of the division of empirical science into allegedly fundamentally separate fields, above all of the division into natural sciences and social sciences (*"Geisteswissenchaften"*), a division which was based on the dualistic metaphysics prevailing at that time in Germany. In contrast to this dualistic conception, our thesis asserted that empirical science, with all its various fields, can be constructed on a uniform basis. Understood in this sense, I still maintain this thesis.

D. Popper's criticism of our anti-metaphysical conception. I come now to the main point of Popper's essay, viz., his criticism of our solution of our problem. In my article on testability [1936-10], I presented a view which differed in several respects from our earlier conception. The influences which led me to revise my views came above all from my Viennese friends, with whom I had many discussions, but also from other philosophers, among them Popper. (I appreciate the influence of Popper's ideas, but I am not sure whether they played quite the central role in the development of my views which he ascribes to them.) I proposed to abandon Wittgenstein's requirement of verifiability as a condition of cognitive significance (meaningfulness) and to replace it by the requirement of confirmability in a wide sense, including indirect and incomplete confirmation. My aim was, on the one hand, to make the requirement weak enough to admit as significant all sentences of kinds I and II, but, on the other hand, strong enough to exclude the sentences of kind III. Popper (in §4) offers arguments not only against the particular form of my criterion but generally against criteria of this kind. He tries to show that these criteria would admit certain metaphysical statements as significant. Unfortunately, his objection is based on the fundamental misunderstanding that it had been our intention to solve his problem *A* by means of our various criteria of significance; Popper interprets our thesis that certain metaphysical statements are meaningless as referring to statements of kind II. However, we regarded and still regard, just as he does, statements of kind II as significant and characterize only those of kind III as meaningless.

Popper begins his argument with the remark that a satisfactory language of science would have to contain with each sentence also its negation; hence with the universal sentences also their negations and thus purely existential statements. I certainly agree; I have declared explicitly (in [1936-10] §§24-27) that I regard sentences with any number of universal and existential quantifiers as significant. Then Popper comes to the decisive point: "But this means that it must contain sentences which Carnap, Neurath, and all other anti-metaphysicians always considered to be metaphysical". This shows clearly that he misunderstands our thesis to refer to the boundary *A*; he thinks that we regard the purely existential sentences of a scientific language, which, according to his classification, belong to kind II, as metaphysical and meaningless. He continues: "In order to make this quite clear I choose as an extreme example, what may be called *'the arch-metaphysical assertion'*: 'There exists an omnipotent, omnipresent, and omniscient personal spirit' ". For the terms occurring in the last statement, he gives definitions in a physicalistic language. Thus, the sentence is clearly empirical; it is metaphysical only in Popper's sense (kind II), not in our sense (kind III). It is true that we have sometimes called similar theological sentences metaphysical and meaningless. But we did this only if the context showed that the author of the statement did not intend to give an empirical interpretation to it. I have previously (in §5) mentioned the distinction, first made by Neurath, between mythical (or magical) and metaphysical theology. Popper's theological statement, on the basis of his empirical definitions, obviously belongs to the former.

Even though Popper's argument concerning his particular example is based on a misunderstanding, he might still be right in asserting that empiricists draw the boundary of the language of science, or the boundary of cognitively meaningful statements, in too narrow a fashion. I do not believe that this is the case. I am not aware of any statement which Popper would regard as cognitively meaningful and which we would take as cognitively meaningless.

7. Herbert Feigl on Physicalism

In his essay, Feigl deals with the problem of physicalism, and explains how our present views developed from their original starting point at the time of the Vienna Circle. With some qualifications, which I shall explain presently, I am in agreement with his formulations in all major points. Feigl has given a more detailed presentation of the problem in a later article, which I read in manuscript form.[5] I welcome Feigl's clear exposition of our conception all the more because in recent years I have published almost nothing on physicalism.

Feigl makes two different suggestions for an explication of the concept of factual meaningfulness: first, subjective confirmability, and second, intersubjective confirmability. At the present time I prefer not to emphasize the requirement of intersubjective confirmability as much as we used to do previously, but rather to consider it to be of secondary importance. I regard as meaningful for me whatever I can, in principle, confirm subjectively. This statement may be taken as a rough formulation of the *principle of empiricism.*

Now we come to *physicalism.* I shall briefly outline my position, using some of Feigl's formulations. I, i.e., the knowing subject, accept the reistic language for a description of the world of things. In this world, I find the following features which are empirical but, unlike single facts, belong to what is sometimes called "the all-pervading fundamental features" of the world and of the language in which the world can be described:

(1) There are beings similar to myself with whom I am able to communicate by language.

(2) I find myself able to give to others a signal indicating any kind of experience which I have; or, in case I should be unable to give an intentional signal, others could, under suitable circumstances, infer my state from observable symptoms.

(3) Therefore, everything I know, including what I know by introspection, is in principle confirmable by others on the basis of their observations.

(4) Therefore it is possible, and convenient for practical purposes, to begin the construction of the language with primitive predicates designating properties of things that are intersubjectively observable (e.g., "red", "hot").

Predicates designating properties that are only subjectively observable, though intersubjectively confirmable (as e.g., "angry", "having a toothache") may be introduced derivatively. It should be emphasized

[5] H. Feigl, "The 'Mental' and the 'Physical' ", in: *Minnesota Studies in the Philosophy of Science,* II (1958).

that the difference between these two kinds of thing properties is not a matter of principle, but merely of degree.

The *first thesis of physicalism* may now be formulated in any of the following ways:

(I_1) As the conjunction of the synthetic statements (1), (2), (3) above. Or:

(I_2) "Whatever is subjectively confirmable, is also intersubjectively confirmable".

In other words:

(I_3) "Privacy of knowledge is not absolute, but is only a matter of degree".

I think the thesis may also be stated in the following way which is essentially equivalent to the foregoing formulations:

(I_4) (a) As a proposal of a form of language in which all statements are intersubjectively confirmable,
(b) together with the assertion that this form of language is sufficient for expressing everything that is meaningful for me.
(Assertion (b) follows from I_2.)

Among the various formulations of the *second thesis of physicalism* I should prefer that which refers to the derivability of laws:

(II) All laws of nature, including those which hold for organisms, human beings, and human societies, are logical consequences of the physical laws, i.e., of those laws which are needed for the explanation of inorganic processes.

This thesis does not refer to the laws known to us at present, but to those laws which hold in nature and which our knowledge can only more and more approximate. The thesis may therefore be understood as the hypothesis that in the future it will become possible to an ever greater extent to derive known extra-physical laws from known physical laws.

It is true that these two theses of physicalism go far beyond the present possibility of reducing extra-physical concepts and laws to physical ones. These theses do not represent firmly established knowledge but sweeping extrapolating hypotheses. However, as Feigl has clearly pointed out, the evidence for them is growing stronger due to the progress of research in physics, chemistry, and in the physiology of the central nervous system in recent decades.

As a specific argument against the doctrine of *emergentism,* which has been adopted even by some empiricists, I should like to emphasize in this context the philosophically important fact that scientific investigations demonstrate ever more clearly a *continuity* in the evolution of man. We may think, e.g., of the development of quasi-organic entities from inorganic substances, further of viruses, one-cell organisms, higher organisms, and finally human beings. All empiricists have abandoned the earlier belief that there is a fundamental difference, a "difference in kind", between man and the other animals, and between organisms and the inorganic world. Nobody denies that there are differences and that they are of very great importance both theoretically and practically. But these differences have no sharp boundary lines: they are differences of degree within a continuum. It is possible, of course, to draw a line by definition between human beings and other animals; but any such line is to some extent arbitrary, that is to say, the line might be drawn with just as good reasons somewhat later or somewhat earlier. The traditional discontinuity views had their historical source in certain magical and religious beliefs, and these views lingered on for quite some time after the magical and religious beliefs from which they originated had been abandoned. It seems to me that emergentism has a similar character. There is no doubt that emergentism can be formulated in a non-metaphysical, meaningful, and scientific way. Yet I doubt that there is any good objective reason for drawing a sharp boundary line at some point by declaring: "At exactly this place and time the first sensation (or: the first sensation of red) occurred." Such a declaration may be justified on the basis of a psychophysical dualism, understood not as an ontological thesis, but as a proposal for the use of a dualistic language. Although I would strongly disagree with such a dualistic emergentism, I think it is more coherent than the non-dualistic version of emergentism which is defended by some empiricists. Once dualism is abandoned, there seems to be no good reason for the position which singles out the occurrence of certain new micro-structures from that of others and declares that the former are connected with new qualities or sense-data while the latter are just new physical structures. If we could study the development from inorganic matter to man in detail, down to the physical micro-structure of all bodies, we would find new micro-structures all the time. Many of them show dispositions for responses of higher and higher degrees of integration (in a vague sense not easy to explicate). If the degree of integration is sufficiently high, it is customary to speak of organic responses (again in a vague sense). Finally, there are certain kinds of tissues customarily called nerve tissues; in terrestrial organisms, we find all responses of a very high degree of integration to be connected with tissues of this kind. But we do not know whether this connection holds for all higher organisms in other parts of the universe. Hence, we do not know whether the occurrence of this kind of tissue may be taken as an essential criterion of higher degrees of integration. In any case, the possible degrees of integration form a continuum. Therefore it would be arbitrary to draw a sharp line at one particular value of the degree of integration and to say that from here on all of the more highly integrated responses are accompanied by, or are themselves to be regarded as, "mental" events, (e.g., "sensations") or are "conscious", whereas all responses of lower degree are not. Here, as in the case of the concepts of organism and of man, the discontinuity view, when held by those who have abandoned dualism, seems to be due solely to an after-effect of the abandoned position.[6]

I believe further that, when an adequate explication of the distinction between conscious and unconscious mental processes is found, or, preferably, a degree of consciousness, connected in higher animals with the degree of communicability, e.g., man's ability to verbalize, then this distinction will probably be found to be much less important for the explanation and prediction of behavior than pre-Freudian psychologists thought and some dualistic philosophers still think. It may be a matter of life or death for an animal whether or not its central nervous system receives a signal from a sensory organ indicating an approaching danger, and whether or not this signal leads to an appropriate response. But it may matter relatively little whether or not this process is a "conscious" one or an "unconscious reflex". It seems that emergentism, even in a non-metaphysical version, is in danger of regarding as absolute what is, in fact, gradual, and as fundamental what is only a secondary factor.

In his essay in the present volume, Feigl characterizes his position as *"identity view"*; in his later article (see his footnote 1), he gives more detailed reasons for this designation. According to Feigl, a systemic identity holds between the denotatum of a psychological predicate, say *"P"*, and that of a corresponding neurophysiological term, say *"N"*. (He calls the predicates "phenomenal predicates"; but since he regards them as intersubjectively used, they are, in my terminology, psychological predicates of the reistic language.) Let *"P(a,t)"* say that the individual *a* is at the time *t* in the psychological state *P;* let *"N(a,t)"* say that *a* is at *t* in the neurophysiological state *N*. The identity statement "the process *P(a,t)* is the same as the process *N(a,t)*" is empirical, not logical. Feigl calls it a "systemic" identity because this statement and the law "for every individual *x* and every time *u, P(x,u)* if and only if *N(x,u)*" are based on the postulates and rules of a theoretical system. Although I agree with Feigl in the position itself, I have some doubts about his way of formulating it. The identity statement mentioned is a sentence of the object language; this fact may mislead the reader into believing that the controversy about the identity view concerns a question of fact. This impression may be further strengthened by Feigl's reference to certain facts as "evidence" for the identity view. It seems preferable to me to

[6] For some interesting remarks on the doctrine of discontinuity between the inorganic and the organic, see Felix Mainx, *Foundations of Biology, Encyclopedia of Unified Science,* I, no. 9 (Chicago, 1955).

formulate the question in the metalanguage, not as a factual question about the world, but as a question concerning the choice of a language form. Although we prefer a different language, we must admit that a dualistic language can be constructed and used without coming into conflict with either the laws of logic or with empirically known facts. However, in the dualistic language, the identity statement mentioned above is false; the philosopher who uses this language is therefore justified in denying this statement. Those facts which Feigl proposes as evidence for the identity view are perhaps better regarded as reasons for preferring a monistic language, e.g., the reistic language containing psychological thing predicates. In a certain version of this language, on the basis of suitable postulates and rules, the above identity statement is true; or, as I should prefer to put it, in this language the predicates "*P*" and "*N*", though not L-equivalent, are P-equivalent, i.e., equivalent on the basis of the postulates and rules. To sum up, I am willing to call my position an identity conception in the following sense: in agreement with Feigl I prefer the monistic language, and like him I believe that the evidence available today provides good reasons for the assumption that this language will also function well in the future.

8. A. J. Ayer on Other Minds

Ayer bases his criticism of my views concerning the problem of other minds only on my publications before 1936, and he believes, in particular, that my view of the logical equivalence of a psychological statement about another person and a statement about a physical process in the body of the other person has never changed. However, soon after the publication of the articles mentioned by Ayer, I abandoned (in [1936-10] §15) the positivistic conception as well as the old form of physicalism. According to our earlier positivism, all terms of the reistic language are explicitly definable in terms of the phenomenal (sense-data) language and therefore all sentences of the former are translatable into, i.e., logically equivalent to, sentences of the latter; according to the earlier physicalist thesis, all terms of science, including those of psychology, are explicitly definable in terms of the simple reistic language (thing language without psychological thing predicates) and sentences containing the former are therefore translatable into sentences of the reistic language. In [1938-2] I emphasized again that psychological terms are not definable in terms of the simple reistic language and indicated that a more indirect relation holds ("reducibility"). For example, if, as a result of introspection, I make the statement "I have a toothache", using an intersubjective language, there is a possible behavioristic symptom for the toothache—if no other, then at least the utterance of the sentence mentioned. I emphasized that the state of a person designated by a psychological term is not identical with his overt behavior; the latter is a causal consequence of the former and may therefore be regarded as a symptom. I need not go into further details of the development of my views and their role for the total conception which we call "physicalism", inasmuch as Feigl has explained this matter in detail and with great clarity in his contribution to this volume.

Toward the end of his essay, Ayer formulates two objections against the conceptions I held prior to 1936. My "initial mistake" consists, according to Ayer, in assuming "that there is a natural division of objects into public and private, and that it is only when a statement refers to a public object that it can be publicly understood". But this was most certainly not my view. This division was not made by me; I started from a discussion of this dualistic conception held by other philosophers and attempted to show that it is not compatible with the empiricist principle of intersubjective verifiability.

My "second mistake", according to Ayer, consists in the fact that, due to my method, "the protocol statements which served to describe our experiences are transformed into statements about the condition of our bodies". What exactly does Ayer mean by "protocol statements describing our experiences"? Presumably, he means statements like "I now see green". But, as I pointed out earlier, this sentence can be understood in two different ways. Perhaps Ayer means a statement in the phenomenal language; but in this case the statement would be more adequately formulated as "now green". If a philosopher wishes to use this sentence, say for the confirmation of the sentence "This pencil is green", he may do so; but he must realize that he can speak this sentence only to himself. On the other hand, it may be that Ayer was thinking of a statement in the intersubjective reistic language containing psychological predicates; this interpretation might be suggested by his formulation "*our* experiences". But then the sentence mentioned or, preferably, the sentence "Now Carnap sees green" means as much as "The body Carnap is now in the state of green-seeing"; and this is a statement about a condition of a body. On the basis of my conception, it is not necessary to use the phenomenal language either for psychology or for the confirmation of a sentence of physics or of a thing sentence like "This pencil is green". I believe—and I presume that today many empiricists, if not the majority, share this view—that the reistic language containing psychological predicates is sufficient as a basic language ("protocol language" in the old Vienna terminology), i.e., for the formulation of statements about confirming experiences. Statements like "Now Carnap is green-seeing" are sufficient for this purpose. And if, at the request of another person, I try to give a reason for my assertion "This pencil is green" by describing a confirming experience of mine, I *must* use the form mentioned and I *cannot* use the phenomenal language.

Ayer maintains the legitimacy of inductive inferences by analogy concerning mental processes of other persons. He refers to another article of his[7] in which the argument is developed at greater length. The analogy argument has frequently been used in this context by other philosophers, sometimes in order to affirm the existence of other minds and thereby to refute solipsism. I believe we must distinguish between two fundamentally different questions here. The argument by analogy is not legitimate for the solution of the *philosophical* problem of the existence of other minds; but it is legitimate for obtaining an answer to an empirical question about a specific mental process of another individual.

Before I give my reasons for this view, let us consider the similar problem of the existence of the external world. Here we have to make the same distinction between a philosophical and an empirical question of existence (in the terminology of [1950-1], this is the distinction between an external and an internal question of existence). The philosophical question concerns the allegedly theoretical thesis of realism about the reality of the external world, and that of radical solipsism about the unreality of the external world. As I have often explained, I regard these as pseudo-theses. Therefore I would deny the possibility of using an inductive argument in order to support realism. It seems more fruitful to me to replace the philosophical question by the practical question whether to accept the reistic language. The empirical problem arises only after the reistic language has been accepted and the question has been formulated in this language, e.g., "Is there in this region a mountain having such and such properties?" The affirmative or negative answer to this question can, of course, be inductively confirmed by observations.

In my view, the ontological theses of the existence or non-existence of other minds are likewise pseudo-theses, and therefore no argument by analogy is possible. Here again I propose to replace the philosophical controversy by the discussion of the practical question whether subsequent to the acceptance of the simple reistic language, we wish to accept the conceptual framework of psychological predicates in this language. I should prefer a framework which permits a psychological predicate to be meaningfully attributed to any material object or space-time region. If, in accordance with everyday language, we accept this conceptual framework, then and only then do the empirical problems arise. Among them are not only singular questions such as "Does John now have a

[7]Ayer, "One's Knowledge of Other Minds" (1953); reprinted in *Philosophical Essays* (1954).

toothache?", but also general questions such as "Are there any other beings which, like myself, have experiences of such and such a kind?" or "Does a psychological regularity of such and such a kind hold generally for human beings?" Questions of this kind are to be answered with the help of the rules laid down for the framework according to inductive principles, e.g., by analogy. First, statements about single cases will be obtained, and then, with the help of further inductive steps, general statements about regularities.

III. *Language, Modal Logic, and Semantics*

9. My Conceptions of the Logic of Modalities

Since technical problems of the logic of modalities are discussed in some of the essays, especially in those by Feys, Myhill, and Davidson, I shall indicate my present conceptions of modal logic and the forms in which I would now construct systems of modal logic. These systems are far more comprehensive than those which I have described in my publications.[8] In constructing these systems, I have been aided by valuable ideas from the essays mentioned. Unfortunately the explanations of the systems in this section must be so short that they are perhaps not easily understandable. But I hope to give more detailed expositions in future publications.

I. The logic of extensions. As is customary, I shall understand the *extension of a sentence* to be its truth-value, the *extension of an n-place predicate expression* to be the class of *n*-tuples for which it holds, and the *extension of an individual expression* to be the individual denoted by it.

(1) *L* is an *extensional language* if *L* satisfies the following conditions:

(a) *L* contains *extension variables,* i. e., variables whose values are extensions.

(b) *L* contains a binary connective, say "$\equiv$", such that a sentence containing this symbol as its principal connective is true if and only if the two components have the same extension. This connective is therefore a symbol for the *identity of extensions* (comp. [Meaning] §3).

[8]My article "Modalities and Quantification" [1946-1] describes the modal semantical systems MPL (modal propositional logic) and MFL (modal functional logic of first order), and the corresponding syntactical systems (calculi) MPC and MFC. My book *Meaning and Necessity* [1947-2] discusses in ch. V the interpretation of modal logics which contain quantified variables, but it does not present formal systems. In this chapter III I shall use "[Meaning]" to refer to this book.

(c) Designators with the same extension are interchangeable in every context.[9]

(2) A *logic of extensions* is a system of logical rules for an extensional language. (Note that an extensional language may occur as a part of a non-extensional language; in this case the logic of extensions would be the appropriate part of the full logic for the language.)

I shall now describe the main features of an extensional language L_1, which will later serve as a basis for the modal languages to be described. L_1 is a coördinate language; the individuals are positions corresponding to the natural numbers (comp. [Meaning] §18). For example, the sentence "B(3)" may say that the position 3 is blue. I use a simple type system with the types 0, 1, 2, etc. for all natural numbers (not to be confused with the positions 0, 1, 2, etc.), both for the classification of expressions (individual expressions and class expressions) and also for the analogous classification of the entities referred to by these expressions; these entities are extensions. Let E^n be the class extensions of type n. The E^0 are the individuals; the E^{n+1} are the classes whose elements are E^n. Let v^n be the class of variables of type n. The values of the v^n are the E^n. (L_1 corresponds roughly to the language of *Principia Mathematica* supplemented by a finite number of primitive descriptive predicates of arbitrary types.) Relation sentences are translatable into L_1 in the following way. The ordered n-tuple $<x_1, \ldots, x_n>$ can be defined (by a modification of the Wiener-Kuratowski method) as a certain class whose type is higher than any of the (possibly different) types of the n members. Then an n-place relation can be defined as a class of n-tuples, and a function can be defined as a relation of a special kind.

L_1 contains the customary connectives, universal and existential quantifiers with variables of any type, iota-expressions with variables of type 0 (individual descriptions), and lambda-expressions with variables of any type (abstraction expressions for classes of any type). The iota-expressions and lambda-expressions can always be eliminated according to given rules.

L_1 also contains k primitive descriptive predicate constants; let them be (in a standard order) $c_1, \ldots, c_k$. Let c_i ($i = 1, \ldots, k$) be of the type n_i. As we shall see in §10, we need the concepts of models and value assignments for the semantical rules. We shall now define these two concepts for L_1.

(3) A *model* for L_1 assigns to every primitive descriptive predicate in L_1 one class (of the same type). (See the explanations in §10 II.)

[9]Definitions of "interchangeable", "L-interchangeable", and more exact definitions of "extensional" and "L-extensional" are given in my books [1942-2] §§ 10 and 14, [1943] § 12, [Meaning] § 11.

Suppose that a certain model assigns to the constant c_1 the class C_1, to the constant c_2 the class C_2, and in general, to c_i the class C_i. Then this model can be represented by the k-tuple $<C_1, \ldots, C_k>$, thus by a certain class of higher type than any of the k member-classes. (For the sake of simplicity let us assume here that there are no logical dependencies between the primitive constants; otherwise we should have to express these dependencies by A-postulates. Thus for L_1 A-truth coincides with L-truth, (see §10 I). The models are, so to speak, all the possible states of the universe of discourse of the language L_1.

(4) A *value assignment* assigns to every variable of L_1 one value (here an extension) of the corresponding type.[10]

We assume that *semantical rules* for L_1 are given (see below, §10 I). On the basis of these rules, truth and A-truth in L_1 are defined.

II. The logic of intensions; modalities. (See [Meaning], esp. ch. I and V.) I shall take as a condition of adequacy for any explication of the concept of intension that two designators have the same intension if and only if they are L-equivalent.

(5) L is an *intensional language* if L satisfies the following conditions:

(a) L contains *intension variables,* i.e., variables whose values are intensions.

(b) L contains a binary connective for sentences and other designators, say "$\equiv$", such that a sentence containing this symbol as its principle connective is true if and only if the two components are L-equivalent. This connective is thus a symbol for the *identity of intensions* ([Meaning] p. 177).

(c) L contains the symbol "N" (for logical necessity) such that a sentence of the form $N(S_i)$ is true if and only if the operand S_i is L-true.

(d) L-equivalent designators are L-interchangeable in any context.

(6) A *logic of intensions* or *modal logic* is a system of logical rules for an intensional language.

(7) A connective for designators is called an intensional connective or a *modal sign* if L-equivalence to a designator D_i, but not material equivalence, is sufficient for L-interchangeability with D_i whenever D_i occurs as a component of the connective.

[10] In my book on syntax ([1937-1] § 34c) and still in [Meaning], the values assigned by the semantical rules to variables and descriptive constants were linguistic entities, viz., expressions, classes of expressions, etc. Today I prefer to use as values extra-linguistic entities, e.g., numbers, classes of numbers, etc. In an analogous way I now represent possible states of the universe of discourse by models instead of state-descriptions, which are sentences or classes of sentences.

Thus "≡" and "N" are modal signs. (Each of these two signs is definable on the basis of the other one and "="; see (9) below.)

I shall now describe the main features of two *modal languages* L_2 and L_3. These are formed from L_1 by the addition of the modal signs "*N*" and "≡". But in these two languages, the values of the variables are intensions; in particular, the values of the v^n are here intensions of type n (I^n).[11] The I^0 are individual concepts; the I^n (n>0) are properties of type n. L_2 is a restricted modal language with only a narrow domain of intensions (as values of the variables and as intensions of the designators); L_3 is a richer modal language with a far more comprehensive domain of intensions. The models for L_2 and for L_3 are the same as for L_1 (see (3)), because the possible cases are the same as before. However, it is necessary for the semantical rules for L_2 and L_3, to define the value assignments for the variables in such a way that they assign not extensions, but intensions.

In L_2, the modal signs "*N*" and "≡" are not admitted in the operand of an iota-expression or a lambda-expression (but they are admitted in the operand of a universal or an existential quantifier). The intensions of designators not containing modal signs we call *non-modal intensions*. The non-modal properties are those which, following Russell, are usually called extensional properties. The latter concept can be defined in the object language as follows:

$$(8)\ Extl^{n+2}(x^{n+1}) =_{Df} (x^n_1)(x^n_2)[x^{n+1}(x^n_1) \cdot (x^n_1 \equiv x^n_2) \supset x^{n+1}(x^n_2)].$$

An analysis, which I cannot give here, would show that an extensional I^n can be represented as an assignment by which to every model an extension E^n is assigned.

In L_2 and L_3 propositional variables v^s may occur. In both languages, their values are non-modal intensions (propositional intensions I^s or propositions), because in these languages every modal sentence is L-equivalent to a non-modal sentence. A proposition can be represented as a class of models, viz., the class of those models in which this proposition holds.

In L_3, the modal signs "*N*" and "≡"' are admitted in the operand of a lambda-expression, but still not admitted in that of an iota-expression. The I^0 in L_3 are the same as in L_2. But, whereas L_2 admits only extensional properties, we have in L_3 a more comprehensive domain of intensions I^n for n>0; L_3 includes non-extensional properties (e.g., a

[11] In [Meaning] I distinguished between value intensions and value extensions of the "neutral" variables. But today it seems to me simpler and clearer to regard only intensions as values of the variables in a modal language. Quine suggested this (see the quotation in [Meaning] pp. 196 f.); and Davidson (see § III of his essay and also his footnote 23) says that this was, in effect, already the case in my exposition in the book. Myhill too takes only intensions as values of the higher variables v^n (n>0); but for the v° he takes extensions.

property which is expressible by a lambda-expression with modal signs, but not by one without such signs).

For language L_2 I have formulated semantical rules in an extensional metalanguage M. On the basis of the rules, definitions for L-truth (or A-truth) and truth in L_2 are given. The same can be done for language L_3, but the rules are considerably more complicated.

III. The two identity concepts. In the modal languages L_2 and L_3 we have two connectives between designators which can be regarded as symbols of identity: as in L_1, "$\equiv$" is a symbol for the identity of extensions (material identity); e.g., "$P \equiv Q$" says that the properties P and Q, although they may not be identical, nevertheless have the same extension. On the other hand, "$P \mathrel{\underline{\equiv}} Q$" says that the properties P and Q are themselves identical (strict identity). The latter sign can be defined as follows (comp. [Meaning], 39-6):

(9) $(x^n_1 \mathrel{\underline{\equiv}} x^n_2) =_{\mathrm{Df}} N\,(x^n_1 \equiv x^n_2)$.

The rules of interchange for the two signs are different:

(10) On the basis of a sentence with "$\equiv$" as the principal connective, the two components are interchangeable in *every non-modal context.*

(11) On the basis of a sentence with "$\mathrel{\underline{\equiv}}$" as the principal connective, the two components are L-interchangeable *in any context.*

Two entities are materially identical just in case they have all *non-modal* properties in common; they are strictly identical just in case they have *all* properties in common, including the modal properties. Consequently, in language L_3, in which both modal and non-modal properties are among the values of the variables, the following two theorems hold:

(12) $(x^n_1 \equiv x^n_2) \equiv (x^{n+1})\ [Extl(x^{n+1}) \supset [x^{n+1}(x^n_1) \supset x^{n+1}(x^n_2)]]$.

(13) $(x^n_1 \mathrel{\underline{\equiv}} x^n_2) \equiv (x^{n+1})[x^{n+1}(x^n_1) \supset x^{n+1}(x^n_2)]$.

("$\mathrel{\underline{\equiv}}$" between individual or class expressions could be defined by the right-hand side of (13).)

Ruth Barcan Marcus[12] defined two identity concepts I_m and I, which were apparently intended to explicate material identity and strict identity, respectively. She found, however, that on the basis of her definitions the two concepts are strictly equivalent to each other. This result seemed surprising; other authors also found it paradoxical, among them Prior[13] and Feys (in his essay, § 10c). But the result should be quite obvious. For I_m was defined, by means of an unrestricted predicate variable, as holding between entities having *all* properties in common. Thus, by (13), I_m is

[12] Ruth C. Barcan, "The Identity of Individuals . . .", *J. Symb. Logic,* XII (1947), 12-15.

[13] Arthur N. Prior, *Formal Logic* (Oxford, 1955), 205.

not, as intended, material identity, but strict identity. The relation I was then defined, in effect, as holding whenever the relation I_m holds necessarily. And this is, of course, again strict identity, since "$N(x_1 \equiv x_2)$" is L-equivalent to "$x_1 \equiv x_2$".

IV. Translation of a modal language into an extensional language. The term "translation" is here meant in the weak sense of a transformation of every sentence into an L-equivalent one. In the strong sense of translation, the transformation of every sentence into a synonymous one or the transformation of every *designator* into an L-equivalent one, a translation of a modal language into an extensional language is obviously impossible, since in an extensional language there can be no designator L-equivalent to "N".

I shall here mainly discuss the problem of the translation of the simpler modal language L_2 into L_1. A translation of L_2 into the extensional metalanguage M is already at hand. Let S_1 be an arbitrary sentence in L_2. On the basis of the rules of truth for L_2, there is a sentence in M of the form "S_1 is true in L_2 if and only if - - -", which follows from the rules and therefore is L-true in M. Thus the last component "- - -" is a sentence in M which is L-equivalent to S_1 in L_2. However, "- - -" may contain semantical terms like "model", "value assignment", "variable", "substitution instance", "true", "L-true", and the like; and this is not the kind of translation we are looking for. Nevertheless this is a translation into an extensional language. In view of this fact, I thought that a translation into the extensional *object language* L_1 should also be possible. And I have indeed constructed effective rules which for any sentence in L_2 yield a sentence in L_1 L-equivalent to the former.

I shall now indicate the basic ideas of the translation of L_2 into L_1.[14] If no modal sign occurs, the translation is simple:

(14) A sentence in L_2 without modal signs is L-equivalent to the same sentence in L_1.

This simple rule holds in this case because in L_2 only non-modal intensions occur. The two sentences in L_2 and L_1 hold in the same models and therefore have the same content, i.e., give the same factual information.

The real problem of the translation concerns sentences with modal signs and variables. The values of the variables v^n in L_2 are the extensional I^n. There is a one-one correspondence between the I^n and certain concepts which we shall call the corresponding *quasi-intensions for n* ($QI^{(n)}$), because they may be taken in a certain way as representatives of

[14]These basic ideas (but not the system of the rules of translation themselves) are given in my *Notes* [1955-4].

the intensions. The $QI^{(n)}$ are extensions not of type n but of a higher type. Since they are extensions, they are expressible in L_1. As mentioned earlier, any model for L_1 or L_2 can be represented as a certain k-tuple of classes; and this can in turn be represented as a class of a higher type, say m. Thus every model is represented by an E^m. A proposition can be represented as a class of models, and hence as an E^{m+1}. We now take these classes E^{m+1} as the $QI^{(s)}$, i.e., as QI for propositions. Furthermore, according to the earlier explanations on L_2 (in II above), an extensional I^n, thus any I^n of L_2, can be represented by a function from models to E^n, thus as a class of pairs of the kind $<e^m, e^n>$, where e^m is an E^m and e^n is an E^n. These classes are now taken as $QI^{(n)}$.

The two main problems of the translation concern the variables and the modal sign "N". Let S_2 be a universal sentence in L_2 of the form (v_i^n) (A_j); S_2 says that all I^n of L_2 satisfy the condition expressed by the operand A_j. This means that all $QI^{(n)}$ satisfy a certain corresponding condition. Therefore the universal sentence S_2 of L_2 can be translated into a universal sentence of L_1 with a quantifier containing a variable of the type of the $QI^{(n)}$ and with a modified operand. Further, let S_3 be a sentence in L_2 of the form $N(S_4)$. This sentence says that the proposition expressed by the operand S_4 is necessary, and this means that it holds in all models. Therefore the modal sentence S_3 can be translated into a sentence of L_1 which says that every model satisfies a certain condition. The latter sentence is a universal sentence in L_1 with a quantifier containing a v^m and with an appropriately modified operand.

The basic ideas for the translation of the richer modal language L_3 into L_1 are essentially the same. For the intensions I^n in L_3, the corresponding quasi-intensions $QI^{(n)}$ are again defined as certain classes of a higher type. These definitions and the rules for the translation are similar but more complicated than those for L_2.

The translation of a modal language into an extensional one provides an extensional interpretation of the concepts of logical modalities and of intensions. It is thereby shown that these controversial concepts are unobjectionable and acceptable even to those philosophers who profess to understand only an extensional language, provided they are willing to admit class variables of higher types.

I believe that the informal thinking of the great majority of philosophers and scientists proceeds in terms of intensions, e.g., properties and propositions. It is true that the scientists usually do not use the term "proposition" in this sense, but when they speak of possible cases, events, experimental results, distributions of the electric field or the like, they thereby mean what we call propositions. On the other hand, I agree that the suspicion with which some philosophers and logicians look at intensions had a certain justification as long as no clear and exact explication was given. I myself was previously suspicious of various concepts for similar reasons, e.g., of the concepts of truth and of logical probability. The same held for the concept of intension until I found at least the basic ideas of an interpretation of modalities and intensions as indicated in [Meaning], which gave me the confidence that an exact explication should be possible. This explication, which can only be indicated here, consists in the construction of the comprehensive modal languages L_2 and L_3, whose rules are formulated in an extensional metalanguage, and further in the translations of these modal languages into the extensional language L_1. It seems to me that with this explication the scepticism with respect to intensions loses its basis.

V. Translation of an extensional language into a modal language. As in IV, "translation" is meant here in the weak sense of L-equivalance. The translation of L_1 into L_2 is simple:

(15) Every sentence of L_1 is L-equivalent to the same sentence in L_2. (From (14).)

Translation of L_1 into L_3 is more difficult. We begin with:

(16) A sentence of L_2 without modal signs and without variables is L-equivalent to the same sentence in L_3.

This holds because the intensions of the designators which occur in L_2 are also non-modal intensions in L_3. From (15) and (16) we obtain:

(17) Every sentence of L_1 without variables is L-equivalent to the same sentence in L_3.

It can easily be seen that a sentence without variables in L_1 holds in the same models and thus has the same content as the same sentence in L_3.

The critical problem concerns the translation of sentences with variables, since the values of variables in L_1 are extensions, but those in L_3 are intensions (including modal intensions). I shall illustrate the basic idea of the translation by an example of simplest form, viz., a universal sentence S_2 in L_1 of the form $(v_i^n)(A_j)$, where the operand A_j contains no quantifiers or operators. According to (15), S_2 in L_1 is L-equivalent to the same sentence S_2 in L_2. I shall now show how S_2 in L_2 can be translated into a sentence of L_3. S_2 in L_2 says that all *non-modal* I^n satisfy the condition expressed by A_j; let this condition be C. First we take the case that $n = 0$. In this case, S_2 in L_2 is simply translated into S_2 in L_3, because the values of the v^0 are non-modal intensions in L_3 also. Therefore we have:

(18) A sentence in L_1 of the form S_2 with $n = 0$ is L-equivalent to the same sentence in L_2 and in L_3.

There remains the case that $n>0$. In this case S_2 in L_3 says that all I^n, both non-modal and modal intensions, satisfy the condition C; this is obviously a stronger statement than S_2 in L_2. We have previously defined the concept of a non-modal (extensional) property (see definition (8) in

II). Using this concept, the sentence S_2 in L_2 can be translated into the following sentence of L_3:

(19) $(v^n)[Extl^{n+1}(v^n) \supset A_j]$.

The philosophical importance of the result that the extensional language L_1 is translatable into the modal language L_3 lies in the fact that this result refutes the view that in a language like L_3, where the values of the variables are intensions, the extensions, both individuals and classes of various types, are abandoned or repudiated. Quine originally expressed this view (see the quotation in [Meaning] p. 197). I am not certain of his present opinion. In a conversation in 1949, I understood him to say that he did no longer maintain the previous view since classes are definable in terms of properties (as in *Principia Mathematica*); but he still rejected intensional variables and intensions for other reasons. Later I was surprised to find that he repeated the old assertion.[15] Davidson also expresses the view that extensions are abandoned (in § II of his essay). Further he discusses (in § III) the question of how individuals and other extensions can be dealt with in a modal language. The answer to this question is supplied by the translation of L_1 into L_3. Davidson says in this context that in a modal language an apparently singular sentence like "*Hs*" ("Scott is human") is a disguised universal sentence. But this is not the case; Davidson's transformation is correct, but it shows only the obvious result that the singular sentence is L-equivalent to some universal sentence. A singular sentence in L_3, e.g., "$B(3)$", is genuinely singular, as can be seen from (17); just as the same sentence in L_1, it says simply that the position 3 is blue.

VI. The logic of senses and synonymy. Two designators have the same *sense* (this term understood as with Frege and Church) if they are synonymous. *Synonymy* is here taken as a semantical relation considerably stronger than L-equivalence. In analogy to (5) we have here:

(20) L is a *language of senses,* if L satisfies the following conditions:

- (a) L contains sense-variables, i.e., variables whose values are senses.
- (b) L contains a binary connective for sentences and other designators, say "$=$", such that a sentence containing this symbol as its principal connective is true if and only if the two components are synonymous, i.e., have the same sense. This connective therefore is a symbol for the *identity of senses.*
- (c) Synonymous designators are L-interchangeable in any context.

[15] W. V. Quine, *From a Logical Point of View* (1953), 153ff.

(21) *A logic of senses* is a system of logical rules for a language of senses.

In a language of this kind, we may have semantical rules to the effect that *direct synonymy* holds for certain pairs of designators. (Explicit definitions may be included among these rules of direct synonymy.) We can then define synonymy itself as follows:

(22) The designator D_i is synonymous with the designator D_j if and only if D_i is formed from D_j by replacing designators with directly synonymous designators.

VII. Belief-sentences. Two different methods have been proposed for the reconstruction in a formalized language of belief-sentences like "The person *a* believes that the thing *b* is green".

Method 1. Belief is reconstructed as a relation B_1 between a person and a non-linguistic entity (usually called "proposition"). Example: "$B_1(a, Gb)$", where "Gb" stands for "b is green".

Method 2. Belief is taken as a relation B_2 between a person and a sentence. Example: "$B_2(a, S_1)$", where "S_1" is a name of the sentence "Gb".

In method 1, which is used by Frege and Church, the belief-sentences belong to the object language, but a non-extensional object language is required. This method uses indirect discourse, and is thus closer than method 2 to ordinary language. In method 2, which I proposed earlier (in [Meaning] §15), the belief-sentences belong to the metalanguage *M*, which may be an extensional language. Both methods now seem to me acceptable (see [1955-1]). Only after further investigations have been made, shall we be in a position to judge which of the two methods has greater advantages.

A choice must still be made, in both methods, of the criterion for the identity of beliefs, i.e., the condition of L-interchangeability of the second argument of the relation B_1 or B_2.

Method 1a. Synonymous belief-clauses are L-interchangeable in a B_1- sentence; thus the following holds (i.e., is L-true or A-true):

(23) $B_1(x,p) \cdot (p = q) \supset B_1(x,q)$.

Method 1b. L-equivalent belief-clauses are L-interchangeable in a B_1- sentence; thus the following holds:

(24) $B_1(x,p \cdot (p \equiv q) \supset B_1(x,q)$.

In method 1a, a logic of senses is needed for the belief-sentences; the second-place members of the belief relation are senses of type *s* (called "propositions" by Church). In method 1b, a logic of intensions is used;

the second-place members are intensions of type *s* (called "propositions" by me).

Analogously for method 2; in *method 2a,* the following holds in M:

(25) If $B_2(x,S_i)$ and S_i is *synonymous* with S_j, then $B_2(x,S_j)$.

Similarly in *method 2b:*

(26) If $B_2(x,S_i)$ and S_i is *L-equivalent* to S_j, then $B_2(x,S_j)$.

To the best of my knowledge, up to now only form (a) has been taken into consideration: Church has used 1a, and I have used 2a. However, I believe that form (b) is well worth closer investigation, with both methods, although it deviates more than form (a) from ordinary language.

VIII. Comparison of the logic of intensions and the logic of senses. As I see it, the concept of intension is more important and more fundamental than that of sense. The concept of intension and the corresponding semantical concepts like L-equivalence and L-truth are basic for both deductive logic and mathematics; and in my view also for inductive logic and for the semantical theory of information (comp. [1953-3]). As far as I am aware at the present time, the concept of sense and the corresponding semantical concept of synonymy are used only with respect to certain psychological sentences about so-called epistemic attitudes like belief, doubt, assertion, and the like. These concepts may thus possibly be useful for the theory of knowledge. But, even for these sentences, there are other possible methods (methods 1b and 2b in VII) which avoid the logic of senses, although, to be sure, it is not yet certain whether these methods are entirely adequate.

Today opinions differ on the question whether a logic of intensions or a logic of senses is intuitively clearer or, to put it in terms of semantics, whether logical equivalence or synonymy is intuitively clearer (as an explicandum, before explicit rules are given). I personally find the former clearer. Suppose that each of two sentences in one of the customary formalized languages whose symbols I understand is derivable from the other. If there is a disagreement over the question whether the two sentences can be regarded as logically equivalent in a pre-systematic sense (e.g., disagreement arising because one of the forms of inference used in the derivation is accepted in classical logic but rejected by intuitionism), then in most cases I can decide whether the relation of logical equivalence, as I understand it intuitively, does or does not hold. However, with respect to synonymy the situation is quite different. For example, it is clear to me that two sentences of the forms "$\sim(x)(Px \supset Qx)$" and "$(\exists x)(Px \cdot \sim Qx)$" are not synonymous in the present strong sense of "synonymy", although they are logically equivalent. On the other hand, I am not able to decide whether or not the two sentences "the thing *b* is green and round" and "the thing *b* is round and green" are synonymous and therefore L-interchangeable as clauses in a belief-sentence or in an assertion-sentence. The sentences are accepted as synonymous in ordinary language, even in its most careful use of indirect discourse, for example, in the statement of a witness under oath. On the other hand, Church does not regard them as synonymous. Either of the two views seems acceptable to me. In other words, I have no clear understanding of "synonymy" as an explicandum; the choice of the boundary line seems quite arbitrary. Explicanda, even important ones, have frequently a vagueness of this kind; my intention is not, to deny the usefulness of an explication of the concept of synonymy, but only to point out the lack of intuitive clarity of the explicandum.

10. My Conception of Semantics

I shall briefly describe here the kinds of semantical rules which I would use today for object languages like L_1, L_2, and L_3 (§9, I and II).[16]

I. The extensional metalangauge for semantics M^e. M^e is an extensional language (§9,I). In M^e, semantical rules of the following kinds are formulated for an object language L.

A. The rules of formation give, in the customary way, a recursive definition of "sentential formula in L" and "sentence in L" (and possibly of other kinds of designator formulas and designators).

B. The rules for relative designation give a recursive definition for the relation Des^e_{qr} (where "q" and "r" are variables). A semantical sentence of the form

(1)"$Des^e_{qr}(D_i,E_j)$"

says that the designator formula D_i has the designatum^e (i.e., the extension) E_j relative to the model Mod_q and to the value assignment VA_r. (For the concepts of model and value assignment, see above § 9 I, (3) and (4); for a more general concept of model see II below. As a convenient alternative procedure, the functor "des^e_{qr}" may be used; in which case (1) would be replaced by "$des^e_{qr}(D_i) \equiv E_j$".) For sentences and other closed designators, the value assignment VA_r is irrelevant and the relation is reduced to Des^e_q.

C. The rules of direct designation assign to every primitive descriptive constant in L a designatum of the same type. For example, the rule

(2) "$DDes^e(c_1,Blue)$"

says that the direct designatum of the constant c_1 is the class Blue, i.e., the class of those positions which are blue. By these rules an interpretation of the constants is given (comp. II); for example, the rule (2) says

[16]Rules of the subsequently described kinds for these languages are not contained in my prior publications. But the rules for L_1 (there called "L_3") are completely stated in the *Notes on Semantics* [1955-4].

that the constant c_1 has the meaning Blue. According to the definition of "model" for languages like L_1 (§9 I (3)), the relation $DDes^e$ is a certain descriptively defined model; we may call it *the true model.* Now we define the proper (i.e., non-relative) concept of designation, Des^e. This is defined as designation relative to the true model:

(3) $Des^e =_{Df} Des^e_q$, where Mod_q is the model $DDes^e$.

D. Definition of truth:

(4) An expression A_i is *true* in language $L =_{Df}$ there is a p such that $Des^e(A_i,p)$ and p.

This definition can be stated in general semantics; it is applicable to any language L for which a relation Des^e is defined which includes sentences in its domain.

The form (4) of the definition of truth (which is essentially the same form I gave in [1942-2] D17-C1) refutes the objection sometimes made to the effect that the semantical definition of truth is not general but is given by an enumeration of single cases. Definition (4) presupposes the relations Des^e and $DDes^e$. "Des^e" is also defined in a general form by (3). Only the rules C for "$DDes^e$", as e.g. rule (2), proceed by enumeration; they constitute, so to speak, the dictionary for the primitive constants. And a dictionary, e. g., a German-English dictionary, can usually be given only with the help of an enumeration, not by general rules alone.

E. If logical dependencies hold between the meanings of the primitive descriptive constants of L (which meanings may either be determined by rules C or just be intended informally but not yet stated by explicit rules), then those dependencies are expressed by a list of *meaning postulates* or *A-postulates* (comp. [1952-5]).

F. A model for L is called an *admissible model* if all A-postulates hold in it (i.e., have the truth-value T relative to it).

G. I use "A-true" as a technical term for "analytic" (i.e., logically true in the wider sense). It is defined as follows:

(5) A sentence S is *A-true* in $L =_{Df} S$ holds in all admissible models. This definition can be stated in general semantics.

(6) Theorem. Every A-true sentence in L is true in L.

E and F serve as preparatory steps for G. The rules E, F, and G may be stated before the rules C are stated. This is possible because, for the determination of A-truth, it is not necessary to know the specific meanings of the primitive descriptive constants; it is sufficient to know the logical relations between these meanings (if such relations hold).

II. Models, model structures, and interpretations. It is important to distinguish between these three concepts; unfortunately, for each of them the term "model" is sometimes used. A *model* for a language (in the extensional sense of "model" customary in mathematics, as in the definitions by Tarski, Kemeny, and others) is an assignment of extensions of the following kind: To every type of variables a class of entities of this type is assigned as the range of values, and to every primitive constant of the type system an extension of the same type is assigned. [Sometimes the ranges of values for the kinds of variables and the extensions of the *logical* constants of a language are presupposed as fixed for all models, and therefore in the specification of a model only the extensions assigned to the primitive *descriptive* constants of the language are given. Thus, e.g., I have presupposed in §9 I that, for all models, the values of the variables v^o in L_1 are the natural numbers and the values of the variables v^n for $n > 0$ are the classes of type n based on the natural numbers; furthermore, the extensions of the *logical* constants of the type system (e.g., "0") are fixed by the rules B in the same way for all models. Therefore in the definition of "model" for L_1 (definition (3) in §9 I) I refer only to the primitive *descriptive* constants.]

Two isomorphic models are said to have the same structure. Therefore a *model structure* can be defined as the class of the models isomorphic to a given model.[17]

To give an *interpretation* for a language (or for an axiom system) is to assign meanings to the signs and sentences, either formally by explicit semantical rules or informally by non-technical indications of any form. An interpretation should not be identified with a model, as is sometimes done. It is true that an interpretation can be given by the specification of a model. But there is no one-one correspondence between interpretations and models; two different (i.e., not logically equivalent) descriptions of the *same* model represent two *different* interpretations. In order to illustrate the distinction by some examples, let us suppose that the language L_1 (§9 I) contains as primitive predicates just two one-place predicates of type 1. We assume as before that the domain of individuals is the class of natural numbers, used as coordinates of spatial positions at a given time; each position has certain observable qualities like colors and the like. Now we define for this language some models as ordered pairs of classes:

(7) (a) $Mod_1 =_{\text{Df}} \langle Blue, Red \rangle$,
(b) $Mod_2 =_{\text{Df}} \langle Blue, Red\text{-}or\text{-}(Blue\text{-}and\text{-}Hot) \rangle$,
(c) $Mod_3 =_{\text{Df}} \langle \{2,8,10\},\{3,9\} \rangle$,
(d) $Mod_4 =_{\text{Df}} \langle \{2,3,4\},\{6,8\} \rangle$.

[17]For more exact definitions, especially with respect to axiom systems, see Carnap and Bachmann [1936-9].

First we see without factual information that the models Mod_3 and Mod_4 are isomorphic. The class of all those models (including Mod_3 and Mod_4) in which the first class contains three elements and the second class two other elements, is a model structure. Now let us suppose that, as a matter of fact, just the positions 2, 8, and 10 are blue, and just the positions 3 and 9 are red, and that no position is both blue and hot. Then the class *Blue-and-Hot* is empty, and therefore the models Mod_1 and Mod_2 are identical. However, since the definientia in the definitions (a) and (b) are not logically equivalent, they describe two different interpretations. In the first interpretation, the second predicate has the meaning Red, but in the second interpretation it has the meaning *Red*-or-*(Blue-and-Hot)*. Even if we do not wish to speak of meanings, but formulate the interpretations by rules of direct designation in the extensional metalanguage M^e, there is still a difference between the two interpretations. For the first interpretation the following sentence (a) is taken as a rule, but for the second interpretation the sentence (b) is taken:

(8) (a) "$DDes^e(c_2, Red)$".

(b) "$DDes^e(c_2, Red\text{-or-}(Blue\text{-and-}Hot)$".

These two sentences (a) and (b) are materially equivalent, but not logically equivalent. Therefore a semantical system which contains (a) as a rule is different from a system which instead takes (b) as a rule.

On the basis of our earlier factual assumptions, Mod_3 is also identical with Mod_1 and Mod_2. In a certain sense, the definition (7)(c) also gives an interpretation. According to this interpretation, c_1 is L-equivalent to "$\{2,8,10\}$" and hence to "$(\lambda x)\,[(x \equiv 2) \vee (x \equiv 8) \vee (x \equiv 10)]$"; thus c_1 is a *logical* constant, and so is c_2. Therefore this interpretation would not be of the kind we intended for language L_1, since c_1 and c_2 are to be *descriptive* predicates according to our description of L_1.

III. Non-extensional metalanguages for semantics. Today I would distinguish two non-extensional metalanguages, M^i and M^s.[18] M^i is an intensional language (§9 II). In M^i we have (instead of Des^e) the relation Des^i between a designator and its designatum^i, i.e., its intension, and further the relations Des^i_{qr}, Des^i_q, *and* $DDes^i$. The models, the A-postulates, and the admissible models are the same as in M^e. Furthermore we have in M^i rules and definitions analogous to those of the kinds A, C, (3), (4), and (5) in M^e (but with the superscript "*e*" replaced by "*i*"). The form of the rules B for relative designation depends upon the structure of the object language. For a modal object language these rules are simpler in M^i than in M^e.

[18]These two metalanguages are briefly described and the form of semantical rules in these languages (but not the rules themselves) for a simple object language are given in the *Notes* [1955-4].

A formalized metalanguage of the form M^i has not yet been constructed. But it can easily be formed from the intensional language L_2 (indicated without formal construction in §9 II) by the addition of some customary notations for spelling and of two-place predicates "$Des^{i,o}$" for type 0, "$Des^{i,1}$" for type 1, etc.; "$Des^{i,o}_{qr}$", etc.; "$DDes^{i,o}$", etc.

The metalanguage M^s is a language of senses (§ 9VI), in which we have the two place predicates "$Des^{s,o}$", etc. The relation $Des^{s,o}$ holds between a designator of type 0 and its designatum^s, i.e., its sense.

IV. Comparison of the metalanguages M^e and M^i. I shall not consider here the language M^s because at the present time I do not see sufficient reasons for accepting the greater complications of a language of senses (comp. §9 VIII).

Each of the languages M^e and M^i has certain advantages, just as do extensional languages and intensional languages in general. It is possible to use only the metalanguage M^e, since even the rules for the modal languages L_2 and L_3 can be formulated in M^e. And since the structure of M^e is simpler than that of M^i, and also more customary in contemporary formal logic (though not in ordinary thinking, I believe), it is easily understandable that up to now a metalanguage of the kind M^e has been preferred by most logicians.

In my own investigations I sometimes use M^e and sometimes M^i. My informal thinking about languages frequently proceeds in terms of intensions, e.g., properties, propositions, and the like, and in recent times I have preferred such methods. If I then want to go over from such informal reasoning to more exact formulations in a metalanguage, it is easier to use a language like M^i than one like M^e. For example, suppose I think informally the following:

(9) "The word 'Einhorn' in German means unicorn; it does not mean goblin".

Now let us take "*E*" as short for "The word 'Einhorn' in German". Then in M^e, on the basis of the rule

(10) "$DDes^e$ (*E, Unicorn*)",

the following result holds:

(11) "Des^e (*E, Unicorn*) and Des^e (*E, Goblin*)",

since "*Unicorn*" and "*Goblin*" have the same extension (comp. [1955-3] § 3) and therefore are interchangeable in an extensional language like M^e. In M^i, on the other hand, the following holds:

(12) "Des^i (*E, Unicorn*) and not Des^i (*E, Goblin*)".

And this corresponds exactly to the informal thought (9). A comparison of (12) with (11) shows clearly that "Des^i", but not "Des^e", is similar to the customary usage of the word "designates" or "means".

V. The meaningfulness of semantics. We may divide semantics into two parts, the semantics of extensions and that of intensions (or, more generally, of non-extensional concepts). The former deals with concepts like extension, name-relation, denotation, satisfaction, truth, and the like. The latter deals with concepts like intension, L-truth, sense, synonymy, and the like. Some logicians reject all concepts of the second kind as unclear and incomprehensible, e.g., Quine, who calls the first part "theory of reference" and the second part "theory of meaning".

We shall later (in § 24A) distinguish three concentric languages: the observation language, the (logically) extended observation language, and the full language which also contains theoretical terms. It might perhaps be useful to distinguish three corresponding fields of semantics: *elementary semantics*, (logically) *extended semantics*, and *theoretical semantics*. Elementary semantics is, like the observation language, meaningful and understood in the strictest sense. Extended semantics may be regarded as meaningful in a wider sense, provided sentences with abstract variables (for classes, classes of classes, etc.) are taken to be intelligible. For theoretical semantics, just as for theoretical physics, there is only an incomplete interpretation. For extended semantics we may just as well use an intensional metalanguage, e.g., M^i, as an extensional one. From the point of view of meaningfulness there is no difference, since the former language is translatable into the latter. Therefore the semantics of intensions is here just as legitimate as that of extensions.

If the semantical rules for a given object language are intended to supply information about the interpretation of the object language, then the semantics language itself must be understood. The question as to which kinds of terms are to be regarded as understandable in a narrower sense and which as understandable in a wider sense is not yet sufficiently clarified.

In *pragmatics* we might make similar distinctions. As I indicated in [1955-1] and [1955-6], it seems advisable to introduce some basic concepts of pragmatics as theoretical concepts. This procedure would lead to theoretical pragmatics.

11. Robert Feys on Modalities

In the first part of his essay Feys gives a clear informal exposition of my conception of the logic of modalities. In the second part (§§8-10) he makes critical remarks, points out certain difficulties and unsolved problems, and explains the possibility of other approaches.

My modal propositional calculus corresponds to C. I. Lewis' system S5. Feys mentions (in §8) other interpretations of the logical modalities which would lead to Lewis' system S4. These interpretations are certainly interesting. Especially from an intuitionist point of view, an interpretation of this kind and thus the system form S4 may appear as preferable. However, if our aim is to construct a system of modal logic corresponding to the classical non-intuitionist conception of logic, then the system form S5 seems preferable to me. In the latter case my interpretation, which is based on the correspondence of the modalities with semantical L-concepts, seems to be the most natural one among those which have been proposed so far.

Feys points out correctly that a sharp distinction between logical and factual truth is an essential feature of my conception of semantics and modal logic. He mentions the controversy concerning this problem and declares that he himself is inclined to reject this sharp distinction in a way similar to Tarski, Beth, and Quine. This is an important problem which I discuss in detail elsewhere (see §15, compare also the Autobiography §10).

Feys revives (in §9) the controversy about the alleged paradoxical features of strict implication. Earlier ([1942-2] pp. 65f.) I gave arguments in support of my views that (1) these controversial features depend upon our understanding of the term "logical implication" in a narrower or a wider sense; and (2), if the term is interpreted so as to include the controversial cases (which I represented at the place cited by the postulates P14-14 and P14-15), then the theory of logical deduction becomes considerably simpler than if we exclude these cases. I also referred there to the discussions by Lewis[19] in which he shows that the controversial features actually correspond to the customary classical conception of logical deducibility. Lewis emphasizes that he understands by "deducibility" the *general* concept "deducible by *some* valid mode of inference" in distinction to "logistic deducibility". In view of these statements by Lewis I am inclined to doubt Feys' assertion that Lewis' starting point was the conception that strict implication should correspond to "the syntactical relation of consequence"; I assume that Feys means by the latter phrase derivability in a given calculus. Feys does not discuss either Lewis' or my arguments. Nor have I found in the writings of any other author convincing arguments for the view that the features in question are paradoxical.

Feys also raises the problem of the explication of "if . . ., then . . .", which is certainly important and interesting. However, I was under the impression that there was now fairly general agreement that it is not possible to render adequately the conditional sentences of natural languages in any of the following ways: by material implication, by logical implication (be it L-implication in the metalanguage or strict implication in a modal object language), or by a syntactical relation of deriva-

[19] C. I. Lewis and C. H. Langford, *Symbolic Logic,* 174f., 248ff.

bility in a logical calculus (be it of classical form or of a restricted, e.g., intuitionist form).

At the end of §9 Feys raises the question whether we have to presume "that there is no such thing as an absolute concept of logical consequence, but only a syntactical concept of consequence with respect to various equally acceptable systems". This is a serious and difficult problem, and presumably nobody is today in a position to give a conclusive answer. My feeling on this question is not as pessimistic as that of Feys and other logicians and mathematicians. It is clear that from an intuitionist point of view this sceptical position is inevitable. Furthermore we know from Gödel's result that a general concept of logical consequence cannot be defined constructively. But this does not exclude the possibility, and at the present moment I see no reason for abandoning the hope, that a satisfactory modal logic may be constructed in the future in which the symbol of strict implication can be interpreted in an unrestricted sense, i.e., not restricted by reference to constructively specified rules of deduction.

The problems which Feys discusses in the last section of his essay are indeed serious, and I would agree that they must be solved if a satisfactory system of modal logic is to be constructed. But I believe that none of these difficulties is insuperable and that they are indeed solved in the modal language L_3, whose main features I have briefly indicated in §9.

Feys' first problem (a,b) concerns the status of non-modal expressions in a modal language. Any sentence in the modal language L_3 without modal signs and without variables is L-equivalent to the same sentence in the extensional language L_1 (§9, V (17)). Therefore Feys' example sentence "*Mj*" has the same meaning in a modal language as in an extentional one, namely that John is a man. Thus the sentence is entirely unambiguous, and there is no need for a special symbol designating the actual case. Similarly there is no difference in meaning in L_1 and L_3 for a sentence like "$P \equiv M$" (or for the L-equivalent sentence "(x) $(Px \equiv Mx)$"), provided the predicates "*P*" and "*M*" are either primitive or defined by non-modal expressions. Since "*x*" is a variable of type 0, the universal sentence "(x) $(Px \equiv Mx)$" as a sentence in L_3 is L-equivalent to the same sentence in L_1 (§9, V (18)). Thus this sentence is likewise entirely unambiguous.

In L_3 the predicate "*M*" and the corresponding abstract expression (which I write "(λx) (Mx)") are L-equivalent. They are unambiguous non-modal expressions of the modal object language, and both have the same intension. If one wishes to say that the intension of each of the two expressions is the property of being a man, this must of course, be formulated in the metalanguage.

Feys discusses (in §10c) the problem of the two concepts of identity and the alleged result that factual (or material) identity coincides with necessary (or strict) identity. I have explained my position on this question in §9 III.

Feys analyzes (in § 10d) the sentences "*NAy*" and "$(\hat{x}NAx)y$". I presume that they correspond to the sentences "*NPc*" and "$[(\lambda x)(NPx)](c)$" in my notation (in [Meaning], and similarly in the language L_3), where "*P*" is a predicate, either primitive or defined (non-modal) and "*c*" is an individual constant, either primitive or defined by a non-modal description. In my languages these two sentences are L-equivalent by virtue of the customary rule of λ-conversion. This seems to me to be in agreement with the customary interpretation; at least in my pre-systematic understanding the following sentences have the same meaning: "*c* has the property of necessarily being a P" and "*c* is necessarily a *P*", i.e., "It is necessary that *c* is a *P*". Feys indicates an interpretation by which the two sentences would not be L-equivalent. I do not clearly understand his remarks on this point. He also says that the second sentence is "modally ambiguous". According to my conception the sentence is entirely unambiguous. At the present moment I do not see any reason which would make the abandonment of λ-conversion in a language like L_3 appear either as intuitively plausible or as technically expedient. Feys does not indicate what other rule he would propose to replace the conversion rule.

I agree with Feys that modal individual concepts and modal properties involve particular problems and difficulties. For this reason I have excluded modal individual descriptions (as I did in [Meaning]) and modal λ-expressions from the language L_2. The language L_3, which contains expressions of the latter kind and also predicate variables for which such expressions are substitutable, is indeed considerably more complicated. But the customary rule of λ-conversion also holds in L_3. Thus, in contrast to the system considered by Feys, for the system of modal logic in L_3 it is not the case that it "represents a greater departure from logical common sense than had been supposed hitherto". Nor is it the case for L_3 that "the assertion of a fact becomes ambiguous and hence may no more be handled simply as hard fact". This is seen from my earlier comments on Feys' examples like "*Mj*".

12. *John Myhill on Modal Logic and Semantics*

A. Myhill's objections. Myhill begins his first section by stating three objections against the methods in semantics and modal logic presented in my book [Meaning]. His formulations of the first two objections are very brief, and on these two points I cannot agree with him. The first criticism concerns individual concepts; I shall later reply to this. With respect to the second, which deals with the problem of belief-sentences, see my explanations above, in §9 VII.

The most important of Myhill's objections is the third, which he discusses in detail. I think that on this point Myhill is right. In my book [Meaning] I made the following suggestion. I considered an extension of the language system S_2, which is there explained in detail and which contains only individual variables, to a system S which also contains property variables, e.g. "f". According to my proposal (in [Meaning] p. 182), a property, i.e., a value of these variables, may be represented by an assignment of ranges (classes of state-descriptions) to the individual constants. Myhill points out that this choice of values is too narrow because it does not include modal properties, e.g., the property designated by "$(\lambda x)\ (N(x \equiv a))$". I suppose that my intention in the book was to admit λ-expressions containing "N"; thus my suggestion was not in accord with the intended interpretation. My proposal occurs in the book not within the description of my modal system, but only among the "incidental remarks" in the last paragraph of §40. Therefore one may simply delete my suggestion, or replace it by a more suitable one, without changing anything else in the book. In particular, this error has no influence at all on my general conception of modalities or on the semantical methods discussed in my book.

I have briefly indicated above (in §9 II) two modal languages L_2 and L_3. The specification of the values of property variables of type 1 for L_2 corresponds essentially to the above mentioned proposal in my book. But for language L_2 this choice of values is suitable, because in this language λ-expressions containing "N", e.g., the one mentioned above, do not occur. In contrast, L_3 is sufficiently comprehensive to include λ-expressions of this kind. Therefore the characterization of the values of the variables v^1 in extensional terms, in other words, the definition of the quasi-intensions $QI^{(1)}$ for L_3 (§9 IV) is more complicated and will not be given here.

B. On the choice of a system of modal logic. Myhill has made some interesting remarks about certain possible forms for systems of modal logic. The choice of such a form depends on the answers to two kinds of questions. First there are theoretical questions. For example, the question whether, and in which way, it is possible to construct a modal system which possesses certain specified features. But there are also the practical questions of choosing the features that the system should have. In the discussion of practical questions, in contrast to that of theoretical questions, one cannot give compelling arguments. It is only possible to point out certain consequences of this or that choice (in other words, certain theoretical results), and then to declare one's own subjective preference.

Myhill prefers a modal system in which his principle of modal expression (*PME*) holds, so that his formula I is fulfilled. Myhill believes that this "is by far the most natural course". I am not quite convinced of this. I agree that the system constructed by Myhill, which is a modification of my earlier system *MFL* in [1946-1], is interesting and well worth further investigation. But so are, in my opinion, systems which abandon the principle *PME*. Although I myself had asserted a similar principle in my book ([Meaning] p.200, at the top), I subsequently found that it does not hold generally. It seems to me that in certain modal systems the meaning of a universal sentence with a predicate variable differs from the meaning of the same sentence in a non-modal system. (See the example, in §9 V, following (18), of the sentence S_2, which in L_3 is stronger than in L_2 and in L_1, since in L_3 it refers to *all* properties including modal properties.)

In Myhill's system of modal logic, the possibility of merely contingent identity of individuals is excluded so that his formula III holds. This system has the advantage of greater simplicity, just as my earlier system *MFL* did. On the other hand, it leads to certain features which I now regard as disadvantageous; this was my reason for abandoning *MFL* (see [Meaning] p.183 n.). The main disadvantage is the fact that descriptions are not taken as designators belonging to the system itself, but only as abbreviating devices. Hence the individual constants are the only closed individual expressions. I prefer systems, like L_2 and L_3, containing individual descriptions as designators for which universal instantiation is applicable, systems which therefore admit contingent identity of individuals (so that Myhill's formula III does not hold).

Myhill objects to my introduction of individual concepts as too artificial. I believe that the use of individual concepts appears artificial only because it is less familiar. It is by no means new; what Frege called the sense of an individual expression is similar to what I call an individual concept. It seems to me that assigning intensions to *all* expressions of the hierarchy of types leads to a greater uniformity of the semantical method, especially for language systems which admit compound individual expressions. In systems of this kind we cannot regard individuals as values of the variables. This is possible in Myhill's system only because of its special form.

Myhill's system also differs from my systems of modal logic by the occurrence of a stronger connective of identity "=". From his explanations of this sign it seems to me that he may have in mind a logic of senses (see §9 VI) rather than a logic of intensions. Both kinds of logical systems have certain advantages as I have explained earlier (§9 VII and VIII).

An interesting and valuable feature of Myhill's system is its extension to all finite levels. Today I would do the same, as in the languages L_2 and L_3.

13. Donald Davidson on Modalities and Semantics

I now share Davidson's view that my metalanguage M' (in [Meaning] ch. IV), which I called "neutral" with respect to the distinction between extensions and intensions, is in effect a language of intensions, as I have explained above (in §9 II). Davidson discusses (in §§ II and III) the questions whether by my use of intensions in semantics extensions have been abandoned and how extensions can be dealt with on the basis of my method. I have given my answers to these questions in §9 V.

Davidson compares (in § IV) the method of the name-relation with the method of extension and intension, which I proposed in my book and which I regarded as preferable to the name method. However, the latter judgment referred only to the original form of the name method, not to the form as modified by Frege and Church. It seems to me that today there is general agreement that the old unmodified method of the name-relation is untenable. The Frege-Church method makes significant changes. The development of my method was influenced by the Frege-Church conception. The distinction between these two methods is chiefly a question of practical convenience; I believe that the considerable complication of the Frege-Church method can be avoided. Davidson is right in saying that today my main doubts concerning the method of the name-relation are based on psychological consequences rather than logical consequences. For example, I presume that the erroneous conception which is also maintained by Davidson, that the modal language excludes individuals and other extensions, may be due to a way of thinking deriving from the old method of the name-relation in about this manner: Since in the modal language the designators are names of intensions and the values of the variables are intensions, this language cannot speak about extensions, such as individuals and classes.

In the course of a critical examination of my method of intension and extension, Davidson discusses (in § V) my solution of the paradox of analysis, in which I make use of the concept of intensional isomorphism. His objection to my solution is based on the view that this paradox is quite analogous to the paradox of identity. In both paradoxes, according to this view, what is changed is not the truth-value but only the significance, i.e., the character of being interesting and informative. I cannot agree. The transformation by replacement which leads to the paradox of identity does change the truth-value (see [Meaning] § 31). E.g., in Quine's example, from the true sentence "9 is necessarily greater than 7" we derive the false sentence "the number of planets is necessarily greater than 7". On the other hand, as Davidson has correctly stated, the transformation by replacement which leads to the paradox of analysis does not change the truth-value. Therefore the "complete analogy" between the two paradoxes, which Davidson asserts, does not hold. I think that this argument refutes his objection against my solution of the paradox of analysis.

In my view, the paradox of analysis is not at all similar to the other logical or semantical paradoxes. From what I just said it seems to me to follow that the paradox of analysis is not a genuine antinomy because no contradiction arises. It represents merely a puzzling situation, namely that a trivial L-true sentence is changed into a non-trivial sentence which is likewise L-true but nevertheless in a certain sense informative. Since this sentence is L-true, it cannot be informative in the strong, logical sense of "having a non-null logical content" ("content" to be understood in the sense explained in [1950-4] p.405 and [1953-3]). It is not even entirely clear what exactly is meant by the distinction between trivial and informative (or interesting). In view of the essential difference between the two paradoxes, there is no cogent reason for Davidson's view that the solution of the puzzle of analysis should be analogous to that of the antinomy of identity.

In his discussions of my analysis of belief-sentences, Davidson seems surprised by the fact that I do not deal with modal sentences and belief-sentences in analogous ways. I leave the former in the object language and introduce for their semantical analysis intensions in addition to extensions. For belief-sentences, on the other hand, I do not introduce a third kind of entities (say Church's senses), but I translate them into the metalanguage. In my discussion above (in §9 VII) this is method 2 as against method 1. As I see it today, this is again only a practical question of language engineering, and therefore ought to be solved according to such practical points of view as convenience and simplicity. As I have explained above, I am now inclined to regard the two methods 1 and 2 as both worthy of further investigation. At the beginning of §VI Davidson expresses his requirement in an even stronger way: "It might be contended not only that the analyses [of belief-sentences and of modalities] ought to be similar, but that they ought to be identical; this end could be achieved by rejecting altogether the distinction between the contexts created by belief-sentences and the contexts created by the modal operators". I have quite some sympathy with this end. According to my present conception, the best way to this end would be the method 1b, which takes belief as a relation between persons and propositional intensions. However, if one desires to use method 1a, then he must go beyond a merely modal language, or language of intensions, and adopt the more complicated language of senses.

I cannot agree with Davidson's views, expressed throughout the second paragraph of §VI, concerning my development and motivation in forming semantical concepts like L-truth and similar ones. It is correct that the concept of L-truth plays a fundamental role in my semantics. But the introduction of this concept together with the concept of state-descriptions on which it is based, was not motivated by the aim of giving a semantical analysis of modal languages with variables. At the time of the Vienna Circle we had already developed both concepts by a generalization of Wittgenstein's concepts of tautology and truth-possibilities, respectively. At that time we did not think of modalities or other intensional contexts. For logical empiricism the concept of logical truth was of great philosophical importance, even before it was explicated with respect to formalized languages, because with its help we could overcome one of the main obstacles in the way of empiricism, viz. the lack of a satisfactory account of the nature of logic and mathematics. I certainly do not hold the opinion that "one must know a great deal about what is actual in order to say what is possible". On the contrary, my interpretation of logical possibility and the other logical modalities is of such a kind that statements about them are entirely independent of any knowledge of the actual world.

The recognition of the importance of modal concepts came to me gradually. In my book on syntax I discussed them, but I did this chiefly out of tolerance for a heterodox language form. Only later did I see more and more clearly that this language form has great advantages. In contrast to our views in the Vienna Circle and to that maintained here by Davidson, I believe today that much of what is said by scientists and philosophers informally in ordinary language can be reconstructed in the most natural and most direct way in a language with modalities.

At the end of his essay Davidson raises an important general question of policy for the construction and analysis of a language. He says that the primary goal is "to interpret or rationally reconstruct the language we understand the best and need the most". I would agree with this if it means that the language of formal reconstruction must be such that it serves our needs in the best and most clearly understandable way; but I would not agree if the phrase "we understand the best" means that the language of reconstruction must be as close as possible to the customary form of ordinary language. Davidson thinks that a modal language can't be a candidate for rational reconstruction, because none has ever been constructed as an interpreted system. It is true that no such systems have so far been published. But I have given in the article [1946-1] and in my book [Meaning] the basic features of an interpretation. In the meantime I have constructed semantical systems for much more comprehensive modal languages (as indicated in §9 II); the semantical rules (not given there) provide an interpretation of the modal language in an extensional metalanguage. Finally I have also found a translation (indicated in §9 IV) by which an interpretation in terms of an extensional object language is given. However, I should like to emphasize that such a translation is not necessary for the reconstruction; rules for the use of a new language are sufficient for the purpose of reconstruction. For example, the language of physics (as a theoretical language) is used and understood although it cannot be translated into the ordinary observation language (without higher variables).

Davidson seems to hold the opinion that, if we wish to go beyond the extensional language to a non-extensional one, then the language of modalities would be less natural and less useful than the language with belief-sentences in indirect discourse, thus what I have called above the language of senses. My view is just the opposite of his, as I have explained in §9 VIII.

14. Richard Martin on Semantics

Martin in his essay not only gives a detailed exposition and critical discussion of my semantical method, as far as it is extensional, i.e., does not refer to intensions, but also makes many valuable comments and outlines developments on the basis of his own conception. With some of Martin's criticisms of my semantical theory I am entirely in agreement. Above all, he is certainly right that the metalanguages which I used, both those in syntax and those in semantics, were usually characterized only in an informal way as I have often emphasized myself. This seems to me to be a natural method for the initial stage in the development of syntax and semantics, since in this phase we are chiefly interested in an exact description of the syntactical and the semantical structure of the object language. But I agree with Martin that it is now time to give a formal description of the various metalanguages which are used. This work was begun by Lesniewski, and then continued especially by Tarski. Martin makes valuable contributions in this direction in his § VI, and further in his book on (extensional) semantics.[20] In his formalization Martin puts great weight on the aim of restricting the semantical metalanguage as much as possible, above all with respect to the types of variables to be used. The results which he has found in this respect constitute important progress in comparison with the unrestricted metalanguages which I originally used.

Martin is also correct in stating that the object languages dealt with in my publications on semantics up to now were very elementary. In the meantime I have constructed semantical rules for the much more comprehensive language L_1 (see §10 I, and the first footnote there). In a lan-

20R. M. Martin, *Truth and Denotation* (Chicago and London, 1958).

guage like L_1 it is no longer possible to have expressions for all values of the variables. Therefore in the semantical rules models must be used instead of state-descriptions. Recently I have also constructed, but not yet published, semantical rules for still more comprehensive languages with modalities (see the languages L_2 and L_3 in §9 II).

I am, of course, in agreement with Martin's view that L-truth ought to be a special case of truth. But I do not see how this would make it unnatural or counter-intuitive to define the concepts of L-truth and A-truth independently of the concept of truth. Independent definitions of this kind have the advantage of showing clearly that for the concepts of L-truth and A-truth it is not necessary to presuppose a complete interpretation of the descriptive constants, as is necessary for the concept of truth (comp. §10 I G). When afterwards the concept of truth is defined, it is easy to prove the theorem that every L-true or A-true sentence is true.

While Martin's essay primarily discusses extensional metalanguages, in §VII non-extensional metalanguages which I have described in [Meaning] are also mentioned. As explained above (in §10), I would now distinguish three main forms of semantical metalanguages: one with an extensional logic, another one with an intensional logic, and a third with a logic of senses. The intensional metalanguage seems to me to have certain advantages. Martin is right that it is important to give a formalized description of a metalanguage of this kind. This can easily be done on the basis of the indications which I have given earlier.

Martin asks for a compelling argument that intensions, e.g., propositions, are required in a semantical or philosophical analysis of language. I would not assert that the use of concepts like intension and Des^i are necessary, but their use seems to me convenient and natural for the reasons given earlier (in §9 IV and in §10 IV).

15. W. V. Quine on Logical Truth

A. The linguistic doctrine of logical truth. In the first part of his essay, Quine offers an exposition and a detailed informal discussion of what he calls "the linguistic doctrine of logical truth". I shall first comment on this part, and later discuss his more specific criticisms of my conception of logical truth.

The conception of the nature of logical truth, which was developed in the Vienna Circle on the basis of Wittgenstein's ideas, and which I still maintain in its essential points, was originally, before the construction of a systematic L-semantics, formulated only in informal explanations. Among the various formulations which Quine mentions and discusses critically, there are some which today I would no longer regard as psychologically helpful and would therefore avoid. One of them is the characterization of logical truth as based on "linguistic fiat" or "linguistic conventions". Neither does Quine's choice of the term "linguistic doctrine" seem to be quite suitable for my conception. The term "linguistic convention" is usually understood in the sense of a more or less arbitrary decision concerning language, such as the choice of either centimeter or inch as a unit of length. Sometimes the fact that a certain concept is expressed in a certain language by a certain word is loosely said to be a matter of convention. Although in this case there is no explicit agreement, the term "convention" may nevertheless be employed to express the fact that the usage might be changed by a decision, i.e., that a new word might be chosen instead of the old one, without thereby changing any essential characteristics of the given language. On the other hand, the logical truth of the sentence "all black dogs are dogs" is not a matter of convention even in the looser sense. Once the meanings of the individual words in a sentence of this form are given (which may be regarded as a matter of convention), then it is no longer a matter of convention or of arbitrary choice whether or not to regard the sentence as true; the truth of such a sentence is determined by the logical relations holding between the given meanings. (In the present example, only the meanings of "all" and "are" are relevant.)

A better informal characterization of logical truth mentioned also by Quine describes it as *truth based on meanings.* To ascertain the truth of a given sentence, it is necessary, first, to know the meaning of each part and thereby that of the sentence as a whole; in other words, it is necessary to understand the sentence. To ascertain the truth of some sentences, e.g., "Some dogs are black", it is further necessary to know certain facts of the world. In the case of other sentences, e.g., "all black dogs are black", this is not necessary; to understand them is a sufficient basis for the determination of their truth. Such sentences are called "logically true" or "analytic".

In the following discussion, I shall sometimes be compelled to discuss Quine's views hypothetically, that is to say, on the basis of presumptions about the meanings of his formulations, because I have not been able to determine their meanings with sufficient clarity.

Quine says (in § II) that in a certain sense,

(1) elementary logic is obvious.

I presume that he does not understand the word "obvious" here in the sense in which someone might say: "it is obvious that I have five fingers on my right hand", but rather in the sense in which the word is used in: "it is obvious that, if there is no righteous man in Sodom, then all men in Sodom are non-righteous". In this case, one merely has to think in order to recognize the truth; no observations of the men of Sodom are needed. If Quine has this meaning in mind, we are in agreement. However, Quine says later (in § III) of the linguistic doctrine of elementary logical truth, which I shall call "LD" for short, that

(2) LD "seems to imply nothing that is not already implied by the fact that elementary logic is obvious".

Again I agree. In other words:

(3) Whatever is implied by LD, is implied by (1).

Hence, since LD is implied by LD:

(4) LD is implied by (1).

Thus Quine, having accepted (1), must also accept LD. His argument seems to be not a refutation of LD but rather a proof of it.

Indeed, I have the impression that Quine's critical argument (2) is not meant as a refutation. He himself says soon afterwards: "I do not suggest that the linguistic doctrine is false". I presume that he wants to say that the doctrine is not false. (If so, I wish he had said so!) He nowhere says that the doctrine is meaningless; this also would not accord with his previous statement (2), nor with his remark that the doctrine plays a role analogous to "0 = 0". Therefore we may presume that he regards the doctrine as true. (If so, . . .!) The main point of his criticism seems rather to be that the doctrine is "empty" and "without experimental meaning". With this remark I would certainly agree, and I am surprised that Quine deems it necessary to support this view by detailed arguments. In line with Wittgenstein's basic conception, we agreed in Vienna that one of the main tasks of philosophy is clarification and explication. Usually, a philosophical insight does not say anything about the world, but is merely a clearer recognition of meanings or of meaning relations. If an insight of this kind is expressed by a sentence, then this sentence is, although meaningful (as we would maintain in contrast to Wittgenstein's view), not factual but rather analytic. Thus I would interpret, e.g., the principle of verifiability (or of confirmability), or the empiricist principle that there is no synthetic a priori, as consisting of proposals for certain explications (often not stated explicitly) and of certain assertions which, on the basis of these explications, are analytic. Such philosophical principles or doctrines are sometimes called theories; however, it might be better not to use the term "theory" in this context, in order to avoid the misunderstanding that such doctrines are similar to scientific, empirical theories.

B. Two arguments of Quine's. Now I come to Quine's important arguments (in §§ VIII-X) directed against my present view of the concept of analyticity (or logical truth in the wider sense) as a semantical concept. Quine's objections here should be considered in connection with those in some earlier articles of his, which are reprinted in his book.[21] Some of my arguments are closely related to those made by other authors.[22]

I shall state two arguments by Quine, which were at first rather puzzling to me and, it seems, to other authors. Then I shall explain what I presume to be Quine's basic view, which underlies these two arguments and would make them understandable. Finally, I shall indicate my position with respect to this view. My proposals for the explication of analyticity have always been given for a formalized (codified, constructed) language *L*, i.e., a language for which explicit semantical rules are specified that lead to the concept of truth (e.g., rules of the kinds A, B, C, and D in §10). The explication is given by additional rules, essentially by a list of meaning postulates (A-postulates) and, based upon them, a definition of "A-true" (which I use as a technical term for the explicatum). The first of Quine's critical arguments consists in the remark that the meaning postulates are recognizable only by the label "meaning postulates" and that the sense of this label is not clear (§ X); similarly he said in his book (p. 33f.) that the semantical rules are recognizable only by the heading "Semantical Rules" which itself is meaningless. I was puzzled by this remark because neither Quine nor anybody else has previously criticized the obvious fact that, e.g., the admitted forms of sentences of a formalized language *L* are only recognizable by a label like "Sentence Forms in *L*" preceding a list of forms of expressions, or the fact that the axioms of a logical calculus are only recognizable by the label "Axioms". Why should the same fact be objectionable in the case of meaning postulates?

The second objection consists in Quine's statement that the concept of analyticity is acceptable only if it is not merely explicated by rules in pure semantics, but rather by an empirical criterion in behavioristic terms, applicable to natural languages (§ IX); in his book (pp.56-64) he said the same concerning synonymy. It seemed to me puzzling why for semantical concepts like analyticity or synonymy the definition of a corresponding empirical, pragmatical concept is required, while for other semantical concepts like truth, the name-relation, and the like, a requirement of this kind is not made.

My interpretation of Quine's intention is as follows, formulated in my terminology. It seems to me that Quine's criticism is not directed against the proposed semantical explicata. I believe that he would agree that,

21W. V. Quine, *From a Logical Point of View* (Cambridge, Mass., 1953). In the following, the references to Quine citing page numbers refer to this book; those citing Roman section numbers refer to Quine's essay in the present volume.

22Benson Mates, "Analytic Sentences", *Phil. Review,* LX (1951), 525-34. Richard M. Martin, "On 'Analytic' ", *Phil. Studies,* III (1952), 42-47. H. P. Grice and P. F. Strawson, "In Defense of a Dogma", *Phil. Review,* LXV (1956), 141-158.

e.g., my rules of the above mentioned kinds, leading to the definition of "A-true", are in themselves exact and unobjectionable. His criticism is rather that there is no clear explicandum, in other words, that the customary pre-systematic explanations of analyticity are too vague and ambiguous, and basically incomprehensible. This would make it understandable why he requires for analyticity an empirical criterion, while he does not require it for truth. In Quine's view, there is the following basic difference. In the case of truth he recognizes a sufficiently clear explicandum; i.e., before an explication had been given, the use of this concept had been sufficiently clear, at least for practical purposes. On the other hand, Quine sees no sufficiently clear, pre-systematic concept of analyticity which could be taken as an explicandum. If an empirical criterion for analyticity with respect to natural languages were given, then this concept could serve as an explicandum for a reconstruction of a purely semantical concept of A-truth. This seems to me to be Quine's real motivation in demanding such a criterion. It would also explain Quine's first objection. His remark on recognizability by labels only may be understood, not as a criticism of the semantical rules themselves, but rather as pointing out the lack of an explicandum. He says in his book (p. 33): "The difficulty is simply that the [semantical] rules contain the word 'analytic', which we do not understand!" He proposes to use instead the untendentious term "*K*" for the class determined by the rules because the use of the apparently familiar word "analytic" might give us the illusion that we were in possession of a clear explicandum.

As I now understand Quine, I would agree with his basic idea, namely, that a pragmatical concept, based upon an empirical criterion, might serve as an explicandum for a purely semantical reconstruction, and that this procedure may sometimes, and perhaps also in the present case, be a useful way of specifying the explicandum. On the other hand, I would not think that it is necessary in general to provide a pragmatical concept in order to justify the introduction of a concept of pure semantics.

C. Empirical criteria for intension concepts. Since I agree with Quine's basic idea, I have accepted his challenge to show that an empirical criterion for intension concepts with respect to natural languages can be given. I believe I have shown this in my paper on natural languages [1955-3]. In the original draft of my reply to Quine's present essay, the part dealing with natural languages grew finally beyond the space available in this volume. Therefore, I elaborated this part and published it separately as the above paper.

The basic ideas underlying my intensionalist thesis are simple. It seemed rather plausible to me from the beginning that there should be an empirical criterion for the concept of the meaning of a word or a phrase, in view of the fact that linguists traditionally determine empirically the meanings, meaning differences, and shifts of meanings of words, and that with respect to these determinations they reach a measure of agreement among themselves which is often considerably higher than that reached for results in most of the other fields of the social sciences. Quine's arguments to the effect that the lexicographers actually have no criterion for their determinations did not seem at all convincing to me.

In my paper, I tried to show the possibility of giving operational rules for testing hypotheses concerning the intensions of predicates of a natural language, on the basis of responses by the users of this language. For the sake of simplicity, I shall here take not "intension" but rather "analytic" as an example. Let us suppose that two linguists study the natural language L as used by the person X. Let us suppose that L consists of some English words and English sentences, among them the following sentence:

(S_1) "All ravens are black".

We assume that the two linguists agree on the basis of previous experiments that X uses the words "all" and "are" in the ordinary sense, and that X has repeatedly affirmed the sentence S_1 and hence presumably regards it as true. Now the first linguist states the following hypothesis:

(5) "The sentence S_1 is analytic in language L for person X".

The other linguist denies this hypothesis. In order to obtain evidence relevant for (5), the linguists say to X: "Mr. Smith told us that he had found a raven which is not black but white, and that he will show it to you tomorrow. Will you then revoke your assertion of S_1"? Let us consider the following two of many possible responses by X:

(6) "I would never have believed that there are white ravens; and I still do not believe it until I see one myself. In that case I shall, of course, have to revoke my assertion".

(7) "There cannot be white ravens. If a bird is not black, then I just would not call it a raven. If Mr. Smith says that his raven is not black, then (assuming that he is not lying or joking) his use either of the word 'raven' or of the word 'black' must be different from my use".

It seems obvious to me that a response like (6) would be disconfirming evidence for hypothesis (5), while a response like (7) would be confirming evidence for it. Thus it is clear that (5) is an empirical hypothesis which can be tested by observations of the speaking behavior of X. If anyone is still sceptical about this possibility, I should like to refer him to a recent book by Arne Naess,[23] which shows by numerous examples how

[23]A. Naess, *Interpretation and Preciseness: A Contribution to the Theory of Communication*. Skrifter Norske Videnskaps-Akademi, Oslo, II. Hist.-Philos. Klasse (1953), No. 1.

hypotheses about the synonymy of expressions can be tested by empirical procedures.

Furthermore, in my paper I have shown that it is also possible to determine empirically the intension of a predicate of a language L for a robot who makes observations and can receive and deliver messages in the language L.

D. Analyticity and change of language. Quine shows (in his book, pp. 42-46) that a scientist, who discovers a conflict between his observations and his theory and who is therefore compelled to make a readjustment somewhere in the total system of science, has much latitude with respect to the place where a change is to be made. In this procedure, no statement is immune to revision, not even the statements of logic and of mathematics. There are only practical differences, and these are differences in degree, inasmuch as a scientist is usually less willing to abandon a previously accepted general empirical law than a single observation sentence, and still less willing to abandon a law of logic or of mathematics. With all this I am entirely in agreement. But I cannot follow Quine when he infers from this fact that it becomes folly to seek a boundary between synthetic and analytic statements. I agree that "any statement can be held true come what may". But the concept of an analytic statement which I take as an explicandum is not adequately characterized as "held true come what may". First of all, I should make a distinction between two kinds of readjustment in the case of a conflict with experience, namely, between a change in the language, and a mere change in or addition of, a truth-value ascribed to an indeterminate statement, (i.e., a statement whose truth value it not fixed by the rules of language, say by the postulates of logic, mathematics, and physics). A change of the first kind constitutes a radical alteration, sometimes a revolution, and it occurs only at certain historically decisive points in the development of science. On the other hand, changes of the second kind occur every minute. A change of the first kind constitutes, strictly speaking, a transition from a language L_n to a new language L_{n+1}. My concept of analyticity as an explicandum has nothing to do with such a transition. It refers in each case to just one language; "analytic in L_n" and "analytic in L_{n+1}" are two different concepts. That a certain sentence S is analytic in L_n means only something about the status of S within the language L_n; as has often been said, it means that the truth of S in L_n is based on the meanings in L_n of the terms occurring in S. To be sure, this status has certain consequences in case of changes of the second kind, namely, that analytic sentences cannot change their truth-value. But this characteristic is not restricted to analytic sentences; it holds also for certain synthetic sentences, e.g., physical postulates and their logical consequences.

E. The concept of analyticity in philosophy. I believe that the distinction between analytic and synthetic statements, expressed in whatever terms, is practically indispensable for methodological and philosophical discussions. This is also indicated by the fact that this distinction is made by a large majority of philosophers, including some of those who do not explicitly acknowledge the distinction in these terms or even reject it. As an example, let me refer to a philosopher whose work I esteem very highly, although I cannot agree in all points with his views. This philosopher once undertook to destroy a certain doctrine, propounded by some other philosophers. He did not mean to assert that the doctrine was false; presumably he regarded it as true. But his criticism concerned its particular kind of truth, namely that the truth of the doctrine was of the analytic kind. To be sure, he did not use the word "analytic", which he did not seem to like very much. Instead, he used other expressions which, nonetheless, clearly seem to have essentially the same meaning as "analytic". What he showed was that various attempts to assign an experimental, empirical meaning to this doctrine remained without success. Finally he came to the conclusion that the doctrine, even though not false, is "empty" and "without experimental significance".

16. Herbert G. Bohnert on Definitions and Analyticity

I am in agreement with most points in Bohnert's discussions, in particular, with his arguments against Quine's objections to the concept of analyticity; and I find many of his explanations illuminating. Therefore I shall restrict myself to only a few comments.

I agree with Bohnert's remark (in § II) that today an approach to semiotics by way of a behavioristic sociologism, analogous to the approach of the earlier psychologism, poses a threat to the drawing of precise distinctions in logic. Bohnert believes that Quine's requirement of an empirical criterion for synonymy is an example of this kind of sociologism. This would be the case if, as Bohnert believes, Quine actually had the intention of founding logic upon empirical concepts. Quine's formulations on this point admit of a variety of interpretations, including, perhaps, Bohnert's as well. In my reply (§15) I have given Quine the benefit of the doubt and have suggested a hypothesis about the motivation of Quine's requirement in such a way that I would be able to agree with it. It remains for Quine to make clear which of the interpretations he has in mind.

Bohnert's discussion of what he calls "recipe terms" is clarifying and useful. He is certainly right that in general syntax, and even more in general semantics, some concepts cannot be adequately introduced by exact general definitions for all languages, but only by different recipe definitions for different classes of languages. However, it is possible to give general exact definitions both for A-truth (analyticity) and for truth (see §10 I, D and G) provided that other suitable concepts occurring in these general definitions are introduced by recipe definitions.

Bohnert points out correctly (in § III) that the term "definition" must be introduced as a recipe term, newly defined for each language or class of languages by an enumeration of forms. The situation is similar for the term "meaning postulate". Nevertheless, it is possible, as Bohnert indicates, to give general directives, though not in the form of exact rules, for the formulation of a recipe definition of the term "definition", and for setting up a list of meaning postulates.

17. Wilfrid Sellars on Abstract Entities in Semantics

A. The prescriptive component in syntax and semantics. I am not certain whether I have correctly understood how Sellars distinguishes between descriptive and prescriptive components in statements and concepts, as well as between a priori and empirical statements, and how he intends to apply these distinctions in syntax and semantics. Therefore I shall comment only briefly on these points. Above all, I wish to emphasize that not only pure syntax and pure semantics but also descriptive syntax and descriptive semantics, as I understand them and intend to construct them, do not contain any kind of prescriptive components. It is certainly true that, when a mother teaches her child to speak, or when a reviewer criticizes the style of a book, norms of the use of language are applied either explicitly or implicitly, and therefore the metastatements occurring in these contexts often contain prescriptive components. But in syntax and semantics I deliberately leave aside all prescriptive factors. *Descriptive* syntax and semantics deal with certain features of languages investigated empirically. Even here, the statements about these features are descriptive; what Sellars calls "rule-bound words" do not occur.

Sellars' belief that my descriptive syntax and descriptive semantics contained prescriptive conceptual components is perhaps due to the fact that I used the word "rule" both in syntax and in semantics. Perhaps he understood this term in its everyday sense, i.e., as referring to prescriptive rules, prescriptions, prohibitions, or permissions. However, I use the word "rule" in this field only in order to conform to the customary usage in logic. The so-called rules are meant only as partial conditions of a definition; e.g., as I have often said, the rules of formation for a language *L* together form the definition of "sentence in *L*", and all the rules for *L* together form the definition of "*L*". It seems to me that in the development of modern logic it has become ever more evident that logic, and likewise syntactical and semantical analyses of language, are purely theoretical; the use of terms like "rules", "permitted operations", and "prohibited operations" is here, just as in algebra, merely a psychologically useful way of speaking which should not be understood literally. [When I say that the so-called rules are only definitions, then this could still be misunderstood since some philosophers interpret definitions in a prescriptive sense; Bohnert has clearly criticized this interpretation (in § II of his essay).]

B. Sellars' psychological nominalism. Sellars critically examines the conception that statements like "John perceives this table" and "John is aware of (thinks of, apprehends) the number 13" describe two different but nevertheless similar cases of the *same relation* of awareness between a person (or a mind) and a concrete or abstract object. I agree with Sellars in rejecting this Platonistic conception, as it is represented, e.g., in Sellars' quotation from Alonzo Church. Sellars uses the label "psychological nominalism" for his own position. I have some doubts about the suitability of this term because it might be misunderstood as a rejection of the use of abstract entities, e.g., numbers, in psychology. If I have understood Sellars correctly, this is not what he means. At any rate, I would not agree with such a rejection because it would exclude the application of quantitative magnitudes in psychology.

I would not reject, as Sellars seems to do, all factual or descriptive relations between material objects and abstract entities, at least not if "relation" is understood in the wide sense which is customary in modern logic. In the latter sense, any sentence of arbitrary form containing the names of two entities a and b (of arbitrary, possibly different, logical types or semantical categories) may be said to state that a certain relation holds between a and b. [For example, the sentence "John has a car with four doors" says that a certain relation holds between John and the number four, namely the relation $(\lambda x,n)(x$ has a car with n doors).] Relations between material objects and numbers occur in science whenever measurable magnitudes are applied. If we define:

(1) $M(x,u) =_{\mathrm{Df}}$ the material body x has the mass (in grams) u,

then the physical concept M is a relation between bodies and numbers. This relation is descriptive or factual in the sense that the predicate "M" is a descriptive (i.e., non-logical) constant, and a full sentence, e.g., "$M(a,5)$" is a factual sentence.

I am not certain whether what I have just said contradicts Sellars' view because it is not quite clear to me what he means by a "factual relation". It may be that he understands this term in a very special sense, perhaps in the sense of "causal relation" or in the somewhat wider sense of "relation based on causal connections". It is true that the word "relation" is usually understood in this sense in everyday language, but it seems to me that this does not hold for the technical language of philosophy. Relations of the causal type can indeed hold only among physical objects (or states or processes), not between a physical object and an abstract entity. It seems typical of Platonism, which both Sellars and I reject, that it speaks of relations of this causal type (called "commerce" or "intercourse" or the like) as holding between physical objects (or persons or minds) and abstract entities. My reason for regarding the two sentences "John observes the table" and "John observes (is aware of) the number 13" as not being analogous is just this: the first sentence states a causal relation between the table and John (mediated by light rays, the retina, etc., as Church indicates) but the second does not. Only spatio-temporal objects, not numbers, can have a causal effect on John. On the other hand, it seems to me that some psychological concepts may be regarded or reconstructed as relations (in the wide sense of the logical terminology, not in the causal sense) between a person and an abstract entity; e.g., believing may be taken as a relation between a person and a proposition (as is done by Church, comp. §9 VII), and thinking-of as a relation between a person and a concept (intension or sense) and the like. In particular, there seems to be no objection to the use of relations of this kind *in a theoretical language* (comp. my remarks on semantical concepts in a theoretical language in §10 V).

C. Designation. Let us consider the following sentence in the descriptive semantics of the German language (Sellars' (26)):

(2) (In German) the word "*blau*" designates Blue.

This sentence says that a certain factual (but not causal) relation holds between the word design "*blau*" in German and the property Blue. In pragmatics, the relation of designation is a psychological concept, analogous to the psychological concepts of believing and thinking-of mentioned earlier, and presumably definable on the basis of these and similar psychological concepts. The sentence (2) of descriptive semantics is based on the following sentence of pragmatics:

(3) In the German language community, the German word "*blau*" is mostly used as designating Blue.

The relation of designation in the case just mentioned, either in descriptive semantics or in pragmatics, is not of a Platonistic nature, since it is not meant here as a causal relation. To me the concept seems entirely unobjectionable.

D. Pure and descriptive semantics. Suppose we construct in pure semantics a language system *G* which in a certain way corresponds to a selected part of the German language. First, the relation "directly-designates-in-*G*" or "$DDes_G$" (comp. §10 I C) is defined by an enumeration of pairs, each pair consisting of a predicate in *G* and a property. Motivated by the empirically found result (2), we may, for instance, include the following pair:

(4) "*blau*", Blue.

On the basis of direct designation, the term "designates-in-*G*" or "Des_G" can be defined (cf. § 10 I C). By virtue of these definitions, the following holds as an analytic theorem in the pure semantics of language *G*:

(5) The word "*blau*" designates-in-*G* Blue.

Sellars is right that there is a radical difference between the meaning of the term "designates-in-*G*" in pure semantics and that of the term "designates" in pragmatics and descriptive semantics; this is evident from the nature of their definitions. The two terms have at best the same extension, provided the rules for *G* are chosen in a suitable way; this fact can be expressed by an if-and-only-if-sentence (Sellars' (28) and (39)). It should be noted, however, that this situation does not indicate a defect of the concept of designation in pure semantics. As Sellars aptly expresses it, pure semantics is nothing but a combinatorics of sign designs and extra-linguistical entities. It is therefore possible to define in this field a relation of designation just like the pragmatical, psychological concept of designation; only a corresponding concept can be defined.

The nature of this correspondence may be illustrated by the following example. Let us assume that, on the basis of the definition of "designates-in-*G*" which is given by the rules for the language *G*, the following is an analytic sentence of the pure semantics of *G*:

(6) "Der Mond ist blau" designates-in-*G* the proposition that the moon is blue.

Let us further assume that the predicate "true-in-*G*" is defined in a suitable way (comp. §10 I D). Then the following is likewise an analytic theorem:

(7) The sentence "der Mond ist blau" is true-in-*G* if and only if the moon is blue.

The correspondence between the pure semantics of the language system *G* and the descriptive semantics of any language *L* can now be characterized as follows (where *L* is a language in the ordinary sense, and the relation of designation or meaning is likewise understood in the ordinary sense):

(8) If in any language *L* the relation of designation holds in those pairs which are enumerated in the definition of "directly-designates-in-*G*", and if in *L* the relation of designation satisfies the general conditions stated in the rules for "designates-in-*G*", then the relation of designation in *L* holds in all cases in which "designates-in-*G*" holds, and a truth-condition for any sentence in *G* is a truth-condition for the same sentence in *L*.

Therefore, in particular, the following holds by virtue of (6) and (7) respectively:

(9) If L satisfies the conditions stated in (8), then
(a) the sentence "Der Mond ist blau" in L designates (means, expresses) the proposition that the moon is blue;
(b) the sentence "Der Mond ist blau" in L is true (in the ordinary sense) if and only if the moon is blue.

In this way, pure semantics represents the logical connections among various facts involving the relation of designation in any language, and the connections between these facts, on the one hand, and truth-conditions for the sentences of the same language on the other. But in pure semantics we cannot give an analysis of the concept of designation in its ordinary sense because for this purpose psychological concepts are required. The situation is analogous to the relation between pure geometry and physical geometry (where pure geometry is understood as represented, not by an uninterpreted axiom system, but rather by a purely logical theory concerning a certain structure). In pure geometry, we cannot analyze the physico-spatial concepts, because concepts of physics or of the observation language would be needed for this purpose; but pure geometry can mirror the logical connections holding between physico-geometrical concepts or propositions.

18. E. W. Beth on Constructed Language Systems

Beth emphasizes correctly that, from the beginning, an important aim in my thinking about the foundations of mathematics was the reconciliation of certain philosophical controversies, namely, the controversy between logicism and Cantorism and, still more important, the controversy between logicism and formalism. My view on the latter controversy has had little influence, perhaps because my two main papers on this problem ([1930-5] and [1931-4]) were in German and have so far not been translated into English, while my later comments on the problem of the foundations of mathematics are only brief indications ([1934-6] §84; [1939-1] §20). It seems to me that even today the logicist conception is far too little known.[24] I welcome Beth's emphasis on the

[24]Even the book by Raymond L. Wilder, *Introduction to the Foundations of Mathematics* (1952), which I regard as the best book on the problems of the foundations of mathematics available at the present time, gives only an inadequate exposition of the basic ideas of logicism. Frege's main work *(Die Grundgesetze der Arithmetik,* 2 vols. (1893 and 1903)), is not mentioned at all. And the first, most important step in Frege's reduction of mathematics to logic, viz., the definition of the natural numbers 0, 1, 2, etc. in terms of logic, is not represented. Frege's definition of the general concept of the cardinal number of a class is given (p. 99), but the fact, essential for the point of view of logicism, that this definition uses only concepts of logic, is not mentioned. (Added note, 1962): In the mean time two books have appeared, which give excellent, thorough discussions of the problems of the foundations of mathematics: A. A. Fraenkel and Y. Bar-Hillel. *Foundations of Set Theory* (Amsterdam, 1958); E. W. Beth, *The Foundations of Mathematics* (Amsterdam, 1959).

importance of these problems within the whole of my philosophical conceptions, all the more so since my views on these problems are not discussed in any of the other essays.

Beth (in §5) gives an analysis of my views, in particular those concerning the relation between logicism and formalism, as represented in my book *Logical Syntax* ([1934-6] and [1937-1]; in the present section I shall refer to it as "[Syntax]"). His comments, both on technical questions and also on my motivation in the choice of methods and the forms of systems are very interesting, and in general I agree with them. But it seems to me advisable to make a clearer distinction between formalism and the formalist method. The *formalist method,* or in my terminology the syntactical method, consists in describing a language *L* together with its rules of deduction by reference only to signs and the order of their occurrence in expressions, thus without any reference to meaning. The application of the formalist method in the construction of a language *L* does not in itself exclude adding an interpretation for *L,* but if we do so, this interpretation does not enter into the syntactical rules for *L*. *Formalism,* in the sense of the conception about the nature of mathematics represented by Hilbert and his followers, consists of both the proposal to apply the formalist method and, more essentially, the *thesis of formalism,* that this is the only possible way of constructing an adequate system of mathematics, since it is impossible to give an interpretation for (classical) mathematics. In this assertion the *thesis of logicism,* that all terms of mathematics can be interpreted in terms of logic, is rejected. I accepted the formalist method and developed it in a wider domain, but I did not accept the thesis of formalism and instead maintained that of logicism.

With respect to the *problem of interpretation* I certainly agree with Beth when he says (in §5): "We find in *Logical Syntax* also concepts which, though defined in a purely formal way, are clearly inspired by a non-formal interpretation which, if made manifest, would imply a return to Frege's logicism". And perhaps I would also agree with his further statement: "I think that it is even possible to show that, in the absence of such non-formal, intuitive interpretation, the whole edifice of *Logical Syntax* would miss its purpose".

In order to clarify the situation with respect to different interpretations, Beth introduces a fictitious logician, Carnap*, who interprets the symbolic object language II dealt with in [Syntax] in a way different from Carnap, namely on the basis of a model M^*, different from the normal model M. As I have explained earlier (§10 II), I prefer not to identify models and interpretations; however, an interpretation can be specified by a particular description of a model. Therefore I understand Beth here as saying that Carnap* applies a non-normal interpretation

*Int**, which is given by a certain description of the model *M** and which is therefore different from the normal interpretation *Int* applied by Carnap, which is given by a certain description of the model *M*. Furthermore, Carnap* enlarges the language II to the language II* by adding a new axiom which is true on the basis of *M** though false on the basis of *M*. So far everything is clear. But now Beth proceeds to make a number of further statements about Carnap* which at first glance appear as obviously false, e.g., the statement that the set of all axioms of II* is different for Carnap* and for us, i.e. Carnap and Beth, and the statement that for Carnap* the languages II* and II coincide. These statements certainly do not follow from the sole assumption that Carnap* applies the interpretation *Int** to the object languages. Beth's statements are understandable only on the basis of an additional assumption, namely that Carnap* interprets not only the symbolic object languages but also the metalanguage *ML* in a way different from Carnap. Therefore I suppose that Beth makes this additional assumption, although he does not state it explicitly. And I presume, more specifically, that Beth assumes that the interpretation of *ML* by Carnap* is analogous to his interpretation *Int** of II (and II*). Since the metalanguage *ML* serves as a means of communication between author and reader or among participants in a discussion, I always presupposed, both in syntax and in semantics, that a fixed interpretation of *ML,* which is shared by all participants, is given. This interpretation is usually not formulated explicitly; but since *ML* uses English words, it is assumed that these words are understood in their ordinary senses. The necessity of this presupposition of a common interpreted metalanguage seems to me obvious. If in the rules which constitute language II I use a phrase like "no occurrence of *'x'* ", and a reader were to understand this phrase in the sense of "at least one occurrence of *'x'* ", then there would be no communication between us and he would have in mind not this language II, but an entirely different one. Therefore it seems to me misleading to say that Carnap* has views about the languages II and II* which diverge from our views about these languages. It seems to me more correct to describe the situation as follows: (a) Carnap* does not use the metalanguage *ML,* but a language *ML** which, although it uses the same words and sentences, differs from *ML,* since some of the words and sentences have different meanings; and (b) since the labels "II" and "II*" have in *ML** meanings different from those in *ML,* Carnap* is not talking about the same languages as Carnap.

It seems to be obvious that, if two men wish to find out whether or not their views on certain objects agree, they must first of all use a common language to make sure that they are talking about the same objects. It may be the case that one of them can express in his own language certain convictions which he cannot translate into the common language; in this case he cannot communicate these convictions to the other man. For example, a classical mathematician is in this situation with respect to an intuitionist or, to a still higher degree, with respect to a nominalist.

Beth (in §6) distinguishes two ways in which a natural language may be used. "In *strict usage* we refer to a definite model of the theory to which our statements belong. . . . In *amplified usage* of natural language —and in *all* usage of formalized languages—on the other hand, we refer to *any* model of this theory". Although Beth (in footnote 30) explains his use of the term "model" in the customary sense, in which I too use this term (§10 II), still it seems nonetheless clear from the context that in his explanations of "strict usage" and of "amplified usage" he means the term "model" in the sense of interpretation. Therefore I assume that the strict usage of ordinary language is meant to be the usage based on a fixed interpretation, presumably in such a way that the words are understood in their ordinary meanings; on the other hand, the amplified usage of ordinary language is one in which for a certain word the meanings remain undetermined, as e.g., for the word "point" in Hilbert's axiom system of geometry.

Beth intends now to show that "in *Logical Syntax,* we can find strict usage of natural language" and that this strict usage plays an essential role. If my above interpretation of the term "strict usage" is correct, then Beth's thesis says that it is essential for the purposes of my theory that the English words of my metalanguage *ML* are sometimes used with a fixed interpretation. I emphatically agree; I would even say that this is the case not only sometimes but practically always. For the reasons explained earlier, this seems to me so obvious that I am surprised that Beth should regard it as necessary to demonstrate it by particular examples. It is of course not quite possible to use the ordinary language with a perfectly fixed interpretation, because of the inevitable vagueness and ambiguity of ordinary words. Nevertheless it is possible at least to approximate a fixed interpretation to a certain extent, e.g., by a suitable choice of less vague words and by suitable paraphrases. With regard to this difficulty Beth gives two good examples. First he refers to a passage in [Syntax] (p. 13) which contains in an informal explanation the phrase "and so on" (which, regarded from a strictly logical point of view, is indeed ambiguous), and secondly he refers to a place (p. 113) where I myself point out that phrases like "for all syntactical properties of accented expressions", which occur in syntactical rules, are ambiguous. I would certainly agree if Beth had said about these two examples something like this: "At these two places the requirement of strict usage of natural language, i.e., of a usage of words with fixed meanings, is not fulfilled". Amazingly, he says just the opposite; he introduces the first example with the words: "For instance, we find strict usage of natural language on p. 13 . . .". Later he says: "The term 'and so on' which appears in Carnap's text, is supposed to be univocal". Presumably he means hereby to imply: "but, in fact, it is not univocal"; and with this I would agree.

In [Syntax] I treat only the logical syntax of constructed languages. In the Introduction ([Syntax] p. 2) I point as a reason for this to the fact that it would hardly be feasible in practice to state the syntactical rules for *natural languages,* because in view of their unsystematic and logically incorrect structure the formulation of the syntactical rules would be prohibitively complicated. This attitude has often been criticized as excessively sceptical. Bar-Hillel complains rightly (at the beginning of his essay) that I have given too little encouragement to the logical analysis of natural languages. I am certainly willing to admit that the following is possible: (1) an empirical description of the most important and most frequently used syntactical forms occurring in a natural language, with indications of their frequencies, but without any claim of completeness; or (2) the complete representation of the syntactical structure of a constructed language which is to some extent similar to the syntactical structure (e.g., order of words) of a part of a certain natural language. Work of the first kind has for a long time been carried out by linguists, and that of the second kind is sometimes done by logicians, though only to a very limited extent. I am surprised that Beth criticizes my view from the opposite direction (§6). He is afraid that my remarks in the Introduction might encourage investigations as to the logical structure of natural languages. I would admit that investigations of the kind (1) mentioned above have a character quite different from that of constructed languages; since they are empirical and less exact; but I do not think, as Beth does, that they must necessarily remain futile. I doubt whether Beth is correct when he says that such investigations and even my book might countenance mystical attitudes with regard to natural languages. I rather think that any empirical investigation, in any field, especially if it is careful in its method and clear in the choice of the concepts used, is the best antidote against mystical attitudes.

Beth (in §7) discusses my distinction between *logical and descriptive signs.* He stresses correctly the importance of this distinction for my conception of semantics. Beth then says that it is sometimes extremely difficult to draw the boundary line between these two kinds of signs with respect to a given language system. In contrast, I find this distinction almost always very easy to make, much easier than the distinction between analytic and synthetic sentences. The latter distinction can be based on the former; but for given sentences it can be made only if the meaning relations between the descriptive constants which occur in the sentences are clear; and these relations frequently differ for different reconstructions of the ordinary language within constructed systems (this is the case, e.g., for sentences like "all ravens are black" or "space is three-dimensional", and similar ones). On the other hand, at the present moment I cannot think of any term in a relatively clear language, for which I would be in doubt whether to count it as logical or as descriptive. For example, I would count as logical every constant which is either primitive, or defined, or definable in the system of *Principia Mathematica* or in that of Quine's *Mathematical Logic;* and this covers all constants of pure mathematics. (I do not include, of course, the axiomatic primitive constants of a mathematical axiom system, since they are uninterpreted and thus the distinction does not apply to them at all; but I include the explicit predicate of any axiom system, compare [1929-2] §30b, [1954-3] §42d, and [1958-2] §42d). As an example of the difficulty, Beth refers to the sign "=". He agrees that this sign, if defined as the sign of identity as in Russell's system, is clearly logical. But then he refers to the same sign as occurring within the axiom system of the elementary theory of simple order. It is true that within this system the sign "=" can be defined on the basis of the axiomatic primitive sign "<". But obviously here the question of the classification of the signs can only be raised when an interpretation for the primitive is specified. It is certainly possible to choose the interpretation in such a way that this primitive becomes a descriptive sign; and in this case, the sign "=" is likewise descriptive. But then this sign is not a sign of identity; it is only factually equivalent, not logically equivalent, to the sign of identity, which is logical. (This situation is analogous to the following. If we define *"np"* as "the number of planets", then it is a descriptive sign and is only factually equivalent, not logically equivalent, to the logical sign "9".)

I entirely agree with Beth that the difference between Tarski's method and my method of semantics is to a large extent to be explained by the fact that Tarski deals chiefly with languages for logic and mathematics, thus languages without descriptive constants, while I regard it as an essential task for semantics to develop a method applicable to languages of empirical science. I believe that a semantics for languages of this kind must give an explication for the distinction between logical and descriptive signs and that between logical and factual truth, because it seems to me that without these distinctions a satisfactory methodological analysis of science is not possible.

Beth's criticism (in §9) of the loose use of the words "calculus", "semantical system", and related terms in my books is correct and fair. I thought originally that the context would always make it sufficiently clear whether I meant to refer to expressions of the object language (e.g., with "a sentence of the calculus") or of the metalanguage (e.g., with "a rule of the calculus"). But my experience in teaching has shown that this ambiguous use is often misleading. Beth's suggestions for a terminology seem to me good and helpful. I now use a similar terminology in my courses and in the book [1958-2].

In §10 Beth discusses the problem of so-called *ontological commitments.* I believe today that there is a good deal of truth in his remark that the problems of traditional metaphysics (disregarding here the often anti-scientific attitude in the movement of German idealism) are often closely related to problems of logic and semantics. Beth himself has in other publications clearly pointed out these connections. The earlier anti-metaphysical formulations in our movement, especially during the Vienna period, were often too general. On the other hand, it seems to me still very important to make a clear distinction between genuine questions and pseudo-questions, both in traditional and in contemporary philosophical discussions. It is not quite clear what exactly Beth means by "ontological commitments", and he does not mention explicitly an example of such a commitment. I have the impression that he means existential statements on general kinds of entities (and perhaps also negations of such statements), e.g., "there are classes of classes of objects". More specifically, I presume he is thinking of those statements which I have called *external* existential statements. I have discussed the problem of their interpretation in §4B.

19. P. F. Strawson on Linguistic Naturalism

At the beginning of his essay, Strawson outlines the two competing methods proposed for philosophical clarification, the method of rational reconstruction in a formal language system with exact rules, and the method of describing and analyzing the actual usage of words in everyday language. Strawson calls the adherents of the first method constructionists; the adherents of the second method may be called linguistic naturalists or, within this section for short, naturalists.

By an explication I understand the replacement of a pre-scientific, inexact concept (which I call "explicandum") by an exact concept ("explicatum"), which frequently belongs to the scientific language. (For more details see ch. I of my book on probability [1950-4].) Although explications are often given also by scientists, it seems to me particularly characteristic of philosophical work that a great part of it is devoted to proposing and discussing explications of certain basic, general concepts. The first, preparatory step in an explication consists in the informal *clarification of the explicandum.* (Strawson correctly describes my characterization of the procedure of explication and refers to the chapter mentioned above. He says, however, that my term for this procedure was "clarification" and does not mention the term "explication". Therefore it is not clear in some parts of his discussion of my conception whether he uses the term "clarification" to refer to the explication or to its first step, viz. the clarification of the explicandum.)

Strawson then discusses the specific question, which indeed touches the central point of the controversy, whether an explication given, not in the ordinary language, but in a scientific, technically constructed language could possibly be useful for the solution of a philosophical problem. He declares that the negative answer to this particular question seems "evident" to him and adds that "it seems to require no argument". However, I am firmly convinced of the affirmative answer. But this view does not seem immediately evident to me; I would rather call it an insight, gained on the basis of extended work concerning explications of various kinds. Therefore, arguments on either side do not seem superfluous to me. Frequently, what seems to be a clash between two opposing positions, is actually a difference in the interpretation of a concept. I have the impression that Strawson's view is based on the conception of a sharp separation, perhaps even a gap, between everyday concepts and scientific concepts. I see here no sharp boundary line but a continuous transition. The process of the acquisition of knowledge begins with common sense knowledge; gradually the methods become more refined and systematic, and thus more scientific. To my example of the explication of the qualitative concept Warm by the quantitative concept Temperature, Strawson remarks that the latter concept does not help in solving puzzling questions like "Does it follow from the fact that the same object can feel warm to one man and cold to another that the object really is neither cold nor warm nor cool nor has any such property?" In order to solve this puzzle, we have first to distinguish between the following two concepts: (1) "the thing x feels warm to the person y" and (2) "the thing x is warm", and then to clarify the relation between them. The method and terminology used for this clarification depends upon the specific purpose we may have in mind. First, it is indeed possible to clarify the distinction in a simple way in ordinary language. But if we require a more thorough clarification, we must search for explications of the two concepts. The explication of concept (1) may be given in an improved version of the ordinary language concerning perceptions and the like. If a still more exact explication is desired, we may go to the scientific language of psychology. The explication of concept (2) must use an objective language, which may be a carefully selected qualitative part of the ordinary language. If we wish the explicatum to be more precise, then we use the quantitative term "temperature" either as a term of the developed ordinary language, or as a scientific term of the language of physics.

In his section on pseudo-questions, Strawson ascribes to me the view that "philosophical questions and perplexities cannot really be taken seriously". If this were my view, I would not have devoted the greater part of my life's work to attempts at solving or clarifying such problems. Nor do I "ignore the role of conceptual explanation in resolving philosophical difficulties". A very large part of my philosophical work actually consists just in developing and applying the methods of conceptual explanation—in my terminology, explication. Strawson believes that philosophical problems are raised by people "who know very well how to use the expressions concerned". I should rather say that these people usually believe they know this very well, but often deceive themselves. The first step in helping these people consists in leading them to the insight that something is wrong with their use of certain expressions, that it involves confusions or even inconsistencies. Frequently the puzzle concerns expressions of ordinary language, for example, numerical terms, spatial and temporal terms for the description of motion, terms like "true", "entailment", and the like. These may be terms which in most cases are used without any difficulty. But then it may occur that in certain critical contexts the ordinary usage leads to difficulties, unanswerable questions, even contradictions, demonstrating the surprising fact that people are not completely clear about the correct usage. A misinterpretation of the expressions describing motion led to Zeno's paradoxes; in the antinomy of the liar, the term "true" led to difficulties. With respect to the numerical words "one", "two", etc., the situation might seem different. For thousands of years, many people used these words adequately for all practical purposes, and for several centuries the mathematicians have had a systematically constructed theory involving these words. But even in this case, complete clarity was lacking. Before Frege, nobody was able to give an exact account of the meanings of these words in non-arithmetical terms. By Frege's explication of the numerical words, which I would regard as one of the greatest philosophical achievements of the last century, the logical connection between these words and logical particles like "there is", "not", "or", and "the same as" became completely clear for the first time. Therefore we have to say that in spite of practical skill in usage, people in general, and even mathematicians before Frege, were not completely clear about the meaning of numerical words. Clarity is here understood in a stricter sense than in ordinary language; this sense does not require the ability to give a definition, but it requires that the usage does not lead to logical paradoxes.

An explication replaces the imprecise explicandum by a more precise explicatum. Therefore, whenever greater precision in communication is desired, it will be advisable to use the explicatum instead of the explicandum. The explicatum may belong to the ordinary language, although perhaps to a more exact part of it. Or it may be that it did not belong to the ordinary language originally but was introduced as a scientific term. Even such a term will frequently be accepted later into the everyday language, such as "at 4:30 P.M.", "temperature", "speed" as a quantitative term. In other cases, the explicatum is chiefly used in technical, scientific contexts. The only essential requirement is that the explicatum be more precise than the explicandum; it is unimportant to which part of the language it belongs. However, since exact concepts are more easily found in the scientific part of our language, it will often be useful to define the explicatum in this part. Furthermore, exactness and clarity are best achieved by a certain degree of systematization. Therefore the explicatum usually belongs to a systematic conceptual framework. But the system may be of a rather elementary kind as, for instance, the system of numerical words in everyday language. The use of symbolic logic and of a constructed language system with explicit syntactical and semantical rules is the most elaborate and most efficient method. For philosophical explications the use of this method is advisable only in special cases, but not generally.

The explicatum is intended to take the place of the explicandum, and that means, of course, that it is to be used for the same purpose as the explicandum. Again misled by his sharp distinction between scientific language and ordinary language, Strawson seems to misunderstand this point. He believes that the explicatum is meant to serve a scientific purpose, in distinction to the explicandum which serves a pre-scientific purpose. Suppose the statement "it will probably be very hot tomorrow at noon" is made for the purpose of communicating a future state to be expected, perhaps with regard to practical consequences. The use of the explicatum "temperature" instead of "very hot" in the above statement makes it possible to fulfil the same purpose in a more efficient way: "the temperature tomorrow at noon will probably be about so and so much".

The aim of naturalists and constructionists is basically the same: clarifications and solutions of philosophical problems and perplexities. The two schools would also agree in the point, emphasized by Wittgenstein, that some of these problems and most of these perplexities result from an inappropriate use of language. Here we may distinguish between two kinds of cases, which, however, are not separated by a sharp line. In cases of the first kind, the unsuitable usage does not occur in everyday language, but is introduced by a philosopher in an intentional or unintentional deviation from ordinary language. A philosopher may, for instance, use a certain term of ordinary language in a much more general sense; or he may make a wrong assimilation, as Strawson has explained. In a case of this kind, the method of the analysis of ordinary language may be sufficient for the solution of the ensuing puzzle; the deviation is pointed out, and thereby the perplexity disappears. The constructionist may agree with this procedure; but in some cases of this kind he would suggest an additional step. For example, a philosopher, needing a more general concept for his particular purposes, may change the sense of a term of everyday language because in this language there is no term for the more general concept. In this case, the constructionist may regard it as advisable to choose a different term for the new concept, and to provide more exact directives for its use. The new expression may be formed by the addition of a qualifying adjective to the old term, or by the addition of a subscript, or even a newly coined term may be proposed. (If the reader is shocked or offended by the two last-mentioned procedures, I hasten to assure him that they occur, of course, only in the more barbarous regions, like America, where the sacrilege of tampering with the holy tradition of language is sometimes connived at.)

In cases of the second sort, the misuse of certain expressions occurs in everyday language. Here again, both the naturalist and the constructionist may agree in the diagnosis of the inappropriate usage in question. It may be that both also agree with regard to the therapy, which may consist in the suggestion that the unsuitable way of speaking be replaced by a more suitable one, still belonging to ordinary language. But here it may occur that the constructionist prefers the use of a newly constructed term not belonging to ordinary language. How far he will move away from ordinary language will depend upon what he regards as useful in the given case. I should like to emphasize again that this is a matter of degree. The constructionist may, for example, propose to use, in certain philosophical contexts (not in contexts of everyday life), certain words of everyday language according to certain rules (e.g., to use the word "or" only in the non-exclusive sense), or he may propose a symbol for the new sense. For the rules or the definition of the explicatum—whether it be represented by an old word in a new sense, or by a new word, or by a symbol—he may use either ordinary language, or in addition some scientific terms frequently used in ordinary language, or purely scientific terms. He may merely state a few simple rules, or he may prefer a more or less elaborate procedure, and for this he may or may not use an artificial language.

In my view, the extent to which artificial and elaborate means are used depends on the nature of the philosophical problem in question, and also on the aim of the therapy. The aim may merely be to eliminate an isolated minor difficulty in the simplest way possible. In this case, simple means will suffice. Or the aim may be a more thoroughgoing reform in order to overcome a larger group of interconnected philosophical difficulties. In this case it may be necessary to use more elaborate means and a more comprehensive systematization.

One of Strawson's main arguments for the thesis of naturalism is the following. Since the roots of philosophical difficulties lie in ordinary language, the difficulties must be eliminated by the analysis of ordinary language. To propose for this aim an artificial language or a new scientific explicatum, would be "to do something utterly irrelevant", and to deflect our attention from the original difficulties to entirely different concepts. As I emphasized above, an explicatum serves primarily for the same purpose as the explicandum; therefore, an artificial language as a whole may at first serve the same purpose as ordinary language. Later, of course, the new term or the new language may be used within new contexts. In my view, a language, whether natural or artificial, is an instrument that may be replaced or modified according to our needs, like any other instrument. For the naturalists, ordinary language seems to have an essentially fixed character and therefore to be basically indispensable, just like our body with its organs, to which we may add accessories like eyeglasses, hearing aides, and the like, but which we cannot essentially change or replace. However, a natural language is not an unchangeable function of our body, but something we have learned; therefore we can replace it by another language. Some naturalists seem to think that it is in principle impossible to learn an artificial language in any other way than by a translation into our mother tongue. Some formulations by Strawson might also be interpreted in this sense; but I do not know whether he actually holds this view. At any rate, this view is certainly wrong. The method of learning by translation is indeed sometimes practically convenient, and therefore usually applied in learning an artificial language, especially one used in logic or mathematics. But just as we can learn another natural language without the use of our mother tongue as a metalanguage (e.g., in the Berlitz method), so we can learn a language of the kind used in symbolic logic (but with pronounceable words instead of merely graphic symbols, and with a sufficient vocabulary of non-logical constants) without the help of our mother tongue. Later, after such a language has been learned by the practical, direct method, we might learn explicit rules for it, formulated in this language itself, just as a child in school learns grammatical rules of his mother tongue, formulated in the same language. In this way the artificial language would become a regulated language system. This is explained in detail by Bohnert (§II). My intention in making this point is not, of course, to propose the actual use of this method for learning a logical language, but merely to point out the theoretical possibility of such a procedure, and thereby to refute the wide-spread view that constructed languages are not autonomous, but essentially parasitic, based on natural languages.

A natural language is like a crude, primitive pocketknife, very useful for a hundred different purposes. But for certain specific purposes, special tools are more efficient, e.g., chisels, cutting-machines, and finally the microtome. If we find that the pocket knife is too crude for a given purpose and creates defective products, we shall try to discover the cause of the failure, and then either use the knife more skillfully, or replace it for this special purpose by a more suitable tool, or even invent a new one. The naturalist's thesis is like saying that by using a special tool we evade the problem of the correct use of the cruder tool. But would anyone criticize the bacteriologist for using a microtome, and assert that he is evading the problem of correctly using a pocketknife?

Bertrand Russell,[25] from whom most of us have learned the use of a symbolic language for the clarification and solution of philosophical problems, has recently shown in a delightful way the futility of the tendency to stick to the customary language at any price.

The choice of a method for the solution of a given philosophical problem should be decided in each case by practical considerations. We constructionists should not claim that our method is the only one for the solution of philosophical problems, or necessarily the best in all cases. But naturalists likewise should not make such claims for their method, as some of them, though not Strawson, do.

Let us consider some of the examples mentioned earlier. Frege was able to give his explications of the numerical words "one", "two", etc. in the natural language *(Die Grundlagen der Arithmetik,* 1884). But later he found it advisable and in a certain sense even necessary to formulate these explications in a newly constructed logical language system *(Grundgesetze der Arithmetik,* two volumes, 1893 and 1903). To demonstrate the adequacy of his explications, he had to show that the numerals and the other arithmetical signs, as defined by him, had the properties customarily ascribed to them in arithmetic. For this purpose, it was necessary to show that the basic laws of arithmetic could be proved for his explicata. And in order to assure the cogency and purity of the proofs, it was necessary to formulate them in a system with fixed axioms and rules of inference. It would hardly have been advisable, although theoretically possible, to use the ordinary word language for these operations. The situation is different in the case of Zeno's paradoxes. For their solution, certain parts of mathematics are needed which go far beyond elementary arithmetic, such as the theory of real numbers, the concept of the limit of a series, and finally the proof that certain infinite series are convergent, i.e., that every member of the series is greater than zero and nevertheless the sum of the whole series is finite. In this case, the perplexities were formulated in the natural language. But the diagnosis consists in the demonstration that certain apparently valid forms of inference involving the infinite are fallacious and lead to contradic-

[25]B. Russell, "Logic and Ontology", *J. Phil.* LIV (1957), 225-230.

tions. The therapy consists in the use of a new language, with terms suitable for the formulation of the problem and with rules of deduction preventing the old contradictions. In this case, the old knife and the simple chisel are inadequate; we have to use a more elaborate tool.

I agree with Strawson in the view expressed in his present essay and at another place[26] that the naturalist and the constructionist methods are not necessarily competitive, but rather mutually complementary, since each of them fulfills a certain purpose. To this appeal for cooperation instead of controversy Strawson adds the remark that he himself is partisan; and so am I, on the other side.

A view similar to that in which Strawson and I agree, is held by Nelson Goodman. In the third section of his essay, which deals with constructionism, he gives first a concise, clear exposition of the aims of conceptual constructions. His comparison of this kind of construction with the drawing of a map clears up misunderstandings which are the basis of many criticisms of constructionism. He emphasizes correctly that the reconstruction of a single concept, or of a conceptual system, or of a total language is not intended to copy or picture reality either as a whole, or in part, or on a diminished scale, but to represent the relations among the objects in question by an abstract schema. Then he likewise expresses the view that the activities of the constructionists and the linguistic naturalists (or verbal analysts, as he calls them) are not incompatible but rather complimentary. I share Goodman's feelings when he says that the verbal analyst appears to him "as a valued and respected, if inexplicably hostile ally". (This does not, of course, apply to Strawson.)

It is certainly more fruitful, instead of wasting time in deprecating the method of the other side, to work out some mode of peaceful coexistence of the two movements, and if possible, to cooperate. We all agree that it is important that good analytic work on philosophical problems be performed. Everyone may do this according to the method which seems to be the most promising to him. The future will show which of the two methods, or which of the many varieties of each, or which combinations of both, furnishes the best results.

20. Yehoshua Bar-Hillel on Linguistics and Metatheory

Bar-Hillel makes an appeal for closer collaboration between logicians and linguists. He explains that it would be desirable for logicians to study the logical structure of natural languages too, as he himself, Quine, Reichenbach, and others have begun to do. On the other hand, linguists could use certain methods and results of modern logic to advantage for

26Strawson, "Construction and Analysis" in: Ayer *et al., The Revolution in Philosophy* (London, 1957). Ayer too regards both methods as legitimate and fruitful (*ibid.,* 86).

their own purposes. I am in full sympathy with this appeal. The fact that I myself have given no more than short indications at various places is, as Bar-Hillel remarks, only due to the necessity of a division of labor.

I think, however, that we should be cautious in the specification of those items in logic which might be fruitful for linguistics. I believe that we should less emphasize special results than general points of view and general characteristic traits of the methods of syntax and semantics as developed in logic. These traits would include, e.g., the possibility of representing in a formal way logical meaning relations by syntactical rules of transformation, as Bar-Hillel has pointed out. I myself am not in a position even to try to make these matters clear to the linguists; this is the task of those who, like Bar-Hillel, are familiar with the contemporary methods and tendencies in linguistic investigation. It is always difficult to build a bridge between two fields of knowledge which have developed their methods and terminologies separately, so that even elementary communication is not easy. Bar-Hillel's paper of 1954 (see his footnote 13) seems to have found little echo among linguists so far, although this paper, in contrast to my publications, is written in a generally comprehensible language, is published in a linguistic periodical, and makes direct references to the works of the structural linguists. I was not surprised to find that Chomsky[26a] in his reply to Bar-Hillel's article does not agree with Bar-Hillel's views; I think that Chomsky is to some extent right, because Bar-Hillel claims too much when he speaks about the *immediate* importance of my investigations for linguistics. But, on the other hand, I have the impression that Chomsky failed to grasp the meaning of Bar-Hillel's appeal and also the aim and nature of my theories of syntax and semantics, and this shows the great difficulty of communication between the two fields.

I am in agreement in all essential points with Bar-Hillel's explanation of the replacement of ontological controversies about entities of various kinds by discussions of different language forms. These discussions would include the semantical and pragmatical properties of the language forms and, above all, the usefulness of certain language forms for given purposes. My view on this question is set forth in greater detail in §4A. Bar-Hillel suggests not only to *replace* the ontological theses of the existence of certain kinds of entities by a discussion of practical questions concerning the choice of forms of language, but rather to *interpret* those theses as assertions of the expediency of corresponding language forms for certain purposes. It is true that this procedure would have the advantage that the allegedly theoretical theses of ontology would be in-

[26a]Noam Chomsky, "Logical Syntax and Semantics. Their Linguistic Relevance", *Language,* XXXI (1955), 36-45.

terpreted as genuine theoretical theses. However, I still have the feeling that this reinterpretation deviates too much from the interpretation which the philosophers themselves actually had in mind.

Bar-Hillel is particularly interested in the problem of the logical analysis of *natural languages.* I share, of course, his view that linguists have the task of describing the *actual* use of language (not with respect to individuals but in the average of a language community) and not an improved use that might be proposed by a logician. Thus the linguists would have to say that the meaning of the word "raven" in everyday language is so vague and fluctuating that it is impossible to determine whether or not this meaning implies that of "black".

However, it seems to me that from this fact it by no means follows that the linguist could not or should not use for his task the exact means of logic with its sharp dichotomies. The metalanguage in which he formulates the description of a natural language, is itself not a part of natural language but rather a part of the language of science; therefore this metalanguage should be—and usually is—much more exact than the language which he describes. I have no doubt that the best procedure for this metalanguage would be to use the sharp dichotomies of two-valued logic (certainly not the sometimes proposed "non-Aristotelian" logic). I think the analogy with the situation in geometry is here illuminating. It is clear that the best method for the description of the spatial shapes even of diffuse clouds and of perpetually varying currents in the ocean consists in the use of an exact system of geometry. [The proposal by Johannes Hjelmslev to abandon the customary idealizations of geometry in physics and use instead a "natural geometry" which makes only those distinctions which are actually observable, has not been accepted by physicists. It is true that the concepts of this natural geometry would be closer to the observables and thus also to the concepts of everyday language, but on the whole they would be too complicated and certainly not fruitful.] The metalanguage to be employed in linguistics should, for instance, not use a word as vague and ambiguous as "salt", but instead expressions with clearer meanings, e.g., "kitchen salt" and exact terms of chemistry. With the help of these exact terms the linguist could describe the specific kind of vagueness and ambiguity of the word "salt" of the ordinary language in various contexts e.g.: "Under such and such circumstances, for instance, in kitchen and grocery, the word 'salt' is used almost always in the sense of kitchen salt, i.e., for NaCl, and so forth". Generally speaking, the most efficient form of a metalanguage, even for the description of vague and varying meanings, is a language which enables us to speak about exact meanings. As an example, let us consider meanings of the type of properties of material bodies. For the precise delineation of exact meanings of this type, we need the construction of a suitable (possibly multi-dimensional) logical space of properties. An exact property of maximum specificity corresponds to a *point* in this logical space; an exact meaning of less specificity corresponds to a smaller or larger *region* in this space, but still with a sharp boundary. A vague meaning corresponds to a region without a sharp boundary. Such a region may be described by the specification of three zones: the affirmed interior zone, the negated exterior zone, and the intermediate zone of vagueness. If a more precise description of a vague meaning is desired, then it might be given by the specification of a density distribution (a probability distribution) in the logical space.

For the geometry of the logical space the customary terminology may be applied: for a given region every point either belongs to it or does not belong to it. In a logical space of possible cases ("states" or "models"), every proposition has a range. If the range is universal, the proposition is analytic (logically necessary); if the range is empty, the proposition is contradictory (impossible). Thus it seems to me that it is not at all necessary for the description of vagueness to look for a new metalanguage which abandons the customary logical distinctions. Such a language would be very inefficient. All that is needed is the definition of suitable new concepts within the old logical framework.

Bar-Hillel also discusses the problem of the explication of those concepts which are needed for philosophical investigations and discussions. It is true that in philosophy we often begin with everyday language. But I do not share the view, still maintained by many philosophers especially in England, that philosophy should chiefly be concerned with problems formulated in ordinary language; still less the view that the explication of concepts used for philosophical discussions is always to be given in natural language. It seems to me that in the development of philosophical analyses in recent decades it has become clear that it is often advisable or even necessary to apply terms which do not occur in ordinary language but are taken from science, logic, or metatheory (logical syntax, semantics, pragmatics). I have explained my view on this question in greater detail in my reply to Strawson (§19).

Many of the most important philosophical terms are meta-terms, e.g. "truth" and "logical truth". The majority of those philosophers who are interested in the philosophical analysis of language agree today not only that truth is an important concept, but also that its explication for constructed languages can be given by means of semantical rules. However, there is still disagreement on the question of the object languages for which an explication of truth would be fruitful for the purposes of philosophy, in particular, the philosophy of logic, the philosophy of knowledge, or the philosophy of science. I believe that this object language should be neither the everyday language nor a language like that of *Principia Mathematica* which is not sufficient for the expression of factual assertions. An object language relevant for philosophical discussions would rather be a language that is envisaged or planned but not completely described. It usually suffices to specify only some part of the language or even only some characteristic features of it which are relevant for the philosophical problem to be discussed. Thus the philosopher talks about a proposed, not actually existent, incompletely described language. He will choose that form of language which seems to him most suitable for the problem in question, say the language of natural numbers, of real numbers, of modalities, of certain concepts of physics, or concepts of other branches of science, of belief sentences, of sense data statements, of statements concerning observable events, or anything else. A concept like truth can be explicated by semantical rules for any such partial language as object language, even if it is only incompletely described. These semantical rules can be formulated in a general form so that they are applicable to a comprehensive class of languages (compare the definition of truth in §10 I D).

IV. Concepts and Theories of Empirical Science

21. Nelson Goodman on Der logische Aufbau der Welt

In my first book, *Der logische Aufbau der Welt* [1928-1], I tried to show how the whole system of concepts in science could be constructed on a very simple phenomenalistic basis referring to elementary experiences *("Elementarerlebnisse")*. In my Autobiography (§§2 and 4A) I have outlined the development of my views represented in this book and the thoroughgoing critical examination by Nelson Goodman in his doctor's thesis, in which he proposed not only certain improvements but also an entirely new approach on a different phenomenalistic basis. More recently, Goodman elaborated his thesis in his book *The Structure of Appearance* (1951). In his essay for the present volume Goodman points out that the basic philosophical outlook underlying the *Aufbau* is not essentially new but rather characteristic of a long historical development, beginning with the British empiricists of the eighteenth century. He recognizes clearly, perhaps even overestimates, the strength of the opposition by contemporary philosophers to this reconstructional approach, and he defends the basic features of the general method and, in particular, those of my approach to the problem against these philosophers and, as he adds, even against myself. It is true that I have criticized not only details but also certain basic characteristics of the method developed in the *Aufbau*. I am convinced that progress in philosophy, as in science, can come only through continual mutual criticism, self-criticism, and attempts at improved approaches. But I am indeed gratified that some fundamental features of the method which I helped to develop and which I tried to apply systematically for the first time in my book, are still found to be worth defending and to be worth studying and developing further.

Goodman discusses the two alternative forms for a comprehensive system of concepts: the phenomenalistic form, i.e., a system constructed on the basis of immediate experiences or sense data, and the physicalistic form, i.e., a system constructed on the basis of observable things and their observable properties and relations. The system in the *Aufbau* is phenomenalistic. But since the beginning of physicalism (*ca.*1930) I have chiefly thought about and worked on physicalistic systems. I agree, however, that both system forms are possible. While Goodman prefers a phenomenalistic system, I prefer a physicalistic one because I regard certain features of the latter as more advantageous. Let me mention, on the one hand, the intersubjective character of the physicalistic basic concepts (different observers will in general agree about the observable properties of things in their environments although their subjective experiences might differ), and, on the other hand, the great difficulty of constructing a clearly interpreted, practicable, purely phenomenalistic language, difficulties which have so far not found a satisfactory solution.

I also agree with Goodman's view that every system should, in one way or another, deal with the problem of the relations which, in a phenominalistic system, are characterized as relations between experiences or sense data and perceptible things. He believes that this problem is evaded in a physicalistic system; but this is not the case. The problem appears in such a system in an entirely different form, as a problem concerning human organisms. In particular, it is the problem how an organism is able, on the meager basis of the environmental stimuli received by its sense organs, to recognize and manipulate the things in its environment. While the details of this problem are a matter of physiology and psychology, the general character of these relations is a philosophical problem.

In §4 of his essay, Goodman discusses the relation between definiens and definiendum which must be required for an accurate reconstruction; in my terminology, the problem concerns the relation between explicatum and explicandum which must be required for an adequate explication. It seems justifiable to me to make different requirements for different situations. Although sometimes synonymy in the strong sense might be required, this does not seem necessary to me in general; in most cases logical equivalence is sufficient, and perhaps even this is not necessary. For the system in the *Aufbau* I required identity of extensions. Goodman regards this requirement as too strong and suggests replacing it by a certain kind of isomorphism. This may in many cases be a good requirement. But I should like to emphasize that the correspondence, be it identity of extensions or identity of structures, must fulfil an additional requirement which is hardly ever made explicit, but which seems to be fulfilled in most cases of philosophical explications, as well as in the system of the *Aufbau* (as far as the reconstruction is valid) and in Goodman's system. This additional requirement consists in the condition that the correspondence hold, not merely accidentally, but on the basis of general regularities, e.g., physical laws or empirical generalizations. For example, in a system containing basic concepts of theoretical physics, the color blue (applied to things or light) is reconstructed in terms of electromagnetic wave lengths; this reconstruction is based on laws of physics, physiology and psychology.

Goodman discusses the reduction sentences which I suggested in the article [1936-10] for the introduction of disposition concepts. He says that these sentences are not comparable to definitions, but are merely postulates for the introduction of new primitive terms. Today I would agree that the reduction sentences may be regarded as postulates. They differ, however, from the ordinary postulates of an uninterpreted postulate system, since they contain, in addition to the new primitive term, some interpreted terms and thus contribute to the interpretation of the new term. As I shall explain later (§24D), they may be taken as a special kind of correspondence postulates.

In the *Aufbau,* the basis of the system was extremely limited; I used a certain dyadic relation between elementary experiences (recognition-of-similarity) as the only non-logical primitive. Consequently the reconstruction showed certain defects in the very first steps which led to definitions of sense qualities, e.g., colors. For example, if certain unfavorable circumstances were to occur in the series of elementary experiences then certain colors would be omitted in the reconstruction, although they actually did occur in the visual field of the observer; on the other hand, certain classes would be counted as colors although they did not correspond to actual colors. As Goodman mentions, I explained some of these defects in detail in the *Aufbau* and I stated that additional ones existed. The example concerning "things all alike" which Goodman mentions, is one of those which I discussed in detail (as Goodman states in his book). In addition, Goodman found inadequacies which I had not recognized. I do not believe that these inadequacies are as serious and as disastrous as Goodman thinks. It is clear that most of these defects can easily be avoided by using a more comprehensive basis. But in my system I wanted to find out what could be done with a basis restricted to the minimum.

Today, if I were to construct the schema of a conceptual system on a phenomenalistic basis, I should prefer to use a greater number of primitives. There is a great number of possible system forms from which to choose. Goodman himself takes as individuals, and thus as the only values of the variables, the so-called "qualia"; e.g., if a certain color occurs at a certain position in the visual field at a certain time, then the color, the location, and the time point are three qualia which are regarded as parts constituting the one "concretum". Goodman believes that the nominalistic requirement in this procedure is fulfilled. In a certain sense this is true; but I doubt whether it holds in the ordinary sense of "nominalistic". I should prefer to take as individuals the concreta themselves (e.g., the occurrence of a red spot at a certain position in the visual field at a certain time) and then to use primitive predicates of the following kind: spatial relations (perhaps one is sufficient), a temporal relation, qualitative properties (e.g., red) or qualitative relations (e.g., similarity). Whoever investigates philosophical problems of this kind should mind Goodman's admonition that after some preliminary meta-philosophical discussions the philosophical work itself must be started, in this case, the construction of a system or of parts of a system. For the construction of a system on a phenomenalistic basis, much can be learned from Goodman's thoroughgoing investigations.

At the end of §18 above, I have made some comments on Goodman's constructionism.

22. *Arthur Pap on Dispositions*

A. Reduction sentences. When I originally proposed so-called reduction sentences for the introduction of disposition terms (in [1936-10] §§8-10), I emphasized that these sentences generally combine two different functions. First, they give an interpretation for the disposition terms introduced by them; but, in contrast to definitions, these interpretations are incomplete. Secondly, they make in general a factual assertion. Let C be the conjunction of all reduction sentences for a certain disposition term. I formulated the factual content of C by a certain sentence S which contained only old terms and which I called the representative sentence of C. Later (in [1952-5] §3) I proposed to introduce the disposition term as a new primitive constant by a meaning postulate; but instead of C I took the conditional sentence $S \supset C$ as this postulate (see Hempel's essay, §7, and my Reply, §24D). Thereby a clear separation of the two distinct functions of reduction sentences is achieved. On the basis of the analysis of C into the synthetic postulate S and the analytic meaning postulate $S \supset C$, it becomes possible to apply the dichotomy analytic-synthetic also to sentences with disposition terms introduced in the way described. This procedure refutes Pap's assertion that the dichotomy is not applicable to this case.

If a disposition predicate is introduced as a primitive constant in the way described, then, although only partially interpreted, it is significant in a wider sense since possibilities of confirmation and of disconfirmation are given. This significance is not dependent upon contingent facts but only upon the rules of the given language, including the postulates. I have previously compared a set of reduction sentences to a conditional definition. However, this comparison must not be understood literally; the reduction sentences are postulates rather than definitions. Therefore the logical principles, e.g., that of the excluded middle and that of the excluded contradiction, hold unrestrictedly for terms introduced by reduction sentences. Thus the difficulties which Pap points out in this respect (in §5) do actually not hold for these terms. I shall discuss other theoretical terms later in B.

Pap (§5) believes, surprisingly, that serious difficulties of a similar nature arise even in the basic parts of customary logic. As a first example, Pap refers to individual descriptions introduced according to Russell's method. I shall not discuss the objection that in everyday language phrases like "the wife of John" are not used in exactly the same way as the corresponding symbolic expressions in Russell's constructed language. Like Pap, I shall consider only whether in a constructed language serious difficulties arise which so far have not been entirely solved. Pap discusses the well-known and often-explained difficulties in case the operand of a description does not satisfy the condition of uniqueness *(U)*. The explanations in *Principia Mathematica* (vol. I, ch. III of the Introduction and section *14) make it clear that descriptions cannot generally be treated like individual constants (for example, not in the inference of specification leading from a universal sentence to a substitution instance), but only if condition *U* is satisfied. In my book [1929-2] §7c, I added an explicit warning with respect to this pitfall. Pap points out, no doubt correctly, that "If we allow substitution of definite descriptions for individual variables", we are sometimes led to false conclusions. But then he says himself that Russell's rules do not permit such substitutions (without restrictions). Thus the difficulty disappears, and it is not clear why Pap brings up the whole problem.[27]

The next example discussed by Pap concerns the problem of what Russell called "logically proper names", i.e., those individual constants which are not interpreted as abbreviations for descriptions but are supposed to have simple direct meanings. This was indeed once a serious problem. But this problem too was solved long ago. For example, if a

[27]In his paper "Logic, Existence, and the Theory of Descriptions", *Analysis* XIII (1953), to which he refers in the present footnote 35, Pap discusses at still greater length this "serious puzzle" that has been given "less, if any, attention by logicians". Then he makes the surprising statement (my italics): "If descriptions are substitutable for individual variables, *as they are normally supposed to be,*...." But he gives no reference to any logician who makes this supposition. Compare also the clarifying discussion of Pap's paper by Donald Kalish, *ibid.*, XV (1955).

language form is chosen, following Russell[28] or Quine[29], such that non-logical individual constants do not occur as primitive constants, but, if at all, only as abbreviations for descriptions, then the difficulty discussed by Pap disappears, and significance is no longer dependent upon contingent facts.

Furthermore, methods have been known for many years which make it possible to avoid the bothersome restrictions in the use of descriptions imposed in Russell's theory. This can be achieved if, as was first proposed by Frege, a certain object a^* is chosen once and for all by a suitable convention, and the stipulation is made that any description not satisfying the condition U is to denote the object a^* (comp. [1947-2] §8). If this method is used, then the customary logical inferences—in particular, that of specification—are valid for descriptions without any restriction. [Incidentally, for a language whose individuals are physical things or events, my proposal to take the null thing as a^* still appears very suitable to me. The doubts of some critics about this proposal, and the view that it might lead to contradictions, have no better foundation than the feelings which some beginners in the logic of classes or set theory have against the null class.]

Thus we find that the problems pointed out and discussed in detail by Pap do not involve any serious difficulties. In particular, various methods are known for constructing a language in such a way that the significance of sentences does not depend upon contingent facts.

B. Theoretical concepts. In my article on theoretical concepts [1956-4], which was written after the original version of Pap's essay, but to which he refers in a passage of §2, inserted later, I have explored in detail the general method of introducing theoretical terms by postulates. Let T be the conjunction of the theoretical postulates which connect these terms with one another, and C the conjunction of the correspondence postulates which connect theoretical terms with terms of the observation language. Pap, like Hempel, points out correctly the great difficulty involved in the task of explicating the distinction between *analytic* and *synthetic* in this more general framework. Pap is right in stating that the (incomplete) interpretation of the theoretical terms is given not by T alone but by the total system TC of the T-postulates and the C-postulates. He shows that we arrive at unacceptable consequences if, on the one hand, the C-postulates (sometimes called "coordinative definitions" or "operational definitions") are regarded as genuine definitions and therefore all sentences provable with their help are taken as analytic, and if,

[28]B. Russell *(An Inquiry Into Meaning and Truth* (1940), 117) chooses a language containing names for qualities but not for particulars, i.e., individuals.

[29]W. V. Quine, *Mathematical Logic* (1940), 149ff.

on the other hand, the T-postulates are regarded as having a purely factual character. But these arguments prove merely that this particular method of separating the analytic from the synthetic component is wrong; they do by no means prove that a separation is impossible. Indeed, it seems to me that the new tentative method of separation, which I describe in §24D, is free from the difficulties discussed by Pap. (At the present time, I have not yet seen his publications mentioned in footnote 19, §II of his essay in the present volume, namely, a paper on physical magnitudes and a book on semantics.)

From the point of view of the general framework of a language with theoretical terms, the reduction sentences appear as merely a special, simple form of C-postulates for disposition terms. It would certainly be useful to investigate also other forms, among them, as Pap suggests (§2), probabilistic forms. These may involve the concept of statistical probability. Pap proposes a specific form, whose intended meaning, however, is not clear to me. Of the second probability symbol occurring in his formula, Pap says only that it is "concocted" from Reichenbach's symbol of probability implication (hence statistical probability) and Lewis' symbol of strict implication, and that "it may be read as degree of entailment"; later he says explicitly that it means neither relative frequency nor degree of confirmation in my sense. I agree with Pap's basic idea that the inference from observation sentences to a scientific disposition term (in contrast to "pure disposition terms" in the sense of [1956-4] §X) is in general only a probability inference; the same holds for most theoretical concepts. But it seems to me that for the time being the problem of the best form for C-postulates or C-rules has not yet been sufficiently clarified.

Today I would think like Pap (in §4) that the question of whether a given property is *in itself* a disposition, has no clear meaning. I would prefer to relativize the term "disposition" with respect to a language, as Pap suggests. Disposition terms of a given language are then characterized by the fact that they are introduced into this language in a certain way (e.g., by simple or probabilistic reduction sentences, or by definitions of certain forms involving causal modalities).

C. Causal modalities. I have discussed *logical* modalities in detail in §9. For many problems, among them that of explicating dispositions, it would certainly be of interest to investigate also *causal* modalities. In [1936-10] I did not take them into consideration because then no one had indicated even the very first steps toward an explication or systematization of causal modalities. If I am correct, Arthur Burks was the first to do this.[30] I have the impression that so far nobody has actually refuted the assumption, sometimes called "thesis of extensionality", which says

30 A. Burks, "The Logic of Causal Propositions", *Mind,* LX (1951), 363-382.

that every proposition expressible in a non-extensional language is also expressible in a suitable extensional language (in such a way that the two sentences are logically equivalent). Nevertheless, logical and perhaps also causal modalities, even if they are in principle dispensable, may still be useful and perhaps even practically indispensable. On the other hand, an extensional language has the advantage of having a much simpler logical structure. Only in the future, when the logic of modalities has been investigated much more thoroughly, will it be possible to judge whether an extensional or a modal language has the greater overall advantage.

If an extensional language is chosen, then, among the methods proposed so far, the method of reduction sentences (perhaps as C-postulates, or in the modified form as P- and A-postulates as indicated in §24D) seems yet to be a suitable way of introducing dispositions.

Let us search for a procedure that might be used if a language containing not only logical modalities but also causal modalities is chosen. For the explication of the concept of logical necessity, with whose help all other logical modalities can easily be defined, I found the following procedure useful. The semantical concept corresponding to the modal concept of the logical necessity of a proposition is the logical truth of a sentence. For the latter concept I had found an explication. I proposed the following convention:

(1) If *S* is an extensional sentence and *p* is the proposition designated by *S*, then *p* is *logically necessary* if and only if *S* is logically true.

(This is (39-1) in [1947-2]; today I would use the more general semantical concept of analyticity, i.e., A-truth as explained in §24D.) (1) is not a definition of logical necessity; but it turns out to be useful as a guiding idea for the construction of a system of logical modalities.

I am inclined to think that it may be promising to use an analogous procedure for the explication of causal modalities. (This is only a programmatic idea; I have not yet made detailed systematic studies in this direction.) The concept which I would try to explicate first is the semantical concept of the causal validity of a sentence, corresponding to the modal concept of the causal necessity of a proposition, in other words, the distinction between genuine causal universals (laws) and accidental universals. I would attempt this explication first with respect to an extensional language *L*, comprehensive enough for the purposes of empirical science, especially physics. For this purpose it seems to be essential to distinguish between fundamental laws and derivative laws. *Derivative laws* may have the same semantical nature as accidental universals; therefore we cannot distinguish them directly by a purely semantical analysis of their forms. On the other hand, I believe, although I am not quite certain, that it is possible to explicate the distinction between *fundamental laws* and accidental universals in purely semantical terms.

The central problem so far unsolved is that of explicating the concept of sentences of *nomic form,* i.e., sentences which have the form of a possible fundamental law, irrespective of truth. If this problem were solved, I would proceed as follows. I define:

(2) A sentence *S* in *L* is a *fundamental law* in *L* $=_{\text{Df}}$ *S* has nomic form and is true in *L*.

(3) A sentence *S* in *L* is *causally valid* in *L* $=_{\text{Df}}$ *S* is L-implied (or A-implied in the sense of §24D) by the class of the fundamental laws in *L*.

[Note that the concepts defined in (2) and (3) are semantical concepts which must be clearly distinguished from corresponding (and equally interesting) inductive and epistemological concepts, based not on truth but on high confirmation with respect to a given set of observational data. For the explication of causal modalities we must take the former, not the latter. This is my main objection against Reichenbach's proposal for an explication of "nomological".[31] By analogy to (1), I propose the following convention for a modal language *L′*, which is formed from *L* by adding terms for logical necessity and for causal necessity:

(4) If *S* is a sentence in *L* and *p* is the proposition designated by *S*, then *p* is *causally necessary* if and only if *S* is causally valid.

(4) is not a definition of causal necessity either; but I presume it to be a useful guiding idea for the construction of a system of modal logic containing both logical and causal modalities.

Let *S* be a sentence in a language of physics with a space-time coordinate system. It seems clear that the following is a necessary but not a sufficient condition for *S* having nomic form: *S* must not contain space-time coordinate constants, but only variables, as J. C. Maxwell has first pointed out. Which further conditions must be required for nomic form is today not yet clear.

Once the problem of the explication of nomic form has been solved and a logic of causal modalities has been constructed, it will be possible to use these modalities for the explication of subjunctive and, in particular, of counter-factual conditionals. Presumably it will then also be possible to introduce disposition terms by explicit definitions.

23. *Adolf Grünbaum on the Philosophy of Space and Time*

A. The causal theory of time. In §2 of his essay Grünbaum examines critically the causal theory of time. He raises the question of the relation

[31] H. Reichenbach, *Nomological Statements and Admissible Operations* (Amsterdam, 1954).

between my axiom system of space-time topology[32] and this theory. I doubt whether my axiom system and its underlying epistemological conception can be regarded as a version of the causal theory of time as Grünbaum understands this theory. In my system I take as the two primitive notions the coincidence *C* of world points and a time relation *T*. "*Txy*" means that (1) *x* and *y* are genidentical world points, i.e., moments of the same physical element, e.g., a material particle or a light ray, and (2) *x* is earlier than *y*. It is true that the general time relation is defined in the manner of Einstein by reference to causal or signal chains; a signal chain, however, is nothing but a chain of *T*-segments connected by coincidences. Using these primitives, the whole topology of space is constructed with the help of signal chains. It is essential to note that the epistemological conception underlying the axiom system assumes that the two relations *C* and *T* can be determined by observations. Thus in my construction the asymmetric signal relation is reduced to a locally restricted time relation which is already given as asymmetric. On the other hand, in what is strictly speaking the causal theory of time, the time relation is defined in terms of a causal relation determined independently. Therefore we might say that my system represents a causal theory of *space;* but since a time relation is taken as primitive in it, it seems that we should *not* say that it represents a causal theory of *time* (in the strict sense). For the same reason, the circularity pointed out by Grünbaum does not beset my system. Furthermore, it is not correct, as Grünbaum seems to think, that I have defined the asymmetric time relation according to Reichenbach's method of marking; rather, I am inclined to agree with the criticism of the latter method presented by H. Mehlberg, Grünbaum, and others.

B. The problem of the direction of time. Grünbaum discusses (in §3) at great length the problem of the direction of time and, in particular, the question whether the direction of time can be defined with the help of the concept of entropy. This section explains the main conceptions in Reichenbach's theory[33] and also Grünbaum's own conception which differs from Reichenbach's in certain points. I have not published anything on this problem and the discussion does not refer to any conception of mine. Therefore I shall not go into the details of Grünbaum's discussion. But I should like to express some doubts about the theory.

Reichenbach distinguishes between the problem of the *order* of time and the problem of the *direction* of time. With respect to a given set of

[32]The basic philosophical ideas of the axiom system are explained in [1925]. The axiom system was first published in [1929-2] § 36, later in greater detail in [1954-3] §§ 48-50 in German and in its English translation in [1958-2] §§ 48-50.

[33]For the latest version of this theory see Hans Reichenbach, *The Direction of Time* (Berkeley and Los Angeles, 1956), (posthumously published).

events no two of which are simultaneous, their temporal *order* is fixed if for any three of these events it is determined which of them is between the two others. The temporal *direction* is fixed if for any two events it is determined which is earlier than the other. In the problem of the direction of time it is assumed that the temporal order is given, and a general method is sought of determining, on this basis, the direction of time. Something like this seems to me the main point of the problem, as I understand it. However, the precise sense of the question is not clear to me. Is it meant as a question within the theoretical system of physics or rather a question concerning the operational rules which connect the terms of the theoretical language with those of the observation language? (The relations between these two sub-languages are discussed in §24.) I will briefly indicate three possible interpretations of the question, and thereby of the thesis of the definability of the direction of time in terms of entropy as an answer to the question. The first two interpretations concern the theoretical system only.

First interpretation. Some formulations of the two authors, in particular, many discussions in Reichenbach's book, give the impression that the thesis is meant as a proposal to introduce, in the theoretical system of physics, the direction of time by an explicit definition in terms of entropy (or, more generally, of irreversible processes of some kind); it is not explicitly stated whether in this method entropy is taken as primitive or whether and how it is to be defined on the basis of other primitives. The proposed method differs very much from the one customarily used in physics; in the latter, a space-time coordinate system, and thus the direction of time, belong to the basic concepts.

Boltzmann was the first to propose a definition of the direction of time by the increase of entropy in the universe or in an isolated system. Reichenbach proposes an essential modification in Boltzmann's definition. He refers, not to a single system, but rather to a space-ensemble of simultaneous branch systems. He defines the direction of time by the direction of the increase of entropy in the majority of branch systems. Reichenbach's definition, which is accepted also by Grünbaum, appears to me very problematic. We may criticize Boltzmann's definition by pointing out that the correlation between the direction of time and the increase in entropy holds, not universally, but only with probability. Now it seems to me that an analogous objection holds for Reichenbach's definition.

Second interpretation. Reichenbach's and Grünbaum's discussions of the problem of the direction of time can also be understood in the following sense. Let D be a description of a physical process in theoretical terms; let D^* be the description of the reverse process, i.e., a series of the same states but occurring in the reverse temporal direction. Suppose that we are told only that one of the two descriptions holds, but we are not told which it is. The question is now whether and how one of the two descriptions can be derived from the given information with the help of a given system of physical laws. Perhaps what the authors mean by "determination of the direction of time" is a derivation of this kind. If so, their problem is just the familiar and often discussed question of the irreversibility of processes, and the formulation "the definition of the direction of time" would seem to me misleading. The question explained is not a question of definition but rather a question about the relation between two theoretical concepts both of which are already assumed as given, either as primitive or as defined.

Third interpretation. It may be that Reichenbach and Grünbaum mean the problem of the direction of time as a problem concerning the rules of correspondence between theoretical and observational terms. These rules are often called "operational rules" or "operational definitions"; Reichenbach and Grünbaum call them "coordinative definitions". The formulations by Grünbaum seem to suggest this interpretation, because he frequently refers to "the coordinative definition of the direction of time".[34]

My third interpretation construes Reichenbach's and Grünbaum's thesis as a proposal of the following rule of operation:

(1) "Measure the entropy of each branch system at the time point x, and also at the time point y. If for a majority of the branch systems the entropy value obtained at x is considerably smaller than that at y, then assume that x was earlier than y."

This rule is meant to take the place, at least in important cases, of the customary operational rules for the direction of time, viz. the rule based on the subjective impression of one experience being earlier than another, and the rule referring to the use of a clock.

Rule (1) is based on the correlation between the direction of time and the increase of entropy. The fact that this correlation holds only with high probability, was used earlier as a ground for an objection against basing a *definition* on it. An analogous objection could not be raised

[34]In an earlier version of part B of this section, I explained in greater detail the three interpretations and my reactions to them, especially to the third interpretation, which I regarded as the most likely one. However, Grünbaum, after reading my manuscript, wrote me that he—and, in his opinion, also Reichenbach—had definitely not meant the problem in the sense of the third interpretation but rather "in a sense limited to the first two interpretations". This statement makes it even harder for me to understand the formulations in his essay. Therefore I have decided to restrict part B to some brief remarks. It seems to me that a fruitful discussion of the Reichenbach-Grünbaum theory of time will be possible only when a clearer explanation is given of the sense in which the main question and the main thesis are meant.

against rule (1), because this is not a definition but an operational rule, and an operational rule is not meant to hold without exceptions.

Rule (1) is, of course, not an independent rule; it presupposes other operational rules for the determination of the value of entropy. The question arises whether it is possible to formulate those other rules in such a way that no reference is made either to a clock or to the subjective experience of the direction of time. This possibility would have to be demonstrated if the thesis is meant in the sense of the third interpretation.

C. On the concept of "becoming". I agree with some points in Grünbaum's criticism of Reichenbach's analysis of "becoming" and of "now". However, I rather doubt that Reichenbach actually intended to characterize a *unique* "now", as Grünbaum and Hugo Bergman (as quoted by Grünbaum) accuse him of doing. This idea is so obviously absurd that I cannot believe that anybody would maintain it. But it is true that Reichenbach's use of metaphorical expressions may suggest to some readers an interpretation of this kind. It seems to me unfortunate that in his book Reichenbach used expressions of the following kind (pp. 20 f.): "time goes from the past to the future", "the flow of time", "time is not static, it moves", "we cannot change the past, but we can change the future". Reichenbach admits that these ways of speaking are not precise; he takes them only as explicanda, as formulations of "the conception of the physical world that governs everyday life". But I would think that these expressions are unsuitable even as formulations of the customary prescientific conception. Even the man in the street, at least when he is in a sober, as distinguished from a poetic, mood, is quite able to use clearer ways of expression. The formulations mentioned are so extremely ambiguous that they are almost meaningless.

An entirely different issue is the question whether there exists a fundamental difference between the possibility of our knowledge of the past and that of the future. This is indeed a meaningful and important problem. The answer depends upon the structure of the system of physical laws. Here I shall not enter into the details of this problem; my intention is merely to express my acceptance of the question.

I agree with the contention of Schlick, which is also accepted by Grünbaum, in contrast to that of Reichenbach, that even in a deterministic world, it is meaningful and possible to plan future actions. I think it is not necessary for me to explain this view here, since it has been explained and discussed in great detail and with clarity by a number of authors following Schlick.[35]

[35]See for example the article "The Freedom of the Will" in: University of California Associates, *Knowledge and Society* (New York, 1938); reprinted in H. Feigl and W. Sellars, *Readings in Philosophical Analysis* (New York, 1949).

D. Geometry and empiricism. Grünbaum reports correctly that in my doctor's thesis [1922] I took an empiricist position in regard to *physical* geometry, while following Kant and Husserl in considering our knowledge of the *topological* features of the *"Anschauungsraum"* (intuitive, visual space) as synthetic a priori. Later, especially in the atmosphere of the Vienna Circle, my conception became more consistently one of empiricism. The empiricist conception of geometrical knowledge and, more generally, of our knowledge of the properties of space and time, in which I and the other members of the Vienna Circle agreed with Reichenbach, has found its best exposition in Reichenbach's book of 1928.[36] Although I continued to be interested in the problems of the philosophical foundations of geometry, I have since written very little about it. The main reason for this was the fact that it seemed to me that the main points of this complex of problems had been developed by Reichenbach correctly, clearly, and thoroughly.

I wish to comment on an objection raised by Grünbaum against an assertion in my [1922]. There I had considered a metrization M_e constituting a redefinition of the physical congruence of two segments of the following kind: with respect to this redefinition, coupled with the observational results actually obtained on earth, the surface *E* of the earth is represented to be, not a sphere *S,* as in the customary conception, but a Euclidean plane *P.* (Note that the discussion concerns only the case described on p. 47 and p. 48 to line 7, not the second case described from there to p. 54.) I had asserted that this was only an alternative description *D′* different from the customary description *D,* but that *D′* was in accord with all actual observational results just as much as *D.* Grünbaum believes that this assertion though true in general, does not hold in all cases. I had already remarked myself that the mapping of the sphere *S* onto the Euclidean plane *P*— say by a stereographic projection from the North Pole *N* onto the tangential plane *P* through the South Pole— contains a singularity with respect to one point, namely *N.* Now Grünbaum thinks that this singularity has the consequence that in the description *D′* the point *N* cannot be traversed by a causal chain in any way and that the existence of such a point could be ascertained inductively by observation, at least in principle. But this is not the case. The mapping in my example is bi-unique and bi-continuous with the mere exception of the point *N;* admittedly, the latter is mapped on no point of the open Euclidean plane (or on the infinitely remote points of a projective, closed Euclidean plane). But this fact has no consequences for any possible observational results, since every observation involves a

36Hans Reichenbach, *Philosophie der Raum-Zeit-Lehre* (Berlin, 1928); English translation: *Philosophy of Space and Time* (New York, 1958).

spatial region with a positive extension, however small, but never a single point. This still holds if we think of what is observable "in principle", e.g., if we follow the practice of classical physics and adopt an idealization according to which the precision of observations can be made arbitrarily high (while always remaining finite). Thus, it is assumed classically that the length of any arbitrarily small segment can be measured in terms of arbitrarily small units. Therefore the unusual description D' is compatible with all actual observations made on the earth. For example, let us consider a stone which is moved through the North Pole. In the customary description D we would say that in this process the point N is within the stone during a certain interval of time. By analyzing the situation, we can easily find that in the description D' this process is by no means impossible. But here in D' it is described in such a way that the volume occupied by the stone during the time interval in question is infinite, but appears to our observations as finite. On the basis of the description D', we find exactly the same observations of the stone and of the relation between the stone and other bodies such as measuring rods, as on the basis of the description D. [Reichenbach[37] says, at the place referred to by Grünbaum, that in mathematics, isolated singularities are admitted for topological transformations. But he believes that the same should not be admitted in physics. However, I would think generally that such transformations are also admissible in physics in those cases where no discrepancies with possible observational results can occur.]

My answer to Grünbaum's question on the relation of my view to Schlick's realism is given in §4.

I am happy to find that Grünbaum clarifies Poincaré's conception of geometry, thus counteracting the wide-spread misunderstanding that Poincaré championed a pure conventionalism. Grünbaum shows on the basis of references and quotations from less well known sources that Poincaré, while emphasizing the importance of conventions, quite clearly upholds an empiricist position in regard to physical geometry, a position entirely in agreement with our conception.

24. Carl G. Hempel on Scientific Theories

A. The theoretical language. The discussion in this section concerns a language L which is on the whole similar to the language described in Hempel's essay and in my article [1956-4] on theoretical concepts.[38] The

[37]Reichenbach, *Philosophy of Space and Time,* near the end of § 12.

[38]I shall make use here of my notation of [1956-4], in which "L_O" and "V_O" replace Hempel's "L_B" and "V_B". In contrast to [1956-4], I shall consider all descriptive constants not definable on the basis of V_O as belonging to V_T. Therefore *pure disposition terms will also be taken as theoretical terms* (in contradistinction to [1956-4]

class of descriptive (i.e., non-logical) primitive constants of L is divided into two parts: V_O which contains the *observation terms,* and V_T, which contains the *theoretical terms.* The *observation language* L_O is a sub-language of L; it has a simple logical structure and contains the terms of V_O *but none of* V_T. The *theoretical language* L_T is that sub-language of L which does not contain V_O-terms. The language L, and therefore also L_T, contains a comprehensive system of logic; it also contains, for every constant of V_T, variables for which the constant may be substituted. In contradistinction to the earlier article, I shall also consider that sub-language of L which does not contain any V_T-terms. I shall call this language the *logically extended observation language* L'_O because it may be regarded as being formed from L_O by the addition of the comprehensive logic of L. The two sub-languages L'_O and L_T have this logic in common. But these sub-languages together do not exhaust L, for L also contains *mixed sentences,* i.e., those in which at least one V_O-term and at least one V_T-term occur. Let us assume that logical rules for the language L are given which define the concept of L-truth. A sentence S in L is *L-true in L* (i.e., logically true in the narrower sense) if S is a substitution instance of a logically valid sentence or schema not containing any descriptive constant. I shall write "$\vdash S$" for "S is L-true in L". S_i is said to *L-imply* S_j if and only if $\vdash S_i \supset S_j$; and S_i is said to be L-equivalent to S_j if and only if $\vdash S_i \equiv S_j$. (Note that all terms with the prefix "L-" are used in the narrower sense.) The problem of analyticity (logical truth in the wider sense will be discussed later, and a tentative explication will be given in part D.

It is assumed that the terms of V_O designate directly observable properties or relations, and that their meanings are completely understood. In view of the simple logical structure of L_O it is further assumed that all sentences of this language are completely understood. In contrast, the meanings of the theoretical terms of V_T generally go beyond what is directly observable. However, a partial interpretation of the theoretical terms and of the sentences of L containing them is provided by the following two kinds of postulates: the *theoretical postulates* in which only terms of V_T occur, and the *correspondence postulates* which are mixed sentences. We may assume that the number of postulates of these two kinds is finite, since variables of all required kinds are available. Let T be the conjunction of the theoretical postulates, and C the conjunction of the correspondence postulates. These C-postulates are interpretative sentences in the sense of Hempel (§4). However, in distinction to Hempel, I

§§ IX and X); and the *reduction sentences* by which they are introduced will be regarded as C-postulates. (The extended observation language L'_O *of* [1956-4], which included disposition terms, does not occur in the present discussion; the symbol "L'_O" will now be used in a different sense.)

require that every C-postulate contain at least one V_O*-term* and at least one V_T-term non-vacuously, but I do not require that every term of V_T occur in at least one C-postulate.

We might say that the sentences of L'_O are completely interpreted in a certain sense. These sentences contain as descriptive constants only the completely interpreted terms of V_O. However, it must be admitted that the interpretation of L'_O is not complete in the same strong sense as that of L_O, since L'_O does not satisfy the nominalistic requirement ([1956-4] §II, requirement (3)); sentences of L'_O can be understood only if abstract variables, e.g., variables for classes, for classes of classes, etc., are intelligible.

Hempel discusses (in §5) the following methodological question. Since the purpose of scientific theories is to establish predictive connections between data of experience, is it not possible to avoid the theoretical language and work with observation language alone? In a detailed discussion Hempel gives convincing reasons for the thesis that this is not possible, in other words, that theoretical terms are indispensable for the purposes of science.[39] His main argument is based on the point that a scientific theory has the task of establishing not only deductive relations but also inductive relations among observational data. I believe that Hempel was the first to emphasize clearly this important point. However, the question of the exact way in which the inductive relations should be established in a comprehensive language like L constitutes a difficult and so far unsolved problem.

Hempel points out (especially in §7) that with respect to a language of the kind L, which contains theoretical terms, the difficulties of the following three problems are increased considerably. These problems are: first the empirical significance of terms and sentences, second the "experiential import" of sentences, and finally analyticity. In the remainder of this section I shall discuss these three problems.

B. The problem of empirical significance. Let us seek a criterion or explication of empirical meaningfulness for V_T-terms and for sentences containing such terms. Following Hempel, I use the terms "significance" for the explicatum. The explicandum may be informally explained as follows: a sentence is empirically meaningful if its assumption may, under certain conditions, influence the prediction of observable events.

[39]Frank P. Ramsey ("Theories" (1929), in *The Foundations of Mathematics* (1931), ch. IXA) was among the first to emphasize that the terms of a scientific theory cannot be defined explicitly on the basis of observational terms, in contrast to the logical constructionism of Russell and of my [1928-1]. Ramsey's conception of theories is explained and further developed by Richard S. Braithwaite, *Scientific Explanation* (1953), see ch. III: "The Status of the Theoretical Terms of a Science".

I have discussed this problem of explication in detail and have given a tentative criterion of significance for terms and for sentences in my article [1956-4], especially in sections VI to VIII. These sections may be regarded as an answer to that part of Hempel's essay which deals with the problem of significance. Many points in my article were indeed stimulated by Hempel's essay (I had read its first version of 1954 when I wrote my article) and by conversations and correspondence with Hempel, Feigl, and other members of the Minnesota Center for Philosophy of Science. In the article, I first gave a criterion for the significance of the theoretical *terms* in L. Then I proposed to call an expression E a *significant sentence* in L, if the following two conditions were fulfilled: (a) E is a sentence in L, i.e., E satisfies the rules of formation of L; and (b) every theoretical term in E is significant according to the first criterion.

In his essay Hempel expresses the view that a criterion of significance can be given only for a whole system, not for isolated sentences. Furthermore, he suspects that any criterion of significance which is not too narrow will be too wide in the following sense: a theory which is clearly meaningful, e.g., a postulate system of physics with suitable correspondence rules, will remain significant according to the criterion when further arbitrary postulates, e.g., cognitively meaningless sentences of a metaphysical pseudo-theory, are added. Hempel's reasoning is that, if a derivation of observable predictions from observation sentences is possible in the first theory this possibility remains after the addition of meaningless postulates. Since my criterion is applicable to single terms and thence to single sentences, it does not lead to this undesirable result, as I have shown in the article mentioned (§VII). It would be interesting to consider whether it might be possible to improve or simplify my criterion of significance with the help of the new method which I shall employ for the definition of analyticity (in D).

C. The problem of experiential import. What we learn from a sentence S with respect to possible observable events is called the experiential import of S. In contrast, the problem of the significance of S is not the question of *what* we learn from S, but merely *whether* we learn anything at all about observable events from S. Hempel is correct in maintaining that the concept of experiential import, if it can be defined at all, must be taken as relative to the total theory TC (Hempel's T'), i.e., the conjunction of T and C. For, if S contains only V_T-terms, then obviously we cannot infer from S anything about observable events without the help of the postulates. However, it seems to me that this fact by no means makes the concept useless.

Let us define the following concept for a sentence S in L (analogous definitions can be formulated for a class K of sentences).

(1) (a) The *observational content* or O-content of $S =_{Df}$ the class of all non-L-true sentences in L'_O which are implied by S.

(b) The *O-content* of S *relative to the theory* $TC =_{Df}$ the O-content of $S \cdot TC$.

(2) (a) S' is *O-equivalent* (observationally equivalent) to $S =_{Df} S'$ is a sentence in L'_O, and S' has the same O-content as S.

(b) S' is *O-equivalent* to S *relative to the theory* $TC =_{Df} S'$ is a sentence in L'_O, and S' has the same O-content relative to TC as S.

Hempel gives in a recent article[40] a thorough and illuminating investigation of many logical and methodological questions connected with theoretical concepts. He explains (in a different terminology) that either the O-content of a sentence S or, more simply, a sentence S' which is O-equivalent to S, may serve in certain respects as a substitute for S, namely as far as *deductive* relations among the sentences of L'_O are concerned. But he remarks correctly that the same does not hold for the equally important *inductive* relations, and that therefore the concept of O-content does not furnish a suitable method for dispensing with theoretical terms. In this view I agree with Hempel. However, it seems to me that, although it cannot replace S completely, the O-content of S relative to a given theory TC may still be taken as an explicatum for the experiential import (or, if one prefers, the deductive experiential import) of S.

Furthermore, Hempel explains the method proposed by Ramsey for the effective transformation of any sentence S into a certain O-equivalent sentence. The latter sentence is called by Hempel the *Ramsey-sentence* associated with S; I shall denote it by "^RS". This sentence ^RS is obtained from S by replacing the n theoretical terms occurring in S by n distinct variables not occurring in S, and then prefixing n existential quantifiers with these variables. It is easy to show that, for a given theory TC, the Ramsey-sentence ^RTC is O-equivalent to TC; and for any sentence S, the Ramsey-sentence $^R(S \cdot TC)$ is O-equivalent to S relative to TC. Ramsey proposes to represent a theory in the form ^RTC rather than in the customary form TC. In this way the theoretical terms and sentences, which are only incompletely interpreted, would be avoided. Hempel warns that the Ramsey-sentence ^RTC "avoids reference to hypothetical entities only in letter—replacing . . . constants by . . . variables—, rather than in spirit. For it still asserts the existence of certain entities of the kind postulated by TC, without guaranteeing any more than does TC that those entities are observable or at least fully characterizable in terms

[40]Carl G. Hempel, "The Theoretician's Dilemma: A Study in the Logic of Theory Construction", in vol. II of *Minnesota Studies in Philosophy of Science* (1958). The Ramsey method is described in § 9.

of observables. Hence, Ramsey-sentences provide no satisfactory way of avoiding theoretical concepts. And indeed, Ramsey himself makes no such claim". I agree with Hempel that the Ramsey-sentence does indeed refer to theoretical entities by the use of abstract variables. However, it should be noted that these entities are not unobservable physical objects like atoms, electrons, etc., but rather (at least in the form of the theoretical language which I have chosen in [1956-4] §VII) purely logico-mathematical entities, e.g., natural numbers, classes of such, classes of classes, etc.[41] Nevertheless, ^{R}TC is obviously a factual sentence. It says that the observable events in the world are such that there are numbers, classes of such, etc., which are correlated with the events in a prescribed way and which have among themselves certain relations; and this assertion is clearly a factual statement about the world.

I do not propose to abandon the theoretical terms and postulates, as Ramsey suggests, but rather to preserve them in L_T and simultaneously to give an important function to the Ramsey-sentences in L'_O. Their function is to serve in the explication of experiential import and, more importantly, in the explication of analyticity.

For any sentence S L-implied by TC, including any postulate of TC, the Ramsey-sentence relative to TC, $^{R}(S{\cdot}TC)$, is always L-equivalent to ^{R}TC. But this does not make it impossible to analyze any one of the postulates separately (for instance, for the purpose of deciding to omit or replace it). We simply have to investigate the postulate on the basis of the conjunction of the other postulates of TC.

D. The problem of analyticity. Let us consider the task of finding an explication for the concept of *analytic sentence* for the language L. I shall use "A-true" as the term for the explicatum. The class of the sentences which are analytic (or logically true in the wider sense) is more comprehensive than that of the L-true sentences. It comprises all those sentences whose truth is based, not on contingent facts, but merely on the meanings of the descriptive and logical constants occurring. For the sentences of L_O the problem of explication can be solved with the help of meaning postulates, which I shall call here *"A-postulates"*. Whenever either a logical relation holds among the meanings of the primitive predicates in L_O (e.g., incompatibility between "blue" and "red") or a certain structural property characterizes a two- or more-place primitive predicate of L_O in virtue of its meaning (e.g., the relation "Warmer" is asymmetric and transitive), then these relations and properties are expressed in A-postulates. Let A_O be the conjunction of the A-postulates for O-terms. A_O is formulated in L'_O (it can usually be formulated even in L_O). Let A_T be the conjunction of the A-postulates for theoretical terms;

[41]This is explained in greater detail in [1959-2] § 3.

later I shall explain how these postulates are constructed. Let A be the conjunction of A_O and A_T. For analyticity as the explicandum, I propose the following explication:

(3) S is *A-true* in $L =_{Df} S$ is a sentence in L, and S is L-implied by A $(\vdash A \supset S)$.

I have explained the general role of the A-postulates in greater detail in the paper [1952-5]. The explanation given there is, however, directly applicable only to descriptive constants whose meanings are completely known, thus in language L only to the O-terms. When we introduce new primitive constants by postulates in such a way that the terms are interpreted only incompletely, the situation is entirely different. Hempel has pointed out correctly that the problem of the explication of analyticity is in this case more difficult, because the postulates then have simultaneously two different functions. They serve both for the stipulation of logical meaning relations (relations among the meanings of the new terms and relations between these meanings and the meanings of the old terms) and for the assertion of factual relations. Hempel regarded these difficulties as so great that the concept of analyticity for sentences with theoretical terms appeared to him as quite elusive. During my work on the article (1956-4) and subsequently, I long searched in vain for a solution to this problem; more specifically, for a general method for analyzing the total postulate set TC into two components: analytic meaning postulates A_T for the theoretical terms, and synthetic *P-postulates* P which represent the factual content of the theory TC. I believe now to have found a solution for this problem.

Before I describe the general method, I will mention a solution for a special case which I had found earlier. (It is indicated in [1952-5] at the end of §3, and explained by Hempel in his essay §7.) This solution applies when TC is the conjunction of a set of reduction sentences for a new primitive predicate "Q_3" (compare [1936-10] §10):

(4) (a) "$(x)[Q_1x \supset Q_2x \supset (Q_3x)]$",
(b) "$(x)[Q_4x \supset (Q_5x \supset \sim Q_3x)]$",
(c) "$(x)[Q_1'x \supset (Q_2'x \supset Q_3x)]$",
(d) "$(x)[Q_4'x \supset (Q_5'x \supset \sim Q_3x)]$",
etc.

We take "Q_3" as a theoretical term and the other predicates as observation terms. Thus TC is here simply C, since it consists of mixed sentences, i.e., C-postulates, but contains no T-postulates. Writing "$Q_{1,2}x$" for "$(Q_1x \cdot Q_2x) \vee (Q_1'x \cdot Q_2'x) \vee \ldots$", and "$Q_{4,5}x$" for "$(Q_4x \cdot Q_5x) \vee (Q_4'x \cdot Q_5'x) \vee \ldots$", the conjunction of the reduction sentences (4) is L-equivalent to:

(4′) "$(x)(Q_{1,2}x \supset Q_3x) \cdot (x)(Q_{4,5}x \supset \sim Q_3x)$".

My earlier solution consisted in separating (4′), hence C, into two components S' and $S' \supset C$, where S' is the sentence "$(x) \sim(Q_{1,2}x \cdot Q_{4,5}x)$". C is clearly L-equivalent to the conjunction of S' and $S' \supset C$. I proposed to take the second component $S' \supset C$ as a meaning postulate. In [1936-10] I called the sentence S' the "representative sentence" of the set of given reduction sentences for "Q_3", because it "represents, so to speak, the factual content of the set". S' is a sentence in L_O, and is in general factual. But if the conjunction C of the reduction sentences consists of just one bilateral reduction sentence, then S' is L-true[42] and C itself may be taken as the meaning postulate.[43]

In analogy to the method just described for a simple special case, we can now easily specify a general method applicable to any TC. We decompose TC into two components, the first being the Ramsey-sentence ^{R}TC and the second the conditional sentence $^{R}TC \supset TC$. The method then consists in taking the first component as a P-postulate, and the second as an A-postulate for the theoretical terms in TC, hence as an A_T-postulate. The two components satisfy the following conditions (5):

(5) (a) The two components together are L-equivalent to TC.
(b) The first component is O-equivalent to TC.
(c) The second component contains theoretical terms; but its O-content is null, since its Ramsey-sentence is L-true in L'_O.

These results show, in my opinion, that this method supplies an adequate explication for the distinction between those postulates which represent factual relations between completely given meanings, and those which merely represent meaning relations.

It may be that we wish to establish still further sentences as A_T-postulates in addition to those formed from a theory TC in the way described. But we shall admit as A_T-postulates only sentences whose conjunction satisfies the condition (5c). It then follows that a sentence in L_O is L-implied by $A_O \cdot A_T$ if and only if it is L-implied by A_O alone. Thus:

(6) A sentence S in L'_O is A-true in L if and only if $\vdash A_O \supset S$.

As P-postulates we shall admit only sentences in L'_O. Let P be their conjunction. We define:

(7) S is *P-true* in $L =_{Df}$ S is a sentence in L such that $\vdash A \cdot P \supset S$.

The P-postulates are intended to have factual content. Therefore a sen-

[42] This is what I meant by the sentence [1936-10] p. 452, lines 20-22. Hempel (in his footnote 32) and Pap (§ 2) are right that my formulation was incorrect.

[43] I wish to make an incidental remark on the formula

$(R) \quad (x)(t)[Q_1xt \supset (Q_3xt \equiv Q_2xt)]$,

which I gave in [1936-10] p. 440 as the reduction sentence for the *permanent* disposition "x is soluble in water". R is not a genuine bilateral reduction sentence. Its Ramsey-sentence is L-equivalent to the synthetic sentence

"$(x)[(\exists t)(Q_1xt \cdot Q_2xt) \supset (t)(Q_1xt \supset Q_2xt)]$".

R can be changed into a bilateral reduction sentence for the *instantaneous* disposition "x is soluble in water at the time t" by writing "Q_3xt" instead of "Q_3x".

tence which is known to be A-true will not be taken as a P-postulate. (However, I do not make non-A-truth a requirement for P-postulates, because there is in general no decision procedure for A-truth.)

In the special case when ${}^{R}TC$ is found to be A-true or even L-true, we drop the first component and take TC itself instead of the conditional sentence as an A_T-postulate.

Let us look back at the earlier mentioned case where TC is a conjunction of reduction sentences for "Q_3", as represented by the formulas (4′). In this case ${}^{R}TC$ is as follows:

(8) "$(\exists F)[(x)(Q_{1,2}x \supset Fx) \cdot (x)(Q_{4,5}x \supset \sim Fx)]$".

This is L-equivalent to "$(x)(Q_{1,2}x \supset \sim Q_{4,5}x)$" and therefore to "$(x) \sim(Q_{1,2}x \cdot Q_{4,5}x)$" which was the representative sentence S'. Thus we see that the method for the analysis of a given set of reduction sentences into an A-postulate and a P-postulate, which I proposed in [1952-5], is just a special case of the general method described above which is based on Ramsey's device.

Within the framework of the new method a scientific theory is represented by P-postulates and A_T-postulates. Within this framework, those sentences which in the original method appeared as T-postulates and C-postulates are not taken as postulates but are theorems derived from P and A_T; they are P-true according to definition (7). Since the original terminology, which applies the label "postulates" only to the T-postulates and the C-postulates, may be more customary, it may often seem preferable to keep this terminology and not to use the terms "A_T-postulates" and "P-postulates". If so, we may continue to represent scientific theories by T-postulates and C-postulates and take for "A-true" and "P-true" the following definitions, which take the place of definitions (3) and (7) of the new method and are equivalent to them:

(9) S is *A-true* in $L =_{\mathrm{Df}} S$ is a sentence in L such that $\vdash A_0 \cdot ({}^{R}TC \supset TC) \supset S$.

(10) S is *P-true* in $L =_{\mathrm{Df}} S$ is a sentence in L such that $\vdash A_0 \cdot TC \supset S$.

V. Probability and Induction

25. My Basic Conceptions of Probability and Induction

I shall here briefly summarize my basic conceptions of probability and induction for convenience of reference in the subsequent discussions of the contributions by Kemeny, Burks, Putnam, Nagel and Popper. In what follows I shall use "[Prob.]" to refer to my book *Logical Foundations of Probability* [1950-4] and "[Cont.]" to refer to the monograph *The Continuum of Inductive Methods* [1952-1].

I. Clarification of logical probability as explicandum. I distinguish between two probability concepts as explicanda: logical or inductive probability (also called "probability$_1$") and statistical probability (also called "probability$_2$") which, roughly speaking, means relative frequency in the long run. The aim of my theory is to give an explication of the concept of logical probability, which in my view constitutes the basis of all inductive reasoning.

Before the explication begins, the meaning of the phrase "the logical probability of the hypothesis *h* relative to the evidence *e*" (which we shall here abbreviate by "*P(h,e)*") is explained informally in the following way. Let us suppose that *e* is the total observational knowledge of the person *X* at the time *T;* then the meaning of "*P(h,e)*" is indicated by the following statements (1) through (4).

(1a) *P(h,e)* is the degree to which the hypothesis *h* is confirmed (supported, established, or the like) by the evidence *e* ([Prob.] §41A).

(1b) *P(h,e)* is the degree to which *X* is rationally entitled to believe in *h* on the basis of *e*.

These two tentative explanations are vague and ambiguous. (The first is perhaps even somewhat misleading, because a similar informal explanation can also be given for other concepts, e.g., the amount of increase of the probability of *h* by *e,* as measured by *P(h,e)* — *P(h,t)*, where *t* is the tautology.) Therefore the following explanations (2) through (4) are preferable and are to be regarded as the primary bases of my interpretation of the concept of logical probability.

(2) *P(h,e)* is a fair betting quotient for *X* with respect to a bet on *h* ([Prob.] §41B.)

(3) If *h* is a singular prediction ascribing the property *M* to an individual not mentioned in *e,* then the value of *P(h,e)* is also the value of an estimate for the relative frequency of *M* in any class whose elements are not mentioned in *e* ([Prob.] §41D.)

(4) Suppose that the following offer is made to *X:* the benefit *B* will be bestowed upon him in case the event *h* occurs. If *h* does not occur, he will receive nothing. Then *P(h,e)* is the factor by which the utility of *B* for *X* must be multiplied in order to calculate the rational subjective value for X of the offer. If *X* is given the choice among several offers of this kind, then he must, in order to be rational, choose the offer which has the maximum subjective value.

Formulation (4) gives the fundamental indication of the meaning of "*P*" in its application to practical decisions ([Prob.] §51). [The formulation (2) is only approximate; it holds only if the betting stakes are sufficiently small in relation to the total fortune of *X* (so that the utility may be assumed to be proportional to the money value of the gain). Whenever I refer in the following discussions to a bet, it is tacitly assumed that the stakes are small.] Since (4) is of great importance, I shall explain it in more detail.

II. Utility, subjective value, credence, credibility, and logical probability. [The following is a simplified exposition of the application of logical probability to the determination of practical decisions, as explained in [Prob.] §51. However, the use of the concept of the subjective value of an act, the concepts of credence and credibility, and the distinction between the situations A, B1, B2, and B3 are new.] Suppose that X has at the time T a choice among the possible *acts* of the set a. Let a_i be the i-th act of the set a, and also a sentence asserting that (or the proposition that) X chooses and performs the i-th act. Let us assume that X makes his choice in consideration of the possible *results* which concern himself and which he may value either positively or negatively. Let r be the set of these possible results. A result may for instance consist in X's receiving or losing a certain amount of money or goods. We shall now consider two different kinds of situation distinguished by the certainty of X's knowledge as to what result will ensue from an act of his.

A. Results known with certainty. First we suppose X to know that, for any i, if he performs the act a_i, he will obtain the corresponding result r_i (where r_i includes all consequences of concern to X). For example, he knows that, if he buys this book for five dollars, then he will have the book but will not have the five dollars; and that, if he does not buy it, then he will not have the book but will still have his five dollars. If X's system of valuations (or of preferences as comparative valuations) fulfills certain conditions, then it can be represented by a *utility function* U_X. We consider a certain time period in the life of X, and we assume for the sake of simplicity that X has a utility function U_X which remains unchanged during this period. (So long as we consider only the given person X, we may omit the subscript "X" and write simply "U"; we shall do the same later with other functions.) $U(r)$, i.e., $U_X(r)$, is the utility of the possible result r for X; in more familiar terms, the subjective value of r for X.

We must distinguish between the utility function of X, in other words, his valuations and preferences, on the one hand, and his decisions, his choices of acts, on the other. The former are lasting dispositions, the latter are momentary events. The choice of an act is causally determined by *X's* dispositions and other factors. In a situation of the kind previously indicated, the relation is (in a simplified schematic form, disregarding other factors) as follows:

(5) X performs one of those acts for which the corresponding results have the maximum U-value among the results of the set r.

On the basis of observations of the choices made by X in situations of the kind described, it is possible to ascertain, with the help of (5), equalities and inequalities between values of U (though not yet these values themselves). This is an inductive determination because (5) does not hold strictly. In general, inferences from the observed behavior to dispositions or other traits of a person are inductive and uncertain. If the determination is based, not on acts performed by X, but on answers by X to questions as to what acts he *would* perform in specified situations, much more information is easily obtained, but the inferences are even less reliable.

B. Results not known with certainty. We now consider situations in which the result depends, not only upon the act performed by X, but also upon an event in the environment, an event belonging to a given set H of alternative possible events. Let H_k be the k-th event of the set H, and also the sentence asserting that (or the proposition that) the k-th event occurs. X does not know which of the events of H will occur, but he does know that, if he performs the act a_i and the event H_k occurs, then the result r_{ik} will ensue.

B1. Let us make the simplifying assumption that X's choice of an act (e.g., a bet on H_k) does not have any influence on the occurrence or non-occurrence of the event H_k. We introduce the *credence function* of X, Cr_X; informally speaking, $Cr_X(h,T)$ is the degree of credence or belief which X has in the sentence (or the proposition) h at the time T. We shall now introduce the concept of the *subjective value* of an act a_i for X at the time T, $V_X(a_i,T)$. For situations of the kind considered, V_X is defined as follows:

(6) $V(a_i,T) =_{\text{Df}} \sum_k [U(r_{ik}) \times Cr(H_k,T)]$.

Instead of (5) we have now the following:

(7) At the time T, X performs one of those acts a_i for which $V(a_i,T)$ is a maximum among acts of the set a.

On the basis of observations of X's acts, we can, with the help of (7), inductively ascertain relations between values of V. From these relations and those determined previously for U, we can determine relations for Cr-values. If (6) and (7) are applied to situations in which X has a choice of accepting or rejecting a bet on H_k with various (small) stakes, we find that $Cr(H_k,T)$ is equal to the highest betting quotient with which X is willing to bet on H_k at time T.

Assuming that the functions U and Cr (the latter is usually called "subjective probability", "psychological probability", or "personal probability") fulfill certain conditions (stated in the customary axioms of game theory or the theory of decision making), it is even possible to measure empirically, that is to say, to determine inductively, the numerical values of *X*'s *U*- and *Cr*-functions. The method is complicated and will not be described here. Its basic idea goes back to F. P. Ramsey; work towards developing and improving the method is still going on.[44]

B2. To the assumption made in B1, we now add the assumption that the belief dispositions of *X* are rational in one particular respect (in other respects they may still be quite irrational), namely that the value of $Cr(h,T)$ for any sentence *h* is dependent, not upon irrational factors like wishful or fearful thinking, but only on the totality of *X's* observational knowledge at the time *T*, say the conjunction of those observational results which he has obtained up to the time *T* or which he remembers at the time *T*. Let this conjunction be $K_X(T)$. Let us assume further that, during the time period under consideration, the manner in which $Cr(h,T)$ depends on $K(T)$ remains constant, i.e., that during this period there is in effect one and only one function $Cred_X$ (called the *credibility function* of X) such that the following holds:

(8) (a) If at any time *T* (during the period in question) the total observational knowledge of *X* were *e*, then, for any *h*, $Cr(h,T)$ would be equal to $Cred(h,e)$, the *credibility* of *h* for *X* relative to *e*.

Hence, in particular:

(b) At any time *T*, for any *h*, $Cr(h,T) = Cred(h,K(T))$.

(8a) is a general law, formulated as a subjunctive conditional, applicable to any (non-contradictory) sentence *e*. (8b) is a consequence of (8a), referring for any time *T* to the *actual* knowledge of *X* at *T*.

We see from (8a) and a previous result concerning *Cr*, that $Cred(h,e)$ is equal to the highest betting quotient with which *X would be* willing to bet on *h*, *if* his total knowledge were *e*. Thus, while the function *Cr* represents *X*'s changing actual beliefs, the function *Cred* represents X's permanent disposition for holding beliefs.

Given (6) and (8), we can express the value of *V* in terms of *Cred* instead of *Cr*:

$$(9)\ V(a_i,T) = \sum_k [U(r_{ik}) \times Cred(H_k,K(T)).$$

B3. We shall keep the assumptions of B2. We are now in a position to abandon the restrictive assumption made in B1 and thus to admit even situations in which the chosen act may influence the events *H*. Consequently (9) must be modified in such a way that the credibility of H_k is taken, not simply relative to the actually available observational

44See L. J. Savage, *The Foundations of Statistics* (1954); D. Davidson, P. Suppes, S. Siegel, *Decision Making: An Experimental Approach* (1957).

knowledge $K(T)$, but rather relative to this knowledge together with the assumption that the act a_i will be performed:

(10) $V(a_i,T) = \sum_k [U(r_{ik}) \times Cred(H_k, a_i \cdot K(T))]$.

Informally speaking, the value of *Cred* which occurs here is the betting quotient with which X would be willing to bet on H_k if he knew, in addition to the actual knowledge K, also that he will perform the act a_i. The determination of *X's* choice of an act by the values of V remains the same as that stipulated in (7).

Notice that, although we have assumed that *X*'s credence in h is influenced solely by his knowledge K, we have not made any assumptions about the nature of this influence. Therefore it is still possible that X, although he has a *Cred*-function, has a quite irrational one, i.e., one which according to (10) and (7) leads to entirely unreasonable decisions. Let us now consider *rational Cred-functions*. We shall not assume that there can be only one such *Cred*-function, but rather leave open the possibility that two reasonable persons, or one reasonable person during different periods of his life, may have different *Cred*-functions. We can now give an explanation for logical probability, which is in accord with the earlier explanation (4):

(11) The *logical probability function P* is a rational credibility function.

III. The task of inductive logic. I regard it as the task of inductive logic to explicate the concept of *P*-functions and to construct a theory of *P* on the basis of this explication. As a technical term for the explicatum of relative logical probability I use *"degree of confirmation"*, for which I shall write "d.c.". I take *"c(h,e)"* as a symbolic expression for "the d.c. of the hypothesis *h* on the basis of the evidence *e*" (where the arguments *h* and *e* are either sentences or propositions). The explication can, for example, be effected by stating axioms for *c*-functions; this I shall do in §26. Every axiom expresses a condition which a *c*-function must satisfy in order to represent a rational *Cred*-function. A *c*-function is a logical function of its arguments, that is to say, if a particular *c*-function has been defined, then its value depends merely upon the logical (semantical) properties and relations of the two arguments. Furthermore, the axioms state purely logical properties of the *c*-functions. Therefore the theory of the *c*-functions, based on the axioms, is a part of logic. It is true that the *Cred*-functions are psychological concepts; but it does not follow that the *c*-functions are psychological concepts. The *P*-functions and the *c*-functions are rather *logical* (or purely semantical) concepts which correspond to the *psychological* (or pragmatical) *Cred*-functions in the following way. Any logical function is an adequate *c*-function if and only if it is such that, if it were used as a *Cred*-function, it would lead to rational decisions. [The explanation of the explicandum *P* as a rational *Cred*-function is of the kind which I characterized in [Prob.] §12A as "qualified psychologism". I emphasized that explanations of this kind, e.g., Keynes' explanation of *P* as "the degree of belief which it is rational to entertain under given conditions", by no means make the concept *P* subjectivistic; this holds also for my present explanation.] The explanation of *P* as a rational *Cred*-function has an essential advantage over Keynes' explanation, since it leads to a numerical scale of values. For this reason, the best way of explaining the explicandum *P* is one based on a theory of rational decision making, as Ramsey pointed out.

The following statements hold on the basis of the conception of inductive logic just outlined.

(12) A quantitative *inductive method* can be represented by a *c*-function. If *X* has chosen a particular inductive method, in other words, a particular function *c*, then *inductive reasoning* by *X* concerning the hypothesis *h* on the basis of the evidence *e* is aimed at the determination of the value *c(h,e)*.

For the application of inductive logic by an observer *X* at a certain time *T* the following holds:

(13) *Requirement of total evidence.* If *X* wishes to apply a principle or theorem of inductive logic to his knowledge situation, then he must use as evidence *e* his total observational knowledge *K(T)* ([Prob.] §45B and p. 494).

Let *e* be the evidence available to *X* at a certain time. Then *X* can use the value *c(h,e)*, among other things, as a basis for deciding whether or not to accept the hypothesis *h*. According to a widely held view, it is the proper aim of inductive logic to supply *rules of acceptance*, i.e., rules which determine for given *e* and *h* either that *h* is to be accepted or that it is to be rejected or that it is to be left suspended. I do not agree with this view. My position is rather:

(14) Rules of acceptance as ultimate rules for inductive reasoning are inadequate.

In my view, rules of this kind give in some respect too much, in another respect too little. I shall briefly indicate my main reasons for this opinion.

(a) Suppose that rules of acceptance are given which on the basis of the total evidence *e* available to *X* determine the acceptance of some hypothesis *h*. This means practically that the rules tell *X* to act as if he knew that *h* were true. But such an action may be entirely unreasonable. Therefore the rules say more than they should say. It is impossible to give rational advice for practical action merely on the basis of logical relations between *e* and *h;* for this purpose the expected gains or losses (more exactly, their utilities for *X)* must also be taken into account. (Compare my arguments against the rules R_1 and R_2 in [Prob.] §50 B and C; similar arguments would hold against any rules of acceptance.)

(b) In contrast, there are certain situations in which the rules of acceptance would not provide *X* with any advice on how to act. Suppose, for example, that *X* knows that 100 balls have been drawn from an urn containing black and white balls, and that among them were 60 black balls and 40 white balls. *X* is allowed to choose one of the acts a_1 and a_2; if he chooses a_1 he obtains $100 if the next ball is black *(*H_1*)*, and otherwise nothing; similarly for a_2 with white *(*H_2*)*. Since on the basis of *e* neither H_1 nor H_2 can be predicted with reasonable confidence, rules of acceptance of the customary kind will leave both hypotheses in suspension and therefore will not recommend either of the two acts. But obviously it would be rational for *X* to choose a_1. And suitable rules for logical probability or *c*-functions do indeed lead to the choice of a_1 (e.g., theorem (7) in §26).

I do not deny that sometimes rules of acceptance may be useful. First, they are unobjectionable if they involve reference to gains or losses, as do certain customary rules for decision making. However, in this case the rules are not rules of inductive logic, since they involve non-logical factors. Second, rules of acceptance are frequently used in the methodology of empirical science for the rational reconstruction of scientific method. There is no compelling objection against this use, provided the reconstruction is merely meant as a rough delineation of scientific procedure in purely *theoretical* fields, and especially if the reconstruction is applied only to the acceptance of universal laws. However, when we are concerned with the use of laws and still more that of singular sentences in a field of *practical* application, say in technology, industry, medicine, agriculture, and so on, then rules of acceptance are insufficient for the reasons stated above under (a) and (b).

26. An Axiom System for Inductive Logic

I. Families of predicates. In this section I shall give an axiom system for the most elementary part of inductive logic, which deals with a language containing only one-place primitive predicates.

First I shall briefly indicate an approach, somewhat modified from [Prob.] and [Cont.], with respect to the primitive predicates. These predicates are classified into families (see [Prob.] §18C) in such a way that for each individual exactly one of the predicates of any given family holds. (This is to be stipulated by meaning postulates; comp. [1952-5].) For example, the colors may constitute one family, the odor qualities another, and so on. In the following we shall presuppose that we are dealing with closed families, i.e., that the number of predicates in any family is a given finite number. (It is also possible to deal with open families, for which the number of predicates is indefinite without an upper bound.)

The effect of this modification for the discussions and theorems in my publications is as follows: Everything remains practically unchanged in the systematic part of the body of [Prob.], i.e., in chapters IV through IX, with the exception of a few places (mainly §107A) where the language systems $L\pi$ are used. The discussions and results in these latter places, and also in the Appendix of [Prob.] concerning the function c^*, and those in [Cont.] concerning the λ-system, are now to be regarded as restricted to cases involving predicates of one family only. The number π of independent primitive predicates is now to be disregarded, and the number κ of Q-predicates is to be taken as the number k of predicates of the family in question. If, for example, a result in [Cont.] is applied to three independent primitive predicates, say "P_1", "P_2", and "P_3" (so that the number of Q-predicates is $\kappa = 8$), then I would today describe this situation in terms of three families with two predicates each; the first family would consist of "P_1" and "$\sim P_1$", and similarly for the second and the third. (For this situation a method for three families would have to be used; but we can apply as an approximation a theorem like (7) below with $k = 8$.)[45]

Concerning a further improvement, which became possible on the basis of the new approach, see the comment on A11 below.

II. The general axioms. I shall not give here the axioms A1 through A5, because they correspond to the conventions C53-1 and 2 in [Prob.] and to the customary axioms of the calculus of probability (see Kemeny's essay, §3, (1) through (5)).

A6. In a language with a finite number of models, $c(h,e) = 1$ only if h is a logical consequence of e.

(A6 corresponds to the convention C53-3 in [Prob.].)

(1) A *regular m-function* for the state-descriptions (or models) of a language with a finite domain of individuals is a function such that its value for each state-description is a positive real number and the sum of its values for all state-descriptions is 1. From these m-values, m-values for *any* sentence can be determined according to a given rule ([Prob.] D55-2; see Kemeny's essay, §3).

[45]This modified approach has been the basis of my work in inductive logic since 1951 (after the writing of [Cont.], but before its publication). The axioms which I state below are essentially those which I used in [1955-9] and which will be published in [1959-1], Anhang B. I communicated the new approach to Kemeny and Putnam in 1953. But the essays by Burks and Popper (in 1954) and presumably that by Nagel (in 1957) were written without knowledge of the modification.

(2) A *regular c-function* is a function whose values $c(h,e)$ are determined on the basis of the values of a regular m-function according to a given rule ([Prob.] D55-3 and 4).

(3) *Theorem.* A c-function for a language with a finite number of models is regular if and only if it satisfies the axioms A1 through A6.

The following axioms A7 through A11 are *axioms of invariance.* They represent the valid part of the principle of indifference, whose classical form, e.g., in the system of Laplace, was too general and too strong and was therefore correctly rejected by later authors (comp. [1953-5] pp. 193f., reprinted in [1955-10b] pp. 21f.).

A7. The value of $c(h,e)$ remains unchanged under any finite permutation of the individuals.

This axiom corresponds to the condition of symmetry with respect to individuals ([Prob.] ch. VIII).

A8. The value of $c(h,e)$ remains unchanged under any permutation of the predicates of any family.

A9. The value of $c(h,e)$ remains unchanged under any permutation of families with the same number of predicates.

A10. The value of $c(h,e)$ remains unchanged if the domain of individuals of the language is enlarged, provided no quantifiers occur in e or h.

By virtue of this axiom, it suffices to use an infinite language L_∞, and to abandon the finite languages L_N $(N = 1, 2, \ldots)$. The sentences of L_N, after the elimination of all quantifiers (with the help of [Prob.] T22-3), have the same m-values and c-values as the same sentences in L_∞.

A11. The value of $c(h,e)$ remains unchanged if further families of predicates are added to the language.

With this axiom the requirement of the completeness of the set of primitive predicates of a language ([Prob.] §18B) is abandoned; the value of $c(h,e)$ is now dependent only upon those predicates which occur in h and e, and is independent of any other families of predicates in the language. Therefore we can now admit languages with an infinite number of families of predicates. (Thus no assumption similar to Keynes' principle of limited variety is made.)

III. Special axioms. The subsequent axioms refer to the following special situation: let F be a family of k primitive predicates "P_1", . . . , "P_k". Let e_s be an individual distribution for a sample of s individuals $a_1, \ldots, a_s$, with the cardinal number s_1 for $P_1, \ldots, s_k$ for P_k. Let h_j $(j = 1, \ldots, k)$ say that the individual a_{s+1} has the property P_j; likewise h'_j for a_{s+2}.

A12. Axiom of instantial relevance.

(a) $c(h_j,e_s \cdot h'_j) \geqq c(h_j,e_s)$.

(b) $c(h_j,e_s \cdot h'_j) \neq c(h_j,e_s)$.

[It should be investigated whether (a) can be proved on the basis of the previous axioms. (b) becomes provable if A13, A14, and A15 are accepted as axioms.] With the help of A12 we obtain the following theorems:

(4) $c(h_j,e_s \cdot h'_j) > c(h_j,e_s)$.

(5) $c(h_j,e_s \cdot \sim h'_j) < c(h_j,e_s)$.

(4) is the principle of positive instantial relevance, which I proposed in [1953-1] as an axiom.

(6) If $s_i > s_j$ *then* $c(h_i,e_s) > c(h_j,e_s)$.

A13. Axiom of convergence. Let an infinite sequence $e_1, e_2, \ldots, e_s, \ldots$ be given such that for every s ($s = 1,2, \ldots$) e_s is an individual distribution for s individuals with the predicates of the family F, and e_{s+1} L-implies e_s. For every s, let h_j^{s+1} say that a_{s+1} has the property P_j. Then $\lim_{s \to \infty} \left[c(h_j^{s+1},e_s) - \frac{s_j}{s} \right] = 0$.

This axiom was suggested by Hilary Putnam in a conversation in 1953. (He called it "Reichenbach's axiom"; however, since Reichenbach rejected the concept of d.c., I am doubtful about the suitability of this designation.)

The following two axioms establish the λ-system (first proposed in [Cont.]; see Kemeny's essay §4).

A14. Let e_s be as previously specified, with $k>2$; let i, j, l be three distinct numbers among 1,..., k; let $s_j>0$; let e'_s be like e_s but with $s_j - 1$ instead of s_j and with s_{l+1} instead of s_l. Then $c(h_i,e_s) = c(h_i,e'_s)$.

This axiom corresponds to C9 in [Cont.] §4 ; it seems to be generally accepted, but usually tacitly.

The axioms stated so far yield the following theorem for $k>2$:

(7) $c(h_j,e_s) = \frac{s_j + \lambda/k}{s + \lambda}$, where λ is a parameter (a finite, positive real number) characterizing the function c.

Hence:

(8) For fixed $k>2$ and fixed s, $c(h_j,e_s)$ is a linear function of s_j.

This result suggests the following axiom:

A15. For $k=2$ and fixed s, $c(h_j,e_s)$ is a linear function of s_j.

With this axiom we obtain the result that (7) holds generally (including the case $k = 2$).

(9) The c-function with $\lambda = 0$ violates A6, and the c-function obtained when λ approaches ∞ violates A12 and A13. Therefore these two functions appear unacceptable. (They are discussed in more detail in [Cont.] § 14 and § 13, respectively.)

If a value for λ has been chosen, then the axioms stated so far suffice for the determination of all c-values for sentences containing only predicates of one family. For sentences involving several families, new axioms must be added. Kemeny and I have constructed a solution to this problem for any number of families. The solution uses one parameter in addition to λ. I shall not describe the solution here.[46] For an explanation of the problem, though not the solution, see Kemeny's essay (at the beginning of § 5).

For many c-functions the following holds:

(10) Let l be a universal factual sentence for an infinite domain of individuals. Let e be an arbitrary sentence without quantifiers. then $c(l,e) = 0$.

This result holds not only for c* ([Prob.] §110 F), but also for all c-functions of the λ-system (with positive λ). This result is regarded by many, e.g., by Nagel in §V of his essay, as entirely counter-intuitive. I believe that reasons can be given which make the result appear not entirely implausible (cf. [Prob.] §110 G and H; Nagel quotes from this). On the other hand, I agree that it is of interest to investigate the possibility of c-functions for which (10) would not hold. I have constructed c-functions of this kind, but they are considerably more complicated than those of the λ-system. So far as I know, no other author has given a satisfactory system of logical probability in which (10) does not hold.

IV. Reasons for accepting the proposed axioms. Kemeny (in §3 of his essay) gives reasons for some of the axioms. He shows that certain conditions of adequacy (CA) are intuitively valid. These conditions may serve as reasons for accepting the axioms stated above in the following way: the axioms A1 through A6 are supported by CA1; A7 through A9 by CA3; A10 and A11 by CA2; A12 and A13 by CA4; A14 is supported by the subsequent condition CA5′ or perhaps better by CA6; the reason for A15 is the analogy to (8), which follows from the preceding axioms.

Kemeny himself says of his condition CA5 that it is practically begging the question. I should like to suggest replacing it by the following:

CA5′. If i is intuitively irrelevant for h on the basis of e (i.e., if it is intuitively clear that the addition of i to e can neither increase nor decrease the probability of h) then c should be such that $c(h,e \cdot i) = c(h,e)$.

Furthermore I should like to propose the following additional condition:

CA6. c should be as simple as possible without violating any intuitive requirements. In other words, if c is simpler than c', but there is

[46]The solution for the simplest case, that of two families, is given in [1955-9] § XVII and in [1959-1], Anhang B, § VIII.

no case in which the values of c or the relations between these values appear intuitively less acceptable than those of c', then c is preferable to c'.

I believe that this principle is useful and even necessary in spite of its vagueness. In conformity with it, we would usually prefer one c-function (or the corresponding m-function for individual distributions with a finite number of individuals, or the corresponding m-density-function for structures in an infinite domain) to another, if the first is mathematically simpler than the second. We might consider a more general principle CA6′ containing the weaker phrase "no case is known", instead of "there is no case". Often we cannot judge with certainty the possibility of later finding cases or discovering new points of view which would speak in favor of the less simple function. For example, I believe that axiom A14 is more strongly supported by CA6′ than by CA5′. The reason is that, although A14 leads to a great simplification of the inductive methods, I am not as firmly convinced of its plausibility as I am of that of the preceding axioms. It is conceivable that we might in the future find a vantage point from which it would appear appropriate that $c(h_i,e_s)$ depend not merely on s and s_i, but also on s_j, s_l, etc.

On the controversial problem of the *justification of induction* I shall make only a few brief remarks. I shall discuss only the problem of the justification of a *class* of inductive methods, represented by a class of c-functions which are to serve as rational *Cred*-functions; the class is assumed to be specified by a system of axioms. Thus I understand the problem of the justification of induction as the question as to what kinds of reasons can be given for accepting the axioms of inductive logic. (I shall leave aside the more complicated question of reasons for choosing a particular c-function from the class.) The nature of such reasons can be seen in the examples given above (at the beginning of IV) with respect to the axioms previously stated for our simple language. For more complex languages, of course, additional axioms must be given and perhaps also additional conditions CA. I believe, however, that the general character of the reasons will remain the same. It seems to me that the reasons to be given for accepting any axiom of inductive logic have the following characteristic features (as can be seen by an analysis of Kemeny's explanations):

(11) (a) The reasons are based upon our intuitive judgments concerning inductive validity, i.e., concerning inductive rationality of practical decisions (e.g., about bets).

Therefore:

(b) It is impossible to give a purely deductive justification of induction.

(c) The reasons are a priori.

By (c) I mean that the reasons are independent both of universal synthetic principles about the world, e.g., the principle of the uniformity of the world, and of specific past experiences, e.g., the success of bets which were based on the proposed axioms. If e represents the total experience of X so far, then the value of $c(h,e)$ is certainly dependent upon e, and thus upon the experiences of X. However, the acceptability of the *axioms*, by which the value of $c(h,e)$ is determined or by which certain restrictions are imposed on admissible c-functions, is independent of these experiences.

27. John G. Kemeny on Probability and Induction

Kemeny presents in his essay the basic ideas and the first steps of an explication of the concept of logical probability by a quantitative concept of degree of confirmation (d.c.) with respect to a very simple language. It seems to me that he has been very successful in presenting in nontechnical terms the aims and methods of inductive logic. I hope that Kemeny's discussion will induce those who still have doubts about the possibility of a quantitative inductive logic to reconsider their views.

Since in the body of his essay Kemeny only rarely mentions his own achievements in this field, I should like to emphasize that he has made very essential contributions to the ideas and to the system construction which he describes. In particular, he defined in an earlier article a generalized concept of model, which is applicable to logical systems of very different forms. He then made use of this concept not only for deductive systems, but also in a very fruitful way for inductive logic. With the help of the concept of model, languages of far richer structure can be brought into the range of inductive logic. Kemeny was the first to suggest axioms of a special kind (which I later called "meaning postulates" or "A-postulates") whereby the earlier requirement of the independence of primitive predicates ([Prob.] §18B) can be eliminated. Furthermore, Kemeny has made what seems to me the best investigations of the difficult problem concerning simplicity of laws.[47] In particular, I believe that his analysis of a system of levels of simplicity will be very valuable for the development of an inductive logic for a language containing quantitative magnitudes.

In Princeton, during the year 1952-53, I was very gratified to have the opportunity to collaborate extensively with Kemeny on inductive logic. I had begun to reinterpret the λ-system, so that the original form of the theory, developed in [Cont.], was regarded as restricted to cases involving predicates of one family only (see above, §26 I and III). We worked

[47]Kemeny, "The Use of Simplicity in Induction", *Phil. Review,* LXII (1953), 391-408. (This paper is not listed in his bibliography.)

together chiefly on two problems. The first was the search for a better foundation of the λ-system; in this context, Kemeny found the proof of the important theorems which he explains in §4 of his essay. Most of our effort was devoted to the second problem, on which I had already begun to work, of finding a way of applying the λ-system to two or more families of predicates (see above, §26 III, and Kemeny's §5). Together we developed a solution for any number of families. In addition, Kemeny found at that time the important result (see his footnote 13), that every *c*-function which satisfies the first five axioms is coherent. [Incidentally, I prefer De Finetti's term "coherent" to Kemeny's term "fair". The latter term is customarily used in a narrower sense; a bet is called "fair" if it does not favor either partner ([Prob.] p. 166). A *c*-function satisfying the first five axioms but violating one of the axioms A7, A8, or A9, is coherent, but nevertheless leads to some bets which are not fair in the customary sense, e.g., a bet at even odds on the prediction that the next throw with a given perfect die will be an ace.]

Kemeny states (in §3) conditions of adequacy (CA) for *c*-functions, which may serve as general principles for the construction of a system of inductive logic. The principles which he states comprise those which, either explicitly or implicitly, guided my original work and later our common work. But Kemeny has succeeded in stating the principles in a far more general form. Thereby they become applicable to present and future work on systems of inductive logic for more complex languages. In §26 IV, I have suggested an additional condition CA6, which represents the principle of simplicity.

In his last section Kemeny gives a survey of some of the most important problems of inductive logic which remain to be solved. (Concerning the problem of universal sentences in an infinite domain, see my comments on (10) in §26 III.) I share Kemeny's conviction that solutions for these problems, although they may be complicated, can be found by essentially the same procedure which has been used so far, e.g., for the construction of the original λ-system, and then for its new foundation and extension. The procedure will again consist in the application of general principles like those stated in Kemeny's CA.

28. Arthur W. Burks on the Philosophy of Induction

Burks gives a clear pragmatic analysis of the meaning of elementary probability statements. Their meaning is specified in terms of dispositions to bet and the like. Burks is correct in assuming that I essentially agree with his thesis I (§B) and his pragmatic thesis (§C). Thesis I says that all scientists use (roughly) the same inductive method and that this method is close to that based on my function c^*. (I interpret the last clause in a very liberal sense as saying that this method corresponds to a method of the λ-system with positive finite λ; I presume that Burks would agree with this interpretation.) With the spirit of Burks' pragmatic thesis I certainly agree, but I would prefer a somewhat different formulation in terms of the *Cr*-function and the *Cred*-function of the person *A* (see above, §25 II). In particular, I would prefer instead of "A believes $P(h,e) = x$" to say: "*A* has a *Cred*-function, and this function has the value x for the arguments h and e". This reformulation seems to me essentially in agreement with the way Burks interprets his belief statement (in footnote 33 to §D3).

Burks raises the question (in §C5) what exactly I mean when I propose a certain *c*-function, say c^*, as an explicatum for *P*, i.e., logical probability, and when I claim that c^* is a good explicatum for *P* (in [Prob.] §110). My formulations on this point were indeed somewhat elliptical. A more explicit formulation of what I had in mind is the following. I propose taking as an explicatum for *P* that *P*-function P^* whose values are determined by c^* (i.e., for any h and e, $P^*(h,e) = c^*(h,e)$). The function c^* has been defined in a purely logical way. Therefore, as Burks has stated correctly, the true elementary statements of c^* are accepted by all, irrespective of their inductive methods. On the other hand, P^* is a *P*-function; to propose P^* as an explicatum for *P* means to propose using P^* as a *Cred*-function for the determination of practical decisions (in Burks' terminology: P^* is inductive-method committive, while c^* is not). And I claim that P^* is a good explicatum, which means that the use of P^* (or, which amounts to the same thing, c^*) as a *Cred*-function, leads to rational decisions. A statement of the form (1) "$P^*(h,e) = x$" can therefore in my opinion be analyzed as containing the following two cognitive components: (2) "$c^*(h,e) = x$", and (3) "P^* (and hence c^*) is a rational *Cred*-function". In contrast, what is expressed by the non-cognitive, purely volitional decision statement (4) "Let us henceforth use the function P^* as a *Cred*-function", is, in my opinion, not part of the content of (1). (I discuss the distinction between cognitive and purely optative statements in greater detail in §32 B and C; in terms there used, (4) has the form "Utinam we shall use . . .".) I regard (1) as L-determinate, because according to my conception no factual knowledge is relevant for the question of the truth of (2) or of (3). On (2) Burks agrees. However, the question concerning (3) is a difficult problem. I do not share the widespread view that the rationality of an inductive method depends upon factual knowledge, say, its success in the past. I think that the question of rationality must be answered by purely a priori considerations (see my comments on (11) in §26 IV.)

On the important problem of the justification of induction, which Burks discusses in §D, I said next to nothing in [Prob.]. A few brief comments on the question are made above in §26 IV.

Burks (in §E) points out an interesting parallel to my distinction (in [1950-1]) between internal and external questions of existence of entities, viz., the analogous distinction between internal and external questions of induction. An internal question of induction is a question *within* a given system, e.g., concerning the value of c^* for a given case. The answers to questions of this kind are analytic. On the other hand, an external question of induction is raised *outside* of the inductive system; a question of this kind may concern the choice of an explicatum for probability, in other words, the practical question whether or not to accept a certain *c*-function or at least a class of such functions as supplying the values of *P*. It seems to me that this parallelism indicated by Burks is indeed illuminating. Further, I agree with Burks that important questions of the philosophy of induction belong to the external questions of induction. I regard the external questions themselves, like the examples just mentioned, as practical questions. But still I would agree with Burks, first, that it is an important task of the philosophical clarification of induction to specify the factors which are relevant for a rational decision of a practical external question; and, second, that important *theoretical* questions are involved in the relevant deliberations leading to a practical decision of this kind.

The discussion of the problem of the *presuppositions of induction* in my book ([Prob.] §41F) has sometimes been mistaken as intending to give a solution of the traditional problem of the justification of induction. (At some places in the section mentioned I did use the word "justification"; I think today that this was misleading and should be avoided in such a context.) I had in mind a man *X* who has decided to use as his *Cred*-function a certain *c*-function, say c^*. He is able to give the reason for his conviction that the chosen *c*-function is a rational *Cred*-function. Thus the question raised by *X* is neither the general question of justification of induction nor the specific question of justification of his choice of c^*. *X*'s question can be formulated like this: "I realize that I cannot hope to know with *certainty* that my inductive method will be successful in the long run; therefore I am content if I can establish a high *probability* of success. This I can do if it can be proved that on the basis of evidence presently available to me (and even without any factual evidence) it is very probable that the uniformity of the world is high. My question is whether I can obtain this result." I gave in the section mentioned an affirmative answer to this question of *X*. (In the present case the answer would be formulated in terms of P^*, because that is *X's* explicatum for probability.) What I gave was merely an answer to an *internal* question. I agree with Burks' view that a result of this type cannot be a justification for induction and that the questions of justification of induction in general and of the rationality of a particular inductive method are external questions. Up to this point our views agree. But I do believe that my discussions have shown that *X* does not need any synthetic presuppositions in the application of his chosen inductive method, i.e., in the use of the chosen *c*-function as his *Cred*-function. Maybe Burks would agree with this. But even so, he might object that universal synthetic presuppositions (or at least synthetic presuppositions going beyond the available observational knowledge) are necessary in order to show that a given inductive method is rational. In contrast, as I mentioned before, I believe that questions of rationality are purely a priori.

Burks is right in saying that the method of c^*, as it was described in my previous publications, presupposed that the language fulfills the requirement of completeness and that the number of primitive properties in the universe is finite. In my new approach as described in §26, however, this is no longer the case.

29. Hilary Putnam on Degree of Confirmation and Inductive Logic

Putnam offers interesting new ideas on the problem of inductive logic. He proposes a form of inductive logic based on rules of acceptance. He claims at the beginning of his essay that he will show that an adequate inductive logic in accordance with my method, i.e., based on a quantitative concept of degree of confirmation (d.c.), is not possible. But he does not show this at all. I shall first discuss the method proposed by Putnam and later his criticism of my method.

Putnam uses a language *L,* which refers to a domain of individuals with a discrete, linear order with one initial position, and which contains a finite number of primitive one-place predicates. His inductive method M (§6) consists of rules of acceptance. It is presupposed that the observer may at any time propose new hypotheses (i.e., effective universal laws); no rules for proposing hypotheses are given. The rules of acceptance refer both to the evidence and, in addition, to the proposed hypotheses. Among the rules of the method M is the following:

(ii) *Rule of tenacity*. If a hypothesis *h* is once accepted, it is not subsequently abandoned unless it becomes inconsistent with the data.

As a reason for this rule Putnam points out that scientists usually do not easily abandon a law that has once been accepted, unless a contradiction with the data occurs. It is true that this tendency for retaining hypotheses is often found, especially in the case where the law has already been published and has been used by many other scientists in their work. But it seems to me that this customary tendency ought not to be taken as a general methodological principle. Suppose a scientist finds a new law *h* and accepts it, but then, before he communicates it to anybody, he discovers that another far simpler law h' is likewise compatible with the evidence. Then clearly he should abandon the previously accepted law h in favor of h'. To stick to h in this situation, as method M demands, would not be commendable tenacity, but unreasonable stubbornness. Therefore any method which, like method M, possesses the property of tenacity in Putnam's strong form seems to me not in agreement with the procedure of good scientists and thus unacceptable.

Putnam himself correctly declares that his method M must be supplemented to take account of the simplicity of the laws in question. I would suggest modifying the method M by replacing the rule of tenacity with the following rule:

(ii′) If a hypothesis h is once accepted, it is not subsequently abandoned unless it becomes inconsistent either with the data or with a proposed hypothesis h' (concerning the same molecular property) which is consistent with the data, inconsistent with h, and simpler than h. In the latter case, h is abandoned and h' is accepted.

Putnam proposes (in §6) the following requirement which, he feels, every inductive method for the acceptance of hypotheses must fulfill in order to be adequate:

Requirement III. If h is an effective hypothesis and is true, then h is finally (i.e., after a sufficient number of observations) accepted provided h is ever proposed.

I am not convinced of the validity of this requirement. Putnam does show that his method M satisfies the requirement. But this result is due to the fact that method M contains the rule of tenacity. I believe that, if this rule is replaced by rule (ii′), which seems to me more plausible, then requirement III is no longer generally fulfilled.

My argument against the plausibility of requirement III is as follows. Let us assume that h is a true hypothesis (law) of such a kind that the following holds: at every time-point T, there is another hypothesis h'_T (not necessarily the same for all T), which is formed according to effective rules, is likewise compatible with the given evidence at T, e_T, and which is inductively preferable to h, let us say, simpler than h (leaving aside other factors determining inductive preferability). If the new rule (ii′) is laid down, then at any time T the simpler law h'_T is preferred to h. Therefore h is never accepted, and thus requirement III is not fulfilled. Since rule (ii′) seems to me more plausible than rule (ii), the requirement appears implausible.

Now we have to consider whether there are hypotheses h of the kind just described. I believe that there are. Since we have no generally accepted criterion of simplicity, it is not possible to give compelling examples. However, I shall offer some examples based on certain criteria of simplicity. It is not my intention actually to suggest accepting these criteria of simplicity; but I believe that the examples make it plausible that, once a satisfactory criterion of simplicity is found, there will be hypotheses of the kind described with respect to that criterion.

In the following examples we consider hypotheses (effective laws) h based on an infinite ascending recursive sequence S of numbers $S(1)$, $S(2)$, etc. Let h say that the positions $S(1)$, $S(2)$, etc., are red, and the other positions black. It is assumed that h is true. The evidence e_n is supposed to describe the first n positions. For a given n, let k_n be the number of positions less than or equal to n which are red, i.e. $S(k_n) \leqq n < S(k_n+1)$. Thus e_n describes the positions $S(1), \ldots, S(k_n)$ as red and the other positions up to n as black. We shall consider three examples (A), (B), and (C). In each of these examples, h_n is a hypothesis (law) which is proposed after the observation of e_n, is compatible with e_n, and is simpler than h.

(A). h_n says that $S(1), \ldots, S(k_n)$ are red and all other positions are black. For certain hypotheses h all corresponding hypotheses of the form h_n (with a finite n) will be simpler than h. However, there may be some doubt whether on the basis of e_n a hypothesis of the form of h_n is actually inductively preferable to h. Therefore we shall state other examples in which each hypothesis h_n entails, as does h, that there is an infinite number of red positions.

(B). Let the criterion of simplicity be such that a hypothesis containing a smaller number of quantifiers than another (where successor, sum, and product are taken as the only primitive functions) is regarded as simpler than the other. Let h be Putnam's prime number law; thus S is the sequence of the prime numbers. We now take h_n as saying that a position x is black (non-red) if and only if there is a number y $(1 < y < x)$ such that x is equal either to $yS(1)$ or to $yS(2)$ or to . . . or to $yS(p)$, where $(S(p))^2 \leqq n < (S(p+1))^2$. This h_n contains only two quantifiers and therefore is simpler than h, which contains three.

(C). Let the function S on which h is based be such that (1) S increases faster than any polynomial, (2) S is less simple than any polynomial, (3) for every i, each i-th difference is positive. The conditions (1) and (3) are satisfied, for example, by any geometrical progression. It does not seem implausible to suppose that Putnam's sequence C (§5) satisfies all three conditions (h is then like Putnam's hypothesis (2), but with "black" instead of "red"). We take as h_n the hypothesis based on the following sequence S_n : S_n begins with $S(1), \ldots,$ $S(k_n)$ and then keeps constant the $(k_n - 1)$th difference determined by these k_n numbers. This sequence corresponds to a polynomial of degree $k_n - 1$. Therefore h_n is simpler than h.

So much for Putnam's method M and his requirement III. We come now to the essential part of Putnam's essay, namely, his criticism of quantitative inductive logic, i.e., of the concept d.c. I should like first to emphasize that the difficulties which Putnam discusses do not apply to the inductive methods which I have presented in my publications. These methods refer to languages with an unordered domain of individuals. The difficulties discussed by Putnam apply to languages, e.g., his language *L,* with an ordered domain of individuals. I have developed tentative inductive methods for languages of this kind, but have not published the results. In 1953 I talked with Putnam about these problems and my attempts at solutions. Putnam's objections refer to the methods which we discussed and not to those contained in my publications (although his formulations frequently seem to attack the latter).

Putnam states two requirements, I (in §2) and II (in §5) for d.c. for his language *L.* He first tries to make it appear plausible that each of these requirements is a necessary condition of adequacy for d.c. But he then shows that the requirements I and II cannot both be fulfilled simultaneously. His proof is ingenious and the results are indeed interesting. Putnam believes that hereby he has shown that there cannot be any adequate concept of d.c. But actually his result shows only that the two requirements, in spite of their prima facie appearance of plausibility, are logically incompatible and that therefore at least one of them must be abandoned. I find requirement II fairly plausible, but not requirement I. Putnam's reasons for requirement I are essentially the same as those for requirement III. Requirement I corresponds to III if the convergence of d.c. towards 1 (or in the weaker versions I′ and I″, d.c. $>$ .9 and d.c. $>$ .5, respectively) is taken as a condition of acceptance. The argument against the plausibility of requirement III which I presented earlier is therefore likewise an argument against that of requirement I.

However, I have serious objections against Putnam's whole approach of comparing his method of rules of acceptance with my rules of d.c. He takes as the basis of comparison the correspondence stated above, whereby a certain statement on the d.c. of *h* is transformed into a rule for the acceptance of *h*. But this way of looking at the situation does not do justice to the method of d.c. As I have explained in §25, the purpose of this method is not to supply results in terms of acceptance but rather, to supply *Cred*-values and thereby to determine practical decisions.

Although for the reasons stated earlier I cannot agree with Putnam's view that the method of d.c. should be replaced by the method of acceptance, I nevertheless think that it is worthwhile to consider the possibility of preserving one interesting suggestion which Putnam offers, namely, to make inductive results dependent not only on the evidence but also on the class of actually proposed laws. Putnam applies this suggestion in developing rules of acceptance. My question is whether, in constructing a system of rules of d.c., the use of his idea in some form or other might be advisable. I am not in principle opposed to its use when sufficiently complicated languages are involved. For Putnam's relatively simple language L it seems to me unnecessary, as I shall explain presently. However, for a much richer language, e.g., a language of physics with a continuous space-time system and with quantitative magnitudes possessing continuous scales of values, the new idea might be helpful. This question should be investigated further.

I shall now briefly indicate the general character of the inductive method of d.c. which I would use for languages like L, or preferably a language L' with a discrete series of positions infinite in *both* directions (thus taking all integers as coordinates). Leaving statistical laws aside for simplicity, I would consider only those universal laws l which fulfill the following two conditions:

A. l is *purely general,* i.e., it does not refer to any specified position.
B. l has a *finite span* n (not necessarily the same for all laws).

I say that a universal law in the language L' has the *span* n if n is the smallest number such that l has the following form: "For every x, if certain positions of the interval from x to $x + \text{n} - 1$ have certain properties, then certain other positions of the same interval have certain properties", where the positions are specified by their distances from x and the properties are designated by molecular predicates of L'.

The restrictions (A) and (B) seem to me in agreement with the actual procedure of physicists. Clerk Maxwell already pointed out that a fundamental law of physics never contains temporal or spatial coordinate constants but only coordinate differences. I believe that no physicist would seriously consider a law like Putnam's prime number law as a fundamental (not derivative) physical law. If e is finite evidence and h is a molecular prediction about a single position, then, according to (A) and (B), in the language L' only a finite, effectively determined class of possible laws need be taken into account for the determination of $c(h,e)$. Therefore no explicit reference to those laws is necessary, and the rules determining the value of $c(h,e)$ can be formulated in such a way that this value is effectively computable. My tentative solutions to which I referred earlier were indeed of this kind.

In §8 Putnam emphasizes the indispensability of theories for work in science. On this point I entirely agree with him; his belief that my conception here is "diametrically opposed" to his and Kemeny's is not correct. In my publications I have discussed the problem of inductive logic not for a quantitative theoretical language, but only for simple language forms which may be regarded as constituting part of the qualitative observation language. I also agree with Putnam that, if h is the prediction of the first nuclear explosion and e is the totality of evidence available just before the time in question, where both *h* and *e* are formulated in the observation language, then a system of inductive logic constructed for the observation language will not ascribe to *c(h,e)* a considerable value. But from this it does not follow at all, as Putnam believes, that an adequate method of d.c. is impossible, but rather that for situations of this kind we must construct a new inductive logic which refers to the theoretical language instead of the observation language. I would say that scientists at the time in question would indeed have been willing to bet on the positive success of the first nuclear explosion on the basis of the available evidence, including results of the relevant laboratory experiments. Inductive logic must reconstruct this willingness by ascribing to *c(h,e)* a considerable positive value. And it is indeed my view that the great progress in making successful predictions, from the pre-scientific to the scientific phases of the development of a subject matter, is essentially due to the fact that in the scientific phase a new form of *inductive* logic is used (usually, of course, intuitively; only seldom on the basis of explicit rules). In the inductive logic of the pre-scientific phase some axioms of invariance (e.g., A8 and A9 in §26 II above) refer to the primitive predicates of the observation language. Once theories are constructed, it is possible to use another form of inductive logic in which the analogous axioms of invariance refer, not to observable qualities, but to the fundamental quantitative magnitudes (e.g., by ascribing within a given interval of the scale of a fundamental magnitude equal *m*-values to equal sub-intervals). I cannot enter here into a discussion of the well-known difficulties involved in the problems of probability for continuous scales.

In my article on theoretical concepts [1956-4], which appeared after Putnam wrote his essay, I discussed in detail the relation between the observation language and the theoretical language and emphasized the indispensability of theoretical concepts for the procedure of science. The problem of inductive logic for the theoretical language was, however, not discussed there. I explained there that the interpretation of the theoretical terms, which usually is incomplete, is given by the postulates of the theory and the rules of correspondence connecting the theoretical terms with terms of the observation language. In the construction of a method of inductive logic for the total language of science, consisting of the observation language and the theoretical language, it seems to me that a basic role should be assigned both to the primitive magnitudes of the theoretical language and to the postulates and correspondence rules. Both are given by the rules of the language.

Since I regard d.c. as always relative to a given language, the influence of both factors on the values of d.c. is in accord with my basic conception. In inductive logic, we might consider treating the postulates, although they are generally synthetic, as "almost analytic" ([Prob.] D58-1a), i.e., assigning to them the m-value 1. In this connection it is to be noted that only the fundamental principles of theoretical physics would be taken as postulates, no other physical laws even if they are "well established". What about those laws which are not logical consequences of the postulates, but are "proposed" in Putnams' sense? In my form of inductive logic I would assign to them the m-value 0 (for another alternative see my comments on (10), §26 III); but their instance confirmation may be positive. As mentioned earlier, we could alternatively consider here, in analogy to Putnam's idea, making the rules such that the d.c. of a singular prediction would be influenced not only by the form of the language and thereby by the postulates, but also by the class of proposed laws. At the present moment, however, I am not yet certain whether this would be necessary. At any rate from the features of the customary methods of science, pointed out by Putnam, it does not follow, even for a language containing theoretical terms and postulates, that an inductive logic based on d.c. is impossible.

To sum up, I shall divide Putnam's thesis into two parts. He asserts (1) that an inductive logic based on d.c. is impossible and that instead an inductive logic based on acceptance must be used; and (2) that the rules of inductive logic for a prediction must take into account not only the evidence *e* but also the class of the actually proposed laws which are compatible with *e*. I have rejected the thesis (1) and have given reasons for my view that, on the contrary, the method of d.c. is indispensable and the method of acceptance is inadequate. On the other hand, I believe that Putnam's thesis (2) deserves serious consideration, not for the language discussed in his essay, but perhaps for more complex languages, e.g., the quantitative language of physics.

(Note added in 1962.) All A-postulates (meaning postulates, cf. [1952-5]) obtain in inductive logic the m-value 1. Therefore I should today prefer to give the m-value 1, not to the synthetic postulates TC of a theory, but only to the weaker sentence $^{R}TC \supset TC$, which I have proposed (in §24 D) as the A-postulate for the theoretical terms.

30. Ernest Nagel on Induction

In his introductory remarks Nagel says that I have not given sufficient directives for the application of inductive logic. But, in my view, the rule of maximizing the estimated utility, which I have stated and discussed in great detail in [Prob.] §51, represents the fundamental form of any application of inductive logic, in that all other forms of application are reducible to this form. (The explanations given above in §25 II lead to the same result.) Nagel refers chiefly to applications in theoretical research, and he believes that scientists do not use any numerical values of logical probability in this context. It is true that they usually do not state such values explicitly; but it seems to me that they show, in their behavior, implicit use of these numerical values. For example, a physicist may sometimes bet on the result of a planned experiment; and, more important, his practical decisions with respect to his investment of money and effort in a research project show implicitly certain features not only of his utility function but also of his credibility function and thus of the corresponding *c*-function. If sufficient data about decisions of this kind made by scientists were known, then it would be possible to determine whether a proposed system of inductive logic is in agreement with these decisions. Nagel does indeed try to make a comparison between certain features of my inductive logic and the customary inductive behavior of scientists, though sometimes in a mistaken way, as we shall see.

Nagel says (near the end of §I): "The further assumption in Carnap's system, that even purely logical truths lend a degree of support to empirical hypotheses, does not appear quite so innocuous. For as it turns out, this a priori degree of support for a hypothesis enters fundamentally into the determination of the degree of support that *empirical* evidence gives to the hypothesis". Here Nagel mingles two problems which should be clearly separated. My method of d.c. contains the following steps: (I) introduction of *m*-functions; (IIa) admission of values *c(h,t)* interpreted as d.c. of an empirical hypothesis *h* with respect to tautological evidence; (IIb) stipulation that *c(h,t)* = *m(h)*; (III) calculation of *c(h,e)* where *e* is *empirical,* from certain *m*-values (concerning I and III, see §26 II, (1) and (2), respectively). Step I is unproblematic since the *m*-values are here not yet interpreted; steps II and III involve problems. In the first sentence quoted above, Nagel objects to IIa. His argument obtains some degree of plausibility from his speaking of d.c. in terms of "degree of (evidential) support". Thus, of the informal characterizations of logical probability given in §25 I above, Nagel uses only characterization (1a). If he had also used the slightly different characterization (1b) and still better (2), (3) and (4), which I have emphasized in [Prob.] §41 as being more adequate, then, it seems to me, the plausibility of his argument would disappear. I have explained my reasons for admitting tautological evidence in [Prob.] §§57B and 107A and B. However, if Nagel and others prefer not to use values *c(h,t),* I would not strongly protest. The result would be chiefly that instead of any function *c* in my theory they would use the subfunction *c′* restricted to cases of factual evidence.

However, Nagel's main criticism concerns step III. He seems to believe that this step presupposes step II. But this is not the case. If someone rejects II, as Nagel does, he can still accept step III, using the uninterpreted *m*-values from I. The use of these values in III is simply the use of a certain mathematical concept; therefore it is merely a question of convenience. To object to this is like objecting to the use of imaginary numbers in physical laws, as beginners sometimes do and presumably some philosophers did in the beginning.

In §§II and III Nagel gives good reasons for rejecting two interrelated features of my system based on the function c^* as described in the Appendix of [Prob.]: (1) the requirement of completeness of the class of primitive predicates, and (2) the dependence of the value of c^* upon the number of predicates of the language in question. As I explained above (see my comments on Axiom A11 in §26 II), I agree today with this criticism. From the beginning I felt uneasy about the requirement of completeness. The objections which were raised by Nagel and others in previous conversations helped in stimulating my efforts to find a way of avoiding the requirement. This aim was achieved in the new approach described in §26.

In §IV Nagel expresses doubts about the validity of those principles of my theory which are related to the classical principle of indifference. In the new approach (§26 II) they are represented by the axioms A7, A8, and A9. Nagel raises objections especially against A7 and in this context uses an illustration which refers to samples of water, taken either from different sources or from the same reservoir which is known to be homogeneous, and the like. What Nagel says about these situations and the attitude a scientist would take with respect to such samples is certainly correct, but it is no argument against A7. If the scientist X knows anything about the individuals a_1, a_2, a_4, a_5 other than that they come from the same reservoir, and if he knows either that the water in that reservoir is homogeneous or that it is not, then the knowledge of X is much stronger than the evidence e to which A7 refers. The special case of A7 formulated by Nagel is applicable only if, first, X does not know anything about the individuals a_1, a_2, a_4, a_5 other than that they have the property M and if, second, he does not know with regard to any other individual whether or not it has the property M. Nagel's error here is a case of what I shall later call the fallacy of incomplete evidence. I have discussed the question of the legitimacy of invariance axioms and, in particular, of A7 in more detail in [Prob.] pp. 484f. and 488f. and in [1953-5] pp. 193f.

In §V Nagel expresses doubt about the result that the c-value for a factual universal law on the basis of finite evidence is zero. Concerning this problem, see my comments on (10) in §26 III above.

Nagel gives an interesting discussion of the question whether scientifically established laws might sometimes themselves be included in the evidence, instead of, as I had suggested, only their instances so far observed. The results of the old c^*-method, which he here correctly criticizes, no longer hold on the basis of the new approach. For Nagel's example of three independent predicates, the present rules for several families (which are not yet stated in §26) lead to results which exhibit the inductive influences which he demands. The whole question of the role of laws in inductive logic is too complicated to be discussed here. It must be noted that the situation with respect to a theoretical language with postulates is different from that with respect to empirical generalizations in the observation language. On the question of the theoretical postulates I have said a few words in my reply to Putnam in the preceding section.

I agree with Nagel that it may be useful for the critical examination of a proposed theory of inductive logic based on d.c., to determine whether the c-values given by the theory for certain cases are in accord with the customary way of thinking by scientists. Nagel uses this method often, but repeatedly he makes a certain error in its use, which we might call the *fallacy of incomplete evidence.* I agree in most cases with Nagel's description of the customary procedure used by scientists and also with his assumption that this procedure is rational. But in some of Nagel's examples, the knowledge ascribed to the scientist at the time in question, say e' goes essentially beyond that described in e in the inductive principle or theorem in question. Thus the mistake consists in applying a method of inductive logic, not to the total evidence e', but to an incomplete evidence e; in other words, the requirement of complete evidence is violated (see (13) in §25 III.) Nagel himself states this requirement explicitly (in §V, (ii)). I have mentioned earlier an example of the fallacy; I shall now explain another one. The reader will then easily recognize the same error in still other cases.

Nagel says correctly (in §VII) that the following theorem holds in my inductive logic: Let e_M be a description of the sample S to the effect that the sample consists of s specified individuals and that s_M of them have the property M and the others do not; let h_M be the prediction that a specified individual b not belonging to S will have the property M; let e'_M and h'_M say the same about a sample S' and an individual b', with respect to the same property M and with the same numerical values s and s_M; then $c(h_M,e_M) = c(h'_M,e'_M)$. As an example Nagel considers two samples S and S', each consisting of 10,000 observed cases of human births, and with the number of male births in each sample being 5,300. Against the equality of the two c-values asserted in the theorem, Nagel raises the objection that it is not absurd to believe that the degree of evidential support on the basis of one of the two samples is much higher than on the basis of the other one, because this degree might depend upon the method of sampling employed, on the care with which the data have been collected, and the like. Nobody will disagree with Nagel's view that the logical probability of a prediction or the estimate of a frequency may have different values with respect to the two samples for an observer X who has collected the two samples by different procedures or from different parts of the country. But if X knows of these differences between the samples, then according to the requirement of total evidence he must not use the above theorem. The theorem may be applied by X to his situation only if he does not know anything more about the two samples than is expressed in the two statements e_M and e'_M as specified above; in particular, only if he knows nothing about the methods of sampling used. In a similar way, the fallacy of incomplete evidence vitiates much of Nagel's reasoning about sampling in the first part of §VII. (Incidentally, in his argument based on the sample consisting of just one bird, he seems to have overlooked the qualification "a sufficiently large sample" in my statement.)

Let e_M and h_M be as specified above. My earlier approach was based on the assumption (C10 in [Cont.] §8) that the value of $c(h_M,e_M)$ lies within the closed interval between the relative frequency s_M/s and the relative width of M. Nagel says that this assumption does not seem to him convincing. I agree that it is not immediately convincing. Therefore I have not taken it as an axiom in the new approach. The statement about the interval and also the formula for $c(h_M,e_M)$ which Nagel gives here (it follows immediately from (7) in §26 III above), appear in the new approach as theorems derivable from axioms A1 through A15.

According to my conception of logical probability P, $P(h_M,e_M)$ should be equal to the estimate of the relative frequency of M in any future class K (see above, (3) in §25 I). Nagel raises repeated objections against this proposed equality and, in particular, against the "assumption" that the estimate has the same value for any class K. I am not sure whether he means by the term "evidential support" the same as I mean by "logical probability" (as explained in §25 I, II above and in [Prob.] §41). At any rate, I have proved that $c(h_M, e_M)$ is equal to the estimate mentioned for any class K ([Prob.] T106-1c). This theorem is provable on the basis of my general definition of the estimate of a magnitude ([Prob.] D100-1) and the axioms A1 through A7; these axioms are usually accepted by authors on logical probability.

In §IX Nagel discusses the question of the justification or the reasons which can be given for the validity of proposed inductive rules. His view is that a priori reasons are not sufficient, that the reasons must rather be based on the fact that the rules in question have been successful in the past. I do not agree with this; but, on the other hand, I also do not believe in the possibility of a purely *deductive* justification of inductive rules (see my comments on this problem in §26 IV).

There are many points in Nagel's essay on which I cannot comment here. In particular, I have said nothing or very little on those of Nagel's objections which are directed against conceptions shared by the majority of those authors who have worked on systems of logical probability. Among these conceptions is, for example, the view that logical probability, at least in certain cases, has a value before any empirical evidence is available, in other words, has a value with respect to tautological evidence. A second example is the principle of instantial relevance, i.e., the assertion that the probability for a singular prediction, and likewise for a law referring to a finite domain of individuals, increases whenever a positive instance is added to the evidence (Nagel §VI; compare my theorem (5) in §26 III above and my paper [1953-1]). A third example is the assertion that in a finite domain of individuals the logical probability $P(h_1 \cdot h_2, e)$, where h_2 is not logically implied by $e \cdot h_1$, is less than $P(h_1, e)$; the corresponding theorem for c follows from my axioms A1 through A6.

Quite a number of the statements by Nagel to the effect that a quantitative explicatum for logical probability should or should not have certain properties seem to me counter-intuitive and sometimes even quite obviously wrong. This holds, for example, for the three points mentioned in the preceding paragraph, for some further statements in §VI, in particular those about the urn examples, and for his rejection of the invariance principles (§IV). In view of Nagel's careful, scientifically oriented way of thinking, I was at first rather puzzled by these judgments. But then I remembered that, since the time I began to construct a system of inductive logic, I myself had sometimes to change intuitive judgments on certain properties of logical probability. And this occurs still today when I begin to think about the extension of inductive logic to a new, more complex language form. If Nagel were to try to construct a system of d.c. on the basis of his present intuitive judgments, I am convinced that he would change quite a number of these judgments because he would find that the system would yield many results which would appear to him either as undesirable or even as entirely unacceptable. From experiences with my own intuitive judgments and those of friends whom I often asked for reactions to particular results, I have learned that isolated intuitive judgments are very often unreliable. Of course, the development of inductive logic must be guided by intuitive inductive judgments. But these judgments are more useful if they are made, not on isolated points, but in the context of the tentative construction of a system. Kemeny's essay gives a clear picture of the way in which such a construction may proceed. For a simple language with only one-place predicates, we have at present a tentative axiom system. I am constantly on the lookout for possible improvements, especially with respect to those axioms which I regard as not yet firmly established, e.g., the axioms on which the lambda-system is based (A14 and A15) and the axioms on several families (which are not yet stated in §26). I often ask those who are interested in systematic work in inductive logic for intuitive judgments on modifications under consideration. I said earlier that Nagel's objections to certain features of my original system were correct, and that these features were avoided in the new system by the addition of axiom A11. Among Nagel's numerous other critical comments I have found none which gives me either a new point of view for a possible improvement of the system or even the slightest doubt concerning any one of the axioms or any one of the principles which have guided the choice of the axioms.

I am sorry that my overall reaction to the essay by my dear old friend Ernest Nagel could not be more positive. My convictions on the possibility and the nature of inductive logic, acquired in many years' work and vindicated by constant reexamination, can only be shaken by strong arguments.

31. K. R. Popper on Probability and Induction

In §5 of his essay, Popper presents a critical discussion of my conception of probability and induction. The criticism in this essay as well as those in his published discussion notes are based on a fundamental misunderstanding of my position. Many of the views which Popper ascribes to me and subsequently criticizes, are foreign to me if not diametrically opposed to my own view. It happens not infrequently that one philosopher misunderstands another. What is unusual in Popper's case is the fact that he has persisted in his misunderstanding even after Y. Bar-Hillel, Kemeny, and I had clearly pointed out his mistakes.[48] I shall now make a last attempt to clear up the basic confusion on which Popper's misunderstandings are founded.

The main arguments which Popper brings forward against my conception of degree of confirmation have an interesting common characteristic. They consist in an (unintentional) application of the principle which Frege called the "principle of the nondistinction of the distinct" and whose great fertility he emphasized (see my autobiography §1). The common schema of all these arguments of Popper's is as follows: Carnap asserts that degree of confirmation has a certain property; Popper has shown that degree of confirmation does not have this property; therefore Carnap's assertion is wrong. Both premisses are true, but the conclusion is false, due to the fact that Popper and I use the term "degree of confirmation"

[48]A series of discussion notes was published in the *British Journal for the Philosophy of Science* at the following places (I shall later use for purposes of references the year numbers in brackets as given here): Popper [1954] 5, 143-149; Bar-Hillel [1955] 6, 155-157; Popper [1955] 6, 157-163; Carnap [1956-5] 7, 243-4; Popper [1956a] 7, 244-5; Bar-Hillel [1956] 7, 245-8; Popper [1956b] 7, 249-256. Further, John Kemeny [1955] (a review of Popper [1954]), *Journ. Symb. Logic,* XX, 1955, 304. For other publications by Popper see the first footnote in § 6.

with two entirely different meanings.[49] Sometimes Popper is quite aware of this fact. Nevertheless he continues to present arguments of the form described.

It seems useful for the present discussion to employ two different terms for the two different meanings of "degree of confirmation". I shall use "dc_P" for the concept meant by Popper, and "dc_C" for my own concept.

Let me give one example of Popper's reasoning. He wants to show in his essay "that confirmation, as Carnap himself understands this concept, cannot be logical probability". Thus it is clear that he intends to talk about dc_C. One of his arguments is essentially as follows: Logical probability decreases with increasing content, but the degree of confirmability (he seems to use this term as synonymous with "degree of confirmation" in his sense, hence for dc_P) increases with increasing content. His argument is indeed valid if meant to show that dc_P cannot be logical probability; but he claims to show that dc_C cannot be logical probability. The latter assertion can immediately be seen to be wrong because dc_C "as Carnap himself understands this concept" is nothing but an explicatum of logical probability.

Sometimes Popper seems to see quite clearly not only that dc_C is different from dc_P, but also that dc_C is essentially the same as logical probability. He saw this as early as 1954, thus at the time of writing his essay, before the publication of the notes by Bar-Hillel, Kemeny, and me, mentioned in footnote 49. He says ([1954] pp. 145f.): "I distinguished twenty years ago what I then called the 'degree of confirmation' from both, the logical and the statistical probability. But unfortunately the term 'degree of confirmation' was soon used by others as a new name for (logical) probability". In view of his awareness of the meaning of my term, I was amazed to find Popper making the following statement (in the same paper, footnote 1, referring to my book [Prob.] p. 285): "Carnap uses the multiplication and addition principles as *'conventions on adequacy' for the degree of confirmation*. The only argument he offers in favour of the adequacy of these principles is that 'they are generally accepted in practically all modern theories of probability$_1$' ", (i.e., logical probability).

[49]Popper in his book [*Logik*] has given a detailed analysis of the confirmation (*"Bewährung"*) of theories. He uses (§§ 81 f.) the term "degree of confirmation" (*"Bewährungsgrad"*), but says that it is impossible to define numerical values for this concept. (Only in later publications did he try a quantitative explication.) Many years later I introduced the term "degree of confirmation" for the quantitative concept of logical probability (with numerical values). I did not remember that Popper had earlier used this term in a different sense. I used the term first for a concept in pragmatics, referring to a given person at a given time ([1939-4], 222 and 225; [1942-2] 244), and later for a semantical concept [1945-2] and [1945-3]). Janina Hosiasson used the term in a similar sense in 1939 and 1940.

Furthermore, he himself seems to accept the principles of multiplication and addition for logical probability.

Popper's reasoning reaches the peak of absurdity, when he rejects an assertion of mine about dc_C, while making the same assertion in different words. In my book ([Prob.] §110F, with respect to c^*) I stated the result that dc_C, i.e., logical probability, has the value 0 for a universal law in an infinite domain (compare (10) in §26, and my comments to it). Popper rejects this statement at the beginning of his essay and in his Notes [1955] and [1956b]; his argument is that dc_P cannot have the value 0 in this case. Yet later he states that logical probability does have the value 0 in this case (in the last-mentioned Note, p. 251, with reference to his [Logik]). He continues to talk in this fashion even after Bar-Hillel and Kemeny had repeatedly reminded him that dc_C is not the same as dc_P, but the same as logical probability.

Popper's study of my conception of probability and induction certainly contains other points that involve serious problems and actual disagreements deserving further examination. But a fruitful discussion can only be made if he presents these points in a form which is free of the described confusion.

So far I have assumed that Popper understands the term "logical probability" in essentially the same way as I do; but I am not quite sure of this. The fact that we both accept for logical probability the customary axioms of the calculus of probability is not conclusive because they hold for other concepts, e.g., statistical probability. At any rate, I have made clear the sense in which I use the term (in [Prob.] §§41 and 51; see §25 I above). Thus Popper can easily decide whether he means the same. Unfortunately, in interpreting my concept, Popper always uses only the vague explanation as the degree to which the evidence "confirms" or "supports" or "establishes" a hypothesis ((1) in §25 above). I have stated already in my book (§41) that these explanations are inadequate, and today I would regard it as advisable to avoid them because these informal expressions have quite different meanings for different authors and in different contexts. I meant them in the same sense as the other explanations given above, e.g., as a betting quotient. But, due to the vagueness of the ordinary language, the same expressions may be used correctly with other meanings and have indeed been so used by Popper and other authors. Examples of other concepts formulated in the same vague terms are the various measures of positive relevance (compare [Prob.] §§66f.), e.g., Keynes' relevance quotient and my relevance measure; Popper's "power of support" (which may or may not be the same as positive relevance); Popper's concept dc_P; and finally the concept of factual support, defined by Kemeny and Oppenheim (*Philos. of Science,* XIX, 1952). The fact that ambiguous expressions like "evidential support" are used as non-technical explanations for both dc_P and dc_C, was perhaps a factor contributing to Popper's frequent relapse into the belief that the term "degree of confirmation" is used by us in the same sense. If Popper had paid attention to the other important explanations which I gave for logical probability, e.g., as a rational betting quotient, which he never mentions, then his misinterpretation might have been avoided. Bar-Hillel reminds Popper (in [1956] p. 248) that I consider the characterization of dc_C as a betting quotient to be more adequate than that in terms of evidential support; but Popper takes no notice of this in his reply [1956b].

Popper's discussion of the "content condition" and of my position concerning this condition (see his footnotes 63 and 77) is based on a confusion of two different conditions which are expressible by similar but different formulas. I have shown this in my note [1956-5], point (c). Popper's reply in [1956b] again substitutes dc_P for dc_C.

Some special technical objections by Popper concern the Appendix of [Prob.], which gives a brief summary of the system of the function c^*. The definition of c^*, and other definitions and theorems are formulated in an exact way. However, the accompanying text aims merely at giving informal elucidations. Therefore, a reader may examine the values of c^* which the theorems determine for certain cases, and then state his agreement or criticism, as is done, e.g., by Burks and Nagel in their essays. Popper, unfortunately, bases his discussion of c^* merely on my non-technical explanations. In particular, he has misunderstood my concept of qualified instance confirmation. This error might have been avoided if he had paid attention to the stated definition formula. The criticism made in his essay (written in 1954), including a charge of inconsistency, was published by Popper also in his note [1955] and refuted by Bar-Hillel in his reply ([1956], point (7)). Popper's rejoinder to Bar-Hillel (in [1956b], point (7)) misses the point since it refers again merely to my verbal paraphrasing.[50]

[50]*(Note added in 1960.)* In the meantime an English translation of Popper's [*Logik*], including new appendices has appeared: *The Logic of Scientific Discovery* (1959). In his introductory remarks (pp. 390f) to the reprinting of his note [1954] he claims again, and even more explicitly and emphatically than in [1954], to have shown a "clear self-contradiction" in my theory. He shows correctly that a certain statement (5) holds for logical probability. Then he shows that, if we replace "probability" by "d. of c.", a statement (**) follows, which he declares to be absurd. It is indeed absurd if we interpret it in the sense of dc_P. Since my concept dc_C is the same as logical probability, the statement (**) interpreted in the sense of dc_C is not at all absurd; it is simply a consequence of statement (5) asserted by Popper himself. Popper mentions (*op. cit.,* 392ff) that Bar-Hillel and Kemeny have said that Popper and I have different explicanda in mind when we use the term "d. of c." and that I mean by it logical probability. However, Popper thinks that both are mistaken. I hope that Popper will at last accept their interpretation of my term when I assure him that they are right.

VI. Value Judgments

32. Abraham Kaplan on Value Judgments

A. The thesis of non-cognitivism. As a basis for the subsequent discussion, I shall state some theses concerning statements which are, in some way or other, connected with values or valuations. Theses T1 and T2 are merely stated as a preparation for T3; presumably there is fairly general agreement about them. T3 is the specific thesis of logical empiricism concerning non-cognitivism, stated in a weak form.

T1. Some kinds of statements connected with values or valuations are clearly *factual* statements; among them are the following kinds:

(a) Psychological, sociological, and historical statements on the valuational reactions (or dispositions to such reactions) by a person or a group, e.g., statements of approval, disapproval, or preference of certain actions.
(b) Statements on means-end relationships, e.g., "the action *a* is a means to achieve the aim *b*".
(c) Statements on the utility of a possible event (e.g., receiving a certain amount of money or of certain goods) for a person.

T2. Some kinds of statements connected with values or valuations are clearly analytic if true, otherwise contradictory; among them are the following:

(a) Logically true statements containing as components factual statements of the kinds mentioned in T1.
(b) Statements of pure semantics about meanings or truth-conditions of factual statements of the kinds mentioned in T1.
(c) Statements giving an explication of relevant concepts connected with values or valuations, or consequences of such explications.

T3. Thesis of non-cognitivism. If a statement on values or valuations is interpreted neither as factual nor as analytic (or contradictory), then it is non-cognitive; that is to say, it is devoid of cognitive meaning, and therefore the distinction between truth and falsity is not applicable to it.

This version is obviously a very weak form of the thesis of non-cognitivism since it is stated in a conditional form and does not assert that statements of a specified kind are non-cognitive. This thesis is therefore compatible with Kaplan's thesis that value statements are factual. T3 rejects only those conceptions which regard knowledge of values as a knowledge sui generis, essentially different from factual and logical knowledge. A stronger thesis T4 will be stated later.

My own conception of value statements belongs to the general kind which is customarily labeled "emotivism". However, this term is appropriate only if understood in the wide sense in which Stevenson[51] speaks of "emotive meanings". He warns explicitly (pp. 59f.) that his term does not refer to momentary emotions in the ordinary sense, but rather to attitudes. However, since the term "emotivism" is sometimes associated by critics with too narrow an interpretation which today is rejected by most of the adherents of this conception (see F below), it is perhaps preferable to use a more general term, e.g., "non-cognitivism (with respect to value statements)".

T3 is simply a special case of the general thesis of logical empiricism that there is no third kind of knowledge besides empirical and logical knowledge. The thesis T3 is applicable in the first place to those cases in which an author declares explicitly that a certain value statement is meant neither as factual nor as logical; but also to those cases in which we can infer from the explanations of the author that he would not be willing to accept either a factual or a logical interpretation.

It seems clear that the statements occurring in discussions on values and valuations, even those which their authors themselves regard as value statements, belong to many different kinds. Therefore I shall not try to give a general characterization of the logical and epistemological nature of these statements. Everyone has the right to determine the interpretation of any statement he makes; and the reader has to accept the interpretation of the author unless he finds a discrepancy between the interpretation explicitly stated by the author and that implied in the way in which the author uses the statement or argues about it.

B. The thesis of pure optatives. Kaplan's essay gives an excellent survey of the present problem situation with respect to value statements and a presentation and critical analysis of the view of logical empiricism on this question. I have written almost nothing on the problem of values.[52]

The above formulation of thesis T3 makes clear that I do not hold those views which Kaplan criticizes in his first two objections (in sections II and III). First, I agree that statements of many different kinds, including factual statements, may have normative functions. Therefore it is indeed not permissible to conclude that, if a certain utterance has a normative or optative function, it must be non-cognitive. Secondly, I agree that

[51] Charles L. Stevenson, *Ethics and Language* (1944).

[52] (Note added in September, 1958:)
My formulation in [1935-1] quoted by Kaplan (in his section I) appeared to me long ago obsolete and unsatisfactory. My supplementary remarks [1944-1] are also insufficient.

a given utterance has a cognitive component *if,* on the one hand, it expresses a proposal, command, or the like, and, on the other, logically implies a fact, e.g., a reason for, or a consequence of, the proposed action, as in the following example:

(1) Let us take road *a* rather than road *b,* because *a* is shorter than *b.*

There is a general kind of meaning common to all statements expressing a wish, a proposal, a request, a demand, a command, a prohibition, a permission, a will, a decision, an approval, a disapproval, a preference, or the like, whether or not they also contain meaning components referring to matters of fact. I shall use the term *"optative"* for this general kind of meaning. I shall call a sentence which, among others, has a meaning component of this kind an "optative sentence" or for short "an optative". Thus I am using the term "optative" in a much wider sense than is customary, since there is no term in common use for the intended general sense. The term "emotive" is inappropriate, as mentioned above. The term "imperative" is often used in a generalized sense by philosophers; in such cases, my term "optative" may be regarded as nearly synonymous with it. The term "optative" seems more suitable than the term "imperative" because the conventional meaning of "wish" is wider than that of "command". If I express disapproval of someone's action, then my expression contains the wish, though unfulfillable, that he had not done it. An expression in imperative form would not make sense in this case. Proposals, requests, commands, etc., may be regarded as various modes of optatives.

If an optative, in distinction to (1), does not contain any cognitive component, I shall call it a *pure optative.* In contrast to Kaplan's conception, I assert:

T4. There are pure optatives.

Cognitivism may be defined as the denial of this thesis.

We shall now examine the thesis of pure optatives by means of a simple example. Let us assume that two persons *A* and *B* have decided to walk together to the place *P;* both wish to reach *P* with a minimum expense of time and effort. They now deliberate which of two alternative roads *a* and *b* they are going to take. Suppose that *A* says to *B:*

(2) Let us take road *a* rather than *b.*

This utterance is an optative in the mode of proposal. I would interpret (2) in distinction to (1) as a pure optative. A cognitivist might object to this interpretation and point out that *B,* after hearing *A's* utterance (2), might draw some of the following conclusions:

(3) (a) *A* proposes that road *a* be taken rather than *b.*
(b) *A* believes that it would be more useful for their common purpose to take road *a* rather than *b.*

(c) *A* wishes that *B* accept the proposal to take road *a*.

I agree that it would not only be customary but also correct for *B* to draw these conclusions, and that these statements are factual. However, I wish to emphasize the following two points. First, *B* cannot infer these factual conclusions from (2) but must infer them from the event of *A*'s utterance observed by him, hence from the following factual premiss:

(4) *A* utters (in the tone of a proposal) the sentence: "Let us take road *a* rather than *b*".

Secondly, the sentences (3) can be inferred from premiss (4) only inductively, not deductively, i.e., there is a probability connection between them. Therefore the sentences (3) do not express a part of the meaning of the factual sentence (4), let alone of the optative (2). The sentences (3) are *not logically implied* by (2), but are *merely associated* with (2). Since no other factual sentence is logically implied by (2), the latter is a pure optative.

It might help to clarify the distinction between logical implication and mere association, if we apply this distinction to the utterance of a factual statement rather than to the utterance of an optative. Suppose that *A* says to *B:*

(5) We would reach the place *P* sooner on road *a* than on *b*.

Upon *B*'s question for a reason for (5), *A* answers:

(6) Road *a* is shorter than road *b*.

Anticipating *B*'s wish to hear a reason, *A* may say the following instead of (5);

(7) We would reach *P* sooner on road *a* than on *b*, because *a* is shorter than *b*.

Statement (7) logically implies (6), but (5) does not. From the fact of *A*'s utterance of (5), *B* may conclude the following statements:

(8) (a) *A* asserts that they would reach *P* sooner on road *a* than on road *b*.

(b) *A* believes that they would reach *P* sooner on road *a* than on road *b*.

(c) *A* wishes *B* to accept the assertion (and thus share the belief) that they would reach *P* sooner on road *a* than on road *b*.

However, *B* infers these statements not from (5), but rather from the fact of the utterance, hence from the following premiss:

(9) *A* utters (in an assertive tone) the sentence: "We would reach *P* sooner on road *a* than on *b*".

And even this inference is only inductive. Statements (8) are *not logically implied* by (9), let alone by (5). They are *merely associated* with (5). Their meanings are not parts of the meaning of (5). If we make these results clear to ourselves with respect to the foregoing simple situation, we shall probably find it easier to accept the analogous results for (2) and (3) stated above.

C. *Pure optatives in a constructed language.* A cognitivist would perhaps not agree with my interpretation of optative (2), but would rather assert that the latter contains a factual component, for example, that expressed by the following factual statement:

(10) It is more useful to take road *a* than road *b*.

Let us assume that a psychological and linguistic investigation arrives at the following result (which certainly is not impossible, though it seems unlikely): The majority of English speaking people understand a sentence of the form (2) in such a way that (2) has the same content as the following sentence:

(11) Let us take road *a* rather than *b*, and (or: because) it is more useful to take *a* than *b*.

Thus they understand (2) in such a way that the meaning of (10) is part of the meaning of (2). This would show that, for the majority, (2) is not a pure optative. Let us further assume that the majority does not use any sentence of the English language as a pure optative (this seems even more unlikely to me). Would I, in view of these scientific results, abandon the thesis of pure optatives? I think I would not; just as I would not abandon the thesis of the analytic character of the theorems of logic or of arithmetic if a psychological investigation were to reveal that the majority of people interpret these theorems as containing certain factual components. A *philosophical* thesis on logic or language, in contrast to a psychological or linguistic thesis, is not intended to assert anything about the speaking or thinking habits of the majority of people, but rather something about possible kinds of meanings and the relations between these meanings. In other words, a philosophical thesis does not talk about the haphazard features of natural languages, but about meaning relations, which can best be represented with the help of a constructed language. The thesis on arithmetic, mentioned above, says that it is possible to construct a system of arithmetic in such a way that its theorems (which correspond to the customarily accepted theorems of arithmetic) are analytic statements. Analogously, the thesis of pure optatives is meant as saying that it is possible to construct a language in such a way that it contains pure optatives. A discussion about a thesis of this kind seems to me much more in accord with the spirit of analytic philosophy than a discussion about a thesis interpreted as a psychological empirical assertion. At any rate, my position with respect to the present problem complex may best be characterized, first, by the assertion of the thesis of pure optatives as just interpreted, and second, by the proposal to construct a language with pure optatives and to use it as a basis for the philosophical discussion of value problems.

Let us then imagine that the cognitivist proposes a language L_c for which logical rules are stated in such a way that sentence (2) has the same meaning as (11) or as a similar sentence. ("To have the same meaning" is here always understood, not in the strong sense of synonymy, but in the weaker sense of logical or analytic equivalence.) Thus in L_c, sentence (10) (or a similar sentence) is logically implied by (2). I do not deny that a language L_c of this kind can be constructed without contradictions or ambiguities. On the other hand, I should definitely prefer a language L_O in which a sentence (2′) corresponding to (2) occurs such that (2′) is interpreted as a pure optative so that no factual sentence is logically implied by it. The meaning which (2) has in L_c is expressed in L_O by a sentence (11′) corresponding to (11). On the other hand, L_c does not contain any sentence expressing the meaning which (2′) has in L_O. This shows the disadvantage of a language like L_c.

For the same reason it seems inadvisable to me to interpret the proposal of a definition, as Kaplan does, in such a way that the proposal logically implies the statement of the usefulness of the proposed definition. For example, it seems definitely preferable to me to interpret the optative

(12) Let us introduce '3' as a new sign synonymous with '2 + 1'

as a pure optative. The combined meaning can be expressed more adequately by the following compound sentence:

(13) Let us introduce '3' as a new sign synonymous with '2+1'; and this introduction is useful.

This sentence separates the optative component from the factual component.

For the sake of simplicity, I shall use English words and sentence forms, instead of artificial symbols, in the examples of sentences in L_O. However, English, like all natural languages of which I know, has one serious defect relevant to the present problem. It does not possess a proper grammatical form applicable to optatives in our general sense, including proposals, commands, etc. (English and most of the other natural languages do not even have a special grammatical form for the expression of will or decision. The imperative is applicable only in the second person; in other cases, other sentence forms are borrowed which, in their original and literal sense, have an entirely different meaning.) Therefore, I shall use the Latin word "utinam"; "utinam *p*" (where any declarative sentence may be substituted for "*p*") is to mean approximately the same as "wish that *p*" or "would that *p*". A sentence of this form in L_O is a pure optative; that is, on the basis of the logical rules of this language, no factual sentence is logically implied by it.

The intended meaning of "utinam" is clearer if we take as primitive the use of this word for the expression of a comparative wish, i.e., a

preference. Let "utinam *p* rather than *q*" serve to express (not to describe, which would be done by a declarative sentence) the attitude of preferring the possible state of affairs *p* to *q*. Then we define:
(14) "utinam *p*" for "utinam *p* rather than not-*p*".
Then "utinam not-*p*" expresses the preference of not-*p* to *p*. Note that "not utinam *p*" is weaker than "utinam not-*p*" since it merely expresses the attitude of not preferring *p;* this leaves open whether preference of not-*p* holds, which would be expressed by "utinam not-*p*", or the attitude of indifference to *p,* i.e., neither preference of *p* nor preference of not-*p*.

If *p* is a proposition about the future or a proposition about a state of affairs at the present time with unknown truth-value, then "utinam *p*" expresses a wish in the ordinary sense of this word (in certain modes it may serve to express, in addition, a proposal, a request, a command, or the like). If *p* is a proposition about the past or the present known to be true, then "utinam *p*" expresses the attitude of approval or satisfaction, customarily expressed by sentences like "good that you did this", "good that we had rain yesterday" or the like. "Utinam not-*p*" expresses in this case a counterfactual wish or a disapproval or dissatisfaction about the fact *p,* customarily expressed by sentences like "I wish you had not done this", or "bad that you did this", "I wish there had not been rain" or "a pity that there was rain".

It is well known that the various optative modalities are expressible by combining the optative sign ("utinam" or "!") with the sign of negation (here "not"). For example, if *p* is a possible action of the listener, and "utinam" is understood in the mode of command, then "utinam not-*p*" expresses the prohibition of the action *p,* "not utinam not-*p*" the permission of the action *p,* etc.

Our original example (2) of an optative is thus formulated in L_o as follows (neglecting the special mode, which in (2) was that of a proposal):
(15) Utinam we take road *a* rather than *b*.

D. Belief and attitude. In contrast to Kaplan's view (§IV), it seems to me that the distinction made by Stevenson between belief and attitude and, in particular, between disagreement in belief and disagreement in attitude, is very important and fruitful, both for the theoretical analysis of philosophical formulations and for the practical task of separating the two components. I think that this separation of statements or questions in discussions and deliberations, e.g., on moral or political problems, would lead to greater clarity.

Kaplan explains that a belief and a simultaneous attitude should not be regarded as distinct events, but rather as different aspects or constituents in a given total situation. Strictly speaking, this is true. But we should recognize that most of the concepts of psychology used in describing the state of a person at a given time refer likewise only to a constituent and not to the total state; yet this fact does not diminish their usefulness for the explication of concepts of everyday language and for the explanation of occurring events. In the present problem situation it seems especially important to distinguish between the belief components and the other components (which Stevenson calls collectively "attitude") in the total situation (which Kaplan calls "attitude"). This distinction does not seem to involve any objectionable dualism. In all fields of science, it is customary and useful to distinguish changes of a given system in different respects, and often also to speak of them as if they were different events; for example, changes in the temperature of the blood, in its pressure, in its velocity of flow, in its chemical composition, and so forth. If there are general laws which state functional regularities between the changes of one kind and those of other kinds, then it is customary to speak of causal relations between them. This way of speaking does not imply any hypostatization; nobody will understand this reference to causal relations as asserting that temperature is one part of the blood and the blood pressure another, and so forth. Similarly, there seems to be no serious objection to saying that a belief has a certain effect upon an attitude component, e.g., a wish, or the other way around. Since practically all philosophers, with the exception of dualists of the old Cartesian kind, agree that a belief and a wish are not two substances or things, it seems to me that making the distinction, and even speaking in terms of causal relations, is entirely harmless.

However, the distinction between belief and attitude (the latter always understood as referring to the non-cognitive components) should not be regarded as identical with that between reason and emotion. A belief is often supported on the one hand by reasoning and on the other hand by emotions; and the same holds also for an attitude, e.g., a preference.

I agree with Kaplan's emphasis when he says that the causal analysis is not the only angle from which the relations between an attitude, say, a preference, and a belief on which the attitude is based, may be examined. It is also essential to investigate whether the belief is a valid reason for the preference. For example, it might be the case, that A, asked for a reason for the preference (2), states his belief (5). His intention in making this utterance is not merely to make a contribution to the causal explanation of his preference, but rather to indicate his motivation and to justify his preference. For the purpose of examining A's rationality we shall explore first, whether his belief was obtained in a rational way, i.e., whether it is supported by the evidence available to A, and second, whether the belief constitutes a rational reason for the preference. For example, if A would give as his reason for the preference (2), not (5) but rather:

(16) To take road a would cost more time and more effort than to take b,

we would say that it is irrational for *A* to offer (16) as a reason for his proposal, even if (16) were well confirmed by the evidence. The question of the causes of preferences or decisions, and the question of the reasons for them do not conflict; rather, they point in two different directions of investigation. I do not have the impression that on this point there is an actual disagreement between the conception of Kaplan and that of Stevenson and Reichenbach whom he criticizes.

Kaplan distinguishes between attitudes rooted in beliefs and attitudes not rooted in beliefs. An attitude is said to be rooted in a belief if this belief is not only a cause but also a reason for the attitude. Kaplan regards it as characteristic for emotivism to assert that there are attitudes not rooted in beliefs. I would not make this assertion; and I doubt that Stevenson or Reichenbach meant to make it. Whether this assertion does or does not hold, is a psychological question which is not essential for my interpretation of optatives and value statements. My thesis of pure optatives (T4) says merely that there are optatives which do not logically imply any factual statements; the thesis does not say anything about the *reasons* for the attitude expressed in the optative. For example, if we interpret (2) by sentence (15) in language L_O, then, according to the rules of this language, no factual sentence is logically implied by (2). But this result is perfectly compatible with the possibility that the preference, which *A* expressed by the English sentence (2) and could express by (15) in L_O, was rooted in A's belief in (5). Kaplan's argument is again founded on the assumption that the reason for an attitude is part of the meaning of the optative expressing the attitude; above, I have given arguments against this view.

Kaplan is certainly right in saying that it is illuminating for the problem of ascertaining the reasons for an attitude, to consider the analogous role which reasons play in an epistemological context. For example, *A* might point to the fact (6) as a reason for his belief in (5); and as a reason for his belief in (6), he might refer to a certain complex of observational data which he has experienced during his procedure of measuring the lengths of roads *a* and *b*, and which are stated in a complicated sentence *M*. The data stated in *M* are the observational evidence on which *A*'s belief in (6) is founded. However, *M* is not logically implied by (6). Generally speaking, the observational evidence which a person may or may not have for his belief in a statement describing a physical situation, is not part of the meaning of this statement. Analogously a belief which for *A* is a reason for his attitude, is not necessarily a part of the meaning of the optative expressing this attitude. It is essential for an adequate language about material objects that it contain sentence forms like (6) which state physical properties of objects without stating, in addition, the observational evidence of any observer. Likewise, it is essential for an adequate language about attitudes that it contain pure optatives, optatives which express merely an attitude, without stating any cognitive reason for it.

E. Is difference in attitudes compatible with agreement in all beliefs? Both cognitivists and non-cognitivists agree that beliefs play a very important role in the origin of attitudes and decisions, not only as causes but also as reasons. The core of the controversy lies in the question whether the totality of the beliefs of a perfectly rational person *A* at a certain time uniquely determines the attitudes and decisions of *A*. In contrast to Kaplan, and in agreement with Stevenson and Reichenbach, I would give a negative answer to this question. To put it in Stevenson's terms (see Kaplan's quotation in connection with his footnote 16), our thesis is as follows:

> *T5.* It is logically possible that two persons *A* and *B* at a certain time agree in all beliefs, that their reasoning is in perfect accord with deductive and inductive standards, and that they nevertheless differ in an optative attitude component.

More specifically, let us assume that at a given time *A* and *B* have the same degree of credence for all propositions (see §25 II), but differ in the following respect: Given the choice between two alternative decisions *a* and *b*, *A* prefers *a*, and *B* prefers *b*.

It is clear that the controversy does not concern a situation in which the decision of *A* affects only *A* and that of *B* affects only *B*. For example, it is possible that *A* and *B* have all beliefs in common, including the knowledge that *A* likes dish *a* better than *b*, and that *B* likes dish *b* better than *a*. If they have lunch together and there is a choice between *a* and *b*, then *A* will decide to take *a*, and *B* will choose *b*. In this case there is no real conflict of decisions, merely a difference in individual preferences. Both persons agree in the decision that *A* take dish *a* and *B* take dish *b*.

I shall now illustrate the thesis T5 by two examples. The first is extremely simple, but I think it demonstrates the basic conception on which T5 is founded. However, others may perhaps find it oversimple and unconvincing. We assume that *A* and *B* have decided to share either the activity *a*, say playing chess, or the activity *b*, say listening to music; yet each of them is inclined to give more consideration to his own preference than to that of his partner. If *A* prefers that both do *a*, and *B* prefers that both do *b*, then *A* will vote for *a* and *B* will vote for *b*. In this case there is genuine conflict of attitude components, namely wishes. This conflict can occur in spite of their agreement in all beliefs including the knowledge of their preferences and the knowledge that each is more concerned with his own wishes than with those of his partner.

Let us consider as a second example a situation in which *A* and *B*, together with others, must make an important common decision which does not immediately affect themselves. We assume that *A* and *B* are members of a ruling board which must decide how certain benefits are to be distributed among the members of a community *C* which does not include the ruling board. We presuppose again that *A* and *B* agree in all beliefs including those about the members of *C*, their economic situations, their inclinations, preferences, etc. Then it is nevertheless possible that *A* votes for a different proposal of distribution than *B*. For example, on the basis of a democratic attitude, *A* may wish to give equal rights to all members of *C* and will therefore vote for a distribution in equal amounts, while *B*, on the basis of an aristocratic attitude, favors an elite, a certain small minority group *C′* within *C*, and will therefore vote for a distribution which assigns a considerably higher share to every member of *C′* than to the others. I do not believe like Kaplan (toward the end of his §IV) that such a difference between *A* and *B* is possible only if at least one of them proceeds illogically. In our example, both may have exactly the same relevant evidence, apply the same valid inductive method, and thus come to exactly the same degree of credence for all relevant propositions, e.g., concerning the reactions of the members of *C* and the expectation values of the utilities for these members in the case of either of the distributions. The difference between *A* and *B* in their decisions on how to vote is based, in this case, not on a difference in their theoretical thinking but rather on a difference in their preferences concerning the community *C* and, finally, on a difference in character.

F. Value statements. On the basis of the preceding discussions, we are now prepared to attempt an explication of value statements. First I wish to emphasize that logical empiricists long ago abandoned the formulations of the earlier period (including my formulation quoted by Kaplan at the beginning of his essay) as oversimplifications. We are now in agreement with Dewey's conception (as described by Kaplan in §V) that a value statement expresses more than merely a momentary feeling of desire, liking, being satisfied, or the like, namely satisfaction in the long run. Thus now we agree with Kaplan's criticism in this point (which he calls the fourth difficulty, discussed in his §V).

In spite of our agreement on this point, there remains a disagreement in the interpretation of value statements. In order to clarify the essential issue, I shall simplify the problem by leaving aside some less essential factors. Suppose that the speaker *A* makes the following value statement about the agent *B* who, in a given situation *S*, has a choice between two possible actions *a* and *b*:

(17) In the given situation *S*, in which *B* has a choice between *a* and *b*, it would be better if *B* did *a* rather than *b*.

The word "better" is here understood in a valuative sense (more specifically, in a moral sense), not in the sense of "more useful". The interpretation I shall give for (17) would likewise hold for the statement ". . . , *B* ought to do *a* rather than *b*". According to my earlier explanations, we do not interpret statement (17) as a mere expression of *A*'s momentary feeling of liking *B*'s doing *a* better than *B*'s doing *b*. Let us rather assume that *A* has arrived at the valuation expressed in (17) by careful deliberation and that, asked for his reasons for this valuation, he states the following:

(18) (a) The evidence available to me at the present time and relevant for the present problem is such and such (listing the evidence *E* as a long series of facts known to him).

(b) The possible outcomes of *B*'s action are *a′* and *b′*; both outcomes affect *B* himself and also a third person *C*.

(c) The action *a* by *B* would lead to the consequence *a′*, and *b* would lead to *b′*.

(d) Both outcomes *a′* and *b′* would have a small advantage for *B*, the advantage of *a′* being somewhat smaller than that of *b′*, while for *C*, *a′* would have a considerable advantage, and *b′* a considerable disadvantage.

(e) If an agent *X* has a choice between two actions *p* and *q*, which affect himself and another person *Y*, and the situation is such that in the case of *X*'s doing *p*, *X* would have a somewhat smaller advantage than in the case of his doing *q*, and *Y* would have a considerable advantage in the first case and a considerable disadvantage in the second, than *X*'s doing *p* would be better than his doing *q*.

We assume that (18a) and (18b) state certain facts known to A; that (18c) and (18d) have a high inductive probablity on the basis of the evidence *E;* and that (18e) is a general value principle which together with other principles is accepted by *A* and taken by him as a basis for his value judgments; and that the reasons (a), (b), (c), (d), and (e) together have led *A* to his value judgment (17). On the basis of these assumptions, we would presumably agree that the reasons stated by *A* are good (i.e., rational) reasons for his value judgment (17) (which does not imply that we accept either his value principle (18e) or his value statement (17)).

Our problem is the analysis and interpretation of the complex value statement (17). First we can analyze it into the following two statements (19)(a) and (b), where (a) is clearly factual and (b) is a value statement whose nature is in question:

(19)(a) *B* finds himself in the situation *S* and has the possibility of carry-out either action *a* or action *b*.

(b) It would be better if *B* did *a* rather than *b*. (Or: *B* ought to do *a* rather than *b*.)

It is my view that (19a) states the total factual content of (17), and that (19b) does not contain any factual component and thus is *a pure value statement*. I wish to emphasize that here again, as in analogous cases discussed earlier, the meanings of the factual statements (18)(a), (b), (c), and (d), and the value principle (18)(e), although they were *reasons* for *A*'s judgment (17), are not part of the meaning of (17) since none of those statements is logically implied by (17).

According to Dewey's conception emphasized by Kaplan, a value statement expresses not only momentary satisfaction but rather satisfaction in the long run. Thus, *A*'s value statement (19b) is connected with the following psychological fact:

(20) For any *p* and *q*, if *p* is the totality of the consequences that would occur if *B* were to do *a*, and *q* is the totality of the consequences that would occur if *B* were to do *b*, then *p* is more satisfying for *A* than *q*.

However, statement (20) cannot be taken as an explication of the value statement (19b). It is rather a factual psychological statement about *A*; it has nearly the same relation to (19b) as (3b) has to (2), therefore it is *merely associated* with the value statement (19b). In order to obtain an explication of the pure value statement (19b) in the language L_O, we have to formulate a pure optative analogous to (20):

(21) For any *p* and *q*, if *p* is the totality of consequences that would occur if *B* were to do *a*, and *q* is the totality of consequences that would occur if *B* were to do *b*, then utinam *p* rather than *q*.

Statement (21) may be regarded as merely an expanded version of (19b) which has the same meaning, on the basis of a suitable definition of "better". It is important to note that (21) is in various respects essentially different from the statements (18) of the reasons. First, (21) contains only a general reference to unspecified consequences *p* and *q*, while the statements (18) refer to specified consequences *a′* and *b′* and to specified utilities (advantages or disadvantages) for specified persons. Second, (21) refers to unknown consequences *p* and *q* which would occur in one or the other case, and one of which will actually occur, while the reasons in (17) refer to the consequences *a′* and *b′* which are probable on the basis of the evidence *E* available to *A*, but which may possibly be very different from *p* and *q*.

The essential point is that the second part of our explicatum of (17), formulated first in (19b) and then in (21), is interpreted as having no cognitive content. On the other hand, the question as to the particular kind of non-cognitive content of such a value statement is not essential. In addition to the common basic constituent which we have called optative and which in our example is formulated in (21), we might distinguish components that are volitive (an expression of will or decision), or emotive (an expression of emotions), or motivative (an expression of the intention of influencing attitudes and actions of the listener), and perhaps others. But it is questionable whether clear boundaries can be drawn between these various kinds of components. If it is possible to make distinctions similar to the ones indicated, then an analysis might reveal that usually components of all or most of these kinds occur together.

Stevenson (*op. cit.*, p. 21) gives an approximate interpretation of value statements according to which "*a* is good" means about the same as:

(22) I approve of *a;* do so as well.

The first part has not only the grammatical form of a declarative sentence, but is also interpreted by Stevenson as such a sentence, namely a factual statement about the mental state of the speaker. The second part is intentionally formulated by Stevenson as an imperative in order to make clear that it has no cognitive content but is a pure optative (or imperative, in the wide sense in which Stevenson and others use this word). This is clearly seen from his detailed criticism of the alternative interpretation of the second part as "I want you to do so as well" which he regards as confusing (pp. 24f.). I emphatically agree with this criticism. But for the same reason I would criticize Stevenson's formulation of the first part as a declarative sentence. In my view, this part too would be formulated more adequately as a pure optative:

(23) Utinam *a* happens,

or more explicitly in a form similar to (21) (with "not-*a*" instead of "*b*").

G. The task before us. I entirely agree with Kaplan's view (§VI) that what is lacking on both sides is a more precisely formulated theory, that the present appearance of disagreement may conceal an underlying agreement on many important points, and that a great part of the divergence is no more than a matter of emphasis.

In line with my general tendencies, I would regard it as advisable to propose explications of value statements in standardized forms in a constructed language. I think the fact that standardized forms for cognitive statements, both logical and factual, have existed for a long time, has contributed significantly to our clearer understanding of the nature of these statements and the logical relations between them. I think it will hardly be possible to state precise rules for translating value statements of the ordinary language, including those of the customary philosophical language, into standardized forms, because the customary forms are too vague and ambiguous. The same holds of course for the customary cognitive statements. However, it is important that the meanings of the standardized value statements should be made sufficiently clear, at least for practical purposes, as has been done for cognitive statements. Furthermore, logical rules must be stated for the logical relations, especially for logical implication, both between value statements and between value statements and cognitive statements.

In this reply I could only give some brief indications of the envisaged explication of value statements, but have not carried it out. If I had time to devote myself to this task, I would try to develop explications in the direction indicated, on the basis of the analyses which have been given so far by pragmatists and logical empiricists. The direction of my own work would presumably be closest to that of Stevenson and Reichenbach. As Kaplan has shown, today there is a clearly noticeable convergence between the conception of the empiricists and that of the pragmatists. I share his confidence that progress in the work of explication, undertaken on both sides, will lead to better mutual understanding and increased agreement.

Rudolf Carnap

Department of Philosophy
University of California at Los Angeles

BIBLIOGRAPHY OF THE WRITINGS OF RUDOLF CARNAP

Compiled by

ARTHUR J. BENSON

PREFACE TO THE BIBLIOGRAPHY

The present Bibliography consists of three parts. The longest, Part I (pp. 1018-1056), is an annotated list of the published writings of Rudolf Carnap, with a concluding section of items whose early publication is anticipated. Part II (pp. 1056-1059) provides information about works that have appeared under Carnap's editorship. Part III (pp. 1059-1070) is a list of reviews of Carnap's writings, keyed to Part I.

The description of every item in the Bibliography has been based primarily upon a direct examination of the work itself or, in a few cases, of a photographic reproduction. Where desirable, this has been supplemented with information obtained from the literature or from persons or organizations concerned. In accordance with the practice adopted in most of the previous bibliographies in this series, an analysis of the contents has been included in the notes for the major items. In order to avoid disproportion in the length of such analyses, some or all subheadings have in certain instances been omitted.

The arrangement in Part I is strictly chronological, not only by year but also within the year. The attempt has been made to include every publication of Carnap that might conceivably be of interest to a student of his work. A number of minor pieces, both signed and unsigned, have been deliberately omitted. For the most part these are items occasioned by Carnap's co-editorship of the journal *Erkenntnis* or by his membership in the Organizing Committee for the various International Congresses for the Unity of Science. It seems worth recording here that, although listed for six years as a "contributing editor" of *Philosophic Abstracts,* he never contributed any abstracts to this journal.

It is characteristic of Carnap, as indeed also of other members of the late Vienna Circle, to have devoted considerable energy to the encouragement of a cooperative approach to the problems of philosophy and logic. Part II of the Bibliography describes the periodical and other serial publications with which, especially in the thirties and forties, he has been most intimately connected in an editorial capacity.

In Part III the aim has been to provide a comprehensive list of reviews from the periodical literature. The only principle of selection has been that of length: reviews less than one hundred words long have been omitted, except in special cases. One-third of the reviews listed are more than eight hundred words long. References are given with the names of reviewers and periodicals in abbreviated form, which is explained in two concluding sections. Where the language of a review differs from that suggested by the title of the periodical, the language actually used is indicated in square brackets at the end of the reference.

Although many items in the Bibliography were discovered as a result of systematic search of the literature, full use was naturally made of various standard bibliographical aids. Of these, the most helpful were Alonzo Church's bibliography of symbolic logic in *The Journal of Symbolic Logic* (vol. 1, 1936, pp. 121-218; vol. 3, 1938, pp. 178-212) and the continuing review section of that journal. As mentioned in the note to Item 1955-11 below, an extensive bibliography of writings by and about Carnap was published some years ago by Alberto Pasquinelli; unfortunately, work on the present Bibliography was too far advanced to profit appreciably by his independent labors.

The compiler wishes to express his warm thanks to the Library of the University of California at Berkeley, whose magnificent collection greatly facilitated the preparation of the Bibliography and whose staff members, including those of the Library School, were a constant source of wisdom and advice; to the many publishers, librarians and private individuals, both in this country and abroad, who courteously answered requests for information; and especially to Professor Carnap himself, who, in addition to reading much of the Bibliography in draft, patiently replied to a barrage of written queries.

Information concerning errors of omission or commission in the Bibliography will be welcome and will be incorporated in any future edition of this volume.

ARTHUR J. BENSON

LOS ANGELES STATE COLLEGE
SPRING 1962

I. WRITINGS OF RUDOLF CARNAP

1921

1. DER RAUM. EIN BEITRAG ZUR WISSENSCHAFTSLEHRE. Inaugural-Dissertation zur Erlangung der Doktorwürde der hohen philosophischen Fakultät der Universität Jena. [Jena: Universität Jena, 1921.] 87, [1] pp.

Title page bears prominently displayed *printer's* imprint: Göttingen 1921, Druck der Dieterich'schen Univ.-Buchdruckerei, W. Fr. Kaestner.

"Genehmigt . . . auf Antrag des Herrn Prof. Dr. [Bruno] Bauch . . .

den 1. März 1921" (p. [2]). The degree DR.PHIL. was granted on 9 Dec. 1921.

Contents: Einleitung. Der formale Raum. Der Anschauungsraum. Der physische Raum. Das gegenseitige Verhältnis von formalem, Anschauungs- und physischem Raum. Die Beziehungen zwischen Raumerkenntnis und Erfahrung.—Literaturverzeichnis. Literatur-Hinweise.—Lebenslauf.

1922

1. DER RAUM. EIN BEITRAG ZUR WISSENSCHAFTSLEHRE. "Kant-Studien" Ergänzungshefte, Nr. 56. Berlin: Verlag von Reuther & Reichard, 1922. 87 pp.

Separate issue of preceding item without dissertation statement or "Lebenslauf." Printed by Dieterich, and identical with preceding item except for pp. [1]-[2] and omission of p. [88].

Later distributed by Pan-Verlag Rolf Heise, Berlin; still later, by Pan-Verlag Kurt Metzner, Berlin (later, Leipzig); still later, by Pan-Verlag Rudolf Birnbach, Leipzig.

1923

1. Über die Aufgabe der Physik und die Anwendung des Grundsatzes der Einfachstheit. *Kant-Studien* (Berlin), Bd. 28, H. 1/2 (1923), pp. [90]-107.

1924

1. Dreidimensionalität des Raumes und Kausalität: Eine Untersuchung über den logischen Zusammenhang zweier Fiktionen. *Annalen der Philosophie und philosophischen Kritik* (Leipzig), Bd. 4, H. 3 (1924), pp. [105]-130.

1925

1. Über die Abhängigkeit der Eigenschaften des Raumes von denen der Zeit. *Kant-Studien* (Berlin), Bd. 30, H. 3/4 (1925), pp. [331]-345.

1926

1. PHYSIKALISCHE BEGRIFFSBILDUNG. [Wissen und Wirken, Einzelschriften zu den Grundfragen des Erkennens und Schaffens, Hrsg., Emil Ungerer, Bd. 39.] Karlsruhe: Verlag G. Braun, 1926. [iv], 66 pp.

Contents: Einleitung, die Aufgabe der Physik. Die erste Stufe der physikalischen Begriffsbildung, qualitative Stufe: Wahrgenommene Dinge und Eigenschaften. Die zweite Stufe der physikalischen Begriffsbildung, quantitative Stufe: Die physikalischen Grössen. Die dritte Stufe der physikalischen Begriffsbildung, abstrakte Stufe: Das vierdimensionale Weltgeschehen.—Literatur-Verzeichnis. Sach- und Namenregister.

1927

1. [Literaturbericht:] Rudolf Carnap, *Physikalische Begriffsbildung*. *Annalen der Philosophie und philosophischen Kritik* (Leipzig), Bd. 6, H. 4 (18. Juli 1927), pp. 76*-77* of sep. paged "Literaturberichte."

Signed "Snz.", i.e. "Selbstnotiz." A brief statement of the organization and thesis of preceding item.

2. Eigentliche und uneigentliche Begriffe. *Symposion: Philosophische Zeitschrift für Forschung und Ausprache* (Berlin-Schlachtensee), Bd. 1, H. 4 [1927], pp. 355-374.

1928

1. Der logische Aufbau der Welt. Berlin-Schlachtensee: Weltkreis-Verlag, 1928. xi, 290 pp.

   Later distributed by Wilhelm Benary, Berlin (later, Erfurt) ; still later, by Felix Meiner Verlag, Leipzig.

   For Italian translation and 2nd edition, see "To Appear."

   Contents: Vorwort (Wien, Mai 1928). *Einleitung: Aufgabe und Plan der Untersuchungen.* Die Aufgabe. Plan der Untersuchungen. *Vorbereitende Erörterungen.* Über die Form wissenschaftlicher Aussagen. Überblick über die Gegenstandsarten und ihrer Beziehungen. *Die Formprobleme des Konstitutionssystems.* Die Stufenformen. Die Systemform. (Formale Untersuchungen. Materiale Untersuchungen.) Die Basis. (Die Grundelemente. Die Grundrelationen.) Die Gegenstandsformen. Die Darstellungsformen eines Konstitutionssystems. *Entwurf eines Konstitutionssystems.* Die unteren Stufen: Eigenpsychische Gegenstände. Die mittleren Stufen: Physische Gegenstände. Die oberen Stufen: Fremdpsychische und geistige Gegenstände. *Klärung einiger philosophischer Probleme auf Grund der Konstitutionstheorie.* Einige Wesensprobleme. Das psychophysische Problem. Das konstitutionale oder empirische Wirklichkeitsproblem. Das metaphysische Wirklichkeitsproblem. Aufgabe und Grenzen der Wissenschaft.—Zusammenfassung. Literatur- und Namenregister. Sachregister.

2. Scheinprobleme in der Philosophie: Das Fremdpsychische und der Realismusstreit. Berlin-Schlachtensee: Weltkreis-Verlag, 1928. 46 pp.

   Later distributed by Wilhelm Benary, Berlin (later, Erfurt); still later, by Felix Meiner Verlag, Leipzig.

   For 2nd edition, see "To Appear."

1929

1. [Literaturbericht:] P[aul] Bommersheim, *Beiträge zur Lehre von Ding und Gesetz. Monatshefte für Mathematik und Physik* (Leipzig), Bd. 36, H. 1 (1929), pp. 27-28 of sep. paged "Literaturberichte."

2. Abriss der Logistik, mit besonderer Berücksichtigung der Relationstheorie und ihrer Anwendungen. Schriften zur wissenschaftlichen Weltauffassung, hrsg. von Philipp Frank und Moritz Schlick, Bd. 2. Wien: Verlag von Julius Springer, 1929. vi, 114 pp.

   A contemplated 2nd edition, listed in the Bibliography of the 1st impression of Item 1942-2, was never published. A new work, Item 1954-3, resulted instead.

   Translated into Japanese (in part) as Item 1944-3.

   Contents: Vorwort (Wien, im Jan. 1929). System der Logistik (§§ 1-29). Die Aufgabe der Logistik. Funktionen. Wahrheitsfunktionen. Die Grundsätze. Lehrsätze der Aussagentheorie. Allaussagen und Existenzaussagen. Kennzeichnungen. Klassen. Die Typentheorie. Klassenverknüpfungen. Relationen. Verknüpfungen von Relationen. Die Hierarchie der Typen. Kennzeichnende Funktionen Die Konverse; Bereiche und Feld. Die

Verkettung. Operationen. Drei- und mehrstellige Relationen. Die Klassen 0, 1, 2; Eindeutigkeit. Das Abstraktionsprinzip. Die Kardinalzahlen. Isomorphie; die Relationszahlen. Die *R*-Ketten; Gruppen. Endlich und Unendlich. Verschiedene Zerlegungen einer Relation. Progressionen. Reihen. Grenzbegriffe. Stetigkeit. ANGEWANDTE LOGISTIK. § 30, Über die axiomatische Methode. *Mengenlehre und Arithmetik* (§§ 31-32). AS [Axiomensystem] der Mengenlehre. Peanos AS der natürlichen Zahlen. *Geometrie* (§§ 33-35). AS der Topologie (Umgebungsaxiome). AS der projektiven Geometrie (erste Form: die Geraden als Klassen). AS der projektiven Geometrie (zweite Form: die Geraden als Relationen). *Physik* (§§ 36-37). AS der Raum-Zeit-Topologie. Determination und Kausalität. *Verwandschaftslehre* (§ 38). AS der Verwandschaftsbeziehungen unter Menschen. *Erkenntnisanalyse* (§ 39). Die untersten Stufen des Konstitutionssystems. *Sprachanalyse* (§§ 40-43). Logische Semasiologie einer bestimmten Sprache. Aufstellung des logischen Skeletts vorgelegter Sätze. Masszahlen. Zustände und Vorgänge; Ort und Zeit.—*Anhang* (§§ 44-50). Übungsaufgaben. Übersicht über die wichtigsten logistischen Zeichen. Literaturverzeichnis. Literaturhinweise. Namenregister. Sachregister mit vergleichender Terminologie. Register der logischen Konstanten.

3. [Literaturbericht:] Adolf Fraenkel, *Einleitung in die Mengenlehre,* 3. Aufl. *Annalen der Philosophie und philosophischen Kritik* (Leipzig), Bd. 8, H. 1/2 (15. Mai 1929), p. 10* of sep. paged "Literaturberichte."

   Signed "R.C." For a much longer review of the *Einleitung,* see Item 1929-6.

4. Tagung für Erkenntnislehre der exakten Wissenschaften . . . in Prag. Von Rudolf Carnap, Philipp Frank, Hans Hahn und Hans Reichenbach. *Ibid.,* Bd. 8, H. 4/5 (31. Juli 1929), pp. [113]-114.

   Announcement of the Conference, signed by Carnap, Frank and Hahn for the Verein Ernst Mach, Vienna, and by Reichenbach for the Gesellschaft für empirische Philosophie, Berlin. Held in Prague, 15-17 Sept. 1929, this was the first in a series of nine international meetings (concluding with the Sixth International Congress for the Unity of Science, Chicago, 1-6 Sept. 1941) in which the ideas of logicial empiricism and related movements were to find expression.

   The proceedings of the Conference were published the following year as a triple number of *Erkenntnis* (Bd. 1, H. 2/4, [89]-339 pp.), the journal that superseded the *Annalen* (see "Carnap as Editor"). Contributions by Carnap are listed below as Items 1930-6 to 1930-8.

5. WISSENSCHAFTLICHE WELTAUFFASSUNG: DER WIENER KREIS. [Von Hans Hahn, Otto Neurath und Rudolf Carnap.] Veröffentlichungen des Vereines Ernst Mach, [H. I]. Wien: Artur Wolf Verlag, 1929. 64 pp. (pp. 60-64 advtg. matter).

   Prepared in anticipation of the Conference and dedicated to Moritz Schlick, then at Stanford Univ. as visiting professor. The Geleitwort is signed for the Verein by Hahn, Neurath and Carnap, but their names do not appear on the title page.

   The Bibliographie lists (p. 36) *Von Gott und Seele: Scheinfragen in Metaphysik und Theologie,* the text of a lecture delivered by Carnap in

June 1929 under the auspices of the Verein. Although planned for inclusion in the series "Veröffentlichungen des Vereines Ernst Mach," it was never published. The section of the Bibliographie devoted to Carnap is reprinted as Item 1930-8.

Contents: Geleitwort (Wien, im Aug. 1929). *Der Wiener Kreis der wissenschaftlichen Weltauffassung.* Vorgeschichte. Der Kreis um Schlick. *Die wissenschaftliche Weltauffassung. Problemgebiete.* Grundlagen der Arithmetik. Grundlagen der Physik. Grundlagen der Geometrie. Grundlagenprobleme der Biologie und Psychologie. Grundlagen der Sozialwissenschaften. *Rückblick und Ausblick.—Literaturhinweise. Bibliographie.* Die Mitglieder des Wiener Kreises. Dem Wiener Kreise nahestehende Autoren. Führende Vertreter der wissenschaftlichen Weltauffassung.—Namenregister.

6. [Besprechung:] Adolf Fraenkel, *Einleitung in die Mengenlehre,* 3. Aufl. *Kant-Studien* (Berlin), Bd. 34, H. 3/4 (1929), pp. 428-429.

   See Item 1929-3.

7. [Besprechung:] Karl Menger, *Dimensionstheorie. Ibid.,* pp. 457-458.

1930

1. [Literaturbericht:] H[erbert] Feigl, *Theorie und Erfahrung in der Physik. Monatshefte für Mathematik und Physik* (Leipzig), Bd. 37, H. 1 (1930), p. 6 of sep. paged "Literaturberichte."

2. Die alte und die neue Logik. *Erkenntnis* (Leipzig), Bd. 1, H. 1 [1930], pp. [12]-26.

   Translated into French as Item 1933-2, into Japanese as Item 1942-4, into English as Item 1959-9. For Italian and Spanish translations of Item 1959-9, see note to that item.

3. Einheitswissenschaft auf physischer Basis. *Ibid.,* p. 77.

   Abstract of lecture delivered in 1930 under the auspices of the Verein Ernst Mach. The lecture was not published in full.

4. [Besprechung:] Felix Kaufmann, *Das Unendliche in der Mathematik und seine Ausschaltung. Deutsche Literaturzeitung* (Leipzig), 51. Jahrg. (3. Folge, 1. Jahrg.), H. 35 (30. Aug. 1930), cols. 1674-1678.

5. Die Mathematik als Zweig der Logik. *Blätter für deutsche Philosophie* (Berlin), Bd. 4, H. 3/4 (1930), pp. 298-310.

   Contribution to a symposium on Philosophical Foundations of Mathematics, with six participants, conducted in this issue of the *Blätter,* pp. [259]-381.

6. Diskussion über Wahrscheinlichkeit. Von [Edgar] Zilsel und anderen. *Erkenntnis* (Leipzig), Bd. 1, H. 2/4 (1930), pp. [260]-285.

   Discussion at the First Conference on Theory of Knowledge of the Exact Sciences, Prague, 15-17 Sept. 1929. Carnap's remarks: pp. 268-269 and 282-283.

7. Bericht über Untersuchungen zur allgemeinen Axiomatik. *Ibid.,* pp. [303]-307.

   Abridged version of paper presented at the Conference. Despite the remark that "die Untersuchungen an anderer Stelle in ausführlicher Darstellung veröffentlicht werden sollen" (p. [303], fn.), a longer paper was not published. The material, in changed form, was later incorporated into Items 1934-6 (in part) and 1937-1.

8. [Bibliographie:] Rudolf Carnap. *Ibid.*, pp. [315]-317.

   Annotated auto-bibliography included in the proceedings of the Conference. Reprinted from pp. 33-36 of Item 1929-5.

1931

1. Ergebnisse der logischen Analyse der Sprache. *Forschungen und Fortschritte* (Berlin), 7. Jahrg., Nr. 13 (1. Mai 1931), pp. 183-184.
2. [Besprechung:] A. N. Whitehead and B[ertrand] Russell, *Principia Mathematica,* 2nd ed. *Erkenntnis* (Leipzig), Bd. 2, H. 1 [1931], pp. [73]-75.
3. [Besprechung:] E[ino] Kaila, *Der logistische Neupositivismus. Ibid.,* pp. 75-77.
4. Die logizistische Grundlegung der Mathematik. *Ibid.,* Bd. 2, H. 2/3 (1931), pp. [91]-105.

   Presented at the Second Conference on Theory of Knowledge of the Exact Sciences, Königsberg, 5-7 Sept. 1930.

   For English translation, see "To Appear."
5. Diskussion zur Grundlegung der Mathematik. Von [Hans] Hahn und anderen. *Ibid.,* pp. [135]-149.

   Discussion of preceding item and related Conference papers. Carnap's remarks: pp. 141-144 and 145-146.

1932

1. Überwindung der Metaphysik durch logische Analyse der Sprache. *Erkenntnis* (Leipzig), Bd. 2, H. 4 [1932], pp. [219]-241.

   Revised version of lecture delivered in Nov. 1930 at the Univ. of Warsaw. H. 4 (n.d.) appeared in 1932, although the title page of Bd. 2 is dated "1931".

   Translated into French as Item 1934-8, into Portuguese as Item 1945-4, into Italian (in part) as Item 1950-3, into English as Item 1959-8, into Spanish as Item 1961-2. For Italian translation of Item 1934-8 and Spanish translation of Item 1959-8, see notes to those items.
2. Die Sprache der Physik. *Ibid.,* p. 311.

   Abstract of lecture delivered 1 March 1931, one of a series on Problems of Unified Science, arranged by the Wiener Volksbildungsverein and the Verein Ernst Mach. The lecture was an early version of Item 1932-4.
3. Psychologie in physikalischer Sprache. *Ibid.,* p. 311.

   Abstract of lecture delivered 8 March 1931 in the same series. The lecture was based on Item 1932-5.
4. Die physikalische Sprache als Universalsprache der Wissenschaft. *Ibid.,* Bd. 2, H. 5/6 [1932], pp. [432]-465.

   Revised version of lecture whose abstract is Item 1932-2. H. 5/6 (n.d.) appeared in 1932, although the title page of Bd. 2 is dated "1931".

   Translated into English as Item 1934-4, into Portuguese as Item 1945-5. For contents, see note to Item 1934-4.

   An excerpt from Carnap's letter to Bernhard Bavink—prompted by the latter's review of the present item in *Unsere Welt* (Bielefeld), 24. Jahrg.,

H. 8 (Aug. 1932), pp. 248-251—is quoted on p. 317 of Bavink's review of Item 1934-5, *ibid.*, 26. Jahrg., H. 10 (Okt. 1934), pp. 316-319.

5. Psychologie in physikalischer Sprache. *Ibid.*, Bd. 3, H. 2/3 (30. Dez. 1932), pp. 107-142.

   Revised version of lecture delivered in Nov. 1930 at the Univ. of Warsaw. See note to Item 1932-3.

   Translated into English as Item 1959-10. For Spanish translation thereof, see note to that item.

6. Erwiderung auf die vorstehenden Aufsätze von E. Zilsel und K. Duncker. *Ibid.*, pp. 177-188.

   Reply to Edgar Zilsel's "Bermerkungen zur Wissenschaftslogik," *ibid.*, pp. 143-161, and Karl Duncker's "Behaviorismus und Gestaltpsychologie," *ibid.*, pp. 162-176.

7. Über Protokollsätze. *Ibid.*, pp. 215-228.

   Reply to Otto Neurath's "Protokollsätze," *ibid.*, pp. 204-214.

1933

1. [Besprechung:] Philipp Frank, *Das Kausalgesetz und seine Grenzen. Kant-Studien* (Berlin), Bd. 38, H. 1/2 (1933), p. 275.

2. L'ANCIENNE ET LA NOUVELLE LOGIQUE. Trad. du général Ernest Vouillemin. Introd. de Marcel Boll. Actualités scientifiques et industrielles, 76. Paris: Hermann & Cie, 1933. 36, [1] pp.

   Translation of Item 1930-2 as revised by Carnap. The Literatur-Hinweise are omitted.

3. [Besprechung:] B[ertrand] Russell u. A. N. Whitehead, *Einführung in die mathematische Logik. Erkenntnis* (Leipzig), Bd. 3, H. 4/6 (5. Sept. 1933), pp. 436-437.

   The volume reviewed is a translation by Hans Mokre of the Introductions to the 1st and 2nd editions of *Principia Mathematica.*

1934

1. On the Character of Philosophic Problems. Trans. by W. M. Malisoff. *Philosophy of Science* (Baltimore), vol. 1, no. 1 (Jan. 1934), pp. 5-19; corrections, vol. 1, no. 2 (April 1934), p. 251.

   The original in German was not published.

2. [Besprechung:] Walter Dubislav, *Die Philosophie der Mathematik in der Gegenwart. Erkenntnis* (Leipzig), Bd. 4, H. 1 (8. Mai 1934), pp. 64-65.

3. [Besprechung:] C. I. Lewis and C. H. Langford, *Symbolic Logic. Ibid.*, pp. 65-66.

4. THE UNITY OF SCIENCE. Trans. with an introd. by M[ax] Black. [Psyche Miniatures, General Series, no. 63.] London: Kegan Paul, Trench, Trubner & Co., 1934. 101 pp.

   Translation of Item 1932-4 as revised by Carnap, with added Author's Introduction, pp. 21-29.

   Reprinted (in part) as Item 1961-3. For full reprint, see "To Appear."

   Contents: Introduction, by M. Black. Author's Introduction (Prague, Jan. 1934). Advice to the Reader. *Physics as a Universal Science.* The Heterogeneity of Science. Languages. Protocol Language. The Physical Language as an Intersubjective Language. The Physical Language as a Universal Language. Protocol Language as a Part of Physical Language. Unified Science in Physical Language.

5. Die Aufgabe der Wissenschaftslogik. Einheitswissenschaft, Schriften hrsg. von Otto Neurath in Verbindung mit Rudolf Carnap und Hans Hahn, H. 3. Wien: Verlag Gerold & Co., 1934. 30 pp.

   Translated into French as Item 1935-10*a* and (in part) as Item 1950-6, into Japanese as Item 1942-5. For Italian translation of Item 1935-10*a*, see note to that item.

6. Logische Syntax der Sprache. Schriften zur wissenschaftlichen Weltauffassung, hrsg. von Philipp Frank und Moritz Schlick, Bd. 8. Wien: Verlag von Julius Springer, 1934. xi, 274 pp.

   The Vorwort is dated: Prag, im Mai 1934.

   Translated into English as Item 1937-1. For Italian and Spanish translations thereof, see note to that item.

   For contents, see note to Item 1937-1.

7. Meaning, Assertion and Proposal. *Philosophy of Science* (Baltimore), vol. 1, no. 3 (July 1934), pp. 359-360.

   Reply to John Dewey's "Meaning, Assertion and Proposal," *ibid.,* vol. 1, no. 2 (April 1934), pp. 237-238.

8. La Science et la Métaphysique devant l'Analyse Logique du Langage Trad. du général Ernest Vouillemin. Introd. de Marcel Boll. Actualités scientifiques et industrielles, 172. Paris: Hermann & Cie, 1934. 44, [1] pp.

   Translation of Item 1932-1 as revised by Carnap.

   Translated into Italian (in part) as Item 1952-2.

9. Theoretische Fragen u. praktische Entscheidungen. *Natur und Geist* (Dresden), 2. Jahrg., Nr. 9 (Sept. 1934), pp. 257-260.

10. The Rejection of Metaphysics. *Psyche: An Annual of General and Linguistic Psychology* (Cambridge, Eng., and London), vol. 14 (1934), pp. 100–111.

    Lecture delivered 8 Oct. 1934 at the Univ. of London. A revised version appears in Item 1935–1.

    For a brief account of discussions held during Carnap's visit to London, see pp. 47–48 of C. A. M. Maund and J. W. Reeves's "Report of Lectures on *Philosophy and Logical Syntax . . .* by Professor Rudolf Carnap," *Analysis* (Oxford), vol. 2, no. 3 (Dec. 1934), pp. 42–48.

11. Die Antinomien und die Unvollständigkeit der Mathematik. *Monatshefte für Mathematik und Physik* (Leipzig), Bd. 41, H. 2 (1934), pp. 263-284.

    Received for publication 4 June 1934.

    See note to Item 1937-1.

1935

1. Philosophy and Logical Syntax. [Psyche Miniatures, General Series, no. 70.] London: Kegan Paul, Trench, Trubner & Co., 1935. 100 pp.

Revised version of three lectures delivered on 8, 10 and 12 Oct. 1934 at the Univ. of London. See Items 1934-10 and 1944-1.

Chap. 1 is reprinted as Item 1955-5 and translated into Chinese as Item 1960-3. For other reprints and Spanish translation of the present item, see "To Appear."

Contents: Preface (Prague, Nov. 1934). *The Rejection of Metaphysics.* Verifiability. Metaphysics. Problems of Reality. Ethics. Metaphysics as Expression. Psychology. Logical Analysis. *Logical Syntax of Language.* "Formal" Theory. Formation Rules. Transformation Rules. Syntactical Terms. L-Terms. Content. Pseudo-Object-Sentences. The Material and the Formal Modes of Speech. *Syntax as the Method of Philosophy.* The Material Mode of Speech. Modalities. Relativity in Regard to Language. Pseudo-Questions. Epistemology. Natural Philosophy. What Physicalism Asserts. What Physicalism Does Not Assert. The Unity of Science.—Literature.

2. Formalwissenschaft und Realwissenschaft. *Erkenntnis* (Leipzig), Bd. 5, H. 1 (31. März 1935), pp. 30-37.

Abridged version of paper presented at the Prague Preliminary Conference of the International Congresses for the Unity of Science, 31 Aug. to 2 Sept. 1934. (The Conference dates are incorrectly given as "30. August bis 1. September" on the *covers* of H. 1 and 2/3.)

H. 1 and 2/3 were issued also as a single "Sonderdruck aus *Erkenntnis*": *Einheit der Wissenschaft: Prager Vorkonferenz der internationalen Kongresse für Einheit der Wissenschaft, 1934.* Leipzig: Verlag von Felix Meiner, [1935]. [iv], 204 pp.

The present item is translated into French as Item 1935-10*b*, into Italian (in part) as Item 1950-2, into English as Item 1953-10. For Chinese and Spanish translations of Item 1953-10, see note to that item.

3. Les Concepts psychologiques et les concepts physiques sont-ils foncièrement différents? Trad. par Robert Bouvier. *Revue de synthèse* (Paris), t. 10, n° 1 (avril 1935), pp. [43]-53.

Contribution to a symposium on Psychology and the Natural Sciences, with nine participants, conducted in the pages of the *Revue:* t. 6, n° 2 (oct. 1933), pp. [167]-180; t. 8, n° 2 (oct. 1934), pp. [125]-185; t. 10, n° 1 (avril 1935), pp. [5]-85. The original in German was not published.

4. Ein Gültigkeitskriterium für die Sätze der klassischen Mathematik. *Monatshefte für Mathematik und Physik* (Leipzig), Bd. 42, H. 1 (1935), pp. 163-190.

Received for publication 19 Dec. 1934.

See note to Item 1937-1.

5. [Bibliographie:] Rudolf Carnap. *Erkenntnis* (Leipzig), Bd. 5, H. 2/3 (18. Juni 1935), pp. 187-188.

Annotated, selected auto-bibliography included in the proceedings of the Prague Preliminary Conference (see note to Item 1935-2).

6. [Besprechung:] Willard van Orman Quine, *A System of Logistic. Ibid.,* Bd. 5, H. 4 (31. Juli 1935), pp. 285-287.

7. [Besprechung:] Walter Dubislav, *Naturphilosophie. Ibid.,* pp. 287-288.

8. [Besprechung:] A[rend] Heyting, *Mathematische Grundlagenforschung. Ibid.,* pp. 288-289.

9. [Besprechung:] Karl Popper, *Logik der Forschung. Ibid.,* pp. 290-294.

10. Le Probléme de la logique de la science. Science formelle et science du réel. Trad. du général [Ernest] Vouillemin. Actualités scientifiques et industrielles, 291. Paris: Hermann & Cie, 1935. 37, [1] pp.
   a. Le Problème de la logique de la science: pp. [3]-27.
   b. Science formelle et science du réel: pp. [29]-37.

   Translations of Item 1934-5 (with Literaturverzeichnis and most of Anhang omitted) and Item 1935-2 (with Literatur-Hinweise omitted).

   Item *a* is reprinted (in part) as Item 1950-6 and translated into Italian (in part) as Item 1952-3.

1936

1. Discussion. In *Actes du huitième Congrès international de philosophie, à Prague 2-7 septembre 1934.* Prague: Comité d'organisation du Congrès, 1936. Dépositaire: Orbis, S.A., Prague. (lxxii, 1103 pp.)
   a. Par H[ans] Reichenbach et autres: pp. 31-36.
   b. Par E[rnst]Harms et autres: pp. 117-120.
   c. Par S. A. Kobylecki et autres: pp. 154-160.
   d. Par F. C. S. Schiller et autres: pp. 197-200.
   e. Par R. Carnap et O[tto] Neurath: pp. 244-245.

   Discussion of Congress papers on The Limits of the Natural Sciences (Item *a*) and The Importance of Logical Analysis for Knowledge (Items *b* to *e*). Carnap's remarks (in German): pp. 32, 120, 154, 155-156, 159, 198-199, 244.

2. Die Methode der logischen Analyse. *Ibid.,* pp. 142-145.

   With discussion by Carnap and others, pp. 158-159.

3. Von der Erkenntnistheorie zur Wissenschaftslogik. In *Actes du Congrès international de philosophie scientifique, Sorbonne, Paris 1935,* [fasc.] 1. *Philosophie scientifique et empirisme logique.* Actualités scientifiques et industrielles, 388. Paris: Hermann & Cie, 1936. ([ii], 80, [1] pp.) Pp. [36]-41.

   The Congress, otherwise known as the First International Congress for the Unity of Science, met 15-23 Sept. 1935.

   For a brief account of discussions in which Carnap participated, see Otto Neurath's report on the Congress in *Erkenntnis* (Leipzig), Bd. 5, H. 6 (11. Feb. 1936), pp. 377-406, esp. pp. 382, 386, 388-389, 396-400, 405.

4. Ueber die Einheitssprache der Wissenschaft: Logische Bermerkungen zum Projekt einer Enzyklopädie. *Ibid.,* [fasc.] 2. *Unité de la science.* Actualités . . . , 389. ([ii], 76, [1] pp.) Pp. [60]-70.

5. Wahrheit und Bewährung. *Ibid.,* [fasc.] 4. *Induction et probabilité.* Actualités . . . , 391. ([ii], 64, [1] pp.) Pp.]18]-23.

   Translated into English in Item 1949-1.

6. Truth in Mathematics and Logic. *The Journal of Symbolic Logic* (Menasha, Wis.), vol. 1, no. 2 (June 1936), p. 59.

Abstract of paper presented 1 Sept. 1936 at the Harvard Tercentenary Conference of Arts and Sciences, before a joint session of the Assn. for Symbolic Logic and the American Mathematical Society. The full paper was not published.

For a news story, see p. 16 cols. 4-5 of "New Mathematics Links Two Worlds," *The New York Times,* 2 Sept. 1936, pp. 1 and 16. (The heading refers to another speaker.)

7. Truth in Mathematics and Logic. *Bulletin of the American Mathematical Society* (Menasha, Wis., and New York), vol. 42, no. 9, part 1 (Sept. 1936), p. 642.

Identical with preceding item.

8. Existe-t-il des prémisses de la science qui soient incontrôlables? Trad. par H[enri] Buriot-Darsiles. *"Scientia" (Rivista di scienza)* (Bologna). vol. 60, n. 293 (1 sett. 1936), pp. [129]-135.

Reply to Erwin Schrödinger's "Quelques remarques au sujet des bases de la connaissance scientifique," *ibid.,* vol. 57, n. 275 (1 marzo 1935), pp. 181-191. Carnap's original version in German was not published.

9. Über Extremalaxiome. Von Rudolf Carnap und Friedrich Bachmann. *Erkenntnis* (Leipzig), Bd. 6, H. 3 (31. Okt. 1936), pp. 166-188.

10. Testability and Meaning. *Philosophy of Science* (Baltimore), vol. 3, no. 4 (Oct. 1936), pp. 419-471; vol. 4, no. 1 (Jan. 1937), pp. 1-40.

Reprinted as Item 1950-5 and (in part) as Item 1953-9. For corrections and (chiefly bibliographical) additions, see pp. 40A-40F of Item 1950-5.

For Spanish translation of Item 1953-9, see note to that item.

A paper with the same title was presented on 31 Dec. 1935 at a meeting of the American Philosophical Assn., Eastern Div., at Johns Hopkins Univ. It was reported briefly in a news story, "Offers Problems for Philosophers," *The New York Times,* 1 Jan. 1936, p. 31, col. 4. (The heading refers to another speaker.)

Contents: *Introduction* (§§ 1-4). Our Problem: Confirmation, Testing and Meaning. The Older Requirement of Verifiability. Confirmation Instead of Verification. The Material and the Formal Idioms. *Logical Analysis of Confirmation and Testing* (§§ 5-10). Some Terms and Symbols of Logic. Reducibility of Confirmation. Definitions. Reduction Sentences. Introductive Chains. Reduction and Definition. *Empirical Analysis of Confirmation and Testing* (§§ 11-16). Observable and Realizable Predicates. Confirmability. Method of Testing. Testability. A Remark about Positivism and Physicalism. Sufficient Bases. *The Construction of a Language-System* (§§ 17-28). The Problem of a Criterion of Meaning. The Construction of a Language-System L. Atomic Sentences; Primitive Predicates. The Choice of a Psychological or a Physical Basis. Introduced Atomic Predicates. Molecular Sentences. Molecular Languages. The Critical Problem: Universal and Existential Sentences. The Scale of Languages. Incompletely Confirmable Hypotheses in Physics. The Principle of Empiricism. Confirmability of Predictions.—Bibliography.

1937

1. The Logical Syntax of Language. [Trans. by Amethe Smeaton, Countess von Zeppelin. International Library of Psychology, Philosophy and Scientific Method, gen. ed., C. K. Ogden.] London: Kegan Paul Trench, Trubner & Co., 1937. xvi, 352 pp.

Translation of Item 1934-6 as revised and enlarged by Carnap. Major changes are: inclusion of material originally omitted for lack of space, viz., §§ 16*a*, 34*a-i* (cf. Item 1935-4), 38*a-c*, 60*a-d* and 71*a-d* (both cf. Item 1934-11), 71*e*; deletion of corresponding §§ 34 and 60; and expansion of the Bibliography.

Subsequent impressions (Routledge & Kegan Paul): 1949, 1951, 1954, 1959. Also published in New York (Harcourt Brace & Co., 1937; Humanities Press, 1951) and Paterson, N.J. (Littlefield, Adams & Co., 1959).

Translated into Italian as Item 1961-1. For Spanish translation, see "To Appear."

Contents: Preface to the English Edition (Cambridge, Mass., May 1936). Foreword (Prague, May 1934). *Introduction* (§§ 1-2). What Is Logical Syntax? Languages as Calculi. The Definite Language I. *Rules of Formation for Language I* (§§ 3-9). Predicates and Functors. Syntactical Gothic Symbols. The Junction Symbols. Universal and Existential Sentences. The K-Operator. The Definitions. Sentences and Numerical Expressions. *Rules of Transformation for Language I* (§§ 10-14). General Remarks concerning Transformation Rules. The Primitive Sentences of Language I. The Rules of Inference of Language I. Derivations and Proofs in Language I. Rules of Consequence for Language I. *Remarks on the Definite Form of Language* (§§ 15-16, 16*a*, 17). Definite and Indefinite. On Intuitionism. Identity. The Principle of Tolerance in Syntax. The Formal Construction of the Syntax of Language I (§§ 18-25). The Syntax of I Can Be Formulated in I. The Arithmetization of Syntax. General Terms. Rules of Formation; 1, Numerical Expressions and Sentences. Rules of Formation; 2, Definitions. Rules of Transformation. Descriptive Syntax. Arithmetical, Axiomatic and Physical Syntax. The Indefinite Language II. *Rules of Formation for Language II* (§§ 26-29). The Symbolic Apparatus of Language II. The Classification of Types. Formation Rules for Numerical Expressions and Sentences. Formation Rules for Definitions. *Rules of Transformation for Language II* (§§ 30-33.) The Primitive Sentences of Language II. The Rules of Inference of Language II. Derivations and Proofs in Language II. Comparison of the Primitive Sentences and Rules of Language II with Those of Other Systems. *Rules of Consequence for Language II* (§§ 34*a-i*, 35-36). Incomplete and Complete Criteria of Validity. Reduction. Evaluation. Definition of 'Analytic in II' and 'Contradictory in II'. On Analytic and Contradictory Sentences of Language II. Consequence in Language II. Logical Content. The Principles of Induction and Selection Are Analytic. Language II Is Non-Contradictory. Syntactical Sentences Which Refer to Themselves. Irresoluble Sentences. *Further Development of Language II* (§§ 37-38, 38*a-c*, 39-40). Predicates as Class-Symbols. The Elimination of Classes. On Existence Assumptions in Logic. Cardinal Numbers. Descriptions. Real Numbers. The Language of Physics. General Syntax. *Object-Language and Syntax-Language* (§§ 41-45). On Syntactical Designations. On the Necessity of Distinguishing between an Expression and Its Designation. On the Admissibility of Indefinite Terms. On the Admissibility of Impredicative Terms. Indefinite Terms in Syntax. *The Syntax of Any Language. (a) General Considerations* (§§ 46-52). Formation Rules. Transformation Rules; d-Terms. c-Terms. Content. Logical and Descriptive Expressions; Sub-Languages. Logical and Physical Rules. L-Terms; 'Analytic' and 'Condradictory'. *(b) Variables* (§§ 53-57). Systems of Levels; Predicates and Functors. Substitution; Variables and Constants. Universal and Existential Operators. Range. Sentential Junctions. *(c) Arithmetic; Non-Contradictoriness; the Antinomies* (§§ 58-59, 60*a-d*). Arithmetic. The Non-Contradictoriness and Completeness of a Language. The Antinomies. The Concepts 'True' and 'False'. The Syntactical Antinomies. Every Arithmetic Is Defective. *(d) Translation and Interpretation* (§§ 61-62). Translation from One Language into Another. The Interpretation of a Language. *(e) Extensionality* (§§ 63-71). Quasi-Syntactical Sentences. The Two Interpretations of Quasi-Syntactical Sentences. Extensionality in Relation to Partial Sentences. Extensionality in Relation to Partial Expressions. The Thesis of Extensionality. Intensional Sentences of the Autonymous Mode of Speech. Intensional Sentences of the Logic of Modalities. The Quasi-Syntactical and the Syntactical Methods in the Logic of Modalities. Is an Intensional Logic Necessary? *(f) Relational Theory and Axiomatics* (§§71*a-e*). Relational Theory. Syntactical Terms of Relational Theory. Isomorphism. The Non-Denumerable Cardinal Numbers. The Axiomatic Method. PHILOSOPHY AND SYNTAX. *On the Form of the Sentences Belonging to the Logic of Science* (§§ 72-81). Philosophy Replaced by the Logic of Science. The Logic of Science Is the Syntax of the Language of Science. Pseudo-Object-Sentences. Sentences about Meaning. Universal Words. Universal Words in the Material Mode of Speech. Confusion in Philosophy Caused by the Material Mode of Speech. Philosophical Sentences in the Material and in the Formal Mode of Speech. The Dangers of the Material Mode of Speech. The Admissibility of the Material Mode of Speech. *The Logic of Science as Syntax* (§§ 82-86). The Physical Language. The So-Called Foundations of the Sciences. The Problem of the Foundation of Mathematics. Syntactical Sentences in the Literature of the Special Sciences. The Logic of Science Is Syntax.—Bibliography and Index of Authors. Index of Subjects.

2. Logic. In *Factors Determining Human Behavior* [by Edgar Douglas Adrian and others]. [Harvard Tercentenary Publications.] Cambridge, Mass.: Harvard Univ. Press, 1937. ([2], [ix], 168 pp.) Pp. [107]-118.

Lecture delivered 7 Sept. 1936 at the Harvard Tercentenary Conference of Arts and Sciences, in a symposium on Factors Determining Human Behavior. As one of a number of scholars invited to participate in the Tercentenary Celebration, Carnap was awarded an honorary Sc.D. degree by Harvard Univ. on 18 Sept. 1936.

Reprinted (in part) as Item 1949-4. Also, long excerpts are quoted in cols. 2-3 of the news story, " Holds Modern Man Victim of Machine," *The New York Times,* 8 Sept. 1936, p. 15. (The heading refers to another speaker).

3. Einheit der Wissenschaft durch Einheit der Sprache. In *Travaux du IXe Congrès international de philosophie, Congrès Descartes,* [fasc.] 4. ***L'Unité de la science: la Méthode et les méthodes,*** [Ire partie].

Actualités scientifiques et industrielles, n° 533. Paris: Hermann & Cie, 1937. (222 pp.) Pp. [51]-57.

Includes abstract in French, p. [51].

The proceedings were published in advance of the Congress, which met in Paris, 1-6 Aug. 1937.

4. NOTES FOR SYMBOLIC LOGIC. Chicago, ©1937. Distributed by the Univ. of Chicago Bookstore. [i], 37 pp. (i.e. leaves). Mimeographed.

Notes for a course given at the Univ. of Chicago, fall quarter 1937 and winter quarter 1938. The Second Part did not appear until 1938.

Contents: *First Part.* Use of Letters. Sentential Calculus. Lower Functional Calculus. Transformative Rules. Definitions. Proof and Derivation. Theorems about Demonstrability and Derivability. Theorems about Replacement. Higher Functional Calculus. Functors. *Second Part.* Predicate Expressions; Identity. λ-Expressions. Theory of Relations. Theorems in the Theory of Relations. Cardinal Numbers. Descriptions.—Errata.

1938

1. [Review:] Barkley Rosser, "Gödel Theorems for Non-Constructive Logics." *The Journal of Symbolic Logic* (Menasha, Wis.), vol. 3, no. 1 (March 1938), p. 50.
2. Logical Foundations of the Unity of Science. In *Encyclopedia and Unified Science* by Otto Neurath and others. *International Encyclopedia of Unified Science,* vol. I, no. 1. Chicago: Univ. of Chicago Press, [1938]. (viii, 75 pp.) Pp. 42-62.

Subsequent impressions: 1940, 1946, 1947, 1952, and as Item 1955-7. Also reprinted as Item 1949-3.

Translated into Chinese as Item 1957-1, into Italian as Items 1958-3 and 1958-4.

3. Empiricism and the Language of Science. *Synthese: Maandblad voor het geestesleven van onzen tijd* (Utrecht), 3de jaarg., no. 12 (15 Dec. 1938), pp. 33-35 of sep. paged "Unity of Science Forum."

Abridged version of opening remarks in a symposium on this subject at a meeting of the American Philosophical Assn., Western Div., Knox College, Galesburg, Ill., 23 April 1937.

1939

1. FOUNDATIONS OF LOGIC AND MATHEMATICS. INTERNATIONAL ENCYCLOPEDIA OF UNIFIED SCIENCE, vol. I, no. 3. Chicago: Univ. of Chicago Press, [1939]. viii, 71 pp.

Subsequent impressions: 1945, 1946, 1947, 1949, 1950, 1953, 1957, 1959, and as Item 1955-8. Also reprinted (in part) as Items 1953-11 and 1960-4.

Translated into Japanese as Item 1942-6, into Italian as Item 1956-2. For Spanish translation of Item 1953-11, see note to that item.

Contents: *Logical Analysis of Language: Semantics and Syntax* (§§ 1-9). Theoretical Procedures in Science. Analysis of Language. Pragmatics of Language B. Semantical Systems. Rules of the Semantical System B-S. Some Terms of Semantics. L-Semantical Terms. Logical Syntax. The Calculus B-C. *Calculus and Interpretation* (§§ 10-12). Calculus and Semantical System. On the Construction of a Language System. Is Logic a Matter of Convention?

Calculi and Their Application in Empirical Science (§§ 13-25). Elementary Logical Calculi. Higher Logical Calculi. Application of Logical Calculi. General Remarks about Non-Logical Calculi (Axiom Systems). An Elementary Mathematical Calculus. Higher Mathematical Calculi. Application of Mathematical Calculi. The Controversies over "Foundations" of Mathematics. Geometrical Calculi and Their Interpretations. The Distinction between Mathematical and Physical Geometry. Physical Calculi and Their Interpretations. Elementary and Abstract Terms. "Understanding" in Physics. —Selected Bibliography. Index of Terms.

2. [Review:] Georg Cantor, *Gesammelte Abhandlungen mathematischen und philosophischen Inhalts. The Journal of Unified Science (Erkenntnis)* (The Hague), vol. 8, no. 1/3 (1 June 1939), pp. [182]-183.

   The review is in German.

3. [Review:] D[avid] Hilbert und P[aul] Bernays, *Grundlagen der Mathematik,* Bd. I. *Ibid.,* pp. 184-187.

   The review is in German.

4. SCIENCE AND ANALYSIS OF LANGUAGE. The Hague: W. P. van Stockum & Zoon, [1939]. [221]-226 pp. As from *The Journal of Unified Science (Erkenntnis),* vol. 9.

   Abridged version of paper presented at the Fifth International Congress for the Unity of Science, Cambridge, Mass., 3-9 Sept. 1939. Preprinted for distribution at the Congress, but vol. 9 of the *Journal* was never published.

1940

1. [Review:] S. C. Kleene, *On the Term 'Analytic' in Logical Syntax. The Journal of Symbolic Logic* (Baltimore), vol. 5, no. 4 (Dec. 1940), pp. 157-158.

1942

1. [Dictionary Articles.] In *The Dictionary of Philosophy,* ed. by Dagobert D. Runes. New York: Philosophical Library, 1942. ([viii], 342, [1] pp.)

   a. Anti-Metaphysics: p. 14.
   b. Basic Sentences, Protocol Sentences: p. 35.
   c. Formal: p. 111.
   d. Intersubjective: p. 148.
   e. Meaning, Kinds of: p. 194.
   f. Physicalism: p. 235.
   g. Science of Science: p. 284.
   h. Scientific Empiricism; Unity of Science Movement: pp. 285-286.
   i. Semiotic; Theory of Signs: pp. 288-289.
   j. Verification, Confirmation: p. 332.

   Numerous subsequent impressions with various dates and no date.

   Also published in London (George Routledge & Sons, 1944; Peter Owen & Vision Press, 1951) and in Ames, Iowa (The New Students Outline Series; Littlefield, Adams & Co., 1955, 1956, 1958).

Although corrected in proof, several confusing typographical errors persist in the published version. In this connection see a statement criticizing the editorial policy of the *Dictionary*—signed by 13 contributors, including Carnap—in *The Journal of Philosophy* (Lancaster, Pa.), vol. 39, no. 5 (26 Feb. 1942), p. 139; in *The Philosophical Review* (New York, i.e. Menasha, Wis.), vol. 51, no. 3 (May 1942), p. 341; and in *Mind* (London), n.s., vol. 51, no. 203 (July 1942), p. [296].

The following corrections should be noted: Item *h*, p. 285, after line 5 f.b. insert 'J. Phil. 33, 1936. H. Reichenbach, "Logis-'; Item *h*, p. 286, col. 1, incorporate lines 12-15 (with "1937" altered to "d. 1937") into the next paragraph, after "Berlin Society for Scientific Philosophy"; Item *j*, line 8, for "verification is" read "verification in the strict sense is impossible, at least for universal factual sentences. Therefore, the absolute concept of verification is".

2. INTRODUCTION TO SEMANTICS. [*His* Studies in Semantics, vol. 1.] Cambridge, Mass.: Harvard Univ. Press, 1942. xii, 263 pp.

"The first of a series of small books which will appear under the common title *Studies in Semantics*" (p. ix). Other volumes in the series are Items 1943-1 and 1947-2.

Subsequent impressions: 1946 (with additions to Bibliography), 1948, and as Item 1959-4*a*.

For Italian translation, see "To Appear."

Contents: Preface (Chicago, Dec. 1941). *Semiotic and Its Parts* (§§ 1-6). Object Language and Metalanguage. Signs and Expressions. Sign-Events and Sign-Designs. The Parts of Semiotic: Pragmatics, Semantics, and Syntax. Descriptive and Pure Semantics. Survey of Some Symbols and Terms of Symbolic Logic. *Semantics* (§§ 7-12). Semantical Systems. Truth-Tables as Semantical Rules. Radical Concepts. Further Radical Concepts. Variables. The Relation of Designation. *L-Semantics* (§§ 13-23). Logical and Descriptive Signs. L-Concepts. L-Concepts in Special Semantics. L-Concepts in General Semantics. Correspondence between Semantical and Absolute Concepts. L-Range. The Concept of L-Range in an Extensional Metalanguage. General Semantics Based upon the Concept of L-Range. F-Concepts. Characteristic Sentences. L-Content, *Syntax* (§§ 24-32). Calculi. Proofs and Derivations. The Null Sentential Class in Syntax. Examples of Calculi. C-Concepts (1). Theorems concerning C-Concepts. C-Concepts (2). C-Concepts (3). C-Content and C-Range. *Relations between Semantics and Syntax* (§§ 33-36). True and False Interpretations. L-True and L-False Interpretations. Examples of Interpretations. Exhaustive and L-Exhaustive Calculi.—*Appendix* (§§ 37-39). Terminological Remarks. Outline of Further Semantical Problems. Remarks on "Logical Syntax of Language."—Bibliography. Index.

3. REMARKS ON "LOGICAL SYNTAX OF LANGUAGE." [Cambridge, Mass.:] Harvard Univ. Press, 1942. [i], [246]-250 pp.

Offprint of three-quarters of § 39 of preceding item.

4. Furui ronrigaku to atarashii ronrigaku [The Old Logic and the New Logic]. In *Tōitsu kagaku ronshū,* Vīn-Shikago Gakuha [*Collected Essays in Unified Science,* by the Vienna-Chicago School], trans. [and introd.] by Takeshi Shinohara. Sōgen kagaku sōsho [Sōgen Science

Series, 19]. [Tōkyō: Sōgen Sha, 1942.] ([1], [xi], 285, [1] pp.) Pp. [17]-42.

Translation of Item 1930-2.

The volume in which this and the two following items appear also contains translations, one each, from Moritz Schlick and Hans Reichenbach.

5. Kagaku ronrigaku no kadai [The Task of the Logic of Science]. *Ibid.*, pp. [107]-156.

Translation of Item 1934-5.

6. Ronrigaku to sūgaku no kiso (Foundations of Logic and Mathematics). *Ibid.*, pp. [157]-273.

Translation of Item 1939-1.

1943

1. FORMALIZATION OF LOGIC. [*His* Studies in Semantics, vol. 2.] Cambridge, Mass.: Harvard Univ. Press, 1943. xviii, 159 pp.

Subsequent impressions: 1947 and as Item 1959-4*b*.

For Italian translation, see "To Appear."

Contents: Preface (Santa Fe [N.M.], Nov. 1942). § 1, Introduction: The Problem of a Full Formalization of Logic. *The Propositional Calculus (PC)* (§§ 2-9). The Calculus PC_1. Propositional $Connections_C$ in PC. Forms of PC. Elementary Theorems concerning PC. Extensible Rules. General Theorems concerning $Disjunction_C$. General Theorems concerning $Negation_C$. General Theorems concerning Other $Connections_C$. *Propositional Logic* (§§ 10-13). The Normal Truth-Tables (NTT). The Connections in NTT. Extensionality. Theorems Concerning Particular Connections. *Interpretations of PC* (§§ 14-18). NTT as an L-True Interpretation for PC. Non-Normal Interpretations of Signs of $Negation_C$ and $Disjunction_C$. Non-Normal Interpretations in General. Examples of Non-Normal Interpretations. PC Is Not a Full Formalization of Propositional Logic. *Junctives* (§§ 19-24). Syntactical Concepts of a New Kind Are Required. C-Falsity. Junctives in Semantics. Application of L-Concepts to Junctives. Junctives in Syntax. Rules of Deduction for Junctives. *Full Formalization of Propositional Logic* (§§ 25-27). Junctives in Propositional Logic. The Calculus PC*. PC* Is a Full Formalization of Propositional Logic. *Full Formalization of Functional Logic* (§§ 28-32). The Functional Calculus (FC). Transfinite Junctives. The Calculus FC*. FC^*_I Is a Full Formalization of Functional Logic. Involution.—Bibliography. Index.

1944

1. [Remarks on Ethics.] In *Verifiability of Value* by Ray Lepley. [Columbia Studies in Philosophy, no. 7.] New York: Columbia Univ. Press, 1944. ([xi], 267 pp.) Pp. 137-138.

In footnote 14. Direct quotation of note of 9 May 1943, in clarification of views expressed in Item 1935-1. (Title supplied by the Bibliographer.)

See also *ibid.*, p. 9, fn. 34.

2. The Problem of a World Language. *Books Abroad* (Norman, Okla.), vol. 18, no. 3 (Summer 1944), pp. 303-304.

Letter to the Editor concerning Pierre Delattre's "A Foreigner Views Basic English," *ibid.*, vol. 18, no. 2 (Spring 1944), pp. [115]-119. With the author's reply, "Professor Delattre Clarifies His Position," *ibid.*, vol. 18, no. 3, p. 304.

3. Kigō ronrigaku no taikei [System of Symbolic Logic]. Trans. by Tomoharu Hirano. In *Kagaku ronrigaku*, Vīn Gakudan [*The Logic of Science*, by the Vienna Circle], [ed. and introd. by] Katsumi Nakamura, [trans. by] Tomoharu Hirano and others. [Tōkyō:] Nisshin Shoin, [1944]. ([xi], 400, [1] pp.) Pp. [143]-248.

Translation of two-thirds of Item 1929-2, consisting of the Vorwort, the entire "System der Logistik" (§§ 1-29), and part of the Anhang (§§ 46-47, 45, 50). With translator's preface (pp. [145]-146) and autographed porttrait of Carnap.

The volume in which this item appears also contains translations from Karl Menger, Walter Dubislav (2), Jan Łukasiewicz (2), Karl Popper, and Hans Hahn.

1945

1. Hall and Bergmann on Semantics. *Mind: A Quarterly Review of Psychology and Philosophy* (London), n.s., vol. 54, no. 214 (April 1945), pp. [148]-155.

Reply to Everett W. Hall's "The Extra-Linguistic Reference of Language (II): Designation of the Object-Language," *ibid.*, vol. 53, no. 209 (Jan. 1944), pp. [25]-47, and Gustav Bergmann's "Pure Semantics, Sentences, and Propositions," *ibid.*, vol. 53, no. 211 (July 1944), pp. [238]-257.

2. On Inductive Logic. *Philosophy of Science* (Baltimore), vol. 12, no. 2 (April 1945), pp. 72-97.

3. The Two Concepts of Probability. *Philosophy and Phenomenological Research* (Buffalo), vol. 5, no. 4 (June 1945), pp. 513-532.

Includes abstract in Spanish, p. 532.

Items 1945-3, 1946-2 and 1946-3 were contributions to a symposium on Probability, with eight participants, conducted in the pages of *PPR:* vol. 5, no. 4 (June 1945), pp. 449-532; vol. 6 no. 1 (Sept. 1945), pp. 11-86; vol. 6, no. 4 (June 1946,), pp. 590-622.

The present item is reprinted as Items 1949-2, 1953-12 and (in part) 1959-5.

For Spanish translation of Item 1953-12, see note to that item.

4. Superação da metafísica pela análise lógica da linguagem. *Seara nova* (Lisboa), ano 24, n.º 942 (1 set. 1945), pp. 4-7; n.º 943 (8 set. 1945), pp. 25-27.

Anonymous translation of Item 1932-1 with minor omissions.

5. A Linguagem física como linguagem universal da ciência. *Ibid.*, ano 24, n.º 946 (29 set. 1945), pp. 75-77; n.º 947 (6 out. 1945), pp. 85-87; n.º 948 (13 out. 1945), pp. 99-102.

Anonymous translation of Item 1932-4 with footnotes omitted.

1946

1. Modalities and Quantification. *The Journal of Symbolic Logic* (Baltimore), vol. 11, no. 2 (June 1946), pp. 33-64.

Received for publication 26 Nov. 1945.

This item constitutes the entire issue.

Contents: The Problems of Modal Logic. Propositional Logic (PL) and Propositional Calculus (PC). P.-Reduction. Modal Propositional Logic (MPL) and Modal Propositional Calculus (MPC). MP-Reduction. Relations between MPC and MPL. Functional Logic (FL). Functional Calculus (FC). Modal Functional Logic (MFL). Modal Functional Calculus (MFC). MF-Reduction. Relations between MFC and MFL.

2. Remarks on Induction and Truth. *Philosophy and Phenomenological Research* (Buffalo), vol. 6, no. 4 (June 1946), pp. 590-602.

See note to Item 1945-3.

Reprinted (in part) in Item 1949-1.

3. Rejoinder to Mr. Kaufmann's Reply. *Ibid.*, pp. 609-611.

Reply to Felix Kaufmann's "On the Nature of Inductive Inference," *ibid.*, pp. 602-609.

4. Theory and Prediction in Science. *Science* (Lancaster, Pa.), vol. 104, no. 2710 (6 Dec. 1946), pp. 520-521.

Opening remarks in a symposium on this subject, joint session of the American Assn. for the Advancement of Science, Section L, and the American Philosophical Assn., St. Louis, 28 March 1946.

1947

1. Probability as a Guide in Life. *The Journal of Philosophy* (Lancaster, Pa.), vol. 44, no. 6 (13 March 1947), pp. 141-148.

Presented at a meeting of the American Philosophical Assn., Western Div., Univ. of Chicago, 9 May 1946. (The year is incorrectly given as "1945" on p. 141, fn. 1.)

Reprinted as Item 1948-2.

2. Meaning and Necessity: A Study in Semantics and Modal Logic. [*His* Studies in Semantics, vol. 3.] Chicago: Univ. of Chicago Press, [1947]. viii, 210 pp.

"This book may be regarded as a third volume of the series . . . 'Studies in Semantics' " (p.v). Unlike Items 1942-2 and 1943-1, however, it does not carry a series title on the half-title page.

Second impression, 1948. For 2nd edition, see Item 1956-3.

For Italian and (in part) Japanese translations, see "To Appear."

Contents: Preface (Chicago, Nov. 1946). *The Method of Extension and Intension* (§§ 1-16). Preliminary Explanations. L-Concepts. Equivalence and L-Equivalence. Classes and Properties. Extensions and Intensions. Extensions and Intensions of Sentences. Individual Descriptions. Frege's Method for Descriptions. Extensions and Intensions of Individual Expressions. Variables. Extensional and Intensional Contexts. The Principles of Interchangeability. Sentences about Beliefs. Intensional Structure. Applications of the Concept of Intensional Structure. Lewis' Method of Meaning Analysis. *L-Determinacy* (§§ 17-23). L-Determinate Designators. The Problem of L-Determinacy of Individual Expressions. Definition of L-Determinacy of Individual Expressions. L-Determinacy of Predicators. Logical and Descriptive Signs. L-Determinate Intensions. Reduction of Extensions to Intensions. *The Method of the Name-Relation* (§§ 24-32). The Name-Relation. An Ambiguity in the Method of the Name-Relation. The Unnecessary Duplication of Names. Names of Classes. Frege's Distinction between Nominatum and Sense. Nominatum and Sense: Extension and

Intension. The Disadvantages of Frege's Method. The Antinomy of the Name-Relation. Solutions of the Antinomy. *On Metalanguages for Semantics* (§§ 33-38). The Problem of a Reduction of the Entities. The Neutral Metalanguage M′. M′ Is Not Poorer than M. Neutral Variables in M′. On the Formulation of Semantics in the Neutral Metalanguage M′. On the Possibility of an Extensional Metalanguage for Semantics. *On the Logic of Modalities* (§§ 39-45). Logical Modalities. Modalities and Variables. Semantical Rules for the Modal System S_2. Modalities in the Word Language. Quine on Modalities. Conclusions.—Bibliography. Index.

3. On the Application of Inductive Logic. *Philosophy and Phenomenological Research* (Buffalo), vol. 8, no. 1 (Sept. 1947), pp. 133-148.
   Includes abstract in Spanish, pp. 147-148.

1948

1. Reply to Nelson Goodman. *Philosophy and Phenomenological Research* (Buffalo), vol. 8, no. 3 (March 1948), pp. 461-462.
   Reply to Goodman's "On Infirmities of Confirmation-Theory," *ibid.*, vol. 8, no. 1 (Sept. 1947), pp. 149-151.
2. Probability as a Guide in Life. *ETC.: A Review of General Semantics* (Bloomington, Ill.), vol. 5, no. 4 (Summer 1948), pp. 263-267.
   Reprint of Item 1947-1 with fns. 6 and 7 omitted.
3. Reply to Felix Kaufmann. *Philosophy and Phenomenological Research* (Buffalo), vol. 9, no. 2 (Dec. 1948), pp. 300-304.
   Reply to Kaufmann's "Rudolf Carnap's Analysis of 'Truth'," *ibid.*, pp. 294-299.

1949

1. Truth and Confirmation. In *Readings in Philosophical Analysis,* sel. and ed. by Herbert Feigl and Wilfrid Sellars. [The Century Philosophy Series.] New York: Appleton-Century-Crofts, [c1949]. (x, 626 pp.) Pp. 119-127.
   Adapted by Carnap from Item 1936-5, as translated by Feigl, and § 3 of Item 1946-2 ("On the Concept of Truth," pp. 598-602).
   For reprint see "To Appear."
2. The Two Concepts of Probability. *Ibid.,* pp. 330-348.
   Reprint of Item 1945-3 with Spanish abstract omitted.
3. Logical Foundations of the Unity of Science. *Ibid.,* pp. 408-423.
   Reprint of Item 1938-2.
4. The Condition of Clarity. In *The Language of Wisdom and Folly: Background Readings in Semantics,* ed. and with an introd. by Irving J. Lee. New York: Harper & Brothers, [c1949]. (xxii, 361 pp.) Pp. 44-47.
   Reprint of pp. [107]-112 of Item 1937-2, with minor omissions.
5. A Reply to Leonard Linsky. *Philosophy of Science* (Baltimore), vol. 16, no. 4 (Oct. 1949), pp. 347-350.
   Reply to Linsky's "Some Notes on Carnap's Concept of Intensional Isomorphism and the Paradox of Analysis," *ibid.*, pp. 343-347.
   The intended title of this item was "Remarks on the Paradox of Analysis: A Reply to Leonard Linsky." The main title was omitted in printing.

1950

1. Empiricism, Semantics, and Ontology. *Revue internationale de philosophie* (Bruxelles), 4e année, no 11 (15 janv. 1950), pp.]20]-40.

Contribution to a symposium on Logical Empiricism, with five participants, conducted in this issue of the *Revue,* pp. [3]-102.

Reprinted as Items 1952-4, 1953-4 and 1954-2, and in Item 1956-3. For another reprint, see "To Appear."

For Chinese and Italian translations of Item 1953-4, see note to that item.

2. Scienza formale e scienza reale. Trad. di Enzo Paci. In *Il pensiero scientifico contemporaneo,* [a cura] di Enzo Paci. [Biblioteca enciclopedica Sansoniana, 13.] Firenze: G. C. Sansoni, [1950]. (214 pp.) Pp. 169-172.

Translation of pp. 30-32 and 35-36 of Item 1935-2, with omissions.

3. La scienza e la metafisica. Trad. di Enzo Paci. *Ibid.,* pp. 173-175.

Translation of pp. [219]-220 and 238-240 of Item 1932-1, with omissions.

4. LOGICAL FOUNDATIONS OF PROBABILITY. [Chicago:] Univ. of Chicago Press, [1950]. xvii, 607 pp.

Second impression, 1951, with minor additions to the Preface (p. xii). Also published in London (Routledge & Kegan Paul, 1951). For 2nd edition, see "To Appear."

Sections 41-43 and 49-51 are reprinted as Item 1951-2.

Approximately one-third of the book is translated into German in Item 1959-1.

Although the present item is described (p. vii) as "the first in a projected two-volume work, *Probability and Induction,"* it is now unlikely that vol. 2 will materialize.

Contents: Preface (Univ. of Chicago, March 1950). *On Explication* (§§ 1-6). Introduction: Our Problems. On the Clarification of an Explicandum. Requirements for an Explicatum. Classificatory, Comparative, and Quantitative Concepts. Comparative and Quantitative Concepts as Explicata. Formalization and Interpretation. *The Two Concepts of Probability* (§§ 8-12). The Semantical Concepts of Confirmation. The Two Concepts of Probability. The Logical Nature of the Two Probability Concepts. Psychologism in Deductive Logic. Psychologism in Inductive Logic. *Deductive Logic* (§§ 14-29, 31-35, 37-38, 40). Preliminary Explanations. The Signs of the Systems **L**. The Rules of Formation. Rules of Truth. State-Descriptions (**Z**) and Ranges (**R**). Theorems on State-Descriptions and Ranges. L-Concepts. Theorems of Propositional Logic. Theorems on General Sentences. Theorems on Replacements. Theorems on Identity. On Predicate Expressions and Divisions. Isomorphic Sentences; Individual and Statistical Distributions. Structure-Descriptions (**Str**). Correlations for Basic Matrices. Some Numbers Connected with the Systems **L**. The Systems $\mathbf{L}^{\pi}$; the *Q*-Predicates. Logical Width. The *Q*-Normal Form. The *Q*-Numbers. Some Numbers Connected with the Systems $\mathbf{L}^{\pi}$. Simple Laws. Simple Laws of Conditional Form. Some Mathematical Definitions and Theorems. *The Problem of Inductive Logic* (§§ 41-54). The Logical Concept of Probability. (Probability$_1$ as a Measure of Evidential Support. Probability$_1$ as a Fair Betting Quotient. Probability$_1$ and Relative Frequency. Probability$_1$ as an Estimate of Relative Frequency. Some Comments on Other Conceptions. Presuppositions of Induction.) Probability$_1$ and Probability$_2$. Inductive and Deductive Logic. Logical and

Methodological Problems. Abstraction in Inductive Logic. Is a Quantitative Inductive Logic Impossible? Some Difficulties Involved in the Problem of Degree of Confirmation. Is Probability$_1$ Used as a Quantitative Concept? The Question of the Usefulness of Inductive Logic. The Problem of a Rule for Determining Decisions. The Rule of Maximizing the Estimated Utility. (The Rule of Maximizing the Estimated Utility. Daniel Bernoulli's Law of Utility. Consequences of Bernoulli's Law.) On the Arguments of Degree of Confirmation. Some Conventions on Degree of Confirmation. Reduction of the Problem of Degree of Confirmation. *The Foundation of Quantitative Inductive Logic: The Regular **c**-Functions* (§§ 55-62). Regular **m**- and **c**-Functions for Finite Systems. Regular Functions for the Infinite System. Null Confirmation; Fitting Sequences. Almost L-True Sentences. Theorems on Regular **c**-Functions. Confirmation of Hypotheses by Observations; Bayes's Theorem. Confirmation of a Hypothesis by a Predictable Observation. On Some Axiom Systems by Other Authors. *Relevance and Irrelevance* (§§ 65-76). The Concepts of Relevance and Irrelevance. The Relevance Quotient. The Relevance Measure. Relevance Measures for Two Observations and Their Connections. The Possible Relevance Situations for Two Observations and Their Connections. The Relevance Measures for Two Hypotheses and Their Connections. The Possible Relevance Situations for Two Hypotheses and Their Connections. Relevance Measures of State-Descriptions; First Method: Disjunctive Analysis. Second Method: Conjunctive Analysis. Extreme Relevance. Complete Relevance. Relations between Extreme and Complete Relevance. *Comparative Inductive Logic* (§§ 79-88). The Problem of a Comparative Concept of Confirmation. Requirements of Adequacy. Definition of the Comparative Concept of Confirmation **MC**. Some Concepts Based on **MC**. Further Theorems on Comparative Concepts. Maximum and Minimum Confirmation. Correspondence between Comparative and Quantitative Theorems. The Concept of Confirming Evidence. Hempel's Analysis of the Concept of Confirming Evidence. Hempel's Definition of Confirming Evidence. *The Symmetrical **c**-Functions* (§§ 90-92, 94-96). Symmetrical **m**-Functions. Symmetrical **c**-Functions. Theorems on Symmetrical **c**-Functions. The Direct Inductive Inference. The Binomial Law. Bernoulli's Theorem. *Estimation* (§§ 98-100, 102-107). The Problem of Estimation. A General Estimate-Function. Definition of the **c**-Mean Estimate-Function. The Problem of the Reliability of an Estimate. The Estimated Square Error of an Estimate. Estimation of Frequencies. Direct Estimation of Frequencies. Predictive Estimation of Frequencies. Further Theorems on Predictive Estimation of Relative Frequency.—*Appendix* (§ 110). Outline of a Quantitative System of Inductive Logic. (The Function **c***. The Direct Inference. The Predictive Inference. The Inference by Analogy. The Inverse Inference. The Universal Inference. The Instance Confirmation of a Law. Are Laws Needed for Making Predictions? The Variety of Instances. Inductive Logic as a Rational Reconstruction.)—Glossary. Selected Bibliography. Index.

5. TESTABILITY AND MEANING. New Haven, Conn.: Graduate Philosophy Club, Yale Univ., 1950. [i], [419]-471, 2-40, 40A-40F pp.

Photo-offset reprint of Item 1936-10, with appended corrections and (chiefly bibliographical) additions.

Second impression (Whitlock's, Inc., for the Graduate Philosophy Club of Yale Univ.), 1954.

6. Le Problème de la logique de la science. Trad. par Ernest Vouillemin. In *Philosophie des sciences,* [manuel et lectures choisies] par Simone Daval et Bernard Guillemain. Cours de philosophie et textes choisis. Paris: Presses Universitaires de France, 1950. Pp. 36-44.
   a. In *Philosophie des sciences: Classe[s] de philosophie et de mathématiques, préparation aux grandes écoles.* (viii, 555 pp.)
   b. In *Philosophie des sciences: Classe de sciences expérimentales.* (xxxii, 563 pp.)

   Reprint of pp. [3]-13 of Item 1935-10*a*. The "*b*" version of the book includes added initial and final sections on anthropology and psychology.

   Second edition, 1951, with unchanged pagination.

   For the 3rd edition, 1955, the volume was extensively revised. Among those readings deleted was the present item, which had proved to be too difficult for the pupils concerned.

7. Rejoinder to Linsky. *Philosophical Studies* (Minneapolis), vol. 1, no. 6 (Dec. 1950), p. 83.

   Reply to Leonard Linsky's "A Note on Carnap's 'Truth and Confirmation'," *ibid.,* pp. 81-82.

1951

1. [Letter on Academic Freedom.] In *Interim Report of the Committee on Academic Freedom to the Academic Senate, Northern Section, of the University of California.* [Berkeley:] Univ. of California, 1951. (58, [1] pp.) P. 40.

   Letter of 22 Oct. 1950 to Robert Gordon Sproul, then President of the University, declining a lecture invitation during the "loyalty oath" controversy.

   The *Interim Report* is subtitled (p. [3]): *The Consequences of the Abrogation of Tenure: An Accounting of Costs.* The original impression (Feb. 1951) was intended solely for members of the Academic Senate, officials of the University, etc. A 2nd impression, for public distribution, was authorized by the Senate on 6 March 1951. Minor revisions were made, none of which affect the present item.

   A substantial excerpt from this letter is quoted on p. [71] of "What the Loyalty Oath Did to the University of California," *Look* (Des Moines), vol. 16, no. 3 (29 Jan. 1952), pp. 69-[71].

2. THE NATURE AND APPLICATION OF INDUCTIVE LOGIC, CONSISTING OF SIX SECTIONS FROM *LOGICAL FOUNDATIONS OF PROBABILITY.* Chicago: Univ. of Chicago Press, [1951]. viii, 161-202, 242-279 pp.

   Photo-offset reprint of §§ 41-43 and 49-51 of Item 1950-4, and parts of the Preface and Bibliography; with an added Introduction. The final paragraph of § 43 is omitted.

   These six sections are among those translated into German in Item 1959-1 (cf. §§ 7-9 and 11-13).

3. The Problem of Relations in Inductive Logic. *Philosophical Studies* (Minneapolis), vol. 2, no. 5 (Oct. 1951), pp. 75-80.

   Reply to Yehoshua Bar-Hillel's "A Note on State-Descriptions," *ibid.,* pp. 72-75.

1952

1. THE CONTINUUM OF INDUCTIVE METHODS. [Chicago:] Univ. of Chicago Press, [1952]. v, 92 pp.

Described (p. iii) as a preliminary version of part of a projected sequel to Item 1950-4, but see note to that item.

Approximately one-third of the book is translated into German in Item 1959-1.

Contents: Preface (Univ. of Chicago, Nov. 1951). Summary. *The λ-System* (§§ 1-18). The Situation in the Theory of Inductive Methods. Our Task: The Construction of a Continuum of Inductive Methods. Preliminary Explanations. The Characteristic Function of an Inductive Method. A Characteristic Function Gives a Complete Characterization. Methods of Estimation. The Empirical Factor and the Logical Factor. An Interval for Values of *G*. The λ-Functions. A λ-Function Gives a Complete Characterization. Inductive Methods of the First Kind: λ Is Independent of κ. The Nonextreme Methods. The First Extreme Method: $\lambda = \infty$. The Second Extreme Method: $\lambda = 0$; the Straight Rule. Inductive Methods of the Second Kind: λ Is Dependent upon κ. The Difference between the Two Kinds of Inductive Methods. Complete Inductive Methods. The Choice of an Inductive Method. *Comparison of the Success of Inductive Methods* (§§ 19-24). Sampling Distributions. The Mean Square Error as a Measure of Success. The Mean Square Error with Respect to All *Q*-Properties. The Optimum Inductive Method for a Given State-Description. Are Unbiased Estimate-Functions Preferable? The Problem of the Success in the Actual Universe.—*Appendix* (§ 25). Wald's Theory of Decision Functions and the Minimax Principle.—Index.

2. [La natura della metafisica.] Trad. di Franco Amerio. In *Epistemologi contemporanei,* [a cura di] Franco Amerio. I classici della filosofia. Torino: Società Editrice Internazionale, [1952]. (196 pp.) Pp. 120-123.

Second impression, 1955.

Translation of pp. 37-39 and 42-44 of Item 1934-8, with omissions. (Title supplied by the Bibliographer.)

3. [La sintassi logica.] Trad. di Franco Amerio. *Ibid.,* pp. 123-124.

Translation of pp. 6-9 of Item 1935-10*a*, with omissions, and the concluding paragraph of Item 1935-10*b*. (Title supplied by the Bibliographer.)

4. Empiricism, Semantics, and Ontology. In *Semantics and the Philosophy of Language: A Collection of Readings,* ed. by Leonard Linsky. Urbana: Univ. of Illinois Press, 1952. (ix, 289 pp.) Pp. 208-228.

Photo-offset reprint of Item 1950-1.

5. Meaning Postulates. *Philosophical Studies* (Minneapolis), vol. 3, no. 5 (Oct. 1952), pp. 65-73.

Reprinted in Item 1956-3.

For Italian translation, see "To Appear."

1953

1. On the Comparative Concept of Confirmation. *The British Journal*

for the Philosophy of Science (Edinburgh), vol. 3, no. 12 (Feb. 1953), pp. 311-318.

Received for publication 3 Nov. 1952.

Reply to Yehoshua Bar-Hillel's "A Note on Comparative Inductive Logic," *ibid.*, pp. 308-310.

2. Remarks to Kemeny's Paper. *Philosophy and Phenomenological Research* (Buffalo), vol. 13, no. 3 (March 1953), pp. 375-376.

Reply to John G. Kemeny's "A Contribution to Inductive Logic," *ibid.*, pp. 371-374.

3. An Outline of a Theory of Semantic Information. By Rudolf Carnap and Yehoshua Bar-Hillel. Technical Report No. 247. [Cambridge, Mass.:] Research Laboratory of Electronics, Massachusetts Institute of Technology, 1952 [i.e. 1953]. [ii], 48, [1] pp. With hectographed insert: Additional Corrigenda—Technical Report No. 247.

Although dated "October 27, 1952," this item did not appear until April 1953.

See also Items 1953-6 and 1953-7. For interim reports on the project, see Bar-Hillel's "Semantic Information and Its Measures," *Quarterly Progress Report* (Research Laboratory of Electronics, Massachusetts Institute of Technology), [no. 25] (15 April 1952), pp. 75-77; [no. 26] (15 July 1952), pp. 87-90.

The corrections indicated on the insert are: p. 26, Table III, for "$(n-1)/n$" read "$1-(1/2^n)$"; p. 28, Equation (2), for "c_1 (j)" read "c_1 (i)"; p. 28, line 7 f.b., for "T1b" read "T4b"; p. 31, Table V, transpose the values of cols. 2 and 3. The following additional corrections should be noted: p. 34, line 1 f.b., for "difference" read "difference in number"; p. 38, cancel line 6 (line 5 of proof).

Contents: Abstract. List of Symbols.—The Problem. General Explanations. The Presystematic Concept of Semantic Information. Content-Elements and Content. The Presystematic Concept of Amount of Information. The First Explicatum: Content-Measure (*cont*). The Second Explicatum: Measure of Information (*inf*). Comparison between *cont* and *inf*. *D*-Functions and *I*-Functions. *cont** and *inf**. Estimates of Amount of Information. Semantic Noise; Efficiency of a Conceptual Framework. Conclusions.—Corrigenda.

4. Empiricism, Semantics, and Ontology. In *Readings in Philosophy of Science: Introduction to the Foundations and Cultural Aspects of the Sciences,* arr. and ed. by Philip P. Wiener. New York: Charles Scribner's Sons, [c1953]. (ix, 645 pp.) Pp. 509-522 and 633-634.

Reprint of Item 1950-1, with minor revisions by Carnap "to the effect that the term 'framework' is now used only for the system of linguistic expressions, and not for the system of the entities in question" (p. 509, fn.).

Reprinted as Item 1954-2 and in Item 1956-3. For another reprint, see "To Appear."

Translated into Chinese as Item 1961-4. For Italian translation, see "To Appear."

5. Inductive Logic and Science. *Proceedings of the American Academy*

of Arts and Sciences (Boston), vol. 80, no. 3 (March [i.e. May] 1953), pp. [189]-197.

Presented at a symposium on Philosophy of Science, joint session of the American Physical Society and the Philosophy of Science Assn., Chicago, 27 Oct. 1951.

Vol. 80 of the *Proceedings* (1951-54) was published in cooperation with the Institute for the Unity of Science, Boston, and bears the subtitle: *Contributions to the Analysis and Synthesis of Knowledge.*

The present item is reprinted as Item 1955-10*b*. See also note to Item 1959-1.

6. Semantic Information. By Yehoshua Bar-Hillel and Rudolf Carnap. In *Communication Theory: Papers Read at a Symposium on "Applications of Communication Theory" Held at the Institution of Electrical Engineers, London, September 22nd-26th 1952,* ed. by Willis Jackson. London: Butterworths Scientific Publications, 1953. (xii, 532 pp.) Pp. 503-511.

   Based on Item 1953-3 and presented at the symposium by Bar-Hillel. With discussion by Bar-Hillel and D. M. MacKay, pp. 511-512.

   Also published in New York (Academic Press, 1953).

7. Semantic Information. By Yehoshua Bar-Hillel and Rudolf Carnap. *The British Journal for the Philosophy of Science* (Edinburgh), vol. 4, no. 14 (Aug. 1953), pp. 147-157.

   Received for publication 23 Oct. 1952.

   Revised version of preceding item.

8. What Is Probability? *Scientific American* (New York), vol. 189, no. 3 (Sept. 1953), pp. 128-130, 132, 134, 136, 138.

   Contribution to a symposium on Fundamental Questions in Science, with nine participants, conducted in this issue of *Scientific American.* The original, considerably longer version was later published as Item 1955-10*a*.

   The present item is translated into Italian as Item 1953-13, into French as Item 1954-1.

9. Testability and Meaning. In *Readings in the Philosophy of Science,* Herbert Feigl and May Brodbeck, eds. New York: Appleton-Century-Crofts, [c1953]. (ix, 811 pp.) Pp. 47-92.

   Reprint of Item 1936-10 with omissions amounting to some 30 pp., but incorporating revisions indicated in Item 1950-5. Sections omitted: 2, 3 (in part), 4, 6, 14, 21-25.

   For Spanish translation, see "To Appear."

10. Formal and Factual Science. Trans. by Herbert Feigl and May Brodbeck. *Ibid.,* pp. 123-128.

   Translation of Item 1935-2 with Literatur-Hinweise omitted.

   For Chinese and Spanish translations of the present item, see "To Appear."

11. The Interpretation of Physics. *Ibid.,* pp. 309-318.

   Reprint of §§ 23-25 (pp. 56-69) of Item 1939-1.

   For Spanish translation, see "To Appear."

12. The Two Concepts of Probability. *Ibid.*, pp. 438-455.

Reprint of Item 1945-3 with Spanish abstract omitted and with minor revisions by Carnap.

For Spanish translation, see "To Appear."

13. Che cos'è la probabilità? *L'Industria: Rivista di economia politica* (Milano), [vol. 67] (1953), n. 4, pp. 567-575.

Anonymous translation of Item 1953-8 with minor revision of the opening paragraph. Accompanied by an anonymous summary in English, p. 739.

1954

1. Qu'est-ce que la probabilité? *Atomes: Tous les aspects scientifiques d'un nouvel âge* (Paris), 9e année, no 95 (fév. 1954), pp. 48-50.

Anonymous translation of Item 1953-8 with minor revision of the opening paragraph.

For brief remarks "destinées à éclairer la validité respective" of two inductive probability methods described in this item, see Marcel Boll, "A propos de probabilité," *ibid.*, 9e année, no 96 (mars 1954), p. 100.

2. Empiricism, Semantics, and Ontology. In *Contemporary Philosophy: A Book of Readings,* ed. by James L. Jarrett and Sterling M. McMurrin. New York: Henry Holt & Co., [c1954]. (xvii, 524 pp.) Pp. 377-390.

Reprint of Item 1953-4.

Second impression, 1957.

3. EINFÜHRUNG IN DIE SYMBOLISCHE LOGIK, MIT BESONDERER BERÜCKSICHTIGUNG IHRER ANWENDUNGEN. Wien: Springer-Verlag, 1954. x, 209 pp.

The Vorwort is dated: Princeton, N.J., im Jan. 1954, Institute for Advanced Study.

Carnap's first publication in the German language in 15 years, this book is prefaced with an expression of hope that it "möchte dazu beitragen, das Interesse an der symbolischen Logik in den deutschsprachigen Ländern zu fördern" (p. [v]).

Concerning its relationship to *Abriss der Logistik* (Item 1929-2): "[Eine besondere] Berücksichtigung der logischen Syntax und der Semantik ist es . . . , was dieses Buch—abgesehen von seinem erheblich grösseren Umfang—hauptsächlich von meinem früheren Buch unterscheidet . . . , das . . . in vielem durch die schnelle Entwicklung des Gebietes überholt ist" (p. vi).

Translated into English as Item 1958-2. For contents, see note to that item.

For 2nd German edition, see Item 1960-2. For Spanish translation thereof, see note to that item.

1955

1. On Belief Sentences: Reply to Alonzo Church. In *Philosophy and Analysis: A Selection of Articles Published in ANALYSIS between 1933-40 and 1947-53,* ed. with an introd. by Margaret Macdonald. Oxford: Basil Blackwell, 1954 [i.e. 1955]. (viii, 296 pp.) Pp. 128-131.

Also published in New York (Philosophical Library, 1954 [i.e. 1955]).

Reply to Church's "On Carnap's Analysis of Statements of Assertion and

Belief," *ibid.*, pp. 125-128. The latter first appeared in the journal *Analysis* (Oxford), vol. 10, no. 5 (April 1950), pp. [97]-99. Carnap's reply was specially written for *Philosophy and Analysis.*

Reprinted in Item 1956-3.

For Italian and Japanese translations, see "To Appear."

2. REMARKS ON PHYSICALISM AND RELATED TOPICS: DISCUSSIONS WITH WILFRID SELLARS, DECEMBER, 1954. [Minneapolis: Minnesota Center for Philosophy of Science, 1955.] [i], 12 pp. (i.e. leaves). Mimeographed.

Based on informal conversations held in Los Angeles, 29 Dec. 1954 to 1 Jan. 1955.

Contents: Physicalism versus Emergentism. Continuity versus Emergentism. Probabilistic Correlation Rules.

3. Meaning and Synonymy in Natural Languages. *Philosophical Studies* (Minneapolis), vol. 6, no. 3 (April 1955), pp. 33-47.

Received for publication 17 Dec. 1954.

Reprinted in Item 1956-3 and as Item 1956-6.

Translated into Italian as Item 1955-11; see also "To Appear." Translated into Spanish as Item 1960-6.

4. NOTES ON SEMANTICS. Los Angeles, 1955. [Distributed by the author.] [i], 54, [3] pp. (i.e. leaves). Hectographed.

Notes for a seminar conducted at the Univ. of California at Los Angeles, spring semester 1955. Subsequently distributed more widely, accompanied by a one-page hectographed memorandum of transmittal dated "June 1955."

For a revised version of the *Notes,* see Item 1959-11.

Contents: *Semiotic* (§§ 1-2). Semiotic and Its Parts. Syntactical Signs. *Logical Syntax* (§§ 3-7). Propositional Calculus PC. The Calculus PC′ (without Variables). Definitions in General Syntax, for Any Calculus C. Examples for PC′. Rules of Tranformation of PC. *Semantics* (§§ 8-29). Terminological Remarks. Semantical Systems. The Semantical System L_1 (without Variables). Some Definitions in General Semantics for a Semantical System L. Interchangeability in Sentences with 'Des'; the Three Des-Relations. Three Metalanguages: M^e, M^i, M^s. The Vocabulary of the Semantical Metalanguage. The Uniqueness of the Designatum. Truth. Denotation. Interpretation in the Extensional Metalanguage M^e. Philosophical Issues concerning the Semantical Concept of Truth. The Semantical System L_2 with Individual Variables. Preliminary Explanations of the Language L_3 with a Type System. Rules of Formation for L_3. Preliminary Explanations of Models for L_3. The L-Concepts for L_3. Preliminary Remarks on Interpretation and Truth for L_3. Rules of Interpretation and Truth for L_3. The Controversy on Meaning and Analyticity. Intensions and Quasi-Intensions. The Controversy about Abstract Entities in Semantics.—Errata. Bibliography.

5. The Rejection of Metaphysics. In *The Age of Analysis,* sel. with introd. and interpretive commentary by Morton White. (253 pp.) Pp. 209-225.

a. In *The Age of Analysis: Twentieth Century Philosophers.* The

Great Ages of Western Philosophy, [vol.] 6. Boston: Houghton Mifflin Co., 1955.

b. In *The Age of Analysis: 20th Century Philosophers.* The Mentor Philosophers; Mentor Book [MD142]. [New York:] New American Library, [1955].

Reprint of chap. 1 of Item 1935-1 with concluding paragraph omitted. Constitutes two-thirds of White's chap. 13, "Logical Positivism: Rudolf Carnap."

The volume in which this item appears was a joint publication of the two firms. Subsequent impressions: HM, 1956 (without date); NAL, 1956, 1957, 1958, 1959, 1960, 1961. Also published in the *"a"* format by George Braziller (New York, 1958).

The item is translated into Chinese as Item 1960-3.

The six-volume series was also issued as a two-volume book. In this format, the present item appeared in: *The Great Ages of Western Philosophy,* vol. 2. *The Age of Enlightenment,* Isaiah Berlin; *The Age of Ideology,* Henry D. Aiken; *The Age of Analysis,* Morton White. Boston: Houghton Mifflin Co., 1962. (vii, 657 pp.) Pp. 609-621.

6. On Some Concepts of Pragmatics. *Philosophical Studies* (Minneapolis), vol. 6, no. 6 (Dec. 1955), pp. 89-91.

Received for publication 9 June 1955.

Reply to Roderick M. Chisholm's "A Note on Carnap's Meaning Analysis," *ibid.,* pp. 87-89.

Reprinted in Item 1956-3.

For Italian translation, see "To Appear."

7. Logical Foundations of the Unity of Science. In *International Encyclopedia of Unified Science,* vol. I, nos. 1-5, ed. by Otto Neurath, Rudolf Carnap, Charles Morris. Chicago: Univ. of Chicago Press, [1955]. (ix, 339 pp.) Pp. 42-62.

Reprint of Item 1938-2.

8. Foundations of Logic and Mathematics. *Ibid.,* pp. [139]-213.

Reprint of Item 1939-1.

9. NOTES ON PROBABILITY AND INDUCTION. Los Angeles, 1955. [Distributed by the author.] [i], 31 [3] pp. (i.e. leaves). Hectographed.

Notes for a seminar conducted at the Univ. of California at Los Angeles, fall semester 1955.

Contents: The Three Main Conceptions of Probability. The Two Explicanda. Preliminary Remarks on Inductive Logic. Some Concepts of Deductive Logic. *The Theory of Degree of Confirmation.* Fundamental Axioms (A1-A5). Regular m-Functions and c-Functions (A6). Coherence. Symmetrical c-Functions (A7). Estimation. The Functions c† and c*. Further Axioms of Invariance (A8-A11). Learning from Experience (A12). The Language L_F with One Family F (A13). The Axiom of Predictive Irrelevance (A14). The λ-System (A15). Various c-Functions in the λ-System. A Language with Two Families (A16). An Infinite Domain of Individuals (A17).—Errata. Bibliography.

10. I. STATISTICAL AND INDUCTIVE PROBABILITY. II. INDUCTIVE LOGIC AND

SCIENCE. Brooklyn, N.Y.: Galois Institute of Mathematics and Art, [c1955]. [ii], 25 pp.

a. Statistical and Inductive Probability: pp. 1-16.

b. Inductive Logic and Science: pp. 17-25.

Item *a* is the original version of, and half again as long as, the article published as Item 1953-8. It is reprinted as Item 1960-1.

Item *b* is a photo-offset reprint of Item 1953-5.

An excerpt from Carnap's letter of 14 May 1949 to Lillian R. Lieber in appreciation of another Galois Institute publication, her *Mits, Wits and Logic* (New York, W. W. Norton & Co., 1947), appears in later editions of the work (rev. ed., Brooklyn, N.Y., Galois Institute Press, 1954, p. [8]; 3rd ed., New York, W. W. Norton & Co., 1960, p. 7).

11. Significato e sinonimità nei linguaggi naturali. Trad. di Alberto Pasquinelli. *Rivista critica di storia della filosofia* (Roma), anno 10, fasc. 5/6 (sett./dic. 1955), pp. [313]-327.

Translation of Item 1955-3. See also "To Appear."

The entire double number of the *Rivista* is devoted to the philosophy of Carnap and includes an extensive bibliography of writings by and about him, compiled by Pasquinelli (pp. [462]-478).

Another Italian philosopher who has paid considerable attention to the thought of Carnap is Francesco Barone. A long excerpt from Carnap's letter of 5 Aug. 1954 to Barone, endorsing the latter's *Il neopositivismo logico* (Torino: Edizioni di "Filosofia," 1953), appears on pp. [17]-18 of *La rivista "Filosofia" e le Edizioni di "Filosofia"*, a 32-page descriptive catalog issued as a "Supplemento" to *Filosofia: Rivista trimestrale* (Torino), anno 6, fasc. 4 (ott. 1955).

1956

1. Committee on Mathematical Biology. By Warren S. McCulloch and others. *Science* (Lancaster, Pa.), vol. 123, no. 3200 (27 April 1956), p. 725.

Received for publication 5 July 1955.

Letter to the Editor, signed by Carnap and seven scientists from diverse fields, expressing concern over "drastic reductions . . . imposed on" the Committee, a quasi-department in the Div. of Biological Sciences, Univ. of Chicago.

2. FONDAMENTI DI LOGICA E MATEMATICA. Introd., trad. e note a cura di Giulio Preti. [Biblioteca di filosofia e pedagogia.] Torino: G. B. Paravia & C., [1956]. [xxxi], 110, [1] pp.

Translation of Item 1939-1 with Index of Terms omitted.

3. MEANING AND NECESSITY: A STUDY IN SEMANTICS AND MODAL LOGIC. [*His* Studies in Semantics, vol. 3.] [Second, enlarged edition.] Chicago: Univ. of Chicago Press, [1956]. x, 258 pp.

Reprint of Item 1947-2 without change in the main body of the book, but with a 46-page Supplement reprinting Items 1953-4, 1952-5, 1955-1, 1955-3 and 1955-6; many additions to the Bibliography; and a brief Preface to the Second Edition (Univ. of California at Los Angeles, Dec. 1955).

Second impression, 1958 (in the Univ. of Chicago Press paperbound series, Phoenix Books).

For Italian and (in part) Japanese translations, see "To Appear." For translations of Supplement components, see notes to those items.

4. The Methodological Character of Theoretical Concepts. In *The Foundations of Science and the Concepts of Psychology and Psychoanalysis,* ed. by Herbert Feigl and Michael Scriven. Minnesota Studies in the Philosophy of Science, vol. 1. Minneapolis: Univ. of Minneapolis Press, [c1956]. (xiv, 346 pp.) Pp. 38-76.

Translated into German as Item 1960-5.

5. Remarks on Popper's Note on Content and Degree of Confirmation. *The British Journal for the Philosophy of Science* (Edinburgh), vol. 7, no. 27 (Nov. 1956), pp. 243-244.

Rejoinder to Karl R. Popper's " 'Content' and 'Degree of Confirmation': A Reply to Dr. Bar-Hillel," *ibid.,* vol. 6, no. 22 (Aug. 1955), pp. 157-163.

6. Meaning and Synonymy in Natural Languages. In *American Philosophers at Work: The Philosophic Scene in the United States,* ed. by Sidney Hook. New York: Criterion Books, [c1956]. (512 pp.) Pp. 58-74.

Reprint of Item 1955-3, with an added footnote.
See note to Item 1958-3.

1957

1. K'o-hsüeh t'ung-i chih lo-chi ti chi-ch'u (Logical Foundations of the Unity of Science). Trans. and annot. by Hai-kuang Yin, *alias* Fu-sheng Yin. *Hsien-tai hsüeh-shu chi-k'an (Contemporary Philosophy and Social Sciences)* (Hong Kong), vol. 1, no. 2 (Feb. 1957), pp. 39-61.

Translation of Item 1938-2.

1958

1. Introductory Remarks to the English Edition. In *The Philosophy of Space and Time* by Hans Reichenbach. Trans. by Maria Reichenbach and John Freund. [Dover Books, S443.] New York: Dover Publications, [1958]. ([4], xvi, [1], 295 pp.) Pp. v-vii.

The Remarks are dated: Univ. of California at Los Angeles, July 1956.
Despite a statement on the title page verso indicating publication in 1957, this translation of *Philosophie der Raum-Zeit-Lehre* did not appear until April 1958.

2. INTRODUCTION TO SYMBOLIC LOGIC AND ITS APPLICATIONS. Trans. by William H. Meyer and John Wilkinson. [Dover Books, S453.] New York: Dover Publications, [1958]. xiv, 241 pp.

Translation of Item 1954-3 as revised and enlarged by Carnap. Major changes are confined to §§ 20, 26, 31, 38, 42, 43, 46 and the Bibliography.
The 2nd German edition, which corresponds to the English version, is Item 1960-2. For Spanish translation thereof, see note to that item.
Contents: Preface to the English Edition (Univ. of California at Los Angeles, May 1957). Preface to the [First] German Edition (Institute for Advanced Study, Princeton, N.J., Jan. 1954). SYSTEM OF SYMBOLIC LOGIC. *The Simple Language A* (§§ 1-19). The Problem of Symbolic Logic. Individual Constants and Predicates. Sentential Connectives. Truth-Tables. L-Concepts.

L-Implication and L-Equivalence. Sentential Variables. Sentential Formulas That Are Tautologies. Universal and Existential Sentences. Predicate Variables. Value-Assignments. Substitutions. Theorems on Quantifiers. L-True Formulas with Quantifiers. Definitions. Predicates of Higher Levels. Identity; Cardinal Numbers. Functors. Isomorphism. *The Language B* (§§ 20-26). Semantical and Syntactical Systems. Rules of Formation for Language B. Rules of Transformation for Language B. Proofs and Derivations in Language B. Theorems on Provability and Derivability in Language B. The Semantical System for Language B. Relations between Syntactical and Semantical Systems. *The Extended Language C* (§§ 27-38). The Language C. Compound Predicate Expressions. Identity; Extensionality. Relative Product; Powers of Relations. Various Kinds of Relations. Additional Logical Predicates, Functors and Connectives. The λ-Operator. Equivalence Classes, Structures, Cardinal Numbers. Individual Descriptions. Heredity and Ancestral Relations. Finite and Infinite. Continuity. APPLICATION OF SYMBOLIC LOGIC. *Forms and Methods of the Construction of Languages* (§§ 39-42). Thing Languages. Coordinate Languages. Quantitative Concepts. The Axiomatic Method. *Axiom Systems (ASs) for Set Theory and Arithmetic* (§§ 43-45). AS for Set Theory. Peano's AS for the Natural Numbers. AS for the Real Numbers. *Axiom Systems (ASs) for Geometry* (§§ 46-47). AS for Topology (Neighborhood Axioms). ASs of Projective, of Affine and of Metric Geometry. *ASs of Physics* (§§ 48-51). ASs of Space-Time Topology: 1, The *C-T* System. (General Remarks. *C, T,* and World-Lines. The Signal Relation. The Structure of Space.) ASs of Space-Time Topology: 2, The *Wlin*-System. ASs of Space-Time Topology: 3, The *S*-System. Determination and Causality. *ASs of Biology* (§§ 52-54). AS of Things and Their Parts. AS Involving Biological Concepts. AS for Kinship Relations.—*Appendix* (§§ 55-57). Problems in the Application of Symbolic Logic. Bibliography. General Guide to the Literature.—Index. Symbols of the Symbolic Language and of the Metalanguage.

3. I fondamenti logici dell'unità della scienza. [Trad. di Alberto Pasquinelli.] In *La filosofia contemporanea in USA: [Metodo, valori, comportamento]*. [Trad. di Alberto Pasquinelli e Enzo Siciliano.] Asti: Arethusa; Roma: Società Filosofica Romana [e] Istituto di Filosofia della Università, [1958]. (702 pp.) Pp. [71]-93.

   Translation of Item 1938-2, undertaken independently of the following item.

   The volume in which this item appears is, in general, a translation of *American Philosophers at Work* (see Item 1956-6), but many essays of the original collection, among them Carnap's, have been replaced by other selections.

4. I fondamenti logici dell'unità della scienza. In *Neopositivismo e unità della scienza* di Otto Neurath e altri [Trad. di Orio Peduzzi.] Introd. di Enzo Paci. Idee nuove [vol. 28]. Milano: Valentino Bompiani, 1958. (263, [3] pp.) Pp. [75]-103.

   Translation of Item 1938-2, undertaken independently of the preceding item.

   The volume in which this item appears is a translation of vol. I no. 1 and vol. II no. 9 of the *International Encyclopedia of Unified Science*.

1959

1. Induktive Logik und Wahrscheinlichkeit. [Übersetzt und] bearbeitet von Wolfgang Stegmüller. Wien: Springer-Verlag, 1959. viii, 261 pp.

Originally planned as a German translation of Item 1951-2 (i.e. six sections from Item 1950-4), the present item in final form consists of the following: (*a*) an introductory essay by Stegmüller (pp. [1]-11), which includes the content of Item 1953-5; (*b*) a translation, in part paraphrastic, of approximately one-third of the text of Items 1950-4 (pp. [12]-206) and 1952-1 (pp. [207]-232); (*c*) a summary of certain discussions that followed publication of Item 1950-4 (pp. [233]-242); (*d*) a new axiom system for *c*-functions (pp. 242-252), hitherto unpublished except for inclusion in Carnap's seminar notes, Item 1955-9.

The following corrections to the Vorwort should be noted: p. v, line 7 of fine print, for "13" read "14"; line 8, for "14" read "15"; line 9, for "15 bis 18" read "16 bis 19"; line 10, for "von Kapitel VI" read "von Kapiteln III und VIII,".

Contents: Vorwort (im Dez. 1958), von R.C. und W.S. Einleitung, Carnaps Auffassung der induktiven Logik, von W.S. Philosophische Grundlegung der induktiven Logik. *Die beiden Wahrscheinlichkeitsbegriffe* (§§ 1-6). Über die Explikation von Begriffen; klassifikatorische, komparative und quantitative Begriffe. Axiomatisierung und Interpretation. Die beiden Wahrscheinlichkeitsbegriffe. Der logische Charakter der beiden Wahrscheinlichkeitsbegriffe. Der Psychologismus in der deduktiven und induktiven Logik. Die L-Begriffe. *Das Problem der induktiven Logik* (§§ 7-10). Der logische Begriff der Wahrscheinlichkeit. (Wahrscheinlichkeit$_1$ als Stützungsmass. Wahrscheinlichkeit$_1$ als fairer Wettquotient. Wahrscheinlichkeit$_1$ und relative Häufigkeit. Wahrscheinlichkeit$_1$ als Schätzung der relativen Häufigkeit. Einige Bemerkungen zu anderen Auffassungen. Voraussetzungen der Induktion.) Wahrscheinlichkeit$_1$ und Wahrscheinlichkeit$_2$. Induktive und deduktive Logik. Weitere vorbereitende Überlegungen zur induktiven Logik. *Die Anwendung der induktiven Logik* (§§ 11-13). Die Frage nach dem Nutzen der induktiven Logik. Das Problem einer Regel für das Fassen von Entschlüssen. Die Regel der Maximalisierung des geschätzten Nutzens. Grundriss des formalen Aufbaus der induktiven Logik. Übersicht. *Grundlegung der quantitativen induktiven Logik* (§§ 14-19). Die semantischen Systeme **L**. Reduktion des Problems des Bestätigungsgrades. Die regulären Mass- und Bestätigungsfunktionen. Lehrsätze für die Nullbestätigung. Lehrsätze für die regulären *c*-Funktionen. Bestätigung von Hypothesen durch Beobachtungen; das Theorem von Bayes. *Die symmetrischen Bestätigungsfunktionen* (§§ 20-22). Individuelle Verteilungen, Strukturbeschreibungen und *Q*-Prädikate. Die symmetrischen *m*- und *c*-Funktionen. Der direkte Induktionsschluss und seine Approximationen. *Das Problem der Schätzung* (§§ 23-25). Allgemeines; die *c*-Mittel-Schätzungsfunktion. Das Problem der Zuverlässigkeit von Schätzungen. Häufigkeitsschätzungen. *Das Kontinuum der induktiven Methoden* (§§ 26-28). Die repräsentierende Funktion. Die λ-Funktionen. Das Problem der Wahl einer induktiven Methode. *Anhang A, Weitere Probleme der induktiven Logik.* Das Problem der Relationen in der induktiven Logik; Bedeutungspostulate. Relevanz und Irrelevanz. Der klassifikatorische und der komparative Begriff der Bestätigung. *Anhang B, Ein neues Axiomensystem für die c-Funktionen.* —Literaturverzeichnis. Namen- und Sachverzeichnis.

2. Beobachtungssprache und theoretische Sprache. *Dialectica: Revue internationale de philosophie de science* (Neuchâtel), vol. 12, n° 3/4 (15 sept./15 déc. 1958 [i.e. fév. 1959]), pp. [236]-248.

Includes abstracts in German and English, p. 248.

The entire double number of *Dialectica* is dedicated to Paul Bernays on the occasion of his 70th birthday.

The present item is translated into Italian as Item 1959-7.

The English abstract, with German title, is reprinted in *Philosophy of Science* (Bruges), vol. 26, no. 4 (Oct. 1959), p. 369, and in *The British Journal for the Philosophy of Science* (Edinburgh), vol. 11, no. 42 (Aug. 1960), p. 171.

An anonymous Russian translation of the abstract, under the title "I͡Azyk nabli͡udenii͡a i teoreticheskiĭ," appears as a "rezi͡ume avtora" in *Referativnyĭ zhurnal: Matematika* (Moskva), 1960, no. 8 (Aug.), p. 13, item 8531.

3. Beobachtungssprache und theoretische Sprache. In *Logica: Studia Paul Bernays dedicata,* [a Wilhelm Ackermann et aliis]. Bibliothèque scientifique, 34. Neuchâtel: Éditions du Griffon, [c1959]. (293, [2] pp.) Pp. [32]-44.

Identical with preceding item.

4. INTRODUCTION TO SEMANTICS, AND FORMALIZATION OF LOGIC. [*His* Studies in Semantics, vols. 1 and 2.] Cambridge, Mass.: Harvard Univ. Press, 1959. Two vols. in one. xiv, 259, [v]-xv, 159 pp.

a. Introduction to Semantics.

b. Formalization of Logic.

Reprint of Items 1942-2 and 1943-1 with minor corrections, the bibliographies brought up to date, and a brief Preface to the One-Volume Edition (Univ. of California at Los Angeles, July 1958).

5. The Two Concepts of Probability. In *Contemporary Philosophic Problems: Selected Readings,* ed. by Yervant H. Krikorian and Abraham Edel. New York: Macmillan Co., [c1959]. (xi, 712 pp.) Pp. 173-186.

Reprint of pp. 513-525 of Item 1945-3.

6. Foreword. In *Modern Philosophy of Science: Selected Essays* by Hans Reichenbach. Trans. and ed. by Maria Reichenbach. London: Routledge & Kegan Paul; New York: Humanities Press, [1959]. (ix, 214 pp. Pp. vii-viii.

7. Linguaggio osservativo e linguaggio teorico. Trad. di Pietro Chiodi. *Rivista di filosofia* (Torino), vol. 50, n. 2 (apr. 1959), pp. [135]-145.

Translation of Item 1959-2 with the abstracts omitted.

8. The Elimination of Metaphysics through Logical Analysis of Language. Trans. by Arthur Pap. In *Logical Positivism,* ed. by A. J. Ayer. [The Library of Philosophical Movements.] Glencoe, Ill.: Free Press, [c1959]. (viii, 455 pp.) Pp. 60-81.

Translation of Item 1932-1 with concluding "Zusatz bei der Korrektur" omitted and added Remarks by the Author (1957), pp. 80-81.

For Spanish translation of the present item, see "To Appear."

9. The Old and the New Logic. Trans. by Isaac Levi. *Ibid.*, pp. 133-146.

Translation of Item 1930-2 with Literatur-Hinweise omitted and added Remarks by the Author (1957), p. 146.

For Italian and Spanish translations of the present item, see "To Appear."

10. Psychology in Physical Language. Trans. by George [i.e. Frederic] Schick. *Ibid.*, pp. 165-198.

Translation of Item 1932-5 with minor omissions near the beginning of § 5 and added Remarks by the Author (1957), pp. 197-198. The translator's name is given incorrectly.

For Spanish translation of the present item, see "To Appear."

11. [REVISED NOTES ON SEMANTICS.] [Los Angeles, 1959. Distributed by the author.] 25_n-45_n, $46a_n$-$46b_n$, [55_n], [1]-3 pp. (i.e. leaves). Hectographed.

Revised version of nearly one-half of Item 1955-4 (consisting of §§20-26, an additional erratum sheet, and revised bibliography) for use in a seminar conducted at the Univ. of California at Los Angeles, fall semester 1959. Subsequently distributed more widely, accompanied by a one-page hectographed letter of transmittal dated "February 1960." (Title supplied by the Bibliographer.)

Sections 20 and 24 are retitled: Semantical System for the Language L_2 with Individual Variables; *and* The A-Concepts for L_3.

1960

1. Statistical and Inductive Probability. In *The Structure of Scientific Thought: An Introduction to Philosophy of Science*, [ed. by] Edward H. Madden. Boston: Houghton Mifflin Co., [c1960]. (ix, 381 pp.) Pp. 269-279.

Reprint of Item 1955-10*a*.

Also published in London (Routledge & Kegan Paul, 1960).

2. EINFÜHRUNG IN DIE SYMBOLISCHE LOGIK, MIT BESONDERER BERÜCKSICHTIGUNG IHRER ANWENDUNGEN. Zweite, neubearbeitete und erweiterte Auflage. Wien: Springer-Verlag, 1960. xii, 241 pp.

Revised and enlarged edition of Item 1954-3. The added "Vorwort zur zweiten Auflage" is dated: Los Angeles, im Herbst 1959.

Substantially identical with the English version, Item 1958-2. For contents, see note to that item.

For Spanish translation of the present item, see "To Appear."

3. "Hsüan-hsüeh ch'ü-hsiao-chê"—K'a-na-p'u ti szŭ-hsiang ["The One Who Eliminates Metaphysics"—The Thought of Carnap]. Trans. by Yip-wang Law (Yeh-hung Lo). *Ta-hsüeh shêng-huo (College Life)* (Hong Kong), vol. 5, no. 21 (16 March 1960), pp. 4-11.

Condensed translation of Item 1955-5. Morton White's essay introducing that item was also translated: "Lo-chi ching-yen-lun: K'a-na-p'u [Logical Empiricism: Carnap]," *ibid.*, vol. 4, no. 9 (1 Jan. 1959), pp. 18-21.

4. Elementary and Abstract Terms. In *Philosophy of Science*, readings

sel., ed. and introd. by Arthur Danto and Sidney Morgenbesser. [Meridian Books, M90.] New York: Meridian Books, [1960]. (477 pp.) Pp. [150]-158.

Reprint of §§ 24-25 (pp. 61-69) of Item 1939-1.

5. Theoretische Begriffe der Wissenschaft: Eine logische und methodologische Untersuchung. Übersetzung und Erläuterungen zur Terminologie von Alfred Scheibal. *Zeitschrift für philosophische Forschung* (Meisenheim am Glan), Bd. 14, H. 2 (April-Juni 1960), pp. [209]-233; H. 4 (Okt.-Dez. 1960), pp. [571]-598.

Translation of Item 1956-4.

6. Significado y sinonimia en los lenguajes naturales. Trad. de Emilio O. Colombo. In *Antología semántica,* comp. por Mario Bunge. Colección interciencia, [8]. Buenos Aires: Ediciones Nueva Visión, [1960]. (271, [1] pp.) Pp. 25-44.

Translation of Item 1955-3.

1961

1. SINTASSI LOGICA DEL LINGUAGGIO. [Trad., pref. e note di Alberto Pasquinelli. Collana filosofica, diretta da Enrico Maria Forni.] [Milano:] Silva Editore, [1961]. 476 pp.

Translation of Item 1937-1 with indexes omitted and with various revisions by Carnap, principally in §§11, 30, 43, 50 and 57.

2. LA SUPERACIÓN DE LA METAFÍSICA POR MEDIO DEL ANÁLISIS LÓGICO DEL LENGUAJE. Trad. de C. Nicolás Molina Flores. [Cuadernos del Centro de Estudios Filosóficos,] Cuaderno 10. [México, D.F.:] Centro de Estudios Filosóficos, Universidad Nacional Autónoma de México, 1961. 33, [6] pp.

Translation of Item 1932-1 with concluding "Zusatz bei der Korrektur" omitted and with added author's preface, p. [5], and Notas del Autor (1960), p. [34].

Pages [7]-[35] also numbered 451-479, continuing the paging of the preceding Cuaderno.

3. The Unity of Science. In *Perspectives in Philosophy: A Book of Readings,* [ed. by] Robert N. Beck. New York: Holt, Rinehart and Winston, [c1961]. (x, 405 pp.) Pp. 256-263.

Reprint of pp. 31-40, 42-45 and 93-101 of Item 1934-4, with minor revisions and two added footnotes by Carnap, pp. 258 and 260-261.

4. Ching-yen-lun, yü-yi-hsüeh, yü pên-t'i-lun (Empiricism, Semantics, and Ontology). Trans. by P. C. Chun (Po-chuang Ch'ên) [and Hai-kuang Yin, *alias* Fu-sheng Yin]. In *Mei-kuo chê-hsüeh hsüan (Anthology of American Philosophy),* sel. and ed. by P. C. Chun (Po-chuang Ch'ên). Mei-kuo ts'ung-shu [U.S.A. Series, no. 5]. [Hong Kong:] Chin-jih Shih-chieh Shê (World Today Press), [1961]. ([2], 3, 3, 7, 253 pp.) Pp. 201-209.

Free translation of Item 1953-4 with footnotes omitted.

The "Logical Empiricism" section of the *Anthology* also contains translations, one each, from Philipp Frank, Hans Reichenbach, Carl Hempel, Herbert Feigl, Ernest Nagel and Charles Morris.

5. On the Use of Hilbert's ε-Operator in Scientific Theories. In *Essays on the Foundations of Mathematics, Dedicated to A. A. Fraenkel on His Seventieth Anniversary,* ed. by Y[ehoshua] Bar-Hillel, E. I. J. Poznanski, M. O. Rabin and A[braham] Robinson. Jerusalem: The Magnes Press, The Hebrew University, 1961. (x, 351 pp.) Pp. 156-164.

To Appear: New Works

A. Intellectual Autobiography; *and* Replies and Systematic Expositions. In the present volume.

The "Replies and Systematic Expositions" were distributed in hectographed form two or three years prior to publication of this volume.

B. A Critical Examination of the Statistical Concept of Entropy in Classical Physics.

Written in 1953.

C. An Abstract Concept of Entropy and Its Use in Inductive Logic.

Written in 1953.

D. Philosophical Foundations of Physics. By Rudolf Carnap with Martin Gardner. New York: Basic Books.

Based on a seminar conducted by Carnap at the Univ. of California at Los Angeles, fall semester 1958.

E. On Theoretical Concepts in Science.

Revised version of contribution to a symposium on "Carnap's Views on Theoretical Concepts in Science" at a meeting of the American Philosophical Assn., Pacific Div., Univ. of California at Santa Barbara, 29 Dec. 1959.

F. The Aim of Inductive Logic. In *Logic, Methodology and Philosophy of Science: Proceedings of the 1960 International Congress,* ed. by Ernest Nagel, Patrick Suppes, Alfred Tarski. Stanford, Calif.: Stanford Univ. Press, 1962. (ix, 661 pp.) Pp. 303-318.

Address delivered 25 Aug. 1960 at the International Congress for Logic, Methodology and Philosophy of Science, held at Stanford Univ. under the auspices of the International Union of History and Philosophy of Science.

G. Remarks on Probability. In the journal *Philosophical Studies* (Minneapolis).

Essentially identical with added preface to 2nd edition of Item 1950-4 (see below).

H. Inductive Logic and Rational Decisions; *and* An Axiom System for Inductive Logic. In *Studies in Probability and Inductive Logic,* vol. I, ed. by Rudolf Carnap.

The first essay is an expanded version of "The Aim of Inductive Logic." The volume will also contain two essays by Richard C. Jeffrey and one by John G. Kemeny and Haim Gaifman.

To Appear: Reprints and Translations

A. Der logische Aufbau der Welt. Scheinprobleme in der Philos-

OPHIE. [Zweite Auflage.] Hamburg: Felix Meiner Verlag, [1962]. xx, 336 pp.

a. Der logische Aufbau der Welt: pp. 1-290.

b. Scheinprobleme in der Philosophie: pp. 295-336.

Photo-offset reprint of Items 1928-1 and 1928-2 with added "Vorwort zur zweiten Auflage" (Univ. of California, Los Angeles, März 1961) and "Literaturverzeichnis 1961."

Despite a statement on the title page verso indicating publication in 1961, this volume did not appear until May 1962.

B. DER LOGISCHE AUFBAU DER WELT. (Italian.) Trans. by Emanuele Severino. Bologna: Nicola Zanichelli.

Translation of Item 1928-1.

C. The Old and the New Logic. (Italian.) Trans. by Francesco Adorno. In an anthology of contemporary logic and epistemology. Firenze: Felice Le Monnier.

Translation of Item 1959-9.

D. On the Logicist Foundations of Mathematics; *and* Empiricism, Semantics, and Ontology. In *Readings in the Philosophy of Mathematics,* ed. by Paul Benacerraf and Hilary Putnam. Englewood Cliffs, N.J.: Prentice-Hall.

Translation of Item 1931-4 and reprint of Item 1953-4.

E. The Unity of Science; Philosophy and Logical Syntax; *and* Truth and Confirmation. In *Readings in Twentieth Century Philosophy,* ed. by William P. Alston and George Nakhnikian. New York: Free Press of Glencoe.

Reprint of Items 1934-4 and 1935-1 with extensive terminological and stylistic revisions and added remarks by Carnap, and unaltered reprint of Item 1949-1.

F. The Rejection of Metaphysics. In *Introduction to Philosophy: Readings in Epistemology, Metaphysics, Ethics, Philosophy of Religion,* ed. by Arthur Smullyan, Paul Dietrichson, David Keyt, Leonard Miller. Belmont, Calif.: Wadsworth Publishing Co., [c1962]. (ix, [1], 418 pp.) Pp. 16-25.

Reprint of chap. 1 of Item 1935-1 with concluding paragraph omitted, and with minor revisions and an added footnote by Carnap, p. 21.

G. FILOSOFÍA Y SINTAXIS LÓGICA. Trad. de C. Nicolás Molina Flores. In the series, Cuadernos del Centro de Estudios Filosóficos. Universidad Nacional Autónoma de México.

Translation of Item 1935-1.

H. LA SINTAXIS LÓGICA DEL LENGUAJE. Trad. de Rafael Ruíz Harrel. In the series, Cuadernos del Centro de Estudios Filosóficos. Universidad Nacional Autónoma de México.

Translation of Item 1937-1.

I. INTRODUCTION TO SEMANTICS. (Italian.) Milano: Arnoldo Mondadori.

Translation of Item 1942-2.

J. FORMALIZATION OF LOGIC. (Italian.) Milano: Arnoldo Mondadori.
Translation of Item 1943-1.

K. MEANING AND NECESSITY. (Italian.) Trans. by Alberto Pasquinelli. Milano: Giangiacomo Feltrinelli.
Translation of Item 1956-3, i.e. of Items 1947-2, 1953-4, 1952-5, 1955-1, 1955-3 and 1955-6.

L. The Method of the Name-Relation; Sentences about Beliefs; *and* Reply to Church. (Japanese.) In *Studies in Semantics,* trans. and ed. by Hiromichi Takeda. Kyōto: Minerva Press.
Translation of §§24-32 and 13-15 of Item 1947-2, and Item 1955-1.

M. LOGICAL FOUNDATIONS OF PROBABILITY. [Second edition.] [Chicago:] Univ. of Chicago Press, [1962]. xxvii, 613 pp.
Reprint of Item 1950-4 with minor corrections and substantial added preface and bibliog. Also to be pub. in London (Routledge & Kegan Paul).

N. Testability and Meaning; Formal and Factual Science; The Interpretation of Physics; *and* The Two Concepts of Probability. (Spanish.) In a translation of *Readings in the Philosophy of Science,* Herbert Feigl and May Brodbeck, eds. Editorial de la Universidad de Buenos Aires.
Translation of Items 1953-9 to 1953-12.

O. Hsing-shih k'o-hsüeh yü shih-chih k'o-hsüeh [Formal Science and Factual Science]. Trans. by Ching-yüeh Lin. *Min-chu p'ing-lun (The Democratic Review)* (Hong Kong), vol. 13, no. 3 (1 Feb. 1962), pp. 14-15, 18.
Translation of Item 1953-10.
Pages also numbered 62-63, 66, continuing the paging of the preceding issue.

P. La eliminación de la metafísica mediante el análisis lógico del lenguaje; La antigua y la nueva lógica; *y* Psicología y lenguaje físico. In *Positivismo lógico,* comp. por A. J. Ayer. Trad. por Florentino M. Torner. México, D. F.: Fondo de Cultura Economica.
Translation of Items 1959-8 to 1959-10.

Q. EINFÜHRUNG IN DIE SYMBOLISCHE LOGIK. (Spanish.) Editorial de la Universidad de Buenos Aires.
Translation of Item 1960-2.

II. CARNAP AS EDITOR

ERKENNTNIS, ZUGLEICH ANNALEN DER PHILOSOPHIE. Hrsg. von Rudolf Carnap und Hans Reichenbach. Leipzig: Felix Meiner Verlag, 1930-37; The Hague: W. P. van Stockum & Zoon, 1938-40. 8 vols., av. 440 pp.

Journal, each vol. comprising six nos, published at irregular intervals. Superseded *Annalen der Philosophie und philosophischen Kritik* and continued its vol. numbering as a secondary scheme through *Erkenntnis* Bd. 7, *zugleich Annalen der Philosophie* Bd. 15. Organ of the Gesellschaft für empirische (*later,* wissenschaftliche) Philosophie, Berlin, and the Verein Ernst Mach, Vienna, through Bd. 3. Cover title for some issues: *Erkenntnis*

(Annalen der Philosophie). With vol. 8, assumed title: *The Journal of Unified Science (Erkenntnis).* Bd. 7 ed. by Carnap alone; vol. 8, by Carnap and Reichenbach with six assoc. eds. Change of publisher with Bd. 7 H. 2.

Abridged versions of papers presented at the Fifth International Congress for the Unity of Science (Cambridge, Mass., 3-9 Sept. 1939) were preprinted as from vol. 9 and distributed at the Congress, but actual publication of the *Journal* ceased with vol. 8 no. 5/6 (1 April 1940).

Some issues appeared also as "Sonderdruck[e] aus *Erkenntnis,*" e.g., Bd. 5 H. 1 and 2/3 as *Einheit der Wissenschaft* (see note to item 1935-2) and Bd. 6 H. 5/6 as: *Das Kausalproblem: II. internationaler Kongress für Einheit der Wissenschaft, Kopenhagen 1936.* Leipzig: Felix Meiner Verlag; Kopenhagen: Levin & Munksgaard Verlag [*now,* Ejnar Munksgaard], 1937. [ii], 275-450 pp.

BEIHEFTE DER "ERKENNTNIS". Hrsg. von Hans Reichenbach und Rudolf Carnap. Leipzig: Felix Meiner Verlag, 1931. 1 no.

Planned as a series of monographs, but only one was published: WALTER DUBISLAV, *Die Definition.* Dritte, völlig umgearb. u. erw. Aufl. viii, 160 pp. (The earlier editions—*Über die Definition,* Berlin-Schöneberg, H. Weiss, 1926 and 1927—had no connection with the series.)

EINHEITSWISSENSCHAFT. Schriften hrsg. von Otto Neurath in Verbindung mit Rudolf Carnap und anderen. Wien: Verlag Gerold & Co., 1933-35; 's-Gravenhage: Verlag W. P. van Stockum & Zoon, 1938; The Hague: W. P. van Stockum & Zoon, 1939-40. 9 nos.

Series of monographs. With H. 6, assumed title: Einheitswissenschaft, Unified Science, Science Unitaire. With no. 8/9, assumed title: Library of Unified Science, Monograph Series. Other assoc. eds. (variously): Philipp Frank, Hans Hahn, Jørgen Jørgensen, Charles W. Morris.

H. 1. OTTO NEURATH, *Einheitswissenschaft und Psychologie,* 1933. 31 pp. —H. 2. HANS HAHN, *Logik, Mathematik und Naturerkennen,* 1933. 33 pp. —H. 3. RUDOLF CARNAP, *Die Aufgabe der Wissenschaftslogik,* 1934. 30 pp.—H. 4. OTTO NEURATH, *Was bedeutet rationale Wirtschaftsbetrachtung?,* 1935. 46 pp.—H. 5 PHILIPP FRANK, *Das Ende der mechanistischen Physik,* 1935. 35 pp.—H. 6. [OTTO] NEURATH, [EGON] BRUNSWIK, [CLARK L.] HULL, [GERRIT] MANNOURY, [J. H.] WOODGER, *Zur Enzyklopädie der Einheitswissenschaft,* 1938. 42, [1] pp.—H. 7. RICHARD V. MISES, *Ernst Mach und die empiristische Wissenschaftsauffassung,* 1938. 34 pp.—no. 8/9. HEINRICH GOMPERZ, *Interpretation: Logical Analysis of a Method of Historical Research,* [c1939, pub. 1940]. 85 pp.

Hefte 2, 3 and 5 have been published also in translation: *(2) Logique, mathématiques et connaissance de la réalité* (Paris, Hermann & Cie, 1935), "Ronrigaku, sūgaku, oyobi shizen ninshiki" (pp. 351-400 of *Kagaku ronrigaku,* ed. by Katsumi Nakamura; Tōkyō, Nisshin Shoin, 1944), "Logic, Mathematics and Knowledge of Nature" (pp. 147-161 of *Logical Positivism,* ed. by A. J. Ayer; Glencoe, Ill., Free Press, 1959).—*(3)* "Le Problème de la logique de la science" (Item 1935-10*a*), "Kagaku ronrigaku no kadai" (Item 1942-5).—*(5) La Fin de la physique mécaniste* (Paris, Hermann & Cie, 1936).

LIBRARY OF UNIFIED SCIENCE, BOOK SERIES. Ed.-in-chief, Otto Neurath; assoc. eds., Rudolf Carnap, Philipp Frank, Jørgen Jørgensen, Charles W. Morris. The Hague: W. P. van Stockum & Zoon, 1939-46. 2 vols.

Vol. 1. RICHARD VON MISES, *Kleines Lehrbuch des Positivismus,* [c1939].

xii, 467 pp.—vol. 2. HANS KELSEN, *Vergeltung und Kausalität.* [c1941, pub. 1946]. xii, 542 pp.

Both works have been published also in translation: (*1*) *Manuale di critica scientifica e filosofica* (Milano, L. Longanesi e C., 1950), *Positivism* (Cambridge, Mass., Harvard Univ. Press, 1951).—(*2*) *Society and Nature* (Chicago, Univ. of Chicago Press, 1943; London, Kegan Paul, Trench, Trubner & Co. [*now,* Routledge & Kegan Paul], 1946), *Sociedad y naturaleza* (trad. de la edición norteamericana; Buenos Aires, Editorial Depalma, 1945).

INTERNATIONAL ENCYCLOPEDIA OF UNIFIED SCIENCE. Ed.-in-chief, Otto Neurath (*d.* 1945); assoc. eds., Rudolf Carnap, Charles W. Morris. Chicago: Univ. of Chicago Press, 1938 +. 17 nos. to date.

The first 20 nos. will constitute vols. I-II, *Foundations of the Unity of Science.* Since 1949 the *Encyclopedia* project has been under the general direction of the Institute for the Unity of Science, Boston.

Vol. I, no. 1. OTTO NEURATH, NIELS BOHR, JOHN DEWEY, BERTRAND RUSSELL, RUDOLF CARNAP, CHARLES W. MORRIS, *Encyclopedia and Unified Science,* [1938]. viii, 75 pp.—no. 2. CHARLES W. MORRIS, *Foundations of the Theory of Signs,* [1938]. vii, 59 pp.—no. 3. RUDOLF CARNAP, *Foundations of Logic and Mathematics,* [1939]. viii, 71 pp.—no. 4. LEONARD BLOOMFIELD, *Linguistic Aspects of Science,* [1939]. viii, 59 pp.—no. 5. VICTOR F. LENZEN, *Procedures of Empirical Science,* [1938]. vii, 59 pp.—no. 6. ERNEST NAGEL, *Principles of the Theory of Probability,* [1939]. vii, 80 pp.—no. 7. PHILIPP FRANK, *Foundations of Physics,* [1946]. v, 78 pp.—no. 8. E[RWIN] FINLAY-FREUNDLICH, *Cosmology,* [1951]. iii, 59 pp.—no. 9. FELIX MAINX, *Foundations of Biology,* [1955]. iii, 86 pp.—no. 10. EGON BRUNSWIK, *The Conceptual Framework of Psychology,* [1952]. iv, 102 pp.

Vol. II, no. 1. OTTO NEURATH, *Foundations of the Social Sciences,* [1944]. iii, 51 pp.—[no. 2. THOMAS S. KUHN, *The Structure of Scientific Revolutions,* to appear.]—no. 3. ABRAHAM EDEL, *Science and the Structure of Ethics,* [1961]. iv, 100, [1] pp.—no. 4. JOHN DEWEY, *Theory of Valuation,* [1939]. vii, 67 pp.—no. 5. J. H. WOODGER, *The Technique of Theory Construction,* [1939]. vii, 81 pp.—[no. 6. MEYER SCHAPIRO, *Interpretations and Judgement of Art,* to appear.]—no. 7. CARL G. HEMPEL, *Fundamentals of Concept Formation in Empirical Science,* [1952]. iii, 93 pp.—no. 8. GEORGE DE SANTILLANA AND EDGAR ZILSEL, *The Development of Rationalism and Empiricism,* [1941]. viii, 94 pp.—no. 9. JOERGEN JOERGENSEN, *The Development of Logical Empiricism,* [1951]. iii, 100 pp.—[no. 10. HERBERT FEIGL AND WILFRID SELLARS, *Bibliography and Index,* to appear.]

Numerous subsequent impressions with various dates.

In addition to publication in individual paperbound nos., vol. I has been issued in two clothbound parts: INTERNATIONAL ENCYCLOPEDIA OF UNIFIED SCIENCE. Ed. by Otto Neurath, Rudolf Carnap, Charles Morris. Chicago: Univ. of Chicago Press, [1955]. Vol. I, nos. 1-5; ix, 339 pp. Vol. I, nos. 6-10; [v], [341]-760 pp.

Vol. I no. 1 and vol. II no. 9 have been translated as *Neopositivismo e unità della scienza* (see Item 1958-4). Carnap's essay from vol. I no. 1 is available in another Italian translation as Item 1958-3 and in Chinese as Item 1957-1. Morris's essay from vol. I no. 1 has been translated as "K'o-hsüeh-hua ti ching-yen-lun" (pp. 246-253 of *Mei-kuo chê-hsüeh hsüan,* ed. by P. C. Chun; Hong Kong, Chin-jih Shih-chieh Shê, 1961). Vol. II no. 9, except for the "Postscript" by Norman M. Martin, is translated from *Den logiske Em-*

pirismes Udvikling (København, 1948; in the series "Festskrift udgivet af Københavns Universitet . . ." [Bianco Lunos Bogtrykkeri] and also pub. separately by Ejnar Munksgaard).

Vol. I nos. 2 and 3 and vol. II nos. 4 and 7 have also been translated: *(I:2) Lineamenti di una teoria dei segni* ("Biblioteca di filosofia e pedagogia," Torino, G. B. Paravia & C., 1955), *Fundamentos de la teoria de los signos* ("Suplementos del Seminario de Problemas Científicos y Filosóficos, 2a serie, núm. 12," Universidad Nacional de México, 1958).—*(I:3)* "Ronrigaku to sūgaku no kiso" (Item 1942-6), *Fondamenti di logica e matematica* (Item 1956-2).—*(II:4) Teoria della valutazione* ("Pensatori antichi e moderni, 56," Firenze, La Nuova Italia, 1960).—*(II:7) La formazione dei concetti e delle teorie nella scienza empirica* ("Filosofia della scienza, 4," Milano, Feltrinelli Editore, 1961).

III. REVIEWS OF CARNAP'S WRITINGS

A. REFERENCES*

1922-1

B3 UW 15 (1923) 60
D4 UMN 30 (1924) 66-67, 83-87
L8 ZMNU 54 (1923) 238-239
S11 BPDI 3:4 (1925) 44
W8 JFM 48 (1921-22, pub. 1925-28) 631-632
W10 MGMN 24 (1925) 21-22
W12 BAMS 30 (1924) 259

1923-1

A1 Mind 33 (1924) 224
A1 RSPT 13 (1924) 277
B3 UW 15 (1923) 112-113
B3 ZPCU 36 (1923) 200-203
D2 KS 28 (1923) 376-388
R1 PB 4 (1923) 1523

1924-1

A1 Mind 34 (1925) 129

1925-1

A1 PJGG 39 (1926) 203
F7 JFM 51 (1925, pub. 1931-32) 52

1926-1

A1 NFP 23217:Morgenbl. (4. Mai 1929) 10
B3 UW 19 (1927) 94
D3 PZ 28 (1927) 698-699
H3 UMN 33 (1927) 224
H7 JFM 52 (1926, pub. 1934-35) 54-55
L1 ZMNU 62 (1931) 228
M17b SS 31:10 (14. Sept. 1927) 38
P5a Reich. 00 (28. Feb. 1927) 00
S5 ZPC 149 (1930) 335
S12 MMP 35 (1928) 71-72
S19 ZPCU 41 (1928) 157

1927-2

F1 PsA1 (1927) item 2313
H14 JFM 52 (1926, pub. 1934-35) 44

1928-1

B9 APPK 8 (1929) 106*-107*
B20 BDP 4 (1930-31) 117-118
D6 PF 36 (1933) 287-289
D8 PJGG 43 (1930) 131-132
F2 Grundw. 11 (1932) 224-225
H14 JFM 54 (1928, pub. 1931-32) 60-61
K3 ARW 23 (1929-30) 200-202
N2 Kampf 21 (1928) 624-626
P7 SZ 120 (1930-31) 145
R3 KS 38 (1933) 199-201
S6 Naturw. 17 (1929) 550-551
S9 DL 51 (1930) cols. 586-592
S18 LH 65 (1928-29) cols. 585-586
T1 CM 27 (1931) 84-86
W1 NZZ 150:1591 (19. Aug. 1929, Bl. 1) 1; 151:81 (15. Jan. 1930, Bl. 4) 1
W3 Theoria 10 (1944) 216-246 [Eng.]
W9 KF 11 (1933) 183-188

1928-2

B9 APPK 8 (1929) 77*
D8 PJGG 42 (1929) 543-544
H12 Grundw. 9 (1929) 14-24
K1 TW 24 (1930) 244-245
K3 ARW 23 (1929-30) 202
K11 AAZP 2 (1929) 450-451
N2 Kampf 21 (1928) 624-626
P7 SZ 120 (1930-31) 145
S9 DL 51 (1930) cols. 586-592
W9 KF 10 (1932) 142-147

*Key to authors, pp. 1064ff., key to periodicals, pp. 1067ff.

1929-2

B6a EP 4 (1930) 145
C10 JP 27 (1930) 109-110
D4 JDMV 42 (1932-33) *35-36*
D8 JFM 55 (1929, pub. 1931-35) 30
F2 Grundw. 11 (1932) 225
F6 DL 51 (1930) cols. 89-90
H2 MMP 36 (1929) 35
H5 PJGG 43 (1930) 253-254
H11 ZMNU 62 (1931) 223
L4 BDP 3 (1929-30) 433-434
S20 KS 38 (1933) 201
W1 NZZ 151:502 (17. März 1930, Bl. 6) 1
W5 BAMS 35 (1929) 880

1929-5

B3 UW 21 (1929) 331-332
M12a LJD 18 (1929) 135

1930-2

A1 Mind 40 (1931) 267
B13 RPFE 117 (1934) 312
H14 JFM 56 (1930, pub. 1932-35) 44
K6 JPS 6 (1931) 99

1930-5

H13 JDMV 41 (1931-32) *50*
H14 JFM 56 (1930, pub. 1932-35) 43

1930-7

H14 JFM 56 (1930, pub. 1932-35) 44-45

1931-4

G3 ZMG 2 (1931-32) 321
H8 JFM 57 (1931, pub. 1935-39) 52-53

1931-5

H8 JFM 57 (1931, pub. 1935-39) 53-54

1932-1

A1 Mind 41 (1932) 406
B3 UW 24 (1932) 120-123
B13 RPFE 117 (1934) 315
H8 JFM 57 (1931, pub. 1935-39) 60-61
M16 PJGG 47 (1934) 20 37, 154-170
S8 ZMG 3 (1932) 289-290

1932-4

A1 Mind 41 (1932) 406
B3 UW 24 (1932) 248-251
B13 RPFE 117 (1934) 317
H9 JFM 57 (1931, pub. 1935-39) 64
K6 Phil. 8 (1933) 97-98
S23 PF 37 (1934) 91-95

1932-5

A1 Mind 42 (1933) 413-414
B3 UW 25 (1933) 252-256
B13 RPFE 117 (1934) 318
S23 PF 37 (1934) 91-95

1932-6

B3 UW 25 (1933) 252-256

1932-7

B13 RPFE 117 (1934) 319

1933-2

A1 RMM 41:2 (avril 1934) 5-6
B6a EP 9 (1935) 57
B12 MF 245 (1933) 425-427
E2 Scien. 57 (1935) 69-70 [Fr.]
E3 AP 11 (1934-35) 78-79
G5 RQS 105 (1934) 495-496
M7 RSy 6 (1933) 246
M13 Arch. 17 (1935) 333 [Fr.]
S15 PF 37 (1934) 101

1934-1

R2 AP 11 (1934-35) 12

1934-4

A1 TLS 33 (1934) 479
W14 SP 30 (1935-36) 576-577

1934-5

B3 UW 26 (1934) 316-319
B6a EP 8 (1934) 111-112
G6 Erk. 5 (1935-36) 373-374
G7 RSPT 24 (1935) 698-699
H8 DL 56 (1935) col. 410
H8 JFM 61 (1935, pub. 1935-39) 970
N1 JP 31 (1934) 587
S17a NWT 00 (28. April 1935) 00

1934-6

B1 JDMV 45 (1935) *85-88*
B5 PH 5 (1936) 95-96
B5a ZSF 4 (1935) 258-259
B10 Phil. 11 (1936) 110-114
C3 EM 34 (1935) 136-140
D8 JFM 60 (1934, pub. 1934-38) 19-20
F6 SMa 4 (1936) 309-312 [Eng.]
H5 PJGG 54 (1941) 373-374
H8 DL 56 (1935) cols. 405-410
J2 Erk. 4 (1934) 419-422
K2 Theoria 2 (1936) 83-86 [Sw.]
K3 SR 29 (1937) 203-207
K4a GA 2:18 (20. Sept. 1935) 2
M4 NAW 18:3 (1935) 94-97
M14 Scien. 58 (1935) 373-374 [Fr.]

M16 PJGG 48 (1935) 356-357
N1 JP 32 (1935) 49-52
Q1 PRe 44 (1935) 394-397
S11a EP 9 (1935) 138-146
S16 Mind 44 (1935) 499-511
T1 CM 30 (1934) 177-184
V3 ANTWP 29 (1935-36) 62

1934-8

A1 RMM 42:2 (avril 1935) 2-3
B12 MF 256 (1934) 135-136
B14 RSy 12 (1936) 114
B15 Arch. 17 (1935) 334-335 [Fr.]
B18 EM 34 (1935) 128-129
E2 Scien. 60 (1936) 109-110 (Fr.]
G5 RQS 107 (1935) 487-488
N1 PRe 45 (1936) 634-635
P1 RGSPA 46 (1935) 95-96
R2 AP 13 (1937) 13-14
V2 RSc 73 (1935) 249
W1a RIS 15 (1935) 714-716

1934-10

G1a PsA 9 (1935) item 3975

1934-11

G3 ZMG 11 (1935) 1
H8 JFM 60 (1934, pub. 1934-38) 843-844

1935-1

G6 Theoria 3 (1937) 355-357 [Ger.]
H7 JFM 61 (1935, pub. 1935-39) 46
N1 JP 32 (1935) 357
S14 RP 36 (1936) 545-547

1935-2

A1 Mind 45 (1936) 269
H8 JFM 61 (1935, pub. 1935-39) 46
M17 PS 3 (1936) 129

1935-4

A3 JFM 61 (1935, pub. 1935-39) 970
S8 ZMG 12 (1935-36) 145

1935-10

C13 Scien. 62 (1937) 344 [Fr.]
G5 RQS 110 (1936) 165-166
M13 Arch. 18 (1936) 104-105 [Fr.]
N1 JP 33 (1936) 557
S4 Mind 46 (1937) 99
W4 PRe 46 (1937) 563-564

1936-2

N1 JSL 2 (1937) 139

1936-5

H8 JSL 17 (1952) 139

1936-9

A1 Mind 47 (1938) 125
B6 JSL 2 (1937) 42
H8 JFM 62 (1936, pub. 1936-40) 1056-1057
S8 ZMG 15 (1936-37) 49-50

1936-10

A1 Mind 46 (1937) 270-271, 546
H10 JFM 62 (1936, pub. 1936-40) 1052; 63 (1937, pub. 1938-41) 821
K7 KF 14 (1937-38) 55-61
L6 JSL 2 (1937) 49-50
P2b PsA 11 (1937) item 2183

1937-1

A1 TLS 36 (1937) 604
A7 Spec. 158 (1937) 589-590
B10 MG 22 (1938) 90-91
D7 RSPT 27 (1938) 445-449
G4 Nature 143 (1939) 782-783
H4 CR 58 (1936-37) 455-456
K5 JSL 4 (1939) 82-87
L6 Isis 29 (1938) 163-167
M2 BAMS 44 (1938) 171-176
M19 SRL 16:14 (31 July 1937) 19
N1 JP 34 (1937) 303-304
P6 Athen. 24 (1938) 115-117 [Hung.]
S16 Phil. 13 (1938) 485-486
U2 PRe 46 (1937) 549-553
V1 Nation 144 (1937) 599-600
W5 NR 92 (1937) 107-108

1937-2

B2 ASR 2 (1937) 432
G2 SRL 16:6 (5 June 1937) 16
W11 JR 17 (1937) 323-324

1937-3

B8 ANTWP 31 (1937-38) 132-133

1937-4

C6 JSL 4 (1939) 29-30

1938-2

H8 Theoria 6 (1940) 102 [Eng.]
L2 JSL 3 (1938) 157-158
M4a ZSF 8 (1939) 228-229
M5 PRe 50 (1941) 434-436
N1 JP 35 (1938) 691
R7 Logos 22 (1939) 172
S2 RiF 41 (1950) 284-290

1939-1

B8 ANTWP 33 (1939-40) 156, 301
C6 BAMS 45 (1939) 821-822
C8 Isis 33 (1941-42) 721-722

F5 PRe 49 (1940) 678-679
G4 Pers. 21 (1940) 421
H3a ZMG 78 (1958-59) 242 [Eng.]
H8 PA 1:1 (Winter 1939-40) 5
H8 Theoria 6 (1940) 103 [Eng.]
K7 JSL 4 (1939) 117-118
M4a ZSF 8 (1939) 230-232
N1 JP 36 (1939) 636-637
P6 Athen. 26 (1940) 83-84 [Hung.]
S9 JFM 65 (1939, pub. 1941-43) 1099-1100
W5 Ethics 50 (1939-40) 119

1939-4

W3 JSL 4 (1939) 171

1942-2

B10 Mind 54 (1945) 171-175
C6 PRe 52 (1943) 298-304
F5 PPR 4 (1943-44) 450-455
F9 MR 4 (1943) 209
H8 PA 2:11 (Winter 1942-43) 3-4
H15 Nation 154 (1942) 718-719
K7 RuF 16 (1948) 127-135
L2 JSL 8 (1943) 36-37
L8a CI 1 (1945) 174-176
N1 JP 39 (1942) 468-473
R4 PS 9 (1942) 281-282
R5 CPMF 72 (1947) D124-D131
S9 ZMG 35 (1950) 1-3
S17 ZPF 5 (1950-51) 459-464
S21 Isis 34 (1942-43) 229
W6 Thought 18 (1943) 733-735

1943-1

A1 Nature 153 (1944) 8
B4 PA 3:13/14 (Winter 1943-44) 5
B10 Mind 54 (1945) 175-176
C6 PRe 53 (1944) 493-498
F5 PPR 4 (1943-44) 450-455
F9 MR 4 (1943) 209
H8 JSL 8 (1943) 81-83
K7 RuF 16 (1948) 127-135
L8a CI 1 (1945) 174-176
N1 JP 40 (1943) 332-334
R5 CPMF 73 (1948-49) D64-D68
S9 ZMG 35 (1950) 3-4
S17 PL 4 (1952) 42-46
T4 Phil. 20 (1945) 84-86
W6 Thought 18 (1943) 733-735

1945-1

N1 JSL 10 (1945) 104

1945-2

C7 PS 14 (1947) 176
M12 MR 7 (1946) 46
N1 JSL 11 (1946) 19-23

1945-3

C7 PS 14 (1947) 176
K8 MR7 (1946) 189
N1 JSL 11 (1946) 19

1946-1

A1 BAPh 1 (1947) item 2566
A1 BAPr 8 (1947) item 6364
B7 JSL 13 (1948) 218-219
C12 MR 8 (1947) 429

1946-2

A1 BAPh 1 (1947) item 2579
H8 JSL 11 (1946) 124-125
K8 MR 8 (1947) 245-246

1946-3

H8 JSL 11 (1946) 124-125
K8 MR 8 (1947) 246

1946-4

M17a PsA 21 (1947) item 973

1947-2

A1 USQBL 3 (1947) 247
A5 GM 4 (1949) 554-556
B4 PA 11 (1949) 52-53
B7 JSL 14 (1949-50) 237-241
B10 PRe 58 (1949) 257-264
B19 Pers. 29 (1948) 413-414
F1a PL 9 (1956) 367-370
F9 MR 8 (1947) 430
H1 PL 2 (1950-51) 275-279
K7 RuF 16 (1948) 127-135
L7 Mind 58 (1949) 228-238
M6 NL 30:20 (17 May 1947) 11
M10 Sophia 22 (1954) 199-201
N1 JP 45 (1948) 467-472
O1 Thomist 12 (1949) 106-112
R4b Hum. 7 (1947-48) 144-145
R9 Phil. 24 (1949) 69-76
S9 ZMG 34 (1950) 1-3

1947-3

A1 BAPh 2 (1948) item 2655
C7 JSL 13 (1948) 120-121
H7 MR 9 (1948) 323

1948-1

C7 JSL 13 (1948) 121

1948-3

B10 JSL 14 (1949-50) 249

1949-5

Q1 JSL 15 (1950) 149-150

1950-1

A1 BAPh 5 (1951) item 583

C5 JSL 16 (1951) 294-296

1950-4

A1 Scien.* 88 (1953) 65 [Eng.]
A1 TLS 51 (1952) 333
A1 USQBL 6 (1950) 419-420
A2 RPoF 12 (1956) 334
A3a KKK 1 (1954-55) 184-188
A6 RIP 5 (1951) 229-231
B2a Iyyun 2 (1951) 242-243
B6 SMo 72 (1951) 63-64
B17 Schol. 27 (1952) 456-457
B21 JP 48 (1951) 524-535
C2 Meth. 6 (1954) 153-154
C11 PQ 4 (1954) 82-84
D1 Syn. 8 (1950-53) 459-470
F4 JASA 46 (1951) 532-534
G7 RSPT 37 (1953) 484-486
H6 PS 19 (1952) 170-177
H16 PRu 2 (1954-55) 7-16
I1 RZhM (1955) item 1076
J1 Nature 170 (1952) 507-508
K2a PsA 25 (1951) item 5833
K4 JSL 16 (1951) 205-207
K4 RM 5 (1951-52) 145-156
K4 SMa 24 (1959) 161-162 [Eng.]
K10 ZMG 40 (1951) 70-72
L9 JRSS 115 (1952) 435-436
L11 MR 12 (1951) 664-665
M1 Ind. 65 (1951) 467-468
M5 AJS 249 (1951) 459-462
P2 RiF 43 (1952) 338-340
S1a Econ. 20 (1952) 688-690
S17 PL 4 (1952) 268-275
T2 DS 5 (1952) 216
T5 Mind 62 (1953) 86-99
W2 Pers. 33 (1952) 289-290
W13 PPR 13 (1952-53) 103-121
W16 PRe 60 (1951) 362-374

1950-5

K9 JSL 16 (1951) 137 [Ger.]

1950-7

H8 JSL 17 (1952) 139

1951-2

K4 JSL 16 (1951) 287

1951-3

H8 JSL 17 (1952) 214-215

1952-1

A1 Thomist 17 (1954) 121-123
A4 Econ. 23 (1955) 232
A6 RIP 8 (1954) 476-479
B21 JP 50 (1953) 731-734
H6 PRe 62 (1953) 468-472
K4 JSL 18 (1953) 168-169
L11 MR 14 (1953) 4-5
R8 Phil. 28 (1953) 272-273
S1 IMN 8:29/30 (Dez. 1953) 62
S7 MM 57 (1953-54) 89-90
S22 ZMG 47 (1953) 372-373

1952-4

C4 PPR 14 (1953-54) 116-117
H17 BJPS 4 (1953-54) 232-233
I2 RIP 7 (1953) 248

1952-5

A1 BAPh 7 (1953) item 7041
S13 JSL 20 (1955) 188-189

1953-1

A1 BAPh 8 (1954) item 5489
L11 MR 15 (1954) 190
S13 JSL 19 (1954) 300-301
Z1 RZhM 1953 item 16

1953-2

S13 JSL 23 (1958) 77

1953-3

E1 JSL 19 (1954) 230-232

1953-7

A1 BAPh 8 (1954) item 2767
F7 MR 15 (1954) 386
L7a PsA 28 (1954) item 4256
P5 RZhM 1956 item 119

1954-3

B2a Iyyun 6 (1955) 48
B8 ANTWP 47 (1954-55) 168
B11 RPFE 147 (1957) 253
C1 RaSF 8 (1955) 177-184
C9 PQ 6 (1956) 91
C12 MR 16 (1955) 208
F1a Econ. 25 (1957) 385-386
F2a IMN 9:35/36 (Nov. 1954) 67
F3 RPL 53 (1955) 387-390
F7a APA 9 (1954-55) 370-371 [Ger.]
F8 PL 8 (1955) 232-235
G1 RNC 17 (1954-55) 159-160
H14b NZZ 177:2623 (21. Sept. 1956, Bl. 3) 1
H16 PRu 2 (1954-55) 119
L8a CI 11 (1955) 76
M8 PS 22 (1955) 167-168
M9 PPR 17 (1956-57) 280
M18 JSL 20 (1955) 274-277 [Ger.]
R4a Erasmus 10 (1957) cols. 385-386 [Eng.]
R6 Pens. 11 (1955) 473-474
S7 MM 58 (1954) 213

S9 DL 76 (1955) cols. 643-648
S9 ZMG 56 (1955) 6-7
S10 DZP 3 (1955) 260-265
T3 Bijdr. 16 (1955) 341
W15 BJPS 9 (1958-59) 70-72

1955-1

W7 JSL 20 (1955) 296

1955-3

A1 BAPh 11 (1957) item 12460
W7 JSL 20 (1955) 296-297

1955-6

A1 BAPh 10 (1956) item 8612

1955-7

U1 Mind 67 (1958) 572

1955-8

B16 AJP 35 (1957) 65

1956-2

A1 CC 108:1 (1957) 86
D5 Sophia 27 (1959) 387

1956-3

H14a QJS 43 (1957) 83-84
L5 BJPS 9 (1958-59) 249-251
M9 PPR 18 (1957-58) 558-559
M11 Pers. 38 (1957) 283
P4 BP 3 (1956) 110 [Eng.]
Q2 HJ 58 (1959-60) 200-201

1956-4

B2a JSL 25 (1960) 71-74

M1a PRe 67 (1958) 397-398
M3 PPR 17 (1956-57) 562
P3 Phil. 34 (1959) 173
S3 ZPF 12 (1958) 625-636

1958-2

F1b Inquiry 1 (1958) 254-258
L3 JP 57 (1960) 311-313
M15 EPN 14 (1959) 73
P2a IMN 13:62 (Sept. 1959) 48
T3 RQS 130 (1959) 620

1958-4

C1 RaSF 12 (1959) 190-191

1959-1

A6a DL 81 (1960) cols. 393-395
B2a Iyyun 10 (1959) 165
B2a PS 29 (1962) 94-95
B8 ANTWP 52 (1959-60) 32
B12a MM 63 (1959) 401-402
C7a MPS 7 (1960-61) 116-118
F3 RPL 57 (1959) 271-274
F7a APA 13 (1960) 341-343 [Ger.]
G1b Genus 15 (1959) 199
H8 JSL 24 (1959) 272
K5a ACP 159 (1960-61) 162-163
L10 MR 21 (1960) 576-577 [Ger.]

1959-2

B2a JSL 25 (1960) 71-74

1960-1

R6a APA 14 (1961) 242-244 [Ger.]

B. KEY TO AUTHORS

A1. Anonymous
2. Abranches, Cassiano
3. Ackermann, Wilhelm
3a. Akaike, Hirotsugu
4. Anscombe, Francis John
5. Antonelli, Maria Teresa
6. Apostel, Leo
6a. Asser, Günter
7. Ayer, Alfred Jules

B1. Bachmann, Friedrich
2. Bain, Read
2a. Bar-Hillel, Yehoshua
3. Bavink, Bernhard
4. Baylis, Charles Augustus
5. Beck, Maximilian
5a. Benjamin, Walter
6. Bennett, Albert Arnold
6a. Berger, Gaston
7. Bernays, Paul
8. Beth, Evert Willem
9. "Bla."
10. Black, Max
11. Blanché, Robert
12. Boll, Marcel
12a. Brauner, Heinrich
13. Bréhier, Émile
14. Brunet, Lucien
15. Brunet, Pierre
16. Buchdahl, Gerd
17. Büchel, Wolfgang
18. Buhl, Adolfe
19. Bures, Charles Edwin
20. Burkamp, Wilhelm
21. Burks, Arthur Walter

C1. Campanale, Domenico
2. Ceccato, Silvio
3. Chevalley, Claude
4. Chisholm, Roderick Milton
5. Choynowski, Mieczysław
6. Church, Alonzo

7. Churchman, Charles West
7a. Coers, Hellmut
8. Cohen, I. Bernard
9. Cohen, Laurence Jonathan
10. Costello, Harry Todd
11. Cousin, David Ross
12. Curry, Haskell Brooks
13. Cuzzer, Otto

D1. van Dantzig, David
2. Dingler, Hugo
3. Döpel, Robert
4. Doetsch, Gustav
5. Dollo, Corrado
6. Drewnowski, Jan Franciszek
7. Dubarle, Dominique
8. Dubislav, Walter

E1. Elias, Peter
2. Enriques, Federigo
3. Etcheverry, Auguste

F1. Farnsworth, Paul Randolph
1a. Fels, Eberhard
1b. Fenstad, Jens Erik
2. Fernkorn, Carl Maria
2a. Feyerabend, Paul Karl
3. Feys, Robert
4. de Finetti, Bruno
5. Fitch, Frederic Brenton
6. Fraenkel, Abraham Adolf
7. Freudenthal, Hans
7a. Freundlich, Rudolf
8. Frey, Gerhard
9. Frink, Orrin, Jr.

G1. García Bacca, Juan David
1a. Garth, Thomas Russell
1b. Gini, Corrado
2. Ginsburg, Sol Wiener
3. Gödel, Kurt
4. Greenwood, Thomas
5. Grégoire, Auguste
6. Grelling, Kurt
7. Guérard des Lauriers, Michel Louis

H1. Härlen, Hasso
2. Hahn, Hans
3. Hahn, Karl
3a. Hailperin, Theodor
4. Hardie, Charles Dunn
5. Hartmann, Eduard
6. Hay, William Henry
7. Helmer, Olaf
8. Hempel, Carl Gustav
9. Hempel-Ahrends, Eva
10. Hermes, Hans
11. Hertz, Paul
12. Heyde, Johannes Erich
13. Heyting, Arend
14. Hirsch, Kurt August
14a. Hochmuth, Marie
14b. Hoesli, Rudolf J.
15. Hofstadter, Albert
16. Hübner, Kurt
17. Hutten, Ernest Hirschlaff

I1. I͡Anovskai͡a, S. A.
2. Issmann, Samuel

J1. Jeffreys, Harold
2. Jørgensen, Jørgen

K1. "K."
2. Kaila, Eino
2a. Kantor, Jacob Robert
3. Kaufmann, Felix
4. Kemeny, John George
4a. von Kempski, Jürgen
5. Kleene, Stephen Cole
5a. Klug, Ulrich
6. Knight, Helen
7. Kokoszyńska, Maria
8. Koopman, Bernard Osgood
9. Kraft, Victor
10. Kratzer, Adolf
11. Kronfeld, Arthur

L1. Lammert, Berthold
2. Langford, Cooper Harold
3. Leblanc, Hugues
4. Leisegang, Hans
5. Lejewski, Czesław
6. Leonard, Henry Siggins
7. Lewy, Casimir
7a. Lichtenstein, Parker Earl
8. Lietzmann, Walther
8a. Lindemann, Hans Adalbert
9. Lindley, Dennis Victor
10. Lorenzen, Paul
11. Łoś, Jerzy

M1. "E. M."
1a. Mace, Cecil Alec
2. MacLane, Saunders
3. Madden, Edward Harry
4. Mannoury, Gerrit
4a. Marcuse, Herbert
5. Margenau, Henry
6. Margoshes, Adam

7. Mariani, Jean
8. Martin, Norman Marshall
9. Martin, Richard Milton
10. Masellis, Vito
11. Matheson, Gordon
12. McKinsey, John Charles Chenoweth
12a. Merten, Bernhard
13. Metzger, Hélène
14. De Michelis, Enrico
15. Millet, Louis
16. Molitor, Arnulf
17. Morris, Charles William
17a. Mote, Frederick Albert
17b. Müller, Artur
18. Müller, Gert Heinz
19. Munitz, Milton Karl

N1. Nagel, Ernest
2. Neurath, Otto

O1. Oesterle, John Arthur

P1. "L. P."
2. Pasquinelli, Alberto
2a. Peroutka, Franz
2b. Peters, Charles Clinton
3. Peters, Richard
4. Peterson, Svcn Richard
5. Povarov, G. N.
5a. Pozdena, Rudolf
6. Pozsonyi, Frigyes
7. Przywara, Erich

Q1. Quine, Willard Van Orman
2. Quinton, Anthony

R1. Rabel, Gabriele
2. Régnier, Marcel
3. Reichenbach, Hans
4. Reiner, John Maximilian
4a. Reinhardt, Kurt Frank
4b. Reiser, Oliver Leslie
5. Rieger, Ladislav
6. Roig Gironella, Juan
6a. Rollett-Gorbach, Brigitte
7. Rossi, Mario Manlio
8. Russell, Leonard James
9. Ryle, Gilbert

S1. Sagan, Hans
1a. Savage, Leonard Jimmie
2. Scarpelli, Uberto
3. Scheibal, Alfred
4. Schiller, Ferdinand Canning Scott
5. Schiller, Ludwig
6. Schlick, Moritz
7. Schmetterer, Leopold
8. Schmidt, Arnold
9. Scholz, Heinrich
10. Schröter, Karl
11. Sellien, Ewald
11a. Serrus, Charles
12. Sexl, Theodor
13. Shimony, Abner
14. Simon, Yves
15. Sobociński, Bolesław
16. Stebbing, Lizzie Susan
17. Stegmüller, Wolfgang
17a. Stern, Alfred
18. Steuer, Albert
19. Stock, Eugen
20. Sveistrup, Hans
21. Symon, Keith Randolph
22. Szentmártony, Tibor
23. Sztejnbarg, Dina

T1. Tardy, Vladimír
2. Thomas, Ivo
3. De Tollenaere, Maurice
4. Toms, Eric
5. Toulmin, Stephen Edelston

U1. Urmson, James Opie
2. Ushenko, Andrew Paul

V1. Vivas, Eliseo
2. Vouillemin, Ernest
3. Vredenduin, Pieter Gaele Johannes

W1. Walter, Emil Jakob
1a. Warnotte, Daniel
2. Watson, George
3. Wedberg, Anders
4. Weinberg, Julius Rudolph
5. Weiss, Paul
6. Wellmuth, John
7. Wells, Rulon
8. Weyl, Hermann
9. Wiegner, Adam
10. Wieleitner, Heinrich
11. Wieman, Henry Nelson
12. Wiener, Norbert
13. Williams, Donald Cary
14. Wolf, Abraham
15. Woodger, Joseph Henry
16. von Wright, Georg Henrik

Z1. Zykov, A. A.

C. KEY TO PERIODICALS

AAZP	Allgemeine ärztliche Zeitschrift für Psychotherapie und psychische Hygiene (*Leipzig*)
ACP	Archiv für die civilistische Praxis (*Tübingen*)
AJP	Australasian Journal of Philosophy (*Sydney*)
AJS	American Journal of Science (*New Haven, Conn.*)
ANTWP	Algemeen Nederlands Tijidschrift voor Wijsbegeerte en Psychologie (*Assen*)
AP	Archives de philosophie (*Paris*), Supplément bibliographique
APA	Acta Physica Austriaca (*Wien*)
APPK	Annalen der Philosophie und philosophischen Kritik (*Leipzig*), Literaturberichte; [*later* Erk.]
Arch.	Archeion: Archivio di storia della scienza (*Roma*)
ARW	Archiv für Rechts- und Wirtschaftsphilosophie mit besonderer Berücksichtigung der Gesetzgebungsfragen (*Berlin-Grunewald*)
ASR	American Sociological Review (*Menasha, Wis.*)
Athen.	Athenaeum (*Budapest*), Új folyam
BAMS	Bulletin of the American Mathematical Society (*Lancaster, Pa., & New York; Menasha, Wis., & New York*)
BAPh	Bulletin analytique [*later* signalétique] (*Centre national de la recherche scientifique, Paris*), [Troisième partie:] Philosophie
BAPr	Bulletin analytique [*later* signalétique] (*Centre national de la recherche scientifique, Paris*), Première partie
BDP	Blätter für deutsche Philosophie (*Berlin*)
Bijdr.	Bijdragen: Tijdschrift voor Philosophie en Theologie (*Nijmegen & Antwerpen*)
BJPS	The British Journal for the Philosophy of Science (*Edinburgh*)
BP	Bibliographie de la philosophie (*Paris*), [Nouvelle série]
BPDI	Beiträge zur Philosophie des deutschen Idealismus (*Erfurt*)
CC	La civiltà cattolica (*Roma*)
CI	Ciencia e investigación (*Buenos Aires*)
CM	Česká mysl (*Praha*)
CPMF	Časopis pro pěstování matematiky a fysiky (*Praha*)
CR	The Cambridge Review (*Cambridge, Eng.*)
DL	Deutsche Literaturzeitung (*Leipzig; Berlin*)
DS	Dominican Studies (*London*)
DZP	Deutsche Zeitschrift für Philosophie (*Berlin*)
Econ.	Econometrica: Journal of the Econometric Society (*Baltimore*)
EM	L'Enseignement mathématique (*Paris & Genève*)
EP	Les Études philosophiques (*Marseille*)
EPN	Les Études philosophiques (*Paris*), Nouvelle série
Erasmus	Erasmus: Speculum scientiarum (*Darmstadt & Aaru*)
Erk.	Erkenntnis, zugleich Annalen der Philosophie (*Leipzig*)
Ethics	Ethics: An International Journal of Social, Political, and Legal Philosophy (*Chicago*)
GA	Geistige Arbeit (*Berlin & Leipzig*)
Genus	Genus: Organo del Comitato Italiano per lo Studio dei Problemi della Popolazione e della Società Italiana di Genetica ed Eugenica (*Roma*)
GM	Giornale di metafisica (*Torino*)
Grundw.	Grundwissenschaft: Philosophische Zeitschrift der Johannes-Rehmke-Gesellschaft (*Leipzig*)
HJ	The Hibbert Journal (*London*)

Hum.	The Humanist (*Salt Lake City*)
IMN	Internationale mathematische Nachrichten (*Wien*)
Ind.	L'Industria: Rivista di economia politica (*Milano*)
Inquiry	Inquiry: An Interdisciplinary Journal of Philosophy and the Social Sciences (*Oslo*)
Isis	Isis: [An] International Review Devoted to the History of Science and Civilization (*Bruges; Menasha, Wis.; Burlington, Vt.*)
Iyyun	'Iyyun: Riv'on pilosofi (Iyyun: A Hebrew Philosophical Quarterly) (*Yerushalayim*)
JASA	Journal of the American Statistical Association (*Washington, i.e. Menasha, Wis.*)
JDMV	Jahresbericht der Deutschen Mathematiker-Vereinigung (*Leipzig & Berlin*), Zweite Abteilung
JFM	Jahrbuch über die Fortschritte der Mathematik (*Berlin & Leipzig; Berlin*)
JP	The Journal of Philosophy (*Lancaster, Pa.*)
JPS	Journal of Philosophical Studies (*London*); [*later* Phil.]
JR	The Journal of Religion (*Chicago*)
JRSS	Journal of the Royal Statistical Society (*London*), Series A (General)
JSL	The Journal of Symbolic Logic (*Menasha, Wis.; Baltimore; Groningen*)
Kampf	Der Kampf: Sozialdemokratische Monatsschrift (*Wien*)
KF	Kwartalnik filozoficzny (*Kraków*)
KKK	Kagaku kisoron kenkyū (Journal of the Japan Association for Philosophy of Science) (*Tōkyō*)
KS	Kant-Studien (*Berlin*)
LH	Literarischer Handweiser (*Freiburg im Breisgau*)
LJD	Literarischer Jahresbericht des Dürerbundes (*Berlin*)
Logos	Logos: Rivista trimestrale di filosofia e di storia della filosofia (*Roma*)
Meth.	Methodos: Linguaggio e cibernetica (*Milano*)
MF	Mercure de France (*Paris*)
MG	The Mathematical Gazette (*London*)
MGMN	Mitteilungen zur Geschichte der Medizin und der Naturwissenschaften (*Leipzig*)
Mind	Mind: A Quarterly Review of Psychology and Philosophy (*London; Edinburgh*), New Series
MM	Monatshefte für Mathematik (*Wien*)
MMP	Monatshefte für Mathematik und Physik (*Leipzig*), Literaturberichte; [*later* MM]
MPS	Mathematisch-Physikalische Semesterberichte zur Pflege des Zusammenhangs von Schule und Universität (*Göttingen*)
MR	Mathematical Reviews (*Lancaster, Pa.; Providence, R.I.*)
Nation	The Nation (*New York*)
Nature	Nature: A Weekly Journal of Science (*London*)
Naturw.	Die Naturwissenschaften (*Berlin*)
NAW	Nieuw Archief voor Wiskunde (*Groningen*), Tweede Reeks
NFP	Neue Freie Presse (*Wien*)
NL	The New Leader (*New York*)
NR	The New Republic (*New York*)
NWT	Neues Wiener Tagblatt (*Wien*)
NZZ	Neue Zürcher Zeitung (*Zürich*)
PA	Philosophic Abstracts (*New York*)
PB	Physikalische Berichte (*Braunschweig*)

Pens.	Pensamiento: Revista trimestral de investigación e información filosófica (*Madrid*)
Pers.	The Personalist (*Los Angeles*)
PF	Przegląd filozoficzny (*Warszawa*)
PH	Philosophische Hefte (*Prag*)
Phil.	Philosophy: The Journal of the British [*later* the Royal] Institute of Philosophy (*London*)
PJGG	Philosophisches Jahrbuch der Görres-Gesellschaft (*Fulda*)
PL	Philosophischer Literaturanzeiger (*Schlehdorf am Kochelsee; München & Basel*)
PPR	Philosophy and Phenomenological Research (*Buffalo*)
PQ	The Philosophical Quarterly (*St. Andrews*)
PRe	The Philosophical Review (*New York & Menasha, Wis.; New York; Ithaca, N.Y.*)
PRu	Philosophische Rundschau (*Tübingen*)
PS	Philosophy of Science (*Baltimore; Bruges*)
PsA	Psychological Abstracts (*Lancaster, Pa.; Worcester, Mass.; Washington, D.C.*)
PZ	Physikalische Zeitschrift (*Leipzig*)
QJS	The Quarterly Journal of Speech (*Columbia, Mo.*)
RaSF	Rassegna di scienze filosofiche (*Bari; Napoli*)
Reich.	Reichspost (*Wien*)
RGSPA	Revue générale des sciences pures et appliquées (*Paris*)
RiF	Rivista di filosofia (*Milano; Torino*)
RIP	Revue internationale de philosophie (*Bruxelles*)
RIS	Revue de l'Institut de Sociologie (*Bruxelles*)
RM	The Review of Metaphysics (*New Haven, Conn., i.e. Montreal*)
RMM	Revue de métaphysique et de morale (*Paris*), Supplément
RNC	Revista nacional de cultura (*Caracas*)
RP	Revue de philosophie (*Paris*)
RPFE	Revue philosophique de la France et de l'étranger (*Paris*)
RPL	Revue philosophique de Louvain (*Louvain*)
RPoF	Revista portuguesa de filosofia (*Braga*)
RQS	Revue des questions scientifiques (*Louvain & Paris; Louvain*)
RSc	Revue scientifique (*Paris*)
RSPT	Revue des sciences philosophiques et théologiques (*Paris*)
RSy	Revue de synthèse (*Paris*)
RuF	Ruch filozoficzny (*Toruń*)
RZhM	Referativnyĭ zhurnal: Matematika (*Moskva*)
Schol.	Scholastik: Vierteljahresschrift für Theologie und Philosophie (*Freiburg im Breisgau*)
Scien.	"Scientia" (Rivista di scienza) (*Bologna, &c.*)
Scien.*	"Scientia" (Rivista di scienza) (*Bologna, &c.*), Libri ricevuti
SMa	Scripta Mathematica (*New York, i.e. Easton, Pa.*)
SMo	The Scientific Monthly (*Lancaster, Pa.*)
Sophia	Sophia: Rassegna critica di filosofia e storia della filosofia (*Padova*)
SP	Science Progress (*London*)
Spec.	The Spectator (*London*)
SR	The Sociological Review (*London*)
SRL	The Saturday Review of Literature (*New York*)
SS	Sächsische Schulzeitung (*Dresden*), Literarische Beilage
Syn.	Synthese: An International Journal for the Logical and the Psychological Study of the Foundations of Science (*Bussum, Netherlands*)

SZ	Stimmen der Zeit (*Freiburg im Breisgau*)
Theoria	Theoria: Tidskrift för Filosofi och Psykologi [*later subtitle* A Swedish Journal of Philosophy and Psychology] (*Göteborg; Lund*)
Thomist	The Thomist: A Speculative Quarterly Review of Theology and Philosophy (*Washington, i.e. Baltimore*)
Thought	Thought: Fordham University Quarterly (*New York*)
TLS	The Times (*London*), Literary Supplement
TW	Tijdschrift voor Wijsbegeerte (*Haarlem*); [*later* ANTWP]
UMN	Unterrichtsblätter für Mathematik und Naturwissenschaften (*Berlin*)
USQBL	The United States Quarterly Book List [*later* Book Review] (*Washington; New Brunswick, N.J.*)
UW	Unsere Welt (*Detmold; Bielefeld*)
ZMG	Zentralblatt für Mathematik und ihre Grenzgebiete (*Berlin; Berlin, Göttingen & Heidelberg*)
ZMNU	Zeitschrift für mathematischen und naturwissenschaftlichen Unterricht aller Schulgattungen (*Leipzig & Berlin*)
ZPC	Zeitschrift für physikalische Chemie (*Leipzig*), Abteilung A
ZPCU	Zeitschrift für den physikalischen und chemischen Unterricht (*Berlin*)
ZPF	Zeitschrift für philosophische Forschung (*Meisenheim am Glan*)
ZSF	Zeitschrift für Sozialforschung (*Paris*)

INDEX

(Arranged by ROBERT P. SYLVESTER)

C

F

G

H

I

T